D0118929

Oxford Textbook of Psychopathology

OXFORD TEXTBOOKS IN CLINICAL PSYCHOLOGY

Volume 1 *Comprehensive Textbook of Psychotherapy: Theory and Practice* edited by Bruce Bongar and Larry E. Beutler

Volume 2 *Clinical Personality Assessment: Practical Approaches* edited by James N. Butcher

Volume 3 *Ethics in Psychology, Second Edition* by Gerald P. Koocher and Patricia Keith-Spiegel

Volume 4 *Oxford Textbook of Psychopathology* edited by Theodore Millon, Paul H. Blaney, and Roger D. Davis

Oxford Textbook of Psychopathology

Edited by

THEODORE MILLON,
PAUL H. BLANEY & ROGER D. DAVIS

New York Oxford
Oxford University Press
1999

Oxford University Press

Oxford New York
Athens Auckland Bangkok Bogotá Buenos Aires Calcutta
Cape Town Chennai Dar es Salaam Delhi Florence Hong Kong Istanbul
Karachi Kuala Lumpur Madrid Melbourne Mexico City Mumbai
Nairobi Paris São Paulo Singapore Taipei Tokyo Toronto Warsaw

and associated companies in
Berlin Ibadan

Published by Oxford University Press, Inc.
198 Madison Avenue, New York, New York 10016

Oxford is a registered trademark of Oxford University Press

Library of Congress Cataloging-in-Publication Data
Oxford textbook of psychopathology / edited by Theodore Millon,
Paul H. Blaney, and Roger D. Davis
p. cm. — (Oxford textbooks in clinical psychology ; v. 4)
Includes bibliographical references and index.
ISBN 0-19-510307-6
1. Psychology, Pathological. I. Millon, Theodore. II. Blaney,
Paul H. III. Title: Textbook of psychopathology. IV. Series.
[DNLM: 1. Mental Disorders. WM 140 098 1999]
RC454.094 1999
616.89—dc21
DNLM/DLC
for Library of Congress 98-49669

1 3 5 7 9 8 6 4 2

Printed in the United States of America
on acid-free paper

Preface

Whereas most abnormal psychology texts aim for breadth, covering psychotherapy, assessment, personality theory, and perhaps even community psychology and professional ethics, *Oxford Textbook of Psychopathology* aims for depth, focusing almost exclusively on adult psychopathology per se. Where such topics as assessment and treatment are discussed, it is only to inform the understanding of the psychopathology of a given syndrome.

The intended readership consists of graduate students and professionals who are familiar with the field. It is thus assumed that the reader already knows the basic features of the major forms of psychopathology, and that the reader has ready access to a copy of *DSM-IV* while studying this text. Accordingly, the various *DSM-IV* diagnostic entities are not described systematically in this book. Instead, the purpose is to go beyond the descriptive focus of *DSM-IV* by allowing experts to discuss salient issues in the various pathologies that are their expertise. This too sets it apart from other texts in the field.

Indeed, this text may be viewed as companion to the descriptive material given in the *DSM-IV*, with several enhancements. Four chapters address issues cut across all of psychopathology (e.g., chapter 1, on classification). And, among the 23 chapters addressing disorders, each provides a cutting-edge summary of the major theoretical and empirical issues pertaining to that disorder.

The chapters of this book have been organized in terms of the multiaxial model that has been part of the diagnostic system starting with *DSM-III*. That is, following overview material (Part 1), the classic syndromes and symptom disorders of Axis I have been grouped together in Parts II and III, followed by the personality disorder syndromes of Axis II in Part IV. (Exceptions are chapter 13, which incorporates material pertaining to both axes, and chapter 19, which provides a personality disorder overview.) The extensive coverage of Axis II also sets this text apart from most others.

Chapter authors were selected for their expertise, not with an eye to assembling a group of authors who shared a narrow perspective. In moving from one chapter to the next, the reader thus is exposed not only to varied *topics*, but to varied notions of what *approaches* are to be favored, what *issues* are most crucial, and what *forms of discourse* are most informative. While this may be a bit disconcerting at times, it is fundamentally a side-benefit of a multi-authored text, given that it reflects the reality of this heterogeneous field of study.

This book departs from conventional citation style in one major respect. Since at least one of the editions of the *Diagnostic and Statistical Manual* is cited in each chapter, they are simply referred to as *DSM-I, DSM-II,* and so forth. within the body of the text, and they do not appear in chapter References lists. Full bibliographic entries for *DSM-I* (American Psychiatric Association, 1952), *DSM-II*

(American Psychiatric Association, 1968), *DSM-III* (American Psychiatric Association, 1980), *DSM-III-R* (American Psychiatric Association, 1987), and *DSM-IV* (American Psychiatric Association, 1994) are provided below (only). The same applies to *International Classification of Diseases*, for which the current version (World Health Organization, 1992) is simply referred to, without citation, as *ICD-10*. Another acronym that appears often but is not spelled out each time is ECA—for Epidemiologic Catchment Area. The study for which ECA is the abbreviation (cf. Robins & Regier, 1991) is a major census-style survey of the frequency with which various disorders occur in the general population, accounting for its appearance in many chapters of this book.

References

American Psychiatric Association. (1952). *Diagnostic and statistical manual: Mental disorders*. Washington, DC: Author.

American Psychiatric Association. (1968). *Diagnostic and statistical manual of mental disorders (2nd ed.)*. Washington, DC: Author.

American Psychiatric Association. (1980). *Diagnostic and statistical manual of mental disorders (3rd ed.)*. Washington, DC: Author.

American Psychiatric Association. (1987). *Diagnostic and statistical manual of mental disorders (3rd ed.)*. Washington, DC: Author.

American Psychiatric Association. (1994). *Diagnostic and statistical manual of mental disorders (4th ed.)*. Washington, DC: Author.

Robins, L. N., & Regier, D. A., eds. (1991). *Psychiatric disorders in America: The epidemiologic catchment area study.* NY: Macmillan World Health Organization (1992). *ICD-10: The ICD-10 classification of mental and behavioral disorders: Clinical descriptions and diagnostic guidelines*. Geneva: Author.

Contents

Contributors ix

Part I. Foundations

1. Classification 3
   Roger K. Blashfield
   W. John Livesley

2. Developmental Pathogenesis 29
   Theodore Millon
   Roger D. Davis

3. Research Strategies for Studying Psychopathology 49
   Michael L. Raulin
   Scott O. Lilienfeld

Part II. Major Axis I Syndromes

4. Anxiety Disorders: Panic and Phobias 81
   Brian J. Cox
   Steven Taylor

5. Generalized Anxiety Disorder and Obsessive-Compulsive Disorder 114
   Timothy A. Brown

6. Posttraumatic Stress Disorder 144
   Richard J. McNally

7. Affective Disorders: Biological Aspects 166
   Robert H. Howland
   Michael E. Thase

8. Depression: Social and Cognitive Aspects 203
   Rick E. Ingram
   Walter Scott
   Greg Siegle

9. Substance Abuse: Diagnosis, Comorbidity, and Psychopathology 227
   Peter E. Nathan
   Anne Helene Skinstad
   James W. Langenbucher

10. Substance Abuse: Etiological Considerations 249
    R. O. Pihl

11. Schizophrenia: Etiology and Neurocognition 277
    Barbara A. Cornblatt
    Michael F. Green
    Elaine F. Walker

12. Interpersonal Functioning in Schizophrenia 311
    Jill M. Hooley
    Steven F. Candela

13. Paranoid Conditions 339
Paul H. Blaney

Part III. Other Axis I Syndromes

14. Eating Disorders: Anorexia Nervosa and Bulimia Nervosa 365
Howard Steiger
Jean R. Séguin

15. Sleep/Wake Disorders 390
Charles M. Morin
Jack D. Edinger

16. Sexual Dysfunctions and Disorders 410
Daniel N. Weiner
Raymond C. Rosen

17. Somatoform Disorders 444
Theo K. Bouman
Georg H. Eifert
Carl W. Lejeuz

18. Dissociative Disorders 466
Colin A. Ross

Part IV. Axis II Disorders

19. Models of Personality and Its Disorders 485
Roger D. Davis
Theodore Millon

20. Schizoid and Avoidant Personality Disorders 523
David P. Bernstein
Laura Travaglini

21. Dependent and Histrionic Personality Disorders 535
Robert F. Bornstein

22. Psychopathy and Sadistic Personality Disorder 555
Robert D. Hare
David J. Cooke
Stephen D. Hart

23. Obsessive-Compulsive and Negativistic Personality Disorders 585
Joseph T. McCann

24. Schizotypic Psychopathology: Theory, Evidence, and Future Directions 605
Mark F. Lenzenweger

25. Borderline Personality Disorder 628
Joel Paris

26. Depressive and Self-defeating (Masochistic) Personality Disorders 653
Daniel N. Klein
Carina Vocisano

27. Narcissistic Personality Disorder 674
Elsa Ronningstam

Index 694

Contributors

Dr. David Bernstein
Psychology Department
Fordham University
Bronx, NY 10458
(718) 817-3777

Dr. Paul Blaney
Department of Psychology
P.O. Box 248185
Coral Gables, FL 33124-2070
pblaney@umiami.edu

Dr. Roger K. Blashfield
Department of Psychology
Auburn University
Auburn, AL 36849
(334) 844-6465
blashrk@mail.auburn.edu

Dr. Robert F. Bornstein
Department of Psychology
Campus Box 407
Gettysburg College
Gettysburg, PA 17325
bbornste@gettysburg.edu

Dr. Theo K. Bouman
Department of Clinical Psychology
University of Groningen
PO BOX 30.001
9700 RB Groningen
THE NETHERLANDS

Dr. Timothy A. Brown
Center for Stress and Anxiety Disorders
SUNY/Albany
1535 Western Avenue
Albany, NY 12203

Steven F. Candela
Department of Psychology
Harvard University
33 Kirkland Street
Cambridge, MA 02138
scandela@fas.harvard.edu

David J. Cooke
Simon Fraser University
Burnaby, BC V5A 1S6
CANADA
dmcooke@sfu.ca

Dr. Barbara A. Cornblatt
Principal Research Scientist
Hillside Hospital
Psychiatry Research
75-59 263rd Street
Glen Oak, NY 11004
cornblat@lij.edu

Brian J. Cox
Department of Psychology
University of Manitoba
Winnipeg, Manitoba
CANADA R3T 2N2
coxbj@cc.umanitoba.ca

Dr. Roger D. Davis
Institute for Advanced Studies in Personology and Psychopathology
5400 SW 99th Terrace
Coral Gables, FL 33156
rdavis101@aol.com

Dr. Jack D. Edinger
Psychological Services 116 B
VAMC, Durham
508 Fulton Street
Durham, NC 27705
(919) 286-6934

Dr. Georg H. Eifert
Department of Psychology
308C Ogleby HLL
P.O. Box 6040
West Virginia University
Morgantown, WV 26506
geifert@wvu.edu

Dr. Michael F. Green
Department of Psychiatry & Behavioral Science
University of California at Los Angeles
760 Westwood Plaza, C9-420
Los Angeles, CA 90024-1759

Dr. Robert D. Hare
Department of Psychology
University of British Columbia
Vancouver, British Columbia
CANADA V6T 1A1
(604) 531-0273
rhare@unix.ubc.ca

Dr. Steven D. Hart
Department of Psychology
Simon Fraser University
Burnaby, BC V5A 1S6
CANADA
hart@sfu.ca
(604) 291-5584

Dr. Jill M. Hooley
Department of Psychology
Harvard University
33 Kirkland Street
Cambridge, MA 02138
jmh@wjh.harvard.edu

Dr. Robert H. Howland
Department of Psychiatry
Western Psychiatric Institute and Clinic
University of Pittsburgh School of Medicine
Pittsburgh, PA 15213
(412) 624-5330

Dr. Rick E. Ingram
Department of Psychology
San Diego State University
San Diego, CA 92182

Dr. Daniel N. Klein
Department of Psychology and Psychiatry
State University of New York at Stony Brook
Stony Brook, NY 11794

Dr. James W. Langenbucher
Center for Alcohol Studies
Rutgers University
607 Allison Road
Smither's Hall Busch Campus
Piscataway, NJ 08854
lngnbchr@rci.rutgers.edu

Dr. Carl W. Lejeuz
Department of Psychology
P.O. Box 6040
West Virginia University
Morgantown, WV 26506
clejeuz@wvu.edu

Dr. Mark F. Lenzenweger
Department of Psychology
Harvard University
33 Kirkland Street
Cambridge, MA 02138

Dr. Scott O. Lilienfeld
Psychology Department
Psychology Building
Emory University
Atlanta, GA 30322
(404) 727-1125
scott@ss.emory.edu

Dr. W. John Livesley
Professor and Chair
Department of Psychiatry
University of British Columbia
Vancouver, British Columbia
CANADA

Dr. Joseph T. McCann
151 Leroy Street
Binghamton, NY 13905

Dr. Richard McNally
Department of Psychology
Harvard University
33 Kirkland Street
Cambridge, MA 02138

Dr. Theodore Millon
Institute for Advanced Studies
in Personology and Psychopathology
5400 SW 99th Terrace
Coral Gables, FL 33156
iaspp@aol.com
(305) 661-8888

Dr. Charles M. Morin
Université Laval
École de Psychologie
Pavillon F.A. Savard
Ste-Foy, Québec
CANADA G1K 7P4
charles-m.morin@psy.ulaval.ca

Dr. Peter E. Nathan
Department of Psychology
University of Iowa
Iowa City, IA 52242
peter-nathan@uiowa.edu

Dr. Joel Paris
Department of Psychiatry
McGill University
4333 chemin de la côte ste.Catherine
Montreal, Quebec H3T 1E4
CANADA

Dr. R. O. Pihl
Department of Psychology
McGill University
1205 Dr. Penfield Avenue
Montreal, Quebec H3A 1B1
CANADA

Dr. Michael L. Raulin
Psychology Department
SUNY at Buffalo
Buffalo, NY 14260-4110

Dr. Elsa Ronningstam
McLean Hospital
115 Mill Street
Belmont, MA 02178-9106

Dr. Raymond C. Rosen
University Behavioral Health Care
UMDNJ
671 Hoes Lane
Piscataway, NJ 08855
rosen@umdnj.edu

Dr. Colin A. Ross
Charter Behavioral Health Systems of Dallas
6800 Preston Road
Plano, TX 75024

Dr. Walter Scott
Department of Psychology
University of Miami
P.O. Box 248185
Coral Gables, Fl 33124-2070
wscott@umiami.ir.miami.edu

Dr. Jean R. Séguin
6875 Bul LaSalle
Verdun, Quebec H4H 1R3
CANADA
(514) 761-6131 (ext. 2895)

Greg Siegle
The Clarke Institute, 11th Floor, CBT Unit
250 College Street
Toronto, Ontario M5T 1R8
CANADA
gsiegle@psychology.sdsu.edu

Dr. Anne Helene Skinstad
Assistant Professor
Department of Counselor Education
University of Iowa
Iowa City, Iowa 52242

Dr. Howard Steiger
Eating Disorders Program
Douglas Hospital Center
6775 LaSalle Boulevard
Monteal (Verdun) Quebec
H4H 1R3
CANADA
stehow@douglas.mcgill.ca

Dr. Steven Taylor
Department of Psychiatry
University of British Columbia
2255 Westbrook Mall
Vancouver, British Columbia V6T 2A1
CANADA
taylor@unixg.ubc.ca

Dr. Michael E. Thase
Department of Psychiatry
Western Psychiatric Institute and Clinic
University of Pittsburgh School of Medicine
Pittsburgh, PA 15213
(412) 624-5070

Laura Travaglini
Bronx VA Medical Center
130 W. Kingsbridge Road
Bronx, NY 10468

Dr. Elaine F. Walker
Department of Psychiatry
Woodruff Memorial Building
Emory University
Atlanta, GA 30322
(404) 727-0761
walker@ss.emory.edu

Dr. Daniel N. Weiner
Outpatient Services
Butler Hospital
345 Blackstone Boulevard
Providence, RI 02906

Dr. Carina Vocisano
Department of Behavioral Sciences
State University of New York at Stony Brook
Stony Brook, NY 11794

PART I

FOUNDATIONS

1

Classification

ROGER K. BLASHFIELD

W. JOHN LIVESLEY

Compiling glossaries has been a respectable profession since the 2nd century B.C. . . . This is not surprising when the multifarious needs for classification and interpretation are considered. But there is a reverse side to the coin; to "gloss over," or "to gloze," a term derived from the same root as glossary, denotes a disreputable activity. "Classification" likewise has a pejorative as well as a respectable flavour. Psychiatric usage of the relevant terms attests to their ambiguity: "mere labeling," "the neat complacency of classification," "nosological stamp collecting," "a medical hortus siccus." Such damning phrases arise in part from revulsion against the excesses to which classification was pushed in the late 18th and early 19th century.

Sir Aubrey Lewis,
ICD-9, 1978, p. 5

The classification of mental disorders has a lengthy history. The first description of a specific syndrome is usually ascribed to an Egyptian account of dementia about 3000 B.C. The first classification of mental disorders is probably found in the Ayur-Veda, an ancient Indian system of medicine (Menninger, 1963). Ancient Greek and Egyptian writings refer to disorders remarkably similar to concepts of hysteria, paranoia, mania, and melancholia. Since then numerous classifications have emerged, and enthusiasm for classifying mental disorders has waxed and waned. During the last half of the 20th century, classification has been a dominant theme in the study of psychopathology. This period of time saw the publication of five editions of the *Diagnostic and Statistical Manual* (*DSM*), four editions of the mental disorders section of the *International Classification of Diseases* (*ICD*), and numerous books, chapters, and journal articles on classification.

This productivity has not, however, resolved some of the fundamental problems confronting psychiatric nosology. Unresolved issues include the nature of the entities being classified, the definition of mental illness or mental disorder, the nosological principles for organizing psychiatric classifications, and the distinction between normality and pathology. The validity of many diagnoses is not established. Controversies exist regarding the definition and logical status of some diagnoses, and even whether some entities are pathological conditions. For example, heated debates have occurred over whether homosexuality should be considered a mental disorder, and whether a condition such as premenstrual dysphoric disorder belongs in an official classification. Without sound nosological principles, mechanisms for resolving these controversies do not exist.

This chapter provides an overview of some issues associated with the classification of psychopathology. Particular emphasis is placed on the structure of classifications. This will be discussed in terms of (a) the contents or substantive component of classifications with particular reference to the *DSM* system, (b) the evaluative components that can be used to decide how well a classification is functioning, and (c) the formal components that specify the underlying taxonomic principles.

Purpose of Classification

Classification is a necessary and fundamental process (Kendell, 1975). It involves creating and defining the boundaries of concepts (Sartorius, 1990). Through this process, diagnostic entities are defined. Ultimately, the boundaries of the discipline are established. The reason why psychiatric classification has had such an impact is that it has defined the field of psychopathology. A classification of mental disorders stipulates the range of problems to which fields the mental health professions lay claim.

Classifications serve several purposes. These systems (1) provide a *nomenclature* for practitioners; (2) serve as basis for oganizing and *retrieving information*; (3) *describe* the common patterns of symptom presentation; (4) provide the basis for *prediction*; (5) form the basis for the *development of theories*; and (6) serve *sociopolitical functions*.

1. The first major function of a classification is the provision of a standard nomenclature that facilitates description and communication. There are three components to this nomenclature: (a) the definition of mental disorder; (b) definitions of various diagnoses; and (c) definitions of the phenomenology of mental disorders.

2. A classification structures information so that it can be retrieved easily. Information in a science is organized around its major concepts. Knowing a diagnostic concept helps the clinician to retrieve information about such matters as etiology, treatment, and prognosis. A classification shapes the way information is organized, thereby influencing all aspects of clinical practice and research.

3. By providing a nomenclature to describe all levels of psychopathology, a classification establishes the descriptive basis for a science of psychopathology. Most sciences have their origins in description. Only when phenomena are systematically organized into categories is a science in a position to transform accounts of individual cases into principles and generalizations. These descriptions mark the boundaries of events that are considered important and provide the basis for subsequent scientific activities.

4. The fourth goal of classification, prediction, is the most pragmatic from the perspective of clinicians. What a mental health professional typically wants from a diagnosis is prescription regarding the most effective treatment of her patient. In simplest terms, a classification that is useful for prediction is a system in which there is strong evidence that patients with different diagnoses are likely to respond differently to alternative treatments. If treatment outcome is not possible to predict, classifications are also clinically useful if the categories are associated with different clinical courses even if the disorders are not treated.

5. By providing systematic descriptions of phenomena, a classification establishes the foundations for the development of theories. In the natural sciences, especially biology and chemistry, a satisfactory classification proved to be an important precursor for theoretical progress (Hull, 1988). The systematic classification of species by Linnaeus stimulated important questions about the nature of phenomena or processes that accounted for the system—questions that ultimately led to the theory of evolution. For these reasons, classification occupies a central role in research.

6. Finally, a classification of mental disorders has a social-political purpose. By establishing the scope of psychiatry, classifications of mental disorders have a direct impact on related disciplines that are also concerned with the treatment or management of psychopathology leading to a variety of professional boundary questions. A classification system also has broader social consequences by influencing health policy, social policy, forensic decisions, and the economics of the mental health professions. One reason for the recent increased attention to classification is economic. At the end of World War II, psychiatric services in the United

States were either paid for on a fee-for-service basis by individuals who could afford the services or they were provided by governmental institutions such as state hospitals and community mental health centers. Assigning diagnoses in the private and public context of those times was considered relevant, but was not essential to standard clinical practice. With the growth of health insurance and managed care, assigning diagnoses has become an essential part of patient care and has had major consequences for the kind of care made available to American patients.

History of Classification

Although attempts to classify psychopathology date to ancient times, our intent is only to provide a brief overview of major developments, especially those occurring in the last century, as a context for understanding modern classifications. Examining previous classifications shows that many current issues have a long history. For example, writers in the 18th century, like many contemporary authorities, believed that the biological sciences had solved the problems of classification and that biological taxonomies could serve as a model for classifying psychopathology. The Edinburgh physician William Cullen, for example, applied Linnaeus's principles for classifying species to illnesses. The result, published in 1769, was a complex structure involving classes, orders, genera, and species of illness (cited by Kendell, 1990). One class was neurosis (Cullen introduced the concept as a general term for mental disorders) that was subdivided into four orders, 27 genera, and over 100 species. Contemporaneous critics, who believed that there were far fewer diagnoses, dismissed Cullen as a "botanical nosologist." Nonetheless, interest in applying the principles of biological classification to abnormal behavior continues today, as does the debate over the number of diagnoses. "Splitters" seek to divide mental disorders into ever more narrowly defined categories, whereas "lumpers" maintain that a few, broadly defined categories are adequate to represent psychopathology (Havens, 1985).

The features used to classify mental disorders varied substantially across 18th- and 19th-century classifications. Some diagnoses were little more than single symptoms whereas others were broader descriptions resembling syndromes. Many classifications from the last century relied heavily on traditional philosophical analyses of the faculties or attempted to organize disorders around poorly articulated views of etiology. In 1879, Henry Maudsley suggested that classifications should be based on symptoms rather than etiological speculations—an idea not fully implemented until the publication of the *DSM-III* in 1980.

Kraepelin

With the work of Kraepelin, the structure of modern classification began to take shape. Kraepelin was born in 1856, the same year as Freud, an ironic fact considering that they established two very different approaches. Kraepelin was influenced by two traditions (Berrios & Hauser, 1988). The first was the scientific approach to medicine that dominated German medical schools in the late 19th century. Many important medical breakthroughs, especially in bacteriology, occurred in Germany during that period. German psychiatrists of the time generally believed that mental disorders were biological and that psychiatry would gradually be replaced by neurology. Kraepelin was also influenced by early work in experimental psychology (Kahn, 1959). During medical training, he worked for a year in the laboratory of Wundt, one of the first experimental psychologists. In early research, Kraepelin applied Wundt's methods to the study of mental disorders.

Kraepelin's reputation was based on his textbooks of psychiatry. Like most textbook authors, Kraepelin organized his volumes with chapters on each of the major groupings of mental disorders. What has become known as Kraepelin's classifications (Menninger, 1963) are little more than the table of contents to the nine published editions of his textbook. In the sixth edition, Kraepelin included two chapters that attracted considerable international attention. One developed the concept of dementia praecox (now called schizophrenia) that included hebephrenia, catatonia, and paranoia as subtypes. The other discussed manic-depressive insanity—a revolutionary idea that combined mania and melancholia, two concepts that had been considered separate entities since the writings of Hippocrates. The two diagnoses, dementia praecox and manic-depressive psychosis, established a fundamental distinction that forms the lynchpin of contemporary classifications.

ICD-6, DSM-I, ICD-8, *and* DSM-II

In medicine, the official classification of medical disorders is known as the *International Classification of Diseases and Related Health Problems* (World Health Organization, 1992). Historically, this classification began at the end of the nineteenth century when a group named the International Statistical Institute commissioned a committee headed by Jacques Bertillon to generate a classification of causes of death. This classification, initially known as *The Bertillon Classification of Causes of Death*, was adopted as an official international classification of medical disorders at a meeting of 26 countries in France in 1900. The name of the classification was slightly modified in the early 1900s to *The International Classification of Causes of Death* (World Health Organization, 1957). This original version of the *ICD* was revised at subsequent conferences held in 1909, 1920, 1929, and 1938.

After World War II, the World Health Organization met to generate a sixth revision to this classification. A decision was made at that point to expand the classification beyond causes of death and to include all diseases whether those diseases led to death or not (i.e., to include causes of morbidity as well as mortality). The name of the classification was revised accordingly to the *International Classification of Diseases, Injuries, and Causes of Death* (*ICD-6*). Because it focused on all diseases, the *ICD-6* added a section devoted to mental disorders.

Shortly after the publication of the *ICD-6*, the American Psychiatric Association published its first official classification of mental disorders called the *Diagnostic and Statistical Manual of Mental Disorders* (*DSM-I*). The reason for the creation of this classification was that there were four different classifications of psychopathology in use in the United States during World War II, a situation that American psychiatry found embarrassing. Thus, the United States created its ow nomenclature rather than using the *ICD-6*.

Most countries in the world were like the United States. Instead of adopting the *ICD-6* as the official system, the various countries of the world generally had unique classificatory systems. Only five countries in the world adopted the *ICD-6* classification of mental disorders: Finland, New Zealand, Peru, Thailand, and the United Kingdom. To understand why, the World Health Organization asked a British psychiatrist named Stengl to review the classifications of mental disorders that were used in various countries. Stengel's review (1959) was very important because he carefully documented the widespread differences that existed in terminology from country to country (and even within countries). Stengel concluded that a major cause of the failure of clinicians to use a common nomenclature was the etiological implications of many diagnostic concepts and the implicit adoption of different theories of psychopathology across different parts of the classification. Stengel argued that this would lead to psychiatrists' tending to adopt their own diagnostic concepts rather than accept etiological ideas that they did not support. He suggested that the solution was to develop a classification that simply provided operational definitions of mental disorders without reference to etiology. This led to the 8th revision of the mental disorders section of the *International Classification of Diseases*, which was to include a glossary defining the various components of psychopathology to go with the list of diagnoses. Unfortunately this did not happen, although several countries developed their own national glossaries. For instance, the Americans published their version of the *ICD-8* as a second edition of the *DSM* (i.e., the *DSM-II*). The *DSM-II*, like the *DSM-I* but unlike the *ICD-8*, contained short prose definitions of the basic categories in this system. In the *ICD-8* per se, Stengl's plea for operational definitions of categories was ignored.

Criticisms of Psychiatric Classification

During the 1950s and 1960s, concern about the reliability of psychiatric diagnoses surfaced. Problems with levels of diagnostic agreement had been noted in the 1930s. Masserman and Carmichael (1938), for example, reported that 40% of diagnoses in a series of patients followed up one year later required major revision. Ash (1949) compared the diagnoses of three psychiatrists who jointly interviewed 52 individuals applying to work for the CIA. These clinicians agreed on the diagnosis for only 20% of the applicants, and in 30% of the cases, all three psychiatrists made a different diagnosis. Beck (1962) reviewed a series of reliability studies and reported that the highest level of interclinician agreement was 42% for the *DSM-I*. The problem with reliability was further highlighted by the U.K./U.S. Diagnostic Project, which found major differences in diagnostic practice between Britain and the United States (Cooper et al., 1972; Kendell, Cooper, Gourlay, Sharpe, & Gurland, 1971). This study suggested that Americans had an overinclusive concept of schizophrenia and tended to apply the diagnosis to any psychotic patient. British psychiatrists, in contrast, were more specific in the use of schizophrenia as a diagnosis.

Diagnostic unreliability creates major problems for clinical practice and research. It limits the generalizability of research findings: The results of studies on patients with schizophrenia as diagnosed in Britain cannot be generalized to patients diagnosed as having schizophrenia in the United States, if they are based on different applications of the concept of schizophrenia. The problem was not confined to schizophrenia. The reliability studies of the 1960s and 1970s were interpreted as indicating that clinicians had problems achieving high levels of agreement for any area of psychopathology. Most recent commentators on this literature have suggested, however, that the criticisms of diagnostic reliability during this era were overstated (Kirk & Kutchins, 1992).

Concurrent with the empirical studies questioning the reliability of psychiatric diagnosis, psychiatry came under considerable attack from the antipsychiatry movement. Much of this criticism focused on the clinical activities of diagnosis and classification. Szasz (1961) went so far as to argue that mental illness was a myth.

By the late 1960s, three major criticisms of psychiatric classification were popular. First, psychiatric diagnosis was widely thought to be unreliable. Second, classification and diagnosis were considered fundamental components of the medical model that was questioned as the basis for understanding mental disorders. This model clashed with other models, particularly those stemming from psychoanalysis and humanistic perspectives that were influential in clinical and counseling psychology. The medical model of illness was considered inappropriate and in some ways demeaning of patients. Third, widespread concern was expressed particularly among many sociologists and psychologists about the labeling and stigmatizing effects of psychiatric diagnoses (Scheff, 1966, 1975; Goffman, 1959, 1963). Labeling theorists tended to view mental illness and other forms of deviant behavior as largely politically defined and reinforced by social factors and agencies. Psychiatric diagnoses were considered to be self-fulfilling prophecies in which patients adopted the behaviors implied by the label. Their arguments were bolstered by philosophers such as Foucault (1988), who condemned psychiatry as little more than an agent of social control.

A demonstration of these issues was contained in a paper published in *Science* by Rosenhan (1973) titled "On being sane in insane places." In this study, 8 normal persons sought admission to 12 different inpatient units. All accurately reported information about themselves except that they gave false names to avoid a mental hospital record, and they reported hearing an auditory hallucination in which a voice said "thud," "empty," or "hollow." In all instances, the pseudo patients were admitted. Eleven of these admissions were diagnosed as schizophrenia, the other as mania. On discharge, which occurred on average 20 days later, all received the diagnosis of schizophrenia in remission. Rosenhan concluded that mental health professionals were unable to distinguish between sanity and insanity, an observation that was eagerly seized upon by the antipsychiatry movement.

The Neo-Kraepelinians

During the 1970s, a small, but effective, group of researchers emerged in North American psychiatry (Compton & Guze, 1995). These individuals had a major influence first on academic psychiatry and later on research and practice. The movement, usually referred to as the neo-Kraepelinians (Klerman, 1978), sought to reaffirm psychiatry as a branch of medicine. The neo-Kraepelinians emphasized the importance of diagnosis and classification. The movement was a reaction to the antipsychiatrists and the psychoanalytic dominance of North American psychiatry. Klerman summarized the assumptions of the neo-Kraepelinian position by stating values that these researchers upheld:

1. *Psychiatry is a branch of medicine.* Although this statement appears to be a truism, it represented an attempt to refocus psychiatry by emphasizing its medical roots at a time when the antipsychiatric movement and psychoanalytic influences were propelling psychiatry in different directions.
2. *Psychiatry should utilize modern scientific methodologies and base its practice on scien-*

tific knowledge. This proposition needs to be understood in the context of the first: namely, that it represents a further attempt to establish psychiatry as a medical specialty by insisting on a solid empirical foundation.

3. *Psychiatry treats people who are sick and who require treatment for mental illness.* This proposition represents support for the medical model approach to understanding psychopathology. The view has major implications for the direction of psychiatric inquiry. Implicitly, the proposition also asserts the dominance of psychiatry among the mental health professions. Any area of psychopathology that might represent a disease process (e.g., schizophrenia) belongs to psychiatry, whereas other areas could be assigned to ancillary professions such as psychology, social work, and nursing.
4. *There is a boundary between the normal and the sick.* This assumption is part of the attempt to medicalize psychiatric disorders by emphasizing qualitative distinctions between normality and illness. This view contrasts with writers such as Szasz, who considered mental disorders to be problems of living.
5. *There are discrete mental illnesses. Mental illnesses are not myths. There is not one, but many mental illnesses. It is the task of scientific psychiatry, as of other medical specialties, to investigate the causes, diagnoses, and treatment of these medical mental illnesses.* This clearly outlines the agenda for psychiatry—namely, the delineation of these illnesses and the development of appropriate treatments. This assumption of clear distinctions between different forms of disorder places priority on classification and lays the basis for the continued use of a categorical approach to classification.
6. *The focus of psychiatric physicians should be particularly on the biological aspects of mental illness.* This proposition clearly follows from the movement's attempts to reassert the medical basis of psychiatry and represents a try to establish the agenda for psychiatric research and practice. The remedicalization of psychiatry by the neo-Kraepelinians was a clear counterattack to the dispersions aimed by antipsychiatrists such as Szasz (Rogler, 1997).
7. *There should be an explicit and intentional concern with diagnosis and classification.* This position emphasizes the importance of diagnosis as the basis for treatment decisions. Additionally, this claim makes diagnosis the foundation of clinical care. The view contrasts with the approach taken by many psychoanalysts who believe that descriptive classification focused on superficial behavioral aspects of patients' lives (Havens, 1981).
8. *Diagnostic criteria should be codified, and a legitimate and valued area of research should be to validate such criteria by various techniques. Further, the departments of psychiatry in medical schools should teach these criteria and not depreciation them, as has been the case for many years.* This proposition indicates how strongly the neo-Kraepelinians felt the need to counter the influence of psychoanalytic ideas.
9. *In research efforts directed at improving the reliability and validity of diagnoses and classification, statistical techniques should be utilized.* Again, this proposition outlines an agenda—namely, the development of classifications that are reliable and valid.

Reading these propositions more than 20 years later makes one aware of the extent to which the neo-Kraepelinians felt the need to reaffirm the medical and biological aspects of psychiatry. They felt embattled and surrounded by powerful influences that advocated a very different approach. These propositions now seem curiously dated, perhaps indicating the extent to which the neo-Kraepelian movement was successful in achieving its objectives. In many ways these propositions are now widely accepted within the profession, although most would probably express these positions less vehemently. Nevertheless, many of these ideas are part of mainstream psychiatry. Klerman's statements also indicated the importance that the neo-Kraepelinians placed on diagnosis and classification. The way to ensure that their views were adopted was to develop a new classification system. The antipsychiatry movement's concerns about labeling and other negative reactions to psychiatric diagnosis provided an important context that spawned the *DSM-III*, but the neo-Kraepelinian movement provided the agenda (Rogler, 1997).

DSM-III *and Its Successors*

The *DSM-III*, published in 1980, was the culmination of the neo-Kraepelian efforts to reestablish psychiatry as a branch of medicine with diagnosis and classification as fundamental components. The classification took over five years of extensive committee work and consultation to produce. By any criteria, the *DSM-III* was a monumental achievement.

The *DSM-III* differed from the *DSM-II* in four major ways. First, the *DSM-III* adopted diagnostic criteria in order to define the various categories of mental disorders. By using these diagnostic criteria, the intent was to make the diagnostic process more explicit and clearcut, thus improving reliability. Second, the *DSM-III* proposed a multiaxial system of classification. Thus, instead of assigning one diagnosis per patient as was typical with the *DSM-I* and *DSM-II*, clinicians were expected to categorize the patients along five dimensions: (I) symptom picture, (II) personality style, (III) medical disorder, (IV) environmental stressors, and (V) role impairment. Third, the *DSM-III* substantially reorganized the hierarchical arrangement of mental disorder categories. In the *DSM-I* and *DSM-II*, the hierarchical system of organization recognized two fundamental dichotomies: (1) organic vs. nonorganic disorders and (2) psychotic vs. neurotic disorder. The *DSM-III* dropped these dichotomies and instead organized mental disorders under 17 major headings. Fourth, the *DSM-III* was a much larger document than its predecessors. The *DSM-I* contained 108 categories and was 130 pages in length. In contrast, the *DSM-III* had 256 categories and was 494 pages long.

By almost any standard, the *DSM-III* was an astounding success. Financially, it sold very well. As a result of the success of the *DSM-III*, the American Psychiatric Association developed a publication arm of the organization that began to publish a large number of *DSM*-related books and other psychiatric works. Another indication of its success was that the *DSM-III*, although an explicitly American classification, quickly became a more frequently used classification in Europe than did its official international competing classification (*ICD-9*).

Another way of measuring the success of the *DSM-III* is in terms of research. The *DSM-III* stimulated a great deal of research, especially regarding the definitions of the categories proposed in this classification. As a result of this research, the *DSM-III-R* was published in 1987 with the explicit goal of revising the diagnostic criteria for the categories stemming from new research findings. However, like most committee products, the changes from the *DSM-III* to the *DSM-III-R* were not limited to diagnostic criteria. A number of new categories were introduced, especially a group of diagnoses associated with the general category of "sleep disorders." A number of specific categories were revised (e.g., histrionic personality disorder), dropped (attention deficit disorder without hyperactivity), or added (e.g., premenstural syndrome had its name changed and was added to an appendix of the *DSM-III-R*).

Because of the revolutionary impact of the *DSM-III*, the mental disorders section of the *ICD-10* was substantially revised relative to the *ICD-9*. The *ICD-9* had been published in 1977, and the *ICD-9* was very similar to the *ICD-8*. The *ICD-10* represented a substantial change when compared to *ICD-8* or *ICD-9*. The *ICD-10* was published in two versions: a clinical version that contained prose descriptions of categories and a research version that contained diagnostic criteria. However, the *ICD-10* did not adopt a multiaxial system.

As work was progressing on the *ICD-10*, a decision was made to perform another revision of the *DSM-III* that, it was hoped, would make it more similar to the *ICD-10*. The result was the *DSM-IV*, published in 1994. The committee work that went into the creation of the *DSM-IV* was great. The American Psychiatric Association even sponsered special research projects that attempted to empirically resolve important debates that had arisen around classificatory issues. The *DSM-IV* is the largest of the *DSMs* in terms of the shear size of its publication, but it also contains the largest number of categories of any edition of the *DSMs*. Interestingly, different commentators have computed different numbers for the total diagnoses in the *DSM-IV* (cf. Follette & Houts, 1996; Sarbin, 1997; Kutchins and Kirk, 1997; Stone, 1997). Despite the intent of making the *DSM-IV* more like the *ICD-10*, the *DSM-IV* and *ICD-10* are substantially different classifications.

Substantive, Evaulative, and Formal Components of a Classification

Our discussion of contemporary classification will focus on the structure of classifications and on criteria for evaluating them. Regarding structure, a useful distinction is between *substantive* and *for-*

mal components. The *substantive component* describes the domain of mental disorders by defining what a mental disorder is, by identifying individual diagnoses, by formulating diagnostic criteria, and by organizing diagnoses into groups. In contrast, the *formal components* of a classification are concerned with the theoretical principles implicitly and explicitly assumed when creating a classification. The formal components include features such as (1) the organizing principles that structure a classification; (2) the hierarchical structure of a classification; (3) the format used to define specific categories; and (4) the formal procedures used to create and evaluate classificatory systems. The philosopher Gregg (1954), when explicating the characteristics of biological classification, referred to a parallel distinction between taxonomy proper (substantive) and methodological taxonomy (formal).

Besides the formal and structural aspects of a classification, another important aspect is the evaluative component. This refers to the criteria that should be used to assess the utility of a classification for clinical and research purposes. The evaluative components that currently attract attention are reliability, coverage, diagnostic overlap, and validity.

The remainder of this chapter will focus on these three components. The substantive components will be discussed first, followed by the evaluative components because these two domains address relatively practical aspects of classification. The more abstract and complex issue of formal components will be discussed last.

Substantive Components of a Classification

This section will focus on the characteristics of contemporary classifications of psychopathology. Many critical comments of the *DSM-IV*, for instance, can be directed at specific diagnoses. However, our focus will be on the overall characteristics of a classification rather than on features of specific diagnoses within particular classifications. For this reason, the next section focuses on the multiaxial structure of the recent *DSM*s, the use of operational definitions, prose description about the categories, the procedures used to compile the substantive component, and the definition of the concept of "mental disorder."

Multiaxial Classification

An important component of the *DSM-III* and its successors was the use of multiaxial evaluation. Although the concept of multiaxial classification incorporates both substantive and formal components, it is convenient to consider it here. The idea of classifying mental disorders on multiple axes was advanced by Essen-Moller and Wohlfahrt (1947). They proposed separate axes to classify symptoms and etiology because they believed that reliability would be improved by allowing for the classification of cases with a common symptom picture but different etiology. Ottosson and Perris (1973) suggested four axes: symptomatology, severity, course, and etiology. This system, like that proposed by Essen-Moller and Wohlfahrt, replaced traditional diagnostic categories with symptoms and symptom pictures. Rutter, Shaffer, and Sheperd (1975) proposed five axes for classifying childhood disorders: clinical psychiatric syndrome, specific developmental delays, mental retardation and normal intellectual functions, current medical conditions, and current abnormal psychosocial situations. Strauss (1975) also proposed a five-axis system: symptom categories, duration and course, circumstances associated with symptoms (e.g., environmental stresses, physical illness, and substance abuse), quality of relationships, and work functioning.

A multiaxial approach offers several advantages. Coding features on different axes permits a more comprehensive assessment, while separating the different components of the assessment should improve reliability. Given the multidimensional nature of most cases of psychiatric disorder, a major problem is the nature and number of axes. Clearly a balance has to be struck between comprehensiveness, which favors more axes, and pragmatic considerations, which favor fewer axes. The five-axis system for *DSM-III* led to the omission of axes to code features that some clinicians consider important. The failure to include an axis for defenses and coping styles has received the most comment.

The *DSM-III* and subsequent editions proposed the following axes:

Axis I: Clinical syndromes and conditions not attributable to a mental disorderthat are the focus of attention or treatment, and additional codes

Axis II: Personality disorders and specific developmental disorders
Axis III: Physical disorders or conditions
Axis IV: Severity of psychosocial stresses
Axis V: Highest level adaptive functioning in the previous year

Axes I and II provide an exhaustive listing of all mental disorders as understood by the *DSM*. No rationale was offered in *DSM-III* for subdividing mental disorders into clinical syndromes and personality disorders, nor has one been offered in subsequent editions. The reason seems to be an attempt to ensure that personality factors are not overlooked when evaluating patients with florid symptoms that may mask the underlying personality. Millon (1991) suggested that the implicit rationale was that the Axis I disorders were assumed to represent medical disorders for which single, underlying diseases would eventually be identified. In contrast, the Axis II disorders were viewed as representing the entire matrix of the person. However, the lack of a cogent rationale for the Axis I vs. Axis II separation by the authors of the *DSM*s is troublesome, given that subdividing mental disorders into two distinct classes has major theoretical and practical implications.

Operational Definitions

A second major difference between the *DSM-III* and its predecessors was the introduction of specific diagnostic criteria in an attempt to improve reliability. The first "modern" classification system, the *ICD-6*, was a "nomenclature," a list of diagnostic terms sanctioned for use by mental health professionals. None of these categories was defined. The *DSM-I*, published in 1952, and the *DSM-II* offered terse, prose descriptions. The *DSM-II* definition of hysterical (histrionic) personality disorder, for example, was:

> "behavior patterns are characterized by excitability, emotional instability, over-reactivity, and self-dramatization." This self-dramatization is always attention-seeking and often seductive, whether or not the patient is aware of its purpose. These personalities are also immature, self-centered, often vain, and usually dependent upon others. This disorder must be differentiated from Hysterical neurosis. (p. 43)

Because diagnoses were described in general terms, diagnosticians were forced to rely on their own implicit understanding of each diagnosis and their own diagnostic criteria. This inevitably led to diagnostic disagreement.

Hempel (1961) and Stengel (1959) suggested that diagnostic agreement would improve if operational definitions were adopted. As Kendell (1975) commented, the crucial issue was how to reduce the wide range of clinical features to operational definitions. The *DSM-III* solution was to develop both diagnostic criteria sets and rules regarding the number of criteria that needed to be endorsed to establish a diagnosis. The *DSM-III* opted to use polythetic definitions, which list a variety of diagnostic features, only a subset of which must be present to warrant a diagnosis. For instance, the *DSM-III* definition of histrionic personality disorder was:

> The following are characteristic of the individual's current and long-term functioning, are not limited to episodes of illness, and cause either significant impairment in social or occupational functioning or subjective distress.
>
> A. Behavior that is overly dramatic, reactive, and intensely expressed, as indicated by at least three of the following:
>
> 1. Self-dramatization, e.g., exaggerated expression of emotions
> 2. Incessant drawing of attention to oneself
> 3. Craving for activity and excitement
> 4. Overreaction to minor events
> 5. Irrational, angry outbursts or tantrums. (p. 315)

Thus, a major attempt was made to remove the subjective element from diagnosis and to describe criteria precisely by developing more behavioral referents. These developments influenced diagnostic practice and led to improved reliability for many diagnoses. In developing ideas about diagnostic criteria, the *DSM-III* also drew upon the proposals of Feighner and colleagues (1972) that, when necessary, diagnostic criteria include not only features required to make the diagnosis but also features whose presence rules out the diagnosis. By using both inclusion and exclusion criteria it was hoped that the boundaries of each diagnosis would be specified more precisely.

The *ICD*s lagged behind the *DSM*s in the adoption of operational definitions. The first *ICD* to use prose definitions was the *ICD-9*, published in 1978. The *ICD-10*, published in 1992, incorporated diagnostic criteria. Interestingly, the *ICD-10* is published as two manuals: the "green" manual contains diagnostic criteria, and the "blue" manual that contains only prose definitions. The authors of the *ICD-10* believed that the latter would be more user-friendly for clinicians in Third World settings.

Adoption of diagnostic criteria also stimulated the development of semistructured interviews for making diagnoses. The earliest of these interviews, the *Present State Examination*, was developed in the late 1960s (Wing, Cooper, & Sartorius, 1974). Other semistructured interviews became popular after the *DSM-III*, including the *Diagnostic Interview Schedule* (Helzer & Robins, 1988); the *Structured Clinical Interview for the DSM-III-R* (Williams et al., 1992); and the *Structured Interview for the Diagnosis of Personality* (Stangl, Pfohl, Zimmerman, Bowers, & Corenthal, 1985). Semistructured interviews have become standard in research. These interviews are, however, time-consuming to administer and hence they are used infrequently in applied clinical settings. A further problem is that the experience level of the interviewer is important; lay interviewers tend to underdiagnose some conditions and overdiagnose others (Helzer et al., 1985).

Organization of Recent DSMs *by Work Groups*

The process used to formulate and revise the *DSM*s warrants comment. A lengthy consultation process with panels of experts and the profession at large was used to ensure the face or content validity of diagnoses and widespread acceptance of the resulting system. The consultation process was partly a scientific exercise designed to produce a classification based on the best available evidence and expertise, and partly a social-political process designed to ensure the acceptability of the resulting product. Scientific and political objectives often run counter to each other, and compromises were necessary.

With the *DSM-III*, the process was handled by a task force that established advisory committees, each composed of experts whose task was to identify and define diagnostic categories for in their area. Each committee also had a panel of consultants to provide additional advice and information. As the process continued, drafts of *DSM-III* were circulated to the profession for review and comment. Finally, field trials were conducted to evaluate the proposals and identify problems.

While a similar process was used for the *DSM-III-R*, the *DSM-IV* went a stage further. Work groups were established to address specific diagnostic classes. Each group followed a three-stage process. First, comprehensive literature reviews were conducted so that the *DSM-IV* reflected current knowledge. Second, existing data sets were reanalyzed to evaluate diagnostic concepts and to provide information on the performance of diagnostic criteria. Three, extensive field trials were conducted to address specific issues.

There are many laudable features to the process used to revise and develop each edition. Each work group faced a major undertaking that required careful analysis of information and as well as consultation with other experts in the field. This division of labor into work groups probably contributed to the acceptance of the resulting classifications. But there are also problems with the process. The initial structure for the *DSM-III* was established when the work groups were identified. Each was given a defined area of psychopathology. The separation into committees along major topic areas led to both personal and conceptual conflicts. Psychopathology is not readily divisible into discrete areas. Overlap occurred between different committees, leading to dispute. Once a committee was established with a given mandate, however, the committee was reluctant to relinquish domains of psychopathology that might be better classified elsewhere. The superordinate task force was responsible for resolving these disputes and ensuring integration. Inevitably, political processes within and between work groups influenced the solutions adopted.

Definition of Mental Disorder

The definition of the domain to which the *DSM* applies is an important aspect of the substantive component of a classification, one that overlaps with its formal component. The *DSM-III* offers a definition of mental disorder. However, this definition has been extensively criticized (Wakefield, 1993), and the *DSM-III* definition is not used. Lack of a consensual definition of mental disorders has important consequences. Definitions establish boundaries, in this case the boundary regarding what is and what is not a mental disorder, and hence the boundaries of the mental health profession. Without a clear definition of mental disorder, the domain of mental health is fuzzy. Within the profession, the failure to establish an effective definition of the domain leaves the profession without a mechanism to resolve taxonomic disputes about whether a given entity is a mental disorder or not. Thus, as noted earlier, debates have occurred over whether such conditions as homosexuality and masochistic personality disorder are mental disorders. Without an adequate definition of mental disorder such debates can be resolved only by social and political means.

Unfortunately, solutions to this problem are not apparent. Considerable controversy exists not only about the definition of mental disorder but also over whether the conditions classified by psychiatric classifications are mental disorders, mental diseases, or mental illnesses. This situation has prompted some authorities to recommend that the field acknowledge the problem explicitly by recognizing that contemporary classifications are simply classifications of conditions treated by psychiatrists (Guze, 1978; Kendell, 1989).

Evaluative Components of a Classification

Reliability

The reliability of a classification of mental disorders is the degree of diagnostic agreement among users. Reliability is clearly important; diagnoses have little value for communication or prediction if there are high levels of disagreement among clinicians. As Kendell (1975) pointed out, the accuracy of clinical and prognostic decisions based on a diagnosis cannot be greater than the reliability with which the diagnosis is made. Most writers allege that reliability places an upper limit on the validity of a given diagnosis (Spitzer & Fleiss, 1975; Spitzer & Williams, 1980), although Carey and Gottesman (1978) have shown that there are limitations to this assertion.

Reliability is usually evaluated by comparing agreement across several diagnosticians who examine the same patients. Zubin (1967) described three ways of measuring diagnostic reliability: (1) observer agreement, (2) frequency agreement, and (3) consistency. Studies of observer agreement offer the most direct way to assess reliability. Each patient is interviewed by two or more clinicians either conjointly in a single interview, or in separate interviews close together in time. This is the most frequently used method for assessing reliability. Frequency agreement studies compare the proportion of patients allocated to different diagnoses by teams of diagnosticians across two series of patients. If the patients are drawn from similar populations, the frequency of diagnoses should be the same. Studies of consistency compare diagnoses given to a group of patients at two widely separated points of time. Although this method provides useful information, it confounds agreement among clinicians with stability of diagnoses. Problems with either stability or clinician agreement lead to low estimates of reliability.

It is instructive to compare reliability as applied to psychiatric classification with reliability as applied to psychological tests. In test theory, reliability refers to the consistency of scores obtained with the same test on different occasions or with different sets of equivalent items (Anastasi, 1982). If a test is reliable, parallel scales constructed from an equivalent pool of items will yield the same measurement values. The extent to which this does not occur indicates the extent to which measurement is influenced by error.

Traditionally, the reliability of psychological tests is assessed in three ways: (1) The test-retest method assumes that the administration of the same scale at different points in time represents parallel tests. Memory for items is the most common confound with this approach. (2) The alternative form method uses equivalent or parallel measures of the same construct. (3) Internal consistency measures (split-half techniques and coefficient alpha) assume each item on a scale is like a miniature scale. Thus, internal consistency estimates of the extent to which the items in a scale are homogeneous. In psychological testing, this is the most common estimate of reliability. The three methods actually provide different information about the performance of a test. Persons unfamiliar with the psychometric literature often erroneously assume that one method is "better" than another.

These three approaches to reliability can also be applied to the classification of mental disorders. Test-retest measures focus on the temporal stability of psychiatric diagnoses. Unfortunately, the test-retest reliability of diagnoses has received relatively little attention. The relatively few studies on temporal stability are important to note because some disorders, such as the personality disorders, should yield a consistent clinical picture over time.

The homogeneity of diagnoses is also important, but only a few investigators have examined alternative form and internal consistency estimates of diagnostic reliability. Morey (1988) examined the internal consistency of diagnostic criteria for personality disorder, and found low correlations among criteria used to diagnose the same disorder. Steiner, Tebes, Sledge, and Walker (1995) used an alternative form methodology to compare clinical diagnoses based on unstructured interviews with the diagnoses made by different clinicians using a structured interview. Reliability estimates were minimal to low (kappa = .19 to .30).

A diagnosis is usually made after a clinical interview. Kreitman (1961) argued that five sources of variability from interview data can affect diagnostic reliability: (1) variance associated with differences among clinicians making the diagnoses, (2) variance associated with the form of the interview or psychological test, (3) variance across patient characteristics, (4) variance affected by the choice of statistics and methodology to assess reliability, and (5) variance related to the characteristics of the diagnostic system.

1. Variance among clinicians. Traditional sources of variance associated with clinicians include: level of experience, professions training, and personal demographic characteristics. Generally, experience and professional affiliation account for little of the variability in diagnostic decisions. A surprising source of substantial clinician variance has been noted in at least two recent studies. Steiner et al. (1995) compared unstructured and structured interview diagnoses for 100 patients randomly assigned to two treatment settings: an inpatient unit and a day hospital program. The kappa values and the diagnostic distributions were very different in the two settings. Buysse et al. (1994) examined the reliability of *DSM-IV* diagnoses for sleep disorders in five centers in the United States. Again, the kappa estimates and diagnostic frequencies differed markedly across centers. For example, the prevalence of insomnia associated with a mental disorder was 89% in one center and 22% in another. Kappa estimates for interdiagnostician agreement ranged from 0.26 to 0.80 across centers.

2. Variance across forms. Diagnostic disagreement can occur when clinicians have different kinds and amounts of information on which to base diagnosis. This may arise from differences in clinicians' ability to elicit information, the way patients respond to questions, and the availability of information from other sources. Thus, there are important sources of unreliability owing to clinical skill, patient responsiveness, and the diagnostic setting. Most research studies of diagnostic reliability attempt to control for this type of variability by using structured interviews. When these interviews are used, especially by well-trained interviewers, diagnostic reliability can be quite good (Segal, Hersen, & Van Hasselt, 1994). However, studies comparing diagnostic agreement across different structured interviews administered to the same patients have shown lower than expected concordance with kappas in the 0.5 range (Oldham et al., 1992).

3. Variance across patient characteristics. Variations in patient characteristics influence clinicians' diagnostic decisions. For instance, analogue studies, in which clinicians read case histories, show that the sex of the patient can influence the diagnosis of histrionic personality disorder (Warner, 1978; Ford & Widiger, 1988). However, a study in which clinical diagnoses were compared to research diagnoses failed to confirm this result (Morey & Ochoa, 1989). Few studies have examined the influence of variables such as race, older age, and low socioeconomic status on diagnosis. Einfeld and Aman (1995) suggest that reliability in *DSM* diagnoses appears to deteriorate markedly as function of patient IQ scores.

4. Variation across methods. As noted earlier, different methods for assessing reliability are likely to generate different estimates of reliability. Test-retest methods, even over short intervals, can generate different results from case conference or videotape studies. Another source of variability is the statistical procedure used to provide reliability estimates. In earlier years, this was a serious problem (Zubin, 1967). By the mid-1970s, a statistic named kappa became the standard technique for estimating diagnostic reliability. However, a limitation of this statistic is that it is unstable when the base rate of a diagnosis within a sample is less than 5% (Spitznagel & Helzer, 1985).

5. Variation within classificatory systems. Considerable variation in diagnostic reliability occurs across diagnoses. Prior to *DSM-III*, Kreitman (1961)

reported 75% agreement for organic diagnoses, 61% for functional psychosis, and 28% for neurotic disorders. The *DSM-III* led to some improvement (American Psychiatric Association, 1980), but there is still considerable variation across broad categories. For example, in field trials for the most recent edition of the *ICD*, Regier, Kaelber, Roper, Rae, and Sartorius (1994) found average kappa estimates of 0.76, 0.65, and 0.52 for two-point, three-point, and four-point codes in the *ICD-10*. A kappa value of 0.76 is usually considered good to very good (Landis & Koch, 1977). Thus, it appears that the broad diagnostic categories in the *ICD-10* (two-point codes) are used with substantial agreement among clinicians but as diagnoses become more specific (i.e., diagnosing "generalized anxiety disorder" rather than "neurotic disorder"), the typical level of diagnostic agreement decreases. As with the *DSM-III*, the personality disorder diagnoses in the *ICD-10* had the lowest reliability estimates (kappa values of 0.22 to 0.43 for specific personality disorders).

Coverage

The *DSM*, like most classifications, seeks to be exhaustive; diagnostic categories are provided to cover all forms of mental disorder. This is achieved through extensive use of "waste basket" categories such as Anxiety Disorders Not Otherwise Specified (NOS), that ensure all cases can be classified. The use of such categories would not be a problem if they were used infrequently. Unfortunately, this is not the case. For some groups of disorder, the NOS diagnosis is made more frequently than specific diagnoses.

This degree of nonspecificity is a serious problem. It indicates that the system has not developed satisfactory definitions for most conditions that properly fall within the scope of the classification. The problem does not appear to be simply that there are diagnoses that have not been described. Rather, the boundaries of individual diagnoses have not been drawn appropriately and many diagnoses have probably not be conceptualized clearly.

Diagnostic Overlap

Another major problem with the *DSM-IV* and its predecessors is the degree of diagnostic overlap that occurs throughout the classification. For example, about 95% of patients meeting the diagnostic criteria for borderline personality disorder meet the criteria for an additional personality disorder (Widiger et al., 1991). Clearly, the personality disorders diagnoses of *DSM-IV* fail to differentiate among putatively different conditions. This overlap among diagnoses is not unique to personality disorders but occurs across the range of mental disorders.

Validity

The concept of validity as applied to psychiatric classifications has proved more elusive than reliability (McHugh & Slavney, 1983; Spitzer and Williams, 1980). Historically, psychologists faced a similar issue when trying to define the concept of validity as applied to psychological tests. This diversity of ideas about the concept of test validity led the American Educational Research Association, the American Psychological Association, and the National Council on Measurement in Education to join forces to establish a standardized interpretation of types of validity. A manual for evaluating psychological tests, called the *Standards for Educational and Psychological Testing* (American Psychological Association, 1985), organizes validity into three major categories: content, criterion, and construct validity. Because these subtypes of validity are important, they will be described in more detail.

Content Validity

Content validity refers to the extent to which test items represent the behavioral domain measured by the scale. Test items should systematically sample all aspects of the behavioral domain in question. Modern structural approaches to test construction (e.g., Jackson, 1971) use systematic procedures to ensure content validity that involve defining the construct in question and the kinds of behavior believed to represent the construct. Applied to psychiatric disorders, content validity is measured by examining the degree to which the diagnostic criteria represent all symptoms and clinical manifestations of the disorder.

Criterion Validity

Evidence for the criterion validity of psychological tests is usually based on the correlations between scores on the test and scores on outcome or criterion measures. For instance, Zimmerman and Coryell (1987) proposed a brief, 22-item inventory to assess depression, called the Inventory to Diagnose Depression (IDD). When administered with the Beck Depression Inventory and the Hamilton Rating Scale for Depression, the IDD correlated 0.87 and .080 with each measure, respectively. With a psychiatric classification, criterion validity would be determined by correlating diagnostic categories with outcome measures such as treatment response and future clinical status if untreated. Criterion validity is difficult to establish for psychiatric diagnoses partly because treatment specificity is difficult to demonstrate for most mental disorders. Roth and Fonagy (1996) provide an intriguing review of this issue by examining treatment outcome literature for broad categories of psychopathology such as schizophrenia, bipolar disorder, personality disorders, and sexual dysfunctions.

Construct Validity

Construct validity refers to the extent to which a scale measures a construct as that construct is explicated within a particular theory. Loevinger (1957) stated that construct validity "is the whole of validity from a scientific point of view" (p. 636). She suggested that construct validity has three components: substantive, structural, and external. These components are "mutually exclusive, exhaustive of the possible lines of evidence for construct validity, and mandatory." They also incorporate the components of validity discussed above. Others have advanced a similar argument (Guion, 1980; Messick, 1980, 1988). Messick (1988) adopted this perspective when he defined validity as "an integrated, evaluative judgment of the degree to which empirical evidence and theoretical rationales support the *adequacy* and *appropriateness* of *inferences* and *actions* based on test scores or other modes of assessment" (p. 13).

Loevinger's concept of the substantive component resembles content validity. It refers to the degree to which test items are consistent with the theoretical definition of the construct being assessed. Thus, substantive validity encompasses content validity. To evaluate the substantive component of construct validity, an empirical demonstration is required that shows that responses to test items are consistent.

The structural component of construct validity refers to the extent to which structural relationships among test items parallel structural relations of other manifestations of the trait being measured. For most tests, this structure is assumed to be quantitative and correlative; that is, the number of test items endorsed is an index of the degree to which the test is characteristic of the respondent. Therefore, items are expected to intercorrelate. The underlying measurement model usually assumes that the trait in question is continuously distributed, and there is an additional assumption that individuals may be differentiated according to the degree to which the trait is present. Both substantive and structural components of validity deal with the internal structure of the test.

The external component of construct validity is concerned with the correlates of the total test score. External validity rests on evidence that test scores are related to relevant external variables. The type of external relationship that is important is between test scores and other measures of the same construct using different measurement methods. This is usually evaluated using the classical multitrait-multimethod procedure described by Campbell and Fiske (1959). The second type of external relationship is that between test scores and other variables that are predicted on theoretical grounds to be relevant to the construct.

Construct validity can be extended to offer an integrated approach to diagnostic validity. Messick's definition of validity could readily be modified to apply to diagnostic validity: "*Validity is an integrated, evaluative judgment of the degree to which empirical evidence and theoretical rationales support the adequacy and appropriateness of inferences and actions based upon a diagnostic criterion set*" (Messick, 1988, p. 41). Defined in this way, validity is a matter of degree; it is based on the progressive accumulation of evidence. The assessment of validity depends upon the context and purposes for which the diagnosis is made. Kendell (1975) made the same point when he commented that diagnostic validity is largely a matter of the practical value of diagnoses in predicting outcome: "In the last resort all the diagnostic concepts stand all for by the strength of the prospects and therapeutic implications they embody" (p. 140).

As Skinner (1981) noted, the purpose in developing a psychiatric classification is to ensure construct validity. Loevinger's three-component structure to construct validity offers a systematic way to formulate, evaluate, and revise classifications so as to ensure that the objective of a valid system is achieved through an iterative process (Livesley & Jackson, 1991, 1992). The *DSM* system has tended to imply that the first step in compiling a classification was to ensure reliability; validity was assumed to be something to be achieved as reliability is established. The construct validation approach, however, emphasizes the importance of building the conditions for validity into the classification from the outset. This is achieved by developing systematic definitions of diagnoses and using standardized procedures to select diagnostic criteria. Inevitably, this process will lead to findings that are discrepant with the original definition of the diagnosis. Through this iterative process, the definitions of specific mental disorders should consistently increase in validity.

Formal Components of a Classification

Some writers have suggested that biological classification is an example of how classification should be organized, thus the principles of biological classification might provide a model for classifying psychopathology (Meehl, 1995). Biological classification has been successful in providing a structure through which knowledge about living organisms can be organized. An understanding of the reasons for this success and the way biology has approached classification may help to clarify problems in the classification of psychopathology and to identify directions that it may be profitable to pursue. Thus, before discussing the formal components of classifications of psychopathology, a brief overview will be presented about the formal components associated with biological classification.

Formal Components in Biological Classification

There are three different approaches to the classification of living organisms: (1) classical systematics, (2) numerical taxonomy, and (3) cladistics. A fourth approach, ethnobiological classification, deals with the way non-Western cultures classify living things. The implications for classifying psychopathology will be discussed as the formal components of these models are outlined.

Classical Systematics (Set Theory Approach to Classification) With the classical set theory approach, classifications are organized into seven levels or ranks: kingdom, phylum, class, order, family, genus, and species. The classification of humans illustrates this approach:

Kingdom	*Animalia*
Phylum	*Chordate*
Class	*Mammalia*
Order	*Primates*
Family	*Hominidae*
Genus	*Homo*
Species	*Homo sapiens*

Several aspects to this structure should be noted. First, classification has a hierarchical organization. The basic unit of classification is the species. Species are organized into genera that are further organized into families, and so on. The different levels are clearly defined so that the system has an explicit hierarchical structure. Second, the categories are exhaustive and mutually exclusive. Exhaustiveness refers to the fact that categories exist to classify all living things. Exclusiveness refers to the fact that a category at one level of the hierarchy is classified into only one category at a higher level. Exhaustiveness is achieved in biological classifications without the use of "waste basket" categories found in the *DSM*. Third, categories are defined so that the category in question is distinguished from all other categories belonging to the same superordinate category. These categories are usually referred to as a *contrast set*. Thus, definitions focus on distinguishing a group from other groups in its contrast set and not from all other groups in the classification. The *DSM* does not use contrast sets when defining categories at any level. The nearest equivalent is the provision of lists of differential diagnoses for each disorder. Interestingly, these include diagnoses drawn from all parts of the system and not just related diagnoses, as would be the case if contrast sets were used. The strict application of this approach may be difficult to adopt when classifying psychopathology owing to the current state of knowledge. However, this framework may reduce diagnostic overlap for some forms of psychopathology.

A fourth feature of a classical set theory view of biological classification is that there are two broad forms of definition: intensional and extensional. Extensional definitions define a category by listings all members of the set associated with the category. For most categories, it is obviously impractical to list all instances. Intensional definitions, by contrast, define categories by listing the characteristics of individual organisms that are necessary for membership into the categories. Two types of intensional definitions are usually recognized: monothetic and polythetic. Monothetic categories are defined by a set of features that are jointly necessary and sufficient for the diagnosis. For example, a square is defined as having four equal sides and right angles between sides. Polythetic categories are defined by a large number of the attributes, and each member of the category possesses some but not necessarily all of these attributes. Most categories included in the *DSMs* are polythetic. In biology, polythetic categories are defined by a large number of attributes; each member possesses many of these attributes; each attribute is possessed by a large number of members; but no member possesses all attributes (Beckner, 1959). In the *DSM*, categories are defined by a relatively small number of attributes (diagnostic criteria), and the number of diagnostic criteria required to make a diagnosis is specified.

Although classical set theory is often assumed to typify the way biological classification is organized, most biologists reject this approach (Hull, 1988). There are three major problems. The first concerns the way new classifications are created. To develop a new classification using this approach, a set of *characters* would be selected to differentiate among the organisms in question based on characteristics used previously and any other information that was available. This process is potentially circular: characters selected on the basis of current classification of these organisms are used to form a new classification. Not surprisingly, the process tends to yield classifications that are similar to the original. The second difficulty is that the process is highly subjective. Different researchers using the same evidence could generate dissimilar classifications if they interpreted the evidence differently. A third criticism of the classical approach is the limited attention paid to evolutionary theory. In the classical approach, paleontology merely supplies one source of information used to classify species. Many biologists would assert, instead, that the structure of the classification should reflect the course of evolution.

Numerical Taxonomy Numerical taxonomists advocated replacing the circularity and subjectivity inherent in the classical approach with statistical procedures in the form of cluster analysis. Whereas classical systematics uses only a few characteristics when formulating new classifications or new categories, numerical taxonomy takes all available characteristics (variables) and organizes them statistically. From this perspective, the taxa in an ideal taxonomy contain the maximum amount of information because they are based upon as many characteristics as possible (Sokal & Sneath, 1963). Equal weight is given to each characteristic, and the similarity between any two entities is a function of similarities among the variables on which they are compared. Thus, new classifications are the products of empirical investigation that is not influenced by previous, and perhaps mistaken, classifications of the same domain.

The methods of numerical taxonomy yield a hierarchical structure, but this hierarchy has a different organizing principle than the nested-set structure of the classical approach. The hierarchical organization from numerical taxonomy may be represented as a tree diagram in which entities that are most similar fall under the same node in the structure. The hierarchical structure represents degrees of similarity.

Numerical taxonomy was popular in biological classification in the 1960s and 1970s (Sneath & Sokal, 1973) because the use of statistical procedures appeared to avoid bias and theoretical assumptions. These factors also lead to its application to the classification of psychopathology. The emphasis on classifications that were purely empirical and free from theoretical assumptions resonated with similar concerns in the study of psychopathology. Unfortunately, however, difficulties quickly emerged. The concept of similarity, on which the classifications of numerical taxonomy are based, proved to be more complex than was originally thought (Tversky, 1977). In addition, problems emerged with the numerical methods used. Different methods applied to the same data set yielded quite different results. In addition, these numerical methods often failed to identify structure classes in data sets created to contain categories. Interest in numerical taxonomy decreased in both biology and the study of psychopathology. In psychiatry, however, the appeal of a theory free approach to classification continued.

Cladistics The German entomologist Hennig (1950/1966), who believed that the classical approach underemphasized the process of evolution when developing a classification, developed cladistics. With the classical approach, evolutionary data were one source, among many, of information that could be used to develop a classification. With numerical taxonomy, evolutionary processes were not used when developing a classification; rather, they were deduced from the descriptive patterns of similarity that were identified through cluster analytic techniques. In contrast, Hennig maintained that the process of evolutionary change should be at the core of biological classification. Thus, the hierarchical structure of a classificatory system should reflect evolutionary events that led to the emergence of different species. The emergence of a new species must be associated with a new characteristic or set of characteristics that differentiate it from its ancestors. He called these new characteristics *synapomorphies*. Classificatory decisions are made by identifying synapomorphies. The classifications resulting from this approach are hierarchical structures that represent the evolution of the group in question. Cladistics is now the dominant school of biological classification.

The methods and ideas of cladistics cannot easily be applied to the classification of psychopathology. There is, however, one aspect of the cladistic approach that has important implications for classifying psychopathology: the emphasis on theory. For cladistics, theory—evolution—lies at the heart of the classificatory process. This stands in marked contrast to the position adopted by the authors of recent *DSMs*. The fact that cladistics is the dominant school of biological classification suggests that classifications of psychopathology eventually must incorporate theories of psychopathology.

Ethnobiological Classification The last approach to biological classification is ethnobiology, which deals with the way non-Western peoples classify living organisms. Although the relevance of this approach to biological classification initially does not seem plausible, there are remarkable similarities between the structure of folk classifications and the structure of contemporary classifications of mental disorders. Arguably, the *DSMs* show closer resemblance to ethnobiological classifications than to the classifications of scientific biology.

Views on ethnobiological classification are represented most clearly by the work of Berlin (1992). Berlin began studying the classification of living things used by the Tzeltal, a Mayan people living in the Peruvian Andes. Noting that their classification was similar to those described by anthropologists and biologists working with other non-Western peoples, Berlin formulated a set of principles about the way ethnobiological classifications are organized. In particular, he noted that the folk classifications described in diverse studies of non-Western peoples are hierarchical. The universality of hierarchical organization is generally accepted by cultural anthropologists (Atran, 1990).

Berlin claimed this hierarchical structure invariably contains between four and six ranks. These ranks are listed below, along with examples drawn from Western folk classifications.

Kingdom	animal, plant
Life form	tree
Intermediate	evergreen tree
Generic	holly
Specific	live holly
Varietal	variegated holly

The concept of rank parallels the orders, families, genus, species, and so on of the classical approach. Anthropologists debate the actual number of ranks in folk classifications. To understand these ideas, three ranks will be discussed.

1. Generic rank. The generic rank is the most important of the six. Generic categories are the "natural taxa" of folk classifications, and they occur in the middle of the hierarchy of ranks. They usually have a simple one-word or even one syllable name (e.g., "cat," "dog," "pine," "oak"). Generic categories are the most salient categories of living organisms in folk classifications. They are used frequently in everyday discourse because they refer to objects that are common in the environments of the group. These categories are reliably identified by almost speakers of a language, including children. Indeed, the names for these categories are among the first words encountered when learning the language. Further, most generic categories can be unambiguously assigned to superordinate, life-form categories.

Berlin claimed that generic categories typically correspond to genus-level (or, sometimes, species-level) categories in scientific classifications. Thus, the category of "cat" in our folk classification serves as a name for the species *Felis catus*. Dwyer (1977), in his study of the Rofaifo people, found that two thirds of the scientific species of mammals existing in the New Guinea environment of these people corresponded to generic categories in their folk classification.

2. Kingdom rank. The major feature of this rank is its taxonomic properties. Such a category is often called a "unique beginner" because it is the highest level of the classification and includes all other categories. Examples in our folk classification are "plant" and "animal." Users of folk classifications have difficulty defining kingdom-level categories, and most classifications do not have names or even simple phrases for them. When anthropologists inquire about the most inclusive category in botanical classification, they elicit comments such as "those things that do not walk, do not move, possess roots and are all planted in the earth," "all leaves," or "green things that try to reach the sun." Similarly, most mental health professions would have difficulty defining the unique beginner for psychiatric classifications. Is it "mental disorder," "mental illness," "problems in living," or "conditions treated by mental health professionals"?

3. Specific ranks. Categories at this level are subsets of generic categories that are the lowest ranks of ethnobiological classifications. They often have a binomial form of a name that usually includes the generic category name of which it is a subset. Examples are "Persian cat," "Siamese cat" and "Angora cat." Specific categories refer to subsets of generic categories that are particularly important to the users of the classification. The Rofaifo, for example, have three specific categories ("Mi foi," "Mi sevi," and "Mi noi") that refer to subdivisions of Australian possum. These varieties of possum are differentiated by their fur, which has various uses to Rofaifo people.

This structure of ranks is similar to the hierarchical structure of the *DSM-IV*, which also has four to six ranks (e.g., mental disorders → personality disorders → cluster A → schizotypal personality disorder; or mental disorders → mood disorders → bipolar disorder → single manic episode). The users of folk classifications do not have a name for the ranks—it is an implicit structure. Similarly, the ranks in the *DSM* are not defined nor is there a clear understanding of what the different ranks specify. With folk classifications, the hierarchical structure appears to serve the function of cognitive economy. These classifications typically describe 500 categories regardless of the richness of the local fauna and flora. Perhaps, 500 categories is approximately the maximum number of categories that can be retained in memory using a hierarchical structure. As noted, the *DSM-IV* has nearly 400 categories.

The hierarchical structure of folk classifications is irregular for several reasons. First, there are a few categories that do not clearly belong to a particular rank. An example in the Rofaifo classification of small mammals is the category "Yabo" (dog). It is unclear whether this is a life-form or generic category. The category immediately above Yabo is the "unique-beginner" of this classification. However, "Yabo" is not subdivided into generic categories. The *DSM* has similar anomalies. Consider schizophrenia. This term is used as a specific diagnosis and as the name for one of the 17 higher order grouping—"schizophrenia and other psychotic disorders"—listed immediately below the unique beginner of "mental disorders." Moreover, it is unclear whether schizophrenia is a single entity or a group of disorders. Second, the organization of the lower level categories into higher order categories does not necessarily adhere to the principle of "mutual exclusivity." A given category can be subsumed under two or more higher level categories. Similarly, schizoaffective disorder is sometimes classified under mood disorders and sometimes under schizophrenia.

Formal Components of Classifications of Psychopathology

The ideas derived from the summary of biological classification will now be used to comment on two formal components for the classification of psychopathology.

Organizing Principles A fundamental decision when developing a classification concerns the type of diagnostic concepts that should be used to organize information about psychopathology. In concrete terms, this decision often has been seen as reducing to a choice between categories and dimensions. There are, however, other approaches that also warrant attention. The range of psychopathology covered by the *DSM* is extensive. Different types of diagnostic concepts may be required for different forms of psychopathology.

1. Dimensions. With a categorical model, psychopathology is classified using criteria sets that are discrete, mutually exclusive, and exhaustive. Individuals assigned to a given category are assumed to be relatively homogeneous in respect to a given set of characteristics. In contrast, a dimensional system describes psychopathology using a series of reasonably independent dimensions along which individuals are described in quantitative terms. For example, in a categorical system, a person is considered depressed or not depressed, and all depressed persons are considered to be essentially similar. In contrast, in a dimensional system, depression is assessed in terms of degree, with some depressed persons being more depressed than others.

Most classifications of psychopathology employ categories because they offer certain advantages. In everyday life, categorical concepts are used because they are familiar and easy. Clinicians also tend to think in terms of categorical diagnoses, and many clinical decisions are categorical—for example, whether a case needs treatment or not. The tendency to think categorically should not be underestimated. The discussion of folk classifications indicated that categories are used extensively within a hierarchical structure. This suggests that they are the product of universal cognitive mechanisms that evolved as adaptive ways of managing information (Atran, 1990). These adaptations structure experience and thought. It is not surprising, therefore, that people, including clinicians, prefer to use concepts that are the products of these mechanisms or, at least, are consistent with them.

There are, however, substantial disadvantages to using categories. Categorical diagnoses often result in the loss of some information. Because most cases present with features of multiple disorders, categorical systems generate extensive diagnostic overlap—a circumstance that is usually referred to, perhaps somewhat misleadingly, as comorbidity (Regier et al., 1994). These multiple features tend to be overlooked in categorical systems because clinicians usually underestimate the number of diagnostic categories that are appropriate for patients (Morey & Ochoa, 1989). Categorical systems also depend on boundaries or at least points of rarity between syndromes (Kendell, 1975, 1989). But there is little convincing evidence for the existence of discontinuities in psychopathology (Cloninger, Martin, Guze & Clayton, 1985). Instead, categories tend to merge with each other, and the boundaries appear arbitrary (Kendell, 1989). This overlap probably explains why cluster analytic studies have failed to generate consistent results across studies and why the issue of comorbidity has attracted so much attention (Maser & Cloninger, 1990).

These problems have prompted a growing number of authors to argue that dimensional systems are more appropriate ways to represent psychopathology (Eysenck, 1960; Costa & Widiger, 1994). Dimensional systems result in little information loss because patients are evaluated on all dimensions. Such systems do not require discontinuities among syndromes or between normality and pathology. Dimensional systems, however, also have disadvantages. First, these systems are often considered more cumbersome and less user-friendly in clinical settings. The problem with user-friendliness, however, might be obviated by potential increases in reliability. Heumann and Morey (1990), for example, showed that a dimensional system increased the reliability of personality disorder assessment. Second, it is difficult to determine the nature and number of dimensions required to provide an adequate representation of psychopathology. Despite an extensive history of dimensional analyses of psychopathology, there is little consensus on which dimensions are most appropriate. Finally, most clinical decisions are binary (e.g., whether to admit to hospital, and whether to treat with medication). Hence, dimensional evaluations must be converted into functional categories at some point along the continuum.

Initial proposals of dimensional models were made in studies of schizophrenia and the functional psychoses (Moore, 1930; Wittenborn, 1962). More recently, debate over the relative merits of categorical and dimensional models has been most intense for the personality disorders. Multiple lines of evidence converge in support of a dimensional representation of this domain of psychopathology (Widiger, 1993). Nevertheless, *DSM-IV* retained a categorical approach. Political, philosophical, and practical considerations appeared to outweigh scientific evidence when making this decision.

2. Categories. A common view of categories is to think of them as mutually exclusive sets. Class membership is determined by the definition of the categories. If a patient meets definitional criteria, then the patient is said to belong to the set. Two

definitional forms have been used in psychiatric classification: monothetic and polythetic definitions. Before the *DSM-III*, most definitions of specific mental disorders were implicitly monothetic. In the 1960s, numerical taxonomists argued that the categories in biological classification are polythetic (Hull, 1988). The mental health field adopted this approach. Since the publication of the *DSM-III*, polythetic definitions of mental disorders have been standard in psychiatric classifications. Note, however, that although diagnostic concepts used by the *DSM-IV* are described as polythetic, they differ substantially from Beckner's (1959) definition. Most disorders are defined by relatively few criteria. Moreover, some features are shown by only a few cases. Interestingly, as psychiatry began to adopt the polythetic approach, numerical taxonomy was superseded by cladistics. In cladistics, monothetic definitions are standard.

3. Prototypes. An alternative approach has been proposed for diagnoses, especially for the personality disorders. This involves the concept of "prototype" (Cantor & Messich, 1980; Livesley, 1985). Prototypic categories are organized around exemplars (the best examples of the concept) with less prototypical examples forming a continuum of psychological distance from these central cases (Rosch, 1978). Unlike polythetic categories in which category membership is an all or none matter, prototypic categories assume a gradient of membership with some cases being more prototypical of the concept than others. Prototypes appear to capture the way clinicians use diagnostic concepts better than either monothetic or polythetic categories (Livesley, 1985, 1986, 1991). Clinicians frequently refer to patients as a typical case of depressive disorder or a classical borderline personality disorder.

4. Ideal types. The concept of prototype is related to another classificatory concept, the ideal type (Jaspers, 1963; Schwartz, Wiggins, & Norko, 1989; Wiggins & Schwartz, 1994). According to Jaspers, somatic illnesses associated with psychological disturbances are either present or absent. Neuroses and abnormal personality, however, are better classified using the concept of ideal type, a hypothetical construct "denoting the configuration of characteristics which on the basis of theory and observations, are assumed to be interrelated" (Wood, 1969, p. 227). Actual cases that match the ideal in all respects are rare. An ideal typology, according to Jaspers, consists of a series of opposites, such as introversion versus extroversion, or submission versus dominance. By comparing an individual to these contrasting poles, the person's personality and behavior is illuminated. Ideal types sometimes are discussed as if they are categorical diagnoses, but they are not diagnoses in the usual sense (Schneider, 1959). Instead, the typology provides a framework to guide clinical inquiry and to organize an understanding of individual cases.

5. Theoretical, measurement, and diagnostic models. From this brief discussion, the selection of the type of classificatory concept to use is fundamental to the development of a classification. Interestingly, the editions of the *DSM* barely discuss this issue. Polythetic categories are adopted with little exploration of the implications of the decision. The choice of the classificatory concept is fundamental, however, because the different classificatory concepts are associated with different measurement models. When discussing these issues it is important to distinguish three levels of analysis and conceptualization: theoretical, measurement, and diagnostic models (Livesley & Jackson, 1992).

The theoretical model is a conceptualization of the way psychopathology is organized. For example, one might view borderline personality disorder as a distinct entity (category) that is manifested through a series of symptoms or as a trait (dimension) that varies in the extent to which it is present in various individuals. The measurement model describes the structural relationships among diagnostic criteria. In the case of a polythetic categorical model, for example, criteria are summed only until a specified number is deemed to be present, whereupon the diagnosis is said to be present. The presence of more or fewer features than the threshold is not considered to have any significance. The measurement model associated with a dimensional representation of psychopathology has a different structure: the model is cumulative, the number of diagnostic features observed is an index of the degree to which the diagnostic entity is present. Under this model, diagnoses have a specific structure; diagnostic items are expected to intercorrelate. When constructing a criterion set, the object is to compile a criterion set that meets the requirements of a statistical measure of homogeneity.

Measurement and theoretical models should be consistent—a categorical theoretical model implies a categorical measurement model. The diagnostic model specifies the way the diagnosis is represented and communicated. It is useful to distinguish between measurement and diagnostic models because a dimensional model could be converted into a categorical diagnostic model through the use of cutting scores. Thus, the choice of a classificatory concept is associated with choices among the form of theoretical models that researchers might use to explain psychopathology. For classifications of psychopathology to be coherent, the issue of selecting classificatory concepts must be dealt with explicitly.

Jaspers suggested that different classificatory models might be required for different forms of psychopathology. This idea has considerable merit. Some conditions, especially those traditionally described as organic disorders, are similar to diagnoses in physical medicine. These could probably best be represented using a categorical model in which diagnoses are specified by polythetic definitions. Other areas of psychopathology especially the neuroses and personality disorders are probably best represented using a dimensional framework. Theoretical and measurement models for these disorders would be dimensional, and cut-offs would be required for specific treatment decisions. Jaspers's point is important and has a certain plausibility—psychopathology covers a broad spectrum of behaviors. The types of classificatory concepts and associated theoretical issues may not be sufficiently homogeneous to restrict entire systems to a single approach.

Hierarchical Structure Classifications of mental disorders, including *DSM-IV*, are hierarchically organized. For example, the 10 personality disorder diagnoses are organized into three clusters that, in turn, are grouped under the general heading "personality disorder." Similarly, the mood (affective) disorders in the *ICD-10* are divided into manic episode, bipolar affective disorder, depressive episode, recurrent depressive disorder, and persistent mood disorders. Each category is subdivided further. For example, persistent mood disorders are subdivided into cyclothymia and dysthymia. Further subdivisions exist for some categories.

Unfortunately, the reasoning behind the hierarchical structure of both the *DSM-IV* and the *ICD-10* is unclear. The number of levels or ranks in the hierarchy varies substantially according to diagnostic grouping. No explanation is provided for this marked variation in the complexity of the hierarchical schemes. Nor is it clear whether the hierarchical structure reflects fundamental divisions in the way psychopathology is organized or whether it is simply a convenient way to organize information. For example, the reason for organizing personality disorders into three clusters was that the committee on the *DSM-III* felt that 11 disorders were too many to remember easily. Nevertheless, the three clusters have been interpreted as having more substantive meaning than originally intended, and several empirical studies have evaluated this structure (Hyler & Lyons, 1988; Kass, Skodol, Charles, Spitzer, & Williams, 1985).

Higher level categories are inclusive of categories at lower levels. Thus, the category named cluster A includes schizoid, schizotypal, and paranoid personality disorders. This idea is consistent with the set theory approach to biological classification. Categories toward the top of the hierarchies are relatively broad sets that include subsidiary categories as subsets. Thus, every schizoid patient is a member of cluster A.

This hierarchical arrangement is different from other hierarchical organizations of psychopathology. Foulds (1965; Foulds & Bedford, 1975), for example, noted that there is a "pecking order" among diagnostic categories (Kendell, 1975). The first categories that clinicians appear to consider when diagnosing a patient are the organic mental disorders (or cognitive disorders). If the evidence justifies this type of diagnosis, the diagnostic process ends even if the patient shows features of other conditions, such as a depressive disorder, because the presence of an organic mental disorder can explain depression. The second major category considered is schizophrenia and related psychoses. The third category to consider is severe mood disorders. Finally, the neuroses and personality disorders are considered.

With this type of hierarchical structure, diagnosis at a given level excludes the presence of symptoms from higher levels in the hierarchy, but includes possible symptoms at all lower levels. This arrangement has several appealing features. It establishes a formal structure to psychiatric diagnoses that is lacking in classifications such as the *DSM-IV*. It also accounts for diagnostic overlap; a patient with a disorder classified at one of the higher levels is likely to show symptoms associated with disorders lower in the hierarchy. Whereas a patient with a disorder classified at the lowest level is unlikely to show features of higher order diagnoses. While the evidence does not support the specific hierarchy proposed by Foulds, the idea of a hierarchy based on subordinate and superordinate ranks has merit. A similar idea was introduced in parts of the *DSM-III*; some diagnoses excluded the diagnosis of other categories. For instance, a diagnosis of schizophrenia excluded the diagnosis of delusional disorder (First, Spitzer, & Williams, 1990). However, empirical studies did not support these exclusionary rules (Boyd et al., 1984).

Future Directions for Classification

Although psychiatric classification has made considerable progress over the last few decades, there is much to be achieved before a valid system is established. The conceptual problems confronting psychiatric nosology have not received the attention that they deserve and most conceptual issues are unresolved. The brief review of biological classification did not identify a model that psychiatry could directly assume. It did, however, point to several directions that psychiatric classification could profitably pursue. Progress in biological classification is due to two factors. First, the unique beginner (living things) and, what is more important, the entities being classified (species) are clearly understood. Although some disagreement exists about the formal definition of species, major species are readily identified by all. Interestingly, medicine also has the advantage that many basic conditions are manifested through a cluster of symptoms and signs that are readily observed and identified. Once the 18th-century physician Sydenham had proposed the concept of syndrome as a way to organize observations, progress in classification and diagnosis became possible. The mental health disciplines have not, however, resolved the issue of what is being classified—mental disorder, mental illnesses, problems in living, or conditions treated by psychiatrists, to list the main contenders. Unlike most species of living organisms, basic (generic rank) categories of mental disorders are not readily identified. The boundaries between most categories in the *DSM*s are imprecise. These are fundamental problems that must be resolved if further progress can be made in psychiatric nosology.

The second factor responsible for progress in biological classification is the availability of a powerful theory—the theory of evolution—that provides the organizing principles on which the classification is based. The current model of biological classification, cladistics, places theory at the heart of the nosological process. Similarly, the construct validation approach to psychological assessment emphasizes the importance of theory. Theoretical definitions of constructs are the starting points of measurement and the test construction process becomes a vehicle to refine these definitions. The success of biology and the more limited success of psychological assessment raise the question of how long psychiatry can afford to maintain an atheoretical stance. Two major obstacles stand in the way of such developments. First, the success of recent editions of *DSM* in improving reliability has created a climate in which atheoretical approaches to classification appear, with some justification, to be successful; there is little doubt that the *DSM-III* was a substantially improvement. Attempts to move psychiatric classification in the direction of developing a theoretical basis is likely to meet considerable resistance. Second, a theory of psychopathology that could form the basis for such efforts is not available. Moreover, such a theory seems improbable. Psychopathology is too diverse to be explained by a single all-embracing theory. Progress seems more likely if the implications of this diversity are recognized and different approaches are used to deal with the different forms of psychopathology. In this respect, psychiatry may have something to learn from the way physical medicine has dealt with classification and diagnosis.

Medicine has been much less preoccupied with the problem of classification than psychiatry, yet much progress has been made in delineating disorders. Of course, the problems that medicine faces are, in some respects, less complex. The major signs and symptoms of most disorders are readily perceived and identified. In most cases, they are also qualitatively distinct from normality and from each other. Moreover, the etiology, or at least the pathophysiology, of many conditions is known and this knowledge is useful in delineating conditions. Ultimately, progress in psychiatric classification may have to await further progress in understanding the pathophysiology of mental disorders. Meanwhile, other aspects of the approach of medicine may be worth adopting. Progress was achieved by focusing on limited areas and progressively delineating disorders within these areas. This more focal approach has to some extent been successful in psychiatry, but the impact of "official" classifications may hinder the application of this approach. The other major problem that the classification of psychopathology faces is that many of the features of diagnostic entities are not apparent in the way the characteristics of species or the signs of illness are apparent. Many of these features are inferences rather than simple observations. This is one reason the construct validity approach of psychological assessment has relevance. It offers an iterative procedure to define and refine constructs leading to incremental improvements in validity.

Livesley and Jackson (1992) outlined some general principles for developing, evaluating, and revising classifications of personality disorder that apply to the classification of mental disorders generally. First, classifications should be specified in a testable way. This means that the theoretical and conceptual basis of the classification and each diagnosis should be stated and that explicit procedures be used to develop, evaluate, and revise the system. Second, the prerequisites for validity should be incorporated into the system from the outset. Third, the classification should be stated in such a way that it can be revised systematically on the basis of empirical evaluation. Evaluations of *DSM* diagnoses often reveal deficiencies but not specific remedies. An iterative procedure needs to be established whereby criteria sets are developing on the basis of explicit definitions of diagnoses and then subjected to evaluation in ways that lead to modifications in the original formulation. If the classification was defined and structured in this way, the classification could be modified sequentially so that it progressively evolves into an empirically testable system with adequate construct validity. This approach seems more likely to yield useful classification than do current methods that employ committee systems to make intermittent radical revisions of *DSM*s.

References

American Psychiatric Association (1980). *Diagnostic and statistical manual.* (3rd ed.). Washington, DC: Author.

American Psychological Assocation. (1985). *Standards for educational and psychological testing.* Washington, DC: Author.

Anastasi, A. (1982). *Psychological testing* (5th ed.). New York: Macmillan.

Ash, P. (1949). The reliability of psychiatric diagnoses. *Journal of Abnormal and Social Psychology, 44,* 272–276.

Atran, S. (1990). *Cognitive foundations of natural science.* Cambridge: Cambridge University Press.

Beck, A. T. (1962). Reliability of psychiatric diagnoses: A critique of systematic studies. *American Journal of Psychiatry, 119,* 210–216.

Beckner, M. (1959). *The biological way of thought.* New York: Columbia University Press.

Berlin, B. (1992). *Ethnobiological classification: Principles of categorization of plants and animals in traditional societies.* Princeton, NJ: Princeton University Press.

Berrios, G. E., & Hauser, R. (1988). The early development of Kraepelin's ideas on classification: A conceptual history. *Psychological Medicine, 18,* 813–821.

Boyd, J. H., Burke, J. D., Gruenberg, E., Holzer, C. E., Rae, D. S., George, L. K., Karno, M., Stoltzman, R., McEvoy, L., & Nestadt, G. (1984). Exclusion criteria of DSM-III: A study of co-occurrence of hierarchy-free syndromes. *Archives of General Psychiatry, 41,* 983–989.

Buysse, D. J., Reynolds, C. F., Hauri, P. J., Roth, T., Stepanski, E. J., Thorpy, M. J., Bixler, E. O., Kales, A., Manfredi, R. L., Vgontzas, A. N., Stapf, D. M., Houck, P. R., & Kupfer, D. J. (1994). Diagnostic concordance for DSM-IV sleep disorders: A report from the APA/NIMH DSM-IV field trials. *American Journal of Psychiatry, 151,* 1351–1360.

Campbell, D. T., & Fiske, D. W. (1959). Convergent and discriminant validation by the multitrait-multimethod matrix. *Psychological Bulletin, 56,* 81–105.

Cantor, N., Smith, E. E., French, R., & Mezzich, J. (1980). Psychiatric diagnosis as prototype categorization. *Journal of Abnormal Psychology, 89,* 181–193.

Carey G., & Gottesman, I. I. (1978). Reliability and validity in binary ratings. *Archives of General Psychiatry, 35,* 1454–1459.

Cloninger, C. R., Martin, R. L., Guze, S. B., & Clayton, P. J. (1985). Diagnosis and prognosis in schizophrenia. *Archives of General Psychiatry, 42,* 15–25.

Compton, W. M., & Guze, S. B. (1995). The neo-Kraepelinian revolution in psychiatric diagnosis. *European Archives of Psychiatry and Clinical Neuroscience, 245,* 196–201.

Cooper, J. E., Kendell, R. E., Gurland, B. J., Sharpe, L., Copeland, J. R. M., & Simon, R. (1972). *Psychiatric diagnosis in New York and London.* Maudsley Monograph No. 20, London: Oxford University Press.

Costa, P. T., & Widiger, T. A. (Eds.). (1994). *Personality disorders and the five factor model of personality.* Washington, DC: American Psychological Association.

Dwyer, P. D. (1977). An analysis of Rofaifo mammal taxonomy. *American Ethnologist, 4,* 425–445.

Einfeld, S. L., & Amen, M. (1995). Issues in the taxonomy of psychopathology of mental retardation. *Journal of Autism and Developmental Disorders, 25,* 143–167.

Essen-Moller, E., & Wohlfahrt, S. (1947). Suggestions for the amendment of the official Swedish classification of mental disorders. *Acta Psychiatrica Scandinavica, 47* (Suppl.), 551.

Eysenck, H. J. (1961). Classification and the problem of diagnosis. In H. J. Eysenck (Ed.), *Handbook of abnormal psychology.* (pp. 1–31). London: Pitman.

Feighner, J. P., Robins, E., Guze, S. B., Woodruff, R. A., Winokur, G., & Munoz, R. (1972). Diagnostic criteria for use in psychiatric research. *Archives of General Psychiatry, 26,* 57–63.

First, M. B., Spitzer, R. L., and Williams, J. B. W. (1990). Exclusionary principles and the comorbidity of psychiatric diagnoses: A historical review and implications for the future. In J. D. Maser and C. R. Cloninger (Eds.), *Comorbidity of mood and anxiety disorders* (pp. 83–109). Washington, DC: American Psychiatric Press.

Follette, W. C., & Houts, A. C. (1996). Models of scientific progress and the role of theory in taxonomy development: A case study of the DSM. *Journal of Consulting and Clinical Psychology, 64,* 1120–1132.

Ford, M., & Widiger, T. A. (1988). Sex bias in the diagnosis of histrionic and antisocial personality disorders. *Journal of Consulting and Clinical Psychology, 57,* 301–305.

Foucault, M. (1988). *Politics, philosophy, and culture.* London: Routledge.

Foulds, G. A. (1965). *Personality and personal illness.* London: Tavistock Publications.

Foulds, G. A., & Bedford, A. (1975). A hierarchy of classes of mental illness. *Psychological Medicine, 5,* 181–192.

Goffman, E. (1959). The moral career of the mental patient. *Psychiatry, 22,* 123–142.

Goffman, E. (1963). *Stigma.* Englewood Cliffs, NJ: Prentice-Hall.

Gregg, J. R. (1954). *The language of taxonomy.* New York: Columbia University Press.

Guion, R. M. (1980). On trinitarian doctrines of validity. *Professional Psychology, 11,* 385–398.

Guze, S. B. (1978). Nature of psychiatric illness: Why psychiatry is a branch of medicine. *Comprehensive Psychiatry, 19,* 295–307.

Havens, L. (1981). Twentieth-century psychiatry: A view from the sea. *American Journal of Psychiatry, 138,* 1279–1287.

Havens, L. (1985). Historical perspectives on diagnosis in psychiatry. *Comprehensive Psychiatry, 26,* 326–336.

Helzer, J. E., & Robins, L. N. (1988). The diagnostic interview schedule: Its development, evolution, and use. *Social Psychiatry & Psychiatric Epidemiology, 23,* 6–16.

Helzer, J. E., Robins, L. N., McEvoy, L. T., Spitznagel, E. L., Stoltzman, R. K., Farmer, A., & Brockington, I. F. (1985). A comparison of clinical and diagnostic interview schedules: Physician reexamination of lay-interviewed cases in the general population. *Archives of General Psychiatry, 42,* 657–666.

Hempel, C. G. (1961). Introduction to problems of taxonomy. In J. Zubin (Ed.), *Field studies in the mental disorders* (pp. 3–22). New York: Grune & Stratton.

Hennig, W. (1966). *Phytogenic systematics.* (D. D. Davis & R. Zangerl , trans.). Urbana: University of Illinois Press. (Original work published 1950)

Heumann, K. A., & Morey, L. C. (1990). Reliability of categorical and dimensional judgments of personality disorder. *American Journal of Psychiatry, 147,* 498–500.

Hull, D. L. (1988). *Science as a process.* Chicago, IL: University of Chicago Press.

Hyler, S. E., & Lyons, M. (1988). Factor analysis of the DSM-III personality disorder clusters: A replication. *Comprehensive Psychiatry, 29,* 304–308.

Jackson, D. N. (1971). The dynamics of structured personality tests. *Psychological Review, 78,* 229–248.

Jaspers, K. (1963). *General psychopathology.* (J. Hoenig & M. W. Hamilton, Trans.). Manchester: University of Manchester Press.

Kahn, E. (1959). The Emil Kraepelin memorial lecture. In B. Pasamanick (Ed.), *Epidemiology of mental disorders* (pp. 1–38). Washington, DC: AAAS.

Kass, F., Skodol, A. E., Charles, E., Spitzer, R. L., & Williams, J. B. W. (1985). Scaled ratings of DSM-III personality disorders. *American Journal of Psychiatry, 142,* 627–630.

Kendell, R. E. (1975). *The role of diagnosis in psychiatry.* Blackwell: Oxford.

Kendell, R. E. (1989). Clinical validity. In L. N. Robins & J. E. Barrett (Eds.), *The validity of psychiatric diagnosis* (pp. 305–321). New York: Raven Press.

Kendell, R. E. (1990). A brief history of psychiatric classification in Britain. In N. Sartorius, A. Jablensky, D. A. Regier, J. D. Burke Jr., & R. M. A. Hirschfeld (Eds.), *Sources and traditions of psychiatric classification* (pp. 139–151). Toronto: Hogrefe & Huber.

Kendell, R. E., Cooper, J. E., Gourlay, A. J., Sharpe, L., & Gurland, B. J. (1971). Diagnostic criteria of American and British psychiatrist. *Archives of General Psychiatry, 25,* 123–130.

Kirk, S. A., & Kutchins, H. (1992). *The selling of DSM: The rhetoric of science in psychiatry.* Hawthorne, NY: William deGruyter.

Klerman, G. L. (1977). Mental illness, the medical model and psychiatry. *Journal of Medicine and Philosophy,* 2, 220–243.

Klerman, G. L. (1978). The evolution of a scientific nosology. In J. C. Shershow (Ed.), *Schizophrenia : Science and practice* (pp. 104–105). Cambridge, MA.: Harvard University Press.

Kreitman, N. (1961). The reliability of psychiatric diagnosis. *Journal of Mental Science, 107,* 876–886.

Kutchins, H., & Kirk, S. A. (1997). *Making us crazy.* New York: Free Press.

Landis, J. R., & Koch, G. G. (1977). The measurement of observer agreement for categorical data. *Biometrics, 33,* 159–174.

Lewis, A. J. (1978). Preface. In World Health Organization, *Mental disorders: Glossary and guide to their classification in accordance with the Ninth Revision of the International Classification of Diseases.* Geneva: World Health Organization.

Livesley W. J. (1985). The classification of personality disorder: I. The choice of category concept. *Canadian Journal of Psychiatry, 30,* 353–358.

Livesley W. J. (1986). Trait and behavioral prototypes of personality disorder. *American Journal of Psychiatry, 143,* 728–732.

Livesley, W. J. (1991). Classifying personality disorders: Ideal types, prototypes, or dimensions. *Journal of Personality Disorders, 5,* 52–59.

Livesley, W. J., & Jackson, D. N. (1991). Construct validity and the classification of personality disorders. In J. Oldham (Ed.), *Personality disorders: New perspectives on diagnostic validity* (pp. 3-22). Washington, DC: American Psychiatric Press.

Livesley, W. J., & Jackson, D. N. (1992). Guidelines for developing, evaluating, and revising the classification of personality disorders. *Journal of Nervous and Mental Disease, 180,* 609–618.

Loevinger, J. (1957). Psychological tests as instruments of psychological theory. *Psychological Reports, 3,* 635–694.

Maser J. D., & Cloninger, C. R. (Eds.). (1990). *Comorbidity of mood and anxiety disorders.* Washington, DC: American Psychiatric Press.

Masserman, J. H., & Carmichael, H. T. (1938). Diagnosis and prognosis in psychiatry. *Journal of Mental Science, 84,* 893–946.

McHugh, P. R., & Slavney, P. R. (1983). *The perspectives of psychiatry.* Baltimore: John Hopkins University Press.

Meehl, P. E. (1995). Bootstraps taxometrics: Solving the classification problem in psychopathology. *American Psychologist, 50,* 266–275.

Menninger, K. (1963) *The vital balance.* New York: Viking.

Messick, S. (1980). Test validity and the ethics of assessment. *American Psychologist, 11,* 1012–1027.

Messick, S. (1988). Validity. In R. L. Linn (Ed.), *Educational measurement* (3rd ed., pp. 13–103). New York: Macmillan.

Millon, T. (1991). Classification in psychopathology: Rationale, alternatives, and standards. *Journal of Abnormal Psychology, 3,* 245–261.

Moore, T. V. (1930). The empirical determination of certain syndromes underlying praecox and manic-depressive psychoses. *American Journal of Psychiatry, 86,* 719–738.

Morey, L. C. (1988). Personality disorders in the DSM-III and DSM-III-R: Convergence, coverage and internal consistency. *American Journal of Psychiatry, 145,* 573–577.

Morey, L. C., & Ochoa, E. S. (1989). An investigation of clinical adherence to diagnostic criteria: Clinical diagnosis of DSM-III personality disorders. *Journal of Personality Disorders, 3,* 180–192.

Oldham, J. A., Skodol, A. E., Kellman, H. D., Hyler, S. E., Resnick, L., & Davies, M. (1992). Diagnosis of DSM-III-R personality disorders by two structured interviews: Patterns of comorbidity. *American Journal of Psychiatry, 149,* 213–220.

Ottosson, J. O., & Perris, C. (1973). Multidimensional classification of mental disorders. *Psychological Medicine, 3,* 238.

Regier, D. A., Kaelber, C. T., Roper, M. T., Rae, D. S., & Sartorius, N. (1994). The ICD-10 clinical field trial for mental and behavioral disorders: Results in Canada and the United States. *American Journal of Psychiatry, 151,* 1340–1350.

Rogler, L. H. (1997). Making sense of historical changes in the Diagnostic and Statistical Manual of Mental Disorders: Five propositions. *Journal of Health and Social Behavior, 38,* 9–20.

Rosch, E. (1978). Principles of categorization. In E. Rorsch (Ed.), *Cognition and categorization.* Hillsdale, NJ: Lawrence Erlbaum.

Rosenhan, D. (1973). On being sane in insane places. *Science, 114,* 316–322.

Roth, A., & Fonagy, P. (1996). *What works for whom? A critical review of psychotherapy research.* New York: Guilford Press.

Rutter, M., Shaffer, D., & Sheperd, M. (1975). *A multiaxial classification of child psychiatric disorders.* World health Organization: Geneva.

Sarbin, T. R. (1997). On the futility of psychiatric diagnostic manuals (DSMs) and the return of personal agency. *Applied and Preventive Psychology, 6,* 233–243.

Sartorius, N. (1990). Classifications in the field of mental health. *World Health Statistics Quarterly, 43,* 269–272.

Scheff, T. J. (1966). *Being mentally ill: A sociological theory.* Chicago: Aldine.

Scheff, T. J. (1975). *Labeling madness.* Englewood Cliffs, NJ: Prentice-Hall.

Schneider, K. (1959). *Clinical psychopathology* (M. W. Hamilton, Trans). New York: Grune & Stratton.

Schwartz, M. A., Wiggins, O. P., & Norko, M. A. (1989). Prototypes, ideal types, and personality disorders: The return to classical psychopathology. *Journal of Personality Disorders, 3,* 1–9.

Segal, D. L., Hersen, M., & Van Hasselt, V. B. (1994). Reliability of the structured clinical interview for DSM-III-R: An evaluative review. *Comprehensive Psychiatry, 35,* 316–327.

Skinner, H. A. (1981). Toward the integration of classification theory and methods. *Journal of Abnormal Psychology, 90,* 68–87.

Slavney, P. R. (1990). *Perspectives on "hysteria."* Baltimore: Johns Hopkins University Press.

Sneath, P. H. A., & Sokal, R. R. (1973). *Numerical taxonomy.* San Franciso: Freeman.

Sokal, R. R., & Sneath, P. H. A. (1963). *Principles of numerical taxonomy.* San Francisco: W. H. Freeman.

Spitzer, R. L., & Fleiss J. L. (1975). A reanalysis of the reliability of psychiatric diagnosis. *British Journal of Psychiatry, 125,* 341–347.

Spitzer, R. L., & Williams, J. B. W. (1980). Classification in psychiatry. In H. I. Kaplan, A. M. Freeman, & B. J. Sadock. (Eds.), *Comprehensive textbook of psychiatry/III.* (pp. 1035–1072). Baltimore: Williams & Wilkins.

Spitznagel, E. L., & Helzer, J. E. (1985). A proposed solution to the base rate problem in the kappa statistic. *Archives of General Psychiatry, 44,* 1069–1077.

Stangl, D., Pfohl, B., Zimmerman, M., Bowers W., & Corenthal, C. (1985). A structured interview for the personality disorders: a preliminary report. *Archives of General Psychiatry, 42, 591–596.*

Steiner, J. L., Tebes, J. K., Sledge, W. H., & Walker, M. L. (1995). A comparison of the structured clinical interview of DSM-III-R and clinical diagnoses. *Journal of Nervous and Mental Disease, 183, 365–369.*

Stengel, E. (1959). Classification of mental disorders. *Bulletin of the World Health Organization, 21,* 601–663.

Stone, M. H. (1997). *Healing the mind: A history of psychiatry from antiquity to the present.* New York: Norton.

Strauss, J. S. (1975). A comprehensive approach to psychiatric diagnosis. *American Journal of Psychiatry, 132,* 1193.

Szasz, T. S. (1961). *The myth of mental illness.* New York: Hoeber-Harper.

Tversky, A. (1977). Features of similarity. *Psychological Review, 84,* 327–352.

Wakefield, J. C. (1993). Limits of operationalization: A critique of Spitzer and Endicott's (1978) proposed operational criteria for mental disorder. *Journal of Abnormal Psychology, 102,* 160–172.

Warner, R. (1978). The diagnosis of antisocial and hysterical personality disorders. *Journal of Mental and Nervous Disease, 166,* 839–845.

Widiger, T. A. (1993). The DSM-III-R categorical personality disorder diagnoses: A critique and alternative. *Psychological Inquiry, 4,* 75–90.

Widiger, T. A., Frances, A. J., Harris, M., Jacobsberg, L., Fyer, M., & Manning, D. (1991). Comorbidity among the Axis II disorders. In J. Oldham (Ed.), *Personality disorders: New perspectives on diagnostic validity* (pp. 165–194). Washington, DC: American Psychiatric Press.

Wiggens, O. P., & Schwartz, M. A. (1994). The limits of psychiatric knowledge and the problem of classification. In J. Z. Sadler, O. P. Wiggens, & M. A. Schwartz (Eds.), *Philosophical perspectives on psychiatric diagnostic classification* (pp. 89–103). Baltimore: Johns Hopkins University Press.

Williams, J. B. W, Gibbon, M., First, M., Spitzer, R. L., Davies, M., Borus, J., Howes, M. J., Kane, J., Pope, H. G., Rounsaville, B., & Wittchen, H. (1992). The structured clinical interview for DSM-III-R (SCID) II. *Archives of General Psychiatry, 49,* 624–629.

Wing, J. E., Cooper, J. E., & Sartorius, N. (1974). *The description and classification of psychiatric symptoms: An instruction manual for the PSE and Catego system.* London: Cambridge University Press.

Wittenborn, J. R. (1962). The dimensions of psychosis. *Journal of Nervous and Mental Disease, 134,* 117–128.

Wood, A. L. (1969). Ideal and empirical typologies for research in deviance and control. *Sociology and Social Research, 53,* 227–241.

Zimmerman, M., & Coryell, W. (1987). The Inventory to Diagnose Depression (IDD): A self-report scale to diagnose major depressive disorder. *Journal of Consulting & Clinical Psychology, 55, 55–59.*

Zubin, J. (1967). Classification of the behavior disorders. *Annual Review of Psychology, 18,* 373–406.

2

Developmental Pathogenesis

THEODORE MILLON
ROGER D. DAVIS

Possibility is the theme of development: Nothing is inevitable; anything can happen. Epidemiologists, who study the incidence, prevalence, and distribution of disease, have evolved a sophisticated vocabulary that partitions this infinitude of outcomes in a more comprehensible way. The term *etiology* refers to the specific causes of disease, while *pathogenesis* refers to the process by which these causes eventuate in the disease itself. *Vulnerability* reflects an underlying diathesis that requires the interaction of organismic and contextual factors before pathology can develop. While many mental illnesses are believed to be under genetic control, the idea of vulnerability recognizes the role of the environment, whether physical or social, in releasing genetic potentials. A *risk factor* is anything that increases the probability of developing a pathology. The connection between a risk factor and pathology need not be direct, however. A risk factor is simply correlated with the development of pathology, and may not be causally implicated in pathogenesis at all.

Still, there is considerable ambiguity in the scope of what is considered developmental. What is it that develops? And when does development end? Because normality is a necessary reference point whenever pathology is studied, these questions become very important. In the past, development referred to infancy, childhood, and adolescence—the period preceding an organism's physical maturity. More recently, however, developmental psychologists have taken a life-span perspective. Development thus now refers to the totality of changes that occur from birth to death. A similar broadening has taken place within psychopathology. Today, the prevailing model contains axes for both personality and psychosocial functioning, so that pathology, like development, is now considered a property of the whole organism and its ecology. The development of psychopathology, then, need not be limited to the period that precedes diagnosis. Instead, psychopathology may be studied from a life-span perspective on the total person-in-context.

Almost all developmental propositions advanced today are perceptive conjectures that reflect the favorite hypotheses of divergent schools of thought. Such explanations are not confirmed fact, but speculative notions that deserve further empirical evaluation. Moreover, any given empirical study is usually tenuous or inconclusive. Not only are measures of psychopathology and outcome inherently inexact, the variables that interact and result in pathology do so in ways that are often stochastic or nonlinear, and thus not readily amenable to forms of experimental design with which most psychologists are acquainted. Methods such as psychometric and laboratory tests, case histories, clinical observation, and experimental research all inform efforts to unravel the complexities of development. However, they often fail to converge on a single definitive result. Given the manifest difficulties in conducting solid developmental research, especially sound longitudinal studies, we might ask whether answers to developmental questions are even possible. Let us first describe the situation on Axis I.

Taxonomy and Pathogenesis: Axis I

The most vexing developmental problems are taxonomic. Where diagnostic constructs fail to "carve nature at its joints," efforts to specify their developmental antecedents are sabotaged at the outset. Rigorous longitudinal studies are of limited value where the taxonomy itself possesses only dubious validity. Unfortunately, most taxonomies in psychopathology have been developed with the goal of providing detailed descriptions of characteristics and functioning in cross section, at a single point in time. For the most part, the various versions of the *DSM* are excellent examples of cross-sectional taxonomies. Even where diagnostic criteria refer to time, it is usually only to specify the duration that a condition must be present before a particular diagnosis can be assigned. Within six months of suffering a natural disaster, for example, an individual will be diagnosed with acute stress disorder. Only after six months can posttraumatic stress disorder be assigned. Here, time functions only as an exclusionary or inclusionary condition, and the boundary between the two disorders is essentially arbitrary.

In fact, a taxonomy which fails to "carve nature at its joints" is a great hindrance to the goal of identifying developmental characteristics. Moreover, it is unlikely that any taxonomy of psychopathology can ever be valid without specifying "developmental diagnostic criteria," which allow syndromes with similar cross-sectional presentations to be distinguished. The truth of this proposition can be verified through everyday experience. Most readers have visited a physician on several occasions in their lifetime. After inventorying current symptoms and their severity, the doctor usually asks "How did your symptoms develop?" "What were the circumstances?" and "Were you doing anything unusual during this time?" Each question asks for specific content that allows the doctor to rule out a variety of possibilities, until only the one disease or condition that fits current symptoms *and* the facts of their development remains. If the facts do not allow the possibilities to be narrowed down sufficiently, additional tests may be ordered, the purpose of which is literally to test the theory that, for example, your sniffles reflect the common flu, rather than a mysterious and fatal tropical illness with similar symptoms.

The kinds of confounds to which a cross-sectional, descriptive taxonomy are vulnerable are easily schematized. At minimum, individuals within a category should be more clinically similar than individuals from different categories. Similarity is thus the organizing principle on which all taxonomies are constructed. However, similarity itself is a fuzzy notion. In what way are patients who receive the same diagnosis alike? Individuals with similar presentations do not always have the same disease. Thus, two levels of similarity can be distinguished. First, there is the surface similarity of how things appear (observational, cross-sectional, and descriptive). Second, there is the latent similarity of how things really are—a theoretical, developmental, and explanatory similarity. Taxonomies based on surface characteristics often hide latent distinctions. By crossing these two forms of similarity for any two subjects, we obtain the diagram shown in figure 2.1, which illustrates the taxonomic dilemma in psychopathology. Starting in the first quadrant, two presentations that appear similar may indeed be similar. In this case, etiologically similar pathways produce manifestly similar results. Second, two presentations that appear similar may in fact require different diagnoses. Despite etiologic differences, "convergent causality" results in manifestly similar results that are difficult to tease apart. Third, two presentations that appear different many in fact be different. Once again, what you see is what you get. Differences in classification reflect valid differences in etiology. Fourth, two presentations that appear different may in fact be similar. Here, the same disease interacts with individual differences to produce dramatically different presentations, a case of "divergent causality" in development.

A true classification, then, must rest its boundaries where the differences between ostensibly similar persons or conditions actually exist, rather than where appear to exist. The latent situation, however, is never known with certainty, but is always inferred on the basis of available observational methods and practices. For example, in the second quadrant, several categories should be spec-

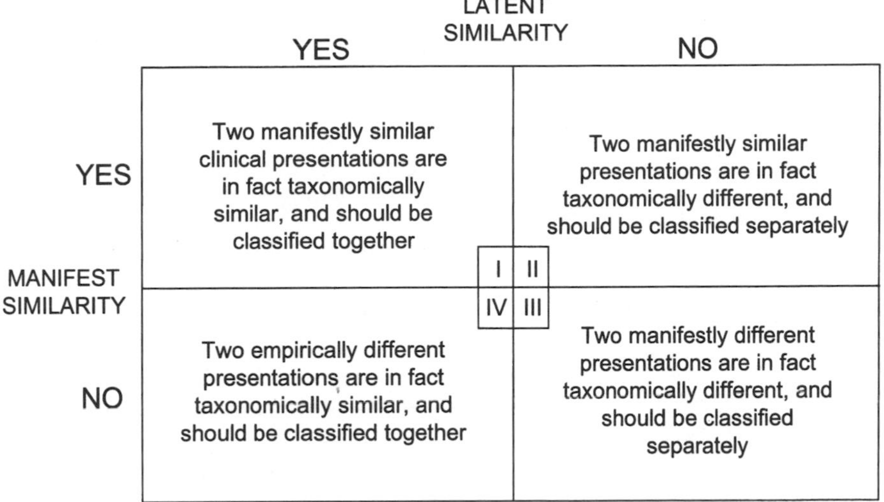

Figure 2.1 Manifest and latent similarity and the taxonomic dilemma.

ified, but only one appears to exist. Here, the covariance of indicators at a manifest level gives the syndrome acceptable internal consistency, providing a further statistical basis for what is in fact a taxonomic illusion. The *DSM* criteria for schizophrenia may represent one such category. In a review of research in the field, Heinrichs (1993, p. 230) noted that "the likelihood that researchers are studying different illnesses without being able to specify these differences must be recognized as the superordinate problem. It is not a subproblem that can be ignored. It is the major obstacle to scientific progress." The problem, of course, is to somehow get beneath surface similarities in order to explore the "latent situation" in a rigorous way. But since the latent situation is never known directly, but only inferred, there is no opportunity for direct feedback, to know how "close" to the truth any given taxonomic hypothesis might be. This is the most frustrating problem in psychopathology, for which no solution is readily forthcoming. Since the *DSM-IV* is a cross-sectional taxonomy, it becomes very difficult to research the development of psychopathology while maintaining a high level of confidence in the validity of the results. Taxonomists are thus caught in a catch-22, attempting to produce a valid cross-sectional taxonomy before developmental research that might validate the taxonomy can even begin.

Degrees of Taxonicity of Axis I Pathologies

In fact, the world is even more complicated. Even where a categorical model is appropriate, not all disorders are equally categorical. Some Axis I disorders are likely to be strongly taxonic, while others are only weakly so. That is, the appropriateness of the categorical model for a given psychopathology is likely to be a matter of degree. *Taxonicity* may be defined as the capacity of a single given illness or condition to coerce other organismic attributes into a characteristic expression or mold. Mongoloidism, for example, is strongly taxonic. All such subjects share certain physical features and a degree of intellectual deficit. Since the interaction with individual differences is minimized, persons with strongly taxonic conditions follow whatever developmental trajectory is set by their disease. Conversely, weakly taxonic conditions are readily influenced by individual differences, so that diverse outcomes are possible. Here, the expression of the disease is changed by the person more than the person is changed by the disease. Earlier we remarked that schizophrenia is possibly an example of an Axis I condition in which several distinct "diseases" are expressed in roughly similar ways. Another explanation is that schizophrenia is so weakly taxonic that individual differences mediate its expression to such an extent that internally consistent diagnostic criteria are difficult to achieve.

Pathogenesis: Axis II

On Axis II, the problem of unraveling developmental antecedents is still more complex. Medical diseases, which the Axis I syndromes more closely resemble, may often be diagnosed with validity even though the exact cause of the condition remains unknown. The developmental course of HIV infection, for example, was known before its cellular mechanisms were uncovered. A history of HIV-related illnesses thus suggests a diagnosis of HIV infection. In contrast, the development of personality and its disorders requires the consideration of at least two additional issues. First, the categorical model may not be appropriate for the personality disorders. Second, theories of normal development, like theories of personality, are typically limited to some circumscribed class of variables. Currently, we have classical theories of cognitive development (Piaget, 1952), of moral development (Kohlberg, 1978), of psychosocial development (Erikson, 1950, 1959), and of psychosexual development (Freud, 1908), as well as accounts of the development of certain specific personality traits and specific personality disorders, but no real theoretical account of the development of personality styles and disorders that interrelates and differentiates the disorders in terms of a single theoretical framework. And it is precisely this possibility that most distinguishes Axis II from Axis I.

Holistic and Categorical Models of Personality

In the *DSM-IV*, personality disorders are given the status of categories. Each category stands on its own, ostensibly unrelated to any other disorder except through what might be discovered by empirical research. Each personality is thus studied as a unitary and discrete disease process with its own unique developmental antecedents. This emphasis has spilled over into developmental psychopathology texts and journals, which feature chapters and articles concerned with the precursors of personality disorders as single taxonomic entities. Theorists have been especially interested in the development of antisocial personality disorder (e.g., Dishion, French, & Patterson, 1995) and borderline personality disorder (e.g., Paris, 1994). Few efforts have been made to study the developmental antecedents of Axis II through theoretical principles that might unify diverse disorders.

Personality and Normal Models of Development

In contrast to the categorical model, which posits unique antecedents for each taxon, theoretical models of normal development, of the kind set forth by Piaget, Kohlberg, Erikson, and Freud, for example, have seldom been concerned with the development of specific kinds of persons (though the character types posited by Freud, Abraham, and Reich may be regarded as the exception). Limited to normality and confined to a single domain of the person, development is described as consisting of stages that progress one to the next, usually as the result of internal maturational processes. Development here is linear and telelogical. For example, Piaget's model (Piaget, 1952) features the Sensorimotor stage, the Preoperational stage, the Concrete-Operations stage, and the Formal Operations stage. Within the model, cognitive development has no choice but to follow this set sequence. No deviation is possible. Neither are mixtures of features from different stages or a range of outcomes within a stage. Stage models thus eliminate individual differences, since individuals are essentially forced into one period of development or another. Since only stages exist, pathology necessarily reflects a failure in progression, which Freud referred to as fixation. Stages are thus much like categories, in that both assume discrete boundaries and internal homogeneity.

Mechanism, Content, and Taxonomy

In contrast to the discreteness of categories and the narrow range of stage models, many contemporary models of personality disorders show nearly seamless variation from one major content characteristic to another. For the interpersonal circle, for example, the variation of characteristics is distributed in a circular pattern, with most individuals falling at the center of the circle, and approximately equal proportions all the way around as one moves toward the edge and toward greater pathology. The circle, then, is dimensional in two different ways, exhibiting continuity not only between normality and pathology but also across its entire range of contents. From within the interpersonal paradigm, the interpersonal space defined by the axes of dominance and communion is assumed to reflect the latent variables around which personality is organized. The same might be said for any structural model of personality, whether Cloninger's (1986, 1987) temperament model, Benjamin's (1993) expansion of the interpersonal circle, or Millon's (1990) evolutionary theory. However, the interpersonal circle includes an important characteristic that distinguishes the idea of development within the interpersonal tradition from most other structural models of personality and from conceptions of development for Axis I: Interpersonal transactions are complementary. Dominance pulls for submission, while friendliness pulls for friendliness, and unfriendliness for unfriendliness. Although the circle is usually defined in terms of its trait dimensions, the complementarity principle is just as fundamental to the taxonomy as its content axes. Complementarity provides an interactional ideal that constrains the interaction of participants in any interpersonal situation.

The elevation of mechanism to a taxonomic status equal to that of content has a further important consequence, again exemplified in the interpersonal tradition. According to Sullivan (1953, pp. 110–111), personality is "the recurrent set of interpersonal situations which characterize a person's life." By definition, personality is concerned with patterns of behavior that span time and situation. However, the phrase "set of situations" does not indicate the level of detail at which personality should be measured. At the most microanalytic level of analysis, personality can be analyzed in terms of the individual act sequences that transpire in the given interpersonal situation. At Leary's (1957) level of public communication, for example, a videotape of patient and therapist might be coded at the level of each utterance. Here, the unit of analysis is the speech turn. The content and intensity of each act would then be plotted on the interpersonal circle, and the entire constellation of acts inspected to determine what personality traits or styles are enacted most frequently. In addition, the entire system of interaction characterizing the participants could be analyzed to determine the chain of responses that eventuates in pathological behavior for a given dyad. Such microanalytic endeavors could be used to study the sequence of behaviors that results in the pathologensis of single episodes of domestic violence, for example. In contrast, where individual behaviors are aggregated and studied in their totality, more general characterizations can be made, but sequential information is sacrificed. An abusive husband might be described as hostile and sadistic, but such trait ascriptions do not explain how any particular episode of abuse occurred. By making mechanisms a taxonomic priority, the relationships between various personality constructs can be examined, individual interactions can be studied, and pathways for personality change are suggested. Future innovations in personality taxonomy are likely to capitalize on this possibility.

In contrast, the *DSM-IV* personality disorders are specified in terms of categories that bear each other no necessary relationship. Their criteria are content rich but mechanism poor. While this reflects the cross-sectional and atheoretical posture of the *DSM-IV*, it also reflects its immaturity as a classification system. A taxonomy must postulate at least one mechanism that explains how its contents interrelate and can be transformed one into the other. Otherwise its explanatory framework is necessarily incomplete: No pathway explains how subjects might move from normality to pathology, a developmental vector, or from pathology back to normality, a therapeutic vector. Vast parts of psychopathology have thus tended to develop autonomously, with little connection between psychopathology and developmental psychology, or between psychopathology and therapy. Psychodiagnostic testing, for example, often yields a neat cross-sectional picture of personality and psychopathology, but less definite ideas about how subjects come to be where they are or what mechanisms might be engaged in their treatment. Until taxonomies begin to give equal priority to both mechanism and content, our conceptual frameworks will remain static constructions that permit development and therapy to remain in independent orbits. If personality is to be genuinely dynamic, mechanism must be recognized as the complement of content. Obviously, taxonomy in psychopathology has not yet matured to this point.

Developmental Relationship of Axis I and Axis II

The development of psychopathology is further complicated by the distinction between Axis I and Axis II. Although research in the development of psychopathology may focus on a single syndrome, in the real world of clinical work Axis I conditions are frequently accompanied by personality disorders. And many subjects who fail to meet criteria for an Axis II disorder nevertheless possess problematic personality traits. Worse, many subjects meet criteria for two or more personality disorders. Since personality disorders and problematic traits often preexist and create the vulnerability through which clinical symptoms emerge, the developmental picture of most Axis I syndromes cannot be complete and ecologically valid until personality contents and mechanisms have been taken into consideration. Moreover, both personality disorders and Axis I syndromes vary in terms of their level of severity, with the result that developmental questions become very complex. Figure 2.2 details various combinations of severity across Axis I and Axis II. In this diagram, normal development, usually thought of as the absence of personality pathology and an absence of clinical symptoms, is restricted to a single cell in the upper left-hand corner. The crucial issue is to what extent developmental accounts in any single cell generalize across the whole diagram. We would almost certainly say that normal development has increasingly little to say as personality and symptom pathology increase. Likewise, accounts of the development of Axis I conditions cannot be complete without an account of personality factors, which might either moderate or speed the development of these conditions. Individuals with an avoidant or compulsive personality disorder, for example, have different inputs into the development of phobic conditions than do normals. Axis I disorders for which personality makes no significant contribution must also be identified.

But must clinical Axis I symptoms be taken into consideration in giving a complete picture of the development of personality pathology? Probably yes. Most personality pathologies of diagnosable severity are unlikely to be found without some accompanying Axis I condition, though the disorder could easily be episodic rather than continuously present. Because interpersonal relationships are so much a part of what it means to be human, it is almost inconceivable that a personality disordered subject could get along well enough in the world to avoid experiences that precipitate anxiety, depression, or an adjustment reaction (the psychopath, whose nonchalence in the face of objective threat is legendary, is a minor exception). Accordingly, empirical studies of the development of Axis I conditions should sample representatively from the entire range of Axis I conditions to have ecological validity. Otherwise, studies of the develop-

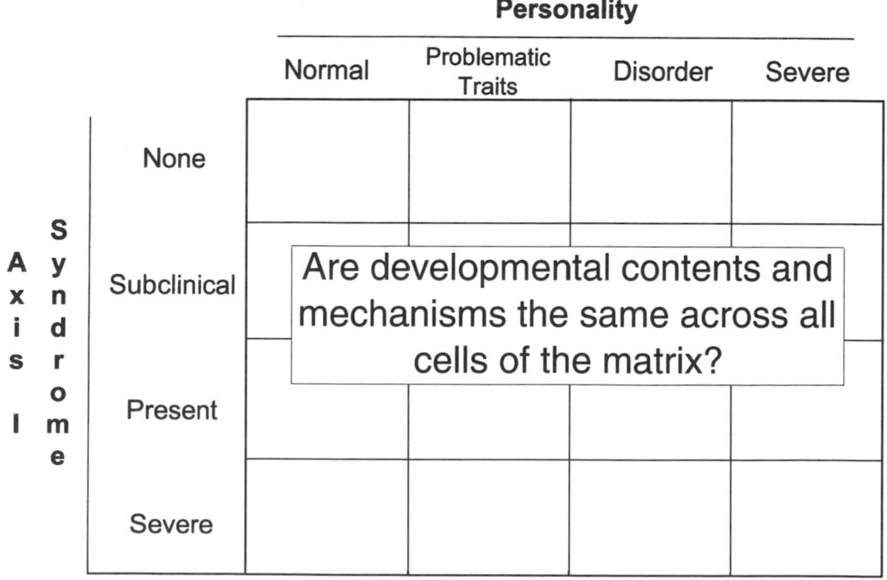

Figure 2.2 Complexity of developmental questions in psychopathology.

mental antecedents of pure personality disordered subjects may have limited generalizability to actual clinical practice.

The complexities explored in the sections above illustrate an important principle: All taxonomies, and all scientific theories, are necessarily simplifications of reality. If it were possible to know the world directly, there would be no distinction between manifest and latent. All knowledge would be tantamount to direct and intuitive mystical knowledge, so that science would need not exist at all. Even given this distinction, however, our scientific mission would be far easier if only psychopathologies did not vary in terms of their degree of taxonicity, in terms of the extent to which they reflect the presumptive disease processes (Axis I) versus pathologies of the entire matrix of the person (Axis II), and finally, in terms of the level of abstraction at which they can be described. But the world is what it is, and the ability of cross-sectional theories and taxonomies to fold its manifest complexities into a finite number of categories that can be understood by a limited cognitive apparatus quickly diminishes when the additional dimension of time becomes involved.

Fortunately, without being able to answer the developmental questions of any particular Axis I or Axis II category directly, we can at least prototype varieties of developmental relationship between personality disorders and Axis I clinical syndromes. Actual clinical cases can then be compared and contrasted to these models to illuminate their developmental background and guide further clinical exploration. A number of models have been discussed in the context of personality and depression by Klein, Wonderlich, and Shea (1993). The *vulnerability model* is the intuitive and classical conception. Here, personality disorders create an enduring diathesis that lowers the threshold at which an Axis I disorder might develop. Thus, Axis II disorders are risk factors for Axis I disorders. Whereas the medical model essentially views Axis II as simply another plane of pathology, in the vulnerability model the function of personality in the larger psychic system is fundamentally immunological, or protective. When coping fails, psychological symptoms ensue.

Many other models are possible. In the *complication model*, a personality disorder and Axis I syndrome are independent, but interweave so that each complicates the clinical status of the other. Individuals experiencing their first schizophrenic episode, for example, sometimes show enough insight into the nature of their illness that they become greatly depressed. Even if successfully medicated, the resulting pessimism could easily become chronic, in effect constituting a personality trait tantamount to a depressive style. The complication model is also referred to as a "scar model," since the second disorder is effectively a scar that may be left over even if the first disorder remits.

Whereas the vulnerability and complication models both conceptualize Axis I and Axis II conditions as relatively distinct, disorders on both axes may be seen as developing from the same underlying constitutional soil, and therefore as existing on a continuum, as in the *spectrum model*. Here, biologically based subclinical traits effectively become the organizing principle for the entire personality, preempting the development of other more adaptive characteristics. Individuals who later develop bipolar disorder, for example, are often found to have possessed as personality characteristics certain subclinical traits that define the syndrome in their more pathological expression. Such persons are often described by family members as having always been energetic, confident, and cognitively expansive. Kraepelin and Kretschmer both endorsed the spectrum model, as does Akiskal (1981) today. Other possible biological spectrums include borderline personality with the affective disorders, and schizoid and schizotypal personalities with schizophrenia.

The spectrum model is perhaps a special case of the more general *mediational model*. In the spectrum model, Axis I and Axis II are correlated, with temperament as an underlying third variable from which both derive. However, underlying third variables need not be limited to biology. Johnson, Quigley, and Sherman (1997) have shown that symptoms of personality disorder mediate the relationship between perception of parental harsh control or inadequate nurturance and Axis I symptomatology. Many other types of mediational models are possible, dependent only on the nature of one's pet variables. Cognitive models are probably excellent candidates, since mediation between contextual inputs and behavior is the essence of the cognitive perspective.

Finally, the pathoplasty model holds that while Axis I and Axis II disorders influence course and clinical status, neither disposes toward the development of the other. While the presentation of one disorder is colored by the other, having one does not increase the risk of acquiring the other. Thus, a paranoid personality may experience depressive feelings in a different way than a histrionic, but having either personality disorder does not make depression more likely.

The Ecology of Development

Early ideas that normal development proceeds according to the unfolding to an intrinsic maturational timetable have since been moderated by a counteremphasis on the ecology of development. The term *ecology* refers to more than just the physical environment. Ecology is the sum total of contextual influences in the living environment in which an organism exists. For animals and plants, the living environment contains mainly other animals and plants, some of which may be predatory and some of which may be symbiotic. For human beings, however, *ecology* refers to a living environment that consists mainly of other human beings, as well as the cultural and societal structures in which the particular person lives and with which he or she transacts. Whereas lower animals must exist and survive in the environment in which they are born, human beings live in contexts that human beings alone create and sustain. Human ecologies feature rich structures, vary across culture, and influence development in unpredictable ways. In the contemporary United States, individuals who see visions of the dead and hear their voices are likely to be diagnosed as schizophrenic and medicated. The same individual, born into American Indian cultures of the past century, might instead have become a shaman and functioned as a respected person whose role included communication with ancestral spirits. Prior to the publication of *DSM-III* in 1980, homosexuality was considered a psychopathology. Today, homosexuality is considered part of normality. Culture thus sets important boundaries for what is considered pathological and for what is not.

Just as important are the structures that compose a culture. Schools, churches, and the family are all structural organizations that subsume the individual and contribute to development. Moreover, taxonomy is just as much an issue at higher levels of organization as it is for mental pathology. We might, for example, posit different types of family structures, family communication styles, disciplinary styles, and so on. Likewise, there are many different kinds of churches and varieties of religious beliefs. Southern Baptists are considered to be strictly fundamental, while Congregationalists are considered more liberal. Sufi Muslims are mystics, while Shiites are fundamental. Such differences contribute to the ritual and ambience of family life. In some cultures, particular structures affect only a few individuals, while in others, the influence of the same structure is pervasive. The draft no longer exists in the United States, but some countries still require extended periods of military training. All of these variables interact with personality development.

The effects of contextual structures on development can be quite strong. Earlier we noted that the taxonicity of a psychopathology must be taken into consideration when predicting developmental outcomes. Strongly taxonic disorders minimize the influence of individual differences. The outcome is the same, regardless of who has the disorder. When the same idea is generalized to environmental influences (Sameroff, 1995), we have the "environtype." Here, the influence of ecological forces on development is so strong that the potential for the full expression of individual differences fails to develop at all. Instead, subjects are canalized toward similar outcomes. Any environmental organization can function as an environtype, including a particular kind of pathological family structure or a particular kind of institutional environment. Introductory developmental texts often tell the story of children raised in intellectually and interpersonally deprived environments. Such children fail to capitalize on their natural cognitive and social potential, an outcome coerced by the impoverished nature of their environment. By failing to experience the full range of environmental possibilities, certain potentials atrophy while others are amplified, contributing to a "sameness" among those who are so exposed. In general, deprivations of many kinds foster increased uniformity of outcomes.

Ecology, like maturation, places important limits on the extent to which personality development can be completely drawn into a grand theory of human nature. However, ecological structures, like maturational ones, have no intrinsic inevitability. Once a form of social organization exists, various influences in its development and demise may be traced by historians in retrospect, but these accounts serve more to document than to explain.

The kibbutz is an example. So are day care, the Head Start program, old folks homes, hospitals, regressive taxes, commuting to work, getting married, and retirement. All of these are part of the structure of life, but nothing in the universe specifically requires their existence. However, once one of these structures exists, social scientists are free to comment on the reciprocal influence between it and other social structures, between it and government, economy, the family, and the individuals.

Intensive study of phenomena at a particular level of organization may even lead some scientists into a "reductionism to the whole." Here, the reciprocal and multilevel influences that transact across all levels of organization and social structures are reduced to one level alone. Many family therapists, for example, deny that individual pathology exists at all. The lesson is that most psychopathologies are likely to be underdetermined at every level of analysis. Only by considering all sources of influence in conjunction can some picture of the development of personality and psychopathology be constructed. And if ecological structures change, developmental scenarios are free to change as well. For Freud, writing during the morally repressive period of Victorian England, hysteria (i.e., *DSM-IV* conversion disorder) was a commonly seen form of mental pathology. Today, however, it is considered uncommon. Like personality, culture, and the ecological structures within a culture, are always dynamic and evolving.

Evolutionary Theory and Personality Development

Through much of its history, psychology has been dominated by various dogmatic schools—the biological, behavioral, cognitive, and psychodynamic movements. As internally consistent perspectives on the field, these highlight the role of their pet variables, but in doing so inevitably discard valid developmental influences from other domains. As such, they encourage linear rather than interactive ways of thinking. Contemporary viewpoints are typically much more informed. Occasionally one still sees opinions that personality is mostly determined by heredity, or by early psychosexual stages of development, and so on. Such explanations are reductionistic. While all psychopathologies are likely to be multidetermined to various extents, the development of the personality disorders is "paradigmatically multidetermined." Because personality is the patterning of variables across the entire matrix of the person, efforts to detail the development of personality and its disorders must necessarily address interactions across all domains of personality, including cognitive, interpersonal, behavioral, psychodynamic, and biophysical variables. While the circular feedback and the serially unfolding character even of the Axis I disorders defies easy simplification, the development of personality disorders is magnitudes more complex.

Putting forward a model of personality development is obviously far different from simply tracing the antecedents of a particular personality trait. Traits are much more narrow in bandwidth than are personality styles or disorders, so much so that only the covariation of many traits, across all domains of personality, may be said to constitute a style or disorder. Moreover, traits may often be predicated to a single domain of personality, while personality styles or disorders cannot. Accordingly, where traits are exclusively interpersonal or exclusively neurobiological, for example, it makes sense to seek primarily interpersonal or neurobiological antecedents as explanations of their development. Thus, traits name "parts" of the whole person and possess developmental accounts that may, but need not necessarily, integrate influences that span multiple domains of the person considered as a whole being. As such, research in the etiology of particular personality traits has the opportunity to specify developmental influences more concretely than should models of the development of the whole person, but also become more narrow in scope, explaining more about the trait and less about the whole person. Developmental explanations must therefore consider the bandwidth of the constructs for which explanations are sought. In a distinctly personological model, developmental explanations cannot be complete until the interactions of contents have been specified at every domain of personality. Obviously, this is also far different from school-oriented models of development, which usually give a stagewise account of personality condensed to a single class of variables.

Instead, a developmental model geared to personality development would address changes that occur across all domains of the person. In chapter 18, three polarities are posited that address the evolutionary imperatives of survival, existence, and reproduction. These necessary and universal polarities, which exist outside personality proper, function as top-down constraints on the contents of the personality domains, which are the contingent product of evolutionary changes occurring across phylogenetic time. Psychology has no answer to the question "Why does personality consist of these particular domains rather than others?" For example, there is no satisfying reason why defense mechanisms must exist as a salient part of personality. Not every fact of development, then, can be drawn into a single theory. Once an ability blossoms, it is available as a basic skill that can be built upon in myriad ways. Speaking, for example, makes possible complex interactions between children, caregivers, and their peers that contributes to interpersonal development over and above the quality of initial attachment relationships. However, if talking did not begin to develop until age 11, the structure of the family and of society, and of human history, would undoubtedly be far different.

The conclusion is that developmental theory must be as informed by particular maturational facts as by theoretical necessity. Moreover, personality development is as much the product of contextual factors—that is, family, society, and culture—as it is the product of organismic factors such as native intelligence or temperament. The behavior of children who grow up in different societies is constrained in different ways. By changing the culture, we change the child. Maturation and culture both reflect the "crystallized accumulation" of historical contingencies, and both influence personality development in ways easily described but not easily assimilated to a single overarching theory. In consequence, accounts of a particular person's development often have a descriptive, chronological, or narrative tone that may be made interesting by the author, but nevertheless tend toward the atheoretical. Such accounts tell what happened, when, and how the person was affected, but do not explore what pathways might be possible given other events, or explain why development proceeded down one pathway rather than another. Instead, most accounts of personality development are elaborate post hoc constructions that portray hindsight as insight. Almost all biographies have this quality.

Development by Domain

In the sections below, we review important developmental considerations within the domains of personality. In the interest of space and relative importance, certain domains have been amplified, while others have been reduced. Temperament has been put under the more encompassing heading of biophysical influences, since the scope of physical structures and processes that influence the development of personality and psychopathology easily exceeds temperament alone. In contrast, the development of defense mechanisms is not discussed, since these constructs are embedded in the difficult language of psychoanalysis. The footprints of the evolutionary polarities are readily seen in several domains, but a full exposition of this thesis is well beyond the scope of this chapter.

Biophysical Influences on Development

Biophysical influences on personality span several levels of analysis. First, personality is a function of the physical properties of the brain, including not only its normal structure and variations but also its defects or lesions, neurotransmitter profile, and genetic composition.

Brain Structure Whereas behavioral psychologists traditionally viewed the mind is a blank slate, modern biological and cognitive scientists now view the brain as active agent that selects, transforms, and registers objective events in accord with its distinctive biological characteristics. Unusual sensitivities in this delicate orienting system can lead to marked distortions in perception and behavior. Any disturbance that produces a breakdown in the smooth integration of functions, or a failure to retrieve previously stored information, is likely to encourage chaos and pathology. Normal psychological functioning depends on the integrity of many areas of biological structure, and any impairment of this substrate may result in disturbed thought, emotion, and behavior. While such dysfunctions or defects may produce the initial break from normality, psychological and social determinants almost invariably shape the form of its expression. Accepting the role of biogenic influences, therefore, does not negate social experience and learning (Eysenck, 1967; Meehl, 1990; Millon, 1969, 1981, 1990).

While an appreciation of the general role of lesions or imbalances can be grasped with only a minimal understanding of the structural organization of the brain, naive misconceptions should be avoided. The belief that behavior and anatomy correspond in a direct fashion resembles phrenology. Just as phrenologists believed that personality could be understood through the configuration of bumps on the head, some theorists have held that personality traits can be precisely localized to particular brain areas. Such ideas simply move phenology inside the skull. Psychological processes such as thought, behavior, and emotion derive from complex and circular feedback properties of brain activity. Unless the intricacy of such pathways is recognized, only simplistic propositions that clinical or personality traits arise as a consequence of specific chemical imbalances or focal lesions will result. The brain is a system, and behavior is a property of the total functioning of this system. Psychological traits and processes must be conceived, therefore, as the product of a widespread and self-regulating pattern of neuronal stimulation.

Genetic Influences The role of nature-versus-nurture has long been a contentious issue in psychopathology. In the past, this debate often held an either-or quality, with strong opinions on both sides and little talk of interaction. The categorical nature of the medical model, which sees syndromes as circumscribed disease entities, has implicitly encouraged this naïve misconception. In the categorical model, pathology is classified as either present or absent. Similarly, in the Mendelian or single-gene model of inheritance, an individual either possesses the gene that leads to a particular characteristic or does not. Indeed, genetic factors do play a definitive role in certain diseases, notably Huntington's, Tourette's syndrome, and Down's syndrome, for example.

Most psychopathologists admit that heredity plays a role in the development of psychopathology, but nevertheless insist that genetic dispositions are modified substantially by environmental factors. Genetic influences do not operates as fixed determinants, but as constraints that often find diverse expressions depending on external circumstances. Genetic factors thus serve as predispositions to the development of certain traits or clinical conditions, so that even similarly affected individuals display important differences in their symptoms and developmental histories. Most psychopathologies, however, are unlikely to be under such strong genetic control. Instead, the combination of many genes probably contributes to the development of many clinical conditions, including bipolar disorders (McGuffin & Katz, 1989; Sharm, Morton, & Rice, 1992), unipolar depression (McGuffin & Katz, 1993), anxiety disorders (Kendler, Neale, Kessler, Heath, Eaves, 1992), schizophrenia (Kendler & Diehl, 1993), and antisocial behavior (Cloninger & Gottesman, 1987).

Moreover, even convinced geneticists make reference to the notion of "phenocopies." Here, a condition or characteristic usually genetic in origin is simulated by environmental factors. Thus, overtly identical forms of pathology may arise from either genetic or environmental sources. Some individuals diagnosed as schizoid personalities, for example, may in fact represent phenocopies. Psychodynamic theorists (Fairbairn, 1954) have speculated that individuals who experience psychological trauma early in life sometimes withdraw almost completely from the social world. Obviously, such individuals look very much like subjects who exhibit extreme introversion as a consequence of their genetic makeup. Same diagnosis, divergent etiology. Even in the contemporary era of relative taxonomic sophistication, the clinical picture of a disorder may provide little evidence to its origins. To complicate matters further, different genes vary in their responsiveness to environmental influences. Some produce uniform effects under all environmental conditions, whereas others can be entirely suppressed in certain environments. In addition, it appears that genes have their effects at particular times of maturation, called "critical periods," and that their interaction with environmental conditions is minimal both before and after. Modern behavioral geneticists have begun to speak of probabilistic genes, many of small effects, which contribute partially to individual differences, rather than deterministic genes that have presumed definitive and universal effects (Plomin, 1990).

Despite these apparent complications, a number of theorists have suggested that certain personality disorders may represent the partial expression of defective genes. The schizotypal personality may possess a schizophrenic genotype, but here the influence of this genotype is moderated by the operation of beneficial modifying genes or favorable environmental experiences (Meehl, 1990).

Temperament Temperament is often regarded as the "native soil" of personality. Each child enters the world with a distinctive pattern of dispositions and sensitivities. Nurses know that infants differ from the moment they are born, and perceptive parents notice distinct differences in their successive offspring. Some twist fitfully in their sleep, while others lie peacefully awake in hectic surroundings. Some are robust and energetic, while others seem perpetually tense and cranky. Investigations of such causal observations have found that infants display a consistent pattern of autonomic system reactivity, with stable differences on such biological measures as sensory threshold, quality and intensity of emotional tone, and consistency in electroencephalographic waveforms. Some infants have a regular cycle of hunger, elimination, and sleep, whereas others vary unpredictably. Moreover, children differ in the intensity of their responses, and even in distractibility and persistence. Such patterns, observed in the first few months of life, are apparently more biogenic than psychogenic in origin, being displayed before postnatal experience can fully account for them.

While individual differences in temperament are now well established, the importance of early temperament to personality rests on the extent to which these differences constrain later development. Several studies have suggested clear relationships between infantile temperament, childhood temperament, and personality traits in adulthood (Ahadi & Rothbart, 1994). Once again, however, outcomes reflect interactive patterns of development. For example, temperamental children often elicit characteristic responses from caretakers. Interpersonal theorists often speak of dyads and triads as systems of reciprocal influence. Although not invariably so, childhood temperament tends to evoke counterreactions from others that confirm and accentuate initial temperamental dispositions (Papousek & Papousek, 1975). Biological moods and activity levels shape not only the child's own behaviors but also those of the child's parents. A cheerful, adaptable, and easily cared-for infant induces a positive reciprocal attitude in caretakers, while a tense and difficult or time-consuming child may produce dismay, fatigue, or hostility. Temperamental dispositions may thus elicit responses that establish an interpersonal foundation, influencing further psychosocial development and identity formation. The child elicits parental reactions that reinforce initial patterns. The influence of temperament may thus "seep" onto a psychological plane, constrain the reaction of caretakers and, consequently, the development of global ideas related to the world, self, and others.

While a particular temperament may strengthen the probability that certain traits will become prepotent, their later expression depends upon contextual factors. For example, highly active and responsive children relate to and rapidly acquire knowledge about events and persons in their environment. The zest and energy of very active children, expressed in a supportive and encouraging environment, may lead to easy personal gratification and the development of self-efficacy expectations. Conversely, in a rigid and condemning environment, active children may experience painful frustrations as insuperable barriers and needless constraints are repetitively encountered (Campbell, 1991). Unable to fulfill their activity needs, some children may strike out in erratic and maladaptive ways. Moreover, temperament also influences the expression of psychological variables such as attachment styles (Belsky & Rovine, 1987). Interaction in development is also the rule for constitutionally passive children. Rather than engage their environment assertively, passive children often tend to avoid conflicts or "step aside" when difficulties arise. While they may thus develop a richer inner life than active children, passive youngsters may also deprive themselves of socially rewarding experiences, and come to feel "left out" by peers. Alternatively, they may come to depend on others to protect or guide them through even the most innocuous events or challenges. Innate dispositions can, of course, be modified or reversed by strong environmental pressures. A cheerful outlook can be crushed by parental contempt and ridicule. Conversely, shy and reticent children may become more self-confident in a thoroughly encouraging family atmosphere (Smith & Pederson, 1988).

Behavioral Principles of Development

According to the classical behavioral perspective, the individual is an empty vessel that becomes filled through environmentally induced contingencies. Organisms possess an intrinsic malleability. Since the behavioral domain produces no strong structural models of personality, it is quite literally a collection of mechanisms. Within the constraints of nervous anatomy lies an unlimited capacity to form new associations between stimuli of almost any kind. The environment, therefore, is free to take development into radically new directions at almost any time. Normality can thus be transformed into pathology, and vice versa. The behavioral perspective includes both classical conditioning and operant conditioning. The more important mechanisms for the development of pathological forms of learning are reviewed below.

Incidental Learning While specific behaviors may be actively taught through instruction or indoctrination, the foundation of many pathological behaviors lies with incidental learning. Young children lack not only the ability to understand their environment but also the mental apparatus necessary to discern logical relationships among its elements. Especially for very young children, the world of objects, people, and events is connected in an unclear and random fashion, associated in ways that have no intrinsic relationship. Clusters of concurrent, but only incidentally connected, stimuli may thus become erroneously fused, resulting in unintended associations. Where these become generalized, the possibility of pathological consequences is increased. A child who is bullied by peers on the way to preschool each morning, for example, may come to associate feeling teased and ridiculed with a learning environment, and come to take an exceedingly submissive attitude in response to legitimate authority figures, who are also seen as bullies.

Modeling Pathological behaviors may also be acquired through modeling. Here, the observer views the behavior of others, together with the consequences of their behaviors, and then decides how favorable or unfavorable the outcome would be if the observer were to behave likewise. Modeling thus requires the development of perspective taking and the calculation of consequences as prerequisite cognitive abilities.

Modeling may occur in almost any venue. The everyday and ordinary activities of caretakers and family members provide children with unintended models to imitate. Children often mirror complex behaviors without understanding their significance. Styles of thinking, loving, relating, and even problem solving may all be adopted vicariously by children observing everyday interactions. Modeling is therefore one of the main pathways through which pathological behaviors may be generationally transmitted. The role of modeling in the transmission of instrumental aggression, for example, has been firmly established. While the family is a cardinal setting, interactions between teacher and peers at school are also prime candidates.

Modeling may transmit not only behaviors with consequences for self but also behaviors that have consequences for others. Antisocial behaviors, for example, usually benefit the self at great expense to others. Prosocial behaviors, in contrast, benefit others, usually at little reward or cost to the subject. Either may be acquired through modeling. As a result, antisocial behaviors probably develop more easily and are more resistant to extinction, whereas prosocial behaviors easily fail to take root. The reinforcement and shaping of positive and adaptive behaviors is thus as important as the extinction of maladaptive actions.

Generalization and Discrimination Behaviors that are adaptive within one setting often prove maladaptive when generalized elsewhere. The roots of such difficulties do not lie in stress, anxiety, or unconscious mechanisms of defense, but rather in the simple learning of cognitions and behaviors that prove troublesome when applied to other venues. Children who are indulged by their parents may learn that passivity is rewarded. Such individuals learn that they can receive assistance by smiling and being pleasant, making their needs known, and then letting others take the initiative. Upon entering the classroom, however, these strategies may be completely frustrated. Although the teacher functions in part as a surrogate caretaker, time and attention are naturally divided among many students, and some self-guided study must be expected. Such children may fail to "learn how to learn," seriously handicapping the development and refinement of more complex skills through autonomous exploration and effort.

Extinction of Adaptive Behaviors Even normal subjects often exhibit a complex mix of adaptive and pathological strategies and behaviors. Fortunately, adaptive strategies usually dominate as strengths that compensate for pathology. Each spouse in a marital relationship, for example, knows that the other possesses certain sensitivities that are best avoided. Like all behaviors, however, adaptive responses require periodic reinforcement to be maintained. Couples who consistently criticize faults without praising genuine good attributes are unlikely to be together long. In addition, individuals vary in the degree to which reinforcement is required to sustain adaptive behaviors. The schizoid personality, for example, presents a basic deficient in hedonic capacity. Such individuals may fail to sustain basic competencies in socialization simply because they find few things in life reinforcing.

Insufficient Learning Insufficient learning is a primary source of pathology. One of the fundamental tasks of development is the acquisition of skills and competencies that foster the individual's capacity to at least meet basic needs and environmental demands. Lack of basic skills is a form of pathological underlearning that may be as severe as those disorders generated either by stressful experiences or by defective or maladaptive learning.

Interpersonal Development

Adaptation and reproduction are luxuries. Survival, however, is a necessity: Unless an organism survives, it cannot adapt or reproduce. The first developments in personality are thus geared toward securing this first evolutionary imperative. At birth, infants are essentially helpless and dependent on others to satisfy their needs and safeguard their survival. In the interpersonal domain, the first relationship concerns the quality of attachment between the infant and its caretakers.

Attachment Trust is one of the most basic orientations to be acquired. For some children, the nurturance, affection, and support of caretakers is assumed to be permanent and reliable. For others, affection and support are nonexistent, sporadic, inconsistent, or contingent. Through the quality and consistency of this support, deeply ingrained feelings of trust or mistrust are etched within the child. Because children's capacities to make fine discriminations are lacking, trust and mistrust easily generalized to other venues, such as the nursery and school, and even to existence itself. Whereas most children receive qualitatively good or poor attention from caretakers, some receive almost none at all. The profound effects of social isolation have been thoroughly studied. Deprived monkeys, for example, are incapable at maturity of relating to peers, of participating effectively in sexual activity, and of assuming adequate roles as mothers (Harlow, 1963). Deprived of warmth and security, they come to mistrust their environment, anticipate further stress, and view others as harsh and undependable. In contrast, children who are given comfort and affection develop a far-reaching trust of others. Recent investigations show that while initial attachments are transformed across development, they remain an important foundation (Sroufe & Fleeson, 1986). Such "internal representational models" become the context within which additional relationships unfold.

Development of Interpersonal Autonomy Toward the end of the first year of life, children begin to achieve some independence from parental support. Holding a drinking cup, taking the first few steps, or uttering a word or two all signify a growing capacity to act autonomously. As the child develops such functions, the attitudes and feelings communicated by others begin to be understood. Rough or tender handling is thus no longer just a variation in the pattern of tactile stimulation. Meanings are now assigned to interpersonal behaviors, which thus acquire a qualitative dimension. In the first year of life, the infant was in its native mode, being comparatively passive and dependent upon parental figures to meet its physical needs. By the second and third years, he is ambulatory and possesses the power of speech and control over many aspects of his own life, having acquired the manipulative skills to venture forth and test his competence to handle events on his own (White, 1960). Rather than remain a passive receptacle for environmental forces, clay to be molded, he acquires competencies that enlarge his vistas and allow him to become a legitimate actor in his environments.

The most significant aspect of children's increasing capacities is the possibility of assuming an active role in doing things on their own, to influence their environments, to free themselves from domination, and to outgrow the dependencies of their first years (Deci & Ryan, 1991). With the development of more autonomous capacities, the child must break out of dependence on parental figures or to perpetuate the dependence of childhood into later years. Children who possess a "secure base" will explore their environments without becoming fearful that their attachment figure cannot be recovered (Ainsworth, 1967). On the other hand, those without such a base tend to remain close to their caretakers, assuming the more passive mode, one likely to ultimately restrict their range of coping resources through decreased or retarded sociocognitive competence.

Needless to say, conflicts and restrictions arise as children assert themselves. These are seen clearly during toilet training, when youngsters often resist submitting to the demands of their parents. A delicate exchange of power and cunning may ensue. Opportunities arise for the child to actively extract promises or deny wishes; in response, parents may mete out punishments, submit meekly, or shift inconsistently. Important precedents for attitudes toward authority, power, and autonomy are generated during this period of parent-child interaction. Overprotected children, who are "spoon-fed," or curtailed in friendships, or repeatedly secured against "danger" may come to see themselves as objects of frailty who must close themselves off from exploration and adventure and submit to the guidance of powerful others. These children may fear abandoning their overlearned dependency upon their parents, believing they are ill-equipped for life's challenges, and becoming timid, helplessly submissive, and depressed when forced to venture out into the world. Conversely, children given free rein with minimal restraint may become irresponsibly undercontrolled. Carried into the wider social context, these behaviors run up against the desires of other children and the restrictions of less permissive adults.

Self-Image

The development of self-image is closely connected to the interpersonal domain. Just as mental representations of others are acquired through interpersonal transactions, the self is also a construct that derives its content through the appraisals of others. Some appraisals are nurturing, valuing, and appropriate, while other appraisals are demeaning. Such attitudes markedly influence future behavior. The esteem in which children are held and affection surrounding their first performances contribute to their confidence in themselves. Severe discipline for transgressions, humiliating comments in response to efforts at self-development, embarrassment over social awkwardness, deprecations associated with poor performances, parental shame as a result of the physical or mental capacities of the child—all influence the development of the self-concept and of self-esteem. Faced with rebuffs and ridicule, children learn to doubt their competence and adequacy. Even children who possess the prerequisite skills for competent performances may simply lack the confidence to apply themselves. Believing their efforts will be ineffectual and futile, these children often adopt a passive attitude toward their environment and future.

In addition to attitudes related to efficacy and passivity, individuals must define themselves as gendered beings and prepare to eventually take on the adult roles of mother or father themselves. The development of gender identity involves further refinements to the sense of self, gained in real and imagined relationships with others. The many crushes and infatuations experienced during adolescence, for example, provide an important source of self-definition. Children turn toward same-sex peers and role models as a means of incorporating behaviors and self-ideals appropriate to their gender role. High school cliques, clubs, and sports activities all aid the development of gender identity by providing sex congruent role models and peer feedback. All these efforts add a psychosocial dimension to the process of gender definition. While most persons remember this period of development as being somewhat difficult, some individuals receive mixed messages from role models and peers, incorporate these into the self, and thus acquire a persistent ambivalence toward their own competencies in relationships and find it difficult to balance what they desire from relationships with the needs of others. Without adequate role models, some adolescents exhibit excessive dependency on peer group sexual habits and values. To protect themselves against the discomforting possibility of peer rejection, they may submerge their own identity to fit whatever roles the group encourages. Where role models are deficient, some adolescents may join neighborhood gangs or deviant subcultures, discarding social norms in favor of peer group norms.

Cognitive Development

Perceptual and cognitive abilities during infancy may be described as diffuse, gross, and undifferentiated. The orientation of the infant is toward sensations that are proportionately broad and undifferentiated. Eventually, however, the maturational timetable of cognitive development unfolds, and children begin to acquire the capacity for symbolic representation and speech. Aimless motor behavior is supplanted by focused movements as children gain feedback by exploring their world.

The essence of the cognitive perspective is that objective realities are mediated, not directly apprehended. Accordingly, cognitive psychologists speak of expectancies, attributions, and cognitive biases. Even language shapes our perceptions of external reality. As Whorf (1956) and others have argued, the words we use transform our experiences in line with their literal meanings. Each family system, for example, forms a microcosm within which characteristic ways of using language affect the development of ways of construing the self, world, and others. Children whose parents regard every minor mishap as devastating interpret similar experiences in a similar way. As a consequence, small setbacks may become major failures, disturbing the development of self-image and self-efficacy expectations. More grossly disturbed individuals may perceive objectively benign events as humiliating, threatening, or punishing, selectively distorting and reforming experience to fit preformed expectancies, which in turn acts to channel attention and magnify irrelevant and insignificant aspects of interactions or events. Such individuals experience neutral events as objectively threatening or painful, where no such correlates exist in reality, intensifying their own miseries as a viscous circle.

Ecological Factors in Personality Development

For most children, the family serves as the primary socialization system for inculcating beliefs and behaviors. Parents transmit a wide range of values and attitudes to their children, through either direct tuition or unintentional commentary. Children learn to think about, be concerned with, and react to certain events and people in prescribed and approved ways. Family figures serve as models for attending, organizing, and reacting to the expressions, thoughts, and feelings of others. Illogical ideas, irrational reactions, and irrelevant and bizarre verbalizations often arise as a consequence of extreme stress. However, their roots as often be traced to defective styles of family communication (Campbell, 1973).

Parenting Styles

Through the family, children are exposed to a variety of role models, both adaptive and maladaptive. They frequently learn different and contrasting sets of perceptions, feelings, attitudes, and behaviors, as well as a mixed set of assumptions about themselves and others. Some family members may be consistently cruel and rejecting, while others are kind and supportive. Children who are the recipients of rejecting cues are usually aware that they are unappreciated or scorned. Some children react with deep and pervasive feelings of isolation in a hostile world. Deprived of security and self-confidence, they fail to venture forth, lose any sense of achievement, and anticipate devaluation by others (Steinberg, Elmen, & Mounts, 1989). As a defense against further pain, children may come to avoid peer contact, using apathy and indifference as a protective cloak to minimize the impact of anticipated ridicule or rejection. Other children may imitate parental abuse, and act in a hostile and vindictive fashion themselves. While other parental attitudes, such as seduction, exploitation, and deception, also contribute to the development of personality pathology, it is usually the sense of being unwanted and unloved that proves to have the most pervasive and shattering of effects (Cicchetti & Beeghly, 1987). Children often tolerate substantial punishment and buffeting from their environment where basic feelings of love and support are present.

Some children have parents who are not overtly abusive, but nevertheless strict, demanding, or overprotective. Some children conform to such pressures and fulfill parental expectations by becoming overly obedient and circumspect, keeping impulses and contrary thoughts in check. Alternatively, children who fail to satisfy excessive parental demands and face continued harassment and punishment may develop pervasive anxieties about self-confidence and personal relationships, leading to hopelessness and discouragement, and ultimately to social avoidance and withdrawal. Others learn to imitate parental harshness and develop hostile and aggressively rebellious behaviors. Some parents so narrowly restrict the experiences to which their children are exposed that these youngsters fail to learn even the basic rudiments of autonomous behaviors (Lewis, 1981). Overprotective mothers, worried that their children are too frail or are unable to care for themselves or make sensible judgments on their own, not only succeed in forestalling the growth of normal competencies but, indirectly, give the child a feeling of inferiority and frailty. Such children then observe their actual inadequacies, verifying their own weakness, ineptness, and dependence on others (Millon, 1981).

Overly permissive, lax, or undisciplined parents allow growing children to assert their every whim.

Such parents provide a model of irresponsibility, fail to control their children, and, by their own lack of discipline, implicitly provide the model of a world that indulges impulses and fails to set limits. Unconstrained by parental control, these youngsters grow up displaying impulsiveness, inconsideration, and egocentrism. At the extreme, they may become exploitive, demanding, uncooperative, and antisocially aggressive. Unless checked by external disciplinary forces, these youngsters may eventually become irresponsible members of society (Millon, 1969). In contrast, some parents rarely punish, but nevertheless expect certain performances before giving love or encouragement. Positive reinforcements are contingent upon approved performance. While such conditions often produce children who are socially pleasant and rewarding to others, an insatiable and indiscriminate need for social approval may also result. Such individuals may experience periods of marked depression unless they are commented upon favorably by others.

Finally, while some degree of variability in parenting is inevitable, some parents display extreme inconsistency of standards and expectations (Maccoby & Martin, 1983). The effects of amorphous, fragmented, or confusing patterns of family communication have been explored by numerous investigators. Communications may be responded to in a vague, erratic, or incidental fashion, and frequently convey equivocal or contradictory meanings. Children who mature in such environments fail to learn consistent adaptive strategies, for their behaviors are paradoxically countermanded by unpredictable parental reactions. Such children may protectively become immobile and noncommittal. Others internalize inconsistency as ambivalence, vacillating from one action or feeling to another. To avoid conflict and confusion, they may distort or deny upsetting signals, or replace these signals with their own tangential or irrational thoughts. Unable to decode the intentions and feelings of others, and faced with inconsistent affection and feedback, they may becomes estranged to their own self.

Sociocultural Influences in Development

Personality and psychopathology are shaped by the institutions, traditions, and values that constitute the cultural context of individual and social. Cultural forces serve as a common framework of formative influences that set limits and establish guidelines for its members. Society and culture, however, are distal influences in development. Both are convenient abstractions that characterize the pattern of relationships and responsibilities shared among group members.

Attention in this "sociocultural" section will focus, not on the more private experiences of particular children in particular families, but on those more public experiences that are shared among members of a societal group. The notion that many of the pathological patterns observed today can best be ascribed to the perverse, chaotic, or frayed conditions of our cultural life has been voiced by many commentators of the social scene (Fromm, 1955; Millon, 1987). These conditions have been characterized in phrases such as "the age of anxiety," "growing up absurd," and "the lonely crowd." First, we will note the operation of forces that compel individuals to surpass the standards to which they were exposed in early life. Second, we will point up the effects of changing, ambiguous, and contradictory social values. And third, we will describe the consequences of the disintegration of social beliefs and goals.

Achievement Striving and Competition Few characterizations of American life are more apt than those that portray our society as upwardly mobile. Ours is a culture that promises material rewards once considered the province only of the aristocracy to those who would work intelligently and hard. This is the "American dream." Implicit in this vision, however, is the expectancy that each person should be measured by the extent to which the dream is fulfilled. Society not only promotes ambition but also expects each of its members to succeed, and judges those who do not. Every aspiring individual is thus confronted with a precarious choice: Along with the promising rewards of success come the devastating consequences of failure. As such, many individuals feel intense competition from their peers and family members. Schoolchildren experience constant testing and grading. Athletes compete for the sake of victory alone. Peers compete for attractive dates, good jobs, the highest income, a status car and home, the richest country club, and so on. Even those who simply have less materialistic goals may experience feelings of guilt for letting others down, for not finishing first. We have been well trained to compete and to seek public achievements without examining their aims, their inevitable frustrations, and their limited rewards.

Unstable and Contradictory Social Standards Competition refers to the struggle among individuals to surpass in achievement. The historical function of cultural traditions is to give meaning and order to social life, to define the tasks and responsibilities of existence, and to guide group members with a system of shared beliefs, values, and goals (Reiss, 1981). These traditions, transmitted from parents to child, provide a blueprint for organizing thoughts, behaviors, and aspirations.

In recent decades, however, the pace of social change has quickened. As a result, many individuals are no longer certain what they should achieve. Ambiguous, and sometimes contradictory, standards are often put forward by groups with diverse ethnic, religious, cultural, and political influences. Under the cumulative impact of rapid industrialization, immigration, urbanization, mobility, technology, and mass communication, traditional values have steadily eroded. Instead of a simple and coherent body of customs and beliefs, we find ourselves confronted with constantly shifting and increasingly questioned standards whose durability is uncertain and precarious. Large segments of our society exist outside the mainstream of American life. Isolated by the unfortunate circumstance of social prejudice or economic deprivation, they struggle less with the problem of achieving in a changing society than with managing the bare necessities of survival. To them, the question is not which of the changing social values should be pursued, but whether social values exist at all. Youngsters exposed to poverty and destitution, provided with inadequate schools, living in poor housing set within decaying communities, raised in chaotic and broken homes, deprived of parental models of "success and attainment," and immersed in a pervasive atmosphere of hopelessness, futility, and apathy cannot help but question the validity of their society.

Harsh cultural and social conditions do not directly cause psychopathology. Instead, they serve as a context within which the immediate experiences of personal life take place, functioning to color or degrade relationships and the quality of life, and to establish maladaptive and pathogenic models for imitation.

Are Developmental Taxonomies Possible?

At the beginning of this chapter, we noted that possibility is the theme of development. Nothing is inevitable, and anything can happen. Development is thus characterized by a remarkable openness that is brought to closure through the maturation of intrinsic potentials and their interaction with chance events and life circumstances, which constitute the ecology of individual life. Ecology is more than just the physical environment, however, and includes all structures within a culture, such as schools, churches, and even governments. Organismic influences on development include brain structure, neurotransmitter profiles, genetic anomalies, normal heredity of other genetic factors, and temperament. Behavioral principles include incidental learning, modeling, inappropriate generalization and discrimination, extinction of adaptive behaviors, and insufficient learning. Interpersonal development begins with attachment, and includes the development of interpersonal autonomy. In turn, the development of self-image is closely connected to the quality of interpersonal relationships, as is cognition. Connections between all domains of personality are to be expected, since personality is a synthetic construct and all domains are part of the whole person. Research designs in psychopathology cannot encompass the interaction of all possible developmental influences simultaneously.

The ultimate issue, however, is the extent to which taxonomies that embrace developmental diagnostic criteria, and thus segregate qualitatively similar presentations in terms of various developmental courses, are even possible at all. The interaction between organismic attributes and contextual structures and events often leads to unpredictable results. Faced with overwhelming adversity, one person becomes Helen Keller, another becomes a serial killer. It is always possible that factors that dispose and protect against adaptive and pathological outcomes will be identified concretely. However, it is also possible that the shear number of bidirectionally interacting causal influences within and across all levels of both organism and context intrinsically lead to complexities so subtle and emergent that they simply do not lend themselves to what we would term "nomothetic knowledge." If this is the case, our inability to construct a taxonomy of psychopathology that resembles a classification of physical diseases, for which the pathways to pathology are mostly already specified, reflects not our ignorance of crucial independent variables but is instead the natural product of a complex world. Nature was not meant to suit our need for a tidy and well-ordered universe. As one moves from the physical world of objects to the social sciences, the phenomena of the subject domain become more loosely boundaried. As the fuzzy domains of family and society interact with the equally fuzzy areas of personality characteristics and biophysical potentials, the resulting tapestry may simply be too finely woven to be understood with much precision. To the extent that this is true, the natural openness and complexity of development places an upper bound on the degree to which psychopathology can break free of cross-sectional taxonomies. If so, the *DSM-IV*, and other taxonomies like it, will be with us for a long, long while.

References

Ahadi, S. S., & Rothbart, M. K. (1994). Temperament, development, and the big five. In C. Halverson, R. Martin, & G. Kohnstamm (Eds.), *The developing structure of temperament and personality from infancy to adulthood* (pp. 189–208). Hillsdale, NJ: Erlbaum.

Ainsworth, M. D. S. (1967). *Infancy in Uganda.* Baltimore: John Hopkins University Press.

Akiskal, H. S. (1981). Subaffective disorders: Dysthymic, cyclothymic, and bipolar-II disorders in the borderline realm. *Psychiatric Clinics of North America, 4,* 25–46.

Belsky, J., & Rovine, M. (1987). Temperament and attachment security in the strange situation: An empirical rapprochement. *Child Development, 58,* 787–795.

Benjamin, L. (1993). *Interpersonal diagnosis and treatment of personality disorders.* New York: Guilford.

Campbell, S. B. (1973). Mother-infant interaction in reflective, impulsive, and hyperactive children. *Developmental Psychology, 8,* 341–349.

Campbell, S. B. (1991). Longitudinal studies of active and aggressive preschoolers: Individual differences in early behavior and in outcome. In D. Cicchetti & S. L. Toth (Eds.), *Rochester Symposium on Developmental Psychopathology: Vol.2. Internalizing and externalizing expressions of dysfunction.* Hillsdale, NJ: Erlbaum.

Cicchetti, D., & Beeghly, M. (1987). Symbolic development in maltreated youngsters: An organizational perspective. In D. Cicchetti and M. Beeghly (Eds.), *Atypical symbolic development.* San Francisco: Jossey-Bass.

Cloninger, R. C. (1986). A unified biosocial theory of personality and its role in the development of anxiety states. *Psychiatric Developments, 3,* 167–226.

Cloninger, R. C. (1987). A systematic method for clinical description and classification of personality variants. *Archives of General Psychiatry, 44,* 573–588.

Cloninger, C. R., & Gottesman, I. I. (1987). Genetic and environmental factors in antisocial behavior. In S. A. Mednick, T. E. Moffitt, & S. A. Stack (Eds.), *Causes of crime: New biological approaches* (pp. 92–109). Cambridge, England: Cambridge University Press

Deci, E. L., & Ryan, R. M. (1991). A motivational approach to self: Integration in personality. In R. Dienstbier (Ed.), *Nebraska Symposium on Motivation: Vol. 38. Perspectives on motivation* (pp. 237–288). Lincoln: University of Nebraska Press.

Dishion, T. J., French, D. C., & Patterson, G. R. (1995). The development and ecology of antisocial behavior. In D. Cicchetti & D. J. Cohen (Eds.), *Developmental psychopathology: Risk, disorder, and adaptation* (Vol 2; pp. 421–471). New York: John Wiley.

Erikson, E. (1950). *Childhood and society.* New York: Norton.

Erikson, E. (1959). Growth and crises of the healthy personality. In G. S. Klein (Ed.), *Psychological issues.* New York: International University Press.

Eysenck, H. J. (1967). *The biological basis of personality.* Springfield, IL: Charles C. Thomas.

Fairbairn, W. (1954). *An object-relations theory of the personality.* New York: Basic Books.

Freud, S. (1908). Character and anal eroticism. In *Collected Papers.* London: Hogarth.

Fromm, E. (1955). *The sane society.* New York: Holt, Rinehart, & Winston.

Harlow, H. (1963). The maternal affectional system. In B. M. Foss (Ed.), *Determinants of infant behavior II.* New York: John Wiley.

Heinrichs, R. (1993). Schizophrenia and the brain: Conditions for a neuropsychology of madness. *American Psychologist, 48,* 221–233.

Johnson, J. G., Quigley, J. F., and Sherman, M. F. (1997). Adolescent personality disorder symptoms mediate the relationship between perceived parental behavior and Axis I symptomatology. *Journal of Personality Disorders, 11,* 381–390.

Kendler, K., & Diehl, S. (1993). The genetics of schizophrenia: A current, geneticepidemiologic perspective. *Schizophrenia Bulletin, 19,* 261–285.

Kendler, K., Neale, M., Kessler, R., Heath, A., & Eaves, L. (1992). A population-based twin study of major depression in women: The impact of varying definitions of illness. *Archives of General Psychiatry, 49,* 257–266.

Klein, K., Wonderlich, and Shea, M. T. (1993). Models of relationships between personality and depression. In B. Klein, D. Kuffer, & M. T. Shea (Eds.), *Personality and depression.* New York: Guilford.

Kohlberg, L. (1978). Revisions in the theory and practice of moral development. In W. Damon (Ed.), *New directions in child development: Moral development* (pp. 83–88). San Francisco: Jossey-Bass.

Leary, T. (1957). *Interpersonal diagnosis of personality: A functional theory and methodology for personality evaluation.* New York: Ronald Press.

Lewis, C. C. (1981). The effects of parental firm control: A reinterpretation of findings. *Psychological Bulletin, 90,* 547–563.

Maccoby, E., & Martin, J. (1983). Socialization in the context of the family: Parentchild interaction. In E. M. Hetherington (Ed.), *Handbook of child psychology, vol. 4: Socialization, personality, and social development.* New York: John Wiley.

McGuffin, P., & Katz, R. (1993). Genes, adversity, and depression. In R. Plomin & G. E. McLearn (Eds.), *Nature, nurture, and psychology* (pp. 217–230). Washington, DC: American Psychological Association.

McGuffin, P., & Katz, R. (1989). The genetics of depression and manic-depressive disorder. *British Journal of Psychiatry, 155,* 294–304.

Meehl, P. E. (1990). Toward an integrated theory of schizotaxia, schizotypy, and schizophrenia. *Journal of Personality Disorders, 4,* 199.

Millon, T. (1969). *Modern psychopathology: A biosocial approach to maladaptive learning and functioning.* Philadelphia: W. B. Saunders.

Millon, T. (1981). *Disorders of personality: DSM-III, Axis II.* New York: John Wiley.

Millon, T. (1987). On the genesis and prevalence of the borderline personality disorder: A social learning thesis. *Journal of Personality Disorders, 1,* 354–372.

Millon, T. (1990). *Toward a new personology: An evolutionary model.* New York: John Wiley.

Papousek, H., & Papousek, M. (1975). Cognitive aspects of preverbal social interaction between human infants and adults. In R. Porter & M. O'Conner (Eds.), *Parentinfant interaction* (pp. 241–260). Amsterdam: Elsevier.

Paris, J. (1994). *Borderline personality disorder : A multidimensional approach.* Washington, DC: American Psychiatric Press.

Piaget, J. (1952). *The origins of intelligence in children.* New York: International Universities Press.

Plomin, R. (1990). The role of inheritance in behavior. *Science, 248,* 183–188.

Reiss, D. (1981). *The families' construction of reality.* Cambridge, MA: Harvard University Press.

Sameroff, A. J. (1995). General system theories and developmental psychopathology. In D. Cicchetti & D. J. Cohen (Eds.), *Developmental psychopathology: Risk, disorder, and adaptation* (vol 2; pp. 659–695). New York: John Wiley.

Sharm, P., Morton, N., & Rice, J. (1992). Segregation analysis of the NIMH Collaborative Study: Family data on bipolar disorder. *Psychiatric Genetics, 2,* 175–184.

Smith, P. B., & Pederson, D. R. (1988). Maternal sensitivity and patterns of infant-mother attachment. *Child Development, 59,* 1097–1101.

Sroufe, L. A, & Fleeson, J. (1986). Attachment and the construction of relationships. In W. Hartup and Z. Rubin. (Eds.), *Relationships and development* (pp. 51–71). Hillsdale, NJ: Erlbaum.

Steinberg, L., Elmen, J. D., & Mounts, N. S. (1989). Authoritative parenting, psychosocial maturity, and academic success among adolescents. *Child Development, 60,* 1424–1436.

Sullivan, H. S. (1953). *The interpersonal theory of psychiatry.* New York: W.W. Norton.

White, R. W. (1960). Competence and the psychosexual stages of development. In M. R. Jones (Ed.), *Nebraska Symposium on Motivation.* Lincoln: University of Nebraska Press.

Whorf, B. (1956). *Language, thought, and reality.* New York: John Wiley.

3

Research Strategies for Studying Psychopathology

MICHAEL L. RAULIN
SCOTT O. LILIENFELD

Few things in life are more frightening, puzzling, or intriguing than psychopathology. The human body and mind are phenomenal evolutionary achievements, but their proper functioning represents a delicate balance. When that balance is upset—whether by external stressors that push the organism beyond its limits, biological aberrations that predispose the organism to respond inappropriately, or cognitive styles that distort everyday experiences—psychopathology may result. In this chapter, we will examine how psychopathology researchers study the causal factors relevant to mental disorders. Each research method has its own strengths and weaknesses. In conjunction, however, these methods have permitted researchers to make substantial progress toward identifying the causes of many mental disorders.

Asking Questions About Psychopathology

One question often asked by new graduate students in clinical psychology is "Why are research designs necessary in psychopathology?" Beginning students often assume that the causes of psychopathological conditions can be identified solely by examining individual patients. So we open this chapter with these two deceptively complex questions: (1) Why can't years of clinical experience provide adequate answers to questions concerning the causes of psychopathology? and (2) Do we really need research designs to obtain these answers?

Why Research Designs Are Necessary in Psychopathology Research

Research designs are necessary largely because the human brain, although remarkably sophisticated, is nonetheless a highly fallible information processor. The same cognitive strategies that are adaptive in everyday life can sometimes lead us astray in our thinking about research problems. Some social cognition theorists (e.g., Gilovich, 1991) have argued that the human brain was "designed" by natural selection to extract meaning and order from its environment. Such a propensity makes good evolutionary sense given that our external surroundings are often complicated and chaotic. Without an innate tendency to organize the world into meaningful groupings—to make "sense out of nonsense"—we would probably be incapable of functioning adequately in the natural environment. Nevertheless, this generally adaptive tendency sometimes results in *cognitive illusions*—errors in thinking that are subjectively compelling (Nisbett & Ross, 1980). We tend to perceive relationships among variables even when such relationships are objectively absent. Like visual illusions, cognitive illusions often appear "real" even after we are told that they are imaginary by-products of our cognitive apparatus. As researchers we must recognize our propensities toward cognitive illusions and learn to compensate for them. Research designs assist researchers with precisely this corrective function. Indeed, the failure to use appropriate research designs has often led psychologists to draw faulty inferences concerning the correlates and causes of psychopathology. Two examples will suffice to make this point.

1. Several authors have argued that patients with schizophrenia tend to come from markedly dysfunctional home backgrounds and that such backgrounds may play an important role in the etiology of schizophrenia. Yet when Schofield and Balian (1959) compared patients with schizophrenia to nonpatient comparison subjects, there were few differences between the samples on such life-history variables as quality of maternal, paternal, or sibling relationships, poverty in the home, and parental discord. Indeed, in several cases comparison subjects exhibited higher levels of adverse environmental variables than the patients!

One factor that may account for many clinicians' and researchers' perceptions of a strong association between schizophrenia and negative life experiences is the *fallacy of positive instances*. This fallacy, which affects all of us, is the error of attending only to data that confirm our hypotheses (see Gilovich, 1991). Thus, individuals who expect to observe a relationship between schizophrenia and negative life experiences may pay attention to confirming evidence while ignoring or downplaying disconfirming evidence. The fallacy of positive instances can be overcome only by using research designs that force us to attend to all relevant evidence.

2. Many clinicians are convinced of the validity of projective tests such as the Draw-A-Person (DAP) test. Yet research on the DAP consistently shows that the signs posited by many clinicians to be diagnostic of specific psychopathological characteristics possess little or no validity. How can we account for this stunning discrepancy? Chapman and Chapman (1967, 1969) hypothesized that individuals are prone to *illusory correlations*—perceived relationships between variables that are, in fact, largely or entirely unrelated—and that this tendency is especially strong when the variables intuitively "seem" to be associated with one another. Chapman and Chapman (1967) tested this hypothesis by showing undergraduates a series of fabricated DAP protocols containing certain features (e.g., large eyes, big head), along with a description of the personality characteristics (e.g., suspicious, concerned about intelligence) of the patient who supposedly produced each drawing. Subjects were then asked to estimate the extent to which these DAP features co-occurred with certain personality characteristics. Unbeknownst to the subjects, there was *no correlation* between the DAP features and personality characteristics in this data set. Yet the subjects consistently perceived certain DAP features to be strongly correlated with certain personality features. Moreover, their errors corresponded to their implicit "theories" concerning which variables go together. For example, subjects reported that patients who produced DAP protocols with large eyes tended to be suspicious and that patients who produced DAP protocols with large genitals tended to concerned about their sexuality. Moreover, Chapman and Chapman found that illusory correlations persisted even when the DAP features and personality characteristics were *negatively* correlated in their data. Chapman and Chapman (1969) replicated these findings with another commonly used projective measure—the Rorschach. Thus, many clinicians' convictions regarding the validity of certain projective tests may stem from cognitive propensities to perceive relationships where none exist and from their inattentiveness to disconfirming evidence.

In summary, one major reason why psychopathologists use research designs is *to prevent themselves from being fooled.* Sophisticated psychopathology researchers are aware of their propensities toward cognitive illusions, and take pains to ensure that such ubiquitous errors in thinking do not influence their results. The research methods discussed in this chapter are designed largely to protect investigators from their own perceptual and inferential biases.

Case Study Methodology

Case studies—the detailed examination of single individuals—do play an important role in psychopathology research. In contrast to the *nomothetic* research designs emphasized in this chapter, which involve the derivation of general laws that apply to large groups of individuals, case studies are *idiographic* in nature. That is, they involve an examination of how the unique patterning of life experiences and personality features within each individual gives rise to that individual's characteristic pattern of thoughts, feelings, and behaviors. Although idiographic approaches can be useful for reconstructing and understanding a given person's life history, they do not provide stringent tests of hypotheses. The distinction between nomothetic and idiographic approaches provides a partial answer to our earlier question of why years of clinical experience cannot provide conclusive answers to questions concerning the etiology of psychological disorders. In general, the case history method lends itself well to a detailed understanding of a given individual's life history, but not to the derivation of general psychological principles.

Case studies are better suited to what philosophers of science call the *context of discovery* than to the *context of justification* (Reichenbach, 1938). Whereas the context of discovery involves hypothesis generation, the context of justification involves hypothesis testing. Thus, although case studies provide a fertile ground for developing interesting hypotheses, they are woefully ill-suited for testing them. Because case studies typically lack the controls found in systematic research, they often result in misleading conclusions. For example, imagine that an individual with bipolar disorder reports that both of her parents were extremely critical of her in childhood. Can we conclude that bipolar disorder is associated with parental criticality? No. Perhaps the parental criticality is specific to this individual. Perhaps most individuals, not just those with bipolar disorder, report that their parents were critical of them in childhood, or perhaps there is something about our interviewing method that tends to elicit reports of parental criticality. No examination of case studies, no matter how meticulous, will permit us to exclude these and other alternative hypotheses. Moreover, because case studies are limited to small numbers of individuals, their generalizability to the broader population is often questionable.

Cause and Effect in Psychopathology Research

The ultimate goal of the psychopathology researcher is to uncover the causes of a disorder. We use the plural (causes) because psychological disorders are probably multiply determined. But what do we mean by cause? Meehl (1977) delineated a number of meanings of causation in the domain of psychopathology, four of which are especially relevant to our discussion. The strongest meaning of the word *cause*—which Meehl calls *specific etiology*—refers to a categorical (all-or-none) variable that is *both necessary and sufficient* for a disorder to emerge. Such cases are probably rare in psychopathology, although they are occasionally found in traditional medicine. For example, a single dominant gene is both necessary and sufficient to produce Huntington's chorea.

A second and weaker form of causation involves a dimensional variable that exerts a *threshold effect*. In other words, only when a critical level of a variable (e.g., a propensity toward anxiety) is exceeded does an individual experience risk for the disorder. Below this threshold, the individual's risk for the disorder is nonexistent. A variant of this second form of causation involves a *step-function*, in which the individual's risk for the disorder increases sharply when a critical level of a variable is exceeded. In a step-function model, unlike a threshold model, the individual's risk for the disorder is low, but not nonexistent, below this critical level.

A third and still weaker form of causation involves a variable that is *necessary but not sufficient* for a disorder to arise. The most common variant of this form of causation is referred to as a *diathesis-stress model*. In a diathesis-stress model, elevated levels of certain variables create a *diathesis*, or vulnerability, to a disorder. This vulnerability, which is often genetically influenced, is actualized only when the individual encounters a psychological or biological stressor. Note that according to a diathesis-stress model, both vulnerability factors and stressors are necessary for a disorder to emerge; neither variable alone can do the trick. Gottesman (1991), for example, argued that the etiology of schizophrenia can best be accommodated within a diathesis-stress model in which a genetic liability to schizophrenia interacts with environmental (e.g., anxiety-provoking life events) and/or biological (e.g., early viral exposure) stressors to produce the disorder.

Finally, a causal factor can be *neither necessary nor sufficient* for psychopathology. Many general risk factors for psychopathology (e.g., excessive reactivity) are probably of this type.

Thus, there are several ways to conceptualize the cause(s) of psychopathology. But what research methods are best suited for inferring these causes?

Experimental vs. Quasi-Experimental Designs

In most research in psychopathology, investigators are placed in a quandary. They want to determine whether one or more factors (e.g., psychosocial stress, early brain trauma) are causes of the psychopathological condition. The design best suited for determining causation is an *experimental design*, in which subjects are randomly assigned to two different conditions, one of which receives the experimental manipulation (the experimental group), whereas the other does not (the control group). In such a design, the experimenter manipulates the independent variable to ascertain its effect on the dependent variable(s) of interest.

But in most research in psychopathology, it is impossible to randomly assign subjects to conditions, and it would be unethical if it were possible. For example, if one wishes to study the personality characteristics of individuals with schizophrenia, one cannot, for obvious practical and ethical reasons, randomly assign individuals to either a schizophrenic experimental group or nonschizophrenic control group. Consequently, most research designs in psychopathology are *quasi-experimental*. In a quasi-experimental design, we compare two or more groups (e.g., depressed vs. nondepressed subjects) that come into our study with certain preexisting characteristics. Because our subjects have not been randomly assigned to conditions, quasi-experimental studies, unlike experimental studies, cannot be used to draw causal inferences. A moment's reflection reveals the reason for this limitation. Because subjects in quasi-experimental designs have not been randomly assigned to groups, the groups often differ on numerous *extraneous*, or *nuisance*, *variables*. For example, if we evaluate the personality characteristics of patients with schizophrenia and comparison subjects, it is virtually inevitable that these two groups will differ on variables other than schizophrenia per se. For example, the patient group may be lower than the comparison group in socioeconomic status (SES), IQ, hygiene, quality of diet, and a host of other variables, many of which could affect scores on dependent variables.

To address this problem, researchers who utilize quasi-experimental designs frequently implement a technique known as *matching*, in which the groups in a quasi-experimental design are equated on potentially relevant variables. By "potentially relevant" we mean variables that could affect the dependent variable. So, in the example above, the investigator could match schizophrenic and nonschizophrenic groups on variables that might influence scores on personality measures, such as SES, IQ, and gender. Some investigators have tried to *statistically control* for these potentially relevant variables by using techniques such as analysis of covariance, but this technique is problematic statistically when used in this manner and is generally not recommended (Chapman & Chapman, 1973; Lord, 1967).

Although matching is a useful strategy in quasi-experimental designs, it has limitations. First, even if the investigator has equated the groups on 100 potentially relevant variables, it is always possible that the groups differ on a 101st variable—a variable that the investigator had not considered. This unpleasant fact explains why quasi-experimental designs cannot be used to draw definitive causal inferences: It is not possible for the investigator to rule out every conceivable nuisance variable.

Second, matching rests on causal assumptions that may be incorrect. Investigators match on variables implicitly assumed to be nuisance variables. But as Meehl (1971) illustrated, variables traditionally considered nuisance variables, such as social class, could easily be a critical element in a complex causal chain. If the variable on which we match is actually a part of the causal chain, matching will distort the picture and bias our interpretations. Although matching is a valuable control for nuisance variables, it should never be applied in a cookbook fashion without considering the potential causal theories for a disorder.

Third, matching on one variable often results in systematic differences between our sample and the general population (Chapman & Chapman, 1973). For example, if we want to match schizophrenic and comparison groups on IQ, we would have to select high-scoring patients to match low-scoring comparison subjects because patients with schizophrenia tend to score lower on almost every task. The resultant patient group will overrepresent paranoid patients because patients with paranoid schizophrenia tend to be brighter and to show less of the thought disorder that would hinder performance on an IQ test. Similarly, selecting the low-scoring comparison subjects would produce a sample of subjects with lower SES, less education, and a different upbringing because all of these variables are correlated with IQ. So in this case, our matching strategy leaves us with unrepresentative patient and/or comparison samples.

Because psychopathology researchers typically must rely on quasi-experimental designs, they are limited in their ability to infer cause-and-effect relations. Researchers who use quasi-experimental designs must instead gradually piece together causal inferences from a variety of forms of circumstantial evidence. Such inferences are necessarily tentative and uncertain.

To a limited extent, the problem of causal inferences can be overcome by examining what are sometimes loosely referred to as experiments of nature, which are sudden and typically unexpected events (e.g., natural disasters) that intrude upon individuals in a more or less random fashion. We say "loosely referred to" because such studies should be technically viewed as quasi-experiments rather than true experiments. This is because subjects cannot be randomly assigned to either experience or not experience these life events. As a consequence, even these studies do not permit definitive cause-and-effect inferences. Nevertheless, psychopathology researchers can sometimes capitalize on the opportunities offered by experiments of nature by comparing the psychology symptoms of individuals who have been exposed to a major stressor with those of individuals who were not exposed to this stressor. In an ideal world, the researcher would also have access to data on the psychological status of both groups of individuals prior to the stressor. But because experiments of nature are almost by definition unpredictable, these data are rarely available.

A good example of such a study was conducted by Wood, Bootzin, Rosenhan, Nolan-Hoeksema, & Jourden (1992), who examined the prevalence and content of nightmares following the 1989 Loma Prieta earthquake among college students in the San Francisco area (who experienced the earthquake) and among a comparison sample of college students from Arizona (who did not experience the earthquake). They found that during the three weeks following the earthquake, approximately 40% of the San Francisco area students reported earthquake-related nightmares, compared to 5% of Arizona students. Wood et al. were not able, of course, to randomly assign subjects to earthquake and nonearthquake conditions. Consequently, we cannot conclusively rule out the possibility that San Francisco area students were more prone to earthquake-related nightmares than Arizona students, and that their higher rates of such nightmares were therefore a consequence of preexisting differences rather than the earthquake itself. Nevertheless, the dramatic difference in the prevalence of these nightmares between groups appears to render this explanation unlikely.

Psychopathology researchers often must reconcile themselves to quasi-experimental designs because they cannot expose subjects randomly to stressful life events. Nevertheless, three major research paradigms in psychopathology are experimental in nature and thus allow relatively unambiguous causal conclusions. First, researchers may utilize *analogue experiments*, which involve attempts to produce variants of psychopathology in either human or animal subjects. Imagine, for example, that an investigator is interested in the hypothesis that depression is characterized by underactivation of the left hemisphere. Rather than obtain a large sample of clinically depressed individuals, the investigator might instead use mood-induction procedures to produce mild analogues of depression, such as having subjects read Velten cards (Velten, 1968), which consist of statements that tend to induce sadness in normal individuals. Alternatively, the investigator might induce *learned helplessness* in subjects by presenting them with insoluble puzzles. In both cases, the investigator would then examine subjects' brain wave activity to test the hypothesis of left hemisphere underactivation. Although analogue experiments can be useful, they do have potential pitfalls. In particular, the investigator who conducts such experiments must assume that the analogue provides an adequate model of the psychopathological condition of interest. If, for example, the mild and transient dysphoria that follows a mood induction procedure differs qualitatively from clinical depression, then generalizing from the former to the latter will be misleading (Coyne, 1994).

One variation of the analogue approach uses *animal models* of psychopathology, which involve attempts to produce a simulated form of a mental disorder in nonhumans. For example, some researchers (e.g., Seligman, 1975) have hypothesized that exposing animals to uncontrollable aversive stimuli produces a state of learned helplessness characterized by apathy, passivity, and loss of appetite—a response that is similar to at least some forms of human depression. Nevertheless, because humans may be different from other animals on variables potentially relevant to psychopathology (e.g., moral development, abstract thinking, language), researchers who use animal models of psychopathology must be cautious in extrapolating their findings to humans. In addition, research using animal models often involves complex ethical considerations (Ulrich, 1991).

Challenge paradigms represent another experimental approach. In the *challenge paradigm*, subjects are randomly presented with stimuli that are thought to trigger a pathological response. Biological challenges, such as CO_2 inhalation, have been used with panic patients to see how reliably and under what circumstances they trigger a panic attack (Barlow, 1988). Of course, challenge paradigms raise ethical issues. They can be used only when the impact on subjects is transitory. Nevertheless, patients will often cooperate with such studies because they want to help advance research that might uncover the mechanisms behind a disorder. In the case of panic, challenge paradigms have given us considerable insight into both the biological and psychological mechanisms behind this disorder (e.g., Gorman, Liebowitz, Fyer, & Stein, 1989).

Finally, researchers interested in the effects of an intervention on a given individual may use *single-subject experimental designs*, in which each subject serves as his or her own control. For example, in an *A-B-A-B*, or *reversal*, design, the investigator measures a relevant aspect of the subject's behavior (e.g., nail biting) at baseline (A) and then again after an intervention (e.g., relaxation training) is introduced (B). To ensure that any change in the subject's behavior at B was not due to factors other than the intervention (e.g., passage of time), the intervention is withdrawn (reversed) in the second A phase and then introduced again in the second B phase. If the subject's behavior improves only after the treatment is presented (i.e., after both B phases), then one can safely conclude that the treatment is effective. This conclusion rests upon several assumptions, however. For example, if the treatment has lasting effects, then one would not expect a return of the subject's behavior to baseline in the reversal phase. Unlike case studies, single-subject designs often permit cause-and-effect inferences because they involve the systematic manipulation of independent variables within a subject. Like case studies, however, these designs are idiographic and are thus often limited in their generalizability.

Most research designs described in this chapter are nonexperimental or quasi-experimental.

Psychometric Issues

The study of any psychological phenomenon, including psychopathology, involves the measurement and interpretation of relevant variables. If we could measure those variables directly and flawlessly, we could proceed immediately to the interpretation stage. But we almost never have that luxury. Therefore, we virtually always need to consider the potential problems introduced by less than perfect measurement.

Reliability

The term *reliability* refers to the consistency of a measure. There are three major types of reliability: *test-retest reliability* (consistency over time), *interrater reliability* (consistency among raters), and *internal consistency reliability* (consistency among the items in the measure). Traditionally, a correlation coefficient is the index of reliability, with +1.00 indicating perfect reliability and 0.00 indicating no reliability. Reliability is the critical first element in evaluating a measure, but as we will see shortly, it does not tell the entire story.

Several types of reliability are relevant in the field of psychopathology. The ability of multiple observers to agree on a diagnosis (assessed by interrater reliability) is critical. This agreement can be indexed with either the traditional correlation or intraclass correlation coefficient (for a continuous variable) or a simple percent agreement index (for a discrete variable). The *Kappa coefficient* (Cohen, 1960) is preferred over a percent agreement index because Kappa takes into account the base rate of the diagnosis. The lower the base rate for a diagnosis, the easier it is for two raters to agree by chance alone. The applicability of test-retest and internal consistency reliability depends on the nature of the variable being measured. For example, some variables are relatively stable over time (e.g., IQ), whereas others are not (e.g., mood). We should expect high test-retest reliability only for stable variables.

The *structured diagnostic interview* represents a critical advance in the reliability of psychiatric diagnoses. Spitzer, Endicott, and Robins (1975) spurred the development of structured interviews, as well as the more detailed and descriptive diagnostic criteria first introduced in *DSM-III*, with their analysis of the sources of diagnostic unreliability. Structured interviews reduce a major contributor to diagnostic unreliability: differences in the information and observations available to different diagnosticians. The combination of structured interviews and more explicit diagnostic criteria improved diagnostic reliability dramatically (Spitzer et al., 1975) and has probably contributed to many of the significant research achievements of the past 20 years. Today, structured diagnostic interviews are the norm in research and increasingly the norm in specialty clinics (Weins, 1990). One commonly used structured interview is the Structured Clinical Interview for DSM-IV (SCID; Fint, Spitzer, Gibbon, & Williams, 1995), which assesses most of the major mental disorders in DSM-IV.

Validity

Validity refers to the extent to which our measure assesses what it purports to measure. Note that although reliability is necessary for validity, it does not guarantee it. Imagine that a researcher claims that the length of a person's neck is a measure of her "intelligence." Such a measure would be reliable (i.e., repeatable over occasions), but it would (we hope!) have no validity as a measure of intelligence. In psychopathology, we rarely have the luxury of a perfect criterion to judge the validity of our measures. As a consequence, our indices of validity often are intertwined with our theories concerning what we are measuring. We judge the validity of IQ tests, for example, by observing how well they predict criteria that are theoretically related to intelligence. We might validate an IQ test by determining how well it predicts grades in school or performance on a task that we believe requires intellectual skill. This approach to validity is referred to as *criterion-related validity*. In criterion-related validity it is necessary to specify the criterion. For example, an IQ test may be a valid predictor of school grades but have no validity when used to predict happiness. Criterion-related validity can refer to how well a test relates to either a criterion that is already available (*concurrent validity*) or to a criterion that will only be available in the future (*predictive validity*).

Cronbach and Meehl (1955) integrated many of the above ideas into a concept called *construct validity*. A construct is an attribute that is not directly observable, such as intelligence, extroversion, or schizophrenia. Cronbach and Meehl argued that in science we are often interested in more than just the reliability or validity of a measure. Instead, we want to know the validity of the theoretical concept that the measure is designed to assess (e.g., an IQ test as a measure of the construct of intelligence). Validating a construct involves a converging operation in which we systematically test predictions derived from our theory. These predictions are embedded within a *nomological network* (an interlocking series of hypotheses derived from one's theoretical understanding of the construct). These predictions may be tested with either reliability or validity indices depending on the nature of the hypothesized relationship. Furthermore, the theory may sometimes predict either strong or weak relationships, so that sometimes we expect large validity coefficients whereas at other times we expect small coefficients. For example, our nomological network of intelligence might include an expectation of stability over time (high test-retest reliability), a generalized ability applicable to many different situations (high internal consistency reliability), strong relationships with current academic achievement (high concurrent validity), and strong relationships with future occupational success (high predictive validity). Construct validity does not yield a single index but rather is evaluated by the broad pattern of theoretically relevant relationships observed. Psychopathology research can be thought of as involving the construct validation of hypothesized theoretical concepts, such as depression and schizophrenia.

Defining and Refining the Syndrome

How do researchers establish the validity of psychopathological syndromes? How can they determine if their definition of a psychopathological syndrome is too broad or too narrow? Like other constructs, psychiatric diagnoses represent latent attributes that are not directly observable. To support the construct validity of a hypothesized diagnosis, psychopathology researchers must accumulate *indirect* evidence. In an influential article, Robins and Guze (1970) delineated a comprehensive approach toward establishing the construct validity of psychiatric diagnoses. They argued that a valid diagnosis must accomplish five things:

1. Describe the clinical syndrome with sufficient clarity to permit high interrater reliability.
2. Predict diagnosed individuals' performance

on laboratory (e.g., cognitive/attentional tasks) and psychometric (e.g., personality questionnaires) indices.
3. Predict diagnosed individuals' natural history (i.e., course and outcome).
4. Predict diagnosed individuals' family history of psychiatric syndromes.
5. Differentiate the diagnosis from other, superficially similar, diagnoses.

In addition, although not mentioned by Robins and Guze, a valid diagnosis should ideally:

6. Predict response to treatment.

Robins and Guze's approach is an application of the principle of construct validation to psychiatric diagnoses. Each of these six pieces of information are components of the nomological network in which one's predictions concerning the relations between the hypothesized syndrome and external variables are embedded (Waldman, Lilienfeld, & Lahey, 1995).

We can best understand the Robins and Guze approach with reference to a specific diagnosis, such as schizophrenia. In the case of schizophrenia, there is evidence from numerous studies that the diagnosis of schizophrenia (1) can be reliably differentiated from other, superficially similar diagnoses (e.g., bipolar disorder); (2) predicts performance on laboratory (e.g., smooth pursuit eye tracking) and psychometric (e.g., MMPI) indices; (3) is generally, but not invariably, associated with a chronic course and poor outcome; (4) is associated with a family history of schizophrenia and "schizophrenia spectrum" disorders (e.g., schizotypal and paranoid personality disorders); (5) differs in its external correlates from other, superficially similar conditions (e.g., psychotic mood disorders); and (6) predicts a positive response to dopamine antagonists (Gottesman, 1991). Thus, according to Robins and Guze's approach, the diagnosis of schizophrenia can be said to possess construct validity.

The Robins and Guze criteria can also be used to refine a syndrome. If a revised definition of a syndrome improves the prediction of one or more of these six criteria, this revision is usually accepted. For example, until the publication of *DSM-III*, schizophrenia was defined more broadly in the United States than in Europe. This broad definition included patients we would now call bipolar. Evidence for differential treatment effects between this narrow definition of schizophrenia and bipolar disorder, as well as differential courses, family histories, and other criteria, provided convincing evidence in support of this revision in diagnostic criteria.

The Robins and Guze approach can also be applied to the examination of the construct validity of multiple syndromes. If, for example, two syndromes are characterized by identical external correlates, such as family history and treatment response, these two syndromes may be manifestations of a single disorder. For example, researchers once distinguished manic-depression (manic episodes plus depressive episodes) from unipolar mania (manic episodes only). Subsequent research indicated, however, that mania with associated depression did not differ from mania alone in terms of natural history, family history, response to treatment, and other correlates (Depue & Monroe, 1978). Consequently, *DSM-IV* regards both mania with associated depression and mania alone as aspects of one overarching syndrome known, perhaps misleadingly, as bipolar disorder.

How should the researcher proceed if a proposed diagnosis fails to meet some or all of the Robins and Guze criteria for construct validity? One possible reason for such low validity is that the proposed diagnosis is too broad—that is, the individuals it encompasses are too *heterogeneous*. A researcher who has either theoretical or empirical reasons to believe that a diagnostic category is heterogeneous can use several approaches to reduce this heterogeneity. First, the researcher may elect to divide the syndrome into one or more subtypes on the basis of rational or theoretical criteria. For example, numerous researchers have argued that the diagnosis of alcohol dependence (alcoholism) is heterogeneous and have proposed ways of meaningfully subdividing this diagnosis. Some have suggested, for instance, that alcoholism that appears prior to another psychiatric disorder (i.e., primary alcoholism) tends to be characterized by an earlier onset and more negative prognosis than alcoholism that appears following another psychiatric disorder (i.e., secondary alcoholism) (Goodwin & Guze, 1989). Once these putative subtypes are proposed, the researcher can use the Robins and Guze framework to determine whether they differ in their external correlates. This was the approach adopted in the earlier example of narrowing the syndrome of schizophrenia.

The researcher may also use statistical techniques to divide the syndrome into narrower and—it is hoped—more etiologically homogeneous, subtypes. For example, the technique of *factor analysis* allows researchers to ascertain whether the relations among symptoms can be accounted for by one or more underlying dimensions and may even shed light on the nature of these dimensions. For example, factor analyses of measures of schizophrenic symptoms suggest that these symptoms may be underpinned by two factors: a positive symptom factor (excesses, such as delusions and hallucations) and a negative symptom factor (deficits, such as flat affect and withdrawal) (Schuldberg, Quinlan, Morganstern, & Glazer, 1990). Such data are consistent with the hypothesis that positive symptom and negative symptom schizophrenia are etiologically distinct conditions, although construct validational studies using Robins and Guze's framework will be needed to further validate this distinction (Andreasen, Flaum, Swayze, Tyrell, & Arndt, 1990).

Another technique used to subdivide syndromes is *cluster analysis*, which can be used to sort symptoms (or, in some cases, patients with these symptoms) into different categories. This sorting procedure is performed by taking mathematical measures of similarity among the variables in question, and creating different clusters that are as homogeneous as possible. Unlike factor analysis, which examines only the variance shared by variables, cluster analysis examines the total variance of these variables. Although cluster analysis can be useful for generating hypotheses concerning the existence of subtypes that may be nested within a broader diagnosis, this technique often yields quite different results depending on the clustering algorithm used (Meehl & Golden, 1982) or the variables selected (Meehl, 1990).

Epidemiological Studies: Gathering Clues to Etiology

What Is Epidemiology and How Is It Relevant to Psychopathology?

How common is a psychological disorder in the general population? What characteristics are associated with its frequency in the general population? How often do cases of this disorder arise and disappear? These questions are addressed by epidemiological methods. Although the term *epidemiology* derives from *epidemic*, epidemiologists concern themselves with far more than the spread of diseases. Epidemiology can be defined as the study of the (1) distribution of disorders in a given population and (2) the variables that are statistically associated with this distribution (Rutter, 1994). Thus, an epidemiological study of antisocial personality disorder (ASPD) would probably focus on the frequency of ASPD in the general population and the factors (e.g., gender, social class, and family history of antisocial behavior) that covary with the frequency of ASPD in the population.

Why do epidemiologists want to know these things? Research on the rate of a disorder in a population provides a baseline for comparison with the rates in various subpopulations. For example, the co-twins of monozygotic ("identical") twins with schizophrenia (see "The Twin Study Paradigm" later in this chapter) have approximately a 50% chance of developing schizophrenia (Gottesman, 1991). This 50% figure takes on full meaning only when compared to the general population prevalence of schizophrenia—approximately 1%. Thus, epidemiological data permit us to determine that having a monozygotic twin with schizophrenia increases one's risk of schizophrenia approximately fiftyfold.

Research on the characteristics that covary with the frequency of a disorder in a population may provide important leads to its etiology. For example, epidemiological studies have revealed that ASPD is more common in males than females, is more common among individuals of lower social class, and is associated with a family history of ASPD and criminality (see *DSM-IV*). Such data might suggest clues to the etiology of ASPD. For example, the finding that ASPD is more common in males than females might point to biological or socialization variables that show marked sex differences and that potentially increase individuals' risk for antisocial behavior. Such variables might include levels of testosterone (Dabbs & Morris, 1990) or adults' tendency to differentially reinforce physical aggression in boys and girls (Serbin, O'Leary, Kent, & Tonick, 1973).

This strategy of identifying factors associated with the frequency of a disorder in the population has yielded several spectacular successes in medicine. For example, the cause of cholera was identified in London in 1848 by Snow (1855), who constructed a detailed map of the distribution of affected cases during an epidemic. In this way, Snow traced the origin of the epidemic to a specific water pump (Tsuang, Tohen, & Murphy, 1988). Subsequent investigators were able to identify the bacterium that produces cholera. Thus far, such remarkable success stories have eluded epidemiologists investigating the causes of psychopathology. For example, although Faris and Dunham's (1939) classic epidemiological study revealed that the rates of schizophrenia in Chicago progressively increased as one moved from the outskirts of the city to its centrally located slums, their investigation and others like it have shed little light on the causes of schizophrenia. Nevertheless, the hope remains that epidemiological research may help to pinpoint risk factors for psychological disorders and may ultimately provide clues to their etiology.

Epidemiology is the study of *who* has *what*, *where*, *when*, and *how* (Costello, 1990). In other words, epidemiologists strive to determine which individuals are affected with which disorders, the geographical distribution of these disorders, the time course of the appearance and spread of these disorders, and (ideally) the processes that give rise to these disorders. The last of these goals,—*how*—is the ultimate goal of epidemiological research because an understanding of the etiology of a disorder often provides the information needed to treat or prevent it.

Critical Concepts and Terms in Epidemiology

Several concepts and terms are crucial for a full understanding of epidemiological methods. The two most critical are prevalence and incidence. *Prevalence* refers to the percentage of a population afflicted with a disorder during a given time period (e.g., one month or one year). *Point prevalence* is defined as the percentage of a population that is afflicted with a disorder at a single point in time (e.g., January 1, 1999). *Period prevalence* is defined as the percentage of a population afflicted with a disorder during a specified time period (e.g., from January 1, 1999, to January 1, 2001). *Lifetime prevalence* is the percentage of the population that develops the disorder sometime during their lifetime. The term *base rate* is often used to refer to lifetime prevalence (Meehl & Rosen, 1955).

Incidence, which is often confused with prevalence, refers to the percentage of *new cases* that arise during a specified time period (Regier & Burke, 1985). For example, if in a population of 1 million individuals, 1,000 individuals develop bipolar disorder during a one-year interval, then the one-year incidence of bipolar disorder in this population is .1%. A moment's reflection leads to the conclusion that prevalence and incidence will be similar only if the disorder in question is brief in duration. Incidence is assessed with a longitudinal design in which a sample of unaffected individuals is followed over time to ascertain what proportion develop the disorder in question.

Two other important epidemiological terms are the comparison group and the case-control method. Epidemiological researchers often select samples of affected individuals from settings in which the rates of a disorder are known to be elevated (e.g., an inpatient unit, a mental health clinic). This strategy is more efficient and economical than sampling affected individuals from the general population, particularly if the prevalence of the disorder is low. For example, if one were interested in examining the characteristics of individuals with autistic disorder, which occurs in no more than 5 out of 10,000 individuals in the general population (*DSM-IV*), one would have to sample 200,000 individuals to obtain a sample of 100 autistic subjects. Instead, one could probably obtain enough autistic subjects by sampling only a handful of inpatient child psychiatry units or mental retardation clinics. Having identified a sample of autistic individuals, one would then need to compare the findings from this sample with those from a sample of individuals without autistic disorder. Because this latter sample serves as a baseline with which the rates of various characteristics in the former group can be compared, it is referred to as a *comparison group*. This group is also sometimes referred to as a *control group*, although this more traditional term is misleading. Unlike a true control group in experimental research, in which extraneous differences between groups are minimized by the process of random assignment, a comparison group often differs from the affected group in many characteristics (e.g., age, gender, social class). The term control group should technically be reserved for groups that have been created by randomly assigning individuals to conditions. Nonetheless, tradition dies hard. The comparison of groups of individuals with and without a disorder (or, in some cases, with a different disorder) is typically referred to as the *case-control design* (even though the term case-comparison design would be more technically accurate).

Methods of Sampling

Thus far, we have discussed how epidemiological researchers examine the distribution of disorders in a population. But unless the population of interest is small, it is not feasible to assess all members of a population. Instead, the investigator must be content to obtain a sample that provides a good approximation to the population from which it is drawn.

How should a population be sampled? The answer to this question is not as simple as it appears, as there are at least three ways in which sampling can be performed. In the first approach, *random sampling*, every individual in the population has an equal chance of being selected. The resulting sample is designed to be as representative as possible of the larger population from which it is drawn. Random sampling is frequently used by political polling organizations to obtain representative samples of registered voters.

The second approach, *stratified random sampling*, is used when the researcher wants to ensure that one or more subgroups within the population are adequately represented in the sample. Imagine, for example, that you were interested in investigating the prevalence of bipolar disorder across different religious groups in the United States. If you used a random sampling approach, there might not be sufficient numbers of individuals in certain religious groups (e.g., Hindu, Shinto) to permit a statistically meaningful examination of the rates of bipolar disorder in such groups. To deal with this problem, you could oversample from these underrepresented religious groups and later apply an adjustment factor to correct for the fact that different religious groups have been sampled in differing proportions. Specifically, you could weight subjects individually based on the probability of their selection in the sample (Regier & Burke, 1985). This approach is called stratified random sampling because the investigator samples extensively from one or more *strata* (i.e., "layers" or subgroups) within the population.

The third approach is called *cluster sampling*, which is typically used when the investigator does not have access to a list of every member of the population. This often occurs when the population is very large. Thus, the researcher can instead sample from clusters of individuals, such as housing projects or apartment complexes. Within clusters, samples of households can then be selected through either random or stratified random sampling (Regier & Burke, 1985).

Potential Biases in Epidemiological Research

Epidemiologists must be careful to avoid biases that may distort the results of their investigations. Perhaps the most crucial of these is *selection bias*, which results when a sample is chosen on the basis of a characteristic that is not representative of the population to which the investigator intends to generalize (Burke & Regier, 1988). An example of this bias can be found in the work of Freeman (1979), who examined the relation between giftedness in children and their risk for psychopathology. When Freeman sampled from an association for the families of intellectually gifted children, she found a high rate of psychological disturbance in these children. But when she sampled gifted children from the general population, she found a low rate. Had she relied exclusively on the former sample, her conclusions would have been misleading. Interestingly, Freeman found that the parents of this sample reported high levels of divorce and conflict. Apparently, parents who join organizations for gifted children are not a random sample of all parents with gifted children. Perhaps high levels of familial dysfunction lead parents to seek out emotional support or camaraderie (Rutter, 1994); or perhaps gifted children with psychopathology tend to increase the likelihood of parental turmoil.

The most common example of selection bias in psychopathology research involves the use of clinical samples drawn from different populations across studies. When this occurs, replication failures often result. For example, Luchins (1982) argued that inconsistent findings across studies of cerebral ventricular enlargement in schizophrenia were a consequence of examining clinical samples drawn from substantially different populations. Luchins noted that the studies that reported enlarged ventricles examined chronic patients with neuropsychological deficits, whereas studies that reported normal ventricles examined acute patients with normal neuropsychological functioning. As another example, Gorenstein (1982) reported that psychopathic personalities exhibited deficits on a number of measures of frontal lobe dysfunction. Hare (1984) failed to replicate Gorenstein's findings despite using the same measures of frontal lobe functioning. Hare explained this discrepancy by noting that Gorenstein's sample, unlike his, was characterized by high rates of alcohol abuse, which can produce frontal lobe damage.

Using clinical samples can also result in misleadingly high estimates of *comorbidity* (Feinstein, 1985)—that is, the overlap of two or more diagnoses within an individual (see Lilienfeld, Waldman, & Israel, 1994). Comorbidity can result from either Berksonian bias (Berkson, 1946), clinical selection bias (du Fort, Newman, & Bland, 1993), or both. *Berksonian bias* is purely mathematical, and results from the fact that an individual with two disorders can seek treatment for either disorder, so that individuals with comorbid disorders will be overrepresented in clinical settings. *Clinical selection bias* results from an increased likelihood of treatment seeking for individuals with one condition because of the presence of another condition. Individuals with alcoholism, for example, may be unlikely to seek treatment unless they are also depressed or anxious (Lilienfeld et al., 1994). Clinical selection bias can be thought of as the "straw that breaks the camel's back" effect. Individuals with a single disorder may not be motivated to obtain help until they find themselves unable to cope with a second disorder. Both of these biases will produce comorbidity rates that are higher in clinical settings than those derived from studies of the general population.

Epidemiological studies are a valuable tool for identifying potential causal or contributory factors. Nevertheless, epidemiological work alone is almost never able to establish specific links between pathology and potential causal influences. But when you are faced with a field filled with haystacks, it is helpful to know which one is likely to hold the needle that you are looking for. Epidemiological studies serve that role well.

Studying Genetic and Environmental Influences

We often take for granted that our family has had an enormous influence on our personalities. We readily point to specific experiences that we feel have shaped our thinking, attitudes, and sense of who we are. Nevertheless, in reality we often have little idea how our families have influenced our development, and more often than not, our impressions leave out one of the most potent family influences—our genetic heritage.

In an intact family, in which biological parents raise their offspring, we are influenced by both the genetic and the environmental contributions of our parents. These independent effects are impossible to separate in a natural environment. Furthermore, it is likely that genetic and environmental influences interact, meaning that individuals with different genetic makeups react differently to different environments. In other words, the dual influence of genes and environment may be more potent than the sum of the individual effects. For example, adoptees with a genetic predisposition toward antisocial behavior are especially likely to develop antisocial behavior if they are reared with antisocial parents (Cadoret, Cain, & Crowe, 1983).

There is now a general consensus that both genetic and environmental influences contribute to virtually every form of psychopathology, but that has not always been the case. From the 1940s well into the 1970s, professionals generally favored exclusively psychogenic theories for most forms of psychopathology. For example, the cause of schizophrenia was attributed to such factors as the "schizophrenogenic mother" (Fromm-Reichman, 1948) or the "double-bind" (Bateson, Jackson, Haley, & Weakland, 1956), even though the data in support of these models were equivocal at best. The Zeitgeist during the middle of the 20th century was to pin the cause of psychopathology on the environment—especially the parents—and the Zeitgeist was maintained in the face of growing evidence of a genetic contribution to a variety of psychopathologies. For example, Kallman (1938) argued that genetics played a significant role in schizophrenia, and he published data consistent with this position. By the early 1960s, there was extensive data supporting the position that genetics played a significant role in schizophrenia (see Gottesman & Shields [1972] for a review). Yet Meehl's classic 1962 paper proposing a genetic diathesis for schizophrenia was considered revolutionary by many and implausible by many more.

Behavior genetics is the study of genetic influences on behavior. The designs discussed below only scratch the surface of the paradigms available.

More behavior genetics research has been conducted on animals than on humans because of the experimental control possible with animal models (Plomin, DeFries, & McClearn, 1990). But even without experimental control, powerful paradigms allow us to probe genetic influences on human behavior. Complete coverage of these approaches is beyond the scope of this chapter. Interested readers are referred to Plomin et al. (1990) for more details.

Demonstrating a Genetic Influence

Behavior genetics uses the concept of *heritability*, which is the extent to which individual differences in a characteristic (e.g., a mental disorder) are attributable to genetic factors. Genetic factors can be subdivided into additive genetic influences and nonadditive genetic influences. *Additive* genetic influences involve the direct effects of genes, whereas *nonadditive* genetic influences involve interactions among genetic elements, including interactions within genes (*dominance*) and interactions among genes (*epistasis*) (Plomin et al., 1990). Because only additive genetic effects are directly transmittable from parent to offspring, these effects are of considerable interest to animal breeders. The distinction between additive and nonadditive genetic influences has implications for the definition of heritability. We use the term *broad heritability* to refer to both additive and nonadditive genetic effects and the term *narrow heritability* to refer to additive genetic effects only (Loehlin, 1992).

Research on the heritability of psychopathological conditions typically uses one of three approaches—the family, twin, or adoption paradigms. Each paradigm has advantages and disadvantages. Traditionally, each paradigm starts by sampling patients with specific characteristics. These initial patients are referred to as *probands*. Probands are selected by both diagnosis and certain nondiagnostic features. For example, if we were conducting a twin study of the genetics of bipolar disorder, we would select probands who have bipolar disorder and who are twins. Once probands are selected, their relevant relatives are identified and diagnosed, where the definition of *relevant* depends on the paradigm. The effectiveness of each of the paradigms rests on how carefully the proband cases are sampled and how accurately the diagnoses of relatives are made.

Sampling is critical because a biased sample will produce biased, and usually erroneous, results. The best sampling technique is random sampling or some variation on this method, although true random sampling is rarely possible. A common strategy is to select all patients admitted to certain treatment facilities during a specified period who meet all the selection criteria. The advantage of this approach is that it avoids subtle biases that may result from less systematic selection procedures, such as having professionals in the community refer suitable cases. For example, professionals may be more likely to refer a case for a study of the genetics of a disorder if they know that there is an unusually high level of pathology in the patient's family. Such cases, although perhaps more clinically interesting, are often unrepresentative of the population. Virtually all sampling techniques have potential biases. Selecting probands from state hospital admissions will overrepresent individuals who lack supportive families or other resources that permit them to stay in the community despite significant pathology, and it will underrepresent individuals who have the financial resources for private treatment. One should always detail the specific sampling procedures to allow other researchers to make reasoned judgments about potential biases.

Once a sample of probands has been gathered, the next task is to identify and diagnose the relatives that are relevant for each paradigm. That task can be formidable. Simply identifying the relatives and tracking them down can be very difficult; some relatives may have moved away and others may have died. Once relatives have been identified and located, the process of diagnosing each relative is far from simple. Three approaches have been used. One approach, the *family history method*, uses the secondary reports of cooperative relatives to make the diagnosis. This is the least expensive procedure, but also the least effective and most biased. Evidence suggests that the family history method tends to produce high false negative rates (not identifying affected family members) but low false positive rates (incorrectly labeling a family member as affected) (Andreasen, Endicott, Spitzer, & Winokur, 1977). Relatives may also be poor observers of relevant behavior and therefore provide the researcher with inadequate information. The two most widely used procedures for obtaining diagnoses are the *individual interview approach* (Gottesman & Shields, 1972) and the *records review approach* (Kety, Rosenthal, Wender, & Schulsinger, 1968). The most valid procedure, but also the most costly and time-consuming, is to interview each relative individually. When relatives are unavailable for an interview, secondary sources of diagnostic information may be used, although traditionally analyses are carried out separately for (1) the primary data (obtained from direct interviews) and (2) the more complete data sets (where some of the data are obtained from these secondary sources). A less costly approach is to rely on standardized records, although such records are not always available. Many behavior-genetic studies have been conducted in countries with socialized medicine, such as Denmark, because these countries maintain extensive standardized medical and psychiatric records. Interviews tend to produce higher estimates of psychopathology than a review of hospital records. Generally, the more extensive the information researchers have available, the more likely they will find evidence of pathology if it exists.

Because each approach varies in its likelihood of uncovering psychopathology, one should include a comparison group and evaluate all subjects blindly (i.e., without knowledge of whether the family member is from the proband or comparison group). Comparison groups are formed by identifying subjects who are similar to the proband sample, except for the diagnostic variable that defined probands, and then finding their relevant family members.

We will briefly describe each of the three most commonly used behavior-genetic paradigms below. We will use schizophrenia as the example in our discussion even though these paradigms have been used to investigate many other disorders.

1. The family study paradigm. The family study paradigm evaluates the prevalence of relevant psychiatric disorders in relatives of patients with a specific disorder. In the study of schizophrenia, the most relevant psychiatric disorder is schizophrenia, although we often probe for related disorders as well (e.g., the so-called schizophrenia-spectrum disorders—schizoaffective disorder, paranoid personality disorder, schizotypal personality disorder). The family study paradigm starts with a sample of proband cases (patients diagnosed with schizophrenia) and proceeds to identify and diagnose as many relatives as possible. We break down the analysis by comparing the rates of schizophrenia, schizophrenia spectrum disorders, or both by the degree of genetic relatedness to the proband case. Parents, children, and full siblings share, on average, 50% of a person's genes and are referred to as *first-degree relatives*. Grandchildren, grandparents, half-siblings, aunts, and uncles (*second-degree relatives*) share, on average, 25% of a person's genes, and first cousins (*third-degree relatives*) share, on average, 12.5% of a person's genes. If schizophrenia is heritable, as the degree of genetic relatedness to the proband drops, we expect the rates of schizophrenia to drop. A comparison group should always be included—in this case, family members of subjects who do not have schizophrenia. And, of course, all diagnostic evaluations should be done blindly (i.e., without knowledge of whether the subject under evaluation is from a proband or comparison family).

The major drawback in family studies is that genetic and environmental influences are confounded. Thus, the finding that psychopathology runs in families does not establish that genetic factors are responsible because environmental influences would produce the same results. On the other hand, a finding that psychopathology does not run in families all but rules out the possibility of genetic influences, although it is remotely possible that certain nonadditive genetic influences may not show up in family studies (Lykken, McGue, Tellegen, & Bouchard, 1992).

2. The twin study paradigm. The twin study paradigm[1] addresses the major weakness of the family study paradigm (the fact that environmental and genetic influences are confounded). Twin studies handle this confounding by attempting to hold environment constant. We begin by identifying probands who have developed schizophrenia and are twins. Co-twins are then located and two classifications are performed. Each twin pair is classified as either identical (also called *monozygotic* or *MZ*) or fraternal (*dizygotic* or *DZ*). MZ twins share 100% of their genes, whereas DZ twins share 50% of their genes on average. Because environment and sex-linked genes can vary dramatically for men and women, typically only same-sex DZ twins are used.[2] When a co-twin of the proband also qualifies for a diagnosis of schizophrenia, the twins are said to be *concordant*. The potential role of genetics is evaluated by comparing the concordance rate for MZ and DZ twins. Because both MZ and DZ twins are raised together, it is assumed that the environmental influences on

these two types of twins are approximately equal (termed the *equal environments assumption*). Therefore, any difference in concordance rates between MZ and DZ twins should be due to the difference in level of shared genes. The raw concordance rates may be corrected statistically to take into account the fact that it is twice as easy to sample a concordant twin pair than a nonconcordant twin pair because a concordant pair has two potential probands in the population from which the sample is drawn.

This paradigm has been used in over a dozen studies of schizophrenia, but perhaps the most influential study was conducted by Gottesman and Shields (1972). These investigators identified 24 MZ twin pairs and 33 DZ twin pairs from the Maudsley Twin Register.[3] After carefully determining zygosity (i.e., MZ or DZ), these investigators obtained extensive clinical information in order to determine concordance rates. In addition to the normal diagnostic information, they obtained case histories, family histories, and MMPIs from most of their subjects. They then obtained independent and blind diagnoses for each of their subjects from six of the best diagnosticians of the time. The comparison between MZ and DZ twins was consistent with previous studies in showing higher MZ than DZ concordance, but the real strength of this study was that the immense wealth of data allowed these investigators to examine potential markers for genetic risk, as well as optimal diagnostic criteria for identifying a homogeneous sample of patients with schizophrenia. These data have shaped selection criteria for hundreds of subsequent studies of schizophrenia, and their influence is clearly evident in the current diagnostic manual.

3. The adoption study paradigm. The adoption paradigm[4] deals with the confounding of environmental and genetic influences by studying individuals who have been separated from their biological relatives. For obvious ethical reasons, the separation from their biological relatives is not under experimental control; hence, this is a quasi-experimental design. Often one begins with probands who have developed schizophrenia and who were adopted at birth. These individuals have both a genetic heritage contributed by their biological family and an environmental heritage contributed by their adoptive family. By comparing the rates of schizophrenia in both biological and adoptive relatives, one can gauge the relative contribution of environment and genetics to the development of the disorder. As with the family study paradigm, a comparison group is selected by finding suitable subjects who have not developed schizophrenia but who were adopted, and the level of psychopathology in their biological and adoptive relatives is evaluated.

Kety et al. (1968) used the adoption study paradigm to study the potential genetic and environmental influences on schizophrenia. Using the remarkably complete record system in Denmark, they identified 33 proband cases who had developed schizophrenia and had been adopted shortly after birth, and they selected a comparison group matched with these subjects on a host of potentially confounding variables (e.g., social class of adoptive and biological parents, age at adoption). They then identified all biological and adoptive relatives for these subjects and obtained their psychiatric records. On the basis of those records, they established that there was an elevated risk for schizophrenia (approximately fivefold) only in the biological relatives of the proband cases. This remarkably rich data set has been reanalyzed over the years from other perspectives (e.g., Kety, Rosenthal, Wender, Schulsinger, & Jacobsen, 1978).

Kety et al.'s approach is known as the *adoptees' relatives approach* because it begins with schizophrenic and nonschizophrenic probands and examines the rates of psychopathology in their relatives. There are other adoption paradigms. For example, Rosenthal et al. (1968) investigated the risk for psychopathology in the adopted offspring of patients with schizophrenia. They found a tenfold increase in the rate of schizophrenia in these offspring relative to the comparison group. This approach is known as the *adoptees' study method* because it begins with schizophrenic and nonschizophrenic parents and examines the rates of psychopathology in their adopted-away offspring.

Cautionary Notes in Using These Paradigms Although the twin and adoption paradigms provide powerful tests of the hypothesis that genetics play a role in the development of schizophrenia, there are limitations to these paradigms. For example, the equal environments assumption in twin studies may not always be strictly true. Nevertheless, this assumption has generally been upheld in a number of studies (Kendler, 1983). An issue with adoption studies is that adoptive parents are not chosen randomly by the social service agencies entrusted with the task of placing children. The screening process likely eliminates potential parents who show obvious signs of psychopathology, which tends to reduce the level of pathology in the adoptive relatives. Presumably this screening process should affect the proband and comparison samples equally. In addition, adoption agencies often place adoptees with parents who are more similar to the adoptees' biological parents than would be expected by chance. Such selective placement can sometimes distort the findings of adoption studies. Researchers can sometimes deal with this problem by measuring the degree of selective placement and correcting for it statistically.

It should also be noted that different behavior-genetic paradigms may yield different estimates of heritability. The heritability estimates for personality traits derived from twin studies, for example, tend to be somewhat higher than those derived from adoption studies (Tellegen et al., 1988). Although several factors may account for this difference, one factor is that twin studies provide estimates of broad heritability, whereas adoption studies provide estimated of narrow heritability (Loehlin, 1992). The heritability estimates derived from twin studies may therefore provide a truer reflection of reality than estimates derived from adoption studies.

Finally, psychopathology researchers never have the experimental control over breeding available to genetic researchers who use animals as subjects. It is unlikely that the random matings assumed by many statistical models are actually occurring. Nonrandom matings (called *assortative matings*) distort estimates of population parameters such as gene frequency. Such assortative matings may be common in the domain of psychopathology; individuals with schizophrenia, for example, are more likely to mate with individuals with schizophrenia-spectrum disorders than would be expected by chance (Gottesman & Shields, 1982).

We have documented several limitations in the paradigms used to study genetic influences on psychopathology. Still, these paradigms have produced reasonably consistent data on genetic influences for many types of psychopathology, including schizophrenia. The convergence of findings from diverse paradigms gives us reasonable confidence in the results, even though each individual paradigm has its weaknesses.

Probing the Nature of Genetic Influences

Population genetics is the study of departures from genetic equilibrium resulting from such factors as selective pressures, mutation, migration, or nonrandom mating. Population genetics relies heavily on the statistical analysis of population base rates and changes in those base rates over generations. A question of interest to population geneticists is the well-documented negative selective pressure in schizophrenia. Patients with schizophrenia have approximately half as many offspring as the general population (Gottesman, 1991), yet the rate of schizophrenia does not appear to be dropping dramatically from generation to generation. Such data make certain genetic models unlikely. For example, if schizophrenia were due to a single dominant gene with complete penetrance, we would expect a 50% drop in the frequency of this gene and the rate of schizophrenia in each generation. Studying factors like this can provide indirect evidence concerning many questions of interest to psychopathology researchers.

Genetic paradigms can also be used to zero in on the exact locations for genetic defects. One such approach is the *linkage study*, in which the pattern of transmission of a disorder is compared with the pattern of transmission of other genetically determined characteristics, where the specific locus on the chromosome of the genetic influence for those characteristics is known (see Schizophrenia Bulletin, 1989, for detailed examples). Using a linkage approach with a sample of families from Iceland and England, Sherrington et al. (1988) isolated a genetic risk factor for schizophrenia on chromosome 5. The families in their study had unusually high rates of schizophrenia, making their *pedigrees* (the chart that shows the genetic relatedness of family members and identifies which individuals have the trait under study) especially informative. The rate of schizophrenia in most families is much lower than in the families included in this study, which raises the issue of whether the latter families are representative.

Linkage studies may soon be much more powerful as the Human Genome Project dramatically increases the number of identified human genes and their specific locations. This information will make the task of identifying linkages easier, and may even allow the use of virtually any pedigree in linkage studies. Such advances may permit us to identify genes that increase risk for specific disorders, although identifying the mechanism for that risk will still require the skills of the psychopathology researcher.

Environmental Studies

Traditionally, psychopathologists have discussed the environment as if it were a monolithic or uniform entity. More recently, however, researchers have recognized two types of environmental influences: shared and nonshared. *Shared environmental influences* make individuals within the same family similar to one another, whereas *nonshared environmental influences* make individuals within the same family different from one another. If a father is highly anxious and succeeds in making all his children anxious by overprotecting them, his anxiety would be a shared environmental influence.[5] Alternatively, if a parent severely mistreats one child but not another, the parental mistreatment would be a nonshared environmental influence. The distinction between these two types of influence is critical in psychopathology research because an increasing body of evidence indicates that nonshared, but not shared, environment plays a major role in the etiology of most mental disorders and personality traits (Bouchard, Lykken, McGue, & Segal, 1990; Plomin, 1990).

1. Behavior-genetic studies. Behavior-genetic designs are often thought of as paradigms for studying genetic influences on psychopathology. Nevertheless, they can also provide a sensitive platform for studying both shared and nonshared environmental influences (Loehlin, 1992). For example, the similarity between adoptive parents and their adopted offspring on a trait can be interpreted, in the absence of selective placement, as an estimate of shared environment on this trait because the only factor accounting for their resemblance is by definition environmental. The discordance rate of MZ twins for a mental disorder can be interpreted as an estimate of nonshared environment on this disorder. Because MZ twins share 100% of their genes, the only factor accounting for their discordance is environmental. Indeed, the study of MZ twins discordant for schizophrenia has provided a fertile ground for the examination of potential nonshared environmental influences on this disorder (Torrey, Bowler, Taylor, & Gottesman, 1994; Wahl, 1976). It should be noted, however, that estimates of nonshared environment typically include errors of measurement (Loehlin, 1992). Thus, if one's diagnoses of schizophrenia are unreliable, this will inflate both the MZ twin discordance rate of schizophrenia and the estimate of nonshared environmental influence on schizophrenia.[6]

2. Correlational studies. Correlational studies can be thought of as extensions of epidemiological studies. In epidemiological studies, one often finds that certain hypothesized causal variables (e.g., age, ethnicity, socioeconomic status, or other demographic variables) are associated with increased risk for a disorder. Demonstrating a correlation between a hypothesized causal element and the presence of psychopathology provides evidence consistent with one's hypothesis. Nevertheless, every undergraduate research methods textbook warns us, and for good reason, that *you cannot infer causation from a correlation.* A and B may be correlated because (1) A causes B, (2) B causes A, (3) or some third variable, C, causes both A and B. Because variable C could be anything, we have a nearly infinite number of possible interpretations of our correlation. Still, it can be tempting to overinterpret a correlation because our favored causal hypothesis seems so plausible. We should note that although correlation does not necessarily imply causation, causation does necessarily imply correlation. Thus, if a variable does not correlate with risk for a given disorder, the hypothesis that this variable is involved in the etiology of this disorder can be effectively excluded.

3. Analogue studies. The most direct test of an environmental hypothesis involves the manipulation of an environmental variable to observe its effects. Ethical and practical constraints make such a manipulation impossible except in very low "doses." We have already discussed the analogue study approach, which often represents an ethically acceptable way to perform this manipulation. The human analogue study attempts to create mild and temporary effects in the direction predicted by the researcher's hypothesis. The effects must be mild and temporary to make this approach ethically viable. This approach has been used to verify that conditions that create the feeling of helplessness will lead to behavior and feelings consistent with depression (e.g., Alloy, Peterson, Abramson, & Seligman, 1984). In addition, a variety of environmental manipulations (e.g., relaxed atten-

tion, speeded performance), referred to as schizomimetic conditions, have been shown to generate, at least temporarily, mild symptoms of psychosis (see Chapman & Chapman, 1973, for a review). A positive finding in such analogue studies indicates that the variable under study could create such symptoms, but never provides evidence that the symptoms normally develop in this way. For example, by providing selective reinforcement and sufficiently powerful incentives, we could probably get college students to bark like dogs, but no one would entertain the notion that dogs bark for similar reasons.

4. Treatment studies. If it is ethically unacceptable or practically impossible to create symptoms, an alternative strategy is to try to alleviate symptoms in individuals with a particular pathology. Such a strategy provides evidence consistent with the hypothesis that an environmental variable plays a role in the etiology or maintenance of psychopathology, but it also has limitations. Taking two aspirin may well relieve a headache, but few people would consider this evidence that headaches are caused by a deficiency in the level of aspirin. This simple example highlights the *ex juvantibus* ("reasoning backward from what helps") error of using treatment response to draw inferences concerning etiology. In spite of this limitation, treatment outcome can provide crucial data if other lines of evidence exist. The role of familial expressed emotion (Vaughn & Leff, 1976) in contributing to relapse in schizophrenia and other psychiatric disorders was rendered more plausible by the finding (Honig et al., 1995; Randolph, Eth, Glynn, & Paz, 1994) that treating the family of patients with schizophrenia reduces the level of expressed emotion and the patients' rate of relapse. Of course, we still need to be cautious in our conclusions because the treatment may have reduced relapse through other mechanisms.

Biological Studies

Biological studies provide invaluable insights into the nature of a disorder and the mechanisms that may underlie it. They may even contribute insights into both biological and psychological treatment strategies. In this section, we will discuss psychophysiological and brain imaging technologies—two approaches that have contributed extensively to our understanding of psychopathology.

Psychophysiological Research Methods

Psychophysiology is the study of individuals' psychological processes as indicated by their involuntary physiological responses (Lykken, 1982). These involuntary physiological responses can be thought of as windows that provide a useful glimpse into individuals' underlying psychological states. But these windows are almost always somewhat foggy, in part because the responses typically studied by psychophysiologists are influenced by many factors other than current psychological state. For example, a subject's brain is engaged in a host of activities (e.g., regulation of breathing and heart beat, maintenance of overall alertness) in addition to responding to the researcher's stimuli.

Psychophysiology can be distinguished from *physiological psychology* in that the former typically uses behavioral independent variables and physiological dependent variables, whereas the latter typically uses physiological independent variables and behavioral dependent variables (Stern, 1964). For example, a psychophysiologist might administer stressful stimuli (e.g., repeated loud tones) to subjects and monitor their levels of skin conductance in response to these stimuli. In contrast, a physiological psychologist might lesion an area of a rat's limbic system and examine the effects of this lesion on aggressive behavior. Psychophysiology should also be distinguished from *psychophysiological* (i.e., psychosomatic) *medicine*, viz., the study of physical disorders that can be caused or exacerbated by psychological factors (e.g., essential hypertension, asthma). Whereas the researcher who studies psychophysiological disorders is typically interested in physiological reactions, such as blood pressure increases and respiratory difficulties, the psychophysiologist is typically interested in these reactions only insofar as they represent *indicators*—albeit fallible indicators—of underlying psychological processes (Lykken, 1982).

The fundamental armamentarium of the modern psychophysiologist includes a polygraph, a variety of electrodes and transducers, and one or more computers. A *polygraph* is a multichannel device that records physiological signals from the subject. The signals arriving from different physiological systems (e.g., heart, brain) are amplified and then filtered to eliminate extraneous noise, such as the ubiquitous 60 cycle per second noise emitted by electrical devices. These signals are routed to pens, which display several simultaneous channels, producing the "squiggles" so familiar to psychophysiologists. Often these signals are simultaneously sent to a computer via an *analogue to digital (A/D) converter*, a device that transforms signals into numerical form. Virtually all modern psychophysiology laboratories are automated, with computers administering the stimuli and recording and analyzing the data.

Polygraph signals come from either electrodes or transducers. *Electrodes* typically are small metal disks that are placed on the subject's skin to record electrical signals—either those produced by the subject (e.g., electroencephalogram or EEG) or those passed through part of the subject's body (e.g., skin conductance or SC). *Transducers* convert changes in temperature, pressure, or other forms of energy to electrical signals that can be detected by a polygraph. A thermister changes its electrical resistance in response to temperature alterations; a strain gauge changes its electrical resistance in response to movement, such as the chest motions occurring during respiration; a pupillometer converts changes in the amount of light reflected by the pupil to voltage (Stern, Ray, & Davis, 1980).

The polygraph can record a variety of physiological reactions including skin conductance (SC), heart rate (HR), blood pressure (BP), brain waves (EEG), muscle activity (electromyogram or EMG), eye movements (electro-oculogram or EOG), respiration, and pupillary dilation. We will focus on SC, HR, and EEG because these are perhaps the three signals most frequently used in psychopathology research. In addition, these three variables have been used to examine a wide variety of disorders and thus have broad applicability in psychopathology research. Because of space constraints, we will not review psychophysiological variables that are relevant primarily to a single disorder. One example of such a variable that has received considerable attention in the past two decades is smooth pursuit eye movement dysfunction (SPEM), which exhibits promise as a biological marker of schizophrenia. The interested reader is referred to Clementz and Sweeney (1990) for an overview of this literature.

Skin Conductance The eccrine sweat glands, which are most densely concentrated on the palms of the hand and soles of the feet, are activated by the sympathetic nervous system and are therefore primarily responsive to psychological stimulation. They differ from the apocrine glands of the armpits and pubic area, which are primarily responsive to temperature changes. Presumably, the eccrine sweat glands evolved in our primate ancestors to facilitate adhesion to tree branches and other dry surfaces. These glands become moist during psychological arousal, including anxiety. Because water facilitates the passage of electrical current, the psychophysiologist passes a weak current (~ .5 volts) between electrodes placed on the fingers and measures the changes in conductance (Lykken & Venables, 1971). The resulting measure (SC) is among the most commonly assessed signals in psychophysiological research.

Several skin conductance measures are available. The skin conductance level (SCL) refers to the slow (*tonic*) changes in electrodermal activity that typically reflect the subject's state of arousal. The skin conductance response (SCR) refers to a rapid (*phasic*) change in electrodermal activity in response to an external stimulus. Fowles (1980) argued that SCR activity is an indicator of sensitivity to signals of punishment or threat. The spontaneous skin conductance response (SSCR) refers to a phasic electrodermal response in the absence of identifiable external stimulation. The frequency of SSCR fluctuations has been interpreted as a marker of arousal, anxiety, or both (Dawson, Schell, & Filion, 1990).

The study of SC has a long history in psychopathology research. For example, a subset of patients with schizophrenia (hyporesponders) exhibit diminished electrodermal reactions to stimuli, whereas another subset (hyperresponders) exhibit excessive electrodermal reactions to stimuli (Katkin & Hastrup, 1982). This finding may help to clarify the etiological heterogeneity of schizophrenia. For example, hyporesponders are more likely to show a negative symptom pattern, whereas hyperresponders are more likely to show a positive symptom pattern (Cannon, Mednick, & Parnas, 1990). SC measures have also been used extensively in the study of psychopathy and criminality. Psychopaths exhibit smaller SCRs in classical conditioning paradigms involving aversive stimuli (Lykken, 1957) and lower SCLs and fewer SSCRs in anticipation of aversive stimuli (e.g., Hare & Craigen, 1974).

Heart Rate The human heart consists of a left and right pump, each including an atrium and ventricle (its upper and lower chambers, respectively). The contraction of the heart—the *systolic* phase—ejects blood into the aorta. This contraction is triggered by a strong electrical impulse. The *diastolic*, or relaxation, phase occurs between successive phases of ventricular contraction. Because heart rate (HR) is such a powerful electrical signal, it can be detected by placing two electrodes between almost any two areas on the subject's body. The most common placement is one electrode on the right arm and one on the left leg (Stern et al., 1980). The pronounced spike (termed *R spike*) of the *electrocardiogram* (EKG) is produced by the electrical innervation of the ventricles, which precedes their contraction by approximately 50 milliseconds (Katkin & Hastrup, 1982). A device known as a *cardiotachometer* calculates the time difference between successive R spikes and outputs a signal inversely proportion to this difference. This signal can be read directly as a measure of HR.

HR, like several other psychophysiological variables, obeys the *law of initial values* (Wilder, 1950). According to this law, there is a negative correlation between individuals' baseline levels and their subsequent responses to stimuli (i.e., the higher subjects' baseline levels, the lower will be their responses). In part, the law of initial values stems from the fact that many physiological systems possess homeostatic mechanisms that set limits on their maximum output (Stern et al., 1980). It should be noted, however, that the "law" of initial values is characterized by numerous exceptions, and does not apply to all psychophysiological systems (Katkin & Hastrup, 1982).

HR measures have been used extensively in psychopathology research. For example, criminal and pre-criminal individuals tend to exhibit lower HRs than other individuals during resting conditions (Raine, 1993), and psychopaths tend to exhibit *larger* HR responses than nonpsychopaths in anticipation of aversive stimuli (Hare & Quinn, 1971). This latter finding superficially runs counter to studies demonstrating lower SCL in psychopaths prior to such stimuli, illustrating a phenomenon known as *directional fractionation* (Lacey, 1967) in which different indicators of arousal change in opposite directions. How can we explain psychopaths' simultaneous high HR levels and low SC levels prior to noxious events? According to the *intake-rejection hypothesis* (Lacey & Lacey, 1978), HR decreases reflect increased attention (i.e., intake) and HR increases reflect decreased attention (i.e., rejection) toward the external environment (for a contrasting view, see Obrist, 1976). Thus, psychopaths' HR increases in anticipation of aversive stimuli may indicate active attempts to reduce environmental input, and their low SC level may indicate that such attempts are successful (Hare, 1978).

EEG The human brain is a three-pound organ consisting of approximately 100 billion neurons. The simultaneous firing of these neurons can be detected by placing electrodes on the subject's scalp. The resulting record, the *EEG*, is an index of the brain's electrical activity. The EEG record is typically subdivided by frequency. *Delta* waves occur in the 1–3 cycle per second (cps) range, *theta* waves in the 4–7 cps range, *alpha* waves in the 8–12 cps range, and *beta* waves at 13 cps or above. These waves are associated with different states of consciousness; delta waves, for example, are commonly observed during slow wave sleep, whereas beta waves are commonly observed during alertness. Although these rhythms can be assessed by inspecting the raw EEG record, modern psychophysiologists almost always use a *Fourier transformation* to analyze brain wave signals. This mathematical transformation decomposes a series of brain waves into its component frequencies (Stern et al., 1980).

Psychophysiologists may examine *resting*, or spontaneous, EEG activity (subjects' brain waves while they are not responding to stimuli delivered by the researcher) or *evoked responses* to discrete stimuli presented to the subject (e.g., tones, lights). Evoked responses are almost never apparent in the raw EEG record because the brain is busily carrying out a multitude of activities in addition to responding to these stimuli. Psychophysiologists measure evoked responses by repeatedly presenting the subject with an identical stimulus, and then averaging the EEG response to this stimulus across all presentations. The rationale underlying this averaging procedure is that the EEG activity irrelevant to the stimulus—which can be thought of as "random" in the sense that its fluctuations constitute unsystematic background noise—will cancel out, whereas the EEG activity relevant to the stimulus will be highlighted. The EEG signal produced by this averaging process is known as an *event-related potential* (ERP) because it is believed to be a relatively "pure" measure of the brain's response to a given event (i.e., stimulus). An ERP typically consists of several wave components, some of which exhibit positive voltages and others negative voltages. ERP wave components are categorized along two parameters: (1) their voltage (positive or negative); and (2) their time lag following the stimulus. An N100 wave component, for example, is a negative voltage occurring approximately 100 milliseconds (msec) following stimulus onset. In general, early ERP components are believed to reflect sensory processing of the stimulus, whereas later ERP components are believed to reflect higher order cognitive processing of the stimulus (Katkin & Hastrup, 1982). One ERP component that has received considerable attention in the psychopathology literature is the *P300.* The P300 is most commonly elicited by means of an "oddball" paradigm, in which an aberrant stimulus (e.g., low frequency tone) is presented periodically, although rarely, amid a large number of identical stimuli (e.g., high frequency tones). Although controversy persists regarding the P300's functional significance, there is an emerging consensus that it reflects context updating—that is, a revision of one's mental model of the environment (Donchin & Coles, 1988). This hypothesis is consistent with the finding that the P300 tends to be elicited by novel or unexpected stimuli.

A number of psychological conditions are characterized by aberrant resting EEG findings. Patients with schizophrenia, for example, tend to exhibit reduced levels of alpha and increased levels of delta in their resting EEG (Iacono, 1982; Sponheim, Clementz, Iacono, & Beiser, 1994), and psychopaths tend to exhibit elevated levels of theta waves in their resting EEG (Syndulko, 1978). Because theta waves are often associated with boredom and drowsiness, however, psychopaths' high levels of theta may reflect only their relative absence of anxiety during EEG examinations. Depressed individuals exhibit less left frontal EEG activation (specifically, alpha activity) than nondepressed individuals (Henriques & Davidson, 1991), a finding that may reflect a deficit in biologically based approach systems among depressed individuals.

Several ERP components show considerable promise in the study of psychopathology. Begleiter, Porjesz, Bihari, and Kissin (1984), for example, found that sons of alcoholics exhibited lower P300s compared to sons of normal parents, although this finding has not been uniformly replicated (e.g., Polich & Bloom, 1988). The meaning of this finding and its specificity to alcoholism are unclear. Jutai and Hare (1983) reported that psychopaths exhibited lower N100s than nonpsychopaths in response to tones while playing a video game. Because the N100 appears to reflect selective attention (Coles, Gratton, & Fabiani, 1990), Jutai and Hare suggested that psychopaths tend to ignore extraneous stimuli while engaged in tasks of immediate interest.

Brain Imaging Technology

In the study of psychopathology, it is extremely helpful to be able to document the structure and functioning of the brain as a means of investigating potential causes of a disorder. Prior to modern imaging techniques, we had to rely on autopsy results and rather crude imaging techniques. Not surprisingly, few patients consent to a premature autopsy, even in the name of science, which limited the effectiveness of this paradigm. Early imaging techniques (e.g., the pneumoencephalogram) produced poor images, were uncomfortable for patients, and carried a significant mortality risk (about 1%). Modern brain imaging technology produces clear images, at a reasonable cost, and with minimal risk and discomfort to the patient. They have contributed significantly to the field of psychopathology and will likely contribute more in the future.

Observing Brain Structure: CAT Scans and MRIs

CAT (computerized axial tomography) *scans* and *MRIs* (magnetic resonance imaging) produce remarkably detailed pictures of the structure of the brain. Both techniques take images from different angles. The images are produced by X-rays in the case of the CAT scan, and by the magnetic properties of certain atoms in the brain in the case of the MRI. A mathematical technique is applied to these multiple images to create a three-dimensional picture of the structure necessary to produce that set of images—a technique ingenious enough to have led to a Nobel Prize. This three-dimensional mathematical model can be manipulated to produce detailed photos of any section of the brain desired. Structural brain imaging techniques have been used to investigate structural abnormalities in schizophrenia (e.g., Sudath, Christison, Torrey, Casanova, & Weinberger, 1990), memory disorders (e.g., Jernigan, 1994), and personality disorders (e.g., Goyer, Konicki, & Schulz, 1994), to name but a few.

Observing Brain Functioning: PET Scans and fMRI Studies Detailed pictures of the brain are of little value unless you suspect that there is a structural abnormality. If the structure is normal but the functioning abnormal, CAT scans and MRIs are uninformative. Instead, we need procedures that can observe brain functioning.

We have already discussed one measure of brain functioning—the EEG. Two additional measures of brain functioning are the *fMRI* (functional MRI) and the *PET* (positron emission tomography) *scan*. The fMRI looks at changes in the magnetic properties of brain regions as an indication of the level of activity. The PET scan utilizes a harmless radioactive isotope, which is absorbed by brain tissue in proportion to its functional activity level. The decay of the isotope releases subatomic particles that collide with electrons to produce the photons that are detected and form the image. All of these measures, including the EEG, allow us to investigate unusual patterns of brain activity in individuals with various forms of psychopathology. Over- or underactivation of a brain region may suggest deficits in that region or a compensatory response to a deficit in another region. These techniques have been used to investigate dysfunctions in depression (e.g., Kravitz & Newman, 1995), schizophrenia (e.g., Liddle, 1995), and Alzheimer's disease (e.g., Foster, 1994), among other conditions.

High-Risk Research Approaches

Longitudinal designs have an advantage over most designs in psychopathology research. Following subjects over time allows one to observe the developmental course of a disorder and to measure the environmental factors that influence that course. But longitudinal designs are costly, especially in the low-yield environment of psychopathology research. The longitudinal design is used frequently in cases in which virtually all subjects are expected to pass through roughly the same developmental course. Therefore, each subject provides valuable data on developmental processes. But few randomly selected individuals will develop a specific psychiatric disorder. The base rates for most psychiatric disorders range from 10% to a fraction of 1%. For a disorder such as schizophrenia, with a base rate near 1%, we would need to follow 10,000 individuals for at least 20 years in order to obtain 100 subjects who develop schizophrenia. This would not be a good choice for a dissertation topic.

An alternative to the traditional longitudinal study is the *high-risk paradigm*. Mednick and Schulsinger (1968) were among the first to propose this strategy. Their idea was simple and elegant—use information about subjects to select those whose risk for developing a particular disorder is substantially above the population base rate. Because schizophrenia runs in families, Mednick and Schulsinger selected first-degree relatives of patients with schizophrenia as their subjects—specifically, offspring of mothers with schizophrenia. One could expect approximately 10% of this group to develop schizophrenia based on available research—a tenfold improvement in the yield of a longitudinal study. The approach used by Mednick and Schulsinger is referred to as the *genetic high-risk paradigm* because it relies on selecting experimental subjects on the basis of their genetic relationship to an individual with a particular disorder. An alternative approach—the *behavioral high-risk paradigm* (e.g., Chapman, Chapman, Raulin, & Edell, 1978)—selects at-risk subjects on the basis of behavioral characteristics.

Genetic High-Risk Paradigm

The genetic high-risk paradigm traditionally assumes a significant genetic contribution to a disorder, although technically this assumption is not needed. All we need to know is that there is an elevated risk in family members, which could be genetically transmitted, environmentally transmitted, or both. Subjects are selected by both their familial relationship to someone with the disorder and their age. Most disorders have well-defined *age-of-risk profiles* (the cumulative frequency graph of the age of the first appearance the disorder). If most people develop a disorder in their 20s, then one wants to select subjects prior to that period of risk. Selecting older subjects will leave out those who have already developed the disorder, and selecting younger subjects will substantially increase the time that one must wait to determine which subjects develop the disorder. A comparison sample is selected, which is usually matched on variables that might confound the results if left uncontrolled (e.g., age, sex, social class). Both groups are then evaluated and followed over time.

The initial evaluation of the at-risk and comparison groups provides a basis for an immediate test of certain hypotheses. Whatever predisposing factors there might be for the disorder should be overrepresented in the at-risk group relative to the comparison group. The sensitivity of this comparison will depend on the proportion of individuals in the at-risk group who are truly "at risk" for the disorder. For example, we know that roughly 10% of the offspring of mothers with schizophrenia will develop schizophrenia. Nevertheless, that figure is likely an underestimate of the number of at-risk individuals because it is unlikely that every at-risk individual will actually develop the disorder. The discordance rate for MZ twins (about 50%) demonstrates that nonshared environmental variables play an important role in the development of schizophrenia. So we would expect at least 20% of the offspring of mothers with schizophrenia to be genuinely at risk because they possess whatever genetic risk factor(s) are specific to schizophrenia. Actually, the figure is probably higher than that because discordant MZ twins presumably share not only the specific genetic risk factor(s) for schizophrenia but also other genetically influenced characteristics—what Meehl (1990) calls polygenic potentiators—which may further increase the risk for psychiatric deterioration. Note that the logic of this paradigm does not depend on our knowing which of the at-risk subjects are truly at risk, only that we know that the experimental group differs from the comparison group in the base rate of the risk factor(s). Having a procedure that reliably identifies groups at differential risk allows us to identify potentially superior selection variables for future studies, a process dubbed *bootstrapping* (lifting oneself up by one's bootstraps) by Dawes and Meehl (1966).

Even through we can use bootstrapping operations without waiting to see who develops the disorder under study, the longitudinal design has some distinct advantages. In the Mednick and Schulsinger (1968) study, for example, subjects were matched in triplets (two at-risk and one comparison subject) on several potentially confounding variables. Because only a small proportion of the at-risk subjects would develop schizophrenia, this procedure provided both a matched comparison subject and a matched at-risk subject for each of the at-risk subjects who later developed schizophrenia.[7] Comparing the at-risk and comparison groups at the initial assessment proved valuable, but the more sensitive comparison was between the subjects who went on to develop schizophrenia and their two matched "controls" (the matched at-risk subject and the matched comparison subject). This powerful and sensitive analysis was not possible until the subjects had been followed long enough to see which of them decompensated.

Behavioral High-Risk Paradigm

Identifying at-risk individuals on the basis of their familial relationship to someone with the disorder is one high-risk approach. Nevertheless, some disorders have weak genetic or familial contributions, rendering the genetic high-risk approach impractical. Even when there is a strong genetic or familial component, the genetic high-risk approach may produce a biased sample. For example, 95% of all patients who develop schizophrenia do not have a schizophrenic parent (Gottesman & Shields, 1972). These patients will not be represented in the genetic high-risk paradigm described above.

The behavioral high-risk paradigm identifies at-risk samples on the basis of behavior or life experiences. Chapman et al. (1978) identified individuals presumed to be at risk for schizophrenia on the basis of traits that Meehl (1964) argued were indicators of genetic risk for schizophrenia (e.g., anhedonia, intense ambivalence, body-image aberration, and magical ideation). A 10–12-year follow-up study (Chapman, Chapman, Kwapil, Eckblad, & Ainser, 1994) confirmed that these subjects are at elevated risk for severe psychopathology, although not necessarily schizophrenia. Nevertheless, long before the follow-up study had been completed, dozens of construct validation studies had been published suggesting that subjects identified by these trait measures exhibited characteristics that one might expect to find in someone at risk for schizophrenia. For example, these subjects showed mild forms of psychotic symptoms (e.g., Chapman et al., 1978), poor social functioning (e.g., Beckfield, 1985), and cognitive processing deficits (e.g., orienting response; Simons, 1981) similar to those reported in patients with schizophrenia. These studies increased confidence in the hypothesis that these subjects were at risk for psychopathology.

The behavioral high-risk strategy has also been used successfully by Depue and his collegues (e.g, Klein & Depue, 1984) in their studies of individuals at risk for bipolar disorder.

Computer Simulations

Parallel distributed processing (PDP) models are mathematical representations, implemented on a computer, of how a heavily interconnected system such as the brain might work. They produce what appears to be rule-based behavior without ever being taught rules, and they seem to learn in much the same way as humans, even to the point of producing similar errors during the learning process.

Cohen and Serban-Schreiber (1992) used PDP models in a series of studies of schizophrenic psychopathology. Because dopamine has been implicated in schizophrenia, they included a "gain" function in each of their simulations (i.e., a mathematical modulator for the overall operation of the model) to simulate the modulatory effect that dopamine would have on the system. They constructed three PDP models to simulate three very different cognitive tasks: (1) the Stroop Effect, (2) the Continuous Performance Test (CPT), and (3) a lexical ambiguity task. The relative performance of patients with schizophrenia had already been well established for the Stroop and CPT tasks. Without going into the technical details, they produced a model to simulate Stroop performance and trained it to perform as normal subjects are known to perform. They then adjusted the gain function until they produced the pattern of results shown by patients with schizophrenia. This first study showed that a systematic manipulation of a single parameter that was designed to simulate the effect of dopamine was sufficient to take a model that reproduced the pattern of results found in normals and make that model reproduce the pattern of results found in patients with schizophrenia. They then built and trained models to reproduce the performance of normals on the CPT, a measure of sustained concentration on which patients with schizophrenia tend to do poorly, and a lexical ambiguity task, on which patients with schizophrenia performed more poorly than normals in one condition but not in another (Cohen, Targ, Kristoffersen, & Spiegel, 1988). As in the Stroop Effect model, Cohen and Serban-Schreiber included a gain parameter in each of these models. They found that adjusting the gain function in these models to the same value that reproduced the pattern of Stroop performance found in patients with schizophrenia also reproduced the pattern of performance on these tasks shown by patients.

The studies reported by Cohen and Serban-Schreiber are an excellent set of construct validation studies. They took what we know about how the brain is wired (i.e., interconnected), what we know about the role of dopamine in normal brain activity (i.e., a modulatory effect), and the fact that dopamine appears to be important in schizophrenia. They then took several areas of cognitive functioning known to be disordered in schizophrenia and simulated each of them with a PDP model. By manipulating the single parameter of gain (designed to be analogous to the action of dopamine), they were able to simulate dramatically different deficits found in schizophrenia. Furthermore, they reproduced the finding in the lexical decision task that patients with schizophrenia are not deficient under certain circumstances, thus ruling out the possibility that the gain parameter simply lowers general performance. This study ties together the research literatures on brain structure and neurochemical and cognitive functioning in both normals and patients with schizophrenia. The manipulation of a single parameter repeatedly reproduced the pattern of findings from previous studies—findings that had previously been explained by invoking different constructs. A single construct (the presumed effect of dopamine) was able to explain each of these disparate findings—clearly an elegant and parsimonious solution to the problem of what underlies the deficits found in schizophrenia. In science, parsimony is considered a virtue (Popper, 1959).

Although the study by Cohen and Serban-Schreiber appears to be radically different from some of the other research approaches discussed in this chapter, it is conceptually identical to the paradigms already presented. The PDP models created by these authors are simply theoretical models of a complex process. These models may be too complex to be diagrammed in a simple flow chart, but they are theoretical models nonetheless. Once created, these computer models can be used to generate specific predictions that can be tested empirically. In effect, that is what Cohen and Serban-Schreiber did, except that the empirical data already existed in the literature. The PDP framework allows us to model complicated cognitive and perceptual processes. In theory at least, this approach could identify promising variables to study in schizophrenia and may even pinpoint variables sufficiently sensitive to the pathology of schizophrenia to serve as markers of the disorder. But even with the "gee wiz" special effects of the computer, it remains a construct validation approach that is dependent on linking the predictions of the models to empirical data.

Conclusion

In this chapter, we reviewed a variety of research methods used by psychopathologists to identify the correlates and causes of mental disorders. Two consistent themes guided this chapter. First, psychopathological conditions are almost certainly multiply determined, and probably involve a complex interplay of both genetic and environmental influences. Second, each methodological approach has its own set of potential advantages and disadvantages. Both of these considerations suggest that the ideal research program in psychopathology incorporates several methodological approaches. By utilizing a number of these approaches in tandem, the researcher seeks to uncover converging evidence across diverse paradigms and thereby triangulate upon the etiology of a given form of psychopathology.

Because each methodological design is best suited for detecting certain potential causal factors, it is unlikely that a single design will ever provide a complete picture of the etiology of any mental disorder. For example, although epidemiological methods are well suited for ascertaining risk factors for psychopathology, they generally provide little information concerning either the genetic or environmental origins of these factors. In turn, although behavior-genetic methods are well suited for ascertaining the relative genetic and environmental influences on risk factors for psychopathology, they generally tell us little about how these influences are linked to the functioning of the central nervous system. For this information, we must instead turn to psychophysiological, neuropsychological, and brain-imaging studies, which, like epidemiological studies, cannot by themselves disentangle the relative contributions of genetic and environmental factors. In addition, because each of the methodological approaches discussed in this chapter is characterized by liabilities and potential biases, an exclusive reliance on one approach will often result in misleading conclusions.

As a result of these limitations, psychopathology investigators have increasingly turned to hybrid designs that simultaneously incorporate multiple methodological approaches. For example, many high-risk researchers have included indices of psychophysiological and neurotransmitter functioning in their investigations. A number of behavior-genetic researchers have included explicit measures of environmental factors in their studies, including those emphasized by epidemiologists (e.g., the social class and education of the adoptive parents). It is only by gradually and painstakingly piecing together evidence from a variety of admittedly imperfect approaches that researchers can hope to arrive at a better understanding of the causes of psychopathology.

Notes

1. A common misconception is that all twin studies involve studying twins that have been reared apart. Although the twins-reared-apart design has been used to study genetic influences, it is impractical in studying genetic influences in most forms of psychopathology because of the low base rate for these disorders.
2. Of course, MZ twins will always be the same sex because sex is genetically determined.
3. The Maudsley Twin Register was compiled from consecutive admissions (1948–1963) of patients to a large outpatient and a short-stay inpatient department at Maudsley Hospital in England.
4. Note that that adoption paradigms used in psychopathology research include all adopted probands and do not restrict their sample to just twins.
5. Of course, to conclusively determine whether this were so, one would have to rule out the possibility that the parent's genes also contribute to the child's anxiety.
6. Note that we tend to think of environment as the social environment of the individual. *Environment* actually refers to any external influence on the individual, and it might well include, for example, differences in diet or medical history.
7. The likelihood of each at-risk subject developing schizophrenia was approximately .10, Therefore, the likelihood of both members of a matched at-risk pair developing schizophrenia is only .01 (.10 × .10).

References

Alloy, L. B., Peterson, C., Abramson, L. Y., & Seligman, M. E. P. (1984). Attributional style and the generalizability of learned helplessness. *Journal of Personality and Social Psychology, 46*, 681–687.

Andreasen, N. C., Endicott, J., Spitzer, R. L., & Winokur, G. (1977). The family history method using diagnostic criteria: Reliability and validity. *Archives of General Psychiatry, 34*, 1229–1235.

Andreasen, N. C., Flaum, M., Swayze, V. W., Tyrell, G., & Arndt, S. (1990). Positive and negative symptoms in schizophrenia: A critical reappraisal. *Archives of General Psychiatry, 47*, 615–621.

Barlow, D. H. (1988). *Anxiety and its disorders: The nature and treatment of anxiety and panic*. New York: Guilford Press.

Bateson, G., Jackson, D. D., Haley, J., & Weakland, J. (1956). Toward a theory of schizophrenia. *Behavioral Science, 1*, 251–264.

Beckfield, D. F. (1985). Interpersonal competence among college men hypothesized to be at risk for schizophrenia. *Journal of Abnormal Psychology, 94*, 397–404.

Begleiter, H., Porjesz, B., Bihari, B., & Kissin, B. (1984). Event-related brain potentials in boys at risk for alcoholism. *Science, 225*, 1493–1496.

Berkson, J. (1946). Limitations of the application of four-fold table analysis to hospital data. *Biometrics, 2*, 247–253.

Bouchard, T. J., Lykken, D. T., McGue, M., & Segal, N. L. (1990). Sources of human psychological differences: The Minnesota study of twins reared apart. *Science, 250*, 223–228.

Burke, J. D., & Regier, D. A. (1988). Epidemiology of mental disorders. In J. A. Talbott, R. E. Hales, & S. C. Yudofsky (Eds.), *The American Psychiatric Press textbook of psychiatry* (pp. 67–89). Washington, DC: American Psychiatric Press.

Cadoret, R. J., Cain, C. A., & Crowe, R. R. (1983). Evidence for gene-environment interaction in the development of adolescent antisocial behavior. *Behavior Genetics, 13*, 301–310.

Cannon, T. D., Mednick, S. A., & Parnas, J. (1990). Two pathways to schizophrenia in children at risk. In L .N. Robins & M. Rutter (Eds.), *Straight and devious pathways from childhood to adulthood* (pp. 328–350). New York: Cambridge University Press.

Chapman, L. J., & Chapman, J. P. (1967). Genesis of popular but erroneous psychodiagnostic observations. *Journal of Abnormal Psychology, 72*, 193–204.

Chapman, L. J., & Chapman, J. P. (1969). Illusory correlation as an obstacle to the use of valid psychodiagnostic signs. *Journal of Abnormal Psychology, 74*, 271–280.

Chapman, L. J., & Chapman, J. P. (1973). *Disordered thought in schizophrenia*. Englewood Cliffs, NJ: Prentice-Hall.

Chapman, L. J., Chapman, J. P., Kwapil, T. R., Eckblad, M., & Ainser, M. C. (1994). Putatively psychosis-prone subjects 10 years later. *Journal of Abnormal Psychology, 103*, 171–183.

Chapman, L. J., Chapman, J. P., Raulin, M. R., & Edell, W. S. (1978). Schizotypy and thought disorder as a high risk approach to schizophrenia. In G. Serban (Ed.), *Cognitive defects in the development of mental illness* (pp. 351–360). New York: Brunner-Mazel.

Clementz, B. A., & Sweeney, J. A. (1990). Is eye movement dysfunction a biological marker for schizophrenia? A methodological review. *Psychological Bulletin, 108*, 77–92.

Cohen, J. A. (1960). A coefficient for agreement for nominal scales. *Educational and Psychological Measurement, 20*, 37–46.

Cohen, J. D., & Serban-Schreiber, D. (1992). Context, cortex, and dopamine: A connectionist approach to behavior and biology in schizophrenia. *Psychological Review, 99*, 45–77.

Cohen, J. D., Targ, E., Kristoffersen, T., & Spiegel, D. (1988). *The fabric of thought disorder: Disturbances in the processing on context*. Unpublished manuscript.

Coles, M. G. H., Gratton, G., & Fabiani, M. (1990). Event-related brain potentials. In J. T. Cacioppo & L. G. Tassinary (Eds.), *Principles of psychophysiology: Physical, social, and inferential elements* (pp. 413–455). New York: Cambridge University Press.

Costello, E. J. (1990). Child psychiatric epidemiology: Implications for clinical research and practice. In B. B. Lahey & A. E. Kazdin (Eds.), *Advances in clinical child psychology* (pp. 53–90). New York: Plenum Press.

Coyne, J. C. (1994). Self-reported distress: Analogue or ersatz depression? *Psychological Bulletin, 116*, 20–45.

Cronbach, L. J., & Meehl, P. E. (1955). Construct validity in psychology tests. *Psychological Bulletin, 52*, 281–301.

Dabbs, J. M., & Morris, R. (1990). Testosterone, social class, and antisocial behavior in a sample of 4,462 men. *Psychological Science, 1*, 209–211.

Dawes, R. M., & Meehl, P. E. (1966). Mixed group validation: A method for determining the validity of diagnostic signs without using criterion groups. *Psychological Bulletin, 66*, 63–67.

Dawson, M. E., Schell, A. M., & Filion, D. L. (1990). The electrodermal system. In J. T. Cacioppo & L. G. Tasinary (Eds.), *Principles of psychophysiology: Physical, social, and in-*

ferential elements (pp. 295–324). New York: Cambridge University Press.

Depue, R. A., & Monroe, S. M. (1978). The unipolar-bipolar distinction in the depressive disorders. *Psychological Bulletin, 85*, 1001–1029.

Donchin, E., & Coles, M. G. (1988). Is the P300 component a manifestation of context updating? *Behavioral and Brain Sciences 11*, 357–427.

duFort, G. G., Newman, S. C., & Bland, R. C. (1993). Psychiatric comorbidity and treatment seeking: Sources of selection bias in the study of clinical populations. *Journal of Nervous and Mental Disease, 181*, 467–474.

Faris, R. E. L., & Dunham, H. W. (1939). *Mental disorders in urban areas.* Chicago: University of Chicago Press.

Feinstein, A. R. (1985). *Clinical epidemiology: The architecture of clinical research.* Philadelphia: W. B. Saunders.

Fint, M. B., Spitzer, R. L., Gibbon, M., & Williams, J. B. W. (1995). *Structured clinical interview for DSM-IV Axis I disorders.* New York: Biometrics Research Department.

Foster, N. L. (1994). PET imaging. In R. D. Terry, R. Katzman, & K. L. Bick (Eds.), *Alzheimer disease* (pp. 87–103). New York: Raven Press.

Fowles, D. C. (1980). The three arousal model: Implications of Gray's two-factor learning theory for heart rate, electrodermal activity, and psychopathy. *Psychophysiology, 17*, 87–104.

Freeman, J. (1979). *Gifted children.* Lancaster: Medical Technical Press.

Fromm-Reichman, F. (1948). Notes on the development of treatments of schizophrenics by psychoanalytic psychotherapy. *Psychiatry, 2*, 263–273.

Gilovich, T. (1991). How we know what isn't so: The fallibility of human reason in everyday life. New York: Free Press.

Goodwin, D. W., & Guze, S. B. (1989). *Psychiatric diagnosis* (4th ed.). New York: Oxford University Press.

Gorenstein, E. E. (1982). Frontal lobe functions in psychopaths. *Journal of Abnormal Psychology, 91*, 368–379.

Gorman,, J. M., Liebowitz, M. R., Fyer, A. j., & Stein, J. (1989). A neuroanatomical hypothesis for panic disorder. *American Journal of Psychiatry, 146*, 148–161.

Gottesman, I. I. (1991). *Schizophrenia genesis: The origins of madness.* New York: W. H. Freeman.

Gottesman, I. I., & Shields, J. (1972). *Schizophrenia and genetics: A twin study vantage point.* New York: Academic Press.

Gottesman, I. I., & Shields, J. (1982). *Schizophrenia: The epigenetic puzzle.* New York: Cambridge University Press.

Goyer, P. F., Konicki, P. E., & Schulz, S. C. (1994). Brain imaging in personality disorders. In K. R. Silk (Ed.), *Biological and neurobehavioral studies of borderline personality disorder. Progress in Psychiatry, No. 45* (pp. 109–125). Washington, DC: American Psychiatric Press.

Hare, R. D. (1978). Electrodermal and cardiovascular correlates of psychopathy. In R. D. Hare & D. Schalling (Eds.), *Psychopathic behaviour: Approaches to research* (pp. 107–143). Chichester: John Wiley.

Hare, R. D. (1984). Performance on psychopaths on cognitive tasks related to frontal lobe function. *Journal of Abnormal Psychology, 93*, 133–140.

Hare, R. D., & Craigen, D. (1974). Psychopathy and physiological activity in a mixed-motive game situation. *Psychophysiology, 11*, 197–206.

Hare, R. D., & Quinn, M. J. (1971). Psychopathy and autonomic conditioning. *Journal of Abnormal Psychology, 71*, 223–235.

Henriques, J. B., & Davidson, R. J. (1991). Left frontal hypoactivation in depression. *Journal of Abnormal Psychology, 100*, 535–545.

Honig, A., Hofman, A., Hilwig, M., Noorthoorn, E., & Ponds, R. (1995). Psychoeducation and expressed emotion in bipolar disorder: Preliminary findings. *Psychiatry Research, 56*, 299–301.

Iacona, W. G. (1982). Bilateral electrodermal habituation-dishabituation and resting EEG in remitted schizophrenics. *Journal of Nervous and Mental Disease, 170*, 91–101.

Jernigan, T. (1994). Magnetic resonance imaging and memory disorders. In L. S. Cermak (Ed.), *Neuropsychological explorations of memory and cognition: Essays in honor of Nelson Butters. Critical issues in neuropsychology* (pp 147–157). New York: Plenum.

Jutai, J. W., & Hare, R. D. (1983). Psychopathy and selective attention during performance of a complex perceptual motor task. *Psychophysiology, 20*, 146–151.

Kallman, F. J. (1938). *The genetics of schizophrenia.* New York: Augustin.

Katkin, E. S., & Hastrup, J. L. (1982). Psychophysiological methods in clinical research. In P. C. Kendall & J. N. Butcher (Eds.), *Handbook of research methods in clinical psychology* (pp. 387-425). New York: John Wiley.

Kendler, K. S. (1983). Overview: A current perspective on twin studies of schizophrenia. *American Journal of Psychiatry, 140*, 1413–1425.

Kety, S. S., Rosenthal, D., Wender, P. H., & Schulsinger, F. (1968). The types and prevalence of mental illness in the biological and adoptive families of adopted schizophrenics. In D. Rosenthal and S. S. Kety (Eds.), *The transmission of schizophrenia* (pp. 345–362). Oxford: Pergamon.

Kety, S. S., Rosenthal, D., Wender, P. H., Schulsinger, F., & Jacobsen, B. (1978). The biological and adoptive families of adoptive individuals who become schizophrenic. In L. C. Wynne, R. L. Cromwell, & S. Matthysse (Eds.), *The nature of schizophrenia* (pp. 25–37). New York: John Wiley.

Klein, D. N., & Depue, R. A. (1984). Continued impairment of persons at risk for bipolar affective disorder: Results of a 19-month follow-up study. *Journal of Abnormal Psychology, 93*, 345–347.

Kravitz, H. M., & Newman, A. J. (1995). Medical diagnostic procedures for depression: An update from a decade of promise. In E. E. Beckham, & W. R. Leber (Eds.), *Handbook of depression* (2nd ed.; pp. 280–301). New York: Guilford.

Lacey, B. C., & Lacey, J. I. (1978). Two-way communication between the heart and the brain. *American Psychologist, 33*, 99–113.

Lacey, J. I. (1967). Somatic response patterning and stress: Some revisions of activation theory. In M. H. Appley & R. Trumbull (Eds.), *Psychological stress: Issues in research* (pp. 14–42). New York: Appleton-Crofts.

Liddle, P. F. (1995). Regional cerebral blood flow and subsyndromes of schizophrenia. In J. A. Den Boer, H. Gerrit, M. Westenberg, & H. M. van Praag (Eds.), *Advances in the neurobiology of schizophrenia* (pp. 189–204). Chichester, England: John Wiley.

Lilienfeld, S. O., Waldman, I. D., & Israel, A. C. (1994). A critical examination of the use of the term and concept of *comorbidity* in psychopathology research. *Clinical Psychology: Science and Practice, 1*, 71–83.

Loehlin, J. C. (1992). *Genes and environment in personality development*. Newbury Park: Sage Publications.

Lord, F. M. (1967). A paradox in the interpretation of group differences. *Psychological Bulletin, 68*, 304–305.

Luchins, D. L. (1982). Computerized tomography in schizophrenia: Disparities in the prevalence of abnormalities. *Archives of General Psychiatry, 39*, 859–860.

Lykken, D. T. (1957). A study of anxiety in the sociopathic personality. *Journal of Abnormal Psychology, 55*, 6–10.

Lykken, D. T. (1982). Psychophysiology. In R. J. Corsini (Ed.), *Encyclopedia of psychology* (pp. 175–179). New York: John Wiley.

Lykken, D. T., McGue, M., Tellegen, A., & Bouchard, T. J. (1992). Emergenesis: Genetic traits that may not run in families. *American Psychologist, 47*, 1565–1577.

Lykken, D. T., & Venables, P. H. (1971). Direct measurement of skin conductance: A proposal for standardization. *Psychophysiology, 8*, 656–672.

Mednick, S. A., & Schulsinger, F. (1968). Some powerful characteristics related to breakdown in children with schizophrenic mothers. In D. Rosenthal and S. S. Kety (Eds.), *The transmission of schizophrenia* (pp. 267–291). Oxford: Pergamon.

Meehl, P. E. (1962). Schizotaxia, schizotypy, schizophrenia. *American Psychologist, 17*, 827–838.

Meehl, P. E. (1964). *Manual for use with checklist of schizotypic signs*. Minneapolis: University of Minnesota Medical School, Medical Research Unit.

Meehl, P. E. (1971). High school yearbooks: A reply to Schwarz. *Journal of Abnormal Psychology, 77*, 143–148.

Meehl, P. E. (1977). Specific etiology and other forms of strong influence: Some quantitative meanings. *Journal of Medicine and Philosophy, 2*, 33–53.

Meehl, P. E. (1990). Toward an integrated theory of schizotaxia, schizotypy, and schizophrenia. *Journal of Personality Disorders, 4*, 1–99.

Meehl, P. E., & Golden, R. R. (1982). Taxometric methods. In P. C. Kendall & J. N. Butcher (Eds.), *Handbook of research methods in clinical psychology* (pp. 127–181). New York: John Wiley.

Meehl, P. E., & Rosen, A. (1955). Antecedent probability and the efficiency of psychometric signs, patterns, or cutting scores. *Psychological Bulletin, 52*, 194–216.

Nisbett, R., & Ross, L. (1980). Human inference: Strategies and shortcomings of social judgment. Englewood Cliffs, NJ: Prentice-Hall.

Obrist, P. A. (1976). The cardiovascular-behavioral interaction—As it appears today. *Psychophysiology, 13*, 95–107.

Plomin, R. (1990). *Nature and nurture*. Pacific Grove, CA: Brooks/Cole.

Plomin, R., DeFries, J. C., & McClearn, G. E. (1990). *Behavioral genetics: A primer (2nd ed.)*. New York: W. H. Freeman.

Polich, J., & Bloom, F. E. (1988). Event-related brain potentials in individuals at high and low risk for developing alcoholism: Failure to replicate. *Alcoholism: Clinical and Experimental Research, 12*, 368–373.

Popper, K. R. (1959). *The logic of scientific discovery.* New York: Basic Books.
Raine, A. (1993). *The psychopathology of crime.* San Diego: Academic Press.
Randolph, E. T., Eth, S., Glynn, S. M., & Paz, G. G. (1994). Behavioral family management in schizophrenia: Outcome of a clinic based intervention. *British Journal of Psychiatry, 164,* 501–506.
Regier, D. A., & Burke, J. D. (1985). Epidemiology. In H. I. Kaplan & B. J. Sadock (Eds.), *Comprehensive textbook of psychiatry* (4th ed.; pp. 295–312). Baltimore: Williams & Wilkins.
Reichenbach, H. (1938). *Experience and prediction.* Chicago: University of Chicago Press.
Robins, E., & Guze, S. B. (1970). Establishment of diagnostic validity in psychiatric illness: Its application to schizophrenia. *American Journal of Psychiatry, 126,* 983–987.
Rosenthal, D., Wender, P. H., Kety, S. S., Schulsinger, F., Welner, J., & Østergard, L. (1968). Schizophrenics' offspring reared in adoptive homes. In D. Rosenthal and S. S. Kety (Eds.), *The transmission of schizophrenia* (pp. 377–391). Oxford: Pergamon.
Rutter, M. (1994). Epidemiologic/longitudinal strategies and causal research in child psychiatry. In J. E. Mezzich, M. R. Jorge, & I. M. Salloum (Eds.), *Psychiatric epidemiology: Assessment concepts and methods* (pp. 139–166). Baltimore: Johns Hopkins University Press.
Schizophrenia Bulletin (1989). Special Issue: Advances in the Genetics of Schizophrenia. *Schizophrenia Bulletin, 15,* 361–464.
Schuldberg, D., Quinlan, D. M., Morganstern, H., & Glazer, W. (1990). Positive and negative symptoms in chronic psychiatric outpatients: Reliability, stability, and factor structure. *Psychological Assessment,* 2, 262–268.
Schofield, W., & Balian, L. (1959). A comparative study of the personal histories of schizophrenia and nonpsychiatric patients. *Journal of Abnormal and Social Psychology, 59,* 216–225.
Seligman, M. E. P. (1975). *Helplessness: On depression, development, and death.* San Francisco: W. H. Freeman.
Serbin, L. A., O'Leary, D. K., Kent, R. N., & Tonick, I. J. (1973). A comparison of teacher response to the preacademic and problem behavior of boys and girls. *Child Development, 44,* 796–804.
Sherrington, R., Brynjolfsson, J., Petursson, H., Potter, M., Wasmuth, J., Dobbs, M., & Gurling, H. (1988). Localization of a susceptibility locus for schizophrenia on chromosome 5. *Nature, 366,* 164–167.
Simons, R. F. (1981). Electrodermal and cardiac orienting in psychometrically defined high-risk subjects. *Psychiatry Research, 4,* 347–356.
Snow, J. (1855). *On the mode of communication with cholera* (2nd ed.). London: Churchill.
Spitzer, R. G., Endicott, J., & Robins, E. (1975). Clinical criteria for diagnosis and DSM-III. *American Journal of Psychiatry, 132,* 1187–1192.
Sponheim, S. R., Clementz, B. A., Iacono, W. G., Beiser, M. (1994). Resting EEG and first-episode and chronic schizophrenia. *Psychophysiology, 31,* 37–43.
Stern, J. A. (1964). Towards a definition of psychophysiology. *Psychophysiology, 1,* 90–91.
Stern, R. M., Ray, W. J., & Davis, C. M. (1980). *Psychophysiological recording.* New York: Oxford University Press.
Sudath, R. L., Christison, G. W., Torrey, E. F., Casanova, M. F., & Weinberger, D. R. (1990). Anatomical abnormalities in the brains of monozygotic twins discordant for schizophrenia. *New England Journal of Medicine, 322,* 789–794.
Syndulko, K. (1978). Electrocortical investigations of sociopathy. In R. D. Hare & D. Schalling (Eds.), *Psychopathic behaviour: Approaches to research* (pp. 145–156). Chichester: John Wiley.
Tellegen, A., Lykken, D. T., Bouchard, T. J., Wilcox, K. J., Segal, N. L., & Rich, S. (1988). Personality similarity in twins reared apart and together. *Journal of Personality and Social Psychology, 54,* 1031–1039.
Torrey, E. F., Bowler, A. E., Taylor, E. H., & Gottesman, I. I. (1994). *Schizophrenia and manic-depressive disorder: The biological roots of mental illness as revealed by the landmark of identical twins.* New York: Basic Books.
Tsuang, M. T., Tohen, M., & Murphy, J. M. (1988). Psychiatric epidemiology. In A. M. Nicholi Jr. (Ed.), *The new Harvard guide to psychiatry* (pp. 761–779). Cambridge, MA: Harvard University Press.
Ulrich, R. E. (1991). Animal rights, animal wrongs, and the question of balance. *Psychological Science,* 2, 197–201.
Vaughn, C. E., & Leff, L. P. (1976). The influence of family and social factors on the course of psychiatric illness: A comparison of schizophrenic and depressed neurotic patients. *British Journal of Psychiatry, 129,* 125–137.
Velten, E. (1968). A laboratory task for induction of mood states. *Behaviour Research and Therapy,* 6, 473–482.

Wahl, O. (1976). Monozygotic twins discordant for schizophrenia: A review. *Psychological Bulletin*, *83*, 91–106.

Waldman, I. D., Lilienfeld, S. O., & Lahey, B. B. (1995). Toward construct validity in the childhood disruptive behavior disorders: Classification and diagnosis in DSM-IV and beyond. In T. H. Ollendick & R. J. Prinz (Eds.), *Advances in clinical child psychology* (Vol. 17; pp. 323–363). New York: Plenum Press.

Weins, A. N. (1990). Structured clinical interviews for adults. In G. Goldstein & M. Hersen (Eds.), *Handbook of psychological assessment* (2nd ed.; pp. 324–341). New York: Pergamon.

Wilder, J. (1950). The law of initial values. *Psychosomatic Medicine*, *12*, 392.

Wood, J. M., Bootzin, R. R., Rosenhan, D., Nolan-Hoeksema, S., & Jourden, F. (1992). Effects of the 1989 San Francisco earthquake on frequency and content of nightmares. *Journal of Abnormal Psychology*, *101*, 219–224.

PART II

MAJOR AXIS I SYNDROMES

4

Anxiety Disorders
Panic and Phobias

BRIAN J. COX
STEVEN TAYLOR

This chapter covers several of the most common and often debilitating anxiety disorders: panic disorder, agoraphobia, social phobia, and specific phobias. Publication trends attest to the rapid growth of anxiety disorders research, especially in the decade of the 1980s (Norton, Cox, Asmundson, & Maser, 1995; Pincus, Henderson, Blackwood, & Dial, 1993). Reasons for this scholarly activity include (1) the detailed description and classification of anxiety disorders introduced in *DSM-III*, and (2) subsequent findings from the large Epidemiological Catchment Area (ECA) survey, which indicated that some of the anxiety disorders were a very common form of mental disorder in community-based adults.

The present chapter will be selective in coverage. In deciding which material should be included, we were guided by several factors. First, only topics that are very salient for a given disorder were covered (e.g., comorbidity issues in relation to panic disorder, structure of fundamental fears in relation to phobic disorders). Second, only seminal theoretical models that have had significant impact on the field or promising new developments were selected. Third, we have also tried to highlight some of the controversial topics and areas where further study are needed. Where appropriate, we have attempted to integrate and reformulate some of the existing knowledge base and to offer new ideas and hypotheses.

Several of these disorders are thought by many to lie on a continuum from normal to abnormal, and we therefore sometimes refer to "nonclinical" data as well. We also hope to convey the heterogeneity of the anxiety disorders, which is often overlooked in the psychopathology literature (e.g., a "clinically anxious" or "anxiety disorder" sample can mean many things and is not a uniform category).

The chapter is divided into two broad sections. The first covers fears and phobias. Many of the principles discussed in relation to fears and phobias will also apply to the latter section on panic disorder. Agoraphobia will also be considered in greater detail in this latter section.

Fears and Phobias

Fears come in a variety of shapes and sizes, ranging from the mundane (e.g., fears of public speaking, spiders, or heights) to the rare and exotic (e.g., fears of balloons, chocolate, or vegetables; see Rachman & Seligman, 1976). Many fears are adaptive responses to danger. Others are excessive or disproportionate, given the objective dangerousness of the situation. In this chapter we will examine the nature and causes of excessive fears, primarily as they occur in humans. We use the term *fear* as a convenient shorthand for excessive fears. In keeping with *DSM-IV*, the term *phobia* is used to refer to a subset of these fears: those in which "the avoidance, fear, or anxious anticipation of encountering the phobic stimulus interferes significantly with the person's daily routine, occupational functioning, or social life, or if the person is markedly distressed about having the phobia" (pp. 405, 411).

DSM-IV Classification

Three classes of phobia are recognized in *DSM-IV*: specific phobia, social phobia, and agoraphobia. Unlike the other phobias, agoraphobia is often a consequence of spontaneous (unexpected) panic attacks (Ballenger & Fyer, 1996). Accordingly, aspects of agoraphobia will be discussed briefly in this section, and in greater depth in the section on panic disorder.

DSM-IV specifies two types of social phobia: generalized (fear of most social situations) and nongeneralized (e.g., fear of a single situation, such as eating in public). Five subtypes of specific phobia are recognized: (1) animal type (e.g., fears of rodents, reptiles, or insects), (2) natural environment type (e.g., fears of storms, heights, or water), (3) blood-injection-injury type (fears of blood or injury, or fear of receiving an injection or other invasive medical procedure), (4) situational type (fears of specific situations such as tunnels, bridges, elevators, flying, or driving), and (5) "other" type (a residual category, including fears of choking, vomiting, illness, loud noises, and falling down). The diagnosis of specific phobia is not made if it appears in the context of a broader disorder, such as agoraphobia, obsessive-compulsive disorder, or hypochondriasis.

Blood-injection-injury phobia deserves special comment. For most fears (including phobias), exposure to the feared stimulus produces heart rate acceleration (Marks, 1987). In contrast, blood-injection-injury phobia is characterized by a dyphasic vasovagal response, consisting of brief acceleration in heart rate, followed by deceleration, bradycardia, and a drop in blood pressure (Page, 1994). This can lead to fainting. However, not all people with these vasovagal reactions develop phobias of blood, injury, or illness. The prevalence of vasovagal reactions is 5–15%, yet the prevalence of blood-injection-injury phobia is 3–6% (Neale et al., 1994; Page, 1994). Vasovagal reactions may be a necessary but not sufficient factor for the development of blood-injection-injury phobia. The other factors contributing to these fears appear similar to those of other fears, which are discussed later in this chapter.

Severe phobias are not trivial afflictions; they can involve marked impairment in functioning and extreme distress. For example, driving phobias can significantly impair one's occupational functioning, and may lead to social isolation (see Taylor & Koch, 1995, for examples of driving phobia). Even common conditions such as spider phobias can be debilitating. To illustrate, one such individual treated by one of the authors (S. T.) displayed extreme fear and avoidance of spiders. She reported being too afraid to enter rooms of her house in which she had seen spiders, and experienced intense panic attacks whenever she was unexpectedly confronted with a spider. She lived in an area in which spiders were commonly encountered, and therefore was chronically hypervigilant for spiders and worried about encountering them. This was associated with persistent tension and irritability. Her fear, avoidance, and preoccupation with spiders significantly interfered with her marital relationship. Fortunately, disorders such as this one are readily treated by behavioral therapies.

In the following sections we will review the basic characteristics of fears, including their prevalence, course, and heritability. These characteristics provide important clues as to the causes of fears, and constitute the basic findings that must be explained by any comprehensive theory. In later sections we will examine the behavioral and cognitive theories in light of these findings.

Prevalence and Course

Common Fears The development of fears is a common but typically transient occurrence in children. There is a predictable pattern of rise and fall of many fears. This has been called the *ontogenetic parade*, and has been extensively reviewed elsewhere (e.g., Marks, 1987; Scarr & Salapatek, 1970). The main findings are as follows: Fear of separation from the caregiver is common at 6–22 months, and typically wanes after 30 months. Fear of unfamiliar adults also is common at 6–9 months; it typically subsides by 20–24 months but may persist as shyness. Fear of unfamiliar peers is common at 20–29 months and often starts to decline by 24 months. Fears of animals, darkness, and imaginary creatures typically emerges between 2 and 6 years, and declines in many (but not all) cases thereafter. Fear of school appears when the child begins attending school (3–6 years); it may gradually decline then reemerge when the child moves from elementary school to high school. Social-evaluative fears often emerge or intensify during adolescence.

The most common fears in children between the ages of 8 and 16 years are those related to physical harm or injury (Bauer, 1976; Ollendick & King, 1991). These include fears of animals, natural environment fears, situational fears, and blood-illness-injury fears. Over 40% of children report "a lot" of fear of such stimuli, as assessed by self-report measures (e.g., Ollendick, Matson, & Helsel, 1985). However, only a fraction of these children would meet criteria for specific phobia.

In adults, common fears include the social fears (e.g., being criticized, speaking before a group); fears pertaining to blood, illness, injury, or death (e.g., automobile accidents, illness or injury to loved ones); fears of animals (e.g., snakes, spiders, stinging insects); and fears of environmental hazards (e.g., deep water, heights; Costello, 1982; Geer, 1965; Kirkpatrick, 1984).

Phobias

Age of Onset and Course. Phobias are similar to fears in that they often emerge in childhood or adolescence, and typically before age 25 (e.g., Craske et al., 1996; Schneier, Johnson, Hornig, Liebowitz, & Weissman, 1992). Despite the trend for onset before early adulthood, there is a considerable variability in age of onset of social and specific phobias, and it appears that both can occur at any point in the life span (Marks, 1987; Rachman, 1990). Compared to subclinical fears, phobias are more likely to be chronic, especially if untreated (Craske et al., 1996; Schneier et al., 1992). Agoraphobia has a later age of onset, typically between 15 and 30 years (*DSM-IV*).

Prevalence The lifetime prevalence of specific phobia has been estimated to be 6–23% (Kessler et al., 1994; Regier et al., 1988; Robins et al., 1984). The estimated lifetime prevalence figures for the subtypes of specific phobia are as follows: animal (11%), blood-injection-injury (3–6%), and situational phobia (12%: e.g., Craske et al., 1996). The lifetime prevalence of the natural environment subtype is unknown. The estimated lifetime prevalence of social phobia ranges from 2 to 19%, and the estimated lifetime prevalence of agoraphobia ranges from 3 to 6% (e.g., Kessler et al., 1994; Schneier et al., 1992; Stein et al., 1994). Despite the wide ranges in estimated prevalence figures, these findings indicate that phobias are common disorders.

The fluctuating course of fears over the life span may be due to maturational factors such as the development of endocrine and other biological systems necessary for fear responses to occur (Bronson, 1965; Hebb, 1946). Developmental milestones (e.g., learning to walk) and developmentally linked life experiences (e.g., starting school) also may play a role in influencing the course of fears. To illustrate, fear of heights appears to arise as the child becomes increasingly mobile (Scarr & Salapatek, 1970), which increases the likelihood of learning to associate heights with danger (e.g., as a result of suffering minor falls). The development of fears also may be influenced by the child's cognitive capacities for recognizing potential dangers, combined with his or her self-perceived ability to control these events (Ollendick, Yule, & Ollier, 1991).

Dimensions of Fear

Factor Analytic Studies To understand the determinants of fears, it is necessary to identify the patterns of covariation of fears. Such patterns are a source of hypotheses about the common and specific causes of fears. Factor analytic studies are the most informative sources of information about such patterns. There have been over 40 factor analytic investigations of fear inventories, such as the Fear Survey Schedule-II (Geer, 1965) and Fear Survey Schedule-III (Wolpe & Lang, 1969). Thirty-eight studies published prior to 1991 were extensively reviewed by Arrindell, Pickersgill, Merckelbach, Ardon, and Cornet (1991). Those authors found that most of the factors could be classified as: (1) social fears (i.e., fears of interpersonal events or situations); (2) fears of death, injury, illness, blood, and surgical procedures; (3) fears of harmless animals; or (4) "agoraphobic" fears (i.e., situational fears, as defined by *DSM-IV*). These categories represent the most common dimensions of self-reported fear, and are invariant across gender, nationality, and sample type (i.e., student, community, and psychiatric samples). The major dimensions of fears roughly correspond to *DSM-IV* classification of phobias. Later studies generally support Arrindell et al.'s (1991) conclusions.

Hierarchical Structure of Fears Evidence suggests that self-reported fears are hierarchically structured, with lower order dimensions loading in higher order dimensions. To illustrate, Staley and O'Donnell (1984) found that the five fear dimensions loaded on a single general factor. Arrindell (1993) reported similar findings, although he found that social fears and agoraphobia loaded on a general factor (neuroticism), whereas animal fears and blood-injury fears did not. Zinbarg and Barlow (1996) demonstrated that the major dimensions of fear (social fears, situational [agoraphobic] fears, animal fears, and blood-injury fears) formed specific factors that tended to load on a single general factor, labeled neuroticism or negative affectivity. Fear dimensions may load on other broad factors. Clark, Watson, and Mineka (1994) proposed that the personality dimension labeled "constraint" may be important in specific phobias, and that low extraversion (also termed low positive affect) may be important in social phobias.

There appear to be several "layers" or levels in the hierarchical structure. Broad dimensions such as neuroticism appear to be composed of factors including the major dimensions of fear (social fears, animal fears, etc.). In turn, the fear dimensions are composed of subdimensions, and the subdimensions composed of still smaller dimensions. For example, the dimension representing situational (agoraphobic) fears appears to be composed of several subdimensions, including fear of public places, fear of open spaces, and claustrophobia (e.g., Arrindell, Cox, van der Ende, & Kwee, 1995). In turn, claustrophobia can be reduced to two dimensions: fear of physical restriction and fear of suffocation (Rachman & Taylor, 1993). Another example comes from a factor analysis of an inventory of 34 different animal fears, which revealed that the dimension of animal fears appears to be composed of at least two subdimensions: (1) animals that can prey on humans (e.g., bear, shark, wolf) and (2) small animals that typically do not prey on humans (i.e., small mammals and insects, which are associated with disgust: e.g., snake, spider, rat; Ware, Jain, Burgess, & Davey, 1994). In turn, the factor representing small, nonpredatory animals can be reduced to two subfactors: invertebrates (e.g., maggot, cockroach, spider) and other small animals (e.g., rat, snake, bat; Davey, 1994).

If we assume that each distinct factor corresponds to a discrete class of causal mechanisms (Cattell, 1978), then the factor structure indicates a hierarchy of causal factors, ranging from relatively nonspecific causes (i.e., those influencing most fears) down to highly specific causes (those influencing a single fear or small class of fears). As in other hierarchical factor models (Clark, Salkovskis, et al., 1994; Lilienfeld, Turner, & Jacob, 1993; Watson, Clark, & Harkness, 1994), the subfactors are nested in the higher order factors. That is, they have their own unique variance, but also share some of their variance with higher order factor(s). Thus, the hierarchical model of fears proposes that fears and phobias arise from combinations of specific and broad (nonspecific) mechanisms.

Genetic and Environmental Factors

Heritabilities of Common Fears Broad-sense heritabilities represent the percent of variation in a trait (e.g., a fear or phobia) that is due to additive and nonadditive genetic factors. The following are estimates of these heritabilities for the following fears: animal fears (range 46–72%; mean = 58%); natural environment fears (range 20–58%; mean = 37%); blood-illness-injury fears (range 14–77%; mean = 43%); social fears (range 12–60%; mean = 37%); situational fears (23%; e.g., Rose & Ditto, 1983; Stevenson, Batten, & Cherner, 1992). The grand mean heritability, across the above-mentioned classes of fears was 40%.

Genetic Contributions to Phobias Kendler et al. (1992) administered a structured interview to assess lifetime history of *DSM-III-R* phobias in 2,163 female twins (MZ and DZ twin pairs), recruited from a population-based twin registry. Four groups of phobias were assessed: animal phobia, social phobia, situational phobia (tunnels, bridges, airplanes, heights), and agoraphobia (going out of the house alone, being in crowds, and being in open spaces). Note that situational phobias were arbitrarily distinguished from agoraphobia. Kendler et al. conducted a series of multivariate analyses of genetic and environmental contributions to these fears. Additive genetic effects (narrow heritabilities) for the best-fitting multivariate models were estimated as follows: animal phobia 32%, situational phobia 0%, agoraphobia 39%, and social phobia 30%. According to the best-fitting models, dominant genetic effects were 0% for each phobia. Thus, up to about a third of the phenotypic variation in phobias were due to additive genetic factors (mean = 25%).Using a subset of the Kendler et al. (1992) sample, Neale et al. (1994) assessed blood-illness-injury phobias (including fears of blood, needles, hospitals, and illness). Results tentatively suggested that additive genetic effects account for up to 30% of the phenotypic variance. Finally, available evidence suggests that phobias and subclinical fear do not differ in the extent that they are genetically determined. This is consistent with the view that phobias are extremes of fear dimensions.

Relative Importance of Shared and Nonshared Environment Several twin studies have found that individual-specific environment, but not shared environment, plays an important role in accounting for phenotypic variance in fears (e.g., Rose & Ditto, 1983) and phobias (Kendler et al., 1992). The hierarchical model of fears suggests that fears arise from a combination of common and specific factors. These may be genetic, environmental, or a combination of both. Kendler et al. found that the best-fitting multivariate genetic model indicated the existence of genetic and individual-specific environmental factors common to all four groups of phobias, and other factors specific for each particular group. Phobia-specific environmental factors were most important for animal and situational phobias, and common environmental factors were more important for agoraphobia and social phobia. Kendler et al. concluded that specific phobias arise from the joint effect of a modest genetic vulnerability and phobia-specific traumatic events in childhood. In comparison, agoraphobia and (to a somewhat lesser extent) social phobia arise from the combined effect of a slightly stronger genetic influence and nonspecific environmental experiences.

These findings are broadly consistent with the hierarchical model of fears, which states that fears (including phobias) arise from combinations of specific and nonspecific (common) factors. The task of future research is to determine what these genetic and environmental factors might be. The broad (nonspecific) genetic factor may have to do with general fear or anxiety proneness (cf. Andrews, 1996). Individual-specific environmental factors may be most important in focusing fear proneness onto fears of particular types of objects or situations.

Theories of Fear: Historical Perspectives

Two-Factor Theory During the 1960s and 1970s the most influential theory of fear was Mowrer's (1939, 1960) two-factor model, which has its origins in the work of Pavlov (1928) and Watson and Rayner (1920). The model proposed that fears are acquired by classical conditioning and maintained by operant conditioning. Classical conditioning is the learning of associations between an unconditioned stimulus (UCS) and conditioned stimulus (CS). In the case of learned fears, UCSs are those stimuli that evoke pain or discomfort in the absence of any prior learning. Pain or discomfort evoked by UCSs are called unconditioned responses (UCRs). Conditioning occurs when a CS is paired with a UCS over one or more trials. Gradually, the organism learns that the CS is premonitory of the UCS. Thus, the CS becomes fear evoking. The fear is referred to as a conditioned response (CR).

To illustrate, dog phobia can arise from a traumatic incident where the person is bitten by a dog. Stimulation of the pain receptors on one's arm might represent the UCS, which evokes pain (UCR). Through the process of associative learning, pain becomes paired to stimuli associated with the UCS (e.g., CSs such as dogs, dog collars, places frequented by dogs). In turn, the CSs become fear evoking (i.e., CR). The strength of the CR is determined by a number of factors, including the intensity of the UCS and the number of repetitions of UCS-CS pairings. Stimuli resembling fear-evoking CSs can become fear evoking in their own right by processes of stimulus generalization and second-order conditioning (Mowrer, 1960; Wolpe & Rachman, 1960).

The link between the CS and UCS tends to decay over successive trials in which the CS is presented without the UCS. As this occurs the CS tends to elicit a weaker or less frequent CR. Given a sufficient number of trials of CS without UCS, the CS eventually ceases to elicit the CR. In the case of many fears, however, this process is blocked from occurring because the person learns that fear can be minimized (at least in the short term) by avoiding or escaping from the CS. In other words, avoidance or escape are operant behaviors under a schedule of negative reinforcement, which prevents the classically conditioned fear from being unlearned. Thus, in addition to eliciting fear, the CS also evokes or motivates escape and avoidance (Mowrer, 1939, 1960).

A good deal of evidence was adduced in support of this theory and has been reviewed in detail elsewhere (e.g., Menzies & Clarke, 1995; Rachman, 1990). However, there are several problems with the two-factor theory (cf., Menzies & Clarke, 1995; Marks, 1987; Rachman, 1990): (1) It sometimes appears that fears are acquired in the absence of conditioning; (2) conditioning theory fails to account for the uneven distribution of fears; i.e., some stimuli are more likely to become feared (e.g., harmless snakes and spiders) compared to others (e.g., guns, knives, electrical outlets); and (3) people sometimes fail to acquire fears in what should be fear-evoking situations (e.g., air raids). Rather than rejecting the two-factor theory, Rachman (e.g., 1976, 1977) and others have attempted to modify the theory to account for these findings. Details of problems, and the major attempts at overcoming them, are as follows.

Pathways to Fear Acquisition To account for fear acquisition in the absence of conditioning, Rachman (1976, 1977) proposed a revised model, which suggested there are other models of fear acquisition. Rachman postulated three pathways: (1) direct conditioning, (2) modeling (e.g., vicarious acquisition due to observational learning), and (3) informational and instructional transmission (e.g., receiving fear-evoking information or misinformation from others). Several retrospective studies of fear onset have assessed the relative importance of these pathways. The results of these studies can be summarized as follows: (1) approximately half of clinical phobias are associated with classical conditioning, with a smaller proportion of phobias associated with modeling (vicarious learning) and fear-relevant instruction or information. A minority of people with phobias appear unable to recall the origins of their fears. This may be because they have forgotten the precipitating events. (2) Conditioning plays a greater role in phobias than in subclinical fears, as suggested by Rachman (1977). However, so-called conditioning events are also found in about a third of nonfearful people. It may be that aversive conditioning experiences are less likely to produce phobias when the person has a history of fearless contact with the stimulus in question. For example, an aversive social experience (e.g., forgetting what to say during a speech) may not be phobogenic when the person has a history of giving successful speeches. This has been called *latent inhibition* (Lubow, 1989) or *fearless familiarity* (Rachman, 1990). Further, it may be that the conditioning experiences in nonfearful people tend to be mild compared to those of people with subclinical fears or phobias.

The conclusions drawn from this research should be regarded as tentative because the studies were based on retrospective accounts, which are subject to a number of biases such as forgetting and "effort after meaning" (i.e., trying to make sense of one's phobia by attributing it to plausible but irrelevant causes). Yet both retrospective reports and findings from twin studies reviewed earlier in this chapter suggest that fortuitous conditioning experiences (i.e., individual-specific environmental effects) are more important than parental modeling or parental instruction (shared environmental effects) in producing fear. Despite the apparent importance of conditioning, it should not be concluded that modeling or instruction are irrelevant to fears. Clearly, further research is needed on the origins of fears.

Prepared Fears Seligman (1970, 1971) claimed that phobias have a number of characteristics that are inconsistent with the two-factor theory of learning, but can be explained by preparedness theory. Phobias, unlike fears conditioned in the laboratory, are said to be (1) rapidly acquired (e.g., single-trial learning), (2) resistant to extinction, (3) "noncognitive" (irrational—i.e., unlike fears conditioned in the laboratory, it is rarely possible to extinguish clinical phobias by informing the person that the UCS will no longer follow the CS—phobias persist even when the person "knows" the stimulus is harmless), and (4) differentially associable with stimuli of evolutionary significance. With regard to the latter, the two-factor theory assumed an equipotentiality of potential fear stimuli; that is, all neutral stimuli can become fear stimuli. In the words of Pavlov, "any natural phenomenon chosen at will may be converted into a conditioned stimulus" (1928, p. 86). Yet some stimuli (e.g., small animals) are more likely to be fear evoking than others (e.g., guns, knives, electrical outlets);

"only rarely, if ever, do we have pyjama phobias, grass phobias, electric-outlet phobias, hammer phobias, even though these things are likely to be associated with trauma in our world" (Seligman, 1971, p. 312).

Seligman (1970, 1971) proposed that people (and other organisms) are biologically prepared to acquire fears of some stimuli. That is, evolution has predisposed organisms to learn easily those associations that facilitate species survival. As a result of a sufficiently long period of natural selection, organisms are prepared ("hard-wired") to fear some events, unprepared for others, and contraprepared for still others. Stimuli such as guns, knives, and electrical outlets have not been around long enough for such preparedness to occur. Seligman's preparedness theory has become widely influential, and has even worked its way into *DSM-IV*: "Feared objects or situations tend to involve things that may actually represent a threat or have represented a threat at some point in the course of human evolution" (p. 408). Seligman conceptualized preparedness as an ease of learning continuum; that is, the relative preparedness for learning about a stimulus is defined by the amount of input (e.g., number of learning trials, bits of information) required in order for an output (responses) to reliably occur.

Preparedness theory has stimulated a large body of research. The most impressive evidence comes from the studies of Rhesus monkeys conducted by Cook and Mineka (1987, 1989, 1990). In these studies the investigators had observer monkeys watch videotapes of monkeys behaving fearfully with toy snakes or a toy crocodile. As a result, the observers acquired a fear of those stimuli. In comparison, observer monkeys who watched videotapes of monkeys showing the identical fear behaviors (via videotape splicing) to artificial flowers or toy rabbits generally did not acquire fears of the flowers or toy rabbit. Thus, there were significant differences in the conditionability of fear to fear-relevant stimuli compared to fear-irrelevant stimuli.

Evidence from human studies has not been so compelling. McNally (1987) conducted an exhaustive review of the literature on humans published up until the mid-to-late 1980s. The typical paradigm for psychophysiological studies testing the theory entailed comparisons between "fear-relevant" stimuli (i.e., putatively prepared stimuli, representing pretechnological fears: e.g., snakes, spiders, angry faces) and fear-irrelevant stimuli (e.g., slides of flowers or mushrooms). These stimuli were used as conditioned stimuli in Pavlovian aversive conditioning paradigms, using measures such as skin conductance to assess fear acquisition. With regard to the hypothesis that prepared associations reflect a primitive, noncognitive form of Pavlovian conditioning, there has been no clear support. Experiments by Ohman and colleagues supported the hypothesis, whereas other studies did not (see Ohman, Dimberg, & Ost (1985).

No conclusive support was found for the hypothesis that preparedness effects are attributable to selective associations between fear-relevant CSs and electric shock. Thus, it remains to be shown that fear-relevance effects are due to differential associability. McNally (1987) found that the evidence most consistent with the theory is enhanced resistance to extinction of electrodermal responses to fear-relevant stimuli. Moreover, it appears that "prepared" phobias are generally no more difficult to treat than "unprepared" phobias (de Silva, Rachman, & Seligman, 1977; Zafiropoulou & McPherson, 1986; but cf. Merckelbach, van den Hout, Hoekstra, & van Oppen, 1988).

It has been suggested that resistance to extinction may be due to ontogenetic (environmental) preparedness rather than phylogenetic (evolutionary) preparedness (Bandura, 1977; Davey, 1995; Delprato, 1980). In other words, cultural factors such as folklore about particular stimuli (e.g., snakes), parental modeling, and other developmental events may prepare otherwise nonfearful people to become fearful of fear-relevant stimuli. The relative importance of ontogenetic and phylogenetic factor remains to be established (see Davey, 1995, and commentaries therein).

It may not be particular stimuli that are "prepared." Rather, it may be that particular stimulus features or combinations of features, are prepared (Bennett-Levy & Marteau, 1984). For example, crawling movements, abrupt movements, sliminess, hairiness, looming shapes. However, it is apparent that none of these fears is necessarily fear evoking (e.g., jelly is slimy but is rarely feared; babies crawl but are infrequently the objects of phobias). It may be that particular stimulus combinations are more likely to be fear evoking. However, if one takes enough features (e.g., crawling, hairy, abrupt movement), then one has an animal (e.g., spider). Thus, it remains to be seen whether the concept of "prepared fear features" is helpful in furthering our understanding of fear.

What we are left with is the fact that there is a nonrandom distribution of fears and phobias: "The only feature of the original [preparedness] model that remains vital today is the concept of selective associations, that is, that organisms may show superior conditioning with certain CS-UCS combinations for reasons other than the simple salience value of the CS or the UCS" (Mineka & Cook, 1995, p. 307). Latent inhibition to stimuli such as hammers, electric outlets, and so forth may account for the rarity of fears of such stimuli. That is, children typically receive parental instruction as to the safe use of such stimuli (Levis, 1979). Common subclinical fears and phobias typically pertain to threats present in a pretechnological era. Yet this does not necessarily mean that they are the direct result of evolutionary selection pressures. The genes for such fears may be adjacent to genes for adaptive behaviors, thus selection for the adaptive behaviors inadvertantly also entails selection for phobias (McNally, 1995).

Retrospective studies of fear development and twin studies support the importance of conditioning as a mechanism of phobia acquisition. An important further question is whether conditioning is the simple associative (reflexlike) process of learning of associations, or whether higher order cognitive processes play a role. Consideration of this possibility has led to the development of neo-conditioning perspectives, which we now consider.

Behavioral and Cognitive Theories: Contemporary Approaches

Neo-Conditioning Neo-conditioning perspectives (Rachman, 1991a; Rescorla, 1988; Rescorla & Wagner, 1972; Wagner & Rescorla, 1972) regard classical and operant conditioning as processes that draw on cognitive mechanisms such as expectations and memory representations of the CS and UCS. Here, UCS-CS links are acquired because CSs are *predictors* of the occurrence of the UCS. To illustrate, a person with a fear of driving might learn that poorly lit, wet roads (CSs) are predictive of a life-threatening motor vehicle accident (UCS; Taylor & Koch, 1995). The strength of the conditioned fear is a function of two factors: the strength of the UCS-CS link (i.e., subjective probability that a given CS will lead to a given UCS), and the perceived aversiveness of the UCS (e.g., perceived dangerousness of motor vehicle accidents).

The neo-conditioning approach also entails a revised view of operant conditioning of avoidance behavior (Seligman & Johnston, 1973). Here, avoidance is not directly determined by the experience of fear, but by the individual's *expectation* of whether a given behavior (e.g., driving in the rain) will lead to an aversive outcome (e.g., a fatal motor vehicle accident). Avoidance behavior is not reinforced by reduction of fear; it is reinforced by full or partial confirmation of one's expectations (e.g., by a "close call" while driving).

According to the neo-conditioning perspective, UCS evaluation (and reevaluation) can influence the acquisition, extinction, and inflation of fears. As noted by Davey (1989):

> When a CS-UCS association has been formed, CS presentation evokes a representation of the UCS. Information about the UCS contained in this presentation is evaluated, and the result of this evaluation process determines the strength of the CR. If the UCS is evaluated as aversive or noxious, this will result in a fear CR. (p. 52)

Thus, mild conditioned fears can escalate into phobias when the UCS is reevaluated. To illustrate, a person might acquire a mild fear of spiders after the person sustains a painful but harmless spider bite. The fear may escalate into a phobia if the person learns that spider bites are often lethal. Thus, the intensity of the UCS is inflated from a harmless painful bite to a painful and potentially life-threatening bite. As a consequence, the nature of the CS changes (i.e., spiders now become predictive of life-endangering events) and the conditioned fear increases accordingly.

Neo-conditioning and Emotional Processing The neo-conditioning model proposes that the CS and UCS are cognitively represented, possibly in networks of interconnections among CSs, CRs, UCSs, and UCRs. According to the network model, fears are represented in networks (fear structures) in long-term memory. The networks contain cognitive representations of feared stimuli (e.g., oncoming trucks, driving at night), response information (e.g., palpitations, trembling, subjective fear, escape behaviors), and meaning information (e.g., the concept of danger). In the network the three types of information are linked (e.g., links between oncoming trucks, danger, and fear). Links can be innate (i.e., UCS-UCR links) or acquired by processes such as conditioning (CS-UCS links and CS-CR links). Fear structures are activated by incoming information that matches information stored in the network. Activation of the network evokes fear and motivates avoidance or escape behavior. According to Foa and colleagues (Foa & Kozak, 1986; Foa, Steketee, & Rothbaum, 1989), fears are reduced by modifying the fear structure through the incorporation of corrective information (e.g., safety information acquired during behavioral exposure exercises). This is called emotional processing.

The neo-conditioning perspective and the emotional processing model are useful ways of conceptualizing fears, and can account for phenomena that are not explained by the two-factor theory (e.g., postconditioning fear inflation due to UCS inflation). A further advantage is that these models are compatible with other cognitive models of fears, such as those discussed in the following sections.

Anxiety Sensitivity In an effort to account for individual differences in conditionability, Reiss's (1980; Reiss & McNally, 1985) theory proposes that anxiety sensitivity (AS) is a fundamental fear than amplifies or exacerbates other (common) fears, such as fears of animals, social situations, blood-illness-injury stimuli, and agoraphobic fears. AS is the fear of anxiety-related sensations (e.g., fears of palpitations, dizziness, and tremulousness), which arises from beliefs that these sensations have aversive somatic, psychological, or social consequences (Reiss, 1991; Reiss & McNally, 1985).

Reiss later revised his theory by proposing that AS is one of three fundamental fears; the others include illness/injury sensitivity (i.e., fear of illness, injury, or death) and fear of negative evaluation. Fundamental fears are said to contribute to, or amplify, many other kinds of fear and phobia, including common fears such as social/evaluative fears and animal fears. Fundamental fears have two features that distinguish them from common fears: They are fears of stimuli that are inherently noxious (at least for most people), and other, "common" fears can be logically reduced to them (Reiss, 1991). With regard to the latter, fundamental fears provide reasons for fearing a variety of stimuli, whereas ordinary fears do not have this property. To illustrate, fear of flying can be exacerbated by, or entirely due to, the following: fear of the plane crashing (illness/injury sensitivity), fear of anxiety evoked by bumpy flights (AS), and fear of embarrassing oneself by becoming airsick (fear of negative evaluation). Thus, a common fear (fear of flying) may be logically reduced to one or more fundamental fears.

Empirical support for this proposition has been provided by a number of studies (McNally & Louro, 1992; McNally & Steketee, 1985). However, the question remains as to whether the fundamental fears can be reduced to still more basic fears. For example, recent evidence suggests that AS—as assessed by the Anxiety Sensitivity Index (ASI; Peterson & Reiss, 1987)—can be reduced to at least three basic fears: (1) fear of anxiety-related somatic sensations (e.g., palpitations), (2) phrenophobia (fear of loss of cognitive control), and (3) fear of publicly observable anxiety reactions (e.g., blushing, trembling; Taylor, Koch, Woody, & McLean, 1996).

Most of the research on fundamental fears has focused on AS, especially in relation to panic attacks and panic disorder (see the later sections in this chapter for details). Several studies have found that ASI scores are correlated with measures of common fears, as measured by subscales from the Fear Survey Schedules and related instruments (Reiss, Peterson, Gursky, & McNally, 1986; Taylor, 1993, 1999). The relationship between common fears and the other fundamental fears (fear of negative evaluation and illness/injury sensitivity) remains to be fully investigated. As expected, fear of negative evaluation is correlated with social fears, and illness/injury sensitivity is correlated with fears of blood, injury, and illness (Taylor, 1993). Further studies, using experimental designs, are needed, however, to show that the fundamental fears are the *causes* rather than mere correlates of common fears.

Consistent with the neo-conditioning approach to fears, some theorists have proposed that exaggerated expectations of danger or "danger schema" may play an important role in motivating fear and avoidance (Beck & Emery, 1985; Davey, 1995). Other types of cognitive factors (e.g., distortions, belief systems) have not played a major role in theories of specific phobia, and are more prominent in theories of agoraphobia and social phobia. People with social phobia tend to be preoccupied with their social presentation and to have heightened public self-consciousness (see Leary & Kowalski, 1995). They also tend to be self-critical, to worry excessively about being criticized or rejected by others, and tend to overestimate the likelihood of aversive social events (Beck & Emery, 1985; Hope, Gansler, & Heimberg, 1989; Lucock & Salkovskis, 1988).

Clark and Wells (1995) have presented a detailed cognitive model of social phobia that describes the hypothesized assumptions and self-schemata characteristic of social phobia (e.g., "I must not show any signs of weakness"), and have hypothesized why social fears may be maintained by cognitive factors (e.g., via an individual's negative "postmortem" analysis of an ambiguous social event). Recent empirical studies support the role of distorted beliefs and appraisals in social phobia (e.g., Lucock & Salkovskis, 1988; Stopa & Clark, 1993), and may be important targets for treatment (Beck & Emery, 1985; Clark & Wells, 1995). However, some models of social phobia borrow heavily on constructs previously linked to depression (e.g., self-criticism, perfectionism), and more work is needed on delineating the psychological boundaries of social phobia and depression, particularly the interpersonal aspects of depression. For example, are the proposed cognitive factors related to social phobia only present with respect to social situations or are these factors more pervasive?

The conditioning model has become increasingly more cognitive in recent years. Thus, neoconditioning accounts of fear are quite compatible with cognitive models of fears (e.g., Beck and Emery, 1985). In the case of phobias, classical and operant conditioning appears to be a function of exaggerated expectations of danger and related beliefs. Deconditioning can be regarded as a process of exposure to corrective information (Foa & Kozak, 1986).

Because of space limitations and the size of the literature on fears and phobias, we have only been able to highlight some of the more important issues. We refer the interested reader to other sources for other important topics in this area, including the debate on whether covariation biases can account for the uneven distribution of fears (Davey, 1995), the role of forgetting of CS and UCS properties in the maintenance of fear (Mineka, 1992), the role of attentional and judgmental biases in maintaining fears (e.g., Merckelbach, de Jong, Muris, & van den Hout, 1996), and the biochemical and neurophysiological bases of fear (e.g., Carr, 1996; Gray, 1982; Shephard, 1986).

As a final point it is worth noting that social phobia is no longer the "neglected anxiety disorder" it was once deemed to be in the early 1980s (Liebowitz, Gorman, Fyer, & Klein, 1985). Although Marks and Gelder (1966) provided detailed earlier accounts of social phobia that closely approximate current diagnostic descriptions, it was not until the appearance of *DSM-III* in 1980 that social phobia was "officially" categorized in the psychiatric nomenclature. Since that time interest in social phobia has continued to grow, and recently two edited books have been published entirely devoted to this anxiety disorder (Heimberg, Liebowitz, Hope, & Schneier, 1995; Stein, 1995).

Panic Disorder with Agoraphobia

As the term suggests, panic disorder with agoraphobia (PDA) largely comprises two related components: panic attacks and agoraphobia. Other components include anticipatory anxiety and dysphoria. Panic attacks are defined as sudden, discrete episodes of very intense anxiety, usually accompanied by feelings of impending doom. In the case of panic disorder, these attacks develop in a spontaneous fashion, at least initially, and are perceived as occurring "out of the blue." Panic attacks are characterized by a number of physical symptoms (e.g., dyspnea, palpitations, dizziness) and psychological symptoms (fears of dying, going crazy, or losing control). Agoraphobia frequently accompanies panic disorder and is seen as a fear of being in places in which escape might be difficult or help not available in the event of sudden incapacitating symptoms such as a panic attack.

PDA is often a severe and very disabling anxiety disorder. It has been associated with a poor quality of life, significant health-care costs, and comorbidity complications. PDA is one of the most common diagnostic entities seen in anxiety disorder clinics (Swinson, Cox, Kerr, Kuch, & Fergus, 1992), and individuals with PDA likely constitute a large proportion of community-based anxiety disorder support groups as well. Boyd (1986), using data from the ECA survey, found that panic disorder led the list of mental disorders for which mental health treatment was sought. Unfortunately, studies suggest that many individuals with PDA either do not receive empirically supported therapies or receive it only after several years of coping with the disorder (Swinson, Cox, & Woszczyna, 1992; Taylor et al., 1989).

DSM-Based Classification of Panic and Agoraphobia

DSM-III and its successors have fostered much of the research cited in this chapter, and important changes have been introduced in the classification of panic and agoraphobia that continue to remain controversial in several quarters. Paralleling the voluminous amount of anxiety disorders research that has accrued since the publication of *DSM-III*, the *DSM-IV* anxiety disorders section has grown to 52 pages in length from the 15 pages found in *DSM-III*. Because of space limitations we will only summarize the changes in diagnostic views of panic and agoraphobia since they were first introduced in *DSM-III*: (1) The fear of panic attacks, rather than the presence or frequency of panic attacks, is now seen as a hallmark feature of panic disorder. (2) There is now an emphasis on differentiating unexpected (uncued) panic attacks, situationally bound (cued), and situationally predisposed panic attacks. (3) Although a diagnosis of panic disorder with comorbid generalized anxiety disorder is now permitted, they are still viewed as qualitatively different types of anxiety experiences and there has been an effort to differentiate the symptoms that constitute these disorders. (4) Agoraphobia has come to be viewed as a secondary complication of panic disorder or is thought to be linked to "panic-like symptoms" (*DSM-IV*, p. 396).

It remains to be seen whether the expanded description in *DSM-IV* will aid the general clinician in establishing an appropriate diagnosis. Others have suggested even further refinement of the definition of panic for research purposes, believing *DSM-IV* definitions are designed primarily for clinicians rather than researchers (Barlow, Brown, & Craske, 1994). The shifting diagnostic framework has obviously influenced research in the area and this fact should be kept in mind when reviewing studies over a multiyear period. *DSM*-based descriptions and criteria are widely accepted and have done much to foster empirical research.

However, there has also been considerable controversy around these issues, particularly among non–North American investigators. Several critical commentaries and reviews of *DSM*-based nomenclature have been published during this time period (e.g., Andrews, 1996; Gelder, 1989; Hallam, 1983, 1991; Tyrer, 1986). In large part, these criticisms concern two central arguments. The first is that panic attacks and generalized anxiety are not qualitatively distinct forms of anxiety. Rather, they represent points on a quantitative continuum of severity, and because they have more similarities than differences, panic disorder and generalized anxiety disorder (GAD) are in fact best thought of as representing part of a "general neurotic syndrome." The second argument is that panic is merely one of several symptoms of agoraphobia, and it is agoraphobia that constitutes the major clinical component in terms of distress and disability. Agoraphobia should therefore not be classified as a secondary complication of panic disorder.

It is beyond the scope of this chapter to review all of the relevant studies addressing these arguments. However, McNally (1994), after having reviewed several relevant empirical papers, concluded that "taken together, most evidence supports the syndromal validity of panic disorder as an entity distinct from GAD, and agoraphobia as a complication of the core disorder of panic" (p. 196). Recent evidence from a large factor analytic study of patients assessed at an anxiety disorders clinic (Zinbarg & Barlow, 1996) supports this position.

Despite considerable empirical support for the panic and agoraphobia classifications in the recent versions of the *DSM*, several issues should be kept in mind. First, agoraphobia is still given prominence in *ICD-10*, a diagnostic nosology widely in use outside of North America. Second, the relegation of agoraphobia as a secondary complication of panic disorder in *DSM-III-R* and *DSM-IV* does not encourage investigation of agoraphobia in its own right, especially in relation to potentially important psychosocial aspects of agoraphobia (e.g., Hallam, 1991).

A third issue is that much of the basic psychopathology research on panic and agoraphobia may have been forced to be somewhat circular. By circular, we mean that it is difficult, if not impossible, to properly investigate the validity of *DSM* classifications and diagnostic criteria, or to subject the latest revisions to empirical testing, if the patients included for study have already been selected (diagnosed) to meet these predetermined criteria. For example, it is difficult to accept findings on the average frequency of panic attacks experienced by panic disorder patients if they had to meet *DSM-III-R* frequency criteria of at least four attacks in four weeks to qualify for a diagnosis of panic disorder and be included in the study in the first place. Few studies have "suspended" or modified the various *DSM* decision rules in order to more fairly evaluate the validity of such rules.

A final cautionary note concerns evaluation of research findings that have emerged during a period of changing criteria for panic disorder. Even subtle changes can effect the makeup of a particular research sample and could influence obtained results (see Klein & Klein, 1989).

Further Phenomenological Considerations

Aside from issues concerning the classification of panic and agoraphobia, several other questions on the nature and clinical features of these disorders often arise. In the following sections we provide examples of the types of questions that psychopathology researchers continue to pursue.

Are All Panic Attacks the Same? In addition to subtypes of panic based on the presence versus absence of situational triggers, the breadth of panic symptoms listed in the *DSM-IV* raises the possibility that there may be identifiable symptom patterns within panic disorder. Also, the fact that panic attacks occur in a variety of disorders raises a similar question.

There is evidence to suggest that meaningful patterns or clusters of symptoms do exist within panic disorder, although a consensus regarding the exact structure of these clusters has not yet been reached. A widely reported finding is that cardiorespiratory distress and dizziness-related symptoms tend to emerge as separate clusters (Argyle, 1988; Cox, Swinson, Endler, & Norton, 1994; Marks, Basoglu, Alkubaisy, Sengun, & Marks, 1991). There is also some suggestion that specific cognitions may be linked with each cluster (e.g., thoughts of dying with cardiorespiratory distress; fears of losing control with dizziness/depersonalization). Lelliott and Bass (1990) found that panic disorder patients with predominantly cardiorespiratory symptoms responded with more distress to voluntary hyperventilation compared to panic disorder patients with predominantly gastrointestinal complaints. Ley (1992) has also suggested that panic disorder may be a heterogeneous condition, and that patients with "classic" panic attacks (i.e., cardiorespiratory distress) may be more suitable for a breathing retraining intervention while patients with "cognitive" panic attacks (catastrophic thinking in the absence of severe physical symptoms) may be more appropriate for cognitive therapy.

Though not yet conclusive, research suggests that subtypes of panic disorder do in fact exist, and this has important clinical implications in regards to tailoring treatments. It also has research implications for studies such as panic provocation experiments that target specific types of symptoms. Further, some studies have provided evidence that there are identifiable subtypes of agoraphobia such as public situations, claustrophobia, and open spaces (e.g., Cox, Swinson, Kuch, & Reichman, 1993). An interesting area for future study is to determine whether congruent patterns exist across panic symptom clusters, catastrophic cognitions, and types of phobic avoidance behavior.

The second possibility of heterogeneity relates to whether all panic attacks are essentially the same and differ only in regards to being expected (cued) versus unexpected (uncued). Although it has been known for some time that panic attacks frequently occur in other anxiety and mental disorders (e.g., Barlow et al., 1985), there appears to be less consensus on whether unexpected panic attacks (which occur in panic disorder) and expected panic attacks (which occur in other disorders) are basically the same type of emotional response, and more direct empirical comparisons appear warranted. After reviewing the available literature, Craske (1991) suggested that expected and unexpected panic attacks are very similar responses. Barlow et al. (1994) also maintain that panic is equivalent to fear and suggest it differs from it only in situational context. In contrast, more cognitively oriented models of panic, which focus on triggers and catastrophic misinterpretations as well as fear, appear to have a fundamentally different view (for a discussion see Rapee, 1993). From the latter perspective, the panic attack experienced by an individual with social phobia would be seen as quite different in regards to trigger, catastrophic thoughts, and perhaps also in symptom pattern, compared to a panic attack in a person with panic disorder. Further research into the nature of the panic experience across different disorders, and especially into the sequence of events that culminate in a full-blown panic attack, is indicated.

Causes of Unexpected Panic Attacks The idea of panic attacks occurring randomly or seemingly out of the blue fits well within a biomedical view of panic disorder, where nonbiological factors are presumed to have little importance. Studying this question is made difficult by the constraint discussed earlier in regards to patient selection and the fact that only those who have already met *DSM*-based criteria for unexpected panic will have been included in a study of panic disorder. Despite this limitation there is some evidence to suggest that initial panic attacks, though perceived as spontaneous by the person experiencing the attack, may in fact follow certain patterns. Although the evidence is mixed, some studies have found that many panic disorder patients, particularly those with agoraphobia, report that their initial "spontaneous" panic attack occurred in what might be termed social/public or classic agoraphobic situations (Faravelli, Pallanti, Biondi, & Scarpato, 1992; Lelliott, Marks, McNamee, & Tobena, 1989; Shulman, Cox, Swinson, Kuch, & Reichman, 1994).

For example, Lelliott et al. (1989) observed that agoraphobic patients were more likely to report initial attacks in public places rather than at home, and Shulman et al. (1994) found that almost 40% of panic disorder patients with extensive agoraphobic avoidance reported that their initial, unexpected panic attacks occurred on either a bus, plane, or subway. Moreover, Fava, Grandi, and Canestrari (1988) reported that in the majority of their (small) PDA sample, some degree of agoraphobic behavior was present *before* the occurrence of the first spontaneous panic attack. It may be that limited symptom attacks, rather than full-blown panic attacks, preceded the onset of agoraphobia in these cases.

A large body of work has focused on precipitating factors that may be associated with the onset of panic attacks and panic disorder, and the results can be briefly summarized as follows. Many, if not most, panic attacks are predated by some negative life event, perceived stressor, anticipation of some future stressful event, or in direct response to an agent such as cocaine. However, the relationship is not one-to-one; major life events can precede a number of forms of psychopathology, such as major depression, and for some individuals these same events can occur without any psychiatric sequelae. Perhaps more important in the case of panic disorder is the fact that recurrent, unexpected panic attacks, and anxious apprehension about these attacks, can persist long after the stressors have ceased. It seems likely that panic disorder is the product of an interaction between some vulnerability factor (diathesis) and an appropriate stressor. Vulnerabilities may include other disorders or psychopathological reactions, such as separation anxiety disorder and other attachment difficulties, behavioral inhibition, "neurotic" temperament, or other psychobiologic factors (see, for example, Anderson, Taylor, & McLean, 1996).

Nocturnal Panic The phenomenon of "nocturnal panic" is highly relevant to the issue of spontaneity of panic attacks. Most of these attacks occur during non-REM sleep, are phenomenologically different from night terrors, and are frequently not precipitated by dreams (McNally, 1994). Thus, nothing could seem more spontaneous than a panic attack occurring while a person is sleeping. It is rare, however, for persons to experience only nocturnal panic and not daytime panic, and in general nocturnal panics are rated as less severe than daytime occurrences (Craske & Barlow, 1989). Little is known about the subjective nature and sequence of events in nocturnal panic. It is possible that a sudden surge in arousal awakens a panic-prone individual who rapidly misinterprets a feared physiological sensation and panics. This would be especially applicable to individuals who have a strong fear of arousal sensations and are prone to daytime catastrophic misinterpretation; some empirical support for this position is available (Craske & Freed, 1995). Another interesting (null) finding is that a known panic-provocation agent, sodium lactate, failed to induce panic attacks in panic disorder patients who were asleep, although it did lead to a greater increase in physiological arousal than among control subjects (Koenigsberg, Pollack, Fine, & Kakuma, 1992). Nocturnal panic will likely continue to attract research attention, and the implications of these studies are of great importance in testing competing hypotheses derived from psychological and biological theories.

Why does Panic Disorder Progress to Panic Disorder with Agoraphobia? Not all people with panic disorder develop agoraphobia; some develop agoraphobic avoidance shortly after the initial panic attack while others live with panic attacks for years without becoming agoraphobic. Some people develop mild phobic avoidance while others become almost completely housebound. Some remain agoraphobic years after panic attacks have dissipated. In the latter scenario, these people may display an increase in panic frequency when beginning in vivo exposure therapy, which includes confronting situations predisposed to panic occurrences that have long been avoided. An irony is that, although very disabled, an individual with this type of disorder may not meet entry criteria for most treatment studies of PDA because of the requirement of frequent panic attacks.

These interesting observations have spawned a significant amount of theory and research into the development of agoraphobia. As noted earlier, however, there has been noticeably less work in this area compared to the attention directed to panic, and the study of agoraphobia has been largely enmeshed with the study of panic.

One of the difficulties in arriving at a consensus from the body of research on this topic is the fact that, although a number of different hypotheses have been proposed and tested, rarely have empirical investigations tested several different hypotheses simultaneously. Thus, while there have been many impressive findings to date, there have also been several failures to replicate. A host of variables have been hypothesized to be influential in the development of agoraphobia, including gender roles, depression, maladaptive coping styles, social evaluation anxiety, feared panic outcomes, effects of unexpected panic, interoceptive/somatic preoccupation, and secondary gain from the environment (for reviews see Clum & Knowles, 1991; Craske & Barlow, 1988). Further, there is often a good rationale for two very different hypotheses: (1) spontaneous, unexpected panic should lead to extensive avoidance behavior because the individual has little idea of when and where the next panic attack will occur; versus (2) expected, situationally predisposed panic should result in phobic avoidance because the person believes various, identifiable situations are now triggering the panic attacks.

Some writers (e.g., McNally, 1994) believe the available evidence indicates the best predictors of agoraphobic avoidance are cognitive in nature (e.g., perceived negative consequences of panic attacks), but the research findings are actually quite mixed. One of the few consistent findings is that panic expectancy is associated with avoidance (e.g., Craske, Rapee, & Barlow, 1988), although evidence for the role of anticipated negative outcomes during panic is mixed. In one study of panic disorder patients with various *DSM-III-R* degrees of agoraphobia (none, mild, moderate, severe), several hypothesized variables were compared simultaneously (Cox, Endler, & Swinson, 1995). The results indicated that cognitive factors such as anxiety sensitivity and fears of dying during a panic attack did not distinguish groups. Rather, the anticipation of panic, specifically in relation to agoraphobic situations, was the best predictor of agoraphobia. Patients also avoided other types of situations (e.g., social) if they anticipated panic there. Cox et al. (1995) concluded that panic and agoraphobia do not share an exclusive relationship. For example, a person with panic disorder characterized by cardiorespiratory distress may avoid any form of strenuous physical exercise. This is obviously a type of panic-related phobic avoidance and yet it is not adequately captured in *DSM* descriptions of agoraphobia.

Apart from anticipation of panic, studies consistently show that the frequency and severity of panic play a minimal role in the development of agoraphobia. The consequence of this arguably narrow focus in our research is that we may now understand more about how agoraphobia can develop (i.e., panic expectancy), but we still know little about why. Writers such as Hallam (1978, 1983) have suggested that agoraphobia is part of a more global coping style or personality feature, and that it is also associated with lower socioeconomic status and other sociocultural variables. Similarly, Craske and Barlow (1988) have postulated that a prior history of mastery and social demand factors may play a significant predisposing role. It is also not uncommon for PDA patients to report agoraphobic-like tendencies (e.g., choosing to sit in aisle seats or near exits, choosing to not be in public places when not feeling well) *before* the onset of full-blown, spontaneous panic attacks. These are valid areas for further study and may help to prevent relapse or to modify existing treatments for individuals who do not respond to exposure-based approaches, terminate therapy prematurely, or do not even choose to enter treatment. (It is worth remembering that in vivo exposure therapy is often very demanding on the individual, even when the exposure is graded.)

The three preceding subsections hopefully give the reader a better sense of some of the phenomenological aspects of panic and agoraphobia, and provide representative examples of some of the many interesting questions awaiting further study.

We turn now to epidemiological findings and comorbidity issues.

Prevalence, Course, and Comorbidity

DSM-IV estimates for the lifetime prevalence of panic disorder (with or without agoraphobia) range from 1.5 to 3.5%, based on several international epidemiological studies. Approximately one half of community samples of individuals with panic disorder also have agoraphobia, and the proportion is much higher in persons seen in clinical settings. At present, agoraphobia without a history of panic attacks is believed to be quite rare. Earlier findings from the ECA survey had suggested otherwise, but it is now thought that assessment weaknesses may have tainted the results. Specifically, many individuals diagnosed with agoraphobia without a history of panic in the ECA survey should have instead been diagnosed with specific phobia (for further discussion see *DSM-IV* and McNally, 1994).

More recent epidemiological findings are available from the National Comorbidity Survey, which employed *DSM-III-R* criteria (Kessler et al., 1994). Anxiety disorders showed the highest one-year prevalence of all the mental disorders (17%). Social phobia was found to be more common than previously believed, and agoraphobia without panic disorder was also not uncommon. Consistent with results from earlier epidemiological studies, women were at least twice as likely to be diagnosed with panic disorder or agoraphobia as men. Men and women who do have these anxiety disorders appear to experience very similar clinical features (e.g., Oei, Wanstall, & Evans, 1990), and it is not clear why women are more often afflicted or, to be accurate, are more often diagnosed with these disorders. It is likely that societal factors are at work here to some extent (e.g., agoraphobia is still a more accepted stereotype for women, self-medication with alcohol is more acceptable for men). Gender-role expectations and their relationship with panic, agoraphobia, and anxiety assessment in general all require further study.

It is important to remember that panic attacks alone do constitute a mental disorder, and far more individuals experience panic attacks than panic disorder. In their review of research on "nonclinical panic," Norton, Cox, & Malan (1992) reported that several studies had obtained a one-year prevalence figure of panic attacks in nonclinical samples of 30% or greater (self-report assessment yielded higher figures). Individuals with nonclinical panic attacks appear to experience an anxiety response similar to that seen in panic disorder patients, but the attacks in nonclinical samples are more often of the cued type rather than spontaneous, and there is considerably less anxious apprehension about future panic occurrences than is present in clinical samples. These differences are hardly surprising because they reflect the very criteria for diagnosing panic disorder. That is, panic disorder is diagnosed by the occurrence of unexpected ("spontaneous") panic attacks, and by the fear of having further attacks.

DSM-IV states that the age of onset for panic disorder ranges considerably, but there does appear to be a large clustering in late adolescence and a second, smaller cluster in the mid-30s. Panic attacks originating in childhood or in late life are not unheard of, but are not common. The typical course of the disorder is chronic, but with waxing and waning of symptoms.

The initial spontaneous panic attack is generally reported by panic disorder patients to be a truly terrifying experience. One individual with panic disorder remarked, "You don't think you are dying, you *know* you are dying." Indeed, over 20% of patients from one sample reported seeking help from a general hospital emergency room (ER) during their first panic attack (Shulman et al., 1994). It has been empirically demonstrated that early and brief behavioral interventions delivered in the ER can have very beneficial effects (Swinson, Soulios, Cox, & Kuch, 1992), but this is not the typical course for panic disorder. A more common pattern for individuals with panic disorder is numerous visits to various medical and other health professionals, medication prescriptions generally in the form of benzodiazepines, and the development of some degree of agoraphobic avoidance, usually within the first year of recurrent, unexpected panic attacks.

Data from the ECA survey indicate that panic disorder is associated with a poor quality of life, as marked by such factors as poor physical health, financial dependency, and alcohol abuse (Markowitz, Weissman, Ouellette, Lish, & Klerman, 1989). There is even some evidence of increased mortality due to cardiovascular disease in panic disorder patients compared to depressed patients (Coryell, Noyes, & Clancy, 1982). However, this finding may be complicated by other associated factors such as an increased rate of smoking.

Panic disorder with or without agoraphobia is frequently comorbid with other mental disorders. Four commonly comorbid Axis I disorders will be discussed here: depressive disorders, alcohol abuse, hypochondriasis, and social phobia (for a review of Axis II comorbidity, see Taylor & Livesley, 1995; Wetzler & Sanderson, 1995). By definition, these comorbid disorders must exist "independently" from panic disorder, and only after the restrictive hierarchical decision rules were abandoned in *DSM-III-R* did most of the research on this topic develop. Another general issue to keep in mind is that when two disorders are found to co-occur (e.g., panic disorder and major depression), it is unclear how one determines which disorder should be considered primary. Some research strategies have relied on chronology (i.e., order of onset), while others have relied more on the predominant clinical concerns at the time of assessment (i.e., the set of symptoms the person is seeking relief from). Comorbidity is an important issue because individuals with multiple comorbid disorders may respond less favorably to treatments than to individuals with only a single disturbance, or may at the least require modification of existing treatment strategies (see Maser & Cloninger, 1990).

Comorbid Depression In their review of panic disorder and depression comorbidity studies, Wetzler and Sanderson (1995) reported that an average of 24% (range = 7–61%) of panic disorder patients have a comorbid depressive disorder (with dysthymia more common than major depression), and prevalence figures for a lifetime history of depression are even higher. Conversely, it is less common for individuals with primary major depression to have comorbid panic disorder (Wetzler & Sanderson estimate the figure at 14%). Many individuals with panic disorder, while not fully meeting diagnostic criteria for a major depressive episode, may still have depression symptoms and elevated scores on measures of depressed mood.

Although individuals with coexisting panic disorder and major depression appear more symptomatic and have a greater overall clinical severity than persons with only one diagnosis, there is evidence to suggest these comorbid patients still respond well to cognitive-behavioral (e.g., Laberge, Gauthier, Cote, Plamondon, & Cormier, 1993; Woody, Taylor, McLean, & Koch, 1996) and pharmacological treatments (e.g., Lesser et al., 1989). The fact that panic disorder and depression frequently co-occur raises the possibility that they represent a single underlying syndrome. However, evidence from a wide range of variables including familial patterns, symptomatology, and biological findings all point to panic disorder and depression as distinct diagnostic entities (for reviews see McNally, 1994; Wetzler & Sanderson, 1995).

Comorbidity with depression also raises the issue of suicidal ideation and attempts associated with panic attacks and panic disorder. Using data from the ECA survey, one study found that 20% of persons diagnosed with panic disorder and 12% of those with panic attacks reported a history of suicide attempts (Weissman, Klerman, Markowitz, & Ouellette, 1989). Weissman et al. also reported that individuals with panic disorder were 18 times more likely to have attempted suicide compared to individuals with no psychiatric disorder, and this increased risk was present even after comorbid depression was controlled for. However, Hornig and McNally (1995) reanalyzed the original ECA dataset used by Weissman et al. (1989) and controlled for combinations of comorbid disorders. The results of this analysis indicated that panic disorder was not associated with increased risk for suicide attempts when comorbidity was controlled for. Similarly, a recent study using the ECA suicide questions (in a self-report format) with panic disorder patients in a clinical setting (Cox, Direnfeld, Swinson, & Norton, 1994) indicated that most suicide attempts reported by panic disorder patients were likely in the context of coexisting depression symptoms.

Comorbid Alcohol Abuse Reviews of existing literature have documented the frequent coexistence of anxiety disorders, including PDA, with alcohol problems (Cox, Norton, Swinson, & Endler, 1990; Kushner, Sher, & Beitman, 1990; Schuckit & Hesselbrook, 1994). Cox et al. noted there was a substantial range in the prevalence of panic disorders in alcoholic samples (10–40%), while the prevalence of alcohol problems in anxiety disorder samples was somewhat more restricted (10–20%). One of the reasons prevalence figures have varied widely is the reliance on *symptoms* of alcohol abuse and panic-related anxiety, versus the assessment of *DSM*-defined disorders.

There may be several mechanisms operating in this pattern of comorbidity. In alcoholic individuals, panic attacks may develop as either a direct response to alcohol abuse (e.g., during a hangover), or as an indirect response to the stressful life events imposed by chronic, heavy drinking. For some individuals the anxiety may be transient while for others a clinical anxiety disorder may develop even if abstinence is obtained. In anxious samples, alcohol abuse may develop as a misguided attempt at coping with clinical anxiety (i.e., a form of self-medication). As noted earlier, it may be more socially acceptable for men to use alcohol as a coping mechanism, while for women an agoraphobic (staying close to home) strategy is more socially acceptable.

Klein (1980) noted that alcohol might reduce anticipatory anxiety in persons with panic disorder, and this could encourage continued drinking, but alcohol was viewed as "completely useless against the spontaneous panic" (p. 413). However, many patients might subjectively perceive self-medication with alcohol to be an effective antipanic coping strategy, despite research findings that individuals who self-medicate have a more serious clinical condition than individuals who do not (Cox et al., 1990).

More research is needed on the prognostic course of these various patterns of panic/alcohol comorbidity. One of the possible reasons for a generally more serious condition in these comorbid cases may be the paucity of treatment services specifically designed for these individuals. A typical scenario for an individual presenting to an anxiety disorders clinic with comorbid PDA and alcohol abuse is the recommendation or subsequent referral for alcohol treatment, and generally abstinence is sought before beginning therapy for panic attacks and agoraphobia. At the same time it is not common for addictions programs to assess and treat a potentially underlying anxiety disorder such as PDA with a cognitive-behavioral or other specialized approach. The presence of PDA may heighten the risk for relapse, or premature termination from treatment, in comorbid individuals treated only for alcohol abuse.

Comorbid Hypochondriasis Panic disorder and hypochondriasis share several features: a significant anxiety component, a fear of certain internal sensations based on the belief these sensations have harmful consequences, and associated interoceptive hypervigilence and sometimes phobic avoidance. It is also possible that a common diathesis such as a pronounced fear of death may underlie these two clinical manifestations. It is therefore not surprising that hypochondriasis *symptoms* are frequently present in panic disorder samples (Fava, Kellner, Zielezny, & Grandi, 1988; Noyes, Reich, Clancy, & O'Gorman, 1986). There is some evidence these hypochondriacal concerns may precede the onset of panic disorder (e.g., Fava, Kellner, et al., 1988), but also that hypochondriasis symptoms decrease along with panic symptoms during successful panic disorder treatment (Noyes et al., 1986).

The fact that many panic disorder patients have elevated scores on hypochondriasis measures is not an unexpected finding given the impact of recurrent, spontaneous panic attacks, but the issue of hypochondriasis coexisting as an independent diagnostic entity in individuals with panic disorder has not been widely studied. Most of the research that has accumulated has focused on psychiatric comorbidity in primary care medical settings (e.g., Barsky, Barnett, & Cleary, 1994; Noyes et al., 1994). Barsky et al. found that in primary care patients who received a diagnosis of panic disorder, 25% also received a comorbid diagnosis of hypochondriasis. Noyes et al. found that the rate of comorbid panic disorder in general medical outpatients with hypochondriasis was 16% (current major depression was the most frequent comorbid disorder at 28%). In a small sample of panic disorder patients, 48% of the patients received a comorbid diagnosis of hypochondriasis, and in the majority of cases the onset of hypochondriasis was determined to have preceded panic disorder (Furer, Walker, Chartier, and Stein, 1997).

From a cognitive perspective (discussed in more detail below), panic disorder and hypochondriasis are differentiated by several factors, including the type of internal sensations feared and the immediacy of the feared catastrophe. It is believed that in panic disorder the internal sensations that trigger the catastrophic spiral are ones that can actually be made worse by increasing anxiety (e.g., accelerated heart rate), whereas this is not true of the feared sensations in hypochondriasis (e.g., skin rash). In regards to the time course of the feared catastrophe, it is believed that in the case of panic disorder the cognitive misinterpretation refers to an immediate catastrophe (e.g., cardiac arrest). Conversely, the feared catastrophic outcome in hypochondriasis is viewed as more progressive and long term (e.g., cancer). These and other predictions have been presented by cognitive theorists such as Salkovskis and Clark (1993), and can be subjected to empirical testing. It is also possible that the two conditions share some underlying features (e.g., death anxiety).

Comorbid Social Phobia Panic disorder (with or without) agoraphobia is frequently associated with other anxiety disorders. One that is challenging in terms of boundary issues is social phobia. In their review of comorbidity studies, Wetzler and Sanderson (1995) reported an average of 17% (range = 10–30%) of panic disorder patients received a comorbid diagnosis of social phobia.

There is substantial overlap between agoraphobia and social phobia, especially in PDA where public situations are commonly feared and avoided. Even when focusing on the different psychological dimensions believed to be underlying the two disorders (fear of negative evaluation in social phobia versus fear of panic attacks in agoraphobia), the boundary is occasionally blurred. This is not surprising if panic disorder and social phobia are regarded as being composed of correlated dimensions rather than being nonoverlapping categories (cf. Zinbarg & Barlow, 1996).

Recognizing this sometimes substantial overlap, Mannuzza, Fyer, Liebowitz, and Klein (1990) emphasized the importance of correctly distinguishing the two for both clinical and research purposes. The "critical features" these authors addressed included the type of panic attacks experienced (spontaneous, situationally predisposed, stimulus bound), and the focus of the fear. To determine these features, Mannuzza et al. stressed the need for careful and comprehensive assessment, and for researchers to be more "clear about how they define 'secondary social phobia,' and not confuse panic patients who simply avoid 'social' situations with those who develop a full social-phobic syndrome" (p. 54).

Other investigators, however, have sometimes found it difficult to apply *DSM*-based diagnostic decision rules in assessing the specific focus of patients' fears, as patients are sometimes not able to be as explicit about the nature of their fears as required (e.g., Stein, Shea, & Uhde, 1989). Consequently, Stein et al. conducted a comorbidity study and suspended the *DSM-III-R* rule of not diagnosing social phobia if it was "unclear" whether the social fear was in relation to the occurrence of panic attacks. The results indicated that of among panic disorder patients, 46% also qualified for an additional diagnosis of social phobia. This finding was by no means a purely academic exercise. A comorbid diagnosis of social phobia was also found to be strongly associated with a history of major depression, whereas severity of agoraphobic avoidance was not associated with major depression. As an aside, this clustering of social phobia and depression again supports the possibility that constructs believed to be related to depression (e.g., self-criticism) may exert a strong influence in social phobia as well.

It does appear that primary panic disorder (with or without agoraphobia) and primary social phobia can be reliably differentiated. However, there is a less common clinical variant that is not "allowed" in the *DSM-IV* (APA, 1994) or its predecessors, and that is panic disorder *with* social phobia (sometimes referred to as secondary social phobia in the research literature). This type of syndrome is distinguished from comorbid panic disorder *and* social phobia because in the former case the two components are intertwined. When social phobia occurs in the context of panic disorder, the current nomenclature implies that only panic disorder is the important and determining feature (i.e., panic is the focus of the fear), and therefore a diagnosis of social phobia should not be made. This may be true in many cases and should result in treatment being targeted toward amelioration of the panic attacks. However, in other cases this may not always capture the clinical picture. In the same way that agoraphobia may persist long after panic attacks have diminished (perhaps because of avoidance behavior), so too might social anxiety and avoidance persist even in the absence of the panic attacks, and for other individuals what once began as a fear of panic in certain situations (in this case social) could develop into a fear of (social evaluation) situations. Several interesting questions remain relatively unanswered, such as: Is it possible that some individuals will experience an initial spontaneous panic attack in a social situation and subsequently develop both social phobia and panic disorder? Can a spontaneous panic attack in a social context act as a catalyst in the development of social phobia in susceptible individuals? Can a fear of negative evaluation or social sensitivity and fear of anxiety symptoms coexist in the same individual and lead to two anxiety disorders?

Research findings indicate that PDA is distinct from, but often comorbid with, other disorders. The latter two disorders reviewed here (hypochondriasis and social phobia) are examples of the boundary issues that arise in diagnostic classification of PDA. These issues may simply reflect the limited success of attempts to impose arbitary boundaries on sets of correlated psychopathological dimensions. If leading anxiety disorder investigators sometimes have difficulty correctly classifying these syndromes, it is likely that clinicians in general practice encounter these occasionally blurred diagnostic boundaries as well. Research into PDA comorbidity was facilitated by the introduction of *DSM-III-R*, but the various diagnostic decision rules can sometimes restrict phenomenological research in this area. It is important for psychopathology researchers to try to understand the psychological meaning of disorders that coexist, and one example is to assess the individual's subjective understanding of the relationship (if any) between the multiple sets of symptoms (see Rachman, 1991b).

Historical Perspectives

In 1871, Westphal introduced the term *agoraphobie* in describing a series of patients who had difficulty walking through streets and squares, bridges and crowds, and suffered from a fear of sudden incapacitation and chronic anticipatory anxiety (see Kuch & Swinson, 1992; Marks, 1987). Kuch and Swinson (1992) noted that Westphal also clearly described situational and spontaneous panic attacks, as well as the catastrophic cognitions associated with panic. Marks (1987) observed that Westphal's conceptualization of agoraphobia as a fear of public places still survives today, although it is an underinclusive description. Interestingly, the vast majority of patients in Westphal's case reports were men; Kuch and Swinson (1992) speculated that social influences of the time dictated that few women would have been required to travel alone if they did not want to.

Much of Freud's writing on "anxiety neurosis" is reflected in current thinking on the nature of PDA as well. In his paper introducing the "new" clinical syndrome of anxiety neurosis, Freud made a clear differentiation between "anxious expectation" and the more severe "anxiety attack" (i.e., panic) (Freud, 1894/1962). He described the spontaneous nature of the panic attack in stating that "it can suddenly break through into consciousness without being aroused by a train of ideas" (p. 93). Freud also noted that while the attack may occur without any associated ideation, there may also be an "interpretation that is nearest to hand, such as ideas of the extinction of life, or of a stroke, or of a threat of madness" (p. 94). As well, many of the symptoms Freud observed are retained in recent versions of the *DSM* (a notable exception is "ravenous hunger"), and he also noted various symptom clusters including "heart action" versus "locomotor vertigo" (pp. 94–95).

Frances and colleagues (1993) have identified the many ways in which Freud's thinking has influenced the classification and description of anxiety disorders in subsequent years. A more recent historical landmark that has greatly influenced current thinking about panic was the seminal work of Donald Klein. Klein (1980) remarked that in 1959 he was studying the clinical effects of the promising new drug imipramine. Because of its normalizing effect on mood, Klein and his colleagues decided to try imipramine with an extremely anxious subgroup of "schizophrenics" who had not responded to other treatments (today these patients would have received a diagnosis of PDA).

At first, patients did not subjectively report improvement in their symptoms. However, the hospital ward staff observed that patients were no longer experiencing severe episodes of anxiety, although their chronic, minor anxiety did not change. From this "pharmacological dissection," Klein (1964) concluded that there were two qualitatively distinct anxiety syndromes. Specifically, spontaneous panic attacks were a distinct form of anxiety that was responsive to imipramine, whereas anticipatory or generalized anxiety was not responsive to imipramine and was therefore believed to not be part of an anxiety-panic continuum. Patients had not reported global improvement because their chronic, anticipatory anxiety was not alleviated. Further, Klein (1980) noted that a distinct pattern of phobic behavior accompanied the panic attacks and anticipatory anxiety and consisted of help-seeking behavior when panic attacks occurred and avoidance of being alone or not being close to an exit in the event of a panic attack occurring.

Essentially, spontaneous panic attacks are central in Klein's model and agoraphobia and chronic anticipatory anxiety are sequelae of the attacks. Klein also specified that the underpinnings of spontaneous panic were biological and involved an evolutionary determined innate alarm system associated with attachment. Interestingly, although

Klein's work is often characterized as exemplifying the biomedical approach, it does in fact contain a strong evolutionary component that is also true of much of the more psychological approaches (see Marks, 1987; Nesse, 1990). Klein's "reconceptualization" of anxiety is very consistent with the changes made in *DSM-III* and its successors. McNally (1994) also critiqued the pharmacological dissection of panic and anxiety in Klein's early work. This research has been used as evidence for the validity of generalized anxiety disorder as a condition distinct from panic disorder. Yet it is worth remembering that there were no GAD patients in the original imipramine investigations. Rather, anticipatory anxiety symptoms were studied in agoraphobic patients.

Contemporary Approaches to Panic Disorder

Alarms: True, False, and Learned Barlow (1988) regarded panic attacks as exemplars of the basic emotion of fear. Fear is an evolutionary "hardwired" response that serves as an adaptive fight-or-flight reaction in the presence of a dangerous, sometimes life-threatening event (i.e., a true alarm). When these alarms are activated in the absence of any specific triggers, the response is viewed as a "false alarm," or spontaneous panic attack. The initial spontaneous panic attack/false alarm is believed to occur in individuals who have a biological vulnerability to such reactions. There is also a stress-diathesis component in Barlow's (1988) model: "It is likely that false alarms are not a direct response to stress. Rather, these alarms are mediated initially by neurobiological responses to stress" (p. 220). Barlow hypothesized a genetic basis for this neurobiological activity. In the case of panic disorder, other factors must come into play in addition to the presence of panic attacks. Specifically, he stated that there must be a type of classical conditioning whereby interoceptive cues become associated with the original false alarm. This interoceptive conditioning occurs in persons who develop anxious apprehension over future panic occurrences and the result is what Barlow referred to as a "learned alarm."

According to Barlow's model there is a hypothesized psychological vulnerability in determining which individuals will develop anxious apprehension. This vulnerability involves a poor sense of control and predictability that are related to negative events in general and emotions in particular (Antony & Barlow, 1996), and this psychological vulnerability was believed to likely originate from developmental experiences. Because of the anxious apprehension, there may be an increased self-awareness or somatic sensitivity in the development of panic disorder.

Antony and Barlow (1996) highlighted a number of areas that they believed provide empirical support for this model. These include the phenomenological similarities between unexpected and expected panic attacks, which they see as providing evidence for the view that panic and fear are not qualitatively different. Family and genetics studies suggest that there is a biological vulnerability to panic (false alarms), consistent with the model. Research on nonclinical panic suggests that people can experience false alarms in reaction to stress, but do not necessarily develop learned alarms (i.e., panic disorder).

In regard to Barlow's proposed psychological vulnerabilities, a study often cited in support the role of controllability and predictability involves a panic provocation experiment (Sanderson, Rapee, & Barlow, 1989). This study used a common biological challenge procedure of 5.5% carbon dioxide–enriched air with panic disorder patients. All of the patients were informed that when a light was illuminated they could turn a dial to decrease the amount of CO_2 they were receiving. For half the light was illuminated and for half it was not, but in fact the dial had no effect and all patients received the same induction. Patients in the "illusion of control" group were significantly less likely to have a panic attack and experienced less anxiety and catastrophic cognitions than patients in the "no illusion of control" group. While this study does support the role of perceived controllability in the development of panic as postulated by Barlow (1988), it is also consistent with predictions from other psychological models that emphasize the importance of safety cues and perception of danger/threat (e.g., Beck & Emery, 1985; Clark, 1986; Rachman, 1984).

Unlike more cognitively oriented approaches (described below), Barlow's (1988) model includes a significant biological component in the development of false alarms, while cognitive processes become more important in the development of learned alarms or panic disorder (e.g., perceived controllability). In this model the catastrophic misinterpretation of a bodily sensation is not required for the initial false alarm. Barlow also views false alarms (spontaneous panic) and true alarms as the same basic emotion of fear, while other leading theorists such as Klein do not hold this view. More direct comparisons on the phenomenology of true alarms and false alarms are required. McNally (1994) noted that, although a sense of control does seem to have importance in our understanding panic, it is also a "vaguely formulated" concept in Barlow's model (p. 136).

Catastrophic Misinterpretations Clark (1986) proposed a cognitive model of panic in which panic attacks are said to arise from the catastrophic misinterpretation of certain bodily sensations (somatic or psychological). That is, these sensations are perceived as much more dangerous than they really are. Sensations that could be misinterpreted include those that are involved in normal anxiety responses (e.g., palpitations, dizziness), and others (e.g., "floaters" in the visual field). As an example, Clark noted that an individual may misinterpret heart palpitations as evidence of impending cardiac failure.

A wide range of stimuli could trigger the catastrophic process, but it is believed the stimuli are more often internal than external. Unlike cognitions associated with hypochondriasis, the threat in panic disorder is seen as an immediate danger or impending catastrophe rather than long term. In contrast to similar "fear of fear" models (e.g., Goldstein & Chambless, 1978), the triggers in Clark's cognitive model are bodily sensations that are not necessarily identified as anxiety per se. Increases in anxiety will not necessarily trigger a panic attack because it is not a fear of anxiety but a fear of certain bodily sensations that drives the process.

Clark (1988) postulated that this tendency to misinterpret bodily sensations is an enduring cognitive trait, one that is amplified in an anxious state. It was not specified how the enduring trait initially develops, however. Clark also stated that, "it is not clear whether this 'trait' antedates the first panic attack" (p. 77).

Clark's (1986) model attempted to explain much of the phenomenology of panic disorder, including the apparently spontaneous nature of panic attacks, by postulating that "in such attacks patients often fail to distinguish between the triggering body sensation and the subsequent panic attack and so perceive the attacks as having no cause and coming 'out of the blue'" (p. 463). In fact, not only could this catastrophic process occur very rapidly, but the catastrophic misinterpretation could even occur at a nonconscious level, and therefore conscious appraisal was not necessary. This could potentially explain the mechanism involved in nocturnal panic.

Clark's model also provided a cognitive framework as a new way of understanding the so-called biological challenges such as sodium lactate in the provocation of panic attacks in panic disorder patients versus control subjects (see also Clark, 1993). In essence, any biological agent that produces the very sensations panic disorder patients are likely to misinterpret (e.g., increased heart rate) may well trigger the catastrophic process and resulting panic attack. This does not indicate a biological basis for panic disorder, but only for the bodily sensations in question. Biological factors are not completely discarded in Clark's model; deficiencies in the autonomic nervous system may well be responsible for physiological surges of arousal. However, it was also stated that cognitive factors will then determine whether these arousal sensations will be catastrophically misinterpreted.

There is a substantial body of empirical work that is consistent with predictions derived from the cognitive perspective on panic, including Clark's model (for reviews see McNally, 1994; Rapee, 1993, 1996b). Lines of support include the effects of cognitive therapy and the role of cognitive mediators in biological induction procedures (for a review see Rapee, 1995).

Clark's (1986) paper has been very influential in the study of panic, and its success is partly due to the fact that it has led to a highly effective treatment for panic disorder (Clark, Salkovskis et al., 1994). However, there have also been several criticisms made of Clark's model (see Klein, 1994b; McNally, 1994). These criticisms include the apparent difficulty in potentially refuting the model when the proposed cognitive processes can occur at a nonconscious level. Another point is that cognitive factors involved in panic may be susceptible to modification by noncognitive therapies, including pharmacotherapy (see Rachman, 1993). Thus, a cognitive basis for panic does not equate to a prescription for cognitive therapy. Finally, the model is not clear about the nature of this "enduring tendency" and instead focuses on the process of catastrophic misinterpretation rather than the underlying trait. The development of agoraphobia, which is so often associated with panic, is not included in this model.

Anxiety Sensitivity As mentioned in the section on phobias, anxiety sensitivity is the fear of anxiety-related sensations, arising from beliefs that these sensations have harmful consequences (Reiss, 1991; Reiss et al., 1986; Reiss & McNally, 1985). Although anxiety sensitivity was originally introduced as part of Reiss and McNally's (1985) expectancy model of fears, and can be associated with a number of forms of clinical anxiety, it has come to be viewed as a cognitive risk factor for panic disorder and may represent the "enduring tendency" in Clark's model (Cox, 1996; Taylor, 1995). Theoretically, the anxiety sensitivity model is also seen as differing somewhat from Clark's cognitive model in that anxiety sensitivity is a fear of anxiety and not a misinterpretation of sensations associated with anxiety that are seen as a sign of an immediate catastrophe (McNally, 1994). Anxiety sensitivity is thought to precede and exist independently of panic attacks, although it is likely amplified by panic experiences.

There are several lines of empirical evidence that support the anxiety sensitivity construct. Studies have found that Anxiety Sensitivity Index (ASI; Peterson & Reiss, 1987) scores are elevated in panic disorder samples, and this measure differentiates panic disorder patients from other anxiety disorder groups, whereas trait anxiety does not (Taylor, Koch, & McNally, 1992). High levels of anxiety sensitivity can exist independently of panic attacks (e.g., Donnell & McNally, 1990), which demonstrates that it is not merely a consequence of panic attacks. Perhaps the two strongest lines of support are the role of anxiety sensitivity in mediating responses to panic provocation procedures and prospective studies of anxiety sensitivity and the development of panic.

In a panic provocation study, Holloway and McNally (1987) compared nonclinical subjects with either high or low ASI scores on a voluntary hyperventilation challenge. Compared to subjects with low ASI scores, individuals with a high level of anxiety sensitivity reported more distress and anxiety following the procedure. McNally and Eke (1996) recently conducted a carbon dioxide challenge study that is a good example of a test of competing theories of panic (in this case anxiety sensitivity versus a suffocation alarm hypothesis, a biological model reviewed in a later section in this chapter). The best predictor of anxiety and bodily sensations in response to this challenge was neither anxiety sensitivity nor a behavioral correlate of suffocation alarms, but rather a measure of fear of suffocation. This result was interpreted as consistent with anxiety sensitivity theory, however, because it showed that fear of sensations, in this case closely matched to the sensations produced by the challenge procedure, is the best predictor of an anxious response (McNally, & Eke, 1996). This finding underscores the importance of examining potential facets within anxiety sensitivity, such as fears of dyspnea. It may be that responses to panic challenges are best predicted by fears of sensations evoked by the challenges.

Prospective studies also support the role of anxiety sensitivity in the prediction of spontaneous panic attacks (Ehlers, 1995; Maller & Reiss, 1992; Schmidt, Lerew, & Jackson, 1997). However, the role of anxiety sensitivity in predicting panic disorder per se requires further investigation.

Neurotransmitter Dysregulation There are a number of different biological models of panic and a vast amount of related research. Several groups of investigators have hypothesized that the dysregulation of the norepinephrine system is responsible for panic in the form of noradrenergic hyperactivity. Dysregulation is believed to originate in the locus coeruleus, an area of the pons that produces much of the brain's norepinephrine. Evidence for noradrenergic dysregulation as the biological underpinning of panic is mixed, however (Asnis & van Praag, 1995b; McNally, 1994). For example, yohimbine, an alpha-2-adrenoceptor antagonist, increases firing of the locus coeruleus. Yohimbine has been found to induce panic attacks more often in panic disorder patients than in control subjects (e.g., Charney, Woods, Goodman, & Heninger, 1987). Yet clonidine, an alpha-2-adrenoceptor agonist, has not been found to have lasting antipanic effects (Uhde et al., 1989).

Other researchers have focused on a metabolite of norepinephrine, 3-methoxy-4-hydroxyphenylglycol (MHPG). This line of research has also yielded mixed findings, with some studies finding elevated levels of MHPG in panic disorder compared to controls and other studies finding lower levels. In one study, PDA patients were exposed to panic-evoking situations and the MHPG changes were compared to those of control subjects; no differences were found (Woods, Charney, McPherson, Gradman, & Heninger, 1987). McNally (1994) concluded that, "although noradrenergic dysfunction may give rise to physiological disturbances in some people, and may trigger panic among those with elevated anxiety sensitivity, evidence for the noradrenergic model of panic is mixed" (p. 64).

Serotonin (5-HT) dysregulation has also been postulated to play a significant role in panic. Much of the support for the role of 5-HT comes from studies investigating animal models of anxiety (for a review see Kahn, Westenberg, & Moore, 1995). Serotonin challenge studies in humans have yielded mixed results, but the overall findings suggest that some panic disorder patients may have hypersensitive postsynaptic serotonin receptors (McNally, 1994). Another line of support comes from work on selective serotonin reuptake inhibitors (SSRIs) such as sertraline and fluvoxamine, which have been found to possess antipanic properties. However, serotonergic dysfunction has been associated with a number of forms of psychopathology, and there is evidence to suggest that serotonin may be linked to anxiety in general rather than panic disorder specifically. This is an important area of ongoing research (e.g., see the special issue of the *Journal of Clinical Psychiatry*, edited by J. H. Greist, 1996).

Another recent development in biologically based research on panic concerns the role of cholecystokinin tetrapeptide (CCK-4). CCK-4 is a neuropeptide that functions like a neurotransmitter or neuromodulator, and it has been found to be a panicogenic agent in laboratory-based induction research (see Bradwejn & Koszycki, 1995). Administration of CCK-4, especially in higher doses, produces panic attacks in a majority of panic disorder patients and in a number of control subjects as well. Because it often produces panic attacks in healthy volunteers, Koszycki, Cox, and Bradwejn (1993) sought to determine whether a cognitive trait (in this case anxiety sensitivity) might mediate responses to CCK-4. The results indicated that individuals with preexisting high levels of anxiety sensitivity experienced more catastrophic cognitions and fear of somatic symptoms following a CCK-4 challenge compared to individuals with low levels of anxiety sensitivity.

Recent work with CCK-4 follows a long line of panic provocation or challenge studies, including sodium lactate (see Cowley, Dager, & Dunner, 1995), carbon dioxide (see Papp & Gorman, 1995), and caffeine (see Uhde, 1995). As McNally (1994) observed, the fact that so many different agents, affecting different neurobiological systems, can seemingly produce panic attacks makes it unlikely that a single biological dysfunction is responsible for panic disorder.

One of the major avenues of biologically driven research involves the biological challenge or panic provocation procedure, and this has been the focus of several psychological critiques (Clark, 1993; Ley, 1988; Rapee, 1995). The basic argument is that biological procedures induce sensations that panic disorder patients fear and this leads to some form of catastrophic misinterpretation and a resulting panic attack. Challenge procedures do induce a variety of sometimes very unpleasant bodily sensations, and control subjects experience this as well, but because of the psychological factors involved in panic disorder these patients will be more likely to experience a full-blown panic attack. There are several studies to support this view. For example, a small study of panic disorder patients who had experienced panic following sodium lactate infusions found that following cognitive-behavioral therapy most did not panic on a subsequent lacate challenge (Shear et al., 1991).

Increasingly, researchers have been examining the interface between psychological and biological factors, and this is an important effort. In traditional provocation studies an inert placebo is often used that does not induce any sensations. We would argue that an active placebo should be used and is a better test of a given provocation agent and its associated neurobiology. Ideally, the active placebo would produce identical symptoms (e.g., cardiorespiratory distress), but would be peripheral and not based in the central nervous system the way the biological agent would be. If both the placebo and agent resulted in panic attacks, this would support a cognitive perspective of physiological arousal and catastrophic misinterpretation. If only the biological agent was panicogenic, this would support a neurobiological hypothesis. Further, the evaluation of a biological challenge solely on the basis of the presence or absence of panic is not an in-depth analysis. The fear of the symptoms experienced and the intensity rating of panic should also be assessed. An assessment of the sequence of symptoms would also be helpful in determining whether catastrophic cognitions are playing an important role or not. At the least, an investigation of the chronology of symptoms would give us a better understanding of the process of the provoked panic attack. Finally, both patients and control subjects should be administered measures such as the ASI, and other preexisting beliefs about the nature of the sensations they will experience should be assessed in order to examine individual differences that may mediate responses.

Suffocation False Alarms Klein (1993) proposed that "many spontaneous panics occur when the brain's suffocation monitor erroneously signals a lack of useful air, thereby maladaptively triggering an evolved suffocation alarm system" (p. 306). Activation of the suffocation alarm is said to produce sudden respiratory distress, panic, brief hyperventilation, and the urge to flee. Unexpected panic attacks occur when the suffocation monitor has a pathologically low threshold for activation, causing it to misfire unpredictably.

Klein's (1993, 1994a) theory minimizes the role of psychological factors. The theory is "physiocentric" in that it "makes a deranged physiological control system central to a broad range of symptomatic precipitants and manifestations" (Klein, 1994a, p. 506). Klein (1993) conceded that suffocation false alarms can be triggered by psychosocial suffocation cues, which serve as reflexlike releasing stimuli: "A no-exit situation or one where stuffy, stale air implies no exit, where there are crowded, immobilized people or someone appears to be smothering, might all elicit panic if the suffocation alarm threshold is pathologically lowered or if the cues are particularly salient" (p. 306). Also, catastrophic thoughts can increase the aversiveness of the panic experience. To illustrate, a suffocation false alarm produces intense dyspnea, which can result in compensatory hyperventilation. "Secondary hyperventilatory symptoms such as chest pain, paresthesias, dizziness, nausea, and derealization may frighten some, perhaps psychologically vulnerable, patients into catastrophic thinking, thus intensifying the panic experience" (Papp, Klein, & Gorman, 1993, p. 1149).

Findings from several studies are consistent with the suffocation false alarm theory. People with panic disorder, compared to people with other anxiety disorders and normal controls, tend to have shorter breath-holding times (Asmundson & Stein, 1994; Zandbergen, Strahm, Pols, & Griez, 1992). This is consistent with the view that people with panic disorder are particularly likely to have lower thresholds for activation of suffocation alarms. Pine et al. (1994) suggested that people who could not perceive elevations of CO_2, compared to healthy controls, would not experience suffocation false alarms, and therefore report fewer anxiety symptoms. This prediction was supported in an assessment of children with congenital central hypoventilation syndrome.

Many of the research findings that are consistent with Klein's theory are also consistent with Clark's (1986) cognitive model. It may be that Klein's theory underestimates the importance of psychological factors in triggering false suffocation alarms (Taylor & Rachman, 1994). Most of the above-mentioned findings also are consistent with Ley's (1989, 1992) dyspneic-fear theory. The latter states that "fear experienced during a hyperventilatory panic attack is a direct response to the sensation of severe dyspnea (i.e., respiratory distress) in the context of a situation in which the sufferer believes that she has little or no control over the conditions that give rise to the dyspnea" (Ley, 1989, p. 549). Ley's dyspneic-fear theory, compared to Klein's theory, may be regarded as more parsimonious in that it doesn't assume a suffocation alarm system (Ley, 1996a, 1996b). However, Ley's theory—at least in its present form (Ley, 1989, 1992)—is not described in much detail, and may not be more parsimonious once its assumptions are fully specified (Taylor & Rachman, 1997). Further research is needed to determine the relative merits of the theories of Klein, Ley, and Clark.

The contrasting treatment implications also need to be tested. Klein's theory suggests two types of panic disorder: one due to a deranged suffocation alarm in which panics are characterized by severe dyspnea, and another milder form of panic disorder in which maladaptive learning plays a greater role. Given the physiocentric emphasis of the suffocation alarm theory, it is predicted that cognitive therapy for panic disorder (derived from Clark's, 1986, model), should be less effective for panic patients with prominent dyspnea symptoms during their panics attacks, compared to panic patient experiencing little or no dyspnea. Results of a recent study failed to support this prediction; both types of panic disorder responded equally to cognitive therapy, with substantial reductions in panic frequency and in associated psychopathology (Taylor, Woody et al., 1996).

A final point for this section is to note that PDA was the most frequently studied anxiety disorder in the past decade (Norton et al., 1995), and the interested reader is referred to several published books that have been exclusively or largely devoted to this topic during this time (Asnis & van Praag; 1995a; Baker, 1989; Ballenger, 1990a, 1990b; Barlow, 1988; Hand & Wittchen, 1986; Katon, 1989; McNally, 1994; Rachman & Maser, 1985; Rapee, 1996b; Walker, Norton, & Ross, 1991; Wolfe & Maser; 1994).

Phobias and Panic: Concluding Comments

Throughout this chapter we have presented, and critically evaluated, many of the important topics and unresolved issues in the study of panic and phobic disorders. This field is an exciting one for psychopathology researchers because tremendous inroads have been made and pressing, unanswered questions have been identified. Along these lines we have stressed the necessity for competing theoretical models to be pitted against each other. All of the theoretical perspectives, and the empirical evaluations to date, have their relative strengths and weaknesses.

We attempted to include some of the biological and psychobiological models and research findings in our discussion, rather than concentrate on purely psychological factors, and to give examples of where the two approaches may interface. Marks (1987) once remarked that nowhere is the need for better integration of the behavioral sciences (i.e., biological vs. psychological) more evident than in the study of fear. Some might argue that this observation is still valid today, where although many writers claim to favor a "psychobiological" or "biopsychosocial" approach, there is still ample evidence of two solitudes in anxiety disorders research.

Another theme we have tried to convey at several points in this chapter is that there may be subtypes of anxiety disorders such as panic disorder, and it is likely that no one theory will account for all of the disorders or perhaps even all of the subtypes within a disorder. Currently, many psychopathology researchers are very interested in the importance of higher order factors. We would still emphasize the importance of lower order phenomenological aspects and level of analysis in order to obtain a more comprehensive understanding of the syndromes; this research must be done before offering a unifying theory that, no matter how appealing, risks being premature and overreaching. Lower order levels of analysis also encourages the scientist-practitioner to tailor treatments to the individual.

A final point is that panic and phobias, and the field of anxiety disorders in general, continues to attract widespread interest. Perhaps in part this is due to the fact that so many of the investigators are not only involved in research and scholarly pursuits in this field but also actively engaged in clinical activities with individuals suffering from anxiety disorders. In many ways the advances made in this area are a testament to the benefits of the scientist-practitioner approach in psychopathology.

References

Anderson, K. W., Taylor, S., & McLean, P. (1996). Panic disorder associated with blood-injury reactivity: The necessity of establishing functional relationships among maladaptive behaviors. *Behavior Therapy, 27*, 463–472.

Andrews, G. (1996). Comorbidity in neurotic disorders: The similarities are more important than the differences. In R. Rapee (Ed.), *Current controversies in the anxiety disorders* (pp. 3–20). New York: Guilford.

Antony, M. M., & Barlow, D. H. (1996). In R. M. Rapee (Ed.), *Current controversies in the anxiety disorders* (pp. 55–76). New York: Guilford.

Argyle, N. (1988). The nature of cognitions in panic disorder. *Behaviour Research and Therapy, 26*, 261–264.

Arrindell, W. A. (1993). The fear of fear concept: Evidence in favour of multidimensionality. *Behaviour Research and Therapy, 31*, 507–518.

Arrindell, W. A., Cox, B. J., van der Ende, J., & Kwee, M. G. T. (1995). Phobic dimensions—II. Cross-national confirmation of the multidimensional structure underlying the Mobility Inventory (MI). *Behaviour Research and Therapy, 33*, 711–724.

Arrindell, W. A., Pickersgill, M. J., Merckelbach, H., Ardon, A. M., & Cornet, F. C. (1991). Phobic dimensions: III. Factor analytic approaches to the study of common phobic fears; an updated review of findings obtained with adult subjects. *Advances in Behaviour Research and Therapy, 13*, 73–130.

Asmundson, G. J. G., & Stein, M. B. (1994). Triggering the false suffocation alarm in panic disorder by using a voluntary breath-holding procedure. *American Journal of Psychiatry, 151*, 264–266.

Asnis, G. M., & van Praag, H. M. (Eds.). (1995a). *Panic disorder: Clinical, biological, and treatment aspects*. New York: John Wiley.

Asnis, G. M., & van Praag, H. M. (1995b). The norepinephrine system in panic disorder. In G. M. Asnis and H. M. van Praag (Eds.), *Panic disorder: Clinical, biological, and treatment aspects* (pp. 119–150). New York: John Wiley.

Baker, R. (Ed.). (1989). *Panic disorder: Theory, research, and therapy*. New York: John Wiley.

Ballenger, J. C. (Ed.). (1990a). *Clinical aspects of panic disorder*. New York: Wiley-Liss.

Ballenger, J. C. (Ed.). (1990b). *Neurobiology of panic disorder*. New York: Wiley-Liss.

Ballenger, J. C., & Fyer, A. J. (1996). Panic disorder and agoraphobia. In T. A. Widiger, A. J. Frances, H. A., Pincus, R. Ross, M. B. First, & W. W. Davis (Eds.), *DSM-IV sourcebook, vol. 2* (pp. 411–471). Washington, DC: American Psychiatric Association.

Bandura, A. (1977). *Social learning theory*. Englewood Cliffs, NJ: Prentice-Hall.

Barlow, D. H. (1988). *Anxiety and its disorders: The nature and treatment of anxiety and panic*. New York: Guilford.

Barlow, D. H., Brown, T. A., & Craske, M. G. (1994). Definitions of panic attacks and panic disorder in the *DSM*-IV: Implications for research. *Journal of Abnormal Psychology, 103*, 553–564.

Barlow, D. H., Vermilyea, J. A., Blanchard, E. B., Vermilyea, B. B., DiNardo, P. A., & Cerny, J. A. (1985). The phenomenon of panic. *Journal of Abnormal Psychology, 94*, 320–328.

Barsky, A. J., Barnett, M. C., & Cleary, P. D. (1994). Hypochondriasis and panic disorder: Boundary and overlap. *Archives of General Psychiatry, 51*, 918–925.

Bauer, D. H. (1976). An exploratory study of developmental changes in children's fears. *Journal of Child Psychology and Psychiatry, 17*, 69–74.

Beck, A. T., & Emery, G. (1985). *Anxiety disorders and phobias: A cognitive perspective*. New York: Basic Books.

Bennett-Levy, J., & Marteau, T. (1984). Fear of animals: What is prepared? *British Journal of Psychology, 75*, 35–42.

Boyd, J. H. (1986). Use of mental health services for the treatment of panic disorder. *American Journal of Psychiatry, 143*, 1569–1574.

Bradwejn, J., & Koszycki, D. (1995). Cholecystokinin and panic disorder. In G. M. Asnis and H. M. van Praag (Eds.), *Panic disorder: Clinical, biological, and treatment aspects* (pp. 233–254). New York: John Wiley.

Bronson, G. (1965). The hierarchical organization of the central nervous system: Implications for learning processes and critical periods in early development. *Behavioral Science, 10*, 7–25.

Carr, J. E. (1996). Neuroendocrine and Behavioural interaction in exposure treatment of phobic avoidance. *Clinical Psychology Review, 16*, 1–15.

Cattell, R. B. (1978). *The scientific use of factor analysis in Behavioral and lifesciences*. New York: Plenum.

Charney, D. S., Woods, S. W., Goodman, W. K., & Heninger, G. R. (1987). Neurobiological mechanisms of panic anxiety: Biochemical and behavioral correlates of yohimbine-induced panic attacks. *American Journal of Psychiatry, 144*, 1030–1036.

Clark, D. M. (1986). A cognitive approach to panic. *Behaviour Research and Therapy, 24*, 461–470.

Clark, D. M. (1988). A cognitive model of panic attacks. In S. Rachman and J. D. Maser (Eds.), *Panic: Psychological perspectives* (pp. 71–89). Hillsdale, NJ: Erlbaum.

Clark, D. M. (1993). Cognitive mediation of panic attacks induced by biological challenge tests. *Advances in Behaviour Research and Therapy, 15*, 75–84.

Clark, D. M., Salkovskis, P. M., Hackmann, A., Middleton, H., Anastasiades, P., & Gelder, M. (1994). A comparison of cognitive therapy, applied relaxation and imipramine in the treatment of panic disorder. *British Journal of Psychiatry, 164*, 759–769.

Clark, D. M., & Wells, A. (1995). A cognitive model of social phobia. In R. G. Heimberg, M. R. Liebowitz, D. A. Hope, & F. R. Schneier (Eds.), *Social phobia: Diagnosis, assessment, and treatment* (pp. 69–93). New York: Guilford.

Clark, L. A., Watson, D., & Mineka, S. (1994). Temperament, personality, and the mood and anxiety disorders. *Journal of Abnormal Psychology, 103*, 103–116.

Clum, G. A., & Knowles, S. L. (1991). Why do some people with panic disorders become avoidant: A review. *Clinical Psychology Review, 11*, 295–313.

Cook, M., & Mineka, S. (1987). Second-order conditioning and overshadowing in the observational conditioning of fear in monkeys. *Behaviour Research and Therapy, 25*, 349–364.

Cook, M., & Mineka, S. (1989). Observational conditioning of fear to fear-relevant versus fear-irrelevant stimuli in rhesus monkeys. *Journal of Abnormal Psychology, 98*, 448–459.

Cook, M., & Mineka, S. (1990). Selective associations in the observational conditioning of fear in rhesus monkeys. *Journal of Experi-*

mental Psychology: Animal Behaviour Processes, 16, 372–389.

Coryell, W., Noyes, R., & Clancy, J. (1982). Excess mortality in panic disorder. *Archives of General Psychiatry, 39,* 701–703.

Costello, C. G. (1982). Fears and phobias in women: A community study. *Journal of Abnormal Psychology, 91,* 280–286.

Cowley, D. S., Dager, S. R., & Dunner, D. L. (1995). The lactate infusion challenge. In G. M. Asnis and H. M. van Praag (Eds.), *Panic disorder: Clinical, biological, and treatment aspects* (pp. 206–232). New York: John Wiley.

Cox, B. J. (1996). The nature and assessment of catastrophic thoughts in panic disorder. *Behaviour Research and Therapy, 34,* 363–374.

Cox, B. J., Direnfeld, D. M., Swinson, R. P., & Norton, G. R. (1994). Suicidal ideation and suicide attempts in panic disorder and social phobia. *American Journal of Psychiatry, 151,* 882–887.

Cox, B. J., Endler, N. S., & Swinson, R. P. (1995). An examination of levels of agoraphobic severity in panic disorder. *Behaviour Research and Therapy, 33,* 57–62.

Cox, B. J., Norton, G. R., Swinson, R. P., & Endler, N. S. (1990). Substance abuse and panic-related anxiety: A critical review. *Behaviour Research and Therapy, 28,* 385–393.

Cox, B. J., Swinson, R. P., Endler, N. S., & Norton, G. R. (1994). The symptom structure of panic attacks. *Comprehensive Psychiatry, 35,* 349–353.

Cox, B. J., Swinson, R. P., Kuch, K., & Reichman, J. T. (1993). Dimensions of agoraphobia assessed by the Mobility Inventory. *Behaviour Research and Therapy, 31,* 427–431.

Craske, M. G. (1991). Phobic fear and panic attacks: The same emotional states triggered by different cues? *Clinical Psychology Review, 11,* 599–620.

Craske, M. G., & Barlow, D. H. (1988). A review of the relationship between panic and avoidance. *Clinical Psychology Review, 8,* 667–685.

Craske, M. G., & Barlow, D. H. (1989). Nocturnal panic. *Journal of Nervous and Mental Disease, 177,* 160–167.

Craske, M. G., Barlow, D. H., Clark, D. M., Curtis, G. C., Hill, E. M., Himle, J. A., Lee, Y. J., Lewis, J. A., McNally, R. J., Ost, L. G., Salkovskis, P. M., & Warwick, H. M. C. (1996). Specific (simple) phobia. In T. A. Widiger, A. J. Frances, H. A., Pincus, R. Ross, M. B. First, & W. W. Davis (Eds.), *DSM-IV sourcebook, vol.* 2 (pp. 473–506). Washington, DC: American Psychiatric Association.

Craske, M. G., & Freed, S. (1995). Expectations about arousal and nocturnal panic. *Journal of Abnormal Psychology, 104,* 567–575.

Craske, M. G., Rapee, R. M., & Barlow, D. H. (1988). The significance of panic-expectancy for individual patterns of avoidance. *Behavior Therapy, 19,* 577–592.

Davey, G. C. L. (1989). Dental phobias and anxieties: Evidence for conditioning processes in the acquisition and modulation of a learned fear. *Behaviour Research and Therapy, 27,* 51–58.

Davey, G. C. L. (1994). Self-reported fears to common indigenous animals in an adult UK population: The role of disgust sensitivity. *British Journal of Clinical Psychology, 85,* 541–554.

Davey, G. C. L. (1995). Preparedness and phobias: Specific evolved associations or a generalized expectancy bias? *Behavioral and Brain Sciences, 18,* 289–325.

Delprato, D. J. (1980). Hereditary determinants of fears and phobias: A critical review. *Behavior Therapy, 11,* 79–103.

de Silva, P., Rachman, S., & Seligman, M. E. P. (1977). Prepared phobias and obsessions: Therapeutic outcome. *Behaviour Research and Therapy, 15,* 65–77.

Donnell, C. D., & McNally, R. J. (1990). Anxiety sensitivity and panic attacks in a nonclinical population. *Behaviour Research and Therapy, 28,* 83–85.

Ehlers, A. (1995). A 1-year prospective study of panic attacks: Clinical course and factors associated with maintenance. *Journal of Abnormal Psychology, 104,* 164–172.

Faravelli, C., Pallanti, S., Biondi, F., Paterniti, S., & Scarpato, M. A. (1992). Onset of panic disorder. *American Journal of Psychiatry, 149,* 827–828.

Fava, G. A., Grandi, S., & Canestrari, R. (1988). Prodromal symptoms in panic disorder with agoraphobia. *American Journal of Psychiatry, 145,* 1564–1567.

Fava, G. A., Kellner, R., Zielezny, M., & Grandi, S. (1988). Hypochondriacal fears and beliefs in agoraphobia. *Journal of Affective Disorders, 14,* 239–244.

Foa, E. B., & Kozak, M. J. (1986). Emotional processing of fear: Exposure to corrective information. *Psychological Bulletin, 99,* 20–35.

Foa, E. B., Steketee, G., & Rothbaum, B. O. (1989). Behavioral/cognitive conceptualizations of post-traumatic stress disorder. *Behavior Therapy, 20,* 155–176.

Frances, A., Miele, G. M., Widiger, T. A., Pincus, H. A., Manning, D., & Davis, W. W. (1993). The classification of panic disorders: From Freud to *DSM-IV. Journal of Psychiatric Research, 27,* (Suppl. 1), 3–10.

Freud, S. (1894/1962). On the grounds for detaching a particular syndrome from neurasthenia under the description 'anxiety neurosis.' In J. Strachey (Ed. & Trans.), *The standard edition of the complete psychological works of Sigmund Freud. Vol. III* (pp. 90–139). London: Hogarth Press and the Institute of Psychoanalysis.

Furer, P., Walker, J. A., Chartier, M. J., & Stein, M. B. (1997). Hypochondriacal concerns and somatization in panic disorder. *Depression and Anxiety, 6,* 78–85.

Geer, J. H. (1965). The development of a scale to measure fear. *Behaviour Research and Therapy, 3,* 45–53.

Gelder, M. G. (1989). The classification of anxiety disorders. *British Journal of Psychiatry, 154* (Suppl. 4), 28–32.

Goldstein, A. J., & Chambless, D. L. (1978). A reanalysis of agoraphobia. *Behavior Therapy, 9,* 47–59.

Gray, J. A. (1982). *The neuropsychology of anxiety.* Oxford: Oxford University Press.

Greist, J. H. (1996). Introduction. Anxiety disorders: The role of serotonin. *Journal of Clinical Psychiatry, 57* (Suppl. 6), 3–4.

Hallam, R. S. (1978). Agoraphobia: A critical review of the concept. *British Journal of Psychiatry, 133,* 314–319.

Hallam, R. S. (1983). Agoraphobia: Deconstructing a clinical syndrome. *Bulletin of the British Psychological Society, 36,* 337–340.

Hallam, R. (1991). A forward look: Psychosocial perspectives. In J. R. Walker, G. R. Norton, & C. A. Ross (Eds.), *Panic disorder and agoraphobia: A comprehensive guide for the practitioner* (pp. 470–503). Pacific Grove, CA: Brooks/Cole.

Hand, I., & Wittchen, H. U. (Eds.). (1986). *Anxiety and panic disorder.* Berlin: Springer.

Hebb, D. O. (1946). On the nature of fear. *Psychological Review, 53,* 259–276.

Heimberg, R. G., Liebowitz, M. R., Hope, D. A., & Schneier, F. R. (1995). *Social phobia: Diagnosis, assessment, and treatment.* New York: Guilford Press.

Holloway, W., & McNally, R. J. (1987). Effects of anxiety sensitivity on the response to hyperventilation. *Journal of Abnormal Psychology, 96,* 330–334.

Hope, D. A., Gansler, D. A., & Heimberg, R. G. (1989). Attentional focus and causal attributions in social phobia: Implications from social psychology. *Clinical Psychology Review, 9,* 49–60.

Hornig, C. D., & McNally, R. J. (1995). Panic disorder and suicide attempt: A reanalysis of data from the Epidemiological Catchment Area study. *British Journal of Psychiatry, 167,* 76–79.

Kahn, R. S., Westenberg, H. G. M., & Moore, C. (1995). Increased serotonin function and panic disorder. In G. M. Asnis and H. M. van Praag (Eds.), *Panic disorder: Clinical, biological, and treatment aspects* (pp. 151–180). New York: John Wiley.

Katon, W. (1989). *Panic disorder in the medical setting.* Washington, DC: National Institute of Mental Health.

Kendler, K. S., Neale, M. C., Kessler, R. C., Heath, A. C., & Eaves, L. J. (1992). The genetic epidemiology of phobias in women: The interrelationship of agoraphobia, social phobia, situational phobia and simple phobia. *Archives of General Psychiatry, 51,* 8–19.

Kessler, R. C., McGonagle, K. A., Zhao, S., Nelson, C. B., Hughes, M., Eshleman, S., Wittchen, H.-U., & Kendler, K. S. (1994). Lifetime and 12-month prevalence of *DSM-III-R* psychiatric disorders in the United States. *Archives of General Psychiatry, 51,* 8–19.

Kirkpatrick, D. (1984). Age, gender and patterns of common intense fears among adults. *Behavior Research and Therapy, 22,* 141–150.

Klein, D. F. (1964). Delineation of two drug-responsive anxiety syndromes. *Psychopharmacologia, 5,* 397–408.

Klein, D. F. (1980). Anxiety reconceptualized. *Comprehensive Psychiatry, 21,* 411–427.

Klein, D. F. (1993). False suffocation alarms, spontaneous panics, and related conditions: An integrative hypothesis. *Archives of General Psychiatry, 50,* 306–317.

Klein, D. F. (1994a). Reply to Taylor and Rachman. *Archives of General Psychiatry, 51,* 506.

Klein, D. F. (1994b). Response to critique of suffocation alarm theory. *Anxiety, 1,* 145–148.

Klein, D. F., & Klein, H. M. (1989). The substantive effect of variations in panic measurement and agoraphobia definition. *Journal of Anxiety Disorders, 3,* 45–56.

Koenigsberg, H. W., Pollack, C. P., Fine, J., & Kakuma, T. (1992). Lactate sensitivity in sleeping panic disorder patients and healthy controls. *Biological Psychiatry, 32,* 539–542.

Koszycki, D., Cox, B. J., & Bradwejn, J. (1993). Anxiety sensitivity and response to cholecystokinin tetrapeptide in healthy volunteers. *American Journal of Psychiatry, 150,* 1881–1883.

Kuch, K., & Swinson, R. P. (1992). Agoraphobia: What Westphal really said. *Canadian Journal of Psychiatry, 37,* 133–136.

Kushner, M. G., Sher, K. J., & Beitman, B. D. (1990). The relation between alcohol problems and the anxiety disorders. *American Journal of Psychiatry, 147,* 685–695.

Laberge, B., Gauthier, J. G., Cote, G., Plamondon, J., & Cormier, H. J. (1993). Cognitive-behavioral therapy of panic disorder with secondary major depression: A preliminary investigation. *Journal of Consulting and Clinical Psychology, 61,* 1028–1037.

Leary, M. R., & Kowalski, R. M. (1995). The self-presentation model of social phobia. In R. G. Heimberg, M. R. Liebowitz, D. A. Hope, & F. R. Schneier (Eds.), *Social phobia: Diagnosis, assessment, and treatment* (pp. 94–112). New York: Guilford Press.

Lelliott, P., & Bass, C. (1990). Symptom specificity in patients with panic. *British Journal of Psychiatry, 157,* 593–597.

Lelliott, P., Marks, I., McNamee, G., & Tobena, A. (1989). Onset of panic disorder with agoraphobia: Toward an integrated model. *Archives of General Psychiatry, 46,* 1000–1004.

Lesser, I. M., Rubin, R. T., Rifkin, A., Swinson, R. P., Ballenger, J. C., Burrows, G. D., Dupont, R. L., Noyes, R., & Pecknold, J. C. (1989). Secondary depression in panic disorder and agoraphobia. II. Dimensions of depressive symptomatology and their response to treatment. *Journal of Affective Disorders, 16,* 49–58.

Ley, R. (1988). Hyperventilation and lactate infusion in the production of panic attacks. *Clinical Psychology Review, 8,* 1–18.

Ley R. (1989). Dyspneic-fear and catastrophic cognitions in hyperventilatory panic attacks. *Behaviour Research and Therapy, 27,* 549–554.

Ley R. (1992). The many faces of Pan: psychological and physiological differences among three types of panic attacks. *Behaviour Research and Therapy, 30,* 347–357.

Ley R. (1996a). Panic attacks: Klein's false suffocation alarm, Taylor and Rachman's data, and Ley's dyspneic-fear theory. *Archives of General Psychiatry, 53,* 83.

Ley R. (1996b). Ondine's curse, false suffocation alarms, trait/state suffocation fear and dyspnea/suffocation fear in panic attacks. *Archives of General Psychiatry.*

Levis, D. J. (1979). A reconsideration of Eysenck's conditioning model of neurosis. *Behavioral and Brain Sciences, 2,* 172–174.

Liebowitz, M. R., Gorman, J. M., Fyer, A. J., & Klein, D. F. (1985). Social phobia: Review of a neglected anxiety disorder. *Archives of General Psychiatry, 42,* 729–736.

Lilienfeld, S. O., Turner, S. M., & Jacob, R. G. (1993). Anxiety sensitivity: An examination of theoretical and methodological issues. *Advances in Behavior Research and Therapy, 15,* 147–182.

Lubow, R. E. (1989). *Latent inhibition and conditioned attention theory.* New York: Cambridge University Press.

Lucock, M. P., & Salkovskis, P. M. (1988). Cognitive factors in social anxiety and its treatment. *Behaviour Research and Therapy, 26,* 297–302.

Maller, R. G., & Reiss, S. (1992). Anxiety sensitivity in 1984 and panic attacks in 1987. *Journal of Anxiety Disorders, 6,* 241–247.

Mannuzza, S., Fyer, A. J., Liebowitz, M. R., & Klein, D. F. (1990). Delineating the boundaries of social phobia: Its relationship to panic disorder and agoraphobia. *Journal of Anxiety Disorders, 4,* 42–59.

Markowitz, J. S., Weissman, M. M., Ouellette, R., Lish, J. D., & Klerman, G. L. (1989). Quality of life in panic disorder. *Archives of General Psychiatry, 46,* 984–992.

Marks, I. M. (1987). *Fears, phobias, and rituals: Panic, anxiety, and their disorders.* New York: Oxford University Press.

Marks, M. P., Basoglu, M., Alkubaisy, T., Sengun, S., & Marks, I. M. (1991). Are anxiety symptoms and catastrophic cognitions directly related? *Journal of Anxiety Disorders, 5,* 247–254.

Marks, I. M., & Gelder, M. G. (1966). Different ages of onset in varieties of phobia. *American Journal of Psychiatry, 123,* 218–221.

Maser, J. D., & Cloninger, C. R. (Eds.). (1990). *Comorbidity of anxiety and mood disorders.* Washington, DC: American Psychiatric Press.

McNally, R. J. (1987). Preparedness and phobias: A review. *Psychological Bulletin, 101,* 283–303.

McNally, R. J. (1994). *Panic disorder: A critical analysis.* New York: Guilford.

McNally, R. J. (1995). Preparedness, phobias, and the Panglossian paradigm. *Behavioral and Brain Sciences, 18,* 303–304.

McNally, R. J., & Eke, M. (1996). Anxiety sensitivity, suffocation fear, and breath-holding duration as predictors of response to carbon dioxide challenge. *Journal of Abnormal Psychology, 105,* 146–149.

McNally, R. J., & Louro, C. E. (1992). Fear of flying in agoraphobia and simple phobia: Distinguishing features. *Journal of Anxiety Disorders, 6,* 319–324.

McNally, R. J., & Steketee, G. S. (1985). The etiology and maintenance of severe animal phobias. *Behaviour Research and Therapy, 23,* 431–435.

Menzies, R. G., & Clarke, J. C. (1995). The etiology of phobias: A nonassociative account. *Clinical Psychology Review, 15,* 23–48.

Merckelbach, H., de Jong, P. J., Muris, P., & van den Hout, M. A. (1996). The etiology of specific phobias: A review. *Clinical Psychology Review, 16,* 337–361.

Merckelbach, H., van den Hout, M. A., Hoekstra, R., & van Oppen, P. (1988). Many stimuli are frightening but some are more frightening than others: The contribution of preparedness, dangerousness, and unpredictability to making a stimulus fearful. *Journal of Psychopathology and Behavioral Assessment, 10,* 355–366.

Miller, P. P., Brown, T. A., DiNardo, P., & Barlow, D. H. (1994). The experimental induction of depersonalization and derealization in panic disorder and nonanxious subjects. *Behaviour Research and Therapy, 32,* 511–519.

Mineka, S. (1992). Evolutionary memories, emotional processing and the emotional disorders. In D. Medin (Ed.), *The psychology of learning and motivation, vol. 28* (pp. 161–206). New York: Academic.

Mineka, S., & Cook, M. (1995). Expectancy bias as sole or partial account of selective associations? *Behavioral and Brain Sciences, 18,* 307–309.

Mowrer, O. H. (1939). Stimulus response theory of anxiety. *Psychological Review, 46,* 553–565.

Mowrer, O. H. (1960). *Learning theory and Behaviour.* New York: John Wiley.

Neale, M. C., Walters, E. E., Eaves, L. J., Kessler, R. C., Heath, A. C., & Kendler, K. S. (1994). Genetics of blood-injury fears and phobias: A population-based twin study. *American Journal of Medical Genetics, 54,* 326–334.

Nesse, R. M. (1990). Evolutionary explanations of emotions. *Human Nature, 1,* 261–289.

Norton, G. R., Cox, B. J., Asmundson, G. J. G., & Maser, J. D. (1995). The growth of research on anxiety disorders during the 1980s. *Journal of Anxiety Disorders, 9,* 75–85.

Norton, G. R., Cox, B. J., & Malan, J. (1992). Nonclinical panickers: A critical review. *Clinical Psychology Review, 12,* 121–139.

Noyes, R., Kathol, R. G., Fisher, M. M., Phillips, B. M., Suelzer, M. T., & & Woodman, C. L. (1994). Psychiatric comorbidity among patients with hypochondriasis. *General Hospital Psychiatry, 16,* 78–87.

Noyes, R., Reich, J., Clancy, J., & O'Gorman, T. W. (1986). Reduction in hypochndriasis with treatment of panic disorder. *British Journal of Psychiatry, 149,* 631–635.

Oei, T. P. S., Wanstall, K., & Evans, L. (1990). Sex differences in agoraphobia. *Journal of Anxiety Disorders, 4,* 317–324.

Ohman, A., Dimberg, U., & Ost, L.-G. (1985). Animal and social phobias: Biological constraints on learned fear responses. In S. Reiss & R. R. Bootzin (Eds.), *Theoretical issues in Behavior therapy* (pp. 123–175). New York: Academic.

Ollendick, T. H., & King, N. J. (1991). Origins of childhood fears: An evaluation of Rachman's theory of fear acquisition. *Behaviour Research and Therapy, 29,* 117–123.

Ollendick, T. H., Matson, J. L., & Helsel, W. J. (1985). Fears in children and adolescents: Normative data. *Behaviour Research and Therapy, 23,* 465–467.

Ollendick, T. H., Yule, W., & Ollier, K. (1991). Fears in British children and their relationship to manifest anxiety and depression. *Journal of Child Psychology and Psychiatry, 32,* 321–331.

Page, A. C. (1994). Blood-injury phobia. *Chemical Psychology Review, 14,* 443–461.

Papp, L. A., & Gorman, J. M. (1995). Respiratory neurobiology of panic. In G. M. Asnis and H. M. van Praag (Eds.), *Panic disorder: Clinical, biological, and treatment aspects.* (pp. 255–275). New York: John Wiley.

Papp, L. A., Klein, D. F., & Gorman, J. M. (1993). Carbon dioxide hypersensitivity, hyperventilation, and panic disorder. *American Journal of Psychiatry, 150,* 1149–1157.

Pavlov, I. P. (1928). *Lectures on conditioned reflexes.* New York: International Publishers.

Peterson, R. A., & Reiss, S. (1987). *Anxiety Sensitivity Index Manual.* Worthington, OH: International Diagnostic Systems.

Pincus, H. A., Henderson, B., Blackwood, D., & Dial, T. (1993). Trends in research in two general psychiatric journals in 1969–1990: Research on research. *American Journal of Psychiatry, 150,* 135–142.

Pine, D. S., Weese-Mayer, D. E., Silvestri, J. M., Davies, M., Whitaker, A. H., & Klein, D. F. (1994). Anxiety and congenital central hypoventilation syndrome. *American Journal of Psychiatry, 151,* 864–870.

Rachman, S. (1976). The passing of the two-stage theory of fear and avoidance: Fresh possibilities. *Behaviour Research and Therapy, 14,* 125–131.

Rachman, S. (1977). The conditioning theory of fear-acquisition: A critical examination. *Behaviour Research and Therapy, 15,* 373–387.

Rachman, S. J. (1984). Agoraphobia: A safety-signal perspective. *Behaviour Research and Therapy, 22,* 59–70.

Rachman, S. (1990). *Fear and courage* (2nd ed.). New York: Freeman.

Rachman, S. (1991a). Neo-conditioning and the classical theory of fear acquisition. *Clinical Psychology Review, 11,* 155–173.

Rachman, S. J. (1991b). A psychological approach to the study of comorbidity. *Clinical Psychology Review, 11,* 461–464.

Rachman, S. (1993). A critique of cognitive therapy for anxiety disorders. *Journal of Behavior Therapy and Experimental Psychiatry, 24,* 279–288.

Rachman, S., & Maser, J. D. (Eds.). (1985). *Panic: Psychological perspectives.* Hillsdale, NJ: Lawrence Erlbaum.

Rachman, S., & Seligman, M. E. P. (1976). Unprepared fears: "Be prepared." *Behaviour Research and Therapy, 14,* 333–338.

Rachman, S., & Taylor, S. (1993). Analyses of claustrophobia. *Journal of Anxiety Disorders, 7,* 281–291.

Rapee, R. M. (1993). Psychological factors in panic disorder. *Advances in Behaviour Research and Therapy, 15,* 85–102.

Rapee, R. M. (1995). Psychological factors influencing the affective response to biological challenge procedures in panic disorder. *Journal of Anxiety Disorders, 9,* 59–74.

Rapee, R. M. (1996a). Information-processing views of panic disorder. In R. M. Rapee (Ed.), *Current controversies in the anxiety disorders* (pp. 77–93). New York: Guilford.

Rapee, R. M. (Ed.). (1996b). *Current controversies in the anxiety disorders.* New York: Guilford.

Regier, D. A., Boyd, J. H., Burke, J. D., Rae, D. S., Myers, J. K., Kramer, M., Robins, L. N., George, L. K., Karno, M., & Locke, B. Z. (1988). One-month prevalence of mental disorders in the United States. *Archives of General Psychiatry, 45,* 977–986.

Reiss, S. (1980). Pavlovian conditioning and human fear: an expectancy model. *Behavior Therapy, 11,* 380–396.

Reiss, S. (1991). Expectancy theory of fear, anxiety, and panic. *Clinical Psychology Review, 11,* 141–153.

Reiss, S., & McNally, R. J. (1985). The expectancy model of fear. In S. Reiss & R. R. Boot zin (Eds.), *Theoretical issues in behavior therapy* (pp. 107–121). New York: Academic Press.

Reiss, S., Peterson, R. A., Gursky, M., & McNally, R. J. (1986). Anxiety sensitivity, anxiety frequency, and the prediction of fearfulness. *Behaviour Research and Therapy, 24,* 1–8.

Rescorla, R. A. (1988). Pavlovian conditioning: It's not what you think it is. *American Psychologist, 43,* 151–160.

Rescorla, R. A., & Wagner, A. R. (1972). A theory of Pavlovian conditioning: Variations in the effectiveness of reinforcement and nonreinforcement. In A. H. Black & W. F. Prokasy (Eds.), *Classical conditioning II: Current research and theory* (pp. 64–99). New York: Appleton-Century-Crofts.

Rimm, D. C., Janda, L. H., Lancaster, D. W., Nahl, M., & Dittmar, K. (1977). An exploratory investigation of the origin and maintenance of phobias. *Behaviour Research and Therapy, 15,* 231–238.

Robins, L. N., Helzer, J. E., Weissman, M. M., Orvaschel, H., Gruenberg, E., Burke, J. D., & Regier, D. A. (1984). Lifetime prevalence of specific psychiatric disorders in three sites. *Archives of General Psychiatry, 41,* 949–958.

Rose, R. J., & Ditto, W. B. (1983). A developmental-genetic analysis of common fears from early adolescence to early adulthood. *Child Development, 54,* 361–368.

Salkovskis, P. M., & Clark, D. M. (1993). Panic disorder and hypochondriasis. *Advances in Behaviour Research and Therapy, 15,* 23–48.

Sanderson, W. C., Rapee, R. M., & Barlow, D. H. (1989). The influence of an illusion of control on panic attacks induced via inhalation of 5.5% carbon dioxide-enriched air. *Archives of General Psychiatry, 46,*157–162.

Scarr, S., & Salapatek, P. (1970). Patterns of fear development during infancy. *Merrill-Palmer Quarterly, 16,* 53–90.

Schmidt, N. B., Lerew, D. R., & Jackson, R. J. (1997). The role of anxiety sensitivity in the pathogenesis of panic: Prospective evaluation of spontaneous panic attacks during acute stress. *Journal of Abnormal Psychology, 106,* 355–364.

Schneier, F. R., Johnson, J., Hornig, C. D., Liebowitz, M. R., & Weissman, M. M. (1992). Social phobia: Comorbidity and morbidity in an epidemiologic sample. *Archives of General Psychiatry, 49,* 282–291.

Schuckit, M. A., & Hesselbrock, V. (1994). Alcohol dependence and anxiety disorders: What is the relationship? *American Journal of Psychiatry, 151,* 1723–1734.

Seligman, M. E. P. (1970). On the generality of the laws of learning. *Psychological Review, 77,* 406–418.

Seligman, M. E. P. (1971). Phobias and preparedness. *Behavior Therapy, 2,* 307–320.

Seligman, M. E. P., & Johnston, J. C. (1973). A cognitive theory of avoidance learning. In F. J. McGuigan & D. B. Lumsden (Eds.), *Contemporary approaches to learning and conditioning* (pp. 69–145). Washington, DC: Winston.

Shear, M. K., Fyer, A. J., Ball, G., Josephson, S., Fitzpatrick, M., Gitlin, B., Frances, A., Gorman, J., Liebowitz, M., & Klein, D. F. (1991). Vulnerability to sodium lactate in panic disorder patients given cognitive-behavioral therapy. *American Journal of Psychiatry, 148, 795–797.*

Shephard, R. A. (1986). Neurotransmitters, anxiety and benzodiazepines: A Behavioural review. *Neuroscience and BioBehavioral Reviews, 10,* 449–461.

Shulman, I. D., Cox, B. J., Swinson, R. P., Kuch, K., & Reichman, J. T. (1994). Precipitating events, locations and reactions associated with initial unexpected panic attacks. *Behaviour Research and Therapy, 32,* 17–20.

Staley, A. A., & O'Donnell, J. P. (1984). A developmental analysis of mothers' reports of normal children's fears. *Journal of Genetic Psychology, 144,* 165–178.

Stein, M. B. (1995) (Ed.). *Social phobia: Clinical and research perspectives.* Washington, DC: American Psychiatric Press.

Stein, M. B., Shea, C. A., & Uhde, T. W. (1989). Social phobic symptoms in patients with panic disorder: Practical and theoretical implications. *American Journal of Psychiatry, 146,* 235–238.

Stein, M. B., Walker, J. R., & Forde, D. R. (1994). Setting diagnostic thresholds for social phobia: Considerations from a community study of social anxiety. *American Journal of Psychiatry, 152,* 408–412.

Stevenson, J., Batten, N., & Cherner, M. (1992). Fears and fearfulness in children and adolescents: A genetic analysis of twin data. *Journal of Child Psychology and Psychiatry, 33,* 977–985.

Stopa, L. & Clark, D. M. (1993). Cognitive processes in social phobia. *Behaviour Research and Therapy, 31,* 255–267.

Swinson, R. P., Cox, B. J., Kerr, S. A., Kuch, K., & Fergus, K. D. (1992). A survey of anxiety disorder clinics in Canadian hospitals. *Canadian Journal of Psychiatry, 37,* 188–191.

Swinson, R. P., Cox, B. J., & Woszczyna, C. B. (1992). Use of medical services and treatment for panic disorder with agoraphobia and for social phobia. *Canadian Medical Association Journal, 147,* 878–883.

Swinson, R. P., Soulios, C., Cox, B. J., & Kuch, K. (1992). Brief treatment of emergency room patients with panic attacks. *American Journal of Psychiatry, 149,* 944–946.

Taylor, C. B., King, R., Margraf, J., Ehlers, A., Telch, M., Roth, W. T., & Agras, W. S. (1989). Use of medication and in vivo exposure in volunteers for panic disorder research. *American Journal of Psychiatry, 146,* 1423–1426.

Taylor, S. (1995). Anxiety sensitivity: Theoretical perspectives and recent findings. *Behaviour Research and Therapy, 33,* 243–258.

Taylor, S. (1993). The structure of fundamental fears. *Journal of Behavior Therapy and Experimental Psychiatry, 24,* 289–299.

Taylor, S. (1999). (Ed.). *Anxiety sensitivity: Theory, research, and treatment of the fear of anxiety.* Lawrence Erlbaum Associates.

Taylor, S., & Koch, W. J. (1995). Anxiety disorders due to motor vehicle accidents: Nature and treatment. *Clinical Psychology Review, 15,* 721–738.

Taylor, S., Koch, W. J., & McNally, R. J. (1992). How does anxiety sensitivity vary across the anxiety disorders? *Journal of Anxiety Disorders, 7,* 249–259.

Taylor, S., Koch, W. J., Woody, S., & McLean, P. (1996). Anxiety sensitivity and depression: How are they related? *Journal of Abnormal Psychology, 105,* 474–479.

Taylor, S., & Livesley, W. J. (1995). The influence of personality on the clinical course of neurosis. *Current Opinion in Psychiatry, 8,* 93–97.

Taylor, S. & Rachman, S. (1994). Klein's suffocation theory of panic. *Archives of General Psychiatry, 51,* 505–506.

Taylor, S., & Rachman, S. (1997). Suffocation fear and theories of panic. *Archives of General Psychiatry, 54,* 677–678.

Taylor, S., Woody, S., Koch, W. J., McLean, P., & Anderson, K. (1996). Suffocation false-alarms and efficacy of cognitive-behavioural therapy for panic disorder. *Behavior Therapy, 27,* 115–126.

Tyrer, P. (1986). Classification of anxiety disorders: A critique of *DSM-III. Journal of Affective Disorders, 11,* 99–104.

Uhde, T. W. (1995). Caffeine-induced anxiety: An ideal chemical model for panic disorder? In G. M. Asnis and H. M. van Praag (Eds.), *Panic disorder: Clinical, biological, and treatment aspects* (pp. 181–205). New York: John Wiley.

Uhde, T. W., Stein, M. B., Vittone, B. J., Siever, L. J., Boulenger, J. P., Klein, E., & Mellman, T. A. (1989). Behavioral and physiologic effects of short-term and long-term administration of clonidine in panic disorder. *Archives of General Psychiatry, 46,* 17–177.

Wagner, A. R., & Rescorla, R. A. (1972). Inhibition in Pavlovian conditioning: Application of a theory. In R. A. Boakes & M. S. Halliday (Eds.), *Inhibition and learning* (pp. 301–336). New York: Academic.

Walker, J. R., Norton, G. R., & Ross, C. A. (Eds.). (1991). *Panic disorder and agoraphobia: A comprehensive guide for the practitioner.* Pacific Grove, CA: Brooks/Cole.

Ware, J. W., Jain, K., Burgess, I., & Davey, G. C. L. (1994). Disease-avoidance model: Factor analysis of common animal fears. *Behaviour Research and Therapy, 32,* 57–63.

Watson, D., Clark, L. A., & Harkness, A. R. (1994). Structures of personality and their relevance to psychopathology. *Journal of Abnormal Psychology, 103*, 18–31.

Watson, J. B., & Rayner, R. (1920). Conditioned emotional reactions. *Journal of Experimental Psychology, 3*, 1–14.

Weissman, M. M., Klerman, G. L., Markowitz, J. S., & Ouellette, R. (1989). Suicidal ideation and suicide attempts in panic disorder and attacks. *New England Journal of Medicine, 321*, 1209–1214.

Westphal, C. (1871–1872). Die agoraphobie: Eine neuropathische erscheinung. *Arch fur Psychiatrie und Nervenkrankheiten, 3*, 138–171, 219–221.

Wetzler, S., & Sanderson, W. C. (1995). Comorbidity of panic disorder. In G. M. Asnis and H. M. van Praag (Eds.), *Panic disorder: Clinical, biological, and treatment aspects* (pp. 80–98). New York: John Wiley.

Wolfe, B. E., & Maser, J. D. (Eds.). (1994). *Treatment of panic disorder: A consensus development conference*. Washington, DC: American Psychiatric Press.

Wolpe, J., & Lang, P. J. (1969). *Fear survey schedule*. San Diego, CA: EdITS.

Wolpe, J., & Rachman, S. (1960). Psychoanalytic evidence: A critique based on Freud's case of Little Hans. *Journal of Nervous and Mental Disease, 131*, 135–145.

Woods, S. W., Charney, D. S., McPherson, C. A., Gradman, A. H., & Heninger, G. R. (1987). Situational panic attacks: Behavioral, physiologic, and biochemical characterization. *Archives of General Psychiatry, 44*, 365–375.

Woody, S. R., Taylor, S., McLean, P., & Koch, W. J. (1996, November). *Comorbid panic and depression: Outcome of cognitive-behavior therapy*. Paper presented in the symposium, "Treatment of panic disorder: New research on efficacy and mechanisms" (Chair: S. Taylor) at the 30th meeting of the Association for the Advancement of Behavior Therapy, Washington, DC.

Zafiropoulou, M., & McPherson, F. M. (1986). "Preparedness" and the severity and outcome of clinical phobias. *Behaviour Research and Therapy, 24*, 221–222.

Zandbergen, J., Strahm, M., Pols, H., & Griez, E. J. L. (1992). Breath-holding in panic disorder. *Comprehensive Psychiatry, 33*, 47–51.

Zinbarg, R. E., & Barlow, D. H. (1996). The structure of anxiety and the anxiety disorders: A hierarchical model. *Journal of Abnormal Psychology, 105*, 181–193.

5

Generalized Anxiety Disorder and Obsessive-Compulsive Disorder

TIMOTHY A. BROWN

Generalized Anxiety Disorder

Overview and History of Generalized Anxiety Disorder

In *DSM-IV*, generalized anxiety disorder (GAD) is defined by the key feature of excessive, uncontrollable worry about a number of life events or activities, accompanied by at least three of six associated symptoms of negative affect or tension (i.e., restlessness or feeling keyed up or on edge, fatigability, concentration difficulties, irritability, muscle tension, sleep disturbance). Differential diagnosis guidelines for *DSM-IV* GAD specify that the disorder should not be assigned if its features are better accounted for by another mental or medical disorder (e.g., worry about future panic attacks in panic disorder should not be counted toward the diagnosis of GAD). In addition, the *DSM-IV* definition of GAD states that the disorder should not be assigned if its features occur exclusively during the course of a mood disorder.

The definition of GAD has evolved across the last three editions of the *DSM*. Indeed, of the anxiety disorders, no diagnostic category has undergone more change over the past 17 years than GAD. These extensive changes to the *DSM* definition of GAD are one reflection of the longstanding controversy surrounding the disorder as to its validity as a distinct diagnostic category. With the publication of *DSM-III* in 1980, the subcategory of anxiety disorders that had been termed "anxiety neurosis" in *DSM-II* became "anxiety states (or anxiety neurosis)." This category contained two new diagnoses: panic disorder and GAD (along with obsessive-compulsive disorder, which existed as "obsessive-compulsive neurosis" in *DSM-II*). In *DSM-III*, diagnostic criteria for GAD required the presence of generalized, persistent anxiety (continuous for a period of at least one month) as manifested by symptoms from at least three of four areas: (1) motor tension (e.g., muscle aches, restlessness); (2) autonomic hyperactivity (e.g., sweating, dizziness, accelerated heart rate); (3) apprehensive expectation (e.g., anxiety, worry, fear); and (4) vigilance and scanning (e.g., concentration difficulties, irritability). However, within the *DSM-III* diagnostic system, GAD was a residual category, meaning that the diagnosis could not be assigned if the patient met criteria for another mental disorder. The residual nature of GAD was probably in part responsible for the unacceptable diagnostic reliability of this category (discussed in a later section). The residual status of GAD had other deleterious effects, such as hindering research on the nature of GAD, on its overlap (e.g., comorbidity) with other disorders, and on the development and evaluation of effective treatments.

Despite the hierarchical rules of *DSM-III*, clinical experience indicated that in addition to patients who experienced generalized anxiety as their primary complaint, many patients evidenced generalized anxiety that was independent of their principal disorder. The important diagnostic consideration in these "comorbid" cases was the differentiation of generalized, nonsituational anxiety from anticipatory anxiety (apprehension focused on future threat-related events or situations), because the latter is always present to varying degrees in the panic and phobic disorders. This differentiation was facilitated by determining whether the focus of apprehension (i.e., worry) was on the core feature of another disorder (e.g., panic, phobic situation) or was focused on an area unrelated to another disorder (Barlow, Blanchard, Vermilyea, Vermilyea, & Di Nardo, 1986; Barlow & Di Nardo, 1991). For example, if a patient presented with anxiety and worry focused exclusively on social situations and possible negative evaluation by others, only social phobia would be assigned. However, if additional pervasive anxiety existed that was independently focused on a number of minor events of everyday life (e.g., finances, job performance), GAD would be assigned as well.

Accordingly, in *DSM-III-R*, the diagnostic criteria for GAD underwent considerable change. GAD was no longer regarded as a residual diagnosis. Rather, the "apprehensive expectation" cluster contained in the *DSM-III* criteria was restructured such that *DSM-III-R* GAD had its own key feature: excessive and/or unrealistic worry in two or more spheres that were unrelated to another Axis I disorder. In addition, the associated symptom criterion was revised to require the presence of at least six symptoms from a list of 18 forming three clusters: Motor Tension, Autonomic Hyperactivity, and Vigilance and Scanning. Based on clinical and empirical considerations (e.g., Breslau & Davis, 1985), the duration criterion was extended from one to six months. Among other reasons, the requirement of pervasive worry more days than not over a period of at least six months was considered to foster the differentiation of GAD from transient reactions to stressful life events (e.g., adjustment disorders).

However, changes to the definition of GAD in *DSM-III-R* did not improve its diagnostic reliability. Consequently, the criteria for GAD were revised further in *DSM-IV* to make them more user-friendly and to more strongly emphasize the pathological features of worry. The requirement of two or more spheres of worry was eliminated. Instead, *DSM-IV* specifies that the worry must be *excessive* (i.e., intensity, duration, and frequency of the worry is out of proportion to the likelihood or impact of the feared event), *pervasive* (i.e., the worry occurs more days than not for at least six months, about a number of events or activities), and *uncontrollable* (i.e., the person finds it difficult to control the worry). Moreover, the 18 ratings constituting the associated symptom criterion were reduced to six; some of the symptoms from the *DSM-III-R* Motor Tension and Vigilance and Scanning clusters were retained, but all of the symptoms from the Autonomic Hyperactivity cluster were eliminated.

Epidemiology, Diagnostic Reliability, Comorbidity, and Presenting Characteristics of Generalized Anxiety Disorder

Epidemiology Studies of the lifetime prevalence for GAD in the general population have provided estimates ranging from 1.9 to 5.4%. The most recent prevalence data for GAD have come from the National Comorbidity Survey (NCS), where over 8,000 persons in the community (ages 15 to 54 years) were evaluated with structured interviews. This study obtained prevalence estimates of 1.6 and 5.1% for current and lifetime GAD, respectively, as defined by *DSM-III-R* criteria (Wittchen, Zhao, Kessler, & Eaton, 1994).[1] A consistent finding in these community surveys is a 2:1 female-to-male preponderance of GAD (e.g., Blazer, George, & Hughes, 1991; Wittchen et al., 1994). In the NCS study, race, religion, education level, or income were not associated with risk for GAD. However, multivariate logistic regression indicated that being older than 24 years, previously married (i.e., separated, divorced, or widowed), unemployed, and holding homemaker status were significant correlates of the disorder (Wittchen et al., 1994). The epidemiology of GAD in older populations awaits future research (cf. Beck, Stanley, & Zebb, 1996; Wisocki, 1994). However, there is some evidence suggesting that GAD may be one of the more common disorders in the elderly. For example, Himmelfarb and Murrell (1984) found that 17% of elderly men and 21.5% of elderly women had sufficiently severe anxiety symptoms to warrant treatment, although it is not clear how many of these individuals actually met criteria for

GAD. Another indicator of the potential prevalence of GAD symptoms in the elderly comes from more recent evidence showing that the use of minor tranquilizers is very high (ranging from 17 to 50%) in this population (Salzman, 1991). In a review of eight published reports of community surveys involving anxiety disorders in persons 60 years of age or older, Flint (1994) concluded that although anxiety disorders are less common in the elderly than in younger adults, GAD and phobias account for most anxiety in later life.

Diagnostic Reliability In part because of its residual status in this edition of the *DSM*, diagnostic reliability of *DSM-III* GAD was quite low. For example, based on two independent administrations of the Anxiety Disorders Interview Schedule, Di Nardo, O'Brien, Barlow, Waddell, and Blanchard (1983) obtained a kappa coefficient for the principal diagnosis of GAD of 0.48, reflecting only fair reliability. However, using a less conservative methodology (independent ratings of videotaped diagnostic interviews), Riskind, Beck, Berchick, Brown, and Steer (1987) obtained a kappa coefficient of 0.79 for *DSM-III* GAD.

Although revised extensively, the *DSM-III-R* definition of GAD was generally not associated with improvements in diagnostic reliability relative to rates of agreement observed for *DSM-III* GAD (cf. Di Nardo, Moras, Barlow, Rapee, & Brown, 1993; Mannuzza et al., 1989; Williams et al., 1992). Among studies examining the test-retest reliability of GAD (i.e., reliabilities based on independent administrations of structured interviews), kappas for *DSM-III-R* GAD ranged from 0.39 to 0.57; however, studies using less stringent methodologies (e.g., independent ratings of audio- or videotaped interviews) obtained higher agreement rates (cf. Skre, Onstad, Torgersen, & Kringlen, 1991). In evaluating the factors contributing to diagnostic unreliability, Mannuzza et al. (1989) observed that, in most cases (72%), disagreements involving GAD were due to variability across interviews in patients' report about the presence, frequency, or duration of symptoms. Di Nardo et al. (1993) noted that many of the disagreements involving GAD were attributable to discrepancies in the relative severity of co-occurring disorders (for example, both interviewers may have agreed that a patient had GAD and social phobia, but they disagreed on which disorder should be assigned as the principal diagnosis). Nevertheless, in cases where interviewers disagreed on the presence of GAD, Di Nardo et al. (1993) reported that these disagreements were most frequently due to whether or not: (1) at least two distinct spheres of worry were present; (2) the worry on each topic was "excessive" or "unrealistic"; and (3) the worry could be better accounted for by the symptoms of another Axis I disorder. The latter source of disagreement is particularly relevant given evidence that the topics of worry commonly associated with GAD are often similar in nature to the concerns of patients with other anxiety and mood disorders. For instance, health-related worries could contribute to several disorders such as GAD, panic disorder, OCD with contamination or somatic obsessions, hypochondriasis, and other somatoform disorders (cf. Brown, 1998).

Because of the substantial reevaluation and redefinition of GAD that occurred in the process of preparing *DSM-IV*, researchers are hopeful that the diagnostic reliability of the category will improve accordingly. Initial evidence suggests that this in fact may be the case (Di Nardo, Brown, Lawton, & Barlow, 1995), although these findings await verification in large-scale studies.

Comorbidity Although GAD had once been regarded as a relatively minor problem lacking the degree of distress and impairment often found in other anxiety disorders (such as panic disorder and obsessive-compulsive disorder), recent data indicate that this is not the case. Findings from NCS indicate that 82% of persons with GAD reported that their problem was associated with significant impairment, as indexed by past treatment-seeking behavior or substantial lifestyle interference (Wittchen et al., 1994; cf. Massion, Warshaw, & Keller, 1993). In addition, research has routinely shown that GAD rarely presents in isolation. Community surveys indicate that 90% of persons with GAD have a history of some other mental disorder at some point in their lives (Wittchen et al., 1994); the NCS estimated that 65% of persons with current GAD had at least one other disorder at the time of their assessment. Studies of clinical samples have found that over 75% of patients with a current principal diagnosis of GAD have other co-occurring anxiety or mood disorders (Brawman-Mintzer et al., 1993; Brown & Barlow, 1992; Massion et al., 1993). The high comorbidity rates obtained in patient samples may actually be *under*-estimates given that the presence of certain disorders (e.g., substance use disorders, disorders involving current suicidality) is an exclusion criterion in many investigations; indeed, data from the NCS suggest that substance use disorders are common (16%) in current GAD. In studies of patient samples, panic disorder, mood disorders (major depression, dysthymia), social phobia, and simple (specific) phobia are typically found to be the most common additional diagnoses. Some studies indicate that GAD is the most common comorbid diagnosis in patients seeking treatment for another anxiety or mood disorder (Brown & Barlow, 1992; Sanderson, Beck, & Beck, 1990). In addition, initial findings suggest that, relative to other anxiety and mood disorders, GAD may be the most commonly occurring disorder in persons presenting for treatment of physical conditions associated with stress (e.g., irritable bowel syndrome, chronic headaches; Blanchard, Scharff, Schwarz, Suls, & Barlow, 1990).

Age of Onset Compared to most of the other anxiety and mood disorders, GAD is more likely to present with a gradual onset or life-long history of symptoms. For example, several studies have found that a large proportion of patients with GAD cannot report a clear age of onset or report an onset dating back to childhood (e.g., Barlow et al., 1986; Noyes, Clarkson, Crowe, Yates, & McChesney, 1987). Many patients with GAD report that they have been worriers or have been tense and anxious all of their lives (Noyes et al., 1992; Sanderson & Barlow, 1990). Thus, in contrast to several other anxiety disorders such as panic disorder, which tends to have a later onset and more acute presentation characterized by exacerbations and remissions, initial evidence suggests that GAD may often have a more characterological presentation (although fluctuations in the course of GAD are noted, often corresponding to the presence and resolution of life stressors). In light of these findings, it is not surprising that GAD has been conceptualized within the context of a personality disorder (Sanderson & Wetzler, 1991). As will be noted later in this chapter, findings that GAD is typically associated with an early age of onset are of considerable significance to many biopsychosocial models of this disorder.

GAD is not exclusively an early-onset condition. For instance, in the NCS study, the lowest prevalence of GAD occurred in the 15- to 24-year age group (Wittchen et al., 1994). However, because prevalence estimates were based on the diagnostic level, they do not necessarily contradict the finding indicating that many patients with GAD report symptoms dating back to childhood (i.e., the extent to which the features of GAD were present at subclinical levels was not examined in this study). Some people with GAD report an onset in adulthood, usually in response to some form of life stress (Blazer et al., 1991; Blazer, Hughes, & George, 1987; Ganzini, McFarland, & Cutler, 1990). In an earlier epidemiological survey of the *DSM-III* disorders, a bimodal distribution in the age of onset of GAD was observed, possibly reflective of two separate pathways to the pathogenesis of this disorder (Blazer et al., 1991). For instance, compared to early-onset GAD, stressful life events may play a stronger role in onsets of GAD occurring later in life. This suggestion is bolstered by the findings of Blazer et al. (1987), who noted that the occurrence of one or more negative life events increased by threefold the risk of developing GAD in the following year.

Conversely, based in part on positions that GAD may be a characterological disturbance (cf. Sanderson & Wetzler, 1991), some researchers have speculated that early-onset GAD should be associated with higher degrees of psychopathology. In efforts to evaluate this hypothesis empirically, the clinical and demographic features of patients with early vs. late onsets of GAD have been compared. In the first of these investigations, Hoehn-Saric, Hazlett, and McLeod (1993) divided a sample of patients with *DSM-III-R* GAD into early- and late-onset groups based on onsets occurring before or after 20 years of age. Consistent with epidemiological findings, late-onset GAD was more likely to develop with a precipitating life event. In contrast, patients with early-onset GAD were younger, had more extensive psychiatric histories, and recalled more parental domestic disturbances and childhood inhibitions and phobias. Moreover, the early-onset group obtained significantly higher scores on measures of trait anxiety, neuroticism, worry, and depression (cf. Shores et al., 1992). However, in a subsequent study of patients with *DSM-III-R* GAD that employed the same early- and late-onset cut-offs as used by Hoehn-Saric et al. (1993), no significant between-groups differences were obtained in measures of current anxiety, depressive, and associated symptoms (Brown, O'Leary, Marten, & Barlow, 1993). As noted by Brown, O'Leary et al. (1993), the methodological approach used in these studies of conducting between-groups comparisons of early- and late-onset groups may be problematic for a variety of reasons, including: (1) it does not take into account the age and duration of the disturbance (e.g., a young adult who had GAD for one year would be placed in a different group than a late adolescent who had GAD for one year, but would be placed in the same group as a middle-aged person who had GAD for 25 years); (2) given that GAD may often be associated with a gradual and insidious onset, retrospective recall of age of onset may be unreliable. Recognizing these methodological issues, Beck et al. (1996) compared a subgroup of their elderly sample of persons with GAD who reported onsets before age 15 or after age 39. Although also using a between-groups comparative strategy, Beck et al. (1996) contended that these analyses were less problematic than those of Hoehn-Saric et al. (1993) because: (1) given that the study was restricted to older adults, the sample was relatively homogeneous in terms of age and duration of disorder; and (2) the 25-year separation between the upper and lower age limits for the early- and late-onset groups, respectively, may have alleviated problems associated with unreliability in retrospective report of age of onset. Despite these methodological refinements, Beck et al. (1996) failed to detect significant differences in measures of anxiety, depression, GAD, and associated symptoms, although all group means were in the direction of greater symptoms in the early-onset patients.

Empirical Basis for Generalized Anxiety Disorder as a Distinct Diagnostic Category

Overview of Issues As discussed in the first section of this chapter, the definition of GAD has changed substantially since its introduction as a residual diagnostic category in *DSM-III*. However, whether GAD should be retained as a formal diagnosis was debated at length during the process of evaluating and revising the diagnoses and diagnostic criteria for *DSM-IV*. Indeed, many researchers argued for the elimination of GAD or moved to place this category in the appendix of disorders in need of further study. A principal argument against the retention of GAD was that in light of its lower diagnostic reliability in the context of other emotional disorders and its high rate of comorbidity, GAD should be subsumed under the diagnoses with which it co-occurs. In other words, findings of low reliability and high comorbidity may be indicative of poor discriminant validity of GAD (e.g., the *DSM* system is erroneously distinguishing the symptoms of GAD as a separate disorder when it would be more parsimonious and more accurate to regard these features as associated symptoms of other disorders; cf. Brown & Chorpita, 1996). The paucity of research on the long-term course of GAD and initial evidence that comorbid GAD often remits upon treatment of another anxiety disorder (Brown, Antony, & Barlow, 1995) may also reflect the tenuous status of this disorder as a distinct diagnostic entity.

This position could be bolstered further by the fact that worry is a somewhat nonspecific feature; that is, worry is present to varying degrees in all of the anxiety and mood disorders (Brown, Barlow, & Liebowitz, 1994). For example, in most psychosocial models of panic disorder, the central maintaining feature of this condition is excessive anxiety and worry about experiencing additional panic attacks (Barlow, Chorpita, & Turovsky, 1996; Clark, 1986). Although these findings may be taken as evidence that the discriminant validity of GAD is poor, conceptual models of anxiety and anxiety disorders have emerged that regard GAD as the "basic" anxiety disorder because its core features may represent the fundamental processes of all emotional disorders (Barlow et al., 1996; Rapee, 1991). This fundamental process has been termed *anxious apprehension* (Barlow et al., 1996). Anxious apprehension is defined as a future-oriented mood state in which one becomes ready or prepared to attempt to cope with upcoming negative events. This is associated with a state of high negative affect and chronic overarousal, a sense of uncontrollability, and an attentional focus on threat-related stimuli (e.g., high self-focused attention, hypervigilance). Whereas the *process* of anxious apprehension is considered to be present in all anxiety disorders, the *content* (focus) of anxious apprehension varies from disorder to disorder (e.g., anxiety over future panic attacks in panic disorder, anxiety over possible negative social evaluation in social phobia). Based on these considerations, it could be asserted that GAD is differentiated from other emotional disorders (and nonpsychopathological states) by the presence of excessive, ubiquitous, and uncontrollable worry.

Measures of Worry GAD, in any case, was retained as a diagnostic category in *DSM-IV* for a variety of reasons (cf. Brown, 1996; Brown, Barlow, & Liebowitz, 1994). For instance, numerous studies have documented that patients with GAD can be differentiated on measures of worry from patients with other anxiety disorders and persons with no mental disorder. Studies examining the nature of worry in patients with GAD vs. nonanxious controls have indicated that, whereas these groups do not differ appreciably on the *content* of worry (e.g., family matters, health, work, finances), considerable differentiation exists on measures reflecting *controllability* of the worry process (e.g., percent day worried, frequency of unprecipitated worry, self-perceptions of controllability of worry, number of worry spheres; cf. Borkovec, 1994; Borkovec, Shadick, & Hopkins, 1991; Craske, Rapee, Jackel, & Barlow, 1989). For example, in a study comparing patients with *DSM-III-R* GAD to nonanxious controls on various potential *DSM-IV* criteria, 100% of the patient group reported difficulties controlling their worry, compared to only 5.6% of the comparison group (Abel & Borkovec, 1995). Such findings guided the revisions to the worry criterion in *DSM-IV* to emphasize the uncontrollable nature of worry as an essential feature of the disorder.

Unlike patients with GAD, nonanxious subjects rarely respond affirmatively to items inquiring about "worry more days than not?" and "worry excessively?," thus highlighting a boundary between normal and pathological worry (Abel & Borkovec, 1995). The content of GAD worries does not differ appreciably from the worries of normal control subjects, although patients report worrying about a greater number of worry topics than controls (e.g., Abel & Borkovec, 1995; Craske et al., 1989). However, studies have consistently shown that patients with GAD are more likely than nonanxious and anxiety control subjects to report worry about minor matters (e.g., Sanderson & Barlow, 1990). Di Nardo (1991) examined the discriminatory power of affirmative responses provided by patients with GAD and patients with other anxiety disorders to the question, "Do you worry excessively about minor matters?," an item in the GAD section of the Anxiety Disorders Interview Schedule-Revised (ADIS-R; Di Nardo & Barlow, 1988). The positive predictive power (specificity) of this question was .36 (the probability of a GAD diagnosis, given an affirmative response); the negative predictive power (sensitivity) was .94 (the probability of not having a GAD diagnosis, given a negative response). Di Nardo (1991) concluded that, although an affirmative response to the question of "excessive worry over minor matters" cannot confirm the diagnosis, a negative response can rule out GAD with confidence. Similarly, Abel and Borkovec (1995) found that, whereas none of the nonanxious comparison subjects reported worrying over minor matters, this item was endorsed frequently (83.5%) by patients with GAD.

Subsequent studies have produced findings that generally support the initial evidence that GAD can be distinguished from other anxiety disorders on measures of excessive or uncontrollable worry. In several studies, patients with GAD obtained significantly higher scores than other anxiety disorder groups and normal controls on the Penn State Worry Questionnaire (PSWQ), a psychometrically validated measure of the trait of worry (e.g., Brown, Antony, & Barlow, 1992; Brown, Moras, Zinbarg, & Barlow, 1993; Meyer, Miller, Metzger, & Borkovec, 1990). Moreover, measures of worry have been found to differentiate patients with *DSM-III-R* GAD from patients with obsessive-compulsive disorder (OCD), which is noteworthy in light of the fact that the potential boundary problems between GAD and OCD (e.g., the distinction between chronic worry and obsessions) were given considerable attention during the preparation of *DSM-IV* (cf. Brown, Dowdall, Côté, & Barlow, 1994; Brown, Barlow, & Liebowitz, 1994; Turner, Beidel, & Stanley, 1992). In addition to observing that GAD and OCD co-occur infrequently, Brown, Moras et al. (1993) found that GAD was distinguished from OCD by PSWQ scores, and items from the GAD section of the ADIS-R (e.g., percentage of the day spent worrying; presence or absence of excessive worry about minor matters). OCD was differentiated from GAD on measures of obsessions and compulsions [e.g., scores on the Maudsley Obsessional Compulsive Inventory (MOCI; Hodgson & Rachman, 1977) and screening items from the OCD section of the ADIS-R]. The GAD and OCD groups did not differ on measures of associated features (e.g., general indices of anxious and depressive symptoms).

Despite initial evidence that GAD and OCD can be differentiated by various measures of key features (e.g., chronic worry, obsessions), it is interesting to note that the behavioral features of these disorders may represent an unstudied point of overlap. Research indicates that the majority of persons with OCD engage in behavioral compulsions that are completed in attempt to neutralize or reduce distress associated with an obsession (Foa & Kozak, 1995). Although not part of the diagnostic definition of GAD, research (e.g., Craske et al., 1989) has indicated that a large percentage of persons with this disorder engage in behaviors that are executed to cope with or prevent a feared outcome associated with their worry (e.g., a person who worries excessively about his or her children's well-being may check on them repeatedly). Because these behaviors are common and are believed to be functionally related to the maintenance of GAD, they are often formal targets of current psychosocial treatments of this disorder (cf. Brown, O'Leary, & Barlow, 1993). Although such safety behaviors are not necessarily unique to GAD (e.g., some patients with panic disorder repetitively check their pulse to allay concerns of cardiac dysfunction), they represent another potential point of overlap with OCD and thus are worthy of future research.

Measures of GAD Associated Symptoms Recently, a number of studies have produced converging evidence that GAD may be allied with a set of associated symptoms that fosters its distinction from the other anxiety disorders. As noted earlier, when GAD was introduced as a nonresidual diagnostic category in *DSM-III-R*, the associated symptom criterion consisted of 18 symptoms forming three clusters (i.e., Autonomic Hyperactivity, Motor Tension; Vigilance and Scanning). However, research conducted after the publication of *DSM-III-R* indicated that, on structured interviews, patients with GAD endorsed symptoms from the Autonomic Hyperactivity cluster (e.g., accelerated heart rate, shortness of breath) less frequently than symptoms from the other two clusters (e.g., Brawman-Mintzer et al., 1994; Marten et al., 1993; Noyes et al., 1992). Indeed, the associated symptoms that were reported by patients with GAD at the highest frequency were irritability, restlessness or feeling keyed up, muscle tension, easy fatigability, sleep difficulties, and concentration difficulties (Marten et al., 1993). Additional research has indicated that, although patients with GAD report autonomic symptoms with some frequency (albeit at a lower rate than symptoms from the other two symptom clusters), these patients could be most strongly differentiated from patients with other anxiety disorders (panic disorder, social phobia, simple phobia, OCD) by the frequency and intensity of symptoms from the Motor Tension and Vigilance and Scanning clusters (Brown, Marten, & Barlow, 1995). In addition, these symptoms correlated more strongly with measures of worry and GAD severity than did symptoms of autonomic arousal. Collectively, these studies guided the decision to revise the associated symptom criterion of GAD in *DSM-IV* by eliminating all of the symptoms from the *DSM-III-R* Autonomic Hyperactivity cluster, but retaining the six symptoms from the Motor Tension and Vigilance and Scanning clusters reported by Marten et al. (1993) as being endorsed most frequently by patients with GAD.

Interestingly, the aforementioned findings based on structured interviews and questionnaires are consistent with the results of several recent psychophysiological studies. For example, the one psychophysiological measure that patients with GAD have been found to evidence *greater* responsiveness than normal controls at baseline and in response to psychological challenge is muscle tension (i.e., frontalis and gastrocnemius EMG; Hazlett, McLeod, & Hoehn-Saric, 1994; Hoehn-Saric, McLeod, & Zimmerli, 1989; cf. Hoehn-Saric & McLeod, 1988), dovetailing with self-report findings that symptoms of tension, irritability, and so on, are most predominant in GAD and most strongly associated with measures of worry. Conversely, initial studies failed to detect differences between worriers and nonworriers (or patients with GAD and normal controls) on cardiovascular indices collected while participants were at rest or were engaging in laboratory-induced worry challenges (e.g., Borkovec, Robinson, Pruzinsky, & DePree, 1983). Thus, the collective findings of these investigations suggested that, although patients with GAD and chronic worriers evidence elevated muscle tension while at rest and in response to laboratory challenges, they do not display a sympathetic activation response that is typically found in other anxiety disorders (cf. Hoehn-Saric & McLeod, 1988).

Subsequent research has indicated that GAD and worry are indeed associated with autonomic inflexibility (Borkovec & Hu, 1990; Borkovec, Lyonfields, Wiser, & Diehl, 1993; Hoehn-Saric et al., 1989). That is, relative to nonanxious comparison subjects, persons with GAD evidence a restricted range of autonomic activity (e.g., lowered heart rate variability) at baseline and in response to laboratory stressors (e.g., periods of worry or exposure to aversive imagery). Moreover, a significant reduction in cardiovascular variability has been observed in nonanxious controls from baseline to aversive imagery induction; however, this reduction in variability was most dramatic during a period of worrisome thinking, suggesting the generalizability of the link between worry and autonomic suppression to nonclinical subjects (Lyonfields, Borkovec, & Thayer, 1995). Although findings of autonomic rigidity in GAD were initially attributed to an inhibition in sympathetic nervous system activity (Hoehn-Saric et al., 1989), more recent findings suggest that this phenomenon may be due to chronic reductions in parasympathetic (vagal) tone (e.g., Lyonfields et al., 1995). Regardless of the underlying mechanisms, these collective findings are consistent with the results of clinical assessment studies (e.g., Brown, Marten, & Barlow, 1995) indicating that GAD is associated with a predominance of symptoms of negative affect/tension (e.g., muscle tension, irritability) and a relative infrequency of autonomic symptoms (e.g., accelerated heart rate). In addition to fostering the distinction between GAD and other anxiety disorders of GAD, these findings are of key salience to current conceptual models of GAD and pathological worry (see "Conceptual Models of GAD" section).

Distinguishability of GAD from the Mood Disorders

Measures of worry and associated symptoms have been less successful at differentiating GAD from the mood disorders (i.e., major depression, dysthymia). For example, Starcevic (1995) reported that patients with a principal diagnosis of *DSM-III-R* major depression obtained virtually identical scores on the Penn State Worry Questionnaire as did patients with GAD (cf. Brown, Anson, & DiBartolo, 1996).

Similarly, GAD cannot be distinguished from the mood disorders on symptoms constituting the associated symptom criterion of *DSM-IV* GAD. As noted earlier, Brown, Marten, and Barlow (1995) found that patients with GAD obtained significantly higher scores on composite measures of the *DSM-IV* associated symptom criterion and *DSM-III-R* Motor Tension and Vigilance and Scanning clusters than did all other anxiety disorder patient groups. However, in this study, patients with GAD did not differ from patients with mood disorders (major depression, dysthymia) on these measures. The GAD group did obtain significantly higher scores than the depression group on the *DSM-III-R* Autonomic Hyperactivity cluster, perhaps supporting some researchers' concerns that the elimination of autonomic symptoms from the *DSM-IV* definition of GAD may obfuscate its boundary with the mood disorders. Indeed, this emerging evidence of the poor discriminability of indices of worry and associated symptoms suggests that the mood disorders may pose greater boundary problems for *DSM-IV* GAD than do other anxiety disorders.

These findings could also be viewed as being highly consistent with the tripartite model of anxiety and depression (Clark & Watson, 1991; Clark, Watson, & Mineka, 1994). In brief, this model forwards a structure of anxiety and depression consisting of: (1) *negative affect* (or general distress), which is shared by both anxiety and mood disorders; (2) *physiological hyperarousal*, which is specific to anxiety disorders; and (3) low *positive affect* (anhedonia), which is specific to mood disorders. In addition to providing a compelling account for the common and unique features of anxiety and depression, the tripartite model may have considerable importance for the understanding of the pathogenesis of anxiety and mood disorders. For example, negative affect, and possibly low positive affect, may represent key vulnerability factors (traits) for the development of anxiety and mood disorders (Clark, Watson, & Mineka, 1994; Costa & McCrae, 1988; Tellegen et al., 1988; Watson & Clark, 1984). Although longitudinal research is needed to explicate the role of these dimensions in the pathogenesis of emotional disorders, several recent cross-sectional studies have produced findings that support the tripartite structure of anxiety and depressive symptoms in clinical populations (e.g., Brown, Chorpita, & Barlow, 1998; Clark, Steer, & Beck, 1994; Joiner, Catanzaro, & Laurent, 1996; Watson et al., 1995).

Given that worry and each of the associated symptoms of *DSM-IV* GAD are considered to be symptoms of negative affect, it may not be surprising that GAD and mood disorders cannot be differentiated on these features because negative affect is common to anxiety and mood disorders, and because of the various emotional disorders, GAD and mood disorders are associated with the highest levels of negative affect (Brown et al., 1998). Similarly, although symptoms of autonomic arousal are regarded in the tripartite model to be specific to anxiety disorders, this may not be true for GAD in light of recent evidence of autonomic suppression in this disorder. Thus, unlike most of the other anxiety disorders (especially panic disorder), autonomic arousal symptoms may not differentiate GAD from mood disorders (although findings from Brown, Marten, & Barlow, 1995, suggest that while autonomic symptoms occur less frequently in GAD, they may still foster its distinction from mood disorders). Rather, consistent with predictions from the tripartite model, emerging data suggest that GAD can be differentiated from depression on indices of low positive affect (anhedonia), although this distinction may be stronger for other disorders than for GAD (Brown et al., 1996; Clark, Beck, & Beck, 1994). Evidence of the close boundary between GAD and depression supports the retention of the *DSM-IV* hierarchy rule specifying that GAD should not be diagnosed if its features occur exclusively during a mood disorder (i.e., co-diagnoses might be redundant given that the defining features of GAD are prevalent associated features of mood disorders) and speak to the need for future investigation on the boundary and distinguishing characteristics of these disorders.

Latent Structure of Dimensions of Anxiety and Depressive Symptoms Most studies addressing the validity of GAD or the validity of current classification systems of anxiety and mood disorders have been conducted at the diagnostic level (e.g., family and twin studies), or have examined dimensional features within a diagnostic category (e.g., across-diagnosis comparisons to determine if a given disorder is distinguished from other disorders on a given dimension). As has been discussed at length elsewhere (e.g., Brown & Chorpita, 1996; Costello, 1992; Livesley, Schroeder, Jackson, & Jang, 1994), the categorical approach to analysis has many limitations. For one, studies conducted at the diagnostic level are restricted by their adherence to the disorders defined by the classification system (i.e., by using diagnoses as the units of analysis, researchers are implicitly accepting or are bound to the nosology they are evaluating). Moreover, if one assumes that the symptoms constituting the various emotional disorders operate on a continuum, analyses at the diagnostic level rely on data that do not reflect the dimensional nature of these features. Categorization of dimensional variables may usually forfeit meaningful information by artificially (and often erroneously) collapsing variability above and below an arbitrary threshold (e.g., presence or absence of a *DSM-IV* disorder). If assessment was performed at the dimensional level, the interrelationships among symptoms and syndromes could be examined, as could the extent to which the latent structure of these features corresponds to how these features are organized in *DSM-IV*.

Studies of this nature that bear on the validity and parameters of GAD have begun to appear (e.g., Zinbarg & Barlow, 1996). For example, we recently examined the relationships of dimensional features of selected *DSM-IV* disorders and dimensions of the tripartite model of anxiety and depression (Clark & Watson, 1991) in a large sample of patients with *DSM-IV* anxiety and mood disorders (Brown et al., 1998). The five *DSM-IV* constructs evaluated in this study (i.e., mood disorders, GAD, panic disorder and agoraphobia, OCD, social phobia) were defined by questionnaires and clinical interview ratings. Results of confirmatory factor analysis supported the discriminant validity of *DSM-IV* for the constructs examined. Outcome of these analyses favored a five-factor model (suggesting that these *DSM-IV* constructs form five distinct factors) over models in which some or all of the *DSM-IV* factors were collapsed (e.g., a model where features of GAD and mood disorders were collapsed under a single factor). Nevertheless, correlations among the five factors highlighted areas of overlap. For instance, the GAD factor was most strongly correlated with the mood disorder factor supporting prior contentions that the features of GAD have the most overlap with the mood disorders. The OCD factor had its strongest correlation with the GAD factor, consistent with the position that the closest "neighbor" to OCD among the emotional disorders is GAD (cf. Turner et al., 1992).

Brown et al. (1998) also evaluated the interrelationships among the five *DSM-IV* factors and the factors from the tripartite model of anxiety and depression (i.e., negative affect, positive affect, autonomic arousal). Consistent with the theoretical predictions discussed earlier (cf. Clark, Watson, & Mineka, 1994), negative affect was significantly related to each of the five *DSM-IV* factors (with strongest relationships with GAD and mood disorder), and positive affect was significantly related to mood disorder and social phobia only. These results are consistent with the tripartite model, which views negative affect as a feature or trait that is shared by anxiety and mood disorders, but has its strongest associations with GAD and mood disorders.

Moreover, results indicated that the GAD and autonomic arousal (AA) factors were inversely related when variance in negative affect was held constant. Thus, findings suggested that the true direct influence of the disorder-specific features of GAD on AA involves a negative relationship (i.e., an increase in worry is associated with a decrease in autonomic symptoms). In addition to supporting current psychosocial models and laboratory studies of GAD, the results may highlight another point of distinction between GAD and the mood disorders (GAD, but not the disorder-specific features of depression, is associated with autonomic suppression).

Family and Genetic Studies Data from family and genetic studies have provided mixed support for the validity of GAD at the diagnostic level. The findings of two studies indicate that *DSM-III* and *DSM-III-R* GAD are discriminable from panic disorder on the basis of the familial aggregation of the two disorders (Noyes et al., 1987, 1992), although these studies are limited by small sample sizes (Noyes et al., 1987), or establishing diagnoses in first-order relatives based solely on proband report (Noyes et al., 1992). No published study to date has examined the extent to which differential familial aggregation patterns exist for GAD relative to disorders that are considered to have the closest or most overlapping boundaries (e.g., mood disorders, OCD).

A number of investigations have examined the genetics of GAD more directly. Although a few early studies failed to find a clear role of genetic factors in *DSM-III* GAD (Andrews, Stewart, Allen, & Henderson, 1990; Torgersen, 1983), more recent findings based on *DSM-III-R* criteria have documented a genetic contribution to GAD (cf. Kendler, Neale, Kessler, Heath, & Eaves, 1992a, 1992b; Kendler et al., 1995; Roy, Neale, Pedersen, Mathé, & Kendler, 1995; Skre, Onstad, Torgersen, Lygren, & Kringlen, 1993). For example, in a study of 1,033 blindly assessed female-female twin pairs from the population-based Virginia Twin Registry, Kendler et al. (1992a) concluded that GAD is a moderately familial disorder, with a heritability estimated at around 30% (the remainder of variance in GAD liability may result from environmental factors not shared by the adult twins). Further research in both all female (Kendler et al., 1992b) and mixed-sex twin samples (Roy et al., 1995) has indicated that whereas a clear genetic influence exists in GAD, the genetic factors in GAD are completely shared with major depression. However, although GAD and major depression share the same genetic factors, their environmental determinants appear to be mostly distinct. Similar results have been obtained in studies evaluating the genetic and environmental contributions to a broader spectrum of disorders (e.g., Kendler et al., 1995) and to anxiety and depression assessed at the symptom (vs. diagnostic) level (Kendler, Heath, Martin, & Eaves, 1987). As elaborated on in the next section, these findings are consistent with conceptual models of emotional disorders (Barlow et al., 1996) which posit that anxiety and mood disorders share common diatheses (i.e., biological vulnerabilities), but differ on important dimensions (e.g., focus of attention, degree of psychosocial vulnerability to environmental experiences of uncontrollability) to the extent that differentiation is warranted.

Conceptual Models of Generalized Anxiety Disorder and Pathological Worry

GAD as Vulnerability to Other Emotional Disorders Although the preceding sections reviewed the extant literature primarily within the framework of the validity of GAD as a diagnostic category, these data have considerable importance to conceptual models of GAD. As noted earlier, GAD as been conceptualized as the "basic" emotional disorder because its constituent features (e.g., worry, negative affect) are present to varying degrees in all anxiety and mood disorders, and because it exemplifies, most purely, the process of anxious apprehension (cf. Barlow et al., 1996; Brown, Barlow, & Liebowitz, 1994). Indeed, the features of GAD are considered to be vulnerability dimensions in leading etiological models of emotional disorders (Clark & Watson, 1991; Clark, Watson, & Mineka, 1994). For instance, GAD is associated with a high level of negative affect (Brown et al., 1998), a construct that is increasingly regarded as a higher order trait that acts as a vulnerability dimension for anxiety and mood disorders (Clark, Watson, & Mineka, 1994). In addition to the evidence reviewed earlier that GAD is typically associated with an early and gradual onset, initial findings indicate that GAD or its symptoms often precede or represent a prodrome for co-occurring disorders such as panic disorder and mood disorders (e.g., Garvey, Cook, & Noyes, 1988; Nisita et al., 1990). These collective findings have been interpreted as indicating that, although feature overlap (poor discriminant validity or diagnostician error) may account in part for the consistent finding that GAD rarely presents isolation of other disorders, the high comorbidity rate associated with GAD may also be due to the fact that the features of GAD, which often seem to emerge long before subsequent disorders, contribute to the predisposition for the development of other anxiety and mood disorders (cf. Brown, Barlow, & Liebowitz, 1994). Furthermore, of the various anxiety disorders, GAD has been the most resistant to psychosocial and pharmacological interventions (cf. Brown, O'Leary, & Barlow, 1993). Findings of poorer treatment outcomes of GAD could also be construed as being consistent with a characterological or vulnerability conceptualization of this disorder; however, this could also be due to fact that it has been only recently that specialized psychosocial treatments have been developed to directly target the key features of GAD (cf. Borkovec & Costello, 1993; Brown, Barlow, & Liebowitz, 1994).

The viability of these conceptual positions requires empirical analysis. Although GAD may well be best conceptualized as a trait or a general vulnerability (as opposed to an Axis I disorder), a substantial body of evidence attests to the construct and discriminant validity of the disorder. Yet, if negative affect and worry are indeed vulnerability dimensions, it is not clear why for some individuals these characteristics simply act as a predisposition for other disorders (e.g., a prodrome to mood disorders), whereas for others, these dimensions become sufficiently prominent to require a separate diagnosis (i.e., GAD) and a specialized treatment. Also, a trait conceptualization may not account for GAD onsets occurring later in life.

Models of the Nature and Functions of Pathological Worry The most widely recognized model of pathological worry has been provided by Borkovec (Borkovec, 1994; Borkovec et al., 1991). Borkovec regards worry as a predominantly conceptual, verbal-linguistic attempt to avoid future aversive events and aversive imagery (i.e., cognitive avoidance of threat); this process is experienced by the worrier as negative-affect laden and uncontrollable. Pathological worry (GAD) is associated with diffuse perceptions that the world is threatening and that one may not be able to cope with or control future negative events (Barlow et al., 1996; Borkovec, 1994). A number of studies have confirmed the notion that worry is characterized by a predominance of thought activity and low levels of imagery (e.g., Borkovec & Inz, 1990; Borkovec & Lyonfields, 1993; cf. East & Watts, 1994). These findings are bolstered by evidence that engaging in worry is associated with an increase in frontal cortical activation, and this activation is greater in the left hemisphere for worriers than for nonworriers (Carter, Johnson, & Borkovec, 1986), consistent with the notion that pathological worry is characterized by repetitious, habitual thought patterns (cf. Tucker, 1981). Borkovec (1994) further postulates that worry is negatively reinforcing because it is associated with the avoidance of or escape from more threatening imagery and more distressing somatic activation. Support for the position that worry may prevent certain somatic experience comes from the host of studies reviewed earlier showing that worry suppresses autonomic activity (e.g., Lyonfields et al., 1995).

According to the Borkovec model, although the avoidant functions of worry provide short-term relief from more distressing levels of anxiety, the long-term consequences of worry include the inhibition of emotional processing and the maintenance of anxiety-producing cognitions (cf. Mathews, 1990). For example, whereas patients with GAD may regard worry as an effective problem-solving strategy that has other benefits (e.g., prevents catastrophe or prepares one to cope with future negative events), it maintains clinical anxiety for a number of reasons. For example, if worry does indeed serve to foster the avoidance of imagery, then emotional processing of threatening material would be prevented because worry inhibits the complete activation of fear structures in memory, a process considered to be *necessary* for permanent anxiety reduction (Foa & Kozak, 1986). The failure to fully access these fear structures may also account for the autonomic inhibition associated with GAD. The avoidant nature of worry would hinder effective problem solving of true life circumstances (e.g., the content of worry often jumps from topic to another without resolution any particular concern). However, because pathological worry is perceived as uncontrollable and because it prevents emotional processing, the afflicted individual is prone to experience heightened negative affect and cognitive intrusions in the future. For instance, research has shown that uncontrollability of negative thinking correlates with the intensity and frequency of such thoughts (e.g., Clark & de Silva, 1985; Parkinson & Rachman, 1981a). Moreover, although the underlying mechanisms are not clear (cf. Borkovec, 1994), a few studies have produced findings indicating that having participants engage in a period of worry prior to and/or following exposure to laboratory stressors (e.g., viewing aversive films, giving a speech) precludes emotional processing (anxiety reduction) and increases subsequent intrusive thinking about these stressors (Borkovec & Hu, 1990; Butler, Wells, & Dewick, 1995).

Models of the Origins of Pathological Worry and GAD

Although initial models of anxiety were basically unidimensional (i.e., purely biological or purely psychosocial), increasingly these conceptualizations are becoming more integrative. In most of these models, GAD is viewed as representing an excess of features (i.e., worry, negative affect) found in persons without mental disorders, with the key differences between pathological and nonpathological states being the frequency, intensity, and uncontrollability of these phenomena (Borkovec, 1994; Borkovec et al., 1991). Assuming that these features operate on a continuum, the issue remains why some individuals develop these symptoms at pathological levels. In addressing this issue, some models (e.g., Barlow et al., 1996) posit that anxiety and depression share a common biological vulnerability that is best characterized as an overactive neurobiological response to life stress. Support for the position that a shared pathophysiology contributes to anxiety and mood disorders comes from the large-scale genetic studies reviewed earlier in this chapter (e.g., Kendler et al., 1992b). Although relatively little empirical attention has been paid to the biology of GAD, several neurotransmitter systems (e.g., GABA-benzodiazepine, noradrenergic, serotonergic) and areas of the limbic system of the brain (e.g., septal-hippocampal system) have been implicated as potentially fruitful directions for further research (Cowley & Roy-Byrne, 1991; Gray, 1982).

However, most current models do not assert that biological factors alone are responsible for the origins of GAD. For example, in one model (Barlow et al., 1996), the processes of GAD are viewed as also being rooted in psychological vulnerabilities that stem from early experiences of uncontrollability. Although the nature of these early experiences may be multifold, Borkovec (1994) has asserted that childhood histories of psychosocial trauma (e.g., death of parent, exposure to physical/sexual abuse) and insecure attachment to primary caregivers may be particularly salient to the origins of this psychological vulnerability. Finally, this psychological vulnerability, combined with a biological vulnerability and triggered by the stress of negative life events, results in clinical anxiety (GAD). Interestingly, the Barlow model also posits that clinical depression may represent "endstate anxiety"; specifically, that depression may reflect a more extreme psychological vulnerability to experiences of uncontrollability. In other words, anxiety may lead to depression depending on the extent of one's psychological and biological vulnerabilities, the severity of current life stressors, and the coping mechanisms at one's disposal. Similar arguments have been forwarded by other researchers (e.g., Alloy, Kelly, Mineka, & Clements, 1990), although the mechanisms of this temporal process vary across models to some degree (e.g., emphasis on a cognitive continuum of helplessness-hopelessness). Although requiring verification by future research, these models provide a plausible account for the temporal sequence of comorbidity often observed at the descriptive level between GAD and the mood disorders.

Obsessive-Compulsive Disorder

Overview and History of Obsessive-Compulsive Disorder

In *DSM-IV*, obsessive-compulsive disorder (OCD) is defined by the presence of recurrent obsessions *or* compulsions that are severe enough to be time-consuming (i.e., take more than an hour per day) or cause significant distress or significant impairment. *Obsessions* are defined by *DSM-IV* as recurrent and persistent thoughts, impulses, or images that are experienced, at some time during the disturbance, as intrusive and inappropriate and that cause marked anxiety and distress. *Compulsions* are defined as repetitive behaviors (e.g., hand washing, checking) or mental acts (e.g., praying, counting) that are engaged in to prevent or reduce anxiety or distress. Although somewhat controversial (see below), the *DSM-IV* criteria state that, in order to qualify for the diagnosis of OCD, the person must at some time during the course of his or her disturbance recognize that the obsessions and compulsions are excessive and unreasonable (a criterion that does not apply in children).

The definition of OCD has undergone less change than has GAD over the last three editions of *DSM*. The symptoms of OCD were classified under "obsessive-compulsive neurosis" in *DSM-II*. In the reorganization of disorders introduced in *DSM-III*, OCD resided in the new subcategory of anxiety disorders termed "anxiety states." In *DSM-III*, diagnostic criteria for GAD required the presence of obsessions or compulsions that were associated with significant distress or impairment and were not due to another mental disorder (e.g., schizophrenia, depression). The definition of OCD was essentially the same in *DSM-III-R*, although the removal of most diagnostic hierarchy rules in *DSM-III* allowed OCD to be assigned more frequently (e.g., the diagnosis could be made even if it occurred during the course of other disorders such as major depression, provided that the OCD symptoms could not be better accounted for by another disorder).

A few important changes were made to the definition of OCD in *DSM-IV*. For the first time, "mental" compulsions were recognized (mental acts, such as silently counting or repeating words or prayers). Prior to *DSM-IV*, a traditional view prevailed in the nosology that regarded obsessions as mental events (e.g., thoughts, images, and impulses) and regarded compulsions as observable, overt behaviors (e.g., checking, washing). However, this conceptualization was inconsistent with more current views that regard obsessions as mental events that *produce distress* and compulsions as either behaviors or mental acts that are performed to *reduce this distress* (Foa & Tillmanns, 1980). Moreover, although the majority of persons with OCD engage in behavioral compulsions that are completed in attempt to neutralize or reduce distress associated with an obsession, research has shown that in up to 25% of cases, compulsive behavior is not evident (Foa & Kozak, 1995). Although these data had been interpreted by some researchers as indicating that a significant minority of persons with OCD do not experience compulsions (note that the diagnostic criteria for OCD do not require the presence of both obsessions *and* compulsions), most of these findings were generated prior to the recognition of mental compulsions in *DSM-IV*. Thus, when mental compulsions are considered, it appears that there actually exists only a very small proportion of persons with OCD who do not evidence any form of compulsions whatsoever (e.g., in one study of a large sample of patients with OCD, only 2.1% were classified as having obsessions without compulsions; Foa & Kozak, 1995).

In addition to its obvious implications for the assessment and diagnosis of OCD, the recognition of mental compulsions may have important ramifications for treatment. Quantitative reviews of the literature have indicated that patients with OCD who do not display overt compulsions are the least responsive to treatment (Christensen, Hadzi-Pavlovic, Andrews, & Mattick, 1987). It has been suggested that this poorer outcome might be related to clinicians' failure to identify and address mental compulsions (Salkovskis & Westbrook, 1989). It is hoped that the acknowledgment of mental compulsions in *DSM-IV* will foster the recognition of these symptoms, resulting in their incorporation into leading interventions of OCD (e.g., exposure and response prevention; cf. Riggs & Foa, 1993).

A major revision to the diagnostic criteria for OCD in *DSM-IV* was the deemphasis on the requirement that persons with OCD recognize that their obsessions and compulsions are senseless (Foa & Kozak, 1995). Indeed, in *DSM-IV* the diagnosis of OCD can now be assigned with the specifier "poor insight type" to reflect cases in which, for most of the time during the disturbance, the person does not recognize that the obsessions and compulsions are excessive or unreasonable. These changes may bear on the distinction between OCD and the delusional and schizophrenic disorders. Whereas researchers had begun to converge on the conclusion that the empirical evidence does not support a relationship between OCD and the schizophrenic disorders (Tynes, White, & Steketee, 1990; cf. Enright, 1996), this revision to the *DSM-IV* criteria for OCD is likely to renew clinical and empirical interest in the potential boundary problems between overvalued obsessions and delusional beliefs. For instance, what are the quantitative or qualitative differences between delusions vs. obsessions that the individual insists are reasonable (cf. Foa & Kozak, 1995; Kozak & Foa, 1994)?

To assist in clarifying this boundary, the *DSM-*

IV definition of OCD includes the requirement that the person must *at some time during the course of his or her disturbance* recognize that the obsessions and compulsions are excessive and unreasonable (although OCD can be assigned with the "with poor insight" specifier for patients who do not currently recognize that their symptoms are senseless).[2] Research findings generally support this criterion because most patients who lack insight at the time of assessment report having insight at an earlier time (Foa & Kozak, 1995). Also, the *DSM-IV* criteria for obsessions require that the person recognize that the obsessions are a product of his or her own mind. This latter specification is important in the differentiation of OCD from psychotic disorders, where intrusive and distressing thoughts or images are often perceived by the individual as being inserted into one's mind from an outside source.

Findings suggest that patients' perceptions of the senselessness of their symptoms are distributed along a continuum (Foa & Kozak, 1995). In response to a structured interview item that inquired about patients' belief intensity of their feared consequence (e.g., contract a disease through germ contamination), only 13% responded that they were certain that their feared consequence would *not* occur; 27% were mostly certain. However, 26% were mostly certain that the consequence *would* occur, and 4% were completely certain that it would occur. Based on another measure used in the study, 8% of the sample were classified as currently having poor insight, and 5% had never recognized the senselessness of their symptoms. These findings were interpreted by Foa and Kozak (1995) as supporting the *DSM-IV* criterion revision that deemphasizes patient recognition of the senselessness of symptoms. In addition to communicating more information about the diagnosis and possibly predicting its response to treatment (cf. Kozak & Foa, 1994), Foa and Kozak (1995) asserted that the inclusion of the "with poor insight" specifier may promote the empirical evaluation of the relationship and boundary of OCD with other aspects of psychopathology (e.g., the psychotic disorders). Initial findings indicate that although the prevalence of schizophrenia in OCD may be slightly higher than the rate of schizophrenia in the general population, there does not appear to be any special association between these disorders (Black & Noyes, 1990; Kozak & Foa, 1994; cf. Enright, 1996).

Epidemiology, Diagnostic Reliability, Comorbidity, and Presenting Characteristics of Obsessive-Compulsive Disorder

Epidemiology Findings from epidemiological studies indicate that the lifetime prevalence of *DSM-III* OCD is 2.5% (Karno & Golding, 1991; Karno, Golding, Sorenson, & Burnam, 1988); six-month prevalence estimates have ranged from 1.3 to 2.0% (Myers et al., 1984). Some researchers believe that these may be underestimates of the true prevalence of OCD, owing to a number of factors such as misdiagnosis, poor screening instruments, and underreport of symptoms by interviewees. Additional evidence suggests that many people experience the symptoms of OCD that, while not meeting the *DSM* definition of the disorder, are nonetheless associated with some degree of distress or lifestyle interference. For example, one study found that 10 to 15% of "normal" college undergraduates reported engaging in some form of checking behavior that was substantial enough to score within the range of patients with OCD (Frost, Sher, & Geen, 1986). Often, subclinical OCD symptoms (e.g., intrusive thoughts, checking) are precipitated by some form of life stress (Parkinson & Rachman, 1981a, 1981b).

Evidence from patient and epidemiological samples indicates that 55 to 60% of patients with OCD are female (Karno & Golding, 1991; Rasmussen & Tsuang, 1986). The average age of onset of the disorder ranges from early adolescence to the mid-20s (Karno et al., 1988), although onsets in childhood and late adulthood are not uncommon (cf. Flament et al., 1988; Flint, 1994; Whitaker et al., 1990). Males have an earlier peak age of onset (i.e., ages 13–15) than do females (ages 20–24; Rasmussen & Eisen, 1990; Swedo, Rapoport, Leonard, Lenane, & Cheslow, 1989). Although acute onset has been noted in some cases, most patients recall a gradual or insidious onset of their OCD (Rasmussen & Eisen, 1990). The untreated course of OCD is usually continuous and "waxing and waning"; often exacerbations in symptoms are related to life stress. However, approximately 10 to 15% of patients show a progressively deteriorating course, and a small percentage (roughly 2–5%) report an episodic course with minimal or no symptoms between episodes (e.g., Rasmussen & Eisen, 1988).

Diagnostic Reliability Unlike GAD, OCD has typically been associated with high levels of diagnostic reliability. For instance, in studies examining the reliability of *DSM-III-R* anxiety disorders, the principal diagnosis of OCD has evidenced excellent diagnostic reliability (calculated on the basis of two independent administrations of the structured interviews such as the ADIS-R), both as a current diagnosis (kappas = .91 and .80 in Mannuzza et al., 1989, and Di Nardo et al., 1993, respectively), and as a lifetime diagnosis (kappa = .89 in Mannuzza et al., 1989). Preliminary evidence based on a limited number of patients with anxiety or mood disorders suggests that the *DSM-IV* diagnosis of OCD is associated with excellent diagnostic reliability as well (kappa = .90; Di Nardo et al., 1995).

Comorbidity In clinical samples, OCD is associated with high rates of diagnostic comorbidity, with at least 50% of patients with a principal diagnosis of OCD having additional anxiety and mood disorders at the time of their evaluation (e.g., Brown & Barlow, 1992; Sanderson, Di Nardo, Rapee, & Barlow, 1990). The mood disorders (major depression, dysthymia), panic disorder, and phobias (social and specific) are particularly common in OCD patient samples (cf. Brown & Barlow, 1992; Rasmussen & Eisen, 1988), a result that is generally consistent with findings from epidemiological studies (Karno et al., 1988). Relative to the other anxiety disorders (except perhaps for GAD and panic disorder with severe agoraphobia; cf. Brown & Barlow, 1992), OCD is more likely to be associated with current or past mood disorders. Roughly two thirds of patients with OCD have a lifetime history of clinical depression, and 30 to 40% have a co-occurring mood disorder at the time of evaluation (Rasmussen & Eisen, 1988). Preliminary evidence bearing on the temporal sequence of these disorders suggests that depression typically follows the onset of OCD (Karno et al., 1988). In child and adolescent patients with OCD, comorbidity with other anxiety disorders, such as specific phobia and overanxious disorder, is more prevalent than with the mood disorders (Swedo et al., 1989).

Personality disorders appear to be very common in OCD as well. It has been consistently found that roughly half of patients with *DSM-III* OCD meet criteria for at least one personality disorder, as determined by structured interviews (e.g., Baer et al., 1990; Black, Noyes, Pfohl, Goldstein, & Blum, 1993) or by self-report questionnaires (Mavissakalian, Hamann, & Jones, 1990a; Steketee, 1990). The most common Axis II diagnoses found in patients with OCD have been avoidant, histrionic, and dependent. In studies assessing personality disorders with questionnaires, schizotypal has been observed to be a somewhat frequent co-occurring diagnosis (e.g., 16% in Mavissakalian et al., 1990a); however, studies using structured interviews have obtained much lower comorbidity rates of OCD and schizotypal personality disorder (e.g., 5–8%; Baer et al., 1990; Stanley, Turner, & Borden, 1990). Interestingly, compulsive personality disorder (renamed obsessive-compulsive personality disorder in *DSM-III-R* and *DSM-IV*) was diagnosed infrequently in most of these studies. As is true for all anxiety disorders, these collective figures may be overestimates of the comorbidity between OCD and Axis II disorders, given the prevalent use of self-report assessment and the inherent overlap in the features constituting the Axis I and II disorders as they are currently defined (cf. Widiger & Shea, 1991). For example, several studies have indicated that pharmacological and psychosocial treatment for OCD produces substantial reductions in personality disorder symptoms and diagnoses (e.g., Mavissakalian, Hamann, & Jones, 1990b; Ricciardi et al., 1992), which could be indicative of overdiagnosis or overlap in the constituent features of these disorders (Brown & Barlow, 1992).

Several studies have shown an association between OCD and the tic disorders such as Tourette's syndrome. Studies of patients with OCD indicate that 20 to 30% report a current or past history of tics (e.g., Pauls, 1989); 5 to 7% of patients with OCD have been found to suffer from the full-blown Tourette's syndrome (Rasmussen & Eisen, 1989). Studies of patients with Tourette's syndrome indicate that 36 to 52% meet criteria for OCD (Leckman & Chittenden, 1990; Pauls, Towbin, Leckman, Zahner, & Cohen, 1986). These results have been interpreted as indicating that OCD and Tourette's syndrome may have a shared genetic basis or underlying pathophysiology (cf. Black & Noyes, 1990). This interpretation is bolstered by recent findings of a study that revealed that the rate of tic disorders was significantly greater among relatives of OCD probands (5%) than among relatives of comparison subjects (1%; Pauls, Alsobrook, Goodman, Rasmussen, & Leckman, 1995).

Presenting Features In *DSM-IV*, obsessions are characterized by recurrent and persistent thoughts, impulses, or images that are experienced as intrusive and inappropriate and that cause marked anxiety or distress, which the person attempts to ignore, suppress, or neutralize with some other thought or action (compulsion). Common types of obsessions include thoughts of contamination (e.g., contracting germs from doorknobs, money, toilets), excessive doubting (e.g., uncertainty if one has locked the door or turned off appliances; concerns that tasks such as managing personal finances were not completed or were completed inaccurately), fear that one has caused accidental harm to oneself or others (e.g., accidentally poisoning someone, unknowingly hitting a pedestrian while driving), nonsensical or aggressive impulses (e.g., undressing in public, hurting oneself or others intentionally), horrific or sexual images or impulses (e.g., images of mutilated bodies, images of having sex with one's parents or a religious figure), need for symmetry or to have things in a certain order, and nonsensical thoughts or images (e.g., numbers, letters, songs, jingles, or phrases).

Results from clinical samples indicate that most patients with OCD experience more than one type of obsession (e.g., 60% in Rasmussen & Eisen, 1988). Using a large sample of patients presenting to a specialty clinic for OCD, Rasmussen and Eisen (1988) determined the most common obsessions to be contamination (45%), pathological doubting (42%), somatic (36%), and need for symmetry (31%). Roughly one quarter of their sample reported aggressive and sexual obsessions as well. In a more recent study, Foa and Kozak (1995) reported the frequency of primary obsessions in a large sample of patients with OCD ("primary" was defined as the obsession associated with the highest frequency and severity). The most common primary obsessions were contamination (41.4%), fear of harming oneself or others (24.2%), and somatic (10.7%). All other types of obsessions were primary in less than 10% of cases.

Compulsions are defined by *DSM-IV* as repetitive behaviors or mental acts that the person feels driven to perform in response to an obsession, or according to rules that must be applied rigidly, which are engaged in to prevent or reduce distress or to prevent a dreaded event or situation. These behaviors or mental acts are not connected in a realistic way with what they are designed to neutralize or prevent, or they are clearly excessive. As noted earlier, *DSM-IV* now formally recognizes mental actions, as well as behavioral rituals, as forms of compulsions. Common types of behavioral compulsions include washing and cleaning, checking (e.g., door locks, appliances, retracing a driving route to ensure that a pedestrian has not been struck, reexamining waste baskets to ensure that important material has not been discarded), hoarding (e.g., collecting things such as newspapers, garbage, or trivial items), reassurance seeking (e.g., demanding assurance that one has not engaged in or failed to complete a feared action such as neglecting to turn off the stove before leaving the house; frequent calls to poison control hotlines to ensure that family members are safe from foods, household/yard objects, etc.), and adhering to certain rules and sequences (e.g., maintaining symmetry such as touching an object with one's left hand if the object had been previously touched with the right hand; adhering to specific routines or order in daily activities, such as putting on clothes in the same order). An atypical form of overt compulsion is "obsessional slowness" (Rachman & de Silva, 1978), a term used to characterize the behavior of patients who expend extraordinary amounts of time to complete daily activities (such as grooming, chores, office work) because each step of the process is carried out with meticulous care. Types of mental compulsions include counting (e.g., certain letters or numbers, objects in the environment), internal repetition of material (e.g., phrases, words, prayers), forming corrective images to "neutralize" unacceptable ideas, and cognitive attempts (e.g., distracting thoughts) to suppress obsessive thoughts or images.

As with obsessions, most patients with OCD present with multiple compulsions (Rasmussen & Eisen, 1988). For example, results of one large-scale study of patients with OCD indicated that nearly 80% of the sample experienced both mental and behavioral compulsions; patients rarely reported that they experienced mental compulsions only (0.2%; Foa & Kozak, 1995). The most common forms of compulsions observed by Rasmussen and Eisen (1988) were checking (63%), cleaning or washing (50%), and counting (36%). Others that occurred at an appreciable frequency included reassurance seeking (31%), symmetry or order (28%), and hoarding (18%). In Foa and Kozak (1995), the most common types of *primary* compulsions were checking (28.5%), cleaning or washing (27.3%), and repetitive actions (10.9%). Mental rituals were the primary form of compulsion in 9.8% of the sample, although, as noted above, they rarely occurred as the sole form of compulsion. Need for order or symmetry, hoarding, and counting were endorsed as primary compulsions infrequently (5.9%, 3.5%, and 2.3%, respectively). Consistent with current conceptual models of OCD (i.e., which assert that compulsions cannot exist without obsessions), results from Foa and Kozak (1995) also indicate that 90% of behavioral rituals and 81% of mental rituals were perceived by patients with OCD to be functionally related to obsessions (i.e., performed in response to an obsession to reduce distress). Only 1.7% of the sample was rated as having compulsions without obsessions.

Empirical Basis for Obsessive-Compulsive Disorder

Overview of Issues Although the subject of less scrutiny than GAD, the discriminant validity of OCD has also been questioned by many investigators. For example, some researchers have suggested that the high rate of co-occurrence between OCD and the mood disorders, as well as evidence that OCD may respond to antidepressant medication, points to the possibility that OCD is not an anxiety disorder but a variant of a mood disorder (e.g., Hudson & Pope, 1990; Insel, Zahn, & Murphy, 1985). In addition, OCD has been considered as being related to or overlapping with a variety of other disorders, including selected anxiety disorders (GAD, specific phobias of illness), somatoform disorders (hypochondriasis, body dysmorphic disorder), habit disorders (trichotillomania), tic disorders (Tourette's disorder), the delusional disorders, and schizophrenia (see Brown, 1998).

Latent Structure As noted earlier, recent studies have examined the latent structure of symptoms making up the various anxiety and mood disorders and found that the dimensions constituting the defining features of OCD form a distinct factor, thereby attesting to the discriminant validity of OCD (Brown et al., 1998; Zinbarg & Barlow, 1996). However, findings from both of these studies indicated that the features of OCD were most strongly associated with the features of GAD (relative to other anxiety and mood disorders). This could be viewed as supporting the contention that the disorder with the closest or most overlapping boundary with OCD is GAD, a result that has been generally upheld in studies that compared various anxiety disorder diagnostic groups on measures of key and associated symptoms (e.g., Steketee, Grayson, & Foa, 1987). However, unlike GAD, studies reviewed earlier suggest that the category of OCD is associated with high rates of diagnostic agreement, lending further support for its discriminant validity.

Family and Genetic Studies Results from genetic and family investigations have provided mixed support for the validity of OCD at the diagnostic level. Several twin studies have produced findings attesting to the genetic aggregation in OCD, with concordance rates higher among monozygotic twins (65%, on average) than among dizygotic twins (15%, on average; see Pauls, Raymond, & Robertson, 1991, and Rasmussen & Tsuang, 1986, for reviews). However, concordance in monozygotic twins is far from perfect, indicating that genetics alone does not account for the origins of this disorder. In addition, other studies have indicated that genetic factors exert a nonspecific influence for the development of anxiety disorders in general rather than risk for OCD specifically (Andrews et al., 1990; Torgersen, 1983).

Although earlier family studies found no significant elevations in risk for OCD in first-order relatives of patients with the disorder (e.g., McKeon & Murray, 1987), recent investigations employing more sophisticated methodologies (e.g., direct interview of relatives) have found the rates of OCD to be higher in relatives of probands compared to relatives of control subjects (e.g., Black, Noyes, Goldstein, & Blum, 1992; Pauls et al., 1995). For example, Pauls et al. (1995) administered structured interviews to first-degree relatives of probands with OCD and to first-degree relatives of persons with no mental disorder. The rates of OCD and subthreshold OCD were significantly greater among the relatives of probands with OCD (10.3% and 7.9%, respectively) than among relatives of comparison subjects (1.9% and 2.0%, respectively). Thus, although more research is needed to reconcile inconsistent findings from earlier studies, evidence from more recent investigations has been largely supportive of the familial nature of OCD.

Conceptual Models of Obsessive-Compulsive Disorder

Early Models Initial psychosocial models of OCD emphasized Mowrer's (1960) two-factor theory for the acquisition and maintenance of fear and avoidance behavior (e.g., Dollard & Miller, 1950). Briefly, Mowrer's theory postulates that fear acquisition occurs through the pairing of a neutral cue (e.g., thought, image, situation, object; the *conditioned stimulus*) with an aversive *unconditional stimulus* that inherently produces distress or fear. In the example of OCD, obsessive fears are posited to acquire the ability to elicit distress through the pairing of an object, thought, or image (e.g., toilets, blasphemous images) with an aversive experience. Maintenance of the obsessive fear occurs through the performance of avoidance and escape behaviors (e.g., compulsions) that reduce distress but perpetuate symptoms owing to negative reinforcement of these maneuvers and the prevention of fear extinction. For example, the compulsion of excessive handwashing may serve to temporarily reduce distress associated with obsessive fears of contamination (negative reinforcement). However, because these actions interfere with the habituation of anxiety, the fear of contamination is maintained or strengthened (akin to the notion that a person with public speaking anxiety can only become comfortable delivering speeches if he or she fully engages in this experience on numerous occasions; avoidance or escape from public speaking opportunities promotes the maintenance of those fears).

Although evidence has supported the second factor of this model (i.e., that ritualistic behaviors are negatively reinforcing because they reduce discomfort associated with obsessions; e.g., Hodgson & Rachman, 1972; Roper & Rachman, 1976), Mowrer's conceptualization of fear acquisition has not garnered much empirical support. For instance, findings indicate that fears can be acquired in multiple fashions other than through traumatic or aversive conditioning (cf. Rachman & Wilson, 1980). Alternative modes of fear acquisition, such as observational and informational learning, seem to be influential in the origins of many cases of OCD (e.g., news reports about AIDS or the multiple sources of germs in the typical household are often implicated by patients as contributing to the emergence of their contamination obsessions). Moreover, a considerable proportion of patients do not recall specific conditioning events associated with the emergence of their OCD symptoms. Although stressful life events often precipitate intrusive thoughts, this association is rarely *immediate* and the content of these intrusions is often unrelated to the stressor, counter to Mowrer's theory.

Cognitive Appraisal Models In part owing to the failings of strictly behavioral theories (e.g., Mowrer's two-factor theory), several cognitive models of OCD have been proposed (e.g., Beck, 1976; Carr, 1974; McFall & Wollersheim, 1979). Generally, these models emphasize obsessions as reflecting overestimations of threat involving common concerns such as those relating to health, welfare of others, religion, and so on (and compulsions as actions that are performed to reduce the chances of the occurrence of these feared outcomes and to alleviate distress). However, these models have been criticized by many researchers (e.g., Riggs & Foa, 1993) because they fail to distinguish pathogenic factors specific to OCD from those of other anxiety disorders (e.g., exaggeration of risk is common to all anxiety-based disorders).

The most elaborate cognitive model of OCD has been forwarded by Salkovskis (1985, 1989, 1996). This model states that negative automatic thoughts, avoidant behavior, and neutralizing behavior are responsible for the maintenance of obsessions. In addition, these features demarcate the boundary between obsessions and normal intrusive thoughts. Prior research has indicated that difficulties in controlling or dismissing obsessions may be positively related to the extent to which an individual finds the obsessions distressing or unacceptable (e.g., Clark & de Silva, 1985; Parkinson & Rachman, 1981a, 1981b). As noted earlier, research on nonclinical participants has shown that the frequency of intrusive thoughts and ritualistic behavior (e.g., washing, checking) increases in response to life stress (e.g., Frost et al., 1986; Parkinson & Rachman, 1981a, 1981b). Indeed, intrusive thoughts occur in nearly 90% of nonclinical samples, yet these phenomena are virtually indistinguishable in terms of content from clinical obsessions (Rachman & de Silva, 1978; Salkovskis & Harrison, 1984). Thus, whereas stress may trigger these symptoms, it is not sufficient for producing a full-blown OCD. Indeed, while many people experience intrusive thoughts or ritualistic behavior after being exposed to stressful life events, most do not go on to develop OCD.

Accordingly, Salkovskis posits that individual differences regarding the cognitive appraisal of normal intrusions are key to determining whether these events develop into a clinical disorder. Although intrusive thoughts are not problematic in themselves, a person's appraisal of these intrusions is viewed in the model as being strongly predictive of the presence or absence of additional OCD symptoms. Unlike individuals with no mental disorder, persons with OCD are prone to interpret intrusive thoughts in a highly negative and threatening manner. Salkovskis claims that these appraisals (negative automatic thoughts) may take the form of exaggerated assumptions about whether actual harm can result from the intrusive thoughts themselves (e.g., thinking about an action may lead to the occurrence of the action; "thought-action fusion"; cf. Shafran, Thordarson, & Rachman, 1996) and about the extent of responsibility for preventing harm to oneself or others (e.g., failing to prevent harm relating to the thought is the same as having caused the harm directly).

Several types of dysfunctional assumptions have been proposed to characterize and differentiate OCD from normal intrusions (see Salkovskis, 1985, 1996); these assumptions emphasize inflated senses of personal responsibility and self-blame in the obsessive-compulsive belief system. In fact, Salkovskis (1989) posits that persons with OCD may not actually overestimate the probability of harm or threat (although risk overestimation is frequently regarded to be a cognitive style characteristic of all anxiety disorders), but rather overestimate their responsibility or blame for harm as a result of their thoughts and images, as described above. Other cognitive styles that have been implicated as characteristic and specific to OCD include indecision or intolerance of uncertainty (e.g., belief that every situation has a "correct" solution, distrust of one's decisions and conclusions; Freeston, Ladouceur, Gagnon, & Thibodeau, 1993), and excessive morality or rigidity (e.g., overvalued religious beliefs about the appropriateness of certain thoughts or behaviors; Steketee, Quay, & White, 1991).

Negative affect, a by-product of obsessions and mediated by negative automatic thoughts, is viewed by Salkovskis as increasing the frequency and intensity of these negative attributions and discomfort. However, anxiety is viewed as eliciting more frequent intrusions. The distress elicited by obsessional phenomena frequently precipitates additional symptoms at the cognitive and behavioral levels. Neutralization refers to any response that is effortfully and intentionally performed in response to cognitive intrusions in order to prevent the processing of these intrusions by means of engaging in incompatible tasks. Of course, neutralization efforts in the form of mental or behavioral compulsions are a predominant feature of OCD, but may also take the form of reassurance seeking and avoidance of situations related to the obsessional thought. Salkovskis has argued that neutralization occurs primarily in the context of negative automatic thoughts pertaining to strong feelings of responsibility or guilt. He maintains that the probability of performing compulsions is greater in patients with OCD who hold strong beliefs in their individual responsibility for the potential consequences of their unwanted thoughts.

Although often resulting in short-term relief of negative affect, attempts to neutralize are conceptualized as maintaining the obsessional pattern in several ways (e.g., prevents disconfirmation of fears of harm, increases acceptance of beliefs about personal responsibility). Moreover, in light of recent claims that neutralization efforts occur to disrupt processing of intrusions and that processing resources are insufficiently distributed to neutralization efforts, they are considered maladaptive responses to pathological intrusions (Edwards & Dickerson, 1987; Freeston, Ladouceur, Thibodeau, & Gagnon, 1992). Misdistribution of these processing resources leads to stereotyped, ineffectual, and seemingly senseless compulsive behaviors and may perpetuate the obsessive-compulsive cycle (see Jakes, 1989 and Salkovskis, 1989, for a critical discussion of the model).

Empirical efforts to evaluate the testable predictions from the Salkovskis model have begun to appear in the literature. Most of these studies have been conducted using nonclinical samples (e.g., Rachman, Thordarson, Shafran, & Woody, 1995; Rhéaume, Freeston, Dugas, Letarte, & Ladouceur, 1995), and only a few clinical investigations on the role of an inflated sense of personal responsibility in OCD have been published thus far. For example, in a recent study of patients with OCD who presented with checking compulsions, an experimental manipulation that decreased perceived responsibility (i.e., the experimenter informed the patient that she or he would take full responsibility for any consequences ensuing from the patient's failure to check) was associated with significant decreases in discomfort, urges to check, and perceived probability and severity of anticipated harm (Lopatka & Rachman, 1995). An experimental manipulation that increased patients' perception of responsibility led to significant increases in perceived panic and likelihood of anticipated criticism. There is evidence that perceived responsibility may be multidimensional (e.g., Rachman et al., 1995), and that it is differentially related to various forms of OCD presentations (e.g., more strongly associated with checking compulsions than with other types of compulsions such as washing or cleaning; cf. Lopatka & Rachman, 1995). Accordingly, much more research is needed to verify the role and explanatory value of perceived responsibility, and other dimensions forwarded by the cognitive model (e.g., thought-action fusion, inflated guilt or self-blame) in the pathogenesis and maintenance of OCD.

A series of studies supports the role of suppression, a type of neutralization, in the origins and maintenance of OCD symptoms (Wegner, 1989). Using nonclinical samples, Wegner's (1989) findings indicated that efforts to suppress particular thoughts produced a rebound effect in that these thoughts recurred more frequently after participants attempted to block them. In line with the Salkovskis model, Wegner suggests that clinical obsessions may emerge after initial efforts to control unwanted thoughts fail, leading to escalated attempts to suppress these thoughts, which in turn highlights the thoughts even further, thereby setting off a vicious cycle of greater negative affect, efforts to control, and frequency and intrusiveness of unwanted thinking.

Cognitive Deficit Models Counter to the Salkovskis model, which underscores the importance of *misappraisals* of aspects of one's mental functioning, some researchers have speculated that the symptoms of OCD (particularly OCD involving checking compulsions) may be accounted for by *deficits* in memory or decision making (e.g., Sher, Frost, Kushner, Crews, & Alexander, 1989; Sher, Frost, & Otto, 1983). For example, a patient's doubt and urge to recheck door locks may be due to actual deficits in memory for having previously completed these actions. The main evidence in support of the cognitive deficit view has come from studies (e.g., Sher et al., 1989) demonstrating negative correlations between measures of OCD and the Wechsler Memory Scale. However, limitations of this conceptualization include the fact that it does not provide a compelling account for many presentations of OCD, such as cases involving cleaning compulsions where memory deficits would not seem relevant. Also, the model does not account for the observation that these so-called memory deficits are highly specific—that is, patients do not show signs of memory problems outside the areas directly linked to their obsessions (e.g., whereas a patient may repeatedly recheck her curling iron to ensure she has turned it off, she never has difficulty with other objects in her house such as water faucets or the television; Salkovskis, 1996). In addition, research has shown that relative to nonanxious controls, patients with OCD evidence *superior* recall for negative (i.e., threat-related) information owing to selective and more elaborate encoding of these stimuli (e.g., Wilhelm, McNally, Baer, & Florin, 1996). Collectively, these observations pose serious challenges to the memory deficit account for certain presentations of OCD. Thus, some researchers (e.g., Frost & Hartl, 1996) have revised this conceptualization to be more along the lines of the Salkovskis model. In these revised conceptualizations, actual memory deficits are deemphasized, but self-appraisals of memory are underscored (e.g., compulsive checking may arise from undue and highly focused concerns about one's ability to remember).

Biological Models Biological models of OCD have implicated both neurochemical and neuroanatomical factors. The most popular neurochemical model of OCD involves deficits in serotonin neurotransmitter system (e.g., Goodman, McDougle, & Price, 1992). Although there are many limitations in making inferences about the etiology of a disorder based on its treatment responses (cf. Salkovskis, 1996), support for this hypothesis has come mainly from studies of the efficacy of serotonergic drugs such as clomipramine (i.e., many studies indicate that clomipramine is more effective than placebo and nonserotonergic drugs in the treatment of OCD; cf. Zohar & Insel, 1987). However, investigations that have directly examined the role of serotonin in OCD have not been conclusive. For example, several studies found no differences in patients with OCD and nonanxious controls in serotonin platelet reuptake (e.g., Insel, Mueller, Alterman, Linnoila, & Murphy, 1985).

Structural theories of OCD have implicated abnormalities in such brain areas as the basal ganglia and orbito-frontal cortex (see Insel, 1992; Pigott, Myers, & Williams, 1996; and Rapoport, 1991). Data indicating higher rates of birth abnormalities, epilepsy, and history of head trauma, encephalitis, or meningitis in persons with OCD versus nondisordered controls have led some researchers to speculate that early physical trauma or certain disease processes may be risk factors for OCD (Hollander, Liebowitz, & Rosen, 1991). In general, studies using imaging technologies (e.g., computed tomography, magnetic resonance imaging, positron emission tomography) have produced mixed results regarding differences in brain structure, function, and metabolism of patients with OCD relative to normal controls or other patient groups (cf. Baxter, Schwartz, & Guze, 1991; Insel & Winslow, 1990). Findings of a potential link between OCD and Tourette's disorder have also been interpreted as possibly reflecting a common neurological basis for these two disorders.

Studies supporting (or rejecting) these positions are far from conclusive. In fact, because a variety of neurochemical and neuroanatomical factors have been implicated in OCD, some researchers have argued that there may be multiple neurobiological pathways to this disorder. Furthermore, these researchers have speculated that these multiple pathways may map meaningfully onto various subtypes of OCD. For instance, whereas some forms of OCD may be linked to deficits in serotonin, psychotic-spectrum OCD (in which obsessions are of delusional intensity) may be due to brain lesions, trauma, or infection (Pigott et al., 1996).

Biopsychosocial Models Similar to the models of GAD reviewed earlier in this chapter, current conceptualizations of the etiology and maintenance of OCD are becoming increasingly integrative. These more comprehensive perspectives may reconcile some of the limitations inherent to unidimensional accounts of OCD. For instance, whereas many researchers concur that the processes highlighted by Salkovskis (1996) are quite plausible in explaining the progression of normal intrusions to obsessions and in accounting for the key maintaining factors of OCD, this strictly cognitive model is limited by its failure to provide a compelling account for the origins of these vulnerability dimensions. In one such integrative model (Barlow et al., 1996), certain biological and psychological vulnerabilities constitute the predisposition to develop OCD. Supported by evidence from genetic studies (e.g., Kendler et al., 1992b), the biological vulnerability for OCD may be shared with all anxiety and mood disorders. Although no specific genetic or biological markers have yet been identified, Barlow considers this vulnerability to be best characterized as an overactive neurobiological response to life stress.

One type of psychological vulnerability that may contribute to the origins of OCD is learning in childhood to regard some thoughts as dangerous or unacceptable. For example, persons raised in devoutly religious families may hold strong beliefs about the appropriateness and acceptability of thoughts relating to such areas as sex and abortion (e.g., thinking about abortion is the moral equivalent of having an abortion). As noted earlier in this chapter, exposure to life stress may elicit intrusive unpleasant thoughts in most individuals. However, coupled with these preexisting vulnerabilities, persons prone to OCD will respond with considerable distress to having thoughts of this nature (owing to their misattributions of these intrusions as being harmful or extremely unacceptable; cf. Salkovskis, 1996). Consequently, they develop anxiety over the possibility of having additional intrusive thoughts. Driven by this anxiety, these individuals try very hard to suppress these thoughts, which has the opposite effect of increasing the intensity and frequency of these intrusions (Salkovskis & Campbell, 1994). Hence, a positive feedback loop emerges where an increase in intrusions leads to increased distress, which results in heightened efforts to suppress (e.g., emergence of compulsive rituals), and so forth. The temporal progression of this feedback loop ultimately is the emergence of full-blown OCD.

Directions for Future Research

Clearly, conceptual models of the nature and etiology of GAD and OCD require evaluation in future research. In addition to investigation of the biology and genetics of these disorders, increased empirical attention should be given to the longitudinal course of these symptoms, in both at-risk and disordered samples. For instance, longitudinal studies would provide a more convincing analysis of the stability of the features (and diagnosis) of GAD and would address whether GAD usually precedes the disorders with which it co-occurs. However, as was discussed earlier in this chapter, such investigations should not be conducted solely at the diagnostic level, but should also involve multiple indicators of the various dimensions of disorder-specific key features, associated symptoms, and variables considered to represent predisposing traits or markers for the emotional disorders (e.g., negative affect, neuroticism, behavioral inhibition, neurotransmitter function). In addition, given the likelihood of shared vulnerability and overlap in constituent symptoms, the pathogenesis and nature of a given disorder should not be examined in isolation from other syndromes.

In tandem with the advances in structural equation modeling, such methodologies would allow researchers to conduct meaningful analyses of important, unresolved issues pertaining to the psychopathology of GAD and OCD. For instance, the high rate of comorbidity associated with GAD could be accounted for by a wide range of explanations that would either support or refute its validity as a distinct diagnostic category. As noted elsewhere (e.g., Blashfield, 1990; Frances, Widiger, & Fyer, 1990), when two disorders are observed to co-occur on a descriptive level, it is difficult to ascertain which interpretation is the most relevant: (1) disorders X and Y are both influenced by another underlying or causal factor Z (i.e., they share the same diathesis); (2) disorder X predisposes or causes disorder Y (or vice versa); (3) disorders X and Y co-occur by chance factors; (4) disorders X and Y are associated because they share overlapping definitional criteria; and (5) disorders X and Y should not be considered comorbid because they are best subsumed into one larger category that has been artificially split into separate parts (see also Brown & Chorpita, 1996; Blashfield & Livesley, this volume). Accordingly, comparative testing of various structural models fit to longitudinal data would offer valuable analyses of these issues. For instance, is a model fit superior for one in which the features of GAD are specified as causal factors of subsequent symptoms, or is the model fit enhanced by subsuming the features of GAD and OCD under other disorders such as major depression?

Moreover, researchers are increasingly underscoring the importance of evaluating the Axis I disorders within the framework of higher order trait dimensions that potentially have more value and parsimony in understanding the pathogenesis, course, and comorbidity of these syndromes (Watson, Clark, & Harkness, 1994). For instance, although some conceptualizations suggest that the features of GAD may act as risk factors for other disorders, it is possible that this influence is due to the fact that, relative to other emotional disorders, GAD has the strongest association with trait vulnerability dimensions (e.g., negative affect; cf. Brown et al., 1998). Hence, the inclusion of personality dimensions in such investigations would allow for the evaluation of features of GAD that are best subsumed under these traits (which would be consistent positions arguing that GAD simply reflects a nonspecific symptom or trait) vs. whether GAD has a distinct latent factor that is perhaps influenced by these higher order dimensions (i.e., GAD is a distinct disorder that is influenced by the same higher order traits influencing the other anxiety and mood disorders). Similarly, given arguments that various cognitions may simply be epiphenomena of a broader overarching trait (e.g., perceptions of helplessness-hopelessness may be better accounted for as a symptom of neuroticism or negative affect), the inclusion of personality measures would be quite valuable in the analysis of leading models of OCD and GAD. For instance, do the cognitive appraisals outlined in the Salkovskis model of OCD account for variance in OCD symptoms above and beyond variability explained for by broader trait dimensions such as negative affect? Although such investigations are time-consuming and expensive, they may provide the strongest and most conclusive tests of the pathogenesis, course, comorbidity, and nature of GAD and OCD.

Notes

1. However, these estimates were made without using the *DSM-III-R* hierarchy rule that GAD should not be diagnosed when it occurs exclusively during the course of a mood disorder or psychotic disorder. When this hierarchy rule was imposed, the lifetime prevalence estimate dropped slightly to 4.8% (an adjusted estimate for current GAD was not reported).

2. In addition, it is stated in *DSM-IV* that the "with poor insight" specifier may be useful for cases that are on the boundary between obsession and delusion. However, in instances where obsessions reach delusion intensity and when reality testing is lost, *DSM-IV* recommends the provision of additional diagnoses such as delusional disorder or psychotic disorder NOS.

References

Abel, J. L., & Borkovec, T. D. (1995). Generalizability of *DSM-III-R* generalized anxiety disorder to proposed *DSM-IV* criteria and cross-validation of proposed changes. *Journal of Anxiety Disorders, 9*, 303–315.

Alloy, L. B., Kelly, K. A., Mineka, S., & Clements, C. M. (1990). Comorbidity of anxiety and depressive disorders: A helplessness-hopelessness perspective. In J. D. Maser & C. R. Cloninger (Eds.), *Comorbidity of mood and anxiety disorders* (pp. 499–543). Washington, DC: American Psychiatric Press.

Andrews, G., Stewart, G., Allen, R., & Henderson, A. S. (1990). The genetics of six neurotic disorders: A twin study. *Journal of Affective Disorders, 19*, 23–29.

Baer, L., Jenike, M. A., Ricciardi, J. N., Holland, A. D., Seymour, R. J., Minichiello, W. E., & Buttolph, M. L. (1990). Standardized assessment of personality disorders in obsessive-compulsive disorder. *Archives of General Psychiatry, 47*, 826–830.

Barlow, D. H., Blanchard, E. B., Vermilyea, J. A., Vermilyea, B. B., & Di Nardo, P. A. (1986). Generalized anxiety and generalized anxiety disorder: Description and reconceptualization. *American Journal of Psychiatry, 143*, 40–44.

Barlow, D. H., Chorpita, B. F., & Turovsky, J. (1996). Fear, panic, anxiety, and disorders of emotion. In D. A. Hope (Ed.), *Perspectives on anxiety, panic, and fear* (Vol. 43; pp. 251–328). Lincoln, NE: University of Nebraska Press.

Barlow, D. H., & Di Nardo, P. A. (1991). The diagnosis of generalized anxiety disorder: Development, current status, and future directions. In R. M. Rapee & D. H. Barlow (Eds.), *Chronic anxiety: Generalized anxiety disorder, and mixed anxiety depression* (pp. 95–118). New York: Guilford Press.

Baxter, L. R., Schwartz, J. M., & Guze, B. H. (1991). Brain imaging: Toward a neuroanatomy of OCD. In J. Zohar, T. Insel, & S. Rasmussen (Eds.), *The psychobiology of obsessive-compulsive disorder.* New York: Springer.

Beck, A. T. (1976). *Cognitive therapy and the emotional disorders.* New York: International Universities Press.

Beck, J. G., Stanley, M. A., & Zebb, B. J. (1996). Characteristics of generalized anxiety disorder in older adults: A descriptive study. *Behaviour Research and Therapy, 34*, 225–234.

Black, D. W., & Noyes, R. (1990). Comorbidity and obsessive-compulsive disorder. In J. D. Maser & C. R. Cloninger (Eds.), *Comorbidity of mood and anxiety disorders* (pp. 305–316). Washington, DC: American Psychiatric Press.

Black, D. W., Noyes, R., Goldstein, R. B., & Blum, N. (1992). A family study of obsessive-compulsive disorder. *Archives of General Psychiatry, 49*, 362–368.

Black, D. W., Noyes, R., Pfohl, B., Goldstein, R. B., & Blum, N. (1993). Personality disorder in obsessive-compulsive volunteers, well comparison subjects, and their first-degree relatives. *American Journal of Psychiatry, 150*, 1226–1232.

Blanchard, E. B., Scharff, L., Schwarz, S. P., Suls, J. M., & Barlow, D. H. (1990). The role of anxiety and depression in the irritable bowel syndrome. *Behaviour Research and Therapy, 28*, 401–405.

Blashfield, R. K. (1990). Comorbidity and classification. In J.D. Maser & C.R. Cloninger (Eds.), *Comorbidity of mood and anxiety disorders* (pp. 61–82). Washington, DC: American Psychiatric Press.

Blazer, D. G., George, L. K., & Hughes, D. (1991). The epidemiology of anxiety disorders: An age comparison. In C. Salzman & B. D. Lebowitz (Eds.), *Anxiety disorders in the elderly* (pp. 180–203). New York: Free Press.

Blazer, D. G., Hughes, D., & George, L. K. (1987). Stressful life events and the onset of the generalized anxiety disorder syndrome. *American Journal of Psychiatry, 144*, 1178–1183.

Borkovec, T. D. (1994). The nature, functions, and origins of worry. In G. Davey & F. Tallis (Eds.), *Worrying: Perspectives on theory, assessment, and treatment* (pp. 5–33). New York: John Wiley.

Borkovec, T. D., & Costello, E. (1993). Efficacy of applied relaxation and cognitive behavioral therapy in the treatment of generalized anxiety disorder. *Journal of Consulting and Clinical Psychology, 61*, 611–619.

Borkovec, T. D., & Hu, S. (1990). The effect of worry on cardiovascular response to phobic imagery. *Behaviour Research and Therapy, 28*, 69–73.

Borkovec, T. D., & Inz, J. (1990). The nature of worry in generalized anxiety disorder: A predominance of thought activity. *Behaviour Research and Therapy, 28*, 153–158.

Borkovec, T. D., & Lyonfields, J. D. (1993). Worry: Thought suppression of emotional processing. In H. Krohne (Ed.), *Vigilance and avoidance* (pp. 101–118). Toronto: Hogrefe & Huber.

Borkovec, T. D., Lyonfields, J. D., Wiser, S. L., & Diehl, L. (1993). The role of worrisome thinking in the suppression of cardiovascular response to phobic imagery. *Behaviour Research and Therapy, 31*, 321–324.

Borkovec, T. D., Robinson, E., Pruzinsky, T., & DePree, J. A. (1983). Preliminary exploration of worry: Some characteristics and processes. *Behaviour Research and Therapy, 21*, 9–16.

Borkovec, T. D., Shadick, R., & Hopkins, M. (1991). The nature of normal and pathological worry. In R. M. Rapee & D. H. Barlow (Eds.), *Chronic anxiety: Generalized anxiety disorder, and mixed anxiety depression* (pp. 29–51). New York: Guilford Press.

Brawman-Mintzer, O., Lydiard, R. B., Crawford, M. M., Emmanuel, N., Payeur, R., Johnson, M., Knapp, R. G., & Ballenger, J. C. (1994). Somatic symptoms in generalized anxiety disorder with and without comorbid psychiatric disorders. *American Journal of Psychiatry, 151*, 930–932.

Brawman-Mintzer, O., Lydiard, R. B., Emmanuel, N., Payeur, R., Johnson, M., Roberts, J., Jarrell, M. P., & Ballenger, J. C. (1993). Psychiatric comorbidity in patients with generalized anxiety disorder. *American Journal of Psychiatry, 150*, 1216–1218.

Breslau, N., & Davis, G. C. (1985). *DSM-III* generalized anxiety disorder: An empirical investigation of more stringent criteria. *Psychiatry Research, 15*, 231–238.

Brown, T. A. (1998). The relationship between obsessive-compulsive disorder and other anxiety-based disorders. In R. P. Swinson, M. M. Antony, S. Rachman, & M. A. Richter (Eds.), *Obsessive-compulsive disorder: Theory, research, and treatment* (pp. 207–226). New York: Guilford Press.

Brown, T. A. (1996). Validity of the *DSM-III-R* and *DSM-IV* classification systems for anxiety disorders. In R. M. Rapee (Ed.), *Current controversies in the anxiety disorders* (pp. 21–45). New York: Guilford Press.

Brown, T. A., Anson, A. M., & DiBartolo, P. M. (1996). *The distinctiveness of DSM-III-R* and *DSM-IV* generalized anxiety disorder from major depression and dysthymia. Unpublished manuscript.

Brown, T. A., Antony, M. M., & Barlow, D. H. (1992). Psychometric properties of the Penn State Worry Questionnaire in a clinical anxiety disorders sample. *Behaviour Research and Therapy, 30*, 33–37.

Brown, T. A., Antony, M. M., & Barlow, D. H. (1995). Diagnostic comorbidity in panic disorder: Effect on treatment outcome and course of comorbid diagnoses following treatment. *Journal of Consulting and Clinical Psychology, 63*, 408–418.

Brown, T. A., & Barlow, D. H. (1992). Comorbidity among anxiety disorders: Implications for treatment and *DSM-IV. Journal of Consulting and Clinical Psychology, 60*, 835–844.

Brown, T. A., Barlow, D. H., & Liebowitz, M. R. (1994). The empirical basis of generalized anxiety disorder. *American Journal of Psychiatry, 151*, 1272–1280.

Brown, T. A., & Chorpita, B. F. (1996). Reply to Andrews: On the validity and comorbidity of the *DSM-III-R* and *DSM-IV* anxiety disorders. In R. M. Rapee (Ed.), *Current controversies in the anxiety disorders* (pp. 48–52). New York: Guilford Press.

Brown, T. A., Chorpita, B. F., & Barlow, D. H. (1998). Structural relationships among dimensions of the *DSM-IV* anxiety and mood disorders and dimensions of negative affect, positive affect, and autonomic arousal. *Journal of Abnormal Psychology, 107*, 179–192.

Brown, T. A., Dowdall, D. J., Côté, G., & Barlow, D. H. (1994). Worry and obsessions: The distinction between generalized anxiety disorder and obsessive-compulsive disorder. In G. C. L. Davey & F. Tallis (Eds.), *Worrying: Perspectives on theory, assessment, and treatment* (pp. 229–246). London: John Wiley.

Brown, T. A., Marten, P. A., & Barlow, D. H. (1995). Discriminant validity of the symptoms constituting the *DSM-III-R* and *DSM-IV* associated symptom criterion of generalized anxiety disorder. *Journal of Anxiety Disorders, 9*, 317–328.

Brown, T. A., Moras, K., Zinbarg, R. E., & Barlow, D. H. (1993). Diagnostic and symptom distinguishability of generalized anxiety disorder and obsessive-compulsive disorder. *Behavior Therapy, 24*, 227–240.

Brown, T. A., O'Leary, T. A., & Barlow, D. H. (1993). Cognitive-behavioral treatment of generalized anxiety disorder. In D. H. Barlow (Ed.), *Clinical handbook of psychological disorders: A step-by-step treatment manual* (2nd ed.; pp. 137–188). New York: Guilford Press.

Brown, T. A., O'Leary, T. A., Marten, P. A., & Barlow, D. H. (1993, November). *Clinical features of generalized anxiety disorder with an early vs. late onset.* Paper presented at the meeting of the Association for Advancement of Behavior Therapy, Atlanta, GA.

Butler, G., Wells, A., & Dewick, H. (1995). Differential effects of worry and imagery after exposure to a stressful stimulus: A pilot study. *Behavioural and Cognitive Psychotherapy, 23*, 44–55.

Carr, A. T. (1974). Compulsive neurosis: A review of the literature. *Psychological Bulletin, 81*, 311–318.

Carter, W. R., Johnson, M. C., & Borkovec, T. D. (1986). Worry: An electrocortical analysis.

Advances in Behaviour Research and Therapy, 8, 193–204.

Christensen, H., Hadzi-Pavlovic, D., Andrews, G., & Mattick, R. (1987). Behavior therapy and tricyclic medication in the treatment of obsessive-compulsive disorder: A quantitative review. *Journal of Consulting and Clinical Psychology, 55*, 701–711.

Clark, D. A., Beck, A. T., & Beck, J. S. (1994). Symptom differences in major depression, dysthymia, panic disorder, and generalized anxiety disorder. *American Journal of Psychiatry, 151*, 205–209.

Clark, D. A., & de Silva, P. (1985). The nature of depressive and anxious intrusive thoughts: Distinct or uniform phenomena? *Behaviour Research and Therapy, 23*, 383–393.

Clark, D. A., Steer, R. A., & Beck, A. T. (1994). Common and specific dimensions of self-reported anxiety and depression: Implications for the cognitive and tripartite models. *Journal of Abnormal Psychology, 103*, 645–654.

Clark, D. M. (1986). A cognitive approach to panic. *Behaviour Research and Therapy, 24*, 461–470.

Clark, L. A., & Watson, D. (1991). Tripartite model of anxiety and depression: Psychometric evidence and taxonomic implications. *Journal of Abnormal Psychology, 100*, 316–336.

Clark, L. A., Watson, D., & Mineka, S. (1994). Temperament, personality, and the mood and anxiety disorders. *Journal of Abnormal Psychology, 103*, 103–116.

Costa, P. T., & McCrae, R. R. (1988). Personality in adulthood: A six-year longitudinal study of self-reports and spouse ratings on the NEO Personality Inventory. *Journal of Personality and Social Psychology, 54*, 853–863.

Costello, C. G. (1992). Research on symptoms versus research on syndromes: Arguments in favour of allocating more research time to the study of symptoms. *British Journal of Psychiatry, 60*, 304–308.

Cowley, D. S., & Roy-Byrne, P. P. (1991). The biology of generalized anxiety disorder and chronic anxiety. In R. M. Rapee & D. H. Barlow (Eds.), *Chronic anxiety: Generalized anxiety disorder, and mixed anxiety depression* (pp. 52–75). New York: Guilford Press.

Craske, M. G., Rapee, R. M., Jackel, L., & Barlow, D. H. (1989). Qualitative dimensions of worry in *DSM-III-R* generalized anxiety disorder subjects and nonanxious controls. *Behaviour Research and Therapy, 27*, 189–198.

Di Nardo, P. A. (1991). *MacArthur reanalysis of generalized anxiety disorder* (Report to the *DSM-IV* Anxiety Disorders Workgroup). Albany, NY: Center for Stress & Anxiety Disorders.

Di Nardo, P. A., & Barlow, D. H. (1988). *Anxiety Disorders Interview Schedule for DSM-III-R* (ADIS-R). Albany, NY: Graywind.

Di Nardo, P. A., Brown, T. A., Lawton, J. K., & Barlow, D. H. (1995, November). *The Anxiety Disorders Interview Schedule for DSM-IV Lifetime Version: Description and initial evidence for diagnostic reliability.* Paper presented at the meeting of the Association for Advancement of Behavior Therapy, Washington, DC.

Di Nardo, P. A., Moras, K., Barlow, D. H., Rapee, R. M., & Brown, T. A. (1993). Reliability of *DSM-III-R* anxiety disorder categories using the Anxiety Disorders Interview Schedule-Revised (ADIS-R). *Archives of General Psychiatry, 50*, 251–256.

Di Nardo, P. A., O'Brien, G. T., Barlow, D. H., Waddell, M. T., & Blanchard, E. B. (1983). Reliability of *DSM-III* anxiety disorder categories using a new structured interview. *Archives of General Psychiatry, 40*, 1070–1074.

Dollard, J., & Miller, N. E. (1950). *Personality and psychotherapy: An analysis in terms of learning, thinking, and culture.* New York: McGraw-Hill.

East, M. P., & Watts, F. N. (1994). Worry and the suppression of imagery. *Behaviour Research and Therapy, 32*, 851–855.

Edwards, S., & Dickerson, M. (1987). On the similarity of positive and negative intrusions. *Behaviour Research and Therapy, 25*, 207–211.

Enright, S. J. (1996). Obsessive-compulsive disorder: Anxiety disorder or schizotype? In R. M. Rapee (Ed.), *Current controversies in the anxiety disorders* (pp. 161–190). New York: Guilford Press.

Flament, M. F., Whitaker, A., Rapoport, J. L., Davies, M., Berg, C. Z., Calico, K., Sceery, W., & Shaffer, D. (1988). Obsessive-compulsive disorder in adolescence: An epidemiological study. *Journal of the American Academy of Child and Adolescent Psychiatry, 27*, 764–771.

Flint, A. J. (1994). Epidemiology and comorbidity of anxiety disorders in the elderly. *American Journal of Psychiatry, 151*, 640–649.

Foa, E. B., & Kozak, M. J. (1986). Emotional processing of fear: Exposure to corrective information. *Psychological Bulletin, 99*, 20–35.

Foa, E. B., & Kozak, M. J. (1995). *DSM-IV* field trial: Obsessive-compulsive disorder. *American Journal of Psychiatry, 152*, 90–96.

Foa, E. B., & Tillmanns, A. (1980). The treatment of obsessive-compulsive neurosis. In A. Goldstein & E. B. Foa (Eds.), *Handbook of behavioral interventions: A clinical guide.* New York: John Wiley.

Frances, A., Widiger, T., & Fyer, M. R. (1990). The influence of classification methods on comorbidity. In J. D. Maser & C. R. Cloninger (Eds.), *Comorbidity of mood and anxiety disorders* (pp. 41–59). Washington, DC: American Psychiatric Press.

Freeston, M. H., Ladouceur, R., Gagnon, F., & Thibodeau, N. (1993). Beliefs about obsessional thoughts. *Journal of Psychopathology and Behavioral Assessment, 15,* 1–21.

Freeston, M. H., Ladouceur, R., Thibodeau, N., & Gagnon, F. (1992). Cognitive intrusions in a nonclinical population: II. Associations with depressive, anxious, and compulsive symptoms. *Behaviour Research and Therapy, 30,* 263–271.

Frost, R. O., & Hartl, T. L. (1996). A cognitive-behavioral model of compulsive hoarding. *Behaviour Research and Therapy, 34,* 341–350.

Frost, R. O., Sher, K. J., & Geen, T. (1986). Psychological and personality characteristics of nonclinical compulsive checkers. *Behaviour Research and Therapy, 24,* 133–143.

Ganzini, L., McFarland, B. H., & Cutler, D. (1990). Prevalence of mental disorders after catastrophic financial loss. *Journal of Nervous and Mental Disease, 178,* 680–685.

Garvey, M. J., Cook, B., & Noyes, R. (1988). The occurrence of a prodrome of generalized anxiety in panic disorder. *Comprehensive Psychiatry, 29,* 445–449.

Goodman, W., McDougle, C., & Price, L. (1992). Pharmacotherapy of obsessive-compulsive disorder. *Journal of Clinical Psychiatry, 53,* 29–37.

Gray, J. S. (1982). *The neuropsychology of anxiety.* New York: Oxford University Press.

Hazlett, R. L., McLeod, D. R., & Hoehn-Saric, R. (1994). Muscle tension in generalized anxiety disorder: Elevated muscle tonus or agitated movement? *Psychophysiology, 31,* 189–195.

Himmelfarb, S., & Murrell, S. A. (1984). The prevalence and correlation of anxiety symptoms in older adults. *Journal of Psychiatry, 116,* 159–167.

Hodgson, R. J., & Rachman, S. J. (1972). The effects of contamination and washing in obsessional patients. *Behaviour Research and Therapy, 10,* 111–117.

Hodgson, R. J., & Rachman, S. J. (1977). Obsessional-compulsive complaints. *Behaviour Research and Therapy, 15,* 389–395.

Hoehn-Saric, R., & McLeod, D. R. (1988). The peripheral sympathetic nervous system: Its role in normal and pathological worry. *Psychiatric Clinics of North America, 11,* 375–386.

Hoehn-Saric, R., Hazlett, R. L., & McLeod, D. R. (1993). Generalized anxiety disorder with early and late onset of anxiety symptoms. *Comprehensive Psychiatry, 34,* 291–298.

Hoehn-Saric, R., McLeod, D. R., & Zimmerli, W. D. (1989). Somatic manifestations in women with generalized anxiety disorder: Psychophysiological responses to psychological stress. *Archives of General Psychiatry, 46,* 1113–1119.

Hollander, E., Liebowitz, M. R., & Rosen, W. G. (1991). Neuropsychiatric and neuropsychological studies in obsessive-compulsive disorder. In J. Zohar, T. Insel, & S. Rasmussen (Eds.), *The psychobiology of obsessive-compulsive disorder.* New York: Springer.

Hudson, J. I., & Pope, H. G. (1990). Affective spectrum disorder: Does antidepressant response identify a family of disorders with a common pathophysiology? *American Journal of Psychiatry, 147,* 552–564.

Insel, T. R. (1992). Neurobiology of obsessive-compulsive disorder: A review. *International Clinical Psychopharmacology,* 7 (Suppl. 1), 31–34.

Insel, T. R., Mueller, E. A., Alterman, I. S., Linnoila, M., & Murphy, D. L. (1985). Obsessive-compulsive disorder and serotonin: Is there a connection? *Biological Psychiatry, 20,* 1174–1188.

Insel, T. R., & Winslow, J. T. (1990). Neurobiology of obsessive-compulsive disorder. In M. A. Jenike, L. Baer, & W. E. Minichiello (Eds.), *Obsessive-compulsive disorders: Theory and management.* Chicago: Year Book Medical.

Insel, T. R., Zahn, T., & Murphy, D. L. (1985). Obsessive-compulsive disorder: An anxiety disorder? In A. H. Tuma & J. D. Maser (Eds.), *Anxiety and the anxiety disorders* (pp. 577–589). Hillsdale, NJ: Erlbaum.

Jakes, I. (1989). Salkovskis on obsessional-compulsive neurosis: A critique. *Behaviour Research and Therapy, 27,* 673–675.

Joiner, T. E., Catanzaro, S. J., & Laurent, J. (1996). Tripartite structure of positive and negative affect, depression, and anxiety in child and adolescent psychiatric inpatients. *Journal of Abnormal Psychology, 105,* 401–409.

Karno, M., & Golding, J. M. (1991). Obsessive-compulsive disorder. In L. N. Robins & D. A. Regier (Eds.), *Psychiatric disorders in America: The Epidemiologic Catchment Area study* (pp. 204–219). New York: Free Press.

Karno, M., Golding, J. M., Sorenson, S. B., & Burnam, A. (1988). The epidemiology of obsessive-compulsive disorder in five US communities. *Archives of General Psychiatry, 45*, 1094–1099.

Kendler, K. S., Heath, A. C., Martin, N. G., & Eaves, L. J. (1987). Symptoms of anxiety and symptoms of depression: Same genes, different environments? *Archives of General Psychiatry, 44*, 451–457.

Kendler, K. S., Neale, M. C., Kessler, R. C., Heath, A. C., & Eaves, L. J. (1992a). Generalized anxiety disorder in women: A population-based twin study. *Archives of General Psychiatry, 49*, 267–272.

Kendler, K. S., Neale, M. C., Kessler, R. C., Heath, A. C., & Eaves, L. J. (1992b). Major depression and generalized anxiety disorder: Same genes, (partly) different environments? *Archives of General Psychiatry, 49*, 716–722.

Kendler, K. S., Walters, E. E., Neale, M. C., Kessler, R. C., Heath, A. C., & Eaves, L. J. (1995). The structure of the genetic and environmental risk factors for six major psychiatric disorders in women: Phobia, generalized anxiety disorder, panic disorder, bulimia, major depression, and alcoholism. *Archives of General Psychiatry, 52*, 374–383.

Kozak, M. J., & Foa, E. B. (1994). Obsessions, overvalued ideas, and delusions in obsessive-compulsive disorder. *Behaviour Research and Therapy, 32*, 342–353.

Leckman, J. F., & Chittenden, E. H. (1990). Gilles de la Tourette's syndrome and some forms of obsessive-compulsive disorder may share a common genetic diathesis. *L'Encephale, 16*, 321–323.

Livesley, W. J., Schroeder, M. L., Jackson, D. N., & Jang, K. L. (1994). Categorical distinctions in the study of personality disorder: Implications for classification. *Journal of Abnormal Psychology, 103*, 6–17.

Lopatka, C., & Rachman, S. (1995). Perceived responsibility and compulsive checking: An experimental analysis. *Behaviour Research and Therapy, 33*, 673–684.

Lyonfields, J. D., Borkovec, T. D., & Thayer, J. F. (1995). Vagal tone in generalized anxiety disorder and the effects of aversive imagery and worrisome thinking. *Behavior Therapy, 26*, 457–466.

Mannuzza, S., Fyer, A. J., Martin, L. Y., Gallops, M. S., Endicott, J., Gorman, J. M., Liebowitz, M. R., & Klein, D. F. (1989). Reliability of anxiety assessment: I. Diagnostic agreement. *Archives of General Psychiatry, 46*, 1093–1101.

Marten, P. A., Brown, T. A., Barlow, D. H., Borkovec, T. D., Shear, M. K., & Lydiard, R. B. (1993). Evaluation of the ratings comprising the associated symptom criterion of *DSM-III-R* generalized anxiety disorder. *Journal of Nervous and Mental Disease, 181*, 676–682.

Massion, A. O., Warshaw, M. G., & Keller, M. B. (1993). Quality of life and psychiatric morbidity in panic disorder and generalized anxiety disorder. *American Journal of Psychiatry, 150*, 600–607.

Mathews, A. (1990). Why worry?: The cognitive function of anxiety. *Behaviour Research and Therapy, 28*, 455–468.

Mavissakalian, M., Hamann, M. S., & Jones, B. (1990a). Correlates of *DSM-III* personality disorder in obsessive-compulsive disorder. *Comprehensive Psychiatry, 31*, 481–489.

Mavissakalian, M., Hamann, M. S., & Jones, B. (1990b). *DSM-III* personality disorders in obsessive-compulsive disorder: Changes with treatment. *Comprehensive Psychiatry, 31*, 432–437.

McFall, M. E., & Wollersheim, J. P. (1979). Obsessive-compulsive neurosis: A cognitive-behavioral formulation and approach to treatment. *Cognitive Therapy and Research, 3*, 333–348.

McKeon, P., & Murray, R. (1987). Familial aspects of obsessive-compulsive neurosis. *British Journal of Psychiatry, 151*, 528–534.

Meyer, T. J., Miller, M. L., Metzger, R. L., & Borkovec, T. D. (1990). Development and validation of the Penn State Worry Questionnaire. *Behaviour Research and Therapy, 28*, 487–495.

Mowrer, O. A. (1960). *Learning theory and behavior.* New York: John Wiley.

Myers, J. K., Weissman, M. M., Tischler, G. L., Holzer, C. E., Leaf, P. J., Orvaschel, H., Anthony, J. C., Boyd, J. H., Burke, J. D., Kramer, M., & Stoltzman, R. (1984). Six-month prevalence of psychiatric disorders in three communities. *Archives of General Psychiatry, 41*, 959–967.

Nisita, C., Petracca, A., Akiskal, H. S., Galli, L., Gepponi, I., & Cassano, G.B. (1990). Delimitation of generalized anxiety disorder: Clinical comparisons with panic and major depressive disorders. *Comprehensive Psychiatry, 31*, 409–415.

Noyes, R., Clarkson, C., Crowe, R. R., Yates, W. R., & McChesney, C. M. (1987). A family study of generalized anxiety disorder. *American Journal of Psychiatry, 144*, 1019–1024.

Noyes, R., Woodman, C., Garvey, M. J., Cook, B. L., Suelzer, M., Clancy, J., & Anderson, D. J. (1992). Generalized anxiety disorder vs. panic disorder: Distinguishing characteristics and patterns of comorbidity. *Journal of Nervous and Mental Disease, 180*, 369–379.

Parkinson, L., & Rachman, S. (1981a). The nature of intrusive thoughts. *Advances in Behaviour Research and Therapy, 3*, 101–110.

Parkinson, L., & Rachman, S. (1981b). Intrusive thoughts: The effects of an uncontrived stress. *Advances in Behaviour Research and Therapy, 3*, 111–118.

Pauls, D. L. (1989). *The inheritance and expression of obsessive-compulsive behaviors*. Proceedings of the American Psychiatric Association, San Francisco, CA.

Pauls, D. L., Alsobrook, J. P., Goodman, W., Rasmussen, S., & Leckman, J. F. (1995). A family study of obsessive-compulsive disorder. *American Journal of Psychiatry, 152*, 76–84.

Pauls, D. L., Raymond, C. L., & Robertson, M. (1991). The genetics of obsessive-compulsive disorder: A review. In J. Zohar, T. Insel, & S. Rasmussen (Eds.), *The psychobiology of obsessive-compulsive disorder*. New York: Springer.

Pauls, D. L., Towbin, K. E., Leckman, J. F., Zahner, G. E., & Cohen, D. J. (1986). Gilles de la Tourette's syndrome and obsessive-compulsive disorder. *Archives of General Psychiatry, 43*, 1180–1182.

Pigott, T. A., Myers, K. R., & Williams, D. A. (1996). Obsessive-compulsive disorder: A neuropsychiatric perspective. In R. M. Rapee (Ed.), *Current controversies in the anxiety disorders* (pp. 134–160). New York: Guilford Press.

Rachman, S., & de Silva, P. (1978). Abnormal and normal obsessions. *Behaviour Research and Therapy, 16*, 233–238.

Rachman, S., Thordarson, D. S., Shafran, R., & Woody, S. R. (1995). Perceived responsibility: Structure and significance. *Behaviour Research and Therapy, 33*, 779–784.

Rachman, S., & Wilson, G. T. (1980). *The effects of psychological therapy*. New York: Pergamon Press.

Rapee, R. M. (1991). Generalized anxiety disorder: A review of clinical features and theoretical concepts. *Clinical Psychology Review, 11*, 419–440.

Rapoport, J. L. (1991). Recent advances in obsessive-compulsive disorder. *Neuropsychopharmacology, 5*, 1–10.

Rasmussen, S. A., & Eisen, J. L. (1988). Clinical and epidemiological findings of significance to neuropharmacologic trials in OCD. *Psychopharmacological Bulletin, 24*, 466–470.

Rasmussen, S. A., & Eisen, J. L. (1989). Clinical features and phenomenology of obsessive-compulsive disorder. *Psychiatric Annals, 19*, 67–73.

Rasmussen, S. A., & Eisen, J. L. (1990). Epidemiology of obsessive-compulsive disorder. *Journal of Clinical Psychiatry, 51*, 10–14.

Rasmussen, S. A., & Tsuang, M. T. (1986). Clinical characteristics and family history in *DSM-III* obsessive-compulsive disorder. *American Journal of Psychiatry, 143*, 317–382.

Rhéaume, J., Freeston, M. H., Dugas, M. J., Letarte, H., & Ladouceur, R. (1995). Perfectionism, responsibility, and obsessive-compulsive symptoms. *Behaviour Research and Therapy, 33*, 785–794.

Ricciardi, J. N., Baer, L., Jenike, M. A., Fischer, S. C., Sholtz, D., & Buttolph, M. L. (1992). Changes in *DSM-III-R* Axis II diagnoses following treatment of obsessive-compulsive disorder. *American Journal of Psychiatry, 149*, 829–831.

Riggs, D. S., & Foa, E. B. (1993). Obsessive-compulsive disorder. In D. H. Barlow (Ed.), *Clinical handbook of psychological disorders: A step-by-step treatment manual* (2nd ed., pp. 189–239). New York: Guilford Press.

Riskind, J. H., Beck, A. T., Berchick, R. J., Brown, G., & Steer, R. A. (1987). Reliability of *DSM-III* diagnoses for major depression and generalized anxiety disorder using the Structured Clinical Interview for *DSM-III*. *Archives of General Psychiatry, 44*, 817–820.

Roper, G., & Rachman, S. (1976). Obsessional-compulsive checking: Experimental replication and development. *Behaviour Research and Therapy, 14*, 25–32.

Roy, M. A., Neale, M. C., Pedersen, N. L., Mathé, A. A., & Kendler, K. S. (1995). A twin study of generalized anxiety disorder and major depression. *Psychological Medicine, 25*, 1037–1040.

Salkovskis, P. M. (1985). Obsessional-compulsive problems: A cognitive-behavioural analysis. *Behaviour Research and Therapy, 23*, 571–583.

Salkovskis, P. M. (1989). Cognitive-behavioural factors and the persistence of intrusive thoughts in obsessional problems. *Behaviour Research and Therapy, 27*, 677–682.

Salkovskis, P. M. (1996). Cognitive-behavioral approaches to understanding obsessional problems. In R. M. Rapee (Ed.), *Current controversies in the anxiety disorders* (pp. 103–133). New York: Guilford Press.

Salkovskis, P. M., & Campbell, P. (1994). Thought suppression induces intrusion in naturally occurring negative intrusive thoughts. *Behaviour Research and Therapy, 32*, 1–8.

Salkovskis, P. M., & Harrison, J. (1984). Abnormal and normal obsessions: A replication. *Behaviour Research and Therapy, 22*, 549–552.

Salkovskis, P. M., & Westbrook, D. (1989). Behaviour therapy and obsessional ruminations: Can failure be turned into success? *Behaviour Research and Therapy, 27,* 149–160.

Salzman, C. (1991). Pharmacologic treatment of the anxious elderly patient. In C. Salzman & B. D. Lebowitz (Eds.), *Anxiety disorders in the elderly* (pp. 149–173). New York: Free Press.

Sanderson, W. C., & Barlow, D. H. (1990). A description of patients diagnosed with *DSM-III-R* generalized anxiety disorder. *Journal of Nervous and Mental Disease, 178,* 588–591.

Sanderson, W. C., Beck, A. T., & Beck, J. (1990). Syndrome comorbidity in patients with major depression or dysthymia: Prevalence and temporal relationships. *American Journal of Psychiatry, 147,* 1025–1028.

Sanderson, W. C., Di Nardo, P. A., Rapee, R. M., & Barlow, D. H. (1990). Syndrome comorbidity in patients diagnoses with a *DSM-III-R* anxiety disorder. *Journal of Abnormal Psychology, 99,* 308–312.

Sanderson, W. C., & Wetzler, S. (1991). Chronic anxiety and generalized anxiety disorder: Issues in comorbidity. In R. M. Rapee & D. H. Barlow (Eds.), *Chronic anxiety: Generalized anxiety disorder, and mixed anxiety depression* (pp. 119–135). New York: Guilford Press.

Shafran, R., Thordarson, D. S., & Rachman, S. (1996). Thought-action fusion in obsessive compulsive disorder. *Journal of Anxiety Disorders, 10,* 379–391.

Sher, K. J., Frost, R. O., Kushner, M., Crews, T. M., & Alexander, J. E. (1989). Memory deficits in compulsive checkers: A replication and extension in a clinical sample. *Behaviour Research and Therapy, 27,* 65–69.

Sher, K. J., Frost, R. O., & Otto, R. (1983). Cognitive deficits in compulsive checkers: An exploratory study. *Behaviour Research and Therapy, 21,* 357–364.

Shores, M. M., Glubin, T., Cowley, D. S., Dager, S. R., Roy-Byrne, P. P., & Dunner, D. L. (1992). The relationship between anxiety and depression: A clinical comparison of generalized anxiety disorder dysthymic disorder, panic disorder, and major depressive disorder. *Comprehensive Psychiatry, 33,* 237–244.

Skre, I., Onstad, S., Torgersen, S., & Kringlen, E. (1991). High interrater reliability for the Structured Clinical Interview for *DSM-III-R* Axis I (SCID-I). *Acta Psychiatrica Scandinavia, 84,* 167–173.

Skre, I., Onstad, S., Torgersen, S., Lygren, S., & Kringlen, E. (1993). A twin study of *DSM-III-R* anxiety disorders. *Acta Psychiatrica Scandinavia, 88,* 85–92.

Stanley, M. A., Turner, S. M., & Borden, J. W. (1990). Schizotypal features in obsessive-compulsive disorder. *Comprehensive Psychiatry, 31,* 511–518.

Starcevic, V. (1995). Pathological worry in major depression: A preliminary report. *Behaviour Research and Therapy, 33,* 55–56.

Steketee, G. (1990). Personality traits and disorders in obsessive-compulsives. *Journal of Anxiety Disorders, 4,* 351–364.

Steketee, G., Grayson, J. B., & Foa, E. B. (1987). A comparison of characteristics of obsessive-compulsive disorder and other anxiety disorders. *Journal of Anxiety Disorders, 1,* 325–335.

Steketee, G., Quay, S., & White, K. (1991). Religion and guilt in OCD patients. *Journal of Anxiety Disorders, 5,* 359–367.

Swedo, S. E., Rapoport, J. L., Leonard, H., Lenane, M., & Cheslow, D. (1989). Obsessive-compulsive disorder in children and adolescents. *Archives of General Psychiatry, 46,* 335–341.

Tellegen, A., Lykken, D. T., Bouchard, T. J., Wilcox, K. J., Segal, N. L., & Rich, S. (1988). Personality similarity in twins reared apart and together. *Journal of Personality and Social Psychology, 54,* 1031–1039.

Torgersen, S. (1983). Genetic factors in anxiety disorders. *Archives of General Psychiatry, 40,* 1085–1089.

Tucker, D. M. (1981). Lateral brain function, emotion, and conceptualization. *Psychological Bulletin, 87,* 380–383.

Turner, S. M., Beidel, D. C., & Stanley, M. A. (1992). Are obsessional thoughts and worry different cognitive phenomena? *Clinical Psychology Review, 12,* 257–270.

Tynes, L. L., White, K., & Steketee, G. S. (1990). Toward a new nosology of obsessive compulsive disorder. *Comprehensive Psychiatry, 31,* 465–480.

Watson, D., & Clark, L. A. (1984). Negative affectivity: The disposition to experience aversive emotional states. *Psychological Bulletin, 96,* 465–490.

Watson, D., Clark, L. A., & Harkness, A. R. (1994). Structures of personality and their relevance to psychopathology. *Journal of Abnormal Psychology, 103,* 18–31.

Watson, D., Clark, L. A., Weber, K., Assenheimer, J. S., Strauss, M. E., & McCormick, R. A. (1995). Testing a tripartite model: II. Exploring the symptom structure of anxiety and depression in student, adult, and patient samples. *Journal of Abnormal Psychology, 104,* 15–25.

Wegner, D. M. (1989). *White bears and other unwanted thoughts*. New York: Viking-Penguin.

Whitaker, A., Johnson, J., Shaffer, D., Rapoport, J. L., Calico, K., Walsh, B. T., Davies, M., Braiman, S., & Dolinsky, A. (1990). Uncommon troubles in young people: Prevalence estimates for selected psychiatric disorders in a nonreferred adolescent population. *Archives of General Psychiatry, 47*, 487–496.

Widiger, T. A., & Shea, T. (1991). Differentiation of Axis I and Axis II disorders. *Journal of Abnormal Psychology, 100*, 399–406.

Wilhelm, S., McNally, R. J., Baer, L., & Florin, I. (1996). Directed forgetting in obsessive-compulsive disorder. *Behaviour Research and Therapy, 34*, 633–641.

Williams, J. B. W., Gibbon, M., First, M. B., Spitzer, R. L., Davies, M., Borus, J., Howes, M. J., Kane, J., Pope, H. G., Rounsaville, B., & Wittchen, H. (1992). The Structured Clinical Interview for *DSM-III-R* (SCID): II. Multisite test-retest reliability. *Archives of General Psychiatry, 49*, 630–636.

Wisocki, P. A. (1994). The experience of worry in the elderly. In G. C. L. Davey & F. Tallis (Eds.), *Worrying: Perspectives on theory, assessment, and treatment* (pp. 247–261). London: John Wiley.

Wittchen, H.-U., Zhao, S., Kessler, R. C., & Eaves, W. W. (1994). *DSM-III-R* generalized anxiety disorder in the National Comorbidity Survey. *Archives of General Psychiatry, 51*, 355–364.

Zinbarg, R. E., & Barlow, D. H. (1996). Structure of anxiety and anxiety disorders: A hierarchical model. *Journal of Abnormal Psychology, 105*, 181–193.

Zohar, J., & Insel, T. (1987). Obsessive-compulsive disorder: Psychobiological approach to diagnoses, treatment, and pathophysiology. *Biological Psychiatry, 22*, 667–687.

6

Posttraumatic Stress Disorder

RICHARD J. MCNALLY

Clinicians have long recognized that traumatic events can produce psychiatric symptoms in previously well-adjusted people, but prevailing opinion held that stress-induced symptoms are transient (Wilson, 1994). Thus, *DSM-I* included a diagnosis called "gross stress reaction" and *DSM-II* included one called "transient situational disturbance." The assumption underlying both categories was that trauma-induced symptoms dissipate; persistent symptoms implied the presence of another characterological or neurotic disturbance.

The psychiatric sequelae of the Vietnam War altered this view of traumatic stress. Although initial reports implied that psychiatric casualties were less common in Vietnam than in previous wars (e.g., Tiffany, 1967), it soon became apparent that many returning combatants continued to experience significant problems long after reentering civilian life. Instead of viewing all impaired veterans as suffering from neuroses or character disorders, clinicians increasingly believed that severe trauma was sufficient to produce long-lasting pathologic consequences.

Clinicians had described neuropsychiatric sequelae of combat after the First and Second World Wars (e.g., "shell shock," "battle fatigue"), but professional attention to these syndromes vanished shortly after cessation of hostilities (Young, 1995). Matters were different after the Vietnam War. The duration and unpopularity of the war mobilized mental health professionals and leaders of veterans' organization to publicize its psychiatric consequences (Scott, 1990). Their observations persuaded them that combat produced a lasting disorder not captured by existing diagnostic categories. Some proposed that "post-Vietnam syndrome" be considered for inclusion in *DSM-III*. The *DSM-III* task force initially rejected this proposal, maintaining that the problems of veterans were already covered by traditional diagnoses. Moreover, a goal of *DSM-III* was to devise a relatively a theoretical system whereby diagnoses are explicitly defined by signs and symptoms without reference to often-debatable etiologies. Ratification of a post-Vietnam syndrome would be clearly inconsistent with this aim.

Nevertheless, members of a *DSM-III* task force examined case studies of combat veterans and survivors of natural and man-made disasters. Their inquiries revealed that a variety of horrific events, such as combat, rape (Burgess & Holmstrom, 1974), internment in concentration camps (Chodoff, 1963), and floods (Rangell, 1976), gave rise to a distinctive syndrome. Their conclusions prompted formal recognition of posttraumatic stress disorder (PTSD) in *DSM-III*. The diagnostic criteria were revised in *DSM-III-R* and *DSM-IV*. Throughout these revisions, PTSD has retained its identity as a syndrome comprising three clusters of characteristic signs and symptoms: (1) recurrent reexperiencing of the trauma (e.g., intrusive recollections, nightmares), (2) avoidance of reminders of the trauma and emotional numbing (e.g., inability to experience positive emotions), and (3) increased arousal (e.g., exaggerated startle, insomnia).

What Counts as a Traumatic Stressor?

Unlike the criteria for most *DSM-IV* disorders, those for PTSD specify an etiology: exposure to a traumatic event. In the absence of a qualifying event, the diagnosis cannot be made. Therefore, what counts as a "traumatic" stressor will affect the estimated prevalence of PTSD, and it may affect who gets diagnosed and treated.

Debate about the definition of a traumatic stressor figured prominently in PTSD deliberations for *DSM-IV*. Some committee members were concerned that a high threshold for affirming an event as traumatic might inadvertently exclude certain individuals from receiving the diagnosis whose symptoms arose in response to a "subtraumatic" stressor. Others held that subjective perception of an event as traumatic ought to determine whether a stressor has in fact occurred. Perhaps "subtraumatic" events (e.g., divorce) are perceived by some people as profoundly stressful, thereby producing PTSD. On the other hand, others argued that inclusion of subjective perception in the definition of a stressor conflates an etiologic agent with the individual's response to it.

Addressing these controversies, the *DSM-IV* PTSD Field Trial was designed to establish what kinds of events give rise to the characteristic signs and symptoms of PTSD in both nonclinical community respondents and trauma clinic patients (Kilpatrick et al., 1991). Assessors administered structured interviews and inventories to determine the prevalence of a wide range of high- and low-magnitude stressors and to determine their relation to the onset of PTSD. High-magnitude stressors included presumably rare events like combat, natural disasters, and rape. Low-magnitude stressors were those not generally viewed as traumatic (such as divorce, ordinary bereavement, and job loss), but that some believed might produce PTSD in certain individuals.

The results revealed that exposure to high-magnitude stressors is almost always necessary for the emergence of PTSD, isolated case reports notwithstanding (e.g., Scott & Stradling, 1994). Only 0.4% of the community participants developed PTSD after having been exposed solely to low-magnitude stressors. Stressors associated with PTSD often had been deliberately inflicted on the victim by another person, and often had involved injury or life threat. These stressors commonly provoked feelings of terror, horror, and helplessness. Criterion A in *DSM-IV* reflects these findings.

Further research has confirmed that subjective perception of danger in the absence of genuine threat is rarely sufficient to cause the disorder. Noting that spontaneous panic attacks are sudden, unpredictable, terrifying events that are often (mis)-perceived as life-threatening (e.g., as a heart attack), McNally and Lukach (1992) hypothesized that panic ought to constitute a traumatic stressor, under the subjective perception view. Their findings revealed, however, that panic disorder patients rarely develop PTSD as a consequence of their most terrifying panic attack.

The field trial data were consistent with previous reports of a "dose-response effect"; in 16 of 19 studies the severity of PTSD was directly proportional to stressor severity as measured by extent of life threat, injury, and so forth (March, 1993). These findings seem broadly consistent with behavioral theories of PTSD that affirm a parallel between stressor severity and intensity of unconditioned stimuli (Keane, Zimering, & Caddell, 1985).

Implicit in discussions of stressor severity is a dimensional dose-response model of causality. This model implies a linear relation between stressor severity and symptomatic response. Whether a person qualifies for the diagnosis would then depend on where one sets the threshold for affirming the presence of disorder, and prevalence rates would vary depending on how strict the cutoff is. A step-functional model is also plausible. This model implies a linear relation between stressor severity and symptomatic response up to a point where a sharp break occurs, marking the presence of disorder. Implicit in this model is a categorical (taxonic) construal of PTSD.

Despite the emphasis on mortal danger, personal exposure to life threat is not the sole pathway to PTSD, as research on Persian Gulf war veterans has shown. Although rates of PTSD among Americans who served in this brief conflict are apparently low (Southwick et al., 1995; Wolfe & Proctor, 1996), this is not true for those who performed graves registration duties. These soldiers were responsible for disposing of the rotting, mutilated remains of the war's victims; they were not themselves exposed to danger. Exposure to the grotesque aftermath of horrific events produced PTSD in 65% of those who did graves registration duty (Sutker, Uddo, Brailey, Vasterling, & Errera, 1994). Being the direct recipient of life-threatening events is clearly not required for PTSD to emerge; vicarious exposure is apparently sufficient for at least some individuals.

Moreover, an emphasis on personal life threat does not wholly capture the moral complexity of trauma. To be sure, many PTSD sufferers are no more than the innocent recipients of extreme stressors. But being the agent of trauma rather than its recipient can also produce posttraumatic symptoms. For example, involvement in atrocities predicts PTSD severity in Vietnam veterans even after the effects of combat exposure are partialled out (Breslau & Davis, 1987; Yehuda, Southwick, & Giller, 1992). As a consequence of murdering their loved ones, civilians have developed PTSD (Harry & Resnick, 1986). Political dissidents, who are forced by their captors to torture other prisoners, sometimes report that torturing others is worse than being tortured oneself (Başoğlu & Mineka, 1992). The traumatogenic effects of violating one's moral code do not fit easily within a framework emphasizing direct personal danger as the core of trauma.

Killing need not involve atrocities for it to be highly traumatogenic for the killer. The psychological cost of killing one's fellow human beings in the line duty for police officers (B. L. Danto, cited in Harry & Resnick, 1986) and for soldiers is far from trivial (Grossman, 1995). The deeply ingrained resistance to taking the lives of others, especially at close range, is evinced by historical research showing that death by bayonet (Grossman, 1995) has almost never occurred throughout military history, and that nonfiring rates of American riflemen during the Second World War approached 80%. Because so many soldiers failed to fire at attacking enemies, the American military changed basic training methods to foster dehumanization of the enemy. The new methods worked: the nonfiring rate in Vietnam was approximately 5% (Grossman, 1995).

Prevalence of PTSD

According to the National Comorbidity Survey (NCS; Kessler, Sonnega, Bromet, Hughes, & Nelson, 1995), the lifetime prevalence of *DSM-III-R* PTSD in the United States is 7.8%. Women are more than twice as likely as men to develop the disorder (10.4% versus 5.0%). In this methodologically sophisticated study, highly trained assessors conducted structured personal interviews with a large, nationally representative sample. A validity study indicated that NCS interviewers slightly underestimated rates of PTSD relative to expert clinicians; thus NCS prevalence estimates are probably a lower bound on the true prevalence (Kessler et al., 1995).

The NCS estimates are in accord with those of Breslau and her associates, who estimated the lifetime prevalence of *DSM-III-R* PTSD in a large sample of Detroit-area men and women (Breslau, Davis, Andreski, & Peterson, 1991). More women developed PTSD than men (11.3% versus 6%).

The aforementioned estimates are higher than those based on *DSM-III* criteria. The Epidemiologic Catchment Area (ECA) team reported lifetime prevalence rates of 1.0% and 1.3% at the St. Louis (Helzer, Robins, & McEvoy, 1987) and North Carolina (Davidson, Hughes, Blazer, & George, 1991) sites, respectively. Lay interviewers used the Diagnostic Interview Schedule (DIS) to assess PTSD.

Two large epidemiologic studies estimated rates of PTSD in Vietnam veterans. Using a slightly modified DIS, lay interviewers in the Vietnam Experience Study (VES) obtained lifetime and current PTSD prevalence rates of 14.7% and 2.2%, respectively, in a random sample of male veterans (Center for Disease Control, 1988). But in striking contrast to these data, researchers conducting the National Vietnam Veterans Readjustment Study (NVVRS) obtained lifetime and current PTSD prevalence rates of 30.9% and 15.2%, respectively, for male veterans, and corresponding rates of 17.5% and 8.5% for female veterans (Kulka et al., 1990). Among veterans exposed to high war-zone stress, 38.5% of the men and 17.5% of the women had current PTSD. Taken together, these data indicate PTSD currently affects about 478,000 of the 3.15 million men and women who served in Vietnam.

There are several reasons why the VES and NVVRS studies yielded such different prevalence rates (Kulka et al., 1988). In the VES, lay interviewers administered the DIS—an instrument whose sensitivity for detecting PTSD in veterans is only 25% (Kulka et al., 1988). In contrast, the NVVRS team used multiple convergent measures to establish PTSD caseness, and approximately 10% of the subjects were administered SCID interviews by a clinical psychologist or psychiatrist expert in the field of PTSD. Accordingly, the NVVRS estimates probably capture the true prevalence of PTSD better than do the CES estimates.

Risk Factors for PTSD

Exposure to traumatic events is required for a diagnosis of PTSD. In one study, retrospectively identified risk factors for exposure to such events included male sex, extraversion, neuroticism, having less than a college education, a history of childhood conduct problems, and a family history of psychiatric disorder (Breslau et al., 1991). A three-year prospective study indicated that extroversion and neuroticism predicted exposure to traumatic events, whereas childhood history of conduct disorder and family history of psychiatric disorder did not (Breslau, Davis, & Andreski, 1995). Blacks had a higher rate of exposure than whites, and being male and having less than a college education marginally predicted exposure.

High-magnitude stressors vary in their capacity to produce PTSD. Epidemiologic data indicate that rape is the most consistently traumatogenic high-magnitude stressor. In Breslau et al.'s (1991) study, 1.6% of the women had been raped, and 80% of them qualified for a lifetime diagnosis of PTSD. Other high-magnitude events produced PTSD at much lower rates. For example, only 22.6% of those who had been nonsexually assaulted developed PTSD, and only 24% of those who had been exposed to other life-threatening events did so.

The NCS also confirmed rape as the most consistently traumatic stressor (Kessler et al., 1995). Both men and women who had been raped cited it as the most distressing thing that had ever happened to them; 9.2% of the women and 0.7% of the men had suffered this trauma. Among rape victims, 65% of the men and 45.9% of the women had developed PTSD. Among people diagnosed with PTSD, the NCS researchers determined what traumatic events were most often responsible. For women with PTSD, 29.9% developed it after rape, and for men with PTSD, 28.8% developed it after combat.

Contrary to *DSM-III*'s implication that highly traumatic stressors are rare events that occur outside the bounds of ordinary experience, recent epidemiologic studies indicate the opposite. Nearly 40% of Breslau et al.'s (1991) sample had been exposed to highly traumatic events, and 60.7% of the men and 51.2% of the women in the NCS study had been similarly exposed (Kessler et al., 1995), as were 93% of the community sample in the *DSM-IV* PTSD field trial (Kilpatrick et al., 1991). Although these data strongly indicate that extreme stressors are far from rare, they also show that traumatic exposure is insufficient to produce PTSD. Indeed, the percentages of trauma-exposed people who developed the disorder are not especially high. Thus, among trauma-exposed people in Breslau et al.'s study, only 23.6% developed PTSD. Likewise, rates of PTSD in trauma-exposed men and women in the NCS were only 8.2% and 20.4%, respectively (Kessler et al., 1995). Only 10.3% of the community respondents in the *DSM-IV* field trial developed the disorder (Kilpatrick et al., 1991). These findings strongly indicate that individual difference variables strongly influence which trauma-exposed people develop PTSD.

The realization that only a minority of people exposed to extreme stressors develop PTSD has prompted research into risk factors for the disorder among those who have been exposed to high-magnitude stressors. Risk factors include female sex (e.g., Breslau et al., 1991; Kessler et al., 1995); neuroticism (e.g., Breslau et al., 1991; McFarlane, 1989); lower social support (e.g., Boscarino, 1995; Davidson et al., 1991; Keane, Scott, Chavoya, Lamparski, & Fairbank, 1985); lower IQ (Macklin et al., 1998; McNally & Shin, 1995); preexisting psychiatric illness, especially mood and anxiety disorders (e.g., Breslau et al., 1991; Smith, North, McCool, & Shea, 1990); having a parent who survived the Holocaust (Solomon, Kotler, & Mikulincer, 1988); childhood physical (Bremner, Southwick, Johnson, Yehuda, & Charney, 1993) or sexual (Engel et al., 1993) abuse; childhood separation from parents (Breslau et al., 1991; Davidson et al., 1991); a family history of mood, anxiety, or substance abuse disorders (Breslau et al., 1991; Davidson, Swartz, Storck, Krishnan, & Hammett, 1985); premilitary traumatic events (King, King, Foy, & Gudanowski, 1996); and family instability (King et al., 1996).

Studying left-wing political activists exposed to horrific tortures in Turkey, Başoğlu et al. (1994) obtained data relevant to factors that might protect against PTSD. These activists had suffered an average of 291 episodes of torture during an average imprisonment of 47 months. Despite this level of trauma, 67% never developed PTSD. Başoğlu et al. identified several potentially protective factors. The less susceptible activists were highly educated, politically committed militants who fully expected to be tortured should their arrest occur. They had considerable social and emotional support from relatives and friends, and were heroes upon their release.

A nonepidemiologic approach to risk assessment is to examine what immediate and short-term responses to traumatic events predict subsequent PTSD. Retrospective studies suggest that peritraumatic dissociation (i.e., occurring at the time of the event) predicts the development of PTSD (Bremner et al., 1992; Marmar et al., 1994). That is, people who reported feeling disconnected from their body, feeling that events were happening in slow motion, and so forth were especially likely to develop PTSD subsequently. A recent prospective study of civilian trauma survivors of automobile accidents, terrorist attacks, and similar events in Israel confirmed these findings (Shalev, Peri, Canetti, & Schreiber, 1996). Peritraumatic dissociation, mainly time distortion and derealization, predicted a PTSD diagnosis six months after the trauma even when Shalev et al. controlled for the intensity of other peritraumatic responses. Although as Marmar et al. (1994) noted, dissociation has often been interpreted as a defense against trauma, its adaptive function must be questioned if it predicts chronic PTSD.

Most researchers have conceptualized predictors of PTSD in terms of risk factors rather than in terms of protective factors. But to say that high neuroticism or lower intelligence are risk factors for PTSD does not necessarily imply that low neuroticism or high intelligence protects a person against the disorder. For example, the degree of protection conferred by an IQ of 15 points above the mean may not be as great as the degree of risk associated with an IQ 15 points below the mean.

Longitudinal Course of PTSD

Although most trauma-exposed people do not develop PTSD, most exhibit at least some acute symptoms after exposure to horrific events. For example, among help-seeking rape survivors, Rothbaum and Foa (1993) found that 95% met PTSD symptom (but not duration) criteria within two weeks of the trauma. Most gradually improved. The proportion still meeting PTSD symptom criteria at one, three, and six months postrape declined to 63.3, 45.9, and 41.7%, respectively. Likewise, among survivors of nonsexual assault, Rothbaum and Foa found that 64.7% met PTSD criteria one week after the crime, whereas the proportion still fulfilling criteria at one, three, six, and nine months postassault declined to 36.7, 14.6, 11.5, and 0%, respectively.

In contrast to single-impact events, such as violent crime, chronic trauma may produce lasting impairment in a significant minority of victims. Forty-year follow-up studies of former World War II prisoners of war reveal chronic impairment in a significant minority (Blank, 1993; Kluznik, Speed, van Valkenburg, & Magraw, 1986; Speed, Engdahl, Schwartz, & Eberly, 1989). Approximately 50 to 67% of these individuals apparently qualified for PTSD at repatriation, and about 20 to 32% still qualified 40 years later.

The overwhelming majority of cases of PTSD begin immediately after the traumatic event; cases of delayed onset are rare (e.g., van Dyke, Zilberg, & McKinnon, 1985). In the *DSM-IV* field trial, 74.4% of the PTSD cases reported symptom onset occurring within one month after trauma exposure; only 11% reported delayed onset of PTSD symptoms (i.e., beginning six months after the trauma).

To study the prevalence of delayed onset PTSD, Solomon and her associates evaluated Israeli veterans who sought psychiatric treatment for combat-related problems between six months and five years after the 1982 Lebanon War (Solomon, Kotler, Shalev, & Lin, 1989). They classified them as follows: (1) delayed help-seeking for chronic PTSD (40%); (2) worsening of subclinical PTSD (33%); (3) reemergence of PTSD in veterans who had recovered from PTSD acquired during the 1973 Yom Kippur War; (4) delayed onset PTSD (10%); (5) other non-PTSD disorders (4%). Cases in the second, third, and fourth categories developed PTSD after exposure to additional nontraumatic stressors (e.g., being summoned for reserve duty, getting married). Even cases of delayed PTSD had been experiencing at least a few symptoms (e.g., nightmares) for years.

Although therapy may hasten remission, a significant minority do not recover regardless of whether they have received treatment (Kessler et al., 1995). In the NCS, the median time to remission for those who received therapy was significantly shorter (36 months) than for those who did not seek therapy (64 months). From 75 to 120 months postonset, however, few individuals remitted, and approximately one third of PTSD sufferers remained symptomatic regardless of whether they had received treatment.

Comorbidity

Doubts about the syndromal validity of PTSD have often been prompted by the very high rates of lifetime and current comorbidity associated with the disorder. Nosologists often assume that a valid disorder ought to appear in pure form, at least some of the time, but in the NVVRS, for example, fully 98.8% of the veterans who qualified for a lifetime diagnosis of PTSD also qualified for at least one other mental disorder relative to 40.6% of those without PTSD (Kulka et al., 1990). In this study, those with PTSD had higher rates of all current and lifetime Axis I disorders than did those without PTSD (Kulka et al., 1990). The most common comorbid disorders in male veterans with PTSD were alcohol abuse, depression, and generalized anxiety disorder (GAD), and the most common comorbid disorders in female veterans were depression, GAD, alcohol abuse, and panic disorder.

Studies on current comorbidity have yielded rates nearly as high as those on lifetime comorbidity. Sierles and his associates found that 84% of outpatient as well as inpatient cases of PTSD qualified for additional disorders, especially alcoholism and antisocial personality disorder (Sierles, Chen, McFarland, & Taylor, 1983; Sierles, Chen, Messing, Besyner, & Taylor, 1986). Interestingly, Lerer et al. (1987) reported no cases of either comorbid substance abuse or antisocial personality disorder among Israeli combat veterans with PTSD. Panic disorder and dysthymia, however, were common additional diagnoses.

Relative to help-seeking Vietnam veterans without PTSD, those with PTSD had higher rates of concurrent major depression, panic disorder, bipolar disorder, and social phobia in Orsillo et al.'s (1996) study. These researchers, however, hastened to add that comorbid disorders are hardly unique to veterans with PTSD; comorbidity was common in help-seeking veterans with other non-PTSD disorders as well.

Comorbidity is prevalent in cases of civilian PTSD, too. Breslau et al. (1991) reported that about 80% of PTSD cases had at least one other disorder at some point in their lives. Likewise, Kessler et al. (1995) reported lifetime comorbidity rates of 88.3% in men and 79% in women with PTSD. Major depression and alcohol dependence were among the most common comorbid conditions. Analyses of age of onset suggested that other anxiety disorders usually preceded PTSD, whereas alcohol and mood disorders usually followed the emergence of PTSD. But not all studies have confirmed this temporal sequence (Keane & Kaloupek, 1997). Although PTSD may sometimes be a risk factor for other disorders, as when people begin to use alcohol to self-medicate their PTSD symptoms, alcoholism, conduct disorder, and so forth may place people in harm's way, thereby increasing their chances of developing PTSD.

Cognitive Aspects of PTSD

People with PTSD report reexperiencing their traumas in the form of intrusive recollections, nightmares, and flashbacks. These phenomenologic reports imply that automatic (i.e., involuntary) cognitive processes underlie traumatic intrusions. To test whether access to traumatic information is automatic in PTSD, researchers have applied versions of the emotional Stroop paradigm (McNally, 1995a).

In this paradigm, subjects are asked to view words of varying emotional significance and to name the colors in which the words are printed while ignoring the meanings of the words (Williams, Mathews, & MacLeod, 1996). "Stroop interference" occurs when the meaning of a word becomes intrusively accessible, thereby slowing the subject's naming of its color. If information related to trauma is, indeed, automatically accessed in PTSD, subjects with the disorder ought to exhibit greater Stroop interference for trauma words relative to other words and relative to people without PTSD. This hypothesis has been repeatedly confirmed in subjects whose PTSD developed from combat (e.g., McNally, Kaspi, Riemann, & Zeitlin, 1990), rape (e.g., Cassiday, McNally, & Zeitlin, 1992), shipwrecks (Thrasher, Dalgleish, & Yule, 1994), and automobile accidents (Bryant & Harvey, 1995). Although interference is automatic in the sense of being involuntary (McNally,

1995b), it is not automatic in the sense of occurring outside awareness; visually masked (i.e., "subliminal") trauma words do not produce Stroop interference in PTSD (McNally, Amir, & Lipke, 1996).

Interference provoked by words related to trauma is more strongly related to severity of PTSD symptoms per se than to severity of the trauma itself (e.g., extent of combat exposure; McNally et al., 1990). Moreover, such interference is more strongly related to self-reported intrusive symptoms than to self-reported avoidance and numbing symptoms (Cassiday et al., 1992). Taken together, these findings suggest that trauma-related interference reflects intrusive cognitive activity associated with PTSD rather than merely reflecting a history of having been exposed to traumatic events.

Interference may reflect changes in clinical state. Patients whose rape-related PTSD has remitted after successful cognitive-behavioral treatment do not exhibit interference for trauma words (Foa, Feske, Murdock, Kozak, & McCarthy, 1991), whereas combat veterans whose PTSD persists continue to exhibit interference for trauma material upon retesting (McNally, English, & Lipke, 1993).

PTSD sufferers typically complain that memories about trauma are remembered all too easily. This suggests that information about trauma is characterized by enhanced accessibility. Consistent with this hypothesis, relative to healthy combat veterans, those with PTSD exhibit superior recall for words related to their traumatic events (Vrana, Roodman, & Beckham, 1995). Likewise, veterans with combat-related PTSD tend to exhibit enhanced implicit memory for sentences related to the Vietnam War relative to neutral sentences and relative to healthy combat veterans (Amir, McNally, & Wiegartz, 1996). Similar effects do not occur on priming tasks (e.g., perceptual identification) that more strongly tap implicit memory for the orthographic rather than the semantic aspects of words (McNally & Amir, 1996).

Like people with depression (e.g., Williams & Dritschel, 1988), those with PTSD often exhibit overgeneral autobiographical memory. That is, when asked to retrieve specific memories in response to valenced cue words (e.g., *happy*), they recall general categories of memories (e.g., "when I am fishing") rather than specific episodes (e.g., "the fishing trip I took last Fourth of July"). Difficulty accessing specific memories from one's past strongly predict failure to recover from major depressive disorder (Brittlebank, Scott, Williams, & Ferrier, 1993) and is linked to deficits in problem solving (Evans, Williams, O'Loughlin, & Howells, 1992).

In one experiment, Vietnam combat veterans with PTSD, but not healthy combat veterans, exhibited overgeneral memories in response to cue words having either positive, negative, or neutral emotional valence (McNally, Litz, Prassas, Shin, & Weathers, 1994). Although each subject had been trained to retrieve specific memories during the preexperimental practice period, those with PTSD slid back into an overgeneral style of retrieval during the experiment. PTSD subjects who had recently viewed an "emotional prime" (i.e., a combat videotape) experienced more difficulties retrieving specific memories than did PTSD subjects who had viewed an emotionally neutral videotape. These data suggest that exposure to reminders of the trauma may preempt cognitive resources, rendering it especially difficult for PTSD patients to use memory effortfully to retrieve specific autobiographical episodes.

In another experiment Vietnam combat veterans with and without PTSD attempted to access specific autobiographical memories exemplifying traits denoted by positive (e.g., *loyal*) and negative (e.g., *guilty*) cue words (McNally, Lasko, Macklin, & Pitman, 1995). PTSD subjects again had difficulty retrieving specific memories, whereas healthy combat subjects did not. Overgeneral memory problems, however, were especially marked among those PTSD subjects who wore Vietnam War regalia to the laboratory (e.g., fatigues, medals, loaded guns). Furthermore, regalia veterans disproportionately recalled memories from the war, unlike other subjects who overwhelmingly recalled memories from the previous few weeks. The striking self-presentational style of wearing military regalia 20 years after the war's end is an apparent marker for autobiographical memory disturbance. The memory problems evident in those PTSD subjects who are "still in Vietnam" may partly underlie the symptom of future foreshortening (i.e., an inability to envision one's future). That is, an inability to remember the past in detail may underlie an inability to envision the future.

Vietnam veterans with PTSD are not the only trauma-exposed group that exhibits overgeneral memory. Kuyken and Brewin (1995) reported that depressed women with histories of childhood sexual abuse experienced difficulties retrieving specific autobiographical memories in response to cue words, whereas depressed women who reported no abuse history did not. These researchers, however, did not assess for PTSD.

Finally, some experts believe that traumatized survivors of childhood sexual abuse are especially adept at disengaging attention from threat cues and thereby forgetting disturbing events (e.g., Terr, 1991). McNally, Metzger, Lasko, Clancy, and Pitman (1998) applied a directed forgetting paradigm to test this hypothesis in women with histories of childhood sexual abuse who either had PTSD or were psychiatrically healthy, and compared their responses to women who had never been traumatized. Subjects viewed a series of trauma words (e.g., *incest*), positive words (e.g., *celebrate*), and neutral words (e.g., *banister*) on a computer screen. Each word was followed by an instruction either to remember or to forget the word. Subjects were later given recall tests for all words, regardless of the original instructions that accompanied each word. Contrary to prediction, PTSD subjects exhibited memory deficits only for positive and neutral words they were supposed to remember, and they remembered trauma words all too well, including those they were instructed to forget. Abuse survivors without PTSD exhibited normal memory performance; they remembered words they were told to remember and forgot those they were told to forget, irrespective of word valence.

Biological Aspects of PTSD

Tonic Autonomic Arousal

Relative to control subjects, PTSD subjects exhibited higher resting heart rate (HR) in 5 out of 13 studies, but did not exhibit higher resting skin conductance in any of 12 studies (Prins, Kaloupek, & Keane, 1995). Prins et al. identified determinants of elevated tonic HR in PTSD. Effects are most apparent when researchers use nonveteran control subjects (e.g., Blanchard, Kolb, Pallmeyer, & Gerardi, 1982), use baseline periods of only several minutes (e.g., Pitman, Orr, Forgue, de Jong, & Claiborn, 1987), and assess tonic arousal before subjects are exposed to trauma-related stimuli (e.g., Pallmeyer, Blanchard, & Kolb, 1986). Effects often disappear or reverse when these conditions are not met. For example, control subjects with other anxiety disorders show higher tonic HR than do those with PTSD (Pitman et al., 1990). When PTSD subjects do not expect exposure to trauma-relevant cues, evidence for tonic arousal usually disappears (McFall, Veith, & Murburg, 1992; Shalev, Orr, Peri, Schreiber, & Pitman, 1992).

The aforementioned studies strongly suggest that elevated tonic arousal in PTSD reflects anticipatory anxiety related to expectation of exposure to trauma cues. One recent study, however, provided evidence of heightened arousal in a trauma-irrelevant context (Gerardi, Keane, Cahoon, & Klauminzer, 1994). Using archival data from routine medical assessments, Gerardi et al. found that Vietnam veterans with PTSD had higher basal HR, systolic blood pressure (BP), and diastolic BP than did era veterans who did not serve in Vietnam. It is unclear whether these data reflect genuine tonic differences or exaggerated reactivity to a relatively mild medical stressor unrelated to combat trauma.

Physiologic Reactivity to Trauma-Related Cues

PTSD subjects exhibit greater physiologic reactivity to trauma cues than do subjects without PTSD. For example, Prins et al. (1995) noted that PTSD subjects had greater HR increases in 11 out of 13 studies, and greater skin conductance increases in 3 out of 7 studies (Prins et al., 1995).

Researchers have assessed reactivity to trauma cues in two ways (Orr, 1994). In the first, subjects are exposed to standardized audiovisual stimuli relevant to traumatic events. Thus, Malloy, Fairbank, and Keane (1983) found that slides and sounds of combat evoked greater HR responses in Vietnam combat veterans with PTSD than in healthy combat veterans or in veterans with other psychiatric disorders. Likewise, Blanchard and his colleagues reported that PTSD subjects exhibit enhanced HR, systolic BP, and electromyographic (EMG) responses to audiotaped battle sounds, and that these enhanced responses do not occur in healthy nonveterans, healthy combat veterans, combat veterans with diagnoses other than PTSD, and nonveterans with specific phobias (Blanchard et al., 1982; Blanchard, Kolb, Gerardi, Ryan, & Pallmeyer, 1986; Pallmeyer et al., 1986). In another study, combat veterans with PTSD exhibited greater HR and diastolic BP increases to a combat film than to a "control" film depicting victims of gruesome automobile accidents, whereas control subjects did not (McFall, Murburg, Ko, & Veith, 1990).

In the second approach, researchers ask subjects to imagine traumatic events recounted in audiotaped scripts. These script-driven imagery studies have revealed that combat veterans with PTSD exhibit greater HR, SCR, and facial EMG (lateral frontalis) responses than do healthy combat veterans (Orr, Pitman, Lasko, & Herz, 1993; Pitman et al., 1987; Pitman et al., 1990); this effect is more pronounced for scripts that recount autobiographical than for generic traumatic events. Pitman et al. (1990), moreover, reported that combat veterans with anxiety disorders other than PTSD do not exhibit the script-driven reactivity exhibited by combat veterans with PTSD. Shalev, Orr, and Pitman (1993) reported similar script-driven imagery findings in a study on Israeli PTSD subjects who had been exposed to a range of traumatic stressors (e.g., automobile accidents, terrorist attacks). Unlike Vietnam veterans who had experienced multiple traumatic events many years ago, Shalev et al.'s subjects had experienced only a single, recent trauma.

HR reactivity to trauma scripts distinguishes PTSD subjects from non-PTSD subjects with a specificity ranging from 61 to 88% and a sensitivity of 100% (Orr et al., 1993; Pitman et al., 1987). Moreover, psychophysiologic reactivity can distinguish between veterans with combat-related PTSD and veterans who are asked to fake PTSD (HR; Gerardi, Blanchard, & Kolb, 1989; EMG; Orr & Pitman, 1993).

Physiologic reactivity differences between PTSD and non-PTSD groups appear confined to trauma-relevant cues (Orr, 1994). The groups do not respond differently to stressors unrelated to trauma (e.g., mental arithmetic Pallmeyer et al., 1986), nor do they respond differently to imagery scripts unrelated to trauma (e.g., Pitman et al., 1987).

Exaggerated Startle Responses

Consistent with self-reports of enhanced startle, sudden, loud tones evoke larger eyeblink EMG responses in combat veterans with PTSD than in healthy combat veterans (Butler et al., 1990; Morgan, Grillon, Southwick, Davis, & Charney, 1996; Orr, Lasko, Shalev, & Pitman, 1995). Likewise, civilians and veterans with PTSD tend to exhibit larger EMG magnitudes than do people with other anxiety disorders or no disorder (Shalev et al., 1992). PTSD and non-PTSD groups, however, do not differ in the rates at which their EMG responses habituate to these repeated tones (Morgan et al., 1996; Orr et al., 1995; Shalev et al., 1992).

Three studies have revealed greater HR responses to loud tones in PTSD groups than in non-PTSD groups (Orr et al., 1995; Paige, Reid, Allen, & Newton, 1990; Shalev et al., 1992). One study reported larger skin conductance responses as well (Shalev et al., 1992), whereas another did not (Orr et al., 1995). Finally, skin conductance response magnitudes habituate more slowly in PTSD than in non-PTSD subjects (Orr et al., 1995; Shalev et al., 1992).

Evidence for enhanced startle has been interpreted in two ways. On the one hand, these data suggest augmentation of unconditioned responses in PTSD (Pitman, Orr, & Shalev, 1993). That is, exposure to traumatic events may sensitize people to startle at any sudden stimulus. On the other hand, sudden, loud noises might best be conceptualized as conditioned stimuli evocative of fear responses, especially for veterans for whom such sounds may resemble gunfire (Prins et al., 1995).

Noradrenergic Dysregulation

Exposure to uncontrollable stressors activates the noradrenergic (NA) system as exemplified by the enhanced release of norepinephrine (NE) by the brainstem locus ceruleus (Charney, Deutch, Krystal, Southwick, & Davis, 1993). Preclinical studies indicate that animals exposed to chronic uncontrollable stressors suffer from hypersensitivity of the NA system (Southwick, Bremner, Krystal, & Charney, 1994), and several lines of evidence suggest that this holds for PTSD sufferers as well. Studies on physiological reactivity to traumatic reminders are consistent with this possibility. More direct evidence was reported by Southwick et al. (1993), who conducted a yohimbine challenge study with Vietnam combat veterans with PTSD and healthy control subjects. Yohimbine antagonizes the alpha-2 autoreceptor. Ordinarily, release of NE activates the autoreceptor, which then brakes further NE release, thereby serving as a negative feedback mechanism. By briefly blocking the autoreceptor, yohimbine enables NE to surge unimpeded. The results revealed that 70% of the PTSD subjects experienced a yohimbine-induced panic attack, and 40% experienced a concurrent flashback. Consistent with the NE dysregulation hypothesis, yohimbine produced more pronounced biochemical and cardiovascular effects in PTSD subjects than in control subjects.

Opioid-Mediated Stress-Induced Analgesia

Exposure to inescapable stress releases endogenous opiates that adaptively blunt sensitivity to pain (Southwick et al., 1994). Pitman and his associates tested whether stimuli reminiscent of traumatic events might evoke a conditioned analgesic response in PTSD (Pitman, van der Kolk, Orr, & Greenberg, 1990). Vietnam combat veterans with and without PTSD twice watched a combat videotape and a neutral videotape, once after having received naloxone (an opiate antagonist) and once after receiving saline placebo. Subjects provided pain ratings in response to standardized thermal stimuli. The results revealed that PTSD patients reported a 30% decrease in pain ratings after the combat videotape when they had been administered placebo but not when they had been administered naloxone. Healthy combat veterans reported no decrease in pain ratings in either condition. Taken together, these findings suggest that exposure to the combat videotape triggered a conditioned release of pain-reducing endogenous opiates in PTSD subjects under placebo, a response blocked by naloxone. Stress-induced analgesia may underlie phasic increases in emotional numbing.

Sleep

Posttraumatic nightmares are among the most disruptive and frightening symptoms of PTSD. After awakening from a nightmare, many people with PTSD experience great difficulty returning to sleep. Fear of nightmares may aggravate sleep-onset insomnia and foster excessive drinking as a means of falling asleep.

Nightmares occurring during Stage 2 or Stage 4 sleep tend to duplicate the content of the traumatic event, whereas those occurring during rapid eye movement (REM) sleep tend to incorporate other elements into the dream sequence (van der Kolk, Blitz, Burr, Sherry, & Hartmann, 1984; van der Kolk & Greenberg, 1987). The first type are "dreamlike" (oneiric) and the second type are "movielike" (eidetic). Interestingly, well-adjusted Holocaust survivors are characterized by very low rates of overall dream recall when awakened during REM sleep in the laboratory (Kaminer & Lavie, 1991).

Sleep studies have also documented increased sleep latency, increased REM latency, decreased REM sleep, decreased Stage 4 (deep) sleep, and diminished sleep efficiency (Hefez, Metz, & Lavie, 1987; Lavie, Hefez, Halperin, & Enoch, 1979; Ross, Ball, Sullivan, & Caroff, 1989; Schlosberg & Benjamin, 1978). It is unclear, however, whether these abnormalities are attributable to PTSD or to an independent sleep disorder. Studying veterans with combat-related PTSD in the laboratory, Brown and Boudewyns (1996) found that 76% qualified for a diagnosis of nocturnal myoclonus, a syndrome characterized by periodic limb movements. Approximately 6% of middle-aged men in the general population suffer from this disorder, and most express complaints of poor sleep. Nocturnal myoclonus may constitute yet another neurologic soft sign resulting from combat trauma (Gurvits et al., 1993).

Hypothalamic-Pituitary-Adrenal (HPA) Axis Abnormalities

Acute stress activates the HPA axis, the function of which is to stimulate adrenal production of glucocorticoids (Yehuda, Giller, Southwick, Lowy, & Mason, 1991). Stress triggers release of the neuropeptide corticotropin-releasing hormone (CRH) from the hypothalamus, which, in turn, controls the synthesis and release of adrenocorticotropic hormone (ACTH) from the anterior pituitary gland. ACTH regulates cortisol synthesis and release from the adrenal cortex. Cortisol and other glucocorticoids suppress immune and metabolic functions, and provide a negative feedback signal to the hippocampus, hypothalamus, and pituitary to regulate further hormone release. The HPA response to stress is adaptive in the short term, but prolonged activation has toxic consequences.

PTSD has often been conceptualized as a normal response to an abnormal stressor, but research on HPA axis abnormalities indicates this view is incorrect (Yehuda, Giller, Levengood, Southwick, & Siever, 1995). Indeed, not only is HPA functioning in PTSD distinct from normal stress responses, it is also distinct from abnormalities associated with major depressive disorder. Although the classic stress response is characterized by elevated cortisol, PTSD is characterized by *low* cortisol levels. Combat veterans with PTSD exhibit lower mean 24-hour urinary cortisol excretion than do either healthy control subjects or patients with major depression, mania, panic disorder, or schizophrenia (Mason, Giller, Kosten, Ostroff, & Podd, 1986; Yehuda, Boisoneau, Mason, & Giller, 1993; Yehuda et al., 1990). Moreover, low cortisol occurs in combat-related PTSD regardless of the presence of comorbid major depressive disorder (Yehuda et al., 1990). Blood draws occurring every 30 minutes for 24 hours have revealed abnormalities in the circadian release of cortisol in patients with combat-related PTSD relative to depressed patients and healthy control subjects (Yehuda, Teicher, Trestman, Levengood, & Siever, 1996). Not only did PTSD patients exhibit significantly depressed plasma cortisol levels, they also tended to exhibit dramatic fluctuations in cortisol. Yehuda et al. (1996) interpreted this circadian pattern as indicative of an HPA system that is hyperresponsive to environmental cues.

Both female and male Holocaust survivors with PTSD exhibit lower cortisol levels than do those without PTSD, Holocaust survivors with past PTSD, or nontrauma-exposed control subjects (Yehuda, Kahana et al., 1995). Importantly, survivors with PTSD exhibit attenuated cortisol levels even though they were well adjusted, nontreatment seeking, and had no history of substance abuse. Taken together, these data strongly indicate that abnormally low cortisol is linked to current PTSD, not merely to a history of having been exposed to traumatic stressors.

Hormones cannot exert their effects unless they bind to steroid receptors. Accordingly, researchers have studied lymphocyte glucocorticoid receptors because of their functional resemblance to those in the brain (Yehuda, Lowy et al., 1995). Consistent with low levels of cortisol, studies have shown that combat veterans with PTSD have lower levels of lymphocyte glucocorticoid receptors than do patients with major depression, schizophrenia, mania, or panic disorder (Yehuda, Boisoneau, Mason, & Giller 1993; Yehuda, Boisoneau, Lowy, & Giller, 1995; Yehuda, Lowy et al., 1991). It is unclear whether upregulation in the number of receptors is a compensatory response to low levels of cortisol or whether low levels of cortisol result from excessive glucocorticoid receptor activity.

Administration of dexamethasone temporarily suppresses cortisol levels in healthy subjects, but not in many patients with major depressive disorder (Carroll et al., 1981). Dexamethasone nonsuppression reflects HPA axis dysfunction. In striking contrast to depression, several studies have shown that PTSD is linked to normal suppression of cortisol in response to dexamethasone administration (e.g., Dinan, Barry, Yatham, Mobayed, & Brown, 1990; Kudler et al., 1987). Moreover, even most PTSD patients with comorbid depression exhibit normal cortisol suppression in response to dexamethasone (Halbreich et al., 1988; Kosten, Wahby, Giller, & Mason, 1990). Administering low doses of dexamethasone, Yehuda and her colleagues discovered that veterans with combat-related PTSD exhibited *hypersuppression* of cortisol (Yehuda, Boisoneau et al., 1995; Yehuda et al., 1993). Hypersuppression occurred even in PTSD patients who had comorbid depression, and it did not occur in healthy combat veterans. Taken together, these data suggest that hypersuppression of cortisol to low doses of dexamethasone may serve as a biological marker of the pathophysiologic process underlying PTSD rather than merely an indicant of a history of exposure to traumatic events (Yehuda, Boisoneau et al., 1995).

Yehuda, Giller et al. (1995) interpret these data as indicating that the HPA system in PTSD is characterized by enhanced negative feedback. A primary deficit in the number of glucocorticoid receptors would foster a stronger negative feedback signal, thereby resulting in lowered ACTH and cortisol levels, plus an enhanced response to dexamethasone. These data suggest that the HPA system is primed to respond maximally to stress.

Genetics

Establishment of the Vietnam Era Twin registry has enabled investigators to study the role of heredity in PTSD. Goldberg, True, Eisen, and Henderson (1990) studied a sample of 2,092 male monozygotic twin pairs who had served in the military during the Vietnam War. There were 715 pairs in which one member had served in Vietnam, whereas the other did not. Goldberg et al. found that, among such pairs, the prevalence of PTSD was 16.8% in cotwins who had served in Vietnam and 5.0% in cotwins who had served elsewhere. Moreover, there was a ninefold increase in the prevalence of PTSD in cotwins who had experienced heavy combat relative to cotwins who had not served in Vietnam. By controlling for genetic variance, Goldberg et al. were able to demonstrate the pathogenic impact of traumatic events.

In a subsequent investigation, True et al. (1993) studied 4,042 male Vietnam era monozygotic (MZ) and dizygotic (DZ) twin pairs to ascertain the relative contributions of heredity, shared environment, and unique environment to variance in PTSD symptoms. The results revealed that MZ twins were more concordant for combat exposure than were DZ twins. Controlling for extent of combat exposure, True et al. found that between 13 and 30% of the variance in reexperiencing symptoms was associated with genetic variation. Likewise, heritability estimates for avoidance symptoms ranged from 30 to 34%, and heritability estimates for arousal symptoms ranged from 28 to 32%. Indices of shared childhood and adolescent environment (e.g., family upbringing, parental socioeconomic status) were unrelated to variance in PTSD symptoms. Taken together, up to one third of the variance in PTSD symptoms is associated with genetic variance, whereas the remaining variance is chiefly associated with unique environmental experiences (e.g., heavy combat).

The fact that about one third of the variance in the PTSD phenotype is associated with genetic variance suggests that definitions of what constitutes a traumatic event cannot wholly be captured by the characteristics of the event itself. Indeed, if the class of "traumatic events" were definitionally clear-cut and casually sufficient to produce disorder, heritability estimates for PTSD would be zero because phenotypic variance would be explained entirely by reference to variance in what one experiences in one's environment (e.g., combat, rape).

Brain-Imaging Studies

Brain-imaging technologies, such as magnetic resonance imaging (MRI) and positron emission tomography (PET), have only recently been applied to the study of PTSD. Several MRI studies indicate diminished hippocampal volume in trauma-exposed patients, especially those with PTSD. Women with histories of severe childhood sexual abuse are characterized by smaller left hippocampi than are women without such histories (Bremner et al., 1997; Stein, Koverola, Hannah, Torchia, & McClarty, 1997). Vietnam veterans with PTSD exhibited smaller right hippocampi than noncombat control subjects in one study (Bremner et al., 1995), whereas in another they exhibited bilateral hippocampal diminution relative both to combat veterans without PTSD and to noncombat control subjects (Gurvits et al., 1996). Hippocampal abnormalities are consistent with problems PTSD patients have when attempting to access explicit, specific autobiographical mmories (e.g., McNally et al., 1995).

It is difficult to interpret the meaning of these findings. Although the Gurvits et al. study shows that hippocampal abnormalities are linked to PTSD and not merely to a history of trauma, it is unclear whether chronic PTSD leads to hippocampal diminution or the latter precedes the development of the disorder. Studies show that chronic exposure to elevated levels of glucocorticoids produces hippocampal damage in nonhuman primates (Sapolsky, Uno, Rebert, & Finch, 1990). However, in contrast to the classic stress response, PTSD is linked to *low* levels of cortisol (Yehuda, Giller et al., 1995). Accordingly, hippocampal diminution may figure as a marker for risk for PTSD. Compromised neurocognitive functioning may hamper a person's ability to cope with traumatic events, thereby increasing the likelihood of PTSD. Consistent with this interpretation, lower intelligence predicts severity of PTSD symptoms even after one controls for the effects of combat exposure (Macklin et al., 1998; McNally & Shin, 1995). Finally, researchers have not ruled out the possibility that hippocampal diminution is the result of comorbid alcoholism.

PET researchers have endeavored to elucidate the functional neuroanatomy of PTSD (Rauch et al., 1996; Shin, McNally et al., in press; Shin, Kosslyn et al., 1997). Using the Pitman-Orr script-driven imagery procedure, Rauch et al. had PTSD subjects with diverse types of traumas listen to audiotapes descriptive of subject-specific (autobiographical) traumatic events and to neutral audiotapes. The results revealed greater activation in right-sided limbic, paralimbic, and visual cortical areas while subjects listened to trauma scripts relative to neutral scripts. More specifically, regions of activation comprised posterior medial orbitofrontal, insular, anterior temporal, medial temporal, and anterior cingulate cortex, in addition to amygdala and right secondary visual cortex. Decreases in activation occurred in left inferior frontal (Broca's area) and left middle temporal cortex. Subjects reported intense reexperiencing symptoms while listening to the trauma scripts, and regions of brain activation were those that mediate intense emotion. Unfortunately, Rauch et al. did not test control subjects.

Also using PET, Shin, Kosslyn et al. (1997) compared the responses of Vietnam combat veterans with and without PTSD to combat-related, generally negative, and neutral pictures and visual images. In contrast to healthy combat veterans, those with PTSD exhibited increased regional cerebral blood flow in ventral anterior cingulate cortex and right amygdala when generating visual images of combat pictures they had previously seen. Also, when viewing these combat pictures, PTSD subjects exhibited decreased activation in Broca's area. As Shin, Kosslyn et al. emphasized, less limbic and paralimbic activation in their study relative to Rauch et al.'s is probably attributable to the latter group's use of audiotapes that described personal traumatic events rather than general trauma-relevant pictures and images.

In another PET study, Shin, McNally et al. (in press) exposed adult female survivors of childhood sexual abuse with and without PTSD to scripts descriptive of their traumatic events plus other nontraumatic events. Shin, McNally et al. also measured peripheral psychophysiology. The results revealed greater blood flow increases in orbitofrontal cortex and anterior temporal poles in the PTSD group than in the control group during imagery of subject-specific abuse events. During trauma imagery, the PTSD group also exhibited greater decreases in Broca's area and in anterior frontal cortex than did the control group. The PTSD group also displayed greater heart rate and diastolic blood pressure responses during trauma imagery than did the control group.

Taken together, these studies suggest that processing of trauma-relevant stimuli is associated with activation in certain limbic and paralimbic regions. Why three studies have shown decreased activation in Broca's area remains unclear.

Theoretical Models

Inescapable Shock

Several theoretical models have been proposed to account for different aspects of PTSD. Among the most prominent has been Maier and Seligman's (1976) animal model of inescapable shock. Originally integral to the learned helplessness theory of depression, today its relevance remains chiefly as a model of PTSD. Some authors have emphasized parallels between the biological consequences of inescapable shock and PTSD (Charney et al., 1993; van der Kolk & Greenberg, 1987), whereas others have elucidated the importance of perceived unpredictability and uncontrollability of aversive events as embodied in this model (Başoğlu & Mineka, 1992; Foa, Zinbarg, & Rothbaum, 1992).

Exposure to stressors stimulates release of NE from the brainstem locus coeruleus LC, and NE increases autonomic arousal, hypervigilance, and fear. NA tracts project widely throughout the central nervous system, including the limbic system and neocortex where NE functions in memory consolidation. Acute stressors trigger cortisol release, which activates metabolic processes essential for responding to stress and for repair of damaged tissue. Release of endogenous opiates blunts sensitivity to pain. Although these processes support an adaptive fight/flight response, severe or chronic exposure to uncontrollable stressors may foster dysregulation in these systems. Indeed, exposure to inescapable shock eventually depletes NE and dopamine, apparently because use exceeds synthesis (van der Kolk & Greenberg, 1987). Escapable shock does not have these effects. Chronic or repeated NE depletion renders central NE receptors hypersensitive to subsequent arousal- or threat-induced NE stimulation. Oscillation between noradrenergic overactivity and noradrenergic depletion may underlie the biphasic phenomenology of PTSD. Startle, angry outbursts, hypervigilance, and psychophysiologic reactivity to traumatic reminders may reflect the phase of noradrenergic hyperreactivity, whereas emotional numbing and apathy may reflect the phase of noradrenergic depletion. Although numbing has sometimes been described as a strategic attempt to block experiencing of painful affect (e.g., Horowitz, Wilner, Kaltreider, & Alvarez, 1980), it may simply be a straightforward consequence of phasic NE depletion (van der Kolk & Greenberg, 1987).

Two-Factor Conditioning Model

Mowrer's (1939) two-factor learning theory has provided another animal model for certain PTSD symptoms, especially psychophysiologic reactivity to reminders of the trauma and avoidance of these reminders (Charney et al., 1993; Keane et al., 1985). The first factor refers to Pavlovian conditioning and the second factor refers to instrumental conditioning. According to this view, initially neutral cues become established as Pavlovian conditioned stimuli for fear by predicting aversive unconditioned stimuli. Therefore, visual, auditory, and olfactory cues present during the original trauma acquire the ability to elicit responses similar to those evoked during the original trauma. These aversive emotional states motivate avoidance of conditioned cues, and reduction in distress negatively reinforces instrumental avoidance responses. PTSD arising from a single horrific event would be akin to "one-trial conditioning" as studied in the animal learning laboratory, whereas PTSD arising from the witnessing of trauma inflicted upon others would be akin to vicarious conditioning.

Relevant to the persistence of conditioned fear in PTSD, behavioral neuroscientists have shown that aversive conditioning involving subcortical thalamic-amygdala circuits is strikingly resistant to extinction, prompting suggestions that such fears are "indelible" (e.g., LeDoux, 1993; LeDoux, Romanski, & Xagoraris, 1989). Moreover, animal researchers have shown that procedures that reduce fear do not erase aversive memories but instead override them with new memories (e.g., Bouton, 1988). Accordingly, dormant fear memories remain subject to reemergence under the appropriate prompting context. Drawing on this research, Charney et al. (1993) have proposed that PTSD may be characterized by deficits in the cortical suppression of subcortical neural circuits that support persistent conditioned fear responses.

Kindling

Although Pavlovian conditioning explains psychophysiologic reactivity to reminders to traumatic events, emotional responses in many PTSD patients are often "not conditional enough" (Pitman et al., 1993, p. 145). That is, intense fear and rage may erupt without any obvious external, trauma-relevant precipitant. Two animal models have been advanced to explain these phenomena: a kindling-like process (Post, Weiss, & Smith, 1995) and emotive biasing (Pitman et al., 1993).

Kindling refers to a process whereby intermittent subconvulsive electrical stimulation of the limbic system eventually results in seizures. Animals that have undergone a kindling procedure exhibit seizures to stimuli that were originally incapable of evoking them. Post et al. (1995) have drawn a parallel between spontaneous paroxysmal discharges of motor circuits in seizures and paroxysmal discharges of memory circuits in flashbacks. Repeated occurrence of frightening reexperiencing events may themselves mimic a kindlinglike process whereby conditioned cues once necessary for provocation of symptoms become unnecessary as the reexperiencing symptoms (e.g., nightmares, flashbacks), like spontaneous seizures, acquire autonomy from triggering stimuli. As Post et al. emphasize, previous exposure to stressors may have a sensitizing or kindlinglike effect in establishing the neural substrate of vulnerability to later stressors that produce full-blown PTSD. Evidence that a history of childhood sexual or physical abuse increases risk for PTSD in war veterans is consistent with this possibility. The neural substrates underlying kindling and sensitization undergo a spatiotemporal evolution. To the extent that similar principles apply to PTSD, one would conclude that PTSD constitutes a continuously unfolding process. The upshot is that the pathophysiology of the disorder may differ depending on the stage of illness studied.

Emotive Biasing

Pitman et al. (1993) have suggested that emotive biasing may better capture PTSD symptoms in that its endpoint is behavioral, not electrophysiological. Emotive biasing procedures involve electrical activation of pathways connecting the amygdala to the ventromedial hypothalamus. Once strengthened, these pathways support enhanced fear responding to a variety of stimuli. Emotive biasing increases the magnitude of unconditioned fear responses, and therefore may underlie nonspecific fear responses such as hypervigilance, startle, and irritability.

Information Processing

Psychopathologists have also advanced information-processing theories of PTSD (e.g., Chemtob, Roitblatt, Hamada, Carlson, & Twentyman, 1988; Foa, Steketee, & Rothbaum, 1989; Litz & Keane, 1989). Inspired by the work of Lang (1985), many theorists have sought to characterize the fear networks that represent traumatic events in memory and support the expression of symptoms. These networks comprise tightly interlocked stimulus, response, and meaning propositions whereby input that activates some elements of the structure leads to activation of the others.

Cognitive theorists also emphasize that persistent PTSD is supported by transformed representations of the world and oneself. Unpredictable traumatic events, in particular, are presumably especially capable of leading PTSD sufferers to assume danger as their default interpretation. For example, Foa et al. (1989) have noted that women who are raped in a place they once believed was safe (e.g., their own bedroom) may be more prone to construe the world as pervasively dangerous than those who were raped elsewhere. Viewing the world as unpredictably hazardous, these individuals chronically are prone to react defensively. Pathologic transformations of the self as unworthy, evil, corrupted, and so forth underlie complex cognitive emotions such as guilt and shame that are not easily captured by biological models that accommodate only basic emotions such as fear.

Is PTSD a Normal Stress Response to an Abnormal Stressor?

Initial theorizing about PTSD was based on the assumption that response to traumatic events constituted an extension of responses to subtraumatic stressors. That is, theorists assumed that PTSD was primarily a normal response to an abnormal stressor. Indeed, *DSM-III* stated that stressors capable of inducing the syndrome were those that would evoke symptoms of distress in almost anybody. Early advocates of the diagnosis wished to emphasize the pathogenic aspects of the event (e.g., war, rape) and to avoid stigmatizing the victim. More recently, during the *DSM-IV* deliberations, discussion concerned issues such as whether women whose intense rape-related symptoms warrant their being considered mentally ill, as a *DSM* diagnosis of PTSD implies. Also, as Başoğlu (1992) has pointed out, political activists and others working with torture survivors are ambivalent about medicalizing or pathologizing the psychological consequences of political repression. Should people who have been traumatized by torture be classified as mentally diseased?

But as Yehuda and McFarlane (1995) have recently observed, subsequent research has indicated that the picture is more complex than early theorists had supposed. Most people exposed to traumatic stressors do not develop PTSD, thereby prompting speculation about vulnerability factors that render some people more likely to fall ill than others. High rates of comorbidity, including disorders preexisting the emergence of PTSD, also point to individual difference variables that modulate the impact of horrific events. Finally, studies on HPA axis dysfunction, for example, validate PTSD as a psychobiological disease entity distinct from other disorders, such as depression, and distinct from the classic stress response. As Yehuda and McFarlane (1995) argued, the concept of stress response needs to be broadened to embrace the pathologic variant embodied in PTSD.

The arguments and data of Yehuda and McFarlane notwithstanding, the boundary between normal and abnormal stress responses remains uncomfortably fuzzy. Matters have been further complicated by the inclusion of acute stress disorder (ASD) as a new entity in *DSM-IV* (Bryant & Harvey, 1997). This diagnosis is assigned to trauma-exposed people who exhibit dissociative, intrusive, avoidance, and arousal symptoms between two days and four weeks following the traumatic event. Victims of motor vehicle accidents who exhibit the ASD symptoms of acute numbing, depersonalization, a sense of reliving the event, and motor restlessness are at enhanced risk for subsequently qualifying for PTSD (Harvey & Bryant, 1998). But it is not obvious that extreme distress immediately following a horrific event necessarily indicates mental illness in the victim. Indeed, as Wakefield (1992a, 1992b) has argued, the range of nonpathological responses to a stressor is probably normally distributed, and classifying all statistically unusual reactions as pathological will lead to incorrectly lumping normal reactions with those that genuinely reflect underlying dysfunction in psychobiological coping mechanisms. Likewise, not all unexpectably intense or prolonged grief reactions necessarily reflect derangements in psychobiological coping mechanisms. Indeed, tremendous cross-cultural variation in what is deemed a "normal" response to the death of a loved one (Kleinman, 1995) underscore the complexity of distinguishing genuine pathology from normal, albeit, uncommon reactions.

In summary, PTSD has been the subject of considerable research since its appearance in the DSM nearly two decades ago. Although confidence in its syndromal validity has grown, it has now become apparent that people exposed to severe stressors do not invariably exhibit this syndrome. Deemphasizing the etiologic significance of the traumatic event per se, researchers in the next century will likely focus on those attributes of victims and their environments that increase or decrease the odds of the disorder emerging. These efforts are likely to become increasingly theoretically motivated as scholars endeavor to specify what psychobiological mechanisms are affected in PTSD. Indeed, only in this way will clinicians manage to discriminate intense but normal responses from those responses that arise from genuine psychopathology.

References

Amir, N., McNally, R. J., & Wiegartz, P. S. (1996). Implicit memory bias for threat in posttraumatic stress disorder. *Cognitive Therapy and Research*, *20*, 625–635.

Başoğlu, M. (1992). Introduction. In M. Başoğlu (Ed.), *Torture and its consequences: Current treatment approaches* (pp. 1–8). Cambridge, UK: Cambridge University Press.

Başoğlu, M., & Mineka, S. (1992). The role of uncontrollable and unpredictable stress in posttraumatic stress responses in torture survivors. In M. Başoğlu (Ed.), *Torture and its consequences: Current treatment approaches* (pp. 182–225). Cambridge, UK: Cambridge University Press.

Başoğlu, M., Paker, M., Paker, Ö., Ozmen, E., Marks, I., Incesu, C., Sahin, D., & Şarlmurat, N. (1994). Psychological effects of torture: A comparison of tortured with nontortured political activists in Turkey. *American Journal of Psychiatry*, *151*, 76–81.

Blanchard, E. B., Kolb, L. C., Gerardi, R. J., Ryan, P., & Pallmeyer, T. P. (1986). Cardiac response to relevant stimuli as an adjunctive tool for diagnosing post-traumatic stress disorder in Vietnam veterans. *Behavior Therapy*, *17*, 592–606.

Blanchard, E. B., Kolb, L. C., Pallmeyer, T. P., & Gerardi, R. J. (1982). A psychophysiological study of post traumatic stress disorder in Vietnam veterans. *Psychiatric Quarterly*, *54*, 220–229.

Blank, A. S., Jr. (1993). The longitudinal course of posttraumatic stress disorder. In J. R. T. Davison & E. B. Foa (Eds.), *Posttraumatic stress disorder: DSM-IV and beyond* (pp. 3–22). Washington, DC: American Psychiatric Press.

Boscarino, J. A. (1995). Post-traumatic stress and associated disorders among Vietnam veterans: The significance of combat exposure and social support. *Journal of Traumatic Stress*, *8*, 317–336.

Bouton, M. E. (1988). Context and ambiguity in the extinction of emotional learning: Implications for exposure therapy. *Behaviour Research and Therapy*, *26*, 137–149.

Bremner, J. D., Randall, P., Scott, T. M., Bronen, R. A., Seibyl, J. P., Southwick, S. M., Delaney, R. C., McCarthy, G., Charney, D. S., & Innis, R. B. (1995). MRI-based measurement of hippocampal volume in combat-related posttraumatic stress disorder. *American Journal of Psychiatry*, *152*, 973–981.

Bremner, J. D., Randall, P., Vermetten, E., Staib, L., Bronen, R. A., Mazure, C., Capelli, S., McCarthy, G., Innis, R. B., & Charney, D. S. (1997). Magnetic resonance imaging-based measurement of hippocampal volume in posttraumatic stress disorder related to childhood physical and sexual abuse: A preliminary report. *Biological Psychiatry*, *41*, 23–32.

Bremner, J. D., Southwick, S., Brett, E., Fontana, A., Rosenheck, R., & Charney, D. S. (1992). Dissociation and posttraumatic stress disorder in Vietnam combat veterans. *American Journal of Psychiatry*, *149*, 328–332.

Bremner, J. D., Southwick, S. M., Johnson, D. R., Yehuda, R., & Charney, D. S. (1993). Childhood physical abuse and combat-related posttraumatic stress disorder in Vietnam veterans. *American Journal of Psychiatry*, *150*, 235–239.

Breslau, N., & Davis, G. C. (1987). Posttraumatic stress disorder: The etiologic specificity of wartime stressors. *American Journal of Psychiatry*, *144*, 578–583.

Breslau, N., Davis, G. C., & Andreski, P. (1995). Risk factors for PTSD-related traumatic events: A prospective analysis. *American Journal of Psychiatry*, *152*, 529–535.

Breslau, N., Davis, G. C., Andreski, P., & Peterson, E. (1991). Traumatic events and posttraumatic stress disorder in an urban population of young adults. *Archives of General Psychiatry*, *48*, 216–222.

Brittlebank, A. D., Scott, L., Williams, J. M. G., & Ferrier, I. N. (1993). Autobiographical memory in depression: State or trait marker? *British Journal of Psychiatry*, *162*, 118–121.

Brown, T. M., & Boudewyns, P. A. (1996). Periodic limb movements of sleep in combat veterans with posttraumatic stress disorder. *Journal of Traumatic Stress*, *9*, 129–136.

Bryant, R. A., & Harvey, A. G. (1995). Processing threatening information in posttraumatic stress disorder. *Journal of Abnormal Psychology*, *104*, 537–541.

Bryant, R. A., & Harvey, A. G. (1997). Acute stress disorder: A critical review of diagnostic issues. *Clinical Psychology Review*, *17*, 757–773.

Burgess, A. W., & Holmstrom, L. L. (1974). Rape trauma syndrome. *American Journal of Psychiatry, 131*, 981–986.

Butler, R. W., Braff, D. L., Rausch, J. L., Jenkins, M. A., Sprock, J., & Geyer, M. A. (1990). Physiological evidence of exaggerated startle response in a subgroup of Vietnam veterans with combat-related PTSD. *American Journal of Psychiatry, 147*, 1308–1312.

Carroll, B. J., Feinberg, M., Greden, J. F., Tarika, J., Albala, A. A., Haskett, R. F., James, N. M., Kronfol, Z., Lohr, N., Steiner, M., de Vigne, J. P., & Young, E. (1981). A specific laboratory test for the diagnosis of melancholia: Standardization, validation, and clinical utility. *Archives of General Psychiatry, 38*, 15–22.

Cassiday, K. L., McNally, R. J., & Zeitlin, S. B. (1992). Cognitive processing of trauma cues in rape victims with post-traumatic stress disorder. *Cognitive Therapy and Research, 16*, 283–295.

Center for Disease Control. (1988). Health status of Vietnam veterans: I. Psychosocial characteristics. *Journal of the American Medical Association, 259*, 2701–2707.

Charney, D. S., Deutch, A. Y., Krystal, J. H., Southwick, S. M., & Davis, M. (1993). Psychobiologic mechanisms of posttraumatic stress disorder. *Archives of General Psychiatry, 50*, 294–305.

Chemtob, C., Roitblatt, H. L., Hamada, R. S., Carlson, J. G., & Twentyman, C. T. (1988). A cognitive action theory of post-traumatic stress disorder. *Journal of Anxiety Disorders, 2*, 253–275.

Chodoff, P. (1963). Late effects of the concentration camp syndrome. *Archives of General Psychiatry, 8*, 323–333.

Davidson, J. R. T., Hughes, D., Blazer, D. G., & George, L. K. (1991). Post-traumatic stress disorder in the community: An epidemiological study. *Psychological Medicine, 21*, 713–721.

Davidson, J., Swartz, M., Storck, M., Krishnan, R. R., & Hammett, E. (1985). A diagnostic and family study of posttraumatic stress disorder. *American Journal of Psychiatry, 142*, 90–93.

Dinan, T. G., Barry, S., Yatham, L. N., Mobayed, M., & Brown, I. (1990). A pilot study of a neuroendocrine test battery in posttraumatic stress disorder. *Biological Psychiatry, 28*, 665–672.

Engel, C. C., Jr., Engel, A. L., Campbell, S. J., McFall, M. E., Russo, J., & Katon, W. (1993). Posttraumatic stress disorder symptoms and precombat sexual and physical abuse in Desert Storm veterans. *Journal of Nervous and Mental Disease, 181*, 683–688.

Evans, J., Williams, J. M. G., O'Loughlin, S., & Howells, K. (1992). Autobiographical memory and problem-solving strategies of parasuicide patients. *Psychological Medicine, 22*, 399–405.

Foa, E. B., Feske, U., Murdock, T. B., Kozak, M. J., & McCarthy, P. R. (1991). Processing of threat-related information in rape victims. *Journal of Abnormal Psychology, 100*, 156–162.

Foa, E. B., Steketee, G., & Rothbaum, B. O. (1989). Behavioral/cognitive conceptualizations of post-traumatic stress disorder. *Behavior Therapy, 20*, 155–176.

Foa, E. B., Zinbarg, R. & Rothbaum, B. O. (1992). Uncontrollability and unpredictability in post-traumatic stress disorder: An animal model. *Psychological Bulletin, 112*, 218–238.

Gerardi, R. J., Blanchard, E. B., & Kolb, L. C. (1989). Ability of Vietnam veterans to dissimulate a psychophysiological assessment for post-traumatic stress disorder. *Behavior Therapy, 20*, 229–243.

Gerardi, R. J., Keane, T. M., Cahoon, B. J., & Klauminzer, G. W. (1994). An in vivo assessment of physiological arousal in posttraumatic stress disorder. *Journal of Abnormal Psychology, 103*, 825–827.

Goldberg, J., True, W. R., Eisen, S. A., & Henderson, W. G. (1990). A twin study of the effects of the Vietnam War on posttraumatic stress disorder. *Journal of the American Medical Association, 263*, 1227–1232.

Grossman, D. (1995). *On killing: The psychological cost of learning to kill in war and society.* Boston, MA: Little, Brown and Company.

Gurvits, T. V., Lasko, N. B., Schachter, S. C., Kuhne, A. A., Orr, S. P., & Pitman, R. K. (1993). Neurological status of Vietnam veterans with chronic posttraumatic stress disorder. *Journal of Neuropsychiatry and Clinical Neuroscience, 5*, 183–188.

Gurvits, T. V., Shenton, M. E., Hokama, H., Ohta, H., Lasko, N. B., Gilbertson, M. W., Orr, S. P., Kikinis, R., Jolesz, F. A., McCarley, R. W., & Pitman, R. K. (1996). Magnetic resonance imaging study of hippocampal volume in chronic, combat-related posttraumatic stress disorder. *Biological Psychiatry, 19*, 433–444.

Halbreich, U., Olympia, J., Glogowski, J., Carson, S., Axelrod, S., & Yeh, C. M. (1988). The importance of past psychological trauma and pathophysiological process as determinants of current biologic abnormalities. *Archives of General Psychiatry, 45*, 293–294.

Harry, B., & Resnick, P. J. (1986). Posttraumatic stress disorder in murderers. *Journal of Forensic Sciences*, *31*, 609–613.

Harvey, A. G., & Bryant, R. A. (1998). The relationship between acute stress disorder and posttraumatic stress disorder: A prospective evaluation of motor vehicle accident survivors. *Journal of Consulting and Clinical Psychology*, *66*, 507–512.

Hefez, A., Metz, L., & Lavie, P. (1987). Long-term effects of extreme situational stress on sleep and dreaming. *American Journal of Psychiatry*, *144*, 344–347.

Helzer, J. E., Robins, L. N., & McEvoy, L. (1987). Post-traumatic stress disorder in the general population: Findings of the Epidemiologic Catchment Area Survey. *New England Journal of Medicine*, *317*, 1630–1634.

Horowitz, M. J., Wilner, N., Kaltreider, N., & Alvarez, W. (1980). Signs and symptoms of posttraumatic stress disorder. *Archives of General Psychiatry*, *37*, 85–92.

Kaminer, H., & Lavie, P. (1991). Sleep and dreaming in Holocaust survivors: Dramatic decrease in dream recall in well-adjusted survivors. *Journal of Nervous and Mental Disease*, *179*, 664–669.

Keane, T. M., & Kaloupek, D. G. (1987). Comorbid psychiatric disorders in PTSD: Implications for research. *Annals of the New York Academy of Sciences*, *821*, 24–34.

Keane, T. M., Scott, W. O., Chavoya, G. A., Lamparski, D. M., & Fairbank, J. A. (1985). Social support in Vietnam veterans with posttraumatic stress disorder: A comparative analysis. *Journal of Consulting and Clinical Psychology*, *53*, 95–102.

Keane, T. M., Zimering, R. T., & Caddell, J. M. (1985). A behavioral formulation of posttraumatic stress disorder in Vietnam veterans. *The Behavior Therapist*, *8*, 9–12.

Kessler, R. C., Sonnega, A., Bromet, E., Hughes, M., Nelson, C. B. (1995). Posttraumatic stress disorder in the National Comorbidity Survey. *Archives of General Psychiatry*, *52*, 1048–1060.

Kilpatrick, D. G., Resnick, H. S., Freedy, J. R., Pelcovitz, D., Resick, P., Roth, S., & van der Kolk, B. (1991). *Report of findings from the DSM-IV PTSD Field Trial: Emphasis on Criterion A and overall PTSD diagnosis*. Paper prepared for the *DSM-IV* Workgroup on PTSD.

King, D. W., King, L. A., Foy, D. W., & Gudanowski, D. M. (1996). Prewar factors in combat-related posttraumatic stress disorder: Structural equation modeling with a national sample of female and male Vietnam veterans. *Journal of Consulting and Clinical Psychology*, *64*, 520–531.

Kleinman, A. (1995). *Writing at the margin: Discourse between anthropology and medicine*. Berkeley, CA: University of California Press.

Kluznik, J. C., Speed, N., van Valkenburg, C., & Magraw, R. (1986). Forty-year follow-up of United States prisoners of war. *American Journal of Psychiatry*, *143*, 1443–1446.

Kosten, T. R., Wahby, V., Giller, E., Jr., & Mason, J. (1990). The dexamethasone suppression test and thyrotropin-releasing hormone stimulation test in posttraumatic stress disorder. *Biological Psychiatry*, *28*, 657–664.

Kudler, H., Davidson, J., Meador, K., Lipper, S., & Ely, T. (1987). The DST and posttraumatic stress disorder. *American Journal of Psychiatry*, *144*, 1068–1071.

Kulka, R. A., Schlenger, W. E., Fairbank, J. A., Hough, R. L., Jordan, B. K., Marmar, C. R., & Weiss, D. S. (1988). *National Vietnam Veterans Readjustment Study (NVVRS): Description, current status, and initial PTSD prevalence estimates*. Research Triangle Park, NC: Research Triangle Institute.

Kulka, R. A., Schlenger, W. E., Fairbank, J. A., Hough, R. L., Jordan, B. K., Marmar, C. R., & Weiss, D. S. (1990). *Trauma and the Vietnam War generation: Report of findings from the National Vietnam Veterans Readjustment Study*. New York: Brunner/Mazel.

Kuyken, W., & Brewin, C. R. (1995). Autobiographical memory functioning in depression and reports of early abuse. *Journal of Abnormal Psychology*, *104*, 585–591.

Lang, P. J. (1985). The cognitive psychophysiology of emotion: Fear and anxiety. In A. H. Tuma & J. D. Maser (Eds.), *Anxiety and the anxiety disorders* (pp. 131–170). Hillsdale, NJ: Erlbaum.

Lavie, P., Hefez, A., Halperin, G., & Enoch, D. (1979). Long-term effects of traumatic war-related events on sleep. *American Journal of Psychiatry*, *136*, 175–178.

LeDoux, J. E. (1993). Emotional networks in the brain. In M. Lewis & J. M. Haviland (Eds.), *Handbook of emotions* (pp. 109–118). New York: Guilford Press.

LeDoux, J. E., Romanski, L., & Xagoraris, A. (1989). Indelibility of subcortical emotional memories. *Journal of Cognitive Neuroscience*, *1*, 238–243.

Lerer, B., Bleich, A., Kotler, M., Garb, R., Hertzberg, M., & Levin, B. (1987). Posttraumatic stress disorder in Israeli combat veterans: Effect of phenelzine treatment. *Archives of General Psychiatry*, *44*, 976–981.

Litz, B. T., & Keane, T. M. (1989). Information processing in anxiety disorders: Application to the understanding of post-traumatic stress disorder. *Clinical Psychology Review, 9,* 243–257.

Macklin, M. L., Metzger, L. J., Litz, B. T., McNally, R. J., Lasko, N. B., Orr, S. P., & Pitman, R. K. (1998). Lower pre-combat intelligence is a risk factor for posttraumatic stress disorder. *Journal of Consulting and Clinical Psychology, 66,* 323–326.

Maier, S. F., & Seligman, M. E. P. (1976). Learned helplessness: Theory and evidence. *Journal of Experimental Psychology: General, 105,* 3–46.

Malloy, P. F., Fairbank, J. A., & Keane, T. M. (1983). Validation of a multimethod assessment of posttraumatic stress disorders in Vietnam veterans. *Journal of Consulting and Clinical Psychology, 51,* 488–494.

March, J. S. (1993). What constitutes a stressor? The "Criterion A" issue. In J. R. T. Davidson & E. B. Foa (Eds.), *Posttraumatic stress disorder: DSM-IV and beyond* (pp. 37–54). Washington, DC: American Psychiatric Press.

Marmar, C. R., Weiss, D. S., Schlenger, W. E., Fairbank, J. A., Jordan, B. K., Kulka, R. A., & Hough, R. L. (1994). Peritraumatic dissociation and posttraumatic stress in male Vietnam theater veterans. *American Journal of Psychiatry, 151,* 902–907.

Mason, J. W., Giller, E. L., Kosten, T. R., Ostroff, R. B., & Podd, L. (1986). Urinary free-cortisol levels in posttraumatic stress disorder patients. *Journal of Nervous and Mental Disease, 174,* 145–149.

McFall, M. E., Murburg, M., Ko, G. N., & Veith, R. C. (1990). Autonomic responses to stress in Vietnam combat veterans with posttraumatic stress disorder. *Biological Psychiatry, 27,* 1165–1175.

McFall, M. E., Veith, R. C., & Murburg, M. M. (1992). Basal sympathoadrenal function in posttraumatic stress disorder. *Biological Psychiatry, 31,* 1050–1056.

McFarlane, A. C. (1989). The aetiology of post-traumatic morbidity: Predisposing, precipitating and perpetuating factors. *British Journal of Psychiatry, 154,* 221–228.

McNally, R. J. (1995a). Cognitive processing of trauma-relevant information in PTSD. *PTSD Research Quarterly, 6*(2), 1–6.

McNally, R. J. (1995b). Automaticity and the anxiety disorders. *Behaviour Research and Therapy, 33,* 747–754.

McNally, R. J., & Amir, N. (1996). Perceptual implicit memory for trauma-related information in post-traumatic stress disorder. *Cognition and Emotion, 10,* 551–556.

McNally, R. J., Amir, N., & Lipke, H. J. (1996). Subliminal processing of threat cues in post-traumatic stress disorder? *Journal of Anxiety Disorders, 10,* 115–128.

McNally, R. J., English, G. E., & Lipke, H. J. (1993). Assessment of intrusive cognition in PTSD: Use of the modified Stroop paradigm. *Journal of Traumatic Stress, 6,* 33–41.

McNally, R. J., Kaspi, S. P., Riemann, B. C., & Zeitlin, S. B. (1990). Selective processing of threat cues in posttraumatic stress disorder. *Journal of Abnormal Psychology, 99,* 398–402.

McNally, R. J., Lasko, N. B., Macklin, M. L., & Pitman, R. K. (1995). Autobiographical memory disturbance in combat-related posttraumatic stress disorder. *Behaviour Research and Therapy, 33,* 619–630.

McNally, R. J., Litz, B. T., Prassas, A., Shin, L. M., & Weathers, F. W. (1994). Emotional priming of autobiographical memory in post-traumatic stress disorder. *Cognition and Emotion, 8,* 351–367.

McNally, R. J., & Lukach, B. M. (1992). Are panic attacks traumatic stressors? *American Journal of Psychiatry, 149,* 824–826.

McNally, R. J., Metzger, L. J., Lasko, N. B., Clancy, S. A., & Pitman, R. K. (1998). Directed forgetting of trauma cues in adult survivors of childhood sexual abuse with and without posttraumatic stress disorder. *Journal of Abnormal Psychology, 107,* 596–601.

McNally, R. J., & Shin, L. M. (1995). Association of intelligence with severity of posttraumatic stress disorder symptoms in Vietnam combat veterans. *American Journal of Psychiatry, 152,* 936–938.

Morgan, C. A., III, Grillon, C., Southwick, S. M., Davis, M., & Charney, D. S. (1996). Exaggerated acoustic startle reflex in Gulf War veterans with posttraumatic stress disorder. *American Journal of Psychiatry, 153,* 64–68.

Mowrer, O. H. (1939). A stimulus-response analysis of anxiety and its role as a reinforcing agent. *Psychological Review, 46,* 553–565.

Orr, S. P. (1994). An overview of psychophysiological studies of PTSD. *PTSD Research Quarterly, 5*(1), 1–7.

Orr, S. P., Lasko, N. B., Shalev, A. Y., & Pitman, R. K. (1995). Physiologic responses to loud tones in Vietnam veterans with posttraumatic stress disorder. *Journal of Abnormal Psychology, 104,* 75–82.

Orr, S. P., & Pitman, R. K. (1993). Psychophysiologic assessment of attempts to simulate posttraumatic stress disorder. *Biological Psychiatry, 33,* 127–129.

Orr, S. P., Pitman, R. K., Lasko, N. B., & Herz, L. R. (1993). Psychophysiological assessment of posttraumatic stress disorder imagery in World War II and Korean combat veterans.

Journal of Abnormal Psychology, 102, 152–159.

Orsillo, S. M., Weathers, F. W., Litz, B. T., Steinberg, H. R., Huska, J. A., & Keane, T. M. (1996). Current and lifetime psychiatric disorders among veterans with war zone-related posttraumatic stress disorder. *Journal of Nervous and Mental Disease, 184*, 307–313.

Paige, S. R., Reid, G. M., Allen, M. G., & Newton, J. E. O. (1990). Psychophysiological correlates of posttraumatic stress disorder in Vietnam veterans. *Biological Psychiatry, 27*, 419–430.

Pallmeyer, T. P., Blanchard, E. B., & Kolb, L. C. (1986). The psychophysiology of combat-induced post-traumatic stress disorder in Vietnam veterans. *Behaviour Research and Therapy, 24*, 645–652.

Pitman, R. K., Orr, S. P., Forgue, D. F., Altman, B., de Jong, J. B., & Herz, L. R. (1990). Psychophysiologic responses to combat imagery of Vietnam veterans with posttraumatic stress disorder versus other anxiety disorders. *Journal of Abnormal Psychology, 99*, 49–54.

Pitman, R. K., Orr, S. P., Forgue, D. F., de Jong, J. B., & Claiborn, J. M. (1987). Psychophysiologic assessment of posttraumatic stress disorder imagery in Vietnam combat veterans. *Archives of General Psychiatry, 44*, 970–975.

Pitman, R. K., Orr, S. P., & Shalev, A. Y. (1993). Once bitten, twice shy: Beyond the conditioning model of PTSD. *Biological Psychiatry, 33*, 145–146.

Pitman, R. K., van der Kolk, B. A., Orr, S. P., & Greenberg, M. S. (1990). Naloxone-reversible analgesic response to combat-related stimuli in posttraumatic stress disorder: A pilot study. *Archives of General Psychiatry, 47*, 541–544.

Post, R. M., Weiss, S. R. B., & Smith, M. A. (1995). Sensitization and kindling: Implications for the evolving neural substrates of post-traumatic stress disorder. In M. J. Friedman, D. S. Charney, & A. Y. Deutch (Eds.), *Neurobiological and clinical consequences of stress: From normal adaptation to post-traumatic stress disorder* (pp. 203–224). Philadelphia: Lippincott-Raven.

Prins, A., Kaloupek, D. G., & Keane, T. M. (1995). Psychophysiological evidence for autonomic arousal and startle in traumatized adult populations. In M. J. Friedman, D. S. Charney, & A. Y. Deutch (Eds.), *Neurobiological and clinical consequences of stress: From normal adaptation to post-traumatic stress disorder* (pp. 291–314). Philadelphia: Lippincott-Raven.

Rangell, L. (1976). Discussion of the Buffalo Creek disaster: The course of psychic trauma. *American Journal of Psychiatry, 133*, 313–316.

Rauch, S. L., van der Kolk, B. A., Fisler, R. E., Alpert, N. M., Orr, S. P., Savage, C. R., Fischman, A. J., Jenike, M. A., & Pitman, R. K. (1996). A symptom provocation study of posttraumatic stress disorder using positron emission tomography and script-driven imagery. *Archives of General Psychiatry, 53*, 380–387.

Ross, R. J., Ball, W. A., Sullivan, K. A., & Caroff, S. N. (1989). Sleep disturbance as the hallmark of posttraumatic stress disorder. *American Journal of Psychiatry, 146*, 697–707.

Rothbaum, B. O., & Foa, E. B. (1993). Subtypes of posttraumatic stress disorder and duration of symptoms. In J. R. T. Davidson & E. B. Foa (Eds.), *Posttraumatic stress disorder: DSM-IV and beyond* (pp. 23–35). Washington, DC: American Psychiatric Press.

Sapolsky, R. M., Uno, H., Rebert, C. S., & Finch, C. E. (1990). Hippocampal damage associated with prolonged glucocorticoid exposure in primates. *Journal of Neuroscience, 10*, 2897–2902.

Schlosberg, A., & Benjamin, M. (1978). Sleep patterns in three acute combat fatigue cases. *Journal of Clinical Psychiatry, 39*, 546–549.

Scott, M. J., & Stradling, S. G. (1994). Post-traumatic stress disorder without the trauma. *British Journal of Clinical Psychology, 33*, 71–74.

Scott, W. J. (1990). PTSD in DSM-III: A case in the politics of diagnosis and disease. *Social Problems, 37*, 294–310.

Shalev, A. Y., Orr, S. P., Peri, T., Schreiber, S., & Pitman, R. K. (1992). Physiologic responses to loud tones in Israeli patients with posttraumatic stress disorder. *Archives of General Psychiatry, 49*, 870–875.

Shalev, A. Y., Orr, S. P., & Pitman, R. K. (1993). Psychophysiologic assessment of traumatic imagery in Israeli civilian patients with posttraumatic stress disorder. *American Journal of Psychiatry, 150*, 620–624.

Shalev, A. Y., Peri, T., Canetti, L., & Schreiber, S. (1996). Predictors of PTSD in injured trauma survivors: A prospective study. *American Journal of Psychiatry, 153*, 219–225.

Shin, L. M., Kosslyn, S. M., McNally, R. J., Alpert, N. M., Thompson, W. L., Rauch, S. L., Macklin, M. L., & Pitman, R. K. (1997). Visual imagery and perception in posttraumatic stress disorder: A positron emission tomographic investigation. *Archives of General Psychiatry, 54*, 233–241.

Shin, L. M., McNally, R. J., Kosslyn, S. M., Thompson, W. L., Rauch, S. L., Alpert, N. M., Metzger, L. J., Lasko, N. B., Orr, S. P., & Pitman, R. K. (in press). Regional cerebral blood flow during script-driven imagery in childhood sexual abuse-related posttraumatic stress disorder: A positron emission tomographic investigation. *American Journal of Psychiatry.*

Sierles, F. S., Chen, J. J., McFarland, R. E., & Taylor, M. A. (1983). Posttraumatic stress disorder and concurrent psychiatric illness: A preliminary report. *American Journal of Psychiatry, 140*, 1177–1179.

Sierles, F. S., Chen, J. J., Messing, M. L., Besyner, J. K., & Taylor, M. A. (1986). Concurrent psychiatric illness in non-Hispanic outpatients diagnosed as having posttraumatic stress disorder. *Journal of Nervous and Mental Disease, 174*, 171–173.

Smith, E. M., North, C. S., McCool, R. E., & Shea, J. M. (1990). Acute postdisaster psychiatric disorders: Identification of persons at risk. *American Journal of Psychiatry, 147*, 202–206.

Solomon, Z., Kotler, M., & Mikulincer, M. (1988). Combat-related posttraumatic stress disorder among second-generation Holocaust survivors: Preliminary findings. *American Journal of Psychiatry, 145*, 865–868.

Solomon, Z., Kotler, M., Shalev, A., & Lin, R. (1989). Delayed onset PTSD among Israeli veterans of the 1982 Lebanon War. *Psychiatry, 52*, 428–436.

Southwick, S. M., Bremner, D., Krystal, J. H., & Charney, D. S. (1994). Psychobiologic research in post-traumatic stress disorder. *Psychiatric Clinics of North America, 17*, 251–264.

Southwick, S. M., Krystal, J. H., Morgan, C. A., Johnson, D., Nagy, L. M., Nicolaou, A., Heninger, G. R., & Charney, D. S. (1993). Abnormal noradrenergic function in posttraumatic stress disorder. *Archives of General Psychiatry, 50*, 266–274.

Southwick, S. M., Morgan C. A., III., Darnell, A., Bremner, D., Nicolaou, A. L., Nagy, L. M., & Charney, D. S. (1995). Trauma-related symptoms of veterans of Operation Desert Storm: A 2-year follow-up. *American Journal of Psychiatry, 152*, 1150–1155.

Speed, N., Engdahl, B., Schwartz, J., & Eberly, R. (1989). Posttraumatic stress disorder as a consequence of the POW experience. *Journal of Nervous and Mental Disease, 177*, 147–153.

Stein, M. B., Koverola, C., Hanna, C., Torchia, M. G., & McClarty, B. (1997). Hippocampal volume in women victimized by childhood sexual abuse. *Psychological Medicine, 27*, 951–959.

Sutker, P. B., Uddo, M., Brailey, K., Vasterling, J. J., & Errera, P. (1994). Psychopathology in war-zone deployed and nondeployed Operation Desert Storm troops assigned to graves registration duties. *Journal of Abnormal Psychology, 103*, 383–390.

Terr, L. C. (1991). Childhood traumas: An outline and overview. *American Journal of Psychiatry, 148*, 10–20.

Thrasher, S. M., Dalgleish, T., & Yule, W. (1994). Information processing in posttraumatic stress disorder. *Behaviour Research and Therapy, 32*, 247–254.

Tiffany, W. J., Jr. (1967). The mental health of army troops in Viet Nam. *American Journal of Psychiatry, 123*, 1585–1586.

True, W. R., Rice, J., Eisen, S. A., Heath, A. C., Goldberg, J., Lyons, M. J., & Nowak, J. (1993). A twin study of genetic and environmental contributions to liability for posttraumatic stress symptoms. *Archives of General Psychiatry, 50*, 257–264.

van der Kolk, B., Blitz, R., Burr, W., Sherry, S., & Hartmann, E. (1984). Nightmares and trauma: A comparison of nightmares after combat with lifelong nightmares in veterans. *American Journal of Psychiatry, 141*, 187–190.

van der Kolk, B. A., & Greenberg, M. S. (1987). The psychobiology of the trauma response: Hyperarousal, constriction, and addiction to traumatic reexposure. In B. A. van der Kolk (Ed.), *Psychological trauma* (pp. 63–87). Washington, DC: American Psychiatric Press.

van Dyke, C., Zilberg, N. J., & McKinnon, J. A. (1985). Posttraumatic stress disorder: A thirty-year delay in a World War II veteran. *American Journal of Psychiatry, 142*, 1070–1073.

Vrana, S. R., Roodman, A., & Beckham, J. C. (1995). Selective processing of trauma-relevant words in posttraumatic stress disorder. *Journal of Anxiety Disorders, 9*, 515–530.

Wakefield, J. C. (1992a). The concept of mental disorder: On the boundary between biological facts and social values. *American Psychologist, 47*, 373–388.

Wakefield, J. C. (1992b). Disorder as harmful dysfunction: A conceptual critique of *DSM-III-R*'s definition of mental disorder. *Psychological Review, 99*, 232–247.

Williams, J. M. G., & Dritschel, B. H. (1988). Emotional disturbance and the specificity of autobiographical memory. *Cognition and Emotion, 2*, 221–234.

Williams, J. M. G., Mathews, A., & MacLeod, C. (1996). The emotional Stroop task and psychopathology. *Psychological Bulletin, 120*, 3–24.

Wilson, J. P. (1994). The historical evolution of PTSD diagnostic criteria: From Freud to

DSM-IV. *Journal of Traumatic Stress, 7,* 681–698.

Wolfe, J., & Proctor, S. P. (1996). The Persian Gulf War: New findings on traumatic exposure and stress. *PTSD Research Quarterly* 7(1), 1–7.

Yager, T., Laufer, R., & Gallops, M. (1984). Some problems associated with war experience in men of the Vietnam generation. *Archives of General Psychiatry, 41,* 327–333.

Yehuda, R., Boisoneau, D., Lowy, M. T., & Giller, E. L., Jr. (1995). Dose-response changes in plasma cortisol and lymphocyte glucocorticoid receptors following dexamethasone administration in combat veterans with and without posttraumatic stress disorder. *Archives of General Psychiatry, 52,* 583–593.

Yehuda, R., Boisoneau, D., Mason, J. W., & Giller, E. L. (1993). Glucocorticoid receptor number and cortisol excretion in mood, anxiety, and psychotic disorders. *Biological Psychiatry, 34,* 18–25.

Yehuda, R., Giller, E. L., Jr., Levengood, R. A., Southwick, S. M., & Siever, L. J. (1995). Hypothalamic-pituitary-adrenal functioning in post-traumatic stress disorder: Expanding the concept of the stress response spectrum. In M. J. Friedman, D. S. Charney, & A. Y. Deutch (Eds.), *Neurobiological and clinical consequences of stress: From normal adaptation to post-traumatic stress disorder* (pp. 351–365). Philadelphia: Lippincott-Raven.

Yehuda, R., Giller, E. L., Southwick, S. M., Lowy, M. T., & Mason, J. W. (1991). Hypothalamic-pituitary-adrenal dysfunction in posttraumatic stress disorder. *Biological Psychiatry, 30,* 1031–1048.

Yehuda, R., Kahana, B., Binder-Brynes, K., Southwick, S., Zemelman, S., Mason, J. W., & Giller, E. L. (1995). Low urinary cortisol excretion in Holocaust survivors with posttraumatic stress disorder. *American Journal of Psychiatry, 152,* 982–986.

Yehuda, R., Lowy, M. T., Southwick, S. M., Shaffer, S., & Giller, E. L., Jr. (1991). Lymphocyte glucocorticoid receptor number in posttraumatic stress disorder. *American Journal of Psychiatry, 148,* 499–504.

Yehuda, R., & McFarlane, A. C. (1995). Conflict between current knowledge about posttraumatic stress disorder and its original conceptual basis. *American Journal of Psychiatry, 152,* 1705–1713.

Yehuda, R., Southwick, S. M., & Giller, E. L., Jr. (1992). Exposure to atrocities and severity of chronic posttraumatic stress disorder in Vietnam combat veterans. *American Journal of Psychiatry, 149,* 333–336.

Yehuda, R., Southwick, S. M., Nussbaum, G., Wahby, V., Giller, E. L., Jr., & Mason, J. W. (1990). Low urinary cortisol excretion in patients with posttraumatic stress disorder. *Journal of Nervous and Mental Disease, 178,* 366–369.

Yehuda, R., Teicher, M. H., Trestman, R. L., Levengood, R. A., & Siever, L. J. (1996). Cortisol regulation in posttraumatic stress disorder and major depression: A chronobiological analysis. *Biological Psychiatry, 40,* 79–88.

Young, A. (1995). *The harmony of illusions: Inventing post-traumatic stress disorder.* Princeton, NJ: Princeton University Press.

7

Affective Disorders
Biological Aspects

ROBERT H. HOWLAND
MICHAEL E. THASE

Historically, various observations of persons with affective disturbances suggested the involvement of abnormal biological processes (Jackson, 1986). The cyclical episodes of depression or mania, with an intensity greater than that seen in normal emotional expressions, suggested an apparently autonomous underlying physiological process. Profound sleep, psychomotor activity, and appetite changes similarly indicated dysfunction of basic vegetative functions. The aggregation of affective disorders within families also was suggestive of an inherited biological vulnerability. The mood and behavior altering effects of various chemicals, plant extracts, and other compounds further pointed to a possible biological connection. Finally, the effectiveness of early physical treatments for severely disturbed behaviors suggested an underlying physical disturbance.

These observations stimulated considerable interest in understanding the biological aspects of affective disorders. During the past 40 years, research efforts have evolved from relatively simple studies of peripheral monoamine metabolites to the use of molecular genetic techniques and other advanced biomedical technologies. Most studies have focused on depression, both because of its greater prevalence and because of the inherent difficulties in studying patients in the midst of a manic episode. In this chapter, the various biological aspects of affective disorders are reviewed. These areas include neurotransmitters and neuroreceptors, cellular second messenger systems, sleep neurophysiology, neuroendocrinology, neuroimaging, chronobiology, and genetics. These findings will also be integrated as a way of understanding the phenomenology and pathogenesis of depressive and manic states as final common outcomes of dysregulated neurobiologic response systems.

Problems in Studying Biological Processes

A number of conceptual and methodological issues must be addressed if one is to study the biology of affective disorders (Thase & Howland, 1995). Research findings may be confounded by the unreliability of clinical diagnoses, possible biological heterogeneity among affective disorders, the inherent heterogeneity of some biological processes, other biological variables (e.g., age and sex), concurrent illnesses and/or drug use, and the type, accuracy, and reliability of biological measurements. Further, a biological abnormality may be an unrelated or secondary illness phenomenon rather than a primary or etiologic finding. Finally, biological abnormalities may be present before the onset of illness (trait or genetic marker), maybe present only during an illness episode (state marker), or persist during recovery (a "scar" or trait marker), and they may be present in never-ill relatives (possible genetic marker).

Neurobiology of Emotional and Vegetative Function

Most biological theories of affective disorders hypothesize disturbances of various central nervous system (CNS) neurotransmitters, especially the catecholamines norepinephrine (NE), epinephrine (E), and dopamine (DA); the indolamine serotonin (5-HT); and acetylcholine (ACH) (see table 7.1). Each has been localized to different tracts and nuclei of the brain, which are involved in the regulation of vegetative function, behavioral activity, and emotional expression (Kandel, Schwarz, & Jessell, 1991).

Neurotransmitters are the mechanism by which nerve cells communicate (Cooper et al., 1997). Stimulation of a nerve cell (the presynaptic neuron) leads to the release of neurotransmitters, which then stimulate or inhibit the function of a second nerve cell (the postsynaptic neuron). Released neurotransmitters are then taken up by the presynaptic neuron (by a reuptake transporter mechanism), where they can be reused, or they are metabolized. Concentrations of these neurotransmitters and their metabolites can be measured in urine, plasma, and/or cerebrospinal fluid (CSF), where they may indirectly reflect abnormal CNS function. The most important metabolites are 3-methoxy-4-hydroxyphenylglycol (MHPG) from NE, 5-hydroxy-indoleacetic acid (5-HIAA) from 5-HT, and homovanillic acid (HVA) from DA.

Neurotransmitters act by binding to receptors located on the neuron, which then initiates a cascade of chemical processes that ultimately affects the function of the neuron (Hyman & Nestler, 1993). Each type of neurotransmitter binds to specific neuroreceptors, which can also exist as different subtypes. For example, NE and E can bind to β_1, β_2, α_1, and α_2 adrenergic receptor subtypes; DA can bind to D_1 and D_2 receptor subtypes; and 5-HT can bind to 5-HT_2 and 5-HT_{1A} receptor subtypes. Receptors are located on both presynaptic neurons, where they typically provide negative feedback inhibiting neurotransmitter release, and on postsynaptic neurons, where they may stimulate or inhibit neuronal function.

Upregulation refers to the phenomenon whereby the binding sensitivity and/or number of receptors is increased, whereas downregulation refers to a decrease in receptor binding sensitivity and/or number. Receptors have usually been studied on blood platelets and lymphocytes, where their number and binding sensitivity can be measured, which

Table 7.1 Abbreviations

CNS	central nervous system
CSF	cerebrospinal fluid
NE	norepinephrine (catecholamine neurotransmitter)
MHPG	3-methoxy-4-hydroxyphenylglycol (NE metabolite)
E	epinephrine (catecholamine neurotransmitter)
DA	dopamine (catecholamine neurotransmitter)
HVA	homovanillic acid (DA metabolite)
5-HT	serotonin (indolamine neurotransmitter)
5-HIAA	5-hydroxy-indoleacetic acid (5-HT metabolite)
ACH	acetylcholine (neurotransmitter)
GABA	aminobutyric acid (inhibitory amino acid neurotransmitter)
NMDA	N-methyl-D-aspartate (excitatory amino acid neuroreceptor)
HPA	hypothalamic-pituitary-adrenal axis
DST	dexamethasone suppression test
ACTH	adrenocorticotropin hormone (pituitary gland hormone)
CRH	corticotropin-releasing hormone (hypothalamic neuropeptide hormone)
HPT	hypothalamic-pituitary-thyroid axis
TRH	thyrotropin-releasing hormone (hypothalamic neuropeptide hormone)
TSH	thyroid stimulating hormone (pituitary gland hormone)
T3	triiodothyronine (thyroid hormone)
T4	thyroxine (thyroid hormone)
GH	growth hormone (pituitary gland hormone)
HPO	hypothalamic-pituitary-ovarian axis
SCN	suprachiasmatic nucleus of the hypothalamus
EEG	electroencephalographic sleep
REM	rapid eye movement EEG sleep
SWS	slow wave EEG sleep
G-proteins	guanine nucleotide-binding proteins (second messenger system)
cAMP	cyclic adenosine monophosphate (a second messenger)
cGMP	cyclic guanine monophosphate (a second messenger)
PET	positron emission tomography brain imaging
SAD	seasonal affective disorder

may indirectly reflect CNS function. Radioactive labeling of the antidepressants imipramine and paroxetine have also been used to study 5-HT reuptake transporter sites on platelets. More recently, brain imaging studies have been able to use radioactively labeled drugs that bind to 5-HT reuptake transporter sites and to different receptor subtypes, enabling their direct study in the CNS.

Antidepressants and other psychotropic drugs have many different pharmacological effects on these neurotransmitter systems. Some bind to neurotransmitter reuptake transporter sites (e.g., serotonin reuptake inhibitor antidepressants). Some affect neurotransmitter metabolism (e.g., monoamine oxidase inhibitor antidepressants). Some bind to different types of presynaptic and postsynaptic receptors (e.g., antipsychotics block DA receptors). Drugs that stimulate receptors are called agonists, whereas drugs that block receptors are called antagonists. Because of the clinical therapeutic effects of these drugs, their known pharmacological properties have been used indirectly to implicate abnormalities among neurotransmitters and/or neuroreceptors that may be relevant to understanding the pathophysiology of affective disorders. Moreover, they have also been used as direct biological probes to study specific neurotransmitters and/or neuroreceptors.

Noradrenergic Systems in Depression

Noradrenergic neurons (containing NE) arising from the locus ceruleus in the brainstem project to the cerebral cortex, limbic system, basal ganglia, hypothalamus, and thalamus (see figure 7.1). Such a diffuse projection is consistent with its role in initiating and maintaining arousal, and modulating the function of other neurotransmitters (Thayer, 1989; Cooper, Bloom, & Roth, 1997). Projections to the medulla of the adrenal gland via the sympathetic nervous system (the sympathoadrenal system) control the release of NE within peripheral circulation, triggering the "fight or flight" response. Cognitive processes can amplify or dampen sympathoadrenal responses to internal or external stimuli (Thayer, 1989). Thus, the perception of stress is relayed from the cortex through the locus ceruleus and sympathoadrenal components, and such heightened CNS arousal elicits cognitive and behavioral correlates of fear and anxiety (Thayer, 1989).

Increased activity of the locus ceruleus occurs following presentation of novel stimuli, whereas decreased activity occurs during vegetative functions, such as feeding or sleeping (Cooper, Bloom, & Roth, 1997). Stimulation of the locus ceruleus also activates the hypothalamic-pituitary-adrenal (HPA) axis (Holsboer, 1995). Noradrenergic projections to the hippocampus have recently been implicated in behavioral sensitization to various stressors, and protracted activation may result in a state of learned helplessness (Petty, Kramer, Wilson, & Jordan, 1994). In severe depression, pathologically increased noradrenergic activity may contribute to anxiety, agitation, poor concentration, decreased appetite, and insomnia (Thase & Howland, 1995).

Stimulation of other noradrenergic pathways, such as the medial forebrain bundle, can produce increased levels of goal-directed behavior (Cooper, Bloom, & Roth, 1997). An abnormal reduction of noradrenergic activity in the medial forebrain bundle may thus contribute to depressive symptoms such as anergia and anhedonia (Carroll, 1991). Sustained stress, for example, may eventually result in decreased noradrenergic activity, resulting in a behavioral state analogous to some forms of depression (Weiss, 1991).

Serotonergic Systems in Depression

Serotonergic neurons arising from the brainstem raphe nuclei project extensively to the cerebral cortex, hypothalamus, thalamus, basal ganglia, septum, and hippocampus (Kandel et al., 1991; see figure 7.2). Serotonergic neurotransmission is proposed to have both inhibitory and facilitatory functions (e.g., Carroll, 1991). For example, much evidence suggests that it is an important regulator of sleep, appetite, and libido (McCarley, 1982; Kandel et al., 1991; Horne, 1993), and it modulates the activity of other neurotransmitters (Cooper et al., 1991; Smith et al., 1997).

Serotonergic neurons projecting to the suprachiasmatic nucleus (SCN) of the hypothalamus may contribute to regulation of circadian rhythms (e.g, sleep-wake cycles, body temperature, and HPA axis function; Wirz-Justice, 1995). Serotonin also facilitates goal-directed motor and consummatory behaviors (Amit, Smith, & Gill, 1991; Jacobs, 1991), and inhibits aggression in primates and humans (Brown & Linnoila, 1990; Higley et al., 1992). Thus, there is considerable evidence that

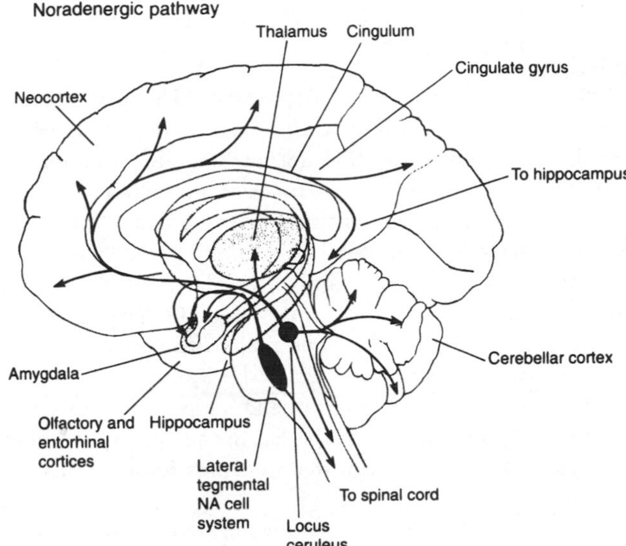

Figure 7.1 The pathway of noradrenergic activity.

pathologic reductions of serotonergic neurotransmission contribute to disturbances of appetite, sleep, and sexual behavior, as well as aggression and suicide (Malone & Mann, 1993).

Recent evidence suggests that basal levels of 5-HT are partly under genetic control (Higley et al., 1993). Acute stress mobilizes 5-HT release, resulting in a transient increase in 5-HT activity, but chronic stress may deplete 5-HT, perhaps in concert with prolonged activation of the HPA axis (Anisman & Zacharko, 1992; Weiss, 1991). Chronic stress may also down regulate of 5-HT receptors in the raphé nucleus, which may lead to reduced 5-HT transmission (Neumaier, Petty, Kramer, Szot, & Hamblin, 1997). It thus seems likely that acute and chronic stress have differential effects on individuals with higher or lower basal serotonergic activity.

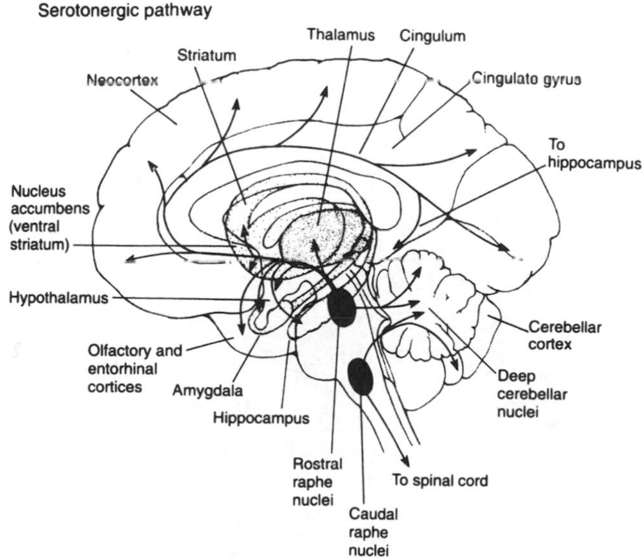

Figure 7.2 The pathway of serotonergic activity.

Dopaminergic Systems in Depression

The dopaminergic system involves four relatively discrete neuronal pathways (Kandel et al., 1991; see figure 7.3). The tuberoinfundibular system originates in the hypothalamus and projects to the pituitary stalk, where it inhibits prolactin secretion. The nigrostriatal system originates in the substantia nigra and projects to the basal ganglia, where it regulates involuntary motor activity. The mesolimbic system originates in the ventral tegmental area and projects throughout the limbic system, including the nucleus accumbens, amygdala, hippocampus, medial dorsal nucleus of the thalamus, and cingulate gyrus. The mesolimbic system modulates emotional regulation, learning and memory, positive reinforcement mechanisms, and hedonic capacity (Swerdlow & Koob, 1987). Finally, the mesocortical system, originating in the ventral tegmental area, projects axons to the orbitofrontal and the prefrontal cortices. This system is involved in motivation, initiation of goal-directed activity, attention, executive cognitive tasks, and social behavior (Swerdlow & Koob, 1987). Together, these Damediated functions may be subsumed within a "behavioral facilitation" system (Depue & Iacono, 1989). Thus, decreased mesocortical and mesolimbic dopaminergic activity may contribute to poor concentration, anhedonia, motivation, psychomotor retardation, and anergia in depression (Depue & Iacono, 1989).

Monoamine Abnormalities in Depression

Norepinephrine in Depression The best studied neurochemical indicator of CNS NE activity is the metabolite MHPG (Schatzberg & Schildkraut, 1995). Several early studies found that a subgroup of patients with major depression had reduced urinary levels of MHPG, suggesting a deficiency of brain NE. Significantly lower levels of plasma NE and MHPG and urinary MHPG have been reported in bipolar I and schizoaffective depressions when compared to either healthy normals or patients with bipolar II and unipolar depressions. There is also evidence that the circadian rhythm of MHPG is dysregulated in depression (Trestman et al., 1995).

Other studies have documented that a subgroup of unipolar patients with more severe, melancholic depressions have increased CSF, plasma, and urinary levels of NE, E, and MHPG as compared to both healthy controls and depressed bipolar patients (Maas et al., 1994; Schatzberg & Schildkraut, 1995). Increased levels of NE and MHPG may be due to an abnormal and sustained activation of the stress-response system, as reflected by overactivation of the locus ceruleus and HPA axis, or deficient 5-HT counter-regulatory control (Thase & Howland, 1995).

There is evidence of abnormal postsynaptic β receptor in function depression, as indicated by

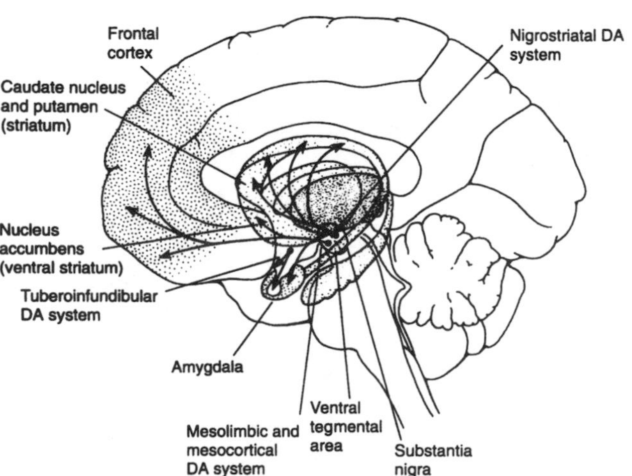

Figure 7.3 Discrete neuronal pathways of the dopaminergic system.

downregulated lymphocyte β receptors (Mazzola-Pomietto, Angrin, Tramoni, & Jenningros, 1994). This finding may be due to the sustained increase in sympathoadrenal activity or to abnormalities associated with the β receptor-linked second messenger system (Avissar, Nechamkin, Roitman, & Schreiber, 1997). A common effect of most antidepressants is to attenuate locus ceruleus activity, which decreases NE and MHPG turnover, downregulates β receptors, and regulates receptor-linked second messenger systems (Lesch & Manji, 1992; Potter, Grossman, & Rudorfer, 1993; Duman, Heninger, & Nestler, 1997). Patients who are responsive to noradrenergic antidepressants do not seem to be vulnerable to the mood-lowering effects of L-tryptophan deletion but, rather, are prone to relapse when NE synthesis is disrupted by α-methyl-paratyrosine (Miller et al., 1992).

A reduced growth hormone response to stimulation with the α_2 receptor agonist drug clonidine is a consistent finding in depression, which also suggests downregulated postsynaptic α_2 receptors (Holsboer, 1995). More recent studies, however, have found evidence of upregulated α-$_2$ receptors on the platelets of depressed patients, perhaps due to second-messenger abnormalities (Karege, Bovier, Rudolph, & Gaillard, 1996). The discrepancy between these findings may be due to the different study methodologies or different patient presentations.

Research in this area clearly demonstrates an interactive, excitatory relationship between the HPA axis and the sympathoadrenal system (Gold, Goodwin, & Chrousos, 1988; Nemeroff, 1992; Stokes, 1995). This suggests that the normally appropriate transient neurohormonal responses to acute stress may be amplified or distorted by failure of feedback to inhibitory systems in severe depressive states.

Serotonin in Depression A relatively consistent finding suggesting 5-HT dysfunction in depression is reduced CSF levels of 5-HIAA in a subgroup of patients (Maes & Meltzer, 1995). Low CSF 5-HIAA levels are more consistently found in patients with a history of violent or impulsive suicidal behavior, but this is also found in other psychiatric disorders (Linnoila & Virkkunen, 1992). Low CSF 5-HIAA levels are also associated with increased HPA axis activity (Stokes, 1995).

Although CSF 5-HIAA levels are not increased by antidepressants, 5-HT neurotransmission is typically enhanced by chronic treatment with antidepressants (Blier, DeMontigny, & Chaput, 1987; Shapira, Cohen, Newman, & Lerer, 1993). Conversely, experimentally induced dietary depletion of 5-HT can induce depressive symptoms in recently remitted patients treated with serotonin reuptake inhibiting antidepressants (Delgado et al., 1990; see figure 7.4).

Most, but not all, studies measuring radioactively labeled platelet imipramine or paroxetine binding sites, which are adjacent to 5-HT reuptake transporter sites, have found reduced levels in depression (Hrdina, Bakish, Chudzik, Ravindran, & Lapierre, 1995; Mellerup & Plenge, 1986; Sheline, Bargdett, Jackson, Newcomer, & Csernansky, 1995). However, it is not clear how well platelet transporter sites reflect CNS 5-HT function, and there are inconsistent findings regarding these binding sites in the brain (Maes & Meltzer, 1995; Little et al., 1997).

Upregulated 5-HT$_2$ receptors have been found in the platelets and the brains of depressed patients (D'haenen et al., 1992; Hrdina et al., 1995; Konopka, Cooper, & Crayton, 1996). Such upregulation is probably a response to chronically reduced presynaptic 5-HT input, and is intensified by hypercortisolism. By contrast, chronic antidepressant treatment typically downregulates 5-HT$_2$ receptors (Maes & Meltzer, 1995).

More recently, there is evidence that depressed patients also have downregulated 5-HT$_{1A}$ autoreceptors, including those located in the hippocampus and amygdala (Cowen, Power, Ware, & Anderson, 1994; Maes & Meltzer, 1995). This is further supported by studies showing a blunted cortisol and prolactin response to 5-HT$_{1A}$ stimulation with agonist drugs such as ipsapirone and buspirone. Increased cortisol levels can downregulate 5-HT$_{1A}$ auto receptors, and antidepressants can upregulate them (Maes & Meltzer, 1995).

Additional research has examined the interaction of 5-HT, NE, and DA. Levels of 5-HT and DA are significantly correlated in the CSF. Effective antidepressant treatment tends to increase the ratio of HVA to 5-HIAA in the CSF, whereas antidepressant nonresponders do not show such an effect (Hsiaso, Agren, Bartko, Rudorfer, Linnoila, & Potter, 1987). Conversely, 5-HT may modulate NE neurotransmission, such that abnormally low 5-HT levels may contribute to NE dyscontrol in response to stress (Anisman & Zacharko, 1992). Said more simply, 5-HT may buffer against excessive noradrenergic activity. Decreased 5-HT func-

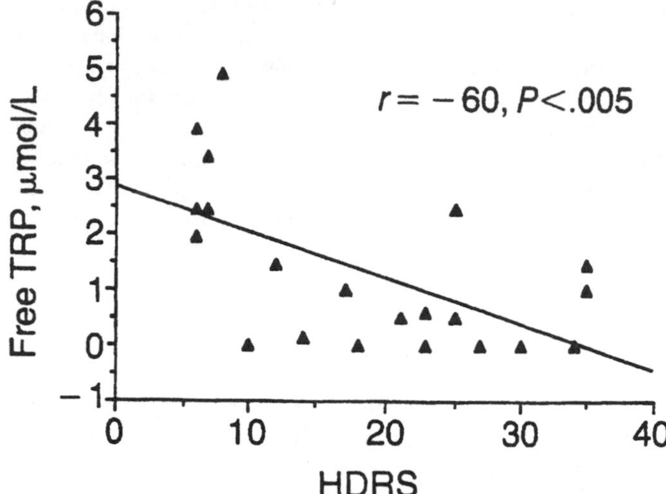

Figure 7.4 Effects of experimentally induced dietary depletion of 5-HT.

tion in the hippocampus may attenuate negative feedback on the HPA axis through decreased synthesis of glucocorticoid receptors, thus contributing to excessive HPA axis activation (Stokes, 1995; Maes & Meltzer, 1995). Conversely, hypercortisolemia may dampen 5-HT neurotransmission, further perpetuating the HPA axis dysregulation.

Dopamine in Depression Research concerning the role of DA in depression has yielded findings that largely complement those from studies of NE and 5-HT (Kapur & Mann, 1992). A functional DA deficit in depression is supported by studies showing decreased CSF and urinary HVA levels and upregulated postsynaptic D_2 receptors (D'haenen & Bossuyt, 1994; Willner, 1995). Drugs that deplete DA, such as reserpine, can lead to a depressed state characterized by psychomotor retardation, anhedonia, amotivation, social withdrawal, and lethargy. Such a state may also be seen during treatment with DA blocking drugs (e.g., antipsychotics) and following the withdrawal of addictive stimulant drugs (e.g., cocaine and amphetamine). Finally, animal models of depression, such as experimentally induced chronic stress or learned helplessness, can lead to decreased mesolimbic DA and behavioral measures of anhedonia (Depue & Iacono, 1989; Muscat, Papp, & Willner, 1992). Chronic antidepressant treatment upregulates presynaptic DA receptors and enhances mesolimbic DA activity (Swerdlow & Koob, 1987; Willner, 1995), which may reverse these behavioral effects.

Acetylcholine in Depression Cholinergic neurons containing ACH are distributed diffusely throughout the cerebral cortex (Cooper, Bloom, & Roth, 1991). There is a reciprocal relationship between ACH and the monoamines in the brain: increased cholinergic function is associated with decreased monoaminergic function and enhanced monoaminergic function may decrease cholinergic function (McCarley, 1982).

A role for abnormal cholinergic functioning in the pathophysiology of depression has been supported by studies of genetical strains of animals bred to have increased cholinergic sensitivity. These animals are more likely to show behavioral despair in response to experimentally induced stress when compared to animals without normal cholinergic function (Orpen & Steiner, 1995). Cholinergic agonist and antagonist drugs also have differential clinical effects in depression and mania (Janowsky & Overstreet, 1995). Agonists can produce lethargy, anergia, and psychomotor retardation in normal subjects, may cause increased symptoms in depressed patients, and may reduce symptoms in manic patients. There is anecdotal evidence that cholinergic antagonists may have mood-elevating effects in normals, alleviate symptoms in depressives, and trigger mania in bipolars, but these observations replicated under experimental conditions and may reflect individual differences in cholinergic sensitivity. Antidepressants, via their serotonergic or adrenergic effects, may decrease cholinergic function, although it is clear that the direct cholinergic antagonist effects of antidepressants are not related to the mechanism of their antidepressant effects (Janowsky & Overstreet, 1995).

In an animal model of depression, cholinergic effects can be attenuated by manipulation of adrenergic activity (Hasey & Hanin, 1991). Conversely, cholinergic agonists can activate the HPA axis, reduce the latency to onset of rapid eye movement (REM) sleep, increase the amount of REM sleep, and increase nocturnal awakenings in normal subjects, that is, changes that are similar to some of the biological features of severe depression (Poland et al., 1997). Depressed patients, remitted bipolar patients, and never-ill persons with a family history of affective disorder appear to be also more sensitive to the effects of cholinergic stimulation relative to normal subjects (Kupfer, Targ, & Stack, 1982; Janowsky & Overstreet, 1995).

Abnormal levels of choline, which is a precursor to ACH, are seen in the brains of some depressed patients (Renshaw et al., 1997). Elevations in red blood cell choline have also been found in depression, bipolar disorder, and schizophrenia (Janowsky & Overstreet, 1995). What is not known, however, is if these changes are primary or if they are compensatory responses to low levels of 5-HT or NE.

Amino Acids in Depression

Gamma-Aminobutyric Acid in Depression The amino acid δ-aminobutyric acid (GABA) is one of the major inhibitory neurotransmitter in the CNS (Petty, 1995). GABA modulates the monoamine pathways described above, including the important mesocortical and mesolimbic systems (Swerdlow & Koob, 1987). Many studies have found reduced plasma, CSF, and brain GABA levels in depression (see Petty, Kramer, & Hendrickse, 1993). Animal studies have also found that chronic stress can reduce or deplete GABA levels (Weiss, 1991). Drugs that stimulate GABA receptors have antidepressant-like effects and antidepressants upregulate GABA receptors (Petty et al., 1993). It is not clear if these effects are strong enough to warrant use of GABA-ergic agents as primary antidepressants, although the efficacy of agents such as divalproex sodium and lamotrigine in bipolar disorder certainly warrants further study.

Glutamate and Glycine in Depression The amino acids glutamate and glycine are the major excitatory neurotransmitters in the CNS (Cotman, Kahle, Miller, Vas, & Bridges, 1995), where they modulate the various monoamine pathways described above. Glutamate and glycine have only recently been investigated in affective disorders (Shader, Fogelman, & Greenblatt, 1997). They bind to closely associated sites on receptor complexes such as the N-methyl-D-aspartate (NMDA) receptor. There is emerging evidence that drugs with antagonist or partial agonist effects on NMDA receptors have antidepressant effects. Antidepressants may also downregulate NMDA receptors.

Excessive glutamate activity has neurotoxic effects in the CNS. Of particular interest to affective disorders, the hippocampus has a high concentration of NMDA receptors. Thus, glutamate may participate in the neurotoxic effects of severe and persistent affective illness. Interactions between glucocorticoid and NMDA might represent one relevant pathway, leading to decreased negative feedback and further activation of the HPA axis via degeneration of hippocampal cortisol receptors (McEwen et al., 1992).

Second-Messenger Systems in Affective Disorders

The binding of neurotransmitters to receptors leads to a physiological response in a neuron by triggering a cascade of chemical processes referred to as second-messenger systems (Hyman & Nestler, 1993; Duman et al., 1997). Neuroreceptors are linked to intracellular second-messenger systems by guanine nucleotide-binding proteins (G-proteins; see figure 7.5). The G-proteins function to connect receptors to various chemical effectors (e.g., adenylate cyclase, phospholipase C, and phosphodiesterase). These effectors then stimulate the formation of second messengers, such as cyclic nucleotides [e.g., cyclic adenosine monophosphate (cAMP) and cyclic guanine monophosphate (cGMP)], phosphatidylinositols (e.g., inositol triphosphate and diacylglycerol), and calcium-calmodulin. These second messengers, in turn, regulate a variety of cellular physiological processes, such as the function of neuronal membrane ion channels, stimulation of neurotransmitter release, and mediation of the activity of protein kinases (which cause protein phos-

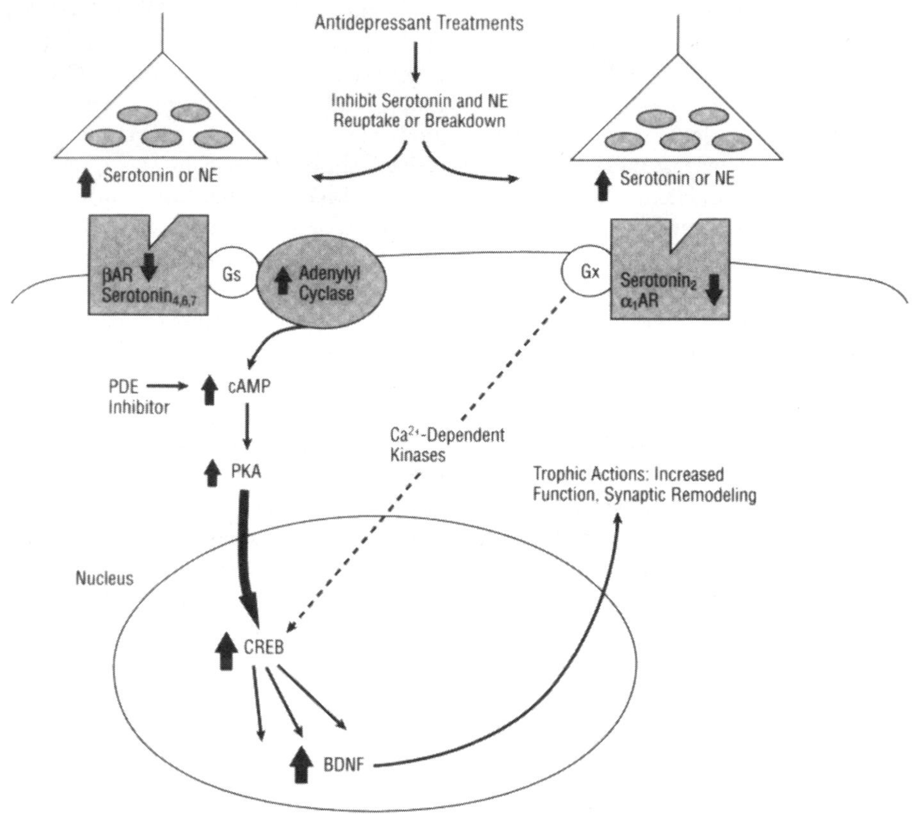

Figure 7.5 Second-messenger sequence.

phorylation). Protein phosphorylation can then regulate the function of many important neuronal proteins. These proteins include enzymes that synthesize and degrade neurotransmitters, neuroreceptors, ion channels, G-proteins, and DNA transcription and messenger-RNA translation factors that regulate gene expression. Second-messenger systems therefore represent a fundamentally important intracellular physiological process that translates neurotransmitter-receptor interactions into a cellular functional response. These mechanisms also explain how environmental experience can activate or inhibit the activity of genes. Research now indicates, for example, that harsh early treatment of rodent pups can have a lasting effect on stress responsiveness (Plotsky et al., 1995).

Recent studies in depression have found abnormalities in platelet adenylate cyclase activity (Menninger & Tabakoff, 1997), phosphoinositide hydrolysis (Karege et al., 1996), intracellular calcium metabolism (Konopka, Cooper, & Crayton, 1996), and G-protein function (Avissar et al., 1997). Such alterations in receptor-linked second-messenger systems probably explain the changes in β, α_2, and 5-HT_2 neuroreceptor responsiveness described above. A central role for abnormal second-messenger systems in depression is consistent with recent studies showing that most antidepressants, regardless of their neurotransmitter effects, directly affect second messengers and gene expression (Lesch & Manji, 1992; Duman et al., 1997).

Recent studies in bipolar disorder have found abnormalities in cell membrane phospholipid composition (Brown, Mallinger, & Renbaum, 1993), increased intracellular calcium concentration and mobilization (Okamoto, Kagaya, Shinno, Motohashu, & Yamawaki, 1994; Emamghoreishi et al., 1997), increased cAMP-dependent phosphorylation (Perez et al., 1995), increased protein kinase C activity (Friedman, Wang, Levinson, Connell, & Singh, 1993; Wang & Friedman, 1996), and increased G-protein levels (Manji, Potter, & Lenox,

1995; Mathews, Li, Young, Kish, & Warsh, 1997; Mitchell, Manji, & Chen, 1997). There is also increasing evidence that the effects of lithium and other antimanic drugs may be mediated through direct effects on G-protein function or other second messengers (Manji et al., 1995; Manji et al., 1996).

Electroencephalographic Sleep Studies in Depression

All-night electroencephalographic (EEG) recording provided one of the earliest windows through which brain activity could be observed. Nearly 50 years of research has led to characterization of sleep patterns during depression and during antidepressant treatment, as well as following remission and among never-ill, high-risk groups. Research has now progressed to the study of specific receptors on sleep and the relationships between alterations of cerebral metabolism and sleep EEG patterns.

Sleep Continuity and Sleep Maintenance in Depression

Sleep continuity disturbances include prolongation of sleep latency, increased number of nocturnal awakenings, and early morning awakening (see figure 7.5). These changes are seen more commonly among hospitalized patients than among outpatients (Thase & Kupfer, 1987). However, sleep continuity disturbances are also seen in many medical and psychiatric conditions, as well as during normal aging (Benca, Obermeyer, Thisted, & Gillin, 1992). Such nonspecific disturbances thus reflect CNS hyperarousal and an age-dependent decline in the ability to buffer or dampen such an effect. Nor suprisingly, sleep continuity disturbances are more pronounced in older depressed patients. Such hyperarousal probably reflects a deficit of 5-HT mediated "quieting," but could also result from increased NE, DA, or HPA activity. Several classes of antidepressants tend to improve sleep continuity disturbances, but this does not necessarily correlate with antidepressant efficacy because other classes of antidepressants (e.g., serotonin reuptake inhibitors and monoamine oxidase inhibitors) often worsen sleep efficiency (Thase, 1998).

A subgroup of patients, most often younger than age 40, sleep too much. Depressed patients with hypersomnia have an extended total sleep time, increased REM time, and/or reduced sleep latency (Nofzinger et al., 1991; Thase, Himmelhoch, Mallinger, Jarrett, & Kupfer, 1989). A pair of recent studies contrasting fluoxetine, a serotonin reuptake inhibitor, and nefazodone, a mixed-action antidepressant that blocks postsynaptic 5-HT_2 receptors, illustrates such differential effects (Armitage, Yonkers, Cole, & Rush, 1997; Gillin, Rapaport, Erman, Winokur, & Albala, 1997). Hypersomnolent patients tend to respond poorly to sedating antidepressants and may, in turn, necessitate treatment with more alerting agents such as the MAOI tranylcypromine or the aminoketone compound bupropion (Thase, 1998).

Slow Wave Sleep in Depression

Slow wave sleep (SWS) comprises sleep Stages 3 and 4, which are characterized by slow, high-amplitude delta EEG waves. Measures of SWS are associated with perceptions of the restfulness or quality of sleep. The density of delta EEG waves is highest in the prefrontal cortex, which may be related to the restorative effects that SWS has on executive cortical functions (Horne, 1993). Decreased SWS is common in depression and may be induced in animals by chronic mild stress (Cheeta, Ruigt, van Proosdiji, & Willner, 1997). Decreased SWS is also seen during normal aging, in chronic medical conditions, and schizophrenia (Benca, Obermeyer, Thisted, & Gillin, 1992).

The deficit in SWS observed in depression and schizophrenia is consistent with reduced serotonergic neurotransmission (Thase & Kupfer, 1987; Benson, Faull, & Zarcone, 1993). Reduced SWS can be induced experimentally by fenfluramine-induced depletion of intraneuronal 5-HT (Myers et al., 1993) or with experimentally induced dietary depletion of 5-HT (Bremner et al., 1997). Reduced SWS in depression is probably not caused by pathologically increased noradrenergic, dopaminergic, or HPA axis activity, however, because slow wave sleep is often normal inmania (Hudson et al., 1992). Regardless of the mechanism, one consequence or correlate of reduced SWS is that non-REM sleep is associated with a significant increase in cerebral metabolism (Ho et al., 1996).

There is some evidence that SWS deficits in depression are relatively traitlike and may be partly under genetic control, such that nondepressed persons with a family history of affective disorders may show decreased SWS (Linkowski et al., 1994; Lauer, Schreiber, Holsboer, & Krieg, 1995). Successful antidepressant treatment typically does not increase visually scored SWS, although more sensitive computer-scored delta EEG wave counts may show improvement (Buysse, Frank, Lowe, Cherry, & Kupfer, 1997). This has potentially important prognostic implications because one study showed that a selective reduction of delta EEG waves in the first non-REM interval was associated with a significantly increased risk of recurrent depression following antidepressant discontinuation (Kupfer, Frank, McEachran, & Grochocinski, 1990). Agents that restore SWS thus have considerable therapeutic potential.

REM Sleep Dysfunction in Depression

In healthy adults, the first REM period typically begins 70 to 90 minutes after sleep onset, with subsequent REM periods of increasing length and activity occurring at 90-minute intervals throughout the night (see figure 7.5). About 20 to 25% of the night is spent in REM sleep, and the ratio of REM activity to REM time (i.e., REM density) typically ranges from 1.0 to 1.7 units/minute. In depression, REM latency is frequently reduced to less than 60 minutes, REM time is shifted into the first 90 minutes of sleep, and REM density is often increased (Thase & Kupfer, 1987).

REM sleep disturbances are most prominent among elders and those with more severe, highly recurrent, and psychotic forms of depression (Thase & Howland, 1995). REM sleep disturbances associated with depression may be divided into two types. Type 1 disturbances, best characterized by reduced REM latency, tend to be state independent or traitlike (Kupfer & Ehlers, 1989). Deficits of SWS and blunted growth hormone release are commonly associated with the Type 1 profile (Kupfer & Ehlers, 1989). Reduced REM latency in depression is, to some extent, an age-dependent process (Lauer et al., 1991) and may partly be genetically controlled (Giles et al., 1987; Lauer et al., 1995). Nondepressed persons with a family history of affective disorders are also more likely to show reduced REM latency in response to cholinergic agonists (Janowsky & Overstreet, 1995). Most, but not all, effective antidepressants prolong REM latency (Sharpley & Cowen, 1995), and this effect may persist for years during maintenance treatment (Kupfer et al., 1994). By contrast, effective psychotherapies are not associated with a prolongation or normalization of REM latency (Buysse, Kupfer, Frank, Monk, & Ritenaur, 1992; Thase et al., 1994; Thase, Fasiczka, Berman, Simons, & Reynolds, 1998). This is important because reduced REM latency is associated with higher long-term rates of relapse (Giles, Jarrett, Roffware, & Rush, 1987; Reynolds, Perel, Frank, Imber, & Kupfer, 1989). In fact, patients with more normal sleep profiles have a much lower risk of recurrrent depressive episodes after successful treatment with cognitive behavior therapy than patients with sleep abnormalities (Thase, Simons, & Reynolds, 1996; see figure 7.6).

The Type 2 REM latency disturbance is associated with increased REM density and sleep continuity disturbances (Thase et al., 1997). This profile is severity dependent and is commonly associated with increased cortisol and sympathoadrenal activity (Kupfer & Ehlers, 1989). Type 2 disturbances thus are more common among inpatients and those with melancholic or psychotic depressions. Recent studies suggest that outpatients with Type 2 disturbances are less responsive to cognitive and interpersonal psychotherapies than patients with more normal sleep profiles (Thase, Simons, & Reynolds, 1996; Thase et al., 1997). When psychotherapy is effective for such patients, the Type 2 disturbances do not normalize fully (Thase et al., 1998), which may explain their higher subsequent risk of recurrence (Thase, Simons, & Reynolds, 1996). Thus, the Type 2 constellation of EEG sleep disturbances may identify a "boundary" of CNS dysfunction, beyond which antidepressants are more effective than psychotherapy.

Neuroendocrine Abnormalities in Depression

Hypothalamic-Pituitary-Adrenocortical Axis Abnormalities

The most common HPA axis abnormalities found in depression are: (1) elevated CSF, plasma, saliva, and/or urine cortisol concentrations; (2) impaired feedback inhibition—that is, the process that normally shuts down the HPA axis after resolution of a transient stressor, which is measured by the dex-

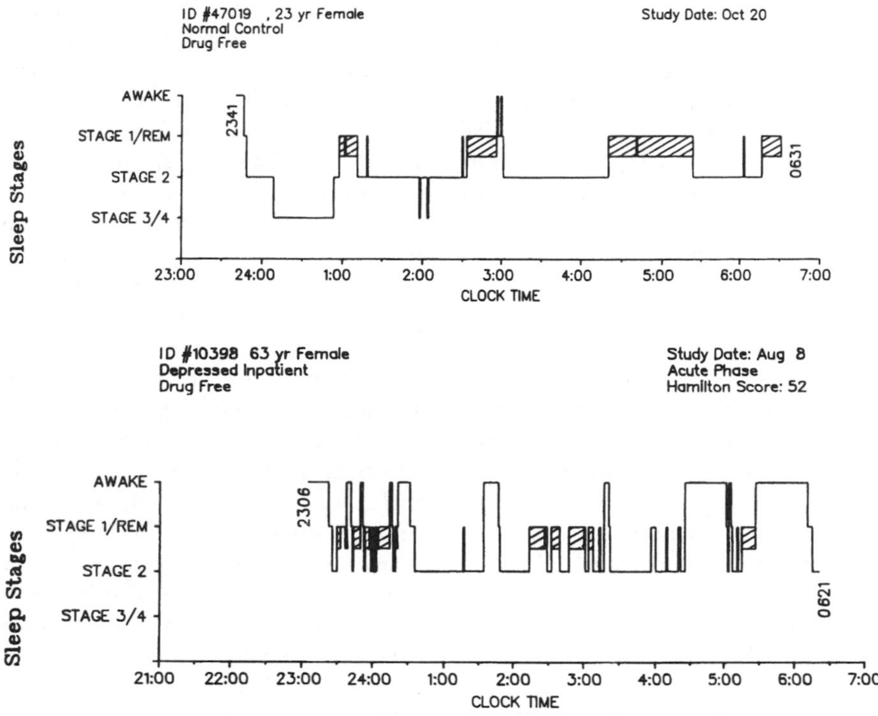

Figure 7.6 Normal versus depressive sleep cycles.

amethasone suppression test (DST); and (3) dysregulation of the HPA axis circadian rhythm, such as a blunting of the daily cortisol rhythm and an abnormally early rise in nocturnal cortisol secretion (Holsboer, 1995).

The activity of the HPA axis is controlled by an intricate feedback inhibition system, which receives input from the limbic system and cerebral cortex. Cortisol secretion from the adrenal cortex is stimulated by adrenocorticotropin hormone (ACTH), which is secreted from the pituitary gland. ACTH secretion is stress responsive and is principally stimulated by the neuropeptide corticotropin-releasing hormone (CRH). CRH is secreted by both the hypothalamus and neurons throughout the prefrontal and limbic cortex (Kandel et al., 1991; Nemeroff, 1992).

The ACTH response to CRH stimulation is attenuated in depression (i.e., a type of downregulation), indicating that the abnormally increased "drive" of the HPA axis originates above the pituitary (Holsboer, 1992). Indeed, depressed patients have increased CSF CRH levels, increased hypothalamic CRH messenger-RNA levels, and downregulated frontal cortex CRH receptors (Nemeroff, 1992; Raadsheer et al., 1995). Moreover, adrenal gland hypertrophy is found in some depressed patients (Rubin, Phillips, McCracken, & Sadow, 1996). This is most likely secondary to chronic excessive HPA axis stimulation in depression.

Feedback inhibition of the HPA axis is regulated primarily by cortisol receptors in the pituitary, hypothalamus, and hippocampus. The release of ACTH is normally inhibited when rising cortisol levels stimulate hippocampal cortisol receptors, but this "fast-feedback" mechanism is blunted in severe depression (Young, Haskett, Murphy-Weinberg, Watson, & Akil, 1991). The number of hippocampal cortisol receptors decreases with age, partly accounting for the greater incidence of increased plasma cortisol in geriatric depression (Holsboer, 1992). Chronic elevations of cortisol may also cause degeneration of hippocampal cortisol receptors, further perpetuating the impairment of HPA feedback inhibition (McEwen et al., 1992; Stokes, 1995). Hippocampal cortisol receptors may be more susceptible to such neurotoxic effects during critical neurodevelopmental periods early in life, perhaps explaining why early life events (such as abuse) are associated with subsequent vulnerability to depression later in life (Gold et al., 1988). Antidepressants can decrease hypothalamic CRH messenger-RNA, decrease CSF CRH levels, increase cortisol receptor messenger-RNA, and increase the synthesis of hippocampal cortisol receptors (Holsboer, 1995; Barden, 1996), which suggests that their antidepressant effects include normalization of HPA axis activity.

The integrity of HPA axis feedback inhibition has been studied most commonly by using the DST. Failure to suppress cortisol levels after ingestion of the potent synthetic glucocorticoid dexamethasone (DST nonsuppression) is an abnormal response. The highest rates of DST nonsuppression are found among depressed inpatients, geriatric patients, and patients with severe, endogenous, melancholic, and psychotic depressions (Thase & Howland, 1995; Rush et al., 1996). Hence, both aging and illness severity are correlated failure of HPA axis feedback inhibition.

Most depressed people with milder symptoms, especially those under age 40, do not have marked HPA abnormalities. The subgroup of patients with atypical depressive symptoms (i.e., anergia and hypersomnia) almost always have normal plasma cortisol levels, suggesting that abnormal HPA activation is a correlate of later stages of recurrent affective illness (Geracioti, Loosen, & Orth, 1997).

Most studies have found that the HPA axis abnormalities in depression are state dependent and typically resolve with clinical remission (Ribeiro, Tandon, Grunhaus, & Greden, 1993). Studies have also found that CSF CRH levels are reduced after successful antidepressant treatment (Plotsky, Owens, & Nemeroff, 1995). Pretreatment DST nonsuppression does not predict a favorable antidepressant response, but the persistence of DST nonsuppression following treatment is associated with a greater risk of earlier relapse (Ribeiro et al., 1993). Therefore, despite clinical improvement, increased HPA activity suggests that an underlying pathological process remains active and, as such, more vigorous treatment is indicated. Further, patients with HPA axis disturbances are less responsive to placebo treatment and, possibly, to psychotherapy (Ribeiro et al., 1993; Thase, Dubé et al., 1996; see figure 7.7).

The HPA axis and sleep-wake cycle are intimately associated. Cortisol and CRH can induce many of the typical sleep abnormalities found in depression (Nemeroff, 1992). However, whereas nearly all patients with increased cortisol have EEG sleep disturbances, whereas only one half with normal HPA axis function have EEG sleep disturbances (Thase & Kupfer, 1987). This suggests a common mechanism of neurobiologic dysfunction in depression, with sleep neurophysiology being more sensitive to perturbation than the HPA axis. Patients manifesting both increased cortisol and EEG sleep disturbances are typically older and are more severely ill (Rush et al., 1997).

Many studies have found that increased cortisol is associated with downregulated adrenergic receptors, suggesting that sustained sympathoadrenal activity also "drives" the HPA axis (Anisman & Zacharko, 1992). Moreover, other studies document a positive correlation between increased NE, E, and MHPG levels and indices of HPA axis hyperactivity (Holsboer, 1992). Finally, CRH increases locus ceruleus activity, and the locus ceruleus stimulates CRH secretion (Anisman & Zacharko, 1992). Thus, with acute stress, adrenergic systems and the HPA axis are reciprocally activated until the stressor is resolved and/or negative feedback inhibition reestablishes homeostasis. The combination of sustained, unresolvable stress and impaired feedback inhibition, therefore, may lead to a deteriorative positive feedback loop, with prolonged pathologic elevations of NE, E, and cortisol, which represents one final common pathway to the development of severe depression, regardless of the initial etiology. Of course, sustained unresolvable stress often places humans in positions of powerlessness and perceived hopelessness, potent cognitive correlates of severe depression. Conversely, among primates the stress of a loss of social dominance reliably induces hypercortisolemia (Sapolsky, 1989).

Much research suggests that increased 5-HT initially stimulates the HPA axis, and that cortisol may transiently enhance 5-HT function (Stokes, 1995). By contrast, chronic stress uncouples this relationship, such that sustained increased cortisol is associated with decreased 5-HT neurotransmission (Weiss, 1991).

Glucocorticoids also have a reciprocal, facilitating relationship with DA systems. For example, activation of the HPA axis is associated with increased HVA levels, agitation, and psychosis, similar to the behavioral effects of ingesting high doses of steroids (Schatzberg et al., 1985, 1987).

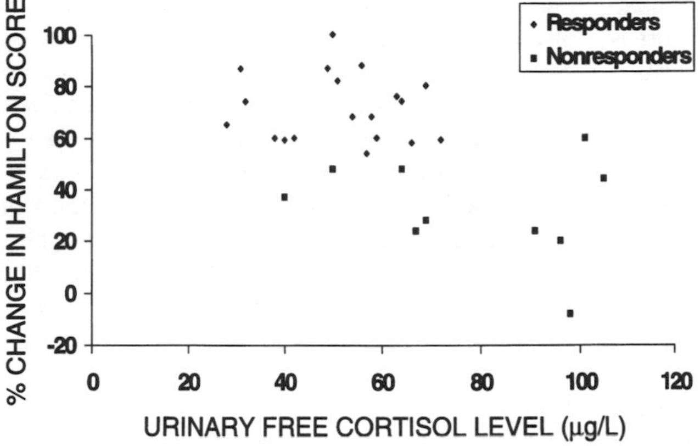

Figure 7.7 Cortisol levels and depression scores.

Hypothalamic-Pituitary-Thyroid Axis Abnormalities

The hypothalamic-pituitary-thyroid (HPT) axis is triggered by the neuropeptide thyrotropin-releasing hormone (TRH), which is secreted from the hypothalamus and stimulates the secretion of thyroid stimulating hormone (TSH) from the pituitary. TSH stimulates the thyroid to secrete its primary hormones triiodothyronine (T_3) and thyroxine (T_4). The HPT axis is regulated primarily by negative feedback inhibition of pituitary TSH secretion by circulating levels of T_3 and T_4. The importance of the HPT axis in affective disorders is supported by evidence that T_3 and TRH receptors are found in the brain, where these hormones function like neurotransmitters, modulate NE and 5-HT receptors, and have antidepressant-like effects (Joffe & Levitt, 1993; Whybrow, 1995). There is also a significant degree of similarity in the genes that code for T_3 receptors and cortisol receptors (Whybrow, 1995). Hence, thyroid dysfunction (i.e., hyperthyroidism and hypothyroidism) leads to significant changes in thyroid hormone levels that may affect CNS function and cause clinically significant affective disorders. A recent brain imaging study of depressed patients found a significant inverse relationship between TSH blood levels and brain metabolism (Marangell et al., 1997). The strongest correlation was found in dorsolateral and mesial prefrontal cortex regions, which are implicated in depression. Increased HPT activation may be a compensatory response to decreased brain metabolism, or a sustained increase in TRH and TSH levels may elicit a counter-regulatory reduction in brain metabolism. Successful antidepressant treatment has consistently been shown to reduce circulating thyroid hormones (Joffe & Levitt, 1993).

Depression has been associated with hyperthyroidism, but this is less common than agitated, manic, or mixed states (Joffe & Levitt, 1993). Although clinical hypothyroidism is often associated with depression, most studies of depressed patients have found low rates of hypothyroidism (e.g., 3–6%; Joffe & Levitt, 1993). Subtle degrees of hypothyroidism, however, may be relatively more common in chronic or treatment-refractory depression, requiring combined treatment with antidepressants and thyroid hormone (Howland & Thase, 1991; Howland, 1993).

In depression, basal TSH levels tend to be lower and show a more blunted circadian rhythm, whereas CSF TRH levels are increased (Joffe & Levitt, 1993). TRH stimulation is used to study HPT axis function. The TRH stimulation test has consistently demonstrated a blunted TSH response in 25 to 40% of depressed patients, which is higher than the rates found in other psychiatric patients or normals (Loosen, Mason, & Prange, 1982). A blunted TSH response is not related to the severity of depression, but persistent TSH blunting after treatment may predict a higher risk of relapse (Langer, Aschauer, Koing, Resch, & Schonbeck, 1983).

Approximately 5 to 10% of newly diagnosed depressed patients have an exaggerated TSH response, and they often do not respond well to antidepressants alone (Joffe & Levitt, 1993). One study found that bipolar depressives were more likely to show an exaggerated TSH response, whereas unipolar depressives had a blunted response (Gold et al.,

1980). This difference may be due to artifact because lithium treatment of the bipolar patients is likely to have dampened thyroid function, eliciting higher TSH responses. By contrast, a blunted TSH response more likely reflects important alterations in neuropeptide function in the brain.

The sustained release of TRH, causing the downregulation of TRH receptors and inhibiting pituitary responsiveness, is the likely cause of TSH blunting (Maeda, Yoshimoto, & Yamadori, 1993; Garbutt et al., 1994). TSH release is stimulated by NE and inhibited by 5-HT and DA (Joffe & Levitt, 1993). Hence, TSH blunting also may result from decreased NE transmission. Finally, cortisol and the neuropeptide somatostatin inhibit TSH secretion (Rush et al., 1997), and there is developing evidence that estrogen may also affect the HPT axis (Whybrow, 1995). The sudden changes in estrogen and thyroid hormones that follow childbirth have been implicated in the high rate of depression and mania that occur during the postpartum period (Whybrow, 1995; Toren, Dor, Rehavi, & Weizman, 1996).

Growth Hormone

Growth hormone (GH) secretion from the pituitary can be stimulated by NE, 5-HT, and DA and inhibited by CRH and the hypothalamic neuropeptide somatostatin (Holsboer, 1995). Studies of GH secretion using DA receptor agonists have not found consistent abnormalities in depression (Checkley, 1992). A more consistent finding in depression is a blunted GH response to the α_2 receptor agonist clonidine and to the adrenergic antidepressant desipramine (Checkley, 1992; Dinan, O'Keane, & Thakore, 1994; Holsboer, 1995). A blunted GH response to the 5-HT precursor tryptophan is also seen in depression (Cowen & Charig, 1987). Among children with depression, the blunted GH response precedes other biological abnormalities (Ryan et al., 1994). Successful treatment with antidepressants does not correct this abnormality, further suggesting traitlike behavior.

The secretion of GH follows a 24-hour circadian rhythm, with a characteristic secretory surge that occurs during the first few hours of sleep. In depression, the circadian rhythm of GH is altered, such that daytime levels are increased and the nocturnal surge is blunted (Holsboer, 1995). Because the surge occurs during the first non-REM period of sleep, the decrease found in depression may be associated with other traitlike abnormalities, including reduced REM latency and decreased SWS. This suggests a common underlying process that is disturbed in depression. As genetic research methodologies become more sophisticated, studies of potential candidate genes may yield better results if they are focused on probands with these traitlike abnormalities.

Somatostatin

The highest concentrations of the neuropeptide somatostatin are found in the hypothalamus, but significant amounts are found elsewhere in the limbic system (e.g., amygdala, hippocampus, and nucleus accumbens), the prefrontal cortex, and the locus ceruleus (Rubinow, Davis, & Post, 1995). Somatostatin is the primary inhibitor of GH, but it also functions like a neurotransmitter, and it can inhibit GABA, CRH, ACTH, and TSH (Rubinow et al., 1995). Somatostatin infusions also can induce many of the typical EEG sleep abnormalities found in depression (Thase & Howland, 1995). Somatostatin CSF levels are lower in depression compared to schizophrenia and normals (Rubinow et al., 1995), whereas normal or high levels have been reported in mania (Sharma, Bissette, Janicak, Davis, & Nemeroff, 1995). The abnormal somatostatin levels tend to normalize with clinical recovery. These findings strongly suggest that abnormalities of somatostatin regulation may play an important role in the pathophysiology and treatment of affective disorders.

Prolactin

The regulation of prolactin in affective disorders is of interest because its secretion from the pituitary is stimulated by 5-HT and inhibited by DA (Checkley, 1992). Most studies of basal and circadian prolactin secretion have not found significant abnormalities in depression (Checkley, 1992). In contrast to basal studies, however, a blunted prolactin response to various 5-HT agonists is a common finding in depression. This abnormality is consistent with a serotonergic deficit (Maes & Meltzer, 1995).

Neuroradiological Abnormalities in Affective Disorders

Structural Studies in Affective Disorders

The computed axial tomography scan is a sensitive, noninvasive method for visualizing brain structure. A magnetic resonance imaging scan is even more sensitive, and can better visualize subcortical tracts and white matter lesions. Many studies have found an increased frequency of abnormal hyperintensities in various subcortical regions (especially the periventricular area, basal ganglia, and thalamus) in affective disorders. These hyperintensities are more common in bipolar I disorder and geriatric depression than in bipolar II disorder or unipolar depression, and they increase in frequency with age (Aylward et al., 1994; Altshuler et al., 1995; Woods, Yorgelum-Todd, Mikulis, & Pillay, 1995; Krishnan, Hays, & Blazer, 1997; see figure 7.8). They are similar to the plaques seen in cerebrovascular disease and multiple sclerosis, and thus may reflect the deleterious neurodegenerative effects of recurrent affective episodes over time (Altshuler, 1993; Dupont et al., 1995).

Most studies have consistently documented ventricular enlargement, cortical atrophy, and sulcal widening in patients with affective disorders compared to normal controls, surprisingly similar to the findings in schizophrenia (Elkis, Friedman, Wise, & Meltzer, 1995). Moreover, such cortical changes have even been found early in the course of bipolar disorder (Strakowski et al., 1993). These findings are not due to medications or electroconvulsive therapy, but they are associated with age, illness severity, chronicity, and increased cortisol (Coffey et al., 1993). Depressed patients also may have reduced frontal lobe and caudate nucleus volumes, which are important structures in the mesocorticolimbic system (Krishnan et al., 1992; Coffey et al., 1993).

Cerebral Metabolism in Affective Disorders

Several methods for measuring cerebral blood flow and brain metabolism have been used to study the neurobiology of affective disorders. Some studies have found global or bifrontal reductions of regional cerebral blood flow, especially in psychotic depression (Sackheim et al., 1990; Silfverskiöld & Risberg, 1989), whereas other studies have suggested more prominent reductions in the left frontal or prefrontal areas (Wu et al., 1992; Philpot, Banerjee, Needham-Bennett, Costa, & Ell, 1993).

Positron emission tomography (PET) scanning is currently the most powerful method for visualizing brain metabolism. The most widely replicated finding in depression has been decreased anterior or frontal brain metabolism (see figure 7.9), which is generally more pronounced on the left side and may be more pronounced in bipolar compared to unipolar disorder (Drevets et al., 1992; Berman, Doran, Pickar, & Weinberger, 1993; Ho et al., 1996).

Other studies of depression have found changes in cerebral blood flow and/or metabolism in many of the specific dopaminergic regions of the mesocortical and mesolimbic systems implicated in depression, such as decreases in the amygdala, striatum, thalamus, cingulate gyrus, and orbitofrontal and prefrontal cortices (Drevets et al., 1992; Ho et al., 1996; Buchsbaum, Someya, Wu, Tang, & Bunney, 1997). There is also evidence that antidepressants may tend to normalize some of these changes (Rubin, Sackeim, Nobler, & Moeller, 1994). Studies of emotional activation in healthy, never mentally ill persons have found decreases in brain activity in many of these same areas (George et al., 1995; Reiman et al., 1997). Furthermore, a recent PET study remitted depressed patients following dietary depletion of 5-HT found decreased metabolism in the dorsolateral prefrontal cortex, thalamus, and orbitofrontal cortex (Bremner et al., 1997).

Bipolar and unipolar depressives tend to show comparable changes in cerebral metabolism, although there are subtle differences (such as more pronounced decreases in the medial dorsal nucleus of the thalamus and the dorsolateral prefrontal cortex in bipolar depressives; Buchsbaum et al., 1997). Curiously, the medial dorsal nucleus of the thalamus contains excitatory glutamate cells and inhibitory GABA cells. Because this area may be preferentially affected in bipolar patients, it might be a potential site for a switch mechanism from depression to mania via activation or inhibition of the mesocorticolimbic system (Buchsbaum et al., 1997).

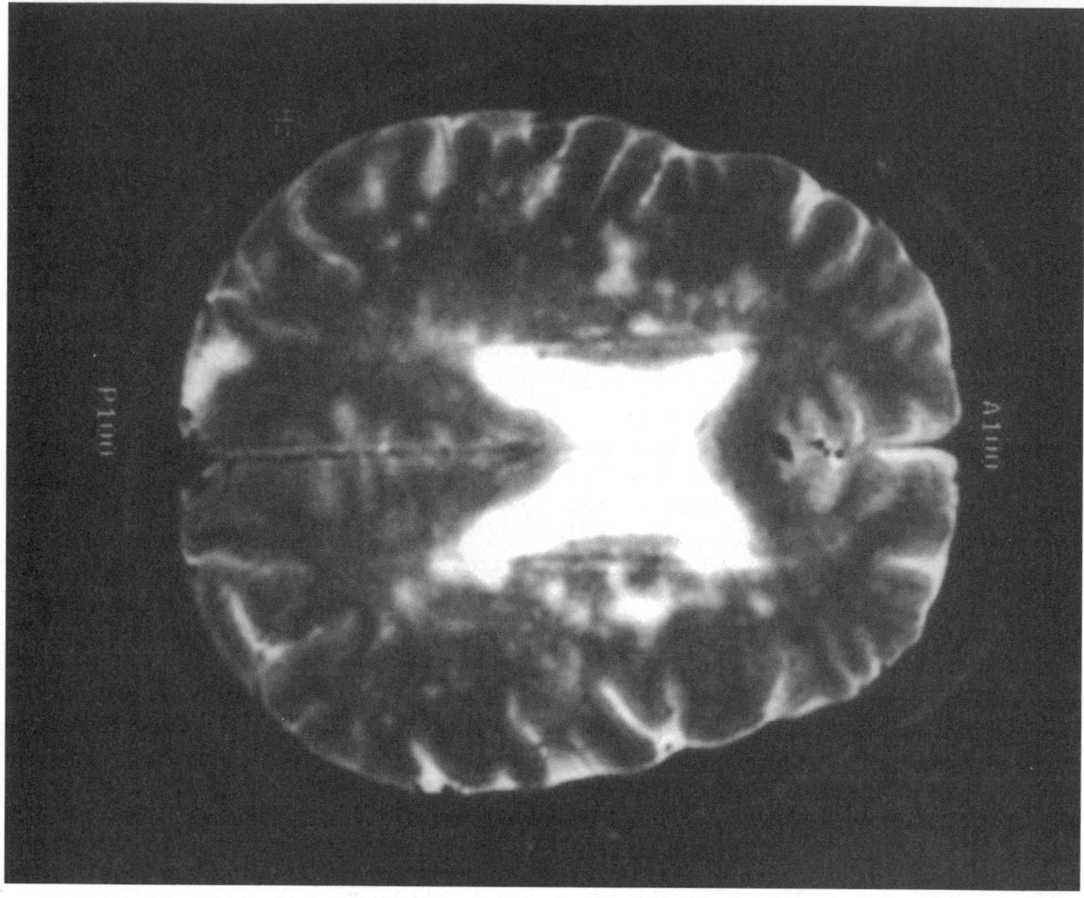

Figure 7.8 A cerebral blood flow image.

There are fewer imaging studies of mania, with some detecting relative decreases in right anterior temporal and orbitofrontal cortices, as well as a reversal of hypofrontality following shifts from depression into hypomania (Baxter et al., 1985; Ketter et al., 1994; Mayberg, 1994; see figure 7.10). There is also evidence that right versus left hemispheric differences in cerebral blood flow or metabolism may distinguish depressed and manic patients, with a greater reduction of left hemisphere blood flow in depression compared to greater right hemisphere changes in mania (Ketter et al., 1994; Mayberg, 1994).

Finally, imaging studies employing magnetic resonance spectroscopy have recently been used to investigate phosphorus metabolism in affective disorders. In contrast to the above studies of cerebral blood flow and metabolism, these studies are able to determine the cerebral levels of various phosphorus metabolites, which would reflect metabolic activity of different second messengers, such as cAMP, cGMP, and phosphatidylinositol. Abnormal and asymmetrical phosphorus metabolism has been found in the frontal lobes of patients with bipolar disorder as compared to normal controls (Deicken, Fein, & Weiner, 1995; Kato et al., 1995). Abnormal phosphorous levels also have been reported in the basal ganglia of patients with unipolar depression (Moore, Christensen, Lafer, Fava, & Renshaw, 1997). One study found decreased phosphorous metabolism in the left frontal lobe of depressed patients compared to normal controls, and decreased metabolism in the right frontal lobe of manic and euthymic patients as compared to normal controls (Kato et al., 1995). These results are consistent with previous studies showing lower glucose metabolism in the left frontal lobe during the depressed phase, in contrast to findings in the

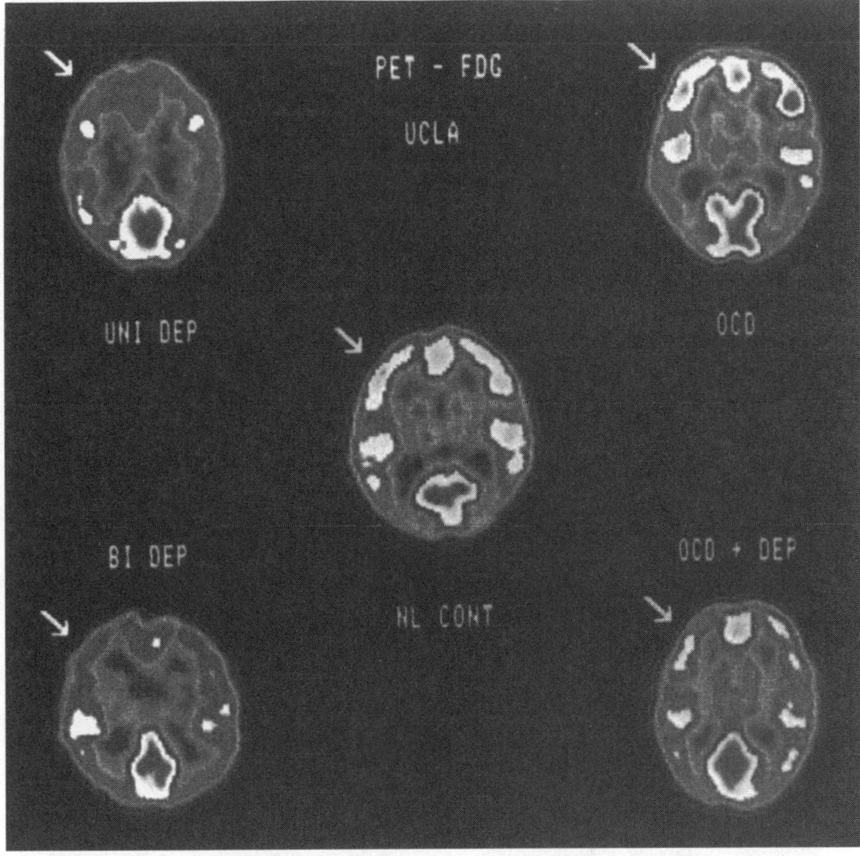

Figure 7.9 Imaging in several clinical syndromes.

right frontal lobe, where metabolism is decreased during the euthymic and manic phases (Ketter et al., 1994). When considered together, there is now compelling evidence of frontal lobe abnormalities in affective disorders (George, Ketter, & Post, 1994; Powell & Miklowitz, 1994), as well as tantilizing hints of differences in functioning in depression and mania.

Chronobiology and Affective Disorders

Most of the biological processes discussed in this chapter, such as cortisol secretion and the sleep-wake cycle, are characterized by regular, periodic 24-hour patterns, referred to as circadian rhythms (Wirz-Justice, 1995). Other biological rhythms, such as the 90-minute REM sleep cycle, are shorter than 24 hours and hence are referred to as ultradian rhythms. These may have some relevance to understanding rapid-cycling bipolar disorder and cyclothymia (Goodwin & Jamison, 1990; Howland & Thase, 1993). Seasonal or yearly patterns (circannual rhythms) also have been described for various biological processes, and may be important to understanding seasonal affective disorder (Goodwin & Jamison, 1990). Because these rhythms are inherently important to the normal function of biological systems, investigating the abnormalities associated with affective disorders may help elucidate fundamental underlying pathophysiological processes.

Circadian rhythms are maintained by a biological "clock" within the CNS, but are normally influenced by external environmental cues (zeitgebers). In the absence of environmental stimuli, circadian rhythms follow a 25-hour cycle, and they can be entrained to follow cycles ranging from 21 to 27 hours with experimental manipulations of

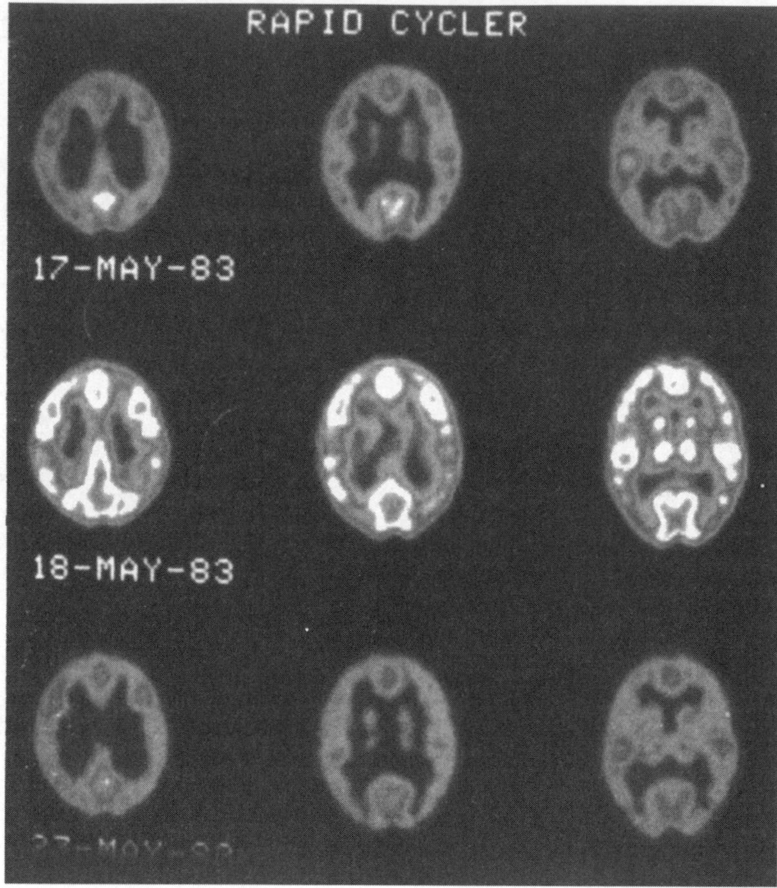

Figure 7.10 Chronobiologic differences among affectively disordered.

the light-dark cycle. The sleep-wake circadian "clock" is located in the suprachiasmatic nucleus (SCN) of the hypothalamus, with neural connections to the retina, pineal gland, and limbic system (Kandel et al., 1991). These connections serve as the pathway by which environmental cues reach the SCN and modulate the sleep-wake cycle. Input from the retina, for example, is relevant to understanding the therapeutic mood effects of bright white light. A second circadian "clock," controlling rhythms for body temperature, REM propensity, and cortisol secretion, also may exist (Wirz-Justice, 1995). These two rhythms can be uncoupled experimentally, and when desynchronized can cause such depression-like symptoms as fatigue, cognitive dulling, and poor sleep quality (Boivin et al., 1997).

The hypothesis that a disorganization of circadian rhythms may result from disrupted social zeitgebers provides a useful model to understand the relationship between psychosocial factors (e.g., life events, social supports) and affective disorders (Ehlers, Frank, & Kupfer, 1988). This effect might be mediated by the neural pathway linking the SCN to the limbic system. One therapeutic implication may be to invoke an artificial control over desynchronized rhythms by helping depressed patents to keep regular meal, sleep, and exercise times.

Another hypothesis suggests that a blunted amplitude of circadian rhythms is the primary chronobiological abnormality in affective disorders, which is supported by studies showing diminished amplitudes of cortisol, melatonin, and body temperature (Thase & Howland, 1995). Such blunting could reflect a state of CNS hyperarousal and/or a deficient dampening or quieting effect.

Finally, a hypothesis that pathological desynchronization (uncoupling) of circadian rhythms (i.e., the advance or delay of various circadian rhythms relative to the sleep-wake rhythm) is associated with affective disorders has been described (Wirz-Justice, 1995). This readily explains the mood-altering effects of transmeridian flight and changing work shifts, which can precipitate more severe manic or depressive episodes in persons with a history of affective disorders. Pathological shifts in biological rhythms also are consistent with the findings from many, but not all, studies that the body temperature, REM propensity, and cortisol rhythms occur earlier (i.e., phase-advanced) relative to the sleep-wake rhythm in depression. The transient antidepressant effect of sleep deprivation also may work by temporarily phase-delaying the sleep-wake cycle relative to the already phase-advanced circadian rhythm, but this has not been firmly established (Goodwin & Jamison, 1990). Conversely, studies of seasonal winter depressions have found that circadian rhythms are phase delayed relative to the sleep-wake cycle (Avery et al., 1997; Schwartz et al., 1997; Teicher et al., 1997).

Biological Studies in Bipolar Disorder

Monoamine Abnormalities in Bipolar Disorder

Patients with bipolar I depression have significantly lower levels of plasma NE and MHPG and urinary MHPG compared to normal controls, bipolar II depression, and unipolar depression (Schatzberg & Schildkraut, 1995). Longitudinal studies of bipolar disorder show increased urinary MHPG levels following shifts from depression into mania. Higher levels of CSF, plasma, and urinary NE, E, and MHPG are found in bipolar disorder during manic periods compared to depressed and euthymic periods, and also compared to normal controls. This may also be true of bipolar patients during dysphoric or mixed manic episodes (Swann et al., 1994). Stimulation of noradrenergic pathways, such as the medial forebrain bundle, can produce increased levels of goal-directed behavior (Cooper, Bloom, & Roth, 1997), suggesting a role for NE in the pathophysiology of hypomanic and manic states (Carroll, 1991). Lithium treatment decreases NE turnover in bipolar patients. These findings support the hypothesis that NE modulates the switch process in bipolar disorder (Bunney, Goodwin, Murphy, House, & Gordon, 1972).

In contrast with studies of depression, there have been far fewer studies examining the role of 5-HT in patients with bipolar disorder. There is indirect evidence from some studies that low levels of 5-HT are associated with a vulnerability to develop manic as well as depressive episodes (Chouinard, Young, Bradwejn, & Annable, 1983). From one perspective (Prange, Wilson, Lynn, Alltop, & Stikeleather, 1974), a deficit of 5-HT has been proposed to create an unstable neuroregulatory state, such that deficits of NE will invoke depression and relative excesses cause mania. This "5-HT permissive" model remains relevant and permits incorporation of both therapeutic effects (e.g., lithium or divalproex) and diverse clinical observations such as rapid cycling, antidepressant-induced cycling, and mixed states.

More direct studies of 5-HT function in mania have yielded inconsistent results, although the overall pattern is similar to studies of depression. Decreased 5-HT has been found in postmortem brain specimens of bipolar patients (Young, Warsh, Kish, Shannak, & Hornykeiwicz, 1994). A recent study found a blunted prolactin response to the 5-HT releasing drug fenfluramine in manic patients (Thakore, O'Keane, & Dinan, 1996), suggesting a 5-HT deficit or state of receptor downregulation similar to that found in unipolar depression. Other studies have reported normal and abnormal findings of platelet 5-HT reuptake and CSF 5-HIAA levels in mania (Thakore et al., 1996). Such findings support the notion that depression and mania may share a common 5-HT dysfunction. Among patients vulnerable to the development of mania, decreased 5-HT function may reflect the failure of inhibitory control over the increases in NE and DA that are associated with the switch in mania (Bunney et al., 1972; Schatzberg et al., 1985).

The mesocortical system, originating in the ventral tegmental area, projects axons to the orbitofrontal and the prefrontal cortices. This system is involved in motivation, initiation of goal-directed activity, attention, executive cognitive tasks, and social behavior (Swerdlow & Koob, 1987). Thus, increased mesocortical and mesolimbic dopaminergic activity may be related to such manic symptoms as euphoria, grandiosity, hyperactivity, hypersexuality, and disinhibited behaviors (Depue & Iacono, 1989). In contrast to nonpsychotic depression, a functional increase in DA has been supported by studies showing increased CSF HVA levels in mania (Schatzberg et al., 1985; Swerdlow & Koob, 1987). Also, brain imaging studies have found that D_2 receptors are upregulated in mania compared to depression, and that D_2 receptor upregulation is greater in psychotic mania than in nonpsychotic mania (Pearlson et al., 1995). Chronic or high-dose treatment with stimulants, which enhance DA function, can also cause a syndrome indistinguishable from mania (Willner, 1995). Patients with bipolar disorder are more susceptible than unipolar patients to the mood-elevating effects of DA drugs, which can often precipitate hypomanic or manic episodes (Bunney et al., 1972; Willner, 1995). Lithium, mood-stabilizing anticonvulsants, and antipsychotic drugs can attenuate some of the DA-stimulated behaviors in animals (Swerdlow & Koob, 1987).

Cholinergic agonist and antagonist drugs also have differential clinical effects in mania (Janowsky & Overstreet, 1995). Agonists may reduce symptoms in manic patients, whereas antagonists may trigger mania in bipolar patients. Remitted bipolar patients and never-ill persons with a family history of affective disorder are also more sensitive to the effects of cholinergic stimulation relative to normal subjects (Janowsky & Overstreet, 1995). One study found an increased growth hormone response to cholinergic stimulation in manic patients compared to normals (Dinan et al., 1994), suggesting that cholinergic sensitivity may not be limited to depression. Interestingly, one study found that bipolar patients with low concentrations of red blood cell choline were more likely to have had previous episodes of mania than depression, whereas those with higher concentrations tended to have similar numbers of manic and depressive episodes, indirectly suggesting an antimanic effect of elevated choline (Janowsky & Overstreet, 1995). Choline has also been used to treat lithium-refractory rapid-cycling bipolar patients (Stoll, Sachs, & Cohen, 1996).

Amino Acids in Bipolar Disorder

Plasma levels of GABA are low in a subgroup of patients with bipolar disorder (Petty, 1995). The levels are similar to those seen in unipolar depression, which differ from the normal levels found in other psychiatric disorders. The low GABA levels also persistent after recovery, suggesting that it may represent a traitlike vulnerability marker for affective disorders. Family studies are needed to determine if decreased GABA levels are an epiphenomenon of chronic stress associated with affective disorders or are a true genetic marker.

Drugs that potently stimulate GABA receptors have antimanic effects, as evidenced by divalproex and related anticonvulsants. There is a reciprocal inhibitory relationship between GABA and the neuropeptide somatostatin, which has proconvulsant effects and contributes to the development of kindled seizures (Rubinow et al., 1995). Kindling is a phenomenon whereby a subthreshold stimulus (e.g., an electrical stimulus too low to induce a seizure) that is repeated over time ultimately can induce a seizure, suggesting sensitization of the CNS. The kindling effect has been proposed to explain the phasic recurrence of manic and depressive episodes (i.e., repeated episodes can sensitize the CNS and increase the vulnerability to future episodes) as well as to explain the antimanic effects of anticonvulsants (Post, 1992). The anticonvulsant carbamazepine increases GABA and decreases somatostatin, which may account for its antikindling antimanic effects (Post, Weiss, & Chuang, 1992).

Electroencephalographic Sleep Studies in Bipolar Disorder

Reduced REM latency and increased REM density are seen in bipolar depression and in mania (Benca et al., 1992; Howland & Thase, 1991; Hudson, Keck, Lipinski, Aizley, & Pope, 1992, 1993; Linkowski et al, 1994). Depressed bipolar patients with hypersomnia have an extended total sleep time, increased REM time, and/or reduced sleep latency (Nofzinger et al., 1991; Thase, Himmelhoch, Mallinger, Jarrett, & Kupfer, 1989). Reduced SWS and poor sleep continuity in nonbipolar depression may be the result of excessive arousal caused by pathologically increased noradrenergic, dopaminergic, or HPA axis activity. Mania is not characterized by decreased SWS (Hudson et al., 1992; Linkowski et al., 1994), however. Such contradictory findings might be explained by regional differences in hyperarousal between severe depression and mania (Ketter et al., 1994).

Neuroendocrine Abnormalities in Bipolar Disorder

The most common HPA axis abnormalities found in depression (i.e., increased cortisol, DST nonsuppression, and HPA axis circadian rhythm dysregulation) are also found in mania, although usually to a less severe degree than in depression (Cookson, 1985; Linkowski et al., 1994; Schmider et al., 1995). Interestingly, the HPA axis may be relatively quiescent in anergic forms of depression, such as bipolar depression (Geracioti et al., 1997), and it may be overactive in mixed, dysphoric, or psychotic mania (Cookson, 1985; Linkowski et al., 1994; Schmider et al., 1995), possibly related to decreased and increased activation, respectively, of the dopaminergic mesocorticolimbic system.

A recent brain imaging study of depressed bipolar patients found a significant inverse relationship between TSH blood levels and brain metabolism (Marangell et al., 1997). The strongest correlation was found in the dorsolateral and mesial prefrontal cortices, which are implicated in affective disorders. Increased HPT activation may be a compensatory response to decreased brain metabolism or a sustained increase in TRH and TSH levels may be a component of a counterregulatory reduction of brain metabolism. Successful anticonvulsant treatment of bipolar disorder has consistently been shown to be associated with a concomitant decrease in circulating thyroid hormones (Joffe & Levitt, 1993).

Mania has been associated with hyperthyroidism, but this is not common (Joffe & Levitt, 1993). Hypothyroidism is also associated with treatment-refractory and rapid-cycling forms of bipolar disorder, especially in women (Whybrow, 1995), and they sometimes respond to high doses of thyroid hormone (Whybrow, 1995).

One study found that bipolar depressives had an exaggerated TSH response, whereas unipolar depressives had a blunted response (Gold et al., 1980). They also found that the switch from depression to mania among bipolar patients was associated with switching from a blunted to an exaggerated TSH response, which is consistent with a possible role for thyroid function in the regulation of circadian rhythms (Bauer, Soloway, Dratman, & Kreider, 1992). Unlike schizophrenia, most TRH studies in mania and depression have found that a significant proportion of patients also have a blunted TSH response, suggesting that TSH blunting may have more relevance and specificity for affective disorders in general (Cookson, 1985; Joffe & Levitt, 1993). A consistent finding in mania is a blunted GH response to the α_2 receptor agonist clonidine and to the adrenergic antidepressant desipramine (Checkley, 1992; Dinan et al., 1994; Holsboer, 1995). Manic patients have a normal GH circadian rhythm (Linkowski et al., 1994).

Most studies of basal, circadian, and stimulated prolactin secretion have not found significant abnormalities in mania (Cookson, 1985; Checkley, 1992; Linkowski et al., 1994).

Seasonal Affective Disorder

Many patients with bipolar disorder have some tendency to cycle with the seasons, and a majority of people with seasonal affective disorder have a history of hypomanias in the spring or summer. The characteristic seasonal mood changes in seasonal affective disorder (SAD) and the apparent effectiveness of bright light therapy have led to particular interest in studying the circadian rhythms in these patients. Most studies have found that circadian rhythms occur later (i.e., phase delayed) relative to the sleep-wake cycle, which generally distinguishes SAD from nonseasonal, melancholic depressions (Avery et al., 1997; Schwartz et al., 1997; Teicher et al., 1997). Patients with SAD typically have reversed vegetative depressive symptoms (hypersomnia, increased appetite, and carbohydrate craving) similar to bipolar depression, and they do not show generally the biological abnormalities associated with melancholia (e.g., EEG sleep abnormalities; Oren & Rosenthal, 1992).

The hormone melatonin has been implicated in SAD because it is secreted by the pineal gland in response to darkness, is suppressed by bright light via the retinal-SCN-pineal neural pathway, and must be effectively suppressed for bright light therapy to be effective. However, there is not strong support for this hypothesis (Oren & Rosenthal, 1992). Patients with SAD have thermoregulatory abnormalities that differ from nonseasonal depressions and normals (Avery et al., 1997; Schwartz et al., 1997), but this is not due to thyroid dysfunction (Lingjaerde, Reichborn-Kjennerud, & Haug, 1995). A more likely explanation may be a 5-HT dysfunction affecting thermoregulation at the hypothalamic level (Schwartz et al., 1997; Neumeister et al., 1997). A deficiency of hypothalamic 5-HT, in the absence of abnormalities of HPA and sympathoadrenal systems, may also account for the characteristic reversed vegetative symptoms (Thase, 1998). The effectiveness of bright light therapy may be serotonergically mediated, and serotoninergic antidepressants may be especially effective in SAD (Neumeister et al., 1997). Although there are many biological differences between SAD and nonseasonal depressions, preliminary brain imaging studies have found prefrontal and orbitofrontal changes in SAD similar to what has been described in other depressed populations (Lam, 1994). Family studies of SAD are described in the section on genetics below.

Rapid-Cycling Bipolar Disorder

Although only a minority of bipolar patients develop a pattern of rapid cycling, it has very important clinical and theoretical implications (Goodwin & Jamison, 1990). Because the clinical symptoms of depression and mania do not differ from nonrapid-cycling bipolar disorder, the phenomenon of rapid cycling may be a good model for specifically investigating underlying processes that may relate to the so-called switch mechanism (Bunney et al., 1972; Bauer et al., 1992). The prevalence of bipolar I and II disorders is relatively equal among patients with rapid cycling, and there is no known association with cyclothymia (Howland & Thase, 1993). Rapid cycling is probably most accurately viewed as a phase of illness rather than a distinct subtype. The most common biological abnormality associated with rapid cycling is hypothyroidism. This finding is consistent with the effects of thyroid function on circadian rhythm regulation (Bauer et al., 1992), the greater prevalence of rapid cycling among women (who are more vulnerable to thyroid dysfunction), and the clinical efficacy of thyroid hormone treatment (Bauer & Whybrow, 1996).

Rapid cycling is also associated with antidepressant use, especially tricyclic antidepressants. This may be related to their adrenergic and/or dopaminergic effects in triggering a switch mechanism (Bunney et al., 1972), particularly if serotonergic inhibitory control is deficient. Finally, rapid cycling is associated with a relatively poorer treatment response to lithium, and such patients may respond better to anticonvulsants such as divalproex and carbamazepine. One reason may be the inhibitory effect of lithium on thyroid function. Also, the differential treatment response to these drugs suggests that investigating and comparing their mechanisms of action (e.g., second-messenger systems, antikindling effects) may shed light on the underlying mechanism in rapid cycling.

Bipolar II Disorder

The validity of bipolar II disorder as a clinical and diagnostic entity distinct from bipolar I and unipolar disorders is a relatively recent development (Dunner, 1993). Perhaps most important, only a minority of patients with bipolar II disorders eventually experience manic episodes during longitudinal follow-up. Findings from numerous studies have found that HPA axis abnormalities, plasma NE and MHPG levels, urinary MHPG levels, and frequency of subcortical hyperintensities in bipolar II were more similar to recurrent (unipolar) major depressive disorder than bipolar I (Dunner, 1993; Altshuler et al., 1995; Schatzberg & Schildkraut, 1995). Finally, family history studies (described in the section on genetics) support a genetic distinction among these affective disorders (Dunner, 1993). Bipolar II patients are also more likely to show a seasonal pattern than either unipolar or bipolar I patients (Dunner, 1993). This suggests the possibility that the serotonergic and circadian rhythm abnormalities seen in SAD may be present in BP II disorder.

Genetics of Affective Disorders

Family studies determine whether affective disorders aggregate within families. Controlled family studies of patients with bipolar disorder have consistently shown a significantly higher relative risk of bipolar disorder (approximately 4–17%) among the relatives of both people with major depressive disorder and bipolar patients compared to the relative risk among the relatives of healthy controls (Merikangas & Kupfer, 1995). The relative risk of major depression among the relatives of bipolar patients (approximately 2–10%) is also significantly greater than that among healthy controls. These results show that the magnitude of the relative risk of bipolar disorder among bipolar patients is greater than that for major depression among bipolar patients. Conversely, a significant minority of people with "depression" have some unexpressed vulnerability to bipolar disorder. The relatives of patients with bipolar disorder also have a greater prevalence of cyclothymia and bipolar II disorder (Howland & Thase, 1993).

Controlled family studies of patients with major depression have also consistently found that the relatives of major depression patients have a significantly greater relative risk of major depression than the relatives of healthy controls. The relative risk of bipolar disorder among relatives of major depression patients is also greater than that seen among the relatives of healthy controls, but the magnitude of relative risk for bipolar disorder in major depression families is much less pronounced than that seen in the bipolar disorder families (Merikangas & Kupfer, 1995). These findings support a genetic contribution to the development of affective disorders, but they also suggest that some degree of genetic specificity distinguishes bipolar and unipolar disorders.

Family studies have found that 35 to 69% of patients with SAD have a family history of affective disorders and 7 to 37% have a history of SAD (Bauer & Dunner, 1996). Although the rate of SAD in families appears to be higher than the estimated population prevalence (Lam, 1994), there have been no family studies comparing SAD and nonseasonal patients.

Finally, family history studies have found higher bipolar I rates in bipolar I probands (than in unipolar or bipolar II probands), higher bipolar I rates in bipolar II probands (than in unipolar probands), high rates of unipolar in all proband groups, and higher rates of bipolar II in bipolar II probands, which supports a genetic distinction among these affective disorders (Dunner, 1993).

The results from numerous twin studies have found an average concordance rate of approximately 60% for bipolar affective disorders among monozygotic twins and approximately 12% for dizygotic twins (Kelsoe, 1997). The rate of concordance for major depression is also greater among monozygotes compared to dizygotes, but the magnitude of this difference is less than that seen for bipolar. These results provide strong evidence that bipolar disorder may have a greater genetic liability than does major depression. However, environmental factors must be invoked to explain why concordance among identical twins is not closer to 100%.

Adoption studies compare the rates of affective disorders among adoptees, their biological parents, and their adoptive parents. Adoption studies have generally found a greater risk for bipolar disorder among the biological parents of bipolar disorder adoptees compared to the risk in the adoptive parents. The magnitude of this difference, however, is somewhat lower than that seen in family studies, again suggesting that there is a significant environmental component to the development of bipolar disorder (Merikangas & Kupfer, 1995).

Association studies compare the prevalence of a genetic marker (e.g., ABO blood type) in groups of persons with or without affective disorders. A large number of association studies have examined various biological markers in affective disorders. The most commonly studied genetic traits have been ABO blood types, human leukocyte antigens, and the enzyme monoamine oxidase, but the studies have not found consistent evidence of an association for any marker (Merikangas & Kupfer, 1995). Recent advances in molecular biology have made it possible to study specific DNA markers, many of which have potential etiological relevance (e.g., tyrosine hydroxylase gene, tryptophan β-hydroxylase gene, dopamine receptor genes, 5-HT reuptake transporter gene; Merikangas & Kupfer, 1995; Bellivier et al., 1997). In addition, it would be informative to study different clinically relevant biological markers, such as REM latency, blunted growth hormone response to clonidine, and G-protein function.

Linkage studies investigate the degree to which a putative affective disorder gene is located near (linked to) a marker gene (that can be easily identified) on the same chromosome, such that the transmission of a marker gene at a particular chromosomal locus can be tracked within a family. Advances in molecular biology have made it possible to examine large numbers of different genetic markers in linkage studies. Numerous studies in bipolar disorder have now reported positive linkage to loci on at least 16 different chromosomes (Kelsoe, 1997). For many of these loci, the linkage is modest or has not been subjected to replication studies. Initial excitement about linkage to chromosomes 11 and X have been tempered by a failure to replicate these findings in subsequent studies, although there is still interest in continuing to study possible linkages to these chromosomes. To date, the strongest evidence for genetic linkage in bipolar disorder is to chromosome 18, because there are several positive studies from independent research groups (Berrettini, Ferraro, & Goldin, 1997; Kelsoe, 1997). Moreover, these findings are important because genes coding for one of the G-protein subunits and for a type of ACTH receptor are located on chromosome 18 (Berrettini et al., 1997). Hence, intensive investigation of other loci on chromosome 18 may be very informative.

Gender Differences in the Biology of Affective Disorders

The incidence and prevalence of major depression is twice as great in women as in men, whereas the rates of bipolar disorder are relatively equal. Moreover, bipolar disorder is much less prevalent than major depression. Why these differences exist among the affective disorders, which have many biological and clinical similarities, may be examined in the context of some of the clear psychosocial and biological differences between men and women. Studies of life events have tended to show that women appear to be more vulnerable to the effects of stressful events in general, although studies that examine many particular life events (such as widowhood, divorce, and financial difficulties) find that women adjust better than men (Kessler, 1995). Other research has found that the rate of first onset of depression is relatively equal for men and women after age 30, such that the doubled risk for depression in women is "created" during the early adult years (Kessler, 1995). Of note, a study of an Amish population found similar rates of unipolar depression in men and women, with an overall rate only one quarter of that found in more secular and heterogeneous communities (Egeland & Hostetter, 1983). These studies suggest that gender differences in the rates of depression may be due to cultural and psychosocial differences rather than biological differences.

Perhaps changes in social support, economic power, and rates of sexual abuse that have accompanied modern life provoke or exaggerate otherwise adaptive gender differences. Nolen-Hoeksema (1991) has summarized a large body of research indicating that women make greater use of emotion-focused and affiliative coping than men. These cognitive-affective ways of responding to distress may have neural counterparts (REF) and, in turn, may be advantageous to child rearing. Unfortunately, devaluation and diffusion of social roles, especially when coupled with inadequate social support and insufficient means to resolve stressful circumstances, may create a state of entrapment that mirrors learned helplessness. In such a circumstance, the evolutionary advantage to experience emotions more intensely may work at cross-purposes, predisposing the dysphoric women to more pervasive periods of depression.

Although there are no significant gender differences in prevalence rates of bipolar disorder, the rapid-cycling subtype is more common among women (Bauer & Whybrow, 1996). Thus, either sex or gender appears to alter the course of this disorder. In addition, recent genetic studies have found significant differences between men and women in the transmission of bipolar disorder, referred to as the parent of origin effect (McInnis, 1997).

The clearest biological differences between men and women that are relevant to affective disorders are found in the HPA, HPT, and hypothalamic-pituitary-ovarian (HPO) axes (Whybrow, 1995; Young, 1995; Toren et al., 1996). There is considerable evidence that estrogens, progesterones, and other components of the HPO axis have significant mood effects that may partly contribute to gender differences in certain affective vulnerabilities (Toren et al., 1996), including postpartum, oral contraceptive–related, menstrual cycle–related, and postmenopausal mood changes. Women normally have higher baseline levels of TSH and are more likely to have various types of thyroid dysfunction, such as hypothyroidism and postpartum thyroid dysfunction (Whybrow, 1995). This may be relevant to such clinical observations as the higher prevalence of rapid-cycling bipolar disorder among women, the superior efficacy of thyroid hormone antidepressant augmentation in women, and the heightened risk for affective disorders during the postpartum period. There is also some evidence of gender differences in HPA axis regulation, especially in later life (Young, 1995). It would appear that during the reproductive years, women are more vulnerable to depressions characterized by normal HPA functions, such as "nonendogenous" or reversed neurovegetative depressions. As estrogens have a pro-5-HT effect, it may be that reversed neurovegetative features actually reflect counterregulatory or compensatory processes that are facilitated by female sex hormones (Thase, Frank, Kornstein, & Yonkers, in press). Premenopausal women have more normal 5-HT and NE mediated responses to pharmacologic probes (REF), as well as more normal levels of slow wave sleep (Reynolds et al., 1990). Conversely, following menopause, the relative deficit of estrogen may permit the more characteristic clinical and neurobiological manifestations of severe depression. Fluctuations of mood in concern with the menstrual cycle thus may represent a "miniature" expression of a more ominous subsequent process. Longitudinal studies conducted across a decade, not months or even years, will be needed to clarify these issues.

Summary of Biological Findings in Affective Disorders

The most common and/or consistently identified abnormalities in affective disorders include: (1) reduced catecholamines in bipolar depression, elevated catecholamines in severe depressions and mania, downregulated α_2 and β receptors in depression, reduced CSF 5-HIAA in depression, downregulated 5-HT_{1A} and upregulated 5-HT_2 receptors in depression, and ACH supersensitivity in depression and mania; (2) excessive activation of the HPA axis and TRH blunting in both depression and mania; (3) decreased CSF GABA in depression and mania; (4) reduced REM latency and increased REM density in depression and mania, and decreased SWS in depression; (5) blunted GH response to clonidine in depression and mania; (6) decreased CSF somatostatin in depression; (7) circadian rhythm disturbances in depression and mania; (8) abnormal second-messenger system function in depression and mania; and (9) abnormal brain metabolism, primarily involving frontal, prefrontal, and limbic regions in depression and mania.

Discussion

The wide range of abnormalities described in this chapter strongly suggest that etiologic theories based primarily on singular systems (e.g., monoamine chemistry, neuroendocrinology, and chronobiology) are too simplistic and cannot fully account for the myriad clinical and biological features of affective disorders. There is increasing evidence that these systems interact in many ways, probably serving to maintain homeostasis by their complex regulatory and compensatory relationships. Affective disorders are, therefore, likely to result from disturbances of major emotional and behavioral systems comprising these smaller components. In addition, some of these abnormalities are seen in depression and in mania. They may represent compensatory responses to disturbances in the different systems involved in these states. Or, they may be part of smaller regulatory components having a particular function, which may have a common use by different systems. For example, second messengers are fundamental to cellular function and are the "keys" that turn the "locks" that regulate gene activity. The manifestations of a second-messenger abnormality, however, will depend on the function of the system it is serving. Therefore, a simultaneous study of different neurochemical, neuroendocrine, and neurophysiological variables is needed to fully understand the interactive and additive nature of smaller underlying disturbances. Moreover, correlating these findings with functional brain imaging studies may ultimately allow us to put each of the pieces together and more clearly identify the fundamental emotional and behavioral systems involved in the pathophysiological states of depression and mania.

Not all patients with affective disorders have significant biological abnormalities. The greatest evidence for neurobiologic dysregulation is found in bipolar I disorder, severe melancholic depression, and psychotic affective disorders. Patients with nonbipolar, nonpsychotic, nonmelancholic major depressions, dysthymia, and cyclothymia are less likely to have multiple biological disturbances, but may still have limited abnormalities such as reduced REM latency (Howland & Thase, 1991; Thase & Howland, 1995).

Some of these neurobiological disturbances are state dependent (e.g., increased cortisol, increased NE activity, downregulated β receptors, poor sleep efficiency, increased REM density, and decreased frontal cortical brain metabolism) and are most consistently seen in severe melancholic and psychotic depressions. Several recent studies suggest that the biological abnormalities that characterize these severe affective states may constitute a "boundary" beyond which psychotheraphy is less effective unless combined with pharmacotherapy (e.g., Thase, Simons, & Reynolds, 1996, Thase, et al., 1996, 1997). At yet a greater level of CNS dysfunction, antidepressant monotherapies may fail and ECT may be necessary. Another set of biological disturbances appear to behave more like traits. These state-independent or traitlike abnormalities include reduced REM latency, diminished SWS, decreased CSF 5-HIAA levels, TRH blunting, blunted GH response, downregulated α_2 receptors, and cholinergic supersensitivity. These parameters may have more relevance to vulnerability or relapse risk.

As was discussed in previous sections of this chapter, there is evidence that the mesocorticolimbic system (Depue & Iacono, 1989) is impaired in some forms of depression, and may be overactivated in mania. Other forms of depression may involve impairment of 5-HT mediated inhibitory functions, which may be referred to as a behavioral quieting system (Gray, 1991). This may result in a state of heightened CNS arousal, characterized by decreased SWS, reduced REM latency, multiple nocturnal awakenings, and blunted adrenergic function, as well as cholinergic supersensitivity. These patients typically have insomnia, weight loss, generalized anxiety, and increased irritability, and they may be prone to violent suicidal behavior (Depue & Spoont, 1986). Impairment of this system also may be involved in the phenomenon of dysphoric or mixed mania (Depue & Iacono, 1989). The illness transduction or kindling model of Post (1992) further suggests that progressively greater abnormalities of behavioral quieting may result from each recurrent episode of depression and mania. Thus, we wonder if measures of cortical atrophy may provide an operational index of the cumulative "wear and tear" of such kindled illnesses.

The effects of stress, of course, would be most evident among people with deficits in behavioral quieting. Traitlike vulnerability thus may predispose to aberrant and sustained CNS stress responses. Exaggerated activation of stress-response systems is the most clearly established disturbance in severe depression, and may play a significant role in the pathogenesis of mania. Sustained activation of stress-response systems, manifested by increased HPA axis and sympathoadrenal activity, may downregulate or inhibit behavioral facilitation. Neurotoxic effects of glucocorticoids, neuropeptides, and excititory amino acids may further impair an overtaxed behavioral quieting system. An abnormal stress response system is most evident in severe episodes of illness, such as melancholic and psychotic depressions. Dysregulation of this system increases with age (especially in postmenopausal women), perhaps contributing to both the onset and severity of late-life depressions.

As discussed in previous sections, disturbances of biological rhythms represent an important neurobiologic process associated with various affective syndromes, such as SAD, rapid cycling, triggering of mania, mood changes associated with shiftwork and jet lag, and possibly mediating the mood effects of psychosocial disturbances.

More recently, abnormalities of the frontal and prefrontal cortical regions of the brain have been implicated in depression, as well as mania. Impairment in the functions normally mediated by these areas may explain many of the cognitive features found in depressed patients, such as poor problem-solving abilities, difficulties utilizing abstraction, and problems mastering more effortful cognitive tasks. Involvement of the frontal lobes would also account for some of the behavioral problems seen in manic patients, such as poor judgment, disinhibited behaviors, and social inappropriateness. As discussed previously, there is evidence that DA, NE, and HPA axis activity may contribute to disturbances related to the frontal and prefrontal pathways.

Second-messenger systems may have a central role in the pathophysiology of affective disorders because they are a common pathway by which limited or distinct abnormalities may be manifested widely, such as abnormalities in multiple neurotransmitter and neuroreceptor systems (Lachman & Papolos, 1995). This common pathway may help explain the phasic recurrence of affective episodes, as well as the triggering of and switching between manic and depressive episodes. All humans may be physiologically capable of experiencing manic or depressive symptoms. Individuals with affective disorders may have a faulty control mechanism that fails to adequately regulate or contain perturbations in mood stability (Gottschalk, Bauer, & Whybrow, 1997). Thus, such persons may be vulnerable to developing an exaggerated affective response to stressors that would ordinarily be restrained, or may be vulnerable to autonomous inexplicable switches that may permit but not necessarily cause an unrestrained progressive evolution of affective symptoms. In patients with bipolar disorder, for example, a faulty second-messenger switch mechanism may turn off and remain locked, disengaging the mesocorticolimbic circuit, effectively shutting down the behavioral facilitation system, which may progressively evolve into a persistent depressed state until the switch is unlocked and the circuit is reopened. Conversely, the switch may turn on and remain locked, opening the mesocorticolimbic circuit, permitting unrestrained activation of the behavioral facilitation system, which may progressively evolve into a persistent manic state until the switch is unlocked and the circuit is closed. Moreover, postulating distinct sites of action of antidepressant and antimanic drugs at different points along the same pathway may also explain their different clinical effects (i.e., mood elevation versus mood stabilization), as well as potential synergistic effects (e.g., combining different psychotropic drugs). This may also account for the similar clinical and biological effects of antidepressants that have different pharmacological properties (e.g., tricyclic compared to serotonin reuptake inhibitor antidepressants). Finally, antidepressants and mood stabilizers may have more persistent and normalizing clinical effects on affective symptoms because they act primarily (though not exclusively) on sites within the regulatory second-messenger system. By contrast, drugs transiently causing affective symptoms (such as stimulants) may not have sustained clinical effects because they act primarily (though not exclusively) on sites outside of the second-messenger system.

Research on the biological aspects of affective disorders has clearly demonstrated the existence of multiple interacting disturbances, ranging from simple neurochemical abnormalities to dysfunction of complex neurobiological systems. A better understanding of the roles and relationships of these disparate findings with respect to the etiology and pathogenesis of depression and mania is beginning to emerge, but is not yet complete. Future efforts should continue to integrate the findings from neurobiological and psychosocial research endeavors, with the ultimate goal of a complete understanding of the etiopathogenesis of affective disorders.

References

Altshuler, L. L. (1993). Bipolar disorder: Are repeated episodes associated with neuroanatomic and cognitive changes? *Biological Psychiatry, 33*, 563–565.

Altshuler, L. L., Curran, J. G., Hauser, P., Mintz, J., Denicoff, K., & Post, R. (1995). T_2 hyperintensities in bipolar disorder: Magnetic resonance imaging comparison and literature meta-analysis. *American Journal of Psychiatry, 152*, 1139–1144.

Amit, Z., Smith, B. R., & Gill, K. (1991). Serotonin uptake inhibitors: effects on motivated consummatory behaviors. *Journal of Clinical Psychiatry, 52*, 55–60.

Anisman, H., & Zacharko, R. M. (1992). Depression as a consequence of inadequate neurochemical adaptation in response to stressors. *British Journal of Psychiatry, 160*, 36–43.

Armitage, R., Yonkers, K., Cole, D., & Rush, A. J. (1997). A multicenter, double-blind comparison of the effects of nefazodone and fluoxetine on sleep architecture and quality of sleep in depressed outpatients. *Journal of Clinical Psychopharmacology, 17*, 161–168.

Avery, D. H., Dahl, K., Savage, M .V., Brengelmann, G. L., Larsen, L. H., Kenny, M. A., Eder, N., Vitiello, M. V., & Prinz, P. N. (1997). Circadian temperature and cortisol rhythms during a constant routine are phase-delayed in hypersomnic winter depression. *Biological Psychiatry, 41*, 1109–1123.

Avissar, S., Nechamkin, Y., Roitman, G., & Schreiber, G. (1997). Reduced G protein functions and immunoreactive levels in mononuclear leukocytes of patients with depression. *American Journal of Psychiatry, 154*, 211–217.

Aylward, E. H., Roberts-Wrillie, J. V., Barta, P. E., Kumar, A. J., Harris, G. J., Geer, M., Peyser, C. E., & Pearlson, G. D. (1994). Basal ganglia volumes and white matter hyperintensities in patients with bipolar disorder. *American Journal of Psychiatry, 151*, 687–693.

Barden, N. (1996). Modulation of glucocorticoid receptor gene expression by antidepressant drugs. *Pharmacopsychiatry, 29*, 12–22.

Bauer, M. S., & Dunner, D. L. (1996). Validity of seasonal pattern as a modifier for recurrent mood disorders in DSM-IV. In T. A. Widiger, A. J. Frances, H. A. Pincus, R. Ross, M. B. First, W. W. Davis (Eds.), *DSM-IV sourcebook* (pp. 281–298). Washington DC: American Psychiatric Association.

Bauer, M. S., Soloway, A., Dratman, M. B., & Kreider, M. (1992). Effects of hypothyroidism on rat circadian activity and temperature rhythms and their response to light. *Biological Psychiatry, 32*, 411–425

Bauer, M. S., Whybrow, P. C. (1996). Validity of rapid cycling as a modifier for bipolar disorder in DSM-IV. In T. A. Widiger, A. J. Frances, H. A. Pincus, R. Ross, M. B. First, W. W. Davis (Eds.), *DSM-IV sourcebook* (pp. 299–314). Washington DC: American Psychiatric Association.

Baxter, L. R., Phelps, M. E., Mazziotta, J. C., Schwartz, J. M., Gerner, R. H., Selin, C. E., & Sumida, R. M. (1985). Cerebral metabolic rates for glucose in mood disorders: Studies with positron emission tomography and fluorodeoxygulcose F18. *Archives of General Psychiatry, 42*, 441–447.

Bellivier, F., Laplanche, J. L., Leboyer, M., Feingold, J., Bottos, C., Allilaire, J. F., & Launay, J. M. (1997). Serotonin transporter gene and manic depressive illness. An association study. *Biological Psychiatry, 41*, 750–752.

Benca, R. M., Obermeyer, W. H., Thisted, R. A., & Gillin, J. C. (1992). Sleep and psychiatric disorders. A meta-analysis. *Archives of General Psychiatry, 49*, 651–668.

Benson, K. L., Faull, K. F., & Zarcone, V. P. Jr. (1993). The effects of age and serotonergic activity on slow-wave sleep in depressive illness. *Biological Psychiatry, 33*, 842–844.

Berman, K. F., Doran, A. R., Pickar, D., & Weinberger, D. R. (1993). Is the mechanism of prefrontal hypofunction in depression the same as in schizophrenia? Regional cerebral blood flow during cognitive activation. *British Journal of Psychiatry, 162*, 183–192.

Berrettini, W. H., Ferraro, T. N., & Goldin, L. R. (1997). A linkage study of bipolar illness. *Archives of General Psychiatry, 54*, 27–35.

Blier, P., DeMontigny, C., & Chaput, Y. (1987). Modifications of the serotonin system by antidepressant treatments: Implications for the therapeutic response in major depression. *Journal of Clinical Psychopharmacology*, 7(Suppl. 7), 245–355.

Boivin, D. B., Czeisler, C. A., Dijk, D. J., Duffy, J. F., Folkard, S., Minors, D. S., Totterdell, P., & Waterhouse, J. M. (1997). Complex interaction of the sleep-wake cycle and circadian phase modulates mood in healthy subjects. *Archives of General Psychiatry, 54*, 145–152.

Bremner, J. D., Innis, R. B., Salomon, R. M., Staib, L. H., Ng, C. K., Miller, H. L., Bronen, R. A., Krystal, J. H., Duncan, J., Rich, D., Price, L. H., Malison, R., Dey, H., Soufer, R., & Charney, D. S. (1997). Positron emission tomography measurement of cerebral metabolic correlates of tryptophan depletion-induced depressive relapse. *Archives of General Psychiatry, 54*, 364–374.

Brown, G. L., & Linnoila, M. I. (1990). CSF serotonin metabolite (5-HIAA) studies in depression impulsivity and violence. *Journal of Clinical Psychiatry, 51*(Suppl. 4), 31–41.

Brown, A. S., Mallinger, A. G., & Renbaum, L. C. (1993). Elevated platelet membrane phosphatidylinositol-4,5-bisphosphate in bipolar mania. *American Journal of Psychiatry, 150*, 1252–1254.

Buchsbaum, M. S., Someya, T., Wu, J. C., Tang, C. Y., & Bunney, W. E. (1997). Neuroimaging bipolar illness with positron emission tomography and magnetic resonance imaging. *Psychiatric Annals, 27*, 489–496.

Bunney, W. E. J., Goodwin, F. K., Murphy, D. L., House, K. M., & Gordon, E. K. (1972). The "switch process" in manic-depressive illness: II: Relationship to catecholamines, REM sleep, and drugs. *Archives of General Psychiatry, 27*, 304–309.

Buysse, D. J., Frank, E., Lowe, K. K., Cherry, C. R., & Kupfer, D. J. (1997). Electroencephalographic sleep correlates of episode and vulnerability to recurrence in depression. *Biological Psychiatry, 41*, 406–418.•

Buysse, D., Kupfer, D. J., Frank, E., Monk, T. H., & Ritenour, A. (1992) Electroencephalographic sleep studies in depressed outpatients treated with interpersonal psychotherapy: II. Longitudinal studies at baseline and recovery. *Psychiatry Research, 40*, 27–40.

Carroll, B. J. (1991) Psychopathology and neurobiology of manic-depressive disorders. In B. J. Carroll & J. E. Barrett (Eds.), *Psychopathology and the brain* (pp. 265–285). New York: Raven Press.

Checkley, S. (1992). Neuroendocrinology. In E. S. Paykel (Ed.), *Handbook of affective disorders*, 2nd ed. (pp. 255–266). New York: Guilford Press.

Cheeta, S., Ruigt, G., van Proosdij, J., & Willner, P. (1997). Changes in sleep architecture following chronic mild stress. *Biological Psychiatry, 41*, 419–427.

Chouinard, G., Young, S. N., Bradwejn, J., & Annable, L. (1983). Tryptophan in the treatment of depression and mania. *Advanced Biological Psychiatry, 10*, 47–66.

Coffey, C. E., Wilkinson, W. E., Weiner, R. D., Parashos, I. A., Djand, W. T., Webb, M. C., Figiel, G. S., & Spritzer, C. E. (1993). Quanititive cerebral anatomy in depression. A controlled magnetic resonance imaging study. *Archives of General Psychiatry, 50*, 7–16.

Coffey, C. E., Wilkinson, W. E., Weiner, R. D., Ritchie, J. C., & Aque, M. (1993). The dexamethasone suppression test and quantitative cerebral anatomy in depression. *Biological Psychiatry, 33*, 442–449.

Cookson, J. C. (1985). The neuroendocrinology of mania. *Journal of Affective Disorders, 8*, 233–241.

Cooper, J. R., Bloom, F. E., & Roth, R. H. (1997). *The biochemical basis of neuropharmacology*, 7th ed. New York: Oxford University Press.

Cotman, C. W., Kahle, J. S., Miller, S. E., Uas, J., & Bridges, R. J. (1995). Excitatory amino acid neurotransmission. In F. E. Bloom, D. J. Kupfer (Eds.), *Psychopharmacology: The fourth generation of progress* (pp. 75–85). New York: Raven Press.

Cowen, P. J., & Charig, E. M. (1987). Neuroendocrine responses to intravenous tryptophan in major depression. *Archives of General Psychiatry, 44*, 958–966.

Cowen, P. J., Power, A. C., Ware, C. J., & Anderson, I. M. (1994). 5-HT_{1A} receptor sensitivity in major depression: A neuroendocrine study with buspirone. *British Journal of Psychiatry, 164*, 372–379.

D'haenen, H. A., & Bossuyt, A. (1994). Dopamine D_2 receptors in depression measured with single photon emission computed tomography. *Biological Psychiatry, 35*, 128–132.

D'haenen, H., Bossuyt, A., Mertens, J., Bossuyt-Piron, C., Gijsemans, M., & Kaufman, L. (1992). SPECT imaging of serotonin 2 receptors in depression. *Psychiatry Research 45*, 227–237.

Deicken, R. F., Fein, G., & Weiner, M. W. (1995). Abnormal frontal lobe phosphorous metabolism in bipolar disorder. *American Journal of Psychiatry, 152*, 915–918.

Delgado, P. L., Charney, D. S., Price, L. H., Aghajanian, G. K., Landis, H., & Heninger, G. R. (1990). Serotonin function and the mechanism of antidepressant action reversal of antidepressant-induced remission by rapid depletion of plasma tryptophan. *Archives of General Psychiatry 47*, 411–418.

Depue, R. A., & Iacono, W. G. (1989). Neurobehavioral aspects of affective disorders. *Annual Review of Psychology 40*, 457–492.

Depue, R. A., & Spoont, M. R. (1986). Conceptualizing a serotonin trait a behavioral dimension of constraint. In J. J. Mann, & M. Stanley (Eds.). Psychobiology of Suicidal Behavior Annals of New York (p. 47–62). New York: Academy of Science.

Dinan, T. G., O'Keane, V., & Thakore, J. (1994). Pyridostigmine induced growth hormone release in mania: Focus on the cholinergic/somatostatin system. *Clinical Endocrinology, 40*, 93–96.

Drevets, W. C., Videen, T. O., Price, J. L., Preskorn, S. H., Carmichael, S. T., & Raichle, M. E. (1992). A functional anatomical study of unipolar depression. *Journal of Neuroscience, 12*, 3628–3641.

Duman, R. S., Heninger, G. R., & Nestler, E. J. (1997). A molecular and cellular theory of depression. *Archives of General Psychiatry 54*, 597–606.

Dunner, D. L. (1993). A review of the diagnostic status of "bipolar II" for the DSM-IV work group on mood disorders. *Depression, 1*, 2–10.

Dupont, R. M., Jernigan, T. L., Heindel, W., Butters, N., Shafer, K., Wilson, T., Hesselink, J., & Gillin, J. C. (1995). Magnetic resonance imaging and mood disorders. Localization of white matter and other subcortical abnormalities. *Archives of General Psychiatry, 52*, 747–755.

Egeland, J. A., & Hostetter, A. M. (1983). Amish study: I. Affective disorders among the Amish. *American Journal of Psychiatry, 140*, 56–61.

Ehlers, C. L., Frank, E., & Kupfer, D. J. (1988). Social zeitgebers and biological rhythms. *Archives of General Psychiatry 45*, 948–952.

Elkis, H., Friedman, L., Wise, A., & Meltzer, H. Y. (1995). Meta-analyses of studies of ventricular enlargement and cortical sulcal prominence in mood disorders. Comparisons with controls or patients with schizophrenia. *Archives of General Psychiatry 52*, 735–746.

Emamghoreishi, M., Schlichter, L., Li, P. P., Parikh, S., Sen, J., Kamble, A., & Warsh, J. J. (1997). High intracellular calcium concentrations in transformed lymphoblasts from subjects with bipolar I disorder. *American Journal of Psychiatry 154*, 976–982.

Friedman, E., Wang, H. Y., Levinson, D., Connell, T. A., & Singh, H. (1993). Altered platelet protein kinase C activity in bipolar affective disorder, manic episode. *Biological Psychiatry, 33*, 520–525.

Garbutt, J. C., Mayo, J. P., Little, K. Y., Gillette, G. M., Mason, G. A., Dew, B., Prange, A. J. (1994). Dose-response studies with protirelin. *Archives of General Psychiatry, 51*, 875–883.

George, M. S., Ketter, T. A., Parekh, P. I., Horwitz, B., Herscovitch, P., & Post, R. M. (1995). Brain activity during transient sadness and happiness in healthy women. *American Journal of Psychiatry, 152*, 341–351.

George, M. S., Ketter, T. A., & Post, R. M. (1994). Prefrontal cortex dysfunction in clinical depression. *Depression, 2*, 59–72.

Geracioti, T. D., Loosen, P. T., & Orth, D. N. (1997). Low cerebrospinal fluid corticotropin-releasing hormone concentrations in eucortisolemic depression. *Biological Psychiatry 42*, 166–174.

Giles, D. E., Jarrett, R. B., Roffwarg, H. P., & Rush, A. J. (1987). Reduced REM latency: A predictor of recurrence in depression. *Neuropsychopharmacology 1*, 33–3.

Gillin, J. C., Rapaport, M., Erman, M. K., Winokur, A., & Albala, B. J. (1997). A comparison of nefazodone and fluoxetine on mood and on objective, subjective, and clinician-related measures of sleep in depressed patients: A double-blind, 8-week clinical trial. *Journal of Clinical Psychiatry, 58*, 185–192.

Gold, P. W., Goodwin, F. K., & Chrousos, G. P. (1988). Clinical and biochemical manifestations of depression: Relation to the neurobiology of stress (part 2). *New England Journal of Medicine, 319*, 413–420.

Gold, P. W., Pottash, A. L. C., Ryan, N., Sweeney, D. R., Davies, R. K., & Martin, D. M. (1980). TRH-induced TSH response in unipolar, bipolar, and secondary depressions: Possible utility in clinical assessment and differential diagnosis. *Psychoneuroendocrinology 5*, 147–155.

Goodwin, F. K., & Jamison, K. R. (1990). *Manic-depressive illness*. New York: Oxford University Press.

Gottschalk, A., Bauer, M. S., & Whybrow, P. C. (1995). Evidence of chaotic mood variation in bipolar disorder. *Archives of General Psychiatry 52*, 947–959.

Gray, J. A. (1991). Neural systems emotion and personality. In J. I. V. Madden (Ed.), *Neurobiology of learning, emotion, and affect* (pp. 273–406). New York: Raven Press.

Hasey, G., & Hanin, I. (1991). The cholinergic-adrenergic hypothesis of depression reexamined using clonidine, metoprolol, and physostigmine in an animal model. *Biological Psychiatry, 29*, 127–138.

Higley, J. D., Mehlman, P. T., Taub, D. M., Higley, S. B., Suomi, S. J., Linnoila, M., & Vickers, J. H. (1992). Cerebrospinal fluid monoamine and adrenal correlates of aggression in free-ranging rhesus monkeys. *Archives of General Psychiatry, 49*, 436–441.

Higley, J. D., Thompson, W. W., Champoux, M., Goldman, D., Hasert, M. F., Kraemer, G. W., Scanlan, J. M., Suomi, S., Linnoila, M. (1993). Paternal and maternal genetic and environmental contributions to cerebrospinal fluid monoamine metabolites in rheus monkeys (macac mulatta). *Archives of General Psychiatry, 50*, 615–623.

Ho, A. P., Gillin, J. C., Buchsbaum, M. S., Wu, J. C., Abel, L., Bunney, W. E. (1996). Brain glucose metabolism during non-rapid eye movement sleep in major depression. *Archives of General Psychiatry, 53*, 645–652.

Holsboer, F. (1992). The hypothalamic-pituitary-adrenocortical system. In E. S. Paykel (Ed.), *Handbook of affective disorders*. New York: Guilford Press, pp. 267–287.

Holsboer, F. (1995). Neuroendocrinology of mood disorders. In F. E. Bloom, & D. J. Kuper (Eds.), *Psychopharmacology: The fourth generation of progress* (pp. 957–969). New York: Raven Press.

Horne, J. A. (1993). Human sleep loss and behavior implications for the prefrontal cortex and psychiatric disorder. *British Journal of Psychiatry, 162*, 413–419.

Howland, R. H. (1993). Thyroid dysfunction in refractory depression: Implications for pathophysiology and treatment. *Journal of Clinical Psychiatry, 54*, 47–54.

Howland, R. H., & Thase, M. E. (1991). Biological studies of dysthymia. *Biological Psychiatry, 30*, 283–304.

Howland, R. H., & Thase, M. E. (1993). A comprehensive review of cyclothymic disorder. *Journal of Nervous Mental Disease, 181*, 485–493.

Hrdina, P. D., Bakish, D., Chudzik, J., Ravindran, A., & Lapierre, Y. D. (1995). Serotonergic markers in platelets of patients with major depression: Upregulation of 5-HT_2 receptors. *Journal of Psychiatry and Neurology, 20*, 11–19.

Hsiao, J. K., Agren, H., Bartko, J. J., Rudorfer, M. V., Linnoila, M., & Potter, W. Z. (1987). Monoamine neurotransmitter interactions and the prediction of antidepressant response. *Archives of General Psychiatry, 44*, 1078–1083.

Hudson, J. I., Keck, P. E., Lipinski, J. F., Aizley, H. G., & Pope, H. G. (1993). Polysomnographic characteristics of bipolar depression. *Depression, 1*, 227–230.

Hudson, J. I., Lipinski, J. F., Keck, P. E. Jr, Aizley, H. G., Lukas, S. E., Rothschild, A. J., Waternaux, C. M., & Kupfer, D. J. (1992). Polysomnographic characteristics of young manic patients: Comparison with unipolar depressed patients and normal control subjects. *Archives of General Psychiatry, 49*, 378–383.

Hyman, S. E., & Nestler, E. J. (1993). *The molecular foundations of psychiatry.* Washington, DC: American Psychiatric Press.

Jackson, S. W. (1986) *Melancholia and depression from Hippocratic times to modern times.* New Haven: Yale University Press.

Jacobs, B. L. (1991). Serotonin and behavior: Emphasis on motor control. *Journal of Clinical Psychiatry, 52*(12), 17–23.

Janowsky, D. S., & Overstreet, D. H. (1995). The role of acetylcholine mechanisms in mood disorders. In F. E. Bloom, & D. J. Kuper (Eds.), *Psychopharmacology: The fourth generation of progress* (pp. 955–956). New York: Raven Press.

Joffe, R. L., & Levitt, A. J. (1993). *The thyroid axis and psychiatric illness.* Washington DC: American Psychiatry Press.

Kandel, E. R., Schwarz, J. H., & Jessell, T. M. (1991). *Principles of neural science*, 3rd ed. New York: Elsevier Press.

Kapur, S., & Mann, J. J. (1992). Role of the dopaminergic system in depression. *Biological Psychiatry, 32*, 1–17.

Karege, F., Bovier, P., Rudolph, W., & Gaillard, J. M. (1996). Platelet phosphoinositide signaling system: An overstimulated pathway in depression. *Biological Psychiatry, 39*, 697–702.

Kato, T., Shioiri, T., Murashita, J., Hamakawa, H., Takahashi, Y., Inubushi, T., & Takahashi, S. (1995). Lateralized abnormality of high energy phosphate metabolism in the frontal lobes of patients with bipolar disorder detected by phase-encoded ^{31}P-MRS. *Psychological Medicine, 25*, 557–566.

Kelsoe, J. R. (1997). The genetics of bipolar disorder. *Psychiatric Annals, 27*, 285–292.

Kessler, R.C. (1995). Sociology and psychiatry. In H. I. Kaplan & B. J. Sadock (Eds.) *Comprehensive textbook of psychiatry, 6th ed.* (pp. 356–365). Baltimore, MD: Walkins.

Ketter, T. A., George, M. S., Ring, H. A., Pazzaglia, P., Marangell, L., Kimbrell, T. A., & Post, R. M. (1994). Primary mood disorders: Structural and resting functional studies. *Psychiatric Annals, 24*, 637–642.

Konopka, L. M., Cooper, R., & Crayton, J. W. (1996). Serotonin-induced increased in platelet cytosolic calcium concentration in depressed, schizophrenic, and substance abuse patients. *Biological Psychiatry, 39*, 708–713.

Krishnan, K. R. R., Hays, J. C., & Blazer, D. G. (1997). MRI-defined vascular depression. *American Journal of Psychiatry, 154*, 497–501.

Krishnan, K. R. R., McDonald, W. M., Escalona, P. R., Doraiswamy, P. M., Na, C., Husain, M. M., Figiel, G. S., Boyko, O. B., Ellinwood, E. H., & Nemeroff, C. B. (1992). Magnetic resonance of the caudate nuclei in depression. *Archives of General Psychiatry, 49*, 553–557.

Kupfer, D. J., & Ehlers, C. L. (1989). Two roads to rapid eye movement latency. *Archives of General Psychiatry, 46*, 945–948.

Kupfer, D. J., Frank, E., McEachran, A. B., & Grochocinski, V. J. (1990). Delta sleep ratio: A biological correlate of early recurrence in unipolar affective disorder. *Archives of General Psychiatry, 47*, 1100–1105.

Kupfer, D. J., Targ, E., & Stack, J. (1982). Electroencephalographic sleep in unipolar depressive subtypes: Support for a biological and familial classification. *Journal of Nervous and Mental Disease, 170*, 494–498.

Kupfer, D. J., Ehlers, C. L., Frank, E., Grochocinski, V. J., McEachran, A. B., & Buhari, A. (1994). Persistent effects of antidepressants: EEG sleep studies in depressed patients during maintenance treatment. *Biological Psychiatry, 35*, 781–793.

Lachman, H. M., & Papolos, D. F. (1995). A molecular model for bipolar affective disorder. *Medical Hypotheses, 45*, 255–264.

Lam, R. W. (1994). Seasonal affective disorders. *Current Opinion in Psychiatry, 7*, 9–13.

Langer, G., Aschauer, H., Koing, G., Resch, F., & Schonbeck, G. (1983). The TSH response to TRH: A possible predictor of outcome to antidepressant and neuroleptic treatment. *Progress in Neuro-psychopharmacology and Biological Psychiatry, 7*, 335–352.

Lauer, C. J., Schreiber, W., Holsboer, F., & Krieg, J. C. (1995). In quest of identifying vulnerability markers for psychiatric disorders by all-night polysomnography. *Archives of General Psychiatry, 52*, 145–153.

Lauer, C. J., Riemann, D., Wiegand, M., & Berger, M. (1991). From early to late adulthood changes in EEG sleep of depressed patients and healthy volunteers. *Biological Psychiatry, 29*, 979–993.

Lesch, K. P., & Manji, H. K. (1992). Signal-transducing G proteins and antidepressant drugs: Evidence for modulation of α subunit gene expression in rat brain. *Biological Psychiatry, 32*, 549–579.

Lingjaerde, O., Reichborn-Kjennerud, T., & Haug, E. (1995). Thyroid function in seasonal affective disorder. *Journal of Affective Disorders, 33*, 39–45.

Linkowski, P., Kerhofs, M., Van Onderbergen, A., Hubain, P., Copinschi, G., L'Hermite-Baleriaux, M., Leclercq, R., Brasseur, M., Mendlewicz, J., & Van cauter, E. (1994). The 24-hour profiles of cortisol, prolactin, and growth hormone secretion in mania. *Archives of General Psychiatry, 51*, 616–624.

Linnoila, V. M., & Virkkunen, M. (1992). Aggression suicidality and serotonin. *Journal of Clinical Psychiatry, 53*, 46–51.

Little, K. Y., McLaughlin, D. P., Rane, J., Gilmore, J., Lopez, J. F., Watson, S. J., Carroll, F. I., & Butts, J. D. (1997). Serotonin transported binding sites and mRNA levels in depressed persons committing suicide. *Biological Psychiatry, 41*, 1156–1164.

Loosen, P. T., Mason, G. A., & Prange, A. J. (1982). The TRH test in normal subjects: Methodological considerations. *Psychoneuroendocrinology, 7*, 147–153.

Maas, J. W., Katz, M. M., Kowlow, S. H., Swann, A., Davis, J. M., Berman, N., Bowden, C. L., Stokes, P. E., & Landis, H. (1994). Adrenomedullary function in depressed patients. *Journal of Psychiatry Research, 28*, 357–367.

Maeda, K., Yoshimoto, Y., & Yamadori, A. (1993). Blunted TSH and unaltered PRL responses to TRH following repeated administration of TRH in neurologic patients: A replication of neuroendocrine features of major depression. *Biological Psychiatry, 33*, 277–283.

Maes, M., & Meltzer, H. Y. (1995). The serotonin hypothesis of major depression. In F. E. Bloom & D. J. Kuper (Eds.), *Psychopharmacology: The fourth generation of progress* (pp. 933–944). New York: Raven Press.

Malone, K., & Mann, J. J. (1993). Serotonin and major depression. In J. J. Mann & D. J. Kupfer (Eds.), *Biology of depressive disorders. Part A: A systems perspective* (pp. 29–44). New York: Plenum Press.
Manji, H. K., Potter, W. Z., & Lenox, R. H. (1995). Signal transduction pathways. *Archives of General Psychiatry, 52*, 531–543.
Manji, H. K., Chen, G., Shimon, H., Hsiao, J. K., Potter, W. Z., & Belmaker, R. H. (1995). Guanine nucleotide-binding proteins in bipolar affective disorder. *Archives of General Psychiatry, 52*, 135–144.
Manji, H. K., Chen, G., Hsiao, J. K., Risby, E. D., Masana, M. I., & Potter, W. Z. (1996). Regulation of signal transduction pathways by mood-stabilizing agents: Implications for the delayed onset of therapeutic efficacy. *Journal of Clinical Psychiatry, 57*(Suppl. 13), 34–46.
Marangell, L. B., Ketter, T. A., George, M. S., Pazzaglia, P. J., Callahan, A. M., Parekh, P., Andreason, P. J., Horwitz, B., Herscovitch, P., & Post, R. M. (1997). Inverse relationship of peripheral thyrotropin-stimulating hormone levels to brain activity in mood disorders. *American Journal of Psychiatry, 154*, 224–230.
Mathews, R., Li, P. P., Young, L. T., Kish, S. J., & Warsh, J. J. (1997). Increased $G\alpha_{q/11}$ immunoreactivity in postmortem occipital cortex from patients with bipolar affective disorder. *Biological Psychiatry, 41*, 649–656.
Mayberg, H. S. (1994). Functional imaging studies in secondary depression. *Psychiatric Annals, 24*, 643–647.
Mazzola-Pomietto, P., Azorin, J. M., Tramoni, V., & Jeanningros, R. (1994). *Biological Psychiatry, 35*, 920–925.
McCarley, R. W. (1982). REM sleep and depression: Common neurobiological control mechanisms. *American Journal of Psychiatry, 139*, 565–570.
McEwen, B. S., Angulo, J., Cameron, H., Chao, H. M., Daniels, D., Gannon, M. N., Gould, E., Mendelson, S., Sakai, R., Spencer, R., & Woolley, C. (1992). Paradoxical effects of adrenal steroids on the brain: Protection versus degeneration. *Biological Psychiatry, 31*, 177–199.
McInnis, M. G. (1997). Recent advances in the genetics of bipolar disorder. *Psychiatric Annals, 27*, 482–488.
Mellerup, E. T., & Plenge, P. (1986). High affinity binding of 3H-imipramine and 3H-paroxetine to rat neuronal membranes. *Psychopharmacology, 89*, 436–439.
Menninger, J. A., & Tabakoff, B. (1997). Forskolin-stimulated platelet adenylyl cyclase activity is lower in persons with major depression. *Biological Psychiatry* 42, 30–38.
Merikangas, K. R., & Kupfer, D. J. (1995). Mood disorders: Genetic aspects. In H. I. Kaplan & B. J. Sadock (Eds.), *Comprehensive textbook of psychiatry*, 6th ed. (pp. 1102–1116). Baltimore, MD: Walkins.
Miller, H. L., Delgado, P. L., Salomon, R. M., Licinio, J., Barr, L. C., & Charney, D. S. (1992). Acute tryptophan depletion: A method of studying antidepressant action. *Journal of Clinical Psychiatry, 53*, 28–35.
Mitchell, P. B., Manji, H. K., & Chen, G. (1997). High levels of Gs Alpha I platelets of euthymic patients with bipolar affective disorder. *American Journal of Psychiatry, 154*, 218–223.
Moore, C. M., Christensen, J. D., Lafer, B., Fava, M., & Renshaw, P. F. (1997). Lower levels of nucleoside triphosphate in the basal ganglia of depressed subjects: A phosphorous-31 magnetic resonance spectroscopy study. *American Journal of Psychiatry, 154*, 116–118.
Muscat, R., Papp, M., & Willner, P. (1992). Antidepressants-like effects of dopamine agonists in an animal model of depression. *Biological Psychiatry, 31*, 937–946.
Myers, J. E., Buysse, D. J., Thase, M. E., Perel, J., Miewald, J. M., Cooper, T. B., Kupfer, D. J., & Mann, J. J. (1993). The effects of fenfluramine on sleep and prolactin in depressed inpatients: A comparison of potential indices of brain serotonergic responsivity. *Biological Psychiatry, 34*, 753–758.
Nemeroff, C. B. (1992). New vistas in neuropeptide research in neuropsychiatry: Focus on corticotropin-releasing factor. *Neuropsychopharmacology, 6*, 69–75.
Neumaier, J. F., Petty, F., Kramer, G. L., Szot, P., & Hamblin, M. W. (1997). Learned helplessness increases 5-hydroxytryptamine$_{1B}$ receptor mRNA levels in the rat dorsal raphe nucleus. *Biological Psychiatry, 41*, 668–674.
Neumeister, A., Praschak-Rieder, N., Heßelmann, B., Rao, M-L., Gluck, J., & Kasper, S. (1997). Effects of tryptophan depletion on drug-free patients with seasonal affective disorder during a stable response to bright light therapy. *Archives of General Psychiatry, 54*, 133–138.
Nofzinger, E. A., Thase, M. E., Reynolds, C. F. III, Himmelhoch, J. M., Mallinger, A., Houck, P., & Kupfer, D. J. (1991). Hypersomnia in bipolar depression: A comparison with narcolepsy using the multiple sleep latency test. *American Journal of Psychiatry, 148*, 1177–1181.
Nolen-Hoeksema, S. (1991). Responses to depression and their effects on the duration of depressive episodes. *Journal of Abnormal Psychology, 100*, 569–582.

Okamoto, Y., Kagaya, A., Shinno, H., Motohashu, N., & Yamawaki (1994). Serotonin-induced platelet calcium mobilization is enhanced in mania. *Life Sciences*, *56*, 327–332.

Oren, D. A., & Rosenthal, N. E. (1992). Seasonal affective disorders. In E. S. Paykel (Ed.), *Handbook of affective disorders*, 2nd ed. (pp. 551–567). New York: Guilford Press.

Orpen, G., & Steiner, M. (1995). The WAGxDA Rat: An animal model of cholinergic supersensitivity. *Biological Psychiatry*, *37*, 874–883.

Pearlson, G. D., Wong, D. F., Tune, L. E., Ross, C. A., Chase, G. A., Links, J. M., Dannals, R. F., Wilson, A. A., Ravert, H. T., Wagner, H. N., & DePaulo, R. (1995). Vivo D_2 dopamine receptor density in psychotic and nonpsychotic patients with bipolar disorder. *Archives of General Psychiatry*, *52*, 471–477.

Perez, J., Zanardi, R., Mori, S., Gasperini, M., Smeraldi, E., & Racagni, G. (1995). Abnormalities of cAMP-dependent endogenous phosphorylation in platelets from patients with bipolar disorder. *American Journal of Psychiatry*, *152*, 1204–1206.

Petty, F. (1995). GABA and mood disorders: A brief review and hypothesis. *Journal of Affective Disorders*, *34*, 275–281.

Petty, F., Kramer, G. L., & Hendrickse, W. (1993). GABA and depression. In J. J. Mann & D. J. Kupfer (Eds.), *Biology of depressive disorders. Part A: A systems perspective.* New York: Plenum Press, pp. 79–108.

Petty, F., Kramer, G., Wilson, L., & Jordan, S. (1994). In vivo serotonin release and learned helplessness. *Psychiatry Research*, *52*, 285–293.

Philpot, M. P., Banerjee, S., Needham-Bennett, H., Costa, D. C., & Ell, P. J. (1993). ^{99m}Tc-HMPAO single photon emission tomography in late life depression: A pilot study of regional cerebral blood flow at rest and during a verbal fluency task. *Journal of Affective Disorders*, *28*, 233–240.

Plotsky, P. M., Owens, M. J., & Nemeroff, C. B. (1995). Neuropeptide alterations in mood disorders. In F. E. Bloom & D. J. Kuper (Eds.), *Psychopharmacology: The fourth generation of progress* (pp. 971–981). New York: Raven Press.

Poland, R. E., McCracken, J. T., Lutchmansingh, P., Lesser, I. M., Tondo, L., Edwards, C., Boone, K. B., & Lin, K. M. (1997). Differential response of rapid eye movement sleep to cholinergic blockade by scopolamine in currently depressed, remitted, and normal control subjects. *Biological Psychiatry*, *41*, 929–938.

Post, R. M. (1992). Transduction of psychosocial stress into the neurobiology of recurrent affective disorder. *American Journal of Psychiatry*, *149*, 999–1010.

Post, R. M., Weiss, S. R. B., & Chuang, D. M. (1992). Mechanisms of action of anticonvulsants in affective disorders: Comparisons with lithium. *Journal of Clinical Psychopharmacology*, *12*(Suppl. 1), 23–35.

Potter, W. Z., Grossman, F., & Rudorfer, M. V. (1993). Noradrenergic function in depressive disorders. In J. J. Mann & D. J. Kupfer (Eds.), *Biology of depressive disorders. Part A: A systems perspective* (pp. 1–27). New York: Plenum Press.

Powell, K. B., & Miklowitz, D. J. (1994). Frontal lobe dysfunction in the affective disorders. *Clinical Psychology Review*, *14*, 525–546.

Prange, A. J., Jr., Wilson, I. C., Lynn, C. W., Alltop, L. B., & Stikeleather, R. A. (1974). L-tryptophan in mania. Contribution to a permissive hypothesis of affective disorders. *Archives of General Psychiatry*, *30*, 56–62.

Raadsheer, F. C., van Heerikhuize, J. J., Lucassen, P. J., Hoogendijk, W. J. G., Tilders, F. J. H., & Swaab, D. F. (1995). Corticotropin-releasing hormone mRNA levels in the paraventricular nucleus of patients with Alzheimer's disease and depression. *American Journal of Psychiatry*, *152*, 1372–1376.

Reiman, E. M., Lane, R. D., Ahern ,G. L., Schwartz, G. E., Davidson, R. J., Friston, K. J., Yun, L.-S., & Chen, K. (1997). Neuroanatomical correlates of externally and internally generated human emotion. *American Journal of Psychiatry*, *154*, 918–925.

Renshaw, P. F., Lafer, B., Babb, S. M., Fava, M., Stoll, A. L., Christensen, J. D., Moore, C. M., Yurgelun-Todd, D. A., Bonello, C. M., Pillay, S. S., Rothschild, A. J., Nierenberg, A. A., Rosenbaum, J. F., & Cohen, B. M. (1997). Basal ganglia choline levels in depression and response to fluoxetine treatment: An invivo proton magnetic resonance spectroscopy study. *Biological Psychiatry*, *41*, 837–843.

Reynolds, C. F. III, Perel, J. M., Frank, E., Imber, S., & Kupfer, D. J. (1989). Open-trial maintenance nortriptyline in late-life depression: Survival analysis and preliminary data on the use of REM latency as a predictor of recurrence. *Psychopharmacology Bulletin*, *25*, 129–132.

Reynolds, C. F. III, Kupfer, D. J., Thase, M. E., Frank, E., Jarrett, D. B., Coble, P. A., Hoch, C. C., Buysse, C. J., Simons, A. D., & Houck, P. R. (1990). Sleep, gender, and depression: An analysis of gender effects on the electroencephalographic sleep of 302 depressed outpatients. *Biological Psychiatry*, *28*, 673–684.

Ribeiro, S. C. M., Tandon, R., Grunhaus, L., & Greden, J. F. (1993). The DST as a predictor of outcome in depression: A meta-analysis. *American Journal of Psychiatry, 150*, 1618–1629.

Rubin, E., Sackeim, H. A., Nobler, M. S., & Moeller, J. R. (1994). Brain imaging studies of antidepressant treatments. *Psychiatric Annals, 24*, 53–658.

Rubin, R. T., Phillips, J. J., McCracken, J. T., & Sadow, T. F. (1996). Adrenal gland volume in major depression: Relationship to basal and stimulated pituitary-adrenal cortical axis function. *Biological Psychiatry 40*, 89–97.

Rubinow, D.R., Davis, C. L., & Post, R. M. (1995). Somatostatin in the central nervous system. In F. E. Bloom & D. J. Kupfer (Eds.), *Psychopharmacology: The fourth generation of progress* (pp. 553–562). New York: Raven Press.

Rush, A. J., Giles, D. E., Schlesser, M. A., Orsulak, P. J., Weissenburger, J. E., Gulton, C. L., Fairchild, C. J., & Roffwarg, H. P. (1997). Dexamethasone response, thyrotropin-releasing hormone stimulation, rapid eye movement latency, and subtypes of depression. *Biological Psychiatry, 41*, 915–928.

Rush, A. J., Giles, D. E., Schlesser, M. A., Orsulak, P. J., Parker, R., Weissenburger, J. E., Crowley, G. T., Khatami, M., & Vasavada, N. (1996). The dexamethasone suppression test in patients with mood disorders. *Journal of Clinical Psychiatry, 57*, 470–48.

Ryan, N. D., Dahl, R. E., Birmaher, B., Williamson, D. E., Iyengar, S., Nelson, B., Puig-Antich, J., & Perel, J. M. (1994). Stimulatory tests of growth hormone in prepubertal major depression: Depressed versus normal children. *Journal of the American Academy of Child and Adolescent Psychiatry, 33*, 824–833.

Sackeim, H. A., Prohovnik, I., Moeller, J. R., Brown, R. P., Apter, S., Prudic, J., Devanand, D. P., & Mukherjee, S. (1990). Regional cerebral blood flow in mood disorders. *Archives of General Psychiatry, 47*, 60–70.

Sapolsky, R. M. (1989). Hypercortisolism among socially subordinate wild baboons originates at the CNS level. *Archives of General Psychiatry, 46*, 1047–1051.

Schatzberg, A. F., Rothschild, A. J., Langlais, P. J., Bird, E. D., & Cole, J. O. (1985). A corticosteroid/dopamine hypothesis for psychotic depression and related states. *Journal of Psychiatry Research, 19*, 57–64.

Schatzberg, A. F., Rothschild, A. J., Langlais, P. J., Lerbinger, J. E., Schildkraut, J. J., & Cole, J. O. (1987). Psychotic and nonpsychotic depressions: II. Platelet MAO activity plasma, catecholamines, cortisol and specific symptoms. *Psychiatry Research, 20*, 155–164.

Schatzberg, A. F., & Schildkraut, J. J. (1995). Recent studies on norepinephrine systems in mood disorders. In F. E. Bloom & D. J. Kuper (Eds.), *Psychopharmacology: The fourth generation of progress* (pp. 911–920). New York: Raven Press.

Schmider, J., Lammers, C. H., Gotthardt, U., Dettling, M., Holsboer, F., & Heuser, J. E. (1995). Combined dexamethasone/corticotropin-releasing hormone test in acute and remitted manic patients, in acute depression, and in normal controls: 1. *Biological Psychiatry, 38*, 797–802.

Schwartz, P. J., Murphy, D. L., Wehr, T. A., Garcia-Borreguero, D., Oren, D. A., Moul, D. E., Ozaki, N., Snelbaker, A. J., & Rosenthal, N. E. (1997). Effects of meta-chlorophenylpiperasine infusions in patients with seasonal affective disorder and healthy control subjects. Diurnal responses and nocturnal regulatory mechanisms. *Archives of General Psychiatry, 54*, 375–385.

Schwartz, P. J., Rosenthal, N. E., Turner, E. H., Drake, C. L., Libert, V., & Wehr, T. A. (1997). Seasonal variation in core temperature regulation during sleep in patients with seasonal affective disorder. *Biological Psychiatry, 42*, 122–131.

Shader, R. I., Fogelman, S. M., & Greenblatt, D. J. (1997). Newer antidepressants: Further reflections. *Journal of Clinical Psychopharmacology, 17*, 75–77.

Shapira, B., Cohen, J., Newman, M. E., & Lerer, B. (1993). Prolactin response to fenfluramine and placebo challenge following maintenance pharmacotherapy withdrawal in remitted depressed patients. *Biological Psychiatry, 33*, 531–535.

Sharma, R. P., Bissette, G., Janicak, P. G., Davis, J. M., & Nemeroff, C. B. (1995). Elevation of CSF somatostatin concentrations in mania. *American Journal of Psychiatry, 152*, 1807–1809.

Sharpley, A. L., & Cowen, P. J. (1995). Effect of pharamcologic treatments on the sleep of depressed patients. *Biological Psychiatry, 37*, 85–98.

Sheline, Y. I., Bargdett, M. E., Jackson, J. L., Newcomer, J. W., & Csernansky, J. G. (1995). Platelet serotonin markers and depressive symptomatology. *Biological Psychiatry, 37*, 442–447.

Silfverskiöld, P., & Risberg, J. (1989). Regional cerebral blood flow in depression and mania. *Archives of General Psychiatry, 46*, 253–259.

Smith, G. S., Dewey, S. L., Brodie, J. D., Logan, J., Vitkun, S. A., Simkowitz, P., Schloesser,

R., Alexoff, D. A., Hurley, A., Cooper, T., & Volkow, N. D. (1997). Serotonergic modulation of dopamine measured with [^{11}C] Raclopride and PET in normal human subjects. *American Journal of Psychiatry, 154*, 490–496.

Stokes, P. E. (1995). The potential role of excessive cortisol induced by HPA hyperfunction in the pathogenesis of depression. *European Neuropsychopharmacology, 17* (Suppl.): 77–82.

Stoll, A. L., Sachs, G., Cohen, B. M. (1996). Choline in the treatment of rapid-cycling bipolar disorder: Clinical and neurochemical findings in lithium-treated patients. *Biological Psychiatry, 40*, 382–388.

Strakowski, S. M., Wilson, D. R., Tohen, M., Woods, B. T., Douglass, A. W., & Stoll, A. L. (1993). Structural brain abnormalities in first-episode mania. *Biological Psychiatry, 33*, 602–609.

Swann, A. C., Stokes, P. E., Secunda, S. K., Maas, J. W., Bowden, C. L., Berman, N., & Koslow, S. H. (1994). Depressive mania versus agitated depression: Biogenic amine and hypothalamic-pituitary-adrenocortical function. *Biological Psychiatry, 35*, 803–813.

Swerdlow, N. R., & Koob, G. F. (1987). Dopamine, schizophrenia, mania, and depression: Toward a unified hypothesis of cortico-straito-pallido-thalamic function. *Behavioral and Brain Sciences, 10*, 197–245.

Teicher, M. H., Gold, C. A., Magnus, E., Harper, D., Benson, G., Krueger, K., & McGreenery, C. E. (1997). Circadian rest-activity disturbances in seasonal affective disorder. *Archives of General Psychiatry, 54*, 124–130.

Thakore, J. H., O'Keane, V., & Dinan, T. G. (1996). d-fenfluramine-induced prolactin responses in mania: Evidence for serotonergic subsensitivity. *American Journal of Psychiatry, 153*, 1460–1463.

Thase, M. E. (1998). Depression, sleep, and antidepressants. *Journal of Clinical Psychiatry, 59* (Suppl. 4), 55–65.

Thase, M. E., Buysse, D. J., Frank, E., Cherry, C. R., Cornes, C. L., Mallinger, A. G., & Kupfer, D. J. (1997). Which depressed patients will respond to interpersonal psychotherapy? The role of abnormal electroencephalographic sleep profiles. *American Journal of Psychiatry, 154*, 502–509.

Thase, M. E., Dubé, S., Bowler, K., Howland, R. H., Myers, J. E., Friedman, E., & Jarrett, D. B. (1996). Hypothalamic-pituitary-adrenocortical activity and response to cognitive behavior therapy in unmedicated, hospitalized depressed patients. *American Journal of Psychiatry, 153*, 886–891.

Thase, M. E., Fasiczka, A. L., Berman, S. R., Simons, A. D., & Reynolds, C. F. III. (1998). Electroencephalographic sleep profiles before and after cognitive behavior therapy of depression. *Archives of General Psychiatry, 55*, 138–144.

Thase, M. E., Frank, E., Kornstein, S., & Yonkers, K. A. (in press). Sex-related differences in response to treatment of depression. In E. Frank (Ed.), *Sex, society, and madness: Gender and psychopathology.* Washington, DC: American Psychiatric Press.

Thase, M. E., Himmelhoch, J. M., Mallinger, A. G., Jarrett, D. B., & Kupfer, D. J. (1989). Sleep EEG and DST findings in anergic bipolar depression. *American Journal of Psychiatry, 146*, 329–333.

Thase, M. E., & Howland, R.H. (1995). Biological processes in depression: An updated review and integration. In E. E. Beckham & W. R. Leber (Eds.), *Handbook of depression* (pp. 213–279). New York: Guilford.

Thase, M. E., & Kupfer, D. J. (1987). Current status of EEG sleep in the assessment and treatment of depression. In G. D. Burrows & J. S. Werry (Eds.), *Advances in human psychopharmacology*, vol. 4. (pp. 93–148). Greenwich CT: JAI Press.

Thase, M. E., Reynolds, C. F. III, Frank, E., Jennings, J. R., Nofzinger, E., Fasiczka, A. L., Garamoni, G., & Kupfer, D. J. (1994). Polysomnographic studies of unmedicated depressed men before and after treatment with cognitive behavior therapy. *American Journal of Psychiatry, 151*, 1615–1622.

Thase, M. E., Simons, A. D., & Reynolds, C. F. III. (1993). Psychobiological correlates of poor response to cognitive behavior therapy: Potential indications for antidepressant pharmacotherapy. *Psychopharmacology Bulletin 29*, 293–301.

Thase, M. E., Simons, A. D., & Reynolds, C. F. III. (1996). Abnormal electroencephalographic sleep profiles in major depression. Association with response to cognitive behavior therapy. *Archives of General Psychiatry, 53*, 99–108.

Thayer, R. E. (1989). *The biopsychology of mood and arousal.* New York: Oxford University Press.

Toren, P., Dor, J., Rehavi, M., & Weizman, A. (1996). Hypothalamic-pituitary-ovarian axis and mood. *Biological Psychiatry, 40*, 1051–1055.

Trestman, R. L., Yehuda, R., Coccaro, E., Horvath, T., Knott, P., Gabriel, S., & Siever, L. J. (1995). Diurnal neuroendocrine and autonomic function in acute and remitted depressed male patients. *Biological Psychiatry, 37*, 448–456.

Wang, H-Y., & Friedman, E. (1996). Enhanced protein kinase C activity and translocation in bipolar affective disorder brains. *Biological Psychiatry, 40*, 568–575.

Weiss, J. M. (1991). Stress-induced depression: Critical neurochemical and electrophysiological changes. In J. I. V. Madden (Ed.), *Neurobiology of learning, emotion, and affect* (pp. 123–154). New York: Raven Press.

Whybrow, P. C. (1995). Sex differences in thyroid axis function: Relevance to affective disorder and its treatment. *Depression, 3*, 33–42.

Willner, P. (1995). Dopaminergic mechanisms in depression and mania. In F. E. Bloom & D. J. Kuper (Eds.), *Psychopharmacology: The fourth generation of progress* (pp. 921–931). New York: Raven Press.

Wirz-Justice, A. (1995). Biological rhythms in mood disorders.In F. E. Bloom & D. J. Kupfer (Eds.), *Psychopharmacology: The fourth generation of progress* (pp. 999–1017). New York: Raven Press.

Woods, B. T., Yurgelum-Todd, D., Mikulis, D., & Pillay, S. S. (1995). Age-related MRI abnormalities in bipolar illness: A clinical study. *Biological Psychiatry, 38*, 846–847.

Wu, J. C., Gillin, J. C., Buchsbaum, M. S., Hershey, T., Johnson, J. C., & Bunney, W. E. (1992). Effect of sleep deprivation on brain metabolism of depressed patients. *American Journal of Psychiatry, 149*, 538–543.

Young, E. A. (1995). Glucocorticoid cascade hypothesis revisited: role of gonadal steroids. *Depression, 3*, 20–27.

Young, E. A., Haskett, R. F., Murphy-Weinberg, V., Watson, S. J., & Akil, H. (1991). Loss of glucocorticoid fast feedback in depression. *Archives of General Psychiatry, 48*, 693–699.

Young, L. T., Warsh, J. J., Kish, S. J., Shannak, K., & Hornykeiwicz, O. (1994). Reduced brain 5-HT and elevated NE turnover and metabolites in bipolar affective disorder. *Biological Psychiatry, 35*, 121–127.

8

Depression

Social and Cognitive Aspects

RICK E. INGRAM
WALTER SCOTT
GREG SIEGLE

Depression is sometimes referred to as the "common cold" of psychopathology. There are a variety of reasons for this label. For one, the term *depression* is widely used to denote feelings of sadness. As with a common cold, this state of feeling depressed is experienced by everyone at one time or another. A second reason may be that forms of depression that are not clinically significant, but that are more severe than simple feelings of sadness (i.e., subclinical depression), are not uncommon. A third reason probably reflects the diversity of different types of depression. For example, *DSM-IV* lists 10 different types of mood disorder. Depression is common in both experience and definition.

Although these are all good reasons to view depression as the psychopathological equivalent of a simple medical illness, the comparison is unfortunate in several regards. In its most serious forms, depression is a disabling disorder that is associated with untold emotional misery, severe social and occupational disruption, increased risk for physical illness, and sometimes death. Unlike the common cold, depression is frequently a chronic disorder that can last for months or even years. Depression also disrupts the lives of those who are close to the sufferer of this disorder. From an economic standpoint, depression accounts for many millions of dollars in year in lost productivity. Comparing depression to the common cold does not do justice to the potential seriousness, and toll, of this condition.

The objective of this chapter is to examine some of the cognitive and social aspects of this disorder. As just noted, *DSM-IV* lists a variety of different types of depression. Although these subtypes are important, the main focus of this chapter is on unipolar depression. To understand the cognitive and social aspects of unipolar depression, it is important to first understand what constitutes depression. Therefore, we begin with an overview of the history of the concept, and then examine issues pertaining to the definition of depression. We then examine subtypes of depression and the epidemiology of unipolar depression. We next assess social aspects from the perspective of the life-event-depression relationship, and then we review behavioral and interpersonal models of depression, and then cognitive models. Cognitive models we examine include schema and information processing models, cognitive subtypes models, and self-regulation models.

Early Conceptions: A Brief History of Depression

The concept of depression is documented in the earliest human records. For example, descriptions of conditions resembling depression can be found in the Bible as well as in Egyptian writings circa 2600 B.C. It was the ancient Greeks, however, who provided the first casual theories of depression. Diseases were characterized as disruptions of balance among four fluids or humors in the body. "Melancholia" (from the Greek, *it melanina chole*) was hypothesized by Hippocrates in the fourth century B.C. to stem from the an imbalance of black bile, "darkening the spirit and making it melancholy." These ideas paved the way for the modern conception of depression, arising with Araetus of Cappadocia around 120 A.D., who characterized melancholia by sadness, a tendency to suicide, feelings of indifference, and psychomotor agitation. In the mid-eighteenth century, Kant turned conceptions of depression back to the body by suggesting that emotions could not cause mental illness. The resulting conception of depression as a somatic ailment prevailed throughout the eighteenth and nineteenth centuries. It was not until the early twentieth century that theorists such as Abraham (1911/1960) and Freud (1917/1950) associated psychological/emotional factors in a causal manner with the onset and maintenance of depression.

One key question in early conceptions of depression regarded the issue of separating mood disorders into their own diagnostic category. Into the beginning of the 20th century, controversy raged over whether the disorders of "mood" should be separated from phenomena traditionally associated with melancholia, characterized by psychosis, and delirium. Kraepelin's (1904/1968) systematic observations of manic and schizophrenic individuals suggested that mania, which was often associated with a depressed state, should be considered a separate disorder from syndromes characterized primarily by psychosis such as schizophrenia. A similar historical debate concerned the distinction between psychopathologies with both manic and depressive states, and just depressive states. However, many of the noted early depression theorists, including Freud, disregarded this distinction. Current evidence suggests that unipolar depression is a qualitatively different phenomenon from the more biologically mediated bipolar disorder.

Another historical distinction concerns the origins of depression. Kraepelin distinguished between "endogenous" or naturally occurring depressions, to which bipolar disorder was assumed to belong, and "psychogenic" depressions, which were assumed to be reactive. This distinction was suggested to have conceptual, treatment, and epidemiological consequences and has been preserved in modern-day distinctions between a depressive personality "trait" and depression as a purely reactive or "state"-like phenomenon. Similar distinctions that have also been preserved are between depressive disorders and the more "normal" reactive state of mourning. Thus, the *DSM-IV* criteria for depression specifically rule out bereavement under most circumstances. This distinction, however, is not as clear-cut as it may seem. Bereavement, for example, is a class of "social exits" (see Brown & Harris, 1978) that have been empirically linked to depressive symptomatology. In this regard, Beckham, Leber, and Youll (1995) have observed the irony that results from the exclusion of bereavement from diagnostic criteria: the woman who experiences depressive symptoms resulting from the death of her husband will not be diagnosed with depression, yet the same woman who experiences depressive symptoms because her husband has left her will be considered to have diagnosable depression. In fact, the underlying processes in these two cases may be identical.

A number of other depression subtype distinctions have led to the formation of the "affective spectrum" of disorders listed in the current *DSM-IV*. The *DSM-IV* distinguishes between traitlike persistent phenomena associated with depressive symptomatology ("dysthymia"), a number of disorders characterized by shifts from depressive to manic states (e.g., cyclothymia, bipolar I, bipolar II disorder), purely reactive phenomena associated with depressive symptomatology (adjustment disorder with depressed mood), and major depression itself. Many other approaches to subtypes of major depression have also been proposed (e.g., distinctions between cognitively and biologically mediated depressions, anxious and nonanxious depressions, etc.). In time, these distinctions, too, may take their place in the discipline's formal diagnostic system.

Definitional Issues

As is apparent from our brief historical overview, depression has been characterized as, and as caused by, many different things. Part of the problem in arriving at a consensual definition is that psychopathological constructs such as depression can be thought of in a variety of different ways. As suggested by several researchers (Compas, Ey, &

Grant, 1993; Kazdin, 1983; Nurcomb, 1992), depression can be thought of as a mood state, a syndrome involving a collection of symptoms irrespective of the presence of other psychological or medical disorders, or as a nosological category with both inclusionary and exclusionary characteristics. Kendall, Hollon, Beck, Hammen, and Ingram (1987) have similarly noted the different levels of reference to which the depression label can refer; the term *depression*

> has several levels of reference: symptom, syndrome, nosological disorder (Beck, 1967; Lehmann, 1959). Depression itself can be a symptom—for example, being sad. As a syndrome, depression is a constellation of signs and symptoms that cluster together (e.g., sadness, negative self-concept, sleep and appetite disturbances). The syndrome of depression is itself a psychological dysfunction but can also be present, in secondary ways, in other diagnosed disorders. Finally, for depression to be a nosological category, careful diagnostic procedures are required during which other potential diagnostic categories are excluded. (p. 290)

The most widely accepted current definition of depression is that specified in the *DSM-IV*, which relies on a categorical conceptualization of mental disorders. The categorical approach has several advantages (e.g., ease of communication between mental health professionals). Alternatively, dimensional approaches assume that depression exists on a continuum from a mild to a severe state and that differences in the degree of depressive symptomatology are a function of different degrees of psychological distress. At present there are no compelling data to suggest the superiority of either the categorical or the dimensional approach to depression, a point that is acknowledged by *DSM-IV*.

Although there are also some disadvantages to the (categorical) *DSM-IV* conceptualization of depression (e.g., the tendency to promote the reification of the construct of depression; Ingram, Miranda, & Segal, 1998), because this operational definition has guided most contemporary research and theorizing, in this chapter we will largely confine our discussion to depression as defined by *DSM-IV*. We also confine our discussion of this disorder to depression in adults. Depression in children is an extremely important problem (Cicchetti & Toth, 1992; Craig & Dobson, 1995; Hammen, 1991; Ingram, et al., 1998), but a thorough examination of this problem is outside the scope of this chapter.

Undoubtedly, a critical issue facing cognitive models of depression (and most likely all models of depression and their empirical evidence) is the issue of causality. Yet definitions of the causality construct are unclear and rarely articulated. For instance, many researchers differentiate between onset and maintenance, and evidence a tendency to identify the onset or appearance of depressive symptomatology as reflecting the cause of depression. Correspondingly, because they are not viewed as causal, relatively little importance is ascribed to the factors that help maintain the state (see Barnett & Gotlib, 1988; Coyne & Gotlib, 1983); such factors are frequently dismissed as epiphenomena or consequences of the depressive state with no corresponding causal relevance. Causality, however, is not synonymous with onset. Depression is a persistent disorder with symptoms frequently lasting for an extended duration (sometimes even with effective treatment). Thus, the factors involved in the perpetuation of depression can be considered to have very real casual significance—not for the onset of the disorder, but for the maintenance of the disorder. This aspect of causality is no less important than causal onset perspectives. Indeed, from a causality standpoint, the entire distinction between onset and maintenance may be more artificial than it is genuinely useful. Thus, our review in this chapter is aimed at social and cognitive factors that are linked to a broadly conceptualized definition of causality; we believe that social and cognitive models have much to say, or at least much that can be inferred, about this view of depression.

Epidemiology of Depression

Prevalence

A caveat in discussing the prevalence of depression concerns the differing expressions of depression over the life span. Because depression may be expressed differently in children than in adults, different assessment procedures are often used with different age groups. Thus, discussion of the lifetime prevalence of the disorder, and the differential prevalence of depression at different ages, may be somewhat confounded by the use of measures that do not assess identical constructs.

Prevalence estimates vary considerably depending upon the aspects of depression whose prevalence is being estimated. Estimates also vary as a function of differences in samples and measurement methods. Flaherty, Gavira, and Val (1982), for instance, reported that, based on different definitions of depression, estimates for point prevalence of depressive states range from 5 to 44% of the population. When depression is defined as a negative mood, most people would probably qualify as having been depressed at some point. Fewer estimates have been attempted to assess the numbers of people with syndromal features indicative of depression. A large number of studies have been conducted to identify numbers of individuals meeting diagnostic criteria for major depressive disorder.

For major depressive disorder, the Epidemiological Catchment Area (ECA) study (Freedman, 1984) found a mean lifetime prevalence rate of 4.9%. Alternatively, the National Comorbidity Survey (NCS; Kessler, Mcgonagle, Zhao, Nelson et al., 1994) found generally higher rates of depression. Lifetime rates of depression were found to be 17.1%, making it one of the most common psychological disorders in both the ECA and the NCS studies. Other prevalence rates are also available. For example, within a given six-month period, some data have estimated that 3 to 5.3% of the population is depressed (Joyce, 1994).

Depression is also generally recurrent, and can be longlasting. The mean number of episodes for individuals experiencing at least one major depression has been estimated at 5 or 6, with previous depression being the best predictor of future depressions. Between 10 and 20% of individuals with major depression display a chronic course. The mean duration of depressive episodes has been estimated at from six months to a year, depending upon the severity of the episode (see Dorzab, Baker, Winokur, & Cadoret, 1971; Keller, Shapiro, Lavori, & Wolfe, 1982).

Sex Differences

Depression is widely recognized to occur approximately twice as frequently in women as in men, a finding that holds up in virtually every country in the world (Culbertson, 1997; Strickland, 1988; Weissman & Klerman, 1977, 1985). In the ECA study, the lifetime rate of major depressive disorder for women is 7.0% and 2.6% for men. Other estimates for lifetime prevalence vary from 10 to 25% for women and 5 to 12% for men (*DSM-IV*). Estimates of the point prevalence of major depression vary from 5 to 9% for women and 2 to 3% for men (*DSM-IV*).

Subtype Prevalence

A number of distinctions may be made among subtypes of major depression that yield differential prevalence estimates. For example, studies suggest that the number of individuals with depression as a primary diagnosis exceeds that of individuals with depression secondary to some other disorder. Likewise, there may be different numbers of individuals suffering from a reactive depression (i.e., in response to a definable loss event) versus an endogenous depression. Although this distinction may be important for the identification and treatment of the disorder, few studies have addressed it epidemiologically. Similarly, some researchers suggest that anxiety and depression share a common substrate of features, often termed negative affectivity (Watson & Clark, 1984; see also Kendall & Watson, 1989), which should be assessed rather than only depression per se. Hence, features predisposing an individual differentially to depression or anxiety may be of minor importance compared to the prevalence of the substrate. Additionally, some researchers suggest that depression in children or the elderly may be "masked" and not include depressed mood (e.g., Posnanski, Cook, & Carrol, 1979). Figures will therefore vary considerably depending upon the population, or the type of depression, that is estimated.

Age and Cohort Effects

The rate of depression also seems to vary with age. The rate of onset of the disorder increases dramatically during adolescence. Depression appears more common in younger than older adults, with rates being highest for individuals from 25 to 45. An individual's first onset of depression most often occurs in the 30s to 40s, with 50% of depressed individuals experiencing the onset of the disorder before age 40. Rates are lower for individuals over 65 years old (Klerman, 1986; Robins, 1984; Weissman & Myers, 1978). The striking gender differences in depression emerges around mid-adolescence, with prepubertal girls and boys being equally affected by the disorder (*DSM-IV*).

These data may be affected by cohort effects; that is, some data suggest that younger generations are currently more prone to depression than comparably aged individuals in the past (Klerman, 1986; Klerman & Weissman, 1989). Indeed, the rate of depression appears to be markedly greater for individuals born after the mid-20th century (Seligman, 1990). For example, individuals born around World War I have a lower rate of depression than individuals born after World War II, despite having a longer period of time in which to experience depression. In addition, rates of depression appear to be increasing most quickly in young men, which is potentially decreasing the discrepancy between the rate of depression in men and women (Joyce et al., 1990; Murphy, 1986). The prevalence of certain symptoms has also increased in recent years. Between 1951 and 1976, for instance, the suicide rate doubled, and the suicide attempt rate quadrupled, a trend that continued into the 1980s (e.g., Skegg & Cox, 1991).

Ethnicity and Nationality

When variables such as socioeconomic status are controlled, current research has not detected markedly different rates of depression for different ethnicities throughout the United States. Even with socioeconomic factors controlled, this observation may still be confounded by a number of variables. For instance, some symptom constellations reminiscent of depression may be specific to certain cultures (e.g., feelings of "imbalance" in Asian cultures, or being "heartbroken" among the Hopi Native Americans; Sandifer, 1972). These syndromes are not typically considered indicative of depression, but may be related to the disorder in a culture-specific manner. Additionally, evidence suggests that certain clusters of symptoms associated with depression are more common in some ethnic groups than others. For example, some researchers have suggested that being Hispanic (Stoker et al., 1968) or Chinese (Flaherty et al., 1982) is more typically associated with somatic symptoms.

Some recent studies of depression outside of North America find slight differences in lifetime and one-year prevalence rates. As noted, in the United States, the ECA study found a mean lifetime prevalence rate of 4.9%. Some research suggests that the rate of depression in Taiwan is generally lower (Hwu et al., 1989). The rate in New Zealand was considerably higher than in the ECA study, with a lifetime prevalence rate of 12.6%. This difference was due to the presence of more depressed older women and younger men in the sample (Oakley-Browne et al., 1989). Estimates of depression in Ghana and Nigeria have been as high as 20% (Flaherty et al., 1982). These differences must be considered cautiously, however, in that they may be due to differences in the samples and methods used to assess depression. Such differences aside, it is nonetheless clear that depression is a major problem worldwide. The prevalence of this disorder has led to the creation of psychological models aimed at explaining some of the important aspects of this debilitating condition.

Models of Depression

Historically, depression models have tended to focus on single causal agents. However, contemporary approaches have increasingly become multifactorial and integrative. This has been necessitated by a growing empirical base. We now know that negative life events, biochemistry, social skills, interpersonal interactions, and cognitive/affective processes are all involved in varying ways and degrees in the onset, maintenance, and relapse of depressive episodes.

As a consequence, distinctions among models have become to some degree blurred. Life event models are no longer simply models about life events; they now explicitly integrate notions of vulnerability, cognitive mediation, and interpersonal behavior. Similarly, in addition to acknowledging the important role of the disruptive capacities of life events, behavioral and interpersonal models explicitly integrate cognitive constructs, and cognitive approaches assign important roles to life events as well as to interpersonal and behavioral functioning. While integration is an exciting and positive trend to facilitate understanding, we will continue in this chapter with the tradition of presenting contemporary approaches according to their single-variable points of origin.

Life Event Models

One might suppose that one reason people get depressed is that bad things happen to them. In many respects, this has been the basic presupposition of life event approaches to depression. Life events refer to sudden, or at least relatively discriminable, changes in the external environment (Paykel & Cooper, 1992). Although earlier research appeared to support a relationship between negative life events and depression, several methodological weaknesses made such findings inconclusive.

Many of these methodological weaknesses stemmed from the use of self-report checklist methods to assess life events (e.g., Holmes & Rahe, 1967). In completing such questionnaires, respondents tended to interpret life event items idiosyncratically, which resulted in a considerable degree of variability in the types of events that were included under life event categories. For example, the life event "serious illness in a close family member" could be interpreted by one person to mean having a child who has had a one-day bout with the flu and by another person to mean having a spouse who suffered a serious heart attack. Clearly, these events should not qualify under the same life event category. In addition to within-event variability, however, these "respondent-based" assessment procedures also suffered reliability problems associated with retrospective reporting methods. Memory processes are both limited and biased and can lead to inaccuracies in reporting of past events. Moreover, the reconstructive nature of memory can limit the validity of self-reports. Finally, respondent-based assessment of life events is not independent of the depression itself. For example, depression is known to cause marital difficulties that can culminate in divorce. In such cases, the negative life event—divorce—is a consequence rather than a cause of the depression. Although it is certainly true that the depression-generated negative life event can contribute to maintaining and even exacerbating the depressed state, it would not have occurred if one were not depressed in the first place.

In an effort to deal with these and other methodological limitations, investigators have developed "investigator-based" assessment procedures that have either taken the form of questionnaires containing specific, narrowly defined items that assess "fateful" events (i.e., events outside the control of the person) or detailed semistructured life event interviews (Brown & Harris, 1978; Paykel, 1983). These more methodologically rigorous studies have clearly established a link between the occurrence of negative life events and depression. For example, Shrout, Link, Dohrenwend, Skodal, Stueve, and Mirotznik (1989) found that individuals with depression were 2.5 times more likely than nondepressed persons to have experienced one or more fateful loss events.

Perhaps the most extensive and influential research using the semistructured interview method has been the work of Brown and Harris (1978, 1986). In prospective studies using the Bedford College Life Events and Difficulties Schedule (LEDS), these investigators have found that only severe events, or events with "marked or moderate long-term threat," are clearly related to the onset of a depressive disorder. An example would be a spouse losing his or her job. In contrast, less severe life events, such as one's spouse only being threatened with a job loss, have appeared insufficient to instigate depression. This is true even when multiple less severe events have been summed (this is termed an additivity effect). Not surprisingly, however, these investigators have found an additivity effect for the occurrence of multiple life events of a severe nature (e.g., the death of a parent and a spouse losing his or her job).

The specific *quality* of an event has also emerged as an important dimension. In particular, severe life events that signify loss appear to be most strongly associated with depression, whereas events that signify danger appear more related to anxiety disorders (Finlay-Jones & Brown, 1981; Paykel, 1982; Smith & Allred, 1989). Finlay-Jones and Brown (1981) found that the "loss" events that were particularly related to depression involved a threat to self-identity and self-worth.

Stressful life events in some cases instigate additional negative life events. For example, research investigating the effects of job loss and unemployment has found that economic hardship can lead to such additional negative life events as child abuse (Justice & Duncan, 1977; Steinberg, Catalano, & Dooley, 1981) and a worsening of the spouse's mental health (Penkower, Bromet, & Dew, 1988). The occurrence of a negative life event can also worsen the quality of a marriage and, in some cases, lead to familial and marital dissolution (Liem & Liem, 1988). In this vein, Vinokur, Price, and Caplan (1996) found that job loss and financial strain resulted in more dysfunctional interactions in couples. Specifically, job loss and financial strain led to increased depression, hostility, and anxiety in both members of the couple. In turn, each member's negative affect was also found to exacerbate depressive symptoms in the other partner. As a result, each partner became less socially supportive and more likely to undermine his or her partner's sense of self-worth. These behaviors had an additional impact on depressive symptomatology, in effect creating a vicious depression-maintaining cycle.

Not all people exposed to even the most severe of negative life events, however, develop a depressive disorder. In reviewing ten studies that used the LEDS in the general population, Brown and Harris (1989) found that three quarters of recently depressed individuals experienced a preceding negative life event. Yet they also found that only one out of five who experienced a negative life event went on to develop depression. Consequently, life event research has attempted to improve the predictive value of life events by examining *matching* and *vulnerability* factors. Evidence suggests, for instance, that severe negative life events that match life domains valued by the person (e.g., marriage, employment, being a parent) are particularly potent instigators of depression (Brown, Andrews, Harris, Adler, & Bridge, 1986; O'Connor & Brown, 1984). Women who experienced a severe life event in a valued domain were found to be three times more likely to develop depression than women who experienced a severe life event in a less valued domain (Brown & Harris, 1989). In addition to these matching strategies, life event researchers have also sought to identify vulnerability factors that make an individual more or less susceptible to the depressing influence of negative life events. In particular, both low social support and low self-esteem have been identified as key vulnerability factors by life event researchers (Brown & Harris, 1989).

Because the association between negative life events and subsequent depressive symptoms has been well established, others have argued that it is important to investigate the opposite path of causality, namely that the depressed person may generate his or her own negative life events and stress (Hammen, 1991; Monroe & Simons, 1991). In a one-year longitudinal study of depressed and nondepressed women, Hammen (1991) found that depressed women experienced more *dependent* negative life events, or negative events in which they were judged to have some contributory role, than did nondepressed women. In particular, these dependent life events involved interpersonal conflict in which depressed women were thought to be partly responsible.

How does depression lead to the generation of dependent negative life events? Some researchers have suggested a role for poor interpersonal problem solving in creating interpersonal stress (Davila, Hammen, Burge, Paley, & Daley, 1995). Others have conjectured that vulnerability factors, specifically the cognitive diathesis, may generate the dependent stressful life events:

> People have been predicted to be differentially susceptible, depending on their particular cognitive vulnerability to achievement or affiliative events. However, given the hypothesized cognitive vulnerabilities to these types of experiences, it is quite plausible that the person navigates a life course that promotes differential exposure to the respective areas of vulnerability. For example, someone with a high affiliative vulnerability may be especially sensitized to interpersonal interactions in key relationships. Vigilant to possible signs of impending rejection, he or she may then make constant demands for assurance and security. Relatively benign interpersonal exchanges may take on major personal meaning; over time the behavior becomes increasingly cloying, and eventually precipitates the very circumstances it was intended to avoid (i.e., rejection). (Monroe & Simons, 1991, p. 411)

In summary, the relationship between severe negative life events and depression is clear. However, the relationship between less severe negative events and depression has not been well supported, even when multiple life events of a less severe nature have been summed. Increasingly, life event researchers have investigated the specific quality of negative life events, as well as matching and vulnerability characteristics of the individual. Negative life events, for instance, that contain qualitative themes of loss, especially loss of self-esteem and self-worth, appear most related to depression. This is particularly true of losses that match valued domains of the person. And such key vulnerability factors as poor social support and low self-esteem have been identified in individuals who are most susceptible to the depressing influence of negative life events. Moreover, researchers have begun to investigate how depressed individuals may in fact generate their own negative life events. Thus, in the face of empirical evidence from well-designed prospective studies using detailed structured interviews, life event models of depression have had to incorporate a variety of new features. For example, the role of cognitive and interpersonal variables, and even the bi-directional nature of the link between depression and life events, must now be appreciated.

Behavioral and Interpersonal Models

Another reasonable position is that people get depressed primarily because of problematic interactions with others. Behavioral and interpersonal models have examined the behaviors and especially the social behaviors of the depressed individual. The most visible of contemporary behavioral models have been the theories of Peter Lewinsohn and James Coyne.

Lewinsohn's Behavioral Model of Depression Lewinsohn's (1974) original model viewed depression as due to a low rate of response-contingent positive reinforcement. When individuals fail to receive positive reinforcement that is dependent on the execution of some behavioral response (e.g., initiating a conversation, driving to the beach), those behavioral responses become extinguished. This subsequent loss of response-based positive reinforcement deprives the individual of pleasure and leads to feelings of dysphoria. Lewinsohn viewed the experience of dysphoria, as well as the low rate of behavioral responding, as driving the other primary symptoms of depression, including low self-esteem and hopelessness. According to Lewinsohn and his colleagues, these depressive symptoms are then reinforced by a social environment that responds with sympathy, interest, and concern, thus rewarding and maintaining the depressed person's low rate of responding and display of dysphoria.

One might experience a low rate of response-contingent positive reinforcement through several pathways. However, the most emphasized and investigated has been a deficit in social skills, leading some to refer to Lewinsohn's theory as a social skill deficit theory of depression (e.g., Segrin & Abramson, 1994). Possessing adequate social skills is crucial if one is to have a chance of obtaining one of the primary sources of response-contingent positive reinforcement, namely the inherent pleasantness of intimate and supportive personal relationships. Lewinsohn maintained that as a result of poor social skills the depressed individual is denied access to the reinforcing properties of social relationships.

In addition to social skills deficits, Lewinsohn's theory posited other factors that might lead to a low rate of response-contingent reinforcement. Specifically, the occurrence of negative life events—particularly events of loss, impoverishment, or excessive aversive events—diminish the supply of potential reinforcers in the individual's environment. Indeed, as reviewed above, severe negative life events, particularly ones in which loss is experienced, do appear to be associated with depression onset. Finally, a decrease in the capacity to enjoy pleasant experiences and/or an increase in sensitivity to negative life events were also seen as contributing to lower rates of response-contingent reinforcement.

Relevant Empirical Evidence There has been a great deal of empirical support for some of the basic tenets of Lewinsohn's original model. For instance, depressed individuals have been found to view themselves as less socially skilled than nondepressed people (Lewinsohn, Mischel, Chaplin, & Barton, 1980; Vanger, 1987; Wierzbicki, 1984; Youngren & Lewinsohn, 1980). Depressed and nondepressed individuals also differ on a variety of specific social skills, such as paralinguistic behaviors, including speech content, gaze, facial expression, and posture and gesture (Segrin & Abramson, 1994), skills that could be important for obtaining and maintaining the positively reinforcing aspects of social interactions. In regard to paralinguistic behaviors, depressed individuals have been found to speak differently from nondepressed individuals, using speech that is slower, lower in volume and pitch, and more monotonous in voice tone. Depressed individuals have also been found to have more silences, hesitancies, and longer latencies when responding to others than nondepressed individuals. In addition, the content of their speech is more negative (Gotlib & Hammen, 1992). They tend to be more self-demeaning, express more negative moods, and verbalize helplessness (Biglan et al., 1985; Hokanson, Sacco, Blumberg, & Landrum, 1980). Depressed individuals also self-disclose more frequently, and they time their self-disclosures less appropriately (Jacobson & Anderson, 1982). In summarizing this and related research, Segrin and Abramson (1994) state "depressed persons show a behavioral pattern of low interpersonal involvement and responsiveness. When the depressive does exhibit a more active behavioral profile, it is typically hostile and aggressive . . . the quality of these behaviors suggests an individual who does not find social interaction to be rewarding and whose enthusiasm for social interaction is near zero" (p. 658).

The notion that a low rate of response-contingent reinforcement will lead to the experience of dysphoria has also received some empirical support. Specifically, dysphoric mood has been negatively correlated with pleasant events. Most of these events appear to require some behavioral response by the person (e.g., going to the beach, having a conversation). Likewise, unpleasant or aversive events have been positively correlated with negative mood (Grosscup & Lewinsohn, 1980; Lewinsohn & Amenson, 1978; Lewinsohn & Graf, 1973; Lewinsohn & Libet, 1973). Depressed individuals have also been found to elicit less social reinforcement (Libet & Lewinsohn, 1973).

Not all aspects of Lewinsohn's behavioral theory have received empirical support. For instance, although negative life events do correlate with depression, Lewinsohn and Hoberman (1982) found in a longitudinal, prospective study that the frequency neither of positive nor negative events predicted future depression, suggesting that life events alone are not a sufficient cause of depression. In addition, his theory had difficulty fully accounting for individual differences in terms of who would become depressed when deprived of response-contingent reinforcement. To increase the predictive power of his theory, Lewinsohn and colleagues formulated a major revision.

Lewinsohn Revised Integrative Model of Depression

This revision (Lewinsohn, Hoberman, Teri, & Hautzinger, 1985) was intended to integrate existing knowledge about life events, cognitive processes, and interpersonal functioning. Indeed, while continuing to emphasize a key feature of the original behavioral theory, it has become integrative to such an extent that it is no longer a distinctively "behavioral" model.

In the revised theory, depression onset is caused by one or more stressful life events occurring in an individual who possesses inadequate coping skills or other such vulnerabilities. In these vulnerable individuals, events that disrupt meaningful but largely automatic behavior such as personal relationships and job tasks lead to an initial negative emotional response. Both life event disruptions and the experience of dysphoric mood lead to a decrease in response-contingent reinforcement. Several cognitive and behavioral consequences then ensue. Cognitively, the individual becomes excessively self-focused, self-critical, pessimistic about future outcomes, and more aware of discrepancies between personal standards and actual accomplishments. Behaviorally, the person withdraws, has more social difficulties, and is less motivated. These cognitive and behavioral consequences combine to spiral the individual into yet a deeper state of depression.

One result of this deepening depressed state is that the individual's processing of information shifts to become excessively negative. Negative thoughts are relatively more accessible and negative information is more efficiently processed. Eventually, this negative information-processing style changes self-knowledge at the structural or schematic level. As a result, the person comes to have more negative self-beliefs. Another result of the negative information-processing style and excessive self-focus is that the individual behaves less competently in social interactions. As a result, he or she is more apt to experience social rejection. This then completes a vicious cycle as the experience of social rejection functions as an additional negative life event that then perpetuates the depressogenic process.

Clearly this model is no longer simply about the role of respondent-based positive reinforcement. However, the advantage of this model is that it is consistent with a broader knowledge base regarding the role of life events, cognition, and interpersonal functioning in depression (Gotlib & Hammen, 1992).

Coyne's Interpersonal Model

In many respects, Coyne's (1976a; Coyne, Burchill, & Stiles, 1991) interpersonal model complements Lewinsohn's original model. The key difference is that Coyne assigns a central role to the manner in which the social environment responds to the interpersonal behavior of the depressed individual.

In Coyne's theory, the occurrence of stressful life events—especially loss of significant relationships—leads to a display of depressive symptoms by the depressed individual. These depressive symptoms include expressions of helplessness and hopelessness, withdrawal from interactions, general slowing, and an irritability and agitation. The goal of the depressed person is to restore social support and gain reassurance regarding his or her self-worth and acceptance by others. Initially, the social environment tends to respond with genuine concern and support, which reinforces the display of depressive symptoms.

The meaning of this social support, however, eventually becomes ambiguous. The depressed person may wonder: Are people responding with support and reassurance because they really believe that I am worthy, or are they doing so merely because it was elicited? The depressed person, caught in this loop of uncertainty, continues to use depressive symptoms in an effort to be reassured. The persistence of such a depressive display, however, eventually is aversive to others, and they begin to have feelings of hostility and resentment. People in the depressed person's social network deal differently with these feelings of hostility and aversion. Some find suitable excuses to avoid any further interactions, which the depressed person tends to interpret, accurately, as rejection. Others, feeling too guilty and inhibited to express their hostility directly, instead offer false reassurance and support. Although this strategy temporarily reduces aversive behavior, the depressed person inevitably recognizes the indirectly expressed hostility and understands that the reassurances and support are insincere. This leads to even further efforts by the depressed person to seek reassurance that he or she is worthwhile and is not being rejected by the person. In short, a cycle based on the perceived or actual rejection by others is generated in the depressed person. This cycle is unpleasant to both the depressed person and to others who continue to remain in the depressed person's social environment.

Relevant Empirical Evidence for Coyne's Interpersonal Model Coyne's (1976a) theory predicts social rejection of depressed individuals. In fact, there is strong evidence that depressed people are rejected by important others in their social environment (Amstutz & Kaplan, 1987; Burchill & Stiles, 1988; Coyne, 1976b; Gotlib & Robinson, 1982; Gurtman, 1986; Hammen & Peters, 1977; Hokanson & Butler, 1992; Joiner & Barnett, 1994; Joiner & Metalsky, 1995; Sacco & Dunn, 1990; Stephens, Hokanson, & Welker, 1987). However, this effect appears to be moderated by features of the depressed person—gender, physical attractiveness, self-esteem—as well as such variables as the length of the depressive episode and the length of the acquaintance with the partner (Segrin & Dillard, 1992).

There has been some disagreement, however, as to why depressed people are rejected by others. Coyne's (1976a) theory specifically predicts that it is reassurance seeking that culminates in feelings of hostility and aversion in others that then leads to rejection. There is, in fact, some evidence that depressed people do engage in excessive reassurance seeking. For instance, Joiner and colleagues (Joiner, Alfano, & Metalsky, 1992; Joiner & Metalsky, 1995) have found that subclinically depressed male college students who more frequently engage in reassurance seeking (in an effort to determine whether significant others actually care for them) are more likely to be rejected by their same-gender college roommates at a later point in time. This effect was not evident for women or for men who indicated high self-esteem. These results were interpreted as supporting Coyne's argument that reassurance seeking leads to eventual rejection.

However, the evidence is mixed with regard to whether it is ultimately feelings of hostility and aversion that lead others to reject the depressed individual. Some researchers have found that interacting with a depressed person leads to feelings of hostility and aversion in the partner (Coyne, 1976b; Coyne et al., 1987; Hokanson & Butler, 1992; Hokanson, Rubert, Welker, Hollander, & Hedeen, 1989; Sacco & Dunn, 1990). For instance, in a study of depressed college students and their roommates, roommates reported experiencing low enjoyment and strong aggressive-competitive reactions toward their depressed roommates (Hokanson et al., 1989). However, other studies have failed to find any evidence of hostility and aversion in partners of depressed individuals (e.g., Burchill & Stiles, 1988; Gotlib & Robinson, 1982; McNiel, Arkowitz, & Pritchard, 1987). Moreover, in mediational analyses, hostility and aversion do not appear to account for the relationship between depression and social rejection (Gurtman, 1986). Thus, although it appears depressed people do seek excessive reassurance and are eventually rejected, the precise mechanism that leads depressed people to be rejected is less clear.

There have been several alternative mechanisms proposed that are more consistent with recent findings. Integrating aspects of Coyne's interpersonal theory with social-cognitive work in self-enhancement and self-consistency theory, Joiner, Alfano, and Metalsky (1992) propose that when the mildly depressed person's reassurance seeking is successfully rewarded by others, he or she is only temporarily satisfied. Specifically, the positive feedback elicited from others conflicts with negative self-beliefs, and consequently the depressed person doubts the validity of the feedback. This leads the depressed person to "flip-flop" and seek negative feedback that is more consistent with current self-beliefs. The combination of depression, reassurance seeking, and negative feedback seeking then causes others to reject. Consistent with this view, Joiner and Metalsky (1995) found that undergraduate males who engaged in both negative feedback seeking and reassurance seeking were more likely to be rejected by their roommates.

Alternatively, depressed people may be socially rejected simply because they lack adequate social skills. Studies in which confederates intentionally interact as if they were depressed (e.g., gazing downward, speaking at a slow rate and low volume, expressing flat affect, inappropriately self-disclosing) consistently indicate that they are viewed as unattractive and undesirable for future interactions (Amstutz & Kaplan, 1987; Gotlib & Beatty, 1985; Gurtman, 1986; Hammen & Peters, 1977, 1978; Howes & Hokanson, 1979; Segrin, 1992). Employing a communication theories analysis, Segrin and Abramson (1994) have integrated these and other empirical findings documenting social skills deficits in depression to argue that depressed people are rejected because they (1) tend to be low in verbal and nonverbal responsiveness to the communicative needs of others, (2) are "impolite" in the sense of failing to satisfy others' needs for approval and validation, and (3) violate others' expectations for nonverbal involvement in the interaction.

In summary, Coyne's theory has focused researchers' efforts on the social consequences of depression. It is clear that the major consequence is social rejection. However, there is some debate concerning the processes that lead the depressed person to be rejected. Although some studies yield support for Coyne's hypothesis that others react to depressive behaviors with aversion and hostility, other studies fail to do so. Alternatively, recent evidence suggests that negative feedback and excessive reassurance seeking may lead to social rejection. Yet another recent integration of the empirical literature suggests instead that social rejection is the result of the depressive's failure to meet the basic communication needs of others.

Cognitive Models

In recent decades, cognitive approaches have arguably had the most influence on psychological research on depression. Cognitive models of depression emphasize that people get depressed primarily because of the way they think. We will first present Beck's (1967, 1987) well-known model and then present a related information-processing model. After reviewing the empirical evidence for these cognitive models of depression, we will review models that specify cognitively based subtypes of depression, including Abramson, Metalsky, and Alloy's (1989) hopelessness theory of depression, as well as self-regulatory theories of depression. Similar to life event and behavioral-interpersonal models, however, cognitive models have become increasingly integrative.

Beck's Cognitive Theory of Depression In Beck's (1967, 1987) model, nonendogenous depression results from the activation of a depressive self-schema. Self-schemas are described as organized representations of an individual's prior experiences, particularly early-childhood experiences. However, schemas have tended to be operationalized as tacit beliefs. For instance, a depressive self-schema might contain the belief: "if I am not loved and accepted by all human beings then I am worthless." In the case of the depression-vulnerable individual, these negative beliefs are primitive, excessive, and rigid.

These self-schemas are viewed as stable but latent until activated by social stressors. A social stressor capable of activating the previous example of a dysfunctional belief might include a life event involving interpersonal rejection. Once a depressive schema is activated by a stressful life event, the activated schema has two consequences, one influencing thinking content and the other influencing thinking processes. First, the content of the depressed person's thinking becomes negative, characterized by a cognitive triad consisting of negative beliefs about the self, the world, and the future. Second, a systematic bias and distortion in information processing results, with the depressed person being particularly prone to committing a variety of cognitive distortions and errors in reasoning (e.g., arbitrary inference, dichotomous thinking, selective abstraction). Although Beck did not view all depressions as caused by depressive self-schemas (i.e., endogenous depression may be an exception), he did view the cognitive triad and negative information-processing bias to be intrinsic features of all depressions.

Information-Processing Models of Depression Since the appearance of Beck's cognitive theory, several cognitive models of depression have emerged that have more explicitly incorporated constructs from experimental cognitive psychology (Ingram, 1984; Kuiper, Olinger, & MacDonald, 1988; Teasdale, 1983, 1988; Teasdale & Barnard, 1993). Information-processing models are similar to Beck's cognitive model in that they describe depression as due to latent structures that have been activated by life event stressors, but these models tend to utilize associated constructs that explain the operation and interaction of these memory structures with other psychological processes.

In Ingram's (1984) information-processing theory, for instance, these latent structures are conceptualized as cognitive-affective networks. These networks consist of primitive emotion nodes (see Bower, 1981) that possess links to affective features of the respective emotion (e.g., facial expressions, action tendencies, physiological responses) and to similarly valenced cognitive-associative networks. In depression, then, an appraisal of loss results in the activation of the sadness emotion node. The experience of sadness results in a process of spreading activation (Norman, 1968) that occurs throughout the associative linkages that make up the entire interconnected affective-cognitive network. The result of spreading activation is the heightened accessibility of the information embedded in the entire network. Upon feeling sad, then, the depression-vulnerable individual becomes more conscious of sad-valenced information (e.g., events, thoughts, evaluations, beliefs that have occurred in past when the individual was sad). Ingram also incorporates a depth-of-processing model (Craik & Lockhart, 1972; Craik & Tulving, 1975) that predicts external information congruent with the primed depressive cognitive-affective structure will be processed at a "deeper" level of analysis. Consequently, the depressed person is expected to exhibit a superiority in attending to, encoding, and recalling negatively valenced self-referent information. This type of negative information processing continues to prime the depressogenic cognitive structure, resulting in a negative "cognitive loop" that both maintains and exacerbates the depressive state.

There are several additional consequences of spreading activation in a well-elaborated negative or "depressogenic" cognitive-affective network. As the spreading activation process primes internal thoughts related to negative aspects of the self, attention becomes extremely self-focused. This tendency of the depressed person to self-absorption (Ingram, 1990) leaves relatively minimal cognitive capacity (see Lachman, Lachman, & Butterfield, 1979) available for attending to the external environment. Consequently, the individual's social interactions suffer, leading to social withdrawal. The subsequent loss of social contacts serves even further yet to prime the depressogenic cognitive-affective structures.

Relevant Empirical Evidence for Beck's Cognitive and Information-Processing Theories There is strong support for the cognitive triad hypothesis that depressed people think more negatively about themselves, the world, and the future (for review see Haaga, Dyck, & Ernst, 1991). In regard to thinking about the self, depressed people report more negative (Kendall, Howard, & Hays, 1989) and less positive automatic self-referent thinking (Ingram, Slater, Atkinson, & Scott, 1990). They are highly self-critical (Cofer & Wittenborn, 1980; Hammen & Krantz, 1976; Kuiper, Derry, & MacDonald, 1982) and are likely to negatively evaluate a variety of stimuli other than the self, including imagined activities (Grosscup & Lewinsohn, 1980) and other people (Hokanson, Hummer, & Butler, 1991; Siegel & Alloy, 1990). Depressed people are also pessimistic about the future (Alloy & Ahrens, 1987). This consistent support for the triad hypothesis has led some reviewers to argue for considering it as a central descriptive feature of depression, equivalent to other such well-acknowledged facts about depression as "high recurrence" and "running in families" (Haaga et al., 1991).

The evidence appears generally supportive of a systematic negative bias in information processing during depressive episodes (Haaga et al., 1991; Ingram & Holle, 1992). For example, there have been numerous studies documenting the fact that depressed people, compared to nondepressed people, display a chronic tendency to direct their attention to internal, rather than external, information (Ingram, 1990). Regarding the selective encoding of negative information, the bulk of the relevant evidence has been from studies that have used the self-referent depth-of-processing paradigm (Rogers, Kuiper, & Kirker, 1977), which has recently been referred to as the *self-referent encoding task* (SRET). This paradigm is based on assumptions that stimuli that match the content of activated and well-elaborated memory structures will be processed at deeper levels of cognitive analysis, leaving a stronger memory trace and thus having a greater likelihood of being retrieved from memory. Procedurally, subjects first rate a series of valenced adjectives (e.g., angry, sad, happy, humorous) in terms of their self-descriptiveness, then incidentally recall the self-referenced information. Consequently, when presented with mixed-valenced information, individuals with depressogenic memory structures are predicted to encode negative information at a deeper level and, as a result, recall more negative adjectives. SRET studies have generally found that depressed individuals appear to selectively encode negative information (for a review see Ingram & Holle, 1992), although a few researchers have failed to find any differences between depressed and nondepressed groups (Clifford & Hemsley, 1987; Myers, Lynch, & Bakal, 1989). Finally, in studies of memory retrieval, depressed individuals have been found to recall more negatively valenced personal memories than the nondepressed. Importantly, the recall advantage fluctuates with diurnal fluctuations in negative mood and disappears entirely when the depressive episode remits (Clark & Teasdale, 1982; Fogarty & Hemsley, 1983; Lewinsohn & Rosenbaum, 1987).

Although cognitions are clearly negative in content, and information processing appears to be biased during episodes of depression, the evidence is decidedly more mixed for cognitive distortions. Gotlib (1983) found that when depressed and nondepressed psychiatric inpatients were given bogus neutral feedback supposedly based on an observation of a dyadic interaction with a stranger, the depressed patients recalled the feedback as more negative than was objectively the case. Depressed people also appear to overestimate self-punishments; Gotlib (1981) found that depressed psychiatric inpatients recalled giving themselves fewer reinforcements than they had delivered to themselves during a verbal recognition task.

Other research done with dysphoric rather than depressed populations has failed to find differences in the accurate processing of information (Dykman, Horowitz, Abramson, & Usher, 1991; Haack, Metalsky, Dykman, & Abramson, 1996). For example, both dysphoric and nondepressed groups appear to utilize objectively valid situational information in making attributions for success and failure experiences (Haack et al., 1996). In other words, neither group appeared to make unwarranted causal inferences. Further, the research on depressive realism suggests that dysphoric individuals' judgments of contingency between performance and outcome are more accurate than were nondepressed people, who possess an "illusion of control" (Alloy & Abramson, 1979, 1988; for a review see Ackermann & DeRubeis, 1991). These findings have led some to argue for reformulations of Beck's theory emphasizing that what distinguishes depressive cognition is negative thought content, not inaccuracy or distorted thought processes per se (Haaga & Beck, 1995). However, these studies need to be replicated with clinically depressed populations before definitive conclusions are warranted. It may be that one of the characteristics that distinguishes clinical depression from subclinical dysphoria is the presence of inaccurate or distorted thought processes.

So far we have reviewed evidence describing the cognitive functioning of depression while the depressed person is in episode. However, both Beck's cognitive model and information-processing theories view cognitive schemata or cognitive-affective structures as causal variables that determine vulnerability to depression. Although generally latent, these structures are presumed to be stable underlying features of the depression-vulnerable individual, becoming active only during episodes of stress or negative mood. Although early attempts to assess the empirical validity of schema and cognitive structure models yielded largely disconfirming findings (for reviews see Gotlib & Hammen, 1992; Haaga et al., 1991; Segal & Ingram, 1994), these studies generally failed to activate or prime these presumed latent but stable structures prior to assessment. More recent studies that have included appropriate priming procedures have generally found evidence supportive of the presence of latent depressogenic cognitive schemas (or cognitive-affective structures) in remitted depressed individuals (Hedlund & Rude, 1995; Ingram, Bernet, & McLaughlin, 1994; Miranda & Persons, 1988; Miranda, Persons, & Byers, 1990; Teasdale & Dent, 1987). For example, Ingram and Ritter (1998) found that when primed with a sad mood, formerly depressed individuals allocated their attentional resources toward negative stimuli, while never-depressed individuals did not. Such processes are not limited to formerly depressed adults. In a study of depressive schema-activation processes in the offspring of depressed mothers, Taylor and Ingram (1998) found that these offspring evidenced significantly more negative information recall when they were primed with a sad mood than did the offspring of mothers who were not depressed. Moreover, Segal, Germer, and Williams (in press) found that recovered patients who evidenced dysfunctional cognition in response to a negative mood experienced more relapse than equally recovered individuals who did not respond with heightened levels of dysfunctional cognition.

Priming procedures other than mood inductions have been reported. For example, Hedlund and Rude (1995) employed a self-focusing procedure to activate the presumed cognitive structures in a formerly depressed and currently depressed patients. Both currently and formerly depressed subjects recalled more negative adjectives on a self-referent depth of processing task and constructed more negative sentences on an unscrambled sentence task. Both of these measures indicate biased information processing. These results, along with other more recent findings, appear to indicate that depressive cognitive processing not only is a concomitant of depressive episodes but also is elicited in formerly depressed patients when appropriate priming procedures are employed (Segal & Ingram, 1994; Ingram et al., 1998).

Learned Helplessness and Cognitive Subtype Theories

One of the most widely known theories of depression is that originally proposed by Seligman (1975). Seligman's model was based on an observation of apparent similarity between the responses of depressed people and the behavior of laboratory dogs who exhibited a lack of escape behavior after they had been unable to control intermittent electrical shocks to their feet. Seligman's theory focused on depressed persons' expectations that they are helpless to control aversive outcomes, and the ensuing behavior that is consistent with these expectations.

Perhaps because of its evident simplicity, the orginal learned helplessness theory generated a tremendous amount of data (Abramson, Seligman, & Teasdale, 1978). Although much of this research supported the fundamental tenets of the model, other research revealed the model's deficiencies. Thus, in 1978 the theory was revised to focus on people's beliefs about the causes of events (Abramson et al., 1978). In this reformulated theory, an attributional style was proposed as the critical causal variable in depression. In particular, making specific, unstable, external attributions for positive events, and global, stable, and internal attributions for negative events was hypothesized to precipitate depression.

Research on the various formulations of the reformulated helplessness/attributional theory of depression have been comparable to that assessing other cognitive approaches; when individuals are depressed, cross-sectional studies show that they do tend to make the types of attributions hypothesized by the theory (Alloy & Abramson, 1988). Additionally, some data show that the tendency to report some of these attributions predicts negative mood reactions in response to negative events. Specifically, two prospective studies indicated that college students who showed a tendency to attribute negative events to stable and global causes experienced a more severe depressed mood after a low midterm grade than did individuals who did not display this attributional style (Metalsky, Halberstadt, & Abramson, 1987; Metalsky, Joiner, Hardin, & Abramson, 1993). As with virtually all cognitive and life event models, however, claims that these kinds of attributional tendencies cause depression have yet to be confirmed.

Many have argued that depression is not a single disorder but actually comprises several subtypes, with each subtype possessing a distinctive cause, course, and symptom complex. Relatively recently, Abramson et al. (1989) have reported a new version of the attributional model, which they have referred to as the *hopelessness theory of depression* (see also Abramson, Alloy, & Hogan, 1997). Their model, however, is more than just a theory of depression; they have also proposed this type of depression as a specific subtype that they refer to as hopelessness depression. The cause of this subtype is the expectation that desired outcomes are unlikely to occur or, conversely, that aversive outcomes are likely and that no response will alter this likelihood.

Earlier studies assessing the relationship between attributional style and depression are consistent with aspects of the model (for reviews see Barnett & Gotlib, 1988; Brewin, 1985; Coyne & Gotlib, 1983; Peterson & Seligman, 1984; Sweeney, Anderson, & Bailey, 1986). This is expected, of course, since the hopelessness model grew out of an earlier attributional approach to depression. Additionally, however, as with the earlier theories, this theory has not yet generated evidence that the putative causal factor—attributional style—is present in ostensibly vulnerable people prior to the onset of depression, although data collected by Alloy and Abramson (1990) may eventually shed light on this issue.

Sociotropic and Autonomous Depression Subtypes

Investigators have described two personality types that constitute specific vulnerabilities for depression (Beck, 1987; Blatt & Zuroff, 1992): sociotropy and autonomy. Sociotropic individuals value interpersonal relationships, intimacy, and acceptance by others as a way of maintaining self-esteem. They are thought to be vulnerable to depression when they experience a loss or rejection in social relationships. In contrast, autonomous individuals are more invested in maintaining independence and achieving their own goals and standards. As a result, they are thought to be more vulnerable to depression when they experience failure in an achievement or individual accomplishment domain, such as a demotion at work or receiving a poor grade. These type of life event–matching hypotheses, however, have yielded equivocal results. In cross-sectional clinical studies, both personality subtypes have shown moderate correlations with self-reported distress, with the sociotropy-dependency correlations being somewhat lower. In longitudinal clinical studies, however, both personality subtypes have had mixed success in predicting subsequent self-reported distress or depression (Coyne & Whiffen, 1995).

Self-Regulatory Approaches to Depression

Another useful approach to depression derives from self-regulatory models that attempt to identify how people regulate their behavior in the relative absence of external reinforcement (Bandura, 1986, 1997; Carver & Scheier, 1981, in press). The ability to self-regulate is decidedly dependent upon cognitive processes. People, for instance, tend to adopt cognitive representations of desired future states that serve as guides and motives for action (Bandura, 1986; Carver & Scheier, 1981, in press; Kanfer, 1970; Lewin, Dembo, Festinger, & Sears, 1944). These *performance standards* or goals serve as the benchmarks against which ongoing behavior is compared and evaluated. In order to understand the specific motivational and affective impact of the goal level adopted, however, two additional cognitive self-regulatory variables must be considered: evaluative judgments and self-efficacy appraisals.

People evaluate the relative successfulness of performance attainments. When performances fall short of standards, the effect can be motivating or disabling, depending partly on the size of the discrepancy between standard and performance. Large discrepancies generally lead to feelings of futility, dysphoria, and low motivation, and small discrepancies spur positive affect, greater persistence, and eventual goal accomplishment (Locke & Latham, 1990). However, the precise motivational effect depends on a third variable: the perceived self-efficacy for the goal-relevant behavior (Bandura, 1977, 1997). *Self-efficacy appraisals* refer to people's assessments of their abilities to organize and execute specific behavioral performances (Bandura, 1986, 1997). When people judge themselves capable of an adequate performance, they may persevere even when their initial performance was substandard and dissatisfying. When people appraise themselves as inefficacious, even small goal-performance discrepancies tend to promote dysphoria and lead to a slackening, or even to an abandoning, of effort altogether (Bandura & Cervone, 1983, 1986; Cervone & Peake, 1986; see also Cervone & Scott, 1995).

Some investigators have proposed that individual differences in these basic self-regulatory mechanisms contribute as vulnerability or maintaining causal factors in depression (Kanfer & Hagerman,

1981; Rehm, 1977). In particular, negative self-evaluations, low self-efficacy, and perfectionistic standard setting have all been identified as putative causal factors in depression. Clearly, one of the most robust findings in the depression literature is that, while in episode, depressed people are in fact particularly self-critical in evaluating performances (Blatt, Quinlan, Chevron, McDonald, & Zuroff, 1982; Cofer & Wittenborn, 1980; Hammen & Krantz, 1976; Roth & Rehm, 1980). However, the evidence regarding the proposed individual differences in the other self-regulatory variables is mixed. Research employing attitudinal or traitlike measures of perfectionism have sometimes found an association with dysphoric and depressive states (Flett, Hewitt, & Mittelstaedt, 1991; Hewitt & Dyck, 1986; Hewitt & Flett, 1991). Other investigators employing different attitudinal measures of goal stringency have found no relation between high standards and dysphoria (Carver, 1997; Carver & Ganellen, 1983; Carver, Ganellen, & Behar-Mitrani, 1985; Carver, La Voie, Kuhl, & Ganellen, 1988). Rather than using such traitlike measures, social-cognitive investigators have assessed goal stringency for specific activities and have obtained similarly mixed results. In these studies, dysphoric and depressed individuals do appear to hold relatively stringent performance standards in that the goals adopted exceed the performance levels judged as accomplishable (Ahrens, 1987). However, whether this discrepancy is due to increased standards, lowered efficacy appraisals, or some combination of both, is presently unclear. Some evidence suggests raised performance standards as the culprit (Golin & Terrell, 1977; Schwartz, 1974), but more recent studies indicate lowered self-efficacy appraisals (Ahrens, 1987; Higgins, Strauman, & Klein, 1986; Kanfer & Zeiss, 1983).

Other self-regulatory theorists have proposed that different types of standard-evaluation discrepancies lead to different types of emotional vulnerabilities (Higgins, 1987; Strauman, 1992, 1996). Specifically, Higgins (1987) proposes that discrepancies between ideal self-standards (representations of the attributes one would ideally like to possess) and evaluated performances lead to dejection-related emotions, such as sadness and dysphoria. In contrast, discrepancies between ought self-standards, or representations of the attributes that one believes should or ought to be possessed, and evaluated performances lead to agitation-related emotions, such as anxiety. Moderate empirical support for these specified relations with both analogue and clinical populations has been found (Higgins, Klein, & Strauman, 1985; Scott & O'Hara, 1993; Strauman, 1992, 1996).

Computational Models of Depression

A relatively new methodology for conceptualizing depression has recently generated interest among researchers. Using computer simulations, computational models tend to focus on aspects of depression rather than on depression as a whole. For example, some computational models have examined the mechanisms by which depressive information processing might become biased. Many such models are created using a framework in which patterns of information processing are theorized to result from networks of simple connected neuronlike units. Models intended to examine the functioning of attentional factors and information-processing biases in depression have been developed by several researchers (Matthews, in press; Siegle & Ingram, 1998; Williams & Oaksford, 1992).

The ultimate value of computational models of depression lies in aiding the conceptualization of cognitive processes by virtue of computer simulation of these processes. Ultimately, however, empirical data are needed to confirm the parameters of models that have been simulated. Because the modeling of depressive cognitive processes is currently in its infancy, extant models are not widely accepted nor are empirical data available to help confirm or disconfirm these models. Nevertheless, computational approaches remain promising for eventually helping to understand important aspects of depression.

Summary and Conclusions

We have sought to examine the relevant theory and data on social and cognitive aspects of depression. To do so, we first provided a brief historical and definitional foundation for assessing these aspects. As noted, depression is a concept with a long history, dating back to the earliest known writings. The phenomenon, however, no doubt existed before its features (and in some cases attendant superstitions) could be put into writing. As this history shows, ideas have also evolved considerably, to the point where the salient characteristics of the depression have been codified in the official psychiatric nonclemanture.

Using the currently accepted criteria, depression has a number of recognized subtypes. The type of depression that constituted the focus of this chapter, unipolar depression, occurs in all countries of the world and, depending on estimates, affects a large percentage of people throughout the world. Sex differences in the rate of depression are also found worldwide, with women being approximately twice as likely as men to report depression. Depression also tends to occur equally across various ethnic groups and subcultures.

Numerous psychological models of depression have been proposed. Many of the most widely accepted models are cognitive in nature, although not exclusively so. For instance, behavioral and interpersonal models have been proposed by several researchers, although even these have evolved to include key cognitive components. Models proposed by cognitive researchers tend to focus on information processing and cognitive structures such as schemas. Schema models have received empirical support in that the factors hypothesized by these models are generally found to be associated with depression. Some research, however, has found that these cognitive factors tend to no longer be detectable when depressed individuals are in remission, a finding that has led some researchers to question the adequacy of all cognitive models. More recent research, however, has found that these cognitive factors again become detectable when vulnerable individuals (e.g., those who have been depressed in the past) encounter situations that are theorized to provoke the resurgence of negative cognitive structures. These studies have the advantage of more closely modeling the diathesis-stress nature of most cognitive theories.

A specific cognitive subtype of depression has been proposed by several researchers. Growing out of the learned helplessness model, the reformulated learned helpless model, and most recently the hopelessness model, have suggested a hopelessness subtype of depression. Although much research has found a link between depression and helplessness, and attributional tendencies, the hopelessness model has not yet received extensive research scrutiny.

Social and cognitive models have contributed significantly to an understanding of several key aspects of depression, although they have not been without criticism. This is particularly true of the cognitive models. Coyne and Gotlib (1983) and Coyne (1992), for instance, have detailed a number of criticisms of both the conceptual and the empirical foundations of cognitive approaches to depression. Nevertheless, many of the valid criticisms of cognitive approaches to depression have proved to be extremely valuable in leading to theoretical refinements and new research paradigms. In addition, acknowledging the inability of existing cross-sectional and correlational research to allow for inferences about causality has been an important outgrowth of this criticism. In fact, such criticisms of the putative causal statements of cognitive models of depression have driven to a large degree the resurgence of interest in issues such as diathesis-stress perspectives and vulnerability (Ingram et al., 1998).

Diathesis-stress perspectives form the core features of models of causality. As we have noted, the various aspects of causality are diverse ranging from determining vulnerability to onset of depression, vulnerability to maintenance, factors impacting treatment, and factors that are relevant to remission in the absence of treatment. Although social and cognitive models have offered various proposals for causality, few data have actually assessed these causal elements. One of the key tasks for researchers in these areas is thus to move beyond the description of social and cognitive features to an understanding of the causal pathways of these factors and how these pathways intersect with pathways from other levels of analysis (e.g., biochemical). This goal may not be obtainable, but it must be an aspiration for continued progress in understanding the social and cognitive aspects of depression.

References

Abraham, K. (1911/1960). Notes on the psychoanalytic investigation and treatment of manic-depressive insanity and allied conditions. In *Selected Papers on Psychoanalysis* (pp. 12–24). New York: Basic Books.

Abramson, L. Y., Alloy, L. B., & Hogan, M. E. (1997). Cognitive/personality subtypes of depression: Theories in search of disorders. *Cognitive Therapy and Research, 21*, 247–266.

Abramson, L. Y., Metalsky, G. I., & Alloy, L. B. (1989). Hopelessness depression: A theory-based subtype of depression. *Psychological Review, 96*, 358–372.

Abramson, L. Y., Seligman, M. E. P., & Teasdale, J. (1978). Learned helplessness in humans: Critique and reformulation. *Journal of Abnormal Psychology, 87*, 49–74.

Ackerman, R., & DeRubeis, R. (1991). Is depressive realism real? *Clinical Psychology Review, 11*, 565–584.

Ahrens, A. H. (1987). Theories of depression: The role of goals and the self-evaluation process. *Cognitive Therapy and Research, 11*, 665–680.

Alloy, L. B., & Abramson, L. Y. (1979). Judgment of contingency in depressed and nondepressed students: Sadder but wiser? *Journal of Experimental Psychology: General, 108*, 441–485.

Alloy, L. B., & Abramson, L. Y. (1988). Depressive realism: Four theoretical perspectives. In L. B. Alloy (Ed.), *Cognitive processes in depression* (pp. 223–265). New York: Guilford Press.

Alloy, L. B., & Abramson, L. Y. (1990). *The Temple-Wisconsin Cognitivie vulnerability to depression project.* Grant from the National Institute of Mental Health.

Alloy, L. B., & Ahrens, A. H. (1987). Depression and pessimism for the future: Biased use of statistically relevant information in predictions for self versus others. *Journal of Personality and Social Psychology, 52*, 366–378.

Amstutz, D. K., & Kaplan, M. F. (1987). Depression, physical attractiveness, and interpersonal acceptance. *Journal of Social and Clinical Psychology, 5*, 365–377.

Bandura, A. (1977). Self-efficacy: Toward a unifying theory of behavioral change. *Psychological Review, 84*, 191–215.

Bandura, A. (1986). *Social foundations of thought and action: A social cognitive theory.* Englewood Cliffs, NJ: Prentice-Hall.

Bandura, A. (1997). *Self-efficacy: The exercise of control.* New York: W. H. Freeman.

Bandura, A., & Cervone, D. (1983). Self-evaluative and self-efficacy mechanisms governing the motivational effects of goal systems. *Journal of Personality and Social Psychology, 45*, 1017–1028.

Bandura, A., & Cervone, D. (1986). Differential engagement of self-reactive influences in cognitive motivation. *Journal of Organizational Behavior and Human Decision Processes, 38*, 92–113.

Barnett, P. A., & Gotlib, I. H. (1988). Psychosocial functioning in depression: Distinguishing among antecedents, concomitants, and consequences. *Psychological Bulletin, 104*, 97–126.

Beck, A. T. (1967). *Depression: Clinical, experimental, and theoretical aspects.* New York: Harper & Row.

Beck, A. T. (1987). Cognitive models of depression. *Journal of Cognitive Psychotherapy: An International Quarterly, 1*, 5–37.

Beckham, E. E., Leber, W. R., & Youll, L. K. (1995). The diagnostic classification of depression. In E. E. Beckham & W. R. Leber (Eds.), *Handbook of depression* (2nd ed.; pp. 36–60). New York: Guilford Press.

Biglan, A., Hops, H., Sherman, L., Friedman, L. S., Arthur, J., & Osteen, V. (1985). Problem-solving interactions of depressed women and their husbands. *Behavior Therapy, 16*, 431–451.

Blatt, S. J., Quinlan, D. M., Chevron, E. S., McDonald, C., & Zuroff, D. (1982). Dependency and self-criticism: Psychological dimensions of depression. *Journal of Consulting and Clinical Psychology, 50*, 113–124.

Blatt, S. J., & Zuroff, D. C. (1992). Interpersonal relatedness and self-definition: Two prototypes for depression. *Clinical Psychology Review, 12*, 527–562.

Bower, G. H. (1981). Mood and memory. *American Psychologist, 36*, 129–148.

Brewin, C. R. (1985). Depression and causal attributions: What is their relation? *Psychological Bulletin, 98*, 297–309.

Brown, G. W., Andrews, B., Harris, T. O., Adler, Z., & Bridge, L. (1986). Social support, self-esteem and depression. *Psychological Medicine, 16*, 813–831.

Brown, G. W., & Harris, T. (1978). *The social origins of depression: A study of psychiatric disorder in women.* New York: Free Press.

Brown, G. W., & Harris, T. (1986). Establishing causal links: The Bedford College studies of depression. In H. Katschnig (Ed.), *Life events and psychiatric disorders: Controversial issues* (pp. 201–285). Cambridge, England: Cambridge University Press.

Brown, G. W., & Harris, T. (1989). *Life events and illness.* New York: Guilford Press.

Burchill, S. A. L., & Stiles, W. B. (1988). Interactions of depressed college students with their roommates: Not necessarily negative. *Journal of Personality and Social Psychology, 55*, 410–419.

Carver, C. S. (1997). Generalization, adverse events, and development of dysphoria.

Carver, C. S., & Scheier, M. F. (1981). *Attention and self-regulation: A control theory approach to human behavior.* New York: Springer-Verlag.

Carver, C. S., & Ganellen, R. J. (1983). Depression and components of self-punitiveness: High standards, self-criticism, and overgeneralization. *Journal of Abnormal Psychology, 92*, 330–337.

Carver, C. S., & Ganellen, R. J., & Behar-Mitrani, V. (1985). Depression and cognitive style: Comparisons between measures. *Journal of Personality and Social Psychology, 49*, 722–728.

Carver, C. S., La Voie, L., Kuhl, J., & Ganellen, R. J. (1988). Cognitive concomitants of depression: A further examination of the roles of generalization, high standards, and self-criticism. *Journal of Social and Clinical Psychology, 7*, 350–365.

Carver, C. S., & Scheier, M. F. (1981). *Attention and self-regulation: A control-theory approach to human behavior.* New York: Springer-Verlag.

Carver, C. S., & Scheier, M. F. (in press). *On the self-regulation of behavior.* New York: Cambridge University Press.

Cervone, D., & Peake, P. K. (1986). Anchoring, efficacy, and action: The influence of judgmental heuristics on self-efficacy judgments and behavior. *Journal of Personality and Social Psychology, 50*, 492–501.

Cervone, D., & Scott, W. D. (1995). Self-efficacy theory of behavioral change: Foundations, conceptual issues, and therapeutic implications. In W. O'Donohue & L. Krasner (Eds.), *Theories of behavior therapy: Exploring behavior change.* Washington, DC: American Psychological Association.

Cicchetti, D., & Toth, S. (Eds.). (1992). *Developmental perspectives on depression.* Rochester, New York: University of Rochester Press.

Clark, D. M., & Teasdale, J. D. (1982). Diurnal variation in clinical depression and accessibility of memories of positive and negative experiences. *Journal of Abnormal Psychology, 91*, 87–95.

Clifford, P. I., & Hemsley, D. R. (1987). The influence of depression on the processing of personal attributes. *British Journal of Psychiatry, 150*, 98–103.

Cofer, D. H., & Wittenborn, J. R. (1980). Personality characteristics of formerly depressed women. *Journal of Abnormal Psychology, 89*, 309–314.

Compas, B. E., Ey, S., & Grant, K. E. (1993). Taxonomy, assessment, and diagnosis of depression during adolescence. *Psychological Bulletin, 114*, 323–344.

Coyne, J. C. (1976a). Toward an interactional description of depression. *Psychiatry, 39*, 28–40.

Coyne, J. C. (1976b). Depression and the response of others. *Journal of Abnormal Psychology, 85*, 186–193.

Coyne, J. C. (1992). Cognition in depression: A paradigm in crisis. *Psychological Inquiry, 3*, 232–235.

Coyne, J. C., Burchill, S. A. L., & Stiles, W. B. (1991). An interactional perspective on depression. In C. R. Snyder & D. R. Forsyth (Eds.), *Handbook of social and clinical psychology* (pp. 327–349). Elmsford, NY: Pergamon Press.

Coyne J. C., & Gotlib, I. H. (1983). The role of cognition in depression: A critical a appraisal. *Psychological Bulletin, 94*, 472–505.

Coyne, J. C., Kessler, R. C., Tal, M., Turnbull, J., Wortman, C. B., & Creden, J. F. (1987). Living with a depressed person. *Journal of Consulting and Clinical Psychology, 55*, 347–352.

Coyne, J. C., & Whiffen, V. E. (1995). Issues in personality as diathesis for depression: The case of sociotropy-dependency and autonomy-self-criticism. *Psychological Bulletin, 118*, 358–378.

Craig, K. D., & Dobson K. S. (Eds.). (1995). *Anxiety and depression in adults and children.* Thousand Oaks, CA: Sage Publications.

Craik, F. I. M., & Lockhart, R. S. (1972). Levels of processing: A framework for memory research. *Journal of Verbal Learning and Verbal Behavior, 11*, 671–684.

Craik, F. I. M., & Tulving, E. (1975). Depth of processing and retention of words in episodic memory. *Journal of Experimental Psychology: General, 104*, 268–294.

Culberston, F. M. (1997). Depression and gender: An international review. *American Psychologist, 52*, 25–31.

Davila, J., Hammen, C., Burge, D., Paley, B., & Daley, S. E. (1995). Poor interpersonal problem solving as a mechanism of stress generation in depression among adolescent women. *Journal of Abnormal Psychology, 104*, 592–600.

Dorzab, J., Baker, M., Winokur, G., & Cadoret, R. J. (1971). Depressive disease: Clinical course. *Diseases of the Nervous System, 32*, 269–273.

Dykman, B. M., Horowitz, L. M., Abramson, L. Y., & Usher, M. (1991). Schematic and situational determinants of depressed and nondepressed students' interpretation of feedback. *Journal of Abnormal Psychology, 100*, 45–55.

Finlay-Jones, R., & Brown, G. W. (1981). Types of stressful life event and the onset of anxiety and depressive disorders. *Psychological Medicine, 11*, 803–815.

Flaherty, J. A., Gavira, F. M., & Val, E. R. (1982). Diagnostic considerations. In E. R. Val, F. M. Gavira, & J. A. Flaherty (Eds.), *Affective disorders: Psychopathology and treatment.* Chicago: Year Book Medical Publishers.

Flett, G. L., Hewitt, P. L., & Mittelstaedt, W. M. (1991). Dysphoria and components of self-punitiveness: A re-analysis. *Cognitive Therapy and Research, 15*, 201–219.

Fogarty, S. J., & Hemsley, D. R. (1983). Depression and the accessibility of memories: A longitudinal study. *British Journal of Psychiatry, 142*, 232–237.

Freedman, D. X. (1984). Psychiatric epidemiology counts. *Archives of General Psychiatry, 41*, 931–933.

Freud, S. (1917/1950). Mourning and melancholia. In *Collected papers* (Vol. 4). London: Hogarth Press.

Golin, S., & Terrell, F. (1977). Motivational and associative aspects of mild depression in skill and chance tasks. *Journal of Abnormal Psychology, 86*, 389–401.

Gotlib, I. H. (1981). Self-reinforcement and recall: Differential deficits in depressed and nondepressed psychiatric inpatients. *Journal of Abnormal Psychology, 90*, 521–530.

Gotlib, I. H. (1983). Perception and recall of interpersonal feedback: Negative bias in depression. *Cognitive Therapy and Research, 7*, 399–412.

Gotlib, I. H., & Beatty, M. E. (1985). Negative responses to depression: The role of attributional style. *Cognitive Therapy and Research, 9*, 91–103.

Gotlib, I. H., & Hammen, C. L. (1992). *Psychological aspects of depression: Toward a cognitive-interpersonal integration*. New York: John Wiley.

Gotlib, I. H., & Robinson, L. A. (1982). Responses to depressed individuals: Discrepancies between self-report and observer-rated behavior. *Journal of Abnormal Psychology, 91*, 231–240.

Grosscup, S. J., & Lewinsohn, P. M. (1980). Unpleasant and pleasant events, and mood. *Journal of Clinical Psychology, 36*, 252–259.

Gurtman, M. B. (1986). Depression and the response of others: Reevaluating there evaluation. *Journal of Abnormal Psychology, 95*, 99–101.

Haack, L. J., Metalsky, G. I., Dykman, B. M., & Abramson, L. Y. (1996). Use of current situational information and causal inference: Do dysphoric individuals make "unwarranted" causal inferences? *Cognitive Therapy and Research, 20*, 309–331.

Haaga, D. A. F., & Beck, A. T. (1995). Perspectives on depressive realism: Implications for cognitive theory of depression. *Behavior Research and Therapy, 33*, 41–48.

Haaga, D. A. F., Dyck, M. J., & Ernst, D. (1991). Empirical status of cognitive theory of depression. *Psychological Bulletin, 110* (2), 215–236.

Hammen, C. (1991). Generation of stress in the course of unipolar depression. *Journal of Abnormal Psychology, 100*, 555–561.

Hammen, C. L., & Krantz, S. (1976). Effects of success and failure on depressive cognitions. *Journal of Abnormal Psychology, 85*, 577–586.

Hammen, C. L., & Peters, S. D. (1977). Differential responses to male and female depressive reactions. *Journal of Consulting and Clinical Psychology, 45*, 994–1001.

Hammen, C. L., & Peters, S. D. (1978). Interpersonal consequences of depression: Responses to men and women enacting a depressed role. *Journal of Abnormal Psychology, 87*, 322–332.

Hedlund, S., & Rude, S. S. (1995). Evidence of latent depressive schemas in formerly depressed individuals. *Journal of Abnormal Psychology, 104*, 517–525.

Hewitt, P. L., & Dyck, D. G. (1986). Perfectionism, stress, and vulnerability to depression. *Cognitive Therapy and Research, 10*, 137–142.

Hewitt, P. L., & Flett, G. L. (1991). Dimensions of perfectionism in unipolar depression. *Journal of Abnormal Psychology, 100*, 98–101.

Higgins, E. T. (1987). Self-discrepancy: A theory relating self and affect. *Psychological Review, 94*, 319–340.

Higgins, E. T., Klein, R., & Strauman, T. J. (1985). Self-concept discrepancy theory: A psychological model for distinguishing among different aspects of depression and anxiety. *Social Cognition, 3*, 51–76.

Higgins, E. T., Strauman, T. J., & Klein, R. (1986). Standards and the process of self-evaluation: Multiple affects from multiple stages. In R. Sorrentino & E. T. Higgins (Eds.), *Handbook of motivation and cognition: Foundations of social behavior.* New York: Guilford.

Hokanson, J. E., & Butler, A. C. (1992). Cluster analysis of depressed college students' social behaviors. *Journal of Personality and Social Psychology, 62*, 273–280.

Hokanson, J. E., Hummer, J. T., & Butler, A. C. (1991). Interpersonal perceptions by depressed college students. *Cognitive Therapy and Research, 15*, 443–457.

Hokanson, J. E., Rubert, M. P., Welker, R. A., Hollander, G. R., & Hedeen, C. (1989). Interpersonal concomitants and antecedents of depression among college students. *Journal of Abnormal Psychology, 98*, 209–217.

Hokanson, J. E., Sacco, W. P., Blumberg, S. R., & Landrum, G. C. (1980). Interpersonal behavior of depressive individuals in a mixed-motive game. *Journal of Abnormal Psychology, 89*, 320–332.

Holmes, T. H., & Rahe, R. H. (1967). The social readjustment rating scale. *Journal of Psychosomatic Research, 11*, 213–218.

Howes, M. J., & Hokanson, J. E. (1979). Conversational and social responses to depressive interpersonal behavior. *Journal of Abnormal Psychology, 88*, 625–634.

Hwu, H., Yeh, E. K., & Chang, L. Y. (1989). Prevalence of psychiatric disorders in Taiwan defined by the Chinese Diagnostic Interview Schedule. *Acta Psychiatrica Scandinavica, 79*, 136–147.

Ingram, R. E. (1984). Toward an information processing analysis of depression. *Cognitive Therapy and Research, 8*, 443–478.

Ingram, R. E. (1990). Self-focused attention in clinical disorders: Review and a conceptual model. *Psychological Bulletin, 107*, 156–176.

Ingram, R. E., Bernet, C. Z., & McLaughlin, S. C. (1994). Attention allocation processes in individuals. *Cognitive Therapy and Research, 18*, 317–332.

Ingram, R. E., & Holle, C. (1992). Cognitive science of depression. In D. J. Stein & J. E. Young (Eds.), *Cognitive science and clinical disorders* (pp. 188–209). San Diego: Academic Press.

Ingram, R. E., Miranda, J., & Segal, Z. V. (1998). *Cognitive vulnerability to depression.* New York: Guilford Press.

Ingram, R. E., & Ritter, J. (1998). *Cognitive reactivity and parental bonding dimensions of vulnerability to depression.* Manuscript submitted for publication.

Ingram, R. E., Slater, M. A., Atkinson, J. H., & Scott, W. D. (1990). Positive automatic cognition in major affective disorder. *Psychological Assessment: A Journal of Consulting and Clinical Psychology, 2*, 209–211.

Jacobson, N. S., & Anderson, E. A. (1982). Interpersonal skill and depression in college students: An analysis of the timing of self-disclosures. *Behavior Therapy, 13*, 271–282.

Joiner, Jr., T. E., Alfano, M. S., & Metalsky, G. I. (1992). When depression breeds contempt: Reassurance-seeking, self-esteem, and rejection of depressed college students by their roommates. *Journal of Abnormal Psychology, 101*, 165–173.

Joiner, Jr., T. E., & Barnett, J. (1994). A test of interpersonal theory of depression in children and adolescents using a projective technique. *Journal of Abnormal Child Psychology, 22*, 595–609.

Joiner, Jr., T. E., & Metalsky, G. I. (1995). A prospective test of an integrative interpersonal theory of depression: A naturalistic study of college roommates. *Journal of Personality and Social Psychology, 69*, 778–788.

Joyce, P. R. (1994). The epidemiology of depression and anxiety. In J. A. den Boer & J. M. A. Sitsen (Eds.), *Handbook of depression and anxiety* (pp. 57–69). New York: Marcel Dekker.

Joyce, P. R., Oakley-Browne, M. A., Wells, J. E., Bushnell, J. A., & Hornblow, A. R. (1990). Birth cohort trends in major depression: Increasing rates and earlier onset in New Zealand. *Journal of Affective Disorders, 18*, 83–89.

Justice, B., & Duncan, D. F. (1977). Child abuse as a work-related problem. *Corrective and Social Psychiatry and Journal of Behavior Technology, Methods and Therapy, 23*, 53–55.

Kanfer, F. H. (1970). Self-regulation: Research, issues, and speculations. In C. Neuringer & L. Michael (Eds.), *Behavior modification in clinical psychology.* New York: Appleton-Century-Crofts.

Kanfer, F. H., & Hagerman, S. (1981). The role of self-regulation. In L. P. Rehm (Ed.), *Behavior therapy for depression: Present status and future directions* (pp. 143–180). New York: Academic Press.

Kanfer, F. H., & Zeiss, A. M. (1983). Depression, interpersonal standard-setting, and judgments of self-efficacy. *Journal of Abnormal Psychology, 92*, 319–329.

Kazdin, A. E. (1983). Psychiatric diagnosis, dimensions of behavior therapy, and child behavior therapy. *Behavior Therapy, 14*, 73–99.

Keller, M. B., Shapiro, R. W., Lavori, P. W., & Wolfe, N. (1982). Relapse in RDC major depressive disorders. Analysis with the life table. *Archives of General Psychiatry, 39*, 911–915.

Kendall, P. C., Hollon, S. D., Beck, A. T., Hammen, C. L., & Ingram, R. E. (1987). Issues and recommendations regarding use of the Beck Depression Inventory. *Cognitive Therapy and Research, 11*, 289–299.

Kendall, P. C., Howard, B. L., & Hays, R. C. (1989). Self-referent speech and psychopathology: The balance of positive and negative thinking. *Cognitive Therapy and Research, 13*, 583–598.

Kendall, P. C., & Watson, D. (1989). *Anxiety and depression: Distinctive and overlapping features.* San Diego: Academic Press.

Kessler, R. C., McGonagle, K. A., Zhao, S., Nelson, C. B., Hughes, M., Eshleman, S., Wittchen, H. U., & Kendler, K. S. (1994). Lifetime and 12 month prevalence of results from the National Comorbidity Survey. *Archives of General Psychiatry, 51*, 8–19.

Klerman, G. L. (1986). The National Institute of Mental Health—Epidemiologic Catchment Area (NIMH-ECA) program: Background, preliminary findings and implications. *Social Psychiatry, 21*, 159–166.

Klerman, G., & Weissman, M. (1989). Increasing rates of depression. *Journal of the American Medical Association, 261*, 2229–2235.

Kraepelin (1904/1968). *Lecturew on clinical psychiatry.* New York: Hafner.

Kuiper, N. A., Derry, P. A., & MacDonald, M. R. (1982). Self-reference and person perception in depression. In G. Weary & H. Mirels (Eds.), *Integrations of clinical and social psychology* (pp. 263–284). New York: Oxford University Press.

Kuiper, N. A., Olinger, L. J., & MacDonald, M. R. (1988). Vulnerability and episodic cognitions in a self-worth contingency model of depression. In L. B. Alloy (Ed.), *Cognitive processes in depression* (pp. 289–309). New York: Guilford Press.

Lachman, R., Lachman, J. L., & Butterfield, E. C. (1979). *Cognitive psychology and formation processing: An introduction.* Hillsdale, NJ: Lawrence Erlbaum.

Lewin, K., Dembo, T., Festinger, L., & Sears, P. S. (1944). Level of aspiration. In J. M. Hunt (Ed.), *Personality and the behavior disorders* (Vol. 1) (pp. 195–217). New York: Ronald Press.

Locke, E. A., & Latham, G. P. (1990). *A theory of goal setting and task performance.* Englewood Cliffs, NJ: Prentice-Hall.

Lehmann, H. J. (1959). Psychiatric concepts of depression: Nomenclature and classification. *Canadian Psychiatric Association Journal Supplement, 4*, 1–12.

Lewinsohn, P. M. (1974). A behavioral approach to depression. In R. J. Friedman & M. M. Katz (Eds.), *The psychology of depression: Contemporary theory and research.* New York: John Wiley.

Lewinsohn, P. M., & Amenson, C. S. (1978). Some relations between pleasant and unpleasant mood-related events and depression. *Journal of Abnormal Psychology, 87*, 644–654.

Lewinsohn, P. M., & Graf, M. (1973). Pleasant activities and depression. *Journal of Consulting and Clinical Psychology, 41*, 261–268.

Lewinsohn, P. M., & Hoberman, H. M. (1982). Depression. In A. S. Bellack, M. Hersen, & A. E. Kazdin (Eds.), *International handbook of behavior modification and therapy.* New York: Plenum.

Lewinsohn, P. M., & Hoberman, H., Teri, L., & Hautzinger, M. (1985). An integrative theory of depression. In S. Reiss & R. R. Bootzin (Eds.), *Theoretical issues in behavior therapy* (pp. 331–361). New York: Academic Press.

Lewinsohn, P. M., & Libet, J. (1973). Pleasant events, activity schedules, and depression. *Journal of Abnormal Psychology, 79*, 291–295.

Lewinsohn, P. M., Mischel, W., Chaplin, C., & Barton, R. (1980). Social competence and depression: The role of illusory self-perceptions. *Journal of Abnormal Psychology, 89*, 203–217.

Lewinsohn, P. M., & Rosenbaum, M. (1987). Recall of parental behavior by acute depressives, remitted depressives, and nondepressives. *Journal of Personality and Social Psychology, 52*, 611–619.

Libet, J., & Lewinsohn, P. M. (1973). The concept of social skill with special reference to the behavior of depressed persons. *Journal of Consulting and Clinical Psychology, 40*, 304–312.

Liem, R., & Liem, J. H. (1988). The psychological effects of unemployment on workers and their families. *Journal of Social Issues, 44* (4), 87–105.

Matthews, G. (Ed.). (in press). *Cognitive science perspectives on personality and emotion.* New York: Elsevier Science.

McNeil, D., Arkowitz, H., Pritchard, B. (1987). The response of others to face-to-face interaction with depressed patients. *Journal of Abnormal Psychology, 96*, 341–344.

Metalsky, G. I., Halberstadt, L. J., & Abramson, L. Y. (1987). Vulnerability to depressive mood reactions: Toward a more powerful test of the diathesis-stress and causal mediation components of the reformulated theory of depression. *Journal of Personality and Social Psychology, 52*, 386–393.

Metalsky, G. I., Joiner, T. E., Hardin, T. S., & Abramson, L. Y. (1993). Depressive reactions to failure in a naturalistic setting: A test of the hopelessness and self-esteem theories of depression. *Journal of Abnormal Psychology, 102*, 101–109.

Miranda, J., & Persons, J. B. (1988). Dysfunctional attitudes are mood-state dependent. *Journal of Abnormal Psychology, 97*, 76–79.

Miranda, J., & Persons, J. B., & Byers, C. N. (1990). Endorsement of dysfunctional beliefs depends on current mood state. *Journal of Abnormal Psychology, 99*, 237–241.

Monroe, S. M., & Simons, A. D. (1991). Diathesis-Stress theories in the context of life stress research: Implications for the depressive disorders. *Psychological Bulletin, 110*, 406–425.

Murphy, J. M. (1986). Trends in depression and anxiety: Men and women. *Acta Psychiatric Scandinavia, 73*, 113–127.

Myers, J. F., Lynch, P. B., & Bakal, D. A. (1989). Dysthymic and hypomanic self-referent effects associated with depressive illness and recovery. *Cognitive Therapy and Research, 13*, 195–209.

Norman, D. A. (1968). Toward a theory of memory and attention. *Psychological Review, 75*, 522–536.

Nurcombe, B. (1992). The evolution and validity of the diagnosis of major depression in childhood and adolescence. In D. Cicchetti & S. L. Toth (Eds.), *Developmental perspectives on depression* (pp. 343–361). Rochester, New York: University of Rochester Press.

Oakley-Browne, M. A., Joyce, P. R., Wells, J. E., & Bushnell, J. A. (1989). Christchurch Psychiatric Epidemiology Study: II. Six month and other period prevalence of specific psychiatric disorders. *Australian and New Zealand Journal of Psychiatry, 23*, 327–340.

O'Connor, P., & Brown, G. W. (1984). Supportive relationships: Fact or fancy? *Journal of Social and Personal Relationships, 1*, 159–175.

Paykel, E. S. (1982). Life events and early environment. In E. S. Paykel (Ed.), *Handbook of affective disorders*. New York: Guilford Press.

Paykel, E. S. (1983). Methodological aspects of life events research. *Journal of Psychosomatic Research, 27*, 341–352.

Paykel, E. S., & Cooper, Z. (1992). Life events and social stress. In E. S. Paykel (Ed.), *Handbook of affective disorders* (2nd ed.) (pp. 292–318). New York: Guilford Press.

Penkower, L., Bromet, E., & Dew, M. (1988). Husbands' layoff and wives' mental health: A prospective analysis. *Archives of General Psychiatry, 45*, 994–1000.

Peterson, C., & Seligman, M. E. (1984). Causal explanations as risk factors for depression: Theory and evidence. *Psychological Review, 91*, 347–374.

Posnanski, E. D., Cook, S. C., & Carrol, B. J. (1979). A depression rating scale for children. *Pediatrics, 64*, 442–450.

Rehm, L. P. (1977). A self-control model of depression. *Behavior Therapy, 8*, 787–804.

Rogers, T. B., Kuiper, N. A., & Kirker, W. S. (1977). Self-reference and the encoding of personal information. *Journal of Personality and Social Psychology, 35*, 677–688.

Roth, D., & Rehm, L. P. (1980). Relationships among self-monitoring processes, memory, and depression. *Cognitive Therapy and Research, 4*, 149–157.

Sacco, W. P., & Dunn, V. K. (1990). Effect of actor depression on observer attributions: Existence and impact of negative attributions toward the depressed. *Journal of Personality and Social Psychology, 59*, 517–524.

Sandifer, M. G. (1972). Psychiatric diagnoses: Cross-national research findings. *Proceedings of the Royal Society of Medicine, 65*, 497–500.

Schwartz, J. L. (1974). Relationship between goal discrepancy and depression. *Journal of Consulting and Clinical Psychology, 42*, 309.

Scott, L., & O'Hara, M. W. (1993). Self-discrepancies in clinically anxious and depressed university students. *Journal of Abnormal Psychology, 102*, 282–287.

Segal, Z. V., Germar, & Williams (1997). *Differential cognitive response to a mood challenge following successful cognitive therapy or pharmacotherapy for unipolar depression.* In press.

Segal, Z. V., & Ingram, R. E. (1994). Mood priming and construct activation in tests of cognitive vulnerability to unipolar depression. *Clinical Psychology Review, 14*, 663–695.

Segrin, C. (1992). Specifying the nature of social skill deficits associated with depression. *Human Communication Research, 19*, 89–123.

Segrin, C., & Abramson, L. Y. (1994). Negative reactions to depressive behaviors: A communication theories analysis. *Journal of Abnormal Psychology, 103* (4), 655–668.

Segrin, C., & Dilliard, J. P. (1992). The interactional theory of depression: A meta-analysis of the research literature. *Journal of Social and Clinical Psychology, 11*, 43–70.

Seligman, M. E. P. (1975). *Helplessness: On depression, development, and death.* San Francisco: Freeman.

Seligman, M. E. P. (1990). Why is there so much depression today? The waxing of the individual and the waning of the common. In R. E. Ingram (Ed.), *Contemporary psychological approaches to depression* (pp. 1–10). New York: Plenum Press.

Shrout, P. E., Link, B. G., Dohrenwend, B. P., Skodol, A. E., Stueve, A., & Mirotznik, J. (1989). Characterizing life evens as risk factors for depression: The role of fateful loss events. *Journal of Abnormal Psychology, 98*, 460–467.

Siegel, S. J., & Alloy, L. B. (1990). Interpersonal perceptions and consequences of depressive-significant other relationships: A naturalistic study of college roommates. *Journal of Abnormal Psychology, 99*, 361–363.

Siegle, G., & Ingram, R. E. (1998). Modeling individual differences in negative information processing biases. In G. Matthews (Ed.), *Cognitive science perspectives on personality and emotion* (pp. 302–353). New York: Elsevier Science.

Skegg, K., & Cox, B. (1991). Suicide in New Zealand 1957–1986: The influence of age, period and birth-cohort. *Australian and New Zealand Journal of Psychiatry, 25*, 181–190.

Smith, T. W., & Allred, K. D. (1989). Major life events in depression and anxiety. In P. C. Kendall & D. Watson (Ed.), *Anxiety and depression: Distinctive and overlapping features* (pp. 205–223). San Diego: Academic Press.

Strauman, T. J. (1992). Self-guides, autobiographical memory, and anxiety and dysphoria: Toward a cognitive model of vulnerability to emotional distress. *Journal of Abnormal Psychology, 101*, 87–95.

Strauman, T. J. (1996). Self-beliefs, self-evaluation, and depression: A perspective on emotional vulnerability. In L. L. Martin & A. Tesser (Eds.), *Striving and feeling: Interactions among goals, affect, and self-regulation* (pp. 67–83). New Jersey: Lawrence Erlbaum.

Steinberg, L., Catalano, R. L., & Dooley, D. (1981). Economic antecedents of child abuse and neglect. *Child Development, 52*, 975–985.

Stephens, R. S., Hokanson, J. I., & Welker, R. (1987). Responses to depressed interpersonal behavior: Mixed reactions in a helping role. *Journal of Personality and Social Psychology, 52*, 1274–1282.

Stoker, D. H., Zurcher, L. A., & Fox, W. (1968). Women in psychotherapy: A cross-cultural comparison. *International Journal of Social Psychiatry, 15*, 5–22.

Strickland, B. R. (1988). Sex-related differences in health and illness. Special Issue: Women's health: Our minds, our bodies. *Psychology of Women Quarterly, 12*, 381–399.

Sweeney, P. D., Anderson, K., & Bailey, S. (1986). Attributional style in depression: A meta-analytic review. *Journal of Personality and Social Psychology, 50*, 974–991

Taylor, L., & Ingram, R. E. (1998). *Cognitive reactivity and depressotypic information processing in the children of depressed mothers.* Manuscript submitted for publication.

Teasdale, J. D. (1983). Negative thinking in depression: Cause, effect, or reciprocal relationship? *Advances in Behavior Research and Therapy, 5*, 3–25.

Teasdale, J. D. (1988). Cognitive vulnerability to persistent depression. *Cognition and Emotion, 2*, 247–274.

Teasdale, J. D., & Barnard, P. J. (1993). *Affect, cognition, and change.* Hillsdale, NJ: Lawrence Erlbaum.

Teasdale, J. D., & Dent, J. (1987). Cognitive vulnerability to depression: An investigation of two hypotheses. *British Journal of Clinical Psychology, 26*, 113–126.

Vanger, P. (1987). An assessment of social skill deficiencies in depression. *Comprehensive Psychiatry, 28*, 508–512.

Vinokur, A. D., Price, R. H., & Caplan, R. D. (1996). Hard times and hurtful partners: How financial strain affects depression and relationship satisfaction of unemployed persons and their spouses. *Journal of Personality and Social Psychology, 71*, 166–179.

Watson, D., & Clark, L. A. (1984). Negative affectivity: The disposition to experience negative emotional states. *Psychological Bulletin, 96*, 465–490.

Weissman, M. M., & Klerman, G. L. (1977). Sex differences and the epidemiology of depression. *Archives of General Psychiatry, 34*, 98–111.

Weissman, M. M., & Klerman, G. L. (1985). Gender and depression. *Trends in Neuroscience, 8*, 416–420.

Weissman, M. M., & Myers, J. K. (1978). Affective disorders in a US urban community: The use of Research Diagnostic Criteria in an epidemiological survey. *Archives of General Psychiatry, 35*, 1304–1311.

Wierzbicki, M. (1984). Social skills deficits and subsequent depressed mood in students. *Personality and Social Psychology Bulletin, 10*, 606–610.

Williams, J. M. G., & Oaksford, M. R. (1992). In D. J. Stein & J. E. Young (Eds.), *Cognitive science and clinical disorders* (pp. 129–150). San Diego: Academic Press.

Youngren, M. A., & Lewinsohn, P. M. (1980). The functional relationship between depression and problematic behavior. *Journal of Abnormal Psychology, 89*, 333–341.

9

Substance Abuse
Diagnosis, Comorbidity, and Psychopathology

PETER E. NATHAN
ANNE HELENE SKINSTAD
JAMES W. LANGENBUCHER

DSM-I, which appeared in 1952, grouped alcoholism and drug addiction, the sexual deviations (now called the paraphilias), and the antisocial and dyssocial reactions (now called antisocial personality disorder) together as the *sociopathic personality disturbances*. The latter phrase was meant to convey the view that persons who act out against society in these ways do so with pathological intent. While the etiology of these conditions was unknown, psychoanalytic explanations were most widely accepted. Alcoholism and drug addiction were also grouped with the personality disorders and the sexual deviations in *DSM-II* (1968), although no longer under the sociopathic umbrella. Clearly, the substance related disorders shared with the sexual deviations and antisocial behavior the distaste the drafters of these early *Diagnostic and Statistical Manuals* felt for behaviors that so seriously transgressed contemporary social norms. Not until publication of *DSM-III* in 1980, after more than a decade of research into genetic/biophysiological explanations, did the antisocial stigmatization begin to lift. Even today, diagnostic characterizations continue to be influenced by social mores and cultural norms, not simply, as many would have it, by objective empirical data (Schacht & Nathan, 1977).

Because of a growing literature pointing to the role of genetic and environmental factors in the etiology of these disorders, *DSM-III* and *DSM-III-R* (published in 1980 and 1987, respectively) eschewed the psychoanalytic flavor of the earlier manuals in favor of empirically based lists of signs and symptoms. Alcohol and drug abuse and dependence were thus separated from the renamed paraphilias and personality disorders. Moreover, the diagnostic manuals also began to distinguish the behavioral consequences of alcohol and drug abuse and dependence from their central nervous system consequences, which include intoxication, withdrawal, and the several alcohol- and drug-related deliria, dementias, personality disorders, and amnestic disorders. The effect was to distinguish more clearly the signs and symptoms of alcohol and drug *abuse* from those of alcohol and drug *dependence*. Previously, the consequences of abusive drinking and drug use, especially tolerance and withdrawal, were more strongly emphasized required. *DSM-III-R*, in contrast, emphasized the complex of behaviors associated with the *substance dependence syndrome*, the term which Edwards and Gross (1976) employed to refer to *preoccupation with* (as opposed to consequences of) the acquisition and consumption of substances. Factors in the development of these disorders were thus placed on an equal footing with their consequences.

The *DSM-IV* Substance Use Disorders Work Group sought to revisit these longstanding diagnostic questions empirically, with an extensive, multisite field trial (Cottler et al., 1995). Four questions asked by the work group are reviewed here. First, *should the new diagnostic criteria reemphasize or deemphasize tolerance and physical withdrawal symptoms?* Results showed that substantial proportions of amphetamine, hallucinogen, inhalant, PCP, and sedative users failed to report tolerance or withdrawal symptoms, even though from 86 to 99% of persons dependent on alcohol, cannabis, cocaine, opiates, sedatives, and nicotine reported one or both symptoms. Unable to generalize across substances, the work group opted instead for the criteria set qualifiers, "with physiological dependence" and "without physiological dependence," as a means of highlighting the issue for further scrutiny in preparation for *DSM-V*.

Second, *should the new diagnostic criteria continue to deemphasize social consequences and occupational impairment as criteria for dependence?* Results showed that substantial numbers of all substance users, except those using cocaine, reported *neither*. After further evaluation, the work group decided that social and occupational consequences of alcohol and drug use better described abuse than dependence, so these criteria became the principal cues to substance abuse.

Third, *could DSM-IV offer a shorter list of criteria for dependence, thereby easing the diagnostic task of clinicians and researchers?* As just observed, the work group moved the social consequences domain from dependence to abuse, so that abuse would represent misuse with adverse social or occupational consequences, but without evidence of compulsive use, tolerance, or withdrawal, while dependence would be signaled by compulsive use, with or without physiological accompaniments. By making these changes, the separate conceptual bases for substance abuse and dependence were clarified.

Fourth, *should abuse be made more distinct (as it was in DSM-III) and not just a residual category (as it became in DSM-III-R)?* As noted above, the work group reconceptualized both abuse and dependence; in doing so, it gave both abuse and dependence specific contexts and distinct sets of criteria, thereby making both more distinct and meaningful.

The Research Diagnostic Project

Other groups have also studied diagnostic issues associated with these disorders. The Research Diagnostic Project (RDP), located at the Center of Alcohol Studies, Rutgers University, has been one of the most productive. The RDP followed subjects at eight sites in five northeastern states, recruiting from four public and four private treatment settings, balanced across inpatient and outpatient facilities. Early RDP studies explored the reliability of lifetime *DSM-IV* diagnoses of alcohol, cannabis, cocaine and opiate abuse and dependence (Langenbucher, Morgenstern, Labouvie, & Nathan, 1994a). In particular, the reliability of the *DSM-IV* decision rules was found to be excellent, with an especially strong relationship observed between the reliability of a symptom and its centrality to the individual abuse pattern. This was true even though many subjects tended to use an unstable guesswork strategy, or even be open to suggestion when asked about less familiar symptoms.

Agreement among diagnostic systems was a particular concern of the drafters of *DSM-IV*, who worked hard to bring that instrument and *ICD-10* into greater diagnostic concordance. Langenbucher, Morgenstern, Labouvie, and Nathan (1994b) examined the diagnostic concordances of *DSM-III, DSM-IV*, and *ICD-10* for alcohol, the amphetamines, cannabis, cocaine, the hallucinogens, the opiates, PCP, and the sedative/hypnotics. Configural frequency analysis permitted a simultaneous look at agreement among the three systems. Langenbucher and his colleagues concluded that *ICD-10* is the most sensitive diagnostic system, diagnosing a larger number of cases than either of the two versions of the *DSM*. Generally satisfactory statistical agreement was found between *ICD-10* "harmful use" and *DSM* "abuse," each of which describes persons whose substance misuse has not reached the severity of dependence. Nonetheless, the three systems disagreed sharply on cases whose symptoms barely reached diagnostic threshold.

One of the most important remaining unanswered questions about the diagnosis of the addictions concerns the predictive validity of tolerance and symptoms of withdrawal (Blaine, Horton, & Towle, 1995; Schuckit, 1996). Although tolerance and withdrawal symptoms have been assumed to be associated with increased risk of medical problems and relapse, two recent reports (Carroll, Rounsaville, & Bryant, 1994; Rounsaville & Bryant, 1992) reported that neither tolerance nor withdrawal symptoms predicted deterioration in physical status or return to substance misuse. To facilitate the collection of data on this question, the drafters of *DSM-IV* specified that a diagnostic distinction be made between individuals with physiological dependence (those meeting at least three dependence criteria including tolerance, withdrawal, or both) and those without physiological dependence (those meeting at least three dependence criteria, none including tolerance or withdrawal).

Langenbucher and his colleagues (in press) compared and contrasted the predictive power of four sets of dependence criteria: the *DSM-IV* criteria for alcohol dependence with and without physiological dependence, an alternative dichotomous criterion for physiological dependence, and a dimensional measure of physiological dependence specifically designed to predict multiple indices of medical problems and relapse behavior. As had previously been reported, *DSM-IV* physiological alcohol dependence failed to predict medical problems or relapse behavior. Langenbucher et al. (in press) blamed this failure on operational problems in *DSM-IV*, rather than on a specific lack of predictive validity for physiological dependence. They concluded that physiological dependence can serve as a course specifier for alcohol problems. However, to serve this purpose, it must be more sensitively scaled than it is in *DSM-IV*, either by using alternative criteria for coding physiological dependence or by using a dimensional measure. In the design of *DSM-V*, these data suggest, it might be wise to choose a multistage or dimensional criterion to replace *DSM-IV*'s dichotomous criterion.

Diagnosticians are called upon to differentiate among cases that vary within as well as those that vary between diagnostic categories. Severity of illness is one of the most important of these within-category descriptive dimensions, influencing patient/treatment matching (McCrady & Langenbucher, 1996), reimbursement for various levels of care (Jencks & Goldman, 1987), and determination of length of stay (Mezzich & Sharfstein, 1985). Langenbucher, Sulesund, Chung, and Morgenstern (1996) compared the predictive efficiency of illness severity (defined as *DSM-IV* symptom count and scores on the Alcohol Dependence Scale and the Addiction Severity Index) with self-efficacy (scores on the Situational Confidence Questionnaire, reflecting patients' estimates of the likelihood of their remaining sober). The Alcohol Dependence Scale predicted four of five relapse indicators; self-efficacy did not contribute to this prediction. In fact, survival analyses found that subjects high on self-efficacy were more rather than less likely to return to drinking quickly following treatment. These findings clearly favor illness severity, particularly severity of physiological dependence, over self-efficacy as the best predictor of posttreatment behavior, thereby suggesting that physiological aspects of dependence may outweigh cognitive mechanisms in controlling relapse behaviors.

The sequential appearance of a disorder's symptoms is often predictable, in which case it contributes to valid diagnoses; when the staging of symptoms is not predictable, the validity of the diagnosis is lower. A study of the onset and staging of symptoms of alcohol abuse and dependence (Langenbucher & Chung, 1995) revealed three discrete stages: alcohol abuse, alcohol dependence, and accommodation to the illness. The model survived a rigorous series of tests for goodness of fit, supporting the construct validity of both alcohol abuse as a discrete first illness phase and alcohol dependence as distinct from and succeeding abuse. These findings support the familiar role for alcohol abuse as a distinct stop along the road to alcohol dependence (Helzer, 1994).

Alcoholism Typologies

Babor (1996) divides the history of typological thinking about alcoholics into three periods: a prescientific era of clinical speculation (1850–1940); the Jellinek period of "review and synthesis" (1941–1960); and the modern period (1960 to the present), characterized by increasingly sophisticated empirical research capable of much more quickly establishing the validity (or lack thereof) of new typologies.

Babor and Lauerman (1986) identify 39 classifications of alcoholics proposed between 1850 and 1940. Representative typologies were Carpenter's (1850), which divided what he called "oinomania" into acute, periodic, and chronic forms; Kerr's (1893), which separated "inebriates" into periodic and habitual varieties; Crothers' (1911), which distinguished among continuous drinkers, explosive inebriates, and periodic drinkers; and Wingfield's (1919), which proposed four main types of alcoholics: pseudodipsomaniacs, chronic sober alcoholics, chronic inebriate alcoholics, and true dipsomaniacs. The most influential of these early typologies was Knight's (1937), which distinguished between essential and reactive alcoholism; this distinction foreshadowed Cloninger's (1987) division of alcoholics into two subtypes, based on their own and their parents' drinking histories as well as their drunken comportment.

In 1960, E. M. Jellinek published one of the classics of the addiction literature, *The Disease Concept of Alcoholism.* It described a typology that continues to influence the field today, despite subsequent empirical advances that have brought a number of Jellinek's conceptualizations and assumptions into question. As table 9.1 shows, Jellinek differentiated among four principal types of alcoholics—alpha, beta, gamma, and delta—by identifying variations in three key factors: etiological elements, alcoholic process elements, and damage elements. Despite the originality of Jellinek's conception of gamma and delta alcoholism, and the ready acceptance of that distinction by clinicians, Jellinek's typology has generated surprisingly little empirical research, either to validate the classification or to relate specific types to specific treatments.

Cloninger's neurogenetic model (1987) is the most influential of the post-Jellinek substance-abuse typologies. Unlike other contemporary typologies, the most prominent of which are Morey and Skinner's hybrid model (1986), Zucker's developmental theory (1987), and Babor and colleagues' vulnerability and severity model (1992), Cloninger's typology has been subjected to extensive independent validation efforts. Developed from observations derived from his prospective adoption studies (Bohman, Sigvardsson, & Cloninger, 1981; Cloninger, Bohman, & Sigvardsson, 1981), Cloninger's theory distinguishes two subtypes of alcoholism, Type 1 and Type 2. This distinction recalls Knight's (1937) essential and reactive alcoholic subtypes, as well as Jellinek's (1960) gamma and delta alcoholics. The alcoholism of Cloninger's Type 1 cases is influenced more by environmental than genetic factors; they experience a later onset of problem drinking, report physical but not psychological dependence, and experience considerable guilt about their alcoholism. Type 2 alcoholics, who typically trace a family history of

Table 9.1 Characteristics of Four of Jellinek's Species of Alcoholism[1,2]

	Species			
Characteristics	Alpha	Beta	Gamma	Delta
Etiological Elements				
Psychological vulnerability	High	Low	High	Low
Physiological vulnerability	Low	Low	High	High
Sociocultural influences	Low/moderate	Low/moderate	Low/moderate	High
Economic influences	Low/moderate	Low/moderate	Low/moderate	High
Alcoholic Process Elements				
Nature of dependence	Psychological	No dependence	Psychological, then physical	Physical, then psychological
Acquired tissue tolerance	Low	Low	High	High
Loss of control	Low[3]	Low	High	Low
Inability to abstain	Low	Low	Low	High
Progression	Slight	Slight	Marked	Slow
Nutritional/physical habits	Good to poor	Poor	Poor	Fair
Damage Elements				
Physical/mental	Low/moderate	High	Low to High	Low to High
Socioeconomic	Low/moderate	Low	High	High

SOURCE: Babor & Dolinsky, 1988, in Babor, 1996, p. 11.

1. Adapted from Jellinek, 1960.
2. Epsilon alcoholism, the fifth species, is not included in this table because Jellinek considered knowledge of that subtype to be too scant to describe in detail.
3. According to Jellinek, alpha alcoholism is characterized by deliberate, undisciplined drinking.

alcoholism, develop extensive alcohol problems early, which are usually accompanied by serious behavioral problems.

Hill (1995a) drew a similar distinction between alcoholic women, separating them into two types that closely parallel Cloninger's Type 1 and Type 2 alcoholism in males. The alcohol abuse of the first type, characterized by late onset (with a peak between the ages of 35 and 49), is influenced most heavily by environmental factors; that of the second has an early onset (between 18 and 24 years of age) and a heavy family loading.

Cloninger differentiated his alcoholic subtypes by distinct personality traits and by the specific neurotransmitter systems that mediate their expression, as well as by behavior and family history. Type 1 alcoholics are low on behavioral activation (novelty seeking) and high on behavioral inhibition (harm avoidance) and behavioral maintenance (reward dependence); Type 2 alcoholics are just the opposite. The principal monoamine neuromodulator for behavioral activation is dopamine; behavioral inhibition is modulated centrally by serotonin; behavioral maintenance is modulated centrally by norepinephrine. This hypothesized linkage among traits of personality and behavior, neurotransmitter systems, and genetic/constitutional factors makes Cloninger's theory broadly explanatory, highly speculative, and especially heuristic. For these reasons, it is not surprising that the theory has generated a number of independent validation efforts. Some have supported aspects of the model (e.g., Farren & Dinan, 1996; Hegerl, Lipperheide, Juckel, Schmidt, & Rommelspacher, 1995), while others have yielded more equivocal findings (e.g., Fils-Aime et al., 1996; Hallman, von Knorring, & Oreland, 1996; Howard, Kivlahan, & Walker, 1997). While Cloninger's complex model has not been consistently supported by independent investigators, their efforts at validation have been sufficiently positive to encourage further efforts.

One of the few typologies proposed for nonalcoholic substance abusers is the cigarette smoker typology proposed by Schiffman, Kassel, Paty, Gnys, and Zettler-Segal (1994) that distinguishes between regular smokers and "chippers" on the basis of smoking pattern and of smoking motive. Regular smokers meet the *DSM-IV* criteria for nicotine dependence. Chippers typically smoke five or fewer cigarettes a day; they are not nicotine dependent and do not meet the criteria for substance abuse. As reflected by self-report scores on the two standard smoking motive scales, chippers scored significantly lower than regular smokers on all smoking motives (Schiffman et al., 1994). In general, they reported their smoking to be influenced primarily by social and sensory motives; the smoking of regular smokers was motivated more by addiction and habit. These findings hold out the possibility that smoker subtypes might prove helpful in designing smoking cessation treatments to help addicted smokers defeat their addictions.

Epidemiology

Between 14 and 16 million Americans meet *DSM-IV* criteria for alcohol abuse or dependence (NIAAA, 1997) while between 4 and 6 million Americans, many of whom also abuse alcohol, abuse or are dependent on illegal drugs (NIDA, 1994). More than 45 million Americans are dependent on the nicotine in cigarettes. Overall, the economic costs to this country of substance abuse totaled more than $200 billion in 1990 (Horgan, 1993).

The annual consumption of alcohol by the average American, a little more than two gallons of ethanol a year, has remained remarkably steady over the past 140 years, with only two deviations—a sharp decline during the Prohibition years of 1919 to 1933 and a modest increase, then an equally modest but continuing decrease, after 1960 (Horgan, 1993). Rates of alcohol abuse and dependence appear to have remained stable over the same period. By contrast, drug abuse rose sharply following the end of World War II, then stabilized in the mid-1970s to the present (NIDA, 1994).

Substance use and abuse vary with age, gender, race, ethnicity, and socioeconomic status (NIAAA, 1997; NIDA, 1994). Rates of substance abuse among men between the ages of 18 and 44 are more than double overall rates, while those for women in the same age range are roughly a quarter of the overall rates. Rates of substance abuse for men and women between 45 and 64 plummet to half the overall rates, even more so beyond the age of 65 (Dawson, Grant, Chou, & Pickering, 1995). At most ages, rates of substance abuse by African Americans and Hispanic Americans of both sexes are slightly higher than for Caucasians.

The NIMH Epidemiologic Catchment Area Study (Eaton et al., 1984), which surveyed the psychiatric status of more than 20,000 residents of five U.S. cities and towns in the early 1980s, found an average lifetime prevalence rate of 17 percent for the substance use disorders in New Haven, Baltimore, and St. Louis (Robins et al., 1984).

The 1992 National Longitudinal Alcohol Epidemiologic Study of almost 43,000 U.S. adults 18 years of age and over, selected at random from a nationally representative sample of households, reported that 44 percent of U.S. adults are current drinkers, 22 percent are former drinkers, and 34 percent are lifetime abstainers (Dawson et al., 1995). Between 5 and 6% of the sample regularly consumed five or more drinks at least once a week. Predictably, men were twice as likely as women to report having drunk five or more drinks at least once, and more than four times as likely to report doing so at least weekly.

The 1984 National Alcohol Survey undertook a detailed comparison of drinking by 723 African-American and 743 Caucasian men (Jones-Webb, Hsiao, & Hannan, 1995). Less affluent black men experienced more drinking problems and more adverse drinking consequences than less affluent white men, while the reverse was true for more affluent black and white men. Explaining their findings, Jones-Webb and colleagues speculate that "black men in the lower classes may be more likely than white men in the lower classes to experience overt forms of discrimination; less affluent black men also may be more likely than less affluent white men to live in communities where there is great police surveillance and fewer health and social resources" (p. 626). As their social class increases, however, African Americans experience a greater reduction in the negative consequences of abusive drinking than Caucasians, perhaps because they monitor their drinking behavior more closely and take more care to avoid drinking situations that might put their hard-won middle-class status at risk.

Sociodemographic factors also affect smoking behavior, as a study by Rose, Chassin, Presson, and Sherman (1996) of young adults who participated in a longitudinal study of the natural history of cigarette smoking suggested. Initial data collection took place between 1980 and 1983, when the 8,503 original subjects were 6th to 12th graders. In 1993–94, a follow-up of 6,223 subjects, now aged 21–34, was completed. Subjects with low educational levels were more likely to smoke, believed less in the negative health effects and more in the positive psychological benefits of smoking, valued a healthy lifestyle less, and reported having more friends who smoked. While gender differences in smoking rates were not found, significant differences between men and women in the mediators that influenced their smoking were: compared with men, smoking among women was more strongly related to the perceived psychological benefits of smoking, number of friends who smoked, and health beliefs about smoking.

Markers of Risk for Substance-Related Disorders

Family History

A family history of alcoholism is the strongest single predictor of heightened risk for alcoholism (Cotton, 1979; Cadoret, 1980). Three different research programs (Cloninger et al., 1981; Goodwin et al., 1974; Kendler, Heath, Neale, Kessler, & Eaves, 1992) have demonstrated that family history of alcoholism increases risk of alcoholism in the children of alcoholics because still unidentified mediators of risk are genetically transmitted, rather than because of the psychological or social environment in which the children are reared. There is also evidence that drug abuse runs in families and that it does so because mediators of risk are genetically transmitted (Cadoret, Troughton, O'Gorman, & Heywood, 1986).

Schuckit and Smith (1996) reported on the results of an 8.2-year follow-up of a group of men in their early 30s, originally evaluated after being chosen at random from lists of university students and nonacademic staff. Fifty-four percent of the men were family history positive (FH+) for paternal alcoholism; in all other relevant respects, the FH+ group was indistinguishable from the matched family history negative (FH–) controls. At the 8.2-year follow-up, the prevalence of *DSM-III-R* alcohol abuse and dependence among the FH+ men was 14.1 and 28.6%, respectively, as compared to 6.6 and 10.8% for the FH– men.

Two smoking behaviors, initiation (whether a nonsmoker becomes a smoker) and persistence (whether a smoker quits smoking or continues to smoke), also appear to be genetically transmitted (Heath & Martin, 1993; Heath et al., 1993). Heath and his colleagues obtained self-report data on smoking initiation from three large American and Australian samples of adult twins; data on smoking persistence were gathered from questionnaire responses by Australian twin pairs. Differences in concordance rates between identical and fraternal twins for both smoking initiation and persistence were so substantial that the genetic contribution to the risk of becoming or remaining a smoker was estimated to be close to 50% in both men and women.

Neurophysiological Factors

ERP: Auditory and Visual P300 Several event-related potential (ERP) studies dating from 1984 have detected diminished P300 amplitudes in response to visual stimuli in both chronic alcoholics (Biggins, Mackay, Poole, & Fein, 1995) and nonalcoholic, FH+ males (Begleiter, Porjesz, Bihari, & Kissin, 1984; O'Connor, Hesselbrock & Tasman, 1986; Hill & Steinhauer, 1993). As a consequence, reduced visually evoked P300 amplitude is now considered a marker of heightened risk for alcohol dependence.

ERP responses to auditory stimuli have not been associated as consistently with P300 amplitude reductions as have visual stimuli. Hill, Steinhauer, and Locke (1995) observed no differences in the amplitude of the P300 component of the ERP to two auditory stimuli among alcoholics from "high-density, multigenerational families," first-degree nonalcoholic relatives from the same families, and nonalcoholic controls from low-density families. This finding contrasts with the same authors' report of reliable visual P300 amplitude differences in high- and low-risk children from the same high- and low-density families.

Ramachandran, Porjesz, Begleiter, and Litke (1996) found differences in the amplitude of the auditory P300 between the young adult sons of alcoholics and age- and sex-matched controls, hypothesizing that reduced auditory and visual P300 amplitudes are signs of cortical inhibition, which interferes with the ability to respond to novel stimuli and reflects a developmental lag or arrest of brain maturation in high-risk youth. Thus, "the P300 seems to be a reliable marker for alcoholism in both the auditory and visual paradigm in both children and young adult males at risk for the development of the disease" (p. 14).

Inborn Tolerance and Level of Reaction to Alcohol and Drugs Nathan and Lipscomb (1979) and Lipscomb, Carpenter, and Nathan (1979) reported that some nonalcoholic individuals given a challenge dose of alcohol showed little body sway in response to the challenge while others swayed substantially. Degree of body sway was associated with subsequent development of tolerance to alcohol: individuals who were relatively unresponsive to the challenge dose turned out to be more likely to demonstrate substantial tolerance following a period of sustained drinking than those who showed significant body sway following ingestion of the challenge dose. Nathan and his colleagues hypothesized that body sway following an alcohol challenge in nonabusive drinkers might be a marker for heightened alcoholism risk.

Schuckit and his colleagues (Schuckit, 1985; Schuckit, 1994a; Schuckit & Gold, 1988) subsequently incorporated a measure of response to alcohol challenge in their longitudinal study of multiple markers of risk of alcoholism development, terming it level of reaction to alcohol (LR). In a follow-up of their longitudinal sample of FH+ and FH– males, Schuckit and Smith (1996) reported that LR at the age of 20 years was significantly associated with later alcoholism. They consider "these data consistent with the conclusion that LR might be a mediator of the alcoholism risk" (p. 202), explaining, as had Nathan and his colleagues, that young drinkers in whom alcohol consumption induces little effect might well drink more over time to achieve a stronger effect than those on whom it has a stronger initial impact to begin with.

Peer Influences

The importance of peer influences on initiation of drinking and drug use by adolescents has been well documented (e.g., Jessor & Jessor, 1977; Newcomb & Bentler, 1986). Delinquent and rebellious behavior and heavy drinking and drug use by peers are significant risk factors in substance abuse; conversely, the decision not to drink or use drugs or not to commit rebellious or delinquent acts appears to be a substantial deterrent to friends' substance use and abuse. A recent study of race and sex differences in the impact of risk factors on substance-use initiation (Gottfredson & Koper, 1996) found that adolescent peer drinking, drug use, rebelliousness, and delinquency were more closely linked to substance-use initiation in Caucasians than in African Americans and in African-American males than in African-American females. Additional confirmatory studies are required before these race and gender differences can be accepted as proven.

Alcohol and Drug Expectancies

One of the most productive foci of psychological research on risk factors for alcoholism during the past decade has been alcohol expectancies, defined as positive and negative expectations of the effects of alcohol intoxication on behavior. Alcohol expectancies appear to interact with personality risk factors to predict drinking behavior and seem to mediate the impact of other risk factors, including family history of alcoholism, on subsequent alcohol consumption (Goldman, Brown, Christiansen, & Smith, 1991).

Smith, Goldman, Greenbaum, and Christiansen (1995) employed a three-wave longitudinal design to study the alcohol expectancies of male and female adolescents ages 12 to 14 years during the two-year period when many of them first tried alcohol. Their expectations of social facilitation from alcohol, as measured by the adolescent form of the Alcohol Expectancy Questionnaire (AEQ; Brown, Goldman, Inn, & Anderson, 1980) and their subsequent drinking influenced each other reciprocally and positively: the more they drank, the more positive their subsequent expectancy endorsement of social facilitation from alcohol; and the more positive their expectancy endorsement, the greater their subsequent drinking. Smith and his colleagues suggested that these findings confirm the value of efforts to change expectancies in the attempt to modify abusive adolescent drinking.

Deckel, Hesselbrock, and Bauer (1995) tested for a relationship between alcohol-related expectancies and anterior and parietal brain functioning in men in their early 20s at risk to develop alcoholism because they were FH+, had received a diagnosis of antisocial personality, or both. None of the subjects had an alcohol or drug abuse history. Neuropsychological test results were found to predict AEQ scores as did left versus right hemisphere difference scores from frontal EEG leads. These findings suggest that alcohol-related expectancies may be biologically determined in part by frontal/prefrontal systems, and that inherited dysfunctions in these systems might function as risk factors for alcohol abuse or dependence.

After developing separate effect expectancy questionnaires for marijuana and cocaine, Schafer and Brown (1991) hypothesized that expectancies for marijuana would be similar to those for alcohol because the pharmacological effects of the two are similar and both are socially facilitative. In contrast, they expected the expectancies for cocaine, a CNS stimulant, to differ substantially from those for either alcohol, a CNS sedative, or marijuana. As predicted, the six marijuana effect expectancies overlapped considerably with those of alcohol; common expectancy domains included social and sexual facilitation, tension reduction, cognitive and behavioral impairment, and cognitive enhancement. While two of the cocaine effect expectancies, global positive effects and relaxation and tension reduction, were similar to those of alcohol and marijuana, two others, anxiety and physiological arousal, both properties of stimulants, were unique to cocaine.

Gender Differences in Substance Use and Abuse

Patterns of Substance Use and Abuse

At every age, men still use and abuse alcohol and drugs at higher rates than women, although these rates have tended to converge in recent years. Thus, the percentage of both men and women who drink or use drugs has declined in recent years; likewise, fewer women and men drink heavily or abuse drugs now than a decade ago (NIAAA, 1997; NIDA, 1994). However, the declines have been smaller for women (Lex, 1996) because rates of abusive drinking and drug use by younger women are higher and have shown smaller reductions than those of older women (Celentano & McQueen, 1984; Curlee, 1970). Much of this difference likely reflects the greater availability of drinking- and drug-related opportunities for younger women as a function of the increasing scope of women's roles in recent decades (Skinstad et al. 1996; Wilsnack & Wilsnack 1995).

Risk Factors for and Social and Familial Consequences of Substance Abuse

In most societies, including our own, substance-abusing women are judged more harshly than substance-abusing men. Women's substance abuse is seen as incompatible with their traditional nurturing roles as wife and mother (Reed, 1985). In some women, this harsh societal judgment maintains or accelerates the progression of substance abuse by augmenting their experience of guilt and sense of alienation from family and friends (Celentano & McQueen, 1984).

Girls are at substantially greater risk of physical and sexual victimization than boys. Moreover, girls who have been physically or sexually victimized are at markedly greater risk than boys to develop adverse psychological and behavioral consequences. Data from a large national survey of women's drinking (Wilsnack & Klassen, 1992; Wilsnack, Vogeltanz, Klassen, & Harris, 1994; Wilsnack, Wilsnack, & Klassen, 1984) reveal that childhood sexual abuse is strongly predictive of heavy episodic drinking, intoxication, drinking-related problems, alcohol-dependence symptoms, use of drugs other than alcohol, depression, binge eating, and vaginismus in adulthood. History of childhood sexual victimization is substantially higher among alcoholic women than either community controls or women arrested for drunken driving (Miller & Downs, 1996). And alcoholic women who have experienced childhood sexual abuse are both more vulnerable to repeated victimization (Miller & Downs, 1996) and more likely to enter into conflictual, violent relationships (Frieze & Schafer, 1984; Skinstad et al., 1996). Although less so than men, substance-dependent women are also more likely to abuse their partners physically than women who are not substance dependent (Frieze & Schafer, 1984).

Blood Alcohol Concentration, Alcohol Metabolism, and Alcohol Effects

Until recently, most studies of the effects of ethanol on the human body involved only males, both because alcoholic males were much more numerous and because it was assumed that men and women did not differ in routes or rates of alcohol metabolism. Recent research, however, has shown that women attain higher blood alcohol concentrations (BACs) than men after ingestion of equivalent amounts of alcohol and that, as a consequence, women experience aversive alcohol effects at higher rates than men at equivalent dosage levels (Arthur, Lee, & Wright, 1984).

The principal reason for this difference between men and women in alcohol metabolism stems from the fact that, more alcohol is metabolized in the stomachs of men than in those of women because men possess more gastric alcohol dehydrogenase than women (Lieber, 1996). Although most ethanol is metabolized by the liver, some alcohol dehydrogenase activity and consequent "first-pass metabolism" takes place in the stomach; metabolism of alcohol in the stomach helps protect against excessive intoxication by reducing the amount of alcohol that enters the bloodstream.

These differences in alcohol metabolism and in body mass between men and women have led experts to define moderate drinking by women as 4 to 9 standard units of alcohol per week and heavy drinking as more than 10 standard units a week (Skinstad et al., 1996); by contrast, moderate drinking by men is generally defined as 7 to 15 standard units a week, heavy drinking as more than 15 standard units. (A 12-ounce beer, 5 ounces of wine, or a 1.5 ounce "shot" of spirits constitutes a standard unit; each contains the equivalent of about one-half ounce of 190 proof ethanol.)

Health Consequences of Alcohol Abuse

The fact that women metabolize alcohol less efficiently and, consequently, reach higher BAC levels than men at equivalent consumption levels helps explain why women are more vulnerable to a variety of medical consequences of alcohol abuse than men. The incidence of chronic liver disease is higher in women (Morgan & Sherlock, 1977): they are more susceptible to liver cirrhosis (Rankin, 1977) and they die from cirrhosis at higher rates than men (Hållen & Krook, 1963). Beyond a certain level, alcohol consumption also seems to increase estrogen levels in alcoholic postmenopausal women; these changes may increase the severity of liver disease (Gavaler, 1995, 1996). Moreover, daily consumption of two or more standard units of alcohol substantially increases the risk of breast cancer in middle-aged women (Hill, 1995b), while chronic excessive alcohol consumption also has a deleterious effect on bone mineral density in older women (Hill, 1995b). By contrast, moderate alcohol consumption is associated with a beneficial decrease in the incidence of various kinds of heart disease in older women (Gavaler, 1996).

Psychiatric Comorbidity

Women who abuse alcohol experience more psychiatric comorbidity than men who abuse alcohol (Robins & Regier, 1991). While 44% of male alcoholics experience one or more additional psychiatric disorders during their lifetimes, 65% of female alcoholics do so (Helzer, Burnam, & McEvoy, 1991). The most common comorbid psychiatric disorders in substance-abusing women are depression (Hesselbrock & Hesselbrock, 1996; Hill, 1995b) and anxiety disorders (Skinstad et al., 1996); the most common psychiatric disorder among substance-abusing men is antisocial personality disorder (Hesselbrock & Hesselbrock, 1996).

Psychopathology of the Substance-Related Disorders

Interpersonal Aggression

One of the most common consequences of amphetamine intoxication is interpersonal aggression (Ray & Ksir, 1996); aggression is also a prominent feature of the paranoid psychosis that sometimes follows chronic amphetamine abuse (Maisto, Galizio, & Connors, 1995).

Cocaine intoxication also leads to interpersonal aggression. When two large treatment samples of cocaine abusers completed the Cocaine Negative Consequences Checklist, they reported that irritability and agitation, suspiciousness and paranoia, and anger were the most common psychological consequences of cocaine use, while arguments with coworkers, arguments with family members, and physical fights were the most common social problems (Michalec et al., 1996).

It is sometimes possible to predict drug-induced violence before it occurs. Frequent early use of drugs, especially alcohol, marijuana, and cocaine, turned out to be a strong predictor of subsequent violent behavior for both men and women in a recent large-scale study of young adult African-American polydrug abusers (Friedman, Kramer, Kreisher, & Granick, 1996).

The case for a link between interpersonal aggression and alcohol use and abuse is also well documented. Alcohol intoxication induces aggression in some persons, probably by disinhibiting usual social constraints against violence and aggressivity (Nathan, 1993). Extensive data tie alcohol intoxication and abuse to criminal behavior and family violence (NIAAA, 1997). Summarizing two decades of research findings, Nathan (1993) concluded that

> the relationship linking alcohol and aggression remains firmly established in our culture. This relationship appears to depend on a balance of expectancies and drug effects. . . . When beverage alcohol consumed in moderate quantities exerts an aggression-inducing effect, it most likely does so because the drinker believes that to be its effect rather than because of any drug-induced effect. (p. 463)

Giancola and Zeichner (1995) examined the cumulative influence of aggressive personality traits, degree of subjective intoxication, and blood alcohol concentration (BAC) on aggression in young adult males and females. Subjects competed against a (nonexistent) "opponent" by giving electric shocks to, and receiving them from, the opponent under both provoking and nonprovoking conditions. Provocation was defined by the strength of the shocks subjects received. Aggression was defined by the intensity of shocks given. For males in the high-provocation condition, aggressive personality traits, subjective intoxication, and BAC all predicted physical aggression. None of these variables was an effective predictor of aggression in women. This latter finding replicates prior failures to observe heightened aggressivity following intoxication among females in experimental settings (e.g., Gustafson, 1991). Heightened aggression might have been observed in intoxicated women if a different laboratory analogue had been used, perhaps one in which the aggression were not as blatantly physical as is shock administration.

Using the same laboratory paradigm, Chermack and Taylor (1995) explored the two principal competing explanations for the effects of alcohol on aggression: the pharmacological explanation and the expectancy/disinhibition explanation. Male college students over the age of 21 were divided into a group already convinced alcohol increases aggression and a group convinced it decreases aggression. Subjects were then randomly assigned to active-placebo (ginger ale and a small amount of alcohol) or high-alcohol dose (in ginger ale) conditions. Subjects who consumed the high-alcohol dose delivered significantly higher levels of shock than those who consumed the active-placebo, regardless of preexisting alcohol expectancies. Intoxicated subjects who believed that alcohol increases aggressive behavior delivered more intense shocks in the high- but not in the low-provocation condition. Chermack and Taylor concluded from these findings that the pharmacological effects of alcohol on aggression play the primary role in the alcohol-aggression nexus. Their use of an analogue aggression measure, however, tempers our acceptance of this explanation: real-world aggression is expressed in a more complex manner.

Moss and Kirisci (1995) examined relations between real-world aggressivity and alcohol consumption in a correlational study of alcohol- and drug-misusing dependent adolescents. Both aggressivity in the real world and the symptoms of conduct disorder, which include overt aggressivity, correlated significantly and positively with alcohol consumption, confirming the link between aggressivity and alcohol consumption observed in the laboratory analogue studies just reviewed.

We conclude that the relationship between interpersonal aggression and substance abuse—especially alcohol, cocaine, and the amphetamines—is strong and that both the pharmacological effects of substances and expectancies/disinhibition associated with their effects mediate this relationship.

Neuropsychological/Cognitive Functioning

Chronic alcohol and drug abuse often lead to cognitive impairment, typically involving visual, spatial, or verbal memory, problem solving, cognitive efficiency, and visuospatial perception (Beatty, Hames, Blanco, Nixon, & Tivis, 1996; Berry, Van Gorp, Herzberg, & Hinkin, 1993; Nixon, Tivis, & Parsons, 1995). Most studies have found that from one third to one half of substance-abusing persons have measureable cognitive deficits (e.g., Fals-Stewart, 1996; Fals-Stewart & Lucente, 1994). Speculations on the etiology of these deficits include substance neurotoxicity (Freund, 1982), heredity (Hegadus, Tarter, Hill, Jacob, & Winsten, 1984), avitaminosis (Victor, Adams, & Collins, 1971), and physical trauma (Wetzig & Hardin, 1990) . Depending on the length and severity of the substance abuse, the length of abstinence, and the age of the abuser, the cognitive dysfunctions may diminish with abstinence and, after a few months, largely or completely disappear (Eckardt, Stapleton, Rawlings, Davis, & Grodin, 1995; O'Malley, Gawin, Heaton, & Kleber, 1989). In older abusers, however, especially those whose abuse histories have been severe, the substance-related cognitive impairments may diminish but never disappear (Goldman, Williams, & Klisz, 1983).

Recently, research on this topic has moved from an exclusive focus on the severe deficits of older chronic alcohol and drug abusers to the more modest impairments of younger social drinkers. Nichols and Martin (1996) recorded ERPs from young, male social drinkers under a drug condition designed to induce mild disorientation and a drug placebo. Subjects includeed both heavy and light social drinkers. The amplitude of the P300 ERP component was significantly lower in heavy than light social drinkers, suggesting that the heavy social drinkers may already have begun to develop an information-processing impairment. Integrated with prior findings indicating that alcoholics typically demonstrate a diminished visual P300, these results suggest that this marker of impairment in information processing may represent an early sign in heavy social drinkers of the serious impairments in cognitive functioning that afflict many chronic alcoholics.

Similarly, after following several hundred adolescents for several years, Scheier and Botvin (1995) found early adolescent drug and alcohol use to be associated with small but significant declines in cognitive and self-management strategies; in middle adolescence, these declines increased. Scheier and Botvin's conclusion: "Early drug use may impede acquisition of critical thinking skills and hinder the learning of important cognitive strategies required for successful transition to adulthood" (p. 379).

Sexual Functioning

Prolonged alcohol and drug abuse impair sexual functioning (Fahrner, 1987; Schiavi, 1990), probably by affecting hormonal mechanisms and, in males, testicular function (Bannister & Lowosky, 1987; Van Thiel et al., 1980).

Schiavi, Stimmel, Mandeli, and White (1995) recently explored the impact of history of alcoholism on sexual function as well as marital adjustment, sleep-related erections, sleep disorders, and hormone levels in a small sample of abstinent males. Two months to three years after achieving stable sobriety, they were compared to a group of nonalcoholic males; both groups of subjects were between 28 and 50 years of age. The subjects and their sexual partners received a thorough psychosexual evaluation, as well as polygraphic assessment of sleep pattern, assessment of nocturnal penile tumescence, and nocturnal sequential blood sampling. The alcoholic men did not differ from the comparison group along any dimension of sexuality or in number of sexual problems, even though their sexual partners reported significant marital dissatisfaction. In other words, despite these men's history of severe alcohol dependence, they had been able to maintain normal sexual function, even in disturbed marriages. Schiavi and his coauthors note the absence of hepatic or gonadal disease or medication regimens in their alcoholic subjects. In prior studies, these factors may have been associated with impaired sexual function.

Substance use also affects safe-sex practices by increasing sexual risk taking. Gordon and Carey (1996) explored the effects of alcohol intoxication on condom use in a laboratory-based inquiry. Young male nonalcoholic subjects, moderate to heavy drinkers, were randomly assigned to either alcohol or alcohol placebo conditions. Subjects in the alcohol condition drank sufficient vodka and tonic to achieve blood alcohol levels of 0.08%; controls drank only tonic. All subjects then completed a battery of self-report measures of condom and AIDS-related knowledge, motivation to use condoms, and behavioral self-efficacy for condom use. Subjects who had consumed alcohol tended to report more negative attitudes toward condom use and lower self-efficacy about their ability to use condoms than subjects who had consumed only tonic.

Parker, Harford, and Rosenstock (1994) also examined relationships between sexual risk taking and drug and alcohol use in a very large group of nonabusing young adults. After controlling for age, education, and family income, they found that quantity and frequency of use of marijuana, cocaine, and alcohol were related significantly to sexual risk taking, defined as the degree to which these men and women failed to take reasonable precautions against unintended pregnancy and sexually transmitted disease. Koopman, Rosario, and Rotheram-Borus (1994) drew the same conclusion in a study of relationships between lifetime and current drug and alcohol use and sexual risk taking among several hundred male and female adolescent runaways, predominantly African American and Hispanic, living in four residential centers in New York City. Greater frequency of substance use, which included alcohol, marijuana, and cocaine, was related significantly to more sexual partners and less frequent condom use. Both behaviors substantially increased risk for HIV/AIDS.

Comorbidity of the Substance-Related Disorders

Substance abusers experience more comorbid psychopathology than do persons with any other psychiatric syndrome (Ross, Glaser, & Germanson, 1988; Wilson, Nathan, O'Leary, & Clark, 1996). Schuckit (1994b) believes the common co-occurrence of substance abuse and other forms of psychopathology—in particular, depression and anxiety—to reflect base rates. Since substance abuse, depression, and anxiety are all very common, chance alone would explain their frequent co-occurrence. Schuckit also suggests that persons with symptoms of two or more disorders—substance abuse and mood or anxiety disorder, for example—are more likely to seek treatment than those with only one disorder and, for that reason, to appear in studies of comorbidity based on treatment populations (Weissman, 1980).

Grant (1995) recently completed a general population survey of the comorbidity of major depression and the *DSM-IV* drug use disorders (including prescription drugs, sedatives, tranquilizers, amphetamines, cannabis, cocaine, and the hallucinogens), reporting pervasive comorbidity between a variety of drug use disorders and major depression. The association between drug dependence and major depression was greater among older than younger subjects, consistent with the use of drugs to self-medicate for depression. Major depression was strongly related to cannabis and hallucinogen abuse. While these two drug classes are not usually associated with depression self-medication, their chronic high-dose use may actually lead to development of amotivational syndrome, whose symptoms are strikingly like those of major depression. The association between drug abuse and major depression was greater for women than for men, perhaps because women's greater vulnerability to stigmatization for drug use coincides with the *DSM-IV* abuse criteria, which emphasize adverse consequences arising from drug use.

Many of the drugs of abuse also produce symptoms that mimic major psychiatric disorders

(Schuckit, 1994b). These behaviors have been studied most extensively in the central nervous system stimulants (the amphetamines and cocaine) and depressants (alcohol, barbiturates, and benzodiazepines).

> intoxication with *brain stimulants* can cause many symptoms of *anxiety*, with intake of larger doses even producing syndromes that can look similar to obsessive-compulsive disorder, panic disorder, and generalized anxiety disorder. Withdrawal from brain stimulants as well as repeated and prolonged intoxication with *brain depressants* can cause sadness that might even produce severe and incapacitating *depression* that resembles a major depressive episode. Withdrawal from brain depressant drugs is likely to produce intense and acute anxiety, with the probability of prolonged, but less severe, anxiety during what might be considered a protracted abstinence syndrome. Repeated stimulant intoxication, especially with amphetamines and cocaine, is likely to produce a syndrome of auditory hallucinations along with paranoid delusions that can temporarily resemble *schizophrenia*. (Schuckit, 1994b, p. 46)

Substance-Related Disorder, Schizophrenia, and Other Psychoses

The ECA study (Regier et al., 1990) revealed that persons diagnosed with schizophrenia experience a 47% lifetime prevalence of substance-related disorder, that about one third of persons with schizophrenia simultaneously experience comorbid substance-related disorder, and that persons diagnosed with schizophrenia are 4.6 times more likely to have a history of substance-related disorder than those without the disorder. All three findings confirm the common co-occurence of substance-related disorder and psychosis, prominently including schizophrenia. These conditions co-occur for several reasons. As noted above, the drugs of abuse—especially the stimulants and, particularly, the amphetamines—precipitate drug-induced psychoses directly (Janowsky & Risch, 1979). Moreover, the stimulants have a tendency to amplify the symptoms of psychosis among persons with preexisting psychoses (Negrete, 1989). Further, as a number of surveys (e.g., Drake, Osher, & Wallach, 1989) have suggested, schizophrenic persons, and those suffering from other psychotic disorders, tend to be intemperate. Finally, as Schuckit (1994b) notes, persons with the dual diagnoses of schizophrenia and substance abuse are substantially more likely to come to the attention of mental health professionals than are those with only one or the other of these disorders.

Substance-Related Disorder and Attention-Deficit/Hyperactivity Disorder (ADHD)

The co-occurrence of ADHD and substance-related disorder has been reported repeatedly (e.g., Kaminer, 1992; Wilens, Biederman, Spencer, & Frances, 1994). Because ADHD is often a feature of the childhood of individuals who develop substance-related disorders as adults, ADHD has even been suggested as a precursor of substance abuse, possibly sharing a common genotype in some individuals (Tarter, McBride, Buonpane, & Schneider, 1977). However, questions remain about whether it is ADHD itself or the mood, anxiety, and conduct disorders that accompany it that is primarily responsible for the comorbidity of substance-related disorders and ADHD.

Biederman and coworkers (1995) compared the behavioral and psychiatric histories of childhood-onset ADHD adults with those of non-ADHD adults. A significantly higher lifetime risk for substance-related disorder (52 versus 27%), as well as significantly higher rates of drug abuse, and combined alcohol and drug abuse, were characteristic of ADHD adults; the two groups did not differ in the rate of alcohol abuse alone. Ball, Carroll, and Rounsaville (1994) assessed large clinical and community samples of cocaine abusers for concurrent psychopathology including ADHD, polysubstance abuse, family history of antisocial behavior, sensation seeking, and substance abuse severity. Overall, a substantially larger percentage of cocaine abusers reported a history of ADHD than base rates would have predicted. Moreover, high-sensation seekers were significantly more likely than low-sensation seekers to report a history of ADHD, as well as a family history of antisocial personality disorder. Pomerleau, Downey, Stelson, and Pomerleau (1995) explored smoking prevalence rates among adult patients diagnosed with ADHD, concluding that ADHD patients overincluded smokers and that they find it especially difficult to quit. These authors hypothesize that, for ADHD smokers, smoking may have begun as an attempt to manage deficits in attention and concentration.

Substance-Related Disorder and Mood Disorder

The mood disorders, including major depressive disorder, dysthymic disorder, and bipolar disorder, are among the most common conditions comorbid with substance-related disorder. In a longitudinal study designed to examine the impact of alcohol use on the course of depressive disorder (Mueller et al., 1994), patients with dual diagnoses of major depression and alcoholism, and patients diagnosed only with major depressive disorder, were followed over a 10-year time span. Intensity analysis reflected transitions between states of major depressive disorder over time. To determine the impact of alcohol abuse on the course of depression, three subtypes based on alcohol usage were created: never alcoholic, not meeting criteria for current alcoholism, and current alcoholism. Depressed patients who had never been alcoholic or were not actively alcoholic at the present time were twice as likely to recover from major depressive disorder as were actively alcoholic patients, strongly indicating that active alcoholism has a decidedly malignant effect on recovery from major depressive disorder.

Brown and her colleagues (1995) had similar goals when they compared changes in the severity of depressive symptoms among men with alcohol dependence, affective disorder, or both over four weeks of inpatient treatment for either alcohol dependence or affective disorder. Symptoms of depression remitted more rapidly in men with primary alcoholism than in those with primary affective disorder. Alcohol dependence in persons suffering from primary affective disorder neither intensified symptoms of depression nor interfered with their resolution in treatment. This finding, in apparent conflict with data from the 1994 study by Mueller and his colleagues, may reflect the fact that Mueller and his colleagues did not distinguish between primary and secondary depression, as did Brown. There also appear to have been differences in the severity of the depressive conditions in the two studies.

Exploring the same issue in a very different population, Camatta and Nagoshi (1995) asked college drinkers to complete a questionnaire asking about alcohol use and alcohol problems. They also completed measures of impulsiveness and adventurousness, depression, life stresses, and proneness to irrational beliefs. While impulsivity and adventurousness were significantly correlated with alcohol use, they were unrelated to alcohol problems. By contrast, depression, stress, and irrational beliefs were significantly correlated with alcohol problems but not with alcohol use. The effects of stress on alcohol problems were mediated by depression, while the effects of depression were mediated by irrational beliefs.

Depression in its many forms—ranging from major depressive disorder to the more benign mood disturbances of late adolescence—is for some individuals an antecedent to and for others a consequence of alcohol use and alcohol abuse. Severe depression exacerbates alcohol problems and makes their effective treatment more difficult. The comorbid behavioral disorder most intimately linked to alcohol abuse and dependence, depression, is also its most troubling accompaniment.

Smoking and major depression also frequently co-occur (Breslau, Kilbey, & Andreski, 1991). Recently, this line of research has focused on the role of depression in outcomes of smoking cessation treatment (Anda et al., 1990; Glassman, 1993). Kinnunen, Doherty, Militello, and Garvey (1996) followed a large group of smokers for three months while they were attempting to quit. Treatment consisted primarily of nicotine gum and brief counseling. One third of the smokers met an established criterion for current depression. Depression played an important role in treatment outcome: depressed smokers reported more stress, fewer coping resources, more physical and psychological symptoms, and more frequent smoking during periods of negative affect. Overall, depressed smokers benefited significantly less from treatment than did the nondepressed smokers.

Withdrawal from the CNS stimulants, including the amphetamines and cocaine, is also commonly accompanied by profound, longlasting, and severely impairing dysphoria (Maisto et al., 1995). A likely consequence of the action of the stimulants on dopamine receptors in the brain during intoxication, the profound depression or "crash" which so often follows stimulant abuse, is a significant clinical phenomenon.

Substance-Related Disorder, Social Anxiety, and Tension Reduction

The tension-reduction hypothesis (TRH) was the first viable alternative to the psychodynamic theory of alcoholism etiology that held sway during the decades immediately preceding World War II. Inspired by anecdotal reports from both social drinkers and alcoholics that alcohol reduces anxiety, the TRH gained additional support from empirical research (e.g., Conger, 1951; Masserman & Yum, 1946) documenting alcohol's capacity to reduce experimentally induced conflict ("anxiety") in rats and cats. The TRH did not fare so well, however, when it was tested in alcoholics. This research (see Cappell, 1974; Langenbucher & Nathan, 1993) revealed that alcoholics do not respond to alcohol in a consistent manner: some experience tension relief, others an increase in tension, and still others show no effect at all.

Several studies (e.g., Abrams & Wilson, 1979; Polivy, Schueneman, & Carlson, 1976; Wilson & Abrams, 1977) have demonstrated the importance of attitudes toward the effects of alcohol on the tension-reducing effects of the drug. The results of this research suggested that the sedative effects of alcohol do tend to reduce tension and anxiety in the short run at low to moderate doses, unless the drinker's attitudes toward drinking are so conflicted (as are those of many alcoholics) that he or she experiences anxiety rather than tension relief when again beginning to drink.

A recent review by Schuckit and Hesselbrock (1994) summarizes findings from contemporary research on alcohol and anxiety. It was motivated by the observation that, although many alcoholics report symptoms of severe anxiety during periods of abstinence, it is unclear whether the anxiety is primarily associated with independent psychiatric syndromes, is largely associated with the abstinence syndrome, or is a combination of the two. Schuckit and Hesselbrock's extensive review led them to conclude the following:

> The available data, while imperfect, do not prove a close relationship between lifelong anxiety disorders and alcohol dependence. Further, prospective studies of children of alcoholics and individuals from the general population do not indicate a high rate of anxiety disorders preceding alcohol dependence. . . . The high rates of comorbidity (of alcohol dependence and anxiety disorder) in some studies likely reflect a mixture of true anxiety disorders among alcoholics at a rate equal to or slightly higher than that for the general population, along with temporary, but at times severe, substance-induced anxiety syndromes. (p. 1723)

These conclusions, pointing to a fairly remote relationship between anxiety and alcohol abuse, contrast sharply with the much closer relationship between alcohol abuse and depression reviewed above.

Anxiety, sometimes intense anxiety, and agitation are common accompaniments of withdrawal from many substances, especially alcohol and the other central nervous system depressants (Schuckit, 1994b). These symptoms are probably consequences, in part, of the disappearance of these substances from the serotonergic and dopaminergic neurotransmitter systems in the brain, the neurotransmitter systems most profoundly affected by dependence on the CNS depressants.

References

Abrams, D. B., & Wilson, G. T. (1979). Effects of alcohol on social anxiety in women: Cognitive versus physiological processes. *Journal of Abnormal Psychology, 88*, 161–173.

Anda, R. F., Williamson, D. F., Esdcobedo, L. G., Mast, E. E., Giovino, G. A., & Remington, P. L. (1990). Depression and the dynamics of smoking. *Journal of the American Medical Association, 264*, 1541–1545.

Arthur, M. J., Lee, A., & Wright, R. (1984). Sex differences in the metabolism of ethanol and acetaldehyde in normal subjects. *Clinical Science, 67*, 397–401.

Babor, T. F. (1996). The classification of alcoholics: Typology theories from the 19th century to the present. *Alcohol Health & Research World, 20*, 6–14.

Babor, T. F., Cooney, N. L., & Lauerman, R. J. (1987). The dependence syndrome concept as a psychological theory of relapse behavior: An empirical evaluation of alcoholic and opiate addicts. *British Journal of Addictions, 82*, 393–405.

Babor, T. F. & Dolinsky, Z. S. (1988). Alcoholic typologies: Historical evolution and empirical evaluation of some common classification schemes. In R. M. Rose & J. Barrett (Eds.), *Alcoholism: Origins and outcome* (pp. 245–266). New York: Raven Press.

Babor, T. F., Hofmann, M., Del Boca, F., Hesselbrock, V., Meyer, R., Dolinsky, Z., & Rounsaville, B. (1992). Types of alcoholics, 1: Evidence for an empirically-derived typology based on indicators of vulnerability and severity. *Archives of General Psychiatry, 49*, 599–608.

Barbor, T. F., & Laverman, R. J. (1986). Classification and forms of inebriety: Historical antecedents of alcoholic typologies. In M. Galanter (Ed.), *Recent developments in alcoholism* (pp. 113–144). New York: Plenum Press.

Ball, S. A., Carroll, K. M., & Rounsaville, B. J. (1994). *Journal of Consulting and Clinical Psychology, 62*, 1053–1057.

Bannister, P., & Lowosky, M. S. (1987). Ethanol and hypogonadism. *Alcohol, 22*, 213–217.

Beatty, W. W., Hames, K. A., Blanco, C. R., Nixon, S. J., & Tivis, L. J. (1996). Visuospatial perception, construction and memory in alcoholism. *Journal of Studies on Alcohol, 57*, 136–143.

Begleiter, H., Porjesz, B., Bihari, B., & Kissin, B. (1984). Event-related brain potentials inboys at risk for alcoholism. *Science, 225*, 1493–1496.

Berry, J., Van Gorp, W. G., Herzberg, D. S., & Hinkin, C. (1993). Neuropsychological deficits in abstinent cocaine abusers: Preliminary findings after two weeks of abstinence. *Drug and Alcohol Dependence, 32*, 231–237.

Biederman, J., Wilens, T., Mick, E., Milberger, S., Spencer, T. J., & Faraone, S. V. (1995). Psychoactive substance use disorders in adults with attention deficit hyperactivity disorder (ADHD): Effects of ADHD and psychiatry comorbidity. *American Journal of Psychiatry, 152*, 1652–1658.

Biggins, C. A., MacKay, S., Poole, N., & Fein, G. (1995). Delayed P3A in abstinent elderly male chronic alcoholics. *Alcoholism: Clinical and Experimental Research, 19*, 1032–1042.

Blaine, J. D., Horton, A. H., & Towle, L. H. (Eds.). (1995). *Diagnosis and severity of drug abuse and drug dependence*. NIH Pub. No. 95-3884. Rockville, MD: National Institute on Drug Abuse.

Bohman, M., Sigvardsson, S., & Cloninger, C. R. (1981). Maternal inheritance of alcohol abuse. *Archives of General Psychiatry, 38*, 965–969.

Breslau, N., Kilbey, M. M., & Andreski, P. (1991). Nicotine dependence, major depression and anxiety in young adults. *Archives of General Psychiatry, 48*, 1069–1074.

Brown, S. A., Goldman, M. S., Inn, A., & Anderson, L. R. (1980). Expectations of reinforcement from alcohol: Their domain and relation to drinking patterns. *Journal of Consulting and Clinical Psychology, 43*, 419–426.

Brown, S. A., Inaba, R. K., Gillin, J. C., Schuckit, M. A., Stewart, M. A., & Irwin, M. R. (1995). Alcoholism and affective disorder: Clinical course and depressive symptoms. *American Journal of Psychiatry, 152*, 45–52.

Cadoret, R. J. (1980). Development of alcoholism in adoptees raised apart from alcoholic biologic relatives. *Archives of General Psychiatry, 37*, 561–563.

Cadoret, R. J., Troughton, E., O'Gorman, T. W., & Heywood, E. (1986). An adoption study of genetic and environmental factors in drug abuse. *Archives of General Psychiatry, 43*, 1131–1136.

Camatta, C. D., & Nagoshi, C. T. (1995). Stress, depression, irrational beliefs, and alcohol use and problems in a college student sample. *Alcoholism: Clinical and Experimental Research, 19*, 142–146.

Cappell, H. (1974). An evaluation of tension models of alcohol consumption. In Y. Israel (Ed.), *Research advances in alcohol and drug problems*. New York: John Wiley.

Carpenter, W. B. (1850). *On the use and abuse of alcoholic liquors in health and disease*. Philadelphia: Lea and Blanchard.

Carroll, K. M., Rounsaville, B. J., & Bryant, K. J. (1994). Should tolerance and withdrawal be required for substance dependence disorders? *Drug and Alcohol Dependence, 36*, 15–22.

Celentano, D. D., & McQueen, D. V. (1984). Multiple substance abuse among women with alcohol-related problems. In S. C. Wilsnack & L. J. Beckman (Eds.), *Alcohol problems in women: Antecedents, consequences, and intervention* (pp. 97–116). New York: Guilford Press.

Chermack, S. T., & Taylor, S. W. P. (1995). Alcohol and human physical aggression: Pharmacological versus expectancy effects. *Journal of Studies on Alcohol, 56*, 449–456.

Cloninger, C. R. (1987). Neurogenetic adaptive mechanisms in alcoholism. *Science, 236*, 410–416.

Cloninger, C. R., Bohman, M., & Sigvardsson, S. (1981). Inheritance of alcohol abuse: Cross-fostering analysis of adopted men. *Archives of General Psychiatry, 38*, 861–868.

Conger, J. J. (1951). The effects of alcohol on conflict behavior in the albino rat. *Quarterly Journal of Studies on Alcohol, 12*, 1–29.

Cottler, L. B., Schuckit, M. A., Helzer, J. E., Crowley, T., Woody, G., Nathan, P. E., & Hughes, J. (1995). The *DSM-IV* field trial for substance use disorders: Major results. *Drug and Alcohol Dependence, 38*, 59–69.

Cotton, N. S. (1979). The familial incidence of alcoholism. *Journal of Studies on Alcohol, 40*, 89–116.

Crothers, T. (1911). *Inebriety: A clinical treatise on the etiology, symptomatology, neurosis, psychosis, and treatment.* Cincinnati: Harvey Publishing.

Curlee, J. (1970). Comparison of male and female patients at an alcoholism treatment center. *Journal of Psychology, 74*, 239–247.

Dawson, D. A., Grant, B. F., Chou, S. P., & Pickering, R. P. (1995). Subgroup variation in U.S. drinking patterns: Results of the 1992 National Longitudinal Alcohol Epidemiologic Study. *Journal of Substance Abuse, 7*, 331–344.

Deckel, A. W., Hesselbrock, V., & Bauer, L. (1995). Relationship between alcohol-related expectancies and anterior brain functioning in young men at risk for developing alcoholism. *Alcoholism: Clinical and Experimental Research, 19*, 476–481.

Drake, R. E., Osher, F. C., & Wallach, M. A. (1989). Alcohol use and abuse in schizophrenia: A prospective community study. *Journal of Nervous and Mental Disease, 177*, 408–414.

Eaton, W. W., Holzer, C. E., Von Korff, M., Anthony, J. C., Helzer, J. E., George, L., Burnam, A., Boyd, J. H., Kessler, L. G., & Locke, B. Z. (1984). The design of the Epidemiologic Catchment Area studies. *Archives of General Psychiatry, 41*, 942–948.

Eckardt, M. J., Stapleton, J. M., Rawlings, R. R., Davis, E. Z., & Grodin, D. M. (1995). Neuropsychological functioning in detoxified alcoholics between 18 and 35 years of age. *American Journal of Psychiatry, 152*, 53–59.

Edwards, G., & Gross, M. M. (1976). Alcohol dependence: Provisional description of a clinical syndrome. *British Journal of Psychiatry, 1*, 1058–1061.

Fahrner, E. M. (1987). Sexual dysfunction in male alcohol addicts: Prevalence and treatment. *Archives of Sexual Behavior, 16*, 247–257.

Fals-Stewart, W. (1996). Intermediate length neuropsychological screening of impairment among psychoactive substance-abusing patients: A comparison of two batteries. *Journal of Substance Abuse, 8*, 1–17.

Fals-Stewart, W., & Lucente, S. (1994). The effect of neurocognitive status and personality functioning on length of stay on residential substance abuse treatment. *Psychology of Addictive Behaviors, 8*, 1–12.

Farren, C. K., & Dinan, T. G. (1996). Alcoholism and typology: Findings in an Irish private hospital population. *Journal of Studies on Alcohol, 57*, 249–252.

Fils-Aime, M.-L., Eckardt, M..J., George, D. T., Brown, G. L., Mefford, I., & Linnoila, M. (1996). Early-onset alcoholics have lower cerebrospinal fluid 5-hydroxyindoleacetic acid levels than late-onset alcoholics. *Archives of General Psychiatry, 53*, 211–216.

Freund, G. (1982). The interaction of chronic alcohol consumption and aging on brain structures and function. *Alcoholism: Clinical and Experimental Research, 6*, 13–21.

Friedman, A. S., Kramer, S., Kreisher, C., & Granick, S. (1996). The relationship of substance abuse to illegal and violent behavior, in a community sample of young adult African American men and women. *Journal of Substance Abuse, 8*, 379–402.

Frieze, I. H., & Schafer, P. C. (1984). Alcohol use and marital violence. Female and male differences in reactions to alcohol. In S. C. Wilsnack & L. J. Beckman (Eds.), *Alcohol problems in women: Antecedents, consequences and intervention* (pp. 260–279). New York: Guilford Press.

Gavaler, J. S. (1995). Alcohol effects on hormone levels in normal postmenopausal women and in postmenopausal women with alcohol-induced cirrhosis. In M. Galanter (Ed.), *Recent developments in alcoholism* (Vol. 12; pp. 199–208). New York: Plenum Press.

Gavaler, J. S. (1996). Alcoholic beverage consumption and estrogenization in normal postmenopausal women. In E. L. Gomberg & T. D. Nirenberg (Eds.), *Women and substance abuse* (pp. 18–41). Norwood, NJ: Ablex Publishing.

Giancola, P. R., & Zeichner, A. (1995). Alcohol-related aggression in males and females: Effects of blood alcohol concentration, subjective intoxication, personality, and provocation. *Alcoholism: Clinical and Experimental Research, 19*, 130–134.

Glassman, A. H. (1993). Cigarette smoking: Implications for psychiatric illness. *American Journal of Psychiatry, 150*, 546–553.

Goldman, M. S., Brown, S. A., Christiansen, B. A., & Smith, G. T. (1991). Alcoholism etiology and memory: Broadening the scope of alcohol expectancy research. *Psychological Bulletin, 110*, 137–146.

Goldman, M. S., Williams, D. L., & Klisz, D. K. (1983). Recoverability of psychological functioning following alcohol abuse: Prolonged visual-spatial dysfunction in older alcoholics. *Journal of Consulting and Clinical Psychology, 51*, 370–378.

Goodwin, D. W., Schulsinger, F., Mollen, N., Hermansen, L., Winokur, G., & Guze, S. B. (1974). Drinking problems in adopted and nonadopted sons of alcoholics. *Archives of General Psychiatry, 31*, 164–169.

Gordon, C. M., & Carey, M. P. (1996). Alcohol's effects on requisites for sexual risk reduction in men: An initial experimental investigation. *Health Psychology, 15*, 56–60.

Gottfredson, D. C., & Koper, C. S. (1996). Race and sex differences in the prediction of drug use. *Journal of Consulting and Clinical Psychology, 64*, 305–313.

Grant, B. F. (1995). Comorbidity between *DSM-IV* drug use disorders and major depression: Results of a national survey of adults. *Journal of Substance Abuse, 7*, 481–497.

Gustafson, R. (1991). Aggressive and nonaggressive behavior as a function of alcohol intoxication and frustration in women. *Alcoholism: Clinical and Experimental Research, 15*, 886–892.

Hållen, J., & Krook, H. (1963). Follow-up studies on unselected ten-year material of 360 patients with liver cirrhosis in one community. *Acta Medica Scandinavia, 173*, 479–493.

Hallman, J., von Knorring, L., & Oreland, L. (1996). Personality disorders according to *DSM-III-R* and thrombocyte monoamine oxidase activity in Type 1 and Type 2 alcoholics. *Journal of Studies on Alcohol, 57*, 155–161.

Heath, A. C., Cates, R., Martin, N. G., Meyer, J., Hewitt, J. K., Neale, M. C., & Eaves, L. J. (1993). Genetic contributions to risk of smoking initiation: Comparisons across birth cohorts and across of cultures. *Journal of Substance Abuse, 5*, 221–246.

Heath, A. C., & Martin, N. G. (1993). Genetic models for the natural history of smoking: Evidence for a genetic influence on smoking persistence. *Addictive Behaviors, 18*, 19–34.

Hegadus, A., Tarter, R., Hill, S., Jacob, T., & Winsten, N. (1984). Static ataxia: A possible marker for alcoholism. *Alcoholism: Clinical and Experimental Research, 8*, 580–582.

Hegerl, U., Lipperheide, K., Juckel, G., Schmidt, L. G., & Rommelspacher, H. (1995). Antisocial tendencies and cortical sensory-evoked responses in alcoholism. *Alcoholism: Clinical and Experimental Research, 19*, 31–36.

Helzer, J. E. (1994). Psychoactive substance abuse and its relation to dependence. In T. A. Widiger, A. J. Frances, H. A. Pincus, M. B. First, R. Ross, & W. Davis (Eds.), *DSM-IV Sourcebook* (Vol. 1; pp. 21–32). Washington, DC: American Psychiatric Association.

Helzer, J. E., Burnam, A., & McEvoy, L. T. (1991). Alcohol abuse and dependence. In L. N. Robins & D. A. Regier (Eds.), *Psychiatric disorders in America: The Epidemiological Catchment Area study* (pp. 81–115). New York: Free Press.

Hesselbrock, M. N., & Hesselbrock, V. M. (1996). Depression and antisocial personality disorder in alcoholism: Gender comparison. In E. L. Gomberg & T. D. Nirenberg (Eds.), *Women and substance abuse* (pp. 142–161). Norwood, NJ: Ablex Publishing.

Hill, S. Y. (1995a). Vulnerability to alcoholism in women: Genetic and cultural factors. In M. Galanter (Ed.), *Recent development in alcoholism* (Vol. 12; pp. 9–28). New York: Plenum Press.

Hill, S. Y. (1995b). Mental and physical health consequences of alcohol use in women. In M. Galanter (Ed.), *Recent developments in alcoholism* (Vol. 12; pp. 181–197). New York: Plenum Press.

Hill, S. Y., & Steinhauer, S. R. (1993). Assessment of prepubertal boys and girls at risk for developing alcoholism with P300 from a visual discrimination task. *Journal of Studies on Alcohol, 54*, 350–358.

Hill, S. Y., Steinhauer, S., & Locke, J. (1995). Event-related potentials in alcoholic men, their high-risk male relatives, and low-risk male controls. *Alcoholism: Clinical and Experimental Research, 19*, 567–576.

Horgan, C. (1993). *Substance Abuse: The nation's number one health problem.* Princeton, NJ: Robert Wood Johnson Foundation.

Howard, M. O., Kivlahan, D., & Walker, R. D. (1997). Cloninger's Tridimensional Theory of personality and psychopathology: Applications to substance use disorders. *Journal of Studies on Alcohol, 58*, 48–66.

Janowsky, D. S., & Risch, C. (1979). Amphetamine psychosis and psychotic symptoms. *Psychopharmacology* (Berlin), *65*, 73–77.

Jellinek, E. M. (1960). *The disease concept of alcoholism.* New Haven, CT: College and University Press.

Jencks, S. F., & Goldman, H. H. (1987). Implications of research for psychiatric prospective payment. *Medical Care, 25*, 542–551.

Jessor, R., & Jessor, S. (1977). *Problem behavior and psychosocial development: A longitudinal study of youth.* New York: Academic Press.

Jones-Webb, R. J., Hsiao, C.-Y., & Hannan, P. (1995). Relationships between socioeconomic status and drinking problems among black and white men. *Alcoholism: Clinical and Experimental Research, 19*, 623–627.

Kaminer, Y. (1992). Clinical implications of the relationship between attention-deficit hyperactivity disorder and psychoactive substance use disorders. *American Journal of Addictions, 1*, 257–264.

Kendler, K. S., Heath, A. C., Neale, M. C., Kessler, R. C., & Eaves, L. J. (1992). A population-based twin study of alcoholism in women. *Journal of the American Medical Association, 268*, 1877–1882.

Kerr, N. (1893). *Inebriety and narcomania.* London: H.K. Lewis.

Kinnunen, T., Doherty, K., Militello, F. S., & Garvey, A. J. (1996). Depression and smoking cessation: Characteristics of depressed smokers and effects of nicotine replacement. *Journal of Consulting and Clinical Psychology, 64,* 791–798.

Knight, R. P. (1937). The dynamics and treatment of chronic alcohol addiction. *Bulletin of the Menninger Clinic, 1,* 233–250.

Koopman, C., Rosario, M., & Rotheram-Borus, M. J. (1994). Alcohol and drug use and sexual behaviors placing runaways at risk for HIV infection. *Addictive Behaviors, 19,* 95–103.

Langenbucher, J. W., & Chung, T. (1995). Onset and staging of *DSM-IV* alcohol dependence using mean age and survival/hazard methods. *Journal of Abnormal Psychology, 104,* 346–354.

Langenbucher, J. W., Chung, T., Morgenstern, J., Labouvie, E., Nathan, P. E., & Bavly, L. (in press). Physiological alcohol dependence as a "specifier" of risk for medical problems and relapse liability in *DSM-IV. Journal of Studies on Alcohol.*

Langenbucher, J. W., Morgenstern, J., Labouvie, E., & Nathan, P. E. (1994a). Lifetime *DSM-IV* diagnosis of alcohol, cannabis, cocaine and opiate dependence: Six-month reliability in a multi-site clinical sample. *Addiction, 89,* 1115–1127.

Langenbucher, J. W., Morgenstern, J., Labouvie, E., & Nathan, P. E. (1994b). Diagnostic concordance of substance use disorders in *DSM-III, DSM-IV* and *ICD-10. Drug and Alcohol Dependence, 36,* 193–203.

Langenbucher, J. W., & Nathan, P. E. (1993). Alcohol, affect, and the tension-reduction hypothesis: The reanalysis of some crucial early data. In W. M. Cox (Ed.), *Why people drink: Parameters of alcohol as a reinforcer.* New York: Gardner Press.

Langenbucher, J. W., Sulesund, D., Chung, T., & Morgenstern, J. (1996). Illness severity and self-efficacy as course predictors of *DSM-IV* alcohol dependence in a multisite clinical sample. *Addictive Behaviors, 21,* 543–553.

Lex, B. W. (1996). Women and illicit drugs: Marijuana, heroin, and cocaine. In E. L. Gomberg & T. D. Nirenberg (Eds.), *Women and substance abuse* (pp. 162–190). Norwood, NJ: Ablex Publishing.

Lieber, C. S. (1996). Women and alcohol: Gender differences in metabolism and susceptibility. In E. L. Gomberg & T. D. Nirenberg (Eds.), *Women and substance abuse* (pp. 1–17). Norwood, NJ: Ablex Publishing.

Lipscomb, T. R., Carpenter, J. A., & Nathan, P. E. (1979). Static ataxia: A predictor of alcoholism? *British Journal of Addiction, 74,* 289–294.

Maisto, S. A., Galizio, M., & Connors, G. J. (1995). *Drug use and abuse* (2nd ed.). Fort Worth: Harcourt Press.

Marshall, A. W., Kingstone, D., Boss, M., & Morgan, M. Y. (1983). Ethanol elimination in males and females: Relationship to menstrual cycle and body composition. *Hematology, 3,* 701–706.

Masserman, J. H., & Yum, K. S. (1946). An analysis of the influence of alcohol and experimental neurosis in cats. *Psychological Medicine, 8,* 36–52.

McCrady, B. S., & Langenbucher, J. W. (1996). Alcoholism treatment and health care system reform. *Archives of General Psychiatry, 53,* 737–746.

Mezzich, J. E., & Sharfstein, S. S. (1985). Severity of illness and diagnostic formulation: Classifying patients for prospective payment systems. *Hospital and Community Psychiatry, 36,* 770–772.

Michalec, E. M., Rohsenow, D. J., Monti, P. M., Varney, S. M., Martin, R. A., Dey, A. N., Myers, M. G., & Sirota, A. D. (1996). A Cocaine Negative Consequences Checklist: Development and validation. *Journal of Substance Abuse, 8,* 181–193.

Miller, B. A., & Downs, W. R. (1996). Violent victimization among women with alcohol problems. In M. Galanter (Ed.), *Recent developments in alcoholism* (Vol. 12; pp. 81–101). New York: Plenum Press.

Morey, L. C., & Skinner, H. A. (1986). Empirically derived classifications of alcohol-related problems. In M. Galanter (Ed.), *Recent developments in alcoholism* (Vol. 5; pp. 145–168). New York: Plenum Press.

Morgan, M. Y., & Sherlock, S. (1977). Sex-related differences among 100 patients with alcoholic liver disease. *British Medical Journal, 1,* 939–941.

Moss, H. B., & Kirisci, L. (1995). Aggressivity in adolescent alcohol abusers: Relationship with conduct disorder. *Alcoholism: Clinical and Experimental Research, 19,* 642-646.

Mueller, T. I., Lavori, P. W., Keller, M. B., Swartz, A., Warshaw, M., Hasin, D., Coryell, W., Endicott, J., Rice, J., & Akiskal, H. (1994). Prognostic effect of the variable course of alcoholism on the 10-year course of depression. *American Journal of Psychiatry, 151,* 701–706.

Nathan, P. E. (1993). Alcoholism: Psychopathology, etiology, and treatment. In P. B. Sutker & H. E. Adams (Eds.), *Comprehensive handbook of psychopathology* (2nd ed.; pp. 451–476). New York: Plenum Press.

Nathan, P. E., & Lipscomb, T. R. (1979). Studies in blood alcohol level discrimination: Etiologic cues to alcoholism. In N. A. Krasnegor (Ed.), *Behavioral analysis and treatment of substance abuse* (pp. 178–190). Washington, DC: NIDA.

National Institute on Alcohol Abuse & Alcoholism. (1997). *Ninth special report to congress on alcohol and health*. Washington, DC: U.S. Department of Health and Human Services.

National Institute on Drug Abuse. (1994). *Fourth triennial report to congress on drug abuse and drug abuse research*. Washington, DC: U.S. Department of Health and Human Services.

Negrete, J. C. (1989). Cannabis and schizophrenia. *British Journal of Addiction, 84*, 349–351.

Newcomb, M. D., & Bentler, P. M. (1986). Substance use and ethnicity: Differential impactof peer and adult models. *Journal of Psychology, 120*, 83–95.

Nichols, J. M., & Martin, F. (1996). The effect of heavy social drinking on recall and event-related potential. *Journal of Studies on Alcohol, 57*, 125–135.

Nixon, S. J., Tivis, R., & Parsons, O. A. (1995). Behavioral dysfunction and cognitive efficiency in male and female alcoholics. *Alcoholism: Clinical and Experimental Research, 19*, 577–581.

O'Connor, S. J., Hesselbrock, V., & Tasman, A. (1986). Correlates of increased risk for alcoholism in young men. *Progress in Neuropsychopharmacology and Biological Psychiatry, 10*, 211–218.

O'Malley, S., Gawin, F. H., Heaton, R. K., & Kleber, H. D. (1989). Cognitive deficits associated with cocaine abuse. Paper at the annual meeting of the American Psychiatric Association, San Francisco, CA.

Parker, D. A., Harford, T. C., & Rosenstock, I. M. (1994). Alcohol, other drugs, and sexual risk-taking among young adults. *Journal of Substance Abuse, 6*, 87–93.

Polivy, J., Schueneman, A. L., & Carlson, K. (1976). Alcohol and tension reduction: Cognitive and physiological effects. *Journal of Abnormal Psychology, 85*, 595–600.

Pomerleau, O. F., Downey, K. K., Stelson, F. W., & Pomerleau, C. S. (1995). Cigarette smoking in adult patients diagnosed with attention deficit hyperactivity disorder. *Journal of Substance Abuse, 7*, 373–378.

Ramachandran, G., Porjesz, B., Begleiter, H., & Litke, A. (1996). A simple auditory oddball task in young adult males at high risk for alcoholism. *Alcoholism: Clinical and Experimental Research, 20*, 9–15.

Rankin, J. G. (1977). The natural history and management of the patient with alcoholic liver disease. In M. M. Fisher & J. G. Rankin (Eds.), *Alcohol and the liver* (pp. 365–381). New York: Plenum Press.

Ray, O., & Ksir, C. (1996). *Drugs, society, and human behavior* (7th ed.). St. Louis: Mosby-Year Book.

Reed, B. G. (1985). Drug misuse and dependency in women: The meaning and implications of being considered a special population or minority. *International Journal of Addictions, 20*, 117–130.

Regier, D. A., Farmer, M. E., Rae, D. S., Locke, B. Z., Keith, S. J., Judd, L. L., & Goodwin, F. K. (1990). Comorbidity of mental disorders with alcohol and other drug abuse: Results from the Epidemiological Catchment Area (ECA) study. *Journal of the American Medical Association, 264*, 2511–2518.

Robins, L. N., Helzer, J. E., Weissman, M. M., Orvaschel, H., Gruenberg, E., Burke, J. D., & Regier, D. A. (1984). Lifetime prevalence of specific psychiatric disorders in three sites. *Archives of General Psychiatry, 41*, 949–958.

Robins, L. N., & Regier, D. A. (Eds.). (1991). *Psychiatric disorders in America: The Epidemiological Catchment Area study*. New York: Free Press.

Rose, J. S., Chassin, L., Presson, C. C., & Sherman, S. J. (1996). Demographic factors in adult smoking status: Mediating and moderating influences. *Psychology of Addictive Behaviors, 10*, 28–37.

Ross, H. E., Glaser, F. B., & Germanson, T. (1988). The prevalence of psychiatric disorders in patients with alcohol and other drug problems. *Archives of General Psychiatry, 45*, 1023–1031.

Rounsaville, B. J., & Bryant, K. J. (1992). Tolerance and withdrawal in the *DSM-III-R* diagnosis of substance dependence: Utility in a cocaine-using population. *American Journal of the Addictions, 1*, 50–60.

Schacht, T., & Nathan, P. E. (1977). But is it good for the psychologists? Appraisal and status of DSM III. *American Psychologist, 32*, 1017–1025.

Schafer, J., & Brown, S. A. (1991). Marijuana and cocaine effect expectancies and drug use patterns. *Journal of Consulting and Clinical Psychology, 59*, 558–565.

Scheier, L. M., & Botvin, G. J. (1995). Effects of early adolescent drug use on cognitive efficiency in early-late adolescence: A developmental structural model. *Journal of Substance Abuse, 7*, 379–404.

Schiavi, R. C. (1990). Chronic alcoholism and male sexual dysfunction. *Journal of Sex and Marital Therapy, 16*, 23–33.

Schiavi, R. C., Stimmel, B. B., Mandeli, J., & White, D. (1995). Chronic alcoholism and male sexual function. *American Journal of Psychiatry, 152*, 1045–1051.

Schiffman, S., Kassel, J. D., Paty, J., Gnys, M., & Zettler-Segal, M. (1994). Smoking typology profiles of chippers and regular smokers. *Journal of Substance Abuse, 6*, 21–35.

Schuckit, M. A. (1985). Ethanol-induced changes in body sway in men at high alcoholism risk. *Archives of General Psychiatry, 42*, 3S., 75–379.

Schuckit, M. A. (1994a). Low level of response to alcohol as a predictor of future alcoholism. *American Journal of Psychiatry, 151*, 184–189.

Schuckit, M. A. (1994b). The relationship between alcohol problems, substance abuse, and psychiatric syndromes. In T. A. Widiger, A. J. Frances, H. A. Pincus, M. B. First, R. Ross, & W. Davis (Eds.), *DSM-IV Sourcebook* (Vol. 1; pp. 45–66). Washington, DC: American Psychiatric Association.

Schuckit, M. A. (1996). *DSM-V*: There's work to be done. *Journal of Studies on Alcohol, 57*, 469–470.

Schuckit, M. A., & Gold, E. O. (1988). A simultaneous evaluation of multiple markers of ethanol/placebo challenges in sons of alcoholics and controls. *Archives of General Psychiatry, 45*, 211–216.

Schuckit, M. A., & Hesselbrock, V. (1994). Alcohol dependence and anxiety disorders: What is the relationship? *American Journal of Psychiatry, 151*, 1723–1734.

Schuckit, M. A., & Smith, T. L. (1996). An 8-year follow-up of 450 sons of alcoholic and control subjects. *Archives of General Psychiatry, 53*, 202–210.

Skinstad, A. H., Eliason, M. J., Gerken, K., Spratt, K. F., Lutz, G. M., & Childress, K. (1996). *Alcohol and drug abuse among Iowa women: Iowa State Needs Assessment project*. Iowa City, IA: The University of Iowa.

Smith, G. T., Goldman, M. S., & Christiansen, B. A. (1989). *The Drinking Styles Questionnaire: Adolescent Drinking Self-Report*. Paper presented at the 97th Annual Convention of the American Psychological Association, New Orleans, LA.

Smith, G. T., Goldman, M. S., Greenbaum, P. E., & Christiansen, B. A. (1995). Expectancy for social facilitation from drinking: The divergent paths of high-expectancy and low-expectancy adolescents. *Journal of Abnormal Psychology, 104*, 32–40.

Tarter, R. E., McBride, H., Buonpane, N., & Schneider, D. U. (1977). Differentiation of alcoholics. *Archives of General Psychiatry, 34*, 761–768.

Thomasson, H. R. (1995). Gender difference in alcohol metabolism: Physiological responses to ethanol. In M. Galanter (Ed.), *Recent developments in alcoholism* (Vol. 12; pp. 163–179). New York: Plenum Press.

Van Thiel, D. H., Gavaler, J. S., Eagan, P. K., Chiao, Y. B., Cobb, C. F., & Lester, R. (1980). Alcohol and sexual function. *Pharmacology and Biochemistry of Behavior, 13* (Suppl. 1), 125–129.

Victor, M., Adams, R. D., & Collins, G. H. (1971). *The Wernicke-Korsakoff syndrome*. Philadelphia: Davis Publishers.

Walker, R. D., Walker, P. S., Maloy, F., Howard, M. O., Lambert, M. D., & Suchinsky, R. T. (1996). Essential and reactive alcoholism: A review. *Journal of Clinical Psychology, 52*, 80–95.

Weissman, M. M. (1980). Alcoholism and depression: Separate entities? Paper presented at the Cambridge Hospital 7th Annual Alcoholism Symposium, Boston, MA.

Wetzig, D., & Hardin, S. I. (1990). Neurocognitive deficits of alcoholism. *Journal of Clinical Psychology, 46*, 219–221.

Wilens, T. E., Biederman, J., Spencer, T. J., & Frances, R. J. (1994). Comorbidity of attention deficit hyperactivity disorder and the psychoactive substance use disorders. *Hospital and Community Psychiatry, 45*, 421–435.

Wilsnack, S. C., & Klassen, A. D. (1992). Childhood sexual abuse and problem drinking in a US national sample of women. Paper presented at the Conference on Women's Issues Related to Alcohol Abuse and Violence. College of Nursing, University of Illinois at Chicago.

Wilsnack, S. C., Vogeltanz, N. D., Klassen, A. D., & Harris, T. R. (1994). Childhood sexual abuse and women's substance abuse: National survey findings. Paper presented at the Annual Meeting of the American Psychological Association, Washington, DC.

Wilsnack, S. C., & Wilsnack, R. W. (1995). Drinking and problem drinking in U.S. women: Patterns and recent trends. In M. Galanter (Ed.), *Recent developments in alcoholism* (Vol. 12; pp. 30–60). New York: Plenum Press.

Wilsnack, R. W., Wilsnack, S. C., & Klassen, A. D. (1984). Women's drinking and drinking problems: Patterns from a 1981 national survey. *American Journal of Public Health, 74*, 1231–1238.

Wilson, G. T., & Abrams, D. B. (1977). Effects of

alcohol on social anxiety and physiological arousal: Cognitive versus pharmacological processes. *Cognitive Therapy and Research, 1*, 195–210.

Wilson, G. T., Nathan, P. E., O'Leary, K. D., & Clark, L. A. (1996). *Abnormal psychology: Integrating perspectives.* Needham Heights, MA: Allyn & Bacon.

Wingfield, H. (1919). *The forms of alcoholism and their treatment.* London: Oxford University Press.

Zucker, R. A. (1987). The four alcoholisms: A developmental account of the etiologic process. In P. C. Rivers (Ed.), *Alcohol and addictive behavior* (pp. 27–83). Lincoln, NE: University of Nebraska Press.

10

Substance Abuse
Etiological Considerations

R. O. PIHL

The Natural History of Drug Abuse

The medical historian Osler wrote "that the only characteristic that distinguishes man from other animals is his propensity to take drugs" (in Bean, 1951). Given current knowledge, Osler might add that there are exceptions to this statement and also that the propensity to "do drugs" is as old as human behavior. In the first instance, animal behaviorists have commonly observed various species ingesting substances for both medicinal and seemingly recreational purposes. Intoxicated behavior is seen in most animals, from elephants to the catnip-consuming pet (Siegal, 1989). Some, like humans, consume hallucinogenic mushrooms—for example, Siberian deer—who then show incoordination and general intoxicated behavior (Furst, 1992). In the second instance, beginning with the earliest indications of human behavior, drugs seem to have been ingested for at least three reasons: to treat disorders both physical and mental, as purgatives, and to alter experience.

Regarding the first reason, in the area of abnormal behavior, pharmacological treatment with behavioral-altering drugs is now the sine qua non of modern psychiatry, and in the future may be even for psychology. This form of treatment was known to the ancient Greeks, who viewed opium as a treatment for grief, and to early inhabitants of India, who used the snakeroot plant, the source of reserpine, a current but seldom used antipsychotic drug, for various disorders. One rather unusual drug employed in the treatment of behavior problems during Shakespeare's time was usnea, made from the moss that grew within the skulls of skeletons. Currently in North America, in excess of 150 million prescriptions are written annually for psychotherapeutic drugs. As a purgative, drugs were and are used as added inducement to reverse consumatory excesses and make one's internal environment uncomfortable for whatever organisms or wicked spirits are thought to be infesting an individual. Consistent with this approach, the ancient Egyptians regularly mixed various forms of excrement with their medicines, which likely gave rise to the frequently heard comment regarding the taste of most drugs.

In terms of altering experience, Rudgley has (1994) argued that Paleolithic drawings that festoon the dark and dank interiors of caves throughout southern Europe were inspired by fly agaric, an hallucinogenic mushroom. It seems many of the drawn geometric symbols, repeated throughout the continent, are strikingly similar to those seen in visual hallucinations produced in today's users. Rudgley also detailed how the opium poppy was cultivated and used by neolithic societies (4th millennium B.C.), as was cannabis. Indian physicians in the first millennium B.C. used cannabis as a surgical anaesthetic, but perhaps the typical use was best cited by the Greek historian Herodotus, who in the fifth century B.C. described cannabis-intoxicated Scythians as "enjoying the drug so much they howl with pleasure." The Indo-Iranians of the second millenium B.C. used a plant called soma, the term later popularized by Huxley in *Brave New World* (1932), which was likely a hallucinogenic mushroom. Rudgley traced the use of fermented beverages (alcohol) to the fourth millennium B.C. Prominent mention of beer occurs in early Sumerian texts, and the Egyptians are described as being heavy users of beer and wine, as well as opium, mandrake root, hempbene, and myhrr, the latter being stimulants and occasional hallucinogens. The discovery of the New World opened new vistas of experience alteration, as some 100 species of hallucinogens have been discovered, a number far exceeding what existed in the Old World. The Incas of Peru chewed daily allotments of coca leaves for intoxication and stimulation, a behavior they inherited from the Nasca culture of approximately 500 A.D. Similarly, the use of peyote derived from a cactus and the use of mushrooms by the Aztecs to induce hallucinations was well known. Rudgley quoted a sixteenth-century Franciscan missionary writing in the *Florentine Codex* who describes the following drug experience:

> At a banquet the first thing the Aztec Indians ate was a black mushroom which they call nanácatl. These mushrooms caused them to become intoxicated, to see visions and also to be provoked to lust. They ate the mushrooms before dawn when they also drank cacao. They ate the mushrooms with honey and when they began to feel excited due to the effect of the mushrooms, the Indians started dancing, while some were singing and others weeping. Thus was the intoxication produced by the mushrooms. Some Indians who did not care to sing, sat down in their rooms, remaining there as if to think. Others, however, saw in a vision that they died and thus cried; others saw themselves being eaten by a wild beast; others imagined that they were capturing prisoners of war; others that they were rich or that they possessed many slaves; others that they committed adultery and had their heads crushed for this offence; others that they had stolen some articles for which they had to be killed, and many other visions. When this mushroom intoxication had passed, the Indians talked over amongst themselves the visions they had seen.

Notably, both positive and negative experiences are described as a result of this polydrug use, as well as overall social reinforcement, a scenario prevalent today.

These historical examples point out the very basic nature of drug-taking behavior for experience-altering reasons. This behavior is part of who we are; it is fundamental yet not necessary. For myriad reasons, societies can and do restrain use. In some, the use of these drugs is relegated to a privileged few: to shamen, to persons in positions of status, to certain age groups or to men. In others, total restriction is the rule, while there are few where use is unfettered. There are those societies, like our own, that attempt to discriminate, arguably poorly and variably, allowing usage of some drugs and disapproving of others, restricting harshly in some instances and benignly in others. Finally, it is important to differentiate between drug use and abuse. For example, relatively few of the approximately 70% of Americans who have tried illicit drugs ever develop drug problems. The challenge is to explain why these few are "the vulnerable ones."

The Importance of Etiology

Attempts to understand the factors that control the occurrence of an event—that is, taking drugs and abusing drugs—presume that causation or etiology is explicable. This is an essential objective, as the ultimate goal in behavior pathology is to treat and prevent. Presently, many treatments are based on no or minimal insight into causality and thus can be ineffective, inefficient, and even dangerous. The current practice of criminalization for some types of drug use encompasses each of these three negative aspects; this is the case also for many of the disastrous treatments of psychiatry past. Even the so-called enlightened treatments, such as Alcoholics' Anonymous, which involve elaborate social manipulations to control general behavior, with some degree of success, basically do so in the absence of knowledge of cause. Perhaps this is also the reason drug abuse disorders such as alcoholism are so frightfully underdiagnosed, with deference often given to other co-morbid disorders. For example, only 5 to 20% of alcoholics are ever treated in their lifetime, and, in those few who are treated, the efficacy of treatment is modest to low (Emrick, 1989; Holder, Longabaugh, Miller, & Rubonis, 1991). In fact, this modest treatment outcome is quite similar across drugs of abuse—that is, alcohol, opiates, cocaine (McLellan et al., 1994), suggesting that treatment is ideological and practitioner driven, rather than determined by patient characteristics; yet, it is precisely these characteristics that should determine what form and amount of treatment are offered.

Terms that are becoming more and more common in the lexicon of the addictions are "heterogeneous," "multifactorial," "interactional," and "interdependent." These terms are increasingly used whenever etiology of drug abuse is the topic, and they denote complexity and obviate current simple linear theories, be they genetic, social, or otherwise. The future will see presently separate areas of analysis—biological, psychological, and social—interacting to contribute explanations for the development of drug abuse problems. As an exemplar, figure 10.1 presents a model of risk factors for alcoholism in those individuals with a positive family history of alcoholism. The point of its inclusion is to illustrate the sheer complexity, and the number of variables and their interactions that are involved, in trying to explain cause. Yet, for all its apparent inclusivity the model lacks both completeness and specificity. Even though focused on only those with a family history of alcoholism, absent from the model are numerous differential biological possibilities for those with a positive family history, which likely involve divergent paths to the disorder. Regarding specificity, questions unanswered are which temperaments, cognitive dysfunctions, life stresses, and so on have an impact, and in which way and for whom. However, expecting any model to fit all possibilities is patently unrealistic. The field is replete with etiological models that are in focus, both complex and simplistic, distal and proximal, linear and reciprocal, and all of which may fail to adequately explain the individual case. The model presented in figure 10.1 is complex, involving many levels of analyses, some far removed (e.g., a drug-condoning culture) and others contiguous with drug use (e.g., being offered drugs by one's peer group). The model is reciprocal in that various factors are seen as interacting and influencing each other. For example, offspring temperament is seen as altering parenting behavior, which in turn is seen as affecting the development of temperament. In contrast, linear models postulate a direct path with one factor presumed to influence another. Explanations that rely on a particular biological state or some societal disadvantage are linear. This approach ignores the multitude of interacting, mediating, and modulating factors that likely are also involved.

A complicating factor for theories or models of drug abuse is that comorbidity, or the presence of another Axis I or II diagnosis, is the rule rather than the exception. When two or more disorders coexist, a distinction is often made between primary and secondary disorders in terms of which disorder is thought to be first and basically responsible for the other disorder. This distinction is deemphasized in this chapter, given that comorbid disorders may share a common etiology, and what follows is a discussion of current factors deemed etiologically significant for substance abuse at the various levels of analysis, beginning with the, until recently, most popularly accepted social and personality explanations.

At the Level of the Society

Culture

One's culture contributes substantially to the use and possible abuse of drugs.The breadth of these nonindividual factors is enormous, constituting at least five areas of influence. First, there is the general cultural environment that affects cultural norms concerning drug use, as well as influencing drug availability. Second, one's specific community affects values and norms and can support differential drug regulations that affect access. Third, subcultures within the community that can involve the workplace, groups at school, gangs, and the like have unique influences. Fourth, family and peers provide immediate models that can be permissive or restrictive, as well as providing direct access. Finally, the drug-using context, the physical and social environment, influences drug-using practices.

The importance of culture is illustrated by perhaps the most consistent finding regarding the use and abuse of various drugs, which is that there is wide variability between cultures. There are cultures in which drug use that our society defines as abnormal is seen as normal and even idealized be-

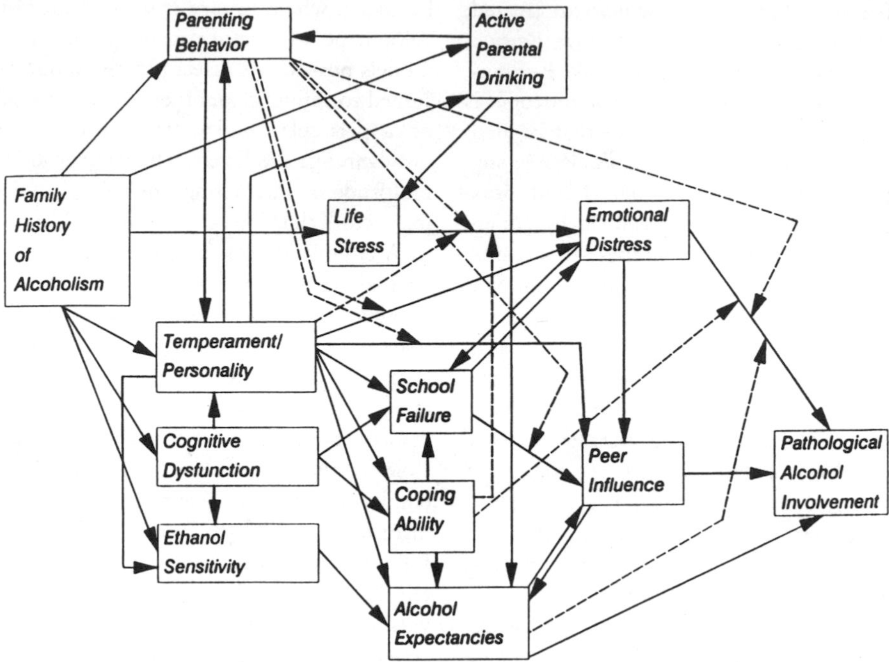

Figure 10.1 Comprehensive model of the relation between family history of alcoholism and pathological alcohol involvement in offspring. Note that most of the variables in the model are assumed to be heterogeneous (i.e., factorially complex). Mediating paths are indicated by solid lines, moderating paths and indicated by dashed lines (from Sher, 1991).

havior—for example, the use of hallucinogenic drugs. Conversely, some drug behaviors (e.g., alcohol) that we consider normative, and which some of our subcultures even idealize, are viewed as highly pathological in other cultures and in some of our subcultures. These differences point to one major nonarguable aspect regarding causation: drug abuse begins with drug use and one can neither try nor abuse that which is unavailable or unaffordable. Concerning alcohol, consumption rates and the frequency of problems have been shown to be related to availability (Smart, 1977; Watts & Rabow, 1983). Increased price reduces alcohol consumption, and increasing the legal drinking age reduces teen DWIs and traffic deaths. These controls are more readily achieved in isolated cultures, where they become interwoven into the basic fabric of societal life. The informational and commercial borderlessness of most western societies predestines such approaches to limited success, as witnessed by the failure of Prohibition, the war on drugs, and the fact that cigarettes and alcohol, although prohibited to minors, are sold to them by most merchants (cigarettes 77% in one study, Radecki & Zdunich, 1993; alcohol, over 50%, Foster, Murray, Wolfson, & Wagenaar, 1995). This reflects the absence of cultural consensus regarding drugs in our patchwork of divergent subcultures.

There are subcultures that promote and those that inhibit drug use and abuse. Drug subcultures emerge from common identities, such as age or perceived and real alienation, which in turn promote group solidarity. Central to each subculture is the development of a set of shared beliefs and practices. Normative beliefs, which are perceptions of the extent to which significant others approve or disapprove of or engage in a behavior themselves, have been shown to be important predictors of drug use, particularly in adolescents and young adults (Grube, Chen, Madden, & Morgan, 1996).

Social networks within subcultures have been described where drug availability and positive expectancies regarding the drug's effect have high promotional value. For example, Delany and Ames

(1995) studied such networks in occupational settings and found that alcohol consumption before and during work is related to the presence or absence of permissive drinking norms and the presence of labor-management antagonism. High levels of drug use, particularly alcohol, by university students represents another interesting example of the role of social networks within subcultures. Psychosocial predictors of drinking by undergraduates (68% are monthly users, though 70% are below the legal drinking age; Johnston, O'Mallery, & Bachman, 1996) include positive alcohol expectancies and peer influences, particularly membership in a fraternity or sorority (Martin & Hoffman, 1993). These same variables plus family drinking (Pullen, 1994), binge drinking in high school (Wechsler, Dondall, Davenport, & Castillo, 1995), a history of family alcoholism (Kushner & Sher, 1993), and nonreligiosity (Cronin, 1995) are related to heavy drinking. Interestingly, drinking levels and problem drinking by students have been quite consistent over time (Wechsler & Isaac, 1992).

One social aspect that has been viewed as a causative factor, and that theoretically could be manipulated, is poverty or neighborhood disorganization. Although poverty per se is a very weak predictor of drug abuse, when combined with neighborhood deterioration and high crime, the prediction increases substantially (Fagen, 1989). The dramatic loss of inner-city jobs, over 60% since the late 1960s in cities like Philadelphia, Chicago, and Detroit, has unfortunately resulted in a situation in which the economic "success" stories (hence models for youths) are often individuals engaged in illegal activities, including the selling of drugs. Further, in this milieu, family deterioriation is prevalent and prosocial training lacking. For the alienated and unemployed, the ostracism and unemployment associated with drug use are of little relevance.

Culture paints the drug-taking context with expectations of response that can also dramatically determine the actual response to the drug. For example, one study (Dobkin de Rios, 1973) illustrated that, when white subjects were compared to Indian subjects in their response to peyote intoxication, the former displayed shifts in mood, the latter stable mood but reverential feelings. Both groups were reflecting the expectations of their particular cultures. Another example concerns the response to cannabis: it has been shown that the intoxicating experience differs geographically (Adamec, Pihl, & Leiter, 1975), between the sexes (Adamec & Pihl, 1978), and with the milieu (Stark-Adamec, Pihl, & Adamec, 1981). These factors are also illustrated in a series of studies conducted in Jamaica in the late 1960s and early '70s. At this time a common belief in North America was that cannabis produced cognitive/neurological deficits, a conclusion supported by many studies. These studies, however, suffered a methodological flaw in that they used clinical, primarily "street" people, who reflected myriad problems as subjects. At this time, the smoking of ganga (cannabis) was almost normative behavior in Jamaica, although the distribution of use was bimodal. In two studies with four populations, none of the expected deleterious effects of very heavy use were found (Bowman & Pihl, 1973). Rather, drug effects seemed dictated by attitude toward the drug. For example, in those who thought one should feel hunger, that occurred; in others who believed satiety was the response, that also occurred. These findings have subsequently been systematically replicated (Rubin & Comitas, 1976).

Cultural variation that influences drug response can even occur in seemingly homogeneous groups. The first "study" of alcohol effects that this author was involved in occurred in the early 1960s. Along with a small group of married college students living adjacent to the football stadium, we sold tickets to drink beer during halftime at our apartment house. This occurred at a small midwestern college where drinking on campus was then prohibited. When the dean of students got wind of this entrepreneurial endeavor, all involved were threatened with expulsion if beer was served. However, tickets had been sold. Consequently, near-beer, an early variant of nonalcoholic beer, was hurriedly purchased from a brewery some 100 miles away, trucked to the apartment building, and bottles were opened and poured into kegs that were then pressurized. During the halftime of the game, those with tickets left the stadium and came to the basement of the apartment house. Experienced drinkers quickly realized that something was wrong, demanded refunds, and returned to the game. However, many individuals, particularly freshmen, displayed drunken behavior, incoordination, falling down, loud exhuberance, and some nausea and vomiting—all of this on a placebo. For these individuals, their expectations and milieu determined their behavior and physical state. Indeed, the examples of cultural variation in response to actual drugs suggest that pharmacologically active substances are also susceptible to this placebo phenomenon.

Within many cultures, psychotropic drugs are often viewed in a spiritual rather than hedonistic way, thus greatly coloring the response. For example, many early AmerIndian societies viewed smoking tobacco as a supernatural aid, and thus the behavior was done communally and to cement agreements. Another good example of cultural determination is in the area of alcohol-related aggression. There is substantial evidence both clinically in crime studies and in laboratory studies that the use of alcohol increases the likelihood of aggression (Pihl, Peterson, & Lau, 1993). Particular pharmacological effects on brain functioning that affect this behavior have been detailed (Pihl & Peterson, 1995a). Yet, there are societies in which, after consumption of considerable alcohol and reaching intoxication, normally sober aggressive individuals display a rather passive demeanor. Further, the behavioral problems frequently associated with excessive alcohol consumption are very rare in cultures where alcohol is considered a food rather than a drug, although health problems resulting from heavy consumption, such as liver disease, remain constant.

The society can model drug use in various ways. In the 1970s, a common explanation for the increased use of drugs conjured up a conspiracy theory. In effect, a de facto collusion between the pharmacological industry and prescribing physicians to promote the use of drugs was proposed (Lennard, Epstein, Bernstein, & Ramson, 1971). The logic was based on the fact that more than half of the individuals seeing physicians were not physically ill but suffered problems in living, which they expressed as physical complaints. Physicians were then seen as prescribing psychotropic drugs to placate the patient and to cement the role of healer. This process was viewed as encouraged by the pharmaceutical industry, where market expansion is accomplished by broadening the definition of problems requiring drug treatment. The evidence for this "conspiracy" included a rapid rise in the prescription of psychotropes, industry advertising that broadened definitions of problems requiring drug treatment, and studies showing the prescribing of psychotropes varied with the training and personality characteristics of doctors. The effect of the "conspiracy" was said to be that focus on the source of the problems per se did not occur, and thus one learned to use drugs to deal with and complement living. In effect, it was argued that an induced pharmacological blindness to reality was produced; a drug culture developed that then generalized from legal to illegal use. Currently, encouraged are the use of drugs are the prolific use and encouragement of use of over-the-counter medications to deal with all forms of child and adult distress, the trend of drug companies to advertise directly to consumers in the popular media, and advocacy of the use of these drugs (e.g., Prozac) to adjust personality (Kramer, 1993).

Cultural examples adroitly illustrate that definitions of problems with drugs often depend on where one resides and who is the user, and that complete models of causation must be multidimensional. Explanations that reside purely within the individual, either physiological or psychological, do not tell the whole story. In fact, a methodological conundrum exists as the application of more science per se cannot solve the problem of shifting definitions, beliefs, and attitudes. Models of etiology are therefore in themselves contextually dependent on the environment and philosophy that constructed them.

The Peer Group

If one has friends who use various drugs, the odds are much higher that one will also. This correlation appears greater if illicit drug use is involved (Swain, Oetting, & Beauvais, 1989), if one is in the initial stages of drug use (Kandel & Yamaguchi, 1985), and if one is white (Newcomb & Bentler, 1986). Specifically, deviancy, lack of achievement, and time spent with friends are important factors in predicting drug use. Dryfoos (1990), in a superb review, listed separately the risk characteristics for the deviant behaviors of drug abuse, delinquency, teenage pregnancy, and school failure and dropout. What appeared was a striking similarity in the list of characteristics that preceded each of these problems. This phenomenon had previously been labeled by researchers (Jessor & Jessor, 1977) as a "problem behavior syndrome." The behaviors included in this predictive basket vary somewhat from study to study, but in approximated decreasing order of inclusion are: conduct problems, slow school achievement and truancy, age at initiation, high peer influence and peer drug use, nonconformity, lack of parental support, sex, parental drug use, lack of resources at home, neighborhood, and health risk behaviors. Generally, a defiance pattern holds; however, as more variables enter the mix the more a multidimensional solution is found (Basen-Engquist, Edmundson, & Parcel, 1996). As an explanation, it is believed that peers reinforce each other for deviant behavior particularly when alienated from convention (Patterson, DeBaryshe, & Ramsey, 1989).

Related to this syndrome is the so-called gateway model, where use from one drug to the next (from legal to illegal drugs) is seen as sequential. Cigarettes, alcohol, marijuana, stimulants, depressants, hallucinogens, cocaine, and heroin are seen hierarchically (Kandel, Kessler, & Margulies, 1978). Obviously, this progression is not inevitable and order is arguable, but exposure to peers who engage in drug use a step beyond one's own is seen as an important determining factor, particularly if one is strongly identified with these peers. This identification is seen as involving expectations regarding positive results from such drug use. Thus, Oetting and Beauvais (1987) suggested that peer factors are central, first in providing the drug, second in developing attitudes about its use and effects, and third in providing an examplar. In fact, their peer cluster theory states not only that peers are the most important predictor of use and progression to abuse and other drugs but also that peers mediate the significance of other risk factors—for example, emotional problems and attitudes about oneself. Some research has confirmed these social learning interpretations, and the consequent argument has been made that interventions should be aimed at peers (Swain et al., 1989). Other research (Fisher & Bowman, 1988; Farrell & Danish, 1993) using longitudinal designs, however, suggests that the relationship is more complex, with the more frequent scenario being peer selection following drug use.

Part of the variability in studying peer and other factors in drug use arises from how *use* is defined. Studies that measure "ever used" may be selecting the wrong population for study. Drug experimentation by adolescents, even with an illegal drug such as marijuana, may be "normative" behavior. One study (Shedler & Block, 1990) found that adolescents who never experimented with drugs, particularly marijuana, showed indications of being more maladjusted than the occasional experimenters. A more recent study (Wills, McNamara, Vaccaro, & Hirky, 1996), however, has found that these experimenters do display some risk factors. In any case, heavy, escalating, and debilitating drug use should be the focus.

Social modeling is a phenomenon often invoked to explain peer effects. Basically one learns by observing, and learning is more likely when the model is similar in age and other characteristics, is looked up to, and the behavior in question is seen as rewarding. Peers alienated from school, parents, and socially conforming peers can readily adopt drug use and create a reinforcing environment where such use achieves priority. Numerous studies on modeling and drinking have shown that one's quantity consumed and drinking style vary with the behavior of one's drinking partner (Collins, Parks, & Marlatt, 1985). Another area where modeling seems to play a role is in the behavior of one's parents and siblings.

The Family

Drug abuse runs in families. Regarding alcoholism, this has been known for centuries. In a very extensive review (Cotton, 1979) it was concluded that this disorder was three to five times more prevalent in relatives of alcoholics than in the general population. Although this may result from genetic factors, environmental variance, or both, this section focuses on how family or parental factors contribute to learning to use drugs through modeling, expectancy, and child abuse and neglect.

Modeling of drug use occurs when parents use drugs of various sorts to relieve negative feelings, cope with stress, provide a social lubricant, and so on. As suggested earlier, this behavior also includes the giving of medications to their children for similar reasons. The most blatant example of modeling is parental abuse of illicit drugs. The recent increase in misuse of drugs by adolescents (Johnston et al., 1996) has been attributed by politicians and the popular press to the fact that the parents of these individuals are at the minimum ambivalent about drug use, and that many parents are models for drug use because of their own use during the 1960s and '70s. Indeed, a number of studies support the conclusion of parental drug use as a risk factor for adolescent initiation and use (Johnson, Schoutz, & Locke, 1984; Brook, Brook, Gordon, Whiteman, & Cohen, 1990). In fact, with the exception of cigarettes, the more family members there are using drugs, the greater the likelihood of use. In the case of cigarettes, all that seems necessary is that there be one smoker, although older brothers are more influential than younger brothers (Brook, Whiteman, Gordon, & Brook, 1988), as modeling explanations would predict. Modeling aside, the simple availability of cigarettes, alcohol, and marijuana within the family seems to be a contributing factor (Resnick et al., 1997). Studies also show that permissive parental attitudes facilitate use (McDermott, 1984; Barnes & Welte, 1986). Poor parental support, defined as lack of ease at talking with one's parents, help on school work, and so on, is another predictor (Wills, McNamara, Vaccaro, & Hirky, 1996). In another study, lack of mother nurturance, measured as maternal support on a series of laboratory tasks, predicted drug use (Dobkin, Tremblay, & Sacchitelle, 1997). In this study, however, early deviancy on the part of the child was also a predictor, raising the possibility that the poor mothering resulted from her child's disruptive behavior.

Stress is a frequent family member in the drug-abusing family. For example, stressors common in families with alcoholism include high conflict and poor communication (Moos & Moos, 1984), marital discord (Wolin, Bennett, Noonan, & Teitelbaum, 1980), coercive interactions (Patterson & Dishion, 1988), physical abuse and neglect (Widom, Ireland, & Glynn, 1995), economic and social deprivation (Dryfoos, 1990), and the extremes of parenting being too authoritarian or too lax (Kempher & DeMarsh, 1985). In risk studies, individuals are at greater risk for drug abuse if they come from a broken home (Baumrind, 1983), there is martial conflict (Simcha-Fagen, Gersten, & Langner, 1986), and or poor parent-child relationships (Baumrind, 1983). Indeed, abusive parenting, ranging from neglect to physical abuse, is commonly thought to be linked to the development of substance abuse, though longitudinal studies of childhood victimization suggest the relationship is weak (Dembo et al., 1990; McCord, 1983). The effect seems more significant in abused girls than boys. In an elegant study (Widom et al., 1995), even when family history of alcoholism was controlled statistically, abused girls remained at risk for drinking problems in adulthood. The opposite situation to a negative family environment, of course, exists. Recently, in a massive national interview study of adolescents from grades 7 to 12 (Resnick et al., 1997), positive family connectedness—defined as feelings of warmth, love, and caring from parents—significantly protected individuals from drug use as well as many other harmful behaviors. Related work with animals (Liu et al., 1997) reveals that more mother-rat pup postnatal contact results in an adult rat with less stress or neuroendocrine reactivity.

A seldom considered but potentially significant family factor in the etiology of drug abuse are teratogenic effects. Drug use by parents can deleteriously affect interuterine development. Well known is fetal alcohol syndrome (FAS) where low birthweight, prematurity, infant mortality, central nervous system dysfunction, and physical anomalies are often described (Streissguth, Bookstein, Sampson, & Barr, 1993). Similar effects are now considered a threat when many drugs are used, particularly drugs of abuse. These include cocaine, amphetamines, cigarettes and opiates, prescribed drugs like barbiturates, and other common tranquilizers. It is often assumed that these effects are exclusive to drug use by pregnant mothers. However, fathers can also affect their nonborn offspring. Human infants fathered by regular drinkers weigh less than those fathered by nondrinkers, after control for maternal ethanol and nicotine use (Little & Sing, 1986). In experimental male animals given alcohol, their offspring are characterized by increased susceptibility to infection, hyperresponsiveness to stress (Abel, Hazlett, Berk, & Mutchnik, 1990), poorer T-maze performance, improved passive avoidance (Abel & Lee, 1988) and reduced active avoidance learning (Abel & Tan, 1988), and changes in noradrenergic, serotonergic, and endorphin brain systems (Nelson, Brighwell, Mackenzie-Taylor, Berg, & Massari, 1988).

How this drug use by parents impacts risk for abuse in offspring is illustrated in a recent well-controlled study. Wakschlay et al. (1997) found that mothers who smoked one half a pack of cigarettes a day or more when pregnant were significantly more likely to have a child who could be diagnosed with conduct disorder than nonsmoking mothers. Similarly, children with FAS are more likely to manifest conduct and attention deficit disorders than nonaffected children. Each of these behavioral profiles, in turn, are known risk factors for drug abuse and dependence. The relationship is illustrated in figure 10.2. Interestingly, potential teratogenic effects are seldom considered, even as a variable to be controlled, in etiological studies. Yet, these effects could account for explanations currently attributed to the family, like modeling and even genetic influences.

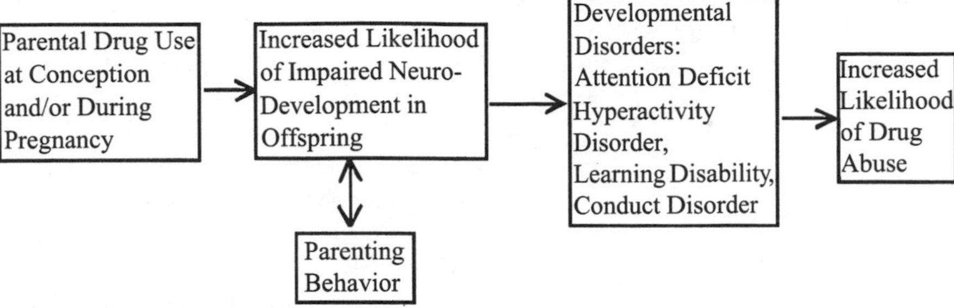

Figure 10.2 Schematic models of possible teratogenic drug effects on subsequent offspring behavior and risk for drug abuse.

Stress and Affective Factors

Irrespective of the source, when asked why they abuse substances, people most frequently report that it is to reduce stress. This is theorized to occur for a number of reasons—for example, as a coping strategy, as an escape, and as a form of self-medication. "Stress response dampening" (Sher, 1987) is a term used to describe the reduction in physiological reactivity to stressors when drinking. Indeed, the rationale for prescribing benzodiazepines to anxious patients is to reduce reactivity, an effect shared by alcohol. A recent study (Kushner et al., 1996) found that in patients with panic disorder, a moderate dose of alcohol decreased anxiety and responses to a panic challenge. The authors conclude, as have many others, that this effect is likely reinforcing and explains the high comorbidity of these types of drugs with panic and anxiety disorders. Panickers, for example, are four times the normal risk for alcoholism (Weissman, 1988), and 15% of alcoholic men and 38% of alcoholic women (compared, respectively, to 10 and 18% of nonalcoholics) have a lifetime anxiety disorder (Helzer & Pryzbeck, 1988).

There is considerable evidence that severe trauma—that is, disaster, assault, combat—greatly increases the risk for drug abuse; unsurprisingly, drug abuse is also a frequent concomitant of posttraumatic stress disorder (PTSD). Although abuse of almost any drug has been reported to be associated with the experiencing, witnessing, or confronting of a physically threatening event (Keane, Gerardi, Lyons, & Wolfe, 1988), alcohol abuse is most frequent. For example, regarding sexual abuse, Stewart (1996), in an extensive review, noted that in any treatment population of alcoholic women, the rates of a history of sexual abuse range from 24 to 85%. One longitudinal study that looked at this relationship (Wilsnack, 1991) found that the onset of problem drinking in women was significantly predicted by sexual abuse. Indeed, there is ample evidence that the typical order is that the sexual abuse precedes the alcohol abuse (Stewart, 1996). Similarly, in Vietnam veterans who had drug abuse problems associated with PTSD, the average was 3½ years between the onset of these symptoms and the development of the drug disorder (Davidson, Swartz, Storck, Krishnan, & Hammett, 1985). This order suggests the reinforcing mechanism that maintains that the drug abuse is related to the anxiety pathology. Although stress or anxiety is an important etiological consideration, two caviats are appropriate. First, even though users say they imbibe to reduce stress, this is not confirmed in laboratory manipulative studies where the results are extremely inconsistent (Pihl & Smith, 1983). Second, the majority of individuals under stress do not turn to drugs for relief. Thus, again, more than a single explanation is required.

Depression is likewise common in cases of drug abuse. For example, more than half of hospitalized alcoholics are also diagnosed as depressed (Merikengas & Gerlanter, 1990): Epidemiological studies suggest that the risk of an alcohol dependency/depression comorbidity is roughly two times what would be normally expected, and it is most problematic and severe in women. A meta-analysis of eight longitudinal studies showed that depression predicted alcohol consumption for women (Hartka et al. 1991). Another study showed that depression tends to precede becoming alcoholic in women (66% of the cases) while for men alcoholism precedes depression (78%; Helzer & Pryzbeck, 1988). Women typically report problems with intimacy and interpersonal stress as the reasons for excessive drug consumption (Frank, Tuer, & Jacobson, 1990; Zucker, 1987).

At the Level of the Individual

Personality

For much of this century, the reasons for drug problems at an individual level were typically ascribed to the presence of an addictive personality. Indeed, a plethora of studies yielded evidence supporting a wide range of topical personality profiles as etiologically significant. In an earlier review (Pihl & Spiers, 1978), it was determined that 93% of this research studied exclusively patients in treatment for various drug abuse problems. Thus, the results may well have reflected the characteristics of individuals who seek or are mandated to treatment, or the concomitants of the problem rather than the cause of the problem. Additionally, in these earlier studies, measures were methodologically questionable. Fortunately, recent years have seen the development of well-constructed measures that are valid predictors tied to limited theoretical notions. These narrow approaches are starting to produce predictive information.

Trull and Sher (1994), studying a large nonclinical sample of young adults, found that those individuals who were subsequently diagnosible with substance use disorders displayed distinctive personality patterns. Specifically, these individuals had significantly higher neuroticism, lower extraversion, higher openness, lower agreeableness, and lower conscientiousness scores than those without a *DSM-III-R* diagnosis. Lifetime alcohol abuse or dependence subjects produced a similar pattern with the exception that they did not show a lower extraversion score. These findings generally fit the pattern of scores achieved with various drug abusing subjects on other measures. For example, a high openness score has been seen as reflecting elevated sensation and novelty seeking (Trull & Sher, 1994). Many studies (Andrucci, Archer, Pancoast, & Gordon, 1989; Zuckerman, 1979) have shown that high scores on tests measuring these traits correlate with drug use in general. In fact, the trait of sensation seeking is a better predictor of drug abuse than self-esteem, mental health, social bonding, or social class. These traits may be involved in the exploratory substance use that precedes abuse, and they may also be linked to biological systems more directly involved in drug reinforcement.

High neuroticism similarly could be linked to other trait characteristics shown to have predictive strength, such as anxiety sensitivity (Sher, 1987). Individuals high in anxiety sensitivity are also at high risk for abuse of alcohol and other anxyliotics (McNally, 1996). When compared to nonanxiety-sensitive subjects, they are more likely to be diagnosed alcohol dependent (Karp, 1993), consume more alcohol per se (Cox, Swinson, Shulman, Kuch, & Reichman, 1993), say they drink to cope (Stewart et al., 1997), and display stress response dampening when intoxicated (Stewart & Pihl, 1994).

Low self-esteem scores, particularly in adolescents, have been linked to drug use (Reid, Martinson, & Weaver, 1987; Sussman et al., 1990), yet many studies have shown no effect (Jessor & Jessor, 1977; Kandel, Kessler, & Margulies, 1978). It may well be that this trait interacts with others to predict use and abuse. It may also be that very low and very high self-esteem both confer a risk for abuse (see Baumeister, Smart, & Boden, 1996).

Genetics

As mentioned above, drug abuse runs in families. The previous discussion illustrated how familial factors like parenting practices and possible teratogenic effects can increase risk vulnerability. In addition, heritability of vulnerability is also a possible explanation for this relationship. In the area of the genetics of drug abuse, alcoholism has received the most attention. Interest in the importance of genes in this area primarily arose in the early 1980s, when a spate of adoption and twin studies appeared in the literature.

Adoption Studies A number of adoption studies (Cloninger, Bohman, & Sigvardson, 1981; Goodwin et al., 1974) indicated that having a biological parent who was alcoholic increases one's risk for alcoholism about 2.5 times, regardless of whether one was raised by that parent. A typology of inherited vulnerability has been extracted from this data where Type 1 inheritance is thought to involve both men and women, be less severe, and result in a later age of onset for the problem as well as being affected by environmental factors. Type 2 is thought to be relatively immune from environmental influences, limited to men, develop at a significantly younger age, and occur in individuals who display, as did their fathers, impulsivity and antisocial behavior (Cloninger, 1987). Subsequently, it has been suggested that there is a group of genetically vulnerable individuals who show the characteristics of Type 2s but without antisocial behavior (Hill, 1992), and that Type 2s cluster according to the presence or absence of particular cardiovascular responsivity when sober and intoxicated (Conrod, Peterson, Pihl, & Mankowski, 1997). In a recent study (Sigvardsson, Bohman, & Cloninger, 1996), Type 2 individuals were found to have a six times increased likelihood of developing the disorder irrespective of the presence or absence of alcoholism in their environment.

Twin Studies A review of 13 earlier twin studies (Cadoret, 1990) showed a greater concordance for the disorder in monozygotic versus dizygotic twins. These studies also demonstrated a genetic influence in quantity and frequency of drinking behavior. More recent twin studies (Carmelli, Heath, & Robinette, 1993; McGue, Pickens, & Svikis, 1992; Kendler, Neal, Kessler, Heath, & Eaves, 1992) have confirmed the importance of heritability, with the most recent and ambitious (Kendler, Prescott, Neale, & Pedersen, 1997) assessing three times the number of affected twins as the next largest study. In this sample, male twins registered with a Swedish Temperance Board indicating problems with alcohol abuse were studied. Concordance rates were, respectively, 47.9% for monozygotic twins and 32.8% for dizygotic twins. Model fitting resulted in attributing 54% to genetic and 14% to familial-environmental risk factors for liability to temperance board registration. These results are generally consistent with the other twin studies. Further, the birth years 1902 to 1949 covered by the study witnessed major social change and marked fluctuations in attitude and law toward alcohol; still, the study found that, when examined over time, genetic and environmental factors remained stable.

Twin studies that have assessed gender differences have shown a stronger genetic influence on early onset alcoholism in males and a lesser influence on alcohol problems in women and late onset problems in men (McGue et al., 1992). However, the data on sex differences should not be construed as suggesting that alcohol problems in women are not heritable. Kendler et al. (1992) have shown that 50 to 61% of the risk for alcoholism in women is the result of genetic influences. Finally, heritability seems more important for problems of alcohol dependence than alcohol abuse (Pickens et al., 1991).

Linkage and Association Studies Which and how many of the 20,000 genes in the human genome thought to be expressed in the central nervous system are involved in drug abuse disorders has become the focus of recent research. One procedure uses chromosomal markers, restriction fragment length polymorphisms (RFLPs), which are short DNA sequences. One such RFLP, the "A1" tag 1 of the D2 dopamine receptor located on chromosome 11 has been linked to alcoholism (Blum et al., 1990). An increased prevalence of the A1 allele was found in the brain tissue of 35 deceased severe alcoholics. A flurry of studies followed this finding with diverse results. The results of 10 studies were summarized by Smith et al. (1992), who noted that 41% of white alcoholics compared to 27% of white controls were A1 positive. When compared to whites, the allele is twice as likely to be found in African Americans and three to four times more likely in an American Indian population (Goldman et al., 1993). It is possible that this A1 gene has multiple effects, and that it influences the course rather than onset of the disorder.

The presence of certain genes not only can indicate increased vulnerability but also can significantly protect against the development of the problem. In the case of alcoholism, many Asians, but not Caucasians, have a form of two liver enzymes that are thought to protect against the disorder. The first, an inactive form of mitochondrial aldehyde dehydrogenas, allows high levels of acetaldehyde to build up in the blood, resulting in negative feelings—that is, flushing; the second, an atypical alcohol dehydrogenase 2 accelerates activity. In one study, the frequencies of these genetic forms successfully separated a population of Japanese alcoholics from nonalcoholics (Higuchi, Matsushita, Murayama, Takagi, & Hayashada, 1995).

Another line of evidence is the discovery of genes involved in behaviors and temperament characteristics seen in drug-vulnerable populations. The trait of novelty seeking has been found, by two research groups, to be related to a polymorphism of the D4 receptor gene on chromosome 11 (Ebstein et al., 1996; Benjamin et al., 1996). As it accounts for only 10% of genetic variation in the trait, it likely represents simply an initial discovery. More recently, dopamine receptor genes have been seen as explaining 20 to 30% of the variance in ADHD individuals, who are also at high risk for drug abuse (La Hoste, Swawnson, Wigal, King, & Kennedy, 1996; O'Brien, 1996).

Animal Studies Until relatively recently, selective breeding was the major animal research methodology. Here, animals selected for a specific behavior (e.g., preference for alcohol) are interbred through many successive generations. Using this procedure, a number of drug-preferring mice and rat strains have been developed. For example, C57BL/6 mice are vulnerable to amphetamines (induced place learning, drug sensitivity, etc.), while mice of the DBA/2 strain are amphetamine resistant (Cabib, Puglisi-Allegra, Le Moal, & Piazza, 1996). There are currently six alcohol-preferring rat strains—that is, rats who consume more alcohol, work to get alcohol even when water and food are present, and develop physical dependence—showing indications of both tolerance and withdrawal (Crabbe, 1989). With such populations, etiological mechanisms are explored, varying from linkage studies to research aimed at determining which biochemical processes are affected to studies of possible gene-environment interactions.

The DNA RFLP marker techniques discussed above are less robust when multiple or "weak" genes are involved than when there is a single gene. Because there is a high likelihood that many genes contribute to an additive vulnerability, techniques for identifying quantitative trait loci (QTL), where a small amount of DNA is believed to effect a trait, have been developed. This approach conforms to the continuous-discontinuous debate regarding diagnoses. That is, unlike qualitative genetic approaches that view traits dichotomously—for example, eye color—the quantitative approach assumes the trait is distributed continuously with expression in degree rather than kind. QTL mapping is the procedure for finding these trait loci. In the area of drug abuse, recent activity has focused on QTL analysis in recombinant mouse strains, in particular those derived from C57 mice and long-sleep (LS alcohol preferring) mice.

To date, it seems that a number of genes are involved in sensitivity to acute effects of alcohol and in withdrawal response to chronic exposure (Dudek & Tritto, 1995). For example, increased sensitivity to alcohol as measured in the loss of the righting reflex in LS mice suggests QTLs on 11 different chromosomes are possibly involved. Thus, we are far from having compelling support for specific genetic involvement in either alcohol or cocaine sensitization (Phillips, 1997). Some specificity regarding QTLs for alcohol withdrawal in mice have recently been reported. Buck, Metten, Belknap, and Crabbe (1997) found genes on chromosomes 1, 4, and 11 that affect severity of withdrawal. In fact, three genes, one involved in the GABA system, the second in the glutamate system, and a third known to effect seizures, collectively account for 68% of the genetic variability in alcohol withdrawal in mice.

Complications On the human level, a variety of additional considerations complicate genetic data. One is assortative mating. Studies show, for example, that alcoholics tend to marry alcoholics (Boye-Beaman, Leonard, & Seuchak, 1991). Another is the previously mentioned fetal drug effects. Finally, gene-environment interactions occur where genes set vulnerability but phenotypic-expression depends on the occurrence of certain environmental events. This probably occurs with most behavioral disorders, and it complicates research at strictly the genetic level, especially in the case for humans with their complex histories and environments.

Even when genes are implicated, we remain a good distance from knowing what is inherited and, most important, how vulnerability is affected. For example, regarding alcoholism, Gordis (1996) has listed some possibilities of what it is that is inherited: "differences in temperament, different initial sensitivity to the rewarding or aversive qualities of alcohol, different rates and routes of alcohol metabolism, different taste preferences, different signaling from peripheral sites to the brain after drinking alcohol and different abilities to relate memories of drinking experiences to their consequences" (p. 199). Hence, once substantial genetic involvement is implicated, the key question is: what is it that the genes in question are doing to enhance vulnerability? Disorders defined on a behavioral level are far removed and under the influence of many other factors than those found at a molecular level.

Biochemistry

In studying the etiology of drug abuse one must attend to the biochemical level of study for at least five reasons. The first reason is that genetic processes are fundamentally biochemical. Second, numerous other factors, (nutrition, stress, etc.) readily affect biochemical functioning and thus, like genes, may alter individual sensitivity to various drugs. Third, increasingly, drug abuse problems are being treated pharmacologically; effective treatment often requires knowledge of etiology, and ideally the therapeutic drug "works" by blocking the biochemical reasons why the abused drug is taken. Fourth, and most obvious, what drugs of abuse do is affect the biochemical systems of an individual; to the degree that this effect is relatively specific, explanations for use and abuse become more explicable. Fifth, drug-induced states such as tolerance and withdrawal actually alter the biochemical functioning of the individual so as to facilitate the continuance and reoccurrence of abuse. Relevant studies appear to focus on neurotransmitter systems including receptors and neuromodulators. Thus, our attention will focus on the dopaminergic, serotonergic, GABAinergic, glutamate, endogenous opioid, and cannaboid and nicotine systems. Although treated separately in what follows, these systems are not independent; they continually interact with each other in facilitating and inhibitory ways.

The Dopaminergic System There are specific areas of the brain for which electrical or chemical stimulation is positively reinforcing, as evidenced by the fact that animals will work to cause such stimulation to occur. The primary focus of this effect, the mesolimbic area (including the ventral tegmental area and the nucleus accumbens) is mediated primarily by dopamine. The rate of self-stimulation is dependent on the density of dopamine neurons, and drugs that block dopamine neurons, like antipsychotics, reduce self-stimulation (Fibiger & Phillips, 1988). Stimulant drugs of abuse operate on this system in one fashion or another. For example, both cocaine and amphetamines block the dopamine reuptake process and thus prolong the effects of released dopamine, and amphetamines may also directly release dopamine as well as norepinephrine (Koob & Bloom, 1988). Alcohol has both stimulative and sedative effects, and has been shown to accelerate the firing of dopaminergic neurons in the ventral tegmental area (Gessa, Muntone, Collu, Vargiu, & Mereu, 1985). Alcohol also results in increased dopamine flux into the nucleus accumbens, as do marijuana and opiates (Leone, Pocock, & Wise, 1991). The effect of marijuana and opiates on this system, however, is likely indirect. Relevant to the previously discussed D2 allele studies, the primary action of psychostimulants appears to be on D2-like dopamine receptors (D2, D3, D4; Sibley & Monsma, 1992), although there is some evidence that even D1-like receptors (D1, D5) may have some involvement (Sibley & Monsma, 1992).

The activation of this dopamine system in the mesolimbic area may explain the high comorbidity between certain forms of drug use. For example, the fact that 84% of cocaine abusers also abuse alcohol (Helzer & Pryzbeck, 1988) may arise from processes in which the use of one drug makes other similar drugs more reinforcing. Interestingly, some environmental stimuli, such as stress, have also been shown to potentiate this sensitivity (Deminiere, Piazza, Le Moal, & Simon, 1989). A related phenomenon may be involved in drug craving and withdrawal. Stimulants chronically taken increase drug-induced dopamine release (Kalivas & Duffy, 1993), while acute short-term use decreases dopamine release (Imperato, Mele, Scrocco, & Puglici-Alegra, 1992).

There may be considerable individual variability with respect to the reinforcing effects that occur when this system is stimulated. For instance, rats bred to prefer alcohol may have an increased inhibition of the dopamine system, and this may explain their elevated alcohol preference (McBride, Murphy, Lumeng, & Li, 1990; Hwang, Lumeng, Wu, & Li, 1988). Sensitivity of the dopamine system in these animals may explain why alcohol enhances locomotor activity (Krimmer & Schecter, 1992). Further, strains of rats such as the Lewis rats, which also self-administer opiates and cocaine, show heightened place preference learning to morphine and cocaine (Guitart, Beitnes-Johnson, & Nestler, 1992).

The Serotonergic System Interest in the neurotransmitter serotonin (5HT) arises from its importance in governing cognitive, affective, and behavioral responses to environmental stimuli, its variations in strains of animals and individuals at risk for various forms of drug abuse, and its response to drugs of abuse. Serotonin is also involved in the regulation of many basic brain functions including circadian rhythms, food and water intake, sexual behavior, and response to pain. From an evolutionary standpoint, this system is ancient as it functions in neuronal development as well as a neurotransmitter and neuromodulator (Whittaker-Azmitia & Peroutka, 1990). The ascending serotonergic projections may be likened to a conductor in an orchestra, responsible for producing music and a harmonious unit out of instrumental sections and talented but individualistic soloists who would otherwise collectively produce noise (Pihl & Peterson, 1995a). It is theorized that optimal 5HT functioning leads to neurosynchrony of affect, cognition, and behavior, while 5HT insufficiency is associated with desynchronization, psychic disharmony, behavioral disregulation, impulsivity, and the production of anxiety as affect (Spoont, 1992). Deviations in the system's functioning appear simultaneously and paradoxically to result in both disinhibition of behavior and heightened sensitivity to stress and threat. These effects presumably account for the use of drugs that affect this system.

Early onset Type 2 alcoholics have generally been found to have lower concentrations of 5HT metabolites in their cerebral spinal fluid (CSF)—a good proxy of brain activity—than various control subjects (Fils-Aime et al., 1996; Ballenger, Goodwin, Major, & Brown, 1979). Similar findings have been reported in antisocial alcoholics with alcoholic fathers (Linnoila, DeJong, & Virkkunen, 1989) and in individuals who comorbidly abuse alcohol and other drugs (Fils-Aime et al., 1996). Further, when Type 2 individuals receive a 5HT 2C receptor antagonist, they display a strong urge to consume alcohol (Benkelfat et al., 1991). Other comorbid disorders linked to alcoholism, such as eating disorders and depression, have also been found to reflect problematic functioning in the 5HT system. In this vein, nonalcoholic depressed patients who have a family history of drinking problems display low CSF 5HT metabolite levels (Rosenthal, Davenport, Cowdry, Webster, & Goodwin, 1980). Reviews of the serotonin and alcohol literatures (LeMarquand, Pihl, & Benkelfat, 1994a, 1994b) support the conclusions that decreased 5HT functioning is related to increased alcohol use while the converse is also true. The 5HT system has also been shown to be involved in altering both the euphorigenic and anxiogenic effects of cocaine (Aronson et al., 1995).

Some hallucinogens, lysergic acid dielhylanide (LSD), N, N-dimethylamine, DMT, psiolocybin, and the phenethylamines (mescaline, methylenedioxy, or MDMA ecstasy) have an affinity for 5HT2 receptors (Titeler, Lyon, & Glenon, 1988). Further, 5HT2 antagonists block the effects of these drugs. Other drugs of abuse also affect 5HT systems in various ways—for example, cocaine blocks 5HT reuptake in the short term, and chronic cocaine use seems to reduce 5HT functioning.

The GABAnergic and Glutamate Systems Benzodiazepines, barbiturates, and alcohol are known to directly affect the gaba amino butyric acid (GABA) system. This widespread system's main action is on inhibitory neurons. The effect is produced by opening chloride ion channels, the major site of action for sedatives and anxiolytic agents (Warneke, 1991; Zorumski & Eisenberg, 1991). In fact, a drug's affinity for this action is directly linked to the sensitivity of the drug effect (Harris & Allen, 1989). One experimental drug, R015-4513 (a derivative of benzodiazepines), antagonizes the behavioral effects of alcohol in rats, and it was popularized as "making drunk animals sober" (Suzduk et al., 1986). Naturally occurring anxiolytics within the brain (Sangameswaran, Fales, Friedrich, & De Blas, 1986) and naturally occurring substances that heighten anxiety (Bodnoff, Suranyi-Cadotte, Quirion, & Meaney, 1989) both have been shown to effect GABA transmission. Directly and indirectly, this inhibition seems to operate on anxyogenic structures like the amygdala (Thomas, 1988). Thus, individuals affected by anxiety for whatever reasons should find the use of these drugs particularly reinforcing. This seems to be the case, as individuals who suffer from phobias, panic disorders, and anxiety sensitivity are at high risk to abuse these drugs.

Although drugs that affect GABA receptors are often used, particularly in Europe, as a pharmacological treatment for alcoholism, they are not generally effective in treating withdrawal symptoms, which can last for a considerable time (Litten & Allen, 1991). An exception to this generalization is the drug acamprosate, which stimulates GABA transmission and reduces glutamate activity. Experiments with rats (Gewiss, Heidbreder, Opsomer, Durbin, & DeWitte, 1991), and trials in Europe with humans (Sass, Sozka, Mann, & Ziezlyunsberger, 1996) support the efficacy of this drug. To explain withdrawal symptoms, researchers have begun to focus on glutamate, a membrane protein that is an excitatory amino acid and a primary neurotransmitter dealing with excitatory neurotransmission. There are a number of glutamate receptors and they are widespread throughout the central nervous system; one that may have specific relevance to the effects of alcohol and other drugs is N-methyl-D-aspartate (NMDA). The hallucinogen phencycladine, for example, binds to the recognition site normally utilized by glutamate. Glutamate receptors facilitate fast neurotransmission but can also have a negative effect, as excessive activation can produce neural degeneration. This system is implicated as the source of damage in a number of neurological disorders, including stroke, Huntington's disease, and Alzheimer's.

Tsai, Gostfriend, and Coyle (1995) have argued that alcohol has three effects on glutamatergic transmission: interfering with excitatory neurotransmission, promoting excitotoxicity, and impairing neurodevelopment (as in fetal alcohol syndrome). These three major effects occur through the NMDA receptor, to which alcohol seems to be an antagonist. Chronic ingestion of alcohol by experimental animals results in an increase in NMDA receptors in both limbic and cortical brain areas. This effect is transient, perhaps an overcompensation of the system being blocked by alcohol; during withdrawal these receptors actually increase, and glutamate functioning in general is accelerated (Gulya, Grant, Valverius, Hoffman, & Tabakoff, 1991; Keller, Cummins, & Hungen, 1983). Tsai et al. (1995) concluded that this specific action of alcohol on the NMDA receptor explains both the symptoms of drug withdrawal and the development of brain damage, which is a common concomittant of heavy alcohol consumption. Specifically, they argue that the supersensitivity that results from alcohol blocking the receptor is displayed when alcohol is not present; in its extreme this can result in glutamate-induced excitotoxicity.

Endogenous Opioid System This system is widespread throughout the body, with at least three types of receptors and three groups of known transmitters. Opioid receptors that have been found in the nucleus accumbens appear to affect this system through the neurotransmitter dopamine. Stimulation appears reinforcing as animals will self-administer opioids (morphine, heroin). The opiates also act both directly and indirectly on dopamine in the ventral tegmental area of the brain. That the endogenous opioid system is involved in the rewarding properties of heroin is exhibited by the fact that treatments aimed specifically at replacing the drug or blocking the receptors are effective. Methadone, introduced in the 1960s, is a long-acting synthetic opioid that, taken orally once daily, serves as a substitute for heroin. Methadone is cross-tolerant to heroin and the treatment is effective but controversial (O'Brien, 1996). A new substitution drug, laam (L-alpha-acetylmethadol), has similar effects. The drug was approved in 1993 and needs to be taken only three times per week. Because regulations require that patients be removed from these substitute drugs according to rather rigid time restrictions, the patients need help reordering their lives if therapy is to be effective (O'Brien, 1996). More evidence that opiate receptors are involved in heroin addictions comes from work with drugs that block these receptors, such as naltrexone and naloxone; in the detoxified addict these drugs prevent heroin from having its positive psychoactive effects. Regrettably, these drugs are generally avoided by addicts.

Recently, naltrexone has been approved by the FDA as a treatment for alcoholism. Clinical studies have shown that naltrexone diminishes the high from alcohol and reduces craving (Volpicelli, Alterman, Hayashida, & O'Brien, 1992; O'Malley et al., 1992), though compliance is a problem (Volpicelli et al., 1997). It should also be noted that naltrexone and naloxone and other opiate antagonists have been shown to decrease ethanol consumption in experimental animals (Frohlich, Zweifel, Hart, Lumeng, & Li, 1991). A working hypothesis is that high-risk individuals have inherited a sensitivity of the opioid system to alcohol, though there is a report (Davidson, Swift, & Fitz, 1996) that naltrexone also reduced the consumption of social drinkers. Thus, perhaps a general anticraving effect is what is operative. Related studies have shown that a moderate dose of alcohol significantly increased plasma beta endorphin (the most potent endogenous opoid peptide) in subjects at high risk for alcoholism, but not in low-risk subjects (Gianoulakis et al., 1989). This has been replicated in a recent study, which also found that the beta endorphin system but not adrenal cortical system is affected (Gianoulakis, Krishnan, & Thourendayil, 1996). Finally, the degree of alcohol-induced release of beta endorphin to alcohol has been shown to correlate with an increased heart rate response to alcohol, thought to indicate positive reinforcement (Peterson et al., 1996).

Cannaboid and Nicotine Systems Specific marijuana receptors exist (Devane, Dysarz, Johnson,

Melvin, & Howlett, 1988). They are widely distributed throughout the brain but are particularly prominent in the cerebellum, cortex, hippocampus, and striatum (Herkenham, 1993). It has also been suggested that there are endogenous cannaboid neurotransmitters/neuromodulators (Di Tomaso, Beltramo, & Plonnelli, 1996). In rats, the active ingredient in marijuana, tetrhydrocanabinol, has been shown to act like stimulant drugs and release dopamine in the nucleus accumbens (Tanda, Pontieri, & Di Chiara, 1997). It has also been found that indications of stress (compulsive grooming, teeth chattering) occur when a cannabinoid antagonist is administered (Rodriguez de Fonseca et al., 1977). These results, while intriguing, should not be seen as putting marijuana on a par with cocaine or amphetamines. Marijuana is quite low on the addiction scale; rats rarely self-administer it or place-condition to it, and in fact it is likely to provoke a stress response. An analogy to certain food effects is also possible. We, for example, know that certain brain lipids bind to the canniboid receptors and can mimic the effects of marijuana on the brain (Devane et al., 1992). Interestingly, chocolate and cocoa powder are shown to elevate the levels of these lipids that have affinity for canniboid receptors, obscuring somewhat the distinction between drugs and foods (Di Tomaso et al., 1996).

Nicotine is the psychoactive substance in cigarette smoke. While the people who manufacture cigarettes have claimed not to know that they contain an addictive drug, central nervous system effects occur within 10 seconds of inhalation: the mesolimbic reward system is activated and the dopamine, endogenous opioid, and glucocorticoid systems among others are affected. Euphoric effects like those resulting from cocaine and morphine are produced (Pomerleau, 1992). These effects are strong enough to support reward-based conditioning (Droungas, Ehrman, Childress, & O'Brien, 1995), and tolerance and withdrawal develop. It is known that D2 receptors are affected, and it is speculated that changes in these receptors are what is reponsible for craving (Li et al., 1995). Recent evidence (Pich et al., 1997) shows that nicotine activates brain areas in a pattern that parallels those affected by cocaine. The strength of nicotine effects is noted in the fact that of all of the drugs of abuse, nicotine is the one most resistant to treatment. Twenty percent or less of individuals who begin smoking cessation treatment are abstinent one year following the program (Fiore, Smith, Jorenby, & Baker, 1994).

Cognitive Aspects

Individual variation in sensitivity to drug effects can also be expressed in terms of structural and functional differences in important brain areas. Human beliefs and experiences are also part of the cognitive context, and expectations of drug effect predict drug use.

Expectancies Luria (1980) has argued that the brain reacts to stimuli in terms of context—past, current, and future. Responses are anchored in experience and learning, which in humans includes culture incorporated through language. Regarding drugs, cultural and social factors as well as individual experience come together to form such a context. We have referred to this elsewhere as the general expectancy set (Pihl et al., 1993). In one study (Stacey, Newcomb, & Bentler, 1991) of a large sample of women and men, who were followed over nine years in a longitudinal study, it was shown that use of alcohol and marijuana could be predicted in adolescence and adulthood based on early expectations of the response of positive feelings to the drugs and the alleviation of negative feelings. According to Bachman, Johnston, and O'Malley (1990), the decline in marijuana and cocaine use in the United States during the 1980s resulted from an increased perception of danger. While this may reflect the success of government information programs at that time, such programs must be credible to be effective. With individuals who have had different experiences (or who have contrary expectations for whatever reason) or are alienated from the source of the information, the effect of such an approach is dubious. Indeed, reviews of general educational drug prevention programs in the United States have been very pessimistic, with some studies demonstrating increased rather than intended decreased use (Dryfoos, 1990).

Expectancies regarding drug effects are far more complex than is implied by describing them as positive or negative (Goldman, Brown, Christiansen, & Smith, 1991). Some expectancies regarding a drug's effect seem completely contradictory—for example, simultaneous alcohol expectancies of social facilitation and social aggression. Alcohol research has shown that expectancy differs with the type of beverage consumed, wine being viewed more positively than beer, which is seen more positively than distilled spirits, even with blood alcohol level controlled (Lang, Kaas, & Barnes, 1983). Relatedly, a greater increase in intoxication-induced aggression has been found in distilled beverage drinkers than in beer drinkers in both laboratory (Pihl et al., 1984) and bar (Murdoch & Pihl, 1988) studies.

Neuroimagery The role of cognitive structural aspects in drug abuse has been assessed through neuroimagery, electrophysiology, and neuropsychology. Neuroimaging technology has been used in only a few studies that directly deal with drug abuse. The techniques have been used more frequently with special populations who display disorders frequently comorbid with drug abuse. Specific to drug abuse, there have been some provocative findings. Research with positron emission tomography (PET) has demonstrated that alcohol is involved with a GABAergic receptor complex (Volkow et al., 1990), and that individuals at high familial risk for alcoholism have lower cerebellar metabolism and a reduced response to a benzodiazepine (Volkow et al., 1995). Generally, lower cerebral metabolic rates have been found with all euphoriant drugs of abuse: morphine, cocaine, amphetamines, and nicotine (London, 1994).

Key issues in assessing drug effects with imaging techniques concern the population being studied. Some drugs, particularly alcohol, taken chronically and in heavy doses, produce marked brain injury. Consequently, magnetic resonance images with such subjects may yield findings that represent the effect of the drug and have little relevance to etiology. For this reason, research is needed that focuses on individuals at risk for drug abuse.

Electrophysiology The measurement of spontaneous brain or electrical activity (electroencephalogram, EEG) and of wave form responses to particular stimuli (event-related evoked potentials, ERP) is often used to assess subtle cognitive impairment. High-frequency fast beta activity has been described in sober sons of alcoholics (Gabrielli et al., 1982), a pattern seen in alcoholics (Mendelson & Mello, 1979); it has been associated with states of tension and anxiety (Kiloh & Osselton, 1961). The consumption of alcohol in family history positive individuals results in a slowing of this activity (Pollock et al., 1983). An increased EEG response to alcohol in family history postive subjects has been generally considered an additional risk factor; however, a recent report of a follow-up of such subjects found that a reduced alpha response was related to later problem development (Volavka et al., 1996).

In research on evoked potentials, by far the most common assessed is the P3, the positive response measured 300 to 500 milliseconds after stimulus presentation. The response is known to originate from a widely distributed cortical network, with the dorsolateral frontal cortex in particular being related to the automated attentional aspects of the response (Knight, 1991). Both visual and auditory stimuli are typically presented, according to a number of varying procedures, in predictable and unpredictable sequences (see Porjesz & Begleiter, 1995). Reduced P3 amplitude has been found in alcoholics and antisocial personalities. Findings regarding children of alcoholics (Polich, Pollock, & Bloom, 1994) support the conclusion of a response of reduced P3 amplitude. One prospective study (Berman, Whipple, Fitch, & Noble, 1993) was able to use this reduced P3 response to successfully predict adolescent substance use.

Neuropsychological Studies There exists a wide variety of behavioral and psychological tests that are thought to represent specific cognitive functions, some implicating specific brain localization and systems. Some at-risk groups (sons of alcoholics) have been particularly implicated in showing mild to moderate impairments on these tests. These impairments have been found in five broad categories of cognitive performance: first, executive functions, which encompass abstracting, planning, and problem-solving abilities; second, language-based skills; third, attentional and memory processing; fourth, psychomotor integration; and fifth, visuo-perceptual analysis and learning (Pihl, Peterson, & Finn, 1990a; Tarter, Jacob, & Bremer, 1989; Wiers, Sergeant, & Gunning, 1994). These deficits have also been found in conduct-disordered and ADHD individuals. In a recent study of aggressive boys (Séguin, Pihl, Harden, Boulerice, & Tremblay, 1995), particular deficits were shown on neuropsychological tests that had been previously demonstrated via PET studies to involve dorsolateral aspects of the frontal cortex. Similar performances in ADHD children have led to a flurry of interest in the role of the frontal lobes in impulse-control problems. Further, certain drugs (particularly alcohol) acutely impair these cognitive functions (Peterson, Finn, & Pihl, 1990). This may be a central factor in explaining the high correlation between intoxicated behavior and violence.

At issue is how these cognitive impairments are involved in the causal process leading to abuse. Initial concern must be with the directionality of cause. Because alcohol consumption results in neuropsychological dysfunction in alcoholics (Parsons & Nixon, 1993) and even in heavy-drinking university freshmen (Sher, Martin, Wood, & Rutledge, 1997), measures can readily represent effect rather than cause. However, studies (Peterson et al., 1992) that have controlled drinking history do find differential neuropsychological functioning in at-risk individuals. It seems apparent that these dysfunctions do not represent a direct cause of drug abuse but rather are typically seen as one element in the complex set of causative variables. As the pattern of impairment seems to cross not only drug abuse but also antisocial personality and conduct and attentional deficit disorders, these impairments are often related to a wide degree of arousal problems in these populations. For example, sons of male alcoholics are hyperreactive to various stimuli, including electric shock, novel tones, unsolvable math problems, and stimulus uncertainty. Alcohol, in an intoxicating dose, has been demonstrated to attenuate this autonomic nervous system activity, an effect which is also produced by benzodiazepines. This reactivity has been viewed as resulting from the cognitive deficits (Peterson & Pihl, 1990), and the dampening of this response may be negatively reinforcing (Pihl, Peterson, & Finn, 1990b). This theorized relationship as well as how other variables may interact is illustrated in figure 10.3.

A current issue of confusion in the literature is whether at-risk individuals show a heightened or diminished response to alcohol. Studies with some of these individuals have shown diminished sensitivity to alcohol effects on measurement of movement, subjective intoxication, and hormone release (Schuckit & Gold, 1988). In addition, this pattern of reduced sensitivity to intoxication has been successful in predicting drinking problems 10 years after testing (Schuckit, 1994). However, a similar population in other studies (Pihl & Peterson, 1995a) shows, if anything, a heightened response to alcohol in the form of increased heart rate reactivity as well as response dampening. The increased sensitivity to alcohol demonstrated in some studies seems to be particularly prominent shortly after an intoxicating dose is consumed, during the arousal phase, and it may well be that the decreased sensitivity occurs later temporally. Thus, differences in protocol would explain the discrepancies. A recent study by Conrod, Peterson, and Pihl (1997) suggests this interpretation is accurate.

Individualized Vulnerability

The myriad facts presented above concerning individual factors suggests the existence of relative anatomical and biochemical uniqueness that can contribute substantially to the likelihood of developing substance abuse problems. Differential motivational systems with individualized drug responsivity have been hypothesized (Pihl & Peterson, 1995a). Externally administered opiates reduce pain or punishment and are profoundly negatively reinforcing. Alcohol and benzodiazepines dampen threat or anxiety and are also highly negatively reinforcing, while amphetamines, cocaine, and (for some individuals) alcohol directly impact dopamine and are associated with positive reinforcement.

Recently, Conrod et al. (1998) tested a large sample of women between the ages of 30 and 50 who, though not in treatment, had self-defined problems with alcohol or prescribed drugs and were willing to complete an extensive battery of tests. The tests involved measures of psychopathology, drug use and abuse of all kinds, the assessment of trait characteristics such as impulsivity, sensitivity to anxiety, depression, coping measures, neuroticism, extroversion, openness, agreeableness, conscientiousness, trait anxiety, and traumatic stress as well as a battery of laboratory tests. When the data were factor analyzed, four factors emerged. The factors predicted comorbid disorders and type of substance dependence: specifically, an impulsive factor was related to simulant and alcohol dependence and to antisocial personality; an anxiety sensitive factor was associated with sedative/anxiolytic dependence and comorbidly to generalized anxiety, panic, simple phobia, and somatization; a sensation-seeking factor to alcohol

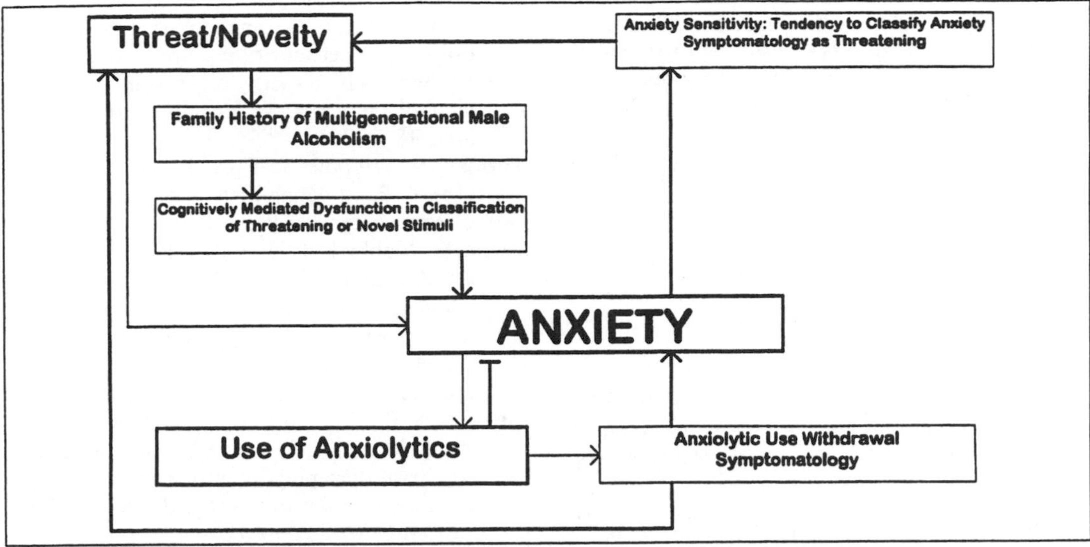

Figure 10.3 A partial schematic model for the predispositional risk of alcoholism in multigenerational sons of male alcoholics and anxiety-sensitive individuals. (Light arrows indicate normal path: threat causes anxiety and heightens tendency to use and appreciate anxiolytics. Heavier arrows indicate manner in which this normal process can be pathologized: cognitive dysfunction, attendant upon familiar history of alcoholism, makes classification of threat and novelty more difficult; anxiolytic withdrawal symptomatology produces anxiety and is threatening as well; anxiety sensitivity makes anxiety symptoms themselves threats. Bar indicates inhibition (from Pihl & Peterson, 1995).

dependence; and a hopeless factor to heroin dependence and mood disorders.

Summary

Diagnoses, particularly when based on purely behavioral definitions, do not explain a phenomenon. A system like the *DSM IV* is designed to produce agreement among observers and does not necessarily point the way to understanding cause or to providing efficient treatment. This chapter has addressed levels of analysis from the cultural to the biochemical, with, in most circumstances, the cause of drug abuse occurring at multiple levels of analysis, all of which can be very individual and highly interactive. Cultural, peer, and family effects all have an impact on the social level that alone, but mostly in combination with individual factors, likely increases vulnerability to abuse. The marked variation that occurs among individuals in terms of susceptibility to develop problems is striking. All substances have users and abusers, and it is the latter that must be of concern. Traditional personality explanations are giving way to molecular-genetic data, which are exploding onto the area and demonstrating an important source of this variability. Specifically, the focus is on how genes affect the functioning of differential biochemical systems. It is these systems that contribute substantially to individual vulnerability to the differential psychopharmacological properties of various drugs. In addition, cognitive factors modulate these and other effects, and can be etiologically significant in their own right. Finally, no discussion of etiology is complete without returning to the issue of definition and societal context. To quote a second historian, Will Durant adroitly observed: "no civilization has found life tolerable without the things that provide at least some brief escape from reality."

References

Abel, E., Hazlett, L., Berk, R., & Mutchnik, M. (1990). Neuroimmunotoxic effects in offspring of paternal alcohol consumption. *Alcohol Immunomodulation and Aids, 1*, 47–55.

Abel, E., & Lee, J. (1988). Paternal alcohol exposure affects offspring behavior but not body organ weights in mice. *Alcoholism Clinical and Experimental Research, 12*, 349–355.

Abel, E., & Tan, S. (1988). Effects of paternal alcohol consumption on pregnancy outcome in rats. *Neurotoxicology & Teratology, 10*, 187–192.

Adamec, C., & Pihl, R. O. (1978). Sex differences in response to marijuana in a social setting. *Psychology of Women Quarterly, 2*, 334–353.

Adamec, C., Pihl, R. O., & Leiter, L. (1975). An analysis of the subjective marijuana experience. *International Journal of the Addictions, 2*, 295–307.

Andrucci, G. L., Archer, R. P., Pancoast, D. L., & Gordon, R. A. (1989). The relationship of MMPI and sensation seeking scales to adolescent drug use. *Journal of Personality Assessment, 53*, 253–266.

Aronson, S., Black, J., McDougle, C., Scanley, E., Jatlow, P., Kosten, T., Heninger, G., & Price, L. (1995). Serotonergic mechanisms of cocaine effects in humans. *Psychopharmacology, 119*, 179–185.

Bachman, J. G., Johnston, L. D., & O'Malley, P. M. (1990). Explaining the recent decline in cocaine use among young adults: Further evidence that perceived risk and disapproval lead to reduced drug use. *Journal of Health and Social Behavior, 31*, 173–184.

Ballenger, J., Goodwin, F., Major, L., & Brown, G. (1979). Alcohol and central serotonin metabolism in man. *Archives of General Psychiatry, 36*, 224–227.

Barnes, G. M., & Welte, J. W. (1986). Adolescent alcohol abuse: Subgroup differences and relationships to other problem behaviors. *Journal of Adolescent Research, 1*, 79–94.

Basen-Ergquest, K., Edmundson, E., & Parcel, G. (1996). Structure of health risk behavior among high school students. *Journal of Consulting and Clinical Psychology, 64*, 764–775.

Baumeister, R., Smart, L., & Boden, J. (1996). Relation of threatened egotism to violence and aggression: The dark side of high self-esteem. *Psychological Review, 103*, 5–33.

Baumrind, D. (1983, October). *Why adolescents take chances—And why they don't.* Paper presented at the National Institute for Child Health and Human Development. Bethesda, MD.

Bean, W. B. (1951). *Osler Aphorisms*. Springfield, IL: Thomas.

Benjamin, J., Li, L., Patterson, C., Greenberg, B., Murphy, D., & Hamer, D. (1996). Population and familial association between the D4 dopamine receptor gene and measures of novelty seeking. *Nature Genetics, 12*, 81–84.

Benkelfat, C., Murphy, D. L., Hill, J. L., George, D. T., Nutt, D., & Linnoila, M. (1991). Ethanol-like properties of the serotonergic partial agonist m-chlorophenylpiperazine in chronic alcoholic patients. *Archives of General Psychiatry, 48*, 383.

Berman, S., Whipple, S., Fitch, R., & Noble, E. (1993). P3 in young boys as a predictor of adolescent substance use. *Alcohol, 10*, 69–70.

Blum, K., Noble, E. P., Sheridan, P. J., Montgomery, A., Ritchie, T., Jagadeeswaran, P., Nogami, H., Briggs, A., & Cohn, J. (1990). Allelic association of human dopamine D2 receptor gene in alcoholism. *JAMA, 263*, 2055–2060.

Bodnoff, S. R., Suranyi-Cadotte, B. F., Quirion, R., & Meaney, M. J. (1989). Role of the central benzodiazepine receptor system in behavioral habituation to novelty. *Behavioral Neuroscience, 103*, 209–212.

Boye-Beamen, J., Leonard, K., & Seuchak, M. (1991). Assortative mating, relationship development, and intimacy among offspring of alcoholics. *Family Dynamics Addiction Quarterly, 1*, 20–33.

Bowman, M., & Pihl, R. O. (1973). Chronic heavy use of cannabis sativa: Psychological effects. *Psychopharmacologia, 23*, 159–170.

Brook, J. S., Brook, D. W., Gordon, A. S., Whiteman, M., & Cohen, P. (1990). The psychosocial etiology of adolescent drug use: A family interactional approach. *Genetic, Social, and General Psychology Monographs, 116*, 111–267.

Brook, J. S., Whiteman, M., Gordon, A. S., & Brook, D. W. (1988). The role of older brothers in younger brothers' drug use viewed in the context of parent and peer influences. *Journal of Genetic Psychology, 151*, 59–75.

Buck, K., Metten, P., Belknap, J., & Crabbe, J. (1997). Quantitative trait loci involved in genetic predisposition to acute alcohol withdrawal in mice. *Journal of Neuroscience, 17*, 3946–3955.

Cabib, S., Puglisi-Allegra, S., LeMoal, M., & Piazza, P. (1996). Strain and stress dependent differences in the affective effects of amphetamines. *Behavioral Pharmacology, 7*, 11–12.

Cadoret, R. J. (1990). Genetics of Alcoholism. In R. Collins, K. Leonard, & J. Searles (Eds.), *Alcohol and the family: Research and clinical perspectives* (pp. 39–78). New York: Guilford Press.

Carmelli, D., Heath, A., & Robinette, D. (1993). Genetic analysis of drinking behavior in World War II veteran twins. *Genetic Epidemiology, 10*, 201–213.

Cloninger, C. R. (1987). Neurogenetic adaptive mechanisms in alcoholism. *Science, 23*, 410–415.

Cloninger, C., Bohman, M., & Sigvardson, S. (1981). Inheritance of alcohol abuse: Cross-fostering analysis of adopted men. *Archives of General Psychiatry, 38*, 861–868.

Collins, R. L., Parks, G., & Marlatt, A. (1985). Social determinants of alcohol consumption: The effects of social interaction and model status on the self-administration of alcohol. *Journal of Consulting and Clinical Psychology, 53*, 189–200.

Conrod, P., Peterson, J., & Pihl, R. (1997). Disinhibited personality and sensitivity to alcohol reinforcement: Individual correlates of drinking behavior in sons of alcoholics. *Alcoholism: Clinical and Experimental Research, 21*, 1320–1332.

Conrod, P. J., Peterson, J., Pihl, R. O., & Mankowski, S. (1997). The biphasic effects of alcohol on heart rate are influenced by alcoholic family history and rate of alcohol ingestion. *Alcoholism: Clinical and Experimental Research, 21*, 140–149.

Conrod, P., Pihl, R., Stewart, S., Mason, H., Fontaine, V., Coté, S., & Dongier, M. (1998). *Subtypes of female substance dependents.* Manuscript submitted for publication.

Cotton, N. (1979). The familial incidence of alcoholism: A review. *Journal of Studies on Alcohol, 40*, 89–116.

Cox, B. J., Swinson, R. P., Shulman, I. D., Kuch, K., & Reichman, J. T. (1993). Gender effects and alcohol use in panic disorder with agoraphobia. *Behavior Research and Therapy, 31*, 413–416.

Crabbe, J. C. (1989). Genetic animal models in the study of alcoholism. *Alcoholism Clinical and Experimental Research, 13*, 120–128.

Cronin, C. (1995). Religiosity, religious affiliation, and alcohol and drug use among American college students living in Germany. *International Journal of the Addictions, 30*, 231–238.

Davidson, D., Swift, R., & Fitz, S. (1996). Naltrexone increases the latency to drink alcohol in social drinkers. *Alcoholism: Clinical and Experimental Research, 20*, 732–739.

Davidson, J. R. T., Swartz, M., Storck, M., Krishnan, R. R., & Hammett, E. (1985). A diagnostic and family study of posttraumatic stress disorder. *American Journal of Psychiatry, 142*, 90–93.

Delaney, W., & Ames, G. (1995). Work team attitudes, drinking norms and workplace drinking. *Journal of Drug Issues, 25*, 275–290.

Dembo, R., Williams, L., La Voie, L., Schmerdler, J., Kern, J., Getren, A., Barry, E., Genuy, L., & Wish, E. (1990). A longitudinal study of the relationship among alcohol use, marijuana/hashish use, cocaine use, and emotional and psychological functioning problems in a cohort of high risk youths. *International Journal of Addictions, 25*, 1314–1382.

Deminiere, J. M., Piazza, P. V., Le Moal, M., & Simon, H. (1989). Experimental approach to individual vulnerability to psychostimulant addiction. *Neuroscience and Biobehavioral Review, 13*, 141–147.

Devane, W. A., Dysarz, F. A., Johnson, M. R., Melvin, L. S., & Howlett, A. C. (1988). Determination and characterization of a cannabinoid receptor in rat brain. *Molecular Pharmacology, 34*, 605–613.

Devane, W. A., Hanus, L., Breuer, A., Pertwee, R. G., Stevenson, L. A., Griffin, G., Mandelbaum, A., Etinger, A., & Mechoulam, R. (1992). Isolation and structure of a brain constituent that binds to the cannabinoid receptor. *Science, 258*, 1946–1949.

Di Tomaso, E., Beltramo, M., & Plonnelli, D. (1996). Brain cannabinoids in chocolate. *Nature, 382*, 677–678.

Dobkin, P., Tremblay, R., & Sacchitelle, C. (1997). Predicting boys' early onset substance abuse from father's alcoholism, son's disruptiveness, and mother's parenting behavior. *Journal of Consulting and Clinical Psychology, 65*, 86–92.

Dobkin de Rios, M. (1973). Curing with ayahuasca in an urban slum. In M. Harner (Ed.), *Hallucinogens and shamanism*, London: Oxford Press, 147–164.

Droungas, A., Ehrman, R. N., Childress, A. R., & O'Brien, C. P. (1995). Effect of smoking cues and cigarette availability on craving and smoking behavior. *Addictive Behaviors, 20*, 657–673.

Dryfoos, J. G. (1990). *Adolescents at risk.* New York: Oxford Press.

Dudek, B., & Tritto, T. (1995). Classical and neoclassical approaches to the genetic analysis of alcohol-related phenotypes. *Alcoholism: Clinical and Experimental Research, 19*, 802–810.

Ebstein, R., Novich, O., Usnansky, R., Priel, B., Osher, Y., Blaine, D., Bennett, E., Nemanov, L., Katz, M., & Belmaker, R. (1996). Dopamine D4 receptor (D4DR) exon III polymorphism associated with the human personality trait of novelty seeking. *Nature Genetics, 12*, 78–80.

Emrick, C. (1989). Alcoholics Anonymous: Membership characteristics and effectiveness as treatment. In M. Galanter (Ed.), *Recent developments in alcoholism* (Vol. 7; pp. 37–53). New York: Plenum Press.

Fagan, J. (1989). The social organization of drug use and drug dealing among urban gangs. *Criminology, 27*, 501–536.

Farrell, A., & Danish, S. (1993). Peer drug associations and emotional restraint: Causes or consequences of adolescents' drug use. *Journal of Consulting and Clinical Psychology, 2*, 327–334.

Fibiger, H. C., & Phillips, A. G. (1988). Mesocorticolimbic dopamine systems and reward. *Annals of the New York Academy of Science, 537*, 206–215.

Fils-Aime, M., Eckardt, M., George, D., Brown, G., Mefford, I., & Linnoila, M. (1996). Early-onset alcoholics have lower cerebrospinal fluid 5-hydroxyincholeacetic acid levels than late onset alcoholics. *Archives of General Psychiatry, 53*, 211–216.

Fiore, M. C., Smith, S. S., Jorenby, D. E., & Baker, T. B. (1994). The effectiveness of the nicotine patch for smoking cessation. *Journal of the American Medical Association, 271*, 1940–1946.

Fisher, L. A., & Bauman, K. E. (1988). Influence and selection in the friend-adolescent relationship: Findings from studies of adolescent smoking and drinking. *Journal of Applied Social Psychology, 18*, 289–314.

Foster, J., Murray, D., Wolfson, M., & Wagenaar, A. (1995). Commercial availability of alcohol to young people. Results of alcohol purchase attempts. *Preventive Medicine, 24*, 342–347.

Frank, S. J., Tuer, M., & Jacobson, S. (1990). Psychological predictors of young adults' drinking behaviors. *Journal of Personality and Social Psychology, 59*, 770–780.

Froehlich, J. C., Zweifel, M., Hart, J., Lumeng, L., & Li, T-K. (1991). Importance of delta opioid receptors in maintaining high alcohol drinking. *Pharmacology and Biochemistry of Behavior, 35*, 385–390.

Furst, P. T. (1992). *Hallucinogens and culture.* London: Chandler & Sharp.

Gabrielli, W. F., Jr., Mednick, S. A., Volavka, J., Pollock, V. E., Schulsinger, F., & Itil, T. M. (1982). Electroencephalograms in children of alcoholic fathers. *Psychophysiology, 19*, 404–407.

Gessa, G. L., Muntone, F., Collu, M., Vargiu, L., & Mereu, G. (1985). Low doses of ethanol activate dopaminergic neurons in the ventral tegmental area. *Brain Research, 348*, 201–203.

Gewiss, M., Heidbreder, C., Opsomer, L., Durbin, P., & DeWitte, P. (1991). Acamprosate and diazepam differentially modulate alcohol-induced behavioral and cortical alterations in rats following chronic inhalation of ethanol vapor. *Alcohol and Alcoholism, 26*, 129–137.

Gianoulakis, C., Beliveau, D., Angelogianni, P., Meaney, M., Thavundayil, J., Tawar, V., & Dumas, M. (1989). Different pituitary B-endorphin and adrenal cortisol response to ethanol in individuals with high and low risk for future development of alcoholism. *Life Science, 45*, 1097–1109.

Gianoulakis, C., Krishnan, B., & Thourendayil, J. (1996). Enhanced sensitivity of pituitary B-endorphin to ethanol in subjects at high risk for alcoholism. *Archives of General Psychiatry, 53*, 250–257.

Goldman, D., Brown, G. L., Albaugh, B., Robin, R., Goodson, S., Trunzo, M., Aktar, L., Lucas-Derse, S., Long, J., Linnoila, M., & Dean, M. (1993). DRD2 dopamine receptor genotype, linkage disequilibrium and alcoholism in American Indians and other populations. *Alcohol: Clinical & Experimental Research, 17*, 199–204.

Goldman, M., Brown, S., Christiansen, B., & Smith, G. (1991). Alcoholism etiology and memory: Broadening the scope of alcohol expectancy research. *Psychological Bulletin, 110*, 137–146.

Goodwin, D. W., Schulsinger, F., Moller, N., Hermansen, L., Winokur, G., & Guze, S. B. (1974). Drinking problems in adopted and nonadopted sons of alcoholics. *Archives of General Psychiatry, 131*, 164–169.

Gordis, E. (1996). Alcohol research; at the cutting edge. *Archives of General Psychiatry, 53*, 199–201.

Grube, J., Chen, M., Madden, P., & Morgan, M. (1996). Predicting adolescent drinking from alcohol expectancy values: A comparison of additive, interactive, and nonlinear models. *Journal of Applied Social Psychology, 25*, 839–857.

Guitart, X., Beitnes-Johnson, D., & Nestler, E. (1992). Fischer and Lewis rat strains differ in basal levels of neurofilament proteins and in their regulation by chronic morphine. *Synapse, 12*, 242–243.

Guyla, K., Grant, K. A., Valverius, P., Hoffman, P. O., & Tabakoff, B. (1991). Brain regional specificity and time-course of changes in the NMDA receptor-ionophore complex during ethanol withdrawal. *Brain Research, 547*, 129–134.

Harris, R. A., & Allan, A. A. (1989). Alcohol intoxication: Ion channels and genetics. *FASEB J., 3*, 1689–1694.

Hartka, E., Johnstone, B., Leino, V., Motoyoshi, M., Temple, M. T., & Fillmore, K. M. (1991). A meta-analysis of depressive symptomatology and alcohol consumption over time. *British Journal of Addictions, 86*, 1283–1298.

Helzer, J. E., & Pryzbeck, T. R. (1988). The occurrence of alcoholism with other psychiatric disorders in the general population and its impact on treatment. *Journal of Studies in Alcohol, 49*, 219–224.

Herkenham, M. A. (1993). Localization of cannabinoid receptors in the brain: Relationship to motor and reward systems. In S. G. Korenman & J. D. Barchas (Eds.), *Biological basis of substance abuse* (Vol. 13; pp. 187–200). New York: Oxford University Press.

Higuchi, S., Matsushita, S., Murayama, M., Takagi, S., & Hayashada, M. (1995). Alcohol and aldehyde dehydrogenase polymorphisms and the risk for alcoholism. *American Journal of Psychiatry, 152*, 1219–1221.

Hill, S. Y. (1992). Absence of paternal sociopathy in the etiology of severe alcoholism: Is there a type III alcoholism? *Journal of Studies on Alcohol, 53*, 161–169.

Holder, H., Longabaugh, R., Miller, W. M., & Rubonis, A. (1991). The cost effectiveness of treatment for alcoholism: A first approximation. *Journal of Studies on Alcohol, 52*, 517–540.

Hwang, B. H., Lumeng, L., Wu, J. Y., & Li, T. K. (1988). GABAergic neurons in nucleus accumbens: A possible role in alcohol preference. *Alcoholism: Clinical and Experimental Research, 12*, 306.

Imperato, A., Mele, A., Scrocco, M., & Puglici-Alegra, S. (1992). Chronic cocaine alters limbic extracellular dopamine. Neurochemical basis for addiction. *European Journal of Pharmacology, 212*, 299–300.

Jessor, R., & Jessor, S. L. (1977). *Problem behavior and psychological development: A longitudinal study of youth*. San Diego, CA: Academic Press.

Johnson, G. M., Schoutz, F. C., & Locke, T. P. (1984). Relationships between adolescent drug use and parental drug behaviors. *Adolescence, 19*, 295–299.

Johnston, L., O'Malley, P., & Bachman, J. (1996). *National Survey Results on Drug Use. From the Monitoring the Future Study, 1975–1994*. Rockville, MD: National Institute on Drug Abuse.

Kalivas, P. W., & Duffy, P. (1989). Similar effects of daily cocaine and stress on mesocorticolimbic dopamine neurotransmission in the rat. *Biological Psychiatry, 25*, 913–928.

Kalivas, P., & Duffy, P. (1993). Time course of extracellular dopamine and behavioral sensitization to cocaine. *Journal of Neuroscience, 13*, 266–275.

Kandel, D. B., Kessler, R. C., & Margulies, R. Z. (1978). Antecedents of adolescent initiation into stages of drug abuse. In D. B. Kandel (Ed.), *Longitudinal research on drug use* (pp. 73–99). New York: John Wiley.

Kandel, D. B., & Yamaguchi, K. (1985). Developmental patterns of the use of legal, illegal, and prescribed drugs. In C. L. Jones & R. J. Battjes (Eds.), *Etiology of drug abuse* (pp. 193–235). Rockville, MD: National Institute on Drug Abuse.

Karp, J. (1993). The interaction of alcohol expectancies, personality, and psychopathology among inpatient alcoholics (Summary). *Dissertation Abstracts International, 53*, 4375B.

Keane, T. M., Gerardi, R. J., Lyons, J. A., & Wolfe, J. (1988). The interrelationship of substance abuse and posttraumatic stress disorder: Epidemiological and clinical considerations. In M. Galanter (Ed.), *Recent developments in alcoholism* (Vol. 6; pp. 27–48). New York: Plenum.

Kempfer, K., & DeMarsh, J. (1985). Family environmental and genetic influences on children's future chemical dependency. *Journal of Children in Contemporary Society, 18*, 49–91.

Kendler, K. S., Neal, M. C., Kessler, R. C., Heath, A. C., & Eaves, L. J. (1992). A population-based twin study of major depression in women: The impact of varying definitions of illness. *Archives of General Psychiatry, 49*, 257–266.

Kendler, K., Prescott, C., Neale, M., & Pedersen, N. (1997). Temperance board registration for alcohol abuse in a national sample of Swedish male twins, born 1902 to 1949. *Archives of General Psychiatry, 54*, 178–184.

Kiloh, L. G., & Osselton, J. W. (1961). *Clinical electroencephalography*. London: Butterworths.

Knight, R. T. (1991). Evoked potential studies of attention capacity in human frontal lobes. In H. S. Levin, H. M. Eisenberg, & A. L. Ben ton (Eds.), *Frontal lobe function and dysfunction* (pp. 139–153). New York: Oxford University.

Koob, G. F., & Bloom, F. E. (1988). Cellular and molecular mechanisms of drug dependence. *Science, 242*, 715–723.

Kramer, P. (1993). *Listening to Prozac*. New York: Viking.

Krimmer, E. C., & Schechter, M. D. (1992). HAD and LAD rats respond differently to stimulating effect but not discriminative effects of alcohol. *Alcoholism, 9*, 71–74.

Kushner, M., MacKenzie, T., Fiszdon, J., Valentiner, D., Foa, E., Anderson, N., & Wangensteen, D. (1996). The effects of alcohol consumption on laboratory-induced panic and state anxiety. *Archives of General Psychiatry, 53*, 264–270.

Kushner, M., & Sher, K. (1993). Comorbidity of alcohol and anxiety disorders among college students: Effects of gender and family history of alcoholism. *Addictive Behaviors, 18*, 543–552.

Kushner, M. G., Sher, K. J., & Beitman, B. D. (1990). The relation between alcohol problems and the anxiety disorders. *American Journal of Psychiatry, 147*, 685–695.

La Hoste, G., Swanson, J., Wigal, S., King, N., & Kennedy, J. (1996). Dopamine D4 receptor gene polymorphism is associated with attention deficit hyperactivity disorder. *Molecular Psychiatry, 1*, 121–124.

Lang, A., Kaas, L., & Barnes, P. (1983). The beverage type stereotype: An unexplored determinant of the effects of alcohol consumption. *Bulletin Society Psychology of Addictive Behaviors, 2*, 46–49.

Le Marquand, D., Pihl, R., & Benkelfat, C. (1994a). Serotonin and alcohol intake abuse and dependence: Animal studies. *Biological Psychiatry, 36*, 395–421.

LeMarquand, D., Pihl, R., & Benkelfat, C. (1994b). Serotonin and alcohol intake, abuse, and dependence: Clinical evidence. *Biological Psychiatry, 36*, 326–337.

Lennard, H., Epstein, L., Bernstein, A., & Ramson, D. (1971). *Mystification and drug misuse*. San Francisco: Jossey-Bass.

Leone, P., Pocock, D., & Wise, R. A. (1991). Morphine-dopamine interaction: Ventral tegmental morphine increases nucleus accumbens dopamine release. *Pharmacology, Biochemistry & Behavior, 39*, 469–472.

Li, X., Zoli, M., Finnman, B. U., LeNovere, N., Changeux, J. P., & Fuxe, K. (1995). A single nicotine injection causes change with a time delay and the affinity of striatal D2 receptors for antagonist, but not for angonist, nor in the D2 receptor MRNA levels in the rat substantia nigra. *Brain Research, 679*, 157–167.

Linnoila, M., DeJong, J., & Virkkunen, M. (1989). Family history of alcoholism in violent offenders and impulsive fire setters. *Archives of General Psychiatry, 46*, 613–616.

Litten, R. Z., & Allen, J. P. (1991). Pharmacotherapies for alcoholism: Promising agents and clinical issues. *Alcoholism: Clinical and Experiment Research, 15*, 620–633.

Little, R. E., & Sing, C. F. (1986). Association of fathers drinking and infants' birth weight. *New England Journal of Medicine, 314*, 1644–1645.

Liu, D., Diorio, J., Tannenbaum, B., Coldji, C., Francis, D., Freedman, A., Sharma, S., Pearson, D., Plotsky, P., & Meaney, M. (1997). Maternal care, hippocampal glucocorticoid receptors, and hypothalamic-pituitary-adrenal responses to stress. *Science, 277*, 1659–1662.

London, E. (1994). Positron Emission Tomography in Studies of Drug Abuse. *NIDA Research Monograph, 138*, 15–24.

Luria, A. R. (1980). *Higher cortical functions in man.* (Basil Haigh, trans.), (2nd ed.) New York: Basic Books.

Martin, C., & Hoffman, M. (1993). Alcohol expectancies, living environment, peer influence, and gender: A model of college-student drinking. *Journal of College Student Development, 34*, 206–211.

McBride, W. J., Murphy, J. M., Lumeng, L., & Li, T. K. (1990). Serotonin, dopamine and GABA involvement in alcohol drinking of selectively rats. *Alcohol, 7*, 199–205.

McCord, J. (1983). A forty year perspective on effects of child abuse and neglect. *Child Abuse and Neglect, 7*, 265–270.

McDermott, D. (1984). The relationship of parental drug use and parent's attitude concerning adolescent drug use to adolescent drug use. *Adolescence, 19*, 89–97.

McGue, M., Pickens, R. W., & Svikis, D. S. (1992). Sex and age effects on the inheritance of alcohol problems: A twin study. *Journal of Abnormal Psychology, 101*, 3–17.

McLellan, T., Alterman, A., Metzger, D., Grissom, G., Woody, G., Lubovsky, L., & O'Brien, C. (1994). Similarity of outcome predictions across opiate, cocaine, and alcohol treatment. *Journal of Clinical and Consulting Psychology, 62*, 1141–1158.

McNally, R. J. (1996). Anxiety sensitivity is distinguishable from trait anxiety. In R. M. Rapee (Ed.), *Current controversies in the anxiety disorders* (pp. 214–227). New York: Guilford Press.

Mendelson, J., & Mello, N. (1979). Biological concomitants of alcoholism. *New England Journal of Medicine, 301*, 912–921.

Merikangas, K. R., & Gelernter, C. S. (1990). Comorbidity for alcoholism and depression. *Psychiatric Clinic of North America, 13*, 613–632.

Moos, R., & Moos, B. (1984). The process of recovery from alcoholism: Comparing functioning in families of alcoholics and matched control families. *Journal of Studies on Alcohol, 45*, 111–118.

Murdoch, D., & Pihl, R. (1988). The influence of beverage type, BAC, and sex of confederate on aggression in males in a natural setting. *Aggressive Behavior, 14*, 325–336.

Nelson, B., Brighwell, W., Mackenzie-Taylor, D., Berg, J., & Massari, V. (1988). Neurochemical, but not behavioral deviations in the offspring of rats following prenatal or paternal inhalation exposure to ethanol. *Neurotoxicology & Teratology 10*, 15–22.

Newcomb, M. D., & Bentler, P. M. (1986). Substance use and ethnicity: Differential impact of peer and adult models. *Journal of Psychology, 120*, 83–95.

O'Brien, C. (1996). Recent developments in the pharmacotherapy of substance abuse. *Journal of Clinical and Consulting Psychology, 64*, 677–686.

Oetting, E. R., & Beauvais, F. (1987). Common elements in youth drug abuse: Peer clusters and other psychosocial factors. *Journal of Drug Issues, 2*, 133–151.

O'Malley, S., Jaffe, A., Chang, G., Schottenfeld, R., Meyer, R., & Rounsaville, B. (1992). Naltrexone and coping skills therapy for alcohol dependence. *Archives of General Psychiatry, 49*, 881–888.

Parsons, O. A., & Nixon, S. (1993). Neurobehavioral sequelae of alcoholism. *Neurologic Clinics, 11*, 205–218.

Patterson, G. R., DeBaryshe, B. D., & Ramsey, E. (1989). A developmental perspective on antisocial behavior. *American Psychologist, 44*, 329–335.

Patterson, G. R., & Dishion, T. J. (1988). Multilevel family process models: Traits, interactions, and relationships. In R. Hinde & J. Stevenson-Hinde (Eds.), *Relationships within families: Mutual influences* (pp. 283–310). Oxford, England: Oxford University Press.

Peterson, J., Finn, P., & Pihl, R. (1990). Cognitive dysfunction and inherited predisposition to alcoholism. *Journal of Studies on Alcohol, 53*, 154–160.

Peterson, J., & Pihl, R. O. (1990). Information processing, neuropsychological function and the inherited predisposition to alcoholism. *Neuropsychology Review, 1*, 343–369.

Peterson, J., Finn, P., & Pihl, R. O. (1992). Cognitive dysfunction and inherited predisposition to alcoholism. *Journal of Studies on Alcohol, 53*, 1059–1075.

Peterson, J., Pihl, R. O., Gianoulakis, C., Conrod, P., Finn, P., Stewart, S., LeMarquand, D., & Bruce, K. (1996). Ethanol-induced change in cardiac and endogenous opiate function and risk for alcoholism. *Alcoholism: Clinical and Experimental Research, 20*, 1542–1552.

Phillips, T. (1997). Behavior genetics of drug sensitization. *Critical Reviews in Neurobiology, 17*, 21–33.

Pich, E. M., Pagluisi, S., Tessari, M., Talabot-Ayer, D., Hofft van Hsuyoduynen, R., & Chiamulera, C. (1997). Common neural substrates for the addictive properties of nicotine and cocaine. *Science, 275*, 83–86.

Pickens, R. W., Svikis, D. S., McGue, M., Lykken, D. T., Hesten, L. L., & Clayton, P. J. (1991). Heterogeneity in the inheritance of alcoholism. *Archives of General Psychiatry, 48*, 19–28.

Pihl, R. O., & Peterson, J. B. (1992). ADHD/conduct disorder and alcoholism: Is there an association? *Alcohol Health and Research World, 15*, 25–31.

Pihl, R. O., & Peterson, J. B. (1995a). Alcoholism: The role of different motivational systems. *Journal of Psychiatry and Neuroscience, 20*, 372–396.

Pihl, R. O., & Peterson, J. (1995b). Drugs and aggression: Correlations, crime and human manipulative studies and some proposed mechanisms. *Journal of Psychiatry & Neuroscience, 20*, 141–149.

Pihl, R. O., Peterson, J. B., & Finn, P. R. (1990a). The inherited predisposition to alcoholism: Characteristics of sons of male alcoholics. *Journal of Abnormal Psychology, 99*, 291–301.

Pihl, R. O., Peterson, J., & Finn, P. (1990b). An heuristic model for the inherited predisposition to alcoholism. *Psychology of Addictive Behavior, 4*, 12–25.

Pihl, R. O., Peterson, J. B., & Lau, M. A. (1993, September). A biosocial model of the alcohol-aggression relationship. *Journal of Studies on Alcohol* (Supp. 11), 128–139.

Pihl, R. O., Smith, M., & Farrell, B. (1984). Alcohol and aggression: A comparison of brewed and distilled beverages. *Journal of Studies on Alcohol, 45*, 273–282.

Pihl, R. O., & Smith, S. (1983). Of affect and alcohol. In L. A. Pohorecky & J. Brick (Eds.), *Stress and alcohol use* (pp. 203–228). New York: Elsevier.

Pihl, R. O., & Spiers, P. (1978). Individual characteristics and drug abuse. In B. Maher (Ed.), *Progress in experimental personality research* (pp. 93–196). New York: Academic Press.

Polich, J., Pollock, V., & Bloom, F. (1994). Meta-analysis of P300 amplitude from males at risk for alcoholism. *Psychological Bulletin, 15*, 55–73.

Pollock, V. E., Volavka, J., Goodwin, D. W., Mednick, S. A., Gabrielli, W. F., Knop, J., & Schulsiger, F. (1983). The EEG after alcohol administration in men at risk for alcoholism. *Archives of General Psychiatry, 40*, 857–861.

Pomerleau, O. (1992). Nicotine and the central nervous system: Biobehavioral effects of cigarette smoking. *American Journal of Medicine, 93*, 2S–7S.

Porjesz, B., & Begleiter, H. (1995). Event-related potentials and cognitive function in alcoholism. *Alcohol Health & Research World, 19*, 108–112.

Pullen, L. (1994). The relationships among alcohol abuse in college students and selected psychological/demographic variables. *Journal of Alcohol and Drug Education, 40*, 36–50.

Radecki, T., & Zdunich, C. (1993). Tobacco sales to minors in 97 U.S. and Canadian communities. *Tobacco Control, 2*, 300–305.

Resnick, M. D., Bearman, P. S., Blum, R., Bauman, K., Harris, K., Jones, J., Tabor, J., Beuhring, T., Sieving, R., Shaw, M., Ireland, M., Bearinger, L., & Udry, R. (1997). Protecting adolescents from harm. *Journal of the American Medical Association, 278*, 823–832.

Reid, L. D., Martinson, O. B., & Weaver, L. C. (1987). Factors associated with the drug use of fifth through eighth grade students. *Journal of Drug Education, 17*, 149–165.

Rodriguez de Fonseca, F., Rocia, M., Carrera, A., Navarro, M., Koob, G., & Weiss, F. (1997). Activation of corticotropin-releasing factors in the limbic system during cannabinoid withdrawal. *Science, 276*, 2050–2054.

Rosenthal, N., Davenport, Y., Cowdry, R., Webster, M., & Goodwin, F. (1980). Monoamine metabolites in cerebrospinal fluid of depressive subgroups. *Psychiatry Research, 2*, 113–119.

Rubin, V., & Comitas, L. (1976). *Ganja in Jamaica: The effects of marijuana*. New York: Doubleday.

Rudgley, R. (1994). *Essential substances*. New York: Kodansha.

Sangameswaran, L., Fales, H. M., Friedrich, P., & De Blas, A. L. (1986). Purification of a benzodiazepine from bovine brain and detection of benzodiazepine-like immunoreactivity in human brain. *Proceedings of the National Academy of Sciences, 83*, 9236–9240.

Sass, H., Sozka, M., Mann, K., & Ziezlyunsberger, W. (1996). Relapse prevention by acamprosate: Results from a placebo-controlled study on alcohol dependence. *Archives of General Psychiatry, 53*, 673–680.

Schuckit, M. A. (1994). Low level of response to alcohol as a predictor of future alcoholism. *American Journal of Psychiatry, 151*, 184–189.

Schuckit, M., & Gold, E. (1988). A simultaneous evaluation of multiple markers of ethanol/placebo challenges in sons of alcoholics and controls. *Archives of General Psychiatry, 45*, 211–216.

Séguin, J., Pihl, R., Harden, P., Boulerice, B., & Tremblay, R. (1995). Cognitive and neuropsychological characteristics of physically aggressive boys. *Journal of Abnormal Psychology, 104*, 614–624.

Shedler, J., & Block, J. (1990). Adolescent drug use and psychological health. *American Psychologist, 45*, 612–630.

Sher, K. J. (1987). Stress response dampening. In H. T. Blane & K. E. Leonard (Eds.), *Psychological theories of drinking and alcoholism* (pp. 227–271). New York: Guilford Press.

Sher, K., Martin, E., Wood, P., & Rutledge, P. (1997). Alcohol use disorders and neuropsychological functioning in first-year undergraduates. *Experimental and Clinical Psychopharmacology, 5*, 304–315.

Sibley, D. R., & Monsma, F. J., Jr. (1992). Molecular biology of dopamine receptors. *Trends in Pharmacology & Science, 13*, 61–69.

Siegal, R. (1989). *Intoxication: Life in pursuit of artificial paradise*. New York: Simon & Schuster.

Sigvardson, S., Bohman, M., & Cloninger, R. (1996). Replication of the Stockholm Adoption Study of Alcoholism. *Archives of General Psychiatry, 53*, 681–687.

Simcha-Fagan, O., Gersten J. C., & Langner, T. (1986). Early precursors and concurrent correlates of illicit drug use in adolescents. *Journal of Drug Issues, 16*, 7–28.

Smart, R. (1977). Effects of two liquor store strikes on drunkenness, impaired driving and traffic accidents. *Journal of Studies on Alcohol, 38*, 1785–1789.

Smith, S., O'Hara, B., Persico, A., Gorelick, D., Newlin, D., Vlahor, D., Solomon, L., Pickens, R., & Uhl, G. (1992). Genetic vulnerability to drug abuse. *Archives of General Psychiatry, 49*, 723–727.

Spoont, M. R. (1992). Modulatory role of serotonin in neural information processing, implications for human psychopathology. *Psychological Bulletin, 12*, 330–350.

Stacy, A., Newcomb, M., & Bentler, P. (1991). Cognitive motivation and drug use: A 9 year longitudinal study. *Journal of Abnormal Psychology, 100*, 502–515.

Stark-Adamec, C., Pihl, R. O., & Adamec, R. (1981). The subjective marijuana experience: Great expectations. *International Journal of Addictions, 51*, 203–206.

Stewart, S. (1996). Alcohol abuse in individuals exposed to trauma: A critical review. *Psychological Bulletin, 120*, 83–112.

Stewart, S., & Pihl, R. (1994). Effects of alcohol administration on psychophysiological and subjective emotional responses to aversive stimulation in anxiety-sensitive women. *Psychology of Addictive Behaviors, 8*, 29–42.

Streissguth, A., Bookstein, F., Sampson, P., & Barr, H. (1993). *The enduring effects of prenatal alcohol exposure on child development*. Ann Arbor: University of Michigan Press.

Sussman, S., Dent, C. W., Stacy, A. W., Burciaga, C., Raynor, A., Turner, G. E., Carlin, V., Craig, S., Hansen, W. B., Burton, D., & Flay, B. R. (1990). Peer-group association and adolescent tobacco use. *Journal of Abnormal Psychology, 99*, 349–352.

Suzduk, P., Glewa, J., Crawley, J., Schwartz, R., Skolnick, P., & Paul, S. (1986). A selective Imidazobenzodiazepine antagonist of ethanol in the rat. *Science, 234*, 1243–1247.

Swain, R. C., Oetting, E. R., & Beauvais, F. (1989). Links from emotional distress to adolescent drug use: A path model. *Journal of Consulting and Clinical Psychology, 57*, 227–231.

Tanda, G., Pontieri, F., & Di Chiara, G. (1997). Cannabinoid and heroin activation of mesolimbic dopamine transmission by a common opioid receptor mechanism. *Science, 276*, 2048–2050.

Tarter, R., Jacob, T., & Bremer, D. (1989). Cognitive states of status of sons of alcoholic men. *Alcoholism: Clinical & Experimental Research, 13*, 232–235.

Thomas, E. (1988). Forebrain mechanisms in the relief of fear: The role of the lateral septum. *Psychobiology, 16*, 36–44.

Titeler, M., Lyon, R., & Glenon, R. (1988). Radiological binding evidence implicates the brain 5-HT2 receptor as a site of action for LSD and phenylisopropylamine hallucinogens. *Psychopharmacology, 94*, 213–215.

Trull, T., & Sher, K. (1994). Relationship between the five-factor model of personality and Axis I disorders in a non-clinical sample. *Journal of Abnormal Psychology, 103*, 350–360.

Tsai, G., Gostfriend, D., & Coyle, J. (1995). The glutamatergic basis of human alcoholism. *American Journal of Psychiatry, 152*, 332–340.

Volavka, J., Czobor, P., Goodwin, D., Gabrielli, W., Penick, E., Mednick, S., Jensen, P., Knop, J., & Schulsinger, F. (1996). The electroencephalogram after alcohol administration in high risk men and the development of alcohol use disorders ten years later. *Archives of General Psychiatry, 53*, 258–263.

Volkow, N. D., Hitzemann, R., Wolf, A. P., Logan, J., Fowler, J. S., Christman, D., Dewey, S. L., Schlyer, D., Burr, G., Vitkun, S., & Hirschowitz, J. (1990). Acute effects of ethanol on regional brain glucose metabolism and transport. *Psychiatry Research, 35*, 39–48.

Volkow, N. D., Wang, G. J., Begleiter, H., Hitzemann, R., Pappas, N., Burr, G., Pascani, K., Wong, C., Fowler, J. S., & Wolf, A. P. (1995). Regional brain metabolic response to lorazepam in subjects at risk for alcoholism. *Alcohol Clinical and Experimental Research, 19* (2), 510–516.

Volpicelli, J., Alterman, A., Hayashida, M., & O'Brien, C. (1992). Naltrexone in the treatment of alcohol dependence. *Archives of General Psychiatry, 49*, 876–880.

Volpicelli, J., Rhines, K., Rhines, J., Volpicelli, L., Alterman, A., & O'Brien, C. (1997). Naltrexone and alcohol dependence. *Archives of General Psychiatry, 54*, 737–742.

Wakschlay, L., Lahey, B., Loeber, R., Green, S., Gordon, R., & Leventhal, B. (1997). Maternal smoking during pregnancy and the risk of conduct disorder in boys. *Archives of General Psychiatry, 54*, 670–676.

Warneke, L. B. (1991). Benzodiazepines: Abuse and new use. *Canadian Journal of Psychiatry, 36*, 194–205.

Watts, R., & Rabow, J. (1983). Alcohol availability and alcohol-related problems in 213 Californian cities. *Alcoholism: Clinical and Experimental Research, 7*, 47–58.

Wechsler, H., Dondall, G., Davenport, A., & Castillo, S. (1995). Correlates of college student binge drinking. *American Journal of Public Health, 85*, 921–926.

Wechsler, H., & Isaac, N. (1992). "Binge" drinkers at Massachusetts Colleges. *Journal of the American Medical Association, 267*, 2929–2931.

Weissman, M. (1988). Anxiety of alcoholism. *Journal of Clinical Psychiatry, 49*, 17–19.

Whitaker-Azmitia, P., & Peroutka, S. J. (Eds.). (1990). *Neuropharmacology of Serotonin.* New York: New York Academy of Science.

Widom, C., Ireland, T., & Glynn, P. (1995). Alcohol abuse in abused and neglected children followed up: Are they at an increased risk? *Journal of Studies on Alcohol, 56*, 207–217.

Wiers, R., Sergeant, J., & Gunning, W. (1994). Psychological mechanisms of enhanced risk of addiction in children of alcoholics: A dual pathway? *Acta Paediatrica Supplement, 404*, 9–13.

Wills, T., McNamara, G., Vaccaro, D., & Hirky, E. (1996). Escalated substance use: A longitudinal grouping analysis from early to middle adolescence. *Journal of Abnormal Psychology, 105*, 166–180.

Wilsnack, S. C. (1991). Sexuality and women's drinking: Findings from a U.S. national study. *Alcohol Health and Research World, 15*, 147–150.

Wolin, S., Bennett, L., Noonan, D., & Teitlebaum, M. (1980). Disrupted family rituals. A factor in the intergenerational transmission of alcoholism. *Journal of Studies on Alcohol, 41*, 199–214.

Zorumski, C. F., & Isenberg, K. E. (1991). Insights into the structure and function of GABA-benzodiazepine receptors: Ion channels and psychiatry. *American Journal of Psychiatry, 148*, 162–173.

Zucker, R. A. (1987). The four alcoholisms: A developmental account of the etiology process. In P. C. Ribers (Ed.), *Nebraska Symposium on Motivation* (pp. 27–83). Lincoln: University of Nebraska Press.

Zuckerman, M. (1979). *Sensation seeking: Beyond the optimal level of arousal*. Hillsdale, NJ: Lawrence Erlbaum.

Zuckerman, M. (1988). Sensation seeking and behavior disorders. *Archives of General Psychiatry, 45*, 502–503.

11

Schizophrenia

Etiology and Neurocognition

BARBARA A. CORNBLATT
MICHAEL F. GREEN
ELAINE F. WALKER

Schizophrenia is the most crippling of the psychiatric disorders. It typically strikes as adulthood is approaching and is likely to be disabling for a lifetime. Schizophrenia occurs in all countries, cultures, and socioeconomic classes. It affects both sexes equally, although, on average, typical age of onset appears to be younger in males (about 21 years of age) than females (closer to 27 years). Contrary to many historical explanations, it is now widely believed that schizophrenia is most often caused by a disease of the brain.

The prevalence of schizophrenia worldwide is commonly accepted to be about 1% of the population. In the United States alone, approximately 2 million individuals are affected with the disorder at any given time, with about 200,000 new cases diagnosed each year. According to these statistics, about one out of every hundred individuals will become schizophrenic at some time in their lives. Because schizophrenia eliminates or severely limits the most productive years of an individual's life and may require lifelong family or institutional care, its costs to society are enormous. In 1988, Kaplan and Sadock reported that in the United States schizophrenia cost more than all of the cancers combined, yet only $14 per patient was spent on schizophrenia research as compared to approximately $300 per patient on cancer research.

The imbalance in funding reflects the fact that schizophrenia has been misunderstood and stigmatized from the time it was first identified until the present. In many cultures, as early as ancient Egypt and as recently as Europe in the Middle Ages, schizophrenic individuals were regarded as being possessed by evil spirits or the devil. In some primitive cultures this has led to such individuals being treated as shamans, but far more often schizophrenic individuals were treated quite brutally. For example, for about 200 years in Europe, dating from the mid-1400s to the mid-1600s, the mentally ill were persecuted, were burned as witches, and, when hospitalized, were "restrained, often by chains; whipped; ill fed; unwashed; and treated with bloodletting, purgatives, and other "curative" tortures. Those who were not hospitalized wandered the countryside unattended, scorned, beaten" (Gottesman, 1991, p. 11). Today, a substantial proportion of the homeless, populating the streets of urban areas, living under bridges, in cardboard boxes, or in subway tunnels, are also schizophrenic.

While many treatment advances have been made in the last half century, schizophrenia remains a chronic debilitating illness with a guarded outcome. Further progress in treating and, perhaps, in preventing this terrible illness requires a more complete understanding of its causes and pathophysiology. While in the past, scientific inquiries have focused on the symptoms of the illness, over the past decade there has been a shift toward studying neurocognitive processes and brain abnormalities.

History of the Clinical Disorder

Emil Kraepelin (1856–1926), a German psychiatrist, is credited with initiating the modern approach to schizophrenia. Kraepelin (1919/1971) spent his career formulating detailed descriptions of the clinical characteristics and course of the different forms of mental illness. He called the disorder "dementia praecox," or early dementia, to reflect what he considered the typical course of the disease—that is, an early onset followed by a progressively deteriorating course leading to dementia. He also recognized that dementia praecox was different from mental illness characterized by an intermittent course and essentially emotionally based symptoms (e.g., euphoria and depression). He labeled the latter illness manic-depression. As concluded by Andreasen (1984a, p. 16), "Kraepelin's recognition of these two illnesses within the confusing array of patients living in the nineteenth and early twentieth-century psychiatric hospitals laid the foundations of modern psychiatry."

It is particularly interesting that Kraepelin viewed the most likely cause of schizophrenia to be some type of physiological disease. He was also the first to establish subtypes of schizophrenia based on differences in symptom patterns. According to his nosology, the illness was divided into catatonic, hebephrenic, and paranoid forms.

Another major historical figure is Eugen Bleuler (1857–1939), a Swiss psychiatrist. Bleuler both added a fourth diagnostic category, simple schizophrenia, to Kraepelin's nosology, and renamed the illness "schizophrenia" in recognition that patients did not all display the deteriorative course defined by Kraepelin. In translation, this has led to a major misunderstanding of the illness. The term *schizophrenia* literally means the "splitting of the mind." In the lay press, and especially in movies, a major misconception is that this implies a "split personality" (or, in more contemporary terms, multiple personality disorder, or dissociative identity disorder). Multiple personality disorder, however, is unrelated to schizophrenia. Rather, Bleuler was referring to a fundamental splitting of various aspects of the mind, such as between thoughts and emotions.

Bleuler adopted a more "psychological" view of schizophrenia than had Kraepelin. Whereas Kraepelin had based diagnosis on symptom course (i.e., poor outcome), Bleuler used the presence of a disordered thought process as the primary criterion, which he considered to consist of a loosening of associations (e.g., connecting unrelated ideas); autism (complete self-centeredness); affective disturbance (inappropriate emotions and actions), and ambivalence (not being able to make up one's mind; Gottesman, 1991). He believed that the symptoms described by Kraepelin, such as hallucinations and delusions, were secondary, resulting from the thought disorder. Bleuler also believed that schizophrenia consisted of a heterogeneous cluster of illnesses—that is, the "group of schizophrenias" (Bleuler, 1950), with different etiologies, symptom clusters, and course. The formulations of both Kraepelin and Bleuler have provided the foundations for much of the research that continues today.

Contemporary Clinical Views

Clinically, schizophrenia is an extremely complex illness. There is no laboratory test for schizophrenia. It is characterized by a diversity of symptoms, no one of which is definitive and many of which overlap with other neurological or psychiatric disorders. The course of the disorder is also variable; it can start either abruptly or insidiously, with outcome ranging from full or partial recovery to total debilitation. Consistent with Bleuler, most researchers continue to regard schizophrenia as likely to be a heterogeneous mix of disorders, with different etiologies, pathophysiologies, and outcome. As a result, diagnostic precision is difficult. This, in turn, greatly complicates the study of the disorder.

Following Kraepelin and Bleuler, there have been a number of more recent attempts to subtype schizophrenia on the basis of symptom patterns in order to reduce the illness to categories more easily studied and understood. For example, in the 1960s, several classifications were based on the longitudinal course of illness and variably divided it into acute vs. chronic, process vs. reactive, or good vs. poor prognosis (Andreasen & Olsen, 1982). These systems, however, were not markedly successful in reflecting etiology and have given way to the more current division of the disorder into positive and negative symptoms.

The distinction between positive and negative symptoms was first discussed in detail by Hughlings-Jackson (1931), a prominent neurologist. This notion was subsequently reintroduced and further developed by Strauss, Carpenter, and Bartko (1974), who added disturbed interpersonal relationships as the third basic symptom dimension. Widespread acceptance of this symptom dichotomy, however, actually began with Crow's (1980) conception of the two-syndrome model. According to Crow's hypothesis, schizophrenia consists of two syndromes with different underlying pathophysiologies. He considered Type I to be essentially a biochemical (dopamine) disorder that was characterized by positive symptoms, acute onset, a good response to medication, and a relatively good prognosis. Type II was viewed, on the other hand, as involving irreversible structural abnormalities of the brain (e.g., enlarged ventricles and cortical atrophy) and characterized by negative symptoms, intellectual impairment, chronicity, poor neuroleptic response, and poor outcome.

In the early 1980s, Andreasen, a leader in the development of modern nosology, and her colleagues developed two scales: the Scale for the Assessment of Negative Symptoms and the Scale for the Assessment of Positive Symptoms (e.g., Andreasen, 1982, 1983, 1984b, 1984c; Andreasen & Olsen, 1982; Andreasen, Olsen, Dennert, & Smith, 1982). These two scales continue to be among the most widely used in measuring positive and negative symptoms today.

The Scale for the Assessment of Positive Symptoms (SAPS) rates five positive symptoms, representing distortions of normal thinking and behavior; the Scale for the Assessment of Negative Symptoms (SANS) rates five negative symptoms, reflecting a loss of a normal function. The positive symptoms consist of hallucinations, delusions, positive thought disorder, bizarre or disorganized behavior, and catatonic motor behavior. The negative symptoms include affective blunting (impoverishment of emotional expression, reactivity, and feeling), alogia (impoverished thinking and cognition), anhedonia (difficulties in experiencing interest or pleasure), avolition-apathy (characteristic lack of energy, drive, and interest), and attentional impairment (difficulties in focusing attention as observed by others).

More recently, based on factor analysis and other correlational studies, Andreasen, Arndt, Alliger, Miller, and Flaum (1995) have empirically found that positive symptoms subdivide into two dimensions: a psychotic factor and a disorganization factor. The psychotic dimension consists of hallucinations and delusions. The disorganizational syndrome consists of disorganized speech, disorganized behavior, and inappropriate affect.

Negative symptoms, the third symptom dimension described by Andreasen et al. (1995), has been consistently upheld by research. However, the nature of the syndrome has been modified by Carpenter and colleagues (e.g., Carpenter, Heinrichs, & Wagman, 1988), who have divided negative symptoms into primary and secondary ones. Primary symptoms are those at the core of the disorder and are referred to as "deficit" symptoms. These include flattened or restrictive affect, anhedonia, poverty of speech, lack of a sense of purpose, and diminished social drive. These symptoms must, in addition, be enduring, not affected by medication, and present for at least the preceding 12 months. Secondary symptoms are those that result from the side effects of medication, especially Parkinsonian symptoms, depression, anxiety, or environmental deprivation.

Reviving the Strauss et al. (1974) approach, some investigators have also included disorder of relating as a fourth independent dimension in schizophrenia (e.g., Cuesta & Peralta, 1995). The extent to which division into the three dimensions (psychotic, disorganized, and negative) or four (with the interpersonal dimension added to the other three) lead to an understanding of etiology and pathophysiology remains to be determined.

Hallucinations and delusions are the most dramatic features and the hallmark characteristics of schizophrenia. Hallucinations involve hearing, seeing, feeling, and smelling things that are not, in reality, present. Of these, the most common type of hallucination consists of hearing voices, one or several, typically making commentaries about the individual or conversing with each other. Delusions are fixed, unshakable beliefs that are not grounded in reality. The most common types of delusions are persecutory (e.g., believing that one is being investigated or followed by the FBI), grandiose (e.g., belief that one has special powers), or somatic (e.g., belief that one's body has been changed in some way).

Etiology of Schizophrenia

It is now widely accepted that schizophrenia is a disease of the brain. However, after close to 100 years of study, the cause of this disease remains a mystery. Throughout this time, it has been well known that schizophrenia runs in families, but whether this is due to shared environment or shared genes has been open to question. For many years, the psychoanalytic tradition guided the search for environmental causes. As a result, a great deal of attention was directed at identifying bad parenting or other family interactions as the source of illness. A leading contender was the influence of the "schizophrenogenic mother," variously described as emotionally cold, distant, rejecting, or as communicating mixed messages (e.g., Fromm-Reichmann, 1948). These notions have now been discarded. No evidence has ever been found to indicate that rearing factors can, in and of themselves, *directly cause* schizophrenia. Similarly, there has been no support that other, quite plausible, negative environmental experiences, such as extreme poverty or severe childhood trauma, can alone induce schizophrenia. On the other hand, a variety of early environmental insults—for example, prenatal viral exposure—have more recently received some preliminary support as possible risk factors for schizophrenia.

Prenatal Environment Risk Factors

Viral Infection The city of Helsinki experienced an A2 influenza epidemic during the autumn of 1957. The epidemic of 1957 was unusual in two respects. First, it was short-lived—five weeks in length with rather clear start and end dates. Second, it was fairly widespread—probably about two thirds of the population experienced some signs of infection. The features of this particular influenza epidemic provide an opportunity for evaluating its long-term effects on risk for schizophrenia.

Mednick and his colleagues (Mednick, Machon, Huttunen, & Bonett, 1988) determined the rates of schizophrenia in offspring who were in utero during the influenza epidemic and compared the rates to those of controls. The sample was divided according to trimester of exposure. Offspring who were born in the three months after the epidemic would have been in their third trimester at the time of the epidemic. Those born four to six months after the epidemic would have been in their second trimester, and those born seven to nine months afterward would have been in their first trimester. These subjects constituted the three "experimental" groups. The control groups were subjects born in the same hospitals during the same months of previous years.

The rates of schizophrenia for offspring of mothers exposed to the influenza virus during the first or third trimesters were not different from those of controls. However, the rates for the offspring exposed during the second trimester were substantially higher than those of controls. The results suggest that the second trimester is a critical period of vulnerability. Studies from other geographic regions have also shown increased risk of schizophrenia with exposure to influenza during the second trimester (Barr, Mednick, & Munck-Jorgenson, 1990; O'Callaghan, Sham, Takei, Glover, & Murray, 1991), but there have been some failures to replicate as well (Crow, 1994). Most of the evidence across studies suggests that a virus may lead to disruption of neural development in the second trimester and that this disruption is linked to the eventual development of schizophrenia.

Influenza epidemics are rare and these viruses probably account for a small proportion of the total number of patients with schizophrenia worldwide. Even with a substantial increase in risk over baseline, only a small minority of mothers who were exposed to the virus in the second trimester gave birth to a pre-schizophrenic child. Nonetheless, the results from the influenza studies are important because they show that a particular environmental factor occurring at a specific time in fetal development can increase risk for schizophrenia.

Studies of Starvation Toward the end of World War II, the Allies invaded France and by September of 1944, they had crossed two branches of the Rhine River. They were, nonetheless, unable to capture key bridges that connected the Netherlands to Germany. The Germans imposed a blockade of western Holland in retaliation for a strike by the Dutch railroad workers. The blockade led to the Dutch Hunger Winter, a severe famine in this region from October 1944 until the end of the war in May 1945. The peak of the famine ran from February to April 1945, during which bread and potatoes formed nearly the entire ration. Just as in the influenza study in Helsinki, it is possible to follow the offspring of women who were pregnant during the Hunger Winter to examine the risk for development of subsequent psychiatric disorders (Susser & Lin, 1992). It is a safe assumption that the women experienced some degree of starvation because pregnant women did not receive any special food supplements during the famine. The offspring of women who were exposed to severe famine had increased rates of hospitalization for schizophrenia compared to controls. Unlike the influenza studies, the increased risk occurred for offspring who were exposed during the first trimester. If starvation exerts its risk at a slightly earlier period of development (i.e., first vs. second trimester), it could indicate that the period of risk varies according to the type of neurodevelopmental stressor.

As in the case of prenatal viral exposure, prenatal starvation interrupting normal brain development accounts for only a very small proportion of individuals becoming schizophrenic. Furthermore, the majority of individuals exposed to such early environmental insults do not develop schizophrenia. Therefore, prenatal exposure to noxious events cannot be the only explanation; in fact, some researchers have argued that these events precipitate illness only in individuals who already have some type of biological predisposition for schizophrenia.

Genetic Factors

In comparison with the still murky environmental picture, a much clearer case can be made for the importance of genetic factors in schizophrenia. During the years that environmental explanations were studied and discarded, a great deal of evidence gradually accumulated indicating that schizophrenia runs in families because it involves a genetic component. This does not imply genetic determinism—but, rather, that an abnormality in one or more genes leads to a biological predisposition or susceptibility for developing the illness. In most cases, this predisposition is not sufficient in itself to cause full-blown schizophrenia, but requires some kind of "trigger," such as the prenatal environmental insults mentioned above. This view is known as the diathesis-stress theory of illness and has been an influential etiological model for at least 20 years. As we will discuss later, it is now increasingly believed that cognitive abnormalities represent a major part of this model.

Family, Twin, and Adoption Studies The classic genetic methodologies—family, twin, and adoption studies—provided the initial evidence for the heritability of schizophrenia.

Family Studies Figure 11.1 (adapted from Gottesman, 1991, p. 96) summarizes the risks for developing schizophrenia in various relatives of an index patient with schizophrenia. This data pools information from about 40 studies conducted in Western Europe from 1920 through 1987. Gottesman explains his exclusive reliance on European studies on the basis that in the countries involved: (1) diagnoses tend to be conservative and based on similar criteria; (2) compared to the United States, the populations are more stable, homogeneous, and, often, more cooperative; and (3) researchers have access to national health registers not available in the United States.

Relatives are shown in order of increasing risk for schizophrenia. As can be seen, this is impressively consistent, with risk for illness increasing as the degree of relatedness to the index subject becomes closer. At the top of the figure are the general population risk of 1% and the similar rate of 2% for spouses of index patients (indicating that there is no increased risk for spouses who share the same environment but do not share any genes with a schizophrenic individual). The risks for second-degree relatives (who share 25% of their genes) range from 2 to 6%, and are therefore only slightly higher than those for individuals unrelated to a person with schizophrenia. First-degree relatives (who share approximately 50% of their genes), by contrast, show a considerably higher risk rate, ranging from 9% for siblings to close to 50% for the offspring of two schizophrenic parents. In the case of monozygotic twins (who share 100% of their genes), risk for schizophrenia is also at the elevated rate of about 50%. However, the fact that the monozygotic twin risk rate is below 100% suggests that environmental factors also play an important role in the expression of illness. Gottesman concludes that:

> Overall, the pattern of risk figures in the relatives of schizophrenics strongly supports the conclusion that the magnitude of the increased risk varies with the amount of gene sharing and not with the amount of experience sharing.

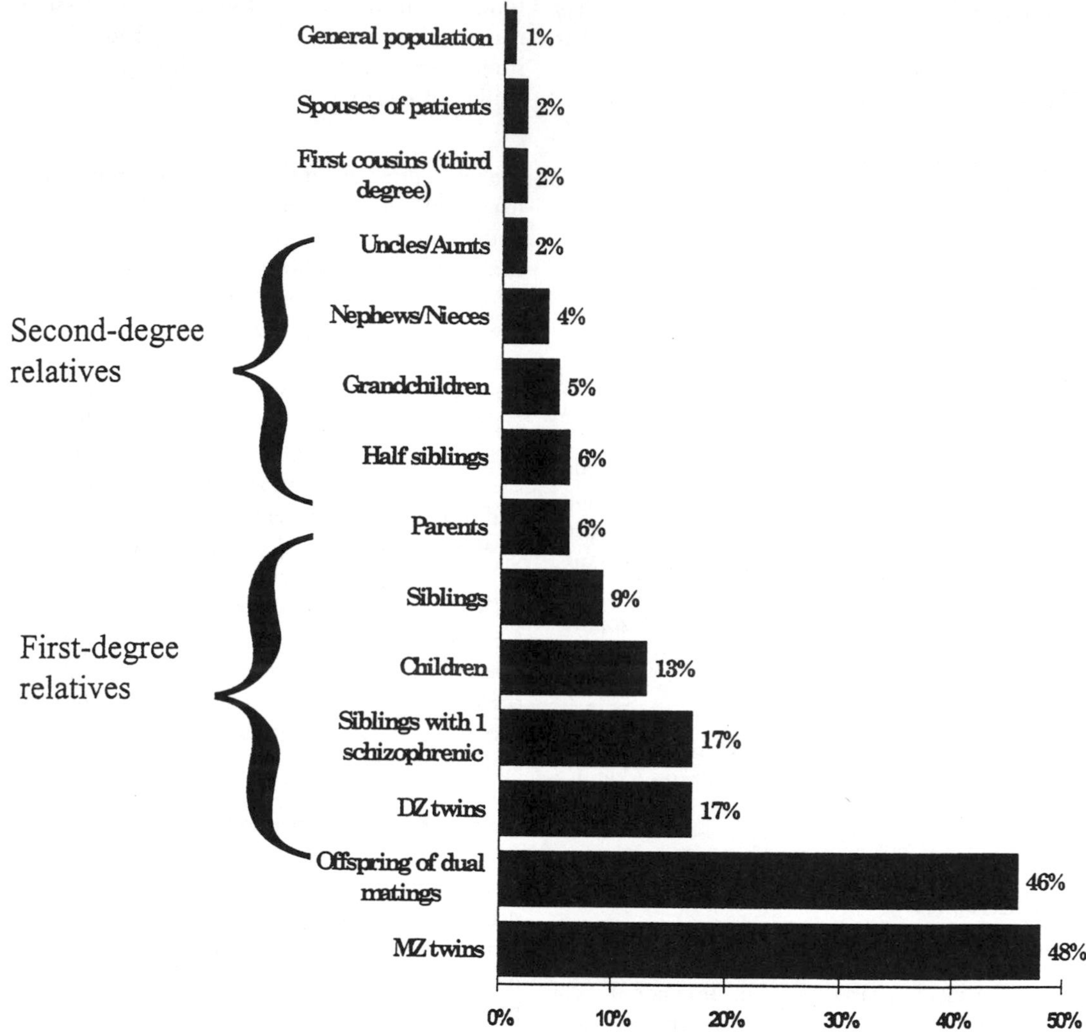

Figure 11.1 Grand average risks for developing schizophrenia compiled from the family and twin studies conducted in European populations between 1920 and 1987 (adapted from Gottesman, 1991).

> Identical twins and offspring of dual matings have higher risks than do first-degree relatives, who have higher risks than do second-degree relatives, who have higher risks than do third-degree relatives, who have higher risks than do spouses and the basic risk of 1 percent in the general population. (Gottesman, 1991, pp. 97–98)

It should be noted that the exception to the approximately 12% risk to first-degree relatives is the unexpectedly low rate of illness in parents of a person with schizophrenia. This finding is well known but not completely understood. It is generally attributed to the fact that schizophrenic patients do not tend to marry or have relationships and typically display reduced fertility. Thus, schizophrenic individuals generally have fewer children than individuals in the general population.

Reanalyses of the original Danish family studies (described in the Adoption Studies section below) to conform to more modern diagnostic criteria (i.e., the *DSM-III*) were conducted by Kendler and colleagues (e.g. Kendler & Diehl, 1993; Kendler & Gruenberg, 1984). Although the new diagnoses changed the sample composition and the base rates of illness, the pattern of increased risk to relatives of a schizophrenic patient remained the same. However, one important result of these studies was the emphasis on the full spectrum of schizophrenia-related disorders that emerged (see Kendler, 1988). The schizophrenia spectrum refers to a cluster of illnesses that are clinically similar to schizophrenia and are found to characterize the relatives of schizophrenic patients. These disorders, typically less severe, are assumed to share a common genetic etiology with the core schizophrenia illness. There is general consensus that schizotypal and paranoid personality disorders fall into this spectrum of disorders (Kendler, 1985). More controversy surrounds the inclusion of other categories of illness, such as schizoid personality disorder and schizoaffective disorder (Levinson & Mowry, 1991).

Twin Studies Because twins with schizophrenia are relatively rare and twin studies of schizophrenia are therefore very difficult to conduct, only a limited number of such studies have been conducted since the early 1900s. Worldwide, six classical twin studies were conducted from 1928 to 1953 and five more since 1963 (see detailed and very interesting descriptions of these in Gottesman, 1991, chap. 6). Findings from the newer studies are often given more weight than the traditional ones, since they adhere to modern diagnostic standards and are considered methodologically more rigorous than the earlier ones. Gottesman (1991, p. 110) reported a concordance rate, summed across studies, of 48% for monozygotic (MZ) twins and 17% for dizygotic (DZ) twins—in close agreement with those previously reported and consistent with a gene X environment interaction model.

In this context, a twin study conducted in Denmark by Gottesman and Bertelson (1989) is particularly supportive of the importance of genetic factors. In this study, the offspring of MZ and DZ twins discordant for schizophrenia, originally evaluated by Fischer (1971), were clinically followed up 18 years later. Gottesman and Bertelson reported the rather extraordinary finding that the rate of schizophrenia among the children of the MZ twins was virtually the same, whether or not the parent twin was schizophrenic. That is, for the MZ twins who were ill, the rate of schizophrenia among their offspring was 16.8%; the rate of illness among offspring of the well MZ cotwins was 17.4%. Therefore, the disease genotype (identical in MZ twins) had the same rate of transmission to the offspring regardless of whether it was clinically expressed in the parent.

However, the same pattern was not found for the discordant DZ twins. In this case, the rate of illness in the offspring of the ill twin was 17.4%, matching the rate for both ill and healthy MZ twins and consistent with the risk to offspring of a parent with schizophrenia, in general. But in this case, there was a dramatic difference in the rate of illness among offspring of the healthy DZ cotwin: only 2.1% of the children of the healthy DZ cotwins became ill, the same as the rate reported for nieces and nephews of schizophrenics (see figure 11.1).

To fully understand these findings, it is important to make a distinction between the genotype and the phenotype. The genotype is the underlying genetic structure of the individual. The phenotype refers to the observable characteristics or behaviors of an individual. The extent to which the genotype is expressed behaviorally (i.e., by the phenotype) depends on a number of additional biological and environmental factors. In the twin study just described, it appears that for the "healthy" MZ cotwins, the disease genotype was present but clinically silent. However, the genotype was transmitted to the next generation to the same extent as it was for the affected MZ parents, resulting in the same rate of illness among offspring, whether the twin parent was phenotypcially sick or healthy. Gottesman thus concludes (1991, p. 124) that "the data we have shown from this unusually well-followed-up sample of Danish schizophrenic twins and their offspring support a strong role for genetic factors in the etiology of schizophrenia. No support is found for the suggestion that rearing by a schizophrenic parent is necessary or sufficient to produce schizophrenia in offspring."

In summary, the results from the twin studies that have been conducted over the past century provide quite strong evidence that schizophrenia is indeed heritable. However, because MZ twins are far from being 100% concordant for illness, genetics can be only part of the explanation. It is clear that some other types of as-yet unidentified factors are also involved.

Adoption Studies A third source of support for the genetics of schizophrenia results from the traditional adoption studies. The first adoption study was conducted by Heston (1966) in Oregon, who assessed the rate of illness in the adult offspring of schizophrenic mothers. All of the children had been adopted or placed in orphanages before they were four days old. Heston found that 10.4% of the 47 adopted-away offspring of schizophrenic mothers were themselves schizophrenic compared to none of the 50 adopted-away offspring of matched normal mothers. Heston's results were subsequently replicated by a team of investigators from the United States and Denmark (e.g., Rosenthal et al., 1968; Lowing, Mirsky, & Pereira, 1983), who reported a higher rate of schizophrenia-related illness among the adopted-away offspring of schizophrenic parents than among adopted-away offspring of normal control parents.

An alternate adoption research strategy was pioneered by Kety and colleagues (Kety, 1988). Also conducted in Denmark, the focus of this study was on the rate of illness among biological relatives of adult adoptees who had become schizophrenic. These investigators found that the rate of schizophrenia-related illness (5.4%) among the adoptive relatives—i.e., the relatives who had raised the schizophrenic index patients—was the same as the rate in the control populations. By contrast, a much higher rate (21.4%) was found for the biological relatives of the patients. In their diagnostically updated reanalysis, Kendler and Gruenberg (1984) again found a significantly higher rate of schizophrenia-related disorders among the biological relatives of the schizophrenic adoptees than among the relatives who had adopted them.

In summary, the above family, twin, and adoption studies have made a solid case for the genetic etiology of schizophrenia within the diathesis-stress model. These early findings paved the way for the more recent linkage studies to be discussed below.

Mode of Transmission Although it is now commonly accepted that schizophrenia involves a genetic component, no simple Mendelian mode of transmission fits the data (McGuffin & Sturt, 1986). The picture is further complicated by the unresolved issue of heterogeneity. It remains to be determined whether schizophrenia is a single disease entity or a cluster of illnesses with different etiologies, some genetic and others environmental (known as phenocopies).

The two types of transmission most frequently hypothesized have been the single gene model and the multifactorial/polygenic model. It has been clear from the earliest family data that a single gene (or single major locus, SML) model is inconsistent with the data. Nevertheless, many researchers have maintained the possibility of a SML by introducing the concept of incomplete penetrance. This is the notion that although the gene is present, it may not be fully expressed clinically (i.e., that not everyone who has the gene will get the illness).

Gottesman introduced the alternative polygenic/multifactorial threshold model into the field of schizophrenia (Gottesman & Shields, 1967). According to this model, a complex illness such as schizophrenia is the result of the interaction of several small genes as well as other factors.

> These polygenes are not different in kind from the major genes that cause Mendelian conditions, but each has only a small effect on trait variation as compared to the total variation for that trait. Therefore, the expression of the trait depends much less on which polygenes in the specific system a person has . . . than on the total number pulling him or her toward an extreme. A feature of special interest in the study of schizophrenia and other major mental disorders is the ability of such polygenic systems to store and conceal genetic contributors to the liability to developing the disorder, somewhat analogous to carrier status for recessive diseases. (Gottesman, 1991, p. 88)

As further explained by McGuffin and Sturt (1986, p. 70):

> In general, it is assumed that there is a single continuous variable, termed liability to develop the disorder, which is contributed by the predominantly additive effects of many genes at different loci. . . . As a result, liability within the population at large tends to follow a normal distribution. Only those individuals whose liability falls beyond a certain threshold manifest the disorder.

In other words, what the individual inherits is a liability or predisposition for developing the disease, not the disease itself. The liability increases the risk that the individual will develop schizophrenia, but whether or not the illness will actually be expressed depends upon many other factors, both biological and environmental, that either worsen or suppress the clinical illness.

This model is consistent with the patterns of familial transmission observed for other complex physical diseases such as diabetes, coronary heart disease, epilepsy, and some forms of mental retardation. Gottesman (1991, p. 88) lists six criteria that distinguish polygenic from Mendelian illnesses as follows:

1. They are not rare in the general population, occurring with a lifetime risk of greater than 1 in 500.
2. There are gradations of severity ranging from mild to severe, whereas Mendelian diseases are either present or absent.
3. Severely ill patients often have more relatives affected than do mildly ill ones.
4. The risk to the next generation increases as a function of the total number of sick relatives in the pedigree.
5. The risk drops sharply rather than by 50% steps as one proceeds by degrees from very close genetic relatives to more remote ones.
6. Affected cases appear on both maternal and paternal sides of the family pedigree.

Schizophrenia appears to meet all of these criteria. As a result, the polygenic/multifactorial model has come to be widely accepted. A major modification adopted by many geneticists involved in linkage studies of schizophrenia, however, is to propose that rather than many small polygenes, it is more likely that the model is oligogenic. That is, it involves only a few genes of major effect (two or more), but that these are influenced by many polygenes of small effect, as well as by other background factors.

Linkage Analysis With the development of modern techniques of molecular genetics, it is now possible to move from questions of whether there is a genetic basis of schizophrenia to identifying the genes. Since restriction fragment length polymorphisms (RFLPs) were discovered in the late 1970s, there has been a rapid proliferation of the number of diseases that have been located on a specific chromosomes. However, the greatest successes have been for Mendelian disorders (i.e., with single major genes), such as cystic fibrosis, Duchene's muscular dystrophy, neurofibromatosis, or Huntington's disease. The early findings for neuropsychiatric disorders, although greeted with much enthusiasm, eventually proved disappointing. For example, Bassett, McGillivray, Jones, and Pantzar (1988) reported a family in which schizophrenia appeared to be associated with a trisomy (three rather than two copies) of a region of chromosome 5. Bassett's finding generated a great deal of interest in that region of chromosome 5 among genetic researchers. For example, Sherrington et al. (1988) shortly thereafter reported evidence for a dominant schizophrenia-susceptibility gene in several Icelandic and English families on a region of chromosome 5 consistent with Bassett's finding. These results created quite a stir in the research world. However, almost immediately, nonreplications of the chromosome 5 finding began to appear throughout the literature (e.g., Kennedy et al., 1988; Detera-Wadleigh et al., 1989; St. Clair et al., 1989), and, currently, there is little confidence that an important gene for schizophrenia will be found on chromosome 5. Furthermore, progress in identifying genes for schizophrenia at other locations has been slow and uneven, although recently several reports have implicated a region of chromosome 6 for a possible subtype of schizophrenia.

A major question can therefore be raised as to why linkage studies have problems with neuropsychiatric disorders. Several answers to this question were provided by the speakers in a 1990 AAAS Symposium on the Genetics of Mental Illness. In an overview of the papers from that session, Cornblatt and Keefe (1991) listed six major issues: (1) the need for more sophisticated linkage methodologies to accommodate complex illnesses; (2) larger sample sizes; (3) improved gene mapping; (4) more stringent criteria for considering a finding to be significant; (5) etiological heterogeneity; and (6) diagnostic dilemmas.

Of these, major strides have been made on the first four. As pointed out by Brzustowicz (in press), several recent technological developments have made it considerably easier to study complex diseases. For example, sparse genetic maps have been replaced by high-density maps with new highly polymorphic markers, improving genetic studies of such complex diseases as insulin-dependent diabetes mellitus, familial breast cancer, and Alzheimer's disease. Furthermore, and of particular importance to schizophrenia, several highly sophisticated methods of analyses have been developed that do not require specification of the mode of inheritance.

However, problems five and six, which are interrelated, continue to plague neuropsychiatric linkage studies. There is considerable controversy about the issue of heterogeneity. A number of proponents feel that etiological heterogeneity fits the data best and has several advantages. For example,

Tsuang, Lyons, and Faraone (1990, p. 17) maintained that:

> If subtypes with distinct aetiologies and pathophysiologies do exist, their identification would greatly facilitate progress in our understanding of schizophrenia. Biochemical or structural abnormalities that occur in some schizophrenics might not be apparent in a schizophrenic sample in which only a fraction had the subtype of schizophrenia associated with the abnormality. Moreover, the identification of subtypes associated with specific pathophysiologies and aetiologies offers the promise of subtype-specific interventions that might treat and prevent the disorder.

On the other hand, if schizophrenia is etiologically heterogeneous, this greatly complicates the task for linkage studies. Risch (1990), for example, explains that heterogeneity is caused by different mutations, either in the same or in different locations, that produce a similar clinical outcome. Complex clinical pictures make it very difficult to develop distinct syndromes that can distinguish among families with different forms of the disorder, especially because specific symptoms rarely breed true to a particular subtype of the illness. None of the clinical systems for dividing patients into systematic subgroups, from the Kraeplinian categories (i.e., paranoid, simple, hebephrenic, catatonic) up to the more contemporary Type I vs. Type II syndrome proposed by Crow (1980), appear to have been successful in identifying etiologically homogeneous subgroups. Linkage studies that combine families that have different forms of schizophrenia will find it difficult, if not impossible, to identify the underlying genes.

Diagnostic precision is a second, closely related problem associated with studying schizophrenia. Inaccurate diagnoses are highly damaging to linkage methodology in that they will distort the computation of the association between marker and disease. This is particularly true of false positive diagnoses, which spuriously weaken evidence for linkage. False negative diagnoses are also a problem, although not as serious, since they function to limit the power of the analysis rather than its accuracy (Levinson & Mowry, 1991).

Identification of affected cases is now based on clinical judgment (even when structured assessments are used). Considerable confusion remains at the boundaries between schizophrenia and other similar disorders (e.g., mood disorders with psychotic features) and between the less severe variants of schizophrenia (e.g., schizotypal personality disorder) and other Axis II disorders (e.g., borderline personality disorder). Among a number of different problems is the tendency for patients to show fluctuations in clinical symptoms over time, sometimes changing from one subtype to another. This increases the chances of false positive and false negative diagnoses. It is possible that clinical symptoms are simply too variable and unreliable to provide a bridge to the underlying biology of schizophrenia.

An alternate strategy for dealing with both heterogeneity and imprecise clinical diagnosis involves the identification of neurocognitive deficits that are potential indicators of the schizophrenia pathophysiology (Tsuang et al., 1990). Such indicators may provide considerable information about the heritability of schizophrenia. For example, they can help to identify carriers of the gene who do not display the full clinical disorder, facilitating linkage studies. In addition, specific indicator profiles might help identify etiologically meaningful subtypes of schizophrenia, either alone or when used in combination with clinical information.

Neurocognition

The recognition of schizophrenia as a brain disease has broadened the field of neurocognition. As elegantly stated by Andreasen, "The aberrations of mental illnesses reflect abnormalities in the brain/mind's interaction with its surrounding world; they are diseases of a psyche (or mind) that resides in that region of the soma (or body) that is the brain" (1997, p. 1586). Neurocognition focuses on both cognitive psychology, the study of the mind, and neuropsychology, the attempt to localize and understand cognitive dysfunctions in the brain. In the field of schizophrenia, neuropsychologists are also expanding their areas of inquiry into structural abnormalities of the brain as measured by brain imaging techniques and into the biochemical mechanisms that are thought likely to interact with structural mechanisms. The sections of the chapter to follow will deal with areas of neurocognition currently most active in schizophrenia research.

Neuropsychology and Cognition

Background

Emil Kraepelin In addition to his influential classification of psychiatric disorders in the late 19th and early 20th century, Kraepelin (1971) also described a rather sophisticated subtyping of attentional dysfunctions in schizophrenia. His training with Wilhelm Wundt, the founder of the first laboratory of psychology in Leipzig, probably instilled this interest in attentional processes. Kraepelin suggested that schizophrenic patients have two types of attentional abnormalities: a disorder in active attention (*aufmerksamkeit*) and in passive attention (*auffassung*). He proposed that these two types of attention relate to the phase of the illness (Nuechterlein & Asarnow, 1989)—that is, that the problem in active attention is relatively consistent over time, but that the disorder in passive attention is present only during the acute and terminal stages of the illness. The notion of active attention is close to the modern definition of sustained attention, and passive attention is similar to selective attention.

Eugen Bleuler Perhaps more than Kraepelin, Bleuler (1950) helped to shape current views of neurocognition in schizophrenia. Bleuler made a key distinction between *fundamental* and *accessory* symptoms of schizophrenia. Accessory symptoms included hallucinations, delusions, and a variety of behavioral and speech abnormalities. Fundamental symptoms were divided into *simple* and *compound* symptoms. Simple fundamental symptoms included disturbances in association, affectivity, and ambivalence. Disturbance in association was considered the abnormality most closely linked to the disease process. Simple fundamental symptoms combined to form compound fundamental symptoms that included disturbances in attention. Bleuler used the term *attention* broadly to refer to lack of responsiveness to the environment: ("the uninterested or autistically encapsulated patients pay very little attention to the outer world," p. 68), as well as a diminution in attentional resources ("the general tendency to fatigue in some cases also causes the rapid dwindling of attention," p. 69).

Bleuler introduced three concepts that form the basis for modern views of neurocognition in schizophrenia. First, he suggested that certain basic dysfunctions (simple symptoms) can be assembled into compound symptoms, including disordered attention. Second, Bleuler considered psychotic symptoms such as hallucinations and delusions to be secondary to fundamental symptoms. This hierarchy of symptoms was not only insightful, but also was counterintuitive: he proposed that the most dramatic features of the illness (i.e., hallucinations and delusions) were one step removed from the disease process. Bleuler suggested that schizophrenia can be best understood by a focus on core features of the illness and not the more noticeable defining features of the disorder. The content of the secondary symptoms are largely based on chance, not predetermined: "Almost the totality of the heretofore described symptomatology of dementia praecox is a secondary, in a certain sense, an accidental one" (p. 349).

A third contribution was his emphasis on the different time courses of fundamental vs. accessory symptoms. Enduring features of the illness were considered more central to the disorder than episodic features: "The primary symptoms are the necessary partial phenomena of a disease; the secondary symptoms may be absent, at least potentially, or they may change without the disease process having to change at the same time" (Bleuler, 1950, p. 349).

Subsequent to the key contributions of Kraepelin and Bleuler, empirical studies of the neurocognition of schizophrenia have emerged from two substantially different traditions: *clinical neuropsychology* and *experimental psychology*.

Clinical Neuropsychology (Brain Pathology) Clinical neuropsychology largely grew out of an interest in the neuropsychology of brain pathology. Many of the clinical neuropsychological assessments are validated by their ability to distinguish between brain-damaged and normal samples. For this reason, it is unsurprising that the clinical neuropsychological approach to schizophrenia began by applying assessments as an aid in differential diagnosis.

In a typical study of this type, a group of psychiatric patients would be compared with a group of neurological patients. Patients' classification would be predicted on the basis of performance (e.g., schizophrenia vs. brain damaged) and the accuracy (hit rates) of classification would be determined. The use of neuropsychological assessments to separate schizophrenia from brain-damaged patients was problematic for several reasons. For one, it did not work. Neuropsychological tests were not much better than chance at distinguishing chronic schizophrenic patients from brain-damaged patients (Heaton, Baade, & Johnson, 1978). Another problem was that the rationale for these studies was flawed. The intention was to distinguish a group with and without brain damage, but schizophrenic patients have a particular type of brain dysfunction. Even if schizophrenia patients perform poorly on neuropsychological tests, we cannot assume that they do so for the same reason as patients with frank lesions (Keefe, 1995; Levy, 1996). There are multiple pathways to poor performance, so schizophrenic and neurologic patients may perform poorly for quite different reasons.

A limitation of earlier attempts at differential diagnosis was the practice of treating all forms of brain damage as a single entity. There may be value in comparing schizophrenic patients with a brain-damaged group that is narrowly defined and well characterized. For example, recent studies have compared schizophrenic patients to neurological patients with clearly defined loci (e.g., left or right temporal lobe epilepsy; Gold et al., 1994). These studies, while more interpretable than previous ones, have not strongly implicated a particular brain region for schizophrenia. Instead, they suggest the relevance of widely distributed brain circuits in schizophrenia.

Another aspect of the neuropsychological approach to schizophrenia has been to look for characteristic cognitive profiles. Clinical neuropsychological batteries often yield profiles of the patients' strengths and weaknesses graphed over various neurocognitive abilities (e.g., attention, language, memory, motor). Brain dysfunction associated with schizophrenia could conceivably have its own neurocognitive profile. But there is a methodological obstacle in searching for a neuropsychological profile in this manner. Compared with normal controls, schizophrenic patients, as a group, generally have poor performance on just about all tasks of higher mental abilities. In the context of a generally suppressed performance, the question becomes whether patients are a little worse than controls on some neuropsychological measures and a lot worse on others. Documenting a *differential deficit* in the presence of an overall deficit is quite hard to do. A greater performance deficiency relative to controls on one type of memory test (e.g., recall) and a much smaller impairment than controls on another (e.g., recognition) may indicate that schizophrenics have a true differential deficit in recall memory, or may simply reflect a difference in test properties—that is, the recall test may be harder and have more power to discriminate between groups than the recognition test. Therefore, in any comparison between neurocognitive tests, differences in psychometric properties must always be considered a possible confound (Chapman & Chapman, 1973).

Despite several efforts to identify a schizophrenia neuropsychological profile, the results have been inconsistent (Blanchard & Neale, 1994; Heaton et al., 1994; Saykin et al., 1991). At this point, there is no agreed-upon neuropsychological profile for schizophrenia. The failure to find a clear schizophrenia profile could be explained by a global generalized deficit, by multiple clusters of patients each with their own profile (Heinrichs & Awad, 1993), or by a weak neurocognitive profile for schizophrenia that is hard to see against the background of a generalized deficit. If schizophrenia is a heterogeneous disorder, it may be unreasonable to expect a single profile. Instead, each etiologically different group may have a specific profile that gets lost when the groups are combined. Alternatively, there may be a limited number of neural circuits that are associated with schizophrenia, and the extent of their compromise may differ from patient to patient owing to a variety of historical and developmental factors.

A related question concerns whether dysfunction in schizophrenia is lateralized to a particular cerebral hemisphere. This topic lies at the interface of phenomenological and empirical approaches, as both have been employed to address the question. Initial interest in a possible lateralized deficit in schizophrenia stems from clinical observations of epilepsy patients. Patients with temporal lobe epilepsy sometimes develop symptoms that appear similar to psychiatric symptoms. Flor-Henry (1976) noticed that, when such experiences occur, schizophrenia-like psychotic features are more common with the left hemisphere, whereas mood-related symptoms are more common with a right hemisphere focus. From this observation, he concluded that it was "abnormal neuronal activity in the dominant temporal lobe and in its hippocampal-amygdaloid-cingular projections which is fundamentally responsible for the schizophrenic syndrome" (p. 390).

Cutting (1994) has also used a phenomenological approach (i.e., one based on symptoms) to examined the clinical characteristics of various neurological conditions, and concluded that the evidence favored right hemisphere involvement in schizophrenia. Cutting observed that some patients with cerebrovascular accidents in the right hemisphere manifest classic schizophrenic symptoms such as disordered self-other boundaries, annihilation of will, and flattened affect. Flor-Henry and Cutting both relied on a phenomenological approach and arrived at opposite sides of the brain, perhaps reflecting the limitations of a phenomenological method for the question of laterality.

The laterality of schizophrenia has been addressed with specialized neurocognitive procedures that involve right vs. left presentation of visual and auditory stimuli (Walker & McGuire, 1982). One advantage of lateralized perceptual tests is that subjects essentially serve as their own controls so that abnormalities in laterality are interpretable even if patients have overall poorer performance (i.e., a generalized performance deficit). Generally, the results of these neurocognitive studies were consistent with the hypothesis of a left hemisphere abnormality. It has also been proposed that this abnormality might involve an overactivation of the left hemisphere (Gur, 1978). In this case, schizophrenic patients would use their left hemisphere to perform mental operations that normally would be conducted more efficiently by the right hemisphere. Despite some suggestions of neurocognitive laterality of the schizophrenia, the issue is unsettled, and it would be a profound oversimplification to describe schizophrenia strictly as a left hemisphere disorder.

Experimental Psychology (Normal Human Cognition)

A second approach has grown from *experimental psychology*, which emphasizes the assessment and understanding of normal human cognition. The experimental psychology approach has evolved steadily over the past 50 years. Modern studies of information processing in schizophrenia have grown out of an influential literature on relatively basic psychological abilities such as reaction time (reviewed in Nuechterlein, 1977). Over the years, experimental psychopathologists have attempted to provide parsimonious accounts for the huge range of cognitive deficits in schizophrenia with overarching explanations, such as deficits in "segmental set" (Shakow, 1962), "filtering" (McGhie & Chapman, 1961), "abstraction" (Goldstein, 1959, or the presence of "overinclusive" thinking (Payne, 1959).

Thus, the experimental approach seeks to document, characterize, and determine the nature of cognitive deficits in the disorder. A neurocognitive deficit in schizophrenia could potentially arise from a number of sources. For example, deficits could arise from the symptoms of the illness, the medications that treat the illness, or the effects of institutionalization. One goal of the experimental psychological approach is to find deficits that indicate a vulnerability or susceptibility to the disorder that are not a result of these other factors. These indicators or markers will be discussed in more detail at the end of the chapter.

Models of Information Processing Studies in the experimental psychology approach tend to be viewed within the models of experimental psychology that are prominent at the time. As the models of human cognition have evolved in the experimental literature, so too have the models that are used to understand deficits in schizophrenia. In the 1970s and '80s, many studies were influenced by two separate, but partially overlapping, models of normal cognition: *capacity models* or *stage models*. The capacity models emphasize the overall processing capacity of the individual (Kahneman, 1973). Deficits in schizophrenia can be attributed to a decrease in the overall amount of processing resources, or to an inefficient allocation of finite resources (Nuechterlein & Dawson, 1984). Stage models involve a series of processing stages; information is transformed at each stage and then fed to subsequent stages. As applied to schizophrenia, the goal of stage models is usually to identify the earliest stage of dysfunction. The notion is that a dysfunction at an early stage will cause poor information to be passed along, disrupting later processing stages. Whether a certain study is using one model vs. the other is often not obvious. Studies of the continuous performance test are often interpreted within capacity models; whereas perceptual techniques such as backward masking are typically viewed within a stage model. The advantage of both of these cognitive models is that they allow for deficits to be mapped on a particular framework.

Integrative models combine features of both and offer considerable value for understanding possible types of attentional dysfunction in schizophrenia (Nuechterlein, Dawson, & Green, 1994). Cowan's (1988) integrative model, for instance has several major components including a brief sensory store, memory components, and a central executive. The initial component of perceptual processing is a very brief sensory store that is experienced as the continuation of sensory input. Activated memory (similar to short-term memory) is a small portion of a long-term memory store that is activated at a given time. Only a subset of activated memory enters conscious awareness and becomes the focus of attention. The central executive controls which items are in the focus of attention, thereby directing the process of voluntary attention.

By using integrated models like the one shown in figure 11.2, one can explain a particular neurocognitive deficit in schizophrenia (Nuechterlein et al., 1994). Deficits in early visual and auditory processing can be explained by sensory/perceptual abnormalities that disrupt the operations of the brief sensory store. Disruptions in the brief sensory store can lead to a failure to activate the correct stimulus code in long-term store. Deficits in frontal systems or selective attention can indicate a malfunction of the central executive's control of voluntary attention. Such models have components that could also explain well-documented psychophysiological abnormalities in orienting and habituation in schizophrenia. For patients who are slow to habituate, stimuli that would normally be ignored capture the focus of attention and pull the central executive off its primary task. For rapid habituators, stimuli that should normally capture the focus of attention fail to do so.

Models from experimental psychology serve a useful purpose: to reduce the apparent randomness of deficits in schizophrenia. By using cognitive models, the experimental psychology approach helps us to map a large variety of deficits on a finite number of model components, and to understand the connections among different components. Without such models, the diversity of neurocognitive deficits in schizophrenia appears haphazard.

Abnormalities Revealed by Structural Neuroimaging

Structural neuroimaging of schizophrenia has employed two primary techniques: computerized tomographic (CT) scans and magnetic resonance im-

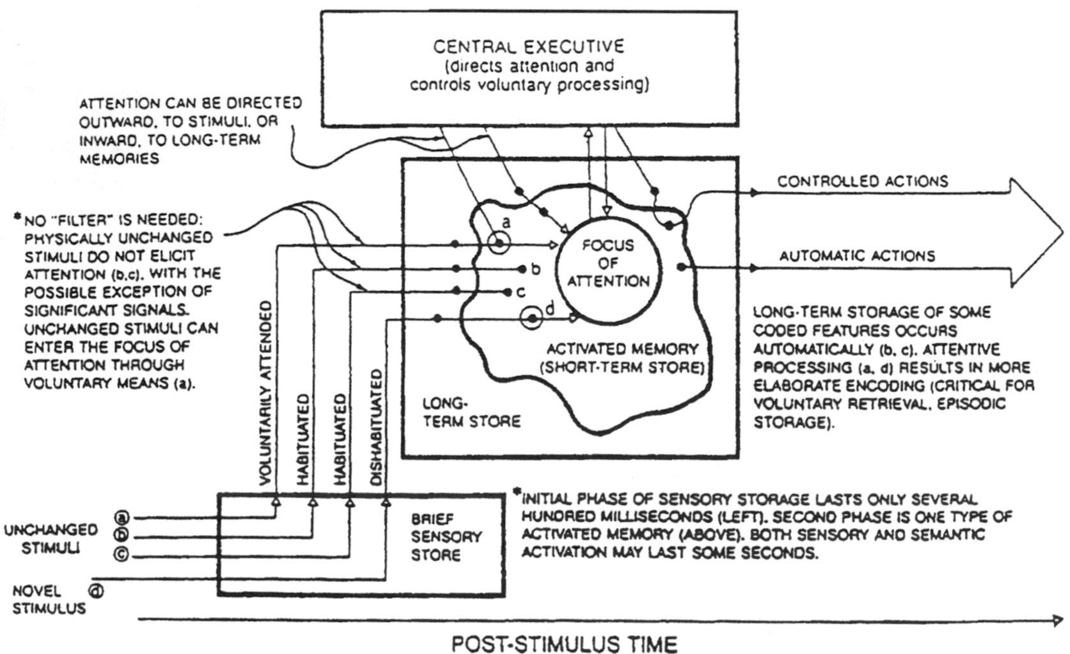

Figure 11.2 Pathways of neurocognitive deficits.

aging (MRI). CT scanning was the predominant imaging procedure from its first applications in the mid-1970s (Johnstone, Crow, Frith, Stevens, & Kreel, 1976) until it was largely replaced by MRI in the late 1980s. MRI has superior spatial resolution compared to CT. Because MRI does not involve any radiation, it is more suited to repeat scans. In general, the findings from these two techniques are comparable. The structural neuroimaging of schizophrenia will be summarized by the type of abnormality and then by the brain region of interest.

Types of Abnormalities in Schizophrenia A few reliable finding can be extracted from the large number of neuroanatomical studies in schizophrenia (Bilder, 1992; Raz & Raz, 1990). First, schizophrenic patients generally have larger ventricles than control subjects with a group difference of roughly 0.70 standard deviations (Raz & Raz, 1990). As described by Andreasen (1984a, p. 268), the ventricles are four structures inside the brain filled with cerebrospinal fluid that apparently function to cushion and nourish. In studies of schizophrenia, the ventricles serve as important indexes of brain atrophy, since they often enlarge to compensate when parts of the brain have atophied. Studies typically use a ratio score of ventricular size divided by brain size (ventricular brain ratio, VBR) to control for individual variability in brain size. The lateral ventricles were selected in most studies, but enlargement of the third ventricle in schizophrenia has been reported as well.

A second reliable finding is that patients tend to have larger sulci (i.e., the fissures between the ridges or "gyri" of the brain) compared to controls. Sulcal enlargement might be independent of ventricular enlargement and could represent a different pathophysiological process. Consistent with this notion is the suggestion that ventricular and cortical abnormalities in schizophrenia derive from different antecedents (Cannon, Mednick, & Parnas, 1989). Cortical abnormalities appear to be associated with family risk for schizophrenia whereas ventricular abnormalities appear more closely associated with obstetric complications.

Third, schizophrenic patients sometimes, but not always, show abnormalities in hemispheric asymmetry. The brain normally extends farther anterior on the right and farther posterior on the left, a pattern of asymmetry described as "torque." Schizophrenic patients sometimes have shown a reduction, or even a reversal, of this normal cerebral asymmetry (Luchins, Weinberger, & Wyatt, 1982). Apart from a possible abnormality in cerebral laterality, some neuroanatomical differences between patients and controls may be primarily restricted to one hemisphere. Sometimes group differences in ventricular enlargement and reduced temporal lobe volumes are significant only in the left side of the brain, consistent with the notion that schizophrenia may primarily involve a dysfunction in the left hemisphere. However, the results have been inconsistent and the laterality of structural abnormalities in schizophrenia remains an open question.

Regions of Interest Much of the attention in structural neuroimaging in schizophrenia has been directed at a few regions (Gur & Pearlson, 1993). The frontal cortex has been studied extensively because of its presumed connection with symptoms and etiology of schizophrenia. The results have been inconsistent, with some but not all studies reporting decreased frontal lobe volume in schizophrenia. It is difficult to draw conclusions from studies of this region owing to the large size and heterogenous nature of the frontal lobe, as well as the difficulty in identifying its boundaries.

The findings have been more consistent for both the temporal cortex and the medial aspects of the temporal lobe. Several studies have reported reduced volume of the superior temporal gyrus for schizophrenic patients. Reduction in size of the posterior temporal gyrus appears to be related to severity of thought disorder (Shenton et al., 1992) and to abnormalities in an electrophysiological index of the processing of novel information (P300; McCarley et al., 1993). Medial temporal lobe structures such as the hippocampus have also been reported to be smaller in schizophrenia (e.g., Breier et al., 1992). Reduced hippocampal size, coupled with the findings of abnormalities from neurohistological studies (Conrad, Abebe, Austin, Forsythe, & Scheibel, 1991), strongly point to abnormalities in the development of this region.

Not all structural abnormalities have been limited to the cortex. The basal ganglia and thalamus have also been the focus of investigation. For the basal ganglia, some studies have found *increases* in the size of basal ganglia structures compared to controls. In a follow-up study, first-episode patients showed an increase in the size of the caudate nuclei over an 18-month period of treatment with conventional neuroleptics (i.e., D2 antagonists), whereas control subjects showed a slight decrease in size over the same time period (Chakos et al., 1994). This finding suggests that enlarged basal ganglia structures in schizophrenia could be a result of the region's response to antipsychotic medications.

One way to study neuroanatomical differences between patients and controls is to combine brain images from multiple subjects and generate an average schizophrenic brain and an average control brain. When this process was applied, specific regional differences between groups were observed in the thalamus and the adjacent white matter (Andreasen et al., 1994). The results were viewed within a neurocognitive framework as support for "a parsimonious explanation for the multiplicity of signs and symptoms: abnormalities in midline structures that mediate attention and information processing, particularly the thalamus and related midline circuitry" (p. 295).

Neurocognitive Associations of Structural Abnormalities Structural abnormalities are reliably found in schizophrenia, but what is the neurocognitive significance of these findings? Neurocognitive correlates of ventricular and sulcal enlargement have been examined using neuropsychological batteries and intellectual measures. In general, ventricular and/or sulcal enlargement is predictably associated with poorer neuropsychological performance. Drawing more specific conclusions is difficult because the brain measures (e.g., ventricular brain ratio) are regionally nonspecific and the neuropsychological measures (e.g., global cutoff scores) are neurocognitively nonspecific.

In contrast to the findings between structural indices and neuropsychological measures, which are as expected, the results regarding structural indices and intellectual functioning have been decidedly mixed. Sometimes results were in the expected direction (i.e., smaller ventricles with higher IQ), some were in the opposite direction, and many studies did not find relationships at all. Variability of the results can be explained by considering that intelligence scales, which are included in neuropsychological batteries, tap different types of intellectual abilities. Some subtests on intelligence scales are sensitive to cognitive decline following brain injury, whereas others change very little with brain injury and are rather good indicators of premorbid ability. The pattern of results appears to depend on the type of subtest that is included. Structural abnormalities in schizophrenia seem to be associated with poor performance on subtests that are sensitive to brain injury such as speeded tasks, but not those that reflect premorbid abilities such as basic information and language (Bilder, 1992).

Neurochemical Aspects of Schizophrenia

It has become increasingly popular to state that schizophrenia is caused by a chemical imbalance of the brain. This typically refers to an imbalance of dopamine, based on early and still very influential findings. As will be discussed in some detail below, the dopamine hypothesis, although still maintained, is now recognized as somewhat oversimplified, and many other neurochemicals have also been implicated in the pathophysiology of schizophrenia.

In general, most current theories propose some type of functional abnormality in neurotransmission that may be a consequence (e.g., Walker, 1994; Weinberger, 1987) or a cause (e.g., Olney & Farber, 1995) of structural brain abnormalities. A variety of neurotransmitters and neurotransmitter receptors are currently under study. Neurotransmitters are the chemicals that enable neurons to communicated with each other. A presynaptic neuron releases neurotransmitters from the vesicles in its nerve ending into the synaptic cleft. The released transmitters then interact with receptors on surrounding postsynaptic neurons; however, receptors are highly specialized and only accept messages from specific target neurochemicals. A number of factors can affect the amount of a transmitter available, including changing the amount released by the presynaptic neuron, influencing regulation in the synaptic space or blocking receptors with other substances. "Reuptake" occurs when a transmitter that has been released is taken back into the presynaptic neuron. Agonists are substances that enhance neurotransmission; antagonists decrease neurotransmission.

Dopamine Dopamine (DA), a monoamine, is one of the catecholamines that functions as a neurotransmitter in the human brain (Nicholls, 1994). Like epinephrine and norepinephrine, DA is synthesized from tyrosine. Although only a small proportion of neurons secrete DA, the extensive projections from these cells result in a widespread release of DA that appears to have a modulating influence on a large number of neurons. This influence can be either excitatory or inhibitory, depending on the subtype of DA receptor that is activated. The three major pathways comprising the DA system are the nigrostriatal, mesolimbic, and mesocortical. Mesocortical and mesolimbic DA neurons originate in the midbrain ventral tegmental area, whereas those in the nigrostriatal pathway originate in the substantia nigra.

The DA hypothesis of schizophrenia is almost entirely based on the effects that various drugs, known to either increase (agonists) or decrease (antagonists) DA, have on psychotic symptoms. By the 1970s, it was clearly established that all effective antipsychotic medications were DA antagonists (Carlsson, 1978). Specifically, the efficacy of the various antipsychotic drugs was shown to vary with their capacity to block DA receptors, so the initial DA hypothesis held that schizophrenia was related to an excess of dopaminergic neuronal activity. Further, it became clear that movement and postural abnormalities, particularly tardive dyskinesia (a writhing and twitching movement of the face and other parts of the body), were the most notable side effect of these drugs. Thus, the term *neuroleptic* gained wide usage as the generic label for antipsychotic medications.

Additional support for the DA hypothesis was based the behavioral effects of DA agonists (e.g., Carlsson, 1995; Davis, Kann, Ko, & Davidson, 1991; Lieberman & Koreen, 1993). DA agonists, such as amphetamine, were observed to induce psychotic symptoms at high doses in some recreational drug users. These symptoms showed a favorable response to antipsychotic drugs (DA antagonists). Similarly, it was well established that neurological patients who receive DA precursors for the treatment of movement disorders, most notably Parkinson's disease, sometimes manifest drug-induced psychotic symptoms.

These and other reports fostered a large number of investigations aimed at determining whether schizophrenia patients were characterized by elevated fluid levels of DA or DA metabolites (e.g., homovanillic acid). Lieberman and Koreen (1993) provide a systematic review of these studies and have suggested that, taken together, the results offer little support for heightened DA levels in schizophrenia. Plasma homovanillic acid (HVA), which partially reflects brain DA turnover, is not elevated in schizophrenia patients. However, many of the results point to neurotransmitter receptors as a possible source of abnormal DA activity in schizophrenia.

Advances in neuroscience have led to the identification of multiple subtypes of DA receptors. To date, two general classes of DA receptors have been localized in the human brain: D1 and D2 (Nicholls, 1994). (Included in the D1 "family" are D1 and D5, while the D2 family includes D2, D3, and D4.) The distinction between these two subtypes of receptors is based on the fact that the D1 subtype of receptor is positively coupled with adenylyl cyclase activation, whereas the D2 subtype inhibits adenylyl cyclase. D1 receptors are more common than D2 receptors, but have a lower affinity for DA.

It has been shown that the D2 subtype of DA receptor is a primary target of typical and atypical antipsychotics (Carlsson, 1995; Busatto, 1995). In an effort to test the hypothesis of DA receptor abnormalities in schizophrenia, several research groups have examined postmortem brain tissue from patients (e g., Reynolds & Czudek, 1988; Toru et al., 1988). The results of these studies suggested an increase in the densities of D2, but not D1, receptors in subcortical regions, particularly the basal ganglia. The findings were mitigated, however, by the fact that many of the brain samples had been obtained from patients who were advanced in age and had received long-term treatment with antipsychotics drugs (Andreasen et al., 1988). Exposure to antipsychotics was considered relevant because some animal studies had revealed that D2 receptor density was increased by drug exposure.

PET technology (positron emission topography, a neuroimaging procedure assessing brain function) provided a means for studying the characteristics of neurotransmitter receptors in vivo, thus allowing investigators to focus on younger patients with no or shorter drug exposure. The findings from this research have not clarified the issue, however, because some studies of drug-naive patients showed elevated D2 receptor densities whereas others did not. (For reviews, see Andreasen et al., 1988; Tune et al., 1993.) The inconsistent findings have generated spirited debates about the influence of various methodological differences (e.g., use of different radioligands and/or receptor quantification procedures) on the study outcomes (Wong, 1992), but there has been no resolution to the DA receptor density controversy.

Several investigators have proposed that it is the ratio of DA receptor subtypes that is abnormal in schizophrenia, rather than the absolute density of a single subtype (Joyce, Lexow, Bird, & Winokur, 1988) Specifically, it has been proposed that schizophrenia is associated with an increased ratio of D2 to D1 receptors. Given the evidence that there are complex synergistic and antagonistic interactions among DA receptor subtypes, this hypothesis seems plausible.

Finally, it should be noted that studies of normal subjects have indicated that DA may be related to attention and memory (cf. Keefe & Harvey, 1994). Since schizophrenic patients have been extensively shown to display deficits in these functions, there may be an association between abnormal DA levels and impaired cognition in schizophrenia.

Norepinephrine As noted, norepinephrine (NE) and DA originate from the same synthetic pathway. Lieberman and Koreen (1993) point out that empirical data linking NE with schizophrenia are limited. Nonetheless, there are several reports of a relation between NE and symptom severity. This is not surprising in light of the biochemical association between NE and DA. Also consistent with the hypothesis that NE is involved in schizophrenia are findings that atypical antipsychotics reduce NE activity (Lieberman, 1994).

Amino Acids The amino acids—glutamate, y-aminobutyrate (GABA), and glycine—act as neurotransmitters at the majority of CNS synapses. Glutamate is an excitatory neurotransmitter. Most projecting glutamatergic pathways originate in the neocortex and the hippocampus. Glutamate is also a major neurotransmitter for interneurons that modulate neurotransmission within brain regions. Within the past decade, researchers have turned their attention to glutamate as a neurochemical factor in schizophrenia (Moghaddam, 1994; Olney & Farber, 1995).

Olney and Farber (1995) proposed that a specific subtype of glutamate receptor, the N-methyl-d-aspartate (NMDA) receptor, is hypofunctional in schizophrenia patients. They base this hypothesis on several research findings. It has been shown that phencyclidine (PCP), which blocks the ion channel of the NMDA receptor, produces a psychotic syndrome that involves both positive and negative symptoms. Further, NMDA antagonists have been shown to cause degeneration of neocortical and limbic regions (e.g., anterior cingulate, parietal, temporal, and entorhinal cortex, hippocampus, and amygdala) in the rat brain. These are the same regions that are reported to be abnormal in studies of schizophrenia patients. Finally, the neurotoxic effects of NMDA receptor antagonism can be blocked by typical and atypical antipsychotics.

Olney and Farber also point out that their NMDA receptor hypofunction hypothesis is compatible with DA theories of schizophrenia, in that DA receptor hyperactivity can result in the inhibition of glutamate release and a consequent hypofunction of NMDA receptors. Thus, NMDA hypofunction might be the primary defect in some cases of schizophrenia, whereas in other patients it might be a secondary consequence of DA overactivity. Other authors have also cited the interaction between glutamate and DA as a factor in schizophrenia (Iverson, 1996; Wan, Geyer, & Swerdlow, 1995).

GABA is the main inhibitory neurotransmitter in the cortex, and GABA cells are predominantly interneurons. Benes (1995) has proposed that a decrease in GABAergic activity, specifically decreased GABAergic innervation of frontal cortex, might be involved in schizophrenia. GABA interneurons (nonpyramidal neurons) are the most common interneurons, and they act to inhibit pyramidal neurons in the cortex. Benes hypothesized a loss of these inhibitory GABA interneurons in the anterior cingulate cortex. This, in turn, produces an upregulation of GABA receptors on pyramidal neurons. In support of this hypothesis, Benes has reported the results of postmortem studies that show an increase in GABA receptor binding on neurons in layers II and III of the cortex in schizophrenia patients.

Serotonin Serotonin (5-HT) is a monoamine that is synthesized from tryptophan and originates in cell bodies located in the raphne nuclei that project to the cortex, striatum, and cerebellum. Several theorists have suggested that schizophrenia may involve excess activity of 5-HT pathways (Carpenter, 1995; Huttenen, 1995; Meltzer, 1991).

Serotonin (5-HT) was originally implicated in schizophrenia because certain psychotomimetic drugs, such as LSD, enhance 5-HT activity. This, in turn, can produce perceptual and ideational distortions similar to the symptoms of schizophrenia. Studies of 5-HT levels in schizophrenia patients have yielded inconsistent results, with some showing elevations and others showing no difference between patients and normals (for a review, see Lieberman & Koreen, 1993).

More recently, hypotheses about 5-HT are based on findings from studies of new antipsychotic agents (Remington, 1995). A new category of medications, the "atypical" antipsychotics, was introduced into clinical use within the past decade. Clozapine was among the first of these drugs, and it has proved to be an effective antipsychotic with few motoric side effects. It has also been shown that clozapine and other "atypical" antipsychotics have a greater 5-HT antagonistic effect, and a somewhat lower DA antagonist effect than typical antipsychotics (Remington, 1995).

These and other findings have led to renewed speculation about the role of serotonin in the production of antipsychotic symptoms. There is recent evidence that certain types of 5-HT (5-HT1) receptors are elevated in schizophrenia (Palacios et al., 1990), while others (5-HT2) are decreased (Arora & Meltzer, 1991). Thus serotonergic receptor abnormalities may confer a heightened sensitivity to 5-HT activity in schizophrenia. Meltzer and Nash (1991) have cited evidence that 5-HT has an inhibitory effect on DA activity in the nigrostriatal pathway, thus explaining the lowered risk for extrapyramidal side effects with atypical antipsychotics.

Adrenal Steroids As discussed above, the diathesis-stress model of schizophrenia continues to be the dominant conceptual framework in the literature on schizophrenia. The hypothalamic-pituitary-adrenal axis is one of the major neural systems mediating the stress response in humans. Following stressful events, a cascade of neurochemical processes culminates in the release of adrenal steroids, most notably cortisol, in human and nonhuman primates.

It has recently been proposed that cortisol may play a potentiating role in the expression of abnormalities in dopaminergic and glutamatergic neurotransmission. As Walker and Diforio (1997) point out, evidence for this comes from several areas of investigation. First, schizophrenia patients show heightened baseline and postdexamethasone cortisol when compared to normals. Second, the hippocampus, which plays a central role in the modulation of the HPA axis, shows reduced volume in schizophrenia patients. Research on nonschizophrenia subjects has shown that hippocampal volume is inversely correlated with cortisol levels. Finally, cortisol acts to enhance DA activity, and recent reports indicate that prenatal exposure to stress hormones may also increase DA receptor density. This suggests a neural basis for the demonstrated effects of psychosocial stress exposure on schizophrenia symptoms.

Neural Circuits

As data have accumulated from the postmortem and neuroimaging studies described above, it has become apparent that a broad range of brain abnormalities are associated with schizophrenia. Many of these abnormalities, particularly reductions in gross and regional volumes and enlargement of the ventricles, have been observed in other disorders, both neurological and psychiatric. Thus, these abnormalities may not reflect the critical neuropathologic feature in schizophrenia. It has been suggested that they may, instead, represent secondary consequences of the same CNS insult that conferred the neural liability for schizophrenia.

Following this line of reasoning, some psychopathology researchers have turned their attention to certain functional neural circuits that have been identified in the human brain. Of greatest interest have been the circuits that link subcortical and cortical regions. A seminal paper by Stevens (1973) was among the first to propose that the striatum might be involved in schizophrenia. She emphasized the role of the limbic striatum (nucleus accumbens, olfactory tubercle, and nucleus of stria terminalis) in filtering signals through the limbic system. Since the publication of Steven's article, interest in limbic system abnormalities has increased. Furthermore, over the past several years, a number of additional, often highly complex models of the neurocircuitry have been proposed as being involved in the neuropathology of schizophrenia (e.g., Swerdlow & Koob, 1987; Walker, 1994; Weinberger, 1987).

It is clear that in any model, the developmental pattern most characteristic of schizophrenia must be explained—that is, why the onset of schizophrenia typically occurs in late adolescence/early adulthood. There are numerous developmental changes in the CNS system during puberty and early adulthood. Among the adolescent changes that have been cited for their relevance to schizophrenia are myelination of cortical pathways (Benes, 1995) and the pruning of synapses (Feinberg, 1982).

Feinberg (1982) pointed out that adolescence is marked by a dramatic acceleration in "synaptic pruning," a process that culminates in the elimination of some synapses. The end result of pruning is presumed to be more efficient neural functioning, owing to the elimination of redundant or nonessential neural connections. Feinberg suggested that excessive or insufficient pruning may result in aberrant interconnections that lead to psychotic symptoms. Along these same lines, Benes (1994, 1995) has shown that myelination of certain limbic pathways extends into early adulthood in normal subjects. She has suggested that an abnormality in the myelination of limbic pathways may play a role in the emergence of the cognitive and affective signs of schizophrenia.

Neurodevelopmental Models of Schizophrenia

As noted above, Kraepelin believed that schizophrenia was an early form of dementia (i.e., dementia praecox) that followed a degenerative course. As a result, for many years, the predominant view of schizophrenia has been that it starts in young adulthood and then becomes progressively worse over time. However, the more recent neurochemical and neuroimaging findings, as well as clinical observations that most patients with schizophrenia do not show the progressive deterioration characteristic of the dementias and that some patients do improve over time, have led to the alternate notion: that schizophrenia is a neurodevelopmental disorder. According to the latter view, the basic biological error leading to schizophrenia occurs very early in development (in many cases, prenatally), is triggered during late adolescence/early adulthood, and may not involve further major deterioration in brain functioning after the initial symptoms have appeared.

For example, neuroanatomical abnormalities in schizophrenia were initially considered to be evidence of brain atrophy, partly because the types of abnormalities (ventricular and sulcal enlargement) are seen in known degenerative disorders. However, structural abnormalities have also been found in untreated, first-episode patients, indicating that long illness and medications were not necessary for their occurrence. Also, studies have generally failed to find evidence of reactive gliosis, the process in mature brains that responds to cell destruction, suggesting that structural changes most likely occurred in an immature brain, long before the onset of illness.

Another way to examine the neurodevelopmental vs. neurodegenerative distinction is through longitudinal studies of repeated brain scans to determine whether ventricular enlargement progresses over time. Most studies have not found any progression of the abnormalities, but a few studies reported an increase in ventricular size over time (Bilder, 1992). The evidence is generally consistent with the view that structural abnormalities in schizophrenia largely reflect neurodevelopmental factors (e.g., hypoplasia) instead of neurodegenerative factors (e.g., atrophy). In some cases, both developmental and deteriorative factors could be operating in the same individual. The majority of the structural abnormalities might be explained by neurodevelopmental processes, with some additional changes occurring after onset of illness. Nevertheless, from the neurodevelopmental perspective, the major brain abnormalities appear to have developed by illness onset.

Interest in the neurodevelopmental view of schizophrenia has been steadily gathering momentum (e.g., Weinbeger, 1986, 1987; Murray, O'Callaghan, Castle, & Lewis, 1992; Jones & Murray, 1991; Canon et al., 1994). According to Weinberger's (1987) highly influential conceptualization:

> Schizophrenia is a neurodevelopmental disorder in which a fixed brain lesion from early in life interacts with certain normal maturational events that occur much later. . . . [T]he lesion itself is static, but its effects on neurologic function change. . . . [I]f a lesion affects a brain structure or region that has yet to mature functionally, the effects of the lesion may remain silent until that structure or system matures. (p. 660)

Weinberger further suggested that there can be numerous causes of the lesion, including heredity and various environmental insults, such as injury, infection, or immunologic disorder, and that different causes may lead to varying levels of pathology and thus clinical severity.

Considerable recent evidence of developmental abnormalities on the cellular level have been reported that can account for this type of neurodevelopmental process (Murray et al., 1992; Jones & Murray, 1991; Weinberger, 1986, 1987). Some examples include abnormal synaptic pruning, axonal myelation, and defects in embryonic cell migration (Kovelman & Scheibel, 1984; Jakob & Beckmann, 1986; Falkai, Bogers, & Rozumek, 1988). As pointed out by several researchers, since the myelination of axons continues well into adolescence, this particular abnormality could directly relate to the delayed clinical expression of schizophrenia.

A Simplified Neurodevelopmental Model

The neurodevelopmental view of schizophrenia, within a diathesis-stress framework, underlies high-risk research, an area concerned with identifying "biobehavioral markers" of the schizophrenia gene and then to use these markers to intervene and, it is hoped, prevent the expression of the schizophrenia illness. A very simplified version of this type of model is presented in figure 11.3.

The starting point of the model is with a genetic error, some type of environmental insult, or a combination of both, that occurs very early in development and leads to a biological susceptibility or vulnerability to schizophrenia. A number of possible causative factors are discussed in the section of this chapter on etiology.

The pathway shown on the figure represents the development of the schizophrenia diathesis, beginning with the earliest etiological factors and ending with the clinical expression of illness. A critical aspect of this model, following Weinberger and others, is that while the underlying pathophysiology causing the susceptibility (sometimes referred to as the "lesion") occurs very early in development, behavior does not become affected until much later. The lesion remains dormant until triggered by some developmental event, at which point the clinical symptoms start to emerge. Findings from high-risk research indicate that, in contrast to clinical symptoms, subtle neurocognitive deficits such as impaired attention appear to be present throughout development, but are only observable when directly measured using highly sensitive procedures.

Susceptibility can take the form of one or more basic brain abnormalities, either structural, functional, or biochemical. Earlier parts of this chapter have presented some possibilities. For example, structural abnormalities may include enlarged ventricals or reduced temporal lobes; abnormal DA levels are a well-established biochemical abnormality. Although not directly discussed here, there is also considerable evidence from PET studies sug-

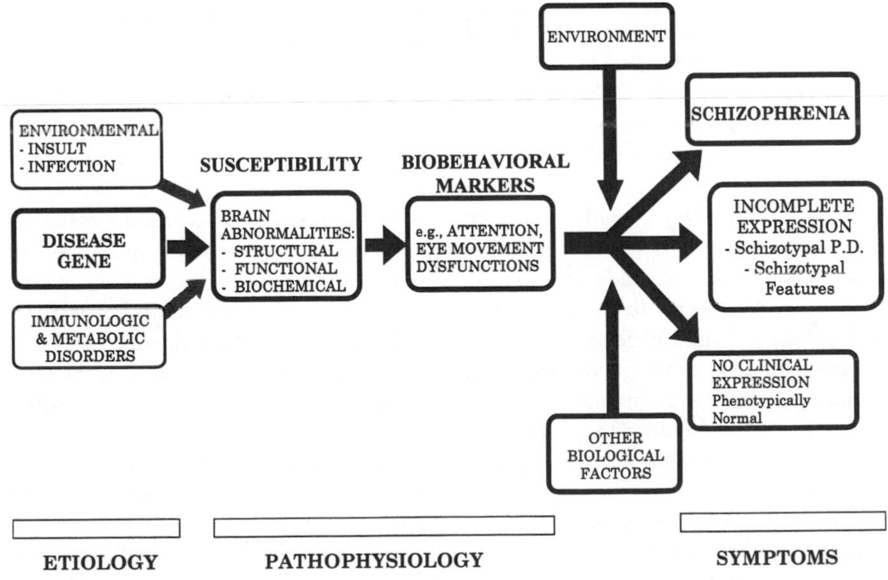

Figure 11.3 Neurodevelopmental model of schizophrenia.

gesting functional impairments of the brain in schizophrenia. Hypofrontality (i.e., underactivity) of the frontal lobes, especially in the dorso-lateral prefrontal cortex, for example, has been consistently reported by Weinberger and his colleagues (e.g., Weinberger & Berman, 1988).

The brain abnormalities are, in turn, thought to be associated with a variety of neurocognitive deficits. In this model, these deficits are called "biobehavioral markers." This type of marker is different from the molecular genetic markers discussed earlier. Biobehavioral markers provide no information about the location of a disease gene. Instead, they indicate the presence of the biological susceptibility for schizophrenia, and provide information about the pathophysiology of the disorder.

The neurocognitive deficits are labeled "biobehavioral" because, as shown in the model, they are considered to be intermediate between basic brain functions (the "bio") and more complex clinical features of the illness (the behaviors). They consist of such things as the ability to process information in the environment (i.e., attention) or to move the eyes smoothly when tracking a moving target. Since they are abnormalities measured on the behavioral level, they are phenotypic (as opposed to genetic) markers. The "markers" part of the label refers to the notion that, if valid, the deficits signal or "mark" the presence of the biological susceptibility to schizophrenia.

The model pathway also illustrates another critical neurodevelopmental point. The cognitive marker deficits can be detected many years before clinical symptoms begin to emerge. These markers therefore can serve as predictors of future illness, paving the way for future intervention programs. That is, once markers have been validated, they can be used to identify individuals with a true susceptibility to illness. This will provide a way to screen at-risk and other populations for individuals most in need of intervention. In addition, because the marker deficits are thought to be involved in the pathophysiology of schizophrenia, they may point to the most effective types of interventions. The goal of such programs is to disrupt the developmental pathway and to eliminate the clinical expression of illness, or, at minimum, to lessen its severity.

At the outcome side of the model, it can be seen that the diathesis can have a number of alternate expressions, ranging from the full-blown illness (sometimes called "core" schizophrenia) through a number of less severe variants of it (e.g., personality disorders or schizophrenia-related features) to no behavioral expression. It has been proposed by several researchers that the diathesis is most likely to be expressed clinically in the form of a nonpsychotic, schizotypal-like personality disorder, with some type of environmental stressor required to trigger psychosis (e.g., Cannon & Mednick, 1993; Cannon et al., 1994; Siever et al., 1990). It is further assumed that a variety of additional factors (environmental, biological, cognitive, personality) can serve as moderators, either exacerbating or reducing the severity of the expressed illness.

As can be seen in the model, at various points along the developmental pathway of the diathesis, it is possible for stressors to come into play. These can be either biological (e.g., abnormal cell migration, excessive axonal pruning) or environmental (e.g., intrauterine trauma, viral exposure, severe malnutrition, birth complications, possibly some type of psychosocial or interpersonal disruptions). However, it should be kept in mind that aspects of the environment considered "stressful" (especially psychosocial, interpersonal) may not be particularly stressful in a normative sense. Rather, "persons who are predisposed to schizophrenia may develop the illness not because of exposure to excessive stress but because they are not protected from normal levels of stress" (Keefe & Harvey, 1994, p. 99).

Applying the Neurodevelopmental Approach: High-Risk Research

A neurodevelopmental view of schizophrenia is the foundation of high-risk research. A major focus of risk researchers is on the identification of developmental abnormalities that act as warning signals of future illness and therefore make intervention possible. Because these abnormalities are detected many years before the appearance of clinical symptoms, they are assumed to be part of the basic pathophysiology of the disorder and not the result of factors associated with having the illness (for example, symptoms, medication, or institutionalization).

The risk for schizophrenia in the general population is about 1%. As a result, if of 1,000 youngsters were randomly selected from the general population and then closely followed for, say, 25 years, only about 10 subjects could be expected to develop fully expressed schizophrenia. Consequently, researchers turned to a population with higher than average risk for developing schizophrenia—the offspring of schizophrenic parents, who are about 12 times as likely to become ill as members of the general population (see figure 11.1).

Pearson and Kley (1957) were the first to recognize the advantages of a prospective design that involved the offspring of schizophrenic parents. Their proposal was followed by the pioneering work of Mednick, who, in 1962, initiated the first offspring high-risk study on a large scale (Mednick & Schulsinger, 1968; Mednick & McNeil, 1968), and then by several additional high-risk studies that were begun between the late 1960s and early '70s. These have been referred to as the "first generation" of high-risk studies.

Many of the first-generation high-risk (HR) projects focused on detecting subtle neurocogntive deficits in the young at-risk offspring under study. In their review of the findings reported by these studies, Cornblatt and Obuchowski (1997) have concluded that: (1) impaired attention appears to be the most promising biobehavioral marker of a susceptibility to schizophrenia; (2) eye-movement dysfunctions also have considerable marker potential, but have not yet been demonstrated to be valid childhood predictors of illness; and (3) there is increasing evidence that neuromotor abnormalities in early childhood may be susceptibility markers.

Biobehavioral Markers

Impaired Attention To be considered a marker candidate, deficits must: (1) be displayed by affected patients more often than by individuals in the general population (i.e., be specific); (2) appear more frequently in the relatives of schizophrenia patients (whether or not the relatives are affected) than in relatives of controls or in members of the general population (i.e., show heritability); and (3) be independent of clinical state (i.e., be a core feature, not a secondary symptom, of the illness). In order to predict illness, such deficits must be reliable, stable, and detectable in as-yet unaffected children or adolescents.

Many of the first-generation high-risk projects emphasized cognition, and many included some version of the Continuous Performance Test (CPT) in their batteries. Although there are many versions of the CPT (see Cornblatt & Keilp, 1994), they are all considered to measure the capacity to focus and sustain attention to a series of rapidly changing stimuli. In the typical CPT paradigm, a computer-generated series of stimuli are flashed in rapid succession on a video monitor. Subjects are required to respond (by pressing a mouse or computer key) whenever a designated target or target sequence occurs in the series. In most CPT versions, there is a relatively low probability (generally around 20%) that a target will appear. Easy versions of the CPT are most often used when testing affected schizophrenic patients. In these CPT tasks, a series of single letters (or, sometimes, single digits) are presented, with the designated target often the letter A (or the digit 0). In a slightly more difficult version, subjects are asked to respond to the letter A only when it follows the letter X.

However, when testing first-degree relatives of a schizophrenic patient, such as at-risk offspring, it is essential that the CPT be considerably more difficult than either the A or AX tasks. This is because most susceptible individuals display very subtle cognitive deficits. An example of a cognitively challenging CPT is the Continuous Performance Test, Identical Pairs version (CPT-IP; see Cornblatt & Keilp, 1994). In the CPT-IP, the stimuli are series of either 150 four-digit numbers or 150 nonsense shapes. In this task, subjects are required to respond when two identical stimuli appear in a row. The CPT-IP is therefore substantially more difficult than either the X or AX tasks, since each complex stimulus be kept in memory until it can be compared with the next stimulus presented.

Results from the studies using various CPTs make a compelling case for impaired attention to be considered a frontrunner among candidate markers. This conclusion is based on the following evidence:

1. Attentional deficits have been widely established to characterize schizophrenic patients compared to both normal and psychiatric controls (Nuechterlein & Dawson, 1984). Although attentional disturbances are also found in patients with major affective disorders and children with attention deficit disorder, particular patterns of impairment appear to be specific to schizophrenia (e.g., Cornblatt et al., 1989; Neuchterlein, 1983).
2. Attentional capacity appears to be heritable both in normal families and in families of schizophrenia probands (Cornblatt, Rish, Faris, Freedman, & Erlenmeyer-Kimling, 1988; Grove et al., 1991).

3. Clinically remitted schizophrenic patients display abnormalities comparable to those characterizing patients who are acutely psychotic. Patients with schizotypal personality disorders or features, who are not psychotic, also display attentional deficits (Lenzenweger, Cornblatt, & Potnick, 1991; Roitman et al., 1997). Moreover, although medication generally improves clinical symptoms, it does not normalize attention. These findings suggest that attention is independent of clinical symptoms (Cornblatt & Keilp, 1994; Cornblatt, Obuchowski, Schnurr, & O'Brien, 1997).
4. Deficits in attention are displayed by children of schizophrenic parents many years before clinical symptoms begin to appear and are therefore not secondary to illness or treatment factors. In the New York High Risk Project, at-risk offspring who displayed impaired attention in childhood (at around age 9), subsequently developed schizophrenia-like behavioral disturbances in mid- to late adolescence, suggesting the predictive potential of attentional marker deficits (Cornblatt & Erlenmeyer-Kimling, 1985). However, since childhood attentional deficits best predicted schizotypal features (i.e., social isolation) in the adult offspring at-risk, it is possible that the attentional trait is a susceptibility marker rather than a marker of the psychotic illness, per se (Cornblatt, Lenzenweger, Dworkin, & Erlenmeyer-Kimling, 1992).
5. Developmentally, impaired attention appears to be a highly stable trait in individuals with a schizophrenia diathesis. That is, when detected in the at-risk offspring of the New York High Risk Project at approximately 9 years of age, deficits continued to be displayed by the same subjects when tested at older ages. Similarly, if not displayed when initially tested, attentional impairments rarely occur at later ages in at-risk offspring (Cornblatt, Lenzenweger, & Erlenmeyer-Kimling, 1989; Winters, Cornblatt, & Erlenmeyer-Kimling, 1991).

Other aspects of attention also appear to have some promise as biobehavioral markers, including early visual processing. For example, researchers using the Span of Apprehension have reported that: (1) performance is impaired in remitted schizophrenic patients (Asarnnow & MacCrimmon, 1978, 1981); (2) deficits are stable across clinical state (Nuechterlein et al., 1992); and (3) they are detectable in high-risk children (Asarnow, Steffy, MacCrimmon, & Cleghorn, 1977). Using backward masking procedures to measure an even earlier component of visual processing, Green, Nuechterlein, and Breitmeyer (1997) found that both symptomatic and asymptomatic adult siblings of schizophrenic patients had poorer performance than normal controls.

Of particular interest in this context is a very recent finding directly related to the use of attentional marker deficits in linkage studies. Schizophrenic patients and some of their relatives have been shown to have a decreased inhibition of the P50 auditory evoked response to the second of a paired of stimuli. P50 is thought to be an early component of attention. Freedman and colleagues (Freedman et al., 1997) recently reported linkage between the P50 abnormality and a nicotine receptor gene. The authors conclude that "despite many schizophrenics' extremely heavy nicotine use, nicotinic receptors were not previously thought to be involved in schizophrenia. The linkage data thus provide unique new evidence that the a7-nicotinic receptor gene may be responsible for the inheritance of a pathophysiological aspect of the illness."

While this finding needs to be replicated and supported by additional studies, it nevertheless provides an excellent example of the potential for attentional and other biobehavioral markers to clarify the etiology of schizophrenia.

Eye-Movement Dysfunctions Eye-movement dysfunctions (EMDs) constitute the second major class of candidate markers (e.g., Holzman, Solomon, Levin, & Waternaux, 1984; Iacono, 1985; and Siever, 1985). Marker status has been primarily derived from the evidence in adult first degree relatives that EMDs are genetically transmitted, biologically based, and specific to schizophrenia (Levy, Holzman, Matthysse, & Mendell, 1994).

Research has focused on smooth pursuit and saccadic eye-movement systems that work interactively during an eye-tracking task. When tracking a moving object with the eyes, saccades are the small jerky movements that bring the target onto the fovea, then the smooth pursuit system holds the moving image there. Disturbances in both types of movements have been demonstrated in schizophrenic patients (Holzman, 1975, 1985, 1987; Levy, Holzman, Matthysse, & Mendell, 1993, 1994).

Between 54 and 86% of schizophrenic patients display EMDs compared to 6 to 8% of the general population (e.g., Clementz, Grove, Iacono, & Sweeney, 1992; Holzman et al., 1984; Shagass, Amadeo, & Overton, 1974). EMDs do not appear to be a product of such confounding factors as long-term medication or frequent hospitalizations, since EMDs are clearly in evidence at the earliest stages of illness (Iacono, Moreau, Beiser, Fleming, & Lin, 1992; Lieberman et al., 1993; Sweeney, Haas, & Li, 1992). Furthermore, comparable abnormalities have been found to characterize subjects with a range of schizophrenia-related disorders, including individuals from the general population with schizotypal personality disorders and features (Siever, Coursey, Alterman, Buchsbaum, & Murphy, 1984; Siever et al., 1989, 1990) and those whose responses on self-report inventories suggest that they may have a predisposition for developing spectrum disorders (Simons & Katkin, 1985).

Although, to date, no research has been conducted assessing EMDs in young at-risk offspring, there are several other lines of support indicating EMDs have considerable marker potential. First, EMDs are displayed by approximately 50% of the older unaffected first-degree relatives of schizophrenic patients, compared to about 10% of the relatives of nonschizophrenic patients (e.g., Clementz, Sweeney, Hirt, & Haas, 1990; Clementz, Grove, Iacono, & Sweeney, 1992; Holzman et al., 1974, 1988; Levy et al., 1983). These findings indicate that EMDs are likely to be involved in the underlying biology of the illness rather than due to symptom expression, treatment, or long-term hospitalization.

Second, although not extensively studied, there is some evidence indicating that EMDS can be reliably measured in adolescents (Ross, Radant, & Hommer, 1993). Third, some preliminary data have been reported suggesting that EMDs in adolescents with schizophrenia are comparable to those known to characterize affected adults (Cegalis & Sweeney, 1981; Obuchowski & Cornblatt, 1995; Schultz et al., 1992). Fourth, a recent report by Rosenberg et al. (in press) provides some preliminary support for applicability of EMDs to high-risk research. However, since eye-tracking has not been studied in at-risk children or adolescents, determination of the predictor potential of EMDs awaits more systematic investigation in future high-risk studies.

Thus, findings indicating that EMDs characterize affected patients across the full schizophrenia spectrum and at all stages of illness can be reliably measured in adolescents, and are found in a substantial proportion of unaffected first-degree relatives of patients, strongly support these deficits to be candidate biobehavioral markers of schizophrenia.

Neuromotor Abnormalities Neuromotor abnormalities represent a third class of potential biobehavioral markers. Fish (1987) was an early proponent of the neurodevelopmental point of view. According to Fish, a neurointegrative defect (genetically transmitted) causes a susceptibility to a schizophrenia-like personality, now known as schizotypal personality disorder. She proposed that an index known as pandysmaturation, a measure of disorganized motor and sensori-motor development, reflects this defect during the first two years of life and can, therefore, serve as an early marker. In her long-term prospective study of a small group of high-risk offspring, Fish (1987; Fish, Marcus, Hans, Auerbach, & Perdue, 1992) found pandysmaturation in infancy and early childhood to be highly predictive of subsequent schizophrenia spectrum disorders.

Although few other researchers focused on neuromotor development, recent findings have reawakened an interest in this area. New support for a relationship between early neurological abnormalities and schizophrenia has been provided by both Walker, Savoie, and Davis (1994) and Jones, Rodgers, Murray, and Marmot (1994). In both studies, motor dysfunctions and delays in early childhood (up to approximately 2 to 3 years of age) were found to characterize children who later developed schizophrenia.

In their study, Walker et al. (1994) used home movies taken during childhood to compare preschizophrenic children (i.e., those who became schizophrenic as adults) with their healthy siblings, preaffective disorder subjects, the healthy siblings of patients with affective disorder, and subjects from families with no mental illness. Preschizophrenic children were significantly differentiated from controls on a number of motor dysfunctions, including dyskinetic signs, motor overflow ("associated" involuntary movements), abnormal hand posture, choreoathetoid movements, and abnormal tonicity. Similar to Fish et al. (1992), a decrease in these abnormalities was observed with age during the premorbid period. However, studies of elderly patients reveal an increase in observable movement abnormalities with advanced age, and this increase does not appear to be solely attributable to neuroleptics (see Walker, 1994). Thus movement abnormalities may fluctuate in intensity across the life course in schizophrenia patients.

Despite these developmental changes in severity, it is important to emphasize that motor dysfunction appears to be associated with schizophrenia across the life span. Both clinical exams and laboratory measures of motor speed, proficiency, steadiness, rhythmicity, and involuntary movement yield evidence of motor dysfunction in patients of all ages (see Lohr & Caligiuri, 1992; Manschreck, 1983; Walker, 1994). The widespread use of neuroleptics in the treatment of schizophrenia has been a major impediment to research on naturally occurring movement abnormalities that accompany this disorder. Nonetheless, retrospective research (using pre-neuroleptic-era archives) and some recent studies of nonmedicated subjects indicate that movement abnormalities, in particular dyskinesias, often accompany schizophrenia (Caligiuri, Lohr, & Jeste, 1993; Casey & Hansen, 1984; Guttman, 1936; Reiter, 1926). For example, screening of medical records from Chestnut Lodge revealed that about 23% of nonmedicated schizophrenia patients manifested readily observable dyskinesia (Fenton, Wyatt, & McGlashan, 1994). A similar study of records from the United Kingdom yielded a figure of 33% (Turner, 1989).Given these and other findings, Khot and Wyatt (1991) argue that some of the movement disorder attributed to neuroleptics in medicated patients may have been preexisting. Consistent with the above findings, research on both child (Nagy & Szatmari, 1986) and adult subjects with Schizotypal Personality Disorder (Siever et al., 1993; Webb & Levinson, 1993) also reveals an elevated rate of motor dysfunction.

Based on these findings, it is possible that childhood neuromotor abnormalities may serve as predictors of later illness. However, in this case, the appropriateness of these particular markers for intervention screening is questionable, since the deficits may be hidden during late childhood and adolescence. Future research will be needed to resolve this issue.

Summary In summary, impaired attention, eye-movement dysfunctions, and neuromotor abnormalities, as well as a number of other neurocognitive functions (e.g., working memory, P50s, negative priming) are now being actively studied as possible biobehavioral markers of the schizophrenia gene (Cornblatt et al., 1997; Cornblatt, Obuchowski, Schnur, & O'Brien, 1998; Cornblatt, Obuchowski, Andreasen, & Smith, in press). The major goal of this research is to use any one or combination of these markers to identify individuals destined to develop schizophrenia or related illnesses. This information can then be used to set up intervention programs, since the markers will indicate who should be receiving early treatment and, it is hoped, what the treatment should consist of.

A major advantage of biobehavioral markers is that they typically employ relatively inexpensive, objective procedures that are easy to administer, score, and quantify. For this reason, they are particularly suitable for screening large numbers of subjects. The question can, however, be asked as to why neuroimaging procedures are not being included, since they have the potential to directly identify brain abnormalities that are likely to be the most valid markers. The answer—at least at the present time—is that neuroimaging procedures are too expensive, labor intensive, and, frequently, too aversive to the subjects to be practical for use in screening procedures.

Conclusions

Understanding schizophrenia remains a formidable task. However, help is on the way. First, in terms of etiology, sophisticated molecular genetic techniques are offering great hope for finding the genes underlying complex illnesses. Furthermore, adding biobehavioral markers to these analyses may facilitate linkage studies of schizophrenia. Second, with regard to pathophysiology, brain imaging is growing by leaps and bounds. Technological advances in brain scans are appearing daily, improving the quality and extending the range of brain scans, thus paving the way to a fuller understanding of brain function, structure, and chemistry. This may result in the identification of the "lesion" leading to schizophrenia in the not too far future. Finally, the study of cognitive mechanisms—the way the working of the mind is disrupted—promises to provide early predictors of the adult illness. This, in turn, will pave the way to feasible intervention programs. We are thus coming closer to an understanding of what causes schizophrenia, what the pathways to illness are, and, we hope, how to prevent or, at least, to better treat it.

References

Andreasen, N. C. (1982). Negative symptoms in schizophrenia: Definition and reliability. *Archives of General Psychiatry, 39*, 784–788.

Andreasen, N. C. (1983). *Comprehensive assessment of symptoms and history: CASH.* Iowa City, IA: University of Iowa.

Andreasen, N. C. (1984a). *The broken brain: The biological revolution in psychiatry.* New York: Harper & Row.

Andreasen, N. C. (1984b). *Scale for the Assessent of Negative Symptoms (SANS).* Iowa City, IA: University of Iowa.

Andreasen, N. C. (1984c). *The Scale for the Assessment of Positive Symptoms (SAPS).* Iowa City: University of Iowa.

Andreasen, N. C. (1997). Linking mind and brain in the study of mental illness: A project for a scientific psychopathology. *Science, 275*, 1586–1593.

Andreasen, N. C., Arndt, S., Alliger, R., Miller, D., & Flaum, M. (1995). Symptoms of schizophrenia. Methods, meanings, and mechanisms. *Archives of General Psychiatry, 52*, 341–351.

Andreasen, N. C., Arndt, S., Swayze II, V., Cizadlo, T., Flaum, M., O'Leary, D., Ehrhardt, J. C., & Yuh, W. T. C. (1994). Thalamic abnormalities in schizophrenia visualized through magnetic resonance image averaging. *Science, 266*, 294–298.

Andreasen, N. C., Carson, R., Diksic, M., Evans, A., Farde, L., Gjedde, A., Hakim, A., Lal, S., Nair, N., & Sedvall, G., et al. (1988). Workshop on schizophrenia PET and dopamine receptors in the human neostriatum. *Schizophrenia Bulletin, 14*, 471–484.

Andreasen, N. C., & Olsen, S. A. (1982). Negative v. positive schizophrenia: Definition and validation. *Archives of General Psychiatry, 39*, 789–794.

Andreasen, N. C., Olsen, S. A., Dennert, J. W., & Smith, M. R. (1982). Ventricular enlargement in schizophrenia: Relationship to positive and negative symptoms. *American Journal of Psychiatry, 139*, 297–302.

Arora, R. C., & Meltzer, H. Y. (1991). Serotonin$_2$(5-HT$_2$) receptor binding in the frontal cortex of schizophrenic patients. *Journal of Neural Transmission, 85*, 19–29.

Asarnow, R. F., & MacCrimmon, D. J. (1978). Residual performance deficit in clinical remitted schizophrenics: A marker of schizophrenia? *Journal of Abnormal Psychology, 87*, 597–608.

Asarnow, R. F., & MacCrimmon, D. J. (1981). Span of apprehension deficits during the postpsychotic stages of schizophrenia. A replication and extension. *Archives of General Psychiatry, 38*, 1006–1011.

Asarnow, R. F., Steffy, R. A., MacCrimmon, D. J., & Cleghorn, J. M. (1977). An attentional assessment of foster children at risk for schizophrenia. *Journal of Abnormal Psychology, 86*, 267–275.

Barr, C. E., Mednick, S. A., & Munck-Jorgenson, P. (1990). Maternal influenza and schizophrenic births. *Archives of General Psychiatry, 47*, 869–874.

Bassett, A. S., McGillivray, B. C., Jones, B., & Pantzar, J. T. (1988). Partial trisomy chromosome 5 cosegregating with schizophrenia, *Lancet, I*, 799–801.

Benes, F. M. (1994). Developmental changes in stress adaptation in relation to psychopathology. *Development and Psychopathology, 6*, 723–739.

Benes, F. M. (1995). Is there a neuroanatomic basis for schizophrenia? An old question revisited. *The Neuroscientist, 1*, 104–115.

Bilder, R. M. (1992). Structure-function relations in schizophrenia: Brain morphology and neuropsychology. *Progress in Experimental Personality & Psychopathology Research, 15*, 183–251.

Blanchard, J. J., & Neale, J. M. (1994). The neuropsychological signature of schizophrenia: Generalized or differential deficit? *American Journal of Psychiatry, 151*, 40–48.

Bleuler, E. (1950). *Dementia praecox or the group of schizophrenias.* New York, NY: International Universities Press.

Botstein, D., White, R. L., Skolnick, M., & Davis, R. W. (1980). Construction of a genetic linkage map in man using restriction fragment length polymorphisms. *American Journal of Human Genetics, 32*, 314–331.

Breier, A., Buchanan, R. W., Ahmed, E., Munson, R. C., Kirkpatrick, B., & Gellad, F. (1992). Brain morphology and schizophrenia: A magnetic resonance imaging study of limbic, prefrontal cortex, and caudate structures. *Archive of General Psychiatry, 49*, 921–927.

Brzustowicz, L. M. (in press). *Molecular genetic approaches to the study of language*. New York: Guilford.

Busatto, G. F., Pilowsky, L. S., Costa, D. C., Ell, P. J., Lingford-Hughes, A., & Kerwin, R. W. (1995). In vivo imaging of GABAA receptors using sequential whole-volume iodine-123 iomazenil single-photon emission tomography. *European Journal of Nuclear Medicine, 22*, 1–26.

Caligiuri, M. P., Lohr, J. B., & Jeste, D. V. (1993). Parkinsonism in neuroleptic–naive schizophrenic patients. *American Journal of Psychiatry, 150*, 1343–1348.

Cannon, T. D., & Mednick, S. A. (1993). The schizophrenia high-risk project in Copenhagen: Three decades of progress. *Acta Psychiatrica Scandinavica, 370* (Suppl.), 33–47.

Cannon, T. D., Mednick, S. A., & Parnas, J. (1989). Genetic and perinatal determinants of structural brain deficits in schizophrenia. *Archives of General Psychiatry, 46*, 883–889.

Cannon, T. D., Mednick, S. A. Parnas, J., Schulsinger, F., Praestholm, J., & Vestergaard, A. (1994). Developmental brain abnormalities in the offspring of schizophrenic mothers: II. Structural brain characteristics of schizophrenia and schizotypal personality disorder. *Archives of General Psychiatry, 51, 955–962.*

Carlsson, A. (1978). Antipsychotic drugs, neurotransmitters, and schizophrenia. *American Journal of Psychiatry, 135*, 164–173.

Carlsson, A. (1995). Towards a new understanding of dopamine receptors. Symposium: Dopamine receptor subtypes in neurological and psychiatric diseases. *Clinical Neuropharmacology, 18* (Suppl.), 6S–13S.

Carpenter, W. T. (1995). Serotonin-dopamine antagonists and treatment of negative symptoms. *Journal of Clinical Psychopharmacology, 15* (1, Suppl. 1), 30S–35S.

Carpenter, W. T. Jr., Heinrichs, D. W., & Wagman, A. M. I. (1988). Deficit and nondeficit types of schizophrenia: The concept. *American Journal of Psychiatry, 145*, 578–583.

Casey, D. E., & Hansen, T. E. (1984). Spontaneous dyskinesias. In D. V. Jeste & R. J. Wyatt (Eds.), *Neuropsychiatric Movement Disorders* (pp. 68–95). Washington, DC: American Psychiatric Press.

Cegalis, J. A., & Sweeney, J. A. (1981). The effect of attention on smooth pursuit eye movements of schizophrenics. *Journal of Psychiatric Research, 16*, 145–161.

Chakos, M. H., Lieberman, J. A., Bilder, R. M., Borenstein, M., Lerner, G., Bogerts, B., Wu, H., Kinon, B., & Ashtari, M. (1994). Increase in caudate nuclei volumes of first-episode schizophrenic patients taking antipsychotic drugs. *American Journal of Psychiatry, 151*, 1430-1436.

Chapman, L. J., & Chapman, J. P. (1973). Problems in the measurement of cognitive deficit. *Psychology Bulletin, 79*, 380–385.

Clementz, B. A., Grove, W. M., Iacono, W. G., & Sweeney, J. A. (1992). Smooth-pursuit eye movement dysfunction and liability for schizophrenia: Implications for genetic modeling. *Journal of Abnormal Psychology, 101*, 117–129.

Clementz, B. A., Sweeney, J. A., Hirt, M., & Haas, G. (1990). Pursuit gain and saccadic intrusions in first-degree relatives of probands with schizophrenia. *Journal of Abnormal Psychology, 99*, 327–335.

Conrad, A. J., Abebe, T., Austin, R., Forsythe, S., & Scheibel, A. (1991). Hippocampal pyramidal cell disarray in schizophrenia as a bilateral phenomenon. *Archives General Psychiatry, 48*, 413–417.

Cornblatt, B., & Erelemeyer-Kimling, L. (1985). Global attentional deviance as a marker of risk for schizophrenia: Specificity and predictive validity. *Journal of Abnormal Psychology, 94*, 470–485.

Cornblatt, B., & Keefe, R. S. E. (1991). Genetics and mental illness: An overview. *Social Biology, 38*, i–v.

Cornblatt, B. A., & Keilp, J. G. (1994). Impaired attention, genetics, and the pathophysiology of schizophrenia. *Schizophrenia Bulletin, 20*, 31–46.

Cornblatt, B., Lenzenweger, M., Dworkin, R. H., & Erlenmeyer-Kimling, L. (1992). Childhood attentional dysfunctions predict social deficits in unaffected adults at risk for schizophrenia. *British Journal of Psychiatry, 161*, 59–64.

Cornblatt, B., Lenzenweger, M., & Erlenmeyer-Kimling, L. (1989). The continuous performance test-identical pairs (CPT-IP): II. Contrasting profiles of attentional deficits in schizophrenic and depressed patients. *Psychiatry Research, 29*, 65–85.

Cornblatt, B., & Obuchowski, M. (1997). Update of high risk research: 1987–1997. *International Review of Psychiatry, 9*, 437–447.

Cornblatt, B. A., Obuchowski, M., Andreasen, A., & Smith, C. (in press). High risk research in schizophrenia: New strategies, new designs. In M. Lenzenweger & R. Dworkin (Eds.), *Origins and development of schizophrenia: Advances in experimental psychopathology.* Washington, DC: American Psychological Association.

Cornblatt, B., Obuchowski, M., Schnurr, D., & O'Brien, J. D. (1997). Attention and clinical symptoms in schizophrenia. *Psychiatric Quarterly, 68*, 343–359.

Cornblatt, B., Obuchowski, M., Schnur, D., & O'Brien, J. D. (1998). The Hillside study of risk and early detection in schizophrenia: An introduction. *British Journal of Psychiatry, 172* (Suppl. 33), 26–32.

Cornblatt, B. A., Rish, N., Faris, G., Freedman, D., & Erlenmeyer-Kimling, L. (1988) The Continuous Performance Test-Identical Pairs (CPT-IP): I. New findings about sustained attention in normal families. *Psychiatry Research, 26*, 223–238.

Cowan, N. (1988). Evolving conceptions of memory storage, selective attention, and their mutual constraints within the human information-processing system. *Psychological Bulletin, 104*, 163–191.

Crow, T. J. (1980). Molecular pathology of schizophrenia: More than one disease process? *British Medical Journal, 280*, 66–68.

Crow, T. J. (1994). Prenatal exposure to influenza as a cause of schizophrenia. *British Journal of Psychiatry, 164*, 588–592.

Cuesta, M. J., & Peralta, V. (1995). Psychopathological dimensions in schizophrenia. *Schizophrenia Bulletin, 21*, 473–482.

Cutting, J. (1994). Evidence for right hemisphere dysfunction in schizophrenia. In A. S. David & J. C. Cutting (Eds.), *The neuropsychology of schizophrenia* (pp. 231–242). London: Lawrence Erlbaum.

Davis, K. L., Khan, R. S., Ko, G., & Davidson, M. (1991). Dopamine in schizophrenia: A review and reconceptualization. *American Journal of Psychiatry, 148*, 1474–1486.

Detera-Wadleigh, S., Goldin, L. R., Sherrington, R., Encio, E., de Miguel, C., Berrettini, W., Gurling, H., & Gershon, E. S. (1989). Exclusion of linkage to 5q11-13 in families with schizophrenia and other psychiatric disorders. *Nature, 340*, 391–393.

Erlenmeyer-Kimling, L., & Cornblatt, B. (1987). The New York High Risk Project: A follow up report. *Schizophrenia Bulletin, 13*, 451–461.

Falkai, P., Bogerts, B., & Rozumek, M. (1988). Limbic pathology in schizophrenia: The entorhinal region-a morphometric study. *Biological Psychiatry, 24*, 518–521.

Feinberg, I. (1982). Schizophrenia: Caused by a fault in programmed synaptic elimination during adolescence? *Journal of Psychiatric Research, 17*, 319–334.

Fenton, W. S., Wyatt, R. J., & McGlashan, T. H. (1994). Risk factors for spontaneous dyskinesia in schizophrenia. *Archives of General Psychiatry, 51*, 643–650.

Fischer, M. (1971). Psychoses in the offspring of schizophrenic monozygotic twins and their normal co-twins. *British Journal of Psychiatry, 118*, 43–52.

Fish, B. (1987). Infant predictors of the longitudinal course of schizophrenic development. *Schizophrenia Bulletin, 13*, 395–409.

Fish, B., Marcus, J. Hans, S. L., Auerbach, J. G., & Perdue, S. (1992). Infants at risk for schizophrenia: Sequelae of a genetic neurointegrative defect. *Archives of General Psychiatry, 49*, 221–235.

Flor-Henry, P. (1976). Lateralized temporal-limbic dysfunction and psychopathology. *Annals New York Academy of Science, 280*, 777–795.

Freedman, R., Coon, H., Myles-Worsley, M., Orr-Urtreger, A., Olincy, A., & Davis, A., et al. (1997). Linkage of a neurophysiological deficit in schizophrenia to a chromosome 15 locus. *Proceeding National Academy of Science, 94*, 587–592.

Fromm-Reichmann, F. (1948). Notes on the development of treatments of schizophrenics by psychoanalytic psychotherapy. *Psychiatry, 2*, 263–273.

Gold, J. M., Herman, B. P., Randolph, C., Wyler, A. R., Goldberg, T. E., & Weinberger, D. R. (1994). Schizophrenia and temporal lobe epilepsy. *Archives of General Psychiatry, 51*, 265–272.

Goldstein, K. (1959). Concerning the concreteness in schizophrenia. *Journal of Abnormal and Social Psychology, 59*, 146–148.

Gottesman, I. I. (1991). *Schizophrenia genesis: The origins of madness.* New York: W.H. Freeman.

Gottesman, I. I., & Bertelsen, A. (1989). Confirming unexpressed genotypes for schizophrenia: Risks in the offspring of Fischer's Danish identical and fraternal discordant twins. *Archives of General Psychiatry, 46*, 867–872.

Gottesman, I. I., & Shields, J. (1967). A polygenic theory of schizophrenia. *Proceeding of the National Academy of Science, 58*, 199–205.

Green, M. F., Nuechterlein, K. H., & Breitmeyer, B. (1997). Backward masking performance in unaffected siblings of schizophrenic patients. Evidence for a vulnerability indicator. *Archives of General Psychiatry, 54*, 465–472.

Grove, W. M., Lebow, B. S., Clementz, B. A., Cerri, A., Medus, C., & Iacono, W. G. (1991). Familial prevalence and coaggregation of schizotypy indicators: A multitrait family study. *Journal of Abnormal Psychology, 100*, 115–121.

Gur, R. E. (1978). Left hemisphere dysfunction and overactivation in schizophrenia. *Journal of Abnormal Psychology, 87*, 226–238.

Gur, R. E., & Pearlson, G. D. (1993). Neuroimaging in schizophrenia research. *Schizophrenia Bulletin, 19*, 337–353.

Guttman, E. (1936). On some constitutional aspects of chorea and on its sequelae. *Journal of Neurology and Psychopharmacology, 17*, 16–26.

Heaton, R. K., Baade, L. E., & Johnson, K. L. (1978). Neuropsychological test results associated with psychiatric disorders in adults. *Psychology Bulletin, 85*, 141–162.

Heaton, R., Paulsen, J. S., McAdams, L. A., Kuck, J., Zisook, S., Braff, D., Harris, J., & Jeste, D. V. (1994). Neuropsychological deficits in schizophrenics. *Archives of General Psychiatry, 51*, 469–476.

Heinrichs, R. W., & Awad, A. G. (1993). Neurocognitive subtypes of chronic schizophrenia. *Schizophrenia Research, 9*, 49–58.

Heston, L. L. (1966). Psychiatric disorders inforster home reared children of schizophrenic mothers. *British Journal of Psychiatry, 112*, 819–825.

Holzman, P. S. (1975). Smooth pursuit eye movements in schizophrenia: Recent findings. In D. X. Freedman (Ed.), *Biology of the major psychoses* (pp. 217–228). New York, NY: Raven Press.

Holzman, P. S. (1985). Eye movement dysfunctions and psychosis. *International Review of Neurobiology, 27*, 179–205.

Holzman, P. S. (1987). Recent studies of psychophysiology in schizophrenia. *Schizophrenia Bulletin, 13*, 49–75.

Holzman, P. S., Kringlen, E., Matthysse, S., Flanagan, S. D., Lipton, R. B., Cramer, G., Levin, S., Lange, K., & Levy, D. L. (1988). A single dominant gene can account for eye tracking dysfunctions and schizophrenia in offspring of discordant twins. *Archives of General Psychiatry, 45*, 641–647.

Holzman, P. S., Proctor, L. R., Levy, D. L., Yasillo, N. J., Meltzer, H. Y., & Hurt, S. W. (1974). Eye tracking dysfunctions in schizophrenic patients and their relatives. *Archives of General Psychiatry, 31*, 143–151.

Holzman, P. S., Solomon, C. M., Levin, S., & Waternaux, C. S. (1984). Pursuit eye movement dysfunctions in schizophrenic patients and their relatives. *Archives of General Psychiatry, 45*, 1140–1141.

Hughlings-Jackson, J. (1931). *Selected writings* (J. Taylor, Ed.) London: Hodder & Stoughton.

Huttunen, M. O. (1989). Maternal stress during pregnancy and the behavior of the offspring. In S. Doxiadis (Ed.), *Early influence shaping the individual* (pp. 175–182). New York: Plenum Press.

Huttunen, M. (1995). The evolution of the serotonin-dopamine antagonist concept. *Journal of Clinical Psychopharmacology, 15* (1, Suppl. 1), 4S–10S.

Iacono, W. G. (1985). Psychophysiologic markers of psychopathology: A review. *Canadian Psychology, 26*, 96–112.

Iacono, W. G., Moreau, M., Beiser, M., Fleming, J. A. E., & Lin, T. (1992). Smooth-pursuit eye tracking in first-episode psychotic patients and their relatives. *Journal of Abnormal Psychology, 101*, 104–116.

Iverson, S. D. (1995). Interaction between excitatory amino acids and dopamine in the forebrain: Implications for schizophrenia and Parkinson's disease. *Behavioral Pharmacology, 6*, 478–491.

Jakob, H., & Beckmann, H. (1986). Prenatal development distrubances in the limbic allocortex in schizophrenics. *Journal of Neural Transmission, 65*, 303–326.

Johnstone, E. C., Crow, T. J., Frith, C. D., Stevens, J., & Kreel, L. (1976). Cerebral ventricular size and cognitive impairment in chronic schizophrenia. *Lancet, 2*, 924–926.

Jones, P., & Murray, R. M. (1991). The genetics of schizophrenia is the genetics of neurodevelopment. *British Journal of Psychiatry, 158*, 615–623.

Jones, P., Rodgers, B., Murray, R., & Marmot, M. (1994). Child developmental risk factors for adult schizophrenia in the British 1946 birth cohort. *Lancet, 344*, 1398–1402.

Joyce, J. N., Lexow, N., Bird, E., & Winokur, A. (1988). Organization of dopamine D1 and D2 receptors in human striatum: Receptor autoradiographic studies in Huntington's disease and schizophrenia. *Synapse, 2*, 546–557.

Kahneman, D. (1973). *Attention and effort*. Englewood Cliffs, NJ: Prentice-Hall.

Kan, Y. W., & Dozy, A. M. (1978). Polymorphism of DNA sequence adjacent to human B-globin structural gene: Relationship to sicle mutation. *Proceedings of the National Academy of Science, 75*, 5631–5635.

Kaplan, H. I., & Sadock, B. J. (1988). *Synopsis of psychiatry* (5th ed.). Baltimore, MD: Williams & Wilkins.

Keefe, R. S. E. (1995). The contribution of neuropsychology to psychiatry. *American Journal of Psychiatry, 152*, 6–15.

Keefe, R., & Harvey, P. D. (1994). *Understanding schizophrenia: A guide to the new research on causes & treatment.* New York: Free Press.

Kendler, K. S. (1985). Diagnostic approaches to schizotypal personality disorder: A historical perspective. *Schizophrenia Bulletin, 11*, 538–553.

Kendler, K. S. (1988). Familial aggregation of schizophrenia and schizophrenia spectrum disorders: Evaluation of conflicting results. *Archives of General Psychiatry, 45*, 377–383.

Kendler, K. S., & Diehl, S. R. (1993). The genetics of schizophrenia: A current genetic-epidemiologic perspective. *Schizophrenia Bulletin, 19*, 261–285.

Kendler, K. S., & Gruenberg, A. M. (1984). An independent analysis of the Copenhagen sample of the Danish adoption study of schizophrenia VI. The pattern of psychiatric illness, as defined by DSM-III in adoptees and relatives. *Archives of General Psychiatry, 41*, 555–564.

Kennedy, J. L., Giuffra, L. A., Moises, H. W., Cavalli-Sforza, L. L., Pakstis, A. J., Kidd, J. R., Castiglione, C. M., Sjorgen, F., Wetterberg, L., & Kidd, K. K. (1988). Evidence against linkage of schizohrenia to markers on chromosome 5 in a northern Swedish pedigree. *Nature, 336*, 167–170.

Kety, S. S. (1988). Schizophrenic illness in the families of schizophrenic adoptees: Findings from the Danish national sample. *Schizophrenia Bulletin, 14*, 217–222.

Khot, V., & Wyatt, R. J. (1991). Not all that moves is tardive dyskinesia. *American Journal of Psychiatry, 148*, 661–666.

Kidd, K. K. (1991). Tiral and tribulations in the search for genes causing neuropsychiatric disorders. *Social Biology, 38*, 163–178.

Kovelman, J. A., & Scheibel, A. B. (1984). A neurohistological correlate of schizophrenia. *Biological Psychiatry, 19*, 1601–1621.

Kraepelin, E. (1919/1971). *Dementia praecox and paraphrenia*. Huntington, NY: Robert E. Krieger.

Lenzenweger, M. F., Cornblatt, B. A., & Putnick, M. (1991). Schizotypy and sustained attention. *Journal of Abnormal Psychology, 100*, 84–49.

Levinson, D. F., & Mowry, B. J. (1991). Defining the schizophrenia spectrum: Issues for genetic linkage studies. *Schizophrenia Bulletin, 17*, 491–514.

Levy, D. L. (1996). Location, location, location: The pathway from behavior to brain locus in schizophrenia. In D. L. Levy, J. Kagan, F. M. Benes, & S. Mathysse (Eds.), *Psychopathology: The evolving science of mental disorder* (pp. 100–126). Cambridge: Cambridge University Press.

Levy, D. L., Holzman, P. S., Matthysse, S., & Mendell, N. R. (1993). Eye tracking dysfunction and schizophrenia: A critical perspective. *Schizophrenia Bulletin, 19*, 461–536.

Levy, D. L., Holzman, P. S., Matthysse, S., & Mendell, N. R. (1994). Eye tracking and schizophrenia: A selective review. *Schizophrenia Bulletin, 20*, 47–62.

Levy, D. L., Yasillo, N. J., Dorus, E., Shaughnessy, R., Gibbons, R. D., Peterson, J., Janicak, P. G., Gaviria, M., & Davis, J. M. (1983). Relatives of unipolar and bipolar patients have normal pursuit. *Psychiatry Research, 10*, 285–293.

Lieberman, J. A. (1994). Clinical biological studies of the atypical antipsychotics: Focus on the serotonin/dopamine system. *Journal of Clinical Psychiatry*, 12, 24–28.

Lieberman, J., Jody, D., Geisler, S., Alvir, J., Loebel, A., Szymanski, S., Woerner, M., & Borenstein, M. (1993). Time course and biologic correlates of treatment response in first-episode schizophrenia. *Archives of General Psychiatry, 50*, 369–376.

Lieberman, J. A., & Koreen, A. R. (1993). Neurochemistry and neuroendocrinology of schizophrenia: A selective review. *Schizophrenia Bulletin, 2*, 371–428.

Lohr, J. B., & Caligiuri, M. P. (1992). Quantitative instrumental measurement of tardive dyskinesia: A review. *Neuropsychopharmacology, 6*, 231–239.

Lowing, P. A., Mirsky, A. F., & Pereira, R. (1983). The inheritance of schizophrenic spectrum disorders A reanalysis of the Danish adoptee study data. *American Journal of Psychiatry, 140*, 1167–1171.

Luchins, D. J., Weinberger, D. R., & Wyatt, R. J. (1982). Schizophrenia and cerebral asymmetry detected by computed tomography. *American Journal of Psychiatry, 139*, 753–757.

Manschreck, T. C. (1983). Psychopathology of motor behavior in schizophrenia. *Progress in Experimental Personality Research, 12*, 53–99.

McCarley, R. W., Shenton, M. E., O'Donnell, B. F., Faux, S. F., Kikinis, R., Nestor, P. G., & Jolesz, F. A. (1993). Auditory P300 abnormalities and left posterior superior temporal gyrus volume reduction in schizophrenia. *Archives of General Psychiatry, 50*, 190–197.

McGhie, A., & Chapman, J. (1961). Disorders of attention and perception in early schizophrenia. *British Journal of Medical Psychology, 43*, 103–116.

McGuffin, P., & Sturt, E. (1986). Genetic markers in schizophrenia. *Human Heredity, 36*, 65–88.

Mednick, S. A., Machon, R. A., Huttunen, M. O., & Bonett, D. (1988). Adult schizophrenia following prenatal exposure to an influenza epidemic. *Archives of General Psychiatry, 45*, 189–192.

Mednick, S. A., & McNeil, T. (1968). Current methodology in research on the etiology of schizophrenia: Serious difficulties which suggest the use of the high-risk group methods. *Psychological Bulletin, 70*, 681–693.

Mednick, S. A., & Schulsinger, F. (1968). Some premorbid characteristics related to breakdown in children with schizophrenic mothers. *Journal of Psychiatry Research, 6*, 267–291.

Meltzer, H. Y. (1991). The mechanism of action of novel antipsychotic drugs. *Schizophrenia Bulletin, 17*, 263–287.

Meltzer, H. Y., & Nash, J. F. (1991). Serotonin and neuropsychiatric disorders: Implications for the discovery of new psychotherapeutic agents, VII: Effects of antipsychotic drugs on serotonin receptors. *Pharmacological Review, 43*, 587–604.

Moghaddam, B. (1994). Recent basic findings in support of excitatory amino acid hypotheses of schizophrenia. *Progress in Neuro-Psychopharmacological and Biological Psychiatry, 18*, 859–870.

Murray, R. M., O'Callaghan, E., Castle, D. J., & Lewis, S. W. (1992). A neurodevelopmetal approach to the classification of schizophrenia. *Schizophrenia Bulletin, 18*, 319–332.

Nagy, J., & Szatmari, P. (1986). A chart review of schizotypal personality disorders in children. *Journal of Autism and Developmental Disorders, 16*, 351–367.

Nicholls, D. G. (1994). *Proteins, transmitters & synapses*. Malden, MA: Blackwell Science.

Nuechterlein, K. H. (1977). Reaction time and attention in schizophrenia: A critical evaluation of the data and theories. *Schizophrenia Bulletin, 3*, 373–428.

Nuechterlein, K. H. (1983). Signal detection in vigilance tasks and behavioral attributes among offspring of schizophrenic mothers and among hyperactive children. *Journal of Abnormal Psychology, 92*, 4–28.

Nuechterlein, K. H., & Asarnow, R. F. (1989). Cognition and perception. In H. I. Kaplan & B. J. Sadock (Eds.), *Comprehensive textbook of psychiatry* (5th ed., Vol. 1). Baltimore: Williams & Wilkins.

Nuechterlein, K. H., & Dawson, M. E. (1984). Information processing and attentional functioning in the developmental course of schizophrenia disorders. *Schizophrenia Bulletin, 10*, 160–203.

Nuechterlein, K. H., Dawson, M. E., Gitlin, M., Ventura, J., Goldstein, M. J., Snyder, K. S., Yee, C. M., & Mintz, J. (1992). Developmental processes in schizophrenic disorders: Longitudinal studies of vulnerability and stress. *Schizophrenia Bulletin, 18*, 387–425.

Nuechterlein, K. H., Dawson, M. E., & Green, M. F. (1994). Information-processing abnormalities as neuropsychological vulnerability indicators for schizophrenia. *Acta Psychiatrica Scandinavica, 90* (Suppl. 384), 71–79.

Obuchowski, M., & Cornblatt, B. (1995). Eye-movement dysfunctions and the neurodevelopmental view of schizophrenia. *Schizophrenia Research, 15*, 182.

O'Callaghan, E., Sham, P., Takei, N., Glover, G., & Murray, R. M. (1991). Schizophrenia after prenatal exposure to 1957 A2 influenza epidemic. *Lancet, 337*, 1248–1250.

Olney, J. W., & Farber, N. B. (1995). Glutamate receptor dysfunction and schizophrenia. *Archives of General Psychiatry, 52*, 998–1007.

Palacios, J. M., Waeber, C., Hoyer, D., & Mengod, G. (1990). Distribution of serotonin receptors: The neuropharmacology of serotonin. *Annual Preceding of the New York Academy of Science, 600*, 36–52.

Payne, R. W., Mattussek, P., & George, E. I. (1959). An experimental study of schizophrenic thought disorder. *Journal of Mental Science, 105*, 627–652.

Pearson, J. S., & Kley, I. B. (1957). On the application of genetic expectancies as age specific base rates in the study of human behavior disorders. *Psychological Bulletin, 54*, 406–420.

Raz, S., & Raz, N. (1990). Structural brain abnormalities in the major psychoses: A quantitative review of the evidence from computerized imaging. *Psychological Bulletin, 108*, 93–108.

Reiter, P. J. (1926). Extrapyramidal motor-disturbances in dementia praecox. *Acta Psychiatrica et Neurologica Scandinavica, 1*, 287–309.

Remington, G. J. (1995). Dopaminergic and serotonergic mechanisms in the action of standard and atypical neuroleptics. In C. L. Shriqui & H. A. Nasrallah (Eds.), *Contemporary issues in the treatment of schizophrenia* (pp. 295–328). Washington, DC: American Psychiatric Press.

Reynolds, G. P., & Czudek, C. (1988). Status of the dopaminergic system in post-mortem brain in schizophrenia. *Psychopharmacology Bulletin, 24*, 345–347.

Risch, N. J. (1990). The role of genetic linkage studies in psychiatry, address presented at *New Developments int he Genetics of Mental Illness*. Symposium of the Annual Meeting of the American Association for the Advancement of Science, New Orleans.

Roitman, S. E. L., Cornblatt, B. A., Bergman, A., Obuchowski, M., Mitropoulou, V., Keefe, R. S. E., Silverman, J. M., & Siever, L. J. (1997). Attentional functioning in schizotypal personality disorder. *American Journal of Psychiatry, 154*, 655–660.

Rosenberg, D. R., Sweeney, J. A., Squires-Wheeler, E., Keshavan, M. S., Cornblatt,

B. A., & Erlenmeyer-Kimling, L. (1977). Eye-tracking dysfunction in offspring from the New York High-Risk Project: Diagnostic specificity and the role of attentional. *Psychiatry Research, 66*, 121–130.

Rosenthal, D., Wender, P. H., Kety, S. S., Schulsinger, F., Welner, J., & Ostergaard, L. (1968). Schizophrenic's offspring reared in adoptive home. In D. Rosenthal & S. S. Kety (Eds.), *The transmission of schizophrenia* (pp. 377–391). Oxford: Pergamon.

Ross, R. G., Radant, A. D., & Hommer, D. W. (1993). A developmental study of smooth pursuit eye movements in normal children from 7 to 15 years of age. *Journal of the American Academy Child and Adolescent Psychiatry, 32*, 783–791.

Saykin, A. J., Gur, R. C., Gur, R. E., Mozley, P. D., Mozley, L. H., Resnick, S. M., Kester, D. B., & Stafiniak, P. (1991). Neuropsychological function in schizophrenia: Selective impairment in memory and learning. *Archives of General Psychiatry, 48*, 618–624.

Schulz, S. C., Goyer, P., Kenney, J., Friedman, L., Semple, W., & Low-Beer, J. (1992). Brain imaging, neuropsychological, and eye-tracking assessments of adolescents with psychosis. Presented at the Annual Meeting of the American College of Neuropsychopharmacology, San Juan, Puerto Rico.

Shagass, C., Amadeo, M., & Overton, D. A. (1974). Eye-tracking performance in psychiatric patients. *Biological Psychiatry, 9*, 245–260.

Shenton, M. E., Kinkinis, R., Jolesz, F. A., Pollack, S. D., LeMay, M., Wible, C. G., Hokama, H., Martin, J., Medcalf, D., Coleman, M., & McCarley, R. W. (1992). Left-lateralized temporal lobe abnormalities in schizophrenia and their relationship to thought disorder: A computerized, quantitative MRI study. *New England Journal of Medicine, 327*, 604–612.

Sherrington, R., Brynjolfsson, J., Petursson, H., Potter, M., Dudleston, K., Barraclough, B., Wasmuth, J., Dobbs, M., & Gurlng, H. (1988). Location of a susceptibility locus for schizophrenia on chromosome 5. *Nature, 336*, 164–167.

Siever, L. J. (1985) Biological markers in schizotypal personality disorder. *Schizophrenia Bulletin, 11*, 564–575.

Siever, L. J., Coursey, R. D., Alterman, I. S., Buchsbaum, M. S., & Murphy, D. L. (1984). Impaired smooth pursuit eye movement: Vulnerability marker for schizotypal personality disorder in a normal volunteer population. *American Journal of Psychiatry, 141*, 1560–1566.

Siever, L. J., Coursey, R., Alterman, I., Zahn, T., Brody, L., Bernad, P., Buchsbaum, M., Lake, C., & Murphy, D. (1989). Clinical, psychophysiological, and neurological characteristics of volunteers with impaired smooth pursuit eye movements. *Biological Psychiatry, 26*, 35–51.

Siever, L. J., Kalus, O. F., Keefe, R. S. (1993). The boundaries of schizophrenia. *Psychiatric Clinics of North America. Vol. 16*, 217–244.

Siever, L. J., Keefe, R., Bernstein, D. P., Coccaro, E. F., Klar, H. M., Zemishlany, Z., Peterson, A. E., Davidson, M., Mahon, T., Horvath, T., & Mohs, R. (1990). Eye tracking impairment in clinically identified patients with schizotypal personality disorder. *American Journal of Psychiatry, 147*, 740–745.

Siever, L. J., Silverman, J. M., Horvath, T. B., Klar, H., Coccaro, E. F., Keefe, R. S. E., Pinkham, L., Rinaldi, P., Mohs, R. C., & Davis, K. L. (1990). Increased morbid risk for schizophrenia-related disorder in relatives of schizotypal personality disorderd patients. *Archives of General Psychiatry, 47*, 634–640.

Simons, R. F., & Katkin, W. (1985). Smooth pursuit eye movements in subjects reporting physical anhedonia and perceptual aberrations. *Psychiatry Research, 14*, 275–289.

St. Clair, D., Blackwood, D., Muir, W., Baillie, D., Hubbard, A., Wright, A., & Evans, H. J. (1989). No linkage of chromosome 5q11-q13 markers to schiziophrenia in Scottish families. *Nature, 339*, 305–309.

Stevens, J. (1973). An anatomy of schizophrenia? *Archives of General Psychiatry, 51*, 177-189.

Straub, R. E., MacLean, C. J., O'Neill, F. A., Burke, J., Murphy, B., Duke, F., Shinkwi, R., Webb, B. T., Zhang, J., Walsh, D., & Kendler, K. (1995). A potential vulnerability locus for schizophrenia on chromosome 6p24-22: evidence for genetic heterogeneity. *Nature Genetics, 11*, 287–293.

Strauss, J. S, Carpenter, W. T. Jr., & Bartko, J. J. (1974). The diagnosis and understanding of schizophrenia. Part III. Speculations on the processes hat underlie schizophrenic symptoms and signs. *Schizophrenia Bulletin, 11*, 61–69.

Susser, E. S., & Lin, S. P. (1992). Schizophrenia after prenatal exposure to the Dutch Hunger Winter of 1944–1945. *Archives of General Psychiatry, 49*, 983–988.

Sweeney, J. A., Haas, G. L., & Li, S. (1992). Neuropsychological and eye movement abnormalities in first-episode and chronic schizophrenia. *Schizophrenia Bulletin, 18*, 283–293.

Swerdlow, N. R., & Koob, G. F. (1987). Dopamine, schizophrenia, mania, and depression: Toward a unified hypothesis of cortico-striato-pallido-thalamic function. *Behavioral and Brain Sciences, 10*, 197–245.

Toru, M., Watanabe, S., Shibuya, H. Nishikawa, T., Noda, K., Mitushio, H., Ichikawa, H., Kurumaji, A., Takashima, M., Mataga, N., & Ogawa, A. (1988). Neurotransmitters, receptors and neuropeptides in post-mortem brains of chronic schizophrenia patients. *Acta Psychiatrica Scandinavica, 78*, 121–137.

Tsuang, M. T., Lyons, M. J., & Faraone, S. V. (1990). Heterogeneity of schizophrenia. Conceptual models and analytic strategies. *British Journal of Psychiatry, 156*, 17–26.

Tune, L. E., Wong, D. F., Pearlson G., Strauss, M., Young, T., Shaya, E. K., Dannals, R. F., Wilson, A. A., Ravert, H. T., Sapp, J., Cooper, T., Chase, G. A., & Wagner, H. N. (1993). Dopamine D2 receptor density estimates in schizophrenia: A positron emission tomography study with 11C-N-Methylspiperone. *Psychiatry Research, 49*, 219–237.

Turner, T. (1989). Rich and mad in Victorian England. *Psychological Medicine, 19*, 29–44.

Walker, E. (1994). Developmentally moderated expressions of the neuropathology underlying schizophrenia. *Schizophrenia Bulletin, 20*, 453–480.

Walker, E., & Diforio, D. (1997). Schizophrenia: A neural diathesis-stress model. *Psychological Review, 104*, 667–685.

Walker, E., & McGuire, M. (1982). Intra- and interhemispheric information processing in schizophrenia. *Psychological Bulletin, 92*, 701–725.

Walker, E., Savoie, T., & Davis, D. (1994). Neuromotor precursors of schizophrenia. *Schizophrenia Bulletin, 20*, 453–480.

Wan, F. J., Geyer, M. A., & Swerdlow, N. R. (1995). Presynaptic dopamine-glutatmate interactions in the nucleus accumbens regulate sensorimotor gating. *Psychopharmacology, 120*, 433–441.

Webb, C. T., & Levinson, D. F. (1993). Schizotypal and paranoid personality disorder in the relatives of patients with schizophrenia and affective disorders: A review. *Schizophrenia Research, 11*, 81–92.

Weinberger, D. R. (1986). The pathogenesis of schizophrenia: A neurodevelopmental theory. In H. Nasrallah & D. R. Weinberger (Eds.), *The neurology of schizophrenia* (pp. 397–406). Amsterdam: Elsevier Science Publishers.

Weinberger, D. (1987). Implications of normal brain development for the pathogenesis of schizophrenia. *Archives of General Psychiatry, 44*, 660–669.

Weinberger, D. R., & Berman, K. F. (1988). Speculation on the meaning of cerebral metabolic hypofrontality in schizophrenia. *Schizophrenia Bulletin, 14*, 157–168.

Windholz, G. (1993). Pavlov's concept of schizophrenia as related to the theory of higher nervous activity. *History of Psychiatry, 4*, 511–526.

Winters, L., Cornblatt, B. A., & Erlenmeyer-Kimling, L. (1991). The prediction of psychiatric disorders in late adolescence. In E. Walker (Ed.), *Schizophrenia: A life-course developmental perspective* (pp. 124–139). New York: Academic Press.

Wong, D. F. (1992). PET studies of neuroreceptors in schizophrenia. *Neuropsychopharmacology, 7*, 69–72.

Wong, D. F., Wagner, H. N. Jr., Tune, L. E., Dannals, R. F., Pearlson, G. D., Links, J. M., Tamminga, C. A., Broussolle, E. P., Ravert, H. T., Wilson, A. A., Toung, J. K. T., Malat, J., Williams, J. A., O'Tuama, L. A., Snyder, S. H., Kuhar, M. J., & Gjedde, A. (1986). Positron emission tomogrophy reveals elevated D2 dopamine receptors in neuroleptic-naive schizophrenics. *Science, 234*, 1558–1563.

Zubin, J., & Spring, B. (1977). Vulnerability: A new view of schizophrenia. *Journal of Abnormal Psychology, 86*, 103–126.

12

Interpersonal Functioning in Schizophrenia

JILL M. HOOLEY
STEVEN F. CANDELA

Impairment in social functioning is a fundamental feature of schizophrenia. Recognized in the early clinical descriptions of the disorder, deterioration of social relations remains one of the defining characteristics of the syndrome. Kraepelin noted the lack of concern for social convention that characterized the schizophrenia patient, remarking that:

> The patients no longer have any regard for their surroundings; they do not suit their behavior to the situation in which they are, they conduct themselves in a free and easy way, laugh on serious occasions, are rude and impertinent towards their superiors, challenge them to duels, lose their deportment and personal dignity; they go about in untidy and dirty clothes, unwashed, unkept, go with a lighted cigar into church, speak familiarly with strangers, decorate themselves with gay ribbons. (Kraepelin, 1896, p. 34)

In a related vein, Bleuler observed:

> It is indeed striking how early those feelings that regulate social intercourse among people are blunted. It hardly makes any difference to the patient whether he is addressing a person in authority or someone more humbly placed, whether a man or a woman. (Bleuler, 1908, p. 49)

Although more contemporary writers might describe the social difficulties of schizophrenia patients less vividly, it is acknowledged that ordinary social encounters often present considerable challenges to those with this disorder. Withdrawal and social isolation form part of the clinical profile of schizophrenia within the *DSM*. Moreover, the sadness that some patients experience as a consequence of their social deficiencies is poignantly illustrated in this comment from a patient with a childhood onset of schizophrenic illness:

> It has always been hard for me to have friends. I want friends, but I don't know how to make them. I always think people are serious when they are just joking around, but I don't figure that out until a lot later. I just don't know how to adapt. . . . After I got back from [my first hospitalization], I really couldn't get along with anyone. That was when kids first began calling me "retard." I am not a retard, but I get confused and I can't figure out what is going on. (Anonymous, 1994a, p. 587)

In this chapter we survey the literature concerning social functioning in schizophrenia, a broad topic that covers a wide range of divergent research areas. Accordingly, a few comments about how the chapter is organized are appropriate. We begin by considering the nature of social exchanges and by talking in general terms about the social problems that schizophrenic patients experience. We then move to a discussion of the factors that are associated with better or worse social functioning, focusing particularly on the role of gender, and positive and negative symptoms. Consideration of the possible link between symptoms and social dysfunction naturally raises the question of whether interpersonal difficulties characterize patients before symptoms even develop. We therefore review the literature concerning social impairments in the premorbid phases of the illness. We also consider the interpersonal functioning of those who are simply at statistically higher risk for the development of the disorder but who are otherwise psychiatrically well.

Once we have established that interpersonal deficits in schizophrenia are important in their own right (i.e., they are not simply correlates of the symptoms of the disorder), we turn our attention to a consideration of what role neurocognitive impairments might play with respect to social functioning. We also highlight some neurocognitive skills that appear to be particularly important in this regard. Following this, we draw readers' attention to the emerging field of social cognition (as opposed to nonsocial cognition) in schizophrenia. Finally, we consider the role of the patient's social environment in the course of schizophrenia, ending with a discussion of the treatment options that are available to help patients and their families to function more effectively in the face of this illness.

Space constraints dictate that our review of all of these areas must be brief. Because our focus is broad, our literature review is more selective than exhaustive, and we are often unable to consider many interesting and important aspects of the topics that we discuss. Wherever possible, however, we draw readers' attention to valuable articles that do provide more detailed consideration of specific issues.

Interpersonal Adjustment and Schizophrenia

How do we know that patients suffering from schizophrenia have problems in the interpersonal domain? At the most obvious level, we know because they tell us. The subjective reports of schizophrenia patients are full of references to the difficulties they experience during ordinary social interactions. These difficulties are also mirrored in the comments of their family members: The ex-wife of "Jon," a schizophrenia patient, puts it this way,

> Some aspects of Jon's illness were particularly puzzling. I knew he was highly intelligent and perfectly at ease when it came to discussing complicated philosophical issues or analyzing the works of sophisticated artists. Why then was he at a loss when it came to dealing with everyday human relationships? He didn't seem to be able to get the feel of people, to interpret their gestures correctly. Instead of relying on that intuitive understanding we usually have of what other people are trying to convey, he built up intricate theories that often led him to erroneous interpretations. It took me a long time to understand that this continuous theorizing might be his way of grappling with his own uncertainty and bewilderment. It was as though some strange deficiency prevented him from understanding some things that seem perfectly obvious to most people. When I finally grasped this, I started spelling out those "obvious" things, even though I started to sound very stilted to myself. It was like explaining the most obvious and familiar aspects of our life on Earth to an extraterrestrial. (Anonymous, 1994b, p. 228)

People with schizophrenia have problems with different sorts of relationships. In the behavioral sciences, relationships have been classified as a function of the interpersonal needs that they serve (Bennis, Schein, Berlew, & Steele, 1964). Instrumental relationships are task oriented and goal driven. Work and service relationships such as purchasing an item in a store, asking for directions, giving appropriate information in a job interview, or dealing with those responsible for processing disability benefits primarily subserve instrumental role needs (see Liberman, 1982).

People with schizophrenia show significant impairment in their instrumental relationships (see Wallace, 1984, for a review of the early literature). For example, those with the illness are frequently unable to finish school or to achieve the level of education they desire. Jeffrey's illness began while he was attending college:

> To say that my freshman year was arduous is an understatement. I didn't finish my first year, my first semester marks were relatively low, and I was placed on academic probation. Although present, the first signs of schizophrenia (loss of motivation, withdrawal from others, and confused thought processes) went undiagnosed. Be-

> cause of this, I failed or withdrew from all college classes. (DeMann, 1994, pp. 579–580)

Another patient describes a problem with an instrumental relationship more specifically: "After graduation I enrolled at a college near home. I stayed only 2 years. It was difficult for me to deal with ordinary situations, such as a problem with a teacher" (Herrig, 1995, p. 339).

Many individuals with schizophrenia are also unable to hold a job for a sustained period of time. Moreover, when they do it is often at an employment level that is lower than that of their parents (see *DSM-IV*). Jon, the patient described earlier, had his first breakdown when he was in the army. He left the army and later found part-time work. Finding that too much, he subsequently gave up work entirely and stayed at home reading, writing, and doing household chores while his wife went out to work (Anonymous, 1994a).

Deficits are also very much apparent in the social-emotional domain. In contrast to the task-oriented or goal-directed nature of instrumental interpersonal relationships, social-emotional aspects of relationships are driven more by the needs of the relationship itself. Social-emotional exchanges might therefore include such things as asking how a spouse or partner feels, greeting a relative, going to an event with a friend, or chatting at a party (Liberman, 1982). Although these sorts of transactions are everyday occurrences for most of us, they are not so routine for the schizophrenia sufferer (Wallace, 1984): "I wanted to blend in in the classroom as though I were a desk. I never spoke. I didn't participate in any extracurricular activities or have any close friends" (Herrig, 1995, p. 339).

Perhaps the most striking evidence that schizophrenia patients are impaired in the social-emotional domain is the fact that the great majority of them never marry. This is conventional wisdom among clinicians. It also is well supported by empirical data. For example, Nanko and Moridaira (1993) found that only 35% of a large sample of outpatients with schizophrenia had ever been married. Interestingly, males with the disorder appear to be particularly unlikely to marry. Using fairly strict diagnostic criteria, Loranger (1984) reported that only 10% of a sample of schizophrenic men had married. In contrast, half of the women with schizophrenia had done so. Although precise rates vary across studies, it is clear that schizophrenia severely reduces the probability of marriage for men, although it compromises it less so in the case of schizophrenic women (Hafner, 1986).

General descriptions of the problems experienced by patients with schizophrenic illness are important and informative. However, they tell us little about what patients with this disorder actually do in social situations. Fortunately, in recent years, researchers have begun to explore the interpersonal deficits associated with schizophrenia in an effort to understand their nature and possible origins. It is to this literature that we now turn.

Measuring Social Behavior

Social Competence

Social competence is "a context-related and more or less subjective judgment or evaluation of observed behavior or social role performance" (Appelo et al., 1992, p. 419; see also McFall, 1982). In general, it reflects how well we consider people to be doing in everyday social situations. Often used interchangeably with terms such as social role functioning or social role adjustment, it is the most molar level of analysis of interpersonal functioning. As we have already seen, subjective accounts and clinical observations make it clear that social competence is often severely compromised in schizophrenia. Studies that have examined social competence more formally have also reached similar conclusions.

An instrument that is frequently used by researchers is the Social Competence Scale (Zigler & Phillips, 1961). This is a rather heterogeneous measure that considers age of onset, education, marital status, occupation, and employment history to yield a composite social functioning score. As might be expected, schizophrenia patients typically score lower on the Social Competence Scale than do psychiatric patients with other disorders (e.g., Schwartz, 1967). Interestingly, adolescents at risk for schizophrenia also appear to score more poorly on this instrument, both relative to nonpsychiatric controls and to adolescents at risk for mood disorders (Dworkin et al., 1990). On other measures of global social functioning, such as the Social Adjustment Scale[1] (SAS-II; Schooler, Hogarty, & Weissman, 1986) and the Quality of Life

Scale[2] (QLS; Heinrichs, Hanlon, & Carpenter, 1984), schizophrenia patients again score worse than either nonpatient controls or patients diagnosed with mood disorders (see Bellack, Morrison, Wixted, & Mueser, 1990). Global difficulties in social competence thus seem to be characteristic of those diagnosed with schizophrenia.

Social Skills

Subsumed within social competence are more specific areas. These include social skills and interpersonal problem solving. McFall (1982) defined social skills as "the specific abilities that enable a person to perform competently at a particular social task" (p. 23). Mueser, Bellack, Morrison, and Wade (1990) further noted that social skills are the "specific verbal, nonverbal and paralinguistic (e.g., voice tone) behavioral components that together form the basis for effective communication" (p. 138). Social skills include the ability to give and obtain information, and to express and exchange attitudes, opinions, and feelings. These skills, which are apparent in the everyday conversations, encounters, and relationships that people have with each other, are thought to be critical to social competence (see also Liberman, 1982).

In the research lab, social skills are often investigated using role-play techniques. In role playing, the patient interacts with a confederate in a prescribed situation. This may range from an exchange with a shopping clerk to a staged argument with a loved one. Thus, a researcher interested in exploring social competence may rate role-playing activities on various dimensions of social skills scales. These more molecular ratings of social behavior may focus raters' attention on specific nonverbal skills such as the appropriateness of gaze, duration of speech, meshing (e.g., the smoothness of turn taking and pauses in the conversation), or the expressiveness and congruence of facial expression (see Mueser, Bellack, Douglas, & Morrison, 1991). Verbal skills, which are evaluated in the context of the social situation being enacted, are also considered.

Role-playing techniques have been widely used by Bellack and his associates. Typically viewed as a measure of response capabilities rather than as a reflection of behavior occurring in the natural environment, role play nevertheless appears to be a valid method for the study of interpersonal behavior. Behavior during role play is strongly correlated with more global measures of social competence, such as the SAS-II and the QLS. Behavior in role-playing situations has also been shown to differentiate schizophrenic, affectively disturbed, and normal control groups. Using a five-point scale of overall social skill, judges blind to diagnosis rated schizophrenia patients as less skilled than mood-disordered patients or nonpatient controls (Bellack, Morrison, Mueser, Wade, & Sayers, 1990). A similar pattern of results was found for judges' ratings of nonverbal behavior.

Social skills research, relying heavily on role-playing tasks, has also provided useful information about more specific deficiencies in the social functioning of schizophrenia patients. For example, in conversation, schizophrenic patients show weaker verbal (e.g., clarity, negotiation, and persistence) and nonverbal skills (e.g., interest, fluency, and affect) than do nonpatient controls (Bellack, Sayers, Mueser, & Bennett, 1994). Compared with mood disordered or nonpatient controls, they also tend to be less assertive when challenged. Moreover, although in the face of criticism normal and psychiatric controls tend to apologize or explain, schizophrenia patients, in contrast, tend to deny making errors or to simply lie (Bellack, Mueser, Wade, Sayers, & Morrison, 1992). In many cases, however, overall social performance in schizophrenia patients is compromised more by mild impairments across a range of component skill areas rather than by marked problems in any one specific domain (see Mueser, Bellack, Douglas, & Morrison, 1991).

Interpersonal Problem Solving

The ability to successfully recognize an interpersonal problem, formulate a solution, and enact that solution is fundamental to social success. Interpersonal problem solving, another element of social competence, can be examined in a number of different ways. In an early series of studies, Platt and Spivak (1972, 1974) administered the Means-Ends Problem Solving (MEPS) procedure to a sample of patients, the majority of whom had been diagnosed with schizophrenia. The MEPS presents subjects with hypothetical interpersonal problem situations and measures how well subjects are then able to conceptualize and generate effective solutions for the resolution of each problem. Compared with a control sample of hospital employees, the schizophrenia patients were less able to provide appropriate and potentially effective solutions to the problems under consideration.

Several important methodological difficulties with these early studies, however, require that the results be viewed in a circumspect manner. Two problems appear to be particularly important. First, because the studies were conducted in the United States prior to the development of *DSM-III*, the diagnostic criteria for schizophrenia are likely to have been especially broad (Professional Staff, 1974). Second, the performance of the schizophrenia patients was compared only with a sample of normal controls. We must also know how schizophrenia patients perform in comparison to patients with diagnoses other than schizophrenia. The interpersonal functioning of schizophrenia patients could be compromised by a variety of factors such as pathology in general, institutionalization, and stigma, to name but three. Comparing schizophrenia patients with patients suffering from other psychiatric disorders provides valuable information about the extent to which any differences found are specific to schizophrenia or characteristic of psychiatric patients in general.

With respect to the first problem, it is now clear that patients diagnosed according to more current diagnostic criteria for schizophrenia also demonstrate problems in the area of interpersonal problem solving. Donahoe et al. (1990) developed the Assessment of Interpersonal Problem-Solving Skills (AIPSS) to examine this issue in depth. The AIPSS consists of 13 brief videotaped interactions, 10 of which depict some form of interpersonal problem. The subject is asked to watch each vignette, identifying with one of the actors in each case. After viewing the videotaped segment, the subject is then asked to identify if there is a problem in the scene and, if so, to describe what the problem is. This aspect of the test is thought to tap *receiving skills*. As an illustration, the subject may watch an actor arrive for a scheduled job interview, only to find out from a receptionist that the interviewer has left for the day. The subject is then asked what he or she would do about the problem. This is considered to be a measure of *processing skills*. Finally, *sending skills* are assessed and subjects are asked to role play what they would do in that specific problem situation. In this respect, of course, the AIPSS shows overlap with other indicators of social competence since the ability to implement and enact a solution to a specified problem necessarily relies on social skills.

As might be expected based on earlier research reports, schizophrenia patients performed poorly on the AIPSS relative to controls (Donahoe et al., 1990). Unfortunately, the results of this study are still difficult to interpret because the control subjects were not matched with patients on either demographic characteristics or IQ. However, using a matched control sample, Bowen and her associates (Bowen et al., 1994) have recently replicated these initial findings. Thus it appears that, relative to normal controls, schizophrenia patients do appear to experience difficulties in the area of interpersonal problem solving.

Whether these difficulties are specific to schizophrenia, however, is open to question. Consistent with the findings discussed above, Bellack and his colleagues (1994) reported that hospital inpatients with schizophrenia performed less well than psychiatrically healthy controls on tasks related to interpersonal problem solving. More specifically, relative to controls, the schizophrenia patients generated solutions that were rated by judges as being less appropriate and less likely to be able to be implemented. The patients were also generally less assertive and tended to be less adequate at recognizing poor problem solutions that were unlikely to work. Importantly, however, these difficulties also characterized patients with bipolar disorder. Both patient groups performed less well than controls, and no significant differences between the patient groups themselves were found.

Because the patients in the Bellack et al. (1994) study were all hospitalized at the time of testing it is not clear whether subsequent testing during a period of remission or greater clinical stabilization might have yielded the same results. Quite possibly the interpersonal difficulties that characterized the schizophrenia patients are more enduring than those that characterized the bipolar patients. In any event, the results of this study remind us that, in the absence of comparisons with other diagnostic groups, we cannot invariably assume that any of the problems identified in schizophrenia patients are unique to this disorder.

In summary, there appears to be ample evidence demonstrating that schizophrenia patients exhibit a wide range of problems across a diverse array of social domains when compared with control subjects. How specific some of these difficulties are to schizophrenia, however, still remains to be investigated. The issue of control groups is extremely important. Although some problems with interpersonal skills do seem to be specific to schizophrenia (e.g., Bellack et al., 1990, 1992), this is not always the case (e.g., Bellack et al., 1994). More data on the extent to which problems remain when patients enter a period of remission would obviously be immensely valuable in this regard. Although Mueser, Bellack, Douglas, and Wade (1991) have provided some indication that social skills deficits may be relatively stable in schizophrenia patients, less is known about the long-term stability of skill deficits in other diagnostic groups.

Gender and Interpersonal Functioning

Gender is a variable often neglected in studies of schizophrenic populations (Lewis, 1992; Wahl & Hunter, 1992). However, a sizable literature now suggests that the course of the illness is more benign in women than in men. For example, female patients have a characteristically later age of onset of the illness (Häfner, Maurer, Löffler, & Riecher-Rössler, 1993). Females also have shorter and less frequent psychotic episodes, and show a better response to treatment than do their male counterparts (e.g. Angermeyer, Kuhn, & Goldstein, 1990; Goldstein, Tsuang, & Faraone, 1989; Hass, Glick, Clarkin, Spencer, & Lewis, 1990; McGlashan & Bardenstein, 1990).

The "advantages" conferred upon female schizophrenics also extend into the interpersonal realm. Evidence suggests that, compared to males, female patients have a milder range of interpersonal problems and are characterized by better social functioning. Both Dworkin (1990) and Perry, Moore, and Braff (1995) have reported that female schizophrenics, as a group, scored significantly better than male schizophrenics on the Social Competency Index (Zigler & Phillips, 1961). In another representative study, Andia and her colleagues (1995) found that women with schizophrenia were more likely than men with the disorder to have been married, to live independently, and to be employed, despite having similar symptom profiles. Moreover, females in this study obtained higher levels of social functioning despite being maintained on lower doses of antipsychotic medication than the male patients. Finally, while more women than men in this study were diagnosed with paranoid schizophrenia (a subtype generally associated with better prognosis), these differences in social functioning were apparent even when only the nonparanoid patients were considered.

Similar gender differences have also been reported by other research groups. Using a role-play test to assess social skill, Mueser and his colleagues reported a clear advantage for female patients across a range of different measures (Mueser et al., 1990). Although they did not differ from male patients with respect to their symptomatology, females with schizophrenia were more skilled than males in the appropriateness of the duration of their speech (very short or very long responses were rated less favorably), their meshing or turn-taking abilities during conversations, aspects of their verbal content in specific role-play scenarios, and their overall social skills. There is also evidence that the relationship between gender and social skill may be specific to schizophrenia. In the Mueser et al. investigation, gender was unrelated to social skill in either the affective control or the normal control group.

It would be misleading to say that gender differences are universally documented. Indeed, in the study just described, no differences were found between the male and female schizophrenia patients on measures of social adjustment such as the SAS-II and the QLS. However, when significant gender differences are found, the results typically point toward better interpersonal functioning in female schizophrenics. Angermeyer et al. (1990) reviewed a series of articles related to schizophrenia and interpersonal functioning, considering studies that focused on occupational status, social integration, and overall global social adaptation. In approximately half of these studies a gender difference was observable. Moreover, in all but two of the studies that did report a significant difference, females were judged to be outperforming male schizophrenics with respect to their interpersonal adjustment.

Why do women look so much better on measures of social adaptation? No definitive explanations to this question are yet available. However, with respect to marriage, the later age of onset of schizophrenic symptoms in women may at least be a partial explanation. At the very least, this would increase the likelihood that they might marry and have children before the development of the disorder. In contrast, because the majority of men with schizophrenia show symptoms before the age of 30 (Loranger, 1984), they are likely to be showing signs of psychological and social impairment at precisely the time that they might otherwise be expected to be meeting possible marriage partners. Moreover, Gold (1984) has suggested that a given degree of psychosocial handicap will have a more detrimental influence on the marriage prospects of men than it will on women. Even in today's modern culture, men are still expected to play a lead role in the courtship process. To the extent that he is lacking in assertiveness, the schizophrenic man is therefore likely to be less successful in dating than the passive schizophrenic women. Related to this point, Planansky and Johnston (1967) have shown that the women who married men with schizophrenia rated themselves as being very much more active in the pursuit of their husbands during courtship than did the wives of men who did not have a psychiatric illness.

Another possibility is that women generally tend to show social competence and social skill advantages compared to men (e.g., Buck, 1984; Hall, 1985). To the extent that this is true, the findings of greater social competence in women with schizophrenia may simply mirror the social competence and social skill advantages found for women in the wider population. However, findings of greater social skills in females relative to males are not invariably reported. In some cases similar levels of social abilities have been reported for both males and females (e.g., Feingold, 1988; Hyde & Linn, 1988). In yet other instances, social advantages have been reported more for males rather than females (e.g., Hollandsworth & Wall, 1977). For these reasons, any global explanations for the social skills advantages of schizophrenic women should perhaps be treated with great caution.

Societal explanations also exist for the female advantage in social functioning. Gender differences in social roles or in society's tolerance for deviant behaviors may result in greater or earlier social morbidity in males. For example, withdrawn behavior or idiosyncratic thought processes may be either detected earlier in males or tolerated less benignly than if they occur in women. This could result in earlier and/or more severe disruption of social roles. As we have already noted, female schizophrenics might find it easier to meet social roles or expectations than do male schizophrenics. However, as Mueser et al. (1990) have correctly pointed out, these advantages may be consequences of, rather than causes of women's greater social skillfulness. In the Mueser et al. study, female patients were evaluated using the same behavioral criteria as those that were applied to the male patients. No social bias was therefore operating in this study. Yet the female patients did show social skills advantages. At the more general level, these advantages may allow them to negotiate their way through the social world in a manner that engenders more tolerance and less hostility than that experienced by their male counterparts. To the extent that we create our social environments, the social environments of female schizophrenics may be more benign than those of male patients.

Finally, the social advantages apparent in female patients may simply reflect the fact that women, for reasons that are not yet clear, tend to have a somewhat milder form of schizophrenic illness. Related to this, some authors have speculated about the role of estrogen in protecting women from excessive dopamine turnover, which has long been implicated as important in the pathogenesis of schizophrenia (Häfner et al., 1993; Seeman, 1983). Others have suggested that the fact that women show greater hemispheric bilaterality of cognitive functioning may work to their advantage (Flor-Henry, 1985). Less lateralization of cognitive abilities may lead to greater sparing of skills in the event that any damage to the brain occurs during the development or course of schizophrenia.

Perhaps most likely is that there is subtle interaction between basic pathology and societal rules, norms, and expectations. Although no unequivocal statements can be made on this issue at present, it is clear that gender is a variable that demands serious consideration in all future research on interpersonal functioning in schizophrenia.

The Relation Between Social Functioning and Clinical Symptoms

To what extent do the symptoms of schizophrenia impair effective social functioning? This is clearly an interesting and important question. Schizophrenia is characterized by a number of symptoms, such as hallucinations, delusions, affective flattening, and anhedonia. Each or all of these might be expected to be associated with interpersonal difficulties. In the section below we examine the current evidence linking problems in interpersonal functioning with positive and negative symptoms.

Developed in an attempt to explain the heterogeneity in schizophrenia, the division between positive and negative symptoms (Andreasen & Olsen,

1982) is based on whether the symptoms of the disorder are florid, or rather represent a "defect" or failure to display a "normal" behavior. Symptoms such as delusions, hallucinations, formal thought disorder, or bizarre behavior would thus be regarded as positive symptoms, while alogia (greatly reduced speech or speech conveying very little information), affective flattening, avolition (apathy), or anhedonia would be considered characteristic negative symptoms.

Positive Symptoms

Positive symptoms in general do not appear to be particularly related to social adjustment (Bellack, Morrison, Wixted, & Mueser, 1990; Jackson et al., 1989; Perry et al., 1995; see also Dworkin, 1990). However, reports of associations between more positive symptoms and impaired social competency can be found in the literature (Appelo et al., 1992; Corrigan & Toomey, 1995). This suggests that intact thought processes may be necessary for effective social functioning. Precisely which symptoms might compromise which domains of interpersonal functioning and under what circumstances, however, are questions that must await further investigation in this area.

Negative Symptoms

Examining the association between negative symptoms and social functioning is not as straightforward as it might appear on first inspection. As Dworkin (1992) has noted, many ratings on the Scale for the Assessment of Negative Symptoms (SANS; Andreasen, 1982) are based on the patient's behavior during an interview. Yet an interview is obviously an interpersonal situation. Moreover, the ratings that are made are based on such things as unchanging facial expression, decreased spontaneous movements, and poor eye contact. These behavioral indicators of negative symptoms could thus actually be the result of social skills deficits.

Recognizing this problem, what does an examination of the current literature tell us about the association between negative symptoms and social adjustment or social skills? Perhaps not surprisingly, negative symptoms do appear to be associated with poorer social functioning, particularly when more global measures of social adjustment are used (e.g., Appelo et al., 1992; Blanchard, Mueser, & Bellack, in press; Jackson et al., 1989; Van der Does, Dingemans, Linszen, Nugter, & Scholte, 1993).

In a specific examination of this issue, Bellack and his colleagues (Bellack, Morrison, Mueser, & Wade, 1989; see also Bellack & Wixted, 1990) administered the SANS to a sample of schizophrenia inpatients. These patients were then further divided into a group that had more severe negative symptoms and a group that had less severe negative symptoms (i.e., positive symptom and mixed symptom patients, see Andreasen & Olsen, 1982). Consistent with prediction, the negative symptom patients were found to be significantly more impaired on the SAS-II and the QLS than were the other schizophrenia patients or the control patients with schizoaffective disorder or bipolar disorder.

Less compelling, however, are the data linking negative symptoms with more specific social deficits. Jackson et al. (1989) report impressive associations between negative symptoms and social skills during a role-play task. Corrigan and his colleagues (Corrigan, Green, & Toomey, 1994), have also found that patients' scores on a scale assessing blunted affect, emotional withdrawal, and motor retardation were negatively correlated with their performance on a social cue recognition task. However Appelo et al. (1992) concluded that negative symptoms did not explain specific skill deficits in their sample of schizophrenia patients, and no compelling links between negative symptoms and problem-solving ability were reported by Bellack et al. (1994). Finally, using the Physical Anhedonia Scale and the Social Anhedonia Scale (see Chapman, Chapman, & Raulin, 1976), Blanchard, Bellack, and Mueser (1994) found no relationship between either of these two anhedonia scales and measures of social skill in their patient samples.

Taken together, these results suggest that, although negative symptoms may not be particularly associated with any clear social skill deficit, negative symptoms do seem to compromise overall social competence. Whether this occurs because of shared measurement variance is not entirely clear. However, given that associations between negative symptoms and social functioning have been found, it becomes reasonable to ask whether the social deficits of schizophrenia patients can be explained solely by negative symptoms.

The answer to this question is "probably not,"

for the following reasons. First, while schizophrenics with negative symptoms generally perform less well than nonnegative symptom schizophrenics on measures of interpersonal skill, nonnegative schizophrenics consistently perform worse than affectively ill or community control groups (Bellack et al., 1989; Bellack, Morrison, Wixted, & Mueser, 1990; Dworkin, 1990; Dworkin et al., 1991) This suggests that social impairments are associated with schizophrenia in general rather than only being linked to the negative symptoms of the disorder in specific.

Second, in Dworkin's (1990) study of schizophrenic twins, male patients exhibited greater asociality and withdrawn behavior, as well as poorer premorbid social competence, than did females. This, as we have seen, is in keeping with the generally better social functioning of female versus male patients. Of particular interest with respect to the current discussion, however, was that Dworkin found no significant differences between the sexes in the symptoms that they exhibited. Thus, the differences in social functioning found in this sample are not easily explained simply by reference to symptoms (see also Andia et al., 1995).

Taken together, these results suggest that negative symptoms and social functioning may reflect different processes in the development and manifestation of schizophrenia. Thus, while it appears likely that negative symptoms may exacerbate the poor interpersonal abilities of schizophrenics, negative symptoms in and of themselves probably do not provide a full explanation for the existence of these interpersonal deficits. Rather, the data point to the likely existence of some more focal deficit that is related to interpersonal functioning. The extant data thus support the early observation made by Strauss, Carpenter, and Bartko (1974) that positive symptoms, negative symptoms, and "disorders of relating" might well represent three distinct dimensions of schizophrenia (see also Lenzenweger, Dworkin, & Wethington, 1991).

Are Interpersonal Deficits Apparent Before the Onset of Schizophrenia?

If the social deficits that characterize schizophrenia are either a consequence of the symptoms of disorder or are iatrogenic, arising from treatment (see Brady, 1984), we would not expect them to be observable prior to the onset of the illness. However, information about patients' interpersonal functioning prior to the development of the disorder suggests that interpersonal difficulties often appear well before any psychiatric illness is diagnosed. A large number of studies employing a wide variety of research designs have demonstrated that schizophrenics display a range of social deficits in the premorbid stages of the illness that are similar to the deficits that characterize them in the morbid phase (see Amminger & Mutschlechner, 1994; Childers & Harding, 1990; Gureje, Aderibigbe, Olley, & Bamidele, 1994). Importantly, interpersonal deficits have also been found to characterize individuals who are simply at a heightened risk for developing the disorder. In other words, although interpersonal problems are frequently apparent in the early stages of the illness, interpersonal difficulties may also predate any signs of illness, often by many years.

One way to examine this issue is to explore the premorbid adjustment of currently diagnosed patients using retrospective reports. An example of a scale that might be used for a study such as this is the Premorbid Adjustment Scale (PAS; Cannon-Spoor, Potkin, & Wyatt, 1982). This is concerned with such issues as how many friends the schizophrenic had in childhood and the nature of his or her interactions with the opposite sex during adolescence. These assessments might be made on the basis of a review of school records or from an interview with the patient or a close relative.

In general, retrospective studies of this type have shown that schizophrenia patients do have poorer premorbid social histories—marked by greater social isolation and inability—than either those with other psychiatric disorders (e.g., Gureje et al., 1994) or healthy controls (e.g., Cannon-Spoor et al., 1982). Furthermore, such studies suggest that the level of premorbid functioning obtained by schizophrenia patients may also have important prognostic significance. Poor premorbid social functioning has been found to be correlated with more chronic and frequent hospitalizations (Cannon-Spoor et al., 1982). In contrast, good premorbid functioning has been shown to be predictive of more complete remissions after an episode of illness (Amminger & Mutschlechner, 1994). Premorbid functioning has also been shown to be predictive of the level of community functioning and adjustment that can be attained once the illness has developed (Childers & Harding, 1990). Thus social difficulties, as indexed via measures of premorbid adjustment, appear to be an important prognostic indicator in schizophrenia.

However, retrospective investigations are not without methodological problems. Of primary concern is the accuracy of the historical reports. Memory does not improve with time. Moreover, potential biases such as the tendency to reinterpret and remember the past in a manner that is more consistent with present events may compromise data obtained from retrospective studies (but see Brewin, Andrews, & Gotlib, 1993; see also Maughan & Rutter, 1977). Because of this, those interested in the premorbid functioning of schizophrenia patients have sought alternative avenues of exploration.

In a creative study, Walker and Lewine (1990) examined home movies of diagnosed schizophrenics and their siblings. These home movies featured the patients and their healthy siblings interacting during childhood, *years before any psychiatric difficulties became apparent in one of the children.* Despite this, independent raters, who were blind to the identity of the child who later became schizophrenic, were able to successfully identify the vulnerable child. This finding is all the more striking when we consider that the Walker and Lewine sample was selected to include patients whose parents reported that their children showed no unusual behavior or signs of illness when they were growing up! Although raters were given no specific instructions about how to evaluate the children in the home movies, they indicated that their decisions were frequently guided by interpersonal aspects of the children's behavior. In particular, such behaviors as decreased social responsiveness, reduced eye contact, and lack of positive affect were mentioned, although other factors, such as motor behavior, also influenced the decisions.

Still more strong evidence for a premorbid social deficit in schizophrenia comes from examinations of high-risk populations. In the classic form of high-risk investigation, the offspring of parents with diagnosed schizophrenic illness are recruited in childhood and then studied prospectively. These children, who are presumed to be at heightened risk for psychiatric disorder themselves, can be followed closely as they mature. In this way, high-risk studies hold the potential to provide valuable information about the manner in which schizophrenia-like social deficits may develop in the absence of overt psychiatric symptoms.[3]

Consistent with results obtained using retrospective reports, data from high-risk studies provide further evidence that those at risk for schizophrenia experience more problems in their social functioning. For example, Dworkin and his colleagues have used the New York High-Risk Project (Erlenmeyer-Kimling et al., 1984) to demonstrate that adolescents at risk for schizophrenia are rated as being lower in social competence than adolescents who are at risk for affective illness (Dworkin et al., 1990, 1991; Dworkin, Lewis, Cornblatt, & Erlenmeyer-Kimling, 1994). These evaluations, which were made by trained raters, were based on information from interviews conducted with the adolescents themselves and from interviews with their parents. More specifically, the adolescents at risk for schizophrenia also reported significantly poorer peer relationships and decreased hobbies and interests relative to the affective controls. Although this study tells us little about why these adolescents had fewer friends, Dworkin et al.'s data do demonstrate that social difficulties may be important in identifying subjects at high risk for the later development of schizophrenia.

No "gold standard" measure exists to assess social competence in all studies. This makes comparisons across different research sites rather difficult. Nonetheless, data from other high-risk projects also confirm that, as a group, children at elevated risk for schizophrenia can be differentiated from both healthy controls and other psychiatric and medical high-risk groups. Although the particular interpersonal problems that characterize these children (assessed from self-reports, parents' reports, and teachers' reports) tend to be quite varied, withdrawn and detached behavior, or defiant and aggressive behavior, or combinations of both, are usually highlighted (Hans, Marcus, Henson, Auerbach, & Mirsky, 1992; Rolf, 1972; Watt, 1978; Watt & Lubensky, 1976; Weintraub, Neale, & Liebert, 1975; Weintraub, Prinz, & Neale, 1978; see also Asarnow, 1988, for a review). However, gender may again be playing an important role. Although some studies report that high-risk males are more likely to be aggressive and disagreeable (Hans et al., 1992; Watt, 1978; Watt & Lubensky, 1976), high-risk females appear to be more likely to be withdrawn (Watt, 1978; Watt & Lubensky, 1976).

High-risk investigations often select subjects based on their genetic relatedness to an identified patient. However, this does not have to be the case. An alternative methodology is simply to select subjects who score high on measures known to be predictive of later schizophrenia. Using this approach, Zborowski and Garske (1993) selected male subjects who scored high on a self-report measure of schizotypic traits involving perceptual abberations and magical ideation (the Per-Mag Scale; see Chapman, Chapman, & Miller, 1982; Chapman, Chapman, Kwapil, Eckblad, & Zinser, 1994). These subjects were then compared to control male undergraduates who scored low on the same self-report scale. Although the two groups were comparable with respect to their age and class rank, the groups differed in important ways when they interacted with a female research assistant in a videotaped interview. Subjects high on the Per-Mag scale showed more odd behavior during the interview. They were also rated as being more avoidant. Interestingly, the female interviewers who interacted with these subjects reported that they felt more anxious, more angry, and less curious when they were interacting with the hypothetically schizophrenia-prone males than did the research assistants who interacted with the control males. These data suggest that undergraduate males who are not psychiatrically ill but who are at statistically higher risk for the development of schizophrenia show interpersonal anomalies during social interactions. Importantly, their odd and avoidant behavior also appears to create social discomfort for those with whom they interact.

In summary, the available evidence from a wide range of studies suggests that interpersonal deficits predate the development of schizophrenia. This means that interpersonal deficits cannot simply be consequences of institutionalization or medication. Interpersonal deficits are also not explained entirely by the presence of positive or negative symptoms. Whether social functioning deficits reflect a vulnerability to the disorder or simply create the kinds of stressful circumstances that might trigger the onset of schizophrenia is not yet clear. Social difficulties may be a manifestation of an underlying diathesis, a behavioral marker that engenders increased social stress (perhaps from irritated peers or family), or both. To the extent that impairments in social functioning appear to characterize both patients with schizophrenia and those at risk of developing the disorder, however, understanding the origins of these social deficits becomes of paramount importance.

Exploring the Role of Cognition in Interpersonal Dysfunction

One of the most active areas of research at the present time centers around the associations among information processing, attention, and interpersonal functioning. The concept of information processing arose from attempts to define the sequence of operations that occurs in response to stimulation in the central nervous system (CNS). More specifically, it refers to a wide set of neurocognitive operations that are necessary to observe, decode, and process incoming information. Attention, difficult to define operationally, is conventionally viewed as having two elements: involuntary attention, which is focused on appetitive needs, and voluntary attention, which is a sort of "vigilance" that requires a conscious and sustained focus on the task at hand.

A large body of literature well documents the difficulties that schizophrenia patients experience in aspects of their neurocognitive functioning relative to healthy controls (see Braff, 1993, for a review). For example, in reaction time studies that require subjects to respond to a stimulus as quickly and appropriately as possible, schizophrenia patients do poorly compared to controls (see Nuechterlein, 1977). They also show deficits on the Continuous Performance Task (CPT; e.g., Cornblatt, Lenzenweger, & Erlenmeyer-Kimling, 1989). This requires the subject to attend to a series of letters or numbers and then to detect an intermittently presented target stimulus that appears on the screen along with other letters or numbers. On the Span of Apprehension tasks (SOA), which are a measure of the number of stimuli that can be attended to, apprehended, and reported in a single brief exposure, schizophrenic patients also perform less well than psychiatric and nonpsychiatric controls (e.g., Neale, 1971; Neale, McIntyre, Fox, & Cromwell, 1969).[4] Finally, in studies that involve working memory (Park, Holzman, & Goldman-Rakic, 1995), backward masking (Green, Nuechterlein, & Mintz, 1994a, 1994b), or other cognitive demands such as sensory gating (e.g., Grillon, Courchesne, Ameli, Geyer, & Braff, 1990), schizophrenia patients also typically perform less well than controls.

At the present time, the weight of evidence suggests that schizophrenics experience problems with the active, functional allocation of attentional resources. Essentially, they are unable to attend well on demand. There is also evidence that attentional dysfunctions may be indicators of a biological susceptibility to at least some forms of schizophrenia (Cornblatt, Lenzenweger, Dworkin, & Erlenmeyer-Kimling, 1992). Not surprisingly, then, it is from within this type of conceptual framework that some of the most promising work in the area of social adjustment in schizophrenia is now being generated.

The idea that attentional deficits and information-processing deficiencies play a role in poor social performance is not new (see Liberman, 1982). It is also intuitively very plausible. The interpersonal skills that most of us take for granted are actually dependent on a wide range of cognitive operations. They are also much more complex than we typically appreciate. For example, entering into a conversation requires us to selectively focus our attention on the appropriate stimulus (our conversational partner) while at the same time filtering out the rest of the background noise that is around us. In addition, to respond appropriately we need to remember what our partner has said, and to generate a comment of our own that is related in some way. This places obvious demands on our memory systems and on higher level information-processing and executive skills. Moreover, all of this must be done while simultaneously processing the multiple verbal and nonverbal cues that our partner generates.

Perhaps we should not, therefore, be too surprised to learn that the conversational abilities of normal subjects can be easily disrupted. In a demonstration of this, Barch and Berenbaum (1994) designed an elegant manipulation that required healthy undergraduates to complete a complex processing task while at the same time talking to an interviewer. The students' performance under this condition was then compared to their performance during a control interview that did not have a concurrent task. Under the condition of reduced processing capacity, the students' conversational skills showed marked impairment. More specifically, they spoke less, showed less syntactic complexity in their language, and said "um" and "ah" significantly more than they did during the control interview. This experimental manipulation thus reveals just how important certain facets of information processing are likely to be to smooth social performance. They also suggest that those who more ordinarily lack sufficient cognitive resources to meet competing demands might well be expected to experience difficulties making sense of and negotiating the interpersonal world. Once again, this struggle is highlighted in the comments of schizophrenia patients themselves:

> I have trouble concentrating and keeping my mind on one thing at a time, especially when I'm with people. I can hear what they're saying, but I can't keep up with them and make sense of the conversation. I lose my grip on being part of the conversation and drift off. It's not so bad when I'm talking with just one other person, but if I'm trying to tune in to a conversation with several people, things come in too fast and I get lost. It's hard for me to contribute to a conversation when the ideas get blurred. (Liberman, 1982, p. 78)

Does Cognitive Task Performance Correlate with Measures of Interpersonal Skill?

This is a central question in efforts to understand social functioning in schizophrenia. However, it is an issue that is only now beginning to attract the attention of researchers. In a review of the literature linking neurocognitive functioning and social competence, Green (1996) noted that only one of the studies that he examined had been conducted before 1990. Green further highlighted the difficulties of drawing conclusions across studies, not least because the cognitive measures used and the assessments of social functioning varied considerably across the different investigations.

Despite this, some interesting findings do appear to be emerging. For example, Lysaker, Bell, and Beam-Goulet (1995) have reported that the performance of schizophrenic and schizoaffective patients on the Wisconsin Card Sort Test (WCST; Heaton, 1981) predicts their functioning and social skills in a work setting one year later. A link has also been made between performance on the WCST and later social adjustment measured using the SAS-II (see Jaeger & Douglas, 1992). Because the WCST is generally thought to tap such skills as executive functioning, concept formation, and cognitive flexibility, these data imply that skills such as these are likely very necessary for social competence.

Memory skills also appear to be important, not only for social competence in general (e.g., Goldman et al., 1993), but also for social skills in particular. Poor memory has been related to greater social skills impairments in both schizophrenic and schizoaffective inpatients but not in patients with affective disorder (Mueser, Bellack, Douglas, & Wade, 1991). Memory has also been found to be linked to the ability to implement solutions in a role play task (Bellack et al., 1994).

The final neurocognitive skill that emerges with some frequency in the neurocognitive literature concerns vigilance. Vigilance is an attentional process, which is very often measured using the Continuous Performance Test. In a representative study, Bowen and her colleagues (1994) administered two measures of visual vigilance (the CPT and the Degraded-Stimulus CPT, or DS-CPT), a measure of immediate recall memory (the Digit Span Distractibility Test, DSDT), and a measure of early visual processing (the Span of Apprehension (SOA) test) to schizophrenia patients and psychiatrically well controls. Performance on these neurocognitive measures was then correlated with interpersonal performance, which was measured using a subset of the items from the AIPSS. As might be expected, significant relationships were found between schizophrenic patients' cognitive functioning and their interpersonal skills. However, the cognitive function that was most related to performance in the role plays of interpersonal skills was vigilance level as measured by the CPT. Because each AIPSS role play began with a brief videotape that created the context, sustained concentration is likely to have been very important with respect to the patient's ability to do the task. Problems in this domain may have resulted in incomplete intake of information and, subsequently, inadequate responding. Thus, memory problems and problems with attention or vigilance appear to be implicated in some of the more specific aspects of interpersonal functioning (see also Corrigan et al., 1994; Penn, Mueser, Spaulding, Hope, & Reed, 1995).

We should further note that the role of attentional dysfunction in the manifestation of interpersonal deficits is also suggested by results of one of the high-risk projects described earlier. As part of a comprehensive assessment battery, subjects from the New York High Risk Project were tested on a wide array of attentional measures allowing a single "attentional index" score to be assigned. Consistent with findings discussed earlier for diagnosed patients, children's attention scores were found to be highly correlated with two factors derived from the Personality Disorders Examination (PDE; Loranger, Susman, Oldham, & Russakoff, 1987) and measured in adulthood. These factors reflected a relative insensitivity to other individuals coupled with an indifference to their feelings and an avoidance of interpersonal interactions whenever possible (see Cornblatt et al., 1992). Thus, children who exhibited deficits in their attentional skills were, as adults, less socially sensitive and more socially indifferent, and also more socially avoidant. Moreover, using data from a second sample in this same project, Dworkin et al. (1993) were further able to demonstrate that poor childhood attentional dysfunction was predictive of significantly poorer social competence when the children reached adolescence. Thus, it appears that even in those simply at high-risk for schizophrenia the link between attention and interpersonal performance is still apparent. In children at risk as well as in schizophrenic adults, deficits in attention are associated with deficits in social competence and social skills.

In summary, the available literature provides evidence that social competence in general and social abilities more specifically are related to patients' abilities to perform well on a number of neurocognitive tasks. These are also some hints in the literature that the link between neurocognitive measures and social functioning may be more important for females than it is for males (see Mueser, Blanchard, & Bellack, 1995; Penn, Mueser, & Spaulding, 1996). Currently, as Green (1996) has noted, the most promising predictors of social competence or community functioning appear to be the WCST and measures of memory—particularly secondary memory. Unlike immediate or short-term memory, secondary memory is the ability to remember information after a time delay. Secondary verbal memory, together with vigilance, also appears to be important with respect to more specific social skills. Although future studies may also support the predictive validity of other neurocognitive measures such as reaction time (see Penn et al., 1995), at the present time measures of vigilance, secondary verbal memory, and the skills tapped by the WCST appear to be the most promising candidates with respect to understanding social functioning in schizophrenia. Again, however, the extent to which these findings are specific to schizophrenia warrants further consideration.

Social Cognition in Schizophrenia

Our understanding of social competence in schizophrenia is likely to be greatly improved by more extensive information about the role of neurocognitive skills such as vigilance and memory. However, it is unlikely that these measures alone will provide all the answers that we need. Penn and his colleagues (Penn, Corrigan, Bentall, Racenstein, & Newman, 1997) have already noted that traditional measures of neurocognition leave much variance in social functioning unaccounted for. What this suggests is that we would also do well to explore other avenues of inquiry in our search for more information about the possible cognitive underpinnings of impaired interpersonal functioning.

An area that is just beginning to attract interest is social cognition. Social cognition involves the perception, interpretation, and processing of social information (Ostrom, 1984). Unlike nonsocial cognition, which involves the kind of stimuli described earlier (reaction time, CPT), social cognition concerns stimuli that are personally relevant. Moreover, although social cognition obviously requires nonsocial cognitive skills, it also involves other skills. It is these skills that are now being viewed as likely to be highly relevant to competent social functioning.

What Kinds of Difficulties in Social Cognition do Schizophrenia Patients Show?

Systematic research in this area is still in its infancy. Already, however, it is clear that schizophrenia patients struggle with some kinds of social processing tasks that most of us perform with relative ease. A case in point is emotion recognition (see Morrison, Bellack, & Mueser, 1988, for a critical review). As well as having difficulty with their own emotions, schizophrenics seem to have problems deciphering the emotional states of others. Whether this is a specific deficit or simply a reflection of the fact that schizophrenic patients generally perform poorly across a wide range of tasks is not yet clear (Chapman & Chapman, 1973; see also Penn et al., 1997). However, several studies have now indicated that schizophrenics have difficulty in correctly identifying emotional expressions in photographs and videotapes (Kerr & Neale, 1993; Mueser et al., 1996), although deficits in this regard are not invariably found (see Joseph, Sturgeon, & Leff, 1992). In some instances, patients with schizophrenia may fail to comment on emotional expression at all (e.g., Cramer, Bowen, & O'Neill, 1992; Hellewell, Connell, & Deakin, 1994). Similar findings have also been demonstrated in psychosis-prone, schizotypic individuals (Altman & Blaney, 1996; Poreh, Whitman, Weber, & Ross, 1994; but see also Toomey & Schuldberg, 1995). Moreover, there is some possibility that these processing deficits are especially marked for expressions involving negative affect (Morrison, Bellack, & Bashore, 1988; Pilowsky & Bassett, 1980).

Interestingly, Mueser et al. (1996) have further reported strong associations between schizophrenia patients' abilities to identify facial emotions from photographs and nurses' ratings of patients' social skills in a hospital setting. This suggests, as Wallace (1984) has previously noted, that social perception may be particularly important with respect to social skill. Mueser et al. (1996) also provide some evidence linking difficulties in emotion recognition to negative rather than to positive symptoms. More specifically, higher Anergia scores on the Brief Psychiatric Rating Scale (Overall & Gorham, 1962) were associated with worse performance on the Facial Emotion Identification Test (Kerr & Neale, 1993). No significant correlations were found between facial emotion recognition and thought disorder, however.

There is also preliminary evidence that schizophrenia patients are less socially knowledgeable than are patients with other psychiatric problems. In an interesting study, Cutting and Murphy (1990) gave patients multiple-choice questions that were designed to tap two knowledge domains. The first concerned practical knowledge (e.g., "Why is it not safe to drink tap water in some countries?"). Patients were also asked questions designed to assess their knowledge in a more social domain (e.g., "How would you tell a friend politely that they had stayed too long?"). For this latter question, the answer choices included saying, "There's no more coffee left," saying, "You'd better go. I'm fed up with you staying too long", or (correct answer), saying, "Excuse me. I've got an appointment with a friend." Compared with manic and depressed controls, the schizophrenia patients showed significant impairment on the social knowledge test. Interestingly, however, the nonsocial knowledge test did not discriminate between the schizophrenics and the manics, although both of these patients groups scored significantly worse than the depressed patients.

As a final example of work in the area of social cognition and schizophrenia, we highlight a study recently completed by Corcoran, Mercer and Frith (1995). This study was designed to examine how well schizophrenia patients and patients with other psychiatric conditions were able to pick up hints made by others. Schizophrenia patients, depressed or anxious psychiatric controls, and normal controls were given brief scenarios that featured interactions between two characters. At the end of each scenario, one of the characters dropped a very obvious hint (e.g., "I want to wear that blue shirt but it's creased."). Subjects were then asked to say what the character meant and what he or she was hinting at. If the subject failed to get the hint, an even more obvious cue was given (e.g., "It's in the ironing basket."). Interestingly, the schizophrenia patients did poorly on this task, scoring significantly lower than subjects in the two control groups. Findings of this nature again bring to mind a comment that we noted earlier. As the ex-wife of "Jon" said, "It was as though some strange deficiency prevented him from understanding some things that seem perfectly obvious to most people."

Thus, across a wide range of social-cognitive tasks, schizophrenia patients appear to do poorly. Not only do they have difficulties with respect to reading emotional cues, but they also appear to be less socially facile. Moreover, they fail to spot the kinds of subtle (or not so subtle) social hints that most of us detect without difficulty. Taken together, these findings suggest that everyday social encounters are unlikely to be smooth for schizophrenia patients and those with whom they interact. As we shall see shortly, this does appear to be the case.

Are Tasks of Social Cognition Better Predictors of Social Behavior than Tasks of Non-Social Cognition?

To the extent that measures of social cognition are more ecologically valid than measures of nonsocial cognition, they might be expected to correlate more strongly with measures of social functioning. In a test of this idea, Corrigan and Toomey (1995) administered a battery of nonsocial cognition measures to a sample of patients with schizophrenia and schizoaffective disorder. The measures of nonsocial cognition included a measure of vigilance (the DS-CPT), a measure of immediate memory (the DSDT), a measure of secondary memory (the Rey Auditory Learning Test), and a measure of conceptual flexibility (the WCST). In addition, a measure of social cognition, the Social Cue Recognition Test (SCRT) was also administered. The SCRT consisted of eight videotaped vignettes that featured two or three people interacting in a social situation. After viewing the vignettes, subjects were asked to answer a series of true-false questions about the interpersonal cues they saw in the interactions. The measures of nonsocial and social cognition were then correlated with performance on the AIPPS (described earlier). Social cue sensitivity was found to be related to receiving (detecting a problem), processing (coming up with a solution), and sending (role-playing the solution) skills. In contrast, none of the nonsocial cognitive variables predicted performance on the AIPSS. These findings suggest that measures of social cognition are more strongly associated with interpersonal problem-solving skills than are measures of nonsocial cognition. The same conclusion was reached by Penn and his colleagues in a similar study conducted the following year (Penn, Spaulding, Reed, & Sullivan, 1996).

Thus, it appears that future researchers would do well to explore the role of social cognition in the interpersonal functioning of schizophrenia patients more fully (see Penn et al., 1997 for a review). Social cognition differs from nonsocial cognition in many ways. Moreover, in the studies that have been conducted to date, measures of social cognition appear to be more valid predictors of social performance than do measures of nonsocial cognition. However, until it can be demonstrated that the two groups of tasks that were used in these studies were equivalent in terms of their psychometric properties and in how difficult they were (see Chapman & Chapman, 1973), this conclusion must obviously remain tentative. Much more remains to be done, although the early findings certainly seem quite promising.

What Are the Social Consequences of Schizophrenic Patients' Interpersonal Difficulties?

So far in this chapter we have focused on the interpersonal functioning of patients diagnosed with schizophrenia. As should now be quite evident, this is a disorder that is characterized by a considerable range of social difficulties. Although the precise form of the social anomalies that are observed tends to vary from study to study, one conclusion can be safely drawn. Schizophrenia patients tend to be less skilled and less fluid in complex interpersonal situations relative to members of the general population. In many cases, they are also more impaired than are patients with other severe psychiatric conditions.

This may be one reason interacting with a person with schizophrenia does not seem to be easy for the average person. Earlier, we described the results of a study in which female interviewers interacted with male college students who scored high on two scales associated with increased risk for schizophrenia (Zborowski & Garske, 1993). Here, it is important to keep in mind that the male students had only schizotypic traits and had not been diagnosed with schizophrenia. Nonetheless, interacting with these males resulted in more anger, increased anxiety, and less interest on the part of the female interviewers than did interactions with males who did not exhibit these schizotypic traits.

In a more recent study, Nisenson, Berenbaum, and Good (1996) had student research assistants form brief friendships with schizophrenic patients at a local inpatient psychiatric facility. Although the students were specifically selected because of their congenial dispositions, over the course of the two weeks of the study, the amount of negativity that the students expressed toward the patients increased significantly. Findings such as these lend credence to the idea that interacting with patients with schizophrenia may present a considerable social challenge.[5]

Blanchard and Panzarella (1998) have further speculated on how affective flattening, one characteristic symptom of schizophrenia, may disrupt interpersonal functioning. More specifically, they hypothesized that diminished emotional expressiveness in the schizophrenic person may be interpreted by others as reflective of a lack of feeling. In other words, family, friends, and coworkers may interpret blunted affect as apathy or insensitivity. To the extent that this is true, this might be expected to damage interpersonal relations. Indeed, Blanchard and Panzarella reported preliminary findings that highlight how readily observers misinterpret the feelings of schizophrenics based on facial cues.

Misinterpretation does, in fact, appear to be the most accurate description of what happens. This is because the literature provides no evidence that the affective flattening that we see in schizophrenia patients represents a lack of true emotional experiences. Certainly schizophrenia patients with flat affect display fewer overt facial expressions than do controls when they view emotional stimuli such as film clips. However, they report experiencing emotion at equal or greater levels (Berenbaum & Oltmans, 1992; Kring, Kerr, Smith, & Neale, 1993; Kring & Neale, 1996). Indeed, in some studies, schizophrenia patients actually appear to be more aroused (as measured by skin conductance) by emotional stimuli than are normals (Kring & Neale, 1996). Thus, there appears to be a lack of congruence between the expressive and the subjective experience response systems of emotion in schizophrenia. This suggests that the lack of affective expression among schizophrenic patients may not be due to an underlying experiential deficiency, but rather may represent a failure to express the emotions that are being experienced in a manner that is detectable by others. Whether this simply reflects a self-monitoring deficit is not yet clear (see Sims & Neale, 1996). Alternatively, these findings could reflect a deficit in motor behavior such that patients find it difficult to express emotions in their facial expressions. The search for the answers to questions such as these is likely to occupy researchers in this area for some years to come.

Interpersonal Stress and the Onset of Schizophrenia

In addition to exhibiting problems in the social domain and making some of the people with whom they interact uncomfortable, schizophrenia patients also appear to be sensitive to the social environments in which they live. This is, of course, an area with a long history. As Hatfield (1987) observes, after World War II the view that problems in child rearing and family environment lay at the root of most adult problems gained ascendancy. By the 1950s, many of the theories of the development of schizophrenia were concerned with pathological family dynamics that were viewed as causally related to the onset of the illness. Fromm-Reichmann (1948), for example, viewed cold mothers who unconsciously conveyed feelings of rejection toward their children as being of such importance in the development of schizophrenia that they were termed "schizophrenogenic" mothers. Bateson and his colleagues, in contrast, focused on problems of communication within the family, developing the notion of the double bind (Bateson, Jackson, Haley, & Weakland, 1956). A double bind is a "mixed message" that contains two or more incompatible communication signals. Thus a mother who claims to have missed her child after a period of separation might stiffen when the child runs to hug her. In the face of continued exposure to such ambiguity, the child is compelled to deny aspects of reality and this later becomes manifest as schizophrenia. In yet another environmental formulation, family dynamics are considered to be so disturbed by chronic discord (marital schism) and disequilibrium (marital skew) that thought disorder is viewed as the consequence for the exposed offspring (Lidz, Fleck, & Cornelison, 1965).

Although theories implicating family factors in the etiology of schizophrenia were popular in the 1950s and '60s, few now believe that pathological family environments play an important causal role in the development of schizophrenic illness. Genetic factors clearly play a major role in the etiology of many cases of schizophrenia (Kendler & Diehl, 1993). Although schizophrenia is an extremely heterogeneous disorder, to the extent that environmental factors are considered relevant, they are more likely to concern exposure to the influenza virus (Mednick, Huttunen, & Machon, 1994), obstetric complications (Verdoux et al., 1997), or severe maternal malnutrition (Susser et al., 1996) than severely disturbed family systems. One recent study does suggest that family factors could be capable of triggering illness in genetically vulnerable individuals (Wahlberg et al., 1997). However, there is no compelling evidence that family factors, in isolation, constitute an environmental risk factor for the onset of schizophrenia.

Interpersonal Stress and Relapse

Families do seem to play a important role in the process of relapse. More than 35 years ago, Brown and his colleagues noticed that the social environment into which schizophrenia patients were discharged after they left the hospital was significantly associated with how well patients fared psychiatrically over the next several months (Brown, Monck, Carstairs, & Wing, 1962). Following up on this observation, Brown and his coworkers attempted to quantify those aspects of the family environment that were associated with patients relapsing or remaining well after a hospital stay. The results of these efforts was the construct of expressed emotion.[6]

Expresssed emotion (EE) reflects the extent to which the relatives of a psychiatric patient talk about that patient in a critical, hostile, or emotionally overinvolved way during an interview conducted in the patient's absence. This interview, which is termed the Camberwell Family Interview (CFI; Brown & Rutter, 1966; Rutter & Brown, 1966; Vaughn & Leff, 1976b), asks the relative a series of semistructured, open-ended questions about the patient's previous and current psychiatric difficulties. Most important, it provides the family member with an opportunity to talk about the index patient's functioning in the months prior to the hospitalization.

The central aspect of EE is criticism. Criticism is rated if there is a statement of frank dislike of something the patients does. This is illustrated in the following comment, which was made to one of the authors (JMH) by the mother of a schizophrenic son: "It gets on my nerves when I tell him to do something and he says 'Yes, I will' and he won't. We'd like to have rules and with him we never have it. It's so aggravating." Criticism can also be rated when, by virtue of changes in voice tone, speed, of speech or other vocal cues, criticism is implicit in what is being said (e.g., "He gets completely out of it and *nasty*."). If the family member makes six or more critical remarks during the CFI or expresses any evidence of hostility (a more extreme form of criticism) or marked emotional overinvolvement toward the patient (a dramatic, overprotective, or excessively self-sacrificing response to the patients illness), he or she is characterized as being high in EE (see Leff & Vaughn, 1985, for more details about EE assessment and measurement).

A series of studies conducted all over the world have well established that high EE (particularly high levels of criticism) is a robust and reliable predictor of early relapse in schizophrenia (see Kavanagh, 1992; Bebbington & Kuipers, 1994; or Butzlaff & Hooley, 1998, for recent reviews). Patients who return home to live with relatives who are rated as being high in EE have relapse rates that are more than double those of patients who return home to live with low EE relatives (e.g., 50–60%

versus 20–30%). Interestingly, this association is not unique to schizophrenia. EE has also been shown to predict poor outcome in patients with mood disorders (e.g., Vaughn & Leff, 1976a; Hooley, Orley, & Teasdale, 1986; Miklowitz et al., 1988), eating disorders (Hodes & Le Grange, 1993) and alcoholism (O'Farrell, Hooley, Fals-Stewart, & Cutter, in press) as well as in certain medical conditions like diabetes (Koenigsberg, Klausner, Pellino, Rosnick, & Campbell, 1993).

Although the prevalence of high EE in families varies across cultures (Jenkins & Karno, 1992), high EE tends to be normative in Europe and the United States. However, it is important to point out that EE is not found only in the relatives of schizophrenia patients. High levels of EE are also prevalent in the families of patients with a wide range of psychiatric and medical problems, as well as in psychiatric staff involved in supervising and treating patients (e.g., Moore, Ball, & Kuipers, 1992; Miklowitz, 1994).

Why high EE attitudes develop is still not entirely clear. In many cases, high levels of EE may be a natural response of families to the stress of prolonged caretaking and continued exposure to psychopathology. EE levels do seem to increase in families where patients have been ill for longer periods of time (Hooley & Richters, 1995). Nisenson et al.'s (1996) findings of increased negativity in the students who visited schizophrenia inpatients also lends credence to this notion that criticism and hostility might develop as a consequence of continued interaction with a disturbed patient.

High EE may also be a reaction to the symptoms (or perhaps the social or behavioral anomalies) of the patients themselves. Hooley and colleagues have demonstrated that the spouses of psychiatric patients who have more negative symptoms are less happy with their relationships than are spouses who are married to patients with more positive symptoms (Hooley, Richters, Weintraub, & Neale, 1987). This may be because negative symptoms, as we have discussed earlier, are associated with more interpersonal deficits on the part of patients and these interpersonal difficulties may generate tension within a marital relationship. Another possibility is that spouses who live with patients who have more pronounced positive symptoms are, because of the unusual nature of the symptoms, more likely to view such patients as being psychiatrically ill and thus remain more sympathetic and understanding (Hooley, 1987). In contrast, one unfortunate consequence of many negative symptoms (e.g., apathy or poor self-care) is that they may not readily be attributed to severe mental illness. Families may thus be more likely to blame patients for negative symptoms in a way that they would not blame them for positive symptoms. Several empirical studies have now provided data consistent with the attributional model (Brewin, MacCarthy, Duda, & Vaughn, 1991; Weissman, Lopez, Karno, & Jenkins, 1993). Moreover, in our current work we are finding that family members are much more likely to complain about patients' generally low levels of activity and lack of cleanliness than they are to complain about delusions or hallucinations. That relatives may be inclined to blame patients for negative symptoms is further suggested by their spontaneous comments: "Always lacking in energy. She's what I call lazy. . . . Sitting around for her is her life." "The problem is he is lazy. He doesn't want to work, that's all."

Finally, characteristics of the relatives themselves may also be important. Hooley (in press) has recently shown that relatives who have a more internally based locus of control make more critical remarks about patients than do relatives with a more external locus of control. Personality characteristics such as flexibility and tolerance also appear to be negatively related to high EE attitudes (Hooley & Hiller, in press). Certain personality characteristics may thus render relatives more or less likely to become high EE in the face of the stress of coping with psychiatric impairment.

How might all of these observations be integrated? Taken together, these findings are consistent with the notion that high EE relatives are people who (not unreasonably) find disturbed behavior difficult to accept. Perhaps because they believe that patients are capable of controlling certain aspects of their symptoms or problem behaviors, these relatives then make efforts to encourage patients to behave differently. These efforts may be well intentioned and designed to help patients function at a higher level. In some cases, these interventions may be helpful and be well received by patients. In other cases, however, patients may be unable (or possibly unwilling) to change in the way that the relative wants. The relative's level of frustration may rise, tolerance may decrease, and, over time, critical attitudes (and later, hostility) may be the inevitable result. According to this formulation, relatives' characteristics and patient factors interact over time to produce high levels of tension in the household and create stress for the relative and the patient alike.

Precisely why patients are more likely to relapse in the face of high EE is still an unanswered and important question. However, within a diathesis-stress framework (Nuechterlein & Dawson, 1984; Zubin & Spring, 1977), EE is generally assumed to be a form of psychosocial stress. One reasonable hypothesis suggests that schizophrenics may be unable to cope with negative affect, perhaps because they lack the social skills to reduce or deflect it. In a recent series of investigations, Bellack and Mueser and their colleagues have begun to explore these issues (Bellack et al., 1992; Mueser et al., 1993). However, their results reveal that schizophrenia patients are not invariably impaired in the face of high-EE type behavior. For example, in a role play in which the confederate takes on different emotional attitudes, schizophrenics were just as likely to lie and not apologize to a benign partner as to a partner mimicking high EE attitudes. However, work such as this is important because it emphasizes the transactional nature of EE (see also Hahlweg et al., 1989). To the extent that patients with highly critical relatives may lack the skills needed to effectively manage affectively charged situations, this may lead to an escalation of negative attitudes, ultimately culminating in relapse.

Psychosocial Approaches to Treatment

Schizophrenia is correctly conceived of as a disorder with a strong biological basis. However, this does not preclude the utility of psychosocial intervention in managing the illness. A diathesis-stress model suggests that interventions that target either the underlying diathesis/diatheses (or their manifestations), or that intervene at the level of the hypothesized stressors could potentially be effective. As this chapter makes apparent, many patients with schizophrenia experience considerable problems in the interpersonal realm. Although no psychosocial strategy alone is sufficient to treat schizophrenia, we echo the view of Bellack and Mueser (1993) that "psychosocial interventions can play a critical role in a comprehensive intervention program and are probably necessary components if treatment is to improve the patient's overall level of functioning, quality of life, and compliance with prescribed treatments" (p. 318).

Developed in the 1970s, one of the most frequently used treatments aimed at the correction of interpersonal deficits in schizophrenia involves *social skills training* (SST). Social skills training programs are designed to teach patients a wide variety of interpersonal skills. These may range from very basic behavioral skills (e.g., eye contact or turn taking) to more elaborate sequences of behaviors, such as those involved in being assertive. In SST, complex social sequences of social behaviors like making friends or interviewing for a job are broken down into their component parts. These parts are then further reduced to more basic elements. After being first taught by instruction and modeling to perform the component elements, patients then learn to combine them in a more smooth and fluid manner through further instruction coupled with reinforcement and feedback.

SST training has been reported to be generally beneficial for schizophrenia (see Bellack & Mueser, 1993, or Penn & Mueser, 1996, for reviews). For example, Benton and Schroeder's (1990) meta-analysis of 27 studies has provided evidence that SST has a strong positive impact on behavioral measures of social skill such as those assessed in role plays. SST also appears to improve patients' self-ratings of assertiveness and to facilitate hospital discharge. Interestingly, however, the benefit of social skills training is somewhat less marked for more global assessments of functioning (Benton & Schroeder, 1990). This highlights the fact that social competence is more than just social skills.

One problem that compromises social skills treatments is the issue of generalizability (Bellack & Mueser, 1993; Corrigan, 1991; Wong et al., 1993). More specifically, do the newly learned skills transfer to more naturalistic settings? Although little formal research has been conducted on this topic, the available evidence suggests that learned skills may well generalize and be maintained in settings other than the one in which the skills were initially taught (Benton & Schroeder, 1990). Although generalizability may be somewhat variable, and dependent on specific tasks and the abilities of the subject, the preliminary evidence in this regard is reasonably encouraging. However, it should not be taken for granted. Efforts to enhance generalizability by training across settings are clearly to be encouraged.

Another problem is that the ability of patients to benefit from social skills training programs is likely (for reasons we have already discussed) to be compromised by the many neurocognitive deficits that characterize schizophrenia patients. Slower reaction times, poorer sustained attention, and more memory impairments have all been found to be related to difficulties in acquiring skills through SST (Bowen et al., 1994; Mueser, Bellack, Douglas, & Wade, 1991). As Bowen et al. (1994) note, "the enduring cognitive dysfunctions that characterize schizophrenia are not only associated with poorer social functioning, but may decrease the efficiency of efforts to improve that functioning" (p. 299).

This suggests that if clinicians and researchers wish to help schizophrenia patients function more effectively in social contexts, they might also need to help patients improve their cognitive skills. Of course, such an approach assumes that we already have a full understanding of which cognitive skills are most important with respect to social behavior (see Bellack, 1992; Green, 1996; Hogarty & Flesher, 1992). It also assumes that these can be modified. Although cognitive rehabilitation in schizophrenia is now attracting attention, the results to date appear somewhat mixed. Benedict, Harris, Markow, and McCormick (1994) attempted to improve the attentional skills of schizophrenia outpatients through repeated practice on computer-administered tasks of vigilance. Although patients did improve on these tasks over time, there was no transfer of cognitive skills to other attentional tasks such as the CPT or the Span of Apprehension. In contrast, Kern, Green and Goldstein (1995) have reported some positive results from training patients with a combination of money and instructional prompts to improve their performance on the Span of Apprehension. Of course, interventions designed to examine the impact of cognitive remediation efforts on social skills or community function remain for the future. At the present time neurocognitive measures might be of most practical value in helping identify those patients who are likely to derive most benefit from conventional social skills training.

Finally, psychosocial interventions targeted at helping families cope with schizophrenia in a loved one deserve mention. As we have already discussed, family attitudes appear to be of considerable importance in the relapse process. To the extent that this is true, families also become a vital resource in efforts to help patients stay well.

Typically these interventions begin with providing information about the symptoms, etiology, treatment, and prognosis of schizophrenia. Families are then provided with family-based therapy, in either an individual family context (e.g., Leff, Kuipers, Berkowitz, Eberlein-Vries, & Sturgeon, 1982, Tarrier et al., 1988) or in a group containing patients and relatives from several families (e.g., McFarlane et al., 1995). Importantly, psychosocial interventions that have involved families of schizophrenia patients have been remarkably successful. Reviews of the existing literature (e.g., Lam, 1991; Penn & Mueser, 1996) indicate that such approaches are generally effective both in reducing relapse rates and in improving patient outcome more generally. Although much still remains to be understood about how such interventions work, the family-based interventions that have been conducted to date obviously provide cause for optimism.

Summary and Concluding Remarks

Difficulties in the interpersonal domain characterize schizophrenia patients in all stages of the illness. Although the extent and nature of social difficulties varies considerably from one individual to another, males appear to be particularly likely to experience difficulties in their social relationships. Moreover, for both males and females, social difficulties frequently predate the illness and remain present even during periods of symptom remission. Interpersonal anomalies are also found in those who are risk for schizophrenia.

Although the symptoms of schizophrenia will inevitably compromise social functioning to some degree, there is reason to believe that the difficulties in relating that are experienced by many schizophrenia patients are important in their own right. Precisely why they are such a central feature of schizophrenic illness is not clear. However, interpersonal impairments seem, at least to some degree, to be related to neurocognitive deficits, particularly those involving attention or vigilance and aspects of memory. Difficulties in these areas may also underlie problems in other more social areas of cognition.

It is also likely that schizophrenia patients' difficulties in relating to and understanding the social world seriously limit the extent to which they can develop supportive interpersonal relationships. Schizophrenia patients do not pick up obvious social hints. They are also often emotionally unexpressive and hard for others to "read." Together, these and other characteristics may conspire to make interactions with schizophrenia patients less rewarding for those who live or work with them. This is unfortunate because schizophrenia patients, like many other patients, appear to be at higher risk of relapse when they live in emotionally stressful home environments. Helping patients improve their social skills and helping families cope with the stress of a schizophrenic relative is clearly important for many reasons.

As this chapter has indicated, we already know much about the problems in interpersonal functioning that are associated with schizophrenia. In the past 15 years there is no doubt that research in this area has come a long way. Yet there is still a great deal to be done. The extent to which particular social difficulties are specific to schizophrenia is not always clear. This speaks to the need for appropriate control samples. We also need much more information about the stability of interpersonal functioning in general and skill deficits in particular. This speaks to the value of longitudinal investigations. Perhaps most important, however, the question of *why* such social deficits characterize schizophrenia patients remains essentially unanswered. Are the skills deficits a consequence of poor learning? Do they reflect a lack of motivation to perform skills that have already been learned adequately? Or are these interpersonal impairments, at least to some degree, the social manifestations of underlying neurocognitive deficits that are essential for the fluid processing of complex stimuli? If the latter, how exactly are social and nonsocial cognition related and how is the pattern of associations between these domains and social functioning influenced by such factors as gender and symptoms? Certainly, these possible explanations are not mutually exclusive. Yet answers to some of the most pressing questions in the area of interpersonal functioning and schizophrenia still await future systematic investigation.

Notes

1. Originally developed for use with affectively disturbed patients (SAS; Weissman, Paykel, Siegal, & Klerman, 1971), the SAS was later revised for use with more chronically ill samples (SAS-II; Schooler, Hogarty, & Weissman, 1986). Using a semistructured interview, 52 items help to measure interpersonal performance in five domains. These include, work, relationships with household members, relationships with other relatives, leisure and recreational activities, and personal well-being.

2. The 21 items on this scale are rated by an interviewer after talking with the patient. Ratings cover four dimensions, including interpersonal relations, instrumental role functioning (primarily occupational, student, or homemaker roles), intrapsychic functioning (that is, cognitive, affective, and motivational functioning), and common objects and activities (which assesses whether the patient reads newspapers, possesses a wallet, or is otherwise involved with the objects and activities of everyday life).

3. High-risk studies are not without methodological concerns of their own. One problem is that many of the studies were begun in the late 1960s and early 1970s. Quite naturally, they used the diagnostic criteria that were available at the time. However, with the publication of *DSM-III*, the diagnostic criteria for schizophrenia narrowed considerably. This resulted in many patients being rediagnosed with bipolar disorder instead of schizophrenia. Because of concerns about the reliability and validity of diagnoses made prior to 1980, the early results from many of the high-risk projects are difficult to interpret. With the subsequent rediagnosis of the patient-parents in the high-risk studies, however, this is no longer such a problem in the more recent literature.

4. Manic patients may also exhibit SOA deficits that are sometimes indistinguishable from those of schizophrenic patients (Strauss, Prescott, Gutterman, & Tune, 1987).

5. Given the extensive literature on the interpersonal consequences of depression, it would be unwise to assume that this is an issue unique to schizophrenia.

6. Other family variables of interest such as affective style (AS) and communication deviance (CD) are reviewed in Miklowitz (1994).

References

Altman, H., & Blaney, P. S. (1996). *Affect recognition in hypothetically psychosis-prone college students*. Poster presented at the 11th annual meeting of the Society for Research in Psychopathology, Atlanta, GA.

American Psychiatric Association. (1994). *Diagnostic and statistical manual of mental disorders* (4th ed.). Washington, DC: Author.

Amminger, G. P., & Mutschlechner, R. (1994). Social competence and adolescent psychosis. *British Journal of Psychiatry, 165*, 273.

Andia, A. N., Zisook, S., Heaton, R. K., Hesselink, J., Jernigan, T., Kuck, J., Morganville, J., & Braff, D. L. (1995). Gender differences in schizophrenia. *Journal of Nervous and Mental Disease, 183* (8), 522–528.

Andreasen, N. C. (1982). Negative symptoms of schizophrenia. *Archives of General Psychiatry, 39*, 782–789.

Andreasen, N. C., & Olsen, S. (1982). Negative v. positive schizophrenia. *Archives of General Psychiatry, 39*, 789–794.

Angermeyer, M. C., Kuhn, L., & Goldstein, J. M. (1990). Gender and the course of schizophrenia: Differences in treated outcomes. *Schizophrenia Bulletin, 16* (2), 293–307.

Anonymous. (1994a). First person account: Life with a mentally ill spouse. *Schizophrenia Bulletin, 20*, 227–229.

Anonymous. (1994b). First person account: Schizophrenia with childhood onset. *Schizophrenia Bulletin, 20*, 587–590.

Appelo, M. T., Woonings, F. M. J., van Nieuwenhuizen, C. J., Emmelkamp, P. M. G., Slooff, C. J., & Louwens, J. W. (1992). Specific skills and social competence in schizophrenia. *Acta Psychiatrica Scandinavica, 85*, 419–422.

Asarnow, J. R. (1988). Children at risk for schizophrenia: Converging lines of evidence. *Schizophrenia Bulletin, 14*, 613–631.

Barch, D., & Berenbaum, H. (1994). The relationship between information processing and language production. *Journal of Abnormal Psychology, 103*, 241–250.

Bateson, G., Jackson, D., Haley, J., & Weakland, J. (1956). Toward a theory of schizophrenia. *Behavioral Science, 1*, 251–264.

Bebbington, P., & Kuipers, L. (1994). The predictive utility of expressed emotion in schizophrenia: An aggregate analysis. *Psychological Medicine, 21*, 1–11.

Bellack, A. S. (1992). Cognitive rehabilitation for schizophrenia: Is it possible? Is it necessary? *Schizophrenia Bulletin, 18*, 43–50.

Bellack, A. S., Morrison, R. L., Mueser, K. T., & Wade, J. (1989). Social competence in schizoaffective disorder, bipolar disorder, and negative and non-negative schizophrenia. *Schizophrenia Research, 2*, 391–401.

Bellack, A. S., Morrison, R. L., Mueser, K. T., Wade, J. H., & Sayers, S. L. (1990). Role play for assessing the social competence of psychiatric patients. *Psychological Assessment, 2*, 248–255.

Bellack, A. S., Morrison, R. L., Wixted, J. T., & Mueser, K. T. (1990). An analysis of social competence in schizophrenia. *British Journal of Psychiatry, 156*, 809–818.

Bellack, A. S., & Mueser, K. T. (1993). Psychosocial treatment for schizophrenia. *Schizophrenia Bulletin, 19*, 317–336.

Bellack, A. S., Mueser, K. T., Wade, J., Sayers, S., & Morrison, R. L. (1992). The ability of schizophrenics to perceive and cope with negative affect. *British Journal of Psychiatry, 160*, 473–480.

Bellack, A. S., Sayers, M., Mueser, K. T., & Bennett, M. (1994). Evaluation of social problem solving in schizophrenia. *Journal of Abnormal Psychology, 103*, 371–378.

Benedict, R. H. B., Harris, A. E., Markow, T., & McCormick, J. A. (1994). Effects of attention training in information processing in schizophrenia. *Schizophrenia Bulletin, 20*, 537–546.

Bennis, W. G., Schein, E. H., Berlew, D. E., & Steele, F. I. (1964). *Interpersonal dynamics: Essays and readings on human interaction.* Homewood, IL: Dorsey Press.

Benton, M. K., & Schroeder, H. E. (1990). Social skills training with schizophrenics: A meta-analytic evaluation. *Journal of Consulting Clinical Psychology, 58*, 741–747.

Berenbaum, H., & Oltmans, T. F. (1992). Emotional experience and expression in schizophrenia and depression. *Journal of Abnormal Psychology, 101*, 37–44.

Blanchard, J. J., Bellack, A. S., & Mueser, K. T. (1994). Affective and social-behavioral correlates of physical and social anhedonia in schizophrenia. *Journal of Abnormal Psychology, 103*, 719–728.

Blanchard, J. J., Mueser, K. T., & Bellack, A. S. (in press). Anhedonia, positive and negative affect, and social functioning in schizophrenia. *Schizophrenia Bulletin.*

Blanchard, J. J., & Panzarella, C. (1998). Affect and social functioning in schizophrenia. To appear in K. T. Mueser & N. Tarrier (Eds.), *Handbook of social functioning*. Needham Heights, MA: Allyn & Bacon.

Bleuler, E. (1908). The prognosis of dementia praecox: The group of schizophrenias. In J. Cutting & M. Shepherd (Eds.), *The clinical roots of the schizophrenia concept. Translations of seminal European contributions on schizophrenia.* Cambridge, UK: Cambridge University Press.

Bowen, L., Wallace, C. J., Glynn, S. M., Nuechterlein, K. H., Lutzker, J. R., & Kuehenl, T. G. (1994). Schizophrenic individuals cognitive functioning and performance in interpersonal interactions and skills training procedures. *Journal of Psychiatric Research, 28* (3), 289–301.

Brady, J. P. (1984). Social skills training for psychiatric patients I. Concepts, methods, and clinical results. *American Journal of Psychiatry, 141* (3), 333–340.

Braff, D. L. (1993). Information processing and attention dysfunctions in schizophrenia. *Schizophrenia Bulletin, 19* (2), 233–257.

Brewin, C. R., Andrews, B., & Gotlib, I. H. (1993). Psychopathology and early experience: A reappraisal of retrospective reports. *Psychological Bulletin, 113*, 82–98.

Brewin, C. R., MacCarthy, B., Duda, K., & Vaughn, C. E. (1991). Attribution and expressed emotion in the relatives of patients with schizophrenia. *Journal of Abnormal Psychology, 100*, 546–554.

Brown, G. W., Monck, E. M., Carstairs, G. M., & Wing, J. K. (1962). Influence of family life on the course of schizophrenic illness. *British Journal of Preventive and Social Medicine, 16*, 55–68.

Brown, G. W., & Rutter, M. (1966). The measurement of family activities and relationships: A methodological study. *Human Relations, 19*, 241–263.

Buck, R. (1984). *The communication of affect*. New York: Guilford.

Butzlaff, R. L., & Hooley, J. M. (1998). Expressed emotion and psychiatric relapse: A meta-analysis. *Archives of General Psychiatry, 55*, 547–552.

Cannon-Spoor, H. E., Potkin, S. G., & Wyatt, R. J. (1982). Measurement of premorbid adjustment in chronic schizophrenia. *Schizophrenia Bulletin, 8*, 470–484.

Chapman, L. J., & Chapman, J. P. (1973). *Disordered thought in schizophrenia*. New York: Appleton-Century-Crofts.

Chapman, L. J., Chapman, J. P., Kwapil, T. R., Eckblad, M., & Zinser, M. (1994). Putatively psychosis-prone subjects ten years later. *Journal of Abnormal Psychology, 103*, 171–183.

Chapman, L. J., Chapman, J. P., & Miller, E. N. (1982). Reliabilities and intercorrelations of eight measures of proneness to psychosis. *Journal of Consulting and Clinical Psychology, 50*, 187–195.

Chapman, L. J., Chapman, J. P., & Raulin, M. L. (1976). Scale for physical and social anhedonia. *Journal of abnormal Psychology, 85*, 374–382.

Childers, S. E., & Harding, C. M. (1990). Gender, premorbid social functioning, and long-term outcome in DSM-III schizophrenia. *Schizophrenia Bulletin, 16*, 309–318.

Corcoran, R., Mercer, G., & Frith, C. D. (1995). Schizophrenia, symptomatology and social inference: Investigating "theory of mind" in people with schizophrenia. *Schizophrenia Research, 17*, 5–13.

Cornblatt, B. A., Lenzenweger, M. F., & Erlenmeyer-Kimling, L. (1989). The continuous performance test, identical pairs version: II. Contrasting attentional profiles in schizophrenic and depressed patients. *Psychiatry Research, 29*, 65–85.

Cornblatt, B. A., Lenzenweger, M. F., Dworkin, R. H., & Erlenmeyer-Kimling, L. (1992). Childhood attentional dysfunctions predict social deficits in unaffected adults at risk for schizophrenia. *British Journal of Psychiatry, 161* (Suppl. 18), 59–64.

Corrigan, P. W. (1991). Social skills training in adult psychiatric populations: A meta-analysis. *Journal of Behavior Therapy and Experimental Psychiatry, 22*, 203–210.

Corrigan, P. W., Green, M. F., & Toomey, R. (1994). Cognitive correlates to social cue perception in schizophrenia. *Psychiatry Research, 53*, 141–151.

Corrigan, P. W., & Toomey, R. (1995). Interpersonal problem solving and information processing in schizophrenia. *Schizophrenia Bulletin, 21*, 395–403.

Cramer, P., Bowen, J., & O'Neill, M. (1992). Schizophrenics and social judgment: Why do schizophrenics get it wrong? *British Journal of Psychiatry, 160*, 481–487.

Cutting, J., & Murphy D. (1990). Impaired ability of schizophrenics, relative to manics or depressives, to appreciate social knowledge about their culture. *British Journal of Psychiatry, 157*, 355–358.

DeMann, J. A. (1994). First person account: The evolution of a person with schizophrenia. *Schizophrenia Bulletin, 20*, 579–582,

Donahoe, C. P., Carter, M. J., Bloem, W. D., Hirsch, G. L, Laasi, N., & Wallace, C. J. (1990). Assessment of interpersonal problem-solving skills. *Psychiatry, 53*, 329–339.

Dworkin, R. H. (1990). Patterns of sex difference in negative symptoms and social functioning consistent with separate dimensions of schizophrenic psychopathology. *American Journal of Psychiatry, 147*, 347–349.

Dworkin, R. H. (1992). Affective deficits and social deficits in schizophrenia: What's what? *Schizophrenia Bulletin, 18*, 59–64.

Dworkin, R. H., Bernstein, G., Kaplansky, L. M., Lipsitz, J. D., Rinaldi, A., Slater, S. L., Cornblatt, B. A., & Erlenmeyer-Kimling, L. (1991). Social competence and positive and negative symptoms: A longitudinal study of children and adolescents at risk for schizophrenia and affective disorder. *American Journal of Psychiatry, 148*, 1182–1188.

Dworkin, R. H., Cornblatt, B. A., Friedmann, R., Kaplansky, L. M., Lewis, J. A., Rinaldi, A., Shilliday, C., & Erlenmeyer-Kimling, L.

(1993). Childhood precursors of affective vs. social deficits in adolescents at risk for schizophrenia. *Schizophrenia Bulletin, 19*, 563–576.

Dworkin, R. H., Green, S. R., Small, N. E. M., Warner, M. L., Cornblatt, B. A., & Erlenmeyer-Kimling, L. (1990). Positive and negative symptoms and social competence in adolescents at risk for schizophrenia and affective disorder. *American Journal of Psychiatry, 147* (9), 1234–1236.

Dworkin, R. H., Lewis, J. A., Cornblatt, B. A., & Erlenmeyer-Kimling, L. (1994). Social competence deficits in adolescents at risk for schizophrenia. *Journal of Nervous and Mental Disease, 182* (2), 103–108.

Erlenmeyer-Kimling L., Marcuse Y., Cornblatt, B., Friedman, D., Rainer, J. D., & Rutschmann, J. (1984). The New York High-Risk Project. In N. F. Watt, E. J. Anthony, L. C. Wynne, & J. E. Rolf (Eds.), *Children at risk for schizophrenia: A longitudinal perspective*. New York: Cambridge University Press.

Feingold, A. (1988). Cognitive gender differences are disappearing. *American Psychologist, 43*, 95–103.

Flor-Henry, P. (1985). Psychiatric aspects of cerebral lateralization. *Psychiatric Annals, 15*, 429–433.

Fromm-Reichmann, F. (1948). Notes on the development of treatment of schizophrenics by psychchoanalytic psychotherapy. *Psychiatry, 11*, 263–273.

Gold, D. D. (1984). Late age of onset schizophrenia: Present but unaccounted for. *Comprehensive Psychiatry, 25*, 225–237.

Goldman, R. S., Axelrod, B. N., Tandon, R., Ribeiro, S. C. M., Craig, K., & Berent, S. (1993). Neuropsychological prediction of treatment efficacy and one-year outcome in schizophrenia. *Psychopathology, 126*, 122–126.

Goldstein, J. M., Tsuang, M. T., & Faraone, S. V. (1989). Gender and schizophrenia: Implications for understanding the heterogeneity of the illness. *Psychiatry Research, 28*, 243–253.

Green, M. F. (1996). What are the functional consequences of neurocognitive deficits in schizophrenia? *American Journal of Psychiatry, 153*, 321–330.

Green, M. F., Nuechterlein, K. H., & Mintz, J. (1994a). Backward masking in schizophrenia and mania: I. Specifying a mechanism. *Archives of General Psychiatry, 51*, 939–944.

Green, M. F., Nuechterlein, K. H., & Mintz, J. (1994b). Backward Masking in schizophrenia and mania: I. Specifying the visual channels. *Archives of General Psychiatry, 51*, 945–951.

Grillon, C., Courchesne, E., Ameli, R., Geyer, M. A., & Braff, D. L. (1990). Increased distractibility in schizophrenic patients: Electrophysiologic and behavioral evidence. *Archives of General Psychiatry, 47*, 171–179.

Gureje, O., Aderibigbe, Y. A., Olley, O., & Bamidele (1994). Premorbid functioning in schizophrenia: A controlled study of Nigerian patients. *Comprehensive Psychiatry, 35*, 437–440.

Häfner, H., Maurer, K., Löffler, W., & Rieche-Rössler, A. (1993). The influence of age and sex on the onset and early course of schizophrenia. *British Journal of Psychiatry, 162*, 80–86.

Häner, H., Riecher-Rössler, A., An Der Heiden, W., Maurer, K., Fätkenheuer, B., & Löffler, W. (1993). Generating and testing a causal explanation of the gender difference in age at first onset of schizophrenia. *Psychological Medicine, 23*, 925–940.

Hafner, R. J. (1986). *Marriage and mental illness: A sex roles perspective*. New York: Guilford Press.

Hahlweg, K., Goldstein, M. J., Nuechterlein, K. H., Magaña, A. B., Mintz, J., Doane, J. A., Miklowitz, D. J., & Snyder, K. S. (1989). Expressed emotion and patient-relative interaction in families of recent onset schizophrenics. *Journal of Consulting & Clinical Psychology, 57*, 11–18.

Hall, J. A. (1985). *Nonverbal sex differences: Communication accuracy and expressive style*. Baltimore, MD: Johns Hopkins University Press.

Hans, S. L., Marcus, J., Henson, L., Auerbach, J. G., & Mirsky, A. F. (1992). Interpersonal behavior of children at risk for schizophrenia. *Psychiatry, 55*, 314–335.

Hass, G. L., Glick, I. D., Clarkin, J. F., Spencer, J. H., & Lewis, A. B. (1990). Gender and schizophrenia outcome: a clinical trial of an inpatient family intervention. *Schizophrenia Bulletin, 16*, 277–292.

Hatfied, A. B. (1987). Families as caregivers: A historical perspective. In A. B. Hatfiled & H. P. Lefley (Eds.), *Families of the mentally ill*. New York: Guilford Press.

Heaton, R. K. (1981). *Wisconsin Card Sort Manual*. Psychological Assessment Resources. Odessa, FL.

Heinrichs, D. W., Hanlon, T. E., & Carpenter, W. T. (1984). The Quality of Life Scale: An instrument for rating the schizophrenic deficit syndrome. *Schizophrenia Bulletin, 12*, 388–398.

Hellewell, J. S. E., Connell, J., & Deakin, J. F. W. (1994). Affect judgment and facial recognition memory in schizophrenia. *Psychopathology, 27*, 255–261.

Herrig, E. (1995). First person account: A personal experience. *Schizophrenia Bulletin, 21*, 339–342.

Hodes, M., & Le Grange, D. (1993). Expressed emotion in the investigation of eating disorders: A review. *International Journal of Eating Disorders, 13*, 279–288.

Hogarty, G. E., & Flesher, S. (1992). Cognitive remediation in schizophrenia: Proceed . . . with caution! *Schizophrenia Bulletin, 18*, 51–57.

Hollandsworth, J. G., & Wall, K. E. (1977). Sex differences in assertive behavior: An empirical investigation. *Journal of Counseling Psychology, 24*, 217–222.

Hooley, J. M. (1987). The nature and origins of expressed emotion. In M. J. Goldstein & K. Hahlweg (Eds.), *Understanding Major Mental Disorder: The Contribution of Family Interaction Research*. New York: Family Process Press.

Hooley, J. M. (1998). Expressed emotion and locus of control. *Journal of Nervous and Mental Disease, 186*, 374–378.

Hooley, J. M., & Hiller, J. B. (in press). *Personality and expressed emotion. Journal of Abnormal Psychology.*

Hooley, J. M., Orley, J., and Teasdale, J. D. (1986). Levels of expressed emotion and relapse in depressed patients. *British Journal of Psychiatry, 148*, 642–647.

Hooley, J. M., & Richters, J. E. (1995). Expressed emotion: A developmental perspective. In D. Cicchetti & S. L. Toth (Eds.), *Rochester Symposium on Developmental Psychopathology, Volume 6: Emotion, Cognition, and Representation.* Rochester, NY: University of Rochester Press.

Hooley, J. M., Richters, J. E., Weintraub, S., & Neale, J. M. (1987). Psychopathology and marital distress: The positive side of positive symptoms. *Journal of Abnormal Psychology, 96*, 27–33.

Hyde, J. S., & Linn, M. C. (1988). Gender differences in verbal ability: A meta-analysis. *Psychological Bulletin, 104*, 53–69.

Jackson, H. J., Minas, I. H., Burgess, P. M., Joshua, S. D., Charisiou, J., & Campbell, I. M. (1989). Negative symptoms and social skills performance in schizophrenia. *Schizophrenia Bulletin, 2*, 457–463.

Jaeger, J., & Douglas, E. (1992). Neuropsychiatric rehabilitation for persistent mental illness. *Psychiatric Quarterly, 63*, 71–94.

Jenkins, J. H., & Karno, M. (1992). The meaning of expressed emotion: Theoretical issues raised by cross-cultural research. *American Journal of Psychiatry, 149*, 9–21.

Joseph, P. L., Sturgeon, D. A., & Leff, J. (1992). The perception of emotion by schizophrenic patients. *British Journal of Psychiatry, 161*, 603–609.

Kavanagh, D. J. (1992). Recent developments in expressed emotion and schizophrenia. *British Journal of Psychiatry, 160*, 601–620.

Kendler, K. S., & Diehl, S. R. (1993). The genetics of schizophrenia: A current, genetic-epidemiologic perspective. *Schizophrenia Bulletin, 19*, 261–285.

Kern, R. S., Green, M. F., & Goldstein, M. J. (1995). Modification of performance on the Span of Apprehension, a putative marker of vulnerability to schizophrenia. *Journal of Abnormal Psychology, 104*, 385–389.

Kerr, S. L., & Neale, J. M. (1993). Emotion perception in schizophrenia: Specific deficit of further evidence of generalized poor performance? *Journal of Abnormal Psychology, 102* (2), 312–318.

Koenigsberg, H. W., Klausner, E., Pellino, D., Rosnick, P., & Campbell, R. (1993). Expressed emotion and glucose control in insulin-dependent Diabetes Mellitus. *American Journal of Psychiatry, 150*, 114–115.

Kraepelin, E. (1896). Dementia Praecox. In J. Cutting & M. Shepherd (Eds.), *The clinical roots of the schizophrenia concept. Translations of seminal European contributions on schizophrenia.* Cambridge, UK: Cambridge University Press.

Kring, A. M., Kerr, S. L., Smith, D. A., & Neale, J. M. (1993). Flat affect in schizophrenia does not reflect diminished subjective experience of emotion. *Journal of Abnormal Psychology, 102*, 507–517.

Kring, A. M., & Neale, J. M. (1996). Do schizophrenic patients show a disjunctive relationship among expressive, experiential, and psychophysiological components of emotion? *Journal of Abnormal Psychology, 105*, 249–257.

Lam, D. H. (1991). Psychosocial family interventions in schizophrenia: A review of empirical studies. *Psychological Medicine, 21*, 423–441.

Leff, J. P., Kuipers, L., Berkowitz, R., Eberlein-Vries, R., & Sturgeon, D. (1982). A controlled trial of social intervention in schizophrenia families. *British Journal of Psychiatry, 141*, 121–134.

Leff, J., & Vaughn, C. (1985). *Expressed emotion in families.* New York: Guilford Press.

Lenzenweger, M. F., Dworkin, R. H., & Wethington, E. (1991). Examining the underlying structure of schizophrenic phenomenology: Evidence for a three-process model. *Schizophrenia Bulletin, 17* (1993), 515–524.

Lewis, S. (1992). Sex and schizophrenia: Vive la diference. *British Journal of Psychiatry, 161*, 445–450.

Liberman, R. P. (1982). Assessment of social skills. *Schizophrenia Bulletin, 8* (2), 62–83.

Lidz, T., Fleck, S., & Cornelison, A. R., (1965). *Schizophrenia and the family.* New York: International Universities Press.

Loranger, A. W. (1984). Sex differences in age at onset of schizophrenia. *Archives of General Psychiatry, 41*, 157–161.

Loranger, A. W., Susman, V. L., Oldham, J. M., & Russakoff, L. M. (1987). The personality disorder examination: A preliminary report. *Journal of Personality Disorders, 1*, 1–13.

Lysaker, P., Bell, M., & Beam-Goulet, J. (1995). Wisconsin Card Sorting Test and work performance in schizophrenia. *Schizophrenia Research, 56*, 45–51.

McFall, R. M. (1982). A review and reformulation of the concept of social skills. *Behavioral Assessment, 4*, 1–33.

McFarlane, W. R., Lukens, E., Link, B, Dushay, R., Deakins, S. A., Newmark, M., Dunne, E. J., Horen, B., & Toran, J. (1995). Multiple-family groups and psychoeducation in the treatment of schizophrenia. *Archives of General Psychiatry, 52*, 679–687.

Maughan, B., & Rutter, M. (1997). Retrospective reporting of childhood adversity: Issues in assessing long-term recall. *Journal of Personality Disorders, 11*, (1), 19–33.

McGlashan, T. H., & Bardenstein, K. K. (1990). Gender Differences in affective, schizoaffective, and schizophrenic disorders. *Schizophrenia Bulletin, 16*, 319–329.

Mednick, S. A., Huttunen, M. O., & Machon, R. A. (1994). Prenatal influenza infections and adult schizophrenia. *Schizophrenia Bulletin, 20*, 263–207.

Miklowitz, D. J. (1994). Family risk indicators in schizophrenia. *Schizophrenia Bulletin, 20*, 137–149.

Miklowitz, D. J., Goldstein, M. J., Nuechterlein, K. H. Snyder, K. S., Mintz, J. (1988). Family factors and the course of bipolar affective disorder. *Archives of General Psychiatry, 45*, 225–231.

Moore, E., Ball, R. A., & Kuipers, L. (1992). Expressed emotion in staff working with the long-term adult mentally ill. *British Journal of Psychiatry, 161*, 802–808.

Morrison, R. L., Bellack, A. S., & Bashore, T. R. (1988). Emotion perception skill among schizophrenic patients. *Journal of Psychopathology and Behavioral Assessment, 10*, 319–332.

Morrison, R. L., Bellack, A. S., & Mueser, K. T. (1988). Deficits in facial-affect recognition and schizophrenia. *Schizophrenia Bulletin, 14*, 67–83.

Mueser, K. T., Bellack, A. S., Douglas, M. S., & Morrison, R. L. (1991). Prevalence and stability of social skill deficits in schizophrenia. *Schizophrenia Research, 5*, 167–176.

Mueser, K. T., Bellack, A. S., Douglas, M. S., & Wade, J. H. (1991). Prediction of social skill acquisition in schizophrenia and major affective disorder patients from memory and symptomatology. *Psychiatry Research, 37*, 281–296.

Mueser, K. T., Bellack, A. S., Morrison, R. L., & Wade, J. H. (1990). Gender, social competence, and symptomatology in schizophrenia: A longitudinal analysis. *Journal of Abnormal Psychology, 99*, 138–147.

Mueser, K. T., Bellack, A. S., Wade, J. H., Sayers, S. L., Tierney, A., & Haas, G. (1993). Expressed emotion, social skill, and response to negative affect in schizophrenia. *Journal of Abnormal Psychology, 102*, 339–351.

Mueser, K. T., Blanchard, J. J., & Bellack, A. S. (1995). Memory and social skill inschizophrenia: The role of gender. *Psychiatry Research, 57*, 141–153.

Mueser, K. T., Doonan, R., Penn, D. L., Blanchard, J. J., Bellack, A. S., Nishith, P., & Deleon, J. (1996). Emotion recognition and social competence in chronic schizophrenia. *Journal of Abnormal Psychology, 105*, 271–275.

Nanko, S., & Moridaira, J. (1993). Reproductive rates in schizophrenic outpatients. *Acta Psychiatrica Scandinavica, 87*, 400–404.

Neale, J. M. (1971). Perceptual span in schizophrenia. *Journal of Abnormal Psychology, 77*, 196–204.

Neale, J. M., McIntyre, C. W., Fox, R., & Cromwell, R. L. (1969). Span of apprehension in acute schizophrenics. *Journal of Abnormal Psychology, 74*, 593–596.

Nisenson, L., Berenbaum, H., & Good, T. (1996, September). *The development of relationships in individuals with schizophrenia: Individual differences among patients and their interaction partners.* Poster presented at the 11th annual meeting of the Society for Research in Psychopathology, Atlanta, GA.

Nuechterlein, K. H. (1977). Reaction time and attention in schizophrenia: A critical evaluation of the data and theories. *Schizophrenia Bulletin, 3*, 373–428.

Nuechterlein, K. H., & Dawson, M. E. (1984). A heuristic vulnerability/stress model of schizophrenic episodes. *Schizophrenia Bulletin, 10*, 300–312.

O'Farrell, T., Hooley, J. M., Fals-Stewart, W., & Cutter, H. S. G. (in press). Expressed emotion and relapse in alcoholic patients. *Journal of Consulting and Clinical Psychology.*

Ostrom, T. M. (1984). The sovereignty of social cognition. In R. S. Wyer & T. K. Srull (Eds.), *Handbook of social cognition* (Vol. 1: 1–37). Hillsdale, NJ: Lawrence Erlbaum.

Overall, J. E., & Gorham, D. R. (1962). The Brief Psychiatric Rating Scale. *Psychological Reports, 10*, 799–812.

Park, S., Holzman, P. S., & Goldman-Rakic, P. S. (1995). Spatial working memory deficits in the relatives of schizophrenic patients. *Archives of General Psychiatry, 52*, 821–828.

Penn, D. L., Corrigan, P. W., Bentall, R. P., Racenstein, J. M., & Newman, L. (1997). Social cognition in schizophrenia. *Psychological Bulletin, 121*, 114–132.

Penn, D. L., & Mueser, K. T. (1996). Research update on the psychosocial treatment of schizophrenia. *American Journal of Psychiatry, 153*, 607–617.

Penn, D., Mueser, K. T., & Spaulding, W. (1996). Information processing, social skill, and gender in schizophrenia. *Psychiatry Research, 59*, 213–220.

Penn, D. L., Mueser, K. T., Spaulding, W., Hope, D. A., & Reed, D. (1995). Information processing and social competence in chronic schizophrenia. *Schizophrenia Bulletin, 21*, 269–281.

Penn, D. L., Spaulding, W. D., Reed, D., & Sullivan, M. (1996). The relationship of social cognition to ward behavior in chronic schizophrenia. *Schizophrenia Research, 20*, 327–335.

Perry, W., Moore, D., & Braff, D. (1995). Gender differences on thought disturbance measures among schizophrenic patients. *American Journal of Psychiatry, 152*, 1298–1301.

Pilowsky, I., & Bassett, D. (1980). Schizophrenia and the response to facial emotions. *Comprehensive Psychiatry, 21*, 236–244.

Planansky, K., & Johnston, R. (1967). Mate selection in schizophrenia. *Acta Psychiatrica Scandinavica, 43*, 397–409.

Platt, J. J., & Spivack, G. (1972). Problem-solving thinking of psychiatric patients. *Journal of Consulting and Clinical Psychology, 39*, 148–151.

Platt, J. J., & Spivack, G. (1974). Means of solving real-life problems: I. Psychiatric patients vs. controls and cross-cultural comparisons of normal females. *Journal of Community Psychology, 2*, 45–48.

Poreh, A., Whitman, D., Weber, M., & Ross, T. (1994). Facial recognition in hypothetically schizotypic college students. *Journal of Nervous and Mental Disease, 182*, 503–507.

Professional Staff of the United States-United Kingdom Cross-National Project. (1974). The diagnosis and psychopathology of schizophrenia in New York and London. *Schizophrenia Bulletin, 1* (Experimental Issue No. 11), 80–102.

Rolf, J. E. (1972). The social and academic competence of children vulnerable to schizophrenia and other behavior pathologies. *Journal of Abnormal Psychology, 80*, 225–243.

Rutter, M., & Brown, G. W. (1966). The reliability and validity of measures of family life in relationships in families containing a psychiatric patient. *Social Psychiatry, 1*, 38–53.

Schooler, N., Hogarty, G. E., & Weissman, M. M. (1986). Social Adjustment Scale II (SAS-II). In W. A. Hargreaves, C. C. Atkinson, & J. E. Sorenson (Eds.), *Resource materials for community mental health program evaluators.* DHEW No. 79-328. Washington, DC: Superintendent of Documents, U.S. Government Printing Office, 290–303.

Schwartz, S. (1967). Diagnosis, level of social adjustment and cognitive deficits. *Journal of Abnormal Psychology, 72*, 446–450.

Seeman, M. V. (1983). Interaction of sex, age, and neuroleptic dose. *Comprehensive Psychiatry, 24*, 125–128.

Sims, R. C., & Neale, J. M. (1996, September). *Self-awareness of affective flattening in schizophrenia.* Poster presented at the 11th annual meeting of the Society for Research in Psychopathology, Atlanta, GA.

Strauss, J. S., Carpenter, W. T., & Bartko, J. J. (1974). The diagnosis and understanding of schizophrenia: Part III. Speculations on the processes that underlie schizophrenic symptoms and signs, *Schizophrenia Bulletin, 1*, 61–69.

Strauss, M. E., Prescott, C. A., Gutterman, D. F., & Tune, L. E. (1987). Span of apprehension deficits in schizophrenia and mania. *Schizophrenia Bulletin, 13*, 699–704.

Susser, E., Neugebauer, R., Hoek, H. W., Brown, A. S., Lin, S., Labovitz, D., & Gorman, J. (1996). Schizophrenia after prenatal famine. *Archives of General Psychiatry, 53*, 25–31.

Tarrier, N., Barrowclough, C., Vaughn, C., Bamrah, J., Porceddu, K., Watts, S., & Freeman, H. (1988). The community management of schizophrenia: A controlled trial of a behavioral intervention with families to reduce relapse. *British Journal of Psychiatry, 153*, 532–542.

Toomey, R., & Schuldberg, D. (1995). Recognition and judgment of facial stimuli inschizotypal subjects. *Journal of Communicable Disorders, 28*, 193–203.

Van der Does, A. J. W., Dingemans, P. M. A. J.,

Linszen, D. H., Nugter, M. A., & Scholte, W. F. (1993). Sympton dimensions and cognitive and social functioning in recent-onset schizophrenia. *Psychological Medicine, 23*, 745–753.

Vaughn, C., & Leff, J. (1976a). The influence of family and social factors on the course of psychiatric illness: A comparison of schizophrenic and depressed neurotic patients. *British Journal of Psychiatry, 129*, 125–137.

Vaughn, C., & Leff, J. (1976b). The measurement of expressed emotion in the families of psychiatric patients. *British Journal of Social and Clinical Psychology, 15*, 157–165.

Verdoux, H., Geddes, J. R., Takei, N., Lawrie, S. M., Bovet, P., Eagles, J. M., Heun, R., McCreadie, R. G., McNeil, T. F., O'Callaghan, E., Stober, Willinger M., U., Wright, P., & Murray, R. M. (1997). Obstetric complications and age at onset in schizophrenia: An international collaborative meta-analysis of individual patient data. *American Journal of Psychiatry, 154*, 1220–1227.

Wahl, O. F., & Hunter, J. (1992). Are gender effects being neglected in schizophrenia research? *Schizophrenia Bulletin, 18*, 313–317.

Walker, E., & Lewine, R. J. (1990). Prediction of adult-onset schizophrenia from childhood home movies of the patients. *American Journal of Psychiatry, 147*, 1052–1056.

Wallace, C. J. (1984). Community and interpersonal functioning in the course of schizophrenic disorders. *Schziophrenia Bulletin, 10*, 233–257.

Watt, N. F. (1978). Patterns of childhood social development in adult schizophrenics. *Archives of General Psychiatry, 35*, 160–165.

Watt, N. F., & Lubensky, A. W. (1976). Childhood roots of schizophrenia. *Journal of Consulting and Clinical Psychology, 44*, 363–375.

Weintraub, S., Neale, J. M., & Liebert, D. E. (1975). Teacher ratings of children vulnerable to psychopathology. *American Journal of Orthopsychiatry, 45*, 838–845.

Weintraub, S., Prinz, R. J., & Neale, J. M. (1978). Peer evaluations of the competence of children vulnerable to psychopathology. *Journal of Abnormal Child Psychology, 6*, 461–473.

Weisman A., Lopez, S. R., Karno, M., & Jenkins, J. (1993). An attributional analysis of expressed emotion in Mexican-American families with schizophrenia. *Journal of Abnormal Psychology, 102*, 601–606.

Weissman, M. M., Paykel, E. S., Siegal, R., & Klerman, G. L. (1971). The social role performance of depressed women: Comparisons with a normal group. *American Journal of Orthopsychiatry, 41*, 390–405.

Whalberg, K-E., Wynne, L. C., Oja, H., Keskitalo, P., Pykalainen, L., Lahti, I., Moring, J., Naarala, M., Sorri, A., Seitamaa, M., Lasky, K., Kolassa, J., & Tienari, P. (1997). Gene-environment interaction in vulnerability to schizophrenia: Findings from the Finnish adoptive family study of schizophrenia. *American Journal of Psychiatry, 154* (3), 355–362.

Wong, S. E., Martinez-Diaz, J. A., Massel, H. K., Edelstein, B. A., Wiegand, W., Bowen, L., & Liberman, R. P. (1993). Conversational skills training with schizophrenic inpatients: A study of generalization across settings and conversants. *Behavior Therapy, 24*, 285–304.

Zborowski, M. J., & Garske, J. P. (1993). Interpersonal deviance and consequent social impact in hypothetically schizophrenia-prone men. *Journal of Abnormal Psychology, 102*, 482–489.

Zigler, E., & Phillips, L. (1961). Social competence and outcome in psychiatric disorder. *Journal of Abnormal and Social Psychology, 63*, 264–271.

Zubin, J., & Spring, B. J. (1977). Vulnerability: A new view of schizophrenia. *Journal of Abnormal Psychology, 86*, 103–126.

13

Paranoid Conditions

PAUL H. BLANEY

The word *paranoid* appears in *DSM-IV* as part of two classification names: schizophrenia, paranoid type (PS; Axis I) and paranoid personality disorder (PPD; Axis II). The condition that arguably lies between them—that involving psychotic delusions in the absence of schizophrenia—is delusional disorder (DD; also Axis I). Whether or not a schizophrenic individual's symptoms warrant a PS diagnosis may depend in part upon when in the course of illness the diagnosis is given, as some individuals who merit PS diagnoses when young eventually settle into a form of chronic schizophrenia less marked by delusions. In DD, as in PPD, the distortions of reality coexist with rational, realistic thinking in multiple realms. Delusions are also mentioned in the *DSM-IV* criteria for brief psychotic disorder, a loosely defined, residual diagnostic grouping.

It is tempting to view PS, DD, and PPD as lying on a continuum; that is, DD is a less thought-disordered variant of PS, while PPD is a less severe variant of DD. The value of such a perspective must not be ignored. It seems likely that qualitatively similar clinical manifestations emerge for the same (or at least overlapping) reasons in the various conditions (cf. Romney, 1988).

Still, there are reasons to suspect that this perspective may be somewhat misleading (cf. Kendler, 1980). For instance, Watt (1985b) has reported data to the effect that the incidence of schizophrenia in families of persons having DD-like disorders is not elevated. In addition, it appears that many PS and most DD patients do not have premorbid PPD (Yassa & Suranyi-Cadotte, 1993). DD with grandiose delusions may have more to do with bipolar disorder than with PS or PPD, and the subpsychotic variant of erotomanic DD is perhaps not PPD but rather a kind of borderline (Meloy, 1990) or obsessional (Segal, 1990) disorder. Varma and Sharma (1993) have reported a low incidence of PPD among first-degree relatives of schizophrenics (subtype unspecified), though the incidence was higher than that seen in families of control subjects (also see Maier, Lichtermann, Minges, & Heun, 1994; Parnas et al., 1993).

A Provisional Prototype

Paranoia has an everyday layman's meaning as well as a *DSM-IV* definition. The two overlap extensively, but there are aspects of the everyday meaning that are not emphasized in *DSM-IV*. With *paranoia*, as with many such terms, one should not assume that the term as used in the research literature and in communications among experienced mental health professionals is so closely tied to *DSM-IV* as to exclude surplus meanings inherent in everyday use.

The following list, gleaned from multiple sources, addresses all of the features that may alert the seasoned clinician to wonder if a client's problems are fundamentally paranoid in nature. The list is not keyed to *DSM-IV*. If it is viewed as a checklist, an individual could have a high "score"—indicating that several of these features characterized him—without its meaning that any of the three paranoid diagnoses (PS, DD, or PPD) was warranted. Several of the features are not central to any of these diagnoses. In fact, with respect to PPD, the list is closer to *ICD-10* than to *DSM-IV*. However, it draws from the same clinical traditions as *DSM-IV* is based upon, and it seems relevant to PS, DD, *and* PPD (with the possible exception of DD somatic type). Similar facets are adjacent so that their differences will be apparent.

1. Suspicious: hyperalert to other persons' anger and to their malevolent and selfish motives.
2. Cynical: ascribes to what might be called an *unjust* world hypothesis.
3. Rivalrous: actively engaged in social comparison.
4. Wronged/jealous: views oneself as the victim of the injustice and/or at the short end of the social comparison.
5. Angry: experiences rage at being wronged and may act on it.
6. Guarded: maintains a self-protective posture; indiscriminately secretive and evasive; reluctant to presume others' good-will.
7. Rigid: impervious to correction on the basis of new data; data *consistent with* prior views are selectively noticed and are taken to be *supportive of* those views.
8. Self-contained: impervious to correction on the basis of the views of others.
9. Intolerant of ambiguity: fixes on one of many plausible explanations; invests it with great import.
10. Humorless: brittle; takes everything seriously; especially unable to laugh at oneself.
11. Conspicuous: views the self as the object of others' attention.
12. Self-important: believes that one's own experience has special significance and is *not mundane*; personalizes neutral events.
13. Self-righteous: certain of one's superior virtue and/or clearer understanding; arrogant.
14. Self-justifying: entitled; views one's own questionable behavior as necessitated by one's unique plight or by others' shortcomings or ill-will.

This list is, like *DSM-IV*, limited to relatively descriptive and behavioral features. See Fenigstein and Vanable (1992) and Livesley and Schroeder (1990) for alternative, overlapping lists. A fine-grained list such as the foregoing reminds us that the various terms usually employed to describe features of paranoia are themselves complex; for instance, while numbers 12 and 13 are distinguishable, they are usually both denoted by the word *grandiose*.

Although all 14 facets are probably somewhat stable (traitlike) characteristics, each may also fluctuate in severity across time within an individual. Each of these facets can exist on various levels of severity or extremity. None of them implies the presence of a delusion. While generally having lots of these facets implies greater severity of paranoia, an individual could be characterized by all of them and still warrant a diagnosis of PPD only if none is of psychotic proportions. In a given individual, they form a single fabric; treating them as distinguishable dimensions reminds us that there are some individuals who have enough of the characteristics to fit a kind of paranoid prototype quite closely but who are conspicuously lacking others. For instance, both Shapiro (1965) and Benjamin (1996) have suggested that within the personality disorder range there are two variants: one more fearful and furtive (see no. 6 above), the other more aggressive and indignant (no. 5)—though intense fear and anger can both be present in agitated delusional states (Kennedy, Kemp, & Dyer, 1992). Millon and Davis (1996) have suggested that there are five subtypes with PPD: fanatic, malignant (i.e., sadistic), obdurate, querulous, and insular.

Differential Diagnosis and History

Mistrust (having a sense of *self against the world*) is a common thread in a number of these facets, and in dealing with a paranoid individual, the diagnostic task is complicated by the fact that mistrust is as likely to be directed at mental health professionals as at anyone else. Some persons may view treatment, assessment, and research activities as aspects of a persecutory plot. For instance, they may view antipsychotic medications as poison or EEG leads as avenues of mind control (Sacks, Carpenter, & Strauss, 1974).

Interpersonal trust may lead to a peculiar clinical paradox. On occasion, paranoid individuals suspect mental health professionals of thinking them paranoid, and consequently present clinically as emphatically *non*paranoid, again introducing obstacles to trustworthy diagnosis. The desire of paranoid individuals not to be judged abnormal[1] and to counteract others' (presumed) watchfulness of them occasionally results in relatively normal behavior, even in the presence of psychotic mentation. Such desires apparently can result in the affirmation of remarkably nonparanoid beliefs as well; for instance, in endorsing some of the items on the empirically derived MMPI paranoia scale, the individual is embracing particularly *un*cynical viewpoints. Sometimes, the therapist's best ally is the patient's desire to appear normal. In one case involving a patient's delusion that he was a spy, the therapist's ploy was to remind the patient: *If you're a secret agent, you'd better keep it a secret.*

While the lack of insight regarding the paranoid nature of one's thoughts is a hallmark of a *psychotic* paranoid condition (PS, DD, or an organically based delusional condition), sometimes insight is fragile and ambivalent. Individuals may even use the word *paranoid* to describe their own thought processes; when this occurs, it suggests not only the presence of aberrant thoughts but also some ability to keep those thoughts in proper perspective. (See Sacks et al.'s, 1974, discussion of the "double awareness phase" of paranoia—a term provided by a patient in describing her own experience.) For an individual whose life has previously been disrupted by psychotic episodes, the awareness that paranoid thoughts are returning can be quite frightening, inasmuch as they signal a resumption of dysfunctionality; this may be the case even if the thoughts are not inherently upsetting. Note that degree of insight regarding delusions is not the same as degree of insight regarding others' views of the strangeness of those beliefs; the two are empirically related, but far from perfectly so (cf. Harrow, Rattenbury, & Stoll, 1988). Finally, while *delusions without insight* suggests PS or DD rather than PPD, it would hardly be right to describe PPD as involving an abundance of insight. While PPD individuals lack delusions, they may also lack the insight that their suspiciousness is excessive. In the words of Cameron's (1963) classic discussion, the paranoid individual, while "forever questioning other people's motivations . . . is incapable of questioning his own" (p. 479).

There are several clinical phenomena for which similarities with, and differences from, paranoid conditions warrant attention.

- *Anxiety.* Reich and Braginsky (1994) have reported 54% comorbidity for PPD in a panic disorder sample, though estimates in other studies have typically been much lower. Individuals with paranoid symptoms are probably at some risk for developing panic disorder—to a greater degree than panic-disordered individuals are to develop paranoia. Comorbidity aside, it is apparent that believing that one faces imminent victimization has the potential of arousing panic. When anxiety arises from a menacing delusion, persons who do not share the delusion commonly discount the anxiety; sometimes the only way to appreciate the fear is to imagine *how I would feel if I experienced the delusion as reality.* In an individual with PS, it is possible that delusional panic may be incremental to a high level of background anxiety commonly seen in schizophrenia. Conversely, panic disorder may foster agoraphobic withdrawal, and paranoid convictions may be fostered by the resulting social isolation. It is unlikely that erotomanic and grandiose delusions entail increased levels of anxiety. However, erotomanic delusions often do have an obsessive quality to them, and there is evidence in delusional conditions more generally that premorbid obsessiveness is a poor prognostic sign (Schanda et al., 1991).
- *Narcissistic Personality Disorder.* While delusions of grandeur (and, as noted above, even persecution) have an obvious narcissistic quality to them, they also are infused with a sense of being wronged not implied by a diagnosis focusing on narcissism. A paranoid overlay on a narcissistic self-image may serve to protect that image from challenge.
- *Avoidant Personality Disorder.* While for both avoidant and paranoid persons mistrust of others is a key element, in the latter case the mistrust is joined with a high level of vigilance and a readiness to see ill will in other individuals.
- *Antisocial Personality Disorder* (ASPD). Both ASPD and PPD persons may behave in ways that harm others, all the while insisting that their attacks were justified by (perhaps preemptive) self-defense.There are individuals who qualify as both. How many PPD criteria

> an individual meets is quite predictive of how many ASPD criteria he will meet (Ekselius, Lindström, von Knorring, Bodlund, & Kullgren, 1994), and in discussing psychopathic types Arieti (1963) suggested that one is the "paranoiac psychopath." Still, of the two, PPD entails distinctly more differentiated—and perhaps genuine—beliefs regarding the intentions of other individuals. In particular cases, it may be difficult to assess the extent to which those beliefs are the *source of* the antisocial behavior, as opposed to the individual's *rationalization for* that behavior.

A review of past versions of *DSM* shows considerable consistency in terminology regarding paranoid disorders. Even *DSM-I* had entries that correspond roughly to *DSM-IV*'s PS, DD, and PPD. Indeed, paranoid is one of only two personality disorders found in both *DSM-I* and *DSM-IV* (the other being schizoid). Though there have also been shifts in PPD criteria (cf. Fenigstein, 1996), the main, relevant change across the years was a narrowing of the criteria for schizophrenia itself. During the days of *DSM-I* and *DSM-II*, in the United States (but not the United Kingdom), most individuals with nonorganic psychoses were given a diagnosis of schizophrenia. As a result, schizophrenia was a category with considerably heterogeneity and limited clinical utility. Among the classic schizophrenic subtypes, only paranoid usually showed substantial frequencies (catatonic and hebephrenic being quite rare), and one common strategy for reducing the heterogeneity of schizophrenic samples was simply to divide them into paranoid and nonparanoid subgroups (the latter consisting mainly of "undifferentiated" cases). This proved quite effective in the sense that the two groups commonly differed dramatically (cf. Nicholson & Neufeld, 1993). In recent versions of *DSM*, the paranoid/nonparanoid distinction within schizophrenia has less to do with the severity of paranoid symptomatology than with its predominance in the clinical picture (cf. Smári, Stefánsson, & Thorgilsson, 1994), and there is ongoing debate about the role delusions should play in the identification of subgroups within schizophrenic samples (cf. Kremen, Seidman, Goldstein, Faraone, & Tsuang, 1994).

As with many other conditions in *DSM-IV*, paranoia and delusionality may define particular disorders (PS, DD, and PPD), but they appear as symptoms of other disorders as well. Paranoia may be precipitated by use of (and withdrawal from) certain psychoactive (and even nonpsychoactive) drugs (e.g., amphetamines), and it is commonly a central feature of a variety of medical conditions, most notably senile dementia (e.g., Alzheimer's). Medical conditions may be contributing factors even when a chronic psychiatric condition is clearly present: cases have been reported in which a chronic ambulatory schizophrenic is apparently precipitated into a short-term paranoid decompensation by a minor illness such as a common cold. In the mid-1980s, it was possible to list over 70 conditions reported to have delusions as one possible symptom (Cummings, 1985); a search of the major indexes for the words *paranoid* and *delusional* in the subsequent decade yields a diverse array of case studies reporting paranoia as a key symptom, so the number has probably increased further. While paranoia may not be as frequently disabling a symptom as anxiety and depression are, its precipitants are at least as many and varied. Given that many of these medical conditions are treatable, correct diagnosis is crucial.

The presence of paranoia in the context of dementia illustrates its role as a symptom. Increased paranoia (e.g., accusing a relative of stealing the family's sterling tableware) may be the first symptom of Alzheimer's to be noticed by family. While this can occur even in an individual not previously characterized by suspiciousness, often there is an apparent continuity between premorbid personality and paranoid decompensation in old age (Howard & Levy, 1993). The fact that paranoid delusions are seen in dementia reflects the perceptiveness behind Morel's and Kraepelin's use of the term *dementia praecox* (or "premature senility") to denote what we now call schizophrenia. In using this term, these writers were presumably noting the strong similarities between the symptoms (including paranoia) seen in youthful schizophrenics and those seen in elderly patients with conditions such as the one we now call Alzheimer's. Differential diagnosis can be a challenge in the elderly, given that DD is often a relatively late-onset condition and that paranoid symptoms are more prevalent among late- than early-onset schizophrenics (cf. Marengo & Westermeyer, 1996).

Diagnostic Boundaries

As Harper (1996) has noted, the presumption that trust is a personal virtue underlies the notion that paranoia is a pathological condition. However, borders between the pathological and the nonpathological are often fuzzy in the domain of psychopathology, and this is particularly the case with respect to paranoia—most notably with respect to the issue of interpersonal trust. Within the normal range, one person's paranoia is another's due caution, and one person's trust is another's gullibility. One does not have to be clinically paranoid to underestimate another person's good-will, nor does one have to be histrionic or dependent to overestimate it. Preceded by near-universal fear of strangers in infancy, normal development entails learning that not everyone who seems trustworthy is trustworthy (as in "Don't take candy from strangers"). It is not uncommon for people—normal individuals who are not notably gullible—to find themselves wishing they had been *less* trusting. Similarly, most psychotherapists can remember at least one client whom they successfully helped to become more trusting, only to see that client's fragile ventures into the social world met by real betrayal. Most of us like to think that by being astute we can protect ourselves from unscrupulous individuals, but anyone who has dealt with a true psychopath knows that mere astuteness is no protection against the dangers such an individual poses. If one is unwilling to risk ever being betrayed, a suspicious, guarded posture is the only option. Moreover, there are harsh environments in which it would arguably be maladaptive not to be somewhat paranoid—for example, if one lives in a police state and has already come to the scornful attention of the authorities, or if one lives in a crime-ridden urban neighborhood in a western democracy. Newhill (1990) has noted the need to differentiate paranoia that is "an adaptive mechanism for coping with a life that is plagued by prejudice and discrimination . . . from paranoia as a functional illness" (p. 177). It seems apparent, however, that this is a matter of degree—that because environments come in all levels harshness, then adaptive vs. illness judgments can hardly be dichotomous.

A measure of vigilance may be adaptive even in environments that are not particularly harsh. Persons for whom risk of victimization is not a daily concern evidently deal with the need for risk-avoidance by maintaining routines that institutionalize or encapsulate their "adaptive paranoia." Mental health professionals buy malpractice insurance and follow self-protective guidelines, then think as little as possible about the prospect of being sued. Businesspersons have attorneys review partnership contracts before signing them, even though they trust the prospective partners fully; in this case, the attorney is the "designated paranoid." A chief executive may hire a somewhat paranoid assistant with the expectation that that assistant's hyperacute antennae may free him (the boss) from himself having to be so alert.

We isolate our paranoia in such ways because we are convinced that being suspicious all the time will surely handicap us unduly. We know, for instance, that the jealous lover may succeed in keeping his partner at his side, but that the jealousy will result in a relationship that is a hollow caricature of one based on mutual trust. Most of us, put simply, would rather risk betrayal than lead a life of simmering suspicion. All of which is to emphasize, however, that there is a *range* of suspiciousness—temporary and trait—that must be viewed as normal. There is for all of us a tradeoff between vigilance and vulnerability, and it is sometimes not obvious whether tilting one way or the other is the healthier. And which of the two is more adaptive depends in part on how benign one's social environment turns out to be. One can view the paranoid as a person who has tilted in the direction of avoiding false positives (failure to detect untrustworthiness) at the expense of incurring many false negatives (failure to correctly identify trustworthiness).

The social context is also relevant in that mistrust—even a sense of being besieged—can be cultivated socially. One variant of this is shared psychotic disorder (SPD), traditionally called *folie à deux*. Typically one of the two individuals (the primary) has clearly led the way into delusional territory (in *DSM-III-R*, SPD was called *induced* psychotic disorder). Often (though not always) the other person (the secondary) is more appropriately described as easily influenced, vulnerable, and isolated rather than as fundamentally paranoid. Indeed, when two psychotically paranoid individuals are married, they typically do *not* share the same delusions (Sacks, 1988). There are case reports in the literature of *folie à trois* (Maizel, Knobler, & Herbstein, 1990) and *folie à quatre* (Mela, Obenbe, & Farmer, 1997). Most cases of SPD in the literature involve persecutory delusions, and the individuals are typically from a single, socially-isolated nuclear family (Silveira & Seeman, 1995); when those affected constitute an entire nuclear family, it is sometimes described as *folie à famille.* SPD may go undetected unless all members of a family are assessed (Sacks, 1988).

Arguably, a number of major historical phenomena can be described in terms of a still larger scale variant of SPD. The recent conflicts in Bosnia and Rwanda both manifest a dynamic focused on shared persecutory beliefs. Indeed, a classic demagogic technique is to get *us* to stand together in opposition to *them* by painting *them* as bent on enslaving or destroying *us.* When the leaders making such dire pronouncements control the media, it is hard for the populace not to believe them—even members of the populace who are not predisposed to suspicions and who would not usually be drawn to a grandiose leader figure. Such talk can be a prelude to real hostilities, as when *our* fear of attack leads us to behave threateningly, instigating suspicion and aggressive intent on the part of *them.*

Thus can paranoia—on both an individual and a communal level—generate prophesies of victimization that are self-fulfilling. And thus are wars started for no more reason than that one nation has a key leader who is himself clinically paranoid—or is so sociopathic that he is willing to cultivate fear of persecution for his own ends. In some cases, the fear of persecution is linked with the personal charisma of the grandiose leader and a widely shared religious (or quasi-religious) ideology that sanctions behaviors that would otherwise be viewed as antisocial (such as murder of those deemed evil). The Branch Davidian tragedy in Waco, Texas, seems to have incorporated all of these aspects—a grandiose leader, an extreme religious ideology, and a focus on persecution that entailed behaviors that elicited *real* "persecution" (from federal agents). (As bizarre and disorganized behavior generally undercut someone's credibility, all things being equal, an individual with DD would have better luck gaining followers than would an individual with florid PS—although presumably PS might emerge *after* the leader gained power.)

Calling a given personage *paranoid* can itself be somewhat demagogic, of course, and at the very least it can be a clever way to give a medical-scientific gloss to one's own arrogance.[2] Interestingly, the opposite epithet—*gullible*—is nearly as nasty and as powerful; some would rather embrace a paranoid view than be thought gullible. But even granting (1) that such words are not to be thrown around lightly; (2) that some paranoia is "explainable" socially; (3) that paranoia can be an adaptive, rational, or even inevitable in some environments; (4) that what beliefs are deemed unacceptable and hence paranoid is partly a function of the prevailing political matrix (Harper, 1996); and (5) that reasonable people may disagree regarding whether a given person's paranoia reflects psychopathology, it is still clear that in some cases paranoia is pathological. For instance, that calling Joseph Stalin paranoid is not merely a case of politically motivated name-calling is seen in the following vignette:

> Of the many letters of condolence that Eleanor Roosevelt received upon her husband's death, the strangest came from Joseph Stalin. After a few lines of sympathy, the Soviet dictator implied that Franklin Delano Roosevelt had been poisoned, and he went on to offer his assistance in any investigation that Mrs. Roosevelt might conduct. . . . From his perspective, even elderly men suffering from severe hypertension and morbid arteriosclerosis do not simply die from these diseases; they are poisoned. (Robins & Post, 1997, pp. 1–2)

It must be emphasized that, as with other disorders having fuzzy boundaries, there is probably no sine qua non of paranoia. Suspiciousness certainly is a key element in *DSM-IV* PPD, and it probably comes closest to being an essential aspect of paranoid conditions more generally. There can be culturally determined differential association between suspiciousness and pathological manifestation. For instance, in the United States, mistrust is apparently more closely associated with depression (as opposed to a paranoid disorder) among black than among white individuals (Whaley, 1997), and trust plays qualitatively different roles in interpersonal relations in the United States and Japan (Yamagishi & Yamagishi, 1994). Note also that not all paranoid individuals are "islands," as evidenced by the phenomenon of SPD (not to mention cults). In this vein, Robins and Post (1997, p. 94) have discussed "the paradoxical solace of belonging to a paranoid group." Even when the group has no grand vision—its purpose may, for instance, be to assert that the lunar landings were hoaxes—a member may take pride in being among the few who are not fooled.

Imperviousness to correction also comes close to being a sine qua non. It may be viewed as a by-product of the unwillingness to risk any false negatives. The quality of mental experience being referred to here is well captured in the following description, pertaining to what is often called the Othello syndrome:

> When the jealousy complex is central to paranoia, the patient is usually gradually overwhelmed by the convictions that the partner is deceiving him or her. Systematization and elaboration inevitably follow. Pseudomemories often abound; the patient remembers incidents that clearly point to infidelity, and reinterprets past actions and previous comments as incontrovertible proof. Misinterpretations abound: The way the husband walks indicates recent intercourse . . . the discarded empty packet of condoms glimpsed in a public park was certainly left by the wife's lover after their tryst in the rhododendrons. (White & Mullen, 1989, p. 211)

Such misinterpretations are not restricted to jealousy but may be present in all kinds of delusional and subdelusional processes. "For example, one patient took the appearance of a police car in a busy thoroughfare as unequivocal evidence that the police were chasing him, neglecting the probability of this event occurring if the police had not interest in him" (Hemsley & Garety, 1986, p. 53). When imperviousness to correction and mistrust are both present, the clinician who expresses skepticism about such "proofs" risks breaching whatever fragile therapeutic alliance might otherwise develop.

Case Vignette

Mr. A., a semiretired businessman, entered therapy with the avowed intention of soliciting the therapist's support in planned malpractice litigation. He presented as very intense, articulate, and of high analytical intelligence. He had already consulted numerous professionals regarding the alleged malpractice and that all of whom had told him he had no case—a pattern he attributed to guild-protective instincts on the part of these individuals. That is, these multiple opinions, from individuals he had judged qualified enough to consult, did not dissuade him from his position. Indeed, he kept his own counsel on all matters. If the therapist made any comment that ventured far from Mr. A.'s prior beliefs, they were ignored or quickly discounted. The therapist soon asserted that he lacked the expertise to assist in the litigation but offered to be helpful in another area that came up in initial discussion: Mr. A.'s marriage, which was in trouble partly because Mrs. A. had tired of his focus on his malpractice grievance. In that context, an extensive history was obtained, including conversations with Mr. and Mrs. A.'s grown children, who now operated the business Mr. A. had started. While acknowledging his quirks, and while indicating that they did not share his views regarding the alleged malpractice, they showed great affection for him. They described an episode years before in which the business had been mysteriously robbed over a period of months. While all involved were upset, Mr. A. was particularly obsessive and suspicious, and it was he who solved the mystery. The crime could have been curtailed promptly; however, the police, having previously noted Mr. A.'s paranoia, initially dismissed his explanation and did not take the preventive action that was suggested by it. That is, the most maladaptive aspect of Mr. A.'s paranoid style—given that he was being genuinely victimized—was that it led other people to discount his views. The therapist addressed the marital problem—all the while avoiding any challenge of Mr. A.'s views regarding the alleged malpractice; presumably, following termination Mr. A. sought out yet another professional for help on that front. It seemed unlikely that such help would be forthcoming—whether or not his case had merit—if only because whomever he consulted would notice his paranoid style and discount his claims.

Such judgments are, of course, fundamentally flawed in that one cannot infer from the fact that a person is paranoid that he has not been wronged. The case is interesting because it is so mixed: paranoid elements were clearly present to a degree that interfered with functioning from time to time over the years. But others are absent—as evidenced by the warm, mutually trusting relationship between Mr. A. and his sons.

Delusions

Delusions are hallmarks of PS (where they are classed as positive symptoms) and of DD, though they appear in other contexts as well. Mood-congruent delusions may be present in affective psychoses: for example, (1) delusions of nihilism (Cotard's syndrome) in psychotic depression, and (2) grandiose delusions in manic states. And a broad range of delusional content is seen in medical and drug-related conditions. Finally, *DSM-IV* does not award a diagnosis of PS to all schizophrenics with delusions, rather only to those who *lack* disorganized speech or behavior, or flat or inappropriate affect.

Delusions in both PS and DD (and subdelusional tendencies in PPD) are commonly seen as involving *grandeur* or *persecution.* Though the two are empirically distinct (cf. Stuart, Malone, Currie, Klimidis, & Minas, 1995) they may reflect alternate expressions of a single undercurrent, as when the person's belief that he is being persecuted is tied to his assumption that he special. For example, the belief that one is being menaced by a team of government operatives involves grandiosity as well as persecution, since only a singularly important person would warrant so much attention. Similarly, one can view one's run-of-the-mill lot in life as evidence of persecution *if* one believes oneself to be special and thus deserving of more. The presence of an overt grandiose (or erotomanic) element within a persecutory belief system may render it especially impermeable and resistant to change (cf. Papernik, Pardes, & Winston, 1975). Of course, persecutory delusions can be part of a psychotic depression as well (as when they are secondary to delusional self-condemnation), but usually only persecution that the individual considers to be unjust is viewed as paranoid (but see Trower & Chadwick, 1995).

DSM-IV actually lists three subtypes of DD beyond grandiose and persecutory, but two of those—*erotomanic* and *jealous*—can be viewed as variants of grandiose and persecutory, respectively. That the erotomanic variant—also called de Clérambault's syndrome—has grandiose overtones is apparent in the fact that the putative lover is always a particularly distinguished or glamorous individual (Segal, 1989). The close link between grandiose and persecutory delusions is sometimes seen even in erotomanic cases, as when the patient believes that he (or, perhaps more often, she) is being kept from the lover by some malevolent force.

The fifth subtype of DD in *DSM-IV* is *somatic.* Pre-*DSM-IV* versions of the *DSM* included the word *paranoid* in the name of what is now called DD. In lay usage (which, as noted above, affects professional usage), the word *paranoid* has persecutory (and, perhaps, grandiose) overtones. It was dropped in *DSM-IV*, perhaps lest its use in this context be seen as claiming that *all* psychotic delusions—even somatic ones—are somehow tied to persecutory or grandiose beliefs. That is, the *DSM-IV* authors were presumably focusing on falsity and resistance to correction as central to the notion of delusions, in which case it makes sense to group severe somatoform delusions with persecutory and grandiose delusions.[3] A reasonable alternative would have been to leave *paranoid* in the name of DD and classify conditions involving somatic delusions as psychotic variants among the somatoform disorders. In so doing, one would be viewing straightforward somatic delusions are more akin to hypochondriasis or body dysmorphic disorder than to, say, persecutory delusions. In this vein, Phillips, McElroy, Keck, Hudson, and Pope (1994) have reported that, among individuals with symptoms of body dysmorphic disorder, those whose symptom was of delusional intensity appeared little different on other variables from those for whom the dysmorphic belief was subdelusional. It is not uncommon for research studies on DD to use samples predominated by individuals whose delusions have persecutory elements (e.g., Bentall & Kaney, 1996), and it is unclear that findings from such studies can be generalized to DD somatic type.

Not mentioned as a DD subtype in *DSM-IV* is the delusional belief that important persons in one's life are imposters—also referred to in the literature as Capgras syndrome or as a kind of misidentification syndrome. Its absence from *DSM-IV* is perhaps warranted by the fact that in many cases it appears to arise from neurological impairments involving visual recognition (cf. Ellis & de Pauw, 1994; Maher & Spitzer, 1993; Silva, Leong, Weinstock, & Wine, 1993). Occasionally, a delusion may qualify as both Capgras and persecutory, as when the individual perceives that an imposter is the source of harassment (e.g., Christodoulou, Margariti, Malliaras, & Alevizou, 1995).

If one assumes that PPD is (in some cases at least) a less severe variant of DD, then a full understanding of delusional processes is central to an understanding of PPD as well. However, as noted above, this is not an assumption that can be accepted without reservations; many individuals with severe PPD never become truly delusional, and DD appears in the absence of PPD. Chapman and Chapman (1988, p. 167) have suggested that "aberrant beliefs" (also described as "delusionlike ideas" and as "attenuated forms of delusions") are on a continuum with—and predispose to the development of—delusions. These include the beliefs that parts of one's body are alien to the self, the belief that psychical energies can be transferred between people, and the tendency to think people are talking about oneself (accompanied, when the condition is *attenuated*, by the willingness to acknowledge that they may not be). Many aberrant beliefs are more in line with schizotypal personality disorder than with PPD. Moreover, it appears likely that the psychotic vulnerability that they confer is not specific to DD (Chapman, Chapman, Kwapil, Eckblad, & Zinser, 1994). However, Chapman and Chapman have noted that psychotic individuals' delusions are often exaggerated versions of delusionlike beliefs they held prior to onset of psychosis (see also Harrow et al., 1988).

Diagnostic Boundaries Revisited

The question of what constitutes a delusion is somewhat fraught (see Levy, 1996; Oltmanns, 1988). For a belief to be delusional, must it merely be *false*, or must it be *incredible* and *impossible*? And, in any case, who is to decide? What consideration is to be given as to whether the belief has support within the social milieu? If it has such support, does it matter whether the milieu is heavily populated with troubled individuals? In the absence of strong evidence that a belief is false, does it matter whether or not it is popular? And how is it to be dealt with that some delusional beliefs are essentially irrefutable, either because they lie in the realm of subjective evaluation rather than fact (e.g., that one's poems manifest remarkable artistic merit; Fulford, 1994) or because they pertain to the distant future (Hemsley & Garety, 1986)? For instance, if Unabomber Ted Kaczinski's eccentric beliefs are evaluative and prophetic, hence unfalsifiable, should this eliminate PS and DD as possible diagnoses in his case?

Still, whatever its limitations, the falsity criterion is clearly relevant. Seemingly implausible persecutory fears sometimes prove accurate (e.g., Menuck, 1992), or at least partially so (Kaffman, 1981). Before calling a belief delusional, a professional should in principle obtain an independent assessment of its falsity, though this appears not to be common practice (Maher & Spitzer, 1993). In some cases, as when the patient believes his spouse to be unfaithful, there may be no way to rule out the possibility that the accusation is true; the most one could conclude is that the patient has exaggerated the likelihood of betrayal.

It is especially perilous for a professional who lacks intimate familiarity with a patient's culture to call that patient's beliefs delusional (cf. Gaines, 1988; Newhill, 1990; Westermeyer, 1988), or to declare a false belief bizarre (cf. *DSM-IV*). Consider, for instance, the devout Christian who insists that each week he drinks the blood of a long-since-murdered man whose mother was a virgin and whose father was the creator of the universe: such an person is surely at risk of being viewed as delusional—indeed, bizarrely so—unless whoever makes the diagnosis understands the cultural context. As Levy (1996) has noted, "Against every delusional content, as bizarre and remote as it may look, there exists at least one cultural niche, in which the same content is considered legitimate and reasonable, if not important and dignified" (p. 258).

Obviously, there are gradations of delusionality, and in some ways the more central issues pertain to the severity of other symptoms rather than to the falsity of the belief itself. One cannot assume that *patients* who believe the unbelievable are representative of persons who believe the unbelievable more generally. Even if an individual holds a belief that is truly incredible and unsupported culturally, if he is not preoccupied with it and is a generally high-functioning individual, whether or not the belief qualifies as psychotic is largely academic. Cases have been reported in which psychotropic medications were effective in reducing the individual's passionate engagement in a delusion, hence improving overall functionality and lessening the apparent likelihood of disruptive behavior while leaving untouched the individual's actual beliefs (cf. Taylor et al., 1994; Segal, 1989). See Harrow et al. (1988) for a discussion of *emotional commitment* to delusions.

The subtlety of the paranoia-as-false-beliefs issue is well set forth in the case of the 19th-century physician Ignaz Simmelweis, whose clinical research was important to the modern understanding of microbial disease contagion. His views were at odds with prevailing medical belief, and he faced widespread scorn from contemporary physicians (who, we now know, were infecting their own patients by not following Simmelweis's advice regarding sterilization). He was preoccupied with—and deeply committed to—the rightness of his cause and with the sense that his colleagues' resistance was harming patients and dishonoring him. Sadly, the somewhat paranoid posture that this plight nourished took a malignant turn, and Simmelwies's later years were marked by a deeply paranoid condition. Whether this would have occurred if his contemporaries had been quick to acknowledge the validity of his views cannot be known.

Theoretical Perspectives and Related Research

As is the case with many (perhaps all) forms of severe psychopathology, in explanatory theories of delusions—and of paranoid conditions more generally—one can discern two general classes: *motivational* and *deficit*. Do the faulty beliefs arise from the individual's self-protective needs or from his inability to think more clearly? In the case of delusions, there are two additional models to contend with: that delusions emerge in the context of normal reasoning processes of persons confronted with anomalous information and that paranoia reflects a cognitive bias. A bias hypothesis may be linked to a motivational hypothesis, though it need not be. A sampling of the various kinds of models is provided in this section, motivational models first. See Winters and Neale (1983) and Fenigstein (1996) for more extensive reviews.

At least one writer (Colby, 1977) has argued that, for a persecutory delusion to warrant being called paranoid, it must be purposively constructed and used by the individual to relieve and protect against internal distress—a position in which the motivational model is more a matter of definition than of theory. While Colby adopted this definition as a way of distinguishing paranoid delusions from persecutory beliefs that the individual learns from his cultural milieu, it begs the question of whether PS and DD, as descriptive diagnoses, are appropriately viewed as growing from motivated, defensive processes.

Motivational Approaches

The classic Freudian view is that the individual deals with his own unacceptable impulses by projecting them—that is, by believing those impulses to be present in others. Further, the sensitivity to humiliation was seen as reflecting self-esteem problems. Apparently needing to tie all psychopathology to sexuality (Bone & Oldham, 1994), Freud argued that homosexual impulses lay at the root of paranoia, and that the individual denies the presence of those impulses and projects his own unconscious self-condemnation upon others. Grandiosity was seen as defensive overcompensation. As Colby (1977) noted, the classic homosexuality theory of paranoia seems inapplicable with respect to paranoia in women and in overt homosexuals.

An example of a later psychoanalytic view is that of Shapiro (1965). Writing shortly before the tide of opinion in the mental health professions shifted away from assuming a close link between homosexuality and psychopathology, Shapiro honored Freud's focus on passive-homosexual drives in paranoia by describing it as a "discovery" rather than a point of view. Still, homosexuality was not a major aspect of his own theory—no more so than seems warranted by the fact that some paranoid patients *are* manifestly preoccupied with other's views regarding their sexual orientation (perhaps an especially apt focus of self-doubt in the early 1960s, given that homosexuality was so widely stigmatized then). Rather, Shapiro's focus was on paranoia as a defense against passivity and surrender. That is, the individual deals with his deep sense of vulnerability by projection—by viewing the world as eyeing him menacingly; "the paranoid person is continuously occupied and concerned with the threat of being subjected to some external control or some external infringement of his will" (p. 82). Shapiro noted that suspicious individuals are sometimes insightful observers, but that the intense scanning of the environment entails a bias on attention, especially when linked with the individual's assumption that what is obvious is probably misleading. Shapiro described paranoia as a state of emergency mobilization, requiring that spontaneous responses be replaced with intentional ones and that tender and playful emotions in particular be cast aside. He noted that the individual in this kind of humorless, hyperpurposive state assumes that other persons are as he is—and that others' laughter is purposive rather than spontaneous. Robins and Post (1997, p. 229) have recently made a similar point in their comment that, "because the paranoid thinks constantly about his enemies, [he thinks] they think constantly about him."

Regarding projection, Shapiro offered an eloquent image of the paranoid individual as "in the position of the passenger on a train who, if his attention is fixed on another train alongside and if in addition he does not experience a sensation of his own motion, cannot realize that it is *his* train that is moving" (p. 92).[4] Since Shapiro viewed projection as related to a hyperacute attentional style, he did not assume that what the individual projects onto others is an exact mirror of his own conflicts, only that those conflicts color the individual's perceptions and that their intensity drives the intensity of the delusionality at any given time. Interestingly, though Shapiro assumed that paranoia always arises out of internal conflict, he proposed that, in some cases, it may outlive the original conflict; even "when the individual removes himself from the circumstances and the particular projective object that is involved," the "projective ideas will become a more or less permanent part of the individual's psychology" (p. 101).

A recent entry within the long tradition of models in which paranoid behavior is viewed as fundamentally defensive and compensatory is that offered by Bergner (1993). He proposed two key elements of the paranoid style: the individual perceives himself to be insufficiently autonomous (i.e., to lack the status of an agent) and to be stigmatized (i.e., to have a status which is so low as to be barely intolerable). The lack of autonomy is related to the individual's being uncertain whether his reasons for acting really are *his* reasons. The stigmatization is associated with one's belief that one has a shameful defect that bars one from membership in the community of normal human beings. Both of these features underlie compensatory measures—for example, drastic face-saving endeavors, perhaps involving the adoption of implausible explanations for whatever threatens one's status. The constancy of the lack of perceived autonomy and status necessitates the constant vigilance, the angry retaliation, and the self-exaltation.

Other post-Freudian motivational models have, like Bergner's, viewed paranoia as a means of compensating for some negative self-aspect. They differ in how the negative self-aspect is characterized. For Schwartz (1964), it was helplessness and a sense that one's own thoughts and feelings are meaningless. Zigler and Glick (1988) suggested that PS may be one of several defensive manifestations of an underlying depressive process. Noting that erotomanic delusions typically develop in lonely individuals whose prospects seem dim, various authors have suggested that this condition is compensatory for the lack of romantic or erotic fulfillment (Segal, 1989).

The most extensively researched self-protective model of paranoia is that put forth by Bentall and colleagues (e.g., Kinderman & Bentall, 1996, 1997). The model is fundamentally cognitive. Patients with persecutory delusions tend to make external, global, stable attributions for negative events and internal, global, stable attributions for positive events—at least when their explicit attributions are obtained. This is similar to the self-serving bias shown by many psychologically healthy individuals.[5] However, the attributions may be exaggerated for defensive purposes in paranoia, serving "to maintain consistency between self-perceptions and self-ideals at the expense of contributing to negative perceptions of the intentions of others and, therefore, paranoia" (Kinderman & Bentall, 1996, p. 106).

This model is largely consistent with Zigler and Glick's (1988) proposal that PS is a depressive variant. As expressed by Bentall and Kaney (1996), the proposal is that

> paranoid patients have latent negative self-representations or schemata similar to the more accessible negative self-representations observed in depressed patients. . . . When these negative self-representations are primed by threatening events, leading to discrepancies between the self-representations and self-ideals, external . . . attributions for the threatening events are elicited. These attributions are self-protective in the sense that they reduce the patient's awareness of discrepancies between the self and self-ideals, but carry the penalty of activating schemata that represent threats from others. (p. 1231)

Indeed, on a number of subtle measures paranoid and depressive individuals have been shown to perform similarly. Unlike most theorists who have proposed compensatory and stylistic models for paranoia, Bentall and colleagues have offered empirical evidence consistent with such claims. In particular, they have garnered evidence that attributions are much less self-exonerating when *subtle* measures are obtained, and, more generally, that paranoid individuals have an *implicit* negative self-concept.

However, it should be emphasized that, at least at an explicit level, depressed and nondepressed groups do differ on various parameters. For instance, other research on causal beliefs has suggested that, while depressed and paranoid individuals share a tendency not to see themselves as controlling the important outcomes in their lives, paranoid individuals are distinctive in ascribing control to other persons (Fenigstein & Venable, 1992; Rosenbaum & Hadari, 1985), especially when the event is a negative one (Kinderman & Bentall, 1996). Kaney, Bowen-Jones, Dewey, and Bentall (1997) have presented findings indicating that, while both depressed and deluded individuals have elevated estimates of the frequency with which negative (i.e., interpersonal harassment) experiences occur to the self, paranoid individuals also have elevated estimates of the frequency with which such events occur to others.

False but Reasonable

Maher and colleagues (e.g., 1988; Maher & Spitzer, 1993) have offered a model that, like Bentall et al.'s, draws parallels between normal cognitive processes and those found in paranoia, though the Maher model lacks the focus on defensive self-protection. Also like the model just described, it may be described as having an attributional component, though the term attributional is used in quite different ways in the two cases. In the Bentall model, the attributional focus is on biased assignment of responsibility (external vs. internal) for good and bad events. The Maher model, in contrast, might best be called a misattributional model, and the focus is on delusional development as part of the individual's attempt to make sense of puzzling (often private) experiences.

Maher's central claim is that that paranoid mentation can flourish even in the absence of a noteworthy thought disorder. Delusions are seen as "normal theories." Thus, delusional thinking is not inherently aberrant but results from the same kind of processes that people, including scientists, use to account for the data of observation. In all persons, unexpected or puzzling information calls for an explanation, and when one is forthcoming the individual is relieved, even happy. In anyone, having multiple anomalous experiences—those for which there is no easy explanation—can raise a number of questions: "How is this experience being induced? Who or what is doing the inducing? Why are they doing this to me and not to other people? And (sometimes) Why are other people denying the reality of my experience?" (Maher & Spitzer, 1993, p. 108).

And answers, once established, are not easily abandoned; "nobody changes beliefs easily" (Maher, 1988, p. 31). An explanation is most likely to be judged delusional by others when the person holding it has access to unusual information, when his sensory experience is unusual, or his processes of selective attention are aberrant, causing him to focus on—and be puzzled by—information that other persons ignore. The fact that a large and diverse array of medical conditions—particularly those involving sensory impairments, including a condition so mundane as conductive hearing loss (e.g., Cooper & Curry, 1976)—apparently incur an increased risk for delusions suggests that the common denominator among them is a disturbance in the information coming from the body. In such cases, the individual's "explanation" of his aberrant or confusing experiences may be reasonable (if not accurate). Cases have even been reported in which delusions signaled the presence of a previously undiagnosed sensory defect. In one of the truly experimental studies of paranoia, Zimbardo, Anderson, and Kabat (1981) showed that hypnotic induction of deafness (without awareness thereof) resulted in an temporary increase in a broad range of paranoid symptoms. Note, however, that not all research supports a linkage between hearing loss and paranoia (cf. Moore, 1981; Watt, 1985a).

Maher has suggested that, in the absence of such a physical substratum for delusions, the likely basis is *coincidence*—the individual having noticed some naturally (perhaps randomly) occurring pattern in everyday experience. In further support of his model, Maher has noted that *among normal individuals* it is common to see (1) deficits of logical thinking, (2) readiness to "offer implausible explanations for anomalous experience" (Maher, 1988, p. 27), and, more generally, (3) adherence to faddish, quasi-magical beliefs.

The fact that there is a high incidence of paranoid diagnoses among migrants, particularly refugees—and a tendency for levels of suspiciousness to run high in unselected groups of immigrants—(cf. Westermeyer, 1988) can be accommodated within Maher's model. That is, an immigrant's sense of being looked at, disdained, or taken advantage of may be veridical, such that the individual's experiences may invite explanations involving persecutory intent on the part of others. In many cases, of course, a history of harassment may have been what *led to* the immigration, but the new environment failed to provide a sense of security (cf. Maizel, Knobler, & Herbstein, 1990). It is, however, possible that some of the high rate of paranoid diagnoses among immigrants reflects overdiagnosis on the part of arrival-country clinicians unappreciative of migrants' culture-specific beliefs (Newhill, 1990).

His emphasis on the "normality" of delusions notwithstanding, Maher (1988) did acknowledge that delusions of persecution may be perpetuated by self-fulfilling prophesies, and he suggested that persons who become delusional even though they lack a medical illness may be characterized as hypervigilant (and thus prone to notice puzzling coincidences). Research summarized by Johnson (1988) suggests that, to this, one might add the tendency to rehearse past memories repetitively, perhaps with a focus on memories (veridical or otherwise) that have particular affective valence (cf. David & Howard, 1994). Research reported more recently (cf. Bentall & Kaney, 1996; Mason, Claridge, & Clark, 1997) supports the view that paranoia involves a kind of stylistic hypervigilance, rendering its acknowledgment virtually obligatory within any comprehensive model of paranoia.

It is, of course, a small step from saying that medically ill persons are vulnerable to delusions by virtue of their puzzling experiences to noting that schizophrenic individuals, faced with perceptual experiences that are even more puzzling, have a similar—but probably much greater—vulnerability (cf. Baddeley, Thornton, Chua, & McKenna,1996; Kihlstron & Hoyt, 1988; Maher & Spitzer, 1993). The fact that hallucinations and delusions have been reported to co-occur is relevant; indeed, this co-occurence accounts for the current practice in schizophrenia research of quantifying not delusionality but *positive symptoms*—thus grouping hallucinations and delusions together. Any apparent co-occurence may, however, be partly a function of the way these phenomena are defined: a hallucinatory percept is arguably not a hallucination unless the perceiver believes it to be real, and that belief is itself a delusion (Fulford, 1994)—a view traceable to William James. Moreover, some recent findings (Stuart et al., 1995) have suggested that the grouping of delusions with other positive symptoms on the basis of co-occurence is not warranted. In this vein, while *DSM-IV* treats delusions and auditory hallucinations as interchangeable among PS criteria, Cardno et al. (1996) have reported data suggesting that only "abusive voices" are strongly related to delusions; other auditory hallucinations are not.

Baddeley et al. (1996) have noted that there are various conditions involving perceptual anomalies (e.g., tinnitis, phantom limb syndrome) that appear not to predispose to delusions, and that this is not consistent with Maher's model. Similarly, Chapman and Chapman (1988) have noted that individuals with anomalous perceptual experiences may vary greatly in the attributions they make regarding those events. In their own research, Chapman and Chapman observed some cases in which a delusion arose because the individual had an anomalous perceptual experience that, if the experience was to be accepted as veridical, virtually demanded a delusional belief. Other subjects reported delusions that had some relation to their unusual experiences but were not necessary, or even reasonable, interpretations of those experiences. Still others reported delusions or aberrant beliefs that had no apparent relationship to any unusual experiences (sometimes called primary delusions). Of particular interest is the fact that some individuals who have anomalous experiences develop nondeviant explanations for them. For instance, Chapman and Chapman mentioned an individual who reported hearing critical inner voices but attributed them to his own conscience. Delusional interpretations appeared to arise when the individual treats the anomalous experience "as if it were the only datum available" (p. 176), ignoring even clearly relevant, readily available information. Chapman and Chapman suggested that Maher's model is most plausible only if one also assumes that the delusional process involves an overfocus on the most salient information.

Deficit

Given the cognitive intactness of patients with DD, it would be of great interest to ascertain if specific cognitive deficits could be detected in such individuals. The scarcity of such patients makes such research difficult, and the research addressing the notion that paranoia derives from an information-processing deficit has focused largely on the paranoid-nonparanoid distinction within schizophrenic samples (and much of this research relied on pre-*DSM-III* diagnoses). Across a large number of research paradigms, paranoids have often showed better cognitive functioning than nonparanoids (cf. Chapman & Chapman, 1973; Magaro, 1980; Meissner, 1981; Zigler & Glick, 1988), and they tend to have histories involving greater social competence (Zigler & Levine, 1983).

However, paranoids do worse on some tasks. There is evidence that they do poorly when cognitive flexibility is required—that is, they are tripped up by tasks that require *shifts* in one's working assumptions about how best to proceed (e.g., Abbruzzese, Ferri, & Scarone, 1996), and Young & Jerome, 1972; but see Garety, Hemsley, & Wessely, 1991; Kremen et al., 1994; and Rosse, Schwartz, Mastropaolo, Goldberg, & Deutsch, 1991. Brennan and Hemsley (1984) presented research suggesting that paranoid schizophrenics are especially prone to make the error of viewing uncorrelated events as correlated. In addition, based on a review of prior research, Neufeld (1991) has suggested (1) that studies of stimulus encoding indicate that PS patients are slow to translate presenting stimulation into the kind of cognitive format that facilities working memory; and (2) that studies of short-term memory indicate that PS individuals are particularly susceptible to interference and forgetting. In sum, Neufeld has suggested the following characterization of PS: "Information upon which short memory operations take place . . . may be incomplete or degraded. . . . Also, more simple information relevant to solving problems or drawing conclusions may be missed if encoding of rapidly moving stimulation is prolonged" (p. 252). Neufeld has suggested that this pattern of specific weaknesses, coupled with the individual's assuming the worst when confronted with fractional information, is consistent with the clinical picture seen in PS.

Cognitive Style

Finally, mention should be made of Fenigstein's (e.g., 1995, 1996) model. Like that of Maher and colleagues, this approach looks to behavior commonly seen in normal individuals for an understanding of paranoid pathology. Like that of Bentall and colleagues, this approach focuses on information-processing style, and the research related to it has drawn upon research literatures on social cognition—and upon technologies applied in recent decades to an understanding of cognitive processes in affective disorders. Unlike Bentall's, Fenigstein's model takes no stand regarding underlying motivations or defenses, nor is it sympathetic to the view that paranoia may be a depression-based manifestation.

Its point of contact with paranoid symptomatology is evident in the observations that "almost all paranoid disorders involve personalistic or self-referent interpretations of others' behaviors"; the key stylistic aspect of paranoid cognition is a "*self-as-target bias*" (Fenigstein & Venable, 1992, p. 129). Here the individual's belief that he is the object of others' attention is rooted in his preoccupation with how he is seen by others (i.e., high public self-consciousness). Thus, self-referential ideation is seen as the organizing feature of paranoid behavior. While in nonparanoid individuals focus on the self usually increases the sense that one is the cause of outcomes in one's life, in the case of paranoia the self on which self-focus focuses is "defined in terms of threat from others, control by others, and a sense of personal vulnerability to those external forces" (Fenigstein, 1996, p. 268). That this is a self-schema quite unlike that seen in depression seems to contradict the position taken by Bentall and Kaney (1996) noted above.

Support for this model comes from a number of correlational and experimental studies using unselected students. For instance, Fenigstein and Vanable (1992, Study 3) reported that undergraduates who were induced by a subtle experimental procedure to focus their attention on themselves also showed a tendency to believe that they were being watched by someone else. Similarly, Kramer's (1994, Study 2) research on graduate students employed two variables: induced self-focus and induced ruminativeness; in an ambiguous, quasi-competitive situation, both variables increased individuals' perceptions of being taken advantage of by others. The only study to test this model on psychotic patients yielded partly nonsupportive findings (Smári et al., 1994), though measures of paranoia and *private* self-consciousness were quite strongly related among these subjects. Bodner and Mikulincer (1998) have suggested that, following personal failure, focusing attention on a putative victimizer, rather than on the self, fosters paranoid-like responses, and they have presented extensive experimental evidence in support. While Bodner and Mikulincer's model may seem to contradict Fenigstein's, in both models paranoia is linked with a focus on *self as victimized by other*, which is perhaps fostered by self-focus in some context and by victimizer focus in others.

Stress

There has not been a substantial literature addressing the relation between stressful life events and the development or exacerbation of paranoid disorders, though there are a couple of points that can be made. *ICD-10*, though not *DSM-IV*, suggests stress vulnerability as a criterion for PPD; the long clinical traditional that this comes from has tended to focus on stressors involving the potential for humiliation. It has long been known that life events can affect the course of schizophrenia (e.g., Brown & Birley, 1968) in its various manifestations, and it is becoming increasingly clear that this is true in bipolar disorder as well (e.g., Johnson & Miller, 1997). In one study of a psychiatric sample in which stressor data were reported (Kay, Cooper, Garside, & Roth, 1976), paranoia was associated with *low* levels on this variable—though in comparison with an affective psychosis comparison group. A recent study addressing relapse among young paranoid schizophrenics (Pallanti, Quercioli, & Pazzagli, 1997) has shown that life events scores were elevated during the weeks prior to relapse; in their sample, the relapses of about 61% of individuals appeared to have been precipitated.

Jørgensen and Jensen (1988) have argued that, among psychotically delusional individuals, those with stress-precipitated onset (and brief duration) constitute a distinct subset (about 11% in their sample) for which they suggest the diagnosis of reactive delusional psychosis. Vicente, Ochoa, and Rios (1996) have suggested the term "psychogenic paranoid psychosis" for essentially the same condition; they observed that such cases constitute about 1% of psychiatric inpatients, and that individuals thus classified are subject to full recovery but also to brief relapses (usually also stress precipitated). Consistent with the existence of such a subgroup, Schanda et al. (1991) reported that in a mixed sample of individuals with delusional psychoses, a high level of recent interpersonal stress was a good predictor that the delusion would subside relatively quickly. Within *DSM-IV* brief, precipitated delusional states are diagnosed as brief psychotic disorder (with marked stressor), rather than DD or PS.

Insofar as migration is a stressor, the vulnerability of migrants to paranoid disorders is relevant. However, it appears that in many cases the development of the paranoia is gradual, concomitant with the failure over time to develop a viable social life in the new locale (cf. Maizel et al., 1990), rather than a sudden response to the move. Although cases have been reported in which DD individuals' violent outbursts were arguably precipitated by external events, those events were often not normatively stressful. That is, they became precipitants only through individuals' distortions and hypersensitivity (Kennedy et al., 1992). More generally, it would be no surprise if research were to show that in the chronically paranoid individual, the strength of the normative-stressor/distress relation is unusually weak; malignant interpretations of neutral events may place the individual on such a chronically high level of subjective stress that "real" stressors have no distinctive impact.

Family Issues

Although various authors (e.g. Bone & Oldham, 1994; Benjamin, 1996) have suggested that paranoia, including PPD, has its origins in harsh parenting, few systematic studies have address the childhood experiences of individuals who later become paranoid.

More can be said about the impact of *being* paranoid upon interactions within the family. The key relevant point has been starkly stated by Keefe and Harvey (1994): "extreme paranoia may have a greater impact than any other symptom on those close to a person with schizophrenia. Relatives and friends who may make major sacrifices for the person are accused of being murderers and terrorists plotting doom for him or her. Obviously, these beliefs can be painful to the caring relative or friend. They can also be dangerous" (p. 37).

There are, indeed, cases in the literature of attacks of parents on their children (Anthony, 1986) and of children on parents. In one series of DD individuals who had committed homicide, about two thirds had killed a family member (Benezech, Yesavage, Addad, Bourgeois, & Mills, 1984). In another series of DD individuals remanded for violent behavior, most victims were family members, and most patients had assaulted family members prior to the offense for which they were incarcerated (Kennedy et al., 1992). In some cases, the offender believed the victim was a not his real family member but a "double"—an imposter (Silva et al., 1993), as in Capgras syndrome. (It is not clear how much comfort victims can take from the knowledge that the attacker believed he was attacking someone else.) It should be noted that not all—perhaps not even most—cases of jealous rage directed at a lover are rooted in conditions best described as paranoid. Dutton (1995) has suggested that abusive spouses (usually male) are most commonly characterized as borderline.

The challenge of living with a paranoid individual can be great even if the disorder is of mild PPD proportions and even if physical violence is not an issue. Simply put, it is unpleasant to find one's goodwill doubted and one's intentions misinterpreted repeatedly. If jealousy is involved, efforts to quell the paranoid person's doubts can involve a severe curtailing of one's own behavior (e.g., reduced contact with friends), and it can be tiring at best to find that, even having taken great pains to behave reassuringly, one has fallen short: the suspicions remain. And pervasive suspicion and unwarranted anger can be unpleasant to be around even if it is directed at other persons, rather than at oneself. Faced with the paranoid individual's cynical interpretations of other persons' behavior, one may try to suggest alternative attributions, and the fact that one's suggestions carry so little weight can be demoralizing at best.

In some cases the *self against the world* posture noted above takes the form of *my family against the world*. Here the spouse and children may not be attacked or accused, but the children in particular are at risk by virtue of their constant exposure to the paranoid parent's worldview and the overprotectiveness arising from the paranoid parent's expectation that his children will be victimized (cf. Ulzen & Carpenter, 1997). And when a paranoid parent constantly moves from residence to residence to escape perceived harassment, the children may suffer disruption of friendships and schooling.

Forensic Issues

Among various forms of psychopathology, those involving paranoia are distinctive with respect to the extent to which they involve interaction with the legal system. This is the case in several contexts, both civil and criminal. Each of the following subsections provides a brief discussion of one of them. The ambiguities noted above with regard to the definition of delusions are particularly troublesome in these situations, given the stakes that are involved (see Levy, 1996).

Incompetence

When an individual's behavior is guided by delusions (as in PS or DD), he may be declared legally incompetent to manage his own affairs. There are certainly more individuals who *are* incompetent, and whose affairs are managed by others, than there are persons who are *declared* incompetent. The latter happens only when another person (usually a family member) is distressed by the disturbed person's behavior (e.g., squandering the family fortune) and enlists a court's help in curbing it. Constraints on the freedom of disturbed individuals are often imposed by family in informal, extra-legal ways (e.g., by simply announcing "I'm taking over your finances now"), but this is possible only when the disorder involves passivity or inattentiveness (in which case it is subject to abuse). PS and DD individuals are, of course, usually neither passive nor inattentive, so legal action is especially likely to be necessary with these diagnoses. For a person with PS or DD, a legal declaration of incompetence may be the wrenching culmination of a self-fulfilling prophecy: the individual, perhaps preoccupied with imagined threats to his autonomy, unwittingly behaves in such a way that others are convinced that he must be legally stripped of much of his autonomy.

Competence issues may be involved with respect to whether an individual is capable of creating a valid will. Thornier still is the circumstance in which an existing will is posthumously contested on the grounds that it was based on delusional beliefs (e.g., the decedent, falsely believing that his child has turned against him, disinherited that child). Such cases may involve retrospective diagnosis, which can be especially difficult. In addition, even if it were clear that the decedent was preoccupied with a hateful and delusional belief at the time he signed the will, there is the possibility that the delusional belief in question is the *expression*, rather than the *cause*, of the hatred (Mester, Toren, & Gonen, 1994).

Litigiousness

Some paranoid individuals have extensive contact with the legal system by choice. Some frequently summon police. For some, the main response to feeling persecuted or harassed is the repetitive filing of legal suits (and/or writing to politicians and government officials, etc.) to obtain redress (e.g., Rowlands, 1988; Ungvari, Pang, & Chiu, 1995). Indeed, *litigious* (or *querulous*) could have been included on the list of paranoid features that began this chapter. Individuals with PS are, of course, less likely to be credible litigants than are persons with DD or PPD. Some paranoid individuals develop amateur legal skills to the point that they are able to proceed with litigation that most lawyers would regard as futile and would, absent a considerable retainer, refuse to undertake. It is possible that, lacking the perception of legal recourse, some litigious individuals would become directly violent, such that their abuse of the legal system is the lesser of two evils. It is an occupational hazard of the mental health professions that they entail an increased likelihood of being sued or accused by individuals whom they have met in helping capacities but who, owing to a paranoid disorder, come to see the professionals as having victimized them.

Violence

As noted above, some paranoid individuals—especially when guided by outright persecutory delusions—are angry, self-righteous, and prone to behavior that is asocial, illegal, and/or violent. Schizophrenics in whom delusions are the central symptom are much more commonly represented among those who commit violent crimes than are schizophrenics in whom delusions are secondary or absent (Taylor et al., 1994). Thus while lay perceptions of psychotic individuals typically exaggerate their dangerousness, perception and reality are not so discrepant with severe persecutory paranoia. In light of the possibility that such figures as Joseph Stalin, Adolph Hitler, Pol Pot, and Idi Amin were clinically paranoid (not to mention Jim Jones, Shoko Asahara, David Koresh, Ted Kaczinski, and the ethnic leaders in Rwanda and the former Yugoslavia), it may be that this disorder has played a role in the greatest tragedies of the 20th century (cf. Robins & Post, 1997). The cases one sees in a clinic, too, may be dangerous, if on a smaller scale; often, as noted above, the violence is directed within the family. Of course, the incidence of violent crime is low in virtually all populations, including those with paranoid diagnoses, and studies have been reported in which samples of violent individuals showed no elevation on measures of paranoia (e.g., Katz & Marquette, 1996).

NGRI

When an individual commits a crime as a result of truly delusional beliefs, he arguably should be judged not guilty by reason of insanity (NGRI). It is beyond the scope of this chapter to provide full coverage of the legal complexities involved; various jurisdictions hold to various NGRI standards. One is the M'Naughton rule (named after the defendant in the 19th-century homicide case where the rule was first articulated), which specifies that an individual is to be held NGRI if his mental disease had rendered him unknowing of the nature of his action or of its wrongness. The original Mr. M'Naughton was psychotically paranoid, and the M'Naughton rule, narrow as it is, often encompasses individuals with such conditions. Even NGRI critics who argue that it should be applied only within a very restricted range may include severe psychotic delusional states within that range. The situation becomes murky in cases where, say, a DD patient angrily attacks someone whom he had *not* incorporated into his delusional system (cf. Kennedy et al., 1992).

In some jurisdictions, even when an NGRI defense is not viable or fails, a diagnosis such as PS is a possible "mitigating" consideration in determining punishment. For instance, in the case of Ted Kaczinski, the defense lawyers apparently viewed a guilty verdict as inevitable, and their strategy was to shield him from a death sentence on the basis that he suffered from PS. (Mr. Kaczinski opposed this strategy, though many viewed his doing so as yet another manifestation of his PS.)

Involuntary Commitment

Distinct from issues of competence or guilt is the matter of whether an individual requires involuntary commitment for inpatient psychiatric treatment. Jurisdictions vary, but typically commitment for more than a couple of days requires a court order pursuant to expert judgment that an individual is, by virtue of a mental disorder, of clear danger to himself or others. While danger to oneself obviously suggests suicidal tendencies as in severe depression, danger to others suggests violent tendencies as in aggressive paranoia. As with a declaration of incompetence, commitment may signal to the paranoid individual that his worst fears—loss of autonomy and status—have come true. Ironically, by locking up someone who has the "delusional" belief that others want to lock him up, one renders that belief nondelusional (Fulford, 1994). It would, of course, be inappropriate to use an individual's expressions of anger over the real prospect of commitment as the key "proof" of dangerousness used to justify commitment.

Concluding Comments

The safest conclusion is that paranoia arises in diverse ways. There are apparently multiple risk factors such that the importance of one is reduced when another is present. Cooper, Garside, and Kay (1976), for instance, presented data suggesting that paranoid individuals who are deaf may lack the kinds of predisposing factors present in nondeaf paranoid individuals. In addition, there may be synergy among risk factors. For instance, Satel and Edell (1991) have shown that transient cocaine-induced paranoia occurs mainly in individuals who are characterized by aberrant beliefs (cf. Chapman & Chapman, 1988). Thus, there appear to be multiple risk factors that, working together, contribute to the common outcome.

However, this claim is a starting point and no more. It accommodates *too* diverse a variety of possible empirical findings to have much theoretical specificity. Further, it is supported by any finding indicating that higher levels of impairment incur greater vulnerability, and that is not how the data always emerge; for instance, in Migiorelli et al.'s (1995) study of Alzheimer's patients, there was no difference between delusional and nondelusional subgroups on diverse neuropsychological variables. Apparently, neuropsychological deficits are not additional risk factors for paranoia among Alzheimer's patients.

A good example of one of the many plausible risk factors is social isolation. The rationale for the importance of social isolation is compelling, but it is revealing to consider the complex ways in which it can be involved in the development of paranoia. Any delusional belief, by definition, excludes reality as seen from some broader perspective, and the processes by which that exclusion occurs are varied. The individual may be amply exposed to information contrary to his belief but rejects it. Or the individual may be isolated by his own tendencies to withdraw—perhaps owing to schizoid or avoidant personality, or agoraphobia. Or the individual may be isolated by geography or group membership such that the information about the world that the individual receives is skewed. Whatever the reason for the isolation, the common lack is of the kind of social correction that seems likely to impede the maintenance of paranoid views.

Perhaps the most striking evidence of multiple pathways comes from the diversity of medical and drug conditions in which paranoia—both acute and lasting—can emerge. Given that it seems implausible that these diverse conditions would trigger a common biological mechanism specific to paranoid thinking, the emergence of paranoia in such conditions may suggest that it sometimes serves a compensatory function. As noted above, in the traditional psychoanalytic literature, paranoia was closely tied to the projection of hostility. However, it seems likely that in many cases it is not forbidden hostility but, rather, the incomprehensibility of experience that one must cope with. The latter is apparent, for instance, in the case of paranoia associated with Alzheimer's dementia, where the loss of cognitive function means that one's life is filled with nuisances (lost keys, etc.) that are hard to explain—if one is not to blame personal decline. Rejecting this explanation, the individual favors an account that involves adverse external forces. Among Alzheimer's patients, the most frequently occurring delusions are persecutory (Migliorelli et al., 1995), and even grandiose delusions seem to smack less of narcissism than of an attempt to avoid a collapse of self-respect. The defensive quality of the process may be inferred from its rigidity; the individual does not merely entertain the possibility of a nemesis, he adheres to that explanation with tenacity.

Still, some paranoid states are acute and brief. If they are defensive, the (presumably terrifying) state and the defense are both temporary. Moreover, if a not-otherwise-suspicious individual were to have repeated terror-arousing experiences, it would not be surprising if this were to lead to chronic hypervigilance. Still, key questions would remain: Why does the individual presume that the source of his problems is other people (in contrast to, say, the agoraphobic, who simply withdraws)? Why are puzzling states so readily experienced as so terrifying? And what about the existence of paranoia in individuals who lack apparent exposure to anomalous experiences?

Notes

1. If news reports are to be believed, Ted Kaczinski preferred to plead guilty of murder rather than be portrayed in court as a paranoid schizophrenic.

2. An interesting example is Campbell's (1957) critique of orthodox analytic theory, nicely summarized in the following statements: "The Freudian movement is really a paranoid reaction to civilization" (p. 102); and, "Freud . . . created a systematized delusion in the belief that he was creating a 'science"' (p. 170). In using idioms of paranoia and delusion in an *ad hominem* rhetorical ploy, Campbell was arguably fighting fire with fire. After all, he was attacking a point of view that had its own rhetorical devices for disenfranchising alternative views; for instance, those who disagreed with analytic claims were said to be manifesting *resistance*.

3. On the other hand, the word *paranoid* remains in *DSM-IV* PS even though there is no special focus on persecutory beliefs in the criteria for this subtype. As Kirkpatrick and Amador (1995) have noted, given that they share *paranoid* in their names, it is anomalous for the diagnoses of PS and PPD to differ so greatly regarding emphasis on suspiciousness and persecution. While PPD requires that the individual be suspicious of others, a PS diagnosis can be given even if the only somatic delusions are present, for instance.

4. Frith (1992) has offered a neuropsychological model of schizophrenia that resonates with this analogy. He suggested that delusions in schizophrenia arise from a central defect involving "an impairment in the ability to distinguish changes due to our own actions and changes due to external events" (p. 81). Emprical consideration of such possibilities is likely to benefit from research paradigms developed within the source monitoring tradition (cf. Johnson, 1988; Johnson, Hashtroudi, & Lindsay, 1993).

5. Haynes (1986, p. 272) has suggested that the self-serving bias is so intrinsically reinforcing that it may be necessary for the social environment to reward "nonparanoid alternatives" such as "honest admissions of errors rather than invalid external attributions of blame" if paranoid behaviors are *not* to become prevalent aspects of the individual's behavioral repertoire.

References

Abbruzzese, M., Ferri, S., & Scarone, S. (1996). Performance on the Wisconsin Card Sorting Test in schizophrenia: Perseveration in clinical subtypes. *Psychiatry Research, 64*, 27–33.

Anthony, E. J. (1986). Terrorizing attacks on children by psychotic parents. *Journal of the American Academy of Child Psychiatry, 25*, 326–335.

Arieti, S. (1963). Psychopathic personality: Some views on its psychopathology and psychodynamics. *Comprehensive Psychiatry, 4*, 301–312.

Baddeley, A., Thornton, A., Chua, S. E., & McKenna, P. (1996). Schizophrenic delusions and the construction of autobiographical memory. In D. D. Rubin (Ed.), *Remembering our past* (pp. 384–428). Cambridge, UK: Cambridge University Press.

Benezech, M., Yesavage, J. A., Addad, M., Bourgeois, M., & Mills, M. (1984). Homicide by psychotics in France: A five-year study. *Journal of Clinical Pychiatry, 45*, 85–86.

Benjamin, L. S. (1996). Interpersonal diagnosis and treatment of personality disorders (2nd ed.). New York: Guilford Press.

Bentall, R. P., & Kaney, S. (1996). Abnormalities of self-representation and persecutory delusions: A test of a cognitive model of paranoia. *Psychological Medicine, 26*, 1231–1237.

Bergner, R. M. (1993). Paranoid style: A descriptive and pragmatic account. In R. M. Bergner (Ed.), *Studies in psychopathology* (pp. 89–117). Ann Arbor, MI: Descriptive Psychology Press.

Bodner, E., & Mikulincer, M. (1998). Learned helplessness and the occurrence of depressive-like and paranoid-like responses: The role of attentional focus. *Journal of Personality and Social Psychology, 74*, 1010–1023.

Bone, S., & Oldham, J. M. (1994). Paranoia: Historical considerations. In J. M. Oldham & S. Bone (Eds.), *Paranoia: New psychoanalytic perspectives* (pp. 3–15). Madison, CT: International Universities Press.

Brennan, J. H., & Hemsley, D. R. (1984). Illusory correlations in paranoid and non-paranoid schizophrenia. *British Journal of Clinical Psychology, 23*, 225–236.

Brown, G. W. & Birley, J. L. T. (1968). Crises and life changes and the onset of schizophrenia. *Journal of Health and Social Behavior, 9*, 203–214.

Cameron, N. (1963). *Personality development and psychopathology: A dynamic approach*. Boston: Houghton Mifflin.

Campbell, C. H. (1957). *Induced delusions: The psychopathy of Freudism*. Chicago: Regent House.

Cardno, A. G., Jones, L. A., Murphy, K. C., Asherson, P., Scott, L. C., Williams, J., Owen, M. J., & McGuffin, P. (1996). Factor analysis of schizophrenic symptoms using the OPCRIT checklist. *Schizophrenia Research, 22*, 233–239.

Chapman, L. J., & Chapman, J. P. (1973). *Disordered thought in schizophrenia.* New York: Appleton-Century-Crofts.

Chapman, L. J., & Chapman, J. P. (1988). The genesis of delusions. In T. F. Oltmanns & B. A. Maher (Eds.), *Delusional beliefs* (pp. 167–183). New York: John Wiley.

Chapman, L. J., Chapman, J. P., Kwapil, T. R., Eckblad, M., & Zinser, M. C. (1994). Putatively psychosis-prone subjects 10 years later. *Journal of Abnormal Psychology, 103*, 171–183.

Christodoulou, G. N., Margariti, M. M., Malliaras, D. E., & Alevizou, S. (1995). Shared delusions of doubles. *Journal of Neurology, Neurosurgery and Psychiatry, 58*, 499–501.

Colby, K. M. (1977). Appraisal of four psychological theories of paranoid phenomena. *Journal of Abnormal Psychology, 86*, 54–59.

Cooper, A. F., & Curry, A. R. (1976). The pathology of deafness in the paranoid and affective psychoses of later life. *Journal of Psychosomatic Research, 20*, 97–105.

Cooper, A. F., Garside, R. F., & Kay, D. W. K. (1976). A comparison of deaf and non-deaf patients with paranoid and affective psychoses. *British Journal of Psychiatry, 129*, 532–538.

Cummings, J. L. (1985). Organic delusions: Phenomenology, anatomical correlations, and review. *British Journal of Psychiatry, 146*, 184–197.

David, A. S., & Howard, R. (1994). An experimental phenomenological approach to delusional memory in schizophrenia and late paraphrenia. *Psychological Medicine, 24*, 515–524.

Dutton, D. G. (1995). Male abusiveness in intimate relationships. *Clinical Psychology Review, 15*, 567–581.

Ekselius, L., Lindström, E., von Knorring, L., Bodlund, O., & Kullgren, G. (1994). Comorbidity among the personality disorders in DSM-III-R. *Personality and Individual Differences, 17*, 155–160.

Ellis, H. D., & de Pauw, K. W. (1994). The cognitive neuropsychiatric origins of the Capgras delusion. In A. S. David & J. C. Cutting (Eds.), *The neuropsychology of schizophrenia* (pp. 317–336). Hove, UK: Lawrence Erlbaum.

Fenigstein, A. (1995). Paranoia and self-focused attention. In A. Oosterwegel & R. A. Wicklund (Eds.), *The self in European and North American culture: Development and processes* (pp. 183–192). Amsterdam: Kluwer Academic Publishers.

Fenigstein, A. (1996). Paranoia. In C. G. Costello (Ed.), *Personality characteristics of the personality disordered* (pp. 242–275). New York: John Wiley.

Fenigstein, A., & Vanable, P. A. (1992). Paranoia and self-consciousness. *Journal of Personality and Social Psychology, 62*, 129–138.

Frith, C. D. (1992). *The cognitive neuropsychology of schizophrenia.* Hove, UK: Lawrence Erlbaum.

Fulford, K. W. M. (1994). Value, illness, and failure of action: Framework for a philosophical psychopathology of delusions. In G. Graham & G. L. Stephens (Eds.), *Philosophical psychopathology* (pp. 205–233). Cambridge, MA: MIT Press.

Gaines, A. D. (1988). Delusions: Culture, psychosis and the problem of meaning. In T. F. Oltmanns & B. A. Maher (Eds.), *Delusional beliefs* (pp. 230–258). New York: John Wiley.

Garety, P. A., Hemsley, D. R., & Wessely, S. (1991). Reasoning in deluded schizophrenic and paranoid patients. *Journal of Nervous and Mental Disease, 179*, 194–201.

Harper, D. J. (1996). Deconstructing 'paranoia': Towards a discursive understanding of apparently unwarranted suspicion. *Theory & Psychology, 6*, 423–448.

Harrow, M., Rattenbury, F., & Stoll, F. (1988). Schizophrenic delusions: An analysis of their persistence, of related premorbid ideas, and of three major dimensions. In T. F. Oltmanns & B. A. Maher (Eds.), *Delusional beliefs* (pp. 184–211). New York: John Wiley.

Haynes, S. N. (1986). A behavioral model of paranoid behaviors. *Behavior Therapy, 17*, 266–287.

Hemsley, D. R., & Garety, P. A. (1986). The formation of maintenance of delusions: A Bayesian analysis. *British Journal of Psychiatry, 149*, 51–56.

Howard, R., & Levy, R. (1993). Personality structure in the paranoid psychoses of later life. *European Psychiatry, 8*, 59–66.

Johnson, M. K. (1988). Discriminating the origin of information. In T. F. Oltmanns & B. A. Maher (Eds.), *Delusional beliefs* (pp. 34–65). New York: John Wiley.

Johnson, M. K., Hashtroudi, S., & Lindsay, D. S. (1993). Source monitoring. *Psychological Bulletin, 114*, 3–28.

Johnson, S. L., & Miller, I. (1997). Negative life events and time to recovery from episodes of bipolar disorder. *Journal of Abnormal Psychology, 106*, 449–457.

Jørgensen P., & Jensen, J. (1988). An attempt to operationalize reactive delusional psychosis. *Acta Psychiatrica Scandinavica, 78*, 627–631.

Kaffman, M. (1981). Paranoid disorders: The core of truth behind the delusional system. *International Journal of Family Therapy, 3*, 29–41.

Kaney, S., Bowen-Jones, K., Dewey, M. E., & Bentall, R. P. (1997). Two predictions about paranoid ideation: Deluded, depressed, and normal participants' subjective frequency and consensus judgments for positive, neutral and negative events. *British Journal of Clinical Psychology, 36*, 349–364.

Katz, R. C., & Marquette, J. (1996). Psychosocial characteristics of young violent offenders: A comparative study. *Criminal Behaviour and Mental Health, 6*, 339–348.

Kay, D. W. K., Cooper, A. F., Garside, R. F., & Roth, M. (1976). The differentiation of paranoid from affective psychoses by patients' premorbid characteristics. *British Journal of Psychiatry, 129*, 207–215.

Keefe, R. S. E., & Harvey, P. D. (1994). *Understanding schizophrenia: A guide to the new research on causes and treatment.* New York: Free Press.

Kendler, K. S. (1980). The nosologic validity of paranoia (simple delusional disorder): A review. *Archives of General Psychiatry, 37*, 699–706.

Kennedy, H. G., Kemp, L. I., & Dyer, D. C. (1992). Fear and anger in delusional (paranoid) disorder: The association with violence. *British Journal of Psychiatry, 160*, 488–492.

Kihlstrom, J. F., & Hoyt, I. P. (1988). Hypnosis and the psychology of delusions. In T. F. Oltmanns & B. A. Maher (Eds.), *Delusional beliefs* (pp. 66–109). New York: John Wiley.

Kinderman, P., & Bentall, R. P. (1996). Self-discrepancies and persecutory delusions: Evidence for a defensive model of paranoid ideation. *Journal of Abnormal Psychology, 105*, 106–114.

Kinderman, P., & Bentall, R. P. (1997). Causal attributions in paranoia and depression: Internal, personal, and situational attributions for negative events. *Journal of Abnormal Psychology, 106*, 341–345.

Kirkpatrick, B., & Amador, X. F. (1995). The study of paranoia and suspiciousness. *Biological Psychiatry, 38*, 496–497.

Kramer, R. M. (1994). The sinister attribution error: Paranoid cognition and collective distrust in organizations. *Motivation and Emotion, 18*, 199–230.

Kremen, W. S., Seidman, L. J., Goldstein, J. M., Faraone S. V., & Tsuang, M. T. (1994). Systematized delusions and neuropsychological function in paranoid and nonparanoid schizophrenia. *Schizophrenia Research, 12*, 223–236.

Levy, A. (1996). Forensic implications of the difficulties of defining delusions. *Medicine and Law, 15*, 257–260.

Livesley, W. J., & Schroeder, M. L. (1990). Dimensions of personality disorder: The DSM-III-R Cluster A diagnoses. *Journal of Nervous and Mental Disease, 178*, 627–635.

Magaro, P. A. (1980). *Cognition in schizophrenia and paranoia: The integration of cognitive processes.* Hillsdale, NJ: Lawrence Erlbaum.

Maher, B. A. (1988). Anomalous experience and delusional thinking: The logic of explanations. In T. F. Oltmanns & B. A. Maher (Eds.), *Delusional beliefs* (pp. 15–33). New York: John Wiley.

Maher, B. A., & Spitzer, M. (1993). Delusions. In C. G. Costello (Ed.), *Symptoms of schizophrenia* (pp. 92–120). New York: John Wiley.

Maier, W., Lichtermann, D., Minges, J., & Heun, R. (1994). Personality disorders among the relatives of schizophrenia patients. *Schizophrenia Bulletin, 20*, 481–493.

Maizel, S., Knobler, H. Y., & Herbstein, R. (1990). Folie à trois among two Soviet-Jewish immigrant families to Israel. *British Journal of Psychiatry, 157*, 290–292.

Marengo, J., & Westermeyer, J. F. (1996). Schizophrenia and delusional disorder. In L. L. Carstensen, B. A. Edelstein, & L. Dornbrand (Eds.), *The practical handbook of clinical gerontology.* Thousand Oaks, CA: Sage Publications.

Mason, O., Claridge, G., & Clark, K. (1997). Electrodermal relationships with personality measures of psychosis-proneness in psychotic and normal subjects. *International Journal of Psychophysiology, 27*, 137–146.

Meissner, W. W. (1981). The schizophrenic and the paranoid process. *Schizophrenia Bulletin, 8*, 611–631.

Mela, M., Obenbe, A., & Farmer, A. E. (1997). Folie à quatre in a large Nigerian sub-ship. *Schizophrenia Research, 23*, 91–93.

Meloy, J. R. (1990). Nondelusional or borderline erotomania. *American Journal of Psychiatry, 147*, 820.

Menuck, M. N. (1992). Differentiating paranoia and legitimate fears. *American Journal of Psychiatry, 149*, 140–141.

Mester, R., Toren, P., & Gonen, N. (1994). The delusion based will: The question of validity. *Medicine and Law, 13*, 555–561.

Migliorelli, R., Petracca, G., Tesón, A., Sabe, L., Leiguarda, R., & Sarkstein, S. E. (1995). Neuropsychiatric and neuropsychological correlates of delusions in Alzheimer's disease. *Psychological Medicine, 25*, 505–513.

Millon, T., & Davis, R. D. (1996). *Disorders of personality: DSM-IV and beyond.* New York: Wiley-Interscience.

Moore, N. C. (1981). Is paranoid illness associated with sensory defects in the elderly? *Journal of Psychosomatic Research, 25*, 69–74.

Neufeld, R. W. J. (1991). Memory in paranoid schizophrenia. In P. A. Magaro (Ed.), *Cognitive bases of mental disorders* (pp. 231–261). Newbury Park, CA: Sage Publications.

Newhill, C. E. (1990). The role of culture in the development of paranoid symptomatology. *American Journal of Orthopsychiatry, 60*, 176–185.

Nicholson, I. R., & Neufeld, R. W. J. (1993). Classification of the schizophrenias according to symptomatology: A two-factor model. *Journal of Abnormal Psychology, 102*, 259–270.

Oltmanns, T. F. (1988). Approaches to the definition and study of delusions. In T. F. Oltmanns & B. A. Maher (Eds.), *Delusional beliefs* (pp. 3–11). New York: John Wiley.

Pallanti, S., Quercioli, L., & Pazzagli, A. (1997). Relapse in young paranoid schizophrenic patients: A prospective study of stressful life events, P300 measures, and coping. *American Journal of Psychiatry, 154*, 792–798.

Papernik, D. S., Pardes, H., & Winston, A. (1975). A study of hospitalized paranoid schizophrenics with grandiose symptomatology. *Hospital and Community Psychiatry, 26*, 87–90.

Parnas, J., Cannon, T. D., Jacobsen, B., Schulsinger, H., Schulsinger, F., & Mednick, S. A. (1993). Lifetime *DSM-III-R* diagnostic outcomes in the offspring of schizophrenic mothers. *Archives of General Psychiatry, 50*, 707–714.

Phillips, K. A., McElroy, S. L., Keck, P. E., Hudson, J. I., & Pope, H. G., Jr. (1994). A comparison of delusional and nondelusional body dysmorphic disorder in 100 cases. *Psychopharmacology Bulletin, 30*, 179–186.

Reich, J., & Braginsky, Y. (1994). Paranoid personality traits in a panic disorder population: A pilot study. *Comprehensive Psychiatry, 35*, 260–264.

Robins, R. S., & Post, J. M. (1997). *Political paranoia: The psychopolitics of hatred*. New Haven: Yale University Press.

Romney, D. M. (1988). A simplex model of the paranoid process: Implications for diagnosis and prognosis. *Acta Psychiatrica Scandinavica, 75*, 651–655.

Rosenbaum, M., & Hadari, D. (1985). Personal efficacy, external locus of control, and perceived contingency of parental reinforcement among depressed, paranoid, and normal subjects. *Journal of Personality and Social Psychology, 49*, 539–547.

Rosse, R. B., Schwartz, B. L., Mastropaolo, J., Goldberg, R. L., & Deutsch, S. I. (1991). Subtype diagnosis in schizophrenia and its relation to neuropsychological and computerized tomography measures. *Biological Psychiatry, 30*, 63–72.

Rowlands, M. W. D. (1988). Psychiatric and legal aspects of persistent litigation. *British Journal of Psychiatry, 153*, 317–323.

Sacks, M. H. (1988). Folie à deux. *Comprehensive Psychiatry, 29*, 270–277.

Sacks, M. H., Carpenter, W. T., & Strauss, J. S. (1974). Recovery from delusions. *Archives of General Psychiatry, 30*, 117–120.

Satel, S. L., & Edell, W. S. (1991). Cocaine-induced paranoia and psychosis proneness. *American Journal of Psychiatry, 148*, 1708–1711.

Schanda, H., Wörgötter, G., Berner, P., Gabriel, E., Küfferle, B., Knecht, G., & Kieffer, W. (1991). Predicting course and outcome in delusional psychoses. *Acta Psychiatrica Scandinavica, 83*, 468–475.

Schwartz, D. A. (1964). The paranoid-depressive existential continuum. *Psychiatric Quarterly, 38*, 690–706.

Segal, J. H. (1989). Erotomania revisited: From Kraepelin *to DSM-III-R. American Journal of Psychiatry, 146*, 1261–1266.

Segal, J. H. (1990). Dr. Segal replies. *American Journal of Psychiatry, 147*, 820–821.

Shapiro, D. (1965). *Neurotic styles*. New York: Basic Books.

Silva, J. A., Leong, G. B., Weinstock, R., & Wine, D. B. (1993). Delusional misidentification and dangerousness: A neurobiologic hypothesis. *Journal of Forensic Sciences, 38*, 904–913.

Silveira, J. M., & Seeman, M. V. (1995). Shared psychotic disorder: A critical review of the literature. *Canadian Journal of Psychiatry, 40*, 389–395.

Smári, J., Stefánsson, S., & Thorgilsson, H. (1994). Paranoia, self-consciousness, and social cognition in schizophrenics. *Cognitive Therapy and Research, 18*, 387–399.

Stuart, G. W., Malone, V., Currie, J., Klimidis, S., & Minas, I. H. (1995). Positive and negative symptoms in neuroleptic-free psychotic inpatients. *Schizophrenia Research, 16*, 175–188.

Taylor, P. J., Garety, P., Buchanan, A., Reed, A., Wessely, S., Ray, K., Dunn, G., & Grubin, D. (1994). Delusions and violence. In J. Monahan & H. J. Steadman (Eds.), *Violence and mental disorder* (pp. 161–182). Chicago: University of Chicago Press.

Trower, P., & Chadwick, P. (1995). Pathways to defense of the self: A theory of two types of paranoia. *Clinical Psychology: Science and Practice, 2*, 263–278.

Ulzen, T. P. M., & Carpentier, R. (1997). The delusional parent: Family and multisystemic issues. *Canadian Journal of Psychiatry, 42*, 617–622.

Ungvari, G. S., Pang, A. H. T., & Chiu, H. F. K. (1995). Delusional disorder, litigious type. *Clinical Gerontologist, 16*, 71–73.

Varma S. L., & Sharma, I. (1993). Psychiatric morbidity in the first-degree relatives of schizophrenic patients. *British Journal of Psychiatry, 162*, 672–678.

Vicente, N., Ochoa, E., & Rios, B. (1996). Psychogenic paranoid psychosis: An empirical study. *European Psychiatry, 11*, 180–184.

Watt, J. A. G. (1985a). Hearing and premorbid personality in paranoid states. *American Journal of Psychiatry, 142*, 1453–1455.

Watt, J. A. G. (1985b). The relationship of paranoid states to schizophrenia. *American Journal of Psychiatry, 142*, 1456–1458.

Westermeyer, J. (1988). Some cross-cultural aspects of delusions. In T. F. Oltmanns & B. A. Maher (Eds.), *Delusional beliefs* (pp. 212–229). New York: John Wiley.

Whaley, A. L. (1997). Ethnicity/race, paranoia, and psychiatric diagnoses: Clinician bias versus sociocultural difference. *Journal of Psychopathology and Behavioral Assessment, 19*, 1–20.

White, G. L., & Mullen, P. E. (1989). *Jealousy: Theory, research and clinical strategies*. New York: Guilford Press.

Winters, K. C., & Neale, J. M. (1983). Delusions and delusional thinking in psychotics: Review of the literature. *Clinical Psychology Review, 3*, 227–253.

Yamagishi, T., & Yamagishi, M. (1994). Trust and commitment in the United States and Japan. *Motivation and Emotion, 18*, 129–166.

Yassa, R., & Suranyi-Cadotte, B. (1993). Clinical characteristics of late-onset schizophrenia and delusional disorder. *Schizophrenia Bulletin, 19*, 701–707.

Young, M. L., & Jerome, E. A. (1972). Problem-solving performance of paranoid and nonparanoid schizophrenics. *Archives of General Psychiatry, 26*, 442–444.

Zimbardo, P. G., Anderson, S. M., & Kabat, L. G. (1981). Induced hearing deficit generates experimental paranoia. *Science, 212*, 1529–1531.

Zigler, E., & Glick, M. (1988). Is paranoid schizophrenia really camouflaged depression? *American Psychologist, 43*, 284–290.

Zigler, E., & Levine, J. (1983). Hallucinations *vs.* delusions: A developmental approach. *Journal of Nervous and Mental Disease, 171*, 141–146.

PART III

OTHER AXIS I SYNDROMES

14

Eating Disorders

Anorexia Nervosa and Bulimia Nervosa

HOWARD STEIGER
JEAN R. SÉGUIN

Anorexia and bulimia nervosa are polysymptomatic syndromes, defined by maladaptive attitudes and behaviors around eating, weight, and body image, but typically accompanied by disturbances of self-image, mood, impulse regulation, and interpersonal functioning. In this chapter, we review the pathognomonic features of the eating disorders (EDs) and findings on comorbid psychopathology. We provide an overview on sociocultural, biological, psychological, and developmental factors thought to act in ED etiology. We then elaborate a multidimensional (biopsychosocial) perspective on ED causality that attempts to account for some of the more salient aspects of ED phenomenology.

Defining Characteristics

Anorexia Nervosa

The essence of anorexia nervosa (AN) is a relentless pursuit of thinness (presumably driven by a central disturbance in bodily experience) and a phobia of the consequences of eating (usually expressed as a dread of weight gain or obesity). The result is a willful (and often dramatic) restriction of food intake, with the sufferer becoming underweight or (in the extreme) dangerously emaciated. In AN, "weight-gain phobia" is so intense that actual (or possible) weight gain, in an already thin or emaciated sufferer, can provoke profound anxiety, irritability, and/or feelings of loss of control. The sufferer thus avoids eating, and incrementally loses further weight.

The anorexic's eating behaviors often appear quite bizarre: She[1] may eat a restricted range of "safe" (usually low-calorie) foods, or may avoid social eating situations, so that there will be no interference in ritualized eating habits. Foods may be eaten in prescribed order, or in painstakingly metered, hypocaloric amounts. In some cases, the sufferer's anxiety mounts so intensely after eating that, to appease fears that she may have overeaten, she purges through vomiting, misuse of laxatives, or other means. Appetite becomes so suppressed that about half of sufferers eventually develop binge eating—that is, periodic dyscontrol over eating, or incapacity to satiate (DaCosta & Halmi, 1992). Given inconsistent presence of binge/purge behaviors in AN, a distinction is usually made between two anorexic subtypes: (a) the Restricting subtype, in which the sufferer limits food intake but does not engage in binge eating or purging (i.e., self-induced vomiting, or misuse of laxatives, diuretics, or enemas); (b) the Binge-eating/Purging subtype, in which (as the name implies) binge or purge episodes are prominent. The presence or absence of binge/purge behaviors in AN has been thought to correspond to important phenomenological and etiological differences (DaCosta & Halmi, 1992), upon which we will elaborate in subsequent sections.

Bulimia Nervosa

In apparent contrast to the overcontrolled eating behavior seen in AN, the main feature of bulimia nervosa (BN) is *dyscontrol* over eating. BN is diagnosed in relatively normal-weight or overweight individuals (not anorexics) who display recurrent eating binges (or bulimic episodes), following which the sufferer feels compelled to compensate through self-induced vomiting, laxative misuse, intensive exercise, fasting, or other means. Binge episodes can provoke a terrifying sense of loss of control and profound feelings of shame, anxiety, or depression. When binging, bulimics often experience dramatic self-disparagement—in some cases, to the point of self-damaging or suicidal feelings.

While the overeating seen in BN may seem to be antithetical to the rigid suppression of food intake seen in AN, both syndromes are believed to be causally linked to excessive or compulsive dieting. The putative causal relationship between dietary restraint and binge eating is formally addressed by Polivy and Herman (1985, 1993), who postulate that prolonged dieting and chronically restrictive attitudes around eating potentiate a breakdown of physiological and cognitive controls over consummatory behaviors—and eventual binge episodes. Consistent with this notion, naturalistic studies show bulimics' typical pattern of eating to be to avoid eating (or to eat minimalistically) through much of the day, only to lose control over restrained appetites in the evening (e.g., Davis, Freeman, & Garner, 1988). To understand this relationship, imagine what happens after holding your breath for a minute or two. The inevitable need to gasp for air is much like a bulimic's eating binge. In other words, even though the most evident eating anomaly in BN is binge eating, as in AN, the disorder is believed to hinge upon compulsive *dieting*. (Given its explicative value for binge-eating syndromes, we discuss dietary restraint further in a later section on individual psychological features.)

Other Eating Syndromes

Other variations on eating disorders occur that are classified in *DSM-IV* as eating disorder not otherwise specified (EDNOS). For example, some normal-weight individuals purge after eating small or normal amounts of food, without ever binge eating. Others show regular eating binges without compensatory behaviors (like vomiting, laxative abuse, or exercise). The latter syndrome, often associated with obesity, is usually labeled binge eating disorder (BED). The specific etiology of BED, and its relationship to BN, both require clarification. Similarly, obesity in the absense of binge eating (which is not classified as an ED in *DSM-IV*) is probably quite a heterogeneous entity, with variable causality, variable association with underlying psychopathology, and uncertain relationship to anorexia and bulimia nervosa—both, to some extent, syndromes of dietary overcontrol (versus excess). Given the preceding, we do not discuss BED or obesity in detail in this chapter.

The Restricter/Binger Distinction

Diagnostic convention and nosology differentiate AN from BN, but many clinicians and theorists have preferred an alternative distinction, between those ED patients (always anorexic) who restrict food intake without binging and purging, and those (sometimes anorexic, sometimes bulimic) who binge and purge (see DaCosta & Halmi, 1992). This distinction between restricters and bingers/purgers has been thought to correspond to important phenomenological and etiological differences, including differences as to predominant personality features, family-interaction styles, associations with neurobiological abnormalities, and patterns of genetic transmission (all reviewed below). Such differences imply that the restricter/binger distinction may isolate meaningful subgroups of ED sufferers, perhaps more than does the distinction between AN and BN. Where relevant, throughout this chapter we will address findings bearing upon the restricter/binger concept, clarifying the rationale for this distinction progressively further.

History

Widespread popular awareness of the EDs has developed over only the past few decades, so that it may be a common belief that the EDs are relatively recent creations. However, reports on well-defined syndromes corresponding to modern-day AN are found over at least three centuries, and suggestive records of self-starvation syndromes (occurring in the context of religious or ascetic self-purification rites) date back to the pre-Christian era. The relevance of early self-starvation (the so-called holy anorexics of the Middle Ages, for example) to modern AN is difficult to ascertain (Bemporad, 1996; Gordon, 1990), and our discussion will emphasize accounts referring unambiguously to the ED syndromes we know today.

The first clear accounts of AN are believed to have been provided in 1689 by Thomas Morton, an English physician, who documented two cases of "nervous consumption": one in a 16-year-old boy, the other in an 18-year-old girl (Gordon, 1990, p. 12). Characteristics of both cases included "want of appetite" and weight loss, in the absence of any apparent medical cause. Both patients were noted to be highly studious, and to display prominent anxiety and sadness. Morton's female patient ultimately died after refusing treatment. Well-elaborated reports on AN emerged again in an 1860 description by the French physician Marcé and the simultaneous reports (published in 1870) of Sir William Gull and Charles Lasègue. Gull is credited with introduction of the term anorexia nervosa; Marcé referred to a "hypochondriacal delirium," Lasègue a variation on "hysteria." Regardless, all three described a syndrome that closely resembled modern-day AN, including refusal to eat, onset in adolescence, amenorrhea, restlessness, and lack of concern for consequences of food refusal (Bemporad, 1996; Gordon, 1990). All three assumed underlying psychological causes, and Marcé and Gull (cited in Treasure & Holland, 1995) postulated hereditary factors. Intriguingly, while reports on AN become more frequent through the 19th and 20th centuries, a pivotal diagnostic element—weight-gain phobia—is first acknowledged in accounts emerging well into the 20th century. This may suggest that the weight-phobia characteristic may not be as central a construct in AN as has been believed—perhaps constituting a contemporary rationale for instances of self-starvation, shaped by contemporary cultural values.

Having been acknowledged formally only in the 1970s, BN is widely thought to be a more recent variant of ED than is AN. However, Ziolko (1996) has noted reports of syndromes characterized by unbridled hunger, dating back to Greek records of the 4th and 5th centuries B.C. Likewise, he noted that Galen, in the 2nd century A.D., referred to "bulimos," a generally debilitating syndrome characterized by episodes of overeating, vomiting, and fainting. Ziolko reviewed similar case descriptions, some reporting alternating under- and overeating, found in medical treatises dating through the 4th to the 17th centuries, and again in various 19th- and early 20th-centuries accounts. Marked mood manifestations, and preoccupation with food and eating, become prominent in the latter descriptions. All of these suggest that BN may be less linked to the contemporary era than has been believed. The process of defining bulimia as a distinct syndrome culminated in the roughly concurrent accounts, published in 1979, by Igoin in French, Boyadjieva and Achkova in Bulgarian, and by Robert Palmer and by Gerald Russell in English (Vandereycken, 1994).

Epidemiology

AN and BN occur more frequently in industrialized nations than in less economically developed areas. In Western nations, both syndromes are alarmingly common. Reported prevalences of strictly defined AN in Western school-aged females generally fall between .5 and 1% (Wakeling, 1996), while BN may afflict from 1 to 2% of the same at-risk, female group (e.g., Fairburn & Beglin, 1990; Garfinkel et al., 1995). In subthreshold forms, diagnosed using less-stringent criteria, EDs are believed to affect even larger numbers (Garfinkel et al., 1995; Shisslak, Crago, & Estes, 1995), and it is probably not an exaggeration to assume that 10% (or more) of Western school-aged females may display partial anorexic or bulimic syndromes, associated with significant dietary (and psychological) distress. Although stereotype may conjure images of a young-adolescent sufferer, actual peak prevalences of EDs are obtained in a young-adult age group—likely reflecting the tendencies of EDs to run a chronic course, and of BN to develop later than AN, during the transition to adulthood. Both syndromes are rarer in males—each apparently being roughly 1/10th as common in men as in women (Fairburn & Beglin, 1990; Wakeling, 1996). Similarly, EDs seem to occur less frequently in certain racial groups—for example, less among Black- and Asian- than Caucasian-American females (Crago, Shisslak, & Estes, 1996).

ED incidence appears to have increased over past decades (Wakeling, 1996). Reviewing annual incidence rates for AN in the United States published between the early 1960s and the mid-1980s, Mitchell and Eckert (1987) concluded that there had been a progressive increase, from 0.35 to 4.06 per 100,000, and corresponding increases in the incidence of BN are noted during a comparable period (e.g., Fairburn & Beglin, 1990). We are aware, however, of one study that notes a small decrease (over the past 10 years) in maladaptive eating practices among U.S. college students (Heatherton, Nichols, Mahamedi, & Keel, 1995). Optimism about a reduction in the incidence of EDs may be premature, but such observations could imply that a rising incidence of EDs may have plateaued.

It is a popular notion that EDs are disorders of affluent, urban society. While early reports associated AN distinctly with upper socioeconomic standing, systematic evidence of such a trend in recent data is mixed at best (Gard & Freeman, 1996). Furthermore, if a bias toward upper socioeconomic status exists at all, it almost certainly applies more strongly to AN than to BN, for which data suggest a rather even distribution across socioeconomic classes (Gard & Freeman, 1996). It is probably safe to assume that Western middle- and upper-class values placed upon slimness contribute to risk of ED development, but act less focally than has previously been thought. For example, mass media may communicate values that originate within affluent groups effectively enough across all social groups to tend to erase influences of socioeconomic status. Likewise, EDs are found in unexpectedly high numbers in rural communities, suggesting that EDs are not as much an urban phenomenon as may once have been believed.

Comorbidity with Other Psychiatric Syndromes

EDs frequently co-occur with other psychiatric syndromes, notably affective, anxiety, substance-abuse, and personality disorders (Brewerton, Lydiard, Herzog, Brotman, O'Neil, & Ballenger, 1995; Holderness, Brooks-Gunn, & Warren, 1994; Herzog, Keller, Sacks, Yeh, & Lavori, 1992; Vitousek & Manke, 1994). To follow, we review findings on prominent comorbid tendencies in the EDs. We call attention, in advance, to a tendency for psychiatric comorbidity to be broader in bulimic (binge/purge) ED variants than in restrictive ones. This tendency may imply that restrictive AN constitutes a more circumscribed type of pathology or is associated with a more focal causality.

Mood Disorders

EDs frequently include mood manifestations, and it is therefore not surprising that comorbidity of mood disorders (MDs) in the EDs is very marked (see Herzog et al., 1992; Strober & Katz, 1988). Available findings suggest that about 25 to 50% of anorexics will display a concurrent major depression, while 50 to 75% will suffer a depression in their lifetimes. In one recent study on AN, rates for comorbid (current) major depression and overall MDs were reported to be 40 and 70%, respectively, whereas lifetime rate of MD exceeded 90% (Råstam, 1992). Data suggest that binge/purge syndromes display a similar, or even more pronounced, affinity for MDs. A recent study on BN reports 41% of bulimics to be clinically depressed (Brewerton et al., 1995); another reports concurrent and lifetime rates of depression to be 20 and 38%, respectively (Garfinkel et al., 1995); a third, comparing point prevalences of major depression across restricter and binger/purger anorexics, notes the disorder in about 30% of restricters and in 53% of bingers/purgers (Herzog et al., 1992). Recent evidence has been consistent with a strong additional association of BN with seasonal affective disorder (SAD). In one study, 69% of BN patients were noted to show signs of comorbid SAD (Levitan, Kaplan, Levitt, & Joffe, 1994), while in another, 25% of SAD patients were noted to have an ED, most often BN (Gruber & Dilsaver, 1996).

Various areas of etiological overlap can be postulated to explain convergence of eating and mood disorders: Both are believed to depend upon similar underlying psychological and family/developmental substrates (developmental neglect or familial overprotection, for example); both have been thought to have similar neurobiological substrates, associated with serotonergic, norepinephrinergic, and other neurotransmitter abnormalities; both have been thought to constitute stress responses to social pressures detrimental to sufferers' sense of control or self-worth (see Strober & Katz, 1988). In addition, in considering sources for the convergence of MDs with EDs, it is necessary to contemplate secondary effects (psychological and neurobiological) of an active ED upon mood regulation. ED sequelae, related to malnutrition and other factors, have been postulated to heighten susceptibility to mood disturbances (e.g., Strober & Katz, 1988), and may in part explain the propensity of actively eating-disordered individuals, if not to fulfill mood disorder criteria, to display prominent mood manifestations.

Anxiety Disorders

Anxiety disorders are also common in ED sufferers. Rates of comorbid anxiety disorder in AN reportedly vary from 20% (Herzog et al., 1992) to around 75% (Deep, Nagy, Weltzin, Rao, & Kaye, 1995). In BN, corresponding rates vary from from 13% (Herzog et al., 1992) to about 60% (Garfinkel et al., 1995). Studies report presence in the EDs of generalized anxiety disorder, social and simple phobias, agoraphobia, panic disorder, and especially, obsessive-compulsive disorder. As the structure of the EDs so closely resembles that of obsessive compulsive disorder (OCD)—intrusive obsessions with weight and body image being appeased by apparently compulsive gestures like fasting or purging—we pay particular attention to data on the convergence of OCD with the EDs (e.g., Hsu, Kaye, & Weltzin, 1993). Studies of the lifetime prevalence of OCD in eating-disordered women report some 15 to 70% of anorexics and 10 to 30% of bulimics to display OCD. In corollary, various studies note the EDs (and especially AN) to be unusually common among OCD patients: in 62 OCD patients, Rubenstein, Piggott, L'Heureux, Hill, and Murphy (1992) noted a 13% lifetime prevalence of ED (usually AN) and an 18% prevalence of subthreshold EDs. Common neurobiological (e.g., serotonergic) anomalies have been implicated in both the EDs and OCD (e.g., Hsu et al., 1993), and constitute one of several plausible bases for apparent convergence of these syndromes.

Substance-Abuse Disorders

Studies on substance-abuse problems in women with EDs, or on EDs in substance-abusing women, consistently indicate bulimic ED variants (AN binge-purge subtype and normal-weight BN), but not restrictive AN, to be strongly associated with alcohol and chemical dependencies (see Holderness et al., 1994). According to relevant studies, from 10 to 55% of BN sufferers abuse substances (with a modal figure being about 30%), whereas from 25 to 40% of *female* alcoholics show some form of ED (often in the bulimia spectrum). For restrictive AN, coaggregation with substance abuse is unexceptional, reported prevalences often being comparable to, or even lower than, those obtained in the general population.

Holderness and colleagues (1994) discuss various sources for etiological overlap between bulimic ED variants and substance-abuse disorders: comparable personality traits, constituting a so-called addictive personality (prone to misuse of substances), have been postulated to underlie both types of syndromes. While studies examining personality-trait variations in food- and drug-abusing individuals have suggested that impulsive or sensation-seeking tendencies may be prominent in both syndromes, evidence of a unique personality style that may coaggregate with either eating or substance-abuse disorders is, otherwise, unconvincing. Likewise, while data have associated these disorders with unfavorable family backgrounds, there is no strong evidence of a disorder-specific family constellation for either class of syndrome. It remains viable to consider shared neurobiological substrates underlying substance-abuse and binge-eating behaviors, mediated by brain serotonin, endorphin, or other neurotransmitter or neuroendocrine factors. However, it must still be established whether any such factors are disorder specific or are simply markers of indirect, nonspecific vulnerabilities.

Dissociative Disorders

Dissociative disorders (DDs) are characterized by disturbances in memory (e.g., amnesias) and consciousness (e.g., problems of identity), and by alterations of sensorimotor function (e.g., "conversion" type symptoms). In the extreme, the DD sufferer experiences a marked fragmentation of identity, termed dissociative identity disorder in *DSM-IV* (formerly multiple personality disorder). DDs have traditionally been conceptualized as psychological adaptations to severe trauma (e.g., Putnam, 1985); however, recent evidence has suggested contributing factors of a constitutional nature (e.g., Butler, Duran, Jasiukaitis, Koopman, & Spiegel, 1996). Regardless, several groups have noted that bulimics produce elevated scores, relative to normal subjects, psychiatric comparison subjects, and/or restricter anorexics, on validated self-report instruments measuring dissociation (e.g., Vanderlinden, Vandereycken, van Dyk, & Vertommen,

1993). Relevant to hypotheses concerning post-traumatic effects, Vanderlinden and colleagues (1993) report that sexually abused ED patients show more dissociative symptoms than do those reporting no such experiences. Explorations into this area of comorbidity being recent, it is premature to draw conclusions concerning etiological factors. Nonetheless, dissociative disturbances do seem to occur frequently in a bulimic context, and are suggestive, given that BN sufferers often report feeling "altered" or "not themselves," while binge eating.

Personality Disorders

Another strong comorbid propensity in the EDs is that with personality disorders (PDs). Many studies have accumulated that use validated structured-interview or self-report personality-diagnostic assessments in ED populations, and have been examined in detail in several recent reviews (see Johnson & Wonderlich, 1992; Sohlberg & Strober, 1994; Vitousek & Manke, 1994). Findings on Axis II comorbidity are variable enough to defy generalization. This we attribute to local variations in the application of diagnostic criteria, to sampling differences, to variations in personality assessments applied, and to inherent limitations in the reliability of categorical personality-diagnostic decisions themselves. Nonetheless, available data support several tentative conclusions:

1. Personality disorders are frequent "companions" to anorexic and bulimic syndromes. Estimates of PD prevalences in heterogeneous ED samples vary from roughly 30% to over 90%, with most commonly cited prevalences occupying the 50 to 75% range.
2. Results imply differential coaggregation of PD subtypes with restrictive and bulimic ED variants (see Vitousek & Manke, 1994; Johnson & Wonderlich, 1992), as follows: (a) Restrictive AN seems to be associated with a relatively circumscribed range of PDs, and a high concentration of anxious-fearful PD diagnoses (characterized by anxiousness, orderliness, introversion, and preference for sameness and control). In other words, the dietary overcontrol that characterizes restrictive AN seems to be paralleled by generalized overcontrol, as a personality or adaptive style. (b) ED variants characterized by dietary dyscontrol—i.e., those including binge/purge symptoms—coincide with more heterogeneous PD subtypes than do restrictive forms, and more important, with more pronounced affinity for the dramatic-erratic PDs, notably borderline PD (BPD). Dramatic-erratic PDs implicate prominent attention and sensation seeking, extroversion, mood lability, and proneness to excitability or impulsivity. BPD is a particularly malignant variation on such PDs, characterized by massive dysregulation of affects, impulse controls and identity, chaotic interpersonal functioning, and repeated self-mutilative or parasuicidal acts. According to modal figures, BPD (or an apparent borderline spectrum personality organization, in which impulsivity and parasuicidality may be characteristic) seems to be present in up to a third of bingers/purgers. In other words, the dietary dyscontrol that characterizes binge/purge syndromes seems, in many cases, to be paralleled by generalized dyscontrol. (c) AN binge/purge subtype tends to be associated with the most severe of personality pathologies, its sufferers being reported to often receive simultaneous dramatic-erratic and anxious-fearful diagnoses, and often, borderline PD (Vitousek & Manke, 1994).

Together, results imply elusive restricter/binger differences, coinciding with loadings in the restricter subtype of anxious-fearful PD variants, and in the binger/purger subtype, with broader PD variations, more often including dramatic-erratic PD diagnoses. Such tendencies have inspired speculations on a systematic linkage between restrictive variants of ED and overcontrolled personality subtypes, and between bulimic forms and dyscontrolled personality styles (see Johnson & Wonderlich, 1992; Vitousek & Manke, 1994). Fit is imperfect, however, and important within-subtype heterogenities are noted, especially in bulimic ED variants. We address associations between personality traits and ED subtypes further in a later section on individual psychological features.

Comments on the ED/PD Affinity There is a legitimate concern that very high rates of Axis II (PD) comorbidity reported in ED sufferers may reflect disproportionate sampling, in tertiary-care clinics, from an especially disturbed segment of the ED population. To assess such possibilities, Yager, Landsverk, Edelstein, and Hyler (1989) assessed personality pathology in a large community sample of treatment and nontreatment seeking bulimics. While the self-report measure they applied may assign PD diagnoses liberally, rates of PD comorbidity obtained were not unlike those reported in clinical samples—75% showing a PD and nearly 50% showing BPD.

In addition, EDs are associated with malnutrition and depressed mood, both of which can have adverse effects upon personality functioning (Keys, Brozek, Henschel, Mickelson, & Taylor, 1950; Reich & Green, 1991). Starvation is known, for example, to heighten obsessionality and irritability (Keys et al., 1950). This raises concerns that apparent personality disturbances in ED sufferers may reflect detrimental effects of the ED upon personality functioning—apparent PDs in active ED cases representing "state" disturbances associated with an active ED rather than "trait" tendencies. Numerous findings support just this conception, showing an active ED to often exacerbate latent personality problems or produce features with a characterological coloring (e.g., Ames-Frankel et al., 1992; Garner et al., 1990; Steiger, Leung, Thibaudeau, Houle, & Ghadirian, 1993). Such observations highlight the importance of exercising caution when drawing Axis II diagnoses in sufferers of an active ED.

Various studies indicate, however, that despite any tendencies for ED sequelae to enhance apparent personality disturbances, the EDs often seem to be associated with stable, underlying personality pathologies: (1) Retrospective studies examining premorbid personality in ED sufferers provide "soft" evidence of personality anomalies that may precede onset of eating symptoms. For example, Råstam (1992) estimated that 67% of a group of adolescent anorexics had shown a PD prior to ED onset, the most frequently diagnosed of which (in 35% of cases) was obsessive-compulsive PD. (2) Stability of personality disturbances, and partial independence from ED sequelae, is indicated by prospective studies on recovering patients. Enduring traits of rigidity, overcautiousness, and obsessionality are reported to persist (over several years) in recovered anorexics (Windauer, Lennerts, Talbot, Touyz, & Beumont, 1993), whereas enduring borderline features are reported to occur in recovering bulimics (diagnosed originally as having comorbid BPD), despite clear improvements in eating behaviors (Steiger & Stotland, 1996; Wonderlich, Fullerton, Swift, & Klein, 1994), and after controlling for possible effects attributable to ongoing eating symptoms (Steiger et al., 1993).

Etiology

Given that they are such complex syndromes, with such marked psychiatric comorbidity, contemporary theory on the EDs has tended to invoke a multidimensional, biopsychosocial causality (e.g., Garfinkel & Garner, 1982; Johnson & Connors, 1987; Strober, 1991). Biopsychosocial models postulate that the EDs implicate a "collision" among biological factors (e.g., heritable influences on mood, temperament, and impulse controls), social pressures (promoting body consciousness or generalized self-definition problems), and developmental processes (conducive to self-image or adjustment problems). The following sections elaborate on various biological, psychological, and social factors postulated to create risk for ED development.

Sociocultural Context

The disproportionate occurrence of EDs in Western nations (see section on epidemiology) implies that cultural values that prevail in the West may be especially conducive to ED development. Certainly, Western social values to some extent equate slimness with cultural ideals of "success," "beauty," "power," and "self-control," and this likely underlies the tendency for people in the West—and especially young females—to experience themselves as overweight and to be actively dieting (e.g., Rosen & Gross, 1987). There is little doubt that such factors play a direct role in the development of clinical EDs (see Garfinkel & Garner, 1982). Social values assigned to body image are believed to contribute to higher prevalences of AN in females—women surely being the more strongly socialized to link self-image with body image. Similarly, changing ideals for female body shape are thought to explain (in part) the apparent increase in incidence of EDs that occurred in the West during the decades since 1960 (see section on epidemiology, above). This period coincided with a dramatic shift in cultural ideal—from a "voluptuous" form represented by such celebrities as Marilyn Monroe to a slender (and often relatively androgynous) ideal for female appearance that became popular in the early '60s (and that remains prominent in celebrity and media images in the '90s).

Likewise, we know from the work of Garner and Garfinkel (1980) that AN occurs remarkably frequently in individuals whose social milieu places special emphasis on slimness and weight control (e.g., ballet dancers, models, athletes). In other words, it appears that cultural and "microcultural" pressures that lead to assignment of a positive social value to physical thinness enhance vulnerability to ED development in a predictable fashion. In a related vein, it has been argued that social experiences in Western societies disproportionately impede women's access to means of self-definition, and that such factors may indirectly heighten risk of ED development by heightening experiences of felt dyscontrol or ineffectiveness in females (see Eichenbaum & Orbach, 1983). Thus, gender-specific factors acting in certain segments of Western societies, some linked directly to eating and body image, some more relevant to general adaptation, can be thought to form a backdrop against which eating syndromes flourish in a special way.

Although the preceding associates the EDs with particular social contexts, further work is needed to define the sociocultural boundaries of the EDs. Otherwise, conclusions about the role of culture in the EDs risk being premature. For example, systematic cross-cultural research indicates anorexia-like syndromes, characterized by food refusal, to be prevalent in diverse (nonwestern) contexts (Pate, Pumariega, Hester, & Garner, 1992), and suggests that anorexia-like syndromes may not be as culture bound as once thought. Furthermore, some cross-cultural data reduce emphasis on the role of cultural pressures favoring slimness in ED pathogenesis. Lee, Ho, and Hsu (1993), for example, document a well-constructed study involving anorexics in Hong Kong. All were clearly anorexic according to criteria reflecting self-imposed weight loss, resistance to others' encouragements to eat, and amenorrhea (or loss of libido, in one male case). However, an important phenomenological anomaly was noted: roughly 60% displayed no conscious fear of becoming fat. Instead, a frequent justification from subjects for their refusal to eat was the desire to avoid gastric bloating. Given similar findings from other Asian studies, Lee and colleagues propose that AN may be subject to cross-cultural pathoplastic effects—"fat phobia" being characteristic of Western variants (arising in weight-conscious Western societies), but not definitive of AN at large. Such evidence implies that EDs may have a weaker connection to a Western "culture of thinness" than previously thought. Thus, while EDs are clearly subject to sociocultural influences, and certainly flourish in contemporary industrialized contexts, specific sociocultural influences upon ED development need to be better defined. Furthermore, even given the highly supportable assumption that social factors are a central part of ED pathogenesis, the question still remains: "Why are some individuals so permeable to social influences that they respond to socially prescribed values favoring slimness and dietary control with pathological eating?" Answering this question requires that we consider additional sources of vulnerability, conveyed by various biological and psychological processes.

Biological Factors

Genetics Evidence has supported the view that EDs may have substantial hereditary components. To start, genetic-epidemiological studies have indicated that the EDs are familial in nature—findings consistently indicating increased liability for an ED among the female relatives of ED sufferers than among relatives of control probands (e.g., Strober, Lampert, Morrell, Burroughs, & Jacobs, 1990; Kassett et al., 1989). Sisters of ED sufferers are, for example, found to display six to seven times greater risk of developing an ED themselves than are women in the general population. Furthermore, Strober and colleagues (1990) observed specific familial aggregation for AN, and not for BN, in the relatives of anorexic probands, as would be compatible with selective inheritance.

Available twin data have also suggested that EDs are subject to genetic effects. Studies show considerably stronger concordance for AN among monozygotic (MZ) twin pairs (in the .3 to .65 range) than in dizygotic (DZ) twins, where rates resemble those obtained in any siblings. MZ/DZ differences reportedly become stronger when diagnostic criteria are narrowed to restrictive (versus bulimic) forms of AN, suggesting that genetic influences in restrictive AN may be stronger than are those in bulimic ED variants (Treasure & Holland, 1995). Such findings have led Treasure and Holland (1995) to propose that restrictive and bulimic ED variants may be etiologically distinct—the former having strong genetic determinants, the latter, broader environmental causes.

Cotransmission with Other Syndromes Data such as the foregoing need not imply direct genetic transmission for an ED. Rather, liability for an ED could be conveyed by genetic linkage to another heritable syndrome. Relationships of this type have been explored with respect to various psychological traits and psychiatric syndromes that coincide with the EDs.

Mood Disorders Controlled studies show lifetime prevalences of MDs in relatives of anorexics (Strober et al., 1990) and bulimics (Kassett et al., 1989) to substantially exceed those obtained in control samples. Strongest and most consistent familial aggregation with MDs is, however, almost certainly observed in bulimic syndromes, where liability for MD among sufferers' first-degree relatives is three to four times higher than among relatives of control probands. At the same time, results have suggested that coaggregation for eating and mood syndromes within families does not reflect simple, simultaneous transmission: (1) Studies examining familial coaggregation of MDs with EDs indicate rates of MDs to be elevated in relatives of ED probands who themselves show MD manifestations, but not in those showing no mood disturbances (e.g., Kasset et al., 1989; Strober et al., 1990). In other words, shared liability for eating and mood disorders may exist, but risk of an ED is not increased by the simple presence, in the family, of MD. In further support of this point, Strober and colleagues (1990) found risk of MDs to be elevated in first-degree relatives of AN sufferers, but observed no parallel elevation of AN among the relatives of MD probands. (2) Walters et al. (1992) analyzed the co-occurrence of BN and major depression in 1,033 female twin pairs. Their results suggest shared genetic liabilities for both syndromes, but substantial uncorrelated proportions of liability that would need to be explained by unique genetic and/or environmental factors acting in each disorder.

Alcoholism Family-pedigree studies indicate clear co-aggregation of alcoholism and EDs—especially for bulimic ED variants (see Holderness et al., 1994). This raises the possibility of cotransmission effects that might link alcoholism with eating syndromes characterized by dietary dysregulation. As for mood disorders, however, familial coaggregation seems to be strongest around those eating-disordered probands who themselves have a propensity for substance abuse (Selby & Moreno, 1995). Again, this would suggest some shared component of liability, but also unique genetic and/or environmental determinants for each disorder.

Temperamental Traits Strober (1991) postulated that the "core of Anorexia Nervosa lies in genotypic personality structures that predispose . . . to rigid . . . avoidance behaviors with marked obsessional, anxious-depressive coloring" (p. 11). Conversely, Humphrey (1991) linked bulimia to family-wide "self-soothing" deficits, expressed through instability of affects and impulses. In this light, it becomes reasonable to assume that different ED subtypes may be associated with particular, heritable temperamental traits. Empirical evidence of familial linkage for personality traits in the EDs exists, but findings have been frustratingly inconsistent: Casper (1990) noted that anorexics' sisters tended toward conventionality and control, and Strober, Salkin, Burroughs, and Morrell (1982) documented theoretically relevant differences, on Minnesota Multiphasic Personality Inventory (MMPI) scores, between parents of restricter and bulimic anorexics—the former were emotionally reserved while the latter displayed hostile/depressive tendencies. While such results are suggestive, a number of studies report either negligible differences or no differences when the personality-test scores of parents of anorexics or bulimics are compared to those of normal controls (Carney, Yates, & Cizadlo, 1990; Garfinkel et al., 1983; Steiger, Stotland, Ghadirian, & Whitehead, 1995).

Neurobiology Various neurobiological agents have been postulated to act in the EDs (see Brewerton, 1995; Fava, Copeland, Schweiger, & Herzog, 1989). We address findings on the putative roles of three substances for which a role in the EDs is possible: norepinephrine (NE), a monoamine thought to stimulate eating behavior; cholecystokinin (CCK), a peptidergic neurotransmitter thought to induce satiety; and serotonin (5-hydroxytryptamine; 5-HT), another monoamine thought to inhibit eating behavior. In addition to known roles in the regulation of eating behaviors, NE and 5-HT have been strongly implicated in mood regulation, and the latter, in inhibition of impulsive behavior.

Abnormally low levels of central and peripheral norepinephrine have been reported in eating-disordered patients, both anorexic and bulimic (see Fava et al., 1989). Such anomalies could underlie depressed mood, as well as disturbances in eating behavior. However, evidence shows rapid normalization of NE levels with nutritional rehabilitation, and suggests that NE abnormalities may be secondary to malnutrition or recurrent dieting. In turn, this casts doubt on the belief that NE abnormalities could act causally in the EDs. NE abnormalities that were secondary to malnutrition could, nonetheless, play a perpetuating role in an active ED, or could underlie the heightened susceptibility to depression evinced by active anorexics.

CCK is secreted by the gastrointestinal system and, among many functions, is believed to signal satiety to the brain. Levels of plasma CCK have been found to be lower in normal-weight bulimics after ingesting a high-calorie meal than in anorexic or normal-control subjects (Pirke, Kellner, Frieb, Krieg, & Fichter, 1994). Given its putative role in satiation, abnormal CCK activity could therefore constitute a plausible substrate for the dietary dyscontrol (binge eating) that characterizes BN.

While serotonin abnormalities have been obtained in restricter anorexics, such findings have generally seemed to be attributable to secondary effects of malnutrition on 5-HT levels (Brewerton, 1995), weakening the basis for assuming a causal role of 5-HT anomalies in AN. A more compelling case can, however, be made to support a serotonin hypothesis for bulimic ED variants. In theory, serotonin is thought to act in satiation, and in regulation of mood and impulsivity. Given that bulimic syndromes are often characterized by problems with satiety, mood, and impulse regulation, there is an obvious rationale for assuming an underlying serotonergic factor. Furthermore, empirical findings have linked binge/purge syndromes quite consistently to 5-HT anomalies—showing normal-weight bulimics and bulimic anorexics (relative to restricter anorexics and/or normal controls) to display abnormally low levels of cerebrospinal fluid (CSF) 5-HT and its metabolites (e.g., 5-hydroxyindoleacetic acid), abnormal serotonin contents in blood platelets, or blunted hormonal responses to serotonin agonists (implying problems of serotonergic neurotransmission). To complete a picture linking binge/purge syndromes to 5-HT dysregulation, treatment studies have indicated that selective serotonin reuptake inhibitors (SSRIs), which enhance serotonergic neurotransmission, reduce the frequency of bulimic behaviors (see Brewerton, 1995).

Neuropsychology As for most other psychiatric disorders, it has been postulated that the EDs may be associated with abnormalities in brain function, neuroanatomy, and metabolism. Results of neuropsychological assays have linked anorexic and bulimic ED variants with (generally mild) cognitive impairments, associated with higher level functions like active memory, attention, and problem solving (e.g., Szmukler et al., 1992; Jones, Duncan, Brouwers, & Mirsky, 1991). One study of AN (restricter and binger subtypes) showed improvement in problem solving, attention, and perceptual-motor functions with weight restoration, independent of concurrent variations in depressed mood and substance use (Szmukler et al., 1992). Brain imaging studies have reported anomalous brain asymmetries in BN, in brain metabolism in AN (Hsu, Kaye, & Weltzin, 1993), and brain shrinkage in both AN (Herholz, 1996) and BN (Hoffman et al., 1989). Such effects could be due to an increased permeability of the blood brain barrier (Herholz, 1996) and may account for reversible, state-dependent cognitive and behavioral problems observed during actively eating-disordered phases. While most findings are consistent with problems of neuropsychological status that are secondary to an ED, some neuropsychological impairments observed in ED sufferers have been thought to be results of perinatal brain injury, and could therefore predate ED onset (Jones et al., 1991). Such abnormalities might, in turn, underlie behavioral abnormalities and temperamental vulnerabilities that have been associated with the EDs.

Psychological and Developmental Factors

Individual Psychological Features

Theory Although theories on the psychopathology of the EDs are very diverse, there is some consensus on the notion that there is a systematic linkage between particular psychological characteristics and either restrictive or bulimic ED variants (e.g., Bruch, 1973; DaCosta & Halmi, 1992; Johnson, 1991). For decades, there has been a stereotype of the anorexic restricter as being a compliant, isolated, and anxious girl who gravitates to orderliness or control. Bruch (1973) understood such features to reflect pervasive feelings of low self-worth and ineffectiveness and developmental deficits in awareness of self and feeling states. Similarly, Crisp (1980) emphasized reserved, compliant children with marked conflicts around pubertal demands. He formulated AN as a phobic-avoidance response, reinforced by a literal escape from maturational changes at puberty. Strober's (1991) recently articulated "organismic-developmental" paradigm again addresses pathological adaptations to adolescence, but emphasizes an incompatibility between developmental imperatives surrounding puberty and a heritable temperament characterized by harm avoidance, hyperreactivity to social approval, and preference for sameness.

Thinking on bulimic syndromes (and on anorexic variants that include bulimic symptoms) has emphasized an alternative spectrum of psychopathology: self-regulatory deficits, dramatic fluctuations in self-concept and mood, and erratic efforts to regulate inner tensions (e.g., Humphrey, 1991; Johnson, 1991). Thus, to the extent that restrictive AN has been associated with anxiousness, introversion, and overcontrol, bulimic ED variants have been linked with extroversion, sensation seeking, and dyscontrol. Johnson (1991) provided a nicely integrative view, postulating that restrictive and bulimic ED variants, although they occur along a shared continuum of "self" disturbances, differ as to key aspects of defensive organization. He characterizes defenses in restricters as "paranoid, rigid, and over-determined" attempts to protect a vulnerable ego from external demands (p. 170), and those in bingers as "frantic, diffuse, and chaotic" compensations for inner emptiness and dysphoria (p. 171). In other words, "self" in the restricter is conceptualized as being structured around limiting outside influences, whereas, in the binger, psychological organization is thought to be characterized by a more frantic quest for self soothing and need fulfillment.

Psychometric Findings How well supported are such theoretical differences? To address this question the following section reviews findings from studies employing well-known psychometric instruments to assess psychological traits in ED sufferers.

The first available psychometric studies on AN led to a characterization of ED sufferers as being neurotic, socially anxious, and (often) depressed. More important, they provided initial indices of differences between restricter and binger/purger subtypes—the latter subtype being consistently noted to show greater emotional lability, impulsivity, or oppositionality (see Sohlberg & Strober, 1994). Early studies using the Eysenck Personality Inventory (EPI) showed binger/purger anorexics to display greater extraversion and greater neuroticism, on average, than did restricters (Strober, 1980; Ben Tovim et al., 1979). Studies based on the MMPI tended to reiterate the same theme, often finding bingers/purgers to display more pronounced and broader psychopathological tendencies than restricters. While most findings fail to associate a discriminating profile with either syndrome (see Vitousek & Manke, 1994), some MMPI-based studies support a restricter/binger distinction (e.g., Casper, Hedeker, & McClough, 1992). Others suggest substantial within-subtype heterogeneities that cut across ED subtypes—indicating clusterings within each subtype that are compatible with relatively "intact," "neurotic," and more deeply "characterological" organizations (Strober, 1983).

Evidence derived using other measures contributes to the belief that overcontrolled and disinhibited personality tendencies coincide imperfectly with restricter and binger/purger distinctions: results suggesting more schizoid or avoidant tendencies among restricters and more histrionic tendencies among bingers (normal-weight and anorexic) have been obtained with the Millon Clinical Multiaxial Inventory (e.g., Norman, Blais, & Herzog, 1993). Casper and colleagues (1992) examined personality profiles in eating-disordered inpatients using the Multidimensional Personality Questionnaire (MPQ). They found normal-weight bulimics to be less conforming and more impulsive than were either restricter or binger/purger anorexics, and found anorexic restricters to show strongest loadings on dimensions reflecting self-control, conscientiousness, and emotional inhibition. Parallel trait distinctions have been obtained in subtype comparisons performed with the Tridimensional Personality Questionnaire (TPQ), which measures harm avoidance (preference for predictability or sameness), novelty seeking (behavioral activation), and reward dependence (sensitivity to social approval). Based on convention, the restricter pattern would be expected to coincide with high harm avoidance, high reward dependence, and low novelty seeking, whereas somewhat the converse would be expected in bingers/purgers. Results have provided only partial support for this expectation:

in one study, normal-weight bulimics were found to be more novelty seeking than were restricter or binger anorexics, restricter anorexics were found to be more reward dependent than were bulimic anorexics, but bulimic anorexics were noted to be more harm avoidant than were restricters (Bulik, Sullivan, Weltzin, & Kaye, 1995). In another study, which derived TPQ dimensions from MPQ items, restricter anorexics were observed to be exceptionally low on novelty seeking, but not to differ from bulimic ED subtypes on other dimensions (Casper, Hedeker, & McClough, 1992).

Additional studies have addressed the issue of specificity of psychological traits to eating (versus to other psychiatric) syndromes. Many provide no indications of discriminating psychopathological features when comparing ED sufferers to females suffering other psychiatric disturbances (see Vitousek & Manke, 1994). However, some document suggestive differences: Strober (1980) discriminated adolescent anorexics (in expected directions) from age-matched depressives and conduct disorders on measures reflecting compulsivity, social conformity, obsessionality, interpersonal insecurity, emotional constriction, and stimulus seeking. Studies by our research group have found anorexic and bulimic women to tend toward greater self-criticism (Steiger, Goldstein, Mongrain, & Van der Feen, 1990) and pathological narcissism (Lehoux, Steiger, & Jabalpurwala, in press; Steiger, Jabalpurwala, Champagne, & Stotland, 1997) than do groups composed of women with mixed psychiatric disorders. Our findings are compatible with the concept that ED sufferers may be particularly sensitive to social approval and prone to rapid deflation of self-concept and self-denigration in response to lack of recognition from others. Together, results imply that ED sufferers may be distinguished, not by any disorder-specific psychopathological feature, but by unusually heavy loadings on certain theoretically relevant dimensions (risk avoidance, conformity, self-criticism, narcissistic needs for approval, etc.).

In summary, psychometric findings indicate the EDs to represent heterogeneous personality and psychological features, with few consistent discriminating characteristics when compared to appropriate psychiatric-control groups. This suggests that no single psychological propensity should be regarded as being uniquely conducive to ED development. Assuming this as given, however, available findings have supported theoretically important generalizations: (1) restrictive AN is associated with relatively circumscribed personality characteristics, with particular loadings on traits of rigidity, harm avoidance, emotional constriction, and obsessionality. (2) Binge/purge syndromes, on the other hand, are associated with relatively heterogeneous psychopathological characteristics, implicating both restrained and disinhibited tendencies. Loadings on dimensions suggesting greater behavioral disinhibition and affectivity are, however, much more striking in bingers/purgers than they are in restricters (Johnson & Wonderlich, 1992; Vitousek & Manke, 1994). (3) Although restricter/binger differences are repeatable, findings have also revealed substantial within-subtype heterogeneities. Viewing them as a whole, we interpret findings as reflecting the convergent actions of two opposing tendencies: EDs occur in individuals with relatively heterogeneous psychological traits, but their subtypes (i.e., restrictive or bulimic) do show different affinities for dimensions associated, respectively, with psychological restraint or disinhibition. The combined effects might indeed manifest themselves in the form of unreliable restricter/binger differences, along with substantial heterogeneities, on psychological dimensions, within the population.

Impulsivity To the preceding, we add a brief discussion on the relevance of trait impulsivity to the EDs and to overall severity of eating symptomatology. Observations made with questionnaire-based assessments or structured clinical interviews have indicated that bulimic patients show remarkable propensities toward nonreflectiveness, behavioral disinhibition, self-harming behaviors, or other characteristics thought to imply impulsivity (e.g., Bushnell, Wells, & Oakley-Browne, 1996; Newton, Freeman, & Monro, 1993; Fahey & Eisler, 1993; Wolfe, Jimerson, & Levine, 1994). Almost half of a cohort of normal-weight bulimics studied by Newton and colleagues (1993), for example, met criteria for a "multi-impulsive" syndrome characterized by substance abuse, multiple overdoses, recurrent self-harm, sexual disinhibition, or shoplifting. Such findings corroborate the impression (described earlier) that impulse-control problems are prominent in a substantial subgroup of BN sufferers. Conversely, data reviewed earlier suggest that restricter anorexics, if anything, display the opposite tendency—toward excessive self-control. However, despite marked association between bulimic syndromes and impulse-control problems, and the intuitive appeal of regarding bulimic behaviors as one instance of a generalized dyscontrol over impulsive behaviors, it is intriguing to note that levels of impulsivity do not reliably predict severity of bulimic symptoms in BN sufferers (e.g., Fahey & Eisler, 1993; Wolfe et al., 1994). This suggests that factors underlying impulsivity may be (at least partially) distinct from those controlling severity of eating pathology itself. We elaborate on this point further in the discussion, to follow.

Body-Image Disturbances Disturbance in body image, or excessive impact of perceived body-image upon overall self-evaluation, constitutes the defining characteristic of AN and BN, and is hypothesized to have a fundamental role in the etiology and maintenance of these eating syndromes. Given the preceding, it is surprising to note that there has been ongoing controversy over the importance, and indeed occurrence, of body-image disturbance in AN and BN. Empirical findings have supported conflicting conclusions, with some suggesting clear tendencies of ED sufferers to overestimate bodily proportions or to have unusually harsh attitudes toward their bodies, others yielding negative findings when body-image perceptions and attitudes of ED sufferers are compared to those of relevant controls (see Hsu & Sobkiewicz, 1991).

At present, consensus seems to have been reached on the belief that ED subjects, anorexic and bulimic alike, are prone to marked dissatisfaction with, and negative emotional cathexes in, body image. Resolution of the question of whether or not either of these patient groups actually distort (or misperceive) body image has been complicated by methodological issues bearing upon the measurement of body-image perception. However, the notion that these patients distort bodily appearance has fallen into increasing disfavor and has been gradually replaced by the belief that emotional and attentional factors (and not perceptual ones) explain the ED sufferer's evident preoccupations with her body and body image. This said, the present state of knowledge on body image in the EDs supports a rather unsatisfying generalization: EDs are structured around marked preoccupations with body image, but the origins of these remain largely unknown and have been postulated to include any of several causes—including neurobiological (e.g., Brewerton, 1995) and neuropsychological abnormalities (e.g., Szmukler et al., 1992), social learning factors acting within families (e.g., Pike & Rodin, 1991), developmental trauma impacting upon the bodily experience (e.g., Everill & Waller, 1995), and other processes. We address familial factors thought to influence body attitudes and experience in a following section.

Dietary Restraint Cognitive components of dietary restraint—or "restrictive eating attitudes" (e.g., the belief that one should always eat low-calorie foods or compensate any time one eats more than usual)—are thought to make an important contribution to the development of disinhibited (bingelike) eating behaviors. As mentioned earlier, Polivy and Herman's (1985, 1993) restraint theory specifically postulates that chronic attitudinal restraint of eating potentiates the breakdown of cognitive controls upon appetitive behaviors, and eventual counterregulation (or overeating). Furthermore, it proposes that counterregulation has specific cognitive and emotional triggers. The work of Polivy, Herman, and other investigators (e.g., Baucom & Aiken, 1981; Heatherton & Baumeister, 1991) has led to an impressive catalog of findings, derived mainly from laboratory studies in nonclinical populations, that show that counterregulation of eating behavior can be induced (in attitudinally restrained eaters) by manipulations that generate (1) beliefs that one has exceeded an allowable calorie limit, (2) negative affects, (3) feelings of self-inadequacy, or (4) global disinhibition (as is induced following alcohol consumption). The work of Heatherton and Baumeister (1991) adds a clinically relevant specification—arguing that counterregulation, or disinhibited eating, is explained by transient losses of inhibitory controls (over eating and other behaviors) that occur when cognitive states that serve to divert attention away from painful self-awareness become activated by injuries to self-esteem. Their notion fits BN patients' own descriptions of their binge episodes as "occurring in an altered state of mind" or providing "distraction from painful feelings" and may be relevant to dissociative-type phenomena seen in bulimic patients (discussed earlier).

Assuming that clinical ED sufferers are recurrently (if not constantly) restrictive in their eating attitudes, the concepts described above seem to provide a good fit to patterns evident in clinical binge-eating syndromes. Naturalistic observations of eating behavior in bulimic patients, for example, suggest that binges are often preceded by prolonged undereating, strong negative affects, feelings of personal inadequacy, or situations in which self-imposed dietary limits are felt to have been exceeded (Heatherton & Baumeister, 1991; Polivy & Herman, 1993). An important clinical implication, following from the preceding, is that treatment of binge eating will often require interventions that reduce cognitive dietary restraint in the sufferer.

At the same time, we mention some recent observations that have suggested a subgroup of BN and binge-eating disorder sufferers in whom binge eating develops prior to any history of strict dieting (Mussell et al., 1997; Borman Spurrell, Wilfley, Tanofsky, & Brownell, 1997). Borman Spurrell and her colleagues (1997) noted, further, that people in whom binge eating preceded onset of dieting show more evidence of personality pathology. These findings resonate with some very new data from our research group, suggesting that restraint may be a weaker hour-to-hour antecedent to binge episodes in highly impulsive bulimics than in less-impulsive ones (Steiger, Lehoux, & Gauvin, in press). We interpret these findings as implying that processes associated with impulsivity (e.g., neurobiological factors) may contribute directly to the propensity to binge eat. A main implication, if such findings bear up to further empirical tests, is that dietary restraint may not be an essential antecedent to binge eating in all of its forms.

Family Factors

Theories on Family Dynamics ED symptoms have been thought to reflect adaptations to problematic family-interaction patterns: for example, theorists often construe AN as a "phobic-obsessional" adaptation to familial intrusions and overprotectiveness (e.g., Bruch, 1973; Johnson, 1991), conceptualizing food refusal as a child's means of self-assertion, in the face of excessive familial controls or emotional investment. A related conception (prominent in family systems theories on AN) emphasizes problems around interpersonal boundaries and difficulties with separation and autonomy. The well-known theory of Palazolli (1978), for example, emphasizes familial problems with interpersonal boundaries that draw the anorexic into feeling excessive responsibility for her parents' happiness or guilt around the demands her needs create. The related theory of Minuchin (Minuchin, Rosman, & Baker, 1978) addresses familial enmeshment, overprotectiveness, rigidity, and problems around conflict resolution. Such processes are conceived to cause children to deny their needs or to resort to overcontrolled eating to express frustrations and assert self-control in family environments that otherwise disallow autonomous expressions.

In contrast to the overinvolvement postulated to be characteristic of family environments in which AN develops, family models of BN convey a view of children's frantic struggles to satisfy needs in disengaged or neglectful families. For example, Johnson (1991) linked bulimic symptoms to parental neglect—in his view spanning a continuum from "nonmalevolent" forms (in families in which parents' perfectionistic needs place excessive demands upon children) to "malevolent" forms (occurring in frankly chaotic or abusive families). Humphrey (1991) formulated bulimic syndromes in similar terms, referring to family-wide deficits in nurturance and tension regulation, and systems that ensnare members in mutually destructive, hostile projections (or "blaming"). In both views, bulimic eating patterns are conceived to play a self- and mood-regulatory function and to be metaphors for chaotic family interactions tinged with desperate attempts to affiliate, alternated with hostile rejections and blaming.

Empirical Findings Self-report data from AN sufferers, and from their parents and siblings, have tended to provide partial corroboration of concepts of "enmeshment," "overprotection," "separation problems," and "conflict avoidance." Studies portray families as limiting members' autonomy (Leon, Lucas, Colligan, Ferlinande, & Kemp, 1985), or as showing unusually low levels of conflict (Monck, Graham, Richman, & Dobbs, 1990). More important, observational studies (which, more than self-report measures, may elucidate dynamics of which family members themselves are unaware) often corroborate the "enmeshed, conflict-avoiding family" concept: Crisp, Hsu, Harding, and Hartshorn (1980) reported disturbed parent-child interactions in about half of 102 cases of AN, with enmeshment being the most commonly reported theme. Using coded records of parent-child interactions, Goldstein (1981) discriminated families of hospitalized anorexics from those of hospitalized nonanorexics and adolescents at-risk for schizophrenia on dimensions reflecting requests for protection and conflict avoidance. Similarly, families of anorexics are noted to show unusually low expressed emotion (EE) on observational tasks, indicating low levels of conflictual or dissaproving interactions (Hodes & Legrange, 1993). All of the preceding are compatible with the concept of an enmeshed or underseparated familial organization. In an observational study of families with an eating-disordered daughter, however, Kog, Vertommen, and Vandereycken (1987) identified a subset that indeed displayed boundary problems, rigidity, and low conflict, but found this pattern to coincide with bulimic ED variants as frequently as with restrictive ones. The latter finding raises some doubts about the specificity of the "conflict-avoiding, enmeshed family" concept to AN.

Findings from self-report studies in families of patients with bulimic symptoms (whether at anorexic or normal weight) have pointed toward a different family profile, characterized by overt conflict and distress. For example, Johnson and Flach (1985) used various measures to obtain perceptions of family functioning from adult bulimics and normal controls. Bulimics, relative to controls, were noted to perceive their families as being incohesive, high in conflict, and limited at expressing feelings. Degree of family dysfunction coincided with severity of bulimic symptoms. McNamara and Loveman (1990) obtained comparable results in a comparison of bulimics, repeat dieters, and nondieters. Bulimics rated their families as showing difficulties with affective involvement, affective responsiveness, communication, problem solving, and behavioral control. Other studies measuring the dimension of family cohesion/incohesion show bulimics' families to be less cohesive than are those of controls (see Wonderlich, 1992). Likewise, observational studies have often corroborated the impression that binge/purge syndromes coincide with relatively overt familial discord and hostility. For example, Sights and Richards (1984) documented observations on interactions in small numbers of families with college-age bulimic or nonbulimic daughters. Bulimics' mothers were rated as domineering and demanding of their daughters, and their families were noted to display greater parent-daughter stress. Similar themes are conveyed by Humphrey's work, which has emphasized an intriguing structured observational system based upon object-relations concepts (see Humphrey, 1991; Wonderlich, 1992). In several studies comparing bulimic-anorexic mother-father-daughter triads to those of normal triads, bulimic-anorexic families were noted to be the more blameful, rejecting, and neglectful and less nurturant and comforting. While the preceding corroborates theories on dynamics in binge/purge syndromes described earlier, we note the relative absence of appropriate psychiatric control groups in the available studies to establish specificity of observed patterns to BN. Following a recent review of family data in BN, Schmidt, Tiller, and Treasure (1993) conclude that evidence supports the belief that BN is associated with family disturbance in a high proportion of cases, but that such disturbances may constitute general rather than specific risk factors, perhaps relevant only to bulimic patients showing particular personality or mood problems.

Many studies have explored restricter/binger differences in family functioning using self-report family assessment questionnaires (see Wonderlich, 1992). While inconsistencies exist (perhaps explained by differences in samples, settings, and measures), a recurrent trend suggests that bulimic families display more overt disturbances than do those of restricters. Further refinements upon this view are available: Waller (1994) studied the association between eating symptoms and perceived family-interaction patterns in a series of women suffering either AN or BN. Binge eating was associated with perceptions of families as being incohesive and poor at problem solving. Abnormal dietary restraint was, on the other hand, linked (albeit nonsignificantly) to tendencies toward greater family cohesion and better problem solving. Various observational methods have led to comparable conclusions about restricter/binger family differences: family observations have, for example, indicated expressed emotion (i.e., open conflict) to be greater in bingers' than in restricters' families (Hodes & LeGrange, 1993). A series of observational studies by Humphrey contrasted family processes in females with normal-weight bulimia, bulimic AN, restrictive AN, or no ED. Results implied deficits in parental nurturance and (to some extent) empathy in both bulimic subgroups (see Humphrey, 1991; Wonderlich, 1992). Kog and Vandereycken (1989), however, in observing interaction patterns in families of ED patients and normal controls, noted that anorexic families (restricting and bulimic alike) show boundary problems and conflict avoidance, with families of normal-weight (nonanorexic) bulimics alone showing open disagreement.

Family Data from Community Samples It is possible that selection biases influence findings obtained in samples from specialized ED clinics and cause an artificial association to emerge between presence of eating pathology in children and presence of family-interaction problems. However, various community-based studies link ED-spectrum disturbances to family disturbances resembling those observed in clinic populations (see Wonderlich, 1992). Eme and Damielak (1995) examined the relationship between maladaptive eating attitudes and family relationships among upper-middle-class 15-year-old girls. Girls displaying maladaptive eating reported more dysfunctional family patterns, more problems of autonomy with respect to their fathers, and more problems with both parents on indices of communication and expression of warmth. Similarly, in a study of female undergraduates, Reeves and Johnson (1992) observed likelihood of eating-disordered attitudes and behaviors to be increased in subjects who perceived their families as functioning poorly.

Community studies have also yielded restricter/binger differences on family variables, resembling those obtained in clinical samples. Steiger and colleagues (1991) found that bulimic symptoms were more consistently linked to subject-reported family incohesion than were restrictive ones. Likewise, Smolak and Levine (1993), reporting on community cases believed to display either bulimic or restrictive forms of eating pathology, noted the former group to be "overseparated" from parents (in terms of attitudinal independence), whereas "restricter-like" cases tended to be "underseparated." The resemblance of such findings to those obtained in clinical populations is obvious. However, questions of specificity of family dysfunction for EDs arise in community-based studies, as they do in studies conducted in clinic populations; for example, Brookings and Wilson (1994), in an evaluation of the predictive value of family-environment variables for various symptoms (in female university undergraduates), found family variables to explain generalized emotional or interpersonal problems, but not ED symptoms.

Psychosocial Induction It is appealing to presume that the EDs depend upon psychosocial induction effects, in which maladaptive concerns with body image, weight, and eating are conveyed to children by a family culture of maladaptive eating attitudes. Indeed, studies in nonclinical samples imply that mothers' eating attitudes influence daughters' beliefs and behaviors around eating (e.g., Pike & Rodin, 1991). However, in clinical populations, as many studies report parents of ED sufferers (anorexic and bulimic) to show normal eating and body image attitudes (Hall, Leibrich, Walkley, & Welch, 1986; Garfinkel et al., 1983; Steiger et al., 1995) as report differences (Hall & Brown, 1983; Wold, 1985). Miller, McCluskey-Fawcett, and Irving (1993) compared perceptions of early meal-time experiences across normal eaters, repeat dieters, and bulimics, and found the bulimics to display a differentiating history of eating-related issues in the early family context. Such findings may be sensitive to retrospective reporting biases, but are consistent with the idea that adverse meal-related experiences within the family convey risk for an ED. However, mixed findings on the causal significance of familial eating concerns suggest that such factors will, alone, be insufficient to explain development of clinical EDs.

Sexual Traumata Empirical data indicate the EDs to be alarmingly associated with severe childhood traumata, like sexual abuse (e.g., Connors & Morse, 1993; Everill & Waller, 1995). Modal figures indicate roughly 30% of ED sufferers to report some form of unwanted sexual experience during childhood. Given that they implicate such markedly disturbed bodily experience, it has been thought that EDs may be specifically (and causally) linked to body-relevant trauma occurring during childhood. However, it should be noted that observed rates of trauma in ED sufferers are not consistently found to exceed those obtained in females with other psychiatric problems—a main implication seeming to be that there exists a strong, but nonspecific association, between childhood trauma and the EDs.

Data on prevalences of childhood sexual traumata in restricter and binger subgroups have tended to "echo" findings obtained on other dimensions, suggesting that bulimic ED variants may be associated with the more unfavorable developmental experiences. Findings have consistently associated childhood abuse more strongly with binge/purge than with restrictive ED variations (Steiger & Zanko, 1990; Fullerton, Wonderlich, & Gosnell, 1995). While such observations could reflect greater repression in restricters or protectiveness of the family, the trend in question would also be consistent with an overall portrait of the bulimic family as being the more blatantly destructive, abusive, or neglectful (so as to render children subject either to incestuous or extrafamilial forms of abuse). However, even if childhood traumata are more strongly linked to bulimic than to restrictive ED variants, this need not imply bulimia-specific pathogenic effects. Several studies in BN sufferers have noted, for example, that severity of childhood abuse predicts severity of personality pathology, impulsivity, dissociative potentials, and other forms of comorbid psychopathology far more directly than it does severity of bulimic symptoms per se (e.g., Fullerton et al., 1994; Steiger et al., 1996).

Findings from studies examining the opposite direction of association—namely the presence of disturbed eating in survivors of childhood abuse—tend also to support the conclusion that there exists only an indirect link between the EDs and childhood sexual trauma. Smolak, Levine, and Sullins (1990) noted that sexually abused women report more abnormal eating attitudes and behaviors than nonabused women, but their design did not permit assessment of the specificity of sexual trauma for eating problems. Schaaf and McCanne (1994) found no evidence that childhood sexual or physical abuse was associated with the development of body-image problems or ED symptoms in their subjects. Similarly, Kinzl, Taweger, Guenther, and Biebl (1994) examined the possible implications of negative early family environment and childhood sexual abuse for the later development of ED symptoms in female university students (a group of whom had suffered sexual abuse). Subjects who reported an adverse family background were at significantly higher risk of developing an ED than were subjects reporting a positive family background, but sexual abuse had no specific value as a predictor of eating symptoms.

Toward an Integrated Etiological Concept

If the preceding supports one assertion, it is that the EDs are polysymptomatic syndromes, likely to have diverse causal and maintaining factors. This means that an adequate etiological model needs to explain not only the abnormal eating practices and bodily experiences that characterize the EDs but also the diversity of psychopathological features that coincide with them. The first formal biopsychosocial theory on the EDs was provided by Garfinkel and Garner (1982). Their thinking, and the strongly characterological coloring of comorbid psychopathology in the EDs, inspired subsequent theorists to produce elaborations that attempt to integrate psychobiological conceptions of personality with biopsychosocial perspectives on eating and related disorders (see Johnson & Connors, 1987; Strober, 1991). In general form, their models assume that EDs are multiply-determined by complex interactions among (1) constitutional factors (e.g., biological processes affecting mood, temperament, and appetite); (2) psychological/developmental processes (influencing general personality development and specific attitudes toward eating and body image); (3) social factors (including cultural emphasis on thinness and broad social influences upon self image); and finally (4) the secondary effects, in biological, psychological, and social spheres, of maladaptive eating practices themselves. Much remains to be done, however, before we can claim to have understood the independent or joint contributions of any one, or group, of causal factors.

To help clarify the roles, in ED development, of various putative causal factors discussed in this chapter, we introduce a concept that we believe provides an important heuristic—as it assists with assignment of disorder-specific and nonspecific (but contributing) roles to various factors. This concept, supported by various recent findings, is that severity of comorbid components in the EDs is often surprisingly independent of severity of eating symptoms. In other words, cases displaying severe comorbid disturbances need not display correspondingly severe eating symptoms, and vice versa. This concept, that EDs often implicate semi-autonomous (eating-specific and generalized) components of pathology, was first addressed in the "two-component" model of the EDs proposed by Garner, Olmsted, Polivy, and Garfinkel (1984).

Several types of evidence are consistent with the notion of partial independence of eating-specific and generalized areas of disturbance in ED sufferers:

1. Factor- or path-analytic studies on the structure of ED pathology (e.g., Gleaves, Williamson, & Barker, 1993; Tobin, Johnson, Steinberg, Staats, & Dennis, 1991) have sug-

gested that measures reflecting eating-specific disturbances (e.g., dietary restraint, dietary disinhibition, body-image problems) load onto a latent dimension of pathology (i.e., an underlying psychopathological factor) different from that onto which load measures reflecting generalized psychopathology (e.g., depression, personality, or impulse-control problems). These observations would suggest that severity of generalized psychopathology is controlled by factors that differ, at least partially, from those controlling severity of eating disturbances.
2. Findings on the linkage of eating and personality pathologies have indicated that severe personality disorders, like borderline PD, predict elevations on expected general symptoms (e.g., impulsivity, hostility, mood problems), but *do not* reliably predict more pronounced eating symptoms (e.g., Ames-Frankel et al., 1992; Steiger et al., 1993; Wonderlich et al., 1994). Such findings, too, imply a partial independence of factors contributing to generalized versus eating-specific components.
3. Recent findings converge on the idea that developmental factors (e.g., deficits in family functioning, childhood sexual abuse), while almost certainly associated with ED development, may predict severity of generalized psychopathology in the ED sufferer much more closely than it does severity of his or her eating symptoms (Fullerton et al., 1994; Steiger et al., 1996). This, too, suggests a partial independence of eating-specific and generalized factors.

To permit elaboration on hypothetical causal interactions among eating-specific and generalized components of pathology in the EDs, we have listed biopsychosocial factors thought to be relevant to each component in table 14.1. Hypothetical eating-specific risk factors are listed in the left-hand column of table 14.1. These are presumed to impinge directly on bodily components of self-representation and on eating-specific cognitions and behaviors. They include (1) biological factors related to bodily appearance and appetite regulation, (2) psychological processes linked to concern with body image or weight (e.g., identifications with weight-conscious parents and peers), and (3) social values that heighten concerns with weight and bodily appearance. Together, these factors are presumed to constitute the ingredients, biological, psychological, and social, of marked concerns with eating, weight, and body image. (We assume that various forms of interaction and modulation occur "vertically" among factors shown in table 14.1, and that together, such effects control overall strength of eating-related concerns.) However, we also assume that alone these factors may not create sufficiently strong predisposition to explain development of a clinical ED.

Alternative factors, assumed to be nonspecific to eating (i.e., to underlie generalized disturbances), but to be important components of vulnerability for ED development, are depicted in the right-hand column of table 14.1. These include: (1) biological processes (e.g., serotonin abnormalities, genetic factors) influencing temperament, mood, and impulse regulation, (2) psychological processes that shape general "self" development and self-concept (e.g., familial overprotection, developmental neglect, childhood traumata), and (3) sociocultural influences pertinent to overall self-image. (Again, we assume various forms of interaction, on the vertical dimension, among factors listed in table 14.1—controlling presence and strength of generalized vulnerability and/or maladaption.) While nonspecific, such factors might interact (horizontally and diagonally) with eating-specific agents to contribute to risk of developing a clinical ED, as follows:

1. Constitutional factors (e.g., inherited problems of serotonin neurotransmission) may, along with their predictable effects on mood and impulse regulation, convey vulnerability to disorders of satiation (and hence bulimic eating patterns) in individuals disposed (by factors shown on the left of table 14.1) to restrict their food intake. This might, in part, explain an affinity of bulimic eating syndromes with manifestations suggesting mood or impulse dyscontrol.
2. Given a social context that links body esteem to overall self-esteem (especially in women), generalized self-image problems in females might indirectly heighten susceptibility to dieting and, eventually, to pathological eating practices.
3. Rigid adaptations to parental overprotection or overcontrol (addressed on the right of table 14.1), while alone insufficient to explain

Table 14.1 Putative Bological, Psychological, Developmental, and Social Risk Factors for Eating Disorder Development, Separated into Those Thought to Contribute to "Eating-Specific Pathology" and to "Generalized Psychopathology." Factors Shown Are Meant to be Illustrative, not Exhaustive

	Eating-Specific Factors (Direct Risk Factors)	*Generalized Factors* (Indirect Risk Factors)
Biological Factors	ED-specific genetic risk Physiognomy and body weight Appetite regulation Energy metabolism Gender	Genetic risk for associated disturbance Temperament Impulsivity Neurobiology (e.g., 5-HT mechanisms) Gender
Psychological Factors	Poor body image Maladaptive eating attitudes Maladaptive weight beliefs Specific values or meanings assigned to food, body Overvaluation of appearance	Poor self-image Inadequate coping mechanisms Self-regulation problems Unresolved conflicts, deficits, posttraumatic reactions Identity problems Autonomy problems
Developmental Factors	Identifications with body-concerned relatives, or peers Aversive mealtime experiences Trauma affecting bodily experience	Overprotection Neglect Felt rejection, criticism Traumata Object relationships (interpersonal experience)
Social Factors	Maladaptive family attitudes to eating, weight Peer-group weight concerns Pressures to be thin Body-relevant insults, teasing Specific pressures to control weight (e.g., through ballet, athletic pursuits) Maladaptive cultural values assigned to body	Family dysfunction Aversive peer experiences Social values detrimental to stable, positive self-image Destabilizing social change Values assigned to gender Social isolation Poor support network Impediments to means of self-definition

> ED development, might support the progression from "compulsive dieting" to frank "eating obsession" in a weight-conscious adolescent. Multiple additional interactions between "eating-specific" and "generalized" risk factors can, of course, be considered.

In other words, we assume a "multiple threshold" type of etiology in which risk for development of a clinical ED requires that critical combinations of thresholds be surpassed in key areas of vulnerability, some eating specific, some more generalized. If so, this might account for marked co-occurrence of eating syndromes with comorbid symptoms with a characterological/affective flavor, while allowing for a measure of autonomy between severities of eating-specific and generalized components of disturbance. A main implication of this view is that presence of diffuse psychopathology might enhance vulnerability to ED development, without directly controlling severity of the ED, once it developed.

To elaborate upon this point, we note that we have previously postulated that generalized psychopathology enhances an individual's risk of adopting maladaptive dietary patterns—compulsive dieting playing a role, for example, in consolidating a fragile sense of self-worth or self-control—but that it is dietary behaviors and attitudes toward body image (not generalized psychopathology or personality disturbances) that provoke and maintain clinical eating disturbances (Steiger et al., 1993; Steiger & Stotland, 1996). If so, the severity of an eating disturbance might be a much more direct function of the degree to which maladaptive eating behaviors (e.g., excessive dieting) become entrenched in the sufferer than of the severity of any associated (or underlying) psychopathology. In turn, an ED might become quite self-perpetuating and, in time, quite divorced from psychopathological factors that may originally have contributed to it.

Conclusions

If EDs are indeed as multiply determined as biopsychosocial etiological theory would have it, pathways to them will likely be immensely heterogeneous, and singularly biological, psychological, or social models will, at best, provide partial explanations. Following from this line of thinking, we propose that what may be of greatest interest about the EDs is, in fact, their tendency to have diverse and interleaved causes. The study of the EDs may inform theory on the way in which many forms of psychopathology represent a collision between sociocultural pressures and psychobiological vulnerabilities. In other words, in understanding the pathogenesis of the EDs, we may be learning generally about psychobiological processes that render affected individuals so permeable to social influences and values that maladaptive effects may ensue. In Western social contexts, such vulnerabilities may often become manifest in the form of extreme susceptibility, especially in young females, to social ideals of thinness, self-control, and achievement. However, the same generalized vulnerabilities may (in other contexts and life stages) account for diverse maladaptive investments that may equally reflect the adverse impacts of social ideals upon generalized "self" disturbances.

Note

1. Recognizing different proportions of EDs among females and males, we use feminine personal pronouns. This convention is not to disregard eating syndromes in males.

References

Ames-Frankel, J., Devlin, M. J., Walsh, B. T., Strasser, T. J., Sadik, C., Oldham, J. M., & Roose, S. P. (1992). Personality disorder diagnoses in patients with bulimia nervosa: Clinical correlates and changes in treatment. *Journal of Clinical Psychiatry, 53*, 90–96.

Baucom, D. H., & Aiken, P. A. (1981). Effect of depressed mood on eating among obese and nonobese dieting persons. *Journal of Personality and Social Psychology, 41*, 577–585.

Bemporad, J. R. (1996). Self-starvation through the ages: Reflections on the pre-history of anorexia nervosa. *International Journal of Eating Disorders, 19*, 217–237.

Ben-Tovim, D. I., Marilov, V., & Crisp, A. H. (1979). Personality and mental state (P.S.E.) within Anorexia Nervosa. *Journal of Psychosomatic Research, 23*, 321–325.

Borman Spurrel, E. B., Wilfley, D. E., Tanofsky, M. B., & Brownell, K. D. (1997). Age of onset for binge eating: Are there different pathways to binge eating? *International Journal of Eating Disorders, 21*, 55–65.

Brewerton, T. D. (1995). Toward a unified theory of serotonin dysregulation in eating and related disorders. *Psychoneuroendocrinology, 20*, 561–590.

Brewerton, T. D., Lydiard, R. B., Herzog, D. B., Brotman, A. W., O'Neil, P. M., & Ballenger, J. C. (1995). Comorbidity of Axis I psychiatric disorders in bulimia nervosa. *Journal of Clinical Psychiatry, 56*, 77–80.

Brookings, J. B., & Wilson, J. F. (1994). Personality and family-environment predictors of self-reported eating attitudes and behaviors. *Journal of Personality Assessment, 63*, 313–326.

Bruch, H. (1973). *Eating disorders: Obesity, anorexia nervosa and the person within*. New York: Basic Books.

Bulik, C. M., Sullivan, P. F., Weltzin, T. F., & Kaye, W. H. (1995). Temperament in eating disorders. *International Journal of Eating Disorders, 17*, 251–261.

Bushnell, J. A., Wells, J. E., & Oakley-Browne, M. A. (1996). Impulsivity in disordered eating, affective disorder and substance use disorder. *British Journal of Psychiatry, 169*, 329–333.

Butler, L. D., Duran, R. E. F., Jasiukaitis, P., Koopman, C., & Spiegel, D. (1996). Hypnotizability and traumatic experience: A diathesis-stress model of dissociative symptomatology. *American Journal of Psychiatry, 153* (Suppl.), 42–63.

Carney, C. P., Yates, W. R., & Cizadlo, B. (1990). A controlled family study of personality in normal-weight bulimia nervosa. *International Journal of Eating Disorders, 9*, 659–665.

Casper, R. (1990). Personality features of women with good outcome from restricting anorexia nervosa. *Psychosomatic Medicine, 52*, 156–170.

Casper, R. C., Hedeker, D., & McClough, J. F. (1992). Personality dimensions in eating disorders and their relevance for subtyping. *Jour-*

nal of the American Academy of Child and Adolescent Psychiatry, 31, 830–840.

Connors, M., & Morse, W. (1993). Sexual abuse and eating disorders: A review. *International Journal of Eating Disorders, 13*, 1–11.

Crago, M., Shisslak, C. M., & Estes, L. S. (1996). Eating disturbances among American minority groups: A review. *International Journal of Eating Disorders, 19*, 239–248.

Crisp, A. H. (1980). *Anorexia nervosa: Let me be*. London: Academic Press.

Crisp, A. H., Hsu, L., Harding, B., & Hartshorn, J. (1980). Clinical features of anorexia nervosa: A study of a consecutive series of 102 female patients. *Journal of Psychosomatic Research, 24*, 179–191.

DaCosta, M., & Halmi, K. A. (1992). Classifications of anorexia nervosa: Question of subtypes. *International Journal of Eating Disorders, 11*, 305–313.

Davis, R., Freeman, R. J., & Garner, D. M. (1988). A naturalistic investigation of eating behavior in bulimia nervosa. *Journal of Consulting and Clinical Psychology, 56*, 273–279.

Deep, A. L., Nagy, L. M., Weltzin, T. E., Rao, R., & Kaye, W. H. (1995). Premorbid onset of psychopathology in long-term recovered anorexia nervosa. *International Journal of Eating Disorders, 17*, 291–297.

Eichenbaum, L., & Orbach, S. (1983). Understanding women: A feminist and psychoanalytic approach. New York: Basic Books.

Eme, R. F., & Damielak, M. H. (1995). Comparison of fathers of daughters with and without maldaptive eating attitudes. *Journal of Emotional and Behavioral Disorders, 3*, 40–45.

Everill, J., & Waller, G. (1995) Reported sexual abuse and eating psychopathology: A review of evidence for a causal link. *International Journal of Eating Disorders, 18*, 1–11.

Fahey, T., & Eisler, I. (1993). Impulsivity and eating disorders. *British Journal of Psychiatry, 162*, 193–197.

Fairburn, C. G., & Beglin, S. J. (1990). Studies of the epidemiology of bulimia nervosa. *American Journal of Psychiatry, 147*, 401–408.

Fava, M., Copeland, P. M., Schweiger, U., & Herzog, D. (1989). Neurochemical abnormalities of anorexia nervosa and bulimia nervosa. *American Journal of Psychiatry, 146*, 963–971.

Fullerton, D. T., Wonderlich, S. A., & Gosnell, B. A. (1995). Clinical characteristics of eating disorder patients who report sexual or physical abuse. *International Journal of Eating Disorders, 17*, 243–254.

Gard, M. C. E., & Freeman, C. P. (1996). The dismantling of a myth: A review of eating disorders and socioeconomic status. *International Journal of Eating Disorders, 20*, 1–12.

Garfinkel, P., & Garner, D. (1982). *Anorexia nervosa: A multidimensional perspective*. New York: Brunner/Mazel.

Garfinkel, P. E., Garner, D., Rose, J., Darby, P., Brandes, J. S., O'Hanlon, J., & Walsh, N. (1983). A comparison of characteristics in the families of patients with anorexia nervosa and normal controls. *Psychological Medicine, 13*, 821–828.

Garfinkel, P. E., Lin, E., Goering, P., Spegg, C., Goldbloom, D. S., Kennedy, S., Kaplan, A. S., & Woodside, D. B. (1995). Bulimia nervosa in a Canadian community sample: Prevalence and comparison of subgroups. *American Journal of Psychiatry, 152*, 1052–1058.

Garner, D. M., & Garfinkel, P. E. (1980). Sociocultural factors in the development of anorexia nervosa. *Psychological Medicine, 10*, 647–656.

Garner, D. M., Olmsted, R., Davis, R., Rockert, W., Goldbloom, D., & Eagle, M. (1990). The association between bulimic symptoms and reported psychopathology. *International Journal of Eating Disorders, 9*, 1–16.

Garner, D., Olmsted, M., Polivy, J., & Garfinkel, P. (1984). Comparison between weight preoccupied women and anorexia nervosa. *Psychosomatic Medicine, 46*, 255–266.

Gleaves, D. H., Williamson, D. A., & Barker, S. E. (1993). Confirmatory factor analysis of a multidimensional model of bulimia nervosa. *Journal of Abnormal Psychology, 102*, 173–176.

Goldstein, H. J. (1981). Family factors associated with schizophrenia and anorexia nervosa. *Journal of Youth and Adolescence, 10*, 385–405.

Gordon, R. A. (1990). *Anorexia and bulimia: Anatomy of a social epidemic*. Cambridge, MA: Blackwell.

Gruber, N. P., & Dilsaver, S. C. (1996). Bulimia and anorexia nervosa in winter depression: Lifetime rates in a clinical sample. *Journal of Psychiatry and Neuroscience, 21*, 9–12.

Hall, A., & Brown, L. B. (1983). A comparison of the attitudes of young anorexia nervosa patients and non-patients with those of their mothers. *British Journal of Medical Psychology, 56*, 39–48.

Hall, A., Leibrich, J., Walkley, F., & Welch, G. (1986). Investigation of "weight pathology" of 58 mothers of anorexia nervosa patients and 204 mothers of schoolgirls. *Psychological Medicine, 16*, 71–76.

Heatherton, T. F., & Baumeister, R. F. (1991). Binge eating as escape from self-awareness. *Psychological Bulletin, 110*, 86–108.

Heatherton, T. F., Nichols, P., Mahamedi, F., & Keel, P. (1995). Body weight, dieting, and eating disorder symptoms among college students, 1982 to 1992. *American Journal of Psychiatry, 152*, 1623–1629.

Herholz, K. (1996). Neuroimaging in anorexia nervosa. *Psychological Reports, 62*, 105–110.

Herzog, D. B., Keller, M. B., Sacks, N. R., Yeh, C. J., & Lavori, P. W. (1992). Psychiatric comorbidity in treatment-seeking anorexics and bulimics. *Journal of the American Academy of Child and Adolescent Psychiatry, 31*, 810–818.

Hodes, M., & LeGrange, D. (1993). Expressed emotion in the investigation of eating disorders: A review. *International Journal of Eating Disorders, 13*, 279–288.

Hoffman, G. W., Ellinwood, E. H., Rockwell, W. J., Herfkens, R. J., Nishita, J. K., & Guthrie, L. F. (1989). Cerebral atrophy in bulimia. *Biological Psychiatry, 25*, 894–902.

Holderness, C., Brooks-Gunn, J., & Warren, M. (1994). Co-morbidity of eating disorders and substance abuse: Review of the litertaure. *International Journal of Eating Disorders, 16*, 1–34.

Hsu, L. K. G., Kaye, W., & Weltzin, T. (1993). Are the eating disorders related to obsessive compulsive disorder? *International Journal of Eating Disorders, 14*, 305–318.

Hsu, L. K. G., & Sobkiewicz, T. A. (1991). Body image disturbance: Time to abandon the concept for eating disorders. *International Journal of Eating Disorders, 10*, 15–30.

Humphrey, L. L. (1991). Object relations and the family system: An integrative approach to understanding and treating eating disorders. In C. Johnson (Ed.), *Psychodynamic treatment of anorexia nervosa and bulimia* (pp. 322–353). New York: Guilford Press.

Johnson, C. (1991). Treatment of eating-disordered patients with borderline and false-self/narcissistic disorders. In C. Johnson (Ed.), *Psychodynamic treatment of anorexia nervosa and bulimia* (pp. 165–193). New York: Guilford Press.

Johnson, C., & Connors, M. (1987). *The etiology and treatment of bulimia nervosa*. New York: Basic Books.

Johnson, C., & Flach, A. (1985). Family characteristics of 105 patients with bulimia. *American Journal of Psychiatry, 142*, 1321–1324.

Johnson, C., & Wonderlich, S. (1992). Personality characteristics as a risk factor in the development of eating disorders. In J. H. Crowther, D. L. Tennenbaum, S. E. Hobfell, & M. A. P. Stephens (Eds.), *The etiology of bulimia nervosa: The individual and family context* (pp. 179–198). Bristol: Hemisphere Publishing.

Jones, B. P., Duncan, C. C., Brouwers, P., & Mirsky, A. F. (1991). Cognition in eating disorders. *Journal of Clinical and Experimental Neuropsychology, 13*, 711–728.

Kassett, J. A., Gershon, E. S., Maxwell, M. E., Guroff, J. J., Kazuba, D. M., Smith, A. L., Brandt, H. A., & Jimerson, D. C. (1989). Psychiatric disorders in the first-degree relatives of probands with bulimia nervosa. *American Journal of Psychiatry, 146*, 1468–1471.

Keys, A., Brozek, J., Henschel, A., Mickelson, O., & Taylor, H. (1950). *The biology of human starvation*. Minneapolis: University of Minnesota Press.

Kinzl, J. F., Trawager, C., Guenther, V., & Biebl, W. (1994). Family background and sexual abuse associated with eating disorders. *American Journal of Psychiatry, 151*, 1127–1131.

Kog, E., & Vandereycken, W. (1989). Family interaction in eating disorder patients and normal controls. *International Journal of Eating Disorders, 8*, 11–23.

Kog, E., Vertommen, H., & Vandereycken, W. (1987). Minuchin's psychosomatic family model revised: A concept validation study using a multitrait-multimethod apporach. *Family Process, 26*, 235–253.

Lee, S., Ho, P., & Hsu, L. K. G. (1993). Fat phobic and non-fat phobic anorexia nervosa: A comparative study of 70 Chinese patients in Hong Kong. *Psychological Medicine, 23*, 999–1017.

Lehoux, P., Steiger, H., & Jabalpurwala, S. (in press). State/trait distinctions in bulimia nervosa. *International Journal of Eating Disorders*.

Leon, G., Lucas, A., Colligan, R., Ferlinande, R., & Kamp, J. (1985). Sexual, body-image, and personality attitudes in anorexia nervosa. *Journal of Abnormal Child Psychology, 13*, 245–258.

Levitan, R. D., Kaplan, A. S., Levitt, A. J., & Joffe, R. T. (1994). Seasonal fluctuations in mood and eating behavior in bulimia nervosa. *International Journal of Eating Disorders, 16*, 295–299.

McNamara, H., & Loveman, C. (1990). Differences in family functioning among bulimics, repeat dieters and nondieters. *Journal of Clinical Psychology, 46*, 518–523.

Miller, D. A., McCluskey-Fawcett, K., & Irving, L. M. (1993). Correlates of bulimia nervosa: Early mealtime experiences. *Adolescence, 28*, 621–635.

Minuchin, S., Rosman, B. L., & Baker, L. (1978). *Psychosomatic families: Anorexia nervosa in context*. Cambridge, MA: Harvard University Press.

Mitchell, J. E., & Eckert, E. D. (1987). Scope and significance of eating disorders. *Journal of Consulting and Clinical Psychology, 55*, 628–634.

Monck, E., Graham, P., Richman, N., & Dobbs, R. (1990). Eating and weight-control problems in a community population of adolescent girls aged 15–20 years. In H. Remschmidt & M. H. Schmidt (Eds.), *Anorexia nervosa* (pp. 1–12). Toronto: Hogrefe and Huber Publishers.

Mussell, M. P., Mitchell, J. E., Fenna, C. J., Crosby, R. D., Miller, J. P., & Hoberman, H. M. (1997). A comparison of onset of binge eating versus dieting in the development of bulimia nervosa. *International Journal of Eating Disorders, 21*, 1–8.

Newton, J. R., Freeman, C. P., & Munro, J. (1993). Impulsivity and dyscontrol in bulimia nervosa: Is impulsivity an independent phenomenon or a marker of severity? *Acta Psychiatrica Scandinavia, 87*, 389–394.

Norman, D. K., Blais, D., & Herzog, D. (1993). Personality characteristics of eating-disordered patients as identified by the Millon Clinical Multiaxial inventory. *Journal of Personality Disorders, 7*, 1–9.

Palazolli, M. (1978). *Self-starvation: From individual to family therapy in the treatment of anorexia nervosa.* New York: Jason Aronson.

Pate, J. E., Pumariega, A. J., Hester, C., & Garner, D. M. (1992). Cross-cultural patterns in eating disorders: A review. *Journal of the American Academy of Child and Adolescent Psychiatry, 31*, 802–809.

Pike, K. M., & Rodin, J. (1991). Mothers, daughters, and disordered eating. *Journal of Abnormal Psychology, 100*, 198–204.

Pirke, K. M., Kellner, M. B., Frie, E., Krieg, J.-C., & Fichter, M. M. (1994). Satiety and cholecystokinin. *International Journal of Eating Disorders, 15*, 63–69.

Polivy, J., & Herman, C. P. (1985). Dieting and binging: A causal analysis. *American Psychologist, 40*, 193–201.

Polivy, J., & Herman, C. (1993). Etiology of binge eating: Psychological mechanisms. In C. G. Fairburn & G. T. Wilson (Eds.), *Binge eating: Nature, assessment, and treatment* (pp. 173–205). New York: Guilford Press.

Putnam, F. W. (1985). Dissociation as a response to extreme trauma. In R. P. Kluft (Ed.), *The childhood antecedents of multiple personality.* Washington: American Psychiatric Press.

Råstam, M. (1992). Anorexia nervosa in 51 Swedish adolescents: Premorbid problems and comorbidity. *Journal of the American Academy of Child and Adolescent Psychiatry, 31*, 819–829.

Rathner, G. (1993). Detection of eating disorders in a small rural town: An epidemiological study. *Psychological Medicine, 23*, 175–184.

Reeves, P. C., & Johnson, M. E. (1992). Relationship between family-of-origin functioning and self-preceived correlates of eating disorders among female college students. *Journal of College Student Development, 33*, 44–49.

Reich, J. R., & Green, A. I. (1991). Effect of personality disorders on outcome of treatment. *Journal of Nervous and Mental Disease, 179*, 74–82.

Rosen, J., & Gross, J. (1987). Prevalence of weight reducing and weight gaining in adolescent girls and boys. *Health Psychology, 6*, 131–147.

Rubenstein, C. S., Pigott, T. A., L'Heureux, F., Hill, J. L., & Murphy, D. L. (1992). A preliminary investigation of the lifetime prevalence of anorexia and bulimia nervosa in patients with obsessive compulsive disorder. *Journal of Clinical Psychiatry, 53*, 309–314.

Schaaf, K. K., & McCanne, T. R. (1994). Childhood abuse, body image disturbance and eating disorders. *Child Abuse and Neglect, 18*, 607–615.

Schmidt, U., Tiller, J., & Treasure, J. (1993). Psychosocial factors in the origins of bulimia nervosa. *International Review of Psychiatry, 5*, 51–59.

Selby, M. J., & Moreno, J. K. (1995). Personal and family substance misuse patterns among eating disordered and depressed subjects. *International Journal of the Addictions, 30*, 1169–1176.

Shisslak, C. M., Crago, M., & Estes, L. S. (1995). The spectrum of eating disturbances. *International Journal of Eating Disorders, 18*, 209–219.

Sights, J. R., & Richards, H. C. (1984). Parents of bulimic women. *International Journal of Eating Disorders, 3*, 3–13.

Smolak, L., & Levine, M. P. (1993). Separation-individuation difficulties and the distinction between bulimia nervosa and anorexia nervosa in college women. *International Journal of Eating Disorders, 14*, 33–41.

Smolak, L., Levine, M. P., & Sullins, E. (1990). Are childhood sexual experiences related to eating-disordered attitudes and behaviors in a college sample? *International Journal of Eating Disorders, 9*, 167–178.

Sohlberg, S., & Strober, M. (1994). Personality in anorexia nervosa: An update and a theoretical integration. *Acta Psychiatrica Scandinavica, 89* (Suppl. 378), 1–15.

Steiger, H., Goldstein, C., Mongrain, M., & Van der Feen, J. (1990). Description of eating-disordered, psychiatric and normal women on cognitive and psychodynamic measures. *International Journal of Eating Disorders, 9*, 129–140.

Steiger, H., Jabalpurwala, S., & Champagne, J. (1996). Axis-II comorbidity and developmental adversity in bulimia nervosa. *Journal of Nervous and Mental Disease, 184*, 555–560.

Steiger, H., Jabalpurwala, S., Champagne, J., & Stotland, S. (1997). A controlled study of trait narcissism in anorexia and bulimia nervosa. *International Journal of Eating Disorders, 22*, 173–178.

Steiger, H., Lehoux, P., & Gauvin, L. (in press). Impulsivity, dietary restraint, and the urge to binge in bulimic eating syndromes. *International Journal of Eating Disorders.*

Steiger, H., Leung, F., Thibeaudeau, J., Houle, L., & Ghadirian, A. M. (1993). Comorbid features in bulimics before and after therapy: Are they explained by Axis II diagnoses, secondary effects of bulimia, or both? *Comprehensive Psychiatry, 34*, 45–53.

Steiger, H., Puentes-Neuman, G., & Leung, F. (1991). Personality and family features of adolescent girls with eating symptoms: Evidence for restricter/binger differences in a nonclinical population. *Addictive Behaviors, 16*, 303–314.

Steiger, H., & Stotland, S. (1996). Prospective study of outcome in bulimics as a function of Axis-II comorbidity: Long-term responses on eating and psychiatric symptoms. *International Journal of Eating Disorders, 20*, 149–162.

Steiger, H., Stotland, S., Ghadirian, A. M., & Whitehead, V. (1995). Controlled study of eating concerns and psychopathological traits in relatives of eating-disordered probands: Do familial traits exist? *International Journal of Eating Disorders, 18*, 107–118.

Steiger, H., & Zanko, M. (1990). Sexual traumata in eating-disordered, psychiatric and normal female groups: Comparison of prevalences and defense styles. *Journal of Interpersonal Violence, 5*, 74–86.

Strober, M. (1980). Personality and symptomatological features in young nonchronic anorexia nervosa patients. *Journal of Psychosomatic Research, 24*, 353–359.

Strober, M. (1983). An empirically derived typology of anorexia nervosa. In P. L. Darby, P. E. Garfinkel, D. M. Garner, & D. V. Coscina (Eds.), *Anorexia nervosa: Recent developments in research* (pp. 185–196). New York: Alan R. Liss.

Strober, M. (1991). Disorders of the self in anorexia nervosa: An organismic-developmental paradigm. In C. Johnson (Ed.), *Psychodynamic treatment of anorexia nervosa and bulimia* (pp. 354–373). New York: Guilford Press.

Strober, M., & Katz, J. (1988). Depression in the eating disorders: A review and analysis of descriptive, family, and biological findings. In D. Garner & P. Garfinkel (Eds.), *Diagnostic issues in anorexia nervosa and bulimia nervosa* (pp. 80–118). New York: Brunner/Mazel.

Strober, M., Lampert, C., Morrell, W., Burroughs, J., & Jacobs, C. (1990). A controlled family study of anorexia nervosa: Evidence of familial aggregation and lack of shared transmission with affective disorders. *International Journal of Eating Disorders, 9*, 239–253.

Strober, M., Salkin, B., Burroughs, M., & Morrell, W. (1982). Validity of the bulimic-restricter distinction in anorexia nervosa: Parental personality characteristics and family morbidity. *Journal of Nervous and Mental Disease, 170*, 345–351.

Szmukler, G. I., Andrewes, D., Kingston, K., Chen, L., Stargatt, R., & Stanley, R. (1992). Neuropsychological impairment in anorexia nervosa: Before and after refeeding. *Journal of Clinical and Experimental Neuropsychology, 14*, 347–352.

Tobin, D. L., Johnson, C., Steinberg, S., Staats, M., & Dennis, A. B. (1991). Multifactorial assessment of bulimia nervosa. *Journal of Abnormal Psychology, 100*, 14–21.

Treasure, J., & Holland, A. J. (1995). Genetic factors in eating disorders. In G. Szmukler, C. Dare, & J. Treasure (Eds.), *Handbook of eating disorders: Theory, treatment and research* (pp. 65–81). New York: John Wiley.

Vandereycken, W. (1994). Emergence of bulimia nervosa as a separate diagnostic entity: Review of the literature from 1960 to 1979. *International Journal of Eating Disorders, 16*, 105–116.

Vanderlinden, J., Vandereycken, W., van Dyk, R., & Vertommen, H. (1993). Dissociative experiences and trauma in eating disorders. *International Journal of Eating Disorders, 13*, 187–194.

Vitousek, K., & Manke, F. (1994). Personality variables and disorders in anorexia nervosa and bulimia nervosa. *Journal of Abnormal Psychology, 103*, 137–147.

Wakeling, A. (1996). Epidemiology of anorexia nervosa. *Psychiatry Research, 62*, 3–9.

Waller, G. (1994). Bulimic women's perceptions of interaction within their families. *Psychological Reports, 74*, 27–32.

Walters, E. E., Neale, M. C., Eaves, L. J., Heath, A. C., Kessler, R. C., & Kendler, K. S. (1992). Bulimia nervosa and major depression: A study of common genetic and environmental factors. *Psychological Medicine, 22*, 617–622.

Windauer, U., Lennerts, W., Talbot, P., Touyz, S., & Beumont, P. (1993). How well are "cured" anorexia nervosa patients? An investigation of 16 weight-recovered anorexic patients. *British Journal of Psychiatry, 163*, 195–200.

Wold, P. N. (1985). Family attitudes toward weight in bulimia and affective disorders—a pilot study. *The Psychiatric Journal of the University of Ottawa, 10*, 162–164.

Wolfe, B. E., Jimerson, D. C., & Levine, J. M. (1994). Impulsivity ratings in bulimia nervosa: Relationship to binge eating behaviors. *International Journal of Eating Disorders, 15*, 289–292.

Wonderlich, S. A. (1992). Relationship of family and personality factors in bulimia. In J. H. Crowther, D. L. Tennenbaum, S. E. Hobfell, & M. A. P. Stephens (Eds.), *The etiology of bulimia nervosa: The individual and family context* (pp. 103–128). Bristol: Hemisphere Publishing.

Wonderlich, S. A., Fullerton, D., Swift, W. J., & Klein, M. H. (1994). Five-year outcome from eating disorders: Relevance of personality disorders. *International Journal of Eating Disorders, 15*, 233–244.

Yager, J., Landsverk, J., Edelstein, C. K., & Hyler, S. E. (1989). Screening for Axis II personality disorders in women with bulimic eating disorders. *Psychosomatics, 30*, 255–262.

Ziolko, H.-U. (1996). Bulimia: A historical outline. *International Journal of Eating Disorders, 20*, 345–358.

15

Sleep/Wake Disorders

CHARLES M. MORIN
JACK D. EDINGER

Sleep/wake disorders are common and debilitating conditions that contribute to emotional distress, social or occupational dysfunction, increased risks for injury, and, in some instances, serious medical illnesses (Mitler, Dinges, & Dement, 1994; National Commission on Sleep Disorders Research, 1993). Although it has long been recognized that sleep disturbances are common symptoms of various psychopathological conditions, their significance as distinct clinical entities has been minimized or ignored by psychologists and other health care providers. However, over the past three decades, research has increasingly pointed to the importance of sleep disturbances both as central factors in the etiology of many psychiatric disorders and as primary disorders that often warrant independent clinical attention. This chapter highlights those sleep/wake disturbances that present either as primary, independent syndromes or as etiologically important symptoms in the development of other forms of psychopathology. The initial section describes the brief history of classification systems for sleep/wake disorders. The second section considers the epidemiology, clinical features and etiology of primary sleep disorders, whereas, the third, fourth, and fifth sections, respectively, consider the sleep disturbances that occur in association with common psychiatric, medical, and substance-abuse disorders. Subsequently, the comorbidity between sleep and psychiatric disorders is discussed. The concluding section considers limitations of previous research and provides suggestions for future research.

Sleep/Wake Disorders Classification

Unlike the relatively long history of nosological systems developed for the diagnostic classification of mental disorders, nosologies for the diagnostic classification of sleep/wake disturbances have become available only within the past two decades. During this time period, several rather divergent approaches for sleep/wake disorders classification have been proposed. Unfortunately, given the relatively short evolutionary histories of these nosologies, research supporting their reliability and validity has been extremely limited. Nonetheless, each has heuristic appeal and provides a basis for further research. Hence, the ensuing discussion describes the evolution of these nosologies and discusses the merits and limitations of the two systems currently in use.

In 1979, the Association of Sleep Disorders Centers (ASDC) spawned initial interest in formal sleep/wake disorders classification with the publication of their monograph entitled *Diagnostic Classification of Sleep and Arousal Disorders—DCSAD* (ASDC, 1979). This system categorized sleep/wake disorders primarily on the basis of patients' presenting complaints. There were four global categories: disorders of initiating and maintaining sleep (DIMS), disorders of excessive daytime somnolence (DOES), sleep/wake schedule disorders, and parasomnias. Included within the DIMS were seven insomnia subtypes arising from underlying psychiatric, behavioral, or medical/neurological causes. The DOES included a variety of diagnoses reserved for sleep/wake disturbances associated with primary complaints of excessive daytime sleepiness. Sleep/wake schedule disorders included several conditions resulting from a mismatch of individuals' endogenous *circadian* rhythms and their desired sleep/wake schedules. Finally, the parasomnias included various unusual events (e.g., seizures) or aberrant behaviors (e.g., sleep walking) that occur during sleep.

Several years following the publication of the *DCSAD*, the *DSM-III-R* included 15 diagnoses of sleep/wake disorders. Within the *DSM-III-R* system, insomnias were subdivided into four categories (i.e., insomnia due to another mental disorder, insomnia due to a known organic factor, primary insomnia, and insomnia not otherwise specified—NOS) whereas the diagnoses of breathing-related sleep disorder, narcolepsy, primary hypersomnia, hypersomnia related to another mental disorder, hypersomnia related to a known organic factor, and hypersomnia NOS were reserved for those conditions characterized primarily by complaints of excessive daytime sleepiness. Also included within the *DSM-III-R* were four diagnoses (sleep walking, night terror, nightmare, and parasomnia NOS) for the parasomnias and one diagnosis, sleep/wake schedule disorder, which subsumed all types of circadian rhythm disorders (e.g., jet lag, shift work). Whereas the *DSM-III-R* and *DCSAD* classification schemes both categorized sleep/wake disorders primarily on the basis of patients' presenting complaints, the DSM-III-R system represented a far more global approach that allowed for significantly less diagnostic specificity.

Unlike these earlier nosologies, currently used classification systems such as the *International Classification of Sleep Disorders* (*ICSD*; American Sleep Disorders Association, 1990) and *DSM-IV* group sleep disorders primarily on the basis of their underlying pathophysiologies. For example, the *DSM-IV* nosology includes a total of 22 disorders that are presumed to represent either primary sleep/wake disorders or predominant secondary symptoms arising from other psychiatric, medical, or substance-abuse disorders. Included among the primary sleep disorders are various sleep disturbances arising from abnormalities in the biological, sleep-wake system and complicated by such factors as conditioned arousal, poor sleep hygiene practices, and the development of secondary medical illnesses. Within this broad category are several dyssomnias resulting from abnormalities in the timing, amount, or quality of sleep, and parasomnias characterized by abnormal events (nightmares) or unusual behaviors (sleep walking) arising out of sleep. In contrast, those sleep disorders related to another mental disorder involve a prominent sleep complaint attributable to a coexisting mental disorder such as a mood or anxiety disorder. Sleep disorders related to a general medical condition include disturbances directly arising from the effects (e.g., pain, seizures) of an active medical illness whereas substance-induced sleep disorders arise from inappropriate use of medications, illicit drugs, stimulants or alcohol. Like the *DSM-IV*, the *ICSD* classifies sleep disorders on the basis of their underlying pathophysiologies but includes a total of 84 specific disorders and, hence, allows for much greater diagnostic specificity.

From a practical standpoint, the *ICSD* nosology appears best suited to the needs of sleep disorders specialists, whereas the *DSM-IV* system is likely to be more familiar and, perhaps, more user-friendly to most psychologists and other mental health professionals. However, inasmuch as both of these systems were derived primarily on the basis of the sleep experts' clinical experiences and opinions, the reliability and validity of both systems remain questionable. In fact, initial attempts to establish the reliability and validity of these nosologies have been limited in number and disappointing in their results. Buysse et al. (1994), for example, noted only modest diagnostic agreement both among general practitioners and among sleep specialists during a preliminary field trial for the *DSM-IV* sleep/wake diagnoses. Similarly, Edinger et al. (1996) found only a moderate degree of concordance between insomniac subgroups identified via an empirical cluster analysis and diagnostic subgroups defined on the basis of either *DSM* or *ICSD* criteria. As a consequence, neither of these systems may accurately characterize the range of sleep disturbances encountered in clinical settings. Nonetheless, studies that have focused on specific disorders have attested to the reliability and validity of many of the sleep/wake disorder subtypes described in both the *DSM-IV* and *ICSD* nosologies (see Kryger, Roth, & Dement, 1994). Hence, although future research likely will lead to refinements in the diagnostic criteria and categories included in these nosologies, currently there is general consensus among sleep experts that various distinctive sleep disorders exist and merit attention. The ensuing portions of this chapter provide detailed descriptions of those sleep disorders included in *DSM-IV*.

Primary Sleep Disorders: Dyssomnias

Primary Insomnia

Primary insomnia, characterized by a chronic difficulty initiating and/or maintaining sleep or persistent poor quality sleep, is a relatively common form of sleep disturbance. This condition may cooccur with psychiatric and/or medical disorders, but it is viewed as an independent disorder that is etiologically unrelated to any other coexisting conditions. Indeed, individuals suffering from primary insomnia often complain of mild anxiety, mood disturbances, concentration/memory dysfunction, somatic concerns, and general malaise, but such clinical findings are viewed as common symptoms rather than causes of their sleep disturbances (Mellinger, Balter, & Uhlenhuth, 1985).

Although transient insomnia due to episodic stress or sudden disruption in the usual sleep/wake schedule is experienced by most individuals at one time or other, between 9 and 12% of adults report chronic, unrelenting forms of such sleep difficulty (Ford & Kamerow, 1989; Gallup Organization, 1995; Mellinger et al., 1985). Epidemiological surveys have shown that insomnia complaints are age related, with an increased prevalence among middle-aged and older adults (Mellinger et al., 1985; Ohayon, 1996). In addition, sleep-onset difficulties are more common among young adults whereas difficulties maintaining sleep and poor quality sleep occur more commonly among middle-aged and older individuals. Moreover, several studies have shown that women more often than men complain of insomnia (Gallup Organization, 1995), but it is not known whether such findings reflect reporting biases or actual gender differences. Unfortunately, the "true" prevalence of primary insomnia remains unknown since previous epidemiological surveys have queried respondents about general sleep symptoms (e.g., difficulty falling asleep, difficulty staying asleep) and have not included questions that would allow diagnostic categorization of such complaints. However, data compiled by sleep experts suggest that primary insomnia is fairly prevalent inasmuch as approximately one in five patients who present to specialty sleep disorders centers seemingly meet criteria for this diagnosis (Buysse et al., 1994; Coleman et al., 1982).

The most widely accepted etiological theory regarding primary insomnia attributes this condition to a special confluence of endogenous *predisposing characteristics*, sleep-disruptive *precipitating events*, and *perpetuating behaviors or circumstances* (Spielman, 1986). According to this theory, vulnerabilities such as a proneness to worry, repression of disturbing emotion, physiological hyperarousal, and/or an innate propensity toward light, fragmented sleep may all predispose certain individuals to a primary sleep disturbance. Subsequently, insomnia may develop among such individuals given sufficient stress or disruption from a precipitating event (e.g., loss of a loved one, undergoing a painful medical procedure, frequent disruptions in the normal sleep-wake schedule). Primary insomnia may then persist when conditioned environmental cues, repetitive sleep-disruptive habits, and dysfunctional cognitions serve to perpetuate sleep disturbance long after the initial precipitating circumstances are resolved.

Clinical observations have provided much support for this etiological model. Many primary insomniacs report an intense preoccupation with sleep and a heightened arousal as bedtime approaches (Hauri, 1994; Morin, 1993). Indeed, such patients frankly report that they view bedtime as the worst time of day. A vicious cycle seemingly emerges in which repetitive unsuccessful sleep attempts reinforce the insomniac's anticipatory anxiety that, in turn, contributes to more insomnia. Through their repetitive association with unsuccessful sleep efforts, the bedroom environment and pre-sleep rituals often become cues or stimuli for poor sleep. Moreover, in some cases, formerly benign habits such as watching television, eating, or reading in bed may also reduce the stimulus value of the bed and bedroom for sleep and may further exacerbate the sleep problem. Consequently, it is not unusual for primary insomniacs to report improved sleep in novel settings where conditioned environmental cues are absent and usual pre-sleep rituals are obviated.

In addition, many primary insomniacs admit to poor sleep habits that initially may emerge as a means of combating their sleep disturbances. For example, poor sleep at night may lead to daytime napping or sleeping late on weekends in efforts to catch up on lost sleep. Alternatively such individuals may lie in bed for protracted periods trying to force sleep only to find themselves becoming more and more awake. Such findings are particularly common among middle-aged and older adults due to an increase in sleep fragmentation and shortening of their natural biological sleep-wake rhythm due to aging (Miles & Dement, 1980). In addition, other practices such as routinely engaging in physically or mentally stimulating activities shortly before bed or failing to adhere to a regular sleep-wake schedule may emerge due to lifestyle choices or perceived social obligations and also may contribute to the sleep difficulty.

Several empirical studies have corroborated these clinical findings by suggesting that dispositional characteristics, stressful life events, and perpetuating behaviors or circumstances may all play a role in the etiology of primary insomnia. Psychometric studies have suggested that insomniacs are particularly prone to show psychological profiles characterized by mild anxiety, depression, and a proneness toward worrying and the internalization of disturbing affect (Edinger, Stout & Hoelscher, 1988; Freedman & Sattler, 1982; Kales & Kales, 1984). In addition, laboratory studies have shown that primary insomniacs evidence less diurnal sleepiness and higher heart rates, core body temperature, and metabolic activity during the night than do age- and gender-matched controls (Bonnet & Arand, 1995; Freedman & Sattler, 1982; Stepanski, Zorick, Roehrs, Young, & Roth, 1988). Collectively, such studies give credibility to the assumption that predisposing characteristics (i.e., hyperarousal, worrying, repressive tendencies) may predispose certain individuals to insomnia problems. Similarly, appropriate precipitating circumstances appear etiologically important inasmuch as approximately 65% of insomniacs report that a stressful life event preceded and led to their insomnia problems (Healey et al., 1981). Finally, numerous treatment studies (for reviews see Lichstein & Riedel, 1994; Morin, Culbert, & Schwartz, 1994; Murtagh & Greenwood, 1995) have demonstrated the efficacy of behavioral treatments to eliminate poor sleep hygiene practices and conditioned arousal at bedtime, thus lending support to the presumed significance of those perpetuating mechanisms in sustaining primary insomnia.

Although these studies provide indirect support for the above-described etiological model for primary insomnia, they fall short of confirming it. Studies of predisposing and precipitating factors either failed to include appropriate control groups or employed either cross-sectional or retrospective methodologies. As a result, these studies fail to substantiate a cause-effect relationship between such factors and primary insomnia. Moreover, whereas behavioral treatment studies provide seemingly more compelling support for the importance of conditioned arousal and poor sleep hygiene as perpetuating mechanisms for primary insomnia, such studies have generally failed to demonstrate that sleep improvements occurred in conjunction with elimination of these sustaining factors (see Morin & Wooten, 1996). Hence, it is possible that such treatments are effective because they address some yet-to-be-identified dispositional characteristic and/or perpetuating agents germane to primary insomnia. In addition, factors other than those noted above may play a significant role in sustaining the sleep difficulties of at least some primary insomniacs. Results reported by Buysse et al. (1994), for example, showed that psychiatric disorders often coexist with primary insomnia. As a consequence, some writers (e.g., Vgontzas, Kales, Bixler, & Vela-Buelo, 1993) have argued that such psychiatric conditions play central etiological roles in the development of most who meet criteria for this disorder. Furthermore, some rare primary insomniacs present characteristics that argue for alternate etiological explanations.

Whereas *DSM-IV* recognizes only one form of primary insomnia, the *ICSD* nosological classification distinguishes among at least three different subtypes: psychophysiological insomnia, which is essentially the *DSM-IV* equivalent of primary insomnia; sleep-state misperception; and idiopathic (childhood-onset) insomnia. Sleep-state misperception, also called subjective insomnia, is a genuine complaint of poor sleep that is not corroborated by objective findings. For example, a patient may perceive very little sleep (e.g., 1–2 hours per night) whereas EEG recordings show normal or near-normal sleep duration and quality. This sleep-state misperception condition is not the result of an underlying psychiatric disorder or of malingering. To some degree, all insomniacs tend to overestimate the time it takes them to fall asleep and to underestimate the time they actually sleep. In sleep-state misperception, however, the subjective complaint of poor sleep is clearly out of proportion with any objective finding. Some authors have suggested that sleep-state misperception may be a prodromal phase for more objectively verifiable insomnia (Salin-Pascual, Roehrs, Merlotti, Zorick, & Roth, 1992). However, this condition is still poorly understood and some have suggested that it should not even be considered a separate diagnostic entity (Trinder, 1988). The main problem with this diagnosis is that most clinicians do not have the benefit of objective data to confirm or refute the patient's subjective complaint. Thus, this condition may be underdiagnosed.

Idiopathic insomnia is, by definition, of unknown origin. One of the most persistent forms of insomnia, it presents an insidious onset in childhood, unrelated to psychological trauma or medical disorders, and has a chronic course throughout the adult life. It does not present the nightly variability observed with other forms of primary insomnia. A mild defect of the basic neurological sleep/wake mechanisms may be a predisposing factor (Hauri & Olmstead, 1980); this hypothesis comes from the observations that patients with this condition often have a history of learning disabilities or similar conditions associated with minimal brain dysfunctions.

Although idiopathic insomnia and sleep-state misperception would meet *DSM-IV* criteria for primary insomnia, they may differ qualitatively from the more conventional primary insomnias and may also require different treatment. Patients with sleep-state misperception may require treatments that specifically correct their sleep misperceptions since they typically are less responsive to behavioral interventions that are effective with other primary insomniacs (McCall & Edinger, 1992). Moreover, the occurrence of such cases supports the *ICSD* system, which delineates various primary insomnia subtypes and suggests that insomnia represents a heterogeneous mixture of etiologically distinctive sleep/wake disorders. However, as noted previously (Edinger et al., 1996), the *ICSD* may not provide a perfect characterization of primary or other forms of insomnia. Thus, much more research is needed to ascertain the number of etiologically distinctive primary insomnia subtypes that warrant clinical attention.

Narcolepsy

The term narcolepsy was first used in 1880 by the French neuropsychiatrist Gelineau to describe a syndrome characterized by recurrent, irresistible daytime sleep episodes that, in some patients, were accompanied by sudden falls or *astasias*. Slightly over 50 years later, Daniels (1934) identified four symptoms that commonly co-occur and are currently regarded as the classic tetrad indicative of narcolepsy: (1) *excessive daytime sleepiness* and unintended sleep episodes occurring during situations (e.g., driving, at work, during conversations) when most persons typically are able to remain awake; (2) *cataplexy*, which consists of an abrupt and reversible decrease or loss of muscle tone (without loss of consciousness) precipitated most often by such emotions as laughter, anger, surprise, or exhilaration; (3) *sleep paralysis*, which involves an awakening from nocturnal or diurnal sleep with an inability to move; and (4) *hypnagogic hallucinations*, consisting of vivid images and dreams, usually just as sleep develops, but sometimes intruding into wakefulness (Parkes, 1985).

Individuals with narcolepsy complain of frequent overwhelming episodes throughout the day during which they feel compelled to sleep despite having obtained a seemingly adequate amount of sleep during the previous night. Excessive daytime sleepiness (EDS) is typically the first symptom to present and usually develops during adolescence or young adulthood. However, this symptom may first occur as late as the fifth decade of life for some individuals. Other symptoms of the disorder may develop several years after the onset of EDS or not at all. Although daytime naps are often momentarily restorative, excessive sleepiness may return shortly thereafter. As the syndrome progresses, naps may lose their restorative value and even nocturnal sleep may become disturbed (Parkes, 1985).

Narcolepsy is a relatively rare condition, with about 5 cases in 10,000, and a slightly higher prevalence among men. Cross-cultural comparisons indicate its prevalence varies substantially across ethnic groups and such findings, along with studies of narcoleptic canines, point to genetic transmission of this syndrome via single autosomal or complex polygenic mechanisms. However, nongenetic mechanisms such as developmental accidents or central nervous system (CNS) trauma have been implicated as causative factors in some cases of posttraumatic narcolepsy (Guilleminault, 1989; Lankford, Wellman, & O'Hara, 1994). Current theoretical models attribute narcolepsy to abnormalities in CNS areas controlling rapid eye movement sleep and neuropharmacologic studies suggesting hyperactivity of CNS cholinergic systems along with hypoactivity of CNS catecholaminergic systems lend support to this theory.

Life events may, at times, precipitate the onset of this disorder (Orellana et al., 1994) and, although they are not viewed as causative factors, psychosocial disturbances may present as a noteworthy associated features of narcolepsy. Depressed mood, impaired occupational and social functioning, and marital discord may all be caused by the excessive daytime sleepiness arising from this syndrome. In addition, many narcoleptics engage in volitional emotional constriction or avoid situations that might arouse even pleasant emotions in an effort to control their cataplectic attacks. Hence, despite its physiological basis, narcolepsy may contribute to significant psychosocial dysfunction.

Breathing-Related Sleep Disorders

A variety of breathing-related sleep disorders (BRSDs) may produce significant nocturnal sleep disruption and result in sleep/wake complaints. Patients suffering form *obstructive sleep apnea* experience repetitive partial (hypopneas) or complete (apneas) obstructions of their upper airways during sleep despite a continued diaphragmatic effort to breathe. There are several variations of obstructive sleep apnea, but whatever their exact form, such BRSDs lead to repeated arousals from sleep (to restart normal breathing) and a consequent diminution in sleep quality and restorative value (Guilleminault, 1989).

The main symptoms of sleep apnea are loud snoring, pauses in breathing, and excessive daytime sleepiness. Although some patients complain of insomnia, most complain of excessive daytime sleepiness and unintentional sleep episodes occurring while watching T.V., reading, conversing, driving, and, in severe cases, standing. Additional symptoms may include gasping for breath during sleep, frequent dull headaches upon awakening and *automatic behaviors* (i.e., carrying out activities without being aware of one's actions). BRSDs may result in such secondary psychological symptoms as dysphoria, memory disturbance, concentration problems, and enhanced irritability. In addition, they may produce serious medical consequents including hypertension, cardiac arrhythmias, sexual dysfunction, nocturnal enuresis, and hearing loss (Stoohs & Guilleminault, 1992).

BRSDs are far more prevalent than is narcolepsy. Obstructive sleep apnea, the most common BRSD, is found most frequently among middle-aged (ages 30 to 60 years) men, with estimated prevalence among this group ranging between 1 and 5% (Partinen, 1994; Young et al., 1993). BRSDs are relatively rare among young and middle-aged women, but may be found with greater frequency in the postmenopausal years. Among older adults, BRSDs may be particularly common, although the clinical significance of mild sleep apnea in this population is unclear.

Current etiological theories of BRSDs vary as a function of the particular condition in question. Anatomic factors such as a small oropharynx, presence of excessive or obstructive tissues in the upper airway, or intrusion of the mandible into the upper airway space have been implicated in the development of obstructive sleep apnea and upper airway resistance syndrome. More research designed to uncover the causes of BRSDs is needed since their etiologies are not yet fully understood. Although it clearly represents a physical condition, BRSDs are included as an Axis I in the *DSM-IV* to facilitate the differential diagnosis of hypersomnia.

Circadian Rhythm Sleep Disorders

Individuals with circadian rhythm sleep disorders (CRSDs) experience persistent or recurrent sleep/wake difficulties as a result of a mismatch between their endogenous, circadian sleep-wake rhythms and the sleep-wake schedules imposed upon them by occupational or social demands. Alterations of the usual sleep-wake pattern due to *jet lag*, rotating shift work, or social/recreational pursuits may all lead to CRSDs. In some individuals, CRSDs are intermittent or recurrent as a function of frequently changing work or travel schedules. For others, aberrant bedtimes may, over a period of time, lead to a persistent shift (either an advance or delay) in the underlying circadian mechanisms that control when sleep occurs. To meet criteria for this disorder, an individual must demonstrate significant distress or impairment and not have symptoms exclusively during the course of another sleep or mental disorder.

Individuals with CRSDs typically complain that their sleep is disrupted and/or does not occur at a time that is consistent with their desired sleep-wake schedule. In addition, they often report insomnia at certain times of day and excessive sleepiness at other times. Among individuals engaged in rotating shift work, alterations in sleep-wake schedules between work days and days off may perpetuate the sleep/wake complaints. In other cases, the person appears to obtain a normal amount of sleep if it is allowed to occur ad lib and not at the time chosen in response to actual or perceived external demands (Edinger & Erwin, 1992; Roehrs & Roth, 1994).

There is limited information regarding the prevalence of and pathophysiological mechanisms responsible for CRSDs. Estimates from clinical case series (Coleman et al., 1982) suggest that CRSDs account for approximately 2% of all patients seen at sleep disorders centers. Investigations concerning etiological factors contributing to CRSDs have implicated the involvement of neural and endocrine mechanisms that serve as 24-hour pacemakers and synchronizers. Speculations derived from this research suggest that CRSDs arise either from a disruption in: (1) the neural/endocrine systems that serve as 24-hour pacemakers; (2) the coupling mechanisms that link endogenous pacemakers to each other; or (3) those systems that synchronize endogenous circadian rhythms with externally prescribed sleep/wake schedules. The extent to which these dysfunctions are primary or secondary to behavioral and environmental factors is often uncertain. In fact, there is some debate as to whether sleep difficulties arising from conditions such as jet lag and shift work should be considered primary sleep disorders since behavioral and environmental factors play such a prominent etiological role in those disorders (Regestein & Monk, 1994).

Primary Sleep Disorders: Parasomnias

Parasomnias are disorders of arousal during sleep or dysfunctions associated with particular sleep stages. These disorders are manifestations of abnormal or excessive activation of the central nervous system. Parasomnias do not necessarily lead to a complaint of insomnia or hypersomnia, although in their most severe forms either one of these difficulties may be present. While they are often simply undesirable phenomena, some parasomnias may cause physical injuries (sleepwalking) and significant distress (sleep terror).

Nightmare Disorder

Nightmare disorder is characterized by repeated awakenings from nocturnal sleep or daytime naps precipitated by disturbing dreams. Typically such dreams involve threats to the individual's physical, psychological, and/or emotional well-being. Upon awakening, the individual appears fully alert, oriented and cognizant of the arousing dream's content. Subsyndromal anxiety and depressed mood often develop as secondary features of the nightmares, leading the individual to seek clinical attention. Moreover, inasmuch as nightmares are common to children, college students, and many noncomplaining normal adults (Wood & Bootzin, 1990), nightmare disorder is a diagnosis reserved for those whose disturbing dreams lead to impairment of emotional, social, or occupational functioning.

Individuals with nightmare disorder complain of repeated disturbing dreams that arouse them from their sleep. Since nightmares arise during rapid eye movement (REM) sleep, individuals with nightmare disorder typically report nightmare-induced awakenings during the latter half of the night when REM sleep becomes longer and more vivid. Careful interview may reveal dream content that reflects a recurrent theme of underlying conflicts, characteristic fears, or more general personality characteristics (Kales, Soldatos, Caldwell, Charney et al., 1980). For example, individuals with obsessive-compulsive traits often report recurrent nightmares during which they find themselves repeatedly unable to finish an important assignment despite their persistent efforts to do so. In addition, individuals with nightmare disorder usually complain of anxiety and sleep disturbance caused by the nightmares, as well as resultant disruption of their normal day-to-day functioning.

The prevalence of nightmare disorder in the general population is estimated at approximately 1% (*ICSD*, 1990). Nightmares are reported two to four times more often by women than by men, but it is unclear whether this finding is attributable to actual gender-specific prevalence differences (*DSM-IV*; Hartmann, 1984). Such findings may instead represent differences between women and men in regard to their willingness to report nightmares. The frequency of nightmares decreases slightly with aging (Hartmann, 1994), but it is unclear whether this is due to poorer dream recall in aging individuals. It is also noteworthy that some cultures attribute nightmares to spiritual or supernatural phenomena whereas other cultures regard nightmares as indicative of psychopathology. Consequently, nightmare disorder may be diagnosed more freely in some cultures than in others.

Early psychoanalytic theory attributed nightmares and other dreams to subconscious drives related to conflict resolution and wish fulfillment. However, inasmuch as the role dreaming, per se, plays in human psychological and biological functioning remains poorly understood, our knowledge regarding the etiology of nightmare disorder remains rudimentary. Some research has suggested that individuals who evidence frequent nightmares tend to be open, trusting, creative, and vulnerable to other mental disorders (Hartmann, 1984). In addition, studies have suggested that nightmare sufferers have thin or permeable *ego boundaries* whereas those with rigid, solid and obsessional characteristics are less prone to frequent nightmares (Hartmann, 1984). Finally, clinical observations of nightmares occurring following exposure to traumatic events has led to the speculation that nightmares represent efforts to connect new memories to old so as to integrate and synthesize such events (Hartmann, 1994). Given our limited understanding of nightmares, it is safe to assume that nightmare disorder represents a cluster of symptoms that may have a variety of etiological origins.

Sleep Walking and Night Terrors

In approximately 15% of all patients presenting to sleep centers, aberrant nocturnal behaviors disrupt normal sleep (Coleman et al., 1982). Among the more common of these are sleep walking and night terrors (Kales, Kales, Soldatos, et al., 1980; Kales, Soldatos, Caldwell, et al., 1980). Both of these phenomena occur early in the sleep period and appear to represent incomplete arousals from the deepest stages of sleep (stages 3–4), known as slow wave sleep (SWS). Sleep walking and night terror can occur together or in isolation. Individuals with sleep walking disorder arise from bed in a stuporous state and amble about their homes or even out of doors. Typically such sleep walking episodes involve behaviors that are relatively routine or of low complexity, such as using the bathroom, eating, talking, or walking aimlessly. In contrast, individuals with night terror disorder display episodes during which they suddenly emit a shrill scream, usually after sitting up in bed. Since neither of these conditions is associated with REM sleep, the affected individual usually does not report dream content in association with the event. Moreover, the patient is usually difficult to arouse from the episode and typically has no recall of the event the next morning. At a minimum, such events cause embarrassment and may contribute to avoidance of certain situations (e.g., going on trips, overnight visits to friends' homes). In more severe cases, these parasomnias may result in injury to the affected individual or bed partner.

Epidemiological studies suggest that between 1.4 and 2.5% of the adult population report sleep walking episodes (Bixler, Kales, Soldatos, Kales, & Healey, 1979). The prevalence of sleep terrors among adults is currently unknown but is estimated to be less than 1%. These parasomnias are more prevalent in children than in adults. Gender appears to play a role in the development of night terrors inasmuch as these phenomena are more common in men than in women.

Research related to the causes of these parasomnias has suggested myriad etiological factors. Genetic factors likely play a role in their development in that the presence of such parasomnias in one or both parents dramatically increases the likelihood of such phenomena in their offspring (Kales, Soldatos, Bixler et al., 1980). Psychological trauma such as combat exposure or childhood abuse are commonly reported by individuals who present these parasomnias. In addition, one study (Crisp, Matthews, Oakley, & Crutchfield, 1990) found that psychometric indices of anxiety were elevated among those with night terrors whereas measures of externally directed hostility were elevated among sleep walkers. Among children, night terrors and sleep walking are developmental phenomena that are typically outgrown by mid-adolescence. Psychopathology is more likely to be (but is not always) present, when these conditions persist and particularly begin during adulthood. Among older adults, cardiovascular medications often are viewed as significant contributors to the development of these parasomnias, particularly when such individuals show a recent, de novo onset (Keefauver & Guilleminault, 1994). Collectively, these various findings suggest that, like nightmare disorder, these parasomnias most probably result from multiple etiological pathways.

Sleep Disorders Related to Another Mental Disorder

Sleep disturbances are common clinical features of several forms of psychopathology. By definition, the diagnosis of sleep disturbances related to another mental disorder implies that the sleep problem is temporally and causally related to the underlying psychopathology and that it is of sufficient concern to the patient to warrant independent clinical attention. In fact, sleep disturbance is often what prompts a person to seek professional attention. Estimates from clinical case series suggest that between 35 and 44% of patients presenting with a complaint of insomnia to sleep disorders centers meet diagnostic criteria for "insomnia related to another mental disorder" (Buysse et al., 1994; Coleman et al., 1982; Edinger et al., 1989). In contrast, psychiatric disorders account for a much smaller proportion (4%) of hypersomnia complaints (Coleman et al., 1982). The most common diagnoses associated with sleep/wake disorders are mood disorders (major depression and dysthymia), anxiety disorders (especially generalized anxiety disorders), and substance-induced sleep disorder (alcohol abuse). Comorbid Axis II diagnoses such as borderline, histrionic, and obsessive-compulsive personality disorders have been reported, although few empirical data are available on the exact prevalence of those diagnoses. In this section, we review typical subjective sleep/wake complaints and objective (EEG) sleep disturbances associated with selected psychopathologies.

Mood Disorders

Subjective sleep/wake complaints in mood disorders involve primarily insomnia and, much less frequently, hypersomnia. Major depression and dysthymia are characterized by difficulty falling asleep, frequent and/or prolonged nocturnal awakenings, and premature awakening in the morning with an inability to return to sleep. The early morning awakening is often seen as a classic symptom of major depression, although it is by no means specific to this condition. Most patients with major depression present mixed difficulties initiating and maintaining sleep. In bipolar patients, insomnia is more typical of the manic phase whereas excessive sleep is more characteristic of the depressive cycles. In mania, there is a perception of reduced need for sleep, which is not seen as problematic by the patient. However, the sleep-wake schedule is often disorganized, with the much reduced need for sleep at night being compensated for by excessive sleep during the day. When excessive daytime sleepiness is involved, it is not as severe as the hypersomnia associated with primary sleep disorders such as narcolepsy (Nofzinger et al., 1991). Individuals with atypical mood disorders (e.g., seasonal depression) may complain of hypersomnolence that is manifested by extended nocturnal sleep periods, frequent but unrefreshing napping, and feelings of fatigue and lethargy (Walsh, Moss, & Sugerman, 1994). However, not all patients with seasonal depression present these clinical features (Shapiro, Devins, Feldman, & Levitt, 1994). In fact, not all subjects complaining of excessive daytime sleepiness associated with mood disorders show objective evidence of hypersomnia (Billard, Partinen, Roth, & Shapiro, 1994); for some, this subjective complaint may simply reflect the underlying state of anergia.

Approximately 50% of outpatients and up to 90% of inpatients with major depression show some form of objective nocturnal sleep disturbances (Reynolds & Kupfer, 1987). The most consistent findings across studies include sleep continuity disturbances (increased sleep latency and time awake after sleep onset, more frequent awakenings, and diminished total sleep time), and alteration of the sleep architecture (Benca, Obermeyer, Thisted, & Gillin, 1992; Nofzinger, Buysse, Reynolds, & Kupfer, 1993). Of all forms of psychopathology, depression seemingly has the most pronounced effects on sleep architecture in general and on REM sleep in particular. Compared to normal, nondepressed individuals, depressed patients typically show a shorter latency between sleep onset and their first REM episode, an increased proportion of the night spent in REM sleep, and an altered temporal distribution of REM sleep and slow wave (stages 3–4) activity across the night. The first REM sleep period is longer and more intense (increased frequency of rapid eye movements) among depressed patients, whereas much of their deep sleep (stages 3–4) is delayed and occurs after the first REM episode. These abnormal findings are less pronounced in dysthymia relative to major depression (Reynolds & Kupfer, 1987).

The diagnostic specificity, sensitivity, and clinical utility of REM latency in depression are controversial. Although earlier findings suggested that a short REM latency might be a biological marker for major depression (Kupfer & Foster, 1972), more recent studies have shown that reduced REM sleep latency and increased percentages of REM sleep occur in other psychopathologies (Zarcone, Benson, & Berger, 1987). Thus, the REM abnormalities noted above may be sensitive to depression, but indicators such as reduced REM latency are not necessarily specific to this condition. Also, not all depressed patients show a reduced REM latency or increased percentage of REM sleep. Several factors affect REM sleep including age, the severity of the depressive illness, and the subtype of depression. For instance, REM latency decreases slightly with aging and a shortened REM latency may be less of a specific marker of depression in late life. Changes in REM appear more reliable in well-defined clinical inpatients with more severe endogenous depression (Reynolds & Kupfer, 1987). Another issue is whether REM abnormalities are temporally specific to the acute phase of depression or represent a trait marker of a greater vulnerability to recurring depressive episodes (Cartwright, 1983; Rush et al., 1986). Some evidence suggests that several abnormal features of REM sleep persist even after clinical remission of depressive symptoms (Rush et al., 1986).

Anxiety Disorders

Almost all anxiety disorders, with the exception of simple phobias, are associated with complaints of sleep disturbances. Difficulties falling asleep and increased awakenings are quite common, especially in generalized anxiety disorder (GAD). Once asleep, anxious patients show an essentially normal distribution of sleep stages across the night, but they may display prolonged awakenings due to their heightened arousal levels. The differential diagnosis between primary (psychophysiological) insomnia and insomnia secondary to GAD is not always easily made. In primary insomnia, the patient's focus of attention is essentially on his or her inability to sleep and on the resulting daytime consequences; in GAD, sleeplessness is only one among several sources of preoccupations or apprehensions.

As for depression, anxiety may increase the perception of disrupted sleep more so than the standard EEG variables reflect. Nonetheless, objective sleep abnormalities are typically present among anxious patients. For instance, GAD patients take longer to fall asleep, wake up more frequently and spend more time awake at night, achieve lower sleep efficiencies, and spend less time in deep (stages 3–4) sleep and more time in light (stage 1) sleep (Reynolds, Shaw, Newton, Coble, & Kupfer, 1983). As a group, GAD patients display sleep continuity disturbances fairly similar to those observed in major depression, with the exception that patients with a primary depression have a shorter REM sleep latency and a higher REM percentage (Papadimitriou, Linkowski, Kerkhofs, Kempenaers, & Mendlewicz, 1988). However, this latter finding has not been completely reliable in that one study found that GAD patients also had a short REM sleep latency (Rosa, Bonnet, & Kramer, 1983). One problem with comparing these two groups is that separation of anxious and depressed patients into diagnostic subgroups without overlapping symptoms is difficult if not impossible.

Patients with obsessive-compulsive disorders (OCD) may report trouble falling asleep and staying asleep. These difficulties are often associated with excessive worries and checking rituals. Sleep laboratory data suggest the presence of sleep fragmentation, reduced total sleep time, and increase movement time among OCD patients (Insel et al., 1982). However, these findings are not different from those in other anxiety disorders or even in other psychopathologies. Part of this problem is that the few studies of sleep abnormalities in anxiety disorders have been conducted with a heterogeneous group of patients often presenting mixed clinical features of various anxiety disorders.

In panic disorder, panic attacks can arise from sleep and lead to insomnia symptoms, especially sudden awakenings (Stein, Enns, & Kryger, 1993). Difficulties initiating sleep may also develop secondarily because of the anticipatory anxiety of having nocturnal panic attacks. Other sleep abnormalities associated with panic disorder are similar to those of other anxiety disorders; they include reduced sleep efficiency and total sleep time. Sleep architecture outside the attacks is not remarkably affected (Hauri, Friedman, & Ravaris, 1989), and there is no characteristic changes in REM sleep. Panic awakenings typically occur from non-REM sleep, particularly in the transition period between stages 2 and slow wave (stages 3–4) sleep (Mellman & Uhde, 1989). These attacks appear different from the sleep terror, which originate from slow wave sleep, in that they are less stereotyped and less intense. Since psychological factors presumably play a very limited role in triggering nocturnal panic attacks, the distinction between these attacks and those occurring during wakefulness may help delineate the biological bases of panic attacks. There is currently no clear distinction between these two forms of panic attacks. However, when panic attacks occur exclusively in sleep, it is important to consider other diagnoses such as sleep terrors, sleep apnea, laryngospasm, sleep choking, and gastroesophageal reflux.

In posttraumatic stress disorder (PTSD), patients often experience various forms of sleep disturbances including insomnia, nightmares, and sleep terrors (Ross, Ball, Sullivan, & Caroff, 1989). Recurring traumatic dreams, the most characteristic sleep features of PTSD, can be quite marked and disabling. PTSD patients exhibit excessive body movements during sleep and awakenings that are accompanied with startle or paniclike features often related to threatening dreams (Mellman, Kulick-Bell, Ashlock, & Nolan, 1995). Most studies do report some change in REM sleep parameters, but the direction of the change varies. Some reports indicate a shortened REM latency and others indicating a lengthened REM latency. The arousals from sleep in PTSD patients do not always arise from REM sleep. Anxiety, depression, poor sleep hygiene, and other factors contribute to the findings of disturbed sleep and are difficult to tease out from the posttraumatic stress disorder.

Schizophrenia

Sleep disturbances are very prevalent in schizophrenia and other psychoses, although individuals with such disorders rarely complain or report sleep as their primary difficulties. The sleep-wake cycle is often disorganized or delayed in that patients exhibit significant difficulties falling asleep but often sleep until late in the morning. These difficulties are in part, although not exclusively, the result of poor sleep hygiene. Chronic use of and withdrawal from neuroleptic drugs can also alter sleep patterns. Sleep disturbances are more pronounced during acute psychotic decompensation (Neylan, van Kammen, Kelley, & Peters, 1992); however, there is significant variability of sleep disruptions across patients and within patients over the course of a psychotic exacerbation. Persistent disruptions of sleep in chronic and even remitted psychotic patients are quite frequent as well.

The hallucinatory experiences of schizophrenics once were hypothesized to be the result of intrusions of dreaming into wakefulness. Empirical data have not supported this interpretation. In some very specific cases, however, there may be confusion between the schizophrenic hallucinations and the REM-sleep-induced hallucinations of some narcoleptic patients. Diagnostic sleep studies on a small number of schizophrenics found two who met the criteria for narcolepsy and whose psychosis improved with treatment for narcolepsy (Douglass et al., 1993).

The literature on sleep architecture abnormalities of schizophrenic patients has yielded few reliable findings distinguishing this disorder from normal controls or other psychiatric disorder. A significant decrease in slow wave (stages 3–4) sleep has been noted (Hiatt, Floyd, Katz, & Feinberg, 1985), but this finding has also been reported for several other disorders. It is also unclear the extent to which this reduction of deep sleep at night is due to poor sleep habits (e.g., daytime napping), to chronic use of neuroleptics, or to the underlying pathophysiological mechanisms of schizophrenia. Like the shortened REM sleep latency in patients with major depression, a shortened REM latency does occur in some schizophrenic patients, although their REM intensity is not as high as in major depression. When psychotic patients with and without a history of suicidal tendencies were compared, patients with suicidal behavior had increased REM intensity (Keshavan et al., 1994). One sleep feature distinguishing schizophrenic patients from normal controls is that following sleep deprivation schizophrenic patients do not show the typical rebound of REM sleep observed in healthy subjects; the clinical significance of this finding is unclear.

Alzheimer's Dementia

The sleep-wake cycle of demented patients (AD) is often reversed in that nocturnal sleep is frequently interrupted and daytime wakefulness compromised by frequent episodes of intruding sleep (Bliwise,

1994). One naturalistic study of AD patients in a residential care facility found that every single hour of the day was characterized by some microsleep episodes and that every hour of the night was perturbed by some wakefulness (Jacobs, Ancoli-Israel, Parker, & Kripke, 1988).

The sundown syndrome (e.g., agitation, disorientation) is a classic feature of some dementing illness. This may be accompanied by nighttime wandering, which can be very distressing for caregivers. Sleep disturbances in the early phase of a dementing illness can hasten placement in a nursing home facility. In a longitudinal study of community-living older adults, sleep disturbance was the strongest predictor of future nursing home placement, above that of cognitive impairments alone (Pollak, Perlick, Linsner, Wenston, & Hsieh, 1990). The pathophysiology of the sleep disturbance is multifactorial and probably includes alteration of the neurological control of sleep, circadian rhythm disturbances, poor sleep hygiene, and some of the primary sleep disturbances (e.g., sleep disruption related to a breathing-related sleep disorder or periodic limb movements during sleep) seen in middle-aged and older adults. Because of the positive relationship of REM sleep to cholinergic activity, one expectation is that Alzheimer's patients should have reduced REM sleep. However, the results have not been consistent (Bliwise, 1994).

Following sleep deprivation among normal subjects, there is a characteristic rebound or increase of stages 3–4 sleep and of REM sleep during the recovery period. The pattern of sleep rebound from sleep deprivation seems to distinguish elderly patients with depression and dementia from healthy normal controls (Reynolds et al., 1987). Whereas slow wave sleep rebound is comparable across the three groups, REM sleep rebound is more delayed among the depressed subgroup. Some evidence also suggests that a positive, mood-elevating response to sleep deprivation may distinguish patients with depressive pseudodementia from those with primary degenerative dementia (Buysse et al., 1988).

In summary, most psychiatric disorders produce significant sleep/wake complaints that are often corroborated by objective EEG sleep disturbances. These involve sleep continuity disturbances such as trouble falling asleep and staying asleep, with corresponding reductions of sleep efficiency and total sleep time. These abnormalities are quite robust across several psychiatric disorders, especially mood and anxiety disorders, but they are essentially nonspecific. Impairments of the sleep architecture, especially of REM sleep, are more typical of major depression, although it is by no means specific to this syndrome. Thus, it might be concluded that despite the extensive literature on sleep impairments in various mental disorders, the diagnostic yield has been rather limited. The initial interest in finding biological sleep markers of mental disorders has switched to an increased focus on the prognostic significance of sleep disturbances for the evolution of psychopathology. Although this avenue is promising, a great deal more research is needed to delineate further the etiological and prognostic significance of sleep disturbances in major psychopathologies.

Sleep Disorders Related to a General Medical Condition

Sleep/wake disturbances arise in the context of medical disorders that are too numerous to consider herein. Many medical conditions result in secondary sleep disturbances, but the sleep complaints do not dominate their clinical presentation. Nevertheless, a subset of patients with sleep-disruptive medical conditions complain of sleep difficulties to such a degree that these complaints warrant separate clinical attention. It is for this latter group of patients that a diagnosis of sleep disorder due to a general medical condition is reserved. In such cases the associated medical condition is regarded as primary and etiologically responsible for the presenting sleep/wake complaint. As with other sleep disorders, the patient must demonstrate impairment in social and occupational functioning.

The prevalence of sleep disorders related to a general medical condition is unknown. However, there is ample evidence that sleep problems are much more prevalent among individuals with active medical illness than among healthy controls (Gislason & Almqvist, 1987; Hohagen et al., 1993). Medical disorders may produce significant insomnia, hypersomnia, parasomnias, or a mixture of these sleep/wake disturbances. Insomnia, the most common form of sleep impairment, may arise from a variety of medical conditions including vascular headaches, cerebrovascular disease, hyperthyroidism, chronic bronchitis, degenerative neurological conditions, and the pain accompanying rheumatoid arthritis (Mitler, Poceta, Menn, & Erman, 1991; Wooten, 1994). In contrast, conditions such as hypothyroidism, viral encephalitis, fibrositis, and chronic fatigue syndrome may all result in hypersomnia complaints (Wooten, 1994). Among patients with medically based parasomnias, those with sleep-related epileptic seizures compose the largest subgroup. It is also important to note that sleep disturbance can be a side effect of treatments for medical (e.g., beta-blockers for hypertension) or psychiatric disorders (e.g., some SSRI for depression). Regardless of their presenting sleep difficulties, individuals with a medically based sleep disorder require treatment for their underlying medical condition. If stabilization of the medical condition does not alleviate sleep complaints, adjunctive behavioral or medical treatment directly targeting the sleep problem may be necessary (Mitler et al., 1991).

Substance-Induced Sleep Disorder

Alcohol, prescribed and over-the-counter medications, illicit drugs, and a variety of other substances may contribute to sleep/wake disturbances. These substances may produce insomnia, hypersomnia, parasomnias, or a mixture of these symptoms, either while in use or during periods of withdrawal and abstinence. When such sleep/wake disturbances are presented as a predominant clinical complaint, a diagnosis of substance-induced sleep disorder would be warranted as a co-diagnosis in addition to the *DSM-IV* diagnosis descriptive of the substance use problem. Most commonly such a diagnosis would be associated with excessive use of alcohol, sedative-hypnotic medications, and stimulants. Between 4% (Buysse et al., 1994) and 12% (Zorick, Roth, Hartse, Piccione, & Stepanski, 1981) of patients presenting to sleep disorders center are diagnosed with a substance-induced sleep disorders.

Alcohol produces a sedative effect. When it is used around bedtime it may hasten sleep onset and deepen sleep in the first half of the night; however, difficulties maintaining sleep are quite common in the second half of the night after the alcohol is metabolized. Alcohol intoxication may initially produce deeper sleep with very few body movements, but, with falling blood levels, it is soon followed by periods of restlessness, fitful sleep, and awakenings. Behavioral and dietary factors often interact with alcohol abuse in altering the sleep-wake cycles. Heavy alcohol intake may also result in a variety of parasomnias, such as bedwetting, sleep terrors, and sleep walking. Alcohol has a suppressant effect on REM sleep and, during acute withdrawal, vivid, disturbing dreams may emerge due to a REM rebound effect (Gillin, 1994). During acute withdrawal, sleep is frequently interrupted and shortened, and there is a significant loss of deep sleep stages. Among chronic alcohol abusers, sleep disturbances may persist even during prolonged periods of abstinence (Snyder & Karacan, 1985) and serve as the primary catalyst for relapse. Although the exact prevalence of alcohol-related sleep disorders is unknown, such conditions are likely to be relatively common since 10% of men and 3 to 5% of women develop significant alcohol dependence or abuse problems (Shuckit & Irwin, 1988).

Like alcohol, sedative hypnotic medications (e.g., benzodiazepines) may contribute to a substance-induced sleep disorder. Although most sedating medications used as sleep aids are effective for transient sleep disturbances, they lose their effectiveness with repeated use. With short-term use, benzodiazepines improve sleep efficiency and sleep continuity but significantly reduce the amount of stages 3–4 sleep. Individuals who frequently use sedating medications for sleep usually experience a return of their insomnia as they become tolerant to such drugs. When such individuals increase their medication dosages to reestablish drug efficacy, they may suffer from excessive daytime sleepiness, particularly if they are using a long-acting sleep medication. In addition, abrupt withdrawal of some short-acting sedating medications may lead to a period of rebound insomnia during which sleep disturbances worsen (Gillin, 1994). Clinical observations suggest that such withdrawal effects often contribute to a loss of self-efficacy in regard to sleep and encourage many individuals to continue use of hypnotics long after such drugs lose their effectiveness. Also, most benzodiazepines produce anterograde amnesia that may lead to poor recall of the past nights' awakenings upon arising in the morning. Such amnesia, in turn, may explain why some insomniacs continue using these drugs for prolonged periods of time despite loss of efficacy.

Stimulants such as amphetamines, cocaine, caffeine, and nicotine increase daytime alertness and may disrupt nighttime sleep. As a result, insomnia complaints may arise during periods of use. Conversely, complaints of hypersomnia may emerge during periods of withdrawal and abstinence. However, paradoxical symptoms, such as insomnia during nicotine withdrawal and hypersomnia during periods of heavy caffeine use, have also been observed (Gillin, 1994; Regestein, 1989). Most amphetamines and related stimulants also alter the sleep architecture. In addition to insomnia, these substances significantly reduce REM sleep and, upon withdrawal, there is a marked rebound of REM sleep that may be associated with depressed mood. Whatever their exact characteristics, stimulant-related sleep disorders often may persist for prolonged periods after withdrawal given the addictive properties of many of the substances that perpetuate them.

Comorbidity of Sleep Disturbance and Psychopathology

The co-occurrence of sleep disturbances and psychological symptoms and disorders has attracted a great deal of interest in the last few years (Benca et al., 1992; Billard et al., 1994, Morin & Ware, 1996). The question of whether sleep disturbance is strictly a clinical manifestation of an underlying psychiatric condition, a functionally autonomous disorder, or even a marker of vulnerability to develop some form of psychopathology remains unresolved. As such, this issue of comorbidity raises some important implications for differential diagnosis between primary sleep disorders and sleep disorders associated with another mental disorder, as well as for treatment planning and even prevention.

Sleep and Psychiatric Disorders in Clinical Case Series

As noted earlier in this chapter, psychological symptoms (e.g., anxiety, dysphoria, irritability) are extremely common among sleep disorders patients, especially those with chronic insomnia. In their milder forms, these signs are seen as correlates or consequences of chronically disturbed sleep, although definite statements about cause-and-effect relationships may be unwarranted. As also discussed previously, sleep disturbance is a characteristic complaint and even a diagnostic criterion for several psychiatric disorders (e.g., major depression, generalized anxiety disorders). It is not surprising, then, that between 50 and 73% of psychiatric patients experience sleep difficulties during the acute phase of their illnesses (Sweetwood, Grant, Kripke, Gerst, & Yager, 1980). The severity of sleep disturbance is positively related to the intensity of psychiatric symptomatology, although it is not necessarily associated with specific diagnoses. These sleep impairments can be viewed as clinical manifestation of the underlying psychiatric disorder.

Coexisting Sleep and Psychological Symptoms in Community Samples

The relationship between sleep and psychological symptoms has also been documented in randomly selected community samples. In the National Survey of Psychotherapeutic Drug Use (Mellinger et al., 1985), about half (47%) of those who reported significant trouble falling or staying asleep were judged to experience high levels of psychological distress, in comparison to only 11% of those who had never experienced insomnia. When clusters of symptoms were used to approximate *DSM-III* diagnoses, 21% of serious insomniacs (compared to less than 1% of those who never had insomnia) reported symptoms resembling major depression and 13% (vs. 3% for never had insomnia) presented features of generalized anxiety. Severity of reported sleep disturbances and degree of psychological distress were strongly correlated.

In the ECA study (Ford & Kamerow, 1989), the rate of psychiatric disorders was higher among those with sleep complaints. Forty percent of those with insomnia and 47% of those with hypersomnia were diagnosed with a psychiatric disorder compared to a base rate of 16% among those without sleep complaints. The most common disorders in subjects with insomnia complaints were anxiety disorders (24%), major depression (14%), dysthymia (9%), and alcohol abuse (7%) and drug abuse (4%). Sixty percent of insomniacs and 53% of hypersomniacs did not have any psychiatric disorder.

The relationship of insomnia to anxiety and depression was examined in a Swiss cohort of young adults who were interviewed three times over a period of seven years (Vollrath, Wicki, & Angst, 1989). At the third interview, 46% of all subjects with insomnia had suffered from anxiety or depression during the preceding year, in comparison to a base rate of 22% in those without sleep difficulties. Fifty-four percent of insomniacs had not experienced either anxiety or depression during the year their insomnia occurred.

Thus, findings from these studies suggest that between 40 and 47% of community-resident individuals who report sleep disturbances also have psychological symptoms or disorders, whereas about 50% report sleep difficulties without concomitant emotional symptomatology. Because of the cross-sectional nature of these data, it is essentially impossible to determine whether sleep disturbance increases the vulnerability to psychopathology, is part of the clinical manifestation of the disorder, or triggers a latent psychological disorder to become manifest (Van Moffaert, 1994).

Psychological Symptoms as Consequences of Chronic Sleep Disturbance

A few studies have examined the longitudinal relationship of sleep and psychological symptomatology. Participants in the ECA study were questioned twice over a one-year period about sleep complaints and psychiatric symptoms (Ford & Kamerow, 1989). Relative to study participants without persistent insomnia, those who reported insomnia that persisted from the first interview to the subsequent one year follow-up showed an increased risk for developing a new major depression (and to a smaller extent anxiety disorders) during their study participation.A similar pattern occurred in those with continuing hypersomnia, although the incidence of new cases was much smaller.

Several hypotheses might explain the relationship between insomnia and depression. First, because insomnia is one of the diagnostic criteria for depression (and for GAD), this positive relationship may represent an artifact of the measurement process. Second, sleep disturbances might be an epiphenomenon of the underlying psychiatric disorder, and its alteration would not change the course and eventual full manifestation of the depressive/anxiety disorder. Third, and perhaps the most parsimonious hypothesis, is that insomnia represents an early precursor in the clinical course of the disorder. Whether early detection and treatment of insomnia might prevent the development of a full major depression remains an important but unanswered question.

In contrast to the Ford and Kamerow data, findings from the Swiss cohort study (Vollrath et al., 1989), which are based on a relatively small number of incident cases, suggested that the relationship of insomnia to depressive and anxiety disorders reflects a pattern of co-occurrence rather than a sequential or causal pattern. After cases with a history of depression or anxiety prior to the first interview were removed, insomnia neither predicted the subsequent incidence of depression nor of anxiety disorders within the next two years.

The temporal covariation of sleep and mood disturbances has also been documented in two longitudinal studies with older adults. In one study (Rodin, McAvay, & Timko, 1988), depressed affect was found to covary over time with sleep disturbances, and early morning awakening was the sleep problem most consistently related to depressed mood. In a longitudinal study of late-life depression (Kennedy, Kelman, & Thomas, 1991), subjects whose depressive symptoms persisted over a two-year period reported more sleep disturbances than those whose symptoms remitted over the same interval. This finding would suggest that persistence of sleep disturbance might prevent or delay recovery from depression.

Overall, these findings confirm the suspected high rate of comorbidity between sleep and psychiatric disorders, particularly between insomnia and depression and anxiety. However, the nature of this relationship (i.e., causal, covariation) is more complex than is generally assumed. Clearly, additional prospective studies are needed to clarify these relationships and their implications for the (1) differential diagnosis between primary and secondary sleep disturbances, (2) prognostic value of sleep disturbances for predicting the development of and recovery from psychopathology, and (3) prevention/treatment planning.

Conclusions

Sleep disorders are relatively common and often serious conditions that may arise in the context of serious psychopathology or contribute to significant psychological dysfunction. Previous research has provided much information about the prevalence, nature, and etiology of sleep disorders. However, the scientific study of those syndromes discussed herein is yet in its infancy. In fact, so much about sleep/wake disorders remains unknown that it is difficult to prioritize the voluminous research questions that need to be addressed. Nevertheless, some research endeavors pertaining to sleep disturbances and their relationship to other forms of psychopathology seem paramount at this juncture.

As a starting point, it is clear that much more research concerning sleep/wake disorders classification is sorely needed. Although the current nosologies represent conceptual and practical advancements over previous classification systems, little empirical study of these systems has been conducted. As a result, the reliability and validity of many entities described in these nosologies remains questionable. Moreover, it has yet to be empirically demonstrated that any existing classification system accurately characterizes the entire spectrum of sleep/wake disturbances that are encountered in the clinical setting. Until such research is conducted, we will have little basis for the scientific study of many specific sleep/wake disturbances described by such nosological systems.

In addition, cross-sectional and longitudinal epidemiological studies of the various sleep/wake disorders appear critical. As noted herein, the population prevalence of many well-recognized sleep/wake disturbances remains unknown. As a result, it is currently impossible to determine the numbers of adults who may require clinical attention for such conditions. Furthermore, the cause-effect relationship between many sleep/wake disturbances and psychopathology remains controversial. Some writers (Vgontzas et al., 1993), for example, have argued that psychopathology is responsible for most forms of insomnia including primary insomnia, whereas others (Ford & Kamerow, 1989) have suggested that insomnia may serve as a critical etiological prodrome for various forms of psychopathology. Clearly more epidemiologic studies are needed to test the merit of these opposing views.

Finally, little is known about the etiology of many conditions described herein. Whereas many of these conditions appear to be associated with both underlying biological and psychological vulnerabilities, the interplay of such factors in the development of such conditions is currently poorly understood. In the case of primary insomnia, for example, little is known about hypothesized biological factors that contribute to this condition and, as noted above, the role of psychological traits in its etiology has been hotly debated. In contrast, it is generally accepted that sleep/wake disturbances are commonly associated with many psychopathological disorders, but whether specific forms of sleep/wake disruption underlie and contribute to the development of each of these psychiatric conditions is yet to be determined. Thus, much more research with, perhaps, newer technologies and research methods will likely lead to insights into the etiologies of many currently recognized sleep/wake disorders.

At this juncture, the scientific study of sleep/wake disorders and their association to psychopathology remains a relatively new and uncharted field of study. The limited research conducted to date has posed many questions about the interplay of psychological factors and sleep disturbances. However, this research, can be considered only preliminary at best. Indeed, many questions that beckon psychological inquiry remain to be addressed. It is hoped that the discussion presented herein has been both enlightening and sufficiently enticing to encourage some readers to consider future careers devoted to the clinical management and scientific study of sleep/wake pathology.

References

American Sleep Disorders Association. (1990). *International classification of sleep disorders (ICSD): Diagnostic and coding manual.* Rochester, MN: Author.

Association of Sleep Disorders Centers. (1979). Diagnostic classification of sleep and arousal disorders. *Sleep*, *2*, 1–137.

Benca, R. M., Obermeyer, W. H., Thisted, R. A., & Gillin, J. C. (1992). Sleep and psychiatric disorders: A meta-analysis. *Archives of General Psychiatry, 49*, 651–668.

Billard, M., Partinen, M., Roth, T., & Shapiro, C. (1994). Sleep and psychiatric disorders. *Journal of Psychosomatic Research, 38* (Suppl. 1), 1–2.

Bixler, E. O., Kales, A., Soldatos, C. R., Kales, J. D., & Healey, S. (1979). Prevalence of sleep disorders in the Los Angeles metropolitan area. *American Journal of Psychiatry, 136*, 1257–1262.

Bliwise, D. L. (1994). Sleep in normal aging and dementia. *Sleep, 16*, 40–81.

Bliwise, D. L., Friedman, L., & Yesavage, J. A. (1993). Depression as a confounding variable in the estimation of habitual sleep time. *Journal of Clinical Psychology, 49*, 471–477.

Bonnet, M. H., & Arand, D. L. (1995). 24-hour metabolic rate in insomniacs and matched normal sleepers. *Sleep, 18*, 581–588.

Buysse, D. J., Reynolds, C. F., Kupfer, D. J., Houck, P. R., Hoch, C. C., Stack, J. A., & Berman, S. R. (1988). Electroencephalographic sleep in depressive pseudodementia. *Archives of General Psychiatry, 45*, 568–575.

Buysse, D. J., Reynolds, C. F., Kupfer, D. J., Thorpy, M. J., Bixler, E., Manfredi, R., Kales, A., Vgontzas, A., Stepanski, E., Roth, T., Hauri, P., & Mesiano, D. (1994). Clinical diagnoses in 216 insomnia patients using the International Classification of Sleep Disorders (ICSD), DSM-IV and ICD-10 categories: A report from the APA/NIMH DSM-IV field trial. *Sleep, 17*, 630–637.

Cartwright, R. D. (1983). REM sleep characteristics during and after mood-disturbing events. *Archives of General Psychiatry, 40*, 197–201.

Coleman, R. M., Roffwarg, H. P., Kennedy, S. J., Guilleminault, C., Cinque, J., Cohn, M. A., Karacan, I., Kupfer, D. J., Lemmi, H., Miles, L. E., Orr, W. C., Phillips, E. R., Roth, T., Sassin, J. F., Schmidt, H. S., Weitzman, E. D., & Dement, W. C. (1982). Sleep-wake disorders based on a polysomnographic diagnosis: A national cooperative study. *Journal of the American Medical Association, 247*, 997–1003.

Crisp, A. H., Matthews, B. M., Oakley, M., & Crutchfield, M. (1990) Sleepwalking, night terrors and consciousness. *British Medical Journal, 300*, 360–362.

Daniels, L. (1934). Narcolepsy. *Medicine, 13*, 1–122.

Douglass, A. B., Shipley, J. E., Haines, R. F., Scholten, R. C., Dudley, E., & Tapp, A. (1993). Schizophrenia, narcolepsy, and HLA-DR15, DQ6. *Biological Psychiatry, 34*, 773–780.

Edinger, J. D., & Erwin, C. W. (1992). Common sleep disorders: Overview of diagnosis and treatment. *Clinician Reviews, 2*, 60–88.

Edinger, J. D., Fins, A. I., Goeke, J. M., McMillan, D. K., Gersh, T. L., Krystal, A. D., & McCall, W. V. (1996). The empirical identification of insomnia subtypes: A cluster analytic approach. *Sleep, 19*, 398–411.

Edinger, J. D., Hoelscher, T. J., Webb, M. D., Marsh, G. R., Radtke, R. A., & Erwin, C. W. (1989). Polysomnographic assessment of DIMS: Empirical evaluation of its diagnostic value. *Sleep, 12*, 315–322.

Edinger, J. D., Stout, A. L., & Hoelscher, T. J. (1988). Cluster analysis of insomniacs' MMPI profiles: Relation of subtypes to sleep history and treatment outcome. *Psychosomatic Medicine, 50*, 77–87.

Ford, D. E., & Kamerow, D. B. (1989). Epidemiologic study of sleep disturbances and psychiatric disorders: An opportunity for prevention? *Journal of the American Medical Association, 262*, 1479–1484.

Freedman, R. R., & Sattler, H. L. (1982). Physiological and psychological factors in sleep-onset insomnia. *Journal of Abnormal Psychology, 91*, 380–389.

Gallup Organization. (1995). *Sleep in America.* Princeton, NJ: Author.

Gillin, J. C. (1994). Sleep and psychoactive drugs of abuse and dependence. In M. H. Kryger, T. Roth, & W. C. Dement (Eds.), *Principles and practice of sleep medicine* (2nd ed., pp. 934–942). Philadelphia: W. B. Saunders.

Gislason, T., & Almqvist, M. (1987). Somatic diseases and sleep complaints: An epidemiological study of 3201 Swedish men. *Acta Medica Scandinavica, 221*, 475–481.

Guilleminault, C. (1989). Clinical features and evaluation of obstructive sleep apnea. In M. H. Kryger, T. Roth, & W. C. Dement (Eds.), *Principles and practice of sleep medicine* (pp. 552–558). Philadelphia: W. B. Saunders.

Hartmann, E. (1984). *The nightmare: The psychology and biology of terrifying dreams.* New York: Basic Books.

Hartmann, E. (1994). Nightmares and other dreams. In M. H. Kryger, T. Roth, & W. C. Dement (Eds.), *Principles and practice of sleep medicine* (2nd ed., pp. 407–410). Philadelphia: W. B. Saunders.

Hauri, P. J. (1994). Primary insomnia. In M. H. Kryger, T. Roth, & W. C. Dement (Eds.), *Principles and practice of sleep medicine* (2nd ed., pp. 494–499). Philadelphia: W. B. Saunders.

Hauri, P. J., Friedman, M., & Ravaris, C. L. (1989). Sleep in patients with spontaneous panic attacks. *Sleep, 12*, 323–337.

Hauri, P. J., & Olmstead, E. M. (1980). Childhood-onset insomnia. *Sleep, 3*, 59–65.

Healey, E. S., Kales, A., Monroe, L. J., Bixler, E. O., Chamberlain, K., & Soldatos, C. R. (1981). Onset of insomnia: Role of life-stress events. *Psychosomatic Medicine, 43*, 439–451.

Hiatt, J. F., Floyd, T. C., Katz, P. H., & Feinberg, I. (1985). Further evidence of abnormal NREM sleep in schizophrenia. *Archives of General Psychiatry, 42*, 797–802.

Hohagen, F., Rink, K., Kappler, C., Schramm, E., Riemann, D., Weyerer, S., & Berger, M. (1993). Prevalence and treatment of insomnia in general practice: A longitudinal study. *European Archives of Psychiatry and Clinical Neuroscience, 242*, 329–336.

Insel, T. R., Gillin, J. C., Moore, A., Mendelson, W. B., Loewenstein, R. J., & Murphy, D. L. (1982). The sleep of patients with obsessive-compulsive disorder. *Archives of General Psychiatry, 39*, 1370–1377.

Jacobs, D., Ancoli-Israel, S., Parker, L., & Kripke, D. F. (1988). Sleep and wake over 24-hours in a nursing home population. *Sleep Research, 17*, 191.

Kales, A., & Kales, J. D. (1984). *Evaluation and treatment of insomnia*. New York: Oxford University Press.

Kales, J. D., Kales, A., Soldatos, C. R., Caldwell, A. B., Charney, D. S., & Martin E. D. (1980). Night terrors: Clinical characteristics and personality patterns. *Archives of General Psychiatry, 37*, 1413–1417.

Kales, A., Soldatos, C. R., Bixler, E. O., Ladda, R. L., Charney, D. S., Weber, G., & Schweitzer, P. K. (1980). Hereditary factors in sleepwalking and night terrors. *British Journal of Psychiatry, 137*, 111–118.

Kales, A., Soldatos, C. R., Caldwell, A. B., Charney, D. S., Kales, J. D., Markel, D., & Cadieux, R. (1980). Nightmares: Clinical characteristics and personality patterns. *American Journal of Psychiatry, 137*, 1197–1201.

Kales, A., Soldatos, C. R., Caldwell, A. B., Kales, J. D., Humphrey, F. J., Charney, D. S., & Schweitzer, P. K. (1980). Somnambulism: Clinical characteristics and personality patterns. *Archives of General Psychiatry, 37*, 1406–1410.

Keefauver, S. P., & Guilleminault, C. (1994). Sleep terrors and sleepwalking. In M. H. Kryger, T. Roth, & W. C. Dement (Eds.), *Principles and practice of sleep medicine* (2nd ed., pp. 567–573). Philadelphia: W. B. Saunders.

Kennedy, G. J., Kelman, H. R., & Thomas, C. (1991). Persistence and remission of depressive symptoms in late life. *American Journal of Psychiatry, 148*, 174–178.

Keshavan, M. S., Reynolds, C. F., Montrose, D., Miewald, J., Downs, C., & Sabo, E. M. (1994). Sleep and suicidality in psychotic patients. *Acta Psychiatria Scandinavia, 89*, 122–125.

Kryger, M. H., Roth, T., & Dement, W. C. (Eds.). (1994). *Principles and practice of sleep medicine* (2nd ed.). Philadelphia: W. B. Saunders.

Kupfer, D. J., & Foster, F. G. (1972). Interval between onset of sleep and rapid-eye movement sleep as an indicator of depression. *Lancet, 2*, 684–686.

Lankford, D. A., Wellman, J. J., & O'Hara, C. (1994). Posttraumatic narcolepsy in mild to moderate closed head injury. *Sleep, 17*, S25–S28.

Lichstein, K. L., & Riedel, B. W. (1994). Behavioral assessment and treatment of insomnia: A review with an emphasis on clinical application. *Behavior Therapy, 25*, 659–688.

McCall, W. V., & Edinger, J. D. (1992). The validity of sleep state misperception. *Sleep, 15*, 71–73.

Mellinger, G. D., Balter, M. B., & Uhlenhuth, E. H. (1985). Insomnia and its treatment: Prevalence and correlates. *Archives of General Psychiatry, 42*, 225–232.

Mellman, T. A., Kulick-Bell, R., Ashlock, L. E., & Nolan, B. (1995). Sleep events among veterans with combat-related posttraumatic stress disorder. *American Journal of Psychiatry, 152*, 110–115.

Mellman, T. A., & Uhde, T. W. (1989). Electroencephalographic sleep in panic disorder. *Archives of General Psychiatry, 46*, 178–184.

Miles, L. E., & Dement, W. C. (1980). Sleep and aging. *Sleep, 3*, 119–220.

Mitler, M. M., Dinges, D. F., & Dement, W. C. (1994). Sleep medicine, public policy, and public health. In M. H. Kryger, T. Roth, & W. C. Dement (Eds.), *Principles and practice of sleep medicine* (2nd ed.). Philadelphia: W. B. Saunders.

Mitler, M. M., Poceta, S., Menn, & Erman, M. K. (1991). Insomnia in the chronically ill. In P. J. Hauri (Ed.), *Case studies in insomnia* (pp. 223–236). New York: Plenum Press.

Morin, C. M. (1993). *Insomnia: Psychological assessment and management*. New York: Guilford Press.

Morin, C. M., Culbert, J. P., Schwartz, S. (1994). Nonpharmacological interventions for insomnia: A meta-analysis of treatment efficacy. *American Journal of Psychiatry, 151*, 1172–1180.

Morin, C. M., & Ware, J. C. (1996). Sleep and psychopathology. *Applied and Preventive Psychology, 5*, 211–221.

Morin, C. M., & Wooten, V. (1996). Psychological and pharmacological approaches to treating insomnia: Critical issues in assessing their separate and combined effects. *Clinical Psychology Review, 16*, 521–542.

Murtagh, D. R., & Greenwood, K. M. (1995). Identifying effective psychological treatments for insomnia: A meta-analysis. *Journal of Consulting and Clinical Psychology, 63*, 79–89.

National Commission on Sleep Disorders Research. (1993). *Wake up America: A national sleep alert*. Washington, D.C.: Author.

Neylan, T. C., Van Kammen, D. P., Kelley, M. E., & Peters, J. L. (1992). Sleep in schizophrenic patients on and off Haloperidol therapy. *Archives of General Psychiatry, 49*, 643–649.

Nofzinger, E. A., Buysse, D. J., Reynolds, C. F., & Kupfer, D. J. (1993). Sleep disorders related to another mental disorder (Nonsubstance/Primary): A DSM-IV literature review. *Journal of Clinical Psychiatry, 54*, 244–255.

Nofzinger, E. A., Thase, M. E., Reynolds, C. F., Himmelhoch, J. M., Mallinger, A., Houck, P., & Kupfer, D. J. (1991). Hypersomnia in bipolar depression: A comparison with narcolepsy using the multiple sleep latency test. *American Journal of Psychiatry, 148*, 1177–1181.

Ohayon, M. (1996). Epidemiological study on insomnia in the general population. *Sleep, 19*, S7–S15.

Orellana, C., Villemin, E., Tafti, M., Carlander, B., Besset, A., & Billard, M. (1994). Life events in the year preceding the onset of narcolepsy. *Sleep, 17*, S50–S53.

Papadimitriou, G. N., Linkowski, P., Kerkhofs, M., Kempenaers, C., & Mendlewicz, J. (1988). Sleep EEG recordings in generalized anxiety disorder with significant depression. *Journal of Affective Disorders, 15*, 113–118.

Parkes, J. D. (1985). *Sleep and its disorders*. London: W. B. Saunders.

Partinen, M. (1994). Epidemiology of sleep disorders. In M. H. Kryger, T. Roth, & W. C. Dement (Eds.), *Principles and practice of sleep medicine* (2nd ed., pp. 437–452). Philadelphia: W. B. Saunders.

Pollak, C. P., Perlick, D., Linsner, J. P., Wenston, J., & Hsieh, F. (1990). Sleep problems in the community elderly as predictors of death and nursing home placement. *Journal of Community Health, 15*, 123–135.

Regestein, Q. R. (1989). Pathologic sleepiness induced by caffeine. *American Journal of Medicine, 87*, 586–588.

Regestein, Q. R., & Monk, T. (1994). Is the poor sleep of shift workers a disorder? *American Journal of Psychiatry, 148*, 1487–1493.

Reynolds, C. F., & Kupfer, D. J. (1987). Sleep research in affective illness: State of the art circa 1987. *Sleep, 10*, 199–215.

Reynolds, C. F., Kupfer, D. J., Hoch, C. C., Houck, P. R., Stack, J. A., Berman, S. R., Campbell, P. I., & Zimmer, B. (1987). Sleep deprivation as a probe in the elderly. *Archives of General Psychiatry, 44*, 982–990.

Reynolds, C. F., Shaw, D. H., Newton, T. F., Coble, P. A., & Kupfer, D. J. (1983). EEG sleep in outpatients with generalized anxiety: A preliminary comparison with depressed outpatients. *Psychiatry Research, 8*, 81–89.

Rodin, J., McAvay, G., & Timko, C. (1988). A longitudinal study of depressed mood and sleep disturbances in elderly adults. *Journal of Gerontology, 43*, 45–53.

Roehrs, T., & Roth, T. (1994). Chronic insomnias associated with circadian rhythm disorders. In M. H. Kryger, T. Roth, & W. C. Dement (Eds.), *Principles and practice of sleep medicine* (2nd ed., pp. 477–482). Philadelphia: W. B. Saunders.

Rosa, R. R., Bonnet, M. H., & Kramer, M. (1983). The relationship of sleep and anxiety in anxious subjects. *Biological Psychology, 16*, 119–126.

Ross, R. J., Ball, W. A., Sullivan, K. A., & Caroff, S. N. (1989). Sleep disturbance as the hallmark of posttraumatic stress disorder. *American Journal of Psychiatry, 146*, 697–706.

Rush, A. J., Erman, M. K., Giles, D. E., Schlesser, M. A., Carpenter, G., Vasavada, N., & Roffwarg, H. P. (1986). Polysomnographic findings in recently drug-free and clinically remitted depressed patients. *Archives of General Psychiatry, 43*, 878–884.

Salin-Pascual, R. J., Roehrs, T. A., Merlotti, L. A., Zorick, F., & Roth, T. (1992). Long-term study of the sleep of insomnia patients with sleep state misperception and other insomnia patients. *American Journal of Psychiatry, 149*, 904–908.

Schuckit, M. A., & Irwin, M. (1988). Diagnosis of alcoholism. *Medical Clinics of North America, 72*, 1133–1153.

Shapiro, C. M., Devins, G. M., Feldman, B., & Levitt, A. J. (1994). Is hypersomnolence a feature of seasonal affective disorder? *Journal of Psychosomatic Research, 38* (Suppl. 1), 49–54.

Snyder, S., & Karacan, I. (1985). Sleep patterns of sober chronic alcoholics. *Neuropsychobiology, 13*, 97–100.

Spielman, A. J. (1986). Assessment of insomnia. *Clinical Psychology Review, 6*, 11–25.

Stein, M. B., Enns, M. W., & Kryger, M. H. (1993). Sleep in nondepressed patients with panic disorder: II. Polysomnographic assessment of sleep architecture and sleep continuity. *Journal of Affective Disorders, 28*, 1–6.

Stepanski, E., Zorick, F., Roehrs, T., Young, D., & Roth, T. (1988). Daytime alertness in patients with chronic insomnia compared with asymptomatic control subjects. *Sleep, 11*, 54–60.

Stoohs, R., & Guilleminault, C. (1992). Cardiovascular changes associated with the obstructive sleep apnea syndrome. *Journal of Applied Physiology, 75*, 583–589.

Sweetwood, H., Grant, I., Kripke, D. F., Gerst, M. S., & Yager, J. (1980). Sleep disorder over time: Psychiatric correlates among males. *British Journal of Psychiatry, 136*, 456–462.

Trinder, J. (1988). Subjective insomnia without objective findings: A pseudo diagnostic classification? *Psychological Bulletin, 103*, 87–94.

Van Moffaert, M. P. (1994). Sleep disorders and depression: The "Chicken and Egg" situation. *Journal of Psychosomatic Research, 38* (Suppl. 1), 9–13.

Vgontzas, A. N., Kales, A., Bixler, E. O., & Vela-Bueno, A. (1993). Sleep disorders related to another mental disorder (nonsubstance/primary): A DSM-IV literature review. *Journal of Clinical Psychiatry, 54*, 256–259.

Vollrath, M., Wicki, W., & Angst, J. (1989). The Zurich study: VIII. Insomnia: Association with depression, anxiety, somatic syndromes, and course of insomnia. *European Archives of Psychiatry and Neurological Sciences, 239*, 113–124.

Walsh, J. K., Moss, K. L., & Sugerman, J. (1994). Insomnia in adult psychiatric disorders. In M. H. Kryger, T. Roth, & W. C. Dement (Eds.), *Principles and practice of sleep medicine* (2nd ed., pp. 500–508). Philadelphia: W. B. Saunders.

Wood, J. M., & Bootzin, R. R. (1990). The prevalence of nightmares and their independence from anxiety. *Journal of Abnormal Psychology, 99*, 64–68.

Wooten, V. (1994). Medical causes of insomnia. In M. H. Kryger, T. Roth, & W. C. Dement (Eds.), *Principles and practice of sleep medicine* (2nd ed., pp. 509–522). Philadelphia: W. B. Saunders.

Young, T., Palta, M., Dempsey, J., Skatrud, J., Weber, S., & Badr, S. (1993). Occurrence of sleep disordered breathing among middle-aged adults. *New England Journal of Medicine, 328*, 1230–1235.

Zarcone, V. P., Benson, K. L., & Berger, P. A. (1987). Abnormal rapid eye movement latencies in schizophrenia. *Archives of General Psychiatry, 44*, 45–48.

Zorick, F. J., Roth, T., Hartse, K. M., Piccione, P., & Stepanski, E. (1981). Evaluation and diagnosis of persistent insomnia. *American Journal of Psychiatry, 138*, 769–773.

16

Sexual Dysfunctions and Disorders

DANIEL N. WEINER
RAYMOND C. ROSEN

Human sexuality is a highly diverse and complex phenomenon, which is subject to multiple influences from biology, culture, and the social or interpersonal environment. Despite recent advances in our knowledge of developmental origins and psychophysiological mechanisms of sexual response (e.g., Fagot, 1995; Laan & Everaerd, 1995), many aspects of sexuality remain baffling and elusive. This is especially evident in the area of sexual disorders and dysfunctions, where definitions of sexual normality and abnormality are difficult to establish and diagnostic classification is frequently based upon arbitrary or subjective criteria (Hawton, 1992; Rosen & Leiblum, 1995). Moreover, clinical research and practice on this topic are strongly influenced by historical, social, and cultural forces (Tiefer, 1991), which frequently impede or oppose scientific understanding. Perhaps more than any other aspect of human behavior, sexuality is a deeply personal and highly individual experience.

Sexual disorders are broadly classified into three major categories. *Paraphilias* involve sexual arousal in response to nonnormative or deviant stimuli. *Gender identity disorders* involve dissatisfaction with biological gender and a desire to be of the opposite sex. Taken together, these two categories of sexual problems can be broadly considered as deviations in the qualitative aspects of sexuality, or *the direction* of sexual feelings—that is, the nature of the stimuli to which one is responsive or the gender with which one identifies differs categorically from the norm. In contrast, *sexual dysfunctions* encompass alterations or deficiencies in the psychophysiologic changes that characterize the sexual response cycle and can be thought of as *quantitative* problems with the *strength* or *intensity* of sexual drive or arousal (Berlin, 1983; Bancroft, 1989).

Sexual Dysfunctions

Following the pioneering work of Masters and Johnson (1966) and Kaplan (1977), the sexual response cycle in both sexes is often categorized as a four-phase process: the first stage, *sexual desire*, consists of the motivational or appetitive aspects of sexual response. Sexual urges, fantasies and wishes are included in this phase. The second stage, *sexual excitement*, refers to a subjective feeling of sexual pleasure and accompanying physiological changes. This phase includes penile erection in men and vaginal lubrication in women. The third stage, *orgasm* or climax, is defined as the peak of sexual pleasure, with rhythmic contractions of the genital musculature in both men and women, as well as ejaculation in men. The final phase is resolution, during which a general sense of relaxation and well-being is experienced. In men, a refractory period for erection and ejaculation usually occurs during this phase. The sexual dysfunctions can be considered as alterations in one or more phases of the sexual response cycle, and this four-stage model forms the basis for classification of the sexual dysfunctions in *DSM-IV*.

Based upon this model, four major categories of sexual dysfunction are identified by *DSM-IV* as follows (see table 16.1): (1) sexual desire disorders, including hypoactive sexual desire and sexual aversion disorder; (2) sexual arousal disorders, including female sexual arousal disorder and male erectile disorder; (3) orgasmic disorders, including female orgasmic disorder, male orgasmic disorder, and premature ejaculation; (4) sexual pain disorders, including dyspareunia and vaginismus. Additional categories include sexual dysfunction due to a general medical condition, substance-induced sexual dysfunction, and sexual dysfunction not otherwise specified. Examples of the last category include a lack of subjective erotic feelings, despite presence of normal arousal and orgasm, or the presence of a sexual dysfunction of undetermined origin. Additional distinctions are drawn between lifelong and acquired dysfunctions, generalized and situational difficulties, and sexual dysfunctions due to psychological or combined medical and psychological factors. Although alternative multiaxial and problem-oriented diagnostic approaches have been proposed (e.g., Schover, Friedman, Weiler, Heiman, & LoPiccolo, 1982; Segraves & Segraves, 1990), these have not been widely adopted to date.

Despite its broad influence, the sexual response cycle and resulting classification model have been strongly criticized on both theoretical and empirical grounds (Rosen & Beck, 1988; Tiefer, 1991). For example, it has been argued that the distinctions between phases are artificial and fail to represent the cumulative or continuous aspects of sexual response (Robinson, 1976; Bancroft, 1989). The model also lacks distinctions between male and female response patterns, and reinforces a genitally focused, predominantly masculine perspective on sexual performance (Tiefer, 1991). Clinically, many individuals present with multiple diagnoses or problems in more than one phase of the sexual response cycle. In one large-scale study of men and women with a primary diagnosis of hypoactive

Table 16.1 Sexual Response Phases and Associated Dysfunctions

Phase	Characteristics	Dysfunctions
1. Desire	First phase of sexual response. Characterized by subjective feelings of sexual interest or appetite, sexual urges, or fantasies. No identifiable physiological correlates.	Hypoactive sexual desire disorder; sexual aversion disorder.
2. Excitement	Second phase of sexual response. Includes both subjective and physiological concomitants of sexual arousal. Penile erection in males; vaginal engorgement and lubrication in females.	Female sexual arousal disorder; male erectile disorder.
3. Orgasm	Third phase of sexual response. Includes climax or peaking of sexual tension, rhythmic contractions of the genital musculature, and intense subjective involvement.	Female orgasmic disorder; male orgasmic disorder; premature ejaculation
4. Resolution	Final phase of sexual response. Includes a physical release of tension and subjective sense of well-being. Most men have a refractory period for further sexual stimulation.	Sexual pain disorders: dyspareunia; vaginismus

Note: The four-phase sexual response cycle model presented in *DSM-IV* is a synthesis of the earlier sexual response cycle models described by Masters and Johnson (1970) and Helen Kaplan (1977).

sexual desire disorder, 41% of female patients and 47% of male patients had at least one other sexual dysfunction diagnosis (Segraves & Segraves, 1991). Additionally, 18% of the female patients in this study had diagnoses in all three categories of desire, arousal, and orgasm. As illustrated in the following vignette, there is frequently a high degree of overlap between categories of dysfunction.

Case Vignette

Frank G. is a 34-year-old, single male with a lifelong history of sexual dysfunction. He describes himself as always being shy and uncomfortable with women, and has difficulty in forming and maintaining relationships. His first sexual experience took place at age 22, and was accompanied by severe premature ejaculation prior to achieving vaginal penetration. Due to his shame and embarrassment at the incident, he began avoiding intimate and sexual relationships. The frequency of his masturbation and sexual fantasies also declined markedly in the ensuing years. At age 30, Frank became involved with his current partner, whom he describes as sexually active and uninhibited. Despite strong attraction to his partner, he has difficulty in maintaining erections during sexual stimulation and experiences intense performance anxiety. Furthermore, he seldom initiates sexual interaction and has difficulty in communicating his sexual desires. He continues to ejaculate rapidly on most attempts at intercourse.

Traditionally, sexual dysfunctions have been categorized as psychogenically or organically based (Masters & Johnson, 1970; Kaplan, 1974). This distinction has been criticized as simplistic and overly restrictive, and several authors have recommended a multidimensional or interactive approach to classification (e.g., LoPiccolo, 1992; Mohr & Beutler, 1990). Sexual dysfunctions have also been conceptualized as a type of psychophysiological or psychosomatic disorder (Bancroft, 1989), in which both physical symptoms (e.g., pain during intercourse) and psychological determinants (e.g., performance anxiety) are equally emphasized. Finally, interpersonal factors play a major role, as most sexual difficulties occur in the context of a partner relationship. In fact, this concept served as the cornerstone for Masters and Johnson's (1970) approach to the formulation and treatment of all sexual dysfunctions. As noted by these authors: "There is no such thing as an uninvolved partner in any marriage in which there is some form of sexual inadequacy" (1970, p. 2).

Sexual dysfunctions are thought to impact on mood, self-esteem, and overall life satisfaction to varying degrees (Wincze & Carey, 1991; Rosen, Taylor, Leiblum, & Bachmann, 1993). In one recent large-scale study of sexual dysfunction in middle-aged and older men (Feldman, Goldstein, Hatzichristou, Krane, & McKinlay, 1994), a strong correlation was observed between the occurrence of erectile difficulties and self-ratings of depression. Men with partial or complete erectile dysfunction rated themselves as significantly more depressed than those with normal erectile function. Similarly, in a recent population-based survey of sexual behavior in men and women (Laumann, Gagnon, Michael, & Michaels, 1994), more than two thirds of women with sexual arousal or desire difficulties rated themselves as low in overall life satisfaction. Treatment outcome studies frequently show improvements in mood or self-esteem following treatment. However, the direction of causality in these and other studies of the relationship between mood and sexual function is unknown. It is not clear whether sexual dysfunction affects mood or depressed mood affects sexual functioning. One study that experimentally manipulated mood in the laboratory found that negative mood induction diminished sexual arousal in response to erotic stimulation (Mitchell et al., 1992). It is also conceivable that additional factors, such as level of partner intimacy or overall health, may mediate the relationship between mood and sexual functioning. In sum, the association between these variables is likely complex and multidirectional.

In the absence of definitive norms for normal sexual functioning, diagnosis of sexual dysfunctions is highly subjective. Perception of one's own sexual functioning may be distorted by unrealistic expectations based on exaggerations prevalent in the media (e.g., erotic films or books) and other information sources about sex such as "locker room" conversations. Self-diagnosis of sexual performance problems therefore presents much difficulty. It is possible to imagine two people who, in some abstract sense, "perform" identically, but one reports no performance problem while the other reports serious problems because of either unrealistic expectations or partner ineptness. For example, a man who reaches orgasm after 10 minutes of sexual intercourse may think of himself as dysfunctional because he expects to be able to delay his orgasm for 30 minutes. As another example, a woman who rarely has orgasms during sexual encounters with her partner may be quite capable of doing so if her partner paid more attention to her preferences for certain types of stimulation.

As noted above, sexual dysfunctions in both sexes are categorized by *DSM-IV* according to the four stages of the sexual response cycle. In the following sections, we review prevalence, clinical characteristics, and etiological formulations for each category of sexual dysfunction. Male and female dysfunctions are covered separately in some categories (e.g., male erectile disorder, female sexual arousal disorder) and together in others (e.g., hypoactive sexual desire disorder). Both physical and psychological determinants of dysfunction are considered in each category. In the second part of the chapter, we consider the paraphilias and gender identity disorders. Special problems in the definition and classification of these disorders will be addressed, in addition to the social and legal implications of diagnosis. Etiological theories and clinical formulation will also be discussed.

Sexual Desire Disorders

Sexual desire problems were first recognized as a separate clinical entity in the mid-1970s by Harold Lief (1977) and Helen Singer Kaplan (1977). Based upon clinical observation that many individuals presenting with sexual dysfunction could not be adequately classified according to the four-stage model of Masters and Johnson (1970), these authors recommended adding a new category of "inhibited sexual desire." Lief (1977) proposed that this diagnosis be applied to those individuals who chronically fail to initiate or respond to sexual stimuli. The category was incorporated into *DSM-III* and subsequently expanded in *DSM-III-R* to include both hypoactive sexual desire disorder (HSDD) and sexual aversion disorder (SAD). The term hypoactive sexual desire was substituted for inhibited sexual desire as a more theoretically neutral term that avoided the assumption that inhibitory mechanisms are present in all cases (Leiblum & Rosen, 1988). According to *DSM-IV*, HSDD is defined as the persistent lack (or absence) of sexual fantasies or desire for any form of sexual activity. Sexual aversion disorder goes beyond a lack of desire and is characterized by a marked aversion to, and avoidance of, all genital contact with a sexual partner. Poor body image and avoidance of nudity are common characteristics of this disorder (Ponticas, 1992; Katz, Gipson, & Turner, 1992).

Diagnosis of HSDD is highly dependent upon the judgment of the clinican, especially in cases of secondary or situational low desire. There are a wide variety of presenting symptoms or complaints, and the diagnosis is frequently dependent upon partner corroboration (Rosen & Leiblum, 1989). Some individuals have difficulty in initiating sexual contact, whereas others are unresponsive to the sexual initiatives of their partner. Hypoactive desire can be global, in the sense that the individual lacks interest in any or all sexual activity, or the problem may be situational, with lack of desire only for a particular partner or activity. In many instances, HSDD is secondary to another sexual dysfunction, such as anorgasmia in women or erectile dysfunction in men (Wincze & Carey, 1991). It may also result from a wide variety of medical and psychiatric disorders (Rosen & Leiblum, 1995; Schiavi, Schreiner-Engel, White, & Mandeli, 1988), as well as partner conflicts and incompatibilities (Verhulst & Heiman, 1988).

Prevalence Although prevalence rates have varied widely from one study to another (Spector & Carey, 1990), hypoactive sexual desire can be characterized as a highly prevalent sexual disorder in both males and females. It has been estimated that up to 15% of adult males have HSDD (Nathan, 1986), and that the overall population rate for the disorder is about 20% (*DSM-IV*). It is also striking that the number of cases presenting for treatment has increased markedly in the past decade. In one clinic sample (LoPiccolo & Friedman, 1988), the proportion of HSDD cases increased from 32% in the years 1974–76, to approximately 55% of all cases in 1982–84. Data from a recent multicenter trial of pharmacological therapy for sexual dysfunctions (Segraves & Segraves, 1991) indicated that 65% of all patients seeking treatment qualified for a primary diagnosis of HSDD. About 40% of these patients, it should be noted, also had secondary diagnoses of sexual arousal or orgasm disorders.

Most studies have reported higher rates of HSDD in women compared to men. Among clinic samples, the ratio of female to male cases of low desire is typically about 2 : 1 (Renshaw, 1988; Segraves & Segraves, 1991). In a British study (Hawton, Catalan, Martin, & Fagg, 1986), 37% of female patients had a primary diagnosis of hypoactive desire, compared to less than 5% of male patients. The lower rate of HSDD among males in this sample may reflect differences in diagnostic practices or greater reluctance among British males to acknowledge existence of the problem. In accounting for the increased prevalence of HSDD among males in recent U.S. samples, it has been suggested that this may reflect the growing freedom of women to initiate sexual activity. Rather than confronting the anxiety associated with sexual performance fears, men may respond with loss of sexual interest. Alternatively, the change may reflect increased likelihood of hypoactive desire being labeled as a clinical problem in both men and women (Donahey & Carroll, 1993).

The prevalence of SAD is unknown, as none of the studies to date has reported separate prevalence data for this disorder (Rosen & Leiblum, 1995).

Etiological Determinants Little agreement exists concerning the etiological origins of hypoactive desire. The role of biological or hormonal factors is especially controversial, as highly inconsistent findings have been reported in several recent studies. Schiavi and colleagues (Schiavi et al., 1988), for example, evaluated pituitary and gonadal hormones, and nocturnal penile tumescence (NPT) in physically healthy men with HSDD and age-matched controls. Significantly lower levels of plasma testosterone, measured at hourly intervals throughout the night, were observed in low-desire subjects compared to controls, although no differences were found in the pattern of pulsatile release of testosterone or in the levels of free testosterone, SHBG, LH, prolactin, or estradiol. Nocturnal tumescence levels were also significantly depressed in the patient group, many of whom had concomitant erectile difficulties. In a similar study of low-desire women, the same investigator group (Schreiner-Engel, Schiavi, White, & Ghizzani, 1989) found no differences in hormone levels between clinic patients and age-matched controls.

Studies of extreme cases of hormonal deficiency have demonstrated that hormones are essential for normal sexual desire. In several studies, hypogonadal men (i.e., men with congenitally abnormal testes that produce vastly reduced quantities of testosterone) evidenced low or absent sexual desire that was increased with testosterone-replacement therapy (Davidson, Camargo, & Smith, 1979; Skakkebaek, Bancroft, Davidson, & Warner, 1981). Similarly, it has been shown that women who have undergone ovariectomy show diminished sexual desire that is enhanced with hormone replacement treatment (Sherwin, Gelfand, & Brender, 1985). Results of administering hormones to eugonadal individuals (i.e., those with normally functioning gonads) with HSDD have been less consistent, but as in correlational studies, effects have been more reliable in males (Carney, Bancroft, & Matthew, 1978; O'Carroll & Bancroft, 1984). Taken together, these studies suggest that hormonal factors may play a larger role in the etiology of HSDD in males compared to females.

Psychological factors have been shown to affect sexual desire in both clinical and nonclinical samples. In a recent series of laboratory studies by J. G. Beck and colleagues (Beck, Bozman, & Qualtrough, 1991; Bozman & Beck, 1991; Beck & Bozman, 1995), the effects of anger and anxiety on sexual desire were investigated in normal males and females. Although both genders responded negatively to the effects of induced anger and anxiety, female subjects showed greater reductions in sexual desire in the presence of these opposing, possibly intrusive emotions. This was especially noticeable in the anger manipulation condition (Beck & Bozman, 1995), in which audiotapes of sexually coercive situations were used to induce anger prior to presentation of an erotic stimulus. Results were interpreted as supporting Kaplan's (1979) clinical formulation of hypoactive desire as primarily due to the overriding effects of psychological conflict or inhibition.

Among clinical samples, a history of depression appears to be a major concomitant of hypoactive sexual desire. In one study (Schreiner-Engel & Schiavi, 1986), lifetime prevalence of affective disorder was examined in male and female patients with HSDD, compared to age-matched controls. Increased rates of depression were noted in both male and female patients, as 73% of HSDD males met criteria for lifetime histories of affective disorder in contrast to only 32% of the controls. Similar rates of depression were found among female HSDD patients, 71% of whom had a lifetime diagnosis of affective disorder, compared to only 27% of control women. Other authors have reported higher rates of depression in female compared to male patients with low desire, even taking into account base-rate differences in prevalence of depression (Donahey & Carroll, 1993). Female patients in this study were also found to have increased levels of anxiety, hostility, interpersonal sensitivity, and obsessive-compulsiveness. Additionally, female patients reported significantly higher levels of daily stress than their male counterparts.

Other concomitants of HSDD include a history of sexual trauma or abuse (Becker, 1989; Becker, Skinner, Abel, & Cichon, 1986), and marital or relationship distress (Rosen & Leiblum, 1989; Verhulst & Heiman, 1988). Survivors of sexual abuse have been found to have a high incidence of sexual dysfunction generally, including hypoactive desire. According to one large retrospective study of sexual assault survivors (Becker et al., 1986), approximately 85% had subsequent sexual arousal or desire difficulties. For some survivors, sexual contact under any circumstances can reactivate images or memories of the sexual assault, leading to subsequent avoidance of physical intimacy and low sexual desire (Wincze & Carey, 1991).

Case Vignette

Susan P. is a 48-year-old woman presenting for treatment with a lifelong history of low desire. Frequency of sexual contact with her spouse of 17 years had declined markedly in recent years. Psychosexual history revealed that the patient had been sexually molested by her maternal uncle for a two-year period, between the ages of 8 and 10. Although she had confided in her parents, they failed to protect her from further contact with the perpetrator. As a result, she felt betrayed and abandoned by her parents, and experienced consistent difficulty in trusting men and in abandoning herself to any form of sexual or sensual gratification. She had not previously disclosed her abuse to her husband and was surprised at the extent of her recollections in therapy.

Relationship factors play a major role in the genesis or maintenance of both SAD and HSDD, particularly in cases of secondary or situational low desire. Specific relationship factors include lack of trust and intimacy, conflicts over power and control, and lack of physical attraction (Verhulst & Heiman, 1988). In a study comparing women seeking treatment for low desire with controls, Stuart, Hammond, and Pett (1987) found that women with HSDD reported more negative perception of their parents' attitudes about sex and demonstrations of affection, increased frequency of premarital sex, poorer marital adjustment, and diminished feelings of emotional closeness and romanticism toward their partners. In a similar study of married males with low desire (Apt, Hurlbert, & Powell, 1993), interpersonal dependency (i.e., emotional reliance on others) was inversely related to sexual desire levels. Other authors have found that relationship dissatisfaction is more likely to be reported by female patients than by their male counterparts with low desire (Trudel, Boulos, & Matte, 1993).

In summary, sexual desire disorders are a highly prevalent and etiologically diverse category of sexual problems in both males and females. Few conceptual models have been proposed, and there is a general lack of agreement concerning the definitional criteria for diagnosis or classification. Hormonal, psychological, and interpersonal factors have all been implicated as etiological determinants, although research findings to date have been sparse and contradictory. As noted by Bancroft (1989), "Of the various aspects of human sexual experience, sexual desire remains the most resistant to clinical or conceptual analysis" (p. 71).

Sexual Arousal Disorders

Disorders of arousal are characterized by the inability to achieve sufficient physiological or subjective arousal during sexual stimulation. In women, the disorder is referred to as female sexual arousal disorder (FSAD); in men, it is termed male erectile disorder (MED). Female sexual arousal disorder involves failure to attain or maintain an adequate lubrication-swelling response of the vagina and labia for the completion of sexual activity. Although intercourse may be performed, a lack of adequate lubrication frequently results in pain or vaginal irritation. In men, the failure to achieve or maintain erection typically makes intercourse difficult or impossible to complete. In addition to the lack of genital arousal, the diminished arousal must be associated with significant distress or interpersonal difficulty before the diagnosis can be made.

Case Vignette

John R. is a 54-year-old male executive. He has complained of increasing difficulty in achieving or sustaining erections for the past two years, resulting in a complete cessation of sexual activity with his wife for the past several months. History taking reveals that the problem developed during the course of a brief extramarital relationship, of which the patient claims his wife was unaware. Additionally, Mr. R. has been a habitual smoker since his late teens, and consumes two to three alcoholic drinks per day. According to his wife's report, he appeared distracted and irritable during the few occasions recently on which they attempted to have sex. She is also concerned about his frequent bouts of depression and insomnia in recent months.

Although sexual arousal disorders are common in both sexes, males characteristically respond with a greater degree of emotional distress (Zilbergeld, 1992). Possible reasons for this disparity:

1. Erectile failure in men almost invariably leads to an inability to perform sexually, whereas women are more able to compensate, at times with artificial lubricants, for lubrication or arousal difficulties.
2. The term *impotence* is still widely used for male erectile dysfunction, and this term has highly pejorative connotations for most men. Men with the disorder often view themselves as less competent or masculine than other (sexually functional) men, and may compound the problem by withdrawing from other forms of social or sexual interaction (Rosen, Leiblum & Spector, 1994).
3. Since it is possible for women to engage in conventional intercourse without becoming fully lubricated or aroused, arousal difficulties in a woman may be less obvious to her partner or herself. However, either of these problems, if left unaddressed, can lead to significant relationship distress (Leiblum & Rosen, 1992).

Prevalence The reported prevalence of FSAD varies greatly, depending upon the definition of the disorder and type of sample studied (Spector & Carey, 1990). Many women with excitement-phase dysfunctions also have orgasmic difficulties or hypoactive desire, which may result in an underestimate of prevalence in most studies. In one recent study of women attending an outpatient gynecology clinic (Rosen et al., 1993), detailed questions were asked of respondents regarding all phases of the sexual response cycle. Results indicated that 13.6% of women complained of lack of lubrication during most or all sexual activity, while 23.3% had occasional difficulty with lubrication. Among the postmenopausal women in this study, 44.2% reported usually or always having difficulty in lubrication. In an earlier study of "happily married couples," approximately one third of the women reported frequent difficulties in achieving or maintaining adequate excitement during intercourse (Frank, Anderson, & Rubenstein, 1978).

Erectile difficulties in men are believed to be highly prevalent, affecting about 20 to 30 million men in the United States (NIH Consensus Panel, 1993). The frequency of erectile dysfunction increases sharply with age, as shown by data from the recent Massachusetts Male Aging Study (Feldman et al., 1994). In this population-based survey of men aged 40–70 years, the overall incidence of erectile difficulties was 52%, with approximately three times as many men in the older age group reporting moderate to severe erectile dysfunction. Erectile dysfunction is also the most prevalent sexual disorder in males seeking treatment in sexual dysfunction clinics in the United States and abroad (Hawton, 1982; Rosen & Leiblum, 1992), and it may occur in the absence or presence of normal sexual desire (Bancroft, 1989). Although most studies have focused on married couples, erectile difficulties are also common among single and gay men (Paff, 1985; Reynolds, 1991).

Etiological Determinants Both biological and psychosocial factors have been implicated in the etiology of sexual arousal disorders. Among well-known historical examples of men with erectile dysfunction due to medical causes, Louis XVI of France is said to have been unable to consummate his marriage to Marie Antoinette for many years due to "total impotence" (Hastings, 1963). His problem was subsequently traced to an excessively tight foreskin (phimosis), which was surgically corrected with circumcision. In the 19th century, Napolean Bonaparte was reported to have suffered from erectile dysfunction due to an unidentified hormone disorder (Johnson, 1968). Recently, a wide variety of vascular, hormonal, and neurological causes for erectile dysfunction have been identified (Feldman et al., 1994; Krane, Goldstein, & Saenz de Tejada, 1989).

Hormonal factors have been examined in several studies of male and female arousal disorders. Although once thought to be a leading cause of

MED, hormonal deficiencies are now seen as responsible for only a minority of cases (Jones, 1985; Davidson & Rosen, 1992). In fact, findings from several studes indicate that men with low testosterone are able to achieve adequate erections in response to external stimulation (Davidson, Camargo, Smith, & Kwan, 1983), though they may have decreased spontaneous or nocturnal erections (Bancroft & Wu, 1983). In contrast, vaginal lubrication appears to be fully dependent on estrogen (Utian, 1975), although studies in women have not specifically assessed spontaneous versus stimulation-based arousal.

Systemic illnesses, such as diabetes and cardiovascular disease, are also commonly associated with arousal difficulties in both sexes (Schover & Jensen, 1988; Feldman et al., 1994). Prescription drugs, particularly antihypertensives and psychotropic medications, are frequently associated with diminished arousal (Weiner & Rosen, 1997), and smoking and alcohol consumption are additional factors in many studies. Diseases of the small vessels supplying blood to the genital area can adversely affect sexual arousal (Lue, Hriack, Schmidt, & Tanagho, 1986), and spinal cord injuries have been associated with arousal disorders in both sexes (Sipski, 1997; Higgins, 1979). Finally, prostate surgery is a frequent cause of erectile dysfunction in men (Madorsky, Ashamalla, Schussler, Lyons, & Miller, 1976).

Psychosocial determinants of arousal disorders are traditionally divided into immediate and remote causes (Kaplan, 1974). Immediate causes include performance anxiety, or fear of failure, lack of adequate stimulation, and relationship conflicts. Performance anxiety has been especially emphasized as a leading cause of male erectile disorder (Rosen & Leiblum, 1992; Zilbergeld, 1992). As described first by Masters and Johnson (1970), performance anxiety includes the adoption of a "spectator role," in which the individual's attention is focused predominantly on sexual performance and away from erotic stimulation. This distraction from sexually arousing cues was viewed by Masters and Johnson (1970) as central to arousal difficulties in both sexes and formed the basis of their "sensate focus" approach to treatment. Among the remote or early developmental causes of arousal disorders, most authors have emphasized the role of childhood sexual trauma, sexual identity concerns, unresolved parental attachments, and religious orthodoxy (Masters & Johnson, 1970; Kaplan, 1974).

The specific role of cognitive or attentional factors has recently been explored in laboratory studies of sexual arousal (Ackerman & Carey, 1995; Cranston-Cuebas & Barlow, 1990). For example, several studies have shown that increasing the intensity of distracting stimuli presented in conjunction with erotic stimulation markedly attenuates sexual arousal (Adams, Haynes, & Brayer, 1985; Geer & Fuhr, 1975). Furthermore, the effects of anxiety on sexual arousal in men have been shown to be mediated largely by the effects of cognitive factors (Barlow, Sakheim, & Beck, 1983; Beck, Barlow, Sakheim, & Abramson, 1987; Cranston-Cuebas & Barlow, 1990). Similar findings have been reported in recent studies of female arousal disorder (Laan, Everaerd, van Aanhold, & Rebel, 1993; Palace & Gorzalka, 1990, 1992). Interestingly, in these latter studies, women were found to be less susceptible than men to the distracting effects of anxiety or sexual performance demands on sexual arousal (Palace & Gorzalka, 1992). Overall, studies in this area suggest that alterations in perceptual and attentional processes that occur during anxiety can contribute to the initiation or perpetuation of sexual arousal difficulties (Barlow, 1986; Cohen, Rosen, & Goldstein, 1985).

Other psychological or interpersonal factors have been associated with sexual arousal disorders. For example, depressed mood has been shown to reduce both subjective and physiological sexual arousal (Meisler & Carey, 1991; Mitchell et al., 1992), and has been shown to be characteristic of a subtype of men with MED (Sbrocco, Weiner, & Barlow, 1992; Sbrocco et al., 1994). Negative body image has also been associated with reduced sexual arousal (Weiner, Brown, & Barlow, 1993). In women, a past history of sexual abuse has frequently been reported in patients with FSAD (Becker, 1989; Becker et al., 1986), and relationship conflicts have been implicated in many cases of male and female arousal disorders (Hawton, Catalan, & Fagg, 1992; Leiblum & Rosen, 1991). Communication difficulties, lack of intimacy or trust, and power conflicts have been emphasized as frequent concomitants of arousal difficulties in both sexes. In one recent study, couples' ratings of their ability to communicate effectively with one another was the single best predictor of treatment outcome for MED (Hawton et al., 1992).

Modern perspectives take a systemic approach that considers both physiological and psychological processes. Bancroft's (1989) Psychosomatic Circle of Sex model emphasizes an interactive relationship between physical and psychological components. Physical factors such as acute physical illness may cause an initial episode of diminished sexual arousal that triggers worry and expectations of failure during subsequent sexual encounters. If the worry and interference are sufficiently strong, persistent arousal problems result. This formulation also predicts that individuals with mild physiological vulnerability (e.g., minor blockage of the vascular system supplying the penis) are at greater risk for moderate to severe dysfunction when their cognitive reaction to the problem involves a high degree of worry or catastrophizing.

Orgasmic Disorders

Orgasmic disorders include difficulties with the third phase of the sexual response cycle. Male orgasmic disorder (MOD) and female orgasmic disorder (FOD) both refer to a persistent or recurrent difficulty in achieving orgasm, despite adequate stimulation. Some individuals are orgasmic with masturbation or sexual foreplay with a partner, but are unable to reach orgasm during intercourse. This disorder is referred to as situational or secondary orgasmic dysfunction (Masters & Johnson, 1970). Other individuals are unable to achieve orgasm through any means of stimulation, which is termed primary anorgasmia and is more prevalent in women that men (Laumann et al., 1994; Spector & Carey, 1990). In men, the occurrence of rapid and uncontrolled ejaculation is referred to as premature ejaculation (PE). Despite the frequency and importance of this disorder in men, there is no corresponding diagnosis in women.

Female Orgasmic Disorder The definition of orgasmic dysfunction in women is highly controversial, given the wide variability in type and intensity of stimulation required to achieve orgasm in women (Hite, 1975; Laumann et al., 1994). In the absence of reliable norms, the diagnosis is usually based on subjective or clinical criteria. According to *DSM-IV*, female orgasmic disorder is classified as either lifelong or acquired, which corresponds loosely to the categories of primary and secondary anorgasmia, as proposed by Masters and Johnson (1970). According to this distinction, women with primary or lifelong FOD have never succeeded in achieving orgasm through any means of stimulation, including masturbation or sex with a partner.

Anorgasmia is generally regarded as the most frequent sexual dysfunction in women (Heiman & Grafton-Becker, 1989; Spector & Carey, 1990). Among sex therapy clinic samples, the rate of anorgasmia in women has ranged from 24% (Hawton, 1982) to 37% (Renshaw, 1988). Similarly high rates have been reported in nonclinical samples (Laumann et al., 1994; Levine & Yost, 1976; Rosen, Taylor, Leiblum, & Bachmann, 1993). In the latter study, 15.4% of premenopausal and 34.7% of postmenopausal women reported usually or always having difficulty in reaching orgasm during sexual stimulation. Interestingly, the incidence of anorgasmia in the general population appears to be much higher in single, compared to married or cohabiting, women (Laumann et al., 1994). Orgasmic ability has also been associated with sexual assertiveness (Hurlbert, 1991) and comfort with masturbation (Kelley, Strassberg, & Kircher, 1990). In contrast, no relationship has been observed between anorgasmia and race, socioeconomic status, and educational or religious background (Heiman & Grafton-Becker, 1989; Laumann et al., 1994). Moreover, no consistent relationship has been observed between relationship factors and the presence or absence of anorgasmia.

The high prevalence of anorgasmia in women, particularly primary orgasmic dysfunction, has been the subject of much speculation and controversy. Wakefield (1987), for example, has argued that lack of experience with masturbation and inadequate partner stimulation are the major factors underlying the disorder. This author further suggests that the "lack of attainment" criterion in the original Masters and Johnson's (1970) definition of primary anorgasmia has led to serious overdiagnosis of the disorder. In contrast, Morokoff (1989) has emphasized the frequent absence of subjective arousal associated with primary anorgasmia, which suggests that many women with this disorder should be diagnosed with female arousal disorder. The occurrence of intercourse, it is argued, is not sufficient evidence of sexual arousal: "This assumption is based on the erroneous belief that women have intercourse because they are sexually aroused and would not if they were not sexually aroused. However, many women were raised with the belief that a good wife should satisfy her husband, and many have attempted to oblige in the absence of much sexual arousal. Thus, capacity for intercourse, although a good measure of erection in men, is not a good measure of sexual arousal in women" (p. 73).

Relationship and psychological distress factors have been associated with secondary orgasmic dysfunction in women. In one comparison of women with lifelong compared to secondary orgasmic disorder (McGovern, Stewart, & LoPiccolo, 1975), those with secondary anorgasmia were less satisfied with their marital relationships, and reported more rigid and constrained masturbatory practices. Other researchers have found that women with situational or acquired orgasmic dysfunction are more likely than women with generalized or lifelong FOD to have co-occurring psychiatric disorders (Kaplan, 1992). These findings are consistent with the treatment literature indicating poorer outcome in the treatment of secondary compared to primary orgasmic dysfunction (Heiman & Grafton-Becker, 1989; McCabe & Delaney, 1992).

Male Orgasmic Disorder The cardinal feature of male orgasmic disorder is difficulty achieving orgasm following a normal sexual excitement phase. The disorder is relatively rare, occurring in approximately 3 to 8% of clinical samples (Hawton, 1982; Renshaw, 1988; Spector & Carey, 1990). A higher prevalence rate (10–15%) has been reported among homosexual males (Wilensky & Myers, 1987). Delayed or absent ejaculation may be associated with a variety of medical or surgical conditions (e.g., multiple sclerosis, spinal cord injury, surgical prostatecomy), or the use of anti-adrenergic or neuroleptic medications (Rosen, 1991; Segraves, 1989). Psychological and interpersonal factors have been implicated in the development of the disorder, including performance anxiety, conditioning factors, fear of impregnation, and lack of desire or arousal (Apfelbaum, 1989; Dow, 1981; Shull & Sprenkle, 1980; Zgourides & Warren, 1990). However, relatively few studies have systematically examined the relationship between these factors and MOD.

Premature Ejaculation Prevalence data from nonclinical samples indicate that approximately 25–40% of adult males have difficulties with early ejaculation at some time (Spector & Carey, 1990; St. Lawrence & Madakasira, 1992). In their early study of "happily married couples," Frank et al. (1978) found that 36% of males reported difficulty controlling ejaculation or ejaculating too rapidly on most occasions. Similar findings were reported in the National Health and Social Life Survey (Laumann, Gagnon, Michael, & Michaels, 1994) and in a recent study of male medical students (Leiblum, Rosen, Platt, Cross, & Black, 1993). Other surveys have reported that as many as 60% of males have intermittent concerns about rapid ejaculation (Reading & Wiest, 1984). Although there is some evidence of a decline in the number of cases of premature ejaculation (PE) presenting for sexual dysfunction treatment (Spector & Carey, 1990), it continues to be a highly prevalent and potentially disruptive disorder.

A major difficulty in the past has been the lack of a clear-cut definition or diagnostic criteria for "early" ejaculation. Masters and Johnson (1970) initially defined the disorder in terms of the male's inability to delay ejaculation until his partner had been sexually satisfied on at least 50% of intercourse attempts. Other authors have emphasized the average duration of intercourse (Killmann & Auerbach, 1979) or number of thrusts following penetration. A third approach has been to emphasize the degree of voluntary control that the male has over ejaculation (Kaplan, 1974). The definition of PE offered in *DSM-IV* is intended to incorporate elements of each of these earlier definitions. In making the diagnosis, clinicians are expected to take into account contextual and historical factors, such as the patient's age, the novelty or intensity of sexual stimulation, and the time since last sexual activity. Again, in the absence of adequate norms, these considerations are likely to be highly subjective. Despite the difficulty in defining the disorder, the sexual functioning of individuals presenting for treatment for PE differs from control subjects in the following ways: (1) they self-report shorter latencies to ejaculation during sexual activity; and (2) they ejaculate more readily in response to standardized erotic stimulation in the laboratory (Rowland & Slob, 1995).

Several typologies of PE have been proposed. For example, Cooper, Cernovsky, and Colussi (1993) have distinguished between primary or lifelong premature ejaculation, and secondary or situational PE. In support of this distinction, these authors found that men with primary PE were generally younger, had higher levels of sexual anxiety, and had increased libido. In contrast, patients with secondary PE had a higher incidence of erectile dysfunction and other performance difficulties. It has also been suggested that men with primary PE have increased penile sensitivity (Fanciullacci, Colpi, Beretta, & Zanollo, 1988) or a decreased threshold for the bulbocavernosus reflex (Godpodinoff, 1989). These findings were disconfirmed, however, in a recent study of vibrotactile stimulation thresholds in men with PE versus controls (Rowland, Haensel, Blom, & Slob, 1993). Additionally, psychological factors and early conditioning have been emphasized by several authors (e.g., Kaplan, 1974; Masters & Johnson, 1970; St. Lawrence & Madakasira, 1992), although empirical support is again lacking.

Few medical or physiological factors have been implicated in the etiology of PE. PE in association with spinal cord injury at the T-12/L1 level has been reported in several cases (Kuhr, Heiman, Cardenas, Bradley & Berger, 1995), although the phenomenology associated with these cases differs from the typical presentation of PE. Similarly, patients in recovery from alcohol or substance abuse may also complain of severe PE (Rosen, 1991). Overall, with these exceptions, relatively few drugs or illnesses have been associated with PE in the clinical literature.

Sexual Pain Disorders

Dyspareunia, or pain associated with sexual intercourse, is highly prevalent in women but relatively rare in men (Bancroft, 1989; Lazarus, 1989; Steege, 1984). *DSM-IV* criteria indicate that pain may take place before, during, or after intercourse for the diagnosis to be made. In many cases, pain may result from lack of lubrication (Steege & Ling, 1993); however, *DSM* requires that the pain not be solely due to this problem for dyspareunia to be diagnosed. Difficulty in assessing adequate lubrication and the expected co-occurrence of arousal problems in women with sex-related pain limit the usefulness of this distinction (Meana & Binik, 1994). Although there are numerous physical factors that may play a role in dyspareunia, the relative contribution of psychological or interpersonal factors should not be underestimated (Leiblum, 1996).

Vaginismus, or involuntary spasms of the musculature of the outer third of the vagina, is the second major cause of penetration difficulties in women. The disorder is seen relatively frequently in sex therapy clinics, occurring in approximately 15 to 17% of women presenting for treatment (Hawton, 1982; Spector & Carey, 1990). The validity of the diagnostic distinction between vaginismus and dyspareunia has been challenged, since (1) it is difficult in most cases to assess whether it is the pain itself or vaginal contractions that prevent penetration, (2) all pain (including dyspareunic pain) can be accompanied by muscular contractions, and (3) the definition of what constitutes "involuntary" contractions is highly uncertain (Meana & Binik, 1994).

According to *DSM-IV*, a distinction is drawn between generalized vaginismus, which refers to involuntary vaginal spasms in all situations, and situational vaginismus, in which some penetration is possible (e.g., insertion of a tampon). Women with generalized vaginismus typically avoid gynecological examinations and tampon use, in addition to sexual intercourse. Vaginismus can occur in association with vaginal pain due to various medical conditions, although it is more frequently caused by psychological or interpersonal factors (Silverstein, 1989; Wincze & Carey, 1991).

Physiological Factors A wide variety of physical factors have been associated with dyspareunia in women (Black, 1988). These include hymenal scarring, pelvic inflammatory disease, and vulvar vestibulitis (Sandberg & Quevillion, 1987; Steege & Ling, 1993). In men, Peyronie's disease (i.e., an extreme bend in the penis), painful retraction of the foreskin (phimosis), and physical trauma to the genitalia have been associated with painful intercourse (Bancroft, 1989). However, dyspareunia is not a reliable symptom of any particular medical condition (Meana & Binik, 1994), and marked genital abnormalities have been observed in some instances without concomitant dyspareunia (Fordney, 1978). Moreover, anatomical or physiological factors that cause the original pain may not be the same factors responsible for maintaining it. Accordingly, some authors (e.g., Meana & Binik, 1994) have recommended a multidimensional model of physical and psychological determinants of dyspareunia.

Psychosocial Factors Most studies of psychological factors in dyspareunia have been confined to sexual pain problems in women. According to psychodynamic accounts, dyspareunia may be a conversion symptom symbolizing unconscious intrapsychic conflict, or the result of a general aversion to sexuality (Kaplan, 1974; Steege, 1984). Learning theorists have emphasized the role of negative expectations about sex in causing pain (Sotile & Kilmann, 1977). Interpersonal factors such as poor sexual technique and relationship conflicts have also been associated with the disorder (Huffman, 1983; Leiblum, 1996). Other associated factors include depression, religious orthodoxy, low self-esteem, poor body image, inadequate couple's communication, and a history of sexual trauma (Reamy & White, 1985; Wincze & Carey, 1991). Causal relationships between these factors and dyspareunia have yet to be demonstrated. Although elevated levels of psychopathology, notably depression, have been associated with dyspareunia (Beard, Reginald, & Wadsworth, 1988), this may be as much a result as a cause of the disorder.

Among the psychological factors often associated with vaginismus are negative psychosexual upbringing, sexual fears and phobias, and a history of sexual trauma or abuse (Becker et al., 1986; Leiblum, Pervin, & Campbell, 1989). Wincze and Carey (1991) describe a classical conditioning formulation of vaginismus, whereby pain experienced during initial intercourse leads to a self-protective tightening of vaginal musculature. This process may lead to reflexive muscle spasms that generalize to other sex-related stimuli. Subsequent avoidance of sexual activity serves to relieve sex-related anticipatory anxiety. It has also been suggested that specific negative cognitions (e.g., "penetration is difficult and can only be accomplished with great pain, and possibly injury") may play a prominent role in the initiation or maintenance of vaginismus (Leiblum et al., 1989).

In summary, sexual pain disorders are relatively common in women but occur infrequently in men. Dyspareunia is the only female sexual dysfunction in which organic factors have been shown to play a major role, and there is a need for integration of medical and psychological formulations. Vaginismus, on the other hand, is most often associated with psychological and interpersonal determinants. Both disorders are frequently associated with avoidance of sexual contact and marked interpersonal distress.

Paraphilias

Paraphilias (*para* = "beyond"; *philia* = "love") are sexual disorders characterized by persistent and intense fantasies or desires, usually for nonhuman objects; for sexual activities involving pain, dominance or submission; or for nonconsenting partners, such as young children. Diagnosis does not require exclusive dependency on paraphilic stimuli or activities; in some cases, sexual functioning in a nonparaphilic context is possible. However, it is necessary that the paraphilic fantasies, urges, or behaviors cause significant distress or disruption in aspects of the person's functioning, particularly in interpersonal relationships. The defining element of these disorders is the repetitive and persistent character of the sexual fantasies or urges, which may involve common elements with obsessive-compulsive disorders (Bradford, Boulet, & Pawlak, 1992; Stein et al., 1992). Accordingly, the paraphilias are sometimes referred to as disorders of sexual compulsivity or impulsivity (Kafka & Prentky, 1992). The paraphilias also typically interfere with interpersonal relationships or normal pair-bonding in varying degrees (Freund & Blanchard, 1986; Freund & Watson, 1993).

Prior to *DSM-III*, paraphilias were included in the category of personality disorders, as a subtype of the so-called sociopathic personality. Historically, paraphilias have also been referred to as sexual perversions or deviations, or as atypical sexual behavior. The influence of social or cultural factors in the labeling process is pervasive, as is the response of society to those labeled as sexual deviants. According to Simon (1994), "It is possible that at any one moment a society may contain a wide variety of forms of sexual perversion. Of these, a small number become a special focus of attention and these frequently provoke an intensity of response; their appearances are not merely sanctioned severely but their dangers advertised, and their actual, potential, and suspected practitioners are aggressively pursued" (p. 10). Masturbation and homosexuality, for example, were the predominant sexual perversions of the 18th and 19th centuries, which have been largely "normalized" through the findings of contemporary sex surveys (Kinsey, Pomeroy, & Martin, 1948; 1953; Laumann et al., 1994).

Paraphilias are frequently categorized as either victimless or as involving harm or victimization of a nonconsenting partner. Fetishism or transvestism are examples of the first type, whereas pedophilia or exhibitionism usually result in physical or psychological harm to the victim. From a legal standpoint, these latter paraphilias are also referred to as sex crimes, for which perpetrators are legally prosecuted in most instances. Certain sex crimes (e.g., rape, incest, sexual harrassment) are not categorized as paraphilias, although some authors have argued that compulsive rapists or incest offenders should be included in this category (e.g., Abel & Osborn, 1992). Individuals apprehended for a sex crime are typically labeled as sex offenders, and have been the focus of increasing scientific and public concern in recent years. Diagnosis and treatment of these individuals involves complex legal, ethical, and professional issues, as clinicians are required to balance the individual client's needs with the broader interests and concerns of society. In most states, for example, it is mandatory to report all known cases of child sexual abuse, whether past or present. Moreover, these reporting requirements supercede the normal code of client-therapist confidentiality.

Description of Paraphilias

According to *DSM-IV*, paraphilias are classified according to the type of activities or stimuli found to be sexually arousing. Eight specific paraphilias are listed: exhibitionism, fetishism, frotteurism, pedophilia, sexual masochism, sadism, transvestic fetishism, and voyeurism (see below). Additionally, the category of "paraphilia not otherwise specified" includes a wide range of other deviant behaviors. In the past, these disorders were considered to be discrete syndromes; that is, multiple paraphilic diagnoses in the same individual were thought to be rare (Gebhard, Gognon, Pomeroy, & Christensen, 1965). In fact, recent studies suggest that many if not most paraphilic individuals engage in multiple forms of sexually deviant behavior. Abel, Becker, Cunningham-Rathner, Mittelman, and Rouleau (1988) reported that less than 10% of patients had a single paraphilia. About 20% had two paraphilic diagnoses, another 32% had three to four diagnoses, and the remaining 38% had engaged in five or more concomitant paraphilic behaviors. Most exhibitionists in this study, for example, had engaged in voyeurism or frotteurism, and many showed interests in sadomasochistic behavior, transvestism, or pedophilia. Similarly high rates of multiple paraphilias have been reported in other studies (e.g., Kafka & Prentky, 1992; Bradford et al., 1992). These data support the concept of a generalized sexual compulsivity or impulsivity disorder that might lead the individual to engage in one or more deviant sexual acts at different times or in different situations (Kafka & Prentky, 1992).

Little is known about the epidemiology of the paraphilias, since few individuals with these disorders voluntarily disclose their interests. In fact, much of the prevalence data is derived from reports of victims (e.g., Finkelhor, 1986; Cox & McMahon, 1978). Approximately 20 to 25% of females in these studies report being sexually victimized prior to the age of 18, compared to 8 to 10% of males. In a study of British nurses (Gittelson, Eacott, & Mehta, 1978), 44% reported being a victim of exhibitionism at one time or another. From recent surveys of college students, it appears that young males frequently fantasize about sexually coercive or nonconsenting activities, and almost half have engaged in some form of sexual misconduct, including exhibitionism, voyeurism, frottage, or sexual contact with someone under the age of 14 (Briere & Runtz, 1989; Templeman & Stinnett, 1991). It is uncertain how many of these individuals would meet criteria for adult paraphilias.

In addition to the overall prevalence of these problems, evidence suggests that only a small fraction of paraphilic acts or incidents are ever reported. Abel and Osborn (1992) found that most patients in their sample admitted to high frequencies of paraphilic behavior, including a median of 50 incidents per patient for exhibitionists, and 11 per patient for incestuous pedophiles (see table 16.2). Similarly high rates of pedophilic behavior were reported by Bradford et al. (1992). It is not unusual for paraphilic individuals to commit several hundred paraphilic acts over the course of a lifetime. The age of onset in most cases is prior to age 18 (Abel & Rouleau, 1990).

Lastly, it should be noted that the paraphilias are predominantly, indeed almost exclusively, male disorders. Although some women engage in sadomasochistic or exhibitionistic activities (e.g., stripping), these behaviors seldom meet *DSM-IV* criteria for paraphilias. There is also evidence that a small percentage of children are sexually victimized by adult females (Finkelor, 1984). However, for reasons that are presently unclear, the vast majority of paraphilic individuals are male. Cultural, biological, and psychological explanations have all been proposed at one time or another (Bancroft, 1989; Money, 1994). Following a brief description of each of the major paraphilias as described in

Table 16.2 Median Number of Paraphilic Acts by Paraphilia

Paraphilia	Median # Paraphilic Acts
Pedophilia (incest type)	11.5
Pedophilia (nonincest type)	9.5
Exhibitionism	50.5
Voyeurism	16.5
Frottage	29.5
Fetishistic transvestism	25.0
Fetishism	3.3
Masochism	36.0
Sadism	3.0
Public masturbation	50.0
Telephone scatalogia (obscene phone calls)	30.0

SOURCE: Adapted from Abel & Osborn (1992).

DSM-IV, we will consider several etiological theories for these disorders.

Exhibitionism This disorder involves the recurrent urge for exposure of the genitals to strangers or unsuspecting persons. Some exhibitionists masturbate while exposing themselves or while fantasizing about exposing themselves. Sexual arousal preceding exposure may also be accompanied by a strong sense of restlessness or anxiety, which, according to reports of some exhibitionists, causes them to become oblivious to the social and legal consequences of their behavior (Stevenson & Jones, 1972). The victim's reaction may be important, as many exhibitionists report arousal in response to shock, fear, or embarrassment in the victim. Although exhibitionists have traditionally been viewed as inhibited and relatively "harmless" (Tollison & Adams, 1979), recent evidence suggests that a significant proportion of these individuals also engage in acts of sexual aggression, including rape (Abel et al., 1988). Other reports have noted subtypes of exhibitionists who have antisocial personality traits (Forgac & Michaels, 1982), or heterosocial deficits (Gebhard et al., 1965). These studies suggest that exhibitionism may be associated with a greater degree of psychopathology than originally thought.

The average age of conviction for exhibitionists is approximately 30 years, although onset of the disorder usually occurs before age 18 (Evans, 1970; Abel & Rouleau, 1990). Few arrests for exhibitionism are made past the age of 40, suggesting a possible decline in frequency for older age groups. This decline in frequency may correspond with a general "burning out" of impulsiveness that takes place with age.Exhibitionists are almost exclusively male, and about one-third have never married (Gebhard et al., 1965). Those who are married tend to have unsatisfactory interpersonal relationships (Mohr, Turner, & Jerry, 1964). The overall incidence of exhibition is difficult to estimate since most cases are not reported to legal authorities and do not seek treatment. However, from case reports, it appears to be among the most common sexual offenses (Tollison & Adams, 1979; Abel et al., 1988).

Fetishism This paraphilia involves erotic attraction to nonliving objects, such as women's undergarments or shoes. Fetishes particular to certain materials, such as rubber or fur, are also relatively common (Bancroft, 1989; Chalkley & Powell, 1983). Sexual arousal associated with objects designed for genital stimulation (e.g., an electrical vibrator) is not considered a fetish, despite the dependence of some women on vibrator stimulation for adequate sexual arousal (Devor, 1996). If this dependence causes significant distress, a diagnosis of paraphilia not otherwise specified might be considered. Since fetishistic behavior is unlikely to be reported and often goes untreated, its prevalence is unknown. Fetishes usually begin early in life and, once established, tend to be chronic or lifelong (Coleman, 1972).

The behavioral manifestations of fetishes are widely varied (Tollison & Adams, 1979). Some fetishists masturbate with their preferred object, while others prefer their sexual partners to wear or otherwise incorporate the object into sexual interactions. Some fetishists are unable to become sexually aroused without the presence of the paraphilic object (Wincze, 1989). At times, the object of the fetish is stolen or collected by the individual (Coleman, 1972). "Partial fetishism" refers to the reliance on items of clothing or other nonliving objects for stimulating arousal (Chesser, 1971), in contrast to "complete fetishism," which requires the use of the fetish object to induce orgasm. *DSM-IV* diagnostic criteria do not require complete fetishism, as fantasies or urges, without actual behavior, are sufficient for the diagnosis.

Partialism is a form of fetishistic behavior involving intense erotic attraction to specific parts of the body (e.g., feet, thighs or buttocks). According to Bancroft (1989), this is distinguished from normal erotic attraction to specific body parts by its tendency to override sexual interest in the partner or the partner's body as a whole. Partialism is listed under paraphilias not otherwise specified in *DSM-IV*, which includes other disorders sometimes referred to as fetishes.

Frotteurism This disorder is characterized by the individual's touching or rubbing his genitals against the leg, buttocks, or other body parts of an unsuspecting person. The behavior usually occurs in crowded situations, such as on a bus or subway, and is often undetected by the victim. Frotteurism typically begins during adolescence and declines in frequency after age 25 (Abel & Osborn, 1992). It may be associated with a withdrawn, immature or socially avoidant personality style. As with many paraphilias, the prevalence is largely unknown.

Pedophilia This diagnosis is used to describe adults for whom prepubescent children are the focus of erotic attraction and interest. The specification of ages for the offender and the victim is highly controversial. According to *DSM-IV*, the offender must be at least 16 years of age and at least five years older than the victim, who must be "generally age 13 years or younger" (p. 528). However, as several authors have noted, it may not be meaningful to diagnose as pedophilic an 18-year-old male who engages in sexual activity with a willing, physically mature 13-year-old partner. It is also commonplace in some societies for 13-year-old girls to be betrothed to higher status males, who are frequently much older (Rosen & Hall, 1984). Clearly, cultural and individual circumstances need to be taken into account in making the diagnosis.

Several subtypes of pedophilia have been proposed. Pedophiles may be exclusively attracted to children of one sex or the other, or to both sexes. Although the majority of individuals with pedophilia are attracted to female children, those who target male victims typically engage in a higher frequency of pedophilic acts (Abel & Rouleau, 1990). While some pedophilic contacts involve physical injury to the child, others do not (Knight & Prentky, 1990). Relationship to the victim also varies, as some pedophiles are attracted only to members of their own family (incest type), while others prefer children outside of the immediate family (nonincest type). According to one study, about 12% of paraphilic men engage exclusively in incestuous pedophilic behavior (Abel & Rouleau, 1990). The type of sexual activity engaged in (e.g., penetrative vs. nonpenetrative sex) also varies widely from one offender to another. Finally, several personality subtypes have been proposed (e.g., Groth, Hobson & Gary, 1982; Knight & Prentky, 1990). Pedophiles have been classified as regressive or fixated, for example, depending upon the degree of adult sexual development or compulsivity and repetitiveness of the pedophilic behavior (Knight & Prentky, 1990).

From the results of programatic research, Knight and Prentky (1990) developed a taxonomic model for classification of pedophiles and rapists. Within this model, primary motivation for pedophilic behavior is a major dimension for classification. The motivational types that were derived through factor analysis included: (1) opportunistic, for whom the sexual assault appeared to be impulsive and unplanned; (2) pervasively angry, who appear to be motivated by undifferentiaed rage; and (3) sexual, who are motivated primarily by sexual or sadistic fantasies or preoccupations. In all, the model identified nine types of sexual offenders, highlighting the enormous variation in behavior and motivation within this diagnostic group.

Demographic and background characteristics of pedophiles have been reported in several studies, although results should be viewed cautiously due to selection and reporting biases. One early study noted three distinct age groupings among pedophiles: adolescents, middle-aged men, and elderly offenders (Mohr et al., 1964). These investigators also reported that individuals with pedophilia do not differ from the general population in terms of occupation, race, religion, or marital status, but do report severe marital discord with greater frequency. Abel and Rouleau (1990) reported similar results over two decades later. In addition, these authors noted that about half of the nonincestuous pedophiles in their sample had acquired their sexual interests in children prior to age 18. Controversy exists regarding the psychiatric characteristics of the pedophile. Contrary to prior belief, most individuals with pedophilia are not psychotic or mentally retarded, although many have personality disturbances (Gebhard et al., 1965; Lang, Langevin, Checkly, & Pugh, 1987). As with the other paraphilias, little is known about the true incidence of pedophilia.

Sexual Sadism and Masochism These paraphilias involve sexual excitement in response to the infliction of psychological and physical suffering (sadism), or in response to being humiliated or made to suffer (masochism). Many sadists are able to become aroused in the masochistic role, or vice versa, although some individuals are exclusively one or the other (Spengler, 1977). Sadomasochistic behaviors include beating, restraint, blindfolding, body piercing, and humiliating acts such as forcing the person to crawl or to wear infantile clothing. Autoerotic asphyxiation is an extreme form of masochistic behavior in which intensity of orgasm is heightened by hypoxia, or loss of oxygen to the brain (Friedrich & Gerber, 1994). Hypoxia is usually induced by placing a noose or plastic bag over the head; in some cases, this leads to accidental death (Cesnick & Coleman, 1989; Uva, 1995). Infliction of mild pain (e.g., "love bites," digging fingernails into the back during intercourse) during sexual activity is not uncommon in either sex, but interest in more extreme sadomasochistic acts is usually attributed to males (Bancroft, 1989; Spengler, 1977). Based upon a survey study of subscribers to magazines that specialize in sadomasochistic activities, however, 28% of respondents were found to be female, indicating that unlike other paraphilias, a substantial portion of sadists and masochists are women (Breslow, Evans, & Langley, 1985). Sadomasochistic interest usually develops after the age of 20. As with other paraphilias, the true incidence is difficult to assess due to reluctance to disclose information about such behaviors, even within sadomasochistic clubs (Spengler, 1977).

Transvestic Fetishism This diagnosis applies to heterosexual men for whom dressing in women's clothing is found to be sexually arousing. While cross-dressed, the male typically masturbates while fantasizing about being both a male and the female object of his sexual fantasy. The term autogynephilia refers to the capacity these men have to be sexually aroused by the thought or image of themselves as female (Blanchard, 1989). The diagnosis is not made when cross-dressing occurs exclusively during the course of a gender identity disorder (see next section). Exclusively homosexual men who cross-dress for other reasons are also excluded from the diagnosis, since the motivation for cross-dressing in homosexuals is not typically sexual in nature (Blanchard, 1993). Some homosexual men cross-dress for entertainment (i.e., "camping"), while homosexual prostitutes sometimes cross-dress as a means of attracting heterosexual (i.e., "straight") clients. *DSM-IV* also excludes cross-dressing females from the diagnosis of transvestic fetishism for similar reasons.

The range of behavior associated with transvestic fetishism varies from wearing of a single female undergarment beneath typical masculine attire to dressing up entirely as a woman, sometimes with makeup. Although usually heterosexual in orientation, the male with transvestic fetishism usually has few sexual partners and may engage in homosexual behavior on occasion. Most transvestic fetishists are currently or previously married, about one fifth have appeared in public cross-dressed, and more than half are extremely secretive about their cross-dressing behavior (Prince & Bentler, 1972). The incidence is unknown, as most men with transvestic fetishism do not seek treatment or come into contact with mental health or legal authorities.

Voyeurism Paraphilic voyeurism involves the observation of an unsuspecting person or persons who are nude, disrobing, or engaging in a sexual act. It is also referred to as scopophilia or scoptophilia. An essential feature is the lack of awareness in the victim of being observed, in contrast to consensual forms of voyeurism, such as occurs in sex clubs and X-rated movies. As with most paraphilias, voyeurism is typically associated with multiple paraphilias (Abel & Rouleau, 1990). Earlier research had identified a subtype of pathological voyeurs who are sadistic and aggressive, and may commit other crimes including assault and rape (Yalom, 1960; Gebhard et al., 1965). On the basis of research conducted with convicted offenders, the average individual with voyeurism has little sexual experience, is lacking in heterosocial skills, and has strong feelings of inferiority (Gebhard et al., 1965). Some individuals with voyeurism masturbate during the offense, while others masturbate afterwards while conjuring up memories of the scene. Many have performance difficulties during intercourse with a partner.

Paraphilias Not Otherwise Specified Other types of paraphilias not falling into any of the previous categories are classified under this diagnosis in *DSM-IV*. Generally, little is known about these disorders. They include, with their associated paraphilic stimuli in parentheses, telephone scatalogia (obscene telephone calling), necrophilia (corpses), zoophilia (animals), coprophilia (feces), klismaphilia (enemas), and urophilia (urine). The incidence of these various disorders is unknown, and it is uncertain to what degree they are associated with significant psychopathology in the individuals concerned.

Etiological and Developmental Factors

A wide range of etiological factors have been implicated in the development of the paraphilias. Historically, sexual deviations were attributed to excessive masturbation or nervous system diseases (Krafft-Ebing, 1965). More recently, the role of early sexual trauma, imprinting or conditioning effects, maternal deprivation, and several biological factors have been proposed (Langevin, 1992; Kaplan, 1996). In this section, we review briefly the evidence and arguments for each of these positions.

Conditioning and Social Learning There is general agreement that conditioning factors play an important role in the development and maintenance of deviant sexual arousal (Bancroft, 1989; Abel & Osborn, 1992). In an early British study, McGuire, Carlisle, and Young (1965) reviewed case records from patients with mixed paraphilias and concluded that fantasy rehearsal during masturbation played a key role in the conditioning of deviant arousal in every case. Although early sexual abuse and trauma were also frequently reported, the effects of these experiences were strongly reinforced by fantasy rehearsal during masturbation. Other studies have shown classical conditioning of deviant arousal in normal volunteers (Rachman, 1966; Rachman & Hodgson, 1968). Similarly, Quinn, Harbison, and McAllister (1970) demonstrated operant conditioning of deviant arousal using a positive reinforcement paradigm.

Imprinting, has also been implicated in many cases. There may be a critical period, perhaps about the time of puberty, during which sexual stimuli are especially salient. As noted in one recent account: "Early sexually arousing experiences have an enormous influence in shaping subsequent sexual desires and fantasies. First erotic experiences seem to imprint or program the person's 'love map,' sometimes to the exclusion of any other subsequent input" (Kaplan, 1996, pp. 35–36). The effects of early imprinting are then maintained and reinforced through fantasy arousal during masturbation (Laws & Marshall, 1990).

Sexual abuse or trauma experiences are commonly reported by paraphilic individuals. However, it is unknown whether paraphilic individuals are more likely than the general population to have abusive or traumatic histories. The mechanisms by which these early traumas lead to the development of subsequent paraphilic behavior are not clear. The phrase "eroticization of childhood trauma" has been used by psychoanalytic writers to describe the process by which the abused child gains mastery or control over a painful memory through fantasy rehearsal and masturbation (Money, 1980; Stoller, 1975a). From this perspective, paraphilias are viewed as a type of defense mechanism, which allows the child to reexperience the memory of sexual trauma in a context which permits control and mastery.

Pair-Bonding and Courtship Disturbances Beyond their attraction to deviant sexual stimuli, most paraphilic individuals exhibit deficits in interpersonal or sexual relationships, particularly with a primary partner. From this perspective, the paraphilias have been conceptualized as a form of courtship disorder, in which an intensification or distortion occurs in one phase of the usual courtship sequence (Freund & Watson, 1990, 1993). According to this theory, sexual interaction normally involves the following sequence: (1) location and first appraisal of a suitable partner; (2) pretactile interaction, including looking at and talking to a prospective partner; (3) tactile interaction; and (4) genital union. In the paraphilic individual, sexual behavior is fixated on one of these phases, often to the exclusion of the others. Voyeurism is seen as a distorted version of partner location; exhibitionism reflects a disorder of pretactile interaction; frotteurism is a distortion of tactile interaction; and preferential rape pattern is regarded as a distortion of the phase of genital union. Within this model, early sexual trauma is viewed as etiologically important in determining the type and degree of courtship disturbance (Freund & Watson, 1990). One weakness of this model is its failure to account for certain paraphilic behaviors such as autoerotic asphyxiation.

Personality Factors and Psychopathology Personality factors and comorbid psychopathology have been investigated in several studies of paraphilic patients. From a traditional psychoanalytic perspective, these individuals are seen as suffering from extreme castration or mutilation anxiety, and the paraphilic behavior is seen as a defense against this unconscious castration anxiety (Blair & Lanyon, 1981). For example, the exhibitionist relies on the shocked reaction of his victim to reassure himself that he is not castrated. Others have emphasized the impulsive or obsessional traits found in many paraphiliacs (Kafka & Prentky, 1992, 1994; Stein et al., 1992). Additionally, the terms nonparaphilic sexual addictions and erotomania (Kaplan, 1996) have been applied to individuals with intense and uncontrollable urges for culturally sanctioned forms of sexual behavior.

Is there a specific personality type associated with each of the paraphilias? In one recent study, personality assessments were conducted in a sample of transvestic fetishists compared to other paraphilias (Wise, Fagan, Schmidt, Ponticas, & Costa, 1991). Although both groups of paraphilic patients scored high on the NEO-PI neuroticism scale and impulsiveness subscale compared to nonparaphilic controls, few significant differences were observed between the different paraphilic groups. Not surprisingly, transvestites scored higher on the role identity confusion scale. Similar findings have been reported in other studies (Wilson & Gosselin, 1980; Buhrich, 1981).

High rates of concomitant psychopathology, particularly mood, anxiety, and substance-abuse disorders, have been observed in paraphilic men (Kafka & Prentky, 1994). As shown in table 16.3 below, approximately two thirds of paraphilic patients in this study were diagnosed with mood disorders, about 50% with anxiety disorders, and about 50% with alcohol or substance-abuse problems. Despite the strong association, the causal relationship between paraphilias and comorbid psychopathology is unclear. Mood disorders are especially prevalent in pedophiles and compulsive rapists (McKibben, Proulx, & Lusignan, 1994). The role of negative affect has been emphasized as a potential trigger, stimulus antecedent, or negative reinforcer in many cases of repetitive or compulsive paraphilias (Rosen & Fracher, 1983). In particular, the anxiety-reducing properties of paraphilic behaviors in these individuals may serve to reinforce these behaviors.

Table 16.3 Prevalence of Axis I Diagnoses in Paraphilic Men (N = 34)

Axis I Diagnosis (DSM-III-R)	N	%
Total # Axis I diagnoses	103	
No. Axis I diagnosis	3	8.8
Mood disorder, any	25	73.5
Major depression	14	41.2
Dysthymia	23	67.6
Bipolar	1	2.9
Anxiety disorder, any	16	47.1
Social phobia	7	20.6
Generalized anxiety	6	17.6
Obsessive-compulsive	4	11.8
Panic	4	11.8
Substance abuse, any	16	47.1
Alcohol	14	41.2
Marijuana	10	29.4
Cocaine	6	17.6
Opiates	2	5.9
Impulse disorder, NOS	6	17.6
Gambling	3	8.8
Pyromania	2	5.9
Kleptomania	2	5.9
Psychotic disorder	0	0

SOURCE: Adapted from Kafka & Prentky (1994).

Biological Factors Biological factors, such as abnormal hormone levels or brain function abnormalities, have been implicated in some studies. For example, Berlin (1983) reviewed medical data from a sample of men with paraphilias, primarily pedophilia. Some evidence of biological abnormality was found in each case, although the extent of the abnormality ranged from minor problems, such as dyslexia, to chromosomal disorders and significant cortical atrophy. Hormonal abnormalities, including elevated testosterone and lutenizing hormone levels, were present in approximately 50% of the patients studied. Other authors have reported a high incidence of neuropsychological abnormalities, particularly in left hemisphere function in pedophilic and sexually aggressive patients (Langevin, Bain, Ben-Aron, Coulthard, & Day, 1985; Scott, Cole, McKay, Golden, & Liggett, 1984).

Finally, a neurodevelopmental theory of paraphilias has been proposed by Money and Lamacz (1989). This theory is based on observations in nonhuman species of the essential role of forebrain and limbic structures in the processing of sexual stimuli. This complex neural circuit or program (the "lovemap") is hypothesized to be especially vulnerable to the influence of biological factors during critical periods of prenatal development. According to the authors, the more complex process of prenatal differentiation of the male fetus is associated with a higher proportion of psychosexual developmental errors, or "vandalized lovemaps." These lead, in turn, to a greater incidence of paraphilias among adult males compared to females. Despite its intuitive appeal, this theory is lacking in empirical support.

Gender Identity Disorders

Gender identity disorders are characterized by a chronic or persistent sense of distress with one's biological sex or the corresponding gender role. Individuals with gender identity disorder experience a lasting mismatch or incongruity between sex (biologically defined) and gender (psychologically defined). Although the terms *sex* and *gender* are often used interchangably, in this context their meanings are quite different. According to Stoller (1968), an early pioneer in gender identity research, *sex* is defined as the sum of overt anatomical and physiological differences between male and female. In contrast, *gender* is viewed as a strictly psychological phenomenon and refers to the sum of behavioral or psychological differences between the sexes. Further differentiation is made between *gender role*, which refers to the outward expression or manifestation of one's gender, and *gender identity*, which is defined as the subjective or inner identification as male or female. Whereas gender role may be highly variable from one context or situation to another, gender identity is usually firmly established by age 2, and is perhaps the most fundamental and enduring aspect of psychological identity (Money & Ehrhardt, 1972). Both terms need to be distinguished from *sexual orientation*, which refers to the individual's sexual (or romantic) partner preference (i.e., homosexual, heterosexual, bisexual).[1]

Diagnostic practices and the nosology of gender identity disorders have undergone significant changes in the past two decades. Gender identity diagnoses first appeared in *DSM-III*, along with sexual deviations or paraphilias, under the category of psychosexual disorders. In *DSM-III-R*, gender identity disorders were classified in the category of developmental disorders typically evident in infancy, childhood, or adolescence. This reflected the prevailing view at the time of these disorders representing a form of atypical or abnormal development. *DSM-III-R* also listed four specific types of gender identity disorder: (1) gender identity disorder of childhood; (2) transsexualism; (3) gender identity disorder of adolescence or adulthood, nontranssexual type; and (4) gender identity disorder not otherwise specified. Individuals with a persistent desire for sex-reassignment surgery or other sex change procedures were labeled as transsexuals, whereas those without the desire to undergo biological sex change were labeled as nontranssexuals.

In *DSM-IV*, gender identity disorders are now classified with the paraphilias and sexual dysfunctions in the category of sexual and gender identity disorders. The diagnostic criteria and coding differ depending upon the current age of the individual, although gender disturbances in children and adults are listed under a single diagnostic entity, viz., gender identity disorder (GID). This simplification reflects the current view that gender identity disorders in children and adults are attributable to similar mechanisms or developmental processes (Bradley et al., 1991). Specifically excluded from the diagnosis are physical intersex conditions (e.g., pseudohermaphroditism, Klinefelter's syndrome), which are included in a separate category of GID not otherwise specified.

The primary features of GID are: (1) a strong and persistent desire to be, or the insistence that one is, of the other sex; and (2) distress about one's assigned sex or a sense of inappropriateness in the gender role of that sex. Children with GID show a preoccupation with behaviors or activities traditionally associated with the other sex. For example, a boy with gender identity disorder may show a strong preference for dressing in girls' clothing and playing with dolls. Diminished activity levels and decreased frequency of rough-and-tumble play have also been consistently associated with gender problems in boys (Bates, Bentler, & Thompson, 1973, 1979). Girls with GID may refuse to urinate in a sitting position, to play with feminine toys, or they may show an aversion toward normative female clothing. Adults with gender identity disorder are typically preoccupied with a desire to live as a member of the other sex. This may include seeking hormonal or surgical manipulation to appear more like the other sex (i.e., transsexualism) or adopting the social role of the other sex ("passing").

The effort to resemble or pass as a member of the opposite sex frequently includes dressing in stereotypical clothing of the other sex. In contrast to transvestites, individuals with GID typically derive little or no sexual gratification from cross-dressing. GID adults usually seek out occupations, lifestyles, or recreational activities associated with the other sex, often expressing the belief that they have been "born in the wrong body." Although *DSM-IV* specifically avoids using the term, many GID individuals continue to call themselves "transsexuals." Bancroft (1989) has noted that the issue of sexual orientation is often confusing in individuals with GID. For example, what is the sexual orientation of someone who is biologically female, assigned the female sex at birth, but who thinks of him/herself as essentially male and is sexually attracted only to women? Interestingly, in one early study of GID men and women who underwent sex-reassignment surgery, postoperative self-perceived sexual orientation was heterosexual and consistent with the appearance of postoperative genetalia (Bentler, 1976).

Prevalence Prevalence studies have shown that GID is far more common in males than females. For example, in summarizing the finding of several studies, Meyer-Bahlburg (1985) estimated the occurrence as approximately 1 in 30,000 in men, and 1 in 100,000 in women. One recent Dutch study (Bakker, van Kesteren, Gooren, & Bezemer, 1993) estimated somewhat higher prevalence rates based on the number of persons receiving hormonal treatment for gender problems at a clinical center in the Netherlands. Depite difficulties associated with determining the true prevalence of GID (e.g., a tendency for underreporting due to stigmatization of the disorder), it is generally considered to be relatively rare (Zucker & Bradley, 1995).

Course Gender dysphoria in childhood generally does not persist into adulthood (Green, 1987; Zucker & Bradley, 1995). However, some studies have found that early gender dysphoria predicts homosexual orientation in later life (e.g., Money & Russo, 1979; Zuger, 1978). Similarly, retrospective studies of homosexual adults have reported increased levels of cross-gender behavior in these individuals as children (Bell, Weinberg, & Hammersmith, 1981). Based upon these findings, it has been suggested that early gender dysphoria in some individuals may be resolved through a homosexual identification that is consolidated during later developmental phases. Indeed, some authors (e.g., Zuger, 1988) have speculated that childhood cross-gendered behavior may reflect an immature form of homosexuality. However, the concordance between early gender problems and subsequent homosexuality has not been confirmed in all studies (Green, 1987), suggesting that sexual orientation and gender identity are more likely discrete, but overlapping categories (Zucker & Bradley, 1995).

Etiological Factors in the Development of Gender Identity Disorder

Gender identity development in males and females involves a complex interplay of biological and psychosocial factors (Money & Ehrhardt, 1972; Bancroft, 1989). Most research, however, has focused on the role of specific biological or psychosocial variables in determining the etiology of gender identity disturbances. Significant findings in each of these areas are briefly reviewed as follows. It should be noted that a large proportion of the research is primarily pertinent to homosexuality rather than GID. In the absence of comparable studies on GID, we have chosen to report this body of research from this conceptually related area. It should be noted, however, that these studies are one step removed from studying GID directly, and caution should be used in generalizing the results to the GID population.

Biological Factors The effects of genetic influences, the prenatal hormone environment, and postnatal developmental factors have been implicated in varying degrees as determinants of childhood or adult GID. Despite the obvious appeal of such biological explanations, research findings in this area have been sparse and inconsistent. For example, although there are occasional case reports of sex chromosome abnormalities in GID patients (e.g., Taneja, Ammini, Mohapatra, Saxena, & Kucheria, 1992), the large majority have normal sex chromosomes (Green, 1976; Rekers, Crandall, Rosen, & Bentler, 1979; Chazan, 1995). Simple explanations involving differences in circulating hormone levels have also not been borne out in controlled studies (Meyer-Bahlburg, 1993).

The search for biological determinants has focused recently on the role of genetic factors in the development of sexual orientation, as one component of gender identity. For example, several studies have found higher concordance rates for homosexuality among monozygotic vs. dizygotic twins (Bailey & Pillard, 1991; King & McDonald, 1992). In one highly publicized study, a distinct pattern of maternal gene transmission was identified in a selected sample of male homosexuals (Hamer, Hu, Magnuson, Hu, & Pattatucci, 1993). These authors identified a specific gene location, the Xq28 region of the X chromosome, as concordant in the majority of male homosexual siblings. Although this study has been criticized on methodological and conceptual grounds (e.g., Baron, 1993; King, 1993), it represents an important application of molecular genetics to an aspect of gender identity development. Recent attempts to replicate the findings have met with mixed results (Hamer, 1995; Marshall, 1995).

Similarly, studies of the prenatal hormone environment as a determinant of sexual orientation or gender identity have been inconclusive to date. In general, prenatal hormones influence the development of brain structures associated with later sexual behaviour (e.g., Phoenix, Goy, Gerall, & Young, 1959). Furthermore, studies of the effects of abnormal prenatal hormonal conditions support the connection between prenatal hormone exposure and subsequent gender-related behavior. For example, girls born with congenital adrenal hyperplasia (CAH), a condition associated with increased levels of prenatal androgens, show higher levels of masculinized play behavior (Ehrhardt, Epstein, & Money, 1968; Berenbaum & Hines, 1992). These girls are also more likely to have gender identity disturbances and to take on a masculine gender role later in life (Zucker, 1994). Sexual orientation is also affected, as adult women with CAH are more likely to report homosexual or bisexual fantasies, and are less likely to be married or to have sexual experiences with men (Money, Schwartz, & Lewis, 1984).

Similar evidence for the effects of prenatal hormones on sexual identity development comes from studies of females exposed in utero to diethylstilbesterol (DES), a drug that was widely used in the 1950s to prevent miscarriages and which increases the levels of testosterone to which the developing fetus is exposed. Several studies have shown that females exposed to DES have similar, albeit less strongly masculinized, gender role behaviors and identity compared to those with CAH (Erhardt et al., 1989; Meyer-Bahlburg et al., 1995). Results are inconsistent, however, as some studies have failed to find significant differences between females exposed to DES and controls (Lish, Meyer-Bahlburg, Erhradt, Trvais, & Veridiano, 1992). German researchers (Dorner, Rohde, Seidel, Haas, & Schoft, 1976; Dorner, Rohde, Stahl, Krell, & Masius, 1975) have argued strongly for the effects of prenatal estrogen exposure in males on subsequent gender identity and sexual orientation. Other authors have failed to replicate their results (e.g., Gooren, 1986; Hendricks, Graber, & Rodriguez-Sierra, 1989), and the research has been criticized on methodological and theoretical grounds (Meyer-Bahlburg, 1993; Zucker & Bradley, 1995).

Neuroanatomical differences have also been implicated in some studies of gender or sexual orientation disturbances. The anterior hypothalamus, in particular, is an area of the brain that is significantly involved in the sexual behavior of rodents and monkeys, and has been shown to be sex-dimorphic in humans, with heterosexual men having more cell volume than women (Allen, Hines, Shryne, & Gorski, 1989). In a controversial recent study, LeVay (1991) reported that the volume of INAH-3 cells of the anterior hypothalamus was diminished in homosexual men compared to heterosexual men. The cell volumes (measured postmortem) of homosexual men were found to be comparable to a sample of heterosexual women. Similar results have been reported for the anterior commissure, a tract of nerve fibers connecting the two hemispheres of the brain that had previously been shown to be sexually dimorphic (Allen & Gorski, 1992). This tract is thought to be involved in gender differences in cognitive abilities, and it may play a role in sexual orientation or gender identity disturbances (e.g., Cohen-Kettenis, Doorn, & Gooren, 1992; Tkachuk & Zucker, 1991). Several criticisms have been raised concerning the strength of the neuroanatomical evidence, however. For example, both the LeVay (1991) and the Allen and Gorski (1992) studies were confounded by inclusion of a significant proportion of men who died of AIDS in the homosexual group, which may have influenced cell volume in these individuals (Byne & Parsons, 1993).

Sibling sex ratio (i.e., the ratio of brothers to sisters) and birth order are two biodemographic variables that have been linked to sexual orientation and gender identity in several recent studies. Results have indicated that in comparison to controls, homosexual men, and especially those with gender identity disturbances, tend to have an excess of brothers (Blanchard & Sheridan, 1992; Blanchard & Zucker, 1994). On average, homosexual men are also born later in their families (i.e., have more older siblings) than members of the general population (Blanchard & Zucker, 1994; Hare & Moran, 1979; Slater, 1962). The specific mechanisms responsible for these intriguing findings have yet to be identified. One hypothesis is that antibodies to testosterone are produced by a woman during pregnancy with a male baby. If these antibodies increase over several pregnancies with male babies, then the hormone's biological activity may be reduced, affecting differentiation of the brain structures responsible for sexual orientation and gender identity (McCulloch & Waddington, 1981). Alternatively, there may be subtle differences in child-rearing patterns with younger siblings or male children with several brothers or older siblings.

A final biologic variable of interest associated with GID in several studies is physical attractiveness. Interest in this variable was initially sparked by clinical reports of mothers that their male children with GID were unusually attractive (Stoller, 1975b; Green, 1987). A later study found that college students blind to diagnostic status rated boys with GID as more physically attractive than controls (Zucker, Wild, Bradley, & Lowry, 1993). Several explanations have been offered for this surprising relationship. For example, Green (1974) has hypothesized that parents of feminine boys may dress them and style their hair in ways that are seen as "unmasculine" or "cute." Alternatively, the boys may shape their own appearance to be more feminine (Zucker & Bradley, 1995). In contrast to reports on boys with GID, girls with GID were rated as less physically attractive by college students in a study similar to that described above (Fridell, Zucker, Bradley, & Maing, 1996). It has also been suggested that physical attractiveness may shape parental behavior toward the child, possibly affecting subsequent gender identity development (Stoller, 1975b).

In summary, several biological factors have been associated with GID and other aspects of gender identity development in males and females. The findings to date are inconclusive, however, and many inconsistencies and potential confounds are evident in the studies reported.

Psychosocial Factors Sex assignment, or the process of identification of a newborn child as male or female, has been hypothesized to be the major determinant of gender identity (e.g., Money, Hampson, & Hampson, 1957). In their widely cited study of children born with hermaphroditism, or ambiguous external genitalia, these authors found that sex assignment was clearly the strongest predictor (above and beyond all biological variables measured) of adult gender role and orientation. Later studies confirmed the findings that infants born with intersex conditions could be assigned to either male or female sex, and could develop a gender identity consistent with that assignment (e.g., Money & Dalry, 1976). The authors also emphasized that if sex assignment is not decided early and definitively, gender identity confusion results.

Despite the widespread influence of this position, several sources of contradictory evidence exist. In one early series of studies (Imperato-McGinley, Peterson, Gautier, & Sturla, 1979, 1985) a group of male children in the Dominican Republic with a hormornal disorder known as 5-alpha reductase deficiency (5-ARD) were studied. This condition causes male infants to be born with ambiguous genetalia. In the absence of a complete medical examination, 5-ARD infants are typically assigned the female sex and raised as girls. At puberty, increased androgen production causes male secondary sexual characteristics to appear suddenly in these children, including descent of the testes and growth of a phallus. According to the authors' reports, most children are able to change their gender identities from female to male with little difficulty as these physical changes take place. These findings present a major challenge to those who argue that sex assignment or early rearing are the major determinants of gender identity. Although Money (1976) has questioned the validity of the 5-ARD findings, similar effects have been documented in the natural histories of other endocrine disorders (e.g., Mendonica et al., 1987; Rosler & Kohn, 1983).

Social reinforcement has also been identified as an important contributor to gender identity development. For instance, Fagot and Leinbach (1989) found that increased parental attention to sexually dimorphic behavior (e.g., playing with toy trucks for boys, playing with dolls for girls) predicted earlier ability of children to differentiate gender and increased frequency of sex-differentiated behavior. Green (1974) noted that lack of parental discouragement of cross-sex behavior was frequently associated with GID. Similar findings were reported by Mitchell (1991), who found that mothers of boys with GID were more encouraging of female-typical behavior and less encouraging of male-typical behavior in comparison to normal controls.

The quality of parental interaction has been implicated in some studies of GID. Based upon in-depth clinical interviews, Stoller (1975b) observed that mother-son relationships of boys with GID are often overly close, which he speculated would lead to greater female identification in these children. This hypothesis was not confirmed in a subsequent study by Green (1987), in which mothers of boys with GID recalled spending less time with their sons compared to controls. It could be argued, however, that more subtle aspects are involved in the maternal relationships of GID boys than the amount of time spent together or that mothers of GID boys are unreliable respondents. More recent studies have shown that mothers of GID boys have a higher incidence of psychopathology than controls, including obsessive-compulsive, depressed, and hostile traits; borderline personality disorder; and substance-related disorders (Marantz & Coates, 1991; Zucker & Bradley, 1995). Similarly, mothers of girls with GID have elevated levels of depression (Zucker & Bradley, 1995). These authors have suggested that psychopathology in the mother may impact gender identity formation through diminished parenting skills. For example, mothers who are burdened with their own psychopathology may be less able to set effective limits on their children's behavior, including those aspects that are relevant to gender identity formation. Parental wishes or expectations for a child of the opposite gender have also been implicated in some studies (Zucker & Bradley, 1995).

The specific role of the father has been examined in several studies. Distant or absent fathering has been shown to be related to gender role disturbances (Coates, 1985; Green, 1987), although this effect may be mediated by other factors, such as the age during which paternal absence occurs (Stevenson & Black, 1988). In this latter study, paternal absence prior to 6 years of age predicted later gender-role disturbances, whereas absence of the father after age 6 was not associated with gender-atypical behavior. Paternal psychopathology has also been related to the development of GID in some studies. For example, a high rate of substance abuse, depression, and personality disorders has been observed among fathers of boys with GID (Zucker & Bradley, 1995). As with mothers of GID children, paternal psychopathology may interfere with normal parental bonding, and thereby alter gender identity development in these children (Zucker & Bradley, 1995).

A history of sexual abuse has been implicated in several studies of GID. For example, Cosentino, Meyer-Bahlburg, Alpert, & Gaines (1993) reported that sexually abused girls were more masculine and/or less feminine than control girls. Qualitative analysis suggested that the sexually abused girls tended to feel closer to their fathers than to their mothers and were ambivalent about their status as female. These authors speculated that identification with the aggressor (i.e., the father) might function for the child as a way of avoiding a role that has left her vulnerable in the past. This account fails to explain why a history of sexual abuse is not found in all individuals with GID, and why all individuals with a sexually abusive history do not develop GID. Retrospective studies of both male-to-female and female-to-male transsexuals have also revealed high rates of physical and sexual abuse (Devor, 1994; Pauly, 1974). However, it is unclear from these studies whether these rates differ from baseline.

Finally, it has been suggested that children may influence their own acquisition of gender identity through the effects of self-schemas, or internalized perceptions of self (Zucker & Bradley, 1995). According to this hypothesis, a child with GID is influenced by a rigid self-schema consistent with the opposite sex. This schema negates or inhibits behavioral options that are inconsistent with the child's self-perceptions. Factors such as physical appearance, temperamental differences, and the failure to develop an early understanding of gender invariance might contribute to children misclassifying themselves as members of the other sex. There is limited empirical support for this hypothesis. For example, Fagot, Leinbach, and Hagen (1986) found that toddlers who were able to correctly identify their own biological sex spent more time playing with same-sex peers, supporting the importance of a gender-related self-schema in selecting gender-role behaviors. It has also been shown that children with GID have delayed acquisition of the ability to identify their own biological sex (Zucker & Bradley, 1995).

In summary, there appear to be multiple contributing factors to gender identity and the development of GID in both children and adults. Few authors have attempted to integrate biological and psychosocial determinants, although one recent review has proposed an interactional theory of gender identity and sexual orientation development (Bem, 1996). According to this author, biological factors such as genetics and prenatal hormones determine temperament, not sexual identity or orientation per se. Temperament, in turn, predisposes a child to prefer same-sex or opposite-sex playmates, depending upon the optimal match for his or her temperament. Through increasing interaction, identification with the play group develops and he or she begins to distance from same-sex peers. These feelings of dissimilarity lead to nonspecific autonomic arousal, which in later years may be reinterpreted as erotic/romantic attraction ("exotic becomes erotic"). This model has yet to be empirically tested.

Intersex Conditions

Intersex disorders include a variety of syndromes that result in persons with gross anatomical or physiological features of the opposite sex. Chromosomal abnormalities or prenatal hormonal disturbances are usually implicated in the etiology of these disorders. The most common intersex conditions are Turner's syndrome, in which one sex chromosome is missing (XO); Klinefelter's syndrome, which involves an extra chromosome (XXY); and congenital adrenal hyperplasia (adrenogenital syndrome), in which female fetuses are exposed to excessive quantities of androgen from the adrenal gland. Pseudohermaphroditism refers to a condition in which male or female infants are born with ambiguous genitalia, and a decision is made by the medical staff and parents about which gender to assign. Surgical correction of the ambiguous genitalia usually follows. A detailed description of these syndromes is beyond the scope of the present chapter (see Money, 1994; Zucker and Bradley, 1995 for reviews).

Summary and Conclusion

Sexual dysfunctions and disorders are highly prevalent conditions that are influenced by multiple etiological factors, including biological, social, and cultural determinants. The sexual dysfunctions in both sexes are categorized according to a four-stage model of sexual response; in women, disorders of the desire and orgasmic phases are most common, whereas erectile dysfunction and premature ejaculation are the most prevalent complaints in men. Physical causes are often implicated in male erectile disorder and dyspareunia in women, while other dysfunctions are typically associated with negative conditioning, early sexual trauma, or a history of anxiety or depression. Sexual dysfunctions in both sexes are frequently associated with a high level of individual or relationship distress.

Paraphilias are sexual disorders characterized by deviant sexual interests or behaviors. Among the major categories of paraphilia reviewed in this chapter are exhibitionism, fetishism, frotteurism, pedophilia, sexual masochism, sexual sadism, voyeurism, and transvestic fetishism. Some paraphilias (e.g., fetishism, masochism) are relatively harmless, whereas others (e.g., pedophilia, exhibitionism) involve sexual victimization of other individuals. There is little consensus regarding etiology of these disorders, as a variety of biological and social-learning explanations have been proposed. The prevalence of the paraphilias is likewise uncertain.

Gender identity disorders involve dissatisfaction with one's biological sex or the gender role of that sex. These disorders are more common in males than females, although estimates of the true prevalence vary widely. Childhood GID does not always progress into the adult form of the disorder, although a high proportion of children with GID develop a homosexual sexual orientation as adults. Both biological and psychosocial factors have been implicated in the development of the disorder, and much attention has focused recently on the potential role of chromosomal or neuranatomical determinants. GID is distinguished from intersex conditions, which include individuals with gross anatomical or physiological features of the other sex (e.g., pseudohermaphroditism). GID is often associated with a high level of psychological distress or concomitant psychophathology (e.g., depression).

Note

1. Although homosexuality per se does not appear as a classification in *DSM-IV*, a homosexual person with negative feelings toward his or her sexual orientation might still be diagnosed as sex-

ual disorder not otherwise specified, under which "persistent and marked distress about one's sexual orientation" is listed as an example.

References

Abel, G. G., Becker, J. V., Cunningham-Rathner, J., Mittelman, M., & Rouleau, J. L. (1988). Multiple paraphilic diagnoses among sex offenders. *Bulletin of the American Academy of Psychiatry and the Law, 16*, 153–168.

Abel, G. G., & Osborn, C. (1992). The paraphilias: The extent and nature of sexually deviant and criminal behavior. *Psychiatric Clinics of North America, 15*, 675–687.

Abel, G. G., & Rouleau, J. L. (1990). The nature and extent of sexual assault. In W. L. Marshall, D. R. Laws, & H. E. Barbaree (Eds.), *Handbook of sexual assault: Issues, theories and treatment of the offender* (pp. 9–22). New York: Plenum Press.

Ackerman, M. D., & Carey, M. P. (1995). Psychology's role in the assessment of erectile dysfunction: Historical precedents, current knowledge and methods. *Journal of Consulting and Clinical Psychology, 63*, 862–876.

Adams, A., Haynes, S., & Brayer, M. (1985). Cognitive distraction in female sexual arousal. *Psychophysiology, 22*, 689–696.

Allen, L. S., & Gorski, R. A. (1992). Sexual orientation and the size of the anterior commisure in the human brain. *Procedings of the National Academy of Sciences, 89*, 7199–7202.

Allen, L. S., Hines, M., Shryne, J. E., & Gorski, R. A. (1989). Two sexually dimorphic sex groups in the human brain. *Journal of Neuroscience, 9*, 497–506.

Apfelbaum, B. (1989). Retarded ejaculation: A much-misunderstood syndrome. In S. R. Leiblum & R. C. Rosen (Eds.), *Principles and practice of sex therapy: Update for the 1990's* (pp. 168–206). New York: Guilford Press.

Apt, C., Hurlbert, D. F., & Powell, D. (1993). Men with hypoactive sexual desire: The role of interpersonal dependency and assertiveness. *Journal of Sex Education and Therapy, 19*, 108–116.

Bailey, J. M., & Pillard, R. C. (1991). A genetic study of male sexual orientation. *Archives of General Psychiatry, 48*, 1089–1096.

Bakker, A., van Kesteren, P. J., Gooren, L. J., & Bezemer, P. D. (1993). The prevalence of transsexualism in the Netherlands. *Acta Psychiatrica Scandinavica, 87*, 237–238.

Bancroft, J. H. (1989). *Human sexuality and its problems*. Oxford: Oxford University Press.

Bancroft, J., & Wu, F. (1983). Change in erectile responsiveness during androgen replacement therapy. *Archives of Sexual Behavior, 12*, 59–66.

Barlow, D. H. (1986). Causes of sexual dysfunction: The role of anxiety and cognitive interference. *Journal of Consulting and Clinical Psychology, 54*, 140–148.

Barlow, D. H., Sakheim, D. K., & Beck, J. G. (1983). Anxiety increases sexual arousal. *Journal of Abnormal Psychology, 92*, 49–54.

Baron, M. (1993). Genetic linkage and male homosexual orientation. *British Medical Journal, 307*, 337–338.

Bates, J. E., Bentler, P. M., & Thompson, S. K. (1973). Measurement of deviant gender identity development in boys. *Child Development, 44*, 591–598.

Bates, J. E., Bentler, P. M., & Thompson, S. K. (1979). Gender-deviant boys compared with normal and clinical control boys. *Journal of Abnormal Child Psychology, 7*, 243–259.

Beard, R. W., Reginald, P. W., & Wadsworth, J. (1988). Clinical features of women with chronic lower abdominal pain and pelvic congestion. *British Journal of Obstetrics and Gynecology, 95*, 152–161.

Beck, J. G., Barlow, D. H., Sakheim, D. K., & Abrahamson, D. J. (1987). Shock threat and sexual arousal: The role of selective attention, thought content, and affective states. *Psychophysiology, 24*, 165–172.

Beck, J. G., & Bozman, A. W. (1995). Gender differences in sexual desire: The effects of anger and anxiety. *Archives of Sexual Behavior, 24*, 595–612.

Beck, J. G., Bozman, A. W., & Qualtrough, T. (1991). The experience of sexual desire: Psychological correlates in a college sample. *Journal of Sex Research, 28*, 443–456.

Becker, J. V. (1989). Impact of sexual abuse on sexual functioning. In S. R. Leiblum & R. C. Rosen (Eds.), *Principles and practice of sex therapy: Update for the 1990's* (pp. 298–318). New York: Guilford Press.

Becker, J. V., Skinner, L. J., Abel, G. G., & Cichon, J. (1986). Level of postassault sexual functioning in rape and incest victims. *Archives of Sexual Behavior, 15*, 37–49.

Bell, A. P., Weinberg, M. S., & Hammersmith, S. K. (1981). *Sexual preference: Its development in men and women*. Bloomington: Indiana University Press.

Bem, D. J. (1996). Exotic becomes erotic: A developmental theory of sexual orientation. *Psychological Review, 103*, 320–335.

Bentler, P. M. (1976). A typology of transsexualism: Gender identity, theory and data. *Archives of Sexual Behavior, 5*, 567–584.

Berenbaum, S. A., & Hines, M. (1992). Early androgens are related to childhood sex-typed toy preferences. *Psychological Science, 3*, 203–206.

Berlin, F. S. (1983). Sex Offenders: A biomedical perspective. In J. G. Greer & I. R. Stuart (Eds.), *The sexual aggressor: Current perspectives on treatment* (pp. 83–125). New York: Van Nostrand Reinhold.

Black, J. S. (1988). Sexual dysfunction and dyspareunia in the otherwise normal pelvis. *Journal of Sex and Marital Therapy, 3*, 213–221.

Blair, C. D., & Lanyon, R. I. (1981). Exhibitionism: Etiology and treatment. *Psychological Bulletin, 89*, 439–463.

Blanchard, R. (1989). The classification and labelling of nonhomosexual gender dysphorias. *Archives of Sexual Behavior, 18*, 315–334.

Blanchard, R. (1993). Partial versus complete autogynephilia and gender dysphoria. *Journal of Sex and Marital Therapy, 19*, 301–307.

Blanchard, R., & Sheridan, P. M. (1992). Sibship size, sibling sex ratio, birth order, and parental age in homosexual and nonhomosexual gender dysphorics. *Journal of Nervous and Mental Disease, 180*, 40–47.

Blanchard, R., & Zucker, K. J. (1994). Reanalysis of Bell, Weinberg, and Hammersmith's data on birth order, sibling sex ratio, and parental age in homosexual men. *American Journal of Psychiatry, 151*, 1375–1376.

Bozman, A. W., & Beck, J. G. (1991). Covariation of sexual desire and sexual arousal: The effects of anger and anxiety. *Archives of Sexual Behavior, 20*, 47–60.

Bradford, J. M. W., Boulet, J., & Pawlak, A. (1992). The paraphilias: A multiplicity of deviant behaviors. *Canadian Journal of Psychiatry, 37*, 104–108.

Bradley, S. J., Blanchard, R., Coates, S., Green, R., Levine, S. B., Meyer-Bahlburg, H., Pauly, I. B., & Zucker, K. J. (1991). Interim report of the DSM IV Subcommittee for gender identity disorders. *Archives of Sexual Behavior, 20*, 333–343.

Breslow, N., Evans, L., & Langley, J. (1985). On the prevalence and roles of females in the sadomasochistic subculture: Report of an empirical study. *Archives of Sexual Behavior, 14*, 303–318.

Briere, J., & Runtz, M. (1989). University males' sexual interest in children: Predicting potential indices of "pedophilia" in a nonforensic sample. *Child Abuse and Neglect, 13*, 65–75.

Buhrich, N. (1981). Psychological adjustment in transvestism and transsexualism. *Behavior Research and Therapy, 19*, 407–411.

Byne, W., & Parsons, B. (1993). Human sexual orientation: The biologic theories reappraised. *Archives of General Psychiatry, 50*, 228–239.

Carney, A., Bancroft, J., & Mathews, A. (1978). Combination of hormonal and psychological treatments for female sexual unresponsiveness: A comparative study. *British Journal of Psychiatry, 133*, 339–346.

Cesnick, J. A., & Coleman, E. (1989). Use of lithium carbonate in the treatment of autoerotic asphyxia. *American Journal of Psychotherapy, 43*, 277–286.

Chalkley, A. J., & Powell, G. E. (1983). The clinical description of forty-eight cases of sexual fetishism. *British Journal of Psychiatry, 142*, 292–295.

Chazan, S. E. (1995). *The simultaneous treatment of parent and child.* New York: Basic Books.

Chesser, E. (1971). *Human aspects of sexual deviation.* London: Jerrolds Publishing.

Coates, S. (1985). Extreme boyhood feminity: Overview and new research findings. In Z. DeFries, R. C. Friedman, & R. Corn (Eds.), *Sexuality: New perspectives* (pp. 101–124). Westport, CT: Greenwood.

Cohen, A. S., Rosen, R. C., & Goldstein, L. (1985). EEG hemispheric asymmetry during sexual arousal: Psychophysiological patterns in responsive, unresponsive, and dysfunctional males. *Journal of Abnormal Psychology, 94*, 580–590.

Cohen-Kettenis, P. T., Doorn, C. D., & Gooren, L. J. G. (1992, July). *Cerebral lateralization and spatial ability in transsexuals.* Poster presented at the meeting of the International Academy of Sex Research, Prague.

Coleman, J. C. (1972). *Abnormal psychology and modern life.* New York: Scott, Foresman.

Colpi, G. M., Faniullaci, F., Beretta, G., Negri, L., & Zanollo, A. (1986). Evoked sacral potential in subjects with true premature ejaculation. *Andrologia, 18*, 583–586.

Cooper, A. J., Cernovsky, Z. Z., & Colussi, K. (1993). Some clinical and psychometric characteristics of primary and secondary premature ejaculators. *Journal of Sex and Marital Therapy, 19*, 276–288.

Cosentino, C. E., Meyer-Bahlburg, J. F. L., Alpert, J. L., & Gaines, R. (1993). Cross-gender behavior and gender conflict in sexually abused girls. *Journal of the American Academy of Child and Adolescent Psychiatry, 32*, 940–947.

Cox, D. J., & McMahon, B. (1978). Incidence of male exhibitionism in the United States as reported by victimized female college students. *International Journal of Law and Psychiatry, 1*, 453–457.

Cranston-Cuebas, M. A., & Barlow, D. H. (1990). Cognitive and affective contributions to sexual functioning. *Annual Review of Sex Research, 1*, 119–161.

Davidson, J. M., Camargo, C. A., & Smith, E. R. (1979). Effects of androgens on sexual behaviour of hypogonadal men. *Journal of Clinical Endocrinology and Metaboloism, 48*, 955–958.

Davidson, J. M., Camargo, C. A., Smith, E. R., & Kwan, M. (1983). Maintenance of sexual function in a castrated man treated with ovarian steroids. *Archives of Sexual Behavior, 12*, 263–274.

Davidson, J. M., & Rosen, R. C. (1992). Hormonal determinants of erectile function. In R. C. Rosen & S. R. Leiblum (Eds.), *Erectile disorders: Assessment and treatment* (pp. 72–95). New York: Guilford Press.

Devor, H. (1994). Transsexualism, dissociation, and child abuse: An initial discussion based on nonclinical data. *Journal of Psychiatry and Human Sexuality, 6*, 49–72.

Devor, H. (1996). Female gender dysphoria: Personal problem or social problem? *Annual Review of Sex Research, 7*, 44–89.

Donahey, K. M., & Carroll, R. A. (1993). Gender differences in factors associated with hypoactive sexual desire. *Journal of Sex and Marital Therapy, 19*, 25–40.

Dorner, G., Rohde, W., Seidel, K., Hass, W., & Schott, G. (1976). On the evocability of a positive oestrogen feedback action on LH secretion in transsexual men and women. *Endokrinologie, 67*, 20–25.

Dorner, G., Rohde, W., Stahl, F., Krell, L., & Masius, W. G. (1975). A neuroendocrine predisposition for homosexuality in men. *Archives of Sexual Behavior, 4*, 1–8.

Dow, M. G. (1981). Retarded ejaculation as a function of nonaversive conditioning and discrimination: A hypothesis. *Journal of Sex and Marital Therapy, 7*, 49–53.

Ehrhardt, A. A., Epstein, R., & Money, J. (1968). Fetal androgens and female gender identity in early treated adrenogenital syndrome. *Johns Hopkins Medical Journal, 122*, 160–167.

Ehrhardt, A. A., Meyer-Bahlburg, H. F. L., Rosen, L. R., Feldman, J. F., Veridiano, N. P., Elkin, E. J., & McEwen, B. S. (1989). The development of gender-related behavior in females following prenatal exposure to diethylstilbestrol (DES). *Hormones and Behavior, 23*, 526–541.

Evans, D. R. (1970). Exhibitionism. In C. G. Costello (Ed.), *Symptoms of psychopathology* (pp. 186–204). New York: John Wiley.

Fagot, B. T. (1995). Psychosocial and cognitive determinants of early gender-role development. *Annual Review of Sex Research*, 6, 1–31.

Fagot, B. L., & Leinbach, M. D. (1989). The young child's gender schema: Environmental input, internal organization. *Child Development, 60*, 663–672.

Fagot, B. L., Leinbach, M. D., & Hagan, R. (1986). Gender labeling and the adoption of sex-typed behaviors. *Developmental Psychology, 22*, 440–443.

Fanciullacci, F., Colpi, G. M., Beretta, G., & Zanollo, A. (1988). Cortical evoked potentials in subjects with true premature ejaculation. *Andrologia, 20*, 326–330.

Feldman, H. A., Goldstein, I., Hatzichrisou, D. G., Krane, R. J., & McKinlay, J. P. (1994). Impotence and its medical and psychosocial correlates: Results of the Massachusetts Male Aging Study. *Journal of Urology, 151*, 54–61.

Finkelhor, D. (1986). *A sourcebook on child sexual abuse.* Beverly Hills: Sage.

Finkelhor, D. (1984). *Child sexual abuse: New theory and research.* New York: Free Press.

Fordney, D. S. (1978). Dyspareunia and vaginismus. *Clinical Obstetrics and Gynecology, 21*, 205–221.

Forgac, G. E., & Michaels, E. J. (1982). Personality characteristics of two types of male exhibitionists. *Journal of Abnormal Psychology, 91*, 287–293.

Frank, E., Anderson, A., & Rubenstein, D. (1978). Frequency of sexual dysfunction in "normal" couples. *New England Journal of Medicine, 299*, 111–115.

Freund, K., & Blanchard, R. (1986). The concept of courtship disorder. *Journal of Sex and Marital Therapy, 12*, 79–92.

Freund, K., & Watson, R. (1990). Mapping the boundaries of courtship disorder. *Journal of Sex Research, 27*, 589–606.

Freund, K., & Watson, R. J. (1993). Gender identity disorder and courtship disorder. *Archives of Sexual Behavior, 22*, 13–21.

Friedrich, W. N., & Gerber, P. N. (1994). Autoerotic asphyxia: The development of a paraphilia. *Journal of the American Academy of Child and Adolescent Psychiatry, 33*, 970–974.

Fridell, S. R., Zucker, K. J., Bradley, S. J., & Maing, D. M. (1996). Physical attractiveness of girls with gender identity disorder. *Archives of Sexual Behavior, 25*, 17–31.

Gebhard, P. H., Gagnon, J. H., Pomeroy, W. B., & Christensen, C. V. (1965). *Sex offenders.* New York, Harper and Row.

Geer, J., & Fuhr, R. (1975). Cognitive factors in sexual arousal: The role of distraction. *Journal of Consulting and Clinical Psychology, 44*, 238–243.

Gittelson, N. L., Eacott, S. T., & Mehta, B. M. (1978). Victims of indecent exposure. *British Journal of Psychiatry, 132*, 61–66.

Godpodinoff, M. L. (1989). Premature ejaculation: Clinical subgroups and etiology. *Journal of Sex and Marital Therapy, 15*, 130–134.

Gooren, L. (1986). The neuroendocrine response of leutenizing hormone to estrogen administration in heterosexual, homosexual, and transsexual subjects. *Journal of Clinical Endocrinology and Metabolism, 63*, 583–588.

Green, R. (1974). *Sexual identity conflict in children and adults.* New York: Basic Books.

Green, R. (1976). One-hundred ten feminine and masculine boys: Behavioral contrasts and demographic similarities. *Archives of Sexual Behavior, 5*, 425–446.

Green, R. (1987). *The "sissy boy syndrome" and the development of homosexuality.* New Haven: Yale University Press.

Groth, A. N., Hobson, W. F., & Gary, T. S. (1982). The child molester: Clinical observations. *Social Work and Human Sexuality, 1*, 129–144.

Hamer, D. (1995, May). The role of genes in sexual orientation and sex-typical behavior. Paper presented at the International Behavioral Development Symposium: Biological Basis of Sexual Orientation and Sex-Typical Behaviour, Minot State University, Minot, ND.

Hamer, D. H., Hu, S., Magnuson, V. L., Hu, N., & Pattatucci, A. M. (1993). A linkage between DNA markers on the X chromosome and male sexual orientation. *Science, 261*, 321–327.

Hare, E. H., & Moran, P. A. P. (1979). Parental age and birth order in homosexual patients: A replication of Slater's study. *British Journal of Psychiatry, 134*, 178–182.

Hastings, D. W. (1963). *Impotence and frigidity.* Boston: Little Brown.

Hawton, K. (1992). Sex therapy research: Has it withered on the vine? *Annual Review of Sex Research, 3*, 49–72.

Hawton, K. (1982). The behavioral treatment of erectile dysfunction. *British Journal of Psychiatry, 140*, 94–101.

Hawton, K., Catalan, J., & Fagg, J. (1992). Sex therapy for erectile dysfunction: Characteristics of couples, treatment outcome, and prognostic factors. *Archives of Sexual Behavior, 21*, 161–176.

Hawton, K., Catalan, J., Martin, P., & Fagg, J. (1986). Long-term outcome of sex therapy. *Behavior Research and Therapy, 24*, 665–675.

Heiman, J. R., & Grafton-Becker, V. (1989). Orgasmic disorders in women. In S. R. Leiblum & R. C. Rosen (Eds.), *Principles and practice of sex therapy: Update for the 1990's* (pp. 51–88). New York: Guilford Press.

Hendricks, S. E., Graber, B., & Rodriguez-Sierra, J. F. (1989). Neuroendocrine responses to exogenous estrogen: No differences between heterosexual and homosexual men. *Psychoneuroendocrinology, 14*, 177–185.

Higgins, G. E. (1979). Sexual response in spinal cord injured adults: A review. *Archives of Sexual Behavior, 8*, 173–196.

Hite, S. (1975). *The Hite report: A nationwide study of female sexuality.* New York: Dell Books.

Huffmann, J. W. (1983). Dyspareunia of vulvovaginal origin: Causes and managment. *Postgraduate Medicine, 73*, 287–296.

Hurlbert, D. F. (1991). The role of assertiveness in female sexuality. *Journal of Sex and Marital Therapy, 17*, 183–190.

Imperato-McGinley, J., Peterson, R. E., Gautier, T., & Sturla, E. (1979). Androgens and the evolution of male-gender identity among male pseudohermaphrodites with 5-alphar eductase deficiency. *New England Journal of Medicine, 300*, 1233–1237.

Imperato-McGinley, J., Peterson, R. E., Gautier, T., & Sturla, E. (1985). The impact of androgens on the evolution of male gender identity. In Z. DeFries, R. C. Friedman, & R. Corn (Eds.), *Sexuality: New perspectives* (pp. 125–140). Westport, CT: Greenwood.

Jarvis, G. J. (1994). Dyspareunia. *British Medical Journal, 288*, 1555–1556.

Johnson, J. (1968). *Disorders of sexual potency in the male.* Elmsford, NY: Pergamon Press.

Jones, T. M. (1985). Hormonal considerations in the evaluation of erectile dysfunction. In R. T. Segraves & H. W. Schoenberg (Eds.), *Diagnosis and treatment of erectile disturbances* (pp. 115–158). New York: Plenum Press.

Kafka, M. P., & Prentky, R. (1992). A comparative study of nonparaphilic sexual addictions and paraphilias in men. *Journal of Clinical Psychiatry, 53*, 345–350.

Kafka, M. P., & Prentky, R. A. (1994). Preliminary observations of DSM-III-R Axis I comorbidity in men with paraphilias and paraphilia-related disorders. *Journal of Clinical Psychiatry, 55*, 481–487.

Kaplan, H. S. (1974). *The new sex therapy.* New York: Brunner Mazel.

Kaplan, H. S. (1977). Hypoactive sexual desire. *Journal of Sex and Marital Therapy, 3*, 3–9.

Kaplan, H. S. (1992). Does the CAT technique enhance female orgasm? *Journal of Sex and Marital Therapy, 18*, 285–302.

Kaplan, H. S. (1996). Erotic obsession: Relationship to hypoactive sexual desire disorder and paraphilia. *American Journal of Psychiatry, 153*, 30–41.

Katz, R. C., Gipson, M., & Turner, S. (1992). Brief report: Recent findings on the sexual aversion scale. *Journal of Sex and Marital Therapy, 18*, 141–146.

Kelley, M. P., Strassberg, D. S., & Kircher, J. R. (1990). Attitudinal and experiential correlates of anorgasmia. *Archives of Sexual Behavior, 19*, 165–172.

Killmann, P. R., & Auerbach, R. (1979). Treatments of premature ejaculation and psychogenic impotence: A critical review of the literature. *Archives of Sexual Behavior, 8*, 81–100.

King, D. (1993). Sexual orientation and the X. *Nature, 364*, 228–289.

King, M., & McDonald, E. (1992). Homosexuals who are twins: A study of 46 probands. *British Journal of Psychiatry, 160*, 407–409.

Kinsey, A. C., Pomeroy, W. B., & Martin, C. E. (1948). *Sexual behavior in the human male.* Philadelphia: Saunders.

Knight, R. A., & Prentky, R. A. (1990). Classifying sexual offenders: The development and corroboration of taxonomic models. In W. L. Marshall, D. R. Laws, & H. E. Barbaree (Eds.), *Handbook of sexual assault: Issues, theories, and treatment of the offender* (pp. 23–54). New York: Plenum.

Krafft-Ebing, R. V. (1965). *Psychopathia sexualis.* New York: Putnam Press.

Krane, R. J., Goldstein, I., & Tejada, I. S. (1989). Impotence. *New England Journal of Medicine, 321*, 1648–1659.

Kuhr, C. S., Heiman, J., Cardenas, D., Bradley, W., & Berger, R. E. (1995). Premature emission after spinal cord injury. *Journal of Urology, 153*, 429–431.

Laan, E., & Everaerd, W. (1995). Determinants of female sexual arousal: Psychophysiological theory and data. *Annual Review of Sex Research, 6*, 32–76.

Laan, E., Everaerd, W., van Aanhold, M., & Rebel, M. (1993). Performance demand and sexual arousal in women. *Behavior Research and Therapy, 31*, 25–35.

Lang, R. A., Langevin, R., Checkley, K. L., & Pugh, G. (1987). Genital exhibitionism: Courtship disorder or narcissism? *Canadian Journal of Behavioural Sciences, 19*, 216–232.

Langevin, R. (1992). Biological factors contributing to paraphilic behavior. *Psychiatric Annals, 22*, 307–314.

Langevin, R., Bain, J., Ben-Aron, M., Coulthard, R., & Day, D. (1985). Sexual aggression: Constructing a predictive equation. In R. Langevin (Ed.), *Erotic preference, gender identity, and aggression in men* (pp. 39–76). Hillsdale: Lawrence Erlbaum.

Laumann, E. O., Gagnon, J. H., Michael, R. T., & Michaels, S. (1994). *The social organization of sexuality.* Chicago: University of Chicago Press.

Laws, D. R., & Marshall, W. L. (1990). A conditioning theory of the etiology and maintenance of deviant sexual preference and behavior. In W. L. Marshall, D. R. Laws, & Barbaree (Eds.), *Handbook of sexual assault: Issues, theories, and treatment of the offender* (pp. 209–230). New York: Plenum Press.

Lazarus, A. A. (1989). Dyspareunia: A multimodal perspective. In S. R. Leiblum & R. C. Rosen (Eds.), *Principles and practice of sex therapy: Update for the 1990's* (pp. 89–112). New York: Guilford Press.

Leiblum, S. R. (1996). Sexual pain disorders. In G. O. Gabbard & S. D. Atkinson (Eds.), *Synopsis of treatments of psychiatric disorders* (pp. 805–810). Washington, DC: American Psychiatric Association Press.

Leiblum, S. R., Pervin, L. A., & Campbell, E. H. (1989). The treatment of vaginismus: Success and failure. In S. R. Leiblum & R. C. Rosen (Eds.), *Principles and practice of sex therapy: Update for the 1990's* (pp. 113–140). New York: Guilford Press.

Leiblum, S. R., & Rosen, R. C. (1988). Changing perspectives on sexual desire. In S. R. Leiblum & R. C. Rosen (Eds.), *Sexual desire disorders* (pp. 1–20). New York: Guilford Press.

Leiblum, S. R., & Rosen, R. C. (1991). Couples therapy for erectile disorders: Conceptual and clinical considerations. *Journal of Sex and Marital Therapy, 17*, 147–159.

Leiblum, S. R., & Rosen, R. C. (1992). Couples therapy for erectile disorders: Observations, obstacles and outcomes. In R. C. Rosen & S. R. Leiblum (Eds.), *Erectile disorders: Assessment and treatment* (pp. 226–254). New York: Guilford Press.

Leiblum, S. R., Rosen, R. C., Platt, M., Cross, R. J., & Black, C. (1993). Sexual attitudes and behaviors of a cross-sectional sample of U.S. medical students: Effects of gender, age, and year of study. *Journal of Sex Education and Therapy, 19*, 235–245.

LeVay, S. (1991). A difference in hypothalamic structure between heterosexual and homosexual men. *Science, 253*, 1034–1037.

Levine, S. B., & Yost, M. A. (1976). Frequency of sexual dysfunction in a general gynecological clinic. *Archives of Sexual Behavior, 5*, 229–238.

Lief, H. I. (1977). Inhibited sexual desire. *Medical Aspects of Human Sexuality, 7*, 94–95.

Lish, J. D., Meyer-Bahlburg, H. F. L., Ehrhardt, A. A., Travis, B. G., & Veridiano, N. P. (1992). Prenatal exposure to diethylstilbestrol (DES): Childhood play behaviour and adult gender-role behaviour in women. *Archives of Sexual Behavior, 21*, 423–441.

LoPiccolo, J. (1992). Postmodern sex therapy for erectile failure. In R. C. Rosen & S. R. Lieblum (Eds.), *Erectile disorders: Assessment and treatment* (pp. 171–197). New York: Guilford Press.

LoPiccolo, J., & Friedman, J. M. (1988). Broad-spectrum treatment of low sexual desire: Integration of cognitive, behavioral, and systemic therapy. In S. R. Leiblum & R. C. Rosen (Eds.), *Sexual desire disorders* (pp. 107–144). New York: Guilford Press.

Lue, T. F., Hricak, H., Schmidt, A., & Tanagho, E. A. (1986). Functional evaluation of penile veins by cavernosography and cavernosometry in papaverine induced erections. *Journal of Urology, 135*, 479–482.

Madorsky, I. L., Ashamalla, M. G., Schussler, L., Lyons, H. R., & Miller, G. H. (1976). Post-prostatectomy impotence. *Journal of Urology, 115*, 401–403.

Marantz, S., & Coates, S. (1991). Mothers of boys with gender identity disorder: A comparison of matched controls. *Journal of the American Academy of Child and Adolescent Psychiatry, 30*, 310–315.

Marshall, E. (1995). NIH's "gay gene" study questioned. *Science, 268*, 18–41.

Masters, W. H., & Johnson, V. (1966). *Human sexual response*. Boston: Little, Brown.

Masters, W. H., & Johnson, V. E. (1970). *Human sexual inadequacy.* Boston: Little, Brown.

McCabe, M. P., & Delaney, S. M. (1992). An evaluation of therapeutic programs for the treatment of secondary anorgasmia in women. *Archives of Sexual Behavior, 21*, 69–89.

McCullough, M. J., & Waddington, J. L. (1981). Neuroendocrine mechanisms and the etiology of male and female homosexuality. *British Journal of Psychiatry, 139*, 341–345.

McGovern, K. B., Stewart, R. C., & LoPiccolo, J. (1975). Secondary orgasmic dysfunction: Analysis and strategies for treatment. *Archives of Sexual Behavior, 4*, 265–275.

McGuire, L. S., Carlisle, J. M., & Young, B. G. (1965). Sexual deviations as conditioned behavior: A hypothesis. *Behavior Research and Therapy, 2*, 185–190.

McKibben, A., Proulx, J., & Lusignan, R. (1994). Relationships between conflict, affect and deviant sexual behaviors in rapists and pedophiles. *Behavior Research and Therapy, 32*, 571–575.

Meana, M., & Binik, Y. M. (1994). Painful coitus: A review of female dyspareunia. *Journal of Nervous and Mental Disease, 182*, 264–272.

Meisler, A. W., & Carey, M. P. (1991). Depressed affect and male sexual arousal. *Archives of Sexual Behavior, 20*, 541–554.

Mendonica, B. B., Bloise, W., Arnhold, J. P., Batista, M. C., deAlmeida Toledo, S. P., Drummond, M. C. F., Nicolau, W., & Mattar, E. (1987). Male pseudohermaphroditism due to nonsalt-losing 3-beta-hydroxysteroid dehydrogenase deficiency: Gender role change and absence of gynecomastia at puberty. *Journal of Steroid Biochemistry, 28*, 669–675.

Meyer-Bahlburg, H. F. L. (1985). Gender identity disorder of childhood: Introduction. *Journal of the American Academy of Child Psychiatry, 24*, 681–683.

Meyer-Bahlburg, H. F. L. (1993). Psychobiologic research on homosexuality. *Child and Adolescent Psychiatric Clinics of North America, 2*, 489–500.

Meyer-Bahlburg, H. F. L., Ehrhardt, A. A., Rosen, L. R., Gruen, R. S., Veridiano, N. P., Vann, P. H., & Neuwalder, H. F. (1995). Prenatal estrogens and the development of homosexual orientation. *Developmental Psychology, 31*, 12–21.

Mitchell, J. N. (1991). *Maternal influences on gender identity in boys: Searching for specificity.* Unpublished doctoral dissertation, York University, Downsview, Ontario.

Mitchell, W., Brown, T. A., Barlow, D. H., Weiner, D. N., Sbrocco, T., & Wackett, A. (1992, November). *Sexual responsiveness under affect induction.* Paper presented at the meeting for the Association for Advancement of Behavior Therapy, Boston, MA.

Mohr, D. C., & Beutler, L. E. (1990). Erectile dysfunction: A review of diagnostic and treatment procedures. *Clinical Psychology Review, 10*, 123–150.

Mohr, J. W., Turner, R. E., & Jerry, M. B. (1964). *Pedophilia and exhibitionism.* Toronto: University of Toronto Press.

Money, J. (1976). The development of sexology as a discipline. *Journal of Sex Research, 12*, 83–87.

Money, J. (1980). *Love and love sickness.* Baltimore: Johns Hopkins University Press.

Money, J. (1994). *Sex errors of the body and related syndromes: A guide to counseling children, adolescents, and their families* (2nd ed.). Baltimore, MD: Brookes.

Money, J., & Dalery, J. (1976). Iatrogenic homosexuality: Gender identity in seven 46,XX chromosomal females with hyperadrenocortical hermaphroditism born with a penis, three reared as boys, four reared as girls. *Journal of Homosexuality, 1*, 357–371.

Money, J., & Erhardt, A. A. (1972). *Man and woman, boy and girl*. Baltimore: Johns Hopkins University Press.

Money, J., Hampson, J. G., & Hampson, J. L. (1957). Imprinting and the establishment of gender role. *Archives of Neurology and Psychiatry, 77*, 333–336.

Money, J., & Lamacz, M. (1989). *Vandalized lovemaps*. New York: Prometheus Books.

Money, J., & Russo, A. J. (1979). Homosexual outcome and discordant gender identity/role in childhood: Longitudinal follow-up. *Journal of Pediatric Psychology, 4*, 29–41.

Money, J., Schwartz, M., & Lewis, V. G. (1984). Adult erotosexual status and fetal hormone masculinization and demasculinization: 46,XX congenital adrenal hyperplasia and 46,XY androgen-insensitivity syndrome compared. *Psychoneuroendocrinology, 9*, 405–414.

Morokoff, P. J. (1989). Sex bias and primary orgasmic dysfunction. *American Psychologist, 44*, 73–75.

Nathan, S. G. (1986). The epidemiology of DSM-III psychosexual dysfunctions. *Journal of Sex and Marital Therapy, 12*, 267–281.

NIH Consensus Panel on Impotence. (1993). Impotence. *Journal of the American Medical Association, 270*, 83–90.

O'Carroll, R., & Bancroft, J. (1984). Testosterone therapy for low sexual interest and erectile dysfunction in men: A controlled study. *British Journal of Psychiatry, 145*, 146–158.

Paff, B. A. (1985). Sexual dysfunction in gay men requesting treatment. *Journal of Sex and Marital Therapy, 11*, 3–18.

Palace, E. M., & Gorzalka, B. B. (1990). The enhancing effects of anxiety on arousal in sexually dysfunctional and functional women. *Journal of Abnormal Psychology, 99*, 403–411.

Palace, E. M., & Gorzalka, B. B. (1992). Differential patterns of arousal in sexually functional and dysfunctional women: Physiological and subjective components of sexual response. *Archives of Sexual Behavior, 21*, 135–159.

Pauly, I. B. (1974). Female transsexualism: Part I. *Archives of Sexual Behavior, 3*, 487–507.

Phoenix, C. H., Goy, R. W., Gerall, A. A., & Young, W. C. (1959). Organizing action of prenatally administered testosterone proprionate on the tissues mediating mating behavior in the female guinea pig. *Endocrinology, 65*, 369–382.

Ponticas, Y. (1992). Sexual aversion versus hypoactive sexual desire: A diagnostic challenge. *Psychiatric Medicine, 10*, 273–281.

Prince, V., & Bentler, P. M. (1972). Survey of 504 cases of transvestism. *Psychological Report, 31*, 903–917.

Quinn, J. T., Harbison, J., & McAllister, H. (1970). An attempt to shape human penile responses. *Behavior Research and Therapy, 8*, 27–28.

Rachman, S. (1966). Sexual festishism: An experimental analogue. *Psychological Record, 16*, 293–296.

Rachman, S., & Hodgson, R. J. (1968). Experimentally-induced "sexual fetishism": Replication and development. *Psychological Record, 18*, 25–27.

Reading, A., & Wiest, W. (1984). An analysis of self-reported sexual behavior in a sample of normal males. *Archives of Sexual Behavior, 13*, 69–83.

Reamy, K. J., & White, S. E. (1985). Dyspareunia in pregnancy. *Journal of Psychosomatic Obstetrics and Gynecology, 4*, 263–270.

Rekers, G. A., Crandall, B. F., Rosen, A. C., & Bentler, P. M. (1979). Genetic and physical studies of male children with psychological gender disturbances. *Psychological Medicine, 9*, 373–375.

Renshaw, D. C. (1988). Profile of 2376 patients treated at Loyola Sex Clinic between 1972–1987. *Sexual and Marital Therapy, 3*, 111–117.

Reynolds, B. (1991). Psychological treatment of erectile dysfunction in men without partners: Outcome results and a new direction. *Journal of Sex and Marital Therapy, 17*, 136–146.

Robinson, P. (1976). *The modernization of sex*. New York: Harper and Row.

Rosen, R. C. (1991). Alcohol and drug effects on sexual response: Human experimental and clinical studies. *Annual Review of Sex Research, 2*, 119–180.

Rosen, R. C., & Beck, J. G. (1988). *Patterns of sexual arousal: Psychophysiological processes and clinical applications*. New York: Guilford Press.

Rosen, R. C., & Fracher, J. C. (1983). Tension-reduction training in the treatment of compulsive sex offenders. In J. G. Geer & I. R. Stuart (Eds.), *The sexual aggressor: Current perspectives on treatment* (pp. 144–159). New York: Van Nostrand Reinhold.

Rosen, R. C., & Hall, E. (1984). *Sexuality*. New York: Random House.

Rosen, R. C., & Leiblum, S. R. (1989). Assessment and treatment of desire disorders. In S. R. Leiblum & R. C. Rosen (Eds.), *Principles and practice of sex therapy: Update for the 1990's* (pp. 19–50). New York: Guilford Press.

Rosen, R. C., & Leiblum, S. R. (1992). *Erectile disorders: Assessment and treatment.* New York: Guilford Press.

Rosen, R. C., & Leiblum, S. R. (1995). Treatment of sexual disorders in the 1990s: An integrated approach. *Journal of Consulting and Clinical Psychology, 63,* 877–890.

Rosen, R. C., Leiblum, S. R., & Spector, I. (1994). Psychologically-based treatment for male erectile disorder: A cognitive-interpersonal model. *Journal of Sex and Marital Therapy, 20,* 67–85.

Rosen, R. C., Taylor, J. F., Leiblum, S. R., & Bachmann, G. A. (1993). Prevalence of sexual dysfunction in women: Results of a survey study of 329 women in an outpatient gynecological clinic. *Journal of Sex and Marital Therapy, 19,* 171–188.

Rösler, A., & Kohn, G. (1983). Male pseudohermaphroditism due to 17-beta-hydroxysteroid dehydrogenase deficiency: Studies on the natural history of the defect and effect of androgens on gender role. *Journal of Steroid Biochemistry, 19,* 663–674.

Rowland, D. L., Haensel, S. M., Blom, J. H., & Slob, A. K. (1993). Penile sensitivity in men with premature ejaculation and erectile dysfunction. *Journal of Sex and Marital Therapy, 19,* 189–197.

Rowland, D. L., & Slob, A. K. (1995). Understanding and diagnosing sexual dysfunction: Recent progress through psychophysiological and psychophysical methods. *Neuroscience and Biobehavioral Reviews, 19,* 201–209.

Sandberg, G., & Quevillion, R. P. (1987). Dyspareunia: An integrated approach to assessment and diagnosis. *Journal of Family Practice, 24,* 66–69.

Sbrocco, T., Weiner, D. N., Weisberg, R., Bach, A., & Barlow, D. H. (1992, November). *Behavioral subtypes of sexually dysfunctional males: Preliminary results and treatment implications.* Paper presented at the meeting of the Association for Advancement of Behavior Therapy, Boston, MA.

Sbrocco, T., Weisberg, R., Weiner, D. N., Bach, A. B., & Barlow, D. H. (1994, November). *Psychopathology in individuals presenting with erectile dysfunction.* Paper presented at the meeting of the Association for Advancement of Behavior Therapy, San Diego, CA.

Schiavi, R. C., Schreiner-Engel, P., White, D., & Mandeli, J. (1988). Pituitary-gonadal function during sleep in men with hypoactive sexual desire and in normal controls. *Psychosomatic Medicine, 50,* 304–318.

Schover, L. R., Friedman, J. M., Weiler, S. J., Heiman, J. R., & LoPiccolo, J. (1982). Multiaxial problem-oriented system for sexual dysfunctions: An alternative to DSM-III. *Archives of General Psychiatry, 39,,* 614–619.

Schover, L. R., & Jensen, S. B. (1988). *Sexuality and chronic illness: A comprehensive approach.* New York: Guilford Press.

Schreiner-Engel, P., & Schiavi, R. C. (1986). Life psychopathology in individuals with low sexual desire. *Journal of Nervous and Mental Disease, 174,* 646–651.

Schreiner-Engel, P., Schiavi, R. C., White, D., & Ghizzani, A. (1989). Low sexual desire in women: The role of reproductive hormones. *Hormones and Behavior, 23,* 221–234.

Scott, M. L., Cole, J. K., McKay, S. E., Golden, C. J., & Liggett, K. R. (1984). Neuropsychological performance of sexual assaulters and pedophiles. *Journal of Forensic Sciences, 29,* 1114–1118.

Segraves, R. T. (1989). Effects of psychotropic drugs on human erection and ejaculation. *Archives of General Psychiatry, 46,* 275–284.

Segraves, R. T., & Segraves, K. B. (1990). Categorical and multi-axial diagnosis of male erectile disorder. *Journal of Sex and Marital Therapy, 16,* 208–213.

Segraves, R. T., & Segraves, K. B. (1991). Dianosis of female arousal disorder. *Sexual and Marital Therapy, 6,* 9–13.

Sherwin, B. B., Gelfand, M. M., & Brender, W. (1985). Androgen enhances sexual motivation in females: A prospective, crossover study of sex steroid administration in surgical menopause. *Psychosomatic Medicine, 47,* 339–351.

Shull, G. R., & Sprenkle, D. H. (1980). Retarded ejaculation: Reconceptualization and implications for treatment. *Journal of Sex and Marital Therapy, 6,* 234–246.

Silverstein, J. L. (1989). Origins of psychogenic vaginismus. *Psychotherapy and Psychosomatics, 52,* 197–204.

Simon, W. (1994). Deviance as history: The future of perversion. *Archives of Sexual Behavior, 23,* 1–20.

Skakkebaek, N. E., Bancroft, J., Davidson, D. W., & Warner, P. (1981). Androgen replacement with testosterone undecanoate in hypogondal men: A double-blind controlled study. *Clinical Endocrinology, 14,* 49–67.

Slater, E. (1962). Birth order and maternal age of homosexuals. *Lancet, i,* 69–71.

Sotile, W. M., & Kilmann, P. R. (1977). Treatments of psychogenic female sexual dysfunctions. *Psychological Bulletin, 84,* 619–633.

Spector, I. P., & Carey, M. P. (1990). Incidence and prevalence of the sexual dysfunctions: A critical review. *Archives of Sexual Behavior, 19,* 389–409.

Spengler, A. (1977). Manifest sadomasochism of males: Results of an empirical study. *Archives of Sexual Behavior, 6*, 441–456.

St. Lawrence, J. S., & Madakasira, S. (1992). Evaluation and treatment of premature ejaculation: A critical review. *International Journal of Psychiatry in Medicine, 22*, 77–97.

Steege, J. (1984). Dyspareunia and vaginismus. *Clinics in Obstetrics and Gynecology, 27*, 750–759.

Steege, J., & Ling, F. W. (1993). Dyspareunia: A special type of chronic pelvic pain. *Obstetrics and Gynecology Clinics of North America, 20*, 779–793.

Stein, D. J., Hollander, E., Anthony, D. T., Schneier, F. R., Fallon, B. A., Liebowitz, M. R., & Klein, D. F. (1992). Serotonergic medications for sexual obsessions, sexual addictions, and paraphilias. *Journal of Clinical Psychiatry, 53*, 267–271.

Stevenson, J., & Jones, I. E. (1972). Behavior therapy technique for exhibitionism: A preliminary report. *Archives of General Psychiatry, 27*, 839–841.

Stevenson, M. R., & Black, K. N. (1988). Paternal absence and sex-role development: A meta-analysis. *Child Development, 59*, 793–814.

Stoller, R. J. (1968). *Sex and gender: On the development of masculinity and femininity.* New York: Science House.

Stoller, R. (1975a). *Perversion: The erotic form of hatred.* New York: Pantheon Books.

Stoller, R. J. (1975b). *Sex and gender.* London: Hogarth Press.

Strassberg, D. S., Kelly, M. P., Carroll, C., & Kircher, J. C. (1987). The psychophysiological nature of premature ejaculation. *Archives of Sexual Behavior, 16*, 327–336.

Stuart, F. M., Hammond, D. C., & Pett, M. A. (1987). Inhibited sexual desire in women. *Archives of Sexual Behavior, 16*, 91–106.

Taneja, N., Ammini, A. C., Mohapatra, I., Saxena, S., & Kucheria, K. (1992). A transsexual male with 47,XYY karyotype. *British Journal of Psychiatry, 161*, 698–699.

Templeman, T. L., & Stinnett, R. D. (1991). Patterns of sexual arousal and history in a "normal" sample of young men. *Archives of Sexual Behavior, 20*, 137–150.

Tiefer, L. (1991). Historical, scientific, clinical, and feminist criticisms of "the human sexual response cycle" model. *Annual Review of Sex Research, 2*, 1–23.

Tkachuk, J., & Zucker, K. J. (1991, August). *The relation among sexual orientation, spatial ability, handedness, and recalled childhood gender identity in women and men.* Poster presented at the meeting fo the International Academy of Sex Research, Barrie, Ontario.

Tollison, C. D., & Adams, H. E. (1979). *Sexual disorders: Treatment, theory and research.* New York: Gardner Press.

Trudel, G., Boulos, L., & Matte, B. (1993). Dyadic adjustment in couples with hypoactive sexual desire. *Journal of Sex Education and Therapy, 19*, 31–36.

Utian, W. F. (1975). Effects of hysterectomy, oopherectomy, and estrogen therapy on libido. *International Journal of Obstetrics and Gynecolgy, 84*, 314–315.

Uva, J. L. (1995). Autoerotic asphyxiation in the United States. *Journal of Forensic Sciences, 40*, 574–581.

Verhulst, J., & Heiman, J. R. (1988). A systems perspective on sexual desire. In S. R. Leiblum & R. C. Rosen (Eds.), *Sexual desire disorders* (pp. 243–270). New York: Guilford Press.

Wakefield, J. C. (1987). Sex bias in the diagnosis of primary orgasmic dysfunction. *American Psychologist, 42*, 464–471.

Weiner, D. N., Brown, T. A., & Barlow, D. H. (November, 1993). *An experimental analysis of the influence of body image on male sexual arousal.* Paper presented at the meeting of the Association for Advancement of Behavior Therapy, Atlanta, GA.

Weiner, D. N., & Rosen, R. C. (1997). Pharmacological effects on sexual functioning. In M. Sipski & C. Alexander (Eds.), *Maintaining sexuality with chronic illness* (pp. 85–118). Gaithersburg, MD: Aspen.

Wilensky, M., & Meyers, M. F. (1987). Retarded ejaculation in homosexual partners: A report of nine cases. *Journal of Sex Research, 23*, 85–91.

Wilson, G. D., & Gosselin, C. (1980). Personality characteristics of fetishists, transvestites, and sadomasochists. *Personality and Individual Differences, 1*, 289–295.

Wincze, J. P. (1989). Assessment and treatment of atypical sexual behavior. In S. R. Leiblum & R. C. Rosen (Eds.), *Principles and practice of sex therapy: Update for the 1990's* (pp. 382–404). New York: Guilford Press.

Wincze, J. P., & Carey, M. P. (1991). *Sexual dysfunction.* New York: Guilford Press.

Wise, T. N., Fagan, P. J., Schmidt, C. W., Ponticas, Y., & Costa, P. T. (1991). Personality and sexual functioning of transvestite fetishists and other paraphilias. *Journal of Nervous and Mental Disease, 179*, 694–698.

Yalom, I. D. (1960). Aggression and forbiddenness in voyeurism. *Archives of General Psychiatry, 3*, 305.

Zgourides, G. D., & Warren, R. (1989). Retarded

ejaculation: Overview and treatment implications. *Journal of Psychology and Human Sexuality,* 2, 139–150.

Zilbergeld, B. (1992). *The new male sexuality.* New York: Bantam Books.

Zucker, K. J. (1994). *Gender identity, sexual orientation, and sexual behavior in women with congenital adrenal hyperplasia.* In K. J. Zucker (chair), *Cogenital adrenal hyperplasia: The nature and nurture of psychosexual differentiation.* Symposium presented at the meeting of the International Academy of Sex Research, Edinburgh.

Zucker, K. J., & Bradley, S. J. (1995). *Gender identity disorder and psychosexual problems in children and adolescents.* New York: Guilford Press.

Zucker, K. J., Wild, J., Bradley, S. J., & Lowry, C. B. (1993). Physical attractiveness of boys with gender identity disorder. *Archives of Sexual Behavior,* 22, 23–24.

Zuger, B. (1978). Effeminate behavior present in boys from childhood: Ten additional years of follow-up. *Comprehensive Psychiatry,* 19, 363–369.

Zuger, B. (1988). Is early effeminate behavior in boys early homosexuality? *Comprehensive Psychiatry,* 29, 509–519.

17

Somatoform Disorders

THEO K. BOUMAN

GEORG H. EIFERT

CARL W. LEJUEZ

Somatic symptoms are part and parcel of everyday life. Kellner (1986) summarized results from various studies indicating that as much as 75% of the general population experience some form of mild to severe physical complaints in a month. Yet only a small subgroup contact their doctor to seek care or cure for these symptoms, some of which remain medically unexplained. An Australian study reported that 41% of unselected patients visiting a general practitioner and presenting with somatic complaints were found to have no demonstrable somatic pathology (Pilowsky, Smith, & Katsikitis, 1987). Comparable percentages were reported in U.S. studies on abdominal pain (Harvey, Salih, & Read, 1983) and chest pain (cf. Eifert, 1992). In a hospital setting, Van Hemert, Hengeveld, Bolk, Rooijmans, and Vandenbroucke (1993) found that among new referrals to a general medical outpatient clinic, 52% of patients had symptoms that ultimately remained unexplained.

Many of these patients are satisfied and reassured with negative medical examination results, but a significant subgroup will continue to seek help for the same or different physical symptoms, demand more physical examinations and specialist referrals, undergo costly laboratory tests, and, in some cases, even end up on an operating table. Despite their high prevalence, ambiguous physical problems have received relatively little research attention and remain poorly understood. One of the probable reasons for the lack of knowledge about the somatoform disorders is that persons with such problems are often extremely reluctant to see a psychologist or psychiatrist and prefer to remain within the medical service system.

In the following section introductory remarks will be made on the classification of somatoform disorders, their prevalence, contemporary models, and etiology, along with a discussion of auxiliary constructs. Next, each of the five disorders listed in *DSM-IV* will be discussed in more detail, followed by sections on differential diagnosis and general theoretical perspectives. Over the past decades several theoretical models have been advanced in relation to the process of somatization and the specific somatoform disorders (cf. Kellner, 1991). The central issues of a number of these models will be summarized. Pain and hypochondriasis are specifically highlighted because much of recent research is focused on these conditions.

Introduction

The present chapter departs somewhat from the classification of somatoform disorders put forward in *DSM-IV*. This classification originated from the *DSM-III* task force in an attempt to rid psychiatric taxonomy of the concept of neurosis with its etiological connotations. As a result, disorders previously classified in one category as neuroses (anxiety neurosis, neurotic depression, hypochondriasis, and hysteria) were reclassified in four separate *DSM* categories: anxiety disorders, mood disorders, somatoform disorders, and dissociative disorders (Murphy, 1990).

DSM-IV states: "The common feature of the Somatoform Disorders is the presence of physical symptoms that suggest a general medical condition (hence, the term somatoform) and are not fully explained by a general medical condition, by the direct effects of substance, or by another mental disorder" (p. 445). As a consequence of this definition, somatoform disorders can only be diagnoses of exclusion. These physical symptoms result in substantial personal, social, and occupational impairment, and are not feigned or voluntarily produced as in malingering or factitious disorder.

Overview of Somatoform Disorders

The *DSM-IV* section on somatoform disorders describes criteria for (1) somatization disorder, (2) undifferentiated somatization disorder, (3) conversion disorder, (4) pain disorder, (5) hypochondriasis, and (6) body dysmorphic disorder. According to Comer (1995), somatoform disorders can be clustered in two larger categories: the hysterical disorders and the preoccupation disorders. The classical hysterical disorders (i.e., somatization disorder, conversion, and pain disorder) involve actual loss or alteration of bodily functions. Reports of suffering often exceed symptom reports of patients with known medical illnesses, and the symptoms of distress cannot be sufficiently explained by a medical condition. In addition, physical symptoms are not under voluntary control, although there has to be evidence that psychological factors play a role in the onset, maintenance, or exacerbation of the symptoms. Patients with hysterical disorders typically experience little or no anxiety, whereas persons with preoccupation disorders are excessively concerned with or anxious about the notion that there is something physically wrong with their bodies, either disease (i.e., hypochondriasis) or shape and size (i.e., body dysmorphic disorder). The emphasis *DSM* places on the somatoform disorders is therefore on patients with illness-affirming, rather than illness-denying, presentations (i.e., underreporting of somatic complaints)—a point that we will address later when we discuss abnormal illness behavior.

Although *DSM-IV* provides some information on prevalence rates, reliable information about the prevalence of these conditions is lacking. This is largely due to the fact that earlier studies (cf. Kellner, 1986) often did not adequately differentiate between somatoform and related disorders (e.g., anxiety and depression). Additionally, epidemiological studies used various diagnostic criteria and different samples drawn from the general population or specific medical settings. For instance, a Spanish study (Lobo, García-Campayo, Campos, Marcos, & Pérez-Echeverria, 1996) identified 9.4% of a large primary care sample as somatizers. Another obstacle for establishing reliable prevalence rates in epidemiological studies on somatoform disorders are the low base rates of these conditions in the general population. In general, ethnicity is an understudied but probably important variable in the presentation of somatic symptoms. As an example, Farooq, Gahir, Okyere, Sheikh, and Oyebode (1995) found that Asian patients reported significantly more somatic and depressive symptoms than Caucasians. Finally, women tend to somatize more than men (Wool & Barsky, 1994).

With regard to their etiology, the onset and risk factors of somatoform disorders are mostly obscure and systematic knowledge is lacking. Preliminary consensus is that factors such as parental rearing and childhood development, stressful life events, certain personality variables (i.e., high negative affectivity), and aspects of the relationship and communication between patients and doctors are related to the etiology and development of the somatoform disorders in general. Craig, Boardman, Mills, Daly-Jones, and Drake (1993) found a lack of parental care followed by childhood illness to be the best predictors of adult somatization. In a genetic twin study, Torgerson (1986) concludes that although somatoform disorders may have a familial factor, transmission seems to be environmental. Although in the following sections several factors in relation to the various somatoform disorders will be discussed, it should be noted that most of these factors (e.g., sexual abuse) can play a role in any of the somatoform disorders.

Auxiliary and Historical Concepts

Concepts relating to somatization and somatoform disorders are frequently used interchangeably and remain ill-defined in research and clinical practice. Despite considerable comorbidity and phenomenological overlap between psychological and somatic disorders, Cartesian mind-body dualism is still implicitly or explicitly influential in clinical practice. This may be partly due to the traditional division of labor (at least in the 20th century) between medical and psychological disciplines, each claiming (or hoping) to answer some of the questions in the realm of body and mind. Such reductionist models, however, are a serious obstacle to a full understanding of the complex area described in this chapter. In our view, this dualism is simply outdated and no longer tenable. There is broad agreement among most current researchers that environmental, behavioral, and physiological variables interact at any time. Hence, contemporary theories of somatoform (and indeed most other) disorders seek to account for this interplay—although they may differ in how they account for the specifics of that interplay.

In a similar vein, Lipowsky (1988) defined somatization as a tendency to experience and express psychological distress in the form of somatic symptoms that individuals misinterpret as serious physical illness and for which they seek medical help. Again, this definition reflects the current view of somatization as a complex interactive psychopathological process, rather than a discrete group of disorders. Kellner (1986) stated that somatization is neither a discrete clinical entity nor the result of a single pathological process; instead, it cuts across diagnostic categories, such as depression, anxiety, and somatoform disorders.

Because there has traditionally been much debate on the objective and subjective nature of symptoms and complaints in somatoform disorders, it may be helpful to distinguish between the following constructs. *Disease* is generally defined as the presence of objective biological abnormalities in the structure and/or function of bodily organs and systems, whereas *illness* refers to the subjective perception of being unwell and therefore may be unrelated to the presence of an objectifiable disease. The *sick role* is a sociological construct referring to a role granted to an individual by society with accompanying privileges (e.g., staying home from work) and obligations (e.g., complying with medical instructions). The problem in somatoform disorders is that patients believe they have an illness and hence adopt the sick role in the absence of a disease considered present by medical professionals.

Traditionally, *psychosomatic disorders* have been defined as medical conditions in which psychological factors play a role. The concept of psychosomatic disorders has been criticized as being misleading (Lipowsky, 1988), on the grounds that it presupposes a special class of somatic disorders of psychogenic etiology, as well as monocausal psychological etiology—a view that is incompatible with contemporary multicausal models. A more neutral concept is that of *functional somatic symptoms*, which Kellner (1986) defined as somatic symptoms that are not attributed to organic pathology demonstrable by physical examination or routine laboratory investigations; however, transient physiological changes may be found in some of the disorders.

Somatization Disorder

Clinical Picture

Multiple physical complaints without clear or known physical causes are the main feature of somatization disorder. This condition may last for many years and, in some cases, extend over the entire adult life span. *DSM-IV* requires at least four pain symptoms (e.g., involving back, abdomen, joints), two gastrointestinal symptoms (e.g., diarrhea, food intolerance), one sexual symptom (e.g., irregular menses, indifference to sexual activity), and one pseudoneurological symptom (e.g., poor balance, numbness, paralysis) to make the diagnosis. Symptoms typically start before the age of 30 and lead to frequent and multiple medical consultations, a complex medical history, and alterations of the person's lifestyle. Physical and laboratory findings cannot detect a plausible medical condition to be the cause of the symptoms, and if a cause exists, the patient's reaction to the pathological process seems to be in excess of what would be expected.

Full-blown somatization disorder is a relatively infrequent phenomenon in the general population (*DSM-IV*) with prevalence ratings of 0.2% in men and between 0.2 and 2.0% in women. Lifetime prevalence is estimated at 0.1% in the general population (Robins et al., 1984). Escobar, Burnam, Karno, Forsythe, and Golding (1987) found a lifetime prevalence in the general population as low as 0.03% for the full *DSM-III* somatization disorder, and 4.4% for an abridged and less stringent somatization construct. In the ECA study, prevalence of *DSM-III-R* somatization disorder in the general population was found to be between 0.4

and 4.4%, depending on the number of symptoms used for its estimates (Escobar, Rubio-Stipec, Canino, & Karno, 1989).

Historical Perspectives

Somatization disorder is the present name of arguably the oldest mental health diagnosis, which is "hysteria." The history of the concept of somatization reveals something of its complexity and the relatively arbitrary basis of its definition (Kellner, 1986). The ancient Greeks believed that multiple somatic symptoms were caused by the uterus wandering through the female body. In the middle of the 19th century, the French physician Briquet described a polysymptomatic somatic condition, for many decades known as Briquet's syndrome. Guze and Perley (1963) redefined this syndrome as "somatization disorder" in the 1950s as a precursor of the current diagnostic criteria. In subsequent revisions of the *DSM*, the number of symptoms required to assign the diagnosis has gradually been reduced; for instance, from at least 13 out of 35 symptoms in *DSM-III-R* to only eight symptoms divided over four symptom clusters in *DSM-IV*.

Contemporary Theoretical Perspectives

Patients with somatization disorder are considered to constitute a relatively small subset of patients with multiple functional symptoms (Smith, 1995). Many authors devote their discussion of mechanisms involved in the onset and maintenance of somatization disorder to the broader area of these functional symptoms or to the process of somatization.

Based on a summary of the literature, Kellner (1986) concluded that selective perception of and attention to somatic symptoms may contribute to the acquisition of functional somatic symptoms. Over time, these processes are likely to improve a person's skill to detect sensations that have previously remained below the threshold of perceptibility. Accordingly, the construct of *somatosensory amplification* (Barsky & Wyshak, 1990) has been used to describe the enhanced perceptions of nonpathological bodily sensations and changes. The sensations mentioned in the *DSM-IV* criteria are mostly such bodily changes accompanying anxiety and stress (Bass & Murphy, 1990; Sharpe & Bass, 1992).

Somatization disorder has also been described as a means of communication (cf. Bass & Murphy, 1990), more specifically as a somatic expression of failing to cope with life's stresses (e.g., sexual and physical abuse, neglect, conflict, and daily hassles). The continuous presentation of somatic symptoms may become a self-handicapping strategy (cf. Smith, Snyder, & Perkins, 1983); that is, individuals use poor health as an excuse for poor performance. This inadequate problem solving and attributional strategy is manifested by excessive attention to the somatic consequences of stressors rather than to the stressors themselves (Kellner, 1991).

An important general factor in the maintenance of somatization disorder in particular, and in multiple functional symptoms in general, seems to be the reinforcement of the "sick role." Iatrogenic factors frequently play a role in the formation of somatization disorder. For instance, a physician's failure to recognize psychological factors and the prescription of unnecessary medical drugs and treatments are likely to reinforce the patient's illness beliefs. It is for this reason that recent behavioral treatment approaches particularly focus on the restriction of unnecessary and repeated medical interventions and tests, such as diagnostic procedures, laboratory tests, and surgical procedures (e.g., Smith, Monson, & Ray, 1986; Smith, 1995).

Despite the lack of a specific comprehensive model of somatization disorder, perceptual and behavioral mechanisms seem to play an important role, along with the communicative function of autonomic arousal symptoms.

Etiology and Course

The onset of somatization disorder lies in early adulthood, and the course of the problem is often chronic. Sexual abuse and traumatization are frequently cited as precursors of somatization disorder. For instance, Morrison (1989) found a higher degree of unwanted sexual contact in women with somatization disorder than in women with affective disorder. Pribor, Yutzy, Dean, and Wetzel (1993) found more reports of sexual and physical abuse in female psychiatric patients with somatization disorder than in those with other diagnoses. In addition, Salmon and Calderbank (1996) investigated sexual and physical abuse in undergraduate students and found a higher degree of somatization in abused subjects. Generally, prognosis is poor, and patients are rarely asymptomatic with spontaneous remission being unlikely. Somatization is often correlated with frequent absences from work or school, overuse of medical care, and excessive use of drugs and alcohol (*DSM-IV*).

Conversion Disorder

Clinical Picture

Patients with conversion disorder (CD) present with symptoms suggesting a neurological disorder, although appropriate medical investigations fail to identify a neurological or general medical condition. Patients with CD typically present with pseudoneurological symptoms; these are symptoms that are inconsistent with general neurological knowledge. A classic example is "glove anaesthesia," in with the patient complains of numbness of the hand; however, such a sensation does not conform with the body's innervation pattern. *DSM-IV* describes four subtypes of CD: (1) motor symptoms or deficits (e.g., paralysis), (2) seizures or convulsions, (3) sensory symptom or deficit (e.g., blindness, anaesthesia, and aphonia), and (4) a mixed presentation. An important requirement for the diagnosis is the temporal relation between conversion symptoms and a psychological stressor such as acute grief or victimization. Patients are typically unaware of the psychological basis for their symptoms and report being unable to control them. Although most patients with CD experience extreme distress over their symptoms, some patients manifest an indifference or lack of worry about their symptoms (*la belle indifference*).

The prevalence of CD is unknown. Although common in the 19th century, it has become an exceedingly rare condition with estimates in the general population varying between about 0.001 and 0.3% (*DSM-IV*). CD is usually found in young people and is five times more common in women than in men. The condition is more common in persons living in rural areas and of lower socioeconomic status with limited medical or psychological knowledge. In a retrospective examination of 4,220 records of a psychiatric emergency unit, Fishbain and Goldberg (1991) found no cases of specific conversion symptoms such as paralysis or paresis.

Historical Perspectives

The origin of the contemporary concept of CD can be traced back to the Middle Ages, when "conversio" referred to diseases caused by a "suffocation of the womb." Classic views of somatoform disorders assumed that these disorders have common roots and are somehow related to the female reproductive system. Early psychodynamic theories listed somatoform disorders as "neuroses." The 19th-century French neurologist Charcot demonstrated that "hysterical conversions," involving symptoms such as convulsions and paralysis, could be induced by hypnotic techniques. Based on such observations, he assumed that these symptoms originate from mental rather than physical processes. Physical symptoms were regarded as a defense mechanism against unacceptable unconscious conflicts where massive repression has forced psychic energy to be transformed into bodily symptoms.

Freud (1956) also considered conversion a form of defense in which the resulting symptoms were fixations of physical patterns relating directly to events at the time of a patient's (sexual) trauma (Mace, 1992). Primary gain was seen as the warding off of these forbidden impulses, whereas secondary gain referred to the attention and privileges patients received. The loss of bodily functions in CD was therefore thought either to be the direct effect of the psychological trauma or a symbol of the unconscious conflict. Later psychodynamic writings attempted to link specific conversion symptoms to specific fantasies and thoughts, in the sense of a symbolic body language. This symbolic notion could not be corroborated by empirical research, and was therefore abandoned in contemporary conceptualizations of conversion (Mace, 1992). Although specific psychodynamic notions have been eliminated from the *DSM-IV*, the role of conflict is still mentioned in the conversion disorder section: psychological factors are presumed to be associated with the symptom or deficit because symptom onset or exacerbation is supposedly preceded by conflicts or other stressors.

Contemporary Theoretical Perspectives

There are few theoretical accounts of CD that are supported by research evidence. According to a behavioral model proposed by Ullmann and Krasner (1975) conversion symptoms are learned via modeling (i.e., observation of similar symptoms in others) and are adopted by the individual for a gain. Folks, Ford, and Regan (1984) found CD to be more prevalent in rural residents and people from low socioeconomic status, suggesting sociocultural influences in the etiology of this condition.

Kellner (1991) summarized neurophysiological studies indicating that patients with CD generally fail to habituate to stressful stimuli and show more anxious arousal than other patients. Although they describe themselves as more anxious than other individuals with anxiety disorders, psychiatrists actually rated them as less anxious. Because conversion symptoms occur more on the left rather than right side of the body (cf. Ford & Folks, 1985), they could be linked neurophysiologically to emotional arousal. This assumption is based on findings that the right hemisphere is capable of generating more unpleasant emotions than the left hemisphere (Davison & Neale, 1994). At the present time, however, we must simply concede that we do not have an adequate and empirically examined theory of CD.

Etiology and Course

Isolated conversion symptoms are believed to be fairly common, and symptoms often disappear after a relatively brief period. Although conversion may occur at any age, the onset is typically in late childhood or early adulthood. Onset is often sudden and in response to conflicts or stressful situations such a unresolved grief and (sexual) trauma (Sharma & Chaturvedi, 1995). The course of CD is believed to vary from very brief episodes to several weeks, but it should be noted that such longitudinal data are scarce. Mace and Trimble (1996) reported on a 10-year follow-up of general hospital patients with an original diagnosis of CD and found that 59% had improved. In 15% of these patients, the psychiatric diagnosis had been changed to a medical diagnosis, and some of these patients had been given a provisional neurological diagnosis following initial assessment. In another longitudinal study comparing conversion disorder and somatization disorder, Kent, Tomasson, and Coryell (1995) found patients with conversion disorder to have a better prognosis.

Pain Disorder

Clinical Picture

In pain disorder, severe acute or chronic pain in one or more body parts is not entirely or adequately explained by a known medical condition. Pain is ipso facto a subjective phenomenon, and psychological factors such as mood, anxiety, and attention may be involved in the onset, maintenance, or exacerbation of pain and complicate differential diagnosis. Pain is considered acute if it exists for less than six months and chronic when it persists beyond six months. Chronic pain, in particular, is often associated with major changes in behavior such as decreased activity and somatic preoccupation (Pilowsky, Chapman, & Bonica, 1977).

The exact prevalence of pain disorder in the general population is unknown, but it appears to be relatively common and may occur in adults of all ages. The proliferation of special pain clinics could be seen as another indication of the high number of pain patients seeking professional help. Moreover, pain is the most common complaint of individuals presenting to a physician (Ford, 1995; Margolis, Zimny, & Miller, 1984; Von Korff, Dworkin, & LeResche, 1990). All prevalence figures, however, should be viewed with caution because they include data collapsed from different types of pain.

Historical Perspectives

Throughout history, there has been considerable speculation concerning the nature and cause of pain. For instance, Aristotle thought pain was an emotion as opposed to a sensation; Descartes viewed it as a result of physical stimuli impinging upon the body; Epictetus saw it as the result of cognitive activity; and religious leaders looked at it as a test of faith imposed by God or punishment for sins (Turk, Meichenbaum, & Genest, 1983). A commonality of these early theories is a unidimensional view of pain. Theories were based either upon organic or psychological causes, and few attempted to integrate the two. It was not until the 20th century that Cartesian dualism was seriously questioned and multidimensional theories of pain began to develop.

Contemporary Theoretical Perspectives

Fordyce (1976) formulated a behavioral theory of pain, stating that maladaptive pain behavior is acquired through respondent conditioning ("sensory pain") and maintained through operant conditioning ("psychological pain"). Verbal reports and nonverbal expressions of pain are maintained because of associated positive (e.g., financial benefits, attention, concern, or sympathy) and negative reinforcers (e.g., avoidance of or escape from undesirable stimuli such as work or unwanted social interaction; Fordyce, 1976). Additionally, in the absence of direct exposure to environmental contingencies, pain behavior may be acquired or taught through modeling (Craig, 1986). Although respondent and operant conditioning are different processes, it should be noted that the two may interact from the onset of pain behavior through its development (Rachlin, 1985). For instance, the avoidance of physical activity can lead to muscle fibers shortening and losing elasticity. This can be very painful and, as a consequence, persons tend to avoid or escape from physical activity. Such avoidance and escape are negatively reinforced when they lead to a short-term decrease of pain. On the other hand, a long-term cost is also frequently incurred because avoidance and escape may exacerbate the physical condition of the individual, resulting in a vicious circle (Flor, Birbaumer, & Turk, 1990).

If pain behavior (e.g., verbal complaints, facial contortions) is reinforced more than alternative behavior (e.g., pain coping without complaining), the likelihood of future pain behavior will increase and the likelihood of future healthy behavior will decrease. Conversely, if pain behavior is reinforced less than healthy behavior, preference will shift to the latter alternative. In fact, the proportion of pain behavior to healthy behavior should match the relative reinforcement provided for each of these two alternatives. This relation, referred to as the matching law, is clinically useful because it makes it possible to quantify how much reinforcement is necessary to sustain a particular level of a given behavior. Pain behavior is particularly susceptible to social reinforcement (Cairns & Pasino, 1977; Flor, Kerns, & Turk, 1987). For instance, Fernandez and McDowell (1995) found that the frequency of pain and healthy behavior was sensitive to the relative reinforcement provided for each. Although more pain-related research is necessary, the matching law appears to provide a promising objective approach to the quantification of the subjective phenomenon of pain.

Cognitive-behavioral conceptualizations of pain emphasize that pain behavior is due to negative or unrealistically high expectations about experiencing pain as well as low levels of perceived competence to deal with pain. These cognitions often lead to avoidance of particular situations, which may result in further negative expectations regarding the ability to control future onset and cope with pain (Flor, Birbaumer, & Turk, 1990). Differences in coping style are particularly important for the resultant perception of pain and associated mood states (Turk, Okifuji, & Scharff, 1995) and may also affect the impact of the pain stimulus (Asmundson & Norton, 1995). Perceived competence influences how intense pain is experienced, how much disturbance it elicits, and whether the individual engages in adaptive or maladaptive coping behavior (Schermelleh-Engel, Eifert, Moosbrugger, & Frank, 1997). Coping behavior seems to be directly influenced by a person's perceived level of competence and indirectly through pain intensity and pain-related anxiety and depression. For example, decreasing competence appears to lead to increasing pain intensity and increasing pain emotions, which, in turn, leads to increases in maladaptive behavior. Conversely, individuals who trust in their abilities to cope adequately with pain are more likely to engage in adaptive behavior, irrespective of how anxious they are, and such persons do not suffer as much as individuals with low perceived competence.

There are several biopsychological models emerging that have received a fair amount of empirical attention and that have been helpful for designing integrative treatment approaches. A particularly promising example of a comprehensive psychobiological theory of chronic pain has been proposed by Flor et al. (1990). Pain is viewed as a complex response that comprises subjective-psychological, motor-behavioral, and physiological-organic components. This account of chronic pain integrates concepts and findings from operant, respondent, observational, and cognitive learning and relates them to biological concepts and physiological findings. Flor and her associates (1990) proposed that stress may precipitate and facilitate a particular pain disorder to which the individual is already predisposed on an unlearned and learned basis. The learned aspect of this predisposition consists of a reduced threshold for nociceptive activation due to previous trauma or social learning experiences resulting in a physiological response stereotypy of a specific body system or group of muscles.

As an example, individuals with heart-focused anxiety and noncardiac chest pain may habitually respond to stress and pain with increases in muscular tension and sympathetic activation that may over time lead to learned changes in the nociceptive sensitivity and input of chest muscles (Eifert, 1992). In other words, stress and pain episodes may trigger a host of autonomic and muscular reactions, particularly sympathetic activation and elevated muscle tension levels. If such muscular contractions occur repeatedly, a number of muscular and sympathetic reflexes lead to increases in muscle tension and to sympathetically mediated vasoconstriction. If the muscular contractions are of sufficient intensity, frequency, and duration, there will not be sufficient blood and oxygen in the affected muscles and pain-inducing substances will be released. The ensuing pain experience increases muscular and sympathetic hyperactivity and may thus lead to a vicious circle. As these processes also increase the sensitivity of chemo-nociceptors, the likelihood of future pain also increases.

Etiology and Course

Among pain patients, there is a high frequency of prior physical abuse, sexual abuse, and other trauma. Personality traits also seem to be involved (Ford & Parker, 1990). Engel (1959) described the pain-prone personality as involving frequent depression, pessimism, and an unconscious belief that happiness is not deserved. Occupational factors also seem to influence the development of pain (Flor et al., 1987). For instance, overuse of a body part has been shown to lead to specific pain syndromes (Schuldt, Eckholm, Harms-Ringdahl, Aborelius, & Nemeth, 1987). Although research aimed at determining the prototypical pain patient continues (cf. Gamsa, 1994), there is no compelling empirical evidence that shows pain patients to be a homogenous group of individuals (Turk & Flor, 1984; Love & Peck, 1987). Consequently, in the place of uniformity, many researchers have begun to look for subgroups with different psychological profiles (Jensen, Turner, Romano, & Karoly, 1991).

Hypochondriasis

Clinical Picture

Hypochondriasis is characterized by unjustified fears or convictions that one has a serious and often fatal illness, such as heart disease, cancer, or AIDS. Patients frequently seek reassurance, check their bodies, and avoid illness-related situations. Merely informing the patient of the absence of a disease process or explaining the benign nature of the symptoms only results in temporary reassurance that is followed by renewed worry over symptoms and continuing overuse of medical services. *DSM-IV* requires this condition to last for at least six months and not to be of delusional intensity.

There are presently no consistent prevalence rates for hypochondriasis in the general population. Most prevalence research related to hypochondriasis used specific samples and varying definitions. For example, Kenyon (1976) used a strict definition and determined that 3 to 14% of medical patients were hypochondriacal. Agras, Sylvester, and Oliveau (1969) found that 16% of a sample from the general population had fears of illness and 3.1% qualified as having an illness phobia. Pålson (1988) found 10% of a general practice sample to have questionnaire scores indicative of hypochondriasis. Furthermore, individuals with frequent exposure to medical settings (e.g., medical students) appear to have increased health concerns (Hunter, Lohrenz, & Schwartzman, 1964; Kellner, 1986).

Historical Perspectives

Hypochondriasis—a Greek word meaning "below the cartilage"—was derived from the humoral theories of disease and illness, and considered a special form of melancholia resulting from an excess of black bile. In the 17th century, Thomas Sydenham, an English physician, argued that hypochondriasis occurred only in men and was equivalent to hysteria occurring in females. Freud suggested that hypochondriacal patients direct their libido inwards, whereas healthy persons typically direct their libido at external objects. Eventually, internally directed libido would build up and result in physical symptoms (Freud, 1956). Other psychodynamic theories of hypochondriasis suggested that physical symptoms developed in individuals defending against low self-esteem because a sick body is attached with less stigma than a sick mind. Although psychodynamic theories provided a more comprehensive account of hypochondriasis than earlier pseudo-medical theories, there is virtually no empirical evidence to support any of these theories (Kellner, 1985).

Contemporary Theoretical Perspectives

Behavioral theories of excessive illness fear stipulate that internal cues associated with threat and bodily harm (unconditioned stimuli) can serve as conditioned stimuli (Miller, 1977). In the presence of these stimuli, individuals will begin to exhibit conditioned responses such as anxious behavior and physiological changes. These classically conditioned instances of hypochondriacal behavior can then be maintained and reinforced through operant conditioning. Somatic complaints may lead to attention, sympathy, and escape from or avoidance of undesirable tasks or situations. This may reinforce disingenuous symptom overreporting, or it may reinforce hypochondriacal behavior through selective attention to somatic sensations (Kellner, 1985). If somatic complaints are ignored, hypochondriacal behavior in the presence of family and friends may be extinguished, but it may also lead the patient to constantly seek medical reassurance (hoping to receive attention from a physician instead). These are examples of contingency-shaped hypochondriacal behavior, but observers may also learn to exhibit such behavior through the process of modeling or rule-governed behavior (Eifert & Forsyth, 1996). According to Kellner (1985), the hypochondriacal behavior worsens as the conditioning process repeats.

The major tenet of cognitive theories relating to hypochondriasis pertains to the role of misattributions of somatic symptoms, particularly if such symptoms are difficult to understand. It is argued that patients focus on essentially harmless physical sensations, which they consistently misrepresent and misinterpret as indications of physical illness (Barsky & Klerman, 1983; Warwick & Salkovskis, 1990). According to Warwick and Salkovskis (1990), the onset and maintenance of hypochondriasis involves the complex interaction of several factors. Previous experiences with ill health are often the root of future hypochondriacal behavior and they may result in the formation of dysfunctional assumptions. As a result, harmless incidents or physical symptoms produce more negative assumptions, catastrophic cognitions, and overt illness behavior (e.g., increased avoidance, body checks, and reassurance seeking; Salkovskis & Warwick, 1986) accompanied by physiological arousal, anxiety, and depression (cf. Visser & Bouman, 1992). Hypochondriacal concerns are exacerbated as these processes are perpetuated in a vicious cycle. Repeated cycles of this kind may lead to perceptions of seeing oneself as a sick and incapable individual (Salkovskis, 1996).

According to prominent cognitive theories, perceptual and attentional aspects of bodily sensations play an important role in somatoform disorders. Pennebaker (1982) conducted various studies on the role of attention in symptom perception. As a general conclusion, Pennebaker found that deficient external stimulation and low levels of distraction increase the likelihood that individuals pay attention to somatic symptoms and bodily changes. Studies of anxiety disorders have revealed that anxious patients show an *attentional bias* toward threat-related stimuli (MacLeod & Mathews, 1991). In somatoform disorders, empirical evidence for this type of bias has been studied less. Nearly all studies relate to the role of attentional bias in hypochondriacal patients (Tyrer, Lee, & Alexander, 1980; Barsky, Brener, Coeytaux, & Cleary, 1995) or normal subjects with high scores on a hypochondriasis scale (Hitchcock & Mathews, 1992; Hanback & Revelle, 1978). Results at present are inconclusive in that normal subjects and some hypochondriacal patients show an attentional bias, but others do not. Barsky coined the term *somatosensory amplification*, which refers to the tendency to experience a broad range of bodily sensations as noxious, intense, and disturbing (Barsky & Klerman, 1983). In several studies, Barsky and his colleagues found a substantial positive correlation between somatosensory amplification and hypochondriasis (cf. Barsky & Wyshak, 1990).

Etiology and Course

The onset of hypochondriasis is frequently in early adulthood. Although symptoms may wax and wane, the course is typically chronic and the condition frequently takes on a dominant role in the person's life and relationships. In children, somatic complaints and attention to physical symptoms have been shown to be influenced by attention received from parents (Mechanic, 1964). In addition, adult patients who rate themselves as having high hypochondriacal concerns describe their parents as more caring and overprotective than patients with other psychiatric disorders (Parker & Libscombe, 1980). Studies also found that somatic symptoms of child and adult hypochondriacal patients resemble those of their parents or close relatives (e.g., Eifert & Forsyth, 1996; see also Parkes,

1972). Several researchers have suggested that exposure to disease and display of somatic symptoms in the family, in combination with parental attitudes toward illness, influence the development of hypochondriacal concerns in children (Eifert, 1992; Eifert & Forsyth, 1996; Flor et al., 1990; Kellner, 1985). These concerns are likely to continue into adulthood, particularly when persons experience and selectively attend to symptoms that they cannot easily explain or understand (Bianchi, 1971). These findings suggest that vicarious learning or modeling play an important role in the etiology of at least a subgroup of hypochondriasis. Finally, sexual trauma also has been linked to the development of excessive health anxiety. Barsky, Wool, Barnett, and Cleary (1994) found in a sample of hospital outpatients that hypochondriacal adults recalled more childhood trauma (parental upheaval, sexual trauma, and victimization by violence) before the age of 17 than a control group of patients.

Body Dysmorphic Disorder

Clinical Picture

The preoccupation with an imagined or exaggerated body disfigurement, or an excessive concern that there is something wrong with the shape or appearance of body parts, is the main feature of body dysmorphic disorder (BDD). The presumed abnormality is generally not (or hardly) noticeable to others. Objects of concern typically include the face (nose, teeth), head (amount of hair), sexual characteristics (size of penis, breasts), and general body appearance (length, ugliness). Cognitive features are excessive preoccupation, intrusive thoughts, and sometimes ideas of reference. Typical behaviors include avoidance (e.g., of body exposure, direct social contact, looking in the mirror), concealment of imagined deformities (wearing glasses or make-up), excessive checking, and reassurance seeking.

Although the prevalence of body dysmorphic disorder is largely unknown, preoccupation with body image and dissatisfaction with some aspect of one's appearance are believed to be widespread in the general population. Fitts et al. (1989) found 70% of college students to be dissatisfied with some part of their body, and 46% were preoccupied with that aspect of their appearance. Rosen (1995) found about 1% of a community sample fulfilling the diagnosis of BDD with virtually no sex differences in prevalence, and Connolly and Gipson (1978) reported that 2% of patients who elect plastic surgery can be diagnosed as having BDD. *DSM-IV* states that the disorder may be more common than was previously thought and may be underrecognized in settings where cosmetic procedures are performed. It should be noted, however, that simply being unhappy about one's appearance does not justify a diagnosis of BDD; instead, an individual must believe that those physical features are somehow abnormal.

Historical Perspectives

The concept of dysmorphophobia was coined in the late 19th century by the Italian psychiatrist Enrico Morselli (cited in Berrios & Kan, 1996), who described a condition in which there is a sudden onset and subsequent persistence of an idea that the body is or might become deformed, accompanied by severe anxiety over such an awareness. Morselli stressed the obsessive nature of this condition as well as the strong desire to check the perceived body abnormality. Recent views (cf. Fava, 1992a), however, found an absence of phobic anxiety in this condition. As such, the term dysmorphophobia was abandoned in *DSM-IV* and replaced with the concept of body dysmorphic disorder. This concept is also somewhat misleading, however, because the core of the problem is not an *actual* disfigurement of the body but the individual's *perception* of such an abnormality (Bass & Murphy, 1995).

Contemporary Theoretical Perspectives

There is currently no detailed psychological model of BDD, although Rosen (1995) proposed a comprehensive cognitive-behavioral formulation of BDD. According to this formulation, cognitive and affective features involve a perceptual disturbance in body image, plus a preoccupation with the imagined defect especially in social situations. Thinking may be delusional or obsessional about the presumed abnormality in appearance, and behavioral features include avoidance of social situations, camouflaging, checking, and undertaking beauty remedies. Clinical evidence seems to support this broad model (Philips, 1996), but the model requires further specification and empirical scrutiny.

Etiology and Course

The onset of body dysmorphic disorder may be gradual or sudden, and its course is generally continuous and chronic (though fluctuating in intensity). At present the literature on the origin of this disorder consists of only fragmentary and anecdotal reports on etiological factors (Philips, 1996). In addition, no prospective longitudinal study of body dysmorphic disorder symptoms has been undertaken and no theoretical model of its etiology is widely accepted (Rosen, 1995). Nevertheless, the disorder is usually thought to start in adolescence when preoccupation with physical appearance is very common (Braddock, 1982). Sociocultural factors influencing people's attitudes toward and dissatisfaction with their bodies seem to play a role in determining the extent to which a (real or imagined) physical abnormality becomes a cause for concern and preoccupation. Concepts about ideal physical appearances vary over time and between cultures. Furthermore, some authors found perfectionistic features to be related to this condition (Frost, Williams, & Jenter, 1995).

Factitious Disorder

Clinical Picture

When physical symptoms are produced or feigned intentionally to assume the sick role, the *DSM* diagnosis of factitious disorder with predominantly physical signs and symptoms is applicable. (The category of factitious disorder with predominantly psychological symptoms is beyond the scope of this chapter and will not be discussed here.) These symptoms may be fabrications of subjective complaints (e.g., pain), self-injury, self-inflicted illnesses (e.g., as a result of drug use), injections of infectious materials, automutilation, or an exaggeration of existing physical symptoms. Symptoms are under voluntary control and could apply to any part of the body (cf. Feldman & Ford, 1993). Factitious patients are eager to undergo extensive medical procedures and even surgery, which in turn may lead to further complications.

At some point in their life, patients may be "found out" in the medical care system. This could occur when somatic complaints cannot be explained by medical knowledge, when medical tests yield bizarre outcomes, when unexpected complications emerge, or because an illness lasts exceptionally long. Sometimes symptoms are present only when patients know they are observed by medical staff. Aggressive outbursts may occur when the patient is caught "red-handed" bringing on particular symptoms (e.g., by taking drugs, tampering with wounds). Apart from the presence of fabricated symptoms, the clinical picture consists of a dramatic and sometimes acute, but notably vague, presentation of symptoms. Patients will also frequently lie about the nature of their symptoms and life circumstances in general. The condition has been described as a pathological compulsion to deceive medical professionals (*pseudologia phantastica*). Factitious disorder should be distinguished from malingering, another form of medical deception. A malingering patient intentionally produces symptoms with a recognizable goal such as financial compensation or gaining other privileges (e.g., being exempt from duties). In FD there is no such external goal, and the patient's motive is thought to be psychological in nature.

In chronic cases (referred to as Münchhausen syndrome) patients wander from one hospital or doctor to another. Hospital hopping, doctor shopping, and *pseudologia phantastica* are more prominent in this syndrome than in factitious disorder (Fink & Jensen, 1989). Apart from inflicting illnesses on themselves, some patients, particularly mothers, have been found to fabricate symptoms in their children to get attention from doctors. This condition is know as the Münchhausen-by-proxy-syndrome (Schreier & Libow, 1993), and some authors consider it to be a subtype of the battered-child syndrome.

Although factitious disorder is rarely assigned as a diagnosis, the real prevalence is likely to be higher than generally assumed because many cases go unrecognized. Although the disorder is believed to be more common in men than in women, a significant proportion of cases seems to involve young adult women who possess extensive medical knowledge, such as nurses and medical assistants (Feldman & Ford, 1993; Plassman, 1994a). Bauer and Boegner (1996) found the diagnosis applied to 0.3% of all patients admitted to a neurological clinic over a one-year period, and Sutherland and Rodin (1990) reported 0.8% of consecutively referred patients in a general hospital's psychiatric service meeting criteria for a diagnosis of FD.

Historical and Theoretical Perspectives

The term Münchhausen syndrome was coined by Asher (1951) to describe patients who sought hospitalization at different hospitals under often dramatic circumstances for self-induced or simulated illnesses. Factitious disorder was first mentioned in 1980 as a diagnostic category in *DSM-III* emphasizing the aspect of deception. Over the years, the number of reports and published case studies of this condition has increased (cf. Plassmann, 1994a), but the patients' elusive nature of symptoms has prevented systematic research in this area. At present, there are no specific and empirically validated models of factitious disorders. Several papers have focused on the psychodynamic aspects of factitious disorders assuming that affected parts of the body represent the patient's negative affect and that a highly negative self-concept paves the way to self-destruction (Plassmann, 1994a).

Etiology and Course

Although its etiology is not well understood, many authors point to the patient's need for being taken care of. Significant physical and emotional deprivation and abuse in early life, as well as extreme family tension, is assumed to contribute to the development of FD (Plassman, 1994b). Furthermore, early experience with medical procedures and carrying a grudge against the medial profession have been mentioned as etiological factors.

Onset of the disorder is believed to be in early adulthood, and its course is often chronic. A particularly poor prognosis applies to individuals who wander from hospital to hospital, lack steady relationships and employment, are socially isolated, abuse drugs and alcohol, and display antisocial behaviors that may even result in criminal convictions. Not surprisingly, severe personality disorders, such as borderline personality disorder, are frequently diagnosed in individuals with FD (Freyberger, Nordmeyer, Freyberger, & Nordmeyer, 1994). Legitimizing the subjective experience of distress and evoking responsiveness of a caregiver in a safe, structured context is regarded as a key element in managing and treating the disorder (Spivak, Rodin, & Sutherland, 1994).

Differential Diagnosis and Comorbidity

The diagnostic validity of the somatoform disorders in relation to each other, as well as to other clinical syndromes, is problematic. The authors of *DSM-IV* conceded that the grouping of these disorders in a single section is based on clinical utility rather than on empirical findings suggesting shared etiology or mechanisms. However, a practical problem with these criteria is their reference to normative patterns of behavior that are never clearly outlined. Criteria such as "the person's concern is markedly excessive," "grossly in excess of what would be expected," "slight physical abnormality," and "appropriate medical evaluation" are difficult to objectify. Murphy (1990) also indicated that the disorders are not qualitatively distinct but rather merge into each other. For example, pain may occur in somatization disorder, pain disorder, hypochondriasis, and undifferentiated somatoform disorder. Moreover, there are many similarities in the presentation of persons with somatoform disorders, anxiety disorders, depression, and even personality disorders (Bass & Murphy, 1995). This lack of demarcation is hardly surprising because criteria overlap to a considerable degree, making the delivery of a reliable diagnosis difficult. On the other hand, *DSM* criteria also are very selective and will only diagnose patients with a specific symptom profile (Fink, 1996), particularly in cases of somatization disorder (cf. Escobar et al., 1987).

The overemphasis on physical symptoms as a basis for reliable and valid diagnostic criteria for these disorders seems misleading because behavioral and social aspects of the disorders tend to be neglected (Fink, 1996). A simplistic reliance upon physical symptoms is questionable for diagnosing somatoform disorders and useless for the purpose of designing treatments. Symptom-focused diagnoses may be artifacts biased by patients' suggestibility and clinicians' preoccupation for some disease. We concur with Fink (1996) that patients' interpretations, experience, and responses to this particular symptom constitute the actual psychopathology, rather than the presence of a specific set of physical symptoms. In particular, a somatic attributional style (Robbins & Kirmayer, 1991) may contribute to the translation of personal and social problems into physical symptoms, and may prompt patients to present with somatic distress and to request somatic remedies.

Somatoform Disorders and General Medical Condition

The presence of a general medical condition that could account for the presenting symptoms must be carefully examined and considered in every case where physical problems are the focus of a patient's complaints, because symptoms such as pain or fatigue may be related to a wide array of problems ranging from normal sensations to fatal diseases. Some patients diagnosed with somatoform disorders or "functional problems" are ultimately diagnosed with a demonstrable medical condition and must be regarded as initial false negatives for the actual disorder (Sharma & Chaturvedi, 1995). A particularly poignant example was reported by Fishbain and Goldberg (1991), who found conversion symptoms of extremity paresis/paralysis initially diagnosed in three out of 4,220 cases admitted to a psychiatric emergency service. However, all three patients were eventually diagnosed as suffering from severe organic pathology (leading to the death of one patient), reducing the prevalence rate of conversion in their patients to a dramatic 0%. These findings point to the fact that the diagnosis of any somatoform disorder should be made with caution and only after careful physical examination, because these disorders are rare and may preclude medical treatment. In addition, it is occasionally difficult for both physicians and psychologists to determine the nature or origin of somatic complaints. In a study with patients undergoing cardiac catheterization, Eifert, Edwards, Thompson, Haddad, and Frazer (1998) found that chest pain patients with coronary artery disease could be reliably discriminated from patients without heart disease only after cardiac catheterization data became available *and* when catheterization data were considered together with psychological test results.

Although somatization symptoms often are considered synonymous with "unexplained physical symptoms," several authors point to more or less known (patho)physiological mechanisms underlying these symptoms. Kellner (1991) mentions examples of physiological activity that is accentuated by stress and emotions, such as smooth and striated-muscle contraction, and changes in endocrine secretion and blood flow. Various pathophysiological mechanisms in somatization can be detected by routine or advanced medical evaluation (e.g., in abdominal pain, chest pain, chronic fatigue, breathlessness, irritable bowel syndrome; Sharpe & Bass, 1992). As another example, pelvic venous congestion is now believed to play a role in some women with chronic pelvic pain (Glover & Pearce, 1995). Advances in medical diagnostic procedures (e.g., PET and MRI scans) have resulted in more accurate diagnostic decisions and have reduced the number of false positive diagnoses of somatization disorder (Kent et al., 1995).

These considerations question the unexplainable or "nonorganic" nature of symptoms as well as any attempts to uphold the traditional mind-body dualism. They also point to an inconsistency in *DSM-IV*: its definition of somatoform disorders focuses on the presence of a medical condition that suggests a general medical condition, whereas the essential feature of somatization disorder is a pattern of recurring, multiple, somatic complaints. Thus, *DSM-IV* is inconsistent in its emphasis on either symptoms (disease) or complaints (illness). It follows that a somatoform disorder could be diagnosed in the presence of a well-known pathophysiological process (i.e., disease). What ultimately matters is the individual's coping with (or complaining about) these symptoms (on a cognitive, behavioral, and social level) rather than the presence or absence of disease per se.

Differential Diagnoses of Somatoform Disorders

Differentiating among the various somatoform disorders using *DSM-IV* criteria is difficult because of the considerable overlap in symptoms. In particular, somatization disorder and hypochondriasis merit some discussion.

In somatization disorder, the patient's attention is directed at the somatic symptoms themselves, whereas in hypochondriasis symptoms are generally less elaborate and the patient is concerned about a possible underlying serious illness (Murphy, 1990). As a result, hypochondriacal patients experience higher levels of anxiety, whereas patients with somatization disorder hardly experience any anxiety. Although pain symptoms are included in the diagnostic criteria for somatization disorder, symptoms other than pain must be present before the former diagnosis can be made. In contrast, pain is the predominant (and frequently exclusive) focus of the clinical presentation disorder of a person with pain disorder. Patients with somatization disorder, by definition, report quite a number of different physical symptoms, whereas a person with conversion disorder typically manifests only one symptom.

Although hypochondriasis and body dysmorphic disorder share many presenting symptoms (such as bodily preoccupation, repetitious body checking, reassurance seeking, and medical consultations), persons engage in these behaviors for different reasons. Persons with hypochondriasis are afraid of serious illness, whereas persons with body dysmorphic disorder are concerned about the physical appearance of their body. Finally, pain may be a prominent feature in hypochondriacal patients mainly because of the fear that the pain indicates a fatal disease, whereas in pain disorder pain in itself is the central complaint.

Somatoform Disorders and Depression

The high comorbidity of all somatoform disorders with depression, and to a lesser extent with dysthymic disorder, has been well documented (Katon & Sulivan, 1995). For example, Rief, Hiller, Geissner, and Fichter (1995) found high lifetime comorbidity between various somatoform disorders and depression (86%) and anxiety (43%) (see also McElroy, Philips, Keck, Hudson, & Pope, 1993). When somatoform disorders are not accompanied by other psychiatric disorders (such as anxiety, depression, and addiction), the remission rate is higher than in cases with comorbidity. In addition, somatoform disorders were found to increase the risk for other psychiatric conditions (Rief et al., 1995). Several studies have found a striking relation between pain and major depression or dysthymic disorder, but the specifics of that relation are unclear. For instance, Chaturvedi and Michael (1986) found that in pain patients, dysthymic disorder was observed considerably more frequently than major depression. Moreover, France, Krishnan, Houpt, and Maltbie (1984) found that pain symptoms correlated well with the diagnostic criteria for major depression with melancholia. Unfortunately, these studies do not indicate whether there is a causal, reciprocal, or indirect relation between pain and depression.

Somatoform Disorders and Anxiety Disorders

The degree to which major features are shared among somatoform and anxiety disorders is not clear because somatoform disorders are understudied (Barlow, 1988). Most of the reports on the comorbidity of anxiety and somatoform disorders pertain to hypochondriasis and body dysmorphic disorder.

The considerable symptomatic overlap among hypochondriasis, disease phobia, and panic disorder not only is reflected in reports of high comorbidity rates (Warwick & Salkovskis, 1990) but also has impeded our understanding of somatoform disorders and their complex relation to anxiety disorders. To clarify this confusion, Pilowsky (1967) proposed three hypochondriacal dimensions: disease phobia, disease conviction, and bodily preoccupation. Unfortunately, the *DSM* definition fails to distinguish adequately hypochondriasis as a *fear of* disease from a *conviction of having* a serious disease. A clear separation of the different dimensions of hypochondriasis may contribute to a better understanding and more appropriate treatments. Hypochondriacal patients can be placed on four dimensions:

1. Preoccupation with and excessive awareness of bodily sensations and body functions (even in the absence of physical complaints) constitutes the hypochondriacal core (Starcevic, 1988).
2. Disease suspicion or disease conviction are on a continuum of strength, and in rare cases the conviction may reach delusional intensity.
3. Disease fear implies the fear for having a serious physical disease.
4. Safety-seeking behaviors (such as repeated requests for medical examinations, bodily checking, and reassurance seeking) aim at reducing worry and anxiety over physical illness (Warwick & Salkovskis, 1990). These compulsive behaviors are a direct result of excessive bodily preoccupation and disease suspicion.

Warwick and Salkovskis (1990) report that 59% of their hypochondriacal patients also fulfilled *DSM-III-R* criteria for panic disorder. Other studies (Beitman et al., 1987; Eifert, Hodson, Tracey, Seville, & Gunawardane, 1996) found that between 25 and 50% of persons with cardiophobia also suffer from panic disorder. Panic patients with agoraphobia have been found to score as high as hypochondriacal patients in areas such as somatic preoccupation, disease phobia, and illness conviction (Noyes, Reich, Clancy, & O'Gorman, 1986; Fava, Kellner, Zielezny, & Gurand, 1988). Persons with disease fears tend to report fewer and less severe panic symptoms (Beck, Berisford, Taegtmeyer, & Bennett, 1990) but more pronounced illness behaviors (Eifert, Seville, Antony, Brown, & Barlow, 1992) than persons with panic disorder.

There are similarities between body dysmorphic disorder and obsessive-compulsive disorder in terms of the course, estimated prevalence, age of onset, and comorbidity of both disorders (Hollander, Neville, Frenkel, Josephson, & Liebowitz, 1992). These authors go as far as to argue that body dysmorphic disorder is a subset of obsessive-compulsive disorder. Furthermore, they contend that there is "little evidence linking body dysmorphic disorder to other somatoform disorders and that in individual patients the diagnosis may shift from a somatoform to a delusional disorder" (p. 163). In addition, the lifetime comorbidity between body dysmorphic disorder and social phobia is 54%, and as high as 96% with any mood disorder, with almost 40% of these individuals having attempted suicide (McElroy et al., 1993).

One could also argue that body-dysmorphic disorders is a type of delusional disorder, particularly because *DSM-IV* states that the body flaw may be imagined. Obsessive and compulsive behaviors could the result of a delusional belief about the body. A diagnosis of obsessive-compulsive disorder, however, would imply a greater degree of contact with reality than is commonly seen in body dysmorphic disorder. Nevertheless, the person's problems should be compared with and differentiated from the *DSM-IV* category of delusional disorder, somatic type.

Somatization and Personality

Until recently, somatoform disorders have been regarded solely as clinical syndromes on Axis I of *DSM-IV*. Yet they share many features with personality disorders (Tyrer, 1995; Bass & Murphy, 1995) in terms of their (1) developmental origin; (2) persistent nature; (3) disruptive impact on personal, social, and occupational functioning; and (4) chronic course. This description particularly fits patients with hypochondriasis, somatization disorder, body dysmorphic disorder, and chronic pain. In the same vein, Barsky (1995) states that somatoform disorders may well be regarded as functional somatic symptoms superimposed upon personality disorders. This points to the understudied role of the somatic vocabulary in the development of personality and its disorders (Millon, 1996).

Despite these interesting observations, one should not overstate the overlap between somatization and personality disorders. Indeed, such overlap is not unique to somatization but also applies to other Axis I problems such as anxiety (cf. Barlow, 1988). Patterns of somatization behavior typically have a long history, and as such, somatization behavior can be regarded as a persistent behavioral or personality repertoire (Staats, 1996). Such behavioral repertoires are important for determining how individuals respond to critical situations and challenges in their life. On the other hand, clinical psychologists interested in treatment need to focus on specific observable behavior rather than hypothesized personality repertoires, because when it comes to selecting targets for treatment, all we can focus on is specific observable behavior—and that is what we focus on in this chapter.

General Models of Somatoform Disorders

Abnormal Illness Behavior

Pilowsky (1993, p. 62) defined the concept of abnormal illness behavior as the "persistence of a maladaptive mode of experiencing, perceiving, evaluating, and responding to one's own health status, despite the fact that a doctor has provided a lucid and accurate appraisal of the situation and management to be followed (if any), with opportunities for discussion, negotiation and clarification, based on adequate assessment of all relevant biological, psychological, social and cultural factors." Somatically focused (in contrast to psychologically focused) abnormal illness behavior is divided into illness-affirming and illness-denying behavior. According to Pilowsky, in somatoform disorders the motivation for illness-affirming behavior is supposedly unconscious, as opposed to the conscious motivation in patients with malingering and factitious disorder. In his 1993 paper, Pilowsky stated that abnormal illness behavior is not a diagnosis as such because it refers to the disagreement between the doctor and patient about the sick role to which the patient feels entitled. The concept relates to the sociological concepts of the "sick role" and "illness behavior," and places somatoform disorders in a societal rather than a intraindividual context. Sharpe, Mayou, and Bass (1995) maintained that the concept of abnormal illness behavior has been valuable in drawing attention to the behavioral aspects of all illness, but it is not specific to patients with functional somatic symptoms. Fava (1992b) suggested that the concept of abnormal illness behavior could supplant the somatoform disorders rubric and provide a conceptual framework for disorders that would otherwise be scattered and unrelated in the *DSM* or that would not find a room such as denial of illness. In conclusion, abnormal illness behavior may be regarded as an important (though not unique) dimension in a multidimensional conceptualization of somatoform disorders.

Deficits in Cognitive Processing of Emotion

Initially coined to specify the communicative function of somatic symptoms, the concept of *alexithymia* literally meant "no words for feelings" (Sifneos, 1973). Alexithymia was considered a crucial factor in what Sifneos called psychosomatic illnesses, its key features being "a relative constriction of emotional functioning, poverty of fantasy life, and inability to find appropriate words to describe their emotions" (p. 255). Alexithymic individuals seem to be vulnerable to mounting tension from undifferentiated states of unpleasant emotional arousal. This vulnerability is assumed to be caused by deficits in cognitive processing of emotions independent of their source, one of which may be intrapsychic conflict. In this sense, it is a disturbance in the cognitive processing of emotional awareness that may interfere with the subject's ability to experience and express emotions. Alexithymia has evolved from a psychodynamic construct to a deficit in the cognitive processing of emotions, linking susceptibility to disease with prolonged states of emotional arousal (Taylor, Bagby, & Parker, 1991). For example, in a sample of normal volunteers, Vingerhoets, Van Heck, Grim, and Bermond (1995) found strong negative correlations between alexithymia and the expression of emotions, daydreams and fantasies, and planful and rational actions. Bach and Bach (1995) found high alexithymia scores to be predictive of persistent somatization. Summarizing the present status of alexithymia, Salminen, Saarijävi, and Äärelä (1996) concluded that the concept is not only applicable to patients with "psychosomatic" problems but can be a secondary feature of any kind of psychological trauma (cf. Vingerhoets et al., 1995).

Psychobiological Theories

Earlier in this chapter we discussed a psychobiological theory of chronic pain (Flor et al., 1990) that integrates psychological, biological, and environmental aspects. This type of model seems to be particularly helpful in shedding at least some light on the complex interactions among the various systems involved in the onset and maintenance of somatoform disorders. Another example of such an integrative model relates to the chronic fatigue syndrome (CFS), which is characterized by mental and physical fatigue of at least six months' duration. This syndrome cannot be explained by a known physical disease and occasionally leads to severe disability. Although some researchers believe viral infections could be an important contributing factor to this condition, there is at present no evidence for any specific viral or immunological causation (Wessely, 1993). On the other hand, the lack of such evidence does not preclude that viral or other pathophysiological mechanisms are responsible for this syndrome. Wessely and Sharpe (1995) formulated an integrative biopsychosocial model in which psychological, physiological, and social factors interact. Somatic attributions, inactivity, and depression are hypothesized to perpetuate the problem. CFS patients typically attribute their symptoms to a physical cause, probably because a disease attribution avoids blame and is socially more acceptable. They see rest as an important response to the fatigue, leading to a downward viscious cycle of decreased activity. This cycle leads to neuromuscular deconditioning (i.e., the loss of muscle strength), which may result in painful muscles and a sensation of further fatigue, and frustration (Surawy, Hackmann, Hawton, & Sharpe, 1995). Patients with CFS tend to oscillate between inactivity and bursts of activity, the latter supposedly because of their high achievement standards. It should be noted this theory is largely conjectural and, at this point, there is no firm evidence for or against the involvement of psychological factors in this condition.

In conclusion, psychobiological models hold great future promise because they acknowledge the relative contributions of various aspects of the individual's functioning, rather than seeking to explain somatoform disorders from a single theoretical perspective. However, specific knowledge of the interaction among the various systems is only rudimentary and is available for only a few manifestations of this group of disorders.

Conclusions

The present review of somatoform disorders reveals that there are more questions than answers. Although unexplained and unexplainable somatic symptoms are very common in the general population, it is still unclear why in some people such symptoms develop into an often lifelong distressing condition. We do not even have reliable information on prevalence, distribution across specific group within the population, and sex differences.

We also identified a number of problems regarding the diagnostic criteria for somatoform disorders. Diagnoses are based upon the sophistication and accuracy of medical diagnostic procedures in general and individual cases in particular. Stating that the diagnosis of a somatoform disorder requires the absence of a somatic explanation for the symptoms is an undue simplification of the complex nature of somatoform disorders. Our understanding of these disorders will benefit from taking into account the behaviors, perceptions, cognitions, and social relationships of patients with unexplained physical symptoms, rather than focusing on the absence of somatic abnormalities (cf. Fink 1996). Too much effort has been directed at explaining the *origin* of the somatic complaints and too little at the *consequences* of these complaints once unexplained (cf. Sharpe & Bass, 1992).

An exclusive focus on the absence of physical disease is also problematic because "objective disease states" are difficult to diagnose and quantify. Physiological differences between individuals are likely to interact with objective disease states to produce a range of "valid suffering" from the same disease. Medicine is not a complete science and therefore lacks a comprehensive classification of diseases that can be diagnosed. Individuals often have multiple diseases that interact, and while "norms of suffering" may exist for a disease, these norms must be suspect when there are multiple diseases. Patients with idiosyncratic disease states are likely to be diagnosed somatoform simply because medical science has no pigeonhole to put them in.

Moreover, the validity of any diagnostic category defined mainly by exclusionary conditions is likely to be low. Barlow (1988) stated that classification of any disorder, whether dimensional or categorical, should reliably describe subgroups of symptoms or behaviors that are readily identifiable by independent observers on the basis of operational definitions. There should also be some clinical usefulness or value in identifying these subgroups or dimensions, such as predicting a specific response to treatment, course of the disorder, and tailoring treatment (Eifert, Evans, & McKendrick, 1990). These criteria are not met by the somatoform disorders. It appears that the *DSM-IV* section on somatoform disorders is a somewhat arbitrary amalgam of various conditions relating to bodily functioning and how such functioning is perceived, with fluid boundaries to other psychiatric and medical conditions and processes.

Using a categorical classification system, the boundaries between somatoform disorders, other psychopathology, and general medical conditions cannot be defined to a satisfactory degree. This is partly due to the fact that somatoform disorders share many features with other types of psychological (e.g., anxiety and depression) and functional somatic problems. Their presentations are multifaceted and their understanding can be furthered only from a multidisciplinary rather than a unidimensional perspective, with a biopsychosocial approach showing the greatest promise. This approach is exemplified by the model of Flor and associates (1990) described in this chapter. Another example has been presented by Mayou, Bass, and Sharpe (1995) who have proposed a classification of patients with functional somatic symptoms along five dimensions: (1) number and type of somatic symptoms; (2) mental state, or mood and psychiatric disorder; (3) cognitions, or disease conviction; (4) behavioral and functional impairment, or illness behavior, avoidance, use of health services; and (5) pathophysiological disturbance, or organic diseases, mechanisms such as hyperventilation, neuromuscular deconditioning.

There are several potential avenues for future psychological research on somatoform disorders. For instance, we need more information on the impact of cognitive processes (attribution, attention, and memory) and environmental contingencies (social consequences of illness behavior, medical practice guidelines). We can only speculate what impact health care policies will have on the prevalence of this group of disorders. It is clear, however, that managed care and cost-cutting pressures have the effect of limiting medical access, particularly access to costly medical tests. As a result, patients may be encouraged to exaggerate the seriousness and intensity of symptoms. Furthermore, psychoneuroimmunological models may help clarify the complex nature of what used to be referred to as the "mind-body interface." Studying the specific interactions among psychological, somatic, and social factors, rather than viewing these factors in isolation, should help increase our understanding of this group of disorders. In conclusion, multidimensional classification and integrative psychobiosocial models appear to have the greatest explanatory power and treatment utility.

References

Agras, S., Sylvester, D., & Oliveau, D. (1969). The epidemiology of common fears and phobias. *Comprehensive Psychiatry, 10*, 151–156.

Asher, R. (1951). Münchhausen's syndrome. *Lancet, i*, 339–341.

Asmundson, G. J., & Norton, G. R. (1995). Anxiety sensitivity in patients with physically unexplained chronic back pain. *Behaviour Research and Therapy, 33*, 771–777.

Bach, M., & Bach, D. (1995). Predictive value of alexithymia: A prospective study in somatizing patients. *Psychotherapy and Psychosomatics, 64*, 43–48.

Barlow, D. H. (1988). *Anxiety and its disorders: The nature and treatment of anxiety and panic*. New York: Guilford.

Barsky, A. J. (1995). Somatoform disorders and personality disorders. *Journal of Psychosomatic Research, 39*, 399–402.

Barsky, A. J., Brener, J., Coeytaux, R. R., & Cleary, P. D. (1995). Accurate awareness of heartbeat in hypochondriacal and non-hypochondriacal patients. *Journal of Psychosomatic Research, 39*, 489–497.

Barsky, A. J., & Klerman, G. L. (1983). Overview: Hypochondriasis, bodily complaints, and somatic styles. *American Journal of Psychiatry, 140*, 273–283.

Barsky, A. J., Wool, C., Barnett, M. C., & Cleary, P. D. (1994). Histories of childhood trauma in adult hypochondriacal patients. *American Journal of Psychiatry, 151*, 397–401.

Barsky, A. J., & Wyshak, G. (1990). Hypochondriasis and somatosensory amplification. *British Journal of Psychiatry, 157*, 404–409.

Bass, C. M., & Murphy, M. R. (1990). Somatization disorder: Critique of the concept and suggestions for future research. In C. M. Bass (Ed.), *Somatization. Physical symptoms and psychological illness* (pp. 301–332). Oxford: Blackwell.

Bass, C. M., & Murphy, M. R. (1995). Somatoform and personality disorders: Syndromal comorbidity and overlapping developmental pathways. *Journal of Psychosomatic Research, 39*, 403–427.

Bauer, M., & Boegner, F. (1996). Neurological syndromes in factitious disorder. *Journal of Nervous and Mental Diseases, 184*, 281–288.

Beck, J. G., Berisford, M. A., Taegtmeyer, H., & Bennett, A. (1990). Panic symptoms in chest pain without coronary artery disease: A comparison with panic disorder. *Behavior Therapy, 21*, 241–252.

Beitman, B. D., Basha, I., Flaker, G., DeRosear, L., Mukerji, I. V., Trombka, L., & Katon, W. (1987). Atypical or non-anginal chest pain: Panic disorder or coronary artery disease? *Archives of Internal Medicine, 147*, 1548–1552.

Berrios, G. E., & Kan, C. S. (1996). A conceptual and quantitative analysis of 178 historical cases of dysmorphophobia. *Acta Psychiatrica Scandinavica, 94*, 1–7.

Bianchi, G. N. (1971). Patterns of hypochondriasis: A principle components analysis. *British Journal of Psychiatry, 122*, 541–548.

Braddock, L. E. (1982). Dysmorphophobia in adolescence: A case report. *British Journal of Psychiatry, 140*, 199–201.

Cairns, D., & Pasino, J. (1977). Comparison of verbal reinforcement and feedback in the operant treatment of disability due to chronic low back pain. *Behavior Therapy, 8*, 621–630.

Chaturvedi, S. K., & Michael, A. (1986). Chronic pain in a psychiatric clinic. *Journal of Psychosomatic Research, 30*, 347–354.

Comer, R. J. (1995). *Abnormal psychology* (2nd ed.). New York: Freeman.

Connolly, P. J., & Gipson, M. (1978). Dysmorphophobia—A long-term study. *British Journal of Psychiatry, 132*, 568–570.

Craig, K. D. (1986). Social modelling influences: Pain in context. In R. A. Sternbach (Ed.), *The psychology of pain* (2nd ed.; pp. 67–95). New York: Raven Press.

Craig, T. K. J., Boardman, A. P., Mills, K., Daly-Jones, O., & Drake, H. (1993). The south London somatisation study. I: Longitudinal course and the influence of early life experiences. *British Journal of Psychiatry, 163*, 579–588.

Davison, G. C., & Neale, J. M. (1994). *Abnormal psychology (6th ed.)*. New York: John Wiley.

Eifert, G. H. (1992). Cardiophobia: A paradigmatic behavioral model of heart-focused anxiety and non-anginal chest pain. *Behaviour Research and Therapy, 30*, 329–345.

Eifert, G. H., & Edwards, K., Thompson, R. N., Haddad, J., & Frazer, N. L. (1998). *Panic symptoms and chest pain in cardiology patients with and without coronary artery disease*. Manuscript submitted for publication.

Eifert, G. H., Evans, I. M., & McKendrick, V. (1990). Matching treatments to client problems not diagnostic labels: A case for paradigmatic behavior therapy. *Journal of Behavior Therapy and Experimental Psychiatry, 21*, 163–172.

Eifert, G. H., & Forsyth, J. F. (1996). Heart-focused and general illness fears in relation to parental medical history and separation experiences. *Behaviour Research and Therapy, 34*, 735–739.

Eifert, G. H., Hodson, S. E., Tracey, D. R., Seville, J. L., & Gunawardane, K. (1996). Heart-focused anxiety, illness beliefs, and behavioral impairment: Comparing healthy heart-anxious patients with cardiac and surgical inpatients. *Journal of Behavioral Medicine, 19*, 385–399.

Eifert, G. H., Seville, J. L., Antony, M. M., Brown, T. A., & Barlow, D. H. (November, 1992). *Panic disorder and cardiophobia: An examination of heart-focused anxiety and illness beliefs and behaviors in persons with panic disorder.* Paper presented at the 26th annual conference of the Association for the Advancement of Behavior Therapy, Boston, MA.

Engel, G. E. (1959). Psychogenic pain and the pain-prone patient. *American Journal of Medicine, 16*, 899–918.

Escobar, J. I., Burnam, M. A., Karno, M., Forsythe, A., & Golding, J. M. (1987). Somatization in the community. *Archives of General Psychiatry, 44*, 713–718.

Escobar, J. I., Rubio-Stipec, M., Canino, G., & Karno, M. (1989). Somatic symptoms index (SSI): A new and abridged somatization construct. Prevalence and epidemiological correlates in two large community samples. *Journal of Nervous and Mental Diseases, 177*, 140–146.

Farooq, S., Gahir, M. S., Okyere, E., Sheikh, A. J., & Oyebode, F. (1995). Somatization: A transcultural study. *Journal of Psychosomatic Research, 39*, 883–888.

Fava, G. A. (1992a). Morselli's legacy: Dysmorphophobia. *Psychotherapy and Psychosomatics, 58*, 117–118.

Fava, G. A. (1992b). The concept of psychosomatic disorder. *Psychotherapy and Psychosomatics, 58*, 1–12.

Fava, G. A., Kellner, R., Zielezny, M., & Gurand, S. (1988). Hypochondriacal fears in agoraphobia. *Journal of Affective Disorders, 14*, 239–244.

Feldman, M. D., & Ford, C. V. (1993). *Patient or pretender. Inside the strange world of factitious disorders.* New York: John Wiley.

Fernandez, E., & McDowell, J. J. (1995). Response-reinforcement relationships in chronic pain syndrome: Applicability of Herrnstein's law. *Behaviour Research and Therapy, 33*, 855–863.

Fink, P. (1996). Somatization—Beyond symptom count. *Journal of Psychosomatic Research, 40*, 7–10.

Fink, P., & Jensen, J. (1989). Clinical characteristics of the Münchhausen Syndrome. A review and three new cases. *Psychotherapy and Psychosomatics, 52*, 164–170.

Fishbain, D. A., & Goldberg, M. (1991). The misdiagnosis of conversion disorder in a psychiatric emergency service. *General Hospital Psychiatry, 13*, 177–181.

Fitts, S. N., Gibson, P., Redding, C. A., & Deiter, P. J. (1989). Body dysmorphic disorder: Implications for its validity as a DSM-III-R clinical syndrome. *Psychological Reports, 64*, 655–658.

Flor, F., Birbaumer, N., & Turk, D. C. (1990). The psychobiology of chronic pain. *Advances in Behaviour Research and Therapy, 12*, 47–84.

Flor, F., Kerns, R. D., & Turk, D. C. (1987). The role of spouse reinforcement, perceived pain, and activity levels of chronic pain patients. *Journal of Psychosomatic Research, 31*, 251–259.

Folks, D. G., Ford, C. V., & Regan, W. M. (1984). Conversion symptoms in a general hospital. *Psychosomatics, 25*, 285–295.

Ford, C. V. (1995). Dimensions of somatization and hypochondriasis. *Neurologic Clinics, 13*, 241–253.

Ford, C. V., & Folks, D. G. (1985). Conversion disorder: An overview. *Psychosomatics, 26*, 371–383.

Ford, C. V., & Parker, P. E. (1990). Somatoform disorders. In M. E. Thase, B. A. Edelstein, & M. Hersen (Eds.), *Handbook of outpatient treatment of adults* (pp. 291–307). New York: Plenum Press.

Fordyce, W. E. (1976). *Behavioral methods for chronic pain and illness.* St. Louis: C. V. Mosby.

France, R. D., Krishnan, K. R. R., Houpt, J. L., & Maltbie, A. A. (1984). Differentiation of depression from chronic pain with the dexamethason suppression test and DSM-III. *American Journal of Psychiatry, 141,* 1577–1579.

Freud, S. (1956). *Collected papers.* London: Hogarth.

Freyberger, H., Nordmeyer, J. P., Freyberger, H. P., & Nordmeyer, J. (1994). Patients suffering from factitious disorder in the clinico-psychosomatic consultation liaison service: Psychodynamic procedures, psychotherapeutic initial care and clinico-interdisciplinary cooperation. *Psychotherapy and Psychosomatics, 62,* 108–122.

Frost, R. O., Williams, N., & Jenter, C. (1995). *Perfectionism and body dysmorphic disorder.* Paper presented at the World Congress of Behavioral and Cognitive Therapies, Copenhagen, Denmark.

Gamsa, A. (1994). The role of psychological factors in chronic pain. I. A half century of study. *Pain, 57,* 5–15.

Glover, L., & Pearce, S. (1995). Chronic pelvic pain. In R. Mayou, C. M. Bass, & M. Sharpe (Eds.), *Treatment of functional somatic symptoms* (pp. 313–327). Oxford: Oxford University Press.

Guze, S. B., & Perley, M. J. (1963). Observations on the natural history of hysteria. *American Journal of Psychiatry, 119,* 960–965.

Hanback, J. W., & Revelle, W. (1978). Arousal and perceptual sensitivity in hypochondriasis. *Journal of Abnormal Psychology, 87,* 523–530.

Harvey, R. F., Salih, W. Y., & Read, A. E. (1983). Organic and functional disorders in 2000 gastroenterology outpatients. *Lancet, i,* 632–634.

Hitchcock, P., & Mathews, A. (1992). Interpretation of bodily symptoms in hypochondriasis. *Behaviour Research and Therapy, 30,* 223–234.

Hollander, E., Neville, D., Frenkel, M., Josephson, S., & Liebowitz, M. R. (1992). Body dysmorphic disorder. Diagnostic issues and related disorders. *Psychosomatics, 33,* 156–165.

Hunter, R. C. A., Lohrenz, J. G., & Schwartzman, A. E. (1964). Nosophobia and hypochondriasis in medical students. *Journal of Nervous and Mental Disorders, 139,* 147–152.

Jensen, M. P., Turner, J. A., Romano, J. M., & Karoly, P. (1991). Coping with chronic pain: A critical review of the literature. *Pain, 47,* 249–283.

Katon, W., & Sullivan, M. (1995). Antidepressant treatment of functional somatic symptoms. In R. Mayou, C. M. Bass, & M. Sharpe (Eds.), *Treatment of functional somatic symptoms* (pp. 313–327). Oxford: Oxford University Press.

Kellner, R. (1985). Functional somatic symptoms and hypochondriasis: A survey of empirical studies. *Archives of General Psychiatry, 42,* 821–833.

Kellner, R. (1986). *Somatization and hypochondriasis.* New York: Praeger.

Kellner, R. (1991). *Psychosomatic syndromes and somatic symptoms.* Washington, DC: American Psychiatric Press.

Kent, D. A., Tomasson, K., & Coryell, W. (1995). Course and outcome of conversion and somatization disorders. *Psychosomatics, 36,* 138–144.

Kenyon, F. E. (1976). Hypochondriacal states. *British Journal of Psychiatry, 129,* 1–14.

Lipowsky, Z. J. (1988). Somatization: the concept and its clinical applicability. *American Journal of Psychiatry, 145,* 1358–1368.

Lobo, A., García-Campayo, J., Campos, R., Marcos, G., Pérez-Echeverria, M. J. (1996). Somatization in primary care in Spain. *British Journal of Psychiatry, 168,* 344–353.

Love, A. W., & Peck, C. L. (1987). The MMPI and psychological factors in chronic low back pain: A review. *Pain, 28,* 1–12.

Mace, C. J. (1992). Hysterical conversion. I: A history. *British Journal of Psychiatry, 161,* 369–377.

Mace, C. J., & Trimble, M. R. (1996). Ten-year prognosis of conversion disorder. *British Journal of Psychiatry, 169,* 282–288.

MacLeod, C., & Mathews, A. (1991). Cognitive-experimental approaches to the emotional disorders. In P. R. Martin (Ed.), *Handbook of behavior therapy and psychological science: An integrative approach* (pp. 116–150). New York: Pergamon.

Margolis, R. B., Zimny, G. H., & Miller, D. (1984). Internists and the chronic pain patient. *Pain, 20,* 151–156.

Mayou, R., Bass, C. M., & Sharpe, M. (Eds.). (1995). *Treatment of functional somatic symptoms.* Oxford: Oxford University Press.

McElroy, S. L., Philips, K. A., Keck, P. E., Hudson, J. I., & Pope, H. G. (1993). Body dysmorphic disorder: Does it have a psychotic subtype. *Journal of Clinical Psychology, 54,* 389–395.

Mechanic, D. (1964). The influence of mothers on their children's health attitudes and behavior. *Paediatrics, 33,* 444–453.

Miller, N. E. (1977). The effects of learning on visceral functions. *New England Journal of Medicine, 296*, 1274–1278.
Millon, T. (1996). *Disorders of personality. DSM-IV and beyond*. New York: John Wiley.
Morrison, J. (1989). Childhood sexual abuse of women with somatization disorder. *American Journal of Psychiatry, 146*, 239–241.
Murphy, M. R. (1990). Classification of the somatoform disorders. In C. M. Bass (Ed.), *Somatization. Physical symptoms and psychological illness* (pp. 10–39). Oxford: Blackwell.
Noyes, R., Reich, J., Clancy, J., & O'Gorman, T. W. (1986). Reduction in hypochondriasis with treatment of panic disorder. *British Journal of Psychiatry, 149*, 631–635.
Pålson, N. (1988). Functional somatic symptoms and hypochondriasis among general practice patients: A pilto study. *Acta Psychiatrica Scandinavica, 78*, 191–197.
Parker, G., & Lipscombe, P. (1980). The relevance of early parental experiences to adult dependency, hypochondriasis, and utilization of primary physicians. *British Journal of Medical Psychology, 53*, 355–363.
Parkes, C. M. (1972). *Bereavement: Studies of grief in adult life*. New York: International Universities Press.
Pennebaker, J. W. (1982). *The psychology of physical symptoms*. New York: Springer.
Philips, K. A. (1996). *The broken mirror*. Oxford: Oxford University Press.
Pilowsky, I. (1967). Dimensions of hypochondriasis. *British Journal of Medical Psychology, 113*, 89–93.
Pilowsky, I. (1993). Aspects of abnormal illness behaviour. *Psychotherapy and Psychosomatics, 60*, 62–74.
Pilowsky, I., Chapman, C. R., & Bonica, J. J. (1977). Pain, depression, and illness behavior in a pain clinic population. *Pain, 4*, 183–192.
Pilowsky, I., Smith, Q. P., & Katsikitis, M. (1987). Illness behavior and general practice utilisation: A prospective study. *Psychosomatic Research, 31*, 177–183.
Plassmann, R. (1994a). Münchhausen syndromes and factitious diseases. *Psychotherapy and Psychosomatics, 62*, 7–26.
Plassmann, R. (1994b). The biography of the factitious-disorder patient. *Psychotherapy and Psychosomatics, 62*, 123–128.
Pribor, E. F., Yutzy, S. H., Dean, J. D., & Wetzel, R. D. (1993). Briquet's syndrome, dissociation, and abuse. *American Journal of Psychiatry, 150*, 1507–1511.
Rachlin, H. C. (1985). Pain and behavior. *Behavioral and Brain Sciences, 8*, 43–83.
Rief, W., Hiller, W., Geissner, E., & Fichter, M. M. (1995). A two-year follow-up study of patients with somatoform disorders. *Psychosomatics, 36*, 376–386.
Robbins, J. M., & Kirmayer, L. J. (1991). Attributions of common somatic symptoms. *Psychological Medicine, 21*, 1029–1045.
Robins, L. N., Helzer, J. E., Weissman, M. M., Orvaschel, H., Gruenberg, E., Burke, J. D., & Regier, D. A. (1984). Lifetime prevalence of specific psychiatric disorders in three sites. *Archives of General Psychiatry, 41*, 949–958.
Rosen, J. C. (1995). The nature of body dysmorphic disorder and treatment with cognitive behavior therapy. *Cognitive and Behavioral Practice, 2*, 143–166.
Salkovskis, P. M. (1996). The cognitive approach to anxiety: Threat beliefs, safety-seeking behavior, and the special case of health anxiety and obsessions. In P. M. Salkovskis (Ed.), *Frontiers of cognitive therapy* (pp. 49–74). New York: Guilford.
Salkovskis, P. M., & Warwick, H. M. C. (1986). Morbid preoccupations, health anxiety and reassurance: A cognitive-behavioural approach to hypochondriasis. *Behaviour Research and Therapy, 24*, 597–602.
Salminen, J. K., Saarijävi, S., & Äärelä, E. (1995). Two decades of alexithymia. *Journal of Psychosomatic Research, 39*, 803–807.
Salmon, P., & Calderbank, S. (1996). The relationship of childhood physical and sexual abuse to adult illness behavior. *Journal of Psychosomatic Research, 40*, 329–336.
Schermelleh-Engel, K., Eifert, G. H, Moosbrugger, H., & Frank, D. (1997). Perceived competence and anxiety as determinants of maladaptive and adaptive coping strategies of chronic pain patients. *Personality and Individual Differences, 22*, 1–10.
Schreier, H. A., & Libow, J. A. (1993). *Hurting for love: Münchhausen by proxy syndrome*. New York: Guilford.
Schuldt, K., Ekholm, J., Harms-Ringdahl, K., Aborelius, U., & Nemeth, G. (1987). Influence of sitting postures on neck and shoulder EMG during arm-hand work movements. *Clinical Biomechanics, 2*, 126–139.
Sharma, P., & Chaturvedi, S. K. (1995). Conversion disorder revisited. *Acta Psychiatrica Scandinavica, 92*, 301–304.
Sharpe, M., & Bass, C. M. (1992). Pathophysiological mechanisms in somatization. *International Review of Psychiatry, 4*, 81–97.
Sharpe, M., Mayou, R., & Bass, C. M. (1995). Concepts, theories, and terminology. In R. Mayou, C. M. Bass, & M. Sharpe (Eds.), *Treatment of functional somatic symptoms* (pp. 3–16). Oxford: Oxford University Press.
Sifneos, P. E. (1973). The prevalence of 'alexithymic' characteristics in psychosomatic pa-

tients. *Psychotherapy and Psychosomatics, 22*, 255–262.

Smith, G. R. (1995). Treatment of patients with multiple symptoms. In R. Mayou, C. M. Bass, & M. Sharpe (Eds.), *Treatment of functional somatic symptoms* (pp. 175–187). Oxford: Oxford University Press.

Smith, G. R., Monson, R. A., & Ray, D. C. (1986). Psychiatric consultation in somatization disorder: A randomized, controlled trial. *New England Journal of Medicine, 314*, 1407–1413.

Smith, T. W., Snyder, C. R., & Perkins, S. C. (1983). The self-serving function of hypochondriacal complaints: Physical symptoms as self-handicapping strategies. *Journal of Personality and Social Psychology, 44*, 787–797.

Spivak, H., Rodin, G. M., & Sutherland, A. J. (1994). The psychology of factitious disorder: A reconsideration. *Psychosomatics, 35*, 25–40.

Staats, A. W. (1996). *Behavior and personality.* New York: Springer.

Starcevic, V. (1988). Diagnosis of hypochondriasis: A promenade through the psychiatric nosology. *American Journal of Psychotherapy, 42*, 197–211.

Surawy, C., Hackmann, A., Hawton, K., & Shape, M. (1995). Chronic fatigue syndrome: A cognitive approach. *Behavior Research and Therapy, 33*, 535–544.

Sutherland, A. J., & Rodin, G. M. (1990). Factitious disorder in a general hospital setting: Clinical features and a review of the literature. *Psychosomatics, 31*, 392–399.

Taylor, G. J., Bagby, R. M., & Parker, J. D. A. (1991). The alexithymia construct. A potential paradigm for psychosomatic medicine. *Psychosomatics, 32*, 153–164.

Torgerson, S. (1986). Genetics of somatoform disorders. *Archives of General Psychiatry, 43*, 502–505.

Turk, D. C., & Flor, H. (1984). Etiological theories and treatments for chronic low back pain. II. Psychological models-Interventions. *Pain, 19*, 209–233.

Turk, D. C., Meichenbaum, D., & Genest, M. (1983). *Pain and behavioral medicine: A cognitive-behavioral perspective.* New York: Guilford.

Turk, D. C., Okifuji, A., & Scharff, L. (1995). Chronic pain and depression: Role of perceived impact and perceived control in different age cohorts. *Pain, 61*, 93–101.

Tyrer, P. (1995). Somatoform and personality disorders: Personality and the soma. *Journal of Psychosomatic Research, 39*, 395–397.

Tyrer, P., Lee, I., & Alexander, J. (1980). Awareness of cardiac function in anxious, phobic and hypochondriacal patients. *Psychological Medicine, 10*, 171–174.

Ullman, L., & Krasner, L. (1975). *A psychological approach to abnormal behavior.* Englewood Cliffs, NJ: Prentice-Hall.

Van Hemert, A. M., Hengeveld, M. W., Bolk, J. H., Rooijmans, H. G. M., & Vandenbroucke, J. P. (1993). Psychiatric disorders in relation to medical illness among patients of a general outpatient clinic. *Psychological Medicine, 23*, 167–173.

Vingerhoets, A. J. J. M., Van Heck, G. L., Grim, R., & Bermond, B. (1995). Alexithymia: A further exploration of its nomological network. *Psychotherapy and Psychosomatics, 64*, 32–42.

Visser, S., & Bouman, T. K. (1992). Cognitive-behavioural approaches in the treatment of hypochondriasis: Six single case cross-over studies. *Behaviour Research and Therapy, 30*, 301–306.

Von Korff, M., Dworkin, S. F., & LeResche, L. (1990). Graded chronic pain status: An epidemiologic evaluation. *Pain, 40*, 279–291.

Warwick, H. M. C., & Salkovskis, P. M. (1990). Hypochondriasis. *Behaviour Research and Therapy, 28*, 105–117.

Wessely, S. (1993). Cognitive factigue syndrome: Current issues. *Reviews in Medical Microbiology, 3*, 211–216.

Wessely, S., & Sharpe, M. (1995). Chronic fatigue, chronic fatigue syndrome, and fibromyalgia. In R. Mayou, C. M. Bass, & M. Sharpe (Eds.), *Treatment of functional somatic symptoms* (pp. 285–312). Oxford: Oxford University Press.

Wool, C. A., & Barsky, A. J. (1994). Do women somatize more than men? Gender differences in somatization. *Psychosomatics, 35*, 445–452.

18

Dissociative Disorders

COLIN A. ROSS

The dissociative disorders (DDs) have long been a controversial area of psychopathology. Dissociative identity disorder (DID), formerly called multiple personality disorder, is the most striking, but is one of five DDs listed in the *DSM-IV*. The others are dissociative amnesia, dissociative fugue (see Loewenstein, 1993), depersonalization disorder (see Steinberg, 1995), and DD not otherwise specified. *DSM-IV* defines dissociation (p. 766) as, "A disruption in the usually integrated functions of consciousness, memory, identity or perception of the environment. The disturbance may be sudden or gradual, transient or chronic." This chapter focuses on DID, the only DD for which a substantial empirical literature exists, and perhaps also the most fascinating to professionals and laymen alike.

Dissociation and Cognition

The term dissociation is not limited to abnormal psychology. Experimental cognitive psychologists have used the term dissociation for decades in connection with memory experiments on rats, monkeys, pigeons, humans, and other species. This large literature has produced conclusive evidence for dissociations between declarative and procedural memory in many species, and in normal and brain-damaged humans (see Cohen & Eichenbaum, 1993, for a review). Animal studies consist primarily of hippocampal ablation experiments demonstrating the persistence of procedural memory in the absence of declarative memory. Procedural and declarative memory must thus be considered separate subsystems, a prerequisite of dissociation in the normal brain. The famous case of H.M., considered at length in most introductory neuropsychology texts, provides a ready example. H.M. had both hippocampi surgically removed as a treatment for epilepsy (Cohen & Eichenbaum, 1993). Recall of presurgical events was intact, but new events simply could not be encoded. After meeting a new person fifty times, the fifty-first meeting was still with a complete stranger. Yet, H.M. performed normally on many procedural learning tasks, making substantial improvements with repeated trials. The conclusion is that detailed information processing and learning can occur in procedural memory and have a measurable effect on behavior in the complete absence of declarative memory—that is, without conscious knowledge or awareness. The strange case of H.M. is an outstanding example of how clinical findings inform our knowledge of neurological structures and normal functioning.

Similar dissociations between declarative and procedural memory have been demonstrated in countless experiments across many species with a variety of experimental paradigms. Repetition priming, for example, could not occur without a procedural and declarative dissociation. Here, subjects typically memorize a list of homophonic word pairs such as *reed-read*. They are then asked a question for which only one of the words is the appropriate answer. Subjects so primed misspell their answers much more often than those who are not, even where they cannot remember the homphonic pair in a free recall situation. Repetition priming thus provides conclusive scientific proof that procedural memory can influence behavior, performance, and verbal output in the absence of conscious awareness.

The reconstructive nature of memory allows for other kinds of dissociations as well. Whereas the common person often thinks of memory as a faithful recorder of actual events, in fact memories are reconstructed from some smaller framework of reference elements. In a typical misinformation experiment (Loftus, 1993), two groups of students are shown a video of a car driving through a landscape. One group is asked to describe the landscape with no suggestive cues for misinformation, and a second is asked about a barn in the landscape that does not appear in the video. About one quarter of cued subjects insert the barn into their memories and elaborate on its description in response to postevent misinformation. For the misinformation effect to be an actual cognitive phenomenon, and not a demand artifact, declarative memory of the video must first be imperfect. Otherwise the memory without the barn would be clear. Second, there must be a dissociation between declarative and procedural memory. Otherwise the subject could not be amnestic for the process by which misinformation was spliced into declarative memory. Such dissociations may also eventually explain how memories or selves that become split off from mutual awareness persist as autonomous entities, reconstructing the world from their own unique vantage points and thus perpetuating their own identities by solidifying the underlying architecture upon which individuality rests.

Dissociation and General Systems Theory

Although cognitive psychology has approached dissociation mainly in terms of memory experiments, even more general definitions could be proposed. General systems theory, for example, is in widespread usage in developmental and interactionist psychology. Within cognitive psychology, the mind may be viewed as consisting of a system of modules, which interact at various levels to produce behavior. These modules have a hierarchical structure, with higher level modules integrating inputs from the lower order components they subsume. Normally, the integration of these modules operates as if they formed a single homogenous entity. That is, in normal subjects, their operation is absolutely transparent to the outside observer. For our purposes, the exact nature and number of modules is unimportant; dissociation simply refers to a temporary decoupling of such structures. Dissociated systems are thus composed of subsystems that are no longer functionally integrated. These subsystems fail to share information with each other (they are "mutually amnestic"), behaving as if they are independent systems (in DID the subsystems are called "alter personalities"), and switching suddenly in terms of executive control of the overall organism. In this sense, DDs can be observed in the federal government, large corporations, *DSM-IV*, and the psyches of individual human beings, where the subsystems are actually personified. From a systems organizational point of view, the personification of alter personalities is an incidental feature of DID.

Dissociation as a Clinical Phenomenon

Dissociation has also been studied through self-report measures, such as the Dissociative Experiences Scale (DES; Bernstein & Putnam, 1986). While the term dissociation has historically been associated with a variety of perspectives, mostly psychodynamic, the DES seeks to operationalize dissociation in an atheoretical manner. The motive behind the DES is essentially the same as that which led to the revision of the *DSM-III* in 1980: many schools of thought have considered dissociation, but these account for the phenomenon from a particular perspective, and as such, cannot be as multidetermined as the phenomenon itself. Endorsement of any one perspective would only foreclose further study prematurely. Studies with the instrument show that highly dissociative individuals can be clearly differentiated from the general population (see Carlson, 1994, for review).

Despite its ostensive scientific and experimental underpinnings, many clinicians still believe that neither dissociation nor DID exist. Attempts to study the prevalence rate of the disorder are fraught with methodological entanglements, accusations, and counteraccusations on both sides. Critics have argued that the minority of clinicians account for the vast number of cases of DID. In response, proponents maintain that it is because they are attuned to the subtlety of the phenomenon that they have become more sensitive clinical instruments in detecting its manifestations. Dissociative amnesia and other pathological forms of dissociation have been associated with a wide range of traumatic events for over a hundred years, including combat, rape, incest, natural disaster, plane crash, and internment in Nazi death camps (Loewenstein, 1993; van der Kolk, 1996). Moreover, dissociation has been deliberately induced through coercive persuasion, thought reform, brainwashing, and mind control by destructive cults, interrogators of various kinds, the military, and intelligence agencies around the world (Hassan, 1988; Marks, 1979; Singer, 1995; West & Martin, 1994).

Dissociation and the *DSM-IV*

Dissociation in this chapter incorporates the three meanings outlined above. First, dissociation is a rigorously demonstrated cognitive reality. Second, it is a clinical phenomenon that informs studies of normal cognition. Third, in its broadest usage, it refers to the breakdown of system integration. Taken together, these three senses of the term can used to construct an informative critique of dissociation as presented in the *DSM-IV*.

Lack of Differential Diagnostic Rules

Many authors (Braun, 1988; Cardena, 1994; Kilhstrom, 1994; Ross, 1997) believe that *DSM-IV* arbitrarily limits dissociation to restricted areas of brain functioning. We have already considered dissociation in a cognitive and general systems context above. In contrast, *DSM-IV* limits dissociation to "a disruption in the usually integrated functions of consciousness, memory, identity, or perception of the environment" (p. 477). These functions, however, do not exhaust the entire human organism.

In a broader sense, then, dissociations of sensation and motor function should also be categorized as DDs, and even classic conversion symptoms become prime candidates for dissociative explanation. Conversion disorders feature the dissociation of normal motor function and the absence of a genuine organic cause. That is, knowledge of the true function of the conversion is withheld, or dissociated, from conscious awareness. While such symptoms are common in DID, in the *DSM-IV* they are categorized as somatoform disorders, on the rationale of clinical utility. Given its atheoretical posture, the tendency of *DSM-IV* is to regard general medical conditions and the physical results of substance abuse as distinct from other psychical phenomena. Presumably, positing a single underlying psychological cause for physical symptoms smacks of psychodynamics, a perspective eschewed in the construction of *DSM-III* and considered too speculative and inferential. Historically, conversion symptoms were part of the concept of hysteria, which had fissioned into fragments called histrionic personality disorder, dissociative amnesia, conversion disorder, and somatization disorder by the time *DSM-IV* appeared. Interestingly, the *DSM-IV* symptom list for somatization disorder includes "dissociative symptoms such as amnesia" (p. 449), but no inclusion or exclusion rules are given by which to decide whether amnesia is a symptom of somatization or part of a broader dissociative syndrome. Outside North America, clinicians using *ICD-10* may treat conversion disorders as a branch of the dissociative hierarchy.

Dissociative phenomena are scattered across other disorders as well. In *DSM-IV*, a ninth criterion was added to the *DSM-III-R* criteria set for borderline personality disorder: "transient, stress-related paranoid ideation or severe dissociative symptoms" (p. 654). Yet there are no rules or guidelines for deciding when a dissociative symptom is to be classified as an Axis I or an Axis II symptom. Pathological dissociation currently appears as a prominent feature of two anxiety disorders, namely posttraumatic stress disorder and acute stress disorder, one personality disorder, namely borderline personality disorder, the DDs themselves, and the somatoform disorders. The *DSM-IV*, then, does not account for pathological dissociation in a coherent and consistent fashion. Given classification differences between *DSM-IV* and *ICD-10*, we can conclude that no shared scientific understanding of the DDs exists worldwide.

DID, Comorbidity, and Differential Diagnosis

The differential diagnosis of DID cannot be approached systematically without consideration of the problem of comorbidity. All published research demonstrates that clinically significant, dysfunctional DID is accompanied by extensive lifetime comorbidity for a variety of other mental disorders. In a study using the Structured Clinical Interview for *DSM-III-R* (Spitzer, Williams, Gibbon, & First, 1990), among subjects with clinically diagnosed DID, over nine tenths met lifetime criteria for a mood disorder or an anxiety disorder. Almost three quarters met criteria for a psychotic disorder, two thirds for a substance abuse disorder, and almost two fifths for a somatoform disorder or eating disorder (Ellason, Ross, & Fuchs, 1996). Moreover, borderline personality disorder has been diagnosed in almost 70% of a series of clinically diagnosed DID subjects (Ellason & Ross, unpublished data). Pooling these data show that the average DID inpatient meets lifetime criteria for about 15 different disorders from almost all sections of *DSM-IV* (Ellason, Ross, & Fuchs, 1996), including 3.6 different personality disorders. Thus by *DSM-IV* rules, people with DID have three or four simultaneous different personality structures. This impossible finding is an artifact of the inability of the *DSM-IV* system to account for the pattern of psychopathology in DID. People with DID have only one fragmented personality, not a collection of different people in one body.

On Axis I, about half the comorbid psychotic diagnoses are schizoaffective disorder, with about one fifth being schizophrenia (Ellason, Ross, & Fuchs, 1996). The issue is whether such comorbidity reflects the presence of two discrete disease processes or emerges as an artifact of the nature of DID itself. Simply put, DID patients report more positive symptoms of schizophrenia than people with schizophrenia, including auditory hallucinations, passivity experiences, and thought insertion and withdrawal (Kluft, 1987; Ellason & Ross, 1995). When these symptoms persist in the absence of an active mood disorder, as they commonly do, *DSM-IV* rules result in a diagnosis of schizoaffective disorder. Unlike schizophrenia and schizoaffective disorders, however, these apparently psychotic symptoms go into long-term, stable remission in response to psychotherapy once the individual becomes integrated, and are not accompanied by formal thought disorder or the intractable negative symptoms of schizophrenia. In *DSM-IV*, voices heard commenting on the subject's behavior or conversing with each other are considered so nearly pathognomonic for schizophrenia that when either occurs, only that symptom is required to make the diagnosis. However, both symptoms are the norm for DID, occurring in over nine tenths of all cases.

In spite of its overlap with the psychotic disorders, most comorbid nonpsychotic diagnoses do seem valid. We know that DID rarely occurs as an isolated condition. Instead, it is almost always accompanied by a wide array of psychopathology. The question is how to understand these complex comorbidities. Again, one approach is to dismiss the validity of DID. North, Ryall, Ricci, and Wetzel (1993) argue that DID is secondary to somatization disorder and Axis II pathology. Indeed, DID patients are often described as "really just borderlines" in clinical settings. Here, one set of symptoms is an epiphenomenon of a more fundamental disease process. One syndrome is thus considered primary while all others are considered secondary. Several authors have even proposed that temporal lobe epilepsy can mimic DID (Ross, 1997). This was disproved by a series of studies done in the 1980s (Loewenstein & Putnam, 1988; Putnam, 1986; Ross, Heber, Anderson, et al., 1989). There is no more phenomenological overlap between DID and temporal lobe epilepsy than there is between DID and other neurological disorders. While borderline personality disorder is co-present in about 70% of DID subjects (Horevitz & Braun, 1984; Ross, 1997), borderline personality is neither a necessary nor a sufficient condition for DID, since the other 30% of DID patients do not require a borderline diagnosis. In general, borderline subjects report more severe childhood trauma and more severe symptomatology (Ellason & Ross, 1996). Thus the borderline subset of DID is more seriously disturbed and, hence, perhaps overrepresented in inpatient samples. Other disorders appear in conjunction with DID in a consistent fashion. Almost all DID patients exhibit depression. Eating disorders are intermediate, while bipolar mood disorder and histrionic personality disorder appear less often than what would be expected among general adult inpatients. The rate of histrionic personality disorder among DID subjects is actually less than that of general adult inpatients (Ellason, Ross, & Fuchs, 1996).

Fortunately, the differential diagnosis of DID is straightforward where the clinician actually observes switching of alter personalities that are separated by amnesia barriers or claim different names and ages. In this case, no possibility other than

DID exists. The diagnostic challenge is to inventory the comorbidity and to assign the patient to a presumptive etiological pathway, be it childhood abuse or neglect, factitious or iatrogenic (i.e., cultivated by treatment). These are discussed under etiology and pathogenesis below.

Prevalence

Despite the taxonomic conundrums that beset researchers of DID, a considerable number of studies have been performed in clinical settings. These studies rely on two self-report measures, the DES and the Dissociation Questionnaire (DIS-Q; Vanderlinden, 1993), and two structured interviews, the Dissociative Disorders Interview Schedule (DDIS; Ross, 1997; Ross, Heber, Norton et al., 1989), and the Structured Clinical Interview for DSM-IV Dissociative Disorders (SCID-D; Steinberg, 1995).

Data have been gathered in a variety of settings and in several countries. Two studies in Canada (Horen, Leichner, & Lawson, 1995; Ross, Anderson, Fleisher, & Norton, 1991) two in the United States (Latz, Kramer, & Hughes, 1995; Saxe et al., 1993), one in the Netherlands (Boon & Draijer, 1993), one in Norway (Knudsen et al., 1995), and one in Turkey (Kiziltan et al., 1996) yield the consistent conclusion that undiagnosed DID affects not less than 5% of general adult psychiatric inpatients, while at least 20% of inpatients have some kind of DD. Similar data are available in an eating disorder sample in Japan (Berger et al., 1994). Four studies in chemical dependency inpatient samples also indicate that DDs are common in this setting. These studies include samples from two Veterans Administration settings (Dunn, Paolo, & Ryan, 1993; Leeper, Page, & Hendricks, 1992), an academic hospital (Ross, Kronson et al., 1992), and a private psychiatric hospital in Texas (Ellason, Ross, Sainton, & Mayran, 1996). There is more variability in these studies than among the general adult inpatients, but DDs appear to be common among individuals in treatment for drug and alcohol problems. Averaging the findings of the four studies, DID affects 11.2% of the chemical dependency sample, and the DDs as a whole affect 31.6% in this group. Taken together, these findings show that in clinical settings the DDs are common, but nevertheless rarely diagnosed. These oversights reflect a low index of suspicion and lack of training on how to enter and complete the diagnostic decision tree for DDs.

Information on the prevalence of DID in children and adolescents is currently equivocal (Ross, 1996). Studies in children are fewer in number, have more methodological problems, and involve smaller sample sizes. Nevertheless, the research on children is consistent with that in adults and suggests that DDs can be easily diagnosed in any inpatient adolescent facility if a systematic inquiry is made. A number of standardized screening measures for pathological dissociation in children and adolescents are available or under development.

More limited information is available concerning the epidemiology of the DDs in the general population (Ross, 1991, 1996). The DES was completed by a stratified cluster sample in the city of Winnipeg, Canada (Ross, Joshi, & Currie, 1990, 1991). Analyses indicate that just over 3% of the general population appears to endorse pathological dissociative experiences (Waller & Ross, 1997). While others endorse DES items, these apparently reflect normal absorption experiences, not pathological dissociation. This figure cannot be regarded as a lifetime prevalence, since the DES is based more on recent experiences than on past history. A more precise estimate of lifetime prevalence was obtained by interviewing a subset of the Winnipeg respondents with the DDIS, resulting in a figure of about 11%. About 1% of subjects endorsed *DSM-III-R* criteria for DID and also reported a history of childhood physical and/or sexual abuse. All such subjects would also meet *DSM-IV* criteria for DID. The DID cases in the sample were mild symptomatically and did not include a single case of typical inpatient severity. An additional 2% of subjects endorsed *DSM-III-R* criteria for DID, but had very few symptoms and did not report childhood trauma. However, these subjects were so dissimilar to those seen in actual clinical work that they were assumed to represent false positive cases. In the only international studies worthy of note, DIS-Q data from Europe indicate that about 3% of subjects in the general population of Belgium and the Netherlands may have a DD (Vanderlinden, 1993). The prevalence of DDs has also been studied in college students (Murphy, 1994; Ross, Ryan, Voigt, & Eide, 1991). Lifetime prevalences in representative samples are in the range of 11 to 12%.

Taken together, the tentative conclusion is that DID may have a lifetime prevalence in the general population in the range of about 1%, while the

DDs as a group affect from 3 to 11% of the general population. Estimates vary by methodology. Self-report data support the lower end of this range, while structured interview data support the higher end. Even if the lower figures are roughly accurate, however, DID would be about as common as bipolar mood disorder and schizophrenia, with the other DDs about as common as the anxiety disorders, excluding simple phobias. As with all disorders, undiagnosed cases are milder than those from inpatient settings. None of the subjects in the general population and college student studies reported having received a clinical diagnosis of a DD.

Historical Perspectives

The total number of cases of DID reported in the world literature in 1979 was about 200. The number of diagnosed cases has since mushroomed to somewhere around 30,000 in North America alone. Long series of independent cases have been published, including over 200 by Ross, Norton, and Wozney (1989), and about a hundred each by Ross, Miller, Reagor, Bjornson, Fraser, and Anderson (1990) and Ellason, Ross, and Fuchs (1996).

Skeptics who doubt that DID exists at all claim that the increasing number of cases reflects the creation of the disorder in suggestible patients exposed to leading questions by enthusiasts (Merskey, 1995; Simpson, 1995). Proponents counter that experienced diagnosticians are simply more sensitive measurement instruments, and therefore tend to find otherwise undiscovered cases. Thus far, no systematic research has attempted to differentially diagnose real and created cases. Nor is it certain how this would be accomplished. Only two compelling case studies involving iatrogenic causation have been reported (Coons, 1988; Ross, 1997). These reports notwithstanding, their authors are identified as naive believers by extreme skeptics.

The historical antecedents of contemporary DID are almost impossible to determine, since only a handful of cases have been documented prior to 1850. The issue, therefore, is to identify the core structural features of the disorder that remain constant across time, geography, and culture. The same logic applies to schizophrenia: the content of schizophrenic delusions varies with time and place, but the presence of delusions is universal.

In more anthropological terms, DID is characterized by the presence of intrusive entities that take executive control of the body, colloquially called "possession." All DID patients would be considered demon possessed by the criteria of *Malleus Maleficarum* (Kramer & Sprenger, 1486/1971). The converse is also true: *DSM-IV* would classify historical cases of demon possession as DDs. The difference between DID and demonic possession is not with respect to phenomenology; rather, it pertains to the philosophical systems behind them. The philosophical systems influence the vocabulary of the criteria sets but not their structural properties, which are constant. A large anthropological literature attests to the universal nature of trance and possession states and their linkage to other dissociative experiences such as depersonalization, amnesia, and auditory hallucinations. There is no question that the structural elements of DID are universal, relatively common, and present throughout history. For instance, in a recent Gallup poll, 2% of adult respondents in the United States said that they had channeled another entity through themselves while in a trance state (Ross & Joshi, 1992). The difference between DID and possession is addressed in *DSM-IV* through the inclusion of dissociative trance in the "Appendix on Criteria Sets and Axes Provided for Further Study" (p. 727). According to the provisional criteria for dissociative trance, DID is an exclusion criterion for that diagnosis. The key differentiating feature of the two criteria sets is that in DID the identity states recurrently take executive control while dissociative trance tends to be more often a single episode disorder. However, the *DSM-IV* criteria also state that trance possession can be "episodic."

The lack of clarity in *DSM-IV* rules for differentiating DID from chronic possession states is a good reason to keep dissociative trance in the Appendix. More research on the percentage of possession cases that are chronic, and clear phenomenological rules for differentiating DID and possession states, are required. Additionally, *trance* is a problematic and controversial term in the hypnosis literature, and trance states may not be reliably observable: raters may not be able sufficiently to agree who is and who is not in trance.

Given that the core criteria of DID have been observed throughout history, the really interesting question concerns the high rates of reported childhood trauma in DID patients (Ross, 1997), and the silence of the possession literature on childhood trauma. It is possible that chronic possession states in numerous cultures are highly linked to histories of severe childhood trauma, in which case both dissociative possession and DID are chronic posttraumatic disorders of childhood onset, with variants due to adult-onset trauma.

On the other hand, if pathological possession states as defined by *DSM-IV* dissociative trance are not linked to childhood trauma, another question arises: Why has this capacity of the human mind been harnessed to cope with trauma in DID but not in dissociative trance? There are no data on this question and it has not been addressed at length on a conceptual level in the psychiatric or psychological literatures.

Returning to the iatrogenic model of DID, it is unclear what this model as stated by skeptics is claiming. It is not clear what the word *artifactual* means, given that possession states are always highly colored by culture, always operate on social-psychological principles, are never understood as biomedical disease entities, and are always treated with a culturally prescribed form of individual and/or group psychotherapy. To say that the phenomenon is an "artifact" of culture or social situation has no meaning, since by these criteria the entire field of psychology and the English language are cultural artifacts. The skeptics do not propose that iatrogenic DID is due to conscious malingering.

The underlying assumption of the extreme skeptical model is that to be a legitimate psychiatric disorder a condition must be a biomedical disease. A corollary assumption that this can be taken for granted for depression and psychosis leads to the exclusion of the DDs from the realm of legitimate psychiatric disorders. The exclusion is an artifact of the ascientific assumptions of the bioreductionist model, and cannot be refuted within the philosophical rules of the model. Debate with the extreme skeptic is therefore intellectually sterile, although it is politically important.

The assumption of this chapter is that the DDs should be studied within the rules of the *DSM-IV* system. Diagnoses should be phenomenologically based, and theories of etiology (whether biomedical or social psychological) should not appear among the criteria. From this perspective, the debate about whether DID is "real" is meaningless: the only "reality" *DSM-IV* psychiatric disorders have is that they have defined diagnostic criteria and appear in the manual. These observations and arguments about the reality of DID need to be made only because of ideological hostility to DID in the late 20th century. The same cautions and arguments apply to schizophrenia and obsessive-compulsive disorder, but are not found in other chapters in this text because the political climate does not necessitate them.

A subargument made by the skeptics is that the increase in the average number of alter personalities per patient over the last 100 years is evidence of iatrogenic amplification. The 19th-century cases were mostly dual personality or involved a small number of states, whereas the median number of alter personalities in the 1980s was eight or nine in two large series (Putnam, Guroff, Silberman, Barban, & Post, 1986; Ross, Norton, & Wozney, 1989). Setting aside the modest magnitude of the increase, it is neutral with respect to the two competing hypotheses. Certainly, the increase could be due to iatrogenic amplification. On the other hand, alter personalities could have gone undetected in the 19th century, or the difference could be an artifact of sampling bias. It is impossible to gather valid retrospective data that can determine which of the two models more accurately accounts for the greater number of alter personalities in the late 20th century.

Contemporary Theoretical Perspectives

The Trauma Model

All published research on DID and all clinical experience in specialty programs leads to the conclusion that over 90% of diagnosed DID patients report severe childhood physical and/or sexual abuse (Ross, 1997).

According to the trauma model, DID is a strategy for dealing with severe, chronic childhood trauma. The basic utility of DID is presumably that it insulates the executive self from the full impact of the abuse, thereby preserving function, morale, and normal development. Various elements of the trauma are parceled out to separate selves that are disconnected from each other by amnesia barriers. The barriers are variably porous.

The child draws on normal dissociative capacity, and the theme of transformation of identity is omnipresent in cartoons, books, movies, video games, folklore, and childhood play. The abuse doesn't hurt as much because the child imagines it is happening to someone else. The separate identities are reinforced by the chronic trauma and other interactions of the child with his or her environment. Additionally, overgeneralization of dissociative defenses occurs, with alter personalities being created to deal with nontraumatic aspects of life. The idea that new alter personalities can be created in the social context of psychotherapy is a minor extension of the model.

The small number of studies in which systematic attempts were made to obtain outside corroboration of the abuse indicate that in well over 50% of cases conclusive verification can be obtained. This does not mean that every single detail was accurate, but it means that the identity of the perpetrator, the time frame, and the types of acts perpetrated were corroborated. Clinically, it is not unusual to encounter patients with such corroboration. The surprising thing clinically is how little impact corroboration has on the symptom profile, conflicts, and treatment plan.

A key element of the trauma model is that the DID began in childhood. The natural history may be one of fluctuation in symptom levels, with only intermittent windows of diagnosability, but the individual met criteria for DID prior to age 10. The existence of diagnosable DID in childhood is documented in the literature and best reviewed in a special April 1996 issue of *Child and Adolescent Psychiatric Clinics of North America* on childhood DDs.

The Iatrogenic Model

The basic idea of the model is that DID is an artifact of the doctor-patient relationship. It is caused by leading questions, therapist cues, and other demand characteristics. Elements that preexisted contact with a mental health professional are artifacts of media contamination. By definition, uncontaminated and therefore genuine cases of DID are now impossible because of the attention paid to DID in the popular culture (Merskey, 1995).

This model is not supported by any research data. Most of the opinions of iatrogenic theorists are not expressed in a way that is empirically testable. The key prediction of the model, and the one which is in principle (if not in practice) testable, is that the symptoms of DID did not exist prior to therapy.

A Behavioral Perspective

DID can be conceptualized as a complex phobia whose stimulus is a combination of memories, feelings, and environmental cues. Just as individuals tend to withdraw from the reality of the phobic situation, the executive self tends to retreat behind alters in the presence of phobic stimuli. These could be as concrete as reminders of abuse or as general as the level of anxiety. Treatment would then involve systematic desensitization to these stimuli. This hypothesis is plausible to anyone dealing effectively with DID inpatients. Extensive use of behavioral principles is necessary to contain and manage acting out, regression, and hospital dependency. Moreover, the severe self-mutilation that is common in DID patients can be analyzed and treated in behavioral terms. To provide a rationale for the treatment plan, the therapist can explain that cutting likely results in endorphin release, which modulates the patient's negative mood state and reinforces the cutting. Unfortunately, DID is unpalatable to behaviorists partly because it involves the attribution of mental states and partly because the vocabulary of much of the DID literature is psychoanalytic.

An Object Relations Perspective

No diagnostic category better illustrates the principles of object relations theory than DID. In psychoanalytic discussions about patients, defenses are inferred intrapsychic processes that underlie the speech and behavior of the patient. In the psychotherapy of DID, defenses such as *identification with the aggressor* may be quite tangible, as when the alleged perpetrator of paternal incest takes executive control, claims to own the patient, and expresses hostility toward the therapist and the therapy. Split object relations can be videotaped in DID when an alter personality who idealizes the father describes recent incest with pleasure and positive sentiments, but is soon replaced by a hostile alter who hates the father and denies ownership of the body.

A Cognitive Perspective

DID inpatients are often currently clinically depressed, anxious, or both. Moreover, they endorse all the classic cognitive errors that accompany these disorders. In addition, DID patients make statements that are pathognomonic for DID, including claims that different parts of the self are different people, often with separate physical bodies. Different kinds of alters require different cognitive approaches. For example, the self-mutilating alter must be taught that she lives in the same body as the host personality on whom she is afflicting the cuts and burns. Often the persecutor personality has no cognitive understanding of the fact that her body is also affected by the cutting. However, such cognitive errors are not simply mistakes in thinking. Instead, they serve strategic functions that must also be analyzed and taken into account. For instance, one purpose of the locus of control shift, considered below, is to avoid mourning the loss of the parent the patient never had, a loving and reasonably psychological healthy parent. The shift maintains idealizing cognitions and prevents access to negative feelings that might arise from the neglect and abuse. Another example comes from alter personalities who believe the current year is 1967 or 1973, and who believe that they still live at home under the immediate control of the perpetrators. In the usual mental status sense, this would be consider disorientation. However, it can be corrected by simple explanation.

Another cognitive phenomenon that characterizes DID is the "locus of control shift" (Ross, 1997), a key target of psychotherapy. Here, the blame and responsibility for childhood abuse are shifted from the adult perpetrator to inside the patient herself. This developmentally adaptive childhood distortion is also strategically clever: By shifting the locus of control the child insulates herself from overwhelming feelings of helplessness, powerlessness, and fear, and provides a developmentally protective illusion of mastery and control. In adulthood, however, the locus of control shift becomes maladaptive. Since the patient is now an adult no longer suffering physical and sexual abuse, it is genuine autonomy, not shifts of responsibility, that is adaptive. Often the shift seems to generalize, so that DID patients take responsibility even for things that are not their fault. Such events argue strongly against the idea that most DID patients are malingerers who play the role of multiple personalities as a means of evading responsibility. Characteristically, DID patients avoid responsibility for things they do to themselves, such as self-mutilation, amnesia, or setting themselves up for revictimization. In these scenarios the host personality takes the victim role and wants the therapist to rescue her from her persecuting alter personalities. Simultaneously the persecutor personalities rationalize and justify their actions and want the therapist to stop interfering. The locus of control shift is not specific to the DDs, but is nevertheless a core feature of the cognitive analysis of traumatized individuals, which includes those with DDs.

A Systems Perspective

Family systems theory is directly relevant to understanding and treating DID. The alter personalities clearly form a system, and the system displays all the properties of families described in the family therapy literature. One might compare the internal world of the DID patient to a family living in a house. In this house, the family members are dispersed throughout many different rooms. Some rooms do not connect with the outside world and some do. Some family members have never been on the ground floor and others are not even aware of the existence of those on the third floor. An intermittently and inconsistently functioning intercom system allows some family members to communicate but not others. All these system properties are directly observable in the symptoms, speech, and behavior of the alter personalities.

A Neuropsychological Perspective

Speculative hypotheses relating the neuropsychological interaction of stress and human memory can be constructed from recent works derived from books by Cohen and Eichenbaum (1993) and van der Kolk, McFarlane, and Weisath (1996), and related literature (Siegel, 1996). Chronic stress in experimental mammals causes elevated serum cortisol levels. The cortisol interacts with hippocampal neurons to down-regulate the synthesis of dendritic connections, and can result in actual cell death if extreme. Preliminary evidence indicates that adults with adult-onset posttraumatic stress disorder have reduced hippocampal volume. DID patients report severe, chronic childhood trauma and are likely to have experienced chronic hypercortisolemia in childhood. One would therefore predict that DID patients will manifest hippocampal atrophy on MRI scan and hippocampal hypoactivity on PET scan. However, no empirical literature exists that documents the involvement of the hippocampus in DID.

Developmental Pathogenesis

The concept of different pathways to the same clinical outcome is accepted throughout medicine. For instance, congestive heart failure presents the same way clinically whether the primary problem is in the heart or the lungs. An example from psychiatry is the four pathways to negative symptoms of schizophrenia: the disease process itself, side effects of neuroleptic medication, concurrent depression, and effects of chronic institutionalization. For some diseases or syndromes treatment varies depending on etiological pathway, and for some it does not. The clinical literature, and the author's clinical and forensic experience, suggests four different pathways to DID (childhood abuse, childhood neglect, factitious, and iatrogenic), summarized in table 18.1. Each of these can also be pathways to DDNOS in cases that do not fully crystallize as DID. Each pathway will be described as if it occurs in pure form, which is sometimes the case. In practice, one usually encounters a combination of different pathways in ratios that vary from patient to patient. In the last six years we have had over 1,000 admissions to our Dissociative Disorders Program, now located at Timberlawn Health System of Dallas. As a rough estimate, I would guess that the childhood abuse pathway accounts for about half of the symptomatology we have seen, with each of the other pathways accounting for a third of the remainder.

The Childhood Abuse Pathway

This pathway was described in the section on contemporary theoretical perspectives. Attachment to the perpetrator produces a large proportion of borderline personalities. In object relations terms, the split perceptions of parents who alternate between reasonable and abusive are the primary problem. The internal world of the adult DID patient thus mirrors his or her external childhood world through its dichotomized perceptions, mood states, cognitions and behaviors, and ambivalent attachment to clinicians and loved ones in the present. All existing research indicates that DID patients are often borderline and score at the high end on hypnotizability measures. A large number of studies in many different languages demonstrate that DID patients on average score in the forties or low fifties on the DES (Ross, 1997).

The childhood abuse pathway possesses two key differentiating features. First, chronic, complex dissociative symptoms are present prior to diagnosis. Second, an elaborate medical history is displayed in one subgroup of patients (see table 18.1). All DID patients commonly endorse a variety of somatic symptoms on structured or clinical interviews. These are understood within the model as being dissociated elements of childhood sexual trauma. However, some patients develop complex medical histories when physicians are consulted for help with these symptoms, which are not recognized as being psychosomatic in nature.

The Childhood Neglect Pathway

Children on the neglect pathway child are locked in closets, left at home alone, or ignored by parents who are impaired by character pathology, Axis I disorders (including substance abuse), or both. The neglect pathway features no overt acts of sexual or

Table 18.1 Four Pathways to Dissociative Identity Disorder

Pathway	Predominant Personality Type	Hypnotizability	DES Score	Type of Therapy	Response of DID to Treatment
Childhood Abuse	Borderline	++	40	DID	Integration
Childhood Neglect	Dependent	+	30	Modified DID	?
Factitious Disorder	Antisocial	?	70	Factitious Disorder	Remission/ chronic
Iatrogenic	Dependent	+	70	Cult Exit Counseling	Remission

physical abuse. While inside the closet, the child creates imaginary companions who populate a vivid internal fantasy world intended to fill up the emptiness. In effect, the child is a victim of a sensory deprivation. Initially, the picture is one of DDNOS because fully crystallized alter personalities are not required for transactions with the outside world. The attachment problem is a failure to form human bonds because of the pervasive neglect.

Given the absence of childhood sexual abuse, the neglect pathway produces few or no psychosomatic symptoms. Informal clinical experience indicates that predominantly neglect pathway cases may tend to develop a dependent personality structure. Such individuals are moderately hypnotizable and dissociative—abilities useful to create the inner fantasy world. However, they score lower than abuse pathway cases on standardized measures.

Within the neglect pathway are three subpathways, resulting in a variable pattern of preexisting dissociative symptoms. First, the patient's inner world may remain autistically contained, so that no overt symptoms are produced. Second, the inner characters may at some later time be harnessed to deal with nonabuse problems in the outside world, resulting in a natural evolution from DDNOS to DID, accompanied by active dissociative symptoms. And third, cases that arrive at therapy as DDNOS are sometimes iatrogenically amplified into full DID by bad therapy techniques.

Treatment for neglect cases is based on the fact that their inner fantasy world is a single monolithic defense. Rather than entering the internal dissociative world, as in regular DID therapy, the therapist remains anchored to external reality, challenging the patient on the ongoing cost-benefit of absorption in the inner world. The response to treatment can be either integration or, conversely, retreat into the inner world accompanied by refusal to engage in meaningful therapy. Poor-outcome cases are unwilling to relinquish their attachment to the only stable figures in their lives, their inside people.

The Factitious Pathway

Pure factitious pathway cases of DID are encountered occasionally in the clinic (Feldman & Ford, 1994). Whatever the pathway, however, many DID cases contain at least some factitious elements, often associated with Axis II pathology and due to secondary gain and manipulative interpersonal strategies learned in the family of origin. Consistent with the general literature on medical-surgical factitious disorders (Feldman and Ford, 1994), factitious pathway DID patients are conscious scam artists with antisocial character structures. Unable to form normal attachments, they compensate by assuming the patient role and exaggerating their symptoms—that is, faking bad through manipulative, goal-oriented behaviors. They may claim to miss part of a conversation, to be staring off into space, or to be out of their bodies over 90% of the time. All the while their mental status is unremarkable.

A preexisting medical-surgical factitious disorder is the red flag for factitious DID. Such patients usually have a huge and elaborate medical record. In one case, a woman in her thirties with a medical record about three feet thick was suing therapists to whom she had presented under another name in order to avoid law enforcement agencies in another state. There was no alter personality in her system that had her real name, an absence that would not occur in a genuine case. The falsity of many factitious claims, including cancer, heart attacks, and surgeries in numerous relatives, a variety of life-threatening illnesses and surgeries in herself, and many investigations and tests with inconclusive results, were documented only through a detailed review of her medical record. The factitious DID was just another in a long, long series of lies told to the health care system. I was called as an expert witness by the defense because the woman was suing for false memory syndrome and iatrogenic DID. My conclusion was that this woman had false false memory syndrome. That is, her alleged disorder was one more conscious deception, reinforced by potential massive secondary gain from the legal system.

Factitious pathway cases have one of two outcomes. Either they are willing to drop their DID on confrontation and work on real problems, or they leave and seek DID treatment elsewhere. Some factitious pathway retractors in our program have had a successful outcome with regard to their DID and formed a solid treatment alliance. The agenda of extreme skeptics of DID does not allow for differentiation between the factitious and iatrogenic pathways. The fundamental distinction is that factitious DID is the patient's fault, while iatrogenic cases are the therapist's fault. In practice the distinction is subtle, for even predominantly iatrogenic cases must collude with bad therapy to some degree, otherwise they would be resistors and never develop DID.

The Iatrogenic Pathway

DID cases with significant iatrogenic elements are seen on a regular basis in our Dissociative Disorders Program. Iatrogenic DID is a fulfillment of the therapist's needs and expectations, and is caused by the therapist's cueing, leading questions, suggestions, and reinforcement of iatrogenic symptoms. Not uncommonly, the therapy described meets criteria for a destructive psychotherapy cult (Singer, 1995). Iatrogenic cases can arise from overinterpretation of bipolar mood disorder, overinterpretation of unstructured dissociative symptoms in adults with a real sexual abuse history, through excessive agreement from patients with dependent personality disorder, and from any number of other foundations. A more or less normal attachment pattern is present. The profound ambivalence of childhood abuse cases is lacking. Neither dissociative symptoms nor an elaborate medical history are found prior to diagnosis. In eight cases that received an extensive battery of structured interviews, self-report measures and the Millon Clinical Multiaxial Inventory-II as part of an expert witness assessment, every case had a dependent personality profile. Such dependency makes the patients vulnerable to iatrogenic DID.

During the period of active iatrogenic DID, DES scores are often above the range considered normal for DID. While such patients have the hypnotic capacity to create the disorder in response to iatrogenic pressures, they are not the hypnotic virtuosi of the abuse pathway. The treatment strategy is simple when a case of pure iatrogenic DID is already actively in the retractor phase. However, if the patient is still enmeshed with the therapist and still believes in the reality of the DID and the trauma history, extricating him or her can be extremely difficult. Such patients require a treatment based on cult exit counseling (Hassan, 1988; Singer, 1995), and may in response go into rapid remission. In one case assessed by the author as an expert witness, the therapist admitted in writing and under oath to having lived with her client for five years, to bartering therapy for domestic labor, to being a sexual partner of the client, to using the client as a consultant on other cases, to being a co-client with the client in couples therapy delivered by a friend of the therapist, and to believing absolutely that the client grew up in a Satanic human sacrifice cult. This is the only documented case of ritual sexual abuse the author has personally treated. Ironically, the perpetrator was the therapist, who admitted to having ritualized sex with the client that involved symbols and paraphernalia, chanting, saying words backward, choking the client, and calling out a specific alter personality for sex. The rationale for this activity was to convert a cult alter from allegiance to the cult to allegiance to the therapist. In her defense, the therapist blamed her behavior on the borderline psychodynamics of the client. My assessment of this case was that it was purely iatrogenic with no childhood abuse.

Mixed Pathways

Mixed pathway cases are common, and different symptoms are almost impossible to attribute exclusively to one pathway. None of the items in table 18.1 is pathognomonic for its pathway. For instance, a person can have active DID in childhood, seemingly go into "remission" in adolescence, and then reactivate her system in therapy, a pattern easily misinterpreted as iatrogenic DID. Childhood abuse pathway DID and medical-surgical factitious disorder can also coexist. At the current time, no structured interview or self-report measure of dissociation is able to make pathway designations when used alone. Determinations must be based on clinical judgment, index of suspicion, and alertness to subtle indicators. Moreover, generalizations about any one pathway must be tentative given small case samples, and estimates as to the overall contribution of the four pathways in DID at large are premature. The childhood abuse pathway could account for as little as one quarter or as much as three quarters of the DID symptoms currently in treatment in North America. The same range of possibility applies to the iatrogenic pathway. No one knows the correct percentages.

Other Dissociative Disorders

DDNOS is a heterogeneous and poorly defined group of conditions containing an unknown but probably large number of cases that do not meet full criteria for DID, either because the identity states are not separate and distinct or because there are no clear switches of executive control. Such cases are variants of DID. Little can be said about the phenomenology, epidemiology, or etiology of DDNOS because the category contains so many different subtypes and because there is insufficient published research. In one study comparing subjects with clinical diagnoses of DID and DDNOS on the DDIS (Ross, Anderson, Fraser, et al., 1992), DDNOS subjects endorsed the same symptom profile and types of childhood trauma history as DID subjects, but to a milder degree. Clinically, DDNOS is often used as a provisional diagnosis when it is not yet clear whether the individual has full DID.

Symptoms of the three other DDs all occur in DID. However, DID is an exclusion criterion for those diagnoses. Although *DSM-IV* treats dissociative amnesia and depersonalization disorder as separate disorders, structured interviews with the DDIS often result in both diagnoses being made in the same person. Cases of chronic, recurrent amnesia and depersonalization that fail to meet criteria for DID are perhaps best viewed as DDNOS, though DDNOS can only be diagnosed by *DSM-IV* rules when none of the other DDs are present—yet another evidence that *DSM-IV* deals with these disorders inadequately.

Dissociative amnesia has been described for over a century and is the DD most supported by laboratory research, as reviewed above. The pattern of amnesia usually takes one of two forms. First, a circumscribed amnesia may exist for a single recent traumatic event. Second, amnesia may exist for a large period of childhood. Pathological amnesia for childhood must be differentiated from normal forgetting, but this is not difficult in clear cases. For instance, a patient might describe complete amnesia for three years from ages 9 to 12, but normal memory for time before and after that period. Not uncommonly, cognitively intact adults will describe complete amnesia for all events prior to ages 10, 12, or 14, with a sudden onset of normal memory. Clinically, this form of dissociative amnesia also seems to be traumatic. Amnesia malingered for secondary gain can be extremely difficult or impossible to differentiate from genuine amnesia (Cercy, Schretlen, & Brandt, 1997).

Chronic, disabling depersonalization can occur as a freestanding disorder (Steinberg, 1995) or as a feature of other disorders including schizophrenia, major depressive disorder, panic disorder, and hallucinogen abuse. Unfortunately, no objective method exists by which a limited-symptom panic disorder with prominent depersonalization can be differentiated from depersonalization disorder. However, when it occurs as a freestanding condition, depersonalization disorder does not appear to be linked to reported histories of childhood trauma. No school of psychotherapy claims efficacy for treatment of pure depersonalization disorder.

Dissociative fugue is rarely seen by clinicians, even those to whom DID cases are often referred. Moreover, no DDIS study in college students or the general population has detected a single case of fugue. The lifetime prevalence of the disorder in the general population is apparently less than two tenths of a percent. Sporadic cases have been reported since the 19th century. Clinical experience suggests that the disorder is not related to chronic childhood trauma. Instead, it represents a combined psychological and physical escape from nonspecific current life stresses, including combat, financial problems, or marital conflict. Amnesia in dissociative fugue is much more sudden and radical than that in DID, involving rapid onset of complete autobiographical amnesia, with subsequent complete amnesia for the period of fugue once the condition remits. Curiously, the validity of dissociative fugue is not challenged by extreme skeptics of DID, though fugue requires a more complete and profound dissociation of memory and identity than that claimed in DID. As is true for dissociative amnesia, differentiating malingered from genuine fugue can be difficult or impossible, especially since the condition always represents an avoidance of current circumstances.

Concluding Reflections

The DDs, especially DID, will continue to be controversial in the near future. In fact, DID could disappear from psychiatry entirely. In the late 19th and early 20th centuries, DID was a subject of mainstream interest in psychiatry and psychology, but virtually disappeared for 50 years subsequent to Freud's repudiation of seduction theory, the creation of the diagnosis of schizophrenia, and the rise of behaviorism (Ross, 1997). However, a substantial body of research supports the validity of DID, with contributors from Europe, Turkey, Japan, and North America.

The diagnostic criteria for the DDs require further refinement. As discussed above, dissociative trance is not well differentiated from DID, and no body of structured interview data exists regarding its reliability or prevalence. The main issue for the refinement of the DID criteria set is whether it should become polythetic and incorporate a list of secondary features. These might include auditory hallucinations, disremembered behavior being described to the person by others, changes in handwriting, objects missing and present that cannot be accounted for, or coming out of blank spells in new locations. Another question is whether the identity states should be required to have separate names and ages prior to diagnosis. However, clinicians may not remember additional, cumbersome criteria, and changes are unlikely to increase the interrater reliability of the diagnosis, which has a kappa of 0.90 or greater on structured interviews (Ross, 1997).

Future research should focus on priorities. Larger samples, replications, and refinement of the reliability of dissociative diagnoses other than DID are required. Structured interviews for children must be developed. The epidemiology of the DDs needs much more work, both in North America and throughout the world. Most important of all, treatment outcome studies are sorely needed. In cooperation with anthropologists, a rich field of study concerning normal versus pathological dissociation in different cultures remains to be explored. Finally, DID provides a window into the psychobiology of trauma.

The DDs should be diagnosed and studied using the rules of contemporary mainstream psychiatry and psychology, involving the *DSM* system. DID clinicians and researchers should be held to the same standards as others in the field. Whereas much of the debate concerning DID has been ideological, discussion of its reliability and validity should be empirical and based on the same rules of discourse as apply to anxiety, depression, psychosis, and substance abuse. Approached in this way, DID and the other DDs have a great deal to teach us about general psychopathology.

References

Berger, D., Sato, S., Ono, Y., Tezuka, I., Shirahase, J., Kuboki, T., & Suematsu, H. (1994). Dissociation and child abuse histories in an eating disorder cohort in Japan. *Acta Psychiatrica Scandinavica, 90*, 274–280.

Bernstein, E. M., & Putnam, F. W. (1986). Development, reliability, and validity of a dissociation scale. *Journal of Nervous and Mental Disease, 174*, 727–735.

Boon, S., & Draijer, N. (1993). Multiple personality disorder in the Netherlands. Amsterdam: Swets & Zeitlinger.

Braun, B. G. (1988). The BASK (behavior, affect, sensation, knowledge) model of dissociation. *Dissociation, 1*, 16–23.

Cardena, E. (1994). The domain of dissociation. In S. J. Lynn & L. W. Rhue (Eds.), *Dissociation. Clinical and theoretical perspectives* (pp. 15–31). New York: Guilford.

Carlson, E. B. (1994). Studying the interaction between physical and psychological states with the Dissociative Experiences Scale. In D. Spiegel (Ed.), *Dissociation. Culture, mind, and body* (pp. 41–58). Washington, DC: American Psychiatric Press.

Cercy, S. P., Schretlen, D. J., & Brandt, J. (1997). Simulated amnesia and the pseudo-memory phenomenon. In R. Rogers (Ed.), *Clinical assessment of malingering and deception* (pp. 85–107). New York: Guilford.

Cohen, N. J., & Eichenbaum, H. (1993). *Memory, amnesia, and the hippocampal system.* Cambridge, MA: MIT Press.

Coons, P. M. (1988). Misuse of forensic hypnosis: A hypnotically elicited false confession with apparent creation of multiple personality. *International Journal of Clinical and Experimental Hypnosis, 36*, 1–11.

Dunn, G. E., Paolo, A. M., & Ryan, J. J. (1993). Dissociative symptoms in a substance abuse population. *American Journal of Psychiatry, 150*, 1043–1047.

Ellason, J. W., & Ross, C. A. (1995). Positive and negative symptoms in dissociative identity disorder and schizophrenia. *Journal of Nervous and Mental Disease, 183*, 236–241.

Ellason, J. W., & Ross, C. A. *Borderline and nonborderline subsets of dissociative identity disorder.* Unpublished manuscript.

Ellason, J. W., Ross, C. A., & Fuchs, D. (1996). Assessment of dissociative identity disorder with the Millon Clinical Multiaxial Inventory-II. *Psychological Reports, 76*, 895–905.

Ellason, J. W., Ross, C. A., Sainton, K., & Mayran, L. (1996). Axis I and II comorbidity and childhood trauma history in chemical dependency. *Bulletin of the Menninger Clinic, 60*, 39–51.

Feldman, M. D., & Ford, C. V. (1994). *Patient or pretender: Inside the strange world of factitious disorders.* New York: John Wiley.

Hassan, S. (1988). *Combating cult mind control.* Rochester, VT: Park Street Press.

Horen, S. A., Leichner, P. P., & Lawson, J. S. (1995). Prevalence of dissociative symptoms and disorders in an adult psychiatric population in Canada. *Canadian Journal of Psychiatry, 40*, 185–191.

Horevitz, R. P., & Braun, B. G. (1984). Are multiple personalities borderline? *Psychiatric Clinics of North America, 7*, 69–87.

Kilhstrom, J. F. (1994). One hundred years of hysteria. In S. J. Lynn & J. W. Rhue (Eds.), *Dissociation: Clinical and theoretical perspectives* (pp. 365–394). New York: Guilford.

Kiziltan, E., Ozpulat, T., Sar, V., Tutkun, H., Yanik, M., & Yargic, L. (1996). Frequency of dissociative identity disorder among psychiatric inpatients in a Turkish university clinic. Paper presented at the Fall Meeting of the International Society for the Study of Dissociation, San Francisco.

Kluft, R. P. (1987). First-rank symptoms as a diagnostic clue to multiple personality disorder. *American Journal of Psychiatry, 144*, 293–298.

Knudsen, H., Draijer, N., Haselrud, J., Boe, T., & Boon, S. (1995). Dissociative disorders in Norwegian psychiatric inpatients. Paper presented at the Spring Meeting of the International Society for the Study of Dissociation, Amsterdam, The Netherlands.

Kramer, H., & Sprenger, J. (1486/1971). *The malleus maleficarum*. New York: Dover Publications.

Latz, T. T., Kramer, S. I., & Hughes, D. L. (1995). Multiple personality disorder among female inpatients in a state hospital. *American Journal of Psychiatry, 152*, 1343–1348.

Leeper, D. H., Page, B., & Hendricks, D. E. (1992). *The prevalence of dissociative disorders in a drug and alcohol abusing population of a residential treatment facility in a military medical center.* Unpublished manuscript.

Loewenstein, R. J. (1993). Psychogenic amnesia and psychogenic fugue: A comprehensive review. In D. Spiegel (Ed.), *Dissociative disorders: A clinical review* (pp. 45–77). Lutherville, MD: Sidran Press.

Loewenstein, R. J., & Putnam, F. W. (1988). A comparison study of dissociative symptoms in patients with complex partial seizures, multiple personality disorder, and posttraumatic stress disorder. *Dissociation, 1*, 17–23.

Loftus, E. (1993). The reality of repressed memories. *American Psychologist, 48*, 518–537.

Marks, J. (1979). *The search for the Manchurian candidate*. New York: Norton.

Merskey, H. (1995). The manufacture of personalities: The production of multiple personality disorder. In L. Cohen, J. Berzoff, & M. Elin (Eds.), *Dissociative identity disorder. Theoretical and treatment controversies* (pp. 3–32). Northvale, NJ: Jason Aronson.

Murphy, P. E. (1994). Dissociative experiences and dissociative disorders in a non-clinical university group. *Dissociation, 7*, 28–34.

North, C. S., Ryall, J., Ricci, D. A., & Wetzel, R. D. (1993). *Multiple personalities, multiple disorders*. New York: Oxford University Press.

Putnam, F. W. (1986). The scientific study of multiple personality disorder. In J. M. Quen (Ed.), *Split minds split brains* (pp. 65–97). New York: New York University Press.

Putnam, F. W. (1989). *Diagnosis and treatment of multiple personality disorder.* New York: Guilford.

Putnam, F. W., Guroff, J. J., Silberman, E. K., Barban, L., & Post, R. M. (1986). The clinical phenomenology of multiple personality disorder: Review of 100 recent cases. *Journal of Clinical Psychiatry, 47*, 285–293.

Ross, C. A. (1991). Epidemiology of multiple personality and dissociation. *Psychiatric Clinics of North America, 14*, 503–517.

Ross, C. A. (1996). Epidemiology of dissociation in children and adolescents. *Child and Adolescent Psychiatric Clinics of North America, 5*, 273–284.

Ross, C. A. (1997). *Dissociative identity disorder: Diagnosis, clinical features, and treatment of multiple personality* (2nd ed.). New York: John Wiley.

Ross, C. A., Anderson, D., Fleisher, W. P., & Norton, G. R. (1991). The frequency of multiple personality disorder among psychiatric inpatients. *American Journal of Psychiatry, 148*, 1717–1720.

Ross, C. A., Anderson, G., Fraser, G. A., Reagor, P., Bjornson, L., & Miller, S. D. (1992). Differentiating multiple personality disorder and dissociative disorder not otherwise specified. *Dissociation, 5*, 88–91.

Ross, C. A., Heber, S., Anderson, G., Norton, G. R., Anderson, B., del Campo, M., & Pillay, N. (1989). Differentiating multiple personality disorder and complex partial seizures. *General Hospital Psychiatry, 11*, 54–58.

Ross, C. A., Heber, S., Norton, G. R., Anderson, D., Anderson, G., & Barchet, P. (1989). The Dissociative Disorders Interview Schedule: A structured interview. *Dissociation, 2*, 169–189.

Ross, C. A., & Joshi, S. (1992). Paranormal experiences in the general population. *Journal of Nervous and Mental Disease, 180*, 357–361.

Ross, C. A., Joshi, S., & Currie, R. P. (1990). Dissociative experiences in the general population. *American Journal of Psychiatry, 147*, 1547–1552.

Ross, C. A., Joshi, S., & Currie R. P. (1991). Dissociative experiences in the general population: A factor analysis. *Hospital and Community Psychiatry, 42*, 297–301.

Ross, C. A., Kronson, J., Koensgen, S., Barkman, K., Clark, P., & Rockman, G. (1992). Dissociative comorbidity in 100 chemically dependent patients. *Hospital and Community Psychiatry, 43*, 840–842.

Ross, C. A., Miller, S. D., Reagor, P., Bjornson, L., Fraser, G. A., & Anderson, G. (1990). Structured interview data on 102 cases of multiple personality disorder from four centers. *American Journal of Psychiatry, 147*, 596–601.

Ross, C. A., Norton, G. R., & Wozney, K. (1989). Multiple personality disorder: An analysis of 236 cases. *Canadian Journal of Psychiatry, 34*, 413–418.

Ross, C. A., Ryan, L., Voigt, H., & Eide, L. (1991). High and low dissociators in a college student population. *Dissociation, 4*, 147–151.

Saxe, G. N., van der Kolk, B. A., Berkowitz, R., Chinman, G., Hall, K., Lieberg, G., & Schwartz, J. (1993). Dissociative disorders in psychiatric inpatients. *American Journal of Psychiatry, 150*, 1037–1042.

Siegel, D. J. (1996). Cognition, memory, and dissociation. *Child and Adolescent Psychiatric Clinics of North America, 5*, 509–536.

Simpson, M. (1995). Gullible's travels, or the importance of being multiple. In L. Cohen, J. Berzoff, & M. Elin (Eds.), *Dissociative identity disorder: Theoretical and treatment controversies* (pp. 87–134). Northvale, NJ: Jason Aronson.

Singer, M. (1995). *Cults in our midst: The hidden menace in our everyday lives.* San Francisco: Jossey-Bass.

Spitzer, R. L., Williams, J. B. W., Gibbon, M., & First, M. B. (1990). User's guide for the structured clinical interview for DSM-III-R. Washington, DC: American Psychiatric Press.

Steinberg, M. (1995). *Handbook for the assessment of dissociation: A clinical guide.* Washington, DC: American Psychiatric Press.

van der Kolk, B. A. (1996). The body keeps the score: Approaches to the psychobiology of posttraumatic stress disorder. In B. A. van der Kolk, A. C. McFarlane, & L. Weisath (Eds.), *Traumatic stress: The effects of overwhelming experience on mind, body and society* (pp. 214–241). New York: Guilford.

van der Kolk, B. A., McFarlane, A. C., & Weisath, L. (1996). *Traumatic Stress: The effects of overwhelming stress on mind, body and society.* New York: Guilford.

Vanderlinden, J. (1993). *Dissociative experiences, trauma, and hypnosis.* Delft, Netherlands: Uitgeverij Eburon.

Waller, N., & Ross, C. A. (1997). The prevalence and biometric structure of pathological dissociation in the general: Taxometric and behavior genetic findings. *Journal of Abnormal Psychology, 106*, 499–510.

West, L. J., & Martin, P. (1994). Pseudo-identity and the treatment of personality change in victims of captivity and cults. In S. J. Lynn & J. W. Rhue (Eds.), *Dissociation. Clinical and theoretical perspectives* (pp. 268–288). New York: Guilford.

Whalen, J. E., & Nash, M. R. (1995). Hypnosis and dissociation: Theoretical, empirical, and clinical perspectives. In L. K. Michelson & W. J. Ray (Eds.), *Handbook of dissociation: A clinical guide* (pp. 191–206). New York: Plenum.

PART IV

AXIS II DISORDERS

19

Models of Personality and Its Disorders

ROGER D. DAVIS
THEODORE MILLON

No other area in the study of psychopathology is fraught with more controversy than the personality disorders. First, there is little agreement on the number of personality disorders. Some personalities (schizoid and paranoid), have appeared in every edition of the *DSM* since *DSM-I*, while others have appeared in only one edition. For example, the sadistic and self-defeating (or masochistic) personality disorders appeared in the Appendix of *DSM-III-R*, but are no longer listed in *DSM-IV*, which now includes the new depressive personality disorder. Second, there are arguments concerning the boundaries between various personality disorders and their diagnostic criteria. Anger and impulsivity, for example, characterize many personalities, but for different reasons. Consequently, the very behaviors that most warrant intervention are often those with the most disappointing specificity. Third, there are issues related to the boundaries between the personality disorders and various Axis I disorders. Some theorists see the schizoid and schizotypal personality disorders, for example, as existing on a continuum with schizophrenia. Others have argued that borderline might be categorized with the affective disorders, or that its adult manifestation reflects posttraumatic stress suffered in childhood, that it lies on a continuum with schizophrenia, or even dissociative identity disorder. Likewise, the relationship between the new depressive personality and dysthymia, found on Axis I, is problematic. Fourth, there is disagreement about the nature of individual personality disorders. Borderline again serves as an example. In psychodynamic circles, for example, borderline is often viewed as a level of personality organization that cuts across many different personality disorders. In the *DSM-IV*, it is considered a discrete diagnostic category with no necessary theoretical relationship to any other personality disorder.

Many other controversies could easily be listed, and it is precisely in such controversies that a chapter on models of personality and its disorders finds relevance. In particular, the history of every science may be said to include a prescientific "natural history" phase, where the main questions are "What are the essential phenomena of the field?" and "How can we know them?" Ideally, as more and more data are gathered through increasingly sophisticated methodologies, common sense begins to give way to theoretical accounts that not only integrate and unify disparate observations but also actively suggest directions for future research. The existence of black holes, for example, is predicted by the theory of relativity. Astronomers thus began actively searching these bodies, and the accumulated evidence of several decades now suggests that one or more black holes are likely to exist as the gravitational center of every galaxy. No one, of course, has ever actually "seen" a black hole and no one ever will. Nor will anyone ever hear, touch, or taste one. By necessity, they are purely inferential entities, hidden from all our senses. Nevertheless, many independent lines of evidence now point to their existence. The validation of black holes highlights the function of theory in science: theories present the world to us in ways that go beyond direct experience, but are nevertheless coherent and compelling. The lure of a theory-based classification system that "carves nature at its joints," as Plato said, is that it affords an almost mystical knowledge. Given such a taxonomy, our representational blinders would seem to peel away and the "inner essences" of reality would be revealed to us in a perfect communion between mind and nature. Such knowledge would be intuitive, immediate, absolute, with no need for any intermediate representational system or nomological network. The taxonomy would be completely transparent to the thinker.

Unfortunately, the science of psychopathology has no framework that parallels the theory of relativity. In fact, the atheoretical position adopted with the construction of the *DSM-III* in 1980 may be seen as a required revisitation of the "natural history" phrase of psychopathology, one that launched a renewed and vigorous effort directed toward cataloguing all varieties of mental disorders. Although numerous theories and models of personality and psychopathology have been proposed, our field today is an eclectic mix of partial theories addressed to different levels and kinds of data. This fact has important consequences for our review: although we can describe what perspectives exist today, we cannot know what new and compelling perspectives might be launched tomorrow. In fact, no review can be exhaustive of models that might potentially exist. For the social sciences generally, learning and understanding the science inevitably involves an effort to learn its history because it is the particularities of history that determine the structure and content of the science, and not the guiding force of theory.

For example, what would psychopathology be like if Freud had never been born? The ideas of id, ego, and superego might well be lost to the world. Whole semesters of the graduate curriculum would vanish. Indeed, psychodynamic psychology might not exist at all. Similarly, we can only speculate what figures, their own originality preempted by Freud's influence, might have risen to prominence in his place, what views they might have formulated, and what their unique legacy would be. Such minor variations might easily change the entire content of our science. Essentially, the argument is that the history of psychopathology has much the same formal structure as the history of the individual life, possessing numerous idiographic aspects created by the random walk of chance events. Perspectives come and go, wax and wane, even while scholars maintain that human behavior is explained by psychological laws that are pristine and eternal. In contrast, where the field is a hard science such as physics, the influence of historical contingencies is minimized over time as multiple perspectives within the field converge through experiment and falsification on some more singular and comprehensive view. Where the subject is a social science, however, the falsification of theories is no longer strictly possible as a means of moving the field forward (Meehl, 1978). Instead, perspectives within the field tend to develop to high states of internal consistency, setting their own standards of evidence and experimentation, thus ensuring their indefinite survival. The historical schools of psychology are all solid examples.

While we cannot inventory all the particular models that might be seriously entertained by scientists, we can at least identify a way of approaching the subject so that similar models are sorted together in terms of their essential properties (see figure 19.1). Future models may then be placed within this framework in order to illuminate their strengths, weaknesses, and fundamental assumptions. The major sections of the chapter are presented in a loose progression that ranges from the prescientific or naïve to what is deemed progressively more scientific. The first broad section considers categorical and dimensional models of personality, and associated elaborations of these basic taxonic formats. The second broad section discusses methodologically strong attempts to elaborate these basic ideas in more scientific ways. All of these approaches are inductive, meaning that the scientist first goes to the world and asks what the world has in it, and then develops generalizations based on a presumably thorough and rigorous review. Given their emphasis on inventorying the basic phenomena of personality, methodologically strong approaches are obviously rooted in the natural history stage of science, but attempt to bootstrap themselves into scientific legitimacy through scrupulous observation and methodological rigor. The third section deals with content-strong models, theoretical perspectives on personality, including the behavioral, interpersonal, cognitive, psychoanalytic, and neurobiological or temperament

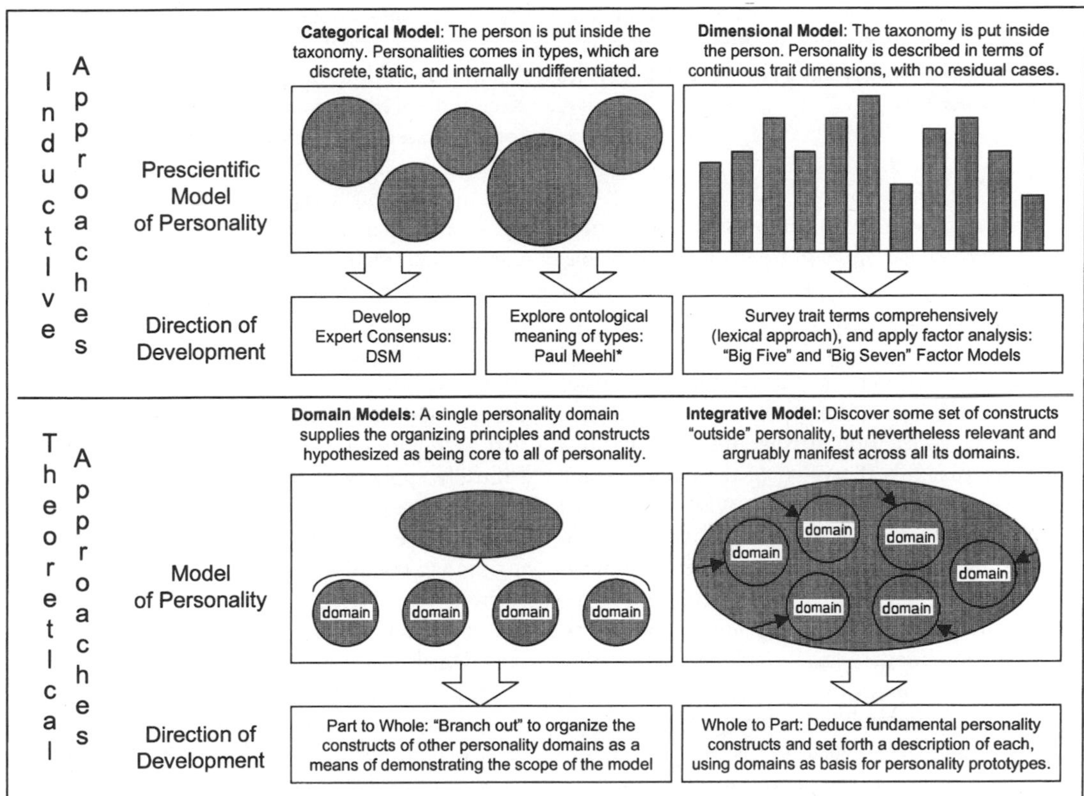

Figure 19.1 Contemporary structure of argumentation in the personality disorders.

models. Each is part of personality and each represents an attempt to make what is only one part the basis for understanding the entire whole of personality. Finally, the last section presents an attempt to develop an evolutionary theory of personality that draws specifically on the synthetic properties of the term in order to integrate its various domains.

Categorical and Dimensional Models of Personality

Strictly speaking, categories and dimensions are taxonomic constructs, not models of personality. Usually, the idea of a model conjures up the work of some theorist, along with arguments to the effect that his or her pet variables or organizing principles constitute the framework through which personality should be organized and discussed. Not surprisingly, psychiatry has favored the so-called medical model of mental disorders, wherein personality disorders (as described in *DSM-IV*) are assumed to be categories of mental illness, with discrete boundaries between normality and pathology and between one personality and another. Psychologists, however, have usually eschewed categories, instead preferring to think in terms of dimensions, which allow a continuous gradient between normality and abnormality. In contrast, the layperson switches easily between categorical and dimensional modes. To the average person, the statement "You're so narcissistic!" is almost identical in meaning to "Your such a narcissist!" The first statement, however, locates the individual at the upper end of a continuous distribution, while the second states that the individual is exemplary of a particular type. In their everyday work, even professionals who strongly believe in the dimensional model often lapse into an implicitly categorical framework. A subject whose test profile has schizoid and compulsive as the highest scales may thus be described as a "schizoid compulsive." Here, the entire personality profile is distilled into two words and rendered as a type, as if other scales were irrelevant.

The Categorical Model

The idea that personalities come in types is probably the most basic model of personality possible, the model of naïve common sense, as in "What personality type are you?" Essentially, it reflects the simple belief that there are things in the world and that these things sort themselves into various kinds, extended to realm of human beings. In this prescientific conception, personality is essentially a substance that fills the vessel of the person, static and internally undifferentiated. Were this model true, various "sections" of the mind would be homogeneous all the way through. There is no dynamism, no speculation about the relationships between various structures of the mind—that is, no "topographic model," as Freud used the term. Moreover, anything can be considered a type, so that there are potentially as many types as there are individuals to be typed. In casual usage, a pensive type is just as plausible as a melancholy type. This gives the idea of types great currency, since kinds can be invented as needed and adapted to any individual person. Everyone can be classified. There are no residual cases. Modern classification systems, which inevitably include a "not otherwise specified" cateogry, cannot say as much. However, the scope of casual usage is exactly what makes it prescientific: no rational basis is set forward to constrain the number of types. The first order of business in graduating from the natural history stage of commonsense observation, then, is to ask which types are fundamental and which are spurious. Three directions have been pursued to answer this question.

First, a theory of personality can be advanced. If our budding scientist is asked why this particular constellation of types exists rather than some other, the reply is that these are preferred because they are anchored to a theory, and that the theory provides a means of understanding the relation of the types both to each other and in terms of the deeper principles on which the theory rests. Many famous figures in the history of psychology have followed this direction. Whatever its real merit, the idea of the oral, anal, phallic, and genital characters represents an effort to derive a system of types from a model of psychosexual development. Likewise, Sheldon (Sheldon & Stevens, 1942) and Kretschmer (1922) developed the idea of the somatotype, classifying individuals in accordance with physical principles as ectomorphs, mesomorphs, or endomorphs. Such types assume a special status because of their link to theory, which ultimately underwrites their very reality. Unfortunately, establishing some constraint on the number of types also introduces another problem. No matter how compelling a particular system of types may be, some individuals are not readily described within the system. Such persons are a nagging reminder that all theories are but partial views and will not fruitfully apply to all instances.

Second, experts in a particular area can be brought together with the formal purpose of deciding among themselves which types the science will address. This is the direction pursued by the *DSM-IV*, and it has its own advantages and shortcomings. On the one hand, the agreement of seasoned experts is to be preferred to naïve common sense. Moreover, requiring consensus from a body of diverse experts ensures that no one theoretical statement can foreclose further speculation and investigation before a more complete, and presumably more valid, theory can be formulated. The *DSM* has yet to officially endorse a set of principles that would relate the Axis II constructs to each other and allow them to be understood in terms of deeper principles. Because it is arbitrated by committee, not derived through a coherent theory or the systematic application of a methodology, the *DSM* cannot completely free itself from its prescientific heritage. Committee consensus does forestall anarchy by putting the official constructs under oligarchical control, but consensus is a means of governing, not a scientific explanation. In the *DSM-IV* deliberations, for example, sadistic personality disorder was dropped in part because it was seldom diagnosed in most clinical settings (Fiester & Gay, 1991). We might ask, however, whether the composition of a taxonomy is to be decided by base rates—that is, by the frequency with which a disorder appears. Chemistry has its periodic table of elements, while physics has what is known as the Standard Model. Both recognize as fundamental taxa elements and particles that are never found in nature, but only in the course of experimentation. Some of these exist only for exceedingly brief moments, perhaps less than a thousandth of a second. Yet it is precisely the effort to account for these rare entities that has been instrumental in driving the science of particle physics forward. Apparently, physicists have yet to appreciate the utility of a category such as esoteric particles NOS.

The third and most sophisticated modern development in the categorical tradition is taxometrics (Meehl & Golden, 1982; Meehl, 1995). Taxometrics explores the ontological aspects of the concept of type—that is, how a type, should it exist, would be manifest and what methods might be used to discover it and refine its detection. When it is suspected that a pathology may be categorical in nature, taxometrics is appropriate. The methodology was developed by Meehl, mainly in conjunction with his theory of schizophrenia and the identification of what are termed "schizotaxics," individuals who possess a genetic predisposition to the development of schizophrenia, but may or may not remain compensated (Meehl, 1962), depending on environmental stressors. Meehl emphasized the heterogeneity of schizophrenia, the fact that interpersonal aversiveness, language abberations, and eye-tracking disturbances all occur together empirically, but without a psychologically compelling reason to do so. Taxometrics is thus intended to evaluate taxonicity on the basis of multiple indicators that co-occur with poor face validity within a particular diagnostic class, but remain largely uncorrelated in other persons. Cutting scores may be derived to classify subjects into catgories on the basis of available indicators, and other indicators may be added to bootstrap the classification system to successively higher levels of validity. Meehl (1995) thus argues that taxometrics solves a chronic problem in history of psychopathology: the absence of a reliable and valid diagnostic criterion. Potentially, its widespread use could replace the use of committees in determining diagnostic standards.

The Dimensional Model

Whereas the categorical model holds that there are discrete boundaries between normality and pathology, and between various personality types, the dimensional model holds instead that personality characteristics are expressed on a continuous gradient. At the prescientific level of common sense, the unit of analysis in the dimensional model is the personality trait, and there are literally thousands of personality traits. In contrast to terms used to describe psychological *states*, such as "mad," "happy," and "angry," *traits* describe enduring characteristics of the person that are stable across time and situational context. Examples would include such terms as "gregarious," "arrogant," "thoughtless," or "helpful" (many terms are used to describe both states and traits, a source of ambiguity and confusion in our discipline). In addition, while types tend to be mutually exclusive, so that an individual cannot be classified within two personality types simultaneously, dimensions readily coexist. Taxonomy and person reverse priority, so that the classification system is literally put inside the person, who receives some score on each trait dimension of the system. Since everyone can be thus dimensionalized, there are no residual cases. Traits thus form a rich vocabulary through which any given person can be described. As before, the problem is to cull from an overwhelming multitude of traits only those that are psychologically fundamental and therefore might serve as a scientific basis for a taxonomy of personality and its disorders.

The dimensional model has a long history in the measurement of psychopathology, dating from the development of the first psychological tests. The best personality instruments consist of many scales that are conjointly normed on large samples of persons. The scores obtained on these scales form a personality profile. For example, the 4-9 codetype (reflecting deviation on the MMPI-2 scales 4 and 9 only) is thought as an indicator of psychopathy. Thus, the profile effectively operationalizes the person, just as a single scale operationalizes the construct that it is intended to measure. As a schematic of the person, the profile carries a considerable burden. An important idea in test construction is the notion of content validity. Nothing important to the definition of a construct should be left out and nothing extra should be thrown in. Likewise, we might speak of the content validity of a personality profile, and ask that the test measure everything that personality is, and nothing more. Obviously, then, the dimensions chosen to constitute the profile should not be selected randomly or casually, but instead chosen with some theoretical or methodological rationale. Ideally, this rationale should serve as a promissory note that the profile not only exhausts human personality but also organizes the resulting clinical information in accordance with principles or domains through which the person can be understood and eventually treated. We now turn to an extended discussion of methodological efforts to answer this question.

Methodology

Theory and methodology form two fundamentally different ways of determining which personality contents are fundamental. Theoretical models usually seek principles that underlie an entire perspective, which is assumed to organize the contents of all other personality domains, which are then cast as peripheral or derivative. Interpersonal theorists, for example, see interpersonal conduct as basic to the development of personality. In contrast, cognitive theorists would argue that, because internal cognitive structures always mediate perception, interpretation, and communication, cognitive theory is the best candidate for an integrative model. And herein lies a principal problem with theoretical approaches to personality: the tendency to reject essential aspects of experience or behavior.

In contrast, methodologically driven models resist making a priori theoretical commitments, and so are free to address any domain of personality for which data are available. First, the universe of personality descriptors is sampled according to some definition of personality. Second, persons may be asked to rate themselves on the resulting of list of traits, called external ratings, or to somehow rate the degree to which different terms are similar to each other, called internal ratings. Third, factor analysis, a multivariate statistical technique which extracts from an observed pattern of correlations a much smaller number of dimensions, is applied in order to telescope hundreds of traits into a parsimonious handful of higher order dimensions. The researcher may have no a priori notion about what dimensions will emerge. Such rationales can be generated at a later date. Structure and sufficiency are thus offered in compensation for lack of a compelling theory.

Factor models provide well-developed examples of an inductive-dimensional approach to personality, and have a number of appealing and interrelated features that form a neat package. First, factor models assume there is no sharp division between normality and pathology, only a smooth unbroken gradation. In contrast, Axis II has been criticized as being archaically categorical (Widiger, 1993). Second, factor models are almost always sufficient, meaning that the model accounts for most of the variation in the data set from which it is developed. The correlation matrix of variables is factored until negligible "residual variance" remains, so that sufficiency is an automatic product of the methodology. Third, where the factors are extracted to be uncorrelated, cognitive economy is further maximized, since the majority of traits are linked to only one factor. The *DSM*, in contrast, assumes that some disorders may have several traits in common, as evidenced by their overlapping criteria sets. Fourth, factor models are almost always parsimonious, extracting between three and seven factors, regardless of the variables factored (Block, 1995). This leads to a fifth premise, the idea that a factor model might serve as a coherent taxonomy to which all of personality psychology can be anchored, thus providing an organizing force for future research. Sixth, since factor models are explicitly constructed to telescope almost all of the variance in a particular domain into a handful of dimensions, they necessarily maximize the possibility of finding statistically significant relationships between some measure of the resulting factors and variables in adjacent domains of study. In contrast, the *DSM* personality disorders constructs exist only within the realm of pathology, with no official endorsement of more normal variants that might encourage their application within related fields. And finally, factor models are explicitly mathematical and provide some assurance that the fuzzy domain of the social sciences can be quantified like the harder sciences of chemistry and physics. Figure 19.2 presents a comparison of recent factor models relevant to the personality disorders.

For its appealing features, it has nevertheless proved extremely difficult within the factor tradition to specify exactly which dimensions should be considered fundamental. Many proponents have concluded that five dimensions are sufficient to account for personality, but disagree about the substance of these five, particularly the nature of the fifth and slimmest factor. Goldberg (1993), for example, has sought to distinguish the "Big Five" model derived from the lexical tradition from the Five-Factor Model of Costa and McCrae (1992). Interested readers are referred to John, Angleitner, and Ostendorf (1988), Digman (1990), John (1990), and Goldberg (1993) for a complete history of these approaches. The following sections are in-

NORMAL PERSONALITY DOMAIN			PATHOLOGICAL PERSONALITY DOMAIN		
Lexical "Big Five" Model	Five-Factor Model	"Big Seven" Model	Livesley & associates	Clark & associates	Harkness & associates
1. Surgency (or Extraversion)	1. Neuroticism	1. Positive Valence	1. Compulsivity	1. Suicide proneness	1. Aggressiveness
2. Agreeableness	2. Extraversion	2. Negative Valence	2. Conduct Problems	2. Self-derogation	2. Psychoticism
3. Conscientiousness	3. Openness to Experience	3. Positive Emotionality	3. Diffidence	3. Anhedonia	3. Constraint
4. Emotional Stability (vs. Neuroticism)	4. Agreeableness	4. Negative Emotionality	4. Identity Problems	4. Instability	4. Negative Emotionality-Neuroticism
5. Intellect (or Culture)	5. Conscientiousness	5. Conscientiousness	5. Insecure Attachment	5. Hypersensitivity	5. Positive Emotionality-Extraversion
		6. Agreeableness	6. Intimacy Problems	6. Anger/Aggression	
		7. Conventionality	7. Narcissism	7. Pessimism	
			8. Suspiciousness	8. Negative affect	
			9. Affective Lability	9. Suspiciousness	
			10. Passive Oppositionality	10. Self-centered Exploitation	
			11. Perceptual Cognitive Distortion	11. Passive-aggressiveness	
			12. Rejection	12. Dramatic Exhibitionism	
			13. Self-Harming Behaviors	13. Grandiose egocentrism	
			14. Restricted Expression	14. Social isolation	
			15. Social Avoidance	15. Emotional coldness	
			16. Stimulus Seeking	16. Dependency	
			17. Interpersonal Disesteem	17. Conventionality-Rigidity	
			18. Anxiousness	18. Dependency	
				19. Impulsivity	
				20. High energy	
				21. Antisocial behavior	
				22. Schizotypal Thought	

Figure 19.2 Factor models of normal and abnormal personality domains.

debted to these papers, which variously detail the rise of the factor tradition, its various models, and the competition between different factor-naming schemes.

The Big Five Model

The Big Five Model (BFM) developed out of research in the lexical tradition, which is based on the assumption that all important individual difference terms are already encoded in the language. Allport and Odbert (1936) were apparently the first to apply the approach in the United States, culling almost 18,000 terms that "distinguish the behavior of one human being from that of another" (p. 24) from 400,000 words listed in the unabridged 1925 edition of *Webster's New International Dictionary*. After the deletion of positively and negatively evaluative terms such as "good," "excellent," or "poor," just over 4,500 terms reflecting "generalized and personalized determining tendencies" (p. 26) remained. The choice to delete evaluative terms has been controversial, and affects the substantive nature of the dimensions extracted.

In the early 1940s, Raymond Cattell set about discovering the latent dimensions of lexical descriptors, culminating ultimately in the Sixteen Personality Factor (16PF) inventory (e.g., Cattell, Eber, & Tatsuoka, 1970). Unfortunately, Cattell's research was hampered by the characteristics of the times. First, microcomputers and their statistical packages did not yet exist. Thus, Cattell was forced to preprocess the Allport and Odbert list on his own in order to produce a smaller number of clusters that could be managed by crude calculation. Eventually, Cattell settled on 35 bipolar dimensions. Subsequent factor calculations were performed by hand or on awkward calculating devices. Mistakes were inevitable (Digman & Takemoto-Chock, 1981). While modern researchers can simply rerun their factor analyses to extract more or fewer factors and examine the various results, the labor involved at the time did not permit such ad hoc studies. Instead, because Cattell (1950) believed that it would be better to extract too many factors than two few, he ultimately extracted narrow and unstable factors, while noting that "only six—A, B, F, H, K, and M—are repeatedly confirmed" (quoted by Digman, 1996). Nevertheless, the 16PF is still used in personality assessment and has a large literature base. Later researchers (Fiske, 1949; Tupes & Christal, 1961) subsequently refactored Cattell's list of personality traits, finding five factors.

In the mid-1970s, Goldberg began anew, starting a lexical research program whose goals was to refind the fundamental factors literally from scratch, thereby avoiding the biases that potentially beset the preprocessed lists. For a decade, Goldberg analyzed data gathered from self and peer ratings and similarity judgments. By the late 1980s, he was convinced: "In each analysis, I would discover some variant of the BFM factors, no two analyses exactly the same, no analysis so different from the rest that I couldn't recognize the hazy outlines of the five domains" (1993, p. 29). Rather than attempt to isolate the single best position of factor axes in five-dimensional space, Goldberg and associates (Peabody & Goldberg, 1989) instead chose to study the determinants of these positions across multiple analyses, demontrate the effect of unipolar versus bipolar adjectives, internal versus external judgments, and so on.

The Five-Factor Model

As reviewed by Block (1995), the origins of the Five-Factor Model (FFM; Costa & McCrae, 1976) lie in a cluster analytic study of Cattell's 16PF. The first two clusters were interpreted as resembling neuroticism and extraversion, respectively, with a slim third cluster marked only by the imaginativeness scale of the 16PF. Similar measures were then added to augment this cluster (Costa & McCrae, 1978), thus creating enough redundant variance to precipitate the emergence of a new factor, openness to experience. As with Cattell, there is a question concerning whether this factor was discovered or simply produced artificially. These three dimensions eventually became the NEO Personality Inventory (Costa & McCrae, 1985). In time the instrument was revised and restructured, with two factors being added, in part reflecting the influence of the lexical Big Five. Items were grouped into 6 facet scales per factor, for a total of 30 facets, giving the instrument a hierarchical structure (Costa & McCrae, 1995). Each facet scale essentially provides a short measure of some trait considered to be an important subsidiary component of its respective factor.

In contrast to the long lexical origins of the Big Five, the Five-Factor Model emerged from questionnaire data (Costa & McCrae, 1992). The Big Five Model is thus the cumulative result of a long tradition, while the FFM is the product of a single set of researchers. Certainly there are similarities between the two, but there are also differences. One concerns the philosophy of the proponents. Goldberg (1993) maintains that the lexical BFM is phenotypic or descriptive, not explanatory. In contrast, McCrae and Costa (1986) believe that factor analysis has the capacity to reveal nature's true structure: traits are real and factors are facts. Perhaps because of their different views, the FFM has been aggressively pushed in many areas of psychology, while the Big Five has not. Whether the BFM or the FFM more closely represents the true structure of personality is an open question at the current time.

The personality disorders have been described in terms of the five factors and facets of the NEO-PI-R by Widiger, Trull, Clarkin, Sanderson, and Costa (1994). Some disorders are uniformly high or low across all or most facets of a factor. Borderline, for example, is high across all facets of neuroticism, histrionic is high across most facets of extraversion, and antisocial is low across most facets of agreeableness, and some facets of conscientiousness. Some have objected, however, that the description of certain disorders in terms of the FFM falls short of providing a complete clinical picture (Kernberg, 1996), and that a refining of the model as analyzed with more pathological descriptors is necessary (Harkness & McNulty, 1994). Others have argued that openness to experience has little relation to personality disorders.

Factor Models in the Abnormal Personality Domain

Whereas five-factor researchers have approached personality disorders through models derived from normal subjects, other researchers have produced factor models specifically within the domain of personality pathology. Clark (1990) factored a pool of descripters that focused on *DSM-III* personality disorder criteria, as well as certain non-*DSM* personality-relevant concepts, including Cleckley's (1964) description of the psychopath and criteria from certain personality-related disorders, namely dysthymia, cyclothymia, and generalized anxiety disorder. Results suggested 22 symptom clusters, listed in figure 19.2. Sixteen of these were then further developed into the Schedule for Nonadaptive and Adaptive Personality (Clark, 1993). The other six were deemed as tapping negative affectivity, positive affectivity, and disinhibition (Clark & Watson, 1990).

Rather than assume the *DSM* to be exhaustive of descriptors for personality pathology, Livesley and associates (1989) sought a logical basis by which to sample the entire domain of personality pathology comprehensively. First, in-depth literature reviews were used to specify and rank-order each personality disorder's prototypal characteristics. The most prototypal characteristic was then assumed to represent a trait category. If the second most prototypal characteristic was judged to be sufficiently similar to the first, it too was placed in the same trait category. If not, it was assumed to sample a different trait characteristic and a new category was generated. Finally, trait categories were examined across *DSM* diagnoses to eliminate redundancies. Seventy-nine trait dimensions were required to represent the 11 personality disorders of *DSM-III-R*. Self-report items were then written and given to two samples from the general population. Items from scales with initially low internal consistency were segregated into separate scales, ultimately increasing the total number of scales to 100, which were then administered to a general population and a personality pathology sample. Fifteen oblique factors were extracted as representing simple structure for both. On the basis of these results, the Dimensional Assessment of Personality Pathology—Basic Questionnaire (DAPP-BQ)—was constructed. Identity disturbance was separated into two scales, identity problems and anxiousness, and suspiciousness and self-harming behaviors were added as scales on rational grounds because of the recognized importance to the abnormal personality domain, resulting in a total of 18 constructs (see figure 19.2). In summarizing analyses of the DAPP-BQ and the NEO-PI, Schroeder, Wormworth, and Livesley (1994) concluded that while neuroticism plays a substantial role in personality pathology, openness to experience is not strongly related.

Yet another point of departure was chosen by Harkness and McNulty (1994). These authors counseled caution in applying models developed with normal samples to personality disorders patients, stating that "structural models are models of the major vectors of variation within a particular population. We contend that adding a strong complement of persons with diagnosable personality disorders could change the list of big variance dimensions" (p. 294). Sixty descriptors consisting of major topics from the *DSM-III-R*, together with markers of primary dimension of normal-range personality, were analyzed via principal components on the basis of similarity and dissimilarity judgments. While solutions ranging from 5 to 20 components were examined for psychological meaningfulness, the authors settled on a five-factor solution, but one with substantial differences from the FFM or BFM (see figure 19.2), which they christened the PSY-5. A comparison of their invention to the Five-Factor model shows constraint and psychoticism as qualitatively distinct: "PSY-5 constraint is not comparable to normal sample-based Conscientiousness. . . . These are two different constructs" (p. 310). Likewise, "psychoticism is a dramatically different construct compared to the so-called 'fifth factor' in normal population five factor models" (p. 310). Harkness and McNulty are perhaps the most successful researchers to date in demonstrating the limits of applicability of normal-range models to clinical populations.

The "Big Seven"

One of the fundamental problems in factor analytic research lies in establishing the boundaries of the personality data to be input for analysis. Change the item sampling criteria and the results may look very different. Tellegen and Waller (1987) have argued that evaluative terms (e.g., ordinary, excellent, evil, or bad), and terms which might refer to both psychological states and traits (e.g., "relaxed" or "anxious"), were systematically excluded by the original lexical researchers, Allport and Odbert (1936). Tellegen and Waller noted, however, that abnormal behavior always contains such positive and negative evaluations. Many personality disorders, for example, are characterized by low self-worth. When 400 personality traits were isolated from the 1985 *American Heritage Dictionary* and factor-analyzed, results indicated a seven-factor model, appropriately christened the "Big Seven." To further strengthen their claim, Almagor, Tellegen, and Waller (1995) researched the cross-cultural validity of the Big Seven in Hebrew, arguing that cultural and linguistic differences between Israel and the United States would provide a strong test of the replicability of the Big Seven. Seven factors were robust across rotation methods and number of factors extracted, with six of the seven present in the previous study. More important, the two largest factors were again positive evaluation and negative evaluation, indicating clear evidence for the replicability of these factors in a culture substantially different from that in which the Big Seven were originally found. The comprehensiveness of the Big Seven provides a considerable challenge to the sufficiency of the BFM and FFM.

Appraisal of Factor Models in Personality

How are factor models of personality to be appraised? First, we might question the lexical hypothesis, which holds that all important characteristics of persons have already be encoded in the natural language. According to this view, every trait that is important to personality is already in the dictionary. Conversely, if it isn't in the dictionary, it can't be part of personality. The general evolution of sciences, however, runs directly counter to this assertion. As science advances, it tends to evolve its own unique jargon that is related to, but becomes increasingly remote from, the vocabulary of the common person. While there are occasional deadends, the process of scientific evolution builds on and adds something new to the commonsense understanding that was its beginning. It is hoped that scientists do not invent new terminologies just for the sociological purpose of setting themselves apart from common folk, who speak the common lexicon and not the language of the illuminati. The lexical hypothesis voids this optimism. If everything in personality from Wundt forward has been "just new wine in old bottles," then that is sad news indeed.

The problem with the lexical hypothesis is, however, only a special case of a more general problem that besets induction as an approach to science. Although factor analysis is elegant as a mathematical means of uncovering the dimensions that underlie a particular correlation matrix, the raw material on which the methodology works must be supplied by the scientist. The attempt to go to the world and inventory its contents, which defines the inductive tradition, is expressed in lexical research through copious studies of personality trait descriptors from many languages, with attempts to show that the derived models can be found across every culture (Digman, 1990). The models of Livesley and associates (1989), Clark (1990), and others reviewed above represent different ways of "sampling the world" as a means of engaging the inductive process. In each case, the goal is to sidestep theoretical speculation, which has lead to the development of numerous historical schools and their excesses, and inquire of nature directly with no biases that might influence the result.

Unfortunately, providing the raw material for any inductive methodology involves critical a priori assumptions. In the lexical tradition, this involves deciding which trait terms belong to personality and which do not. Factor analysis cannot make this decision on its own. As a result, different researchers draw the boundaries in different ways and derive different models, such as the Big Five and the Big Seven. If one agrees with a particular sampling strategy, the results are likely to be persuasive. If one does not agree, the results are not persuasive. Worse, since different factor models disagree at the level of their most basic assumptions—the very raw data of personality—there are no rigorous experiments that can be constructed that might falisfy one model in favor of the other. Paradoxically, then, the most ostensibly rigorous methodological approach to personality, the factor analysis of various lexical terms, intended to avoid the biases of theoretical speculation, has only produced its own species of models, built upon and prejudiced by their own dogmatic assumptions. Factor analysis is attractive in part because it gives us the feeling that something "real" is being uncovered from the data. And this is the principal issue: What is the ontological status of the resulting factors? Are they real, as proponents usually maintain? Or are they but deceptive mathematical fictions?

Theoretical Perspectives on Personality

Personality can be discussed from any number of perspectives. While major viewpoints include the psychodynamic, interpersonal, neurobiological, behavioral, and cognitive, more esoteric conceptions could also be included, including the existential, phenomenological, cultural, and perhaps even religious. Even among the major perspectives, some offer only a particular set of concepts or principles, while others offer strongly structural models that generate entire taxonomies of personality and personality disorder constructs. Whatever their orientation, theorists within each perspective usually maintain that their content area is core or fundamental, drives the development of personality and its structure, and thus serves as the logical basis for the treatment of its disorders. In the earlier dogmatic era of historical systems, psychologists strongly wedded to a particular perspective would either assert that other points of view were peripheral to core processes or just ignore them. Behaviorists, for example, denied the existence of the mental constructs, including self and personality. In contrast, psychodynamic psychologists held that behavior is useful only as a means of inferring the properties and organization of various mental structures, namely the id, ego, and superego, and their "drive derivatives." Most authors probably take this stance for two reasons. First, history remembers only those who father or contribute significantly to the development of a particular point of view. There are no famous eclectics. Second, acknowledgments that other content areas might operate according to their own autonomous principles necessarily impugns the sufficiency of one's own approach. As a result, various perspectives have tended to develop to high states of internal consistency, the dogmatic schools of the history of psychology, and it is not at all clear how one model might falsify another, or how two models might be put against one another experimentally.

Psychodynamic Models

Before there were personality disorders there were character pathologies. In colloquial usage, *character* refers to an individual's respect for moral or social conventions. In psychoanalytic usage, however, *character* refers to the "the habitual mode of bringing into harmony the tasks presented by internal demands and by the external world" by the ego (Fenichel, 1945, p. 467). While Freud's writings focused mainly on the psychosexual roots of specific and narrowly circumscribed symptoms, such as compulsions or conversions, he did suggest that character classification might be based on the structural model of id, ego, and superego (Freud, 1933). In 1932, he sought to devise character types determined by which intrapsychic structure was dominant. The erotic type was governed by the instinctual demands of the id. The narcissistic type was dominated by the ego, so much so that neither other persons nor the id or superego could influence them. The compulsive type was regulated by a strict superego that dominated all other functions. Finally, Freud identified a series of mixed types, combinations in which two of the three intrapsychic structures outweighed the third.

The foundations for an analytic characterology were set forth by Karl Abraham (1927a, 1927b, 1927c) in accord with Freud's psychosexual stages of development. Certain personality traits are believed to be associated with frustrations or indulgences during these stages. For example, the oral period is differentiated into an oral-sucking phase and an oral-biting phase. An overly indulgent sucking stage yields an oral-dependent type, imperturbably optimistic and naively self-assured. Happy-go-lucky and emotionally immature, serious matters do not affect them. An ungratified sucking period yields excessive dependency and gullibility as deprived children learn to "swallow" anything just to ensure they receive something. Frustrations at the oral-biting stage yield aggressive oral tendencies such as sarcasm and verbal hostility in adulthood. These "oral-sadistic characters" are inclined to pessimistic distrust, cantankerousness, and petulance. In the anal stage, children learn control. Their increasing cognitive abilities allow them to comprehend parental expectancies, with the option of either pleasing or spoiling parental desires. "Anal characters" take quite different attitudes toward authority depending on whether resolution occurs during the anal-expulsive or anal-retentive period. The anal-expulsive period is associated with tendencies toward suspiciousness, extreme conceit and ambitiousness, self-assertion, disorderliness, and negativism. Difficulties that emerge in the late anal, or anal-retentive, phase are usually associated with frugality, obstinacy, and orderliness, a hairsplitting meticulousness, and rigid devotion to societal rules and regulations.

With the writings of Wilhelm Reich (1933), the concept of character was expanded. Reich held that the neurotic solution of psychosexual conflicts was accomplished through a total restructuring of the defensive style, ultimately crystallizing in a "total formation" called "character armor." The emergence of specific pathological symptoms now assumed secondary importance, since the impact of early instinctual vicissitudes was no longer limited to symptom formation, but now included the genesis of character itself. Nevertheless, Reich's ideas remained firmly ensconced in the conflict model and did not specify nondefensive ways in which character traits or structures might develop. Character formations, according to Reich, have an exclusively defensive function, forming an inflexible armor against threats from the external and internal worlds. Reich extended Abraham's developments to the phallic and genital stages. In the phallic stage, libidinal impulses normally directed toward the opposite sex may become excessively self-oriented. Frustration leads to a striving for leadership, a need to stand out in a group, and poor reactions to even minor defeats. This "phallic narcissistic character" was depicted as vain, brash, arrogant, self-confident, vigorous, cold, reserved, and defensively aggressive.

Modern analytic thinkers (Kernberg, 1996) regard the psychosexual types to be of value mainly for less severe personality disorders. More severe personality disorders effectively mix aspects from all stages of psychosexual development, thus limiting the heuristic value of any psychosexual characterology. For example, oral conflicts are valuable in understanding the depressive-masochistic personality, while anal conflicts are valuable in understanding the obsessive-compulsive personality. Neither of these personality disorders, however, is considered severe, and the translation of psychosexual conflict into personality type is fairly straightforward. In contrast, individuals functioning at what is termed the "borderline level of personality organization," which includes the paranoid, antisocial, and some narcissistic personalities, variously combine aspects from all psychosexual stages. Prior to the 1950s, such patients were variously labeled as suffering borderline states, or as being psychotic characters, or as ambulatory or pseudoneurotic schizophrenics. Eventually, the idea of a borderline personality was created to fill the gulf between the neuroses and psychoses, particularly schizophrenia.

Kernberg (1984, 1996) advocates classifying various personalities types, some from the *DSM* and some from the psychoanalytic tradition, in terms of three levels of structural organization: psychotic, borderline, and neurotic. Understanding this framework requires some knowledge of the basic principles of contemporary psychoanalysis. The psychoanalytic conception of normality provides a useful point of departure (Kernberg, 1996). Normal personalities are characterized by a cohesive and integrated sense of self, which psychoanalysts term "ego identity." Simply put, most of us know who we are, and our sense of self remains constant over time and situation. We know our likes and dislikes, are conscious of certain core values, and know how we are similar to, and yet different from, others. Ego identity is thus fundamental for self-esteem, and to the pursuit and realization of long-term life goals and desires. You must know who you are to like yourself or to know what you want to become. Likewise, ego identity provides a foundation for intimacy, genuineness, commitment, empathy, and the ability to make valid social appraisals. You cannot know others, or know how others feel, unless you know how they compare and contrast with yourself. Individuals with a well-integrated ego identity are said to possess ego strength, the ability of remain integrated in the face of pressures from internal drives and affects, and external social forces. In addition, normal persons also possess an integrated and mature internalization of social or moral value systems, the superego. Some pathological personalities, particularly the narcissistic and antisocial, exhibit a lack of superego development, while others exhibit an immature and all-condemning superego, reflecting the internalization of harsh parental discipline or abuse. In contrast, normal mature superego development features a stable value system that includes such features as personal responsibility and appropropriate self-criticism. Finally, the ego integration and superego capacities of normal persons allow the management of the basic drives of the analytic perspective, sex and aggression, to be integrated with tender affections and commitment.

With normality as a point of contrast, different levels of personality integration can be described along a continuum ranging from normal to neurotic, then borderline, and finally to psychotic. The neurotic level of personality organization is characterized by a well-developed ego identity, complicated by "unconscious guilt feelings reflected in specific pathological patterns of interaction in relation to sexual intimacy" (Kernberg, 1996, p. 121). In other words, the interpersonal relationships of neurotic personalities are somehow pathologically sexualized, from which guilt feelings follow. The terms used vary somewhat from those of the *DSM-IV*: the neurotic level includes the depressive-masochistic, obsessive-compulsive, and hysterical personalities. The depressive-masochistic character derives primarily from reaction formation—that is, the tendency to do the opposite of unconscious wishes. Thus, the tendency is to deprive or sabotage, rather than indulge, the potential for pleasurable affects. In more pathological and lower level expressions of this personality, aggressive affects may be turned against the self by a punitive superego, culminating in naked displays of self-destructiveness, such as cutting or burning. In contrast, the hysterical personality is more obviously libidinal, featuring some loss of impulse control, some emotional lability, and superficial sexual provocativeness with underlying sexual inhibition. The hysterical personality appears to be a well-integrated example of the neurotic level of personality organization, but exists on a continuum with the so-called infantile personality. Whereas the greater integration of hysterical personalities allows poor impulse control to be restricted to specific situations or venues, lack of impulse control is more pervasive in the infantile personality. Infantile subjects also tend to be demanding in relationships and to display aggression when their needs go unsatisfied. The hysterical and infantile spectrum is one expression of the distinction between neurotic and severe levels of personality organizations.

In contrast to the neurotic level, where ego integration and ego identity are preserved, at the psychotic level of personality organization everything that was achieved in normal maturation of the ego is lost. Whereas normal persons possess a sense of individuating self-distinctiveness, psychotic individuals fuse, or fail to distinguish, between the motivations, affects, and identities of self and others. At times, they may even fail to distinguish between self and the physical environment. Boundaries are diffuse and fluctuating, with loss of reality testing and consequent empathic failures in interpersonal relationships. Unlike the neurotic level, where sexualized relationships and guilt feelings are primary features, the psychotic level is characterized by an intense and inappropriate expression of aggression. No personality disorders described in the *DSM-IV* typically function at the psychotic level.

The borderline level represents a stable ego structure that exists between the neuroses and psychoses. Superficially, their presenting symptoms are often similar to those of neurotics. However, their ego identity is not as integrated. Consequently, while their capacity to test reality is generally good, they may experience transient psychotic episodes and dissociations or identity diffusion under stress, and tend to rely on primitive defenses. "Splitting" is particularly characteristic of the borderline level. In the course of development, children naturally develop cognitive representations of those around them. At first, these representations tend to be either all good or all bad. With additional cognitive development and experience, these representations are eventually integrated and become complex interpersonal apprasials made on a variety of dimensions. Individuals with diffuse ego identity, however, do not achieve this level of qualitative complexity, and as a result, they persist in categorizing themselves and others in all-good or all-bad categories—that is, as angels or devils. Such persons invariably exhibit severe difficulties in their interpersonal relationships, particularly intimate relationships, tend to lack direction in their occupational life, and exhibit various degrees of sexual pathology. Kernberg (1996) holds that borderline and schizoid form the basic personalities of the borderline level of organization, expressing endpoints of a continuum of extraversion-introversion. While both are similar in terms of difficulty in separating and differentiating from caretaker figures, in the borderline, this is expressed through identify diffusion, impulsivity, and affective lability, while in the schizoid, it is expressed as social withdrawl and the overdevelopment of an internal fantasy life (Fairbairn, 1954). The schizotypal, paranoid, hypomanic, narcissistic, and antisocial personality disorders all derive from the basic borderline or schizoid prototypes and fall at this level of personality organization, as shown in figure 19.3. The borderline level is further divided into higher and lower levels of organization. Those at the higher level adapt socially and achieve a degree of interpersonal intimacy and vocational achievement. Included at the higher end are the cyclothymic, sadomasochistic, histrionic, dependent, and some narcissistic personalities. Lower borderline level subjects, like psychotics, tend to express more aggressive pathologies, while those at the higher end are more libidinal.

Behavioral Theories of Personality

The duality of empiricism and rationalism has a long history in philosophy and psychology. Empiricism is most often identified with the English philosophers John Locke and David Hume. Locke emphasized the role of direct experience in knowledge, believing that knowledge must be built up from collections of sensations. Locke's position became known as associationism. Here, learning is seen as occurring through a small collection of processes that associate one sensation with another. Empiricism found a counterpoint in the rationalism of continental philosophers, notably the Dutch philosopher Spinoza, the French philosopher Descartes, and the German philosopher Leibniz. In

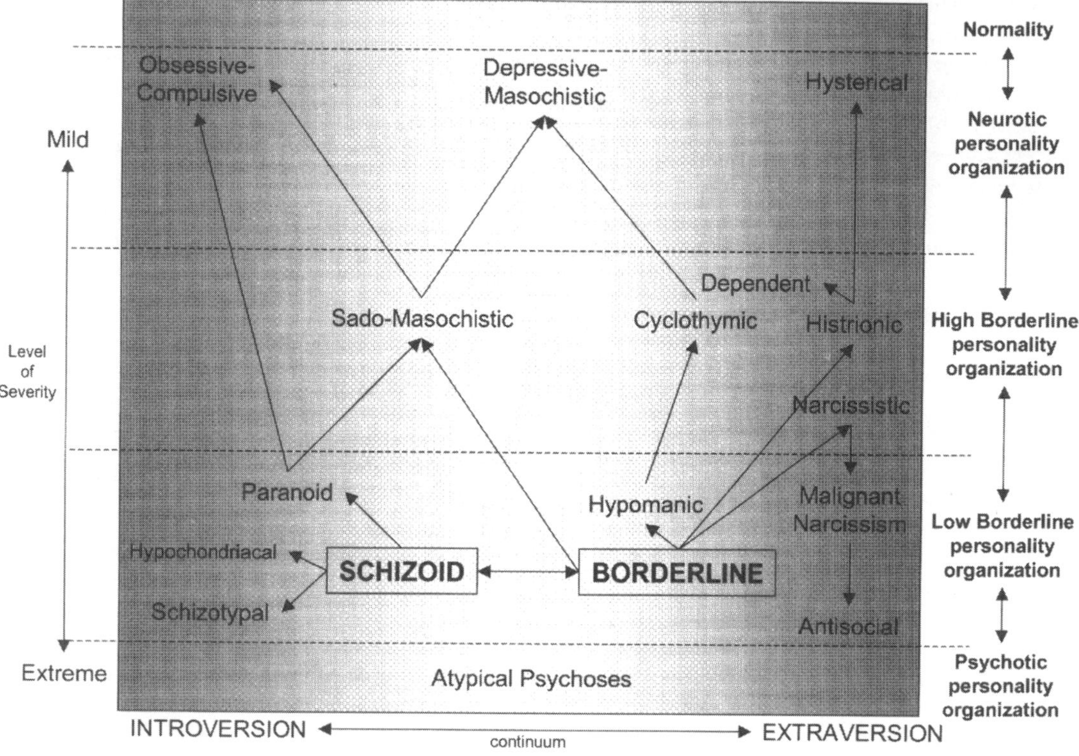

Figure 19.3 Kernberg's levels of personality organization (adapted from Kernberg, 1996).

contrast, the empiricists held that innate ideas could not exist. Locke, for example, maintained that the mind was a tabula rasa, or blank slate, on which experience writes. Eventually, however, the elements of learning were recast in the language of stimulus and response. The foundations of behaviorism are perhaps more associated with J. B. Watson than with any other psychologist, though Watson was preceded by other important figures in the history of learning theory, notably Thorndike and Pavlov. Although a variety of learning theories eventually developed, behaviorism as a formal dogma is most associated with the views of B. F. Skinner.

According to Skinner's strict behaviorism, it is unnecessary to posit the existence of unobservable emotional states or cognitive expectancies to account for behavior and its pathologies. Hypothetical inner states are discarded and explanations are formulated solely in terms of external sources of stimulation and reinforcement. Thus, all disorders become the simple product of environmentally based reinforcing experiences. These shape the behavioral repertoire of the individual, and differences between adaptive and maladaptive behaviors can be traced entirely to differences in the reinforcement patterns to which individuals are exposed. Inner states are regarded as throwbacks to primitive animism. The understanding of an event can be complete only when the contextual factors in which the event is embedded are illuminated. The derivation is relatively simple: if there are no innate ideas, then sensation or stimuli is by definition all that exists. Since sensation originates in the environment, the environment must ultimately control all behavior, however complex. In the absence of innate ideas, the mind is an empty vessel that can contain only what the environment puts there. Hence the emphasis on context or situation, the meaning of the term "stimulus control," and the frequently heard aphorism that "behavior is a function of the environment."

By the mid-1980s, a number of crucial reinterpretations of traditional assessment had been made that allowed clinically applied behavioral approaches to become successively broader and more moderate. Most notably, the diagnoses of Axis I, regarded in psychiatry as substantive disease entities, were reinterepreted with the behavioral paradigm as inductive summaries, labels which bind together a body of observations for the purpose of clinical communication. For example, while depression refers to a genuine pathology in the person for a traditional clinician, a behavioral clinician sees only its operational criteria and their label, not a disease. As a result, behavioral assessment and traditional assessment could thus speak the same tongue, while retaining their respective identities and distinctions. This allowed behavioral therapists to rationalize their use of diagnostic concepts without being untrue to their behavioral core. Likewise, as the cognitive revolution got underway in earnest in the late 1960s and early 1970s, behavioral psychologists began seeking ways to generalize their own perspective in order to bring cognition under the behavioral umbrella. In time, cognitive activity was reinterpreted as covert behavior. Finally, the organism itself began to be seen as a source of reinforcement and punishment, with affective mechanisms viewed as the means through which reinforcement occurs. Contemporary behavioral assessment, then, is no longer focused merely on surface behavior. Instead, behavioral assessment is now seen as involving three "response systems," namely the verbal-cognitive mode, the affective-physiological mode, and the overt-motor response system, a scheme originated by Lang (1968).

Recent behavioral theorists have gone far toward rediscovering personality as a construct in the behavioral paradigm. The relationship between responses across the three response systems, for example, has been extensively studied (see Voeltz & Evans, 1982, for a review). Behavioral psychologists now talk about the organization of behavior, an idea which draws on the conception that the individual person is more than a sum of parts, even where those parts are only behavioral units. An especially seminal thinker, Staats (1986) has developed a more systematic approach to personality that broadens the behavioral tradition. In what he terms "paradigmmatic behaviorism," Staats has sought a "third generation behaviorism" that adds a developmental dimension, arguing that the learning of "basic behavioral repertoires" begins at birth and proceeds hierarchically, with each new repertoire providing the foundation for sucessively more complex forms of learning. Thus, some repertoires must be learned before others. For example, both fine motor movements and the alphabet must be learned before cursive writing can develop. Staats holds that repertoires are learned in the language-cognitive, emotional-motivational, and sensory-motor response systems, and that these systems are interdependent and only pedagogically distinct. Personality thus becomes the total complex hierarchical structure of repertoires and reflects the individual's unique learning history. Different repertoires mediate different responses, so that individual differences simply reflect different learning histories. Thus, the concept of a behavioral repertoire is simultaneously both overt and idiographic, making it acceptable from both behavioral and personality perspectives, and capable of spanning both normality and abnormality.

Nevertheless, paradigmatic behaviorism posits no necessary content to personality and generates no taxonomy. Instead, the principles of the domain are brought to bear on whatever disorders are assumed to exist, as given by forces or committees external to the perspective. Alternatively, proponents of perspectives that do not generate strong structural taxonomies, including the cognitive and psychodynamic, as well as behavioral domains, may also argue that the individual must be understood idiographically as the total product of developmental forces. Accordingly, no taxonomy of personality is required, only a grasp of certain principles specific to the particular domain.

Interpersonal Models

In the previous section, personality was discussed from the behavioral perspective as a patterning of behavioral acts. Although there is no one behaviorism, several core features can nevertheless be summarized. First, behaviorism is contextual. The emphasis is on situations and the stimulus properties of situations that control behavior. No inferences are made about internal dispositions or personality traits. Second, behaviorism is positivistic in the sense that it is focused on events or responses, which are circumscribed in time. Third, behaviorism is idiographic. The unique sequence of situations to which any individual is exposed creates unique patterns of behavior, both normal and pathological.

In contrast, the interpersonal domain argues that personality is best conceptualized as the social product of interactions with significant others. For behavioral psychologists, psychology is the study of behavior. For interpersonalists, behavior is simply one level of information, the raw data from which more complex inferences should be made. While behavior is certainly constrained by the properties of situations, these properties cannot be objectively specified apart from their interpersonal significance. All situations possess a distinctly human import, and so are best conceptualized through principles of human interaction. Very few of our needs can be satisfied, our goals reached, or our potentials fulfilled in a nonsocial world. Even when we are alone, interpersonal theorists argue, the internal representations of significant others continue to populate our mental landscape and guide our actions. We are always, then, transacting either with real others or with our expectations about them. Frances (quoted in Benjamin, 1993) states that "the essence of being a mammal . . . is the need for, and to ability to participate in, interpersonal relationships. The interpersonal dance begins at least as early as birth and ends only with death. Virtually all of the most important events in life are interpersonal in nature and most of what we call personality is interpersonal in expression" (p. v).

Harry Stack Sullivan is regarded as the father of interpersonal perspective. Sullivan's ideas were developed largely as a reaction against the intrapsychic and medical models. Since biographers universally emphasize the stormy nature of Sullivan's own development, he was probably in a unique position to appreciate how these models blame the person without taking into account sources of pathology outside the individual. For example, although Freud's writing indeed contains the seeds of what was later amplified into the object relations approach, the intrapsychic model is based on the resolution of conflict between upwelling sexual and aggressive id instincts and their containment through internalized threats of punishment and condemnation. Other individuals are seen as resources in the selfish pursuit of gratification, not as having their own lives, desires, hopes, and aspirations. Thus, by effectively voiding others of their personhood, Freud kept the location of pathology within the individual. Likewise, the medical model keeps the disease process securely rooted within the person, for it is the person who has the disease. Sullivan's contribution, then, was the realization that some forms of pathology, while perhaps most dramatically manifest within the person, are nevertheless created and perpetuated through maladaptive patterns of interaction between individuals. By relocating pathology as part of a transactional system, Sullivan made room for empathy and humanism in the treatment of psychopathology.

Despite Sullivan's many interesting and brilliant contributions, he is not regarded as a systematic thinker. The personality constructs he proposed are not notably interpersonal, at least by contemporary standards. In an attempt to identify syndromes seen in everyday clinical practice, Sullivan outlined 10 styles, including such dubious conceptions as the nonintegrative personality, the stammerer, and the homosexual personality. While there are obvious relationships between some of these styles and the modern *DSM* personality disorders, the latter two conceptions illustrate the problems inherent when a list of disorders is generated through clinical observation, however astute, where no strong structural model exists. The stammerer confuses a nonspecific symptom with a syndrome, confounding levels of abstraction among psychological phenomena, while the homosexual personality syndromizes cultural prejudice. Sullivan should probably be remembered more for the processes to which he drew clinical attention than the contents he organized as a clinical taxonomy.

Subsequent work in the interpersonal domain has developed in two distinct but interdependent directions (Pincus, 1994), interpersonal theory and the interpersonal circumplex. The circumplex first debued in an article by Freedman, Leary, Ossorio, and Coffey (1951), and was then further developed by Timothy Leary (1957). These theorists crossed two orthogonal dimensions, dominance-submission and hostility-affection (also called love-hate and communion), creating an interpersonal circle further divided into eight segments or themes, each representing a different mix of the two fundamental variables. The dependent, for example, was represented as consisting of approximately equal levels of affection and submission, while the compulsive, which Leary called the responsible-hypernormal, consisted of approximately equal levels of affection and dominance. The four quadrants of the circumplex, Leary suggested, parallel the temperaments or humors of Hippocrates, while the axes of the circle parallel Freud's two basic drives. Each segment of the circle was further differentiated into a relatively normal region, closer to the center, and a relatively pathological region, closer to the edge. Thus, the circumplex may not only be used to generate a taxonomy of personality traits but also to represent continuity between normality and pathology.

The tight links among theory, taxonomy, and normal and abnormal styles of personality is probably the circle's most appealing feature. The ordering of scales reflects the propositions of the interpersonal theory, and bears on the construct validity of all interpersonal inventories. If an instrument does not conform to a circumplex structure, interpersonal propostions cannot be evaluated, compromising the clinical meaningfulness of obtained profiles. In contrast, profiles obtained on most personality inventories are essentially arbitrary (Wiggins & Trobst, 1997). While the "Conversion V," for example, is a well-known MMPI profile, the scales of the MMPI follow no necessary sequence. Change the ordering of the scales, and the profiles are different. In contrast, the trait constructs in the interpersonal circle operationalize interpersonal theory by following a rigorous geometric order. For example, adjacent circle segments within and inventory should be highly correlated, while those at right angles should be independent and those opposite each other should be negatively correlated (Gurtman, 1993). More complex multivariate validational criteria have also been put forward (Wiggins, Steiger, & Gaelick, 1981).

The principles of interpersonal communication have been described in detail by Kiesler (1996). Recall that the goal of interactions is the minimization of anxiety and the enhancement of self-esteem. When two individuals communicate, they seek to engage each other in such a way that both interactants feel validated. Thus, every interpersonal bid seeks to narrow the range of the other's responses to those that confirm our own self-image. Such confirmatory interactions are said to be complementary. According to Kiesler (1983, p. 198), "Our interpersonal actions are designed to invite, pull, elicit, draw, entice, or evoke 'restricted classes' of reactions from persons with whom we interact, especially from significant others." Flexible Individuals are able to offer responses that validate almost anyone. The range of different individuals with whom one may communicate while remaining genuine and spontaneous thus becomes an important criterion distinguishing normal- and pathological-range personality: rigid individuals have a constricted conception of self validated by only a narrow range of interpersonal behaviors. A narcissistic personality whose sense of uniqueness and intelligence must constantly be indulged is an obvious example. Because each person strives to restrict others to responses that are confirmatory, individuals with constricted conceptions of self are often experienced as coercive of particular response patterns. Kiesler (1996) gives the example of the compulsive personality, who presents the image of being rational, logical, and controlled. Others, however, are likely to feel bored, impatient, and evaluated in response. Individuals who are only moderately rigid are likely to encounter a sufficient number of flexible others with whom relations can be mutually confirmatory. In contrast, those who are pathologically rigid are so coercive and restrictive that others seek simply to withdraw. A viscious cycle thus begins whereby the subject tries even harder for confirmation, but makes others want to disengage all the more. Some have suggested that during times of subjective stress (Van Denburg & Kiesler, 1993), individuals may become more rigid as processing load increases, falling back on behaviors that are more automatic and thus even more rigid, a phenomenon referred to as "transactional escalation." As a result, the scope of complementary response is drastically decreased. In effect, the individual has become the driving force behind his or her own pathologies, a defining feature of personality disorder. Kiesler's (1983) version of the interpersonal circle is presented in figure 19.4.

The most radical development of interpersonal theory is Benjamin's (1974, 1986, 1993) Structural Analysis of Social Behavior (SASB), which integrates interpersonal conduct, object relations, and self psychology in a single geometric model (see figure 19.5). Benjamin's point of departure lies in the synthesis of Leary's classic interpersonal circle with Earl Shafer's (1965) circumplex of parental behavior. As every parent knows, there is a fundamental tension between controlling and guiding children and in allowing them to gradually become masters of their own destiny. Parents must either let their children grow up to become genuinely mature beings who realize their own intrinsic potential along a unique developmental path, or else demand submission and deny autonomy, effectively making the child an extension of the parent. Shafer's model thus places autonomy giving at the opposite of control, not submission, as with the Leary circle. The horizontal axis, however, remains the same.

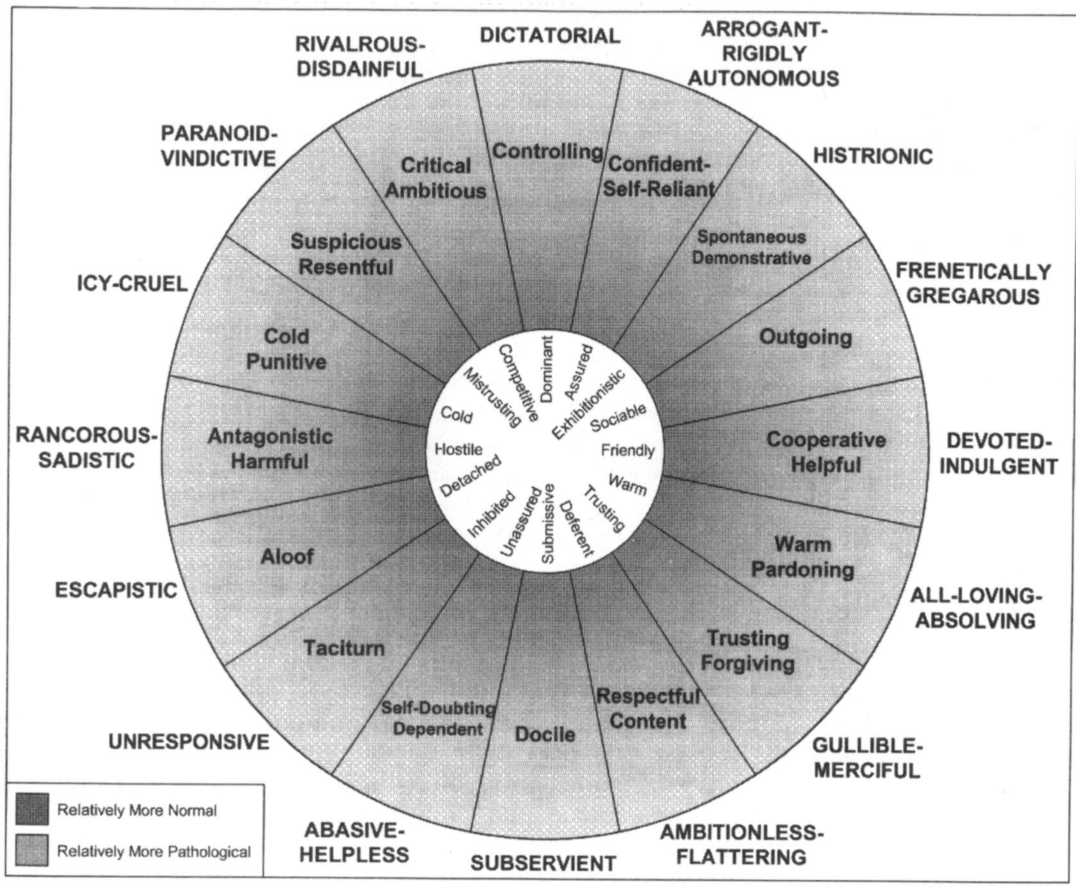

Figure 19.4 Kiesler's 1982 interpersonal circle (adapted from Kiesler, 1986).

The problem lies in reconciling the Leary (1957) and Schaefer (1965) circles. From different perspectives, both make sense. Submission is easily seen as the complement of dominance. When one person dominates, the other tends to submit; when one person submits, the other tends to dominate. One behavior pulls for the other. In contrast, dominance does not pull for autonomy giving. Although submission is the complement of dominance, it is autonomy, referred to by Benjamin as emancipation, which is its opposite. Opposition thus becomes an additional dynamic mechanism that relates the behavior of one person to another. In addition, the SASB provides a unique conception called the focus, which specifies where attention is directed in communcation. By distinguishing between a focus on self and a focus on others, the Leary and Schaefer models may be integrated. Each focus has its own circumplex. The first is focused on parentlike behaviors—that is, what is to be done to or for another person. The second is focused on childlike behaviors—that is, what is to be done to or for the self. The vertical axis always expresses the opposition of control and emancipation. The principle of complementarity is no longer confined to a single circle, but instead relates corresponding points on the focus on other and focus on self circumplices. As a result, the trait content of the Leary circle splits to become the bottom of the two circles. The Leary tradition thus emerges as a personality theory for which enmeshment is a basic assumption. In contrast, the upper half of the focus on other and focus on self circles depicts a new differentiated space, part of which is friendly and part hostile. In addition, the SASB includes a third circumplex to describe the introjected contents of the self. The basic idea is that we tend to treat ourselves the way others have treated us. The

SASB thus includes an explicit means of linking interpersonal transactions and object relations.

Cognitive Models

The cognitive view is extremely popular. Almost all clinical syndromes possess cognitive elements, and surveys show that cognitive therapy is widely practiced among clinicians. When viewed more broadly, the cognitive focus may seen as being essentially identical with the information-processing perspective, so that cognitive models may be highly operationalized and flowcharted. Verbal sources of data feature prominently in cognitive therapies, but only as the final common pathway of beliefs and assumptions, perceptual distortions, heuristic biases, and automatic thoughts that occur across all levels of awareness. The beginning of the *DSM-IV* definition of personality traits as "enduring patterns of perceiving, relating to, and thinking about the environment and oneself" (p. 630) acknowledges the central role of cognition in these constructs.

The cognitive perspective follows the general plan of science, seeking to explain a diversity of instances through the application of a small number of simple rules. Trait theorists, for example, explain individuality in terms of a few personality dimensions, the Five-Factor Model being only one example. Chemists explain the behavior of molecules as combinations of a few chemical elements. Similarly, cognitive therapists hold internal cognitive structures and processes that mediate and explain behavior. Among these structures, the schema holds a particularly prominent place. Given its focus on processes, personality is naturally understood as a tenacious collection of interrelated schemas. Schematic change thus promises potentially sweeping change in a great many problematic behaviors. This provides a point of contrast between the behavioral and the cognitive perspectives: for behavioral therapists, assessment and therapy op-

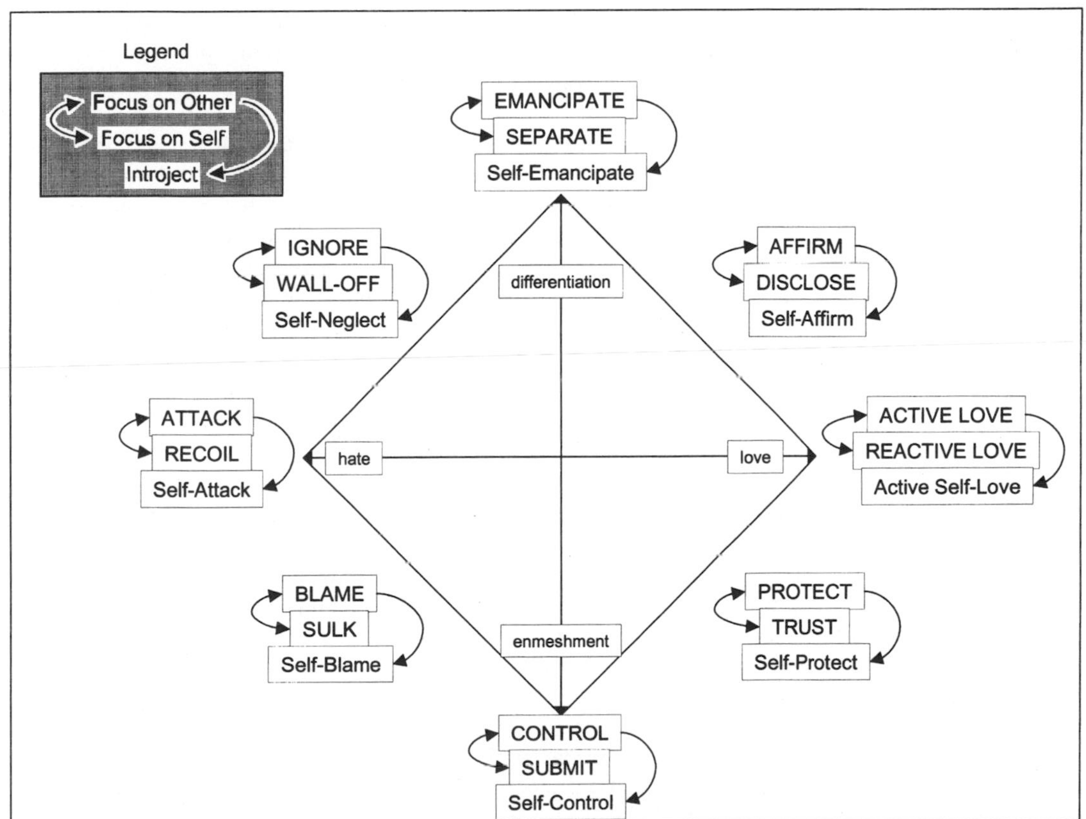

Figure 19.5 Benjamin's simplified SASB model (adapted from Kiesler, 1996).

erate at the same level of information. The behaviors assessed are the very behaviors eventually treated. In contrast, cognitive assessment and therapy occur at two different levels. Assessment is conducted at the level of behavior, but the nature of the inquiry is guided by cognitive theory, which seeks to uncover the maladaptive beliefs, attributions, and other appraisal processes that cause maladaptive behavior. Therapeutic change occurs, not at the level of individual behaviors, but at the level of core cognitive structures. Cognitive therapy seeks to preserve the rigor of behaviorism, but nevertheless maintains that the raw flux of behavior must be ordered in some logical fashion if its significance for personality therapy and change are to be understood.

Historically, the idea of a schema derives from work by Bartlett (1932) and Piaget (1926). Although the term has been defined in different ways, its meaning is obviously related to "scheme" and "schematics." The former suggests a prototypal plan of action that might be elaborated in the performance of any actual activity; the latter suggests a structural pattern that might serve to guide the exploration of some particular instance. Since these models are always available to inform real events, schemas allow the world to be conceptualized with very little cognitive effort. However, the information-processing economy that is won comes with two potential costs. First, information that does not conform to schematic biases is often never perceived. Paranoid, antisocial, and sadistic personalities, for example, easily overlook benign or tender gestures of assistance and support. As such, these personalities suffer a form of "social neglect," in which some schematic structures necessary to process the full range of social interactions are either absent or underdeveloped relative to other schemas that give the disorder its maladaptive character. This leads to the second cost: as the primary unit of cognitive organization, schemas are relatively stable structures that select and organize incoming experience and assign meanings to events. As such, they preempt, displace, and inhibit other interpretive sets. Where schemas are concerned with the transformation of raw sensory information, they serve to coordinate mind with concrete realities. However, schemas operate across all levels of abstraction, from the processing of sensory data, to the perception of objects in consciousness, to the mental construction of individual reality. Like scientific paradigms, preexisting schemas have a kind of conceptual priority by which they dictate the construction of the world. They decrease cognitive load, but also constrain approaches and perspectives. The idea that each personality disorder is driven by a core rubric (Forgus & Schulman, 1979) or a core belief (Beck & Freeman, 1990) expresses this cognitive principle. Here, the core belief becomes the organizing principle that unifies phenomenal awareness and provides ongoing consistency in experience. Perception, then, is one half presumption and the personality disorders are very presumptuous.

Although cognitive psychology would seem to be the natural foundation for theory and research on the role of cognitive constructs in the personality disorders, this has not been the case. Instead, theoretical speculation and research has come mostly from those involved in cognitive therapy. In turn, cognitive therapy, much like the rest of psychotherapy, has developed almost independently semiautonomously from its natural pure science foundations, here cognitive psychology. Ideally, cognitive therapy would thus grow naturally from a pure science foundation, much as engineering grows naturally from its foundation in physics. The still expanding number of psychotherapies provides ample proof that the applied branches of our discipline need not be strongly coupled to a pure science foundation to become progressively more variegated. For example, Aaron Beck is without a doubt a seminal figure in the history of psychotherapy. Almost every book about cognitive therapy written by Beck or his associates includes a paragraph that states that cognitive therapy began in the mid-1950s when Beck was searching for empirical support for the psychodynamic theory of depression. Beck believed the theory was correct, but found depressed subjects, far from having a masochistic need to suffer, actually embraced experiences of success (Alford & Beck, 1997). No mention is made of the cognitive revolution that was occurring simultaneously, or that it influenced Beck's thinking in the least.

Nevertheless, Beck and his associates have been particularly successful in developing cognitive therapies for a wide range of Axis I disorders (Beck, 1976; Beck, Rush, Shaw, & Emery, 1979). More recently, Beck and Freeman (1990) developed a cognitive theory of personality pathology, describing cognitive schemas that shape the experiences and behaviors of individuals with these disorders. Dysfunctional and distorting schemas give rise to maladaptive interaction strategies that, in turn, trigger automatic thoughts that make the individual susceptible to repetitive and pervasive life difficulties (Pretzer & Beck, 1996). Also included are affect and interpersonal behavior, integrated through the central component of cognition, which lead to pathological and self-perpetuating cognitive-interpersonal transaction cycles (Pretzer & Beck, 1996). Beck and Freeman's model (1990) is anchored to evolution, and speculates how personality pathology might relate to strategies that have facilitated survival and reproduction through natural selection. Derivatives of these evolutionary strategies may be identified, according to Beck, in exaggerated form among the Axis I clinical syndromes, and in less dramatic expression among the personality disorders. Further, Beck and Freeman state that these schemas may be either overdeveloped or underdeveloped, inhibiting or even displacing other schemas that may be more adaptive or more appropriate for a given situation. As a result, they introduce a persistent and systematic bias into the individual's processing machinery. For example, the dependent personality is hypersensitive to the possibility of a loss of love and help, and quickly interprets signs of such loss as signifying its reality. Conversely, the antisocial is likely to have an underdeveloped schema to be responsible or to feel guilt for his or her behavioral transgressions. In contrast, obsessive-compulsives are disposed to judge themselves responsible and guilt-ridden, but underdeveloped in the inclination to interpret events spontaneously, creatively, and playfully. A list of "primeval" strategies for some personality disorders was presented by Beck (1992), elaborated as a "cognitive taxonomy" anchored across view of self, view of others, main beliefs, and strategy (reported in Prezler & Beck, 1996).

The theory of cognitive therapy has undergone considerable refinement since the publication of Beck, Freeman, and associates' (1990) classic text on the personality disorders. In particular, the theory has moved in the direction of incorporating advances in cognitive psychology and cognitive science. Thus, in 1990, Beck, Freeman, and associates compare and contrast the psychoanalytic and cognitive approaches by noting that both seek to modify core problems, but that the psychodynamic paradigms regard these as largely unconscious, while cognitive therapy holds that their products "are largely in the realm of awareness and that with special training even more may be accessible to consciousness" (p. 5). By 1997, Alford and Beck, striving to increase the integrative scope of cognitive therapy, noted numerous parallels between the theory of cognitive therapy, as derived from clinical observation, and academic cognitive psychology, including the concept of the cognitive unconscious. Later (p. 106), they state that "cognitive theory is a theory about the role . . . of cognition in the interrelationships among such variables as emotion, behavior, and interpersonal relationships. 'Cognition' includes the entire range of variables implicated in information processing, as well as consciousness of the cognitive products." Modern cognitive therapy, then, which began as a kind of refabricated introspectionism interested only in conscious contents, is now in the process of transition to a fully cognitive therapy with a solid foundation in cognitive psychology. Thus, the applied and pure science branches are becoming closer together, and cognitive therapy has at last escaped the orbit of behaviorism. Had this not occurred, the domain of cognitive therapy would have forever remained restricted to consciousness, since its contents are much more easily verbalized and measured.

Nevertheless, it is possible to take an even broader view of the role of cognition in the personality disorders. Cognitive models of the personality disorders, and most mental disorders generally, have focused on cognitive contents, not structural models of cognition. The emphasis on content is sensible on two counts. First, cognitive contents—that is, actual beliefs, appraisals, attributions, expectations, and so on—are much more open to therapeutic change than are information-processing capacities, which seem fixed in contrast. Bluntly speaking, subjects may change their beliefs, but they are unlikely to raise their IQs, even where willing. Second, personality disorders are themselves pathogenic, and it is largely the terms in which subjects appraise the world around them, its happenings, and its cast of characters, that perpetuate personality disorders. The question "How do particular personality styles construe their world and perpetuate their pathology?" is quite naturally answered in terms of cognitive contents. Cognitive psychology, however, is concerned with mental structures and processes, constraints on these mental structures and processes, and mental contents. For example, academic information-processing psychologists often use flowcharts to schematize the relationship between various cognitive structures and the cognitive processes that link them. They are "average-expectable" models of the mind, assuming, for example, that each person has some quantity of working memory, say Miller's seven chunks plus or minus two (1957) and, further, that each person must move the contents of working memory to long-term storage if information is to be available for retrieval at some future date. While a few individuals may possess extraordinarily accurate memories, or even qualitatively different cognitive abilities like eidetic imagery, most will not. In these models, no mention is made of the contents of memory. Indeed, cognitive scientists have usually been concerned with developing content-free models of the minds, on the assumption that mental content does not influence mental structure.

Both historical and contemporary accounts of several personality disorders stress reciprocity of form and content. The scattered style of the histrionic, for example, serves an adaptive function that prevents all but the most weighty subjects from being considered to any degree. Histrionics simply are not given more to dissocation than to deep existential reflection. The depressive and masochistic ruminate about such matters to no end, but not the histrionic. Such thoughts are stopped, insulating the individual against anxiety, and particularly worry, where the object of concern is constantly held in mind and examined again and again from all angles. At the first signal of anxiety, potential concerns are jettisoned, and the histrionic simply moves on to something lovely, entertaining, and stimulating. Likewise, the compulsive, referred to by Timothy Leary (1957) as the hypernormal personality, lives in constant fear of making a mistake and suffering as a result the disapproval or condemnation of others. As a result, the compulsive becomes, in Piagetian terms, much more of an assimilator than an accommodator. The compulsive desparately wants to do what is expected, and actively resists conceptual innovation, which inevitably requires evaluation from others who must assess its products. Accordingly, the compulsive seeks frames of reference that are common or mundane. Even where intellectually gifted, their minds tend to be encyclopedic repositories of fact. Compulsives make good critics, and narcissistics make better leaders and innovators.

Neurobiological and Temperament Models

Temperament is often referred to as the soil, the biological foundation, of personality. The ontogenetic priority of temperament, the fact that it is the first domain of personality to come into existence in the development of the organism, perhaps gives it a taxonomic priority that other domains lack. The argument is that the contents of all aspects of personality are forever constrained by the first domain to develop. Accordingly, once temperament is determined by the individual's biological constitution, some developmental pathways in other domains are forever excluded while others are reinforced. Thus, while it is not impossible that an irritable and demanding infant will become a diplomat famous for calmly taking the perspectives of others to thereby negotiate resolutions satisfactory to all parties, the odds against it are greater than they would otherwise have been. Similarly, we might expect that children whose personal tempo is somewhat slower than average are unlikely to develop a histrionic personality disorder, and that those who are especially agreeable are unlikely to develop a negativistic personality disorder.

The first explanatory system to specify temperament dimensions was probably the doctrine of body humors posited by the early Greeks some 25 centuries ago. Hippocrates concluded in the fourth century B.C. that all diseases stem from an excess of or imbalance of yellow bile, black bile, blood, and phlegm, the embodiment of earth, water, fire, and air—the declared basic components of the universe according to the philosopher Empedocles. Excesses of these humors led respectively to the choleric, melancholic, sanguine, and phlegmatic temperaments. Modified by Galen centuries later, the choleric temperament was associated with a tendency toward irascibility, the sanguine temperament with optimism, the melancholic temperament with sadness, and the phlegmatic temperament with apathy. The doctrine of humors is today preserved through studies on such topics as neurohormonal chemistry and neurotransmitter systems as its more modern parallels. In the 1920s, Kretschmer (1922) developed a classification system based on thin, muscular, and obese types of physiques. Kretschmer was interested mainly in the relation of physique to psychopathology, and viewed these physiques as discrete types. For his student, Sheldon and his associate Stevens (1942), the three types become the dimensions of ectomorphy, mesomorphy, and endormorphy, as applicable to normal persons as to clinical samples. According to Sheldon, each body type corresponded to a particular temperament, viscerotonia, somatotonia, and cerebrotonia.

Temperament, however, is only one aspect of human biology. Not only are we biological beings, we are also material and chemical beings. Although our experience of our own moment-to-moment existence is one of a continuous and unified consciousness, an anatomical examination of the structure of the nervous system shows that it is composed of many discrete units, called neurons, each of which communicates with many thousands of others through chemical messengers called neurotransmitters, which bridge the gaps between neurons and thus allow the system to work as whole. Since some neurotransmitters seem to be specialized for certain functions rather than others, it makes sense that a taxonomy based on neurotransmitter types might have particular relevance to personality. Ideally, such a model would be put forward so that each neurotransmitter type would relate to some content dimension of personality in a one-to-one fashion. Personality would thus reduce to a profile of neurotransmitter dimensions, and by changing the level of a particular neurotransmitter through a pill or procedure, personality change could be easily effected.

Cloninger (1986, 1987) proposed an elegant theory based on the interrelationship of three genetic neurobiologic trait dispositions, each of which is associated with a particular neurotransmitter system. Specificially, novelty seeking is associated with low basal activity in the dopaminergic system, harm avoidance with high activity in the serotonergic system, and reward dependence with low basal noradrenergic system activity. Novelty seeking is hypothesized to dispose the individual toward exhilaration or excitement in response to novel stimuli, which leads to the pursuit of potential rewards as well as an active avoidance of both monotony and punishment. Harm avoidance reflects a disposition to respond strongly to aversive stimuli, leading the individual to inhibit behaviors to avoid punishment, novelty, and frustrations. Reward dependence is seen as a tendency to respond to signals of reward—verbal signals of social approval, for example—and to resist extinction of behaviors previously associated with rewards or relief from punishment. These three dimensions form the axes of a cube whose corners represent various personality constructs (see figure 19.6). Thus, antisocial personalities, who are often seen as fearless and sensation seeking, are viewed as low in harm avoidance and high in novelty seeking, while the imperturbable schizoid is seen as low across all dimensions of the model. Interesting, the personality disorders generated by Cloninger's model correspond only loosely to those in the *DSM-IV*. A number of *DSM-IV* personality disorders are not represented at all. However, since the *DSM* is itself atheoretical, it cannot be used as a criterion against which any strong structural model can be evaluated. From the standpoint of a theoretical model, it is the disorder categories of the *DSM* that are spurious, and not vice versa.

Recently, Cloninger, Svrakic, and Przybeck (1993) have extended the original model to include a fourth dimension, labeled persistence, and three dimensions of character, which they believe mature in adulthood and influence personal and social effectiveness, as well as the acquistion of self-concepts. The incremental value of adding these dimensions to Cloninger's original three-dimensional model is difficult to determine, however. All scientific theories can be evaluated in terms of their scope and internal consistency, also called coherence. In the social sciences, scope and consistency seem to be inversely related. As theories address a wider range of phenomena, no longer do they integrate multiple variable domains in as great a level of detail as before. Theories of great scope thus tend to deal more with generalities than details, while theories of high internal coherence tend to dig more deeply into the details of a narrow domain. The addition of persistance and character to the neurotransmitter dimensions of the original model would seem to be geared to increasing the scope of the model. However, it is also an admission that the original model is incomplete and thus requires supplementation through principles from other, nearly autonomous domains of personality. Otherwise, persistance and character would be reduceable to the original transmitter dimensions. The revised model therefore becomes somewhat eclectic, borrowing dimensions from here and there without assimilating them into a single coherent framework. Scope is increased, but the waters become somewhat muddied.

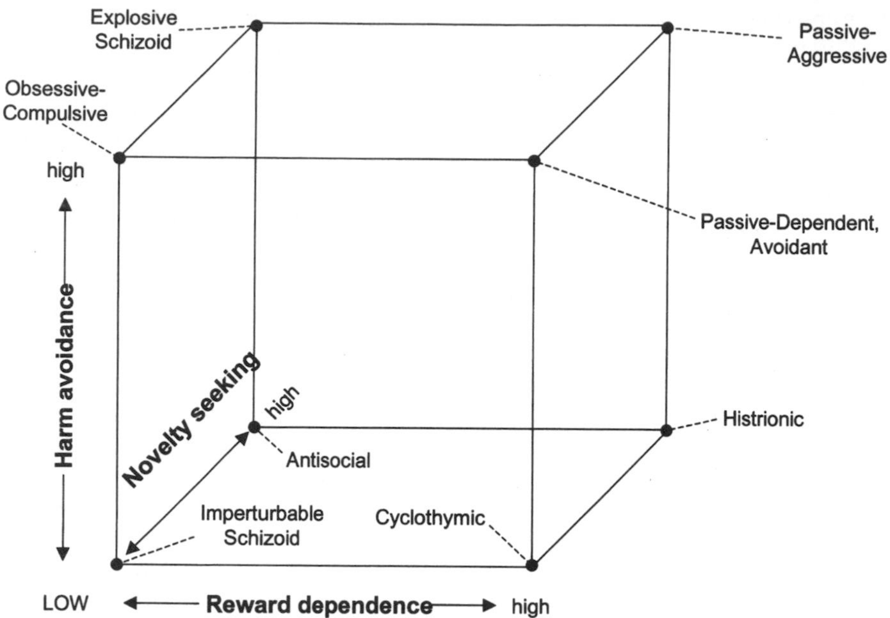

Figure 19.6 Cloninger's neurobiological model of personality disorders.

The theoretical models presented above are all perspectives on personality. These efforts, launched from particular domains of personality, can be said to represent partial views of an intrinsic totality. Throughout the history of psychology, each of these views has attempted to outcompete the others in order to establish itself as the ideal perspective, one with total comprehensiveness of scope and perfect theoretical coherence. Historically, each view has had its turn, recruiting large numbers of adherents who keep the papers flowing into academic journals, and thus keep the perspective at the attention of the psychological community. Eventually, however, enthusiasm fades as explanatory limits gradually come into focus (Meehl, 1978).

Technically, there is nothing wrong with such a progression. In contrast to Karl Popper, who sees scientific theories as being continually subject to threats of falsification, and Thomas Kuhn, who sees paradigms as essentially preempting alternative viewpoints and thus effectively suppressing threats of falsification, Imre Lakatos (1968) holds that science develops through "research programs," a core set of internally consistent ideas deliberately withheld from falsification so that their explanatory potential and boundaries can be programmatically explored. Old theories are thus never really abandoned, just pushed out of vogue as new and more interesting candidates emerge. However, when core beliefs are in fact confronted with potentially falsifying evidence, rationales are constructed that account for findings by adjusting what are termed "auxiliary hypotheses." When Copernicus proposed his heliocentric theory, for example, skeptics argued that the motion of the earth around the sun should result in an apparent motion of the stars against the background of the sky. Rather than give up the theory, Copernicus responded that the stars lie at such vast distances from the earth that no apparent motion can be detected. Instead of discarding the theory, Copernicus altered the universe. In the same way, a researcher who fails to find significance for a pet theory can assert that crucial measures are unreliable, that some systematic sampling bias tainted the results, that research associates are incompetent, and so on. Auxiliary hypotheses thus effectively form a "protective belt" around the core assumptions of every perspective, and can be adjusted as needed whenever the core comes under assault from empirically minded infidels.

The history of psychology contains numerous examples of such adjustments, and so does contemporary personality theory. In laying the foundation for her SASB model, Benjamin (1993) cites

Orford (1986) in noting that efforts to validate the principle of complementarity using the interpersonal circle have often failed. In reply to such critiques, however, Kiesler (1996) presents nine counterpoints, some of which are highly sophisticated. Among them, he notes that Orford examined only studies using the Interpersonal CheckList, which is known to possess a deficient circumplex structure, that the complementarity principle does not state that all interactions will always be complementary, that the evoking power of behaviors of friendship cannot be assumed to be equal to that of hostile behaviors, and that the base rates of various behaviors should be controlled for complementarity to be more strongly demonstrated. All of Kiesler's counterpoints seem well founded. Taken conjointly, however, it is unclear how the principle of complementarity could ever be falsified to the satisfaction of someone steeped in interpersonal theory. The objections are simply impossible to evaluate without a depth of knowledge that can be acquired only by years of experience in the interpersonal perspective. As such, one or more of the various objections would always step forward to salvage the core perspective. In fairness, this may reflect more on the reviewer than on interpersonal theory, since Kiesler's writing is eminently scholarly. Another possible example comes from the competition between the Five-Factor Model and the Seven-Factor models, reviewed above. The stakes here are much higher, since both use the same methodology and proceed from the lexical hypothesis as a fundamental assumption, but start with different definitions of what traits belong to personality, thus leading to dramatically different results.

While the core assumptions of a given perspective may come under assault from many different directions, models sometimes "go on the offensive" by seeking to organize the phenomena of other domains under their own core rubric. Here, a taxonomy originating in one domain encroaches directly on a competitor's turf as a means of pressing foreign variables directly into taxonomic service. Such attempts are as often doctrinal as incidental. In Timothy Leary's 1957 classic on interpersonal theory and the interpersonal circle, Leary (1957), influenced by the psychodynamic idea of levels of consciousness, refers to five "levels" of personality. The first level, public communication, is concerned with what is public and objective. The second level, conscious description, refers to the subjective world of the subject. The third level, private symbolization, refers to unconscious and preconscious material, and is expressed through "projective, indirect fantasy materials" (p. 79), including projectives tests, fantasies, artistic productions, wishes, dreams, and free associations. The fourth level, the unexpressed unconscious, contains material censored from consciousness. And the fifth level is concerned with values, both ideal and realistic. The exact nature of Leary's levels is technically unimportant, since personality can be subdivided in many different ways. What is important is that Leary believed that a single organizing framework, the interpersonal circle, should be used to organize variables at all levels. Contemporary interpersonal theorists have begun to follow through on Leary's dictum. Kiesler (1986) has translated his 1982 interpersonal circle to the level of behavioral acts. Each act may be seen an examplar of the trait that corresponds to its location on the circle, while Benjamin's (1986) has translated her SASB model to both affective and cognitive domains. Obviously, such translations radically extend the scope of their respective models. In the case of the SASB, the attempt is to tie together cognition, affect, object relations, and interpersonal conduct in a single taxonomy. Perspectives on personality must wage successful campaigns of insurgency to secure their longevity.

While the above examples are quite impressive, domains of personality that lack a generative taxonomy also seek to expand their scope in order to coopt the explanatory power of other perspectives. Without a structural taxonomy, however, foreign variables cannot be systematically and directly recruited for support. Usually, proponents of taxonomy-poor perspectives seek to shift the argument to philosophical grounds. Often this amounts to little more than denial, assertion, or misdirection. The behavioral school, for example, held that mental disorders possess no ontological legitimacy. That is, mental disorders cannot exist, since only behavior exists. Any admission to the contrary would have been devastating. If mental disorders are allowed, behavior becomes a means of making diagnostic inference about an entity that overflows behavioral principles and is no longer an end in itself. Likewise, cognitivists have argued that because all knowledge, perception, and feeling ultimately rest on mediating cognitive mechanisms, their domain should be acknowleged as fundamental. Such arguments are typical of perspectives that do not generate strong taxonomies. Without a compelling classification framework, adherents have great difficulty extending their perspective in ways that are empirically convincing. Even if cognitive structures do undergird and mediate the function of constructs from all other perspectives, for example, this does not necessarily mean that cognitive constructs deserve taxonomic or even therapeutic priority. Every cognitive event has a neurochemical basis, but it is unlikely that personality will ever be completely reduced to neurochemistry.

An Evolutionary Theory of Personality

What is personality? Until now, we have hesitated to ask this question explicitly. As an idea, personality must be many thousands of years old. Historically, the word *personality* derives from the Greek term *persona*, originally representing the theatrical mask used by dramatic players. Its meaning has changed through history. As a mask assumed by an actor, it suggested a pretense of appearance—that is, the possession of traits other than those that actually characterized the individual behind the mask. In time, the term persona lost its connotation of pretense and illusion, and began to represent, not the mask, but the apparent, explicit, or manifest features of the person. The third and final meaning that the term personality has acquired delves "beneath" surface impressions and turns the spotlight on the inner, less revealed, and hidden psychological qualities of the individual. Thus, through history the meaning of the term has shifted from external illusion to surface reality, and finally to opaque or veiled inner characteristics. It is this third meaning that comes closest to contemporary use. Personality is seen today as a complex pattern of deeply embedded psychological characteristics that are largely nonconscious and not easily altered, which express themselves automatically in almost every facet of functioning. Intrinsic and pervasive, these traits emerge from the complicated matrix of biological dispositions and experiential learnings that ultimately constitute the individual's distinctive pattern of perceiving, feeling, thinking, coping, and behaving. Personality thus refers to no single aspect of functioning. Instead, personality is best defined as the patterning of variables across the entire matrix of the person. This definition is crucial to an understanding of the theory put forward below.

In contrast to the perspectives outlined above, which appeal to organizing principles that derive from a single domain of personality, we might ask whether there is any theory that honors the nature of personality as the patterning of variables across the entire matrix of the person. Such a theory is necessary for a number of reasons. First, the natural direction of science is toward theories of greater and greater scope. In theoretical physicists, for example, quantum gravity is an attempt to unify quantum mechanics with the theory of relativity. Second, theoretical perspectives presented above do not treat personality in a manner congruent with the formal synthetic properties of the construct itself. Personality is neither exclusively behavioral, exclusively cognitive, or exclusively interpersonal, but instead an integration of all these. Advancement in the hard sciences often occurs through the construction of falsifying experiments. An experimental situation is conceived, the results of which are intended to support one theory, but reject another. In contrast, the social sciences are intrinsically less boundaried, with advancement more often occurring when a heretofore neglected, but nevertheless highly relevant, set of variables surge to the center of scientific interest. Far from overturning established paradigms, the new perspective simply allows a given phenomenon to be studied from an additional angle, becoming a new "research program" in a Lakatosian sense. Agnostic scholars with no strong allegiance may thus avail themselves of a kaleidoscope of views. By turning the kaleidoscope, by shifting paradigmatic sets, the same phenomenon can be viewed from any of a variety of internally consistent perspectives. Eclecticism thus becomes the scientific norm. But no theory that represents a partial perspective on the total phenomenon of personality can be complete. As we have seen, constructs that are considered taxonomically fundamental in one perspective may not emerge as such within another perspectve. The interpersonal model of Lorna Benjamin (1993) and the neurobiological model of Robert Cloninger (1987) are both structurally strong approaches to personality. Yet their fundamental constructs are different. Rather than inherit the construct dimensions of a particular perspective, then, a theory of personality as a total phenomenon should seek some set of principles that can be addressed to the whole person, thereby capitalizing on the synthetic properties of personality as the total matrix of the person. The alternative is an uncomfortable eclecticism of unassimilated partial views.

But how are we to create a theory that breaks free of the "grand theories of human nature" that are all part of the history of psychology? The key lies in finding theoretical principles for personality that fall outside the field of personality proper. Otherwise, we could only repeat the errors of the past by asserting the importance of some new set of variables heretofore unemphasized, building another perspective inside personality as a total phenomenon, but thereby missing a scientific understanding of the total phenomenon itself (Millon, 1990). Herein lies the distinction between the terms "personality" and "personology." Strictly speaking, a science of personality is limited to partial views of the person. These may in fact be highly internally consistent, but they cannot be total. In contrast, personology is from the beginning as a science of the total person. In the absence of falsifying experiments, various perspectives on personality tend to develop to high states of internal coherence, becoming "schools" that intrinsically resist integration and contribute to the fragmentation of psychology as a unified discipline. In so doing, they also create conceptions of personality that intrinsically conflict with the nature of the construct itself. A science of personology ends this long tradition of fractiousness and creates a theoretical basis for a completely unified science of personality and psychopathology. As we will see below, there can be only one science of personology. However, there is probably no limit to the number of variable domains that might call themselves personality.

Evolution and Personality

Evolution is the logical choice as a scaffold upon which to develop a science of personality (Millon, 1990). Just as personality is concerned with the total patterning of variables across the entire matrix of the person, it is the total organism that survives and reproduces, carrying forth both its adaptive and its maladaptive potentials into subsequent generations. While lethal mutations sometimes occur, the evolutionary success of organisms with "average expectable genetic material" is dependent on the entire configuration of the organism's characteristics and potentials. Similarly, psychological fitness derives from the relation of the entire configuration of personality characteristics to the environments in which the person functions. Beyond these analogies, the principles of evolution also serve as principles that lie outside personality proper, and thus form a foundation for the integration of the various historical schools that escapes the part-whole fallacy of the dogmatic past. In creating a taxonomy of personality styles and disorders based on evolutionary principles, we face one central question: How can these processes can best be segmented so that their relevance to the individual person is drawn into the foreground?

The first task of any organism is its immediate survival. Organisms that fail to survive have been selected out, so to speak, and fail to contribute their genes and characteristics to subsequent generations. Whether a virus or a human being, every living thing must protect itself against simple entropic decompensation, predatory threat, and homeostatic misadventure. There are literally millions of ways to die. Evolutionary mechanisms related to survival tasks are oriented toward life enhancement and life preservation. The former are concerned with improvement in the quality of life, and gear organisms toward behaviors that improve survival chances and, it is hoped, lead them to thrive and multiply. The latter are geared toward orienting organisms away from actions or environments that threaten to jeopardize survival. Phenomenologically speaking, such mechanisms form a polarity of pleasure and pain. Behaviors experienced as pleasurable are generally repeated and generally promote survival, while those experienced as painful generally have the potential to endanger life and thus are not repeated. Organisms that repeat painful experiences or fail to repeat pleasurable ones are strongly selected against. Among the various personalities deduced from the theory, we find that some individuals are conflicted in regard to these existential aims. The sadistic personality, for example, finds pleasure in actively establishing conditions that will be experienced as painful. Other personalities possess deficits in these crucial substrates. The schizoid personality, for example, has little capacity to experience pleasurable affects.

The second universal evolutionary task faced by every organism relates to homeostatic processes employed to sustain survival in open ecosystems. To exist is to exist within an environment, and once an organism exists, it must either adapt to its surroundings or adapt its surroundings to conform to and support its own style of functioning. Every organism must satisfy lower order needs related—for example, to nutrition, thirst, and sleep. Mammals and human beings must also satisfy other needs—for example, those related to safety and attachment. Whether the environment is intrinsically bountiful or hostile, the choice is essentially between a passive versus an active orientation—that is, a tendency to accommodate to a given ecological niche and accept what the environment offers, versus a tendency to modify or intervene in the environment, thereby adapting it to oneself. Organisms that fail to adapt to their environment or to restructure their environment to meet their own needs are strongly selected against. These modes of adaptation differ from the first phase of evolution, "being," in that they regard how that which is, endures. Among the various personalities deduced from the theory, we find antisocials, who impulsively affect their environment, often with complete disregard for consequences.

The third universal evolutionary task faced by every organism pertains to reproductive styles that maximize the diversification and selection of ecologically effective attributes. All organisms must ultimately reproduce to evolve. To keep the chain of the generations going, organisms have developed strategies by which to maximize the survivability of the species. At one extreme is what biologists have referred to as the r-strategy. Here, an organism seeks to reproduce a great number of offspring, which are then left to fend for themselves against the adversities of chance or destiny. At the other extreme is the K-strategy, in which relatively few offspring are produced and are given extensive care by parents. Although individual exceptions always exist, these parallel the more male "self-oriented" versus the more female "other nurturing" strategies of sociobiology. Psychologically, the former strategy is often judged to be egotistic, insensitive, inconsiderate, and uncaring, while the latter is judged to be affiliative, intimate, protective, and solicitous (Gilligan, 1981; Millon & Davis, 1996; Rushton, 1985; Wilson, 1978). Organisms that make reproductive investments in many offspring, so that their resources are spread too thin, or who make a long gestational investment but then fail to nurture their offspring, are strongly selected against. Among the various personalities deduced from the theory, we find strong a self orientation among narcissists and a strong other orientation among dependents.

In addition to the three content polarities, the evolutionary theory also posits a content-free dimension that specifies a major pathway along which various personality styles develop and change. Such transformational principles are often important in revealing relationships between diverse personality styles, and also suggest pathways that personality might be changed in therapy. The evolutionary theory incorporates the interpersonal domain through the self and other polarities. In addition, however, it also includes the idea of conflictedness or ambivalence between polarities, a fundamentally psychodynamic construct. By representing self–other and active–passive as orthogonal in a two-dimensional plane, and depicting conflict as a third, vertical dimension, a number of personality disorder constructs can be interrelated and differentiated. The compulsive and negativistic (passive-aggressive) personalities, for example, share an ambivalence concerning whether to put their own priorities and expectations first or to defer to others. The negativistic acts out this ambivalence, repressed in the compulsive. The two personalities are thus theoretically linked, and the theory predicts that if the submerged anger of the compulsive can be confronted consciously, the subject may tend to act out in a passive-aggressive manner until this conflict can be constructively refocused or resolved. Figure 19.7 puts this relationship into a circumplex format and relates these disorders to the "interpersonally-imbalanced" personalities—namely the antisocial, narcissistic, histrionic, and dependent. Looking at the right side of the figure, the negativistic and compulsive shade into each other, while the negativistic shades into the antisocial and histrionic, and the compulsive shades into the narcissistic and dependent. Loosely speaking, to transform a compulsive into a narcissist, therapy should resolve the conflict between self and other toward a preoccupation with the individual's own self-concerns. To transform a compulsive into a dependent, therapy should resolve this conflict in the favor of the needs of others.

Cast in this circumplex format, the comorbidities of these personality disorders begin to make sense as a distortion wrought by the categorical framework into which the disorders have been cast. While the concept of categories pulls for discrete entities, the personalities themselves are obviously related and necessarily share certain common features. Moreover, by depicting the disorders in this manner an element of severity is automatically

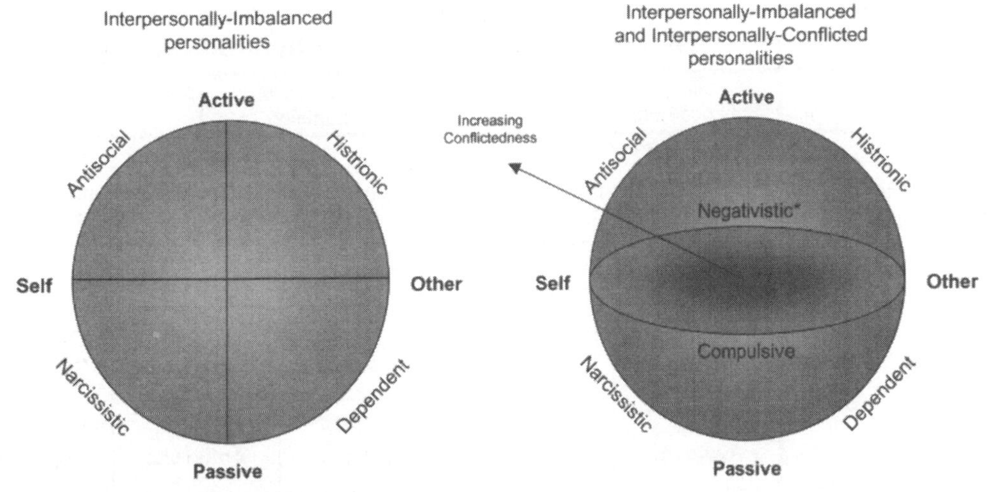

Figure 19.7 Interpersonally imbalanced and interpersonally conflicted personalities.

built into the taxonomy that cannot be reduced to extremity on any content dimension. Some disorders are more severe than others, simply because they include the additional element of conflictedness. Future versions of the *DSM* will likely need to include such content-free dimensions, which are just as fundamental as content-bound dimensions to any personality taxonomy.

While figure 19.7 provides an innovative arrangement of a number of personality disorders, the polarities of the evolutionary theory have most often been schematized in terms of figure 19.8. This diagram illustrates how the constructs of *DSM-III*, *DSM-III-R*, and *DSM-IV* may be derived from the various combinations of the underlying polarities, plus the content-free dimension of conflict. Personalities termed "deficient" lack the capacity to experience or to enact certain aspects of the three polarities (for example, the schizoid has a faulty substrate for both pleasure and pain). Those termed "imbalanced" lean strongly toward one or another extreme of a polarity (for example, the dependent is oriented to passively receive support and nurturance from others). Personalities termed "conflicted" struggle with ambivalences toward opposing ends of a bipolarity (for example, the negativistic vacillates between the expectancies of others and the desires of self). Figure 19.8, diagrammed in a manner similar to the periodic table of elements, illustrates the personality constructs derived from the evolutionary model in their normal and pathological forms.

Domains of Personality

The evolutionary theory offers three levels of content specification. We have already presented the first two, the polarities and their derived personality constructs. The final level is concerned with the manifestation of each construct within the various domains of personality. Understanding this third level requires an understanding of the role of chance and necessity in evolution. Because the polarities are coupled to evolutionary imperatives, the derived personality constructs inherit a quality of necessity: they could not exist otherwise than they do. Whereas the history of psychology may be different in different worlds, these constructs are the same wherever organisms must honor survival, adaptation, and reproduction as the immutable laws of evolution, whether on earth or elsewhere.

In contrast, the various historical schools and their various respective models have no such inevitability. While the personality constructs derived from the evolutionary theory are universal, the historical schools as parts of personality have essentially resulted from the operation of historically contingent processes over phylogenetic time. Consider: Some 60 million years ago, a comet collided with the earth, causing the extinction of the dino-

	Existential Aim		Replication Strategy		
	Life Enhancement	Life Preservation	Reproductive Propagation		Reproductive Nurturance
Polarity	Pleasure - Pain		Self - Other		
Deficiency, Imbalance, or Conflict	Pleasure (low) Pain (low or high	Pleasure Pain (Reversal)	Self (low) Other (high)	Self (high) Other (low)	Self - Other (Reversal)
Adaptation Mode	**DSM Personality Disorders**				
Passive: Accomodation	Retiring **Schizoid Depressive***	Yielding **Masochistic**	Agreeing **Dependent**	Asserting **Narcissistic**	Conforming **Compulsive**
Active: Modification	Hesitating **Avoidant**	Controlling **Sadistic**	Outgoing **Histrionic**	Dissenting **Antisocial**	Complaining **Negativistic**
Structural Pathology	**Schizotypal**	**Borderline, Paranoid**	**Borderline**	**Paranoid**	**Borderline, Paranoid**

*The schizoid is passive and low in both pleasure and pain, the depressive is low in pleasure and high on pain. "Retiring" is the normal variant of the schizoid.

Figure 19.8 Polarity model and its personality style and disorder derivatives.

saurs and setting biological evolution on a completely different course. No amount of theorizing will ever deduce this chance fact of history from some set of abstract theoretical propositions. Collisions between celestial bodies are allowed by the laws of physics, but the particular collision of the earth with a particular comet or asteroid is not an inevitable result of the existence of space, time, matter, and energy. But without that comet, we just wouldn't be here. Perhaps some other form of intelligent life might have evolved, but it would not be us. Their societies and social relationships, their mechanisms of cognition, their brain structures and neurotransmitters, the archetypes lurking in their unconscious, their very senses, and, accordingly, perhaps even the metaphysical categories employed to parse reality, would be far different. Surely they would note differences among themselves as total beings and develop sciences of psychology and personality. But their particular historical schools, being dependent on the unique evolved structure of their minds, might well be far different from anything we can ever imagine. Unless we believe that the psychology of human beings forms a prototype for that of all other sentient beings elsewhere in the cosmos, an anthropocentric delusion, then we must admit that there could well be no equivalents between the content domains of their psychology and those of our own.

Once the role of chance and necessity in the evolution of human psychology is understood, several conclusions readily follow. While the polarities and their derived constructs are necessary and universal, it is highly unlikely that the various content domains of personality will ever be put on a similar footing, one from which a domain of unconscious defenses, a domain of cognitive styles, a domain of interpersonal conduct, and so on, can be derived as an inevitable result. Domains of personality just exist, and the taxonomic principles of these domains are, at least in part, the particular product of our own evolutionary adaptations. As such, they contain specificities that render them unassimilable to any other perspective, including the evolutionary theory, and that justify their very existence as domains. Three important facts of the history of psychology are thus brought together. First, as history has shown, each perspective, once exposed to scientific enthusiasm, perpetuates itself ad nauseum, never becoming truly susceptible to falsification. Instead, it waxes and wanes in accord with the fashion of the times, eventually developing to a highly dogmatic state of internal consistency. Second, once drawn into a particular perspective, clinicians and researchers seem to spend their lives involved in "horizontal refinements," working out the particular problems of their area, even while the generality or clinical importance of their findings to the clinical treatment of the total organism remains unclear. And finally, it explains why the contention between various perspectives never really fades, but never really produces much of anything, either. The "research programs" of Lakatos, then, should not be viewed simply as an inductive fact wrought from an inspection of the history of the social sciences. At least in psychology, Lakatos's conception of "research programs" would seem to have a solid footing in the interplay between chance and necessity in human evolution. We can also conclude that neither the evolutionary theory, nor any other theory, will tell us that defense mechanisms, or any other personality domain, must exist as an inevitable part of the human psyche. Psychology is thus fundamentally different from sciences like physics. Although physics contains numerous universal constants, such as the weight of a proton, the speed of light, and Planck's constant, theoretical physics also explains why these particular values exist as they do and not otherwise. To be complete, a unified theory of the fundamental forces of nature must be able to account for these observed quantities. In contrast, it is doubtful that any "unified field theory" of personality will account for the existence of the various personality domains.

Nevertheless, while specific personality domains "just exist," the evolution of the structure and contents of each has not proceeded with total autonomy, but is instead constrained by the evolutionary imperatives of survival, adaptation, and reproductive success, for it is always the whole organism that is selected and evolves. Accordingly, we should be able to discover the "footprints" of the evolutionary polarities within the history of the major psychological schools, a psychoarcheological record of their role in mental life. This provides some empirical corroboration for the theory, although, as was argued at the beginning of this chapter, the progress of history is contingent and meandering. Figure 19.9 traces the expression of these polarities across three major schools of psychology.

Perhaps the best way to organize the domains of personality draws upon a distinction made in the biological sciences between structure and function. The basic science of anatomy investigates embedded and essentially permanent structures, which serve, for example, as substrates for mood and memory, while physiology examines underlying functions that regulate internal dynamics and external transactions. As an integrated totality, personality must depend on structural and functional domains, as does any organism. In many cases, these domains parallel the major approaches to the field reviewed above. What is new is the theoretical basis through which they may be considered conjointly, rather than singularly, as a means of obtaining a complete representation of any given personality style, one which eschews the past dogmatisms of personality theory. The "expressive acts" domain represents the behavioral legacy of Thorndike, Skinner, and Watson, for example, while the "interpersonal conduct" domain represents the interpersonal tradition, originating with Sullivan and expressed today by Kiesler, Wiggins, and Benjamin, among others. The "cognitive style" domain is obviously intended to represent the cognitive tradition, of which Beck is the most notable modern exponent, while the "regulatory mechanisms" and "object representations" domains parallel the ideas of defense mechanisms and object relations of the psychodynamic school. All of these are legitimate approaches to personality (Millon, 1984, 1986), and through their very existence provide empirical support for the structural paradigm advanced above, that personality pathologies are best thought of as disorders of the entire matrix of the person. The alternative is a reduction of this complex matrix to some one perspective, be it behavioral, cognitive, psychodynamic, or in other words, to treat a part as a substitute for the whole.

Functional Domains

Functional characteristics represent dynamic processes that transpire within the intrapsychic world and between the individual's self and psychosocial environment. For definitional purposes, functional domains represent "expressive modes of regulatory action"—that is, behaviors, social conduct, cognitive processes, and unconscious mechanisms that manage, adjust, transform, coordinate, balance, discharge, and control the give and take of inner and outer life. Four functional domains relevant to personality are briefly described below.

- *Expressive acts*. These attributes relate to the observables seen at the behavioral level of data and are usually recorded by noting what

Subfield of Personality \ Evolutionary Polarities	Pleasure-Pain	Passive-Active	Self-Other
Principles of Learning	Positive and Negative Reinforcers of Learning	Respondent versus Operant Modes of Behavior	Internal versus External Controls of Reinforcement
Psychodynamic Concepts	Instinctual Aims of the ID	Reality Apparatuses of the EGO	Self-Structures versus Object Relations
Components of Motivation and Emotion	Pleasant and Unpleasant Valences of Emotion	Low versus High Intensities of Activation	Competitive versus Cooperative Dispositions of Motivation
Neurobiological Substrates	Substrates of Mood	Substrates of Arousal	Substrates of Gender

Figure 19.9 Manifestation of evolutionary polarities across psychological approaches.

and how the person acts. Through inference, observations of overt behavior enable us to infer either what the person unknowingly reveals about him or herself or, conversely, what he or she wishes others to think or to know about him or her. The range and character of expressive actions not only are wide and diverse but also convey both distinctive and worthwhile clinical information, from communicating a sense of personal incompetence to exhibiting general defensiveness to demonstrating a disciplined self-control.

- *Interpersonal conduct.* A person's style of relating to others is noted essentially at the behavioral data level and may be captured in a number of ways, such as how his or her actions impact on others, intended or otherwise; the attitudes that underlie, prompt, and give shape to these actions; the methods by which he or she engages others to meet his or her needs; or his or her way of coping with social tensions and conflicts. Extrapolating from these observations, the clinician may construct an image of how the patient functions in relation to others, be it antagonistically, respectfully, aversively, or secretively.
- *Cognitive style.* How the individual perceives events, focuses attention, processes information, organizes thoughts, and communicates reactions and ideas to others represent data at a phenomenological level and are among the most useful indices to the clinician of the patient's distinctive way of functioning. By synthesizing these characteristics or symptoms, it may be possible to identify indications of what may be termed an impoverished style, or distracted thinking, or cognitive flightiness, or constricted thought.
- *Regulatory mechanism.* Although "mechanisms" of self-protection, need gratification, and conflict resolution are consciously recognized at times, they derive primarily from an intrapsychic level, and are not open to reflective appraisal. As such, they often contribute to a sequence of events that intensifies the very problems they were intended to avoid. Mechanisms usually represent internal processes and, hence, are more difficult to discern and describe than processes anchored closer to the observable world. Despite the methodological problems they present, the task of identifying which mechanisms are chosen (e.g., rationalization, displacement, reaction formation), and the extent to which they are employed, is extremely useful in a comprehensive personality assessment.

Structural Domains

Structural attributes represent deeply embedded and relatively enduring templates of imprinted memories, attitudes, needs, fears, conflicts, and so on that guide experience and transform the nature of ongoing life events, channeling actions and ex-

	Behavioral Acts	Interpersonal Conduct	Cognitive Style	Regulatory Mechanisms
Schizoid	Impassive	Unengaged	Impoverished	Intellectualization
Avoidant	Fretful	Aversive	Distracted	Fantasy
Depressive	Disconsolate	Defenseless	Pessimistic	Asceticism
Dependent	Incompetent	Submissive	Naive	Introjection
Histrionic	Dramatic	Attention-Seeking	Flighty	Dissociation
Narcissistic	Haughty	Exploitive	Expansive	Rationalization
Antisocial	Impulsive	Irresponsible	Deviant	Acting-Out
Sadistic	Precipitate	Abrasive	Dogmatic	Isolation
Compulsive	Disciplined	Respectful	Constricted	Reaction Formation
Negativistic	Resentful	Contrary	Skeptical	Displacement
Masochistic	Abstinent	Deferential	Diffident	Exaggeration
Schizotypal	Eccentric	Secretive	Autistic	Undoing
Borderline	Spasmodic	Paradoxical	Capricious	Regression
Paranoid	Defensive	Provocative	Suspicious	Projection

Figure 19.10 Functional attributes of personality.

periences into conformity with preformed inclinations and expectancies. Four structural domains relevant to personality will be briefly described below.

- *Self-image.* As the inner world of symbols is mastered through development, the "swirl" of events that buffet the young child gives way to a growing sense of order and continuity. One major configuration emerges to impose a measure of sameness on an otherwise fluid environment—the perception of self-as-object, a distinct, ever-present, and identifiable "I" or "me." Self-identity stems largely from conceptions drawn at the phenomenological level of analysis; it is especially significant in providing a stable anchor to guide and give continuity to changing experience.

	Self-Image	Object Representations	Morphologic Organization	Mood-Temperament
Schizoid	Complacent	Meager	Undifferentiated	Apathetic
Avoidant	Alienated	Vexatious	Fragile	Anguished
Depressive	Worthless	Forsaken	Depleted	Melancholic
Dependent	Inept	Immature	Inchoate	Pacific
Histrionic	Gregarious	Shallow	Disjointed	Fickle
Narcissistic	Admirable	Contrived	Spurious	Insouciant
Antisocial	Autonomous	Debased	Unruly	Callous
Sadistic	Combative	Pernicious	Eruptive	Hostile
Compulsive	Conscientious	Concealed	Compartmentalized	Solemn
Negativistic	Discontented	Vacillating	Divergent	Irritable
Masochistic	Undeserving	Discredited	Inverted	Dysphoric
Schizotypal	Estranged	Chaotic	Fragmented	Distraught or Insentient
Borderline	Uncertain	Incompatible	Split	Labile
Paranoid	Inviolable	Unalterable	Inelastic	Irascible

Figure 19.11 Structural attributes of personality.

While almost everyone holds an implicit sense of "who they are," individuals differ greatly in the clarity and accuracy of their self-introspections.

- *Object representations.* Significant early experiences leave an inner imprint, a structural residue composed of memories, attitudes, and effects that serve as a substrate of dispositions for perceiving and reacting to life's ongoing events. As such, these representations inhere within the phenomenological realm. Analogous to the various organ systems of which the body is composed, both the character and substance of these internalized representations of significant figures and relationships of the past can be differentiated and analyzed for clinical purposes. Variations in the nature and content of this inner world can be associated with various descriptors, including shallow, vexatious, undifferentiated, concealed, and irreconcilable.
- *Morphologic organization.* The overall architecture that serves as a framework for an individual's psychic interior may display weakness in its structural cohesion, exhibit deficient coordination among its components, or possess few mechanisms to maintain balance and harmony, regulate internal conflicts, or mediate external pressures. The concept of morphologic organization refers to the structural strength, interior congruity, and functional efficacy of the personality system. "Organization" of the mind is almost exclusively derived from inferences at the intrapsychic level of analysis; it is a concept akin to and employed in conjunction with current psychoanalytic notions such as borderline and psychotic levels, but this usage tends to be limited, relating essentially to quantitative degrees of integrative pathology, not to variations either in integrative character or configuration.
- *Mood-temperament.* Few observables are clinically more relevant from the biophysical

Functional Domains

Expressively Disciplined (e.g., maintains a regulated, highly structured and strictly-organized life; perfectionism interferes with decision-making and task completion).

Interpersonally Respectful (e.g., exhibits unusual adherence to social conventions and proprieties, as well as being scrupulous and overconscientious about matters of morality and ethics; prefers polite, formal and correct personal relationships, usually insisting that subordinates adhere to personally established rules and methods).

Cognitively Constricted (e.g., constructs world in terms of rules, regulations, schedules and hierarchies; is rigid, stubborn, and indecisive and notably upset by unfamiliar or novel ideas and customs).

Reaction Formation Mechanism (e.g., repeatedly presents positive thoughts and socially commendable behaviors that are diametrically opposite one's deeper contrary and forbidden feelings; displays reasonableness and maturity when faced with circumstances that evoke anger or dismay in others).

Structural Domains

Conscientious Self-Image (e.g., sees self as devoted to work, industrious, reliable, meticulous and efficient, largely to the exclusion of leisure activities; fearful of error or misjudgment and, hence overvalues aspects of self that exhibit discipline, perfection, prudence and loyalty).

Concealed Objects (e.g., only those internalized representations, with their associated inner affects and attitudes that can be socially approved, are allowed conscious awareness or behavioral expression; as a result, actions and memories are highly regulated, forbidden impulses sequestered and tightly bound, personal and social conflicts defensively denied, kept from awareness, maintained under stringent control).

Compartmentalized Organization (e.g., morphologic structures are rigidly organized in a tightly consolidated system that is clearly partitioned into numerous, distinct and segregated constellations of drive, memory, and cognition, with few open channels to permit interplay among these components).

Solemn Mood (e.g., is unrelaxed, tense, joyless and grim; restrains warm feelings and keeps most emotions under tight control).

Figure 19.12 Domain descriptions for the compulsive personality.

level of data than the predominant character of an individual's effect and the intensity and frequency with it is expressed. The "meaning" of extreme emotions is easy to decode. This is not so with the more subtle moods and feelings that insidiously and repetitively pervade ongoing relationships and experiences. Not only are the expressive features of mood and drive conveyed by terms such as "distraught," "labile," "fickle," or "hostile" communicated via self-report, but they are revealed as well, albeit indirectly, in the patient's level of activity, speech quality, and physical appearance.

Operationalizing the Personality Disorders

Having put forward a theory of personality that transcends any particular perspective, we are now in a position to operationalize the constructs derived from the polarities of the evolutionary theory. Essentially, this step makes good on the original definition of personality as the patterning of variables across the matrix of the person. Figures 19.10 and 19.11 present descriptors for all the functional and structural domains across the 14 personality disorders of *DSM-III-R* and *DSM-IV*. Descriptive paragraphs have been developed for each personality those; those for the compulsive personality are presented in figure 19.12. In contrast to the diagnostic criteria of *DSM-IV*, these descriptors have been specifically formulated to be both comprehensive and comparable. Because they refer to the most important domains through which personality has been studied, the claim is that they exhaust all that personality is, describing each construct at an equal level of abstraction across each domain. In contrast, the criteria of *DSM-IV* treat each disorder as a single unitary dimension, much like a trait rather than a style or disorder, and thus neglect some domains while emphasizing others. Moreover, the *DSM-IV* criteria vary in terms of breadth. Some criteria are very wide while others are very narrow. Such a critique is a natural consequence of the matrix definition of personality, perhaps the most natural and intuitive definition possible. Personality is, after all, about the patterning of characteristics. In itself, this definition tells us nothing about the content of personality, but by seeking organizing principles outside personality proper in the evolutionary imperatives of survival, adaptation, and reproduction, a taxonomy of styles and disorders can be constructed. It is hoped, that this taxonomy will allow some resolution of the issues raised at the beginning of this chapter.

References

Abraham, K. (1927a). The influence of oral eroticism on character formation. In *Selected papers on psychoanalysis*. London: Hogarth.

Abraham, K. (1927b). Contributions to the theory of the anal character. In *Selected papers on psychoanalysis*. London: Hogarth. (Original work published 1921.)

Abraham, K. (1927c). In *Selected papers on psychoanalysis*. London: Hogarth. (Original work published 1924.)

Alford, B. A., & Beck, A. T. (1997). *The integrative power of cognitive therapy*. New York: Guilford.

Allport, G. W., & Odbert, H. S. (1936). Trait names: A psycholexical study. *Psychological Monographs, 47* (whole issue).

Almagor, M., Tellegen, A., & Waller, N. G. (1995). The Big Seven Model: A cross-cultural replication and further exploration of the basic dimensions of natural language trait descriptors. *Journal of Personality and Social Psychology, 69*, 300–307.

Bartlett, F. C. (1932). *Remembering*. Cambridge: Cambridge University Press.

Beck, A. T. (1976). *Cognitive therapy and the emotional disorders*. New York: International Universities Press.

Beck, A. T. (1992). Personality disorders (and their relationship to syndromal disorders). *Across-Species Comparisions and Psychiatry Newsletter, 5*, 3–13.

Beck, A. T., & Freeman, A. F. (1990). *Cognitive therapy of personality disorders*. New York: Guilford.

Beck, A. T., Rush, A. J., Shaw, B. F., & Emory, G. (1979). *Cognitive therapy of depression*. New York: Guilford.

Benjamin, L. S. (1993). *Interpersonal diagnosis and treatment of personality disorders*. New York: Guilford.

Benjamin, L. S. (1974). Structured analysis of social behavior. *Psychological Review, 81*, 392–425.

Benjamin, L. S. (1986). Adding social and intrapsychic descriptors to Axis I of DSM-III. In T. Millon & G. L. Klerman (Eds.), *Contemporary directions in psychopathology: Toward the DSM-IV* (pp. 599–638). New York: Guilford.

Block, J. (1995). A contrarian view of the five-factor approach to personality description. *Psychological Bulletin, 117*, 187–215.

Cattell, R. B. (1950). *Personality: A systematic theoretical and factual study.* New York: McGraw-Hill.

Cattell, R. B., Eber, H. W., & Tatsuoka, M. M. (1970). *Handbook for the Sixteen Personality Factor Questionnaire (16PF).* Champaign, IL: Institute for Personality and Ability Testing.

Clark, L. A. (1990). Toward a consensual set of symptom clusters for assessment of personality disorder. In J. N. Butcher & C. D. Spielberger (Eds.), *Advances in personality assessment* (vol. 8; pp. 243–266). Hillsdale, NJ: Lawrence Erlbaum.

Clark, L. A. (1993). *Manual for the Schedule for Nonadaptive and Adaptive Personality (SNAP).* Minneapolis, MN: University of Minnesota Press.

Clark, L. A., & Watson, D. W. (1990). *General Temperament Survey (GTS).* Unpublished manuscript, Southern Methodist University.

Cleckley, H. (1964). *The mask of sanity* (4th ed.), Saint Louis, MO: Mosby.

Cloninger, R. C. (1986). A unified biosocial theory of personality and its role in the development of anxiety states. *Psychiatric Developments, 3*, 167–226.

Cloninger, R. C. (1987). A systematic method for clinical description and classification of personality variants. *Archives of General Psychiatry, 44*, 573–588.

Cloninger, R. C., Svrakic, D. M., & Przybeck, T. R. (1993). A psychobiological model of temperament and character. *Archives of General Psychiatry, 50*, 975–990.

Costa, P. T., Jr., & McCrae, R. R. (1976). Age differences in personality structure: A cluster analytic approach. *Journal of Gerontology, 31*, 564–570.

Costa, P. T., Jr., & McCrae, R. R. (1978). Objective personality assessment. In M. Storandt, I. C. Siegler, & M. F. Elias (Eds.), *The clinical psychology of aging* (pp. 119–143). New York: Plenum.

Costa, P. T., Jr. & McCrae, R. R. (1985). *The NEO Personality Inventory Manual.* Odessa, FL: Psychological Assessment Resources.

Costa, P. T., Jr., & McCrae, R. R. (1992). Revised NEO Personality Inventory (NEO-PI-R) and NEO Five-Factor Inventory (NEO-FFI) professional manual. Odessa, FL: Psychological Assessment Resources.

Costa, P. T., Jr., & McCrae, R. R. (1995). Domains and facets: Hierarchical personality assessment using the Revised NEO Personality Inventory. *Journal of Personality Assessment,* 64, 21–50.

Digman, J. M. (1990). Personality structure: Emergence of the five-factor model. *Annual Review of Psychology, 41*, 417–440.

Digman, J. M. (1996). The curious history of the Five-Factor Model. In J. S. Wiggins (Ed.), *The Five-Factor Model of personality: Theoretical perspectives* (pp. 1–20). New York: Guilford.

Digman, J. M., & Takemoto-Chock, N. K. (1981). Factors in the natural language of personality: Reanalysis and comparison of six major studies. *Multivariate Behavioral Research, 16*, 149–170.

Fairbairn, W. (1954). *An object-relations theory of the personality.* New York: Basic Books.

Fenichel, O. (1945). *The psychoanalytic theory of the neurosis.* New York: Norton.

Fiester, S., & Gay, M. (1991). Sadistic personality disorder: A review of data and recommendations for DSM-IV. *Journal of Personality Disorders, 5*, 376–385.

Fiske, D. W. (1949). Consistency of factorial structure of personality ratings from different sources. *Journal of Abnormal and Social Psychology, 44*, 329–344.

Forgus, R., & Shulman, B. (1979). *Personality: A cognitive view.* Englewood Cliffs, NJ: Prentice-Hall.

Freedman, M. B., Leary, T., Ossorio, A. G., & Coffey, H. S. (1951). The interpersonal dimension of personality. *Journal of Personality, 20*, 143–161.

Freud, S. (1933). *New introductory lectures on psychoanalysis.* New York: Norton.

Gilligan, C. (1981). *In a different voice.* Cambridge, MA: Harvard University Press.

Goldberg, L. R. (1992). The development of markers for the Big-Five factor structure. *Psychological Assessment, 4*, 26–42.

Goldberg, L. R. (1993). The structure of phenotypic personality traits. *American Psychologist, 48*, 26–34.

Gurtman, M. B. (1993). Constructing personality tests to meet a structural criterion: Application of the interpersonal circumplex. *Journal of Personality, 61*, 237–263.

Harkness, A. R., & McNulty, J. L. (1994). The Personality Psychopathology Five (PSY-5): Issues from the pages of a diagnostic manual instead of a dictionary. In S. Strack & M. Lorr (Eds.), *Differentiating normal and abnormal personality* (pp. 291–315). New York: Springer.

John, O. P. (1990). The "Big Five" factor taxonomy: Dimensions of personality in the natural language and in questionnaires. In L. A. Pervin (Ed.), *Handbook of personality theory and research* (pp. 66–100). New York: Guilford.

John, O. P., Angleitner, A., & Ostendorf, F. (1988). The lexical approach to personality: A historical review of trait taxonomic research. *European Journal of Personality, 2*, 171–205.

Kernberg, O. F. (1984). *Severe personality disorders*. New Haven: Yale University Press.

Kernberg, O. F. (1996). A psychoanalytic theory of personality disorders. In J. F. Clarkin & M. F. Lenzenweger (Eds.), *Major theories of personality disorder* (pp. 106–140). New York: Guilford.

Kiesler, D. J. (1983). The 1982 Interpersonal Circle: A taxonomy for complementarity in human transactions. *Psychological Review, 90*, 185–214.

Kiesler, D. J. (1986). The 1982 Interpersonal Circle: An analysis of DSM-III personality disorders. In T. Millon & G. L. Klerman (Eds.), *Contemporary directions in psychopathology: Towards the DSM-IV* (pp. 57–69). New York: Guilford.

Kiesler, D. J. (1996). *Contemporary interpersonal theory and research: Personality, psychopathology, and psychotherapy*. New York: John Wiley.

Kretschmer, E. (1922). *Korperbau und Charakter* (3rd ed.). Berlin: J. Springer.

Lakatos, I. (1968). Criticism and the methodology of scientific research programmes. *Proceedings of the Aristotelian Society, 69*, 149–186.

Lang, P. J. (1968). Fear reduction and fear behavior: Problems in treating a construct. In J. M. Schlien (Ed.), *Research in psychotherapy* (vol. III; pp. 90–102). Washington, DC: American Psychological Association.

Leary, T. (1957). *Interpersonal diagnosis of personality: A functional theory and methodology for personality evaluation*. New York: Ronald Press.

Livesley, W. J., Jackson, D. N., & Schroeder, M. L. (1989). A study of the factorial structure of personality pathology. *Journal of Personality Disorders, 3*, 292–306.

McCrae, R. R., & Costa, P. T., Jr. (1986). Clinical assessment can benefit from recent advances in personality psychology. *American Psychologist, 41*, 1001–1003.

Meehl, P. E. (1962). Schizotaxia, schizotypy, schizophrenia. *American Psychologist, 17*, 827–838.

Meehl, P. E. (1978). Theoretical risks and tabular asterisks: Sir Karl, Sir Ronald, and the slow progress of soft psychology. *Journal of Consulting and Clinical Psychology, 46*, 806–834.

Meehl, P. E. (1995). Bootstraps taxometrics: Solving the classification problem in psychopathology. *American Psychologist, 50*, 266–275.

Meehl, P. E., & Golden, R. R. (1982). Taxometric methods. In P. Kendall & J. Butcher (Eds.), *Handbook of research methods in clinical psychology* (pp. 127–181). New York: John Wiley.

Miller, G. A. (1957). The magical number of seven, plus or minus two. *Psychological Review, 63*, 81–97.

Millon, T. (1984). On the renaissance of personality assessment and personality theory. *Journal of Personality Assessment, 48*, 450–466.

Millon, T. (1986). Personality prototypes and their diagnostic criteria. In T. Millon & G. L. Klerman (Eds.), *Contemporary directions in psychopathology*. New York: Guilford.

Millon, T. (1990). *Toward a new personology: An evolutionary model*. New York: Wiley-Interscience.

Millon, T., & Davis, R. D. (1996). *Disorders of personality: DSM-IV and beyond*. New York: Wiley-Interscience.

Norman, W. T. (1963). Toward an adequate taxonomy of personality attributes: Replicated factor structure in peer nomination personality ratings. *Journal of Abnormal and Social Psychology, 66*, 574–583.

Orford, D. H. (1986). The rules of interpersonal complementarity: Does hostility beget hostility and dominance, submission? *Psychological Review, 93*, 365–377.

Peabody, D., & Goldberg, L. R. (1989). Some determinants of factor structures from personality-trait descriptors. *Journal of Personality and Social Psychology, 57*, 552–567.

Piaget, J. (1926). *The language and thought of the child*. New York: Harcourt Brace.

Pincus, A. L. (1994). The interpersonal circumplex and the interpersonal theory: Perspectives on personality and its pathology. In S. Strack & M. Lorr (Eds.), *Differentiating normal and abnormal personality* (pp. 114–136). New York: Springer.

Pretzer, J. L., & Beck, A. T. (1996). A cognitive theory of personality disorders. In J. F. Clarkin & M. F. Lenzenweger (Eds.), *Major theories of personality disorder* (pp. 36–105). New York: Guilford.

Reich, W. (1933). *Charakteranalyse*. Leipzig: Sexpol Verlag.

Rushton, J. P. (1985). Differential K theory: The sociobiology of individual and group differences. *Personality and Individual Differences, 6*, 441–452.

Schaefer, E. (1965). Configurational analysis of children's report of parent behavior. *Journal of Consulting Psychology, 29*, 552–557.

Schroeder, M. L., Wormworth, J. A., & Livesley, W. J. (1992). Dimensions of personality disorder and their relationships to the Big Five dimensions of personality. *Psychological Assessment, 4*, 47–53.

Sheldon, W. H., & Stevens, S. S. (1942). *The varieties of temperament*. New York: Harper & Row.

Staats, A. W. (1986). Behaviorism with a personality: The paradigmatic behavioral assessment approach. In R. O. Nelson & S. C. Hayes (Eds.), *Conceptual foundations of behavioral assessment* (pp. 242–296). New York: Guilford.

Tellegen, A., & Waller, N. G. (1987, August). *Reexamining basic dimensions of natural language trait descriptors*. Paper presented at the 95th Annual Convention of the American Psychological Association, New York.

Tupes, E. C., & Christal, R. C. (1961). *Recurrent personality factors based on trait ratings* (Tech. Rep. No. ASD-TR-61-97). Lackland Air Force Base, TX: U.S. Air Force.

Van Denburg, T. F., & Kiesler, D. J. (1993). Transactional escalation in rigidity and intensity of interpersonal behaviour under stress. *British Journal of Medical Psychology, 66*, 15–31.

Voeltz, L. M., & Evans, I. M. (1982). The assessment of behavioral interrelationships in child behavior therapy. *Behavioral Assessment, 4*, 131–165.

Widiger, T. A. (1993). The *DSM*-III-R categorical personality disorder diagnoses: A critique and an alternative. *Psychological Inquiry, 4*, 75–90.

Widiger, T. A., Trull, T. J., Clarkin, J. F., Sanderson, C., & Costa, P. T., Jr. (1994). A description of the DSM-III-R and DSM-IV personality disorders with the Five Factor Model of personality. In P. T. Costa, Jr. & T. A. Widiger (Eds.), *Personality Disorders and the Five-Factor Model of Personality* (pp. 41–56). Washington, DC: American Psychological Assocation.

Wiggins, J. S., & Trobst, K. K. (1997). Prospects for the assessment of normal and abnormal interpersonal behavior. In J. A. Schinka & R. L. Greene (Eds.), *Emerging issues and methods in personality assessment* (pp. 113–129). Mahwah, NJ: Lawrence Erlbaum.

Wiggins, J. S., Steiger, J. H., & Gaelick, L. (1981). Evaluating circumplexity in personality data. *Multivariate Behavioral Research, 16*, 263–289.

Wilson, E. O. (1978). *On human nature*. Cambridge: Harvard University Press.

20

Schizoid and Avoidant Personality Disorders

DAVID P. BERNSTEIN
LAURA TRAVAGLINI

Schizoid and avoidant personality disorders are phenomenologically similar diagnostic entities characterized by interpersonal detachment. Both kinds of individuals may appear socially isolated, having few or no close friendships, engage primarily in solitary as opposed to social activities, and remain aloof or inhibited in social situations. Schizoids typically appear emotionally bland and unresponsive and often seem insensitive to the nuances of social interactions. Avoidants experience social interactions as aversive owing to their own propensity for self-criticism and may appear self-conscious in social situations.

A critical distinction between these disorders lies in their motivation or capacity for attachment: schizoid individuals lack the desire or ability to form social relationships, while avoidant individuals desire interpersonal contact but avoid it out of an intense fear of rejection and humiliation. Millon (1981) has described this difference as one of passive (schizoid) versus active (avoidant) detachment. The distinction between the schizoid's passive disinterest in interpersonal relationships and the avoidant's active avoidance of them is of central importance, for both practical and theoretical reasons, since the differential diagnosis between the two disorders hinges on this distinction, as does the discriminant validity of the disorders themselves.

In fact, the classification of schizoid and avoidant personality disorders as separate diagnostic entities is a relatively recent development and remains the subject of much debate. The diagnostic label *schizoid personality*, introduced by Bleuler (1924), has a long history in the clinical and theoretical literature and has traditionally been used to describe individuals who are not psychotic, yet exhibit interpersonal and emotional deficits such as social withdrawal, passivity and aimlessness, and flattened affect or anhedonia. Thus, schizoids were seen as being schizophrenic in its attenuated form. The term *avoidant personality*, on the other hand, was coined by Millon (1981) and was introduced into the *DSM-III* as part of its multiaxial reorganization, with a separate axis for personality disorders. Nevertheless, the *DSM-III* criteria for avoidant personality disorder were also based on an older clinical and theoretical literature that described individuals who were hypersensitive to rejection, highly self-critical, and simultaneously wished for closeness with others and were aversive to it (Kretschmer, 1925; Fenichel, 1945; Rado, 1956; MacKinnon & Michels, 1971). These individuals were sometimes labeled schizoid, but were also referred to by a number of other diagnostic terms, such as the "phobic character" (Fenichel, 1945; Rado, 1956; MacKinnon & Michels, 1971). The decision to include separate diagnostic categories in the *DSM-III* for schizoid and avoidant personality disorders has been criticized on a number of grounds. For example, several authors have noted that traditional descriptions of schizoid character often included the apparently contradictory qualities of superficial insensitivity and aloofness, on the one hand, and underlying hypersensitivity, on the other (Livesley & West, 1986; Akhtar, 1987). Kretchmer (1925) referred to these two poles of the schizoid character as "anesthetic" and "hyperaesthetic," respectively, a classification that informed the distinction between schizoid and avoidant personality disorders in the *DSM-III*. Nevertheless, the presence of these seemingly contradictory traits in the same individuals has raised questions about the justification for considering schizoid and avoidant personality disorders as truly separate diagnostic groups. An alternative conceptualization would be that of a spectrum of socially isolated individuals who vary in their capacity for attachment to others and underlying emotional sensitivity.

Similar questions have been raised about the diagnostic boundaries between schizoid and avoidant personality disorders, on the one hand, and other psychiatric diagnoses on the other. For example, the *DSM-III* introduced a new diagnostic category, schizotypal personality disorder, that shared many phenomenological features with the schizoid diagnosis. Although the *DSM-III* was ostensibly an atheoretical document, based on descriptive features rather than a theory of etiology, the raison d'être of schizotypal personality disorder was its presumed genetic relationship to schizophrenia. The classic Danish adoption studies (Kety et al., 1971) found that relatives of schizophrenics often exhibited symptoms that were reminiscent of schizophrenia, such as peculiar ideas and odd, inappropriate affect, but without the frank breaks with reality that were seen in schizophrenia. In the older clinical descriptive literature, these individuals were often labeled "borderline," "latent schizophrenic," or "ambulatory schizophrenic" (Stone, 1980); in the *DSM-III*, the term schizotypal was adopted to denote individuals with a phenotypic resemblance to schizophrenics, presumably based on a shared underlying genotype (Meehl, 1990; Spitzer, Endicott, & Givvon, 1979). The *DSM* diagnostic criteria for both schizoid and schizotypal individuals thus shared interpersonal and affective features, notably social isolation and odd or inappropriate affect, similar to the "negative" (i.e., deficit) symptoms of schizophrenia. While schizotypal individuals were presumed to exhibit psychotic-like disturbances of cognition and perception ("positive symptoms"), in practice many individuals met criteria for both disorders, raising further questions about their independence (Kalus, Bernstein, & Siever, 1993). After the adoption of the *DSM-III*, many individuals who were formerly labeled schizoid were now classified as schizotypal. In fact, it has been argued that most of the nosological "territory" formerly occupied by schizoid personality disorder has been claimed by the avoidant and schizotypal personality disorders, leaving a restricted version of the schizoid that applies to relatively few individuals. The very low prevalence of schizoid personality disorder in some studies (Kalus et al., 1993) has caused some to wonder whether schizoid personality disorder, in its present form, has been gerrymandered almost out of existence.

Similar concerns have been raised about the diagnostic boundaries between avoidant and dependent personality disorder on Axis II. Dependent personality disorder is characterized by interpersonal submission, neediness, and fears of separation. Although superficially dissimilar from avoidant personality disorder—the avoidant individual shuns interpersonal intimacy, while the dependent individual seeks it—both share an underlying low self-esteem and lack of self-assertion (Reich, 1990; Trull, Widiger, & Frances, 1987). Moreover, as noted earlier, the avoidant individual may actually crave interpersonal contact, but avoid it owing to fears of rejection. Thus, both avoidant and dependent traits may be present in the same individuals.

Likewise, avoidant personality disorder resembles Axis I social phobia, a condition marked by intense fear or avoidance of specific social or performance situations—for example, speaking in public (Herbert, Hope, & Bellack, 1992; Turner, Beidel, Dancee, & Keys, 1986). While avoidant personality disorder reflects a pervasive avoidance of interpersonal interactions, owing to fear of criticism or rejection, social phobia represents a more circumscribed form of impairment. In clinical practice, however, this distinction often becomes blurred because many avoidant individuals also have specific social anxieties. Moreover, research has shown that discrete social phobias are less common than anxieties across a range of social or performance situations (Turner et al., 1986). As a result, *DSM-III-R* adopted a generalized subtype of social phobia, leading to a further blurring of the boundaries with avoidant personality.

In this chapter, we will discuss the clinical presentation of schizoid and avoidant personality disorders, highlighting some of the diagnostic complexities that arise in differentiating these disorders from each other and from other related Axis I syndromes. A case history illustrating many of these diagnostic issues will be presented. We will then examine the epidemiology of schizoid and avoidant personality disorders and weigh the empirical evidence bearing on the issue of their discriminant validity. Finally, we will review the historical and contemporary theoretical literature on these disorders and evaluate the empirical status of various hypotheses concerning their etiology and development.

Clinical Description

Schizoid individuals typically appear passive and detached, as if they were drifting aimlessly through life. They are emotionally bland, cold, unempathic, or unreactive, and seem insensitive to the nuances of social interaction, including praise and criticism. They are frequently experienced by others as dull or boring and are almost always socially isolated, not from social anxiety and an active avoidance of social situations, but from an incapacity for meaningful social engagement. In fact, the incapacity for social relatedness can be considered the cardinal feature of the disorder (Millon, 1981). Closely connected with the lack of affective investment in social relationships is an inability to take pleasure in activities of either a social or a physical nature. Typically pleasurable activities such taking a walk on a beach, listening to a concert, going dancing, and playing sports are usually found wanting. Sex is seen as overrated. Activities that are pursued are usually solitary, involving interactions with inanimate objects rather than people. Occupations, such as computer programming or mail sorting, which involve a minimum of meaningful social interaction, are preferred. The world is experienced in shades of gray rather than in color.

In contrast to the schizoid's insensitivity to social and aesthetic surroundings, the avoidant can be considered overly sensitive, being acutely and painfully self-conscious in social situations, anticipating rejection and humiliation at every turn. Even casual conversations can be excruciating experiences as the seemingly innocuous remarks of others are scrutinized for hints of criticism or disapproval, and one's own interpersonal conduct is dissected for the embarrassing faux pas. In brief, avoidants are their own worst critics, constantly coming up short in their own estimation. As a result they are usually diffident and inhibited in social situations or find them so aversive that they avoid them altogether. Occasionally patients with avoidant personality disorder succeed in forming friendships, but this is usually only after they feel certain that potential friends are unlikely to criticize or reject them. Even in close friendships, these individuals are often reluctant to take risks or make intimate disclosures for fear of embarrassment or betrayal.

As noted, the differential diagnosis between schizoid and avoidant personality disorders can be difficult. Both are superficially socially inhibited or isolated. Accordingly, the distinction between them hinges on the incapacity for meaningful social relationships in the schizoid, and the desire for and conflict over them in the avoidant. In contrast to schizoids, avoidants are often distressed by their social isolation. They desire connections with others, and their inability to achieve this may leave them lonely and depressed. Some authors have observed that the avoidant individual's superficial indifference to social relationships often masks a profound and intense wish for closeness (Guntrip, 1969; Fairbairn, 1952; Winnicott, 1991). Distinguishing between schizoid and avoidant personality disorders thus depends on an inference about the patient's subjective experience of interpersonal interactions.

In the initial diagnostic interview, this distinction may become clear if the patient acknowledges regret over social isolation or a propensity for self-criticism in social situations. Unfortunately, the awkwardness and inhibition of avoidants often make it difficult to obtain accurate information, particularly before the clinician has had the chance to build rapport. Moreover, the avoidant can be secretive during the interview in order to avoid feeling shameful. Conversations with relatives and friends may prove helpful if such informants are available. To further complicate matters, it has been noted that the clinical presentation of schizoid and avoidant patients may change over time. Livesley and West (1986) reported the case of a patient given an initial diagnosis of schizoid personality disorder who, over the course of treatment, began to exhibit more prominent avoidant features. Thus, extended observation sometimes may be required to clarify an otherwise confusing diagnostic picture.

These diagnostic issues are illustrated by the case of Mr. L., a patient who was seen by one of the authors (D.P.B.) in once-a-week group psychotherapy for approximately three years. Mr. L., a 45-year-old Caucasian, unemployed transit worker, presented for treatment of chronic alcohol addiction. At initial evaluation, he reported drinking steadily since age 15, interrupted only by military duty. While he had worked for many years as a toll booth operator, he had recently lost his job and pension benefits owing to alcohol-related tardiness and absences, the precipitant for his seeking treatment. Mr. L. had never married. Instead, he lived with his mother and spent most of his free time alone in his room engaged in solitary hobbies such as stamp and coin collecting. Mr. L. reported no close friends. Even as a child, he preferred to keep to himself because "people are a bother; I would rather be by myself." He denied that feelings of persecution were the basis for his isolation. Although he described a few brief sexual encounters, they ended as soon as they began to get serious, and he claimed they were not missed. While sometimes annoyed by his mother's complaints and habits, he rarely expressed these feelings to her personally. In fact, he claimed to rarely experience intense feelings of any kind, either positive or negative. When questioned by the examiner, he was unable to think of any recreational activity or intellectual pursuit that got him excited. Mr. L. was passive and compliant throughout the interview, displaying an overly deferential attitude. He claimed no specific plans for the future, other than to achieve sobriety and eventually find a new job.

Based on this initial presentation, Mr. L. was given a diagnosis of schizoid personality disorder. He was socially isolated, lacked close friends or confidants (*DSM-IV* criterion 5), and preferred to keep to himself (criterion 1). He seemed to have little interest in sexual experiences (criterion 3). Most of his activities were solitary ones (criterion 2) from which he derived little pleasure (criterion 4). Mr. L. showed little emotional reactivity, and claimed not to experience intense feelings (criterion 7). Mr. L.'s social isolation appeared to reflect a fundamental lack of emotional investment in others, not paranoid ideation or anxiety about others' negative judgments. These disorders therefore were ruled out. Although he exhibited a few of the negative or deficit schizotypal symptoms, such as constricted affect (criterion 6) and lack of friends or confidants (criterion 8), he did not display the more positive, psychotic-like, schizotypal features such as perceptual illusions, self-referential ideas, or odd beliefs. Therefore, schizotypal personality disorder also was ruled out. While Mr. L.'s bland, passive, and constricted demeanor might be mistaken for dysthymia, his mood was better described as flat than as depressed. Moreover, he did not report associated dysthymic features such as appetite or sleep disturbance, poor concentration, or feelings of hopelessness. Nor did he report specific social phobias. In sum, he exhibited the passive, aimless, and disinterested approach to life characteristic of schizoid personality disorder.

While a schizoid diagnosis seems appropriate for Mr. L., it also must be considered in relation to his chronic alcoholism. Untreated alcoholism usually exhibits a downward, deteriorating course. This can result in schizoidlike characteristics, including increasing abandonment of formerly important social, occupational, or recreational activities. For Mr. L., however, social isolation began in childhood, preceding the onset of drinking. Nor was alcoholism an attempt to overcome social inhibitions and become more comfortable in social situations, as is sometimes seen in avoidant individuals. Mr. L. usually drank alone. Social isolation was, therefore, a longstanding personality feature, not a consequence of a progressive deterioration in social functioning due to drinking.

During his first two years in treatment, Mr. L. attended daily therapy groups focused on maintaining sobriety and succeeded in abstaining from alcohol use. He was rarely an active participant in group, however, and formed no new friendships with other patients. Although he was in regular contact with treatment staff, almost nothing was known about his personal life or history. He was a benign, if innocuous presence, the kind of person who "faded into the woodwork." At the recommendation of his individual counselor, Mr. L. was invited to join a once-a-week process-oriented psychotherapy group led by one of the authors. This group was smaller and less structured than the other groups that Mr. L. had attended, and focused on interpersonal relationships, including interactions among the group members themselves.

Over the next year, Mr. L. slowly began to disclose significant aspects of his personal history. His father had been an alcoholic who had died of liver disease. He remembered his father as a man who was prone to become verbally abusive when drunk, but for the most part led a solitary existence, preferring to watch television alone in his bedroom than to be with his family. His mother was an ever-suffering woman, the "family martyr" who used guilt to control her children. Mr. L. suffered an extraordinary degree of social inhibition and self-contempt, describing himself as extremely uncomfortable and self-critical in social situations. He frequently censored himself for fear of appearing foolish. Although objectively pleasant looking, he was ashamed of his appearance and often admonished himself to dress more neatly. Hours were spent chastising himself for past failures, such as losing his transit job. He was convinced that his life would never amount to anything. Nevertheless, Mr. L. had also become more aware of own isolation and began to contemplate the possibility of forming friendships. However, when other members of the group invited him out for coffee or a movie, he always found reasons to decline.

A turning point in Mr. L.'s treatment occurred when his mother died after a brief illness. As her health deteriorated, he increasingly was called to care for her, becoming more and more exasperated by her rigid and controlling behavior. After being repeatedly confronted by the group, he finally admitted feeling angry toward her. This came almost as a revelation, his first recognition of any strong emotion. Shortly thereafter he talked about the absence of pleasure in his life, and the fact that absolutely nothing gave him enjoyment. When his mother finally died, he was unable to cry at her funeral. His incipient access to feelings was replaced by an emotional numbing. About a month after his mother's death, however, he came to a new realization: his mother was a mystery to him. Though he had lived with her nearly every day of his entire life, he knew almost nothing about her. He was thus free to begin the process of mourning, and was able to experience sadness for the first time. His mother's death eventually provided an impetus for greater self-sufficiency. He formed a social relationship with several members of the group. These new friends described him as "a good listener" who rarely revealed much about himself. He now took pride in keeping his refrigerator stocked with food, and took pleasure in his regular Sunday morning routine of coffee and the newspaper. With some trepidation he enrolled in a computer course and, despite some feelings of inadequacy, pursued it to completion. He also appeared to have gained a greater measure of self-acceptance, stating that perhaps he "wasn't so bad" after all.

Five years after his initial diagnosis of schizoid personality disorder, Mr. L. now appeared to meet many of the *DSM-IV* criteria for avoidant personality disorder. He felt unattractive to others (criterion 6), and was tormented by self-criticism (criterion 4). His feelings of inadequacy resulted in marked inhibition in social situations (criterion 5). He was only willing to form friendships (for example, with the other group members) after being certain of approval (criterion 2), but even then showed an undue degree of restraint in interpersonal relationships (criterion 3). He typically avoided any new activities that carried the possibility of embarrassment or criticism (criterion 1), and only embarked on such activities (for example, the computer programming course) after overcoming considerable personal reluctance (criterion 7).

Along with these avoidant features, Mr. L. continued to display many of the traits of schizoid personality disorder, though in somewhat attenuated form. For example, while his demeanor had become more animated—he was now capable of making occasional jokes—he was still emotionally flat and reported difficulties in identifying and expressing feelings. Similarly his range of pleasurable activities, though increased, was still limited, with a need for solitude far in excess of the average person. Thus, Mr. L.'s clinical presentation now comprised a mixture of schizoid and avoidant personality features.

Interestingly, Mr. L.'s history also illustrated many of the risk factors theorized to contribute to the development of both the schizoid and avoidant personalities. His father exhibited a marked tendency toward social avoidance and emotional aloofness, raising the possibility that these schizoid traits were intergenerationally transmitted, through either hereditary or environmental mechanisms—a leading etiological hypothesis since the inception of the schizoid concept. The emotional distance within his family, a father who was grossly uncommunicative, a mother who was more subtly unavailable, is consistent with psychoanalytic theory on the role of emotional deprivation in the development of schizoid personality disorder. The rigid, controlling behavior displayed by his mother is consistent with recent speculation that parental overprotection—that is, excessive control combined with low parental warmth—contributes to the development of avoidant personality disorder. Finally, the verbally abusive behavior of his father is consistent with theory and research suggesting that emotional denigration contributes to low self-esteem, a cardinal feature of avoidant personality disorder. Thus, Mr. L.'s history largely converges with the major hypotheses about the etiology of schizoid and avoidant personality disorders.

The case of Mr. L. also illustrates the point that, although schizoid and avoidant individuals may be initially difficult to engage in treatment, group psychotherapy can be a powerful means of affecting change in these patients by providing corrective feedback regarding their detached interpersonal styles and an opportunity to form attachments in a relatively safe environment. Of course, the schizoid or avoidant person's ability to make use of these experiences will depend on his or her latent capacity for interpersonal closeness and connectedness, which varies greatly across these individuals and may not be immediately apparent.

Prevalence Schizoid personality disorder is a comparatively rare diagnosis in both general population and clinical samples. Avoidant personality disorder is more prevalent. In a large, randomly selected community sample of adolescents, schizoid was among the least common personality disorder diagnoses. Only 1.8% of adolescents were diagnosed as schizoid, compared to 2.7% diagnosed as avoidant (Bernstein, Cohen, & Velez, 1993). Unfortunately, the scarcity of epidemiological studies of personality disorders (Weissman, 1993) makes it difficult to estimate the population prevalence of schizoid and avoidant personality disorders with any certainty. In a review of empirical studies conducted for the *DSM-IV* Work Group on personality disorders, Millon and Martinez (1991) estimated the prevalence of avoidant personality disorder to be about 10% in clinically referred individuals, noting that *DSM-III*'s introduction of the avoidant and schizotypal inadvertently may have reduced the prevalence of schizoid personality disorder. Indeed, another review for the work group found the median prevalence of schizoid personality disorder in clinically referred individuals to be only 1% when studies were based on *DSM-III* diagnostic criteria (Kalus, Bernstein, & Siever, 1993). In contrast, a revision of the schizoid diagnostic criteria in the *DSM-III-R* has increased the prevalence of this disorder, with a median value of 8.5%. Thus, reports of the demise of schizoid personality disorder may have been premature. Some studies have found that schizoid personality disorder is more common in males than females (Kass, Spitzer, & Williams, 1983), perhaps related to the societal tendency for men to be more emotionally constricted. In contrast, a few studies have found that avoidant personality disorder is more prevalent in females (Zimmerman & Coryell, 1989).

Diagnostic Comorbidity

A recent empirical review concluded that, despite considerable variation in rates of comorbidity across studies, schizoid frequently is associated with avoidant and schizotypal personality disorders (Kalus et al., 1993). A median of 53% of avoidants also received a schizoid diagnosis, while 38% of schizotypals were also diagnosed as schizoid. Lesser degrees of comorbidity were shown with paranoid, antisocial, borderline, and passive-aggressive personality disorders.

Avoidant personality disorder also overlaps extensively with dependent personality disorder (Reich, 1990; Trull et al., 1987). In one study of psychiatric inpatients, 71% of avoidants received a diagnosis of dependent personality, while 50% of dependents also received an avoidant diagnosis (Trull et al., 1987).

Not surprisingly, the high degree of diagnostic overlap between schizoid and avoidant personality disorders has raised questions about their status as discrete disorders. Some authors have raised the same issue on theoretical grounds, noting that the historical literature contains descriptions of "schizoid" individuals whose superficial indifference to social relations masks an underlying interpersonal hypersensitivity (Livesley & West, 1986). Several studies have examined this issue by comparing the test performance of patients diagnosed with these disorders. In a small sample, Overholser (1989), for example, found that schizoid and avoidant could not be differentiated by measures of anxiety, depression, psychosis, or introversion. In contrast, Trull et al. (1987) found that patients with avoidant personality disorder could be distinguished from other personality disordered patients on scales measuring anxiety, somatization, and dysthymia, though no direct comparison with schizoid was made. Moreover, all but one of the avoidant personality disorder criteria, social withdrawal, were negatively correlated with the criteria of schizoid personality disorder, strongly supporting the discriminant validity of the disorders. Although the findings of Trull et al. (1987) are reassuring, further studies are needed to determine whether the phenomenological distinction between schizoid and avoidant personality disorders is indeed meaningful.

Interestingly, the differentiation between avoidant and dependent personality disorders is possibly even more problematic. In addition to the disorders' high rate of comorbidity, Trull et al. (1987) found their respective symptoms to be highly correlated. In fact, the criteria for dependent personality disorder were nearly as predictive of an avoidant personality disorder diagnosis as were the criteria for avoidant personality disorder itself. Similarly, Reich (1990) found only minor differences between avoidant and dependent personality disorders across a variety of psychological tests. Patients with dependent personality disorder were more likely to be female, while those with avoidant personality disorder exhibited more self-defeating traits. Despite their superficial dissimilarity, avoidant and dependent personality disorders may lack discriminant validity.

Schizoid and avoidant personality disorders also show comorbidity with several Axis I disorders, particularly social phobia (Alneas & Torgersen, 1988). As Millon and Martinez (1991) have pointed out, the theoretical distinction between avoidant personality disorder and social phobia is that "avoidant personality disorder is essentially a problem of relating to persons, whereas social phobia is largely a problem of performing in situations" (p. 222). In other words, the avoidant individual has a limited range of interpersonal contacts owing to fear of social disapprobation; the social phobic, on the other hand, may have normal friendships, but has specific fears of performing in social settings—for example, speaking or eating in public. Although this distinction appears to be a theoretically meaningful one, research has raised questions about the discriminant validity of avoidant personality disorder and social phobia, particularly since the introduction of a generalized subtype of social phobia in the *DSM-III-R* (i.e., social performance fears in most situations). In one study (Herbert et al., 1992), for example, all subjects diagnosed with avoidant personality disorder also received a diagnosis of generalized social phobia. On the other hand, several studies have suggested that avoidant personality disorder may be associated with greater social impairment and more severe psychopathology than social phobia. Turner et al. (1986) found that, although social phobics showed considerable distress and avoidance, significantly greater impairment was found in avoidant personality disorder, including poorer social skills, more self-reported social avoidance and distress, and greater interpersonal sensitivity. Herbert et al. (1992) found that, compared to subjects with generalized social phobia only, generalized social phobics with a comorbid diagnosis of avoidant personality disorder were more impaired on measures on anxiety, depression, social distress, fear of negative social evaluation, and overall psychopathology. Thus, comorbid avoidant personality disorder diagnosis may indicate a particularly severe variant of social phobia. Further research will be required to determine whether avoidant personality disorder and social phobia are conceptualized validly as distinct disorders or whether they are merely slightly different descriptions of the same disorder, prepared by separate *DSM-IV* work groups.

Historical Perspectives

The earliest descriptions of schizoid personality disorder can be traced to the European phenomenological psychiatrist, Eugene Bleuler. Bleuler (1924) observed that both schizoid and schizophrenic individuals shared an indifference to external reality and an overvaluation of internal life, and therefore viewed schizoid phenomena as forming a continuum with schizophrenia. Bleuler's observations were elaborated by Kretschmer (1925), who introduced the concept of anesthetic (i.e., insensitive) and hyperaesthetic (i.e., hypersensitive) personality traits, forming the basis for the later distinction between schizoid and avoidant personality disorders in *DSM-III*.

Psychoanalytic theorists of the British Object Relations school made major contributions to the elaboration of the schizoid concept. In her seminal writings, Melanie Klein (1996) speculated that the roots of schizoid personality organization could be found in the infant's difficulty integrating the nurturing and depriving aspects of caregiving figures, a phenomenon she referred to as "splitting." Although all infants passed through a "paranoid/

schizoid" phase of psychosocial development, persistent difficulties in achieving a more integrated view of caregiving during this period could lead to lasting fears of persecution and psychological disintegration, along with a subjective sense of emptiness and an inability to experience emotions. Individuals with this developmental history typically appeared withdrawn, detached, and lacking in spontaneity, with a tenuous attachment to others.

Klein's views on schizoid phenomena were further refined by other adherents of the British school, including Fairbairn (1952), Winnicott (1991), and Guntrip (1969). Although Klein did not explicitly link schizoid phenomena to the actual behavior of maternal figures, these later theorists viewed schizoid experience as the result of extreme maternal deprivation—that is, a catastrophic failure of maternal attuneness to the developing infant's needs. Fairbairn (1952) believed that to develop a healthy and spontaneous sense of self, a child needed to be loved unselfishly or unconditionally. When caregivers failed to meet this need, children came to fear that love itself was destructive, that loving would result in them or their love objects being left empty and depleted. Future schizoids, therefore, turned their affective investment inwards, toward the world of ideas and away from human contact. Although they might wish to give and receive love, externally they shunned it. As a result, they often appeared remote, detached, and inhuman, "as if" they were playing a role, but had no real feelings.

Fairbairn's notion of the "as if" personality was further developed by Winnicott (1991), who introduced the concept of the "false self." According to Winnicott, a degree of maternal attuneness to the needs of the infant is necessary to ensure the development of a healthy, spontaneous sense of self—that is, the "true self." The false self, on the other hand, is the adaptive, compliant aspect of the personality that develops in response to inevitable failures of the caregiving environment. The false self serves the necessary and universal function of mediating between the developing person and external social reality. Under normal conditions, the false self serves this necessary protective function and allows the true self to grow and strengthen. When environmental failures are extreme, however, the false self comes to dominate the entire personality, while the true self remains hidden. The developing child thus becomes passive, compliant, and imitative, lacking in spontaneous emotional expression and genuine relatedness. As a result, when interacting with schizoid individuals, one often feels something essential to be missing. Subjectively these persons often feel incomplete and depersonalized.

Guntrip cogently described the experience of the schizoid: "Complaints of feeling cut off, shut off, out of touch, feeling apart or strange, of things being out of focus or unreal, of not feeling one with people, or of the point having gone out of life, interest flagging, things seeming futile and meaningless . . . " (1969, pp. 16–18). He also noted that schizoid persons could appear either anxious and uncomfortable, or cold, reserved, and unfeeling, presaging the distinction between avoidant and schizoid personality disorders in the *DSM-III*. In essence, Guntrip saw schizoids as being starved for love, and as protecting themselves from this longing by denying their needs and withdrawing from relationships. This conflict between intense dependency needs and a powerful fear of them sometimes manifested itself in a flight in and out of relationships, careers, jobs, homes, and so forth.

Whereas the schizoid personality has a long tradition, avoidant personality disorder was introduced by Millon (1981) and first recognized in the *DSM-III*. Although Millon has acknowledged that the literature on the historical antecedents of avoidant personality disorder is sparse, he contended that the historical roots of this concept can be found in descriptions by Kretschmer (1925) of the "hyperaesthetic" temperament; writings on the schizoid personality by adherents of British Object Relations school (Fairbairn, 1952; Winnicott, 1991; Guntrip, 1969); and classic psychoanalytic writings on the "phobic character" (Fenichel, 1945; Rado, 1956; MacKinnon & Michels, 1971). As noted above, Guntrip also described a subgroup of schizoid individuals who appeared anxious and uncomfortable in social situations and who, unlike schizoid persons who were outwardly cold and unfeeling, were aware of their needs for dependency. Several classical psychoanalytic theorists (Fenichel, 1945; Rado, 1956; MacKinnon & Michels, 1971) used the phrase "phobic character" or similar terms to describe individuals for whom avoidance was a predominant defensive mechanism. According to this formulation, avoidance was a means of managing the anxiety stemming from internal conflicts over unacceptable wishes. These individuals often employed elaborate precautions to avoid situations that were potentially anxiety arousing, but were capable of forming interpersonal attachments.

Contemporary Views and Empirical Evidence

Contemporary psychoanalytic perspectives on the schizoid personality have stressed the use of primitive defense mechanisms, such as splitting, or the tendency to see others as either "all good" or "all bad"; and projective identification, or inducing one's own unacceptable feelings in others, that are shared in common with other forms of severe character pathology—for example, borderline personality disorder. Kernberg (1984) conceptualized the schizoid as a form of lower lever ("borderline") character pathology in which impulsiveness predominates over the ability to delay gratification; primitive defenses such as splitting are employed rather than more adaptive means of coping; one's sense of personal identity is confused, fragmented, and diffuse; and moral values are poorly internalized. Similarly, Ahktar (1987) has emphasized the importance of distinguishing between the overt and covert manifestations of schizoid personality disorder. Thus, patients with schizoid and borderline personality disorder may be superficially dissimilar (e.g., the schizoid appears cold and unemotional, while the borderline shows exaggerated emotionality), but share an underlying lower level personality organization in which splitting and identity diffusion are central. In fact, for Ahktar (1987), the discrepancy between the inner and outer person is the defining characteristic of schizoid personality disorder. For example, while schizoids may appear overtly asexual, their sexual fantasy lives are often elaborate and perverse. Similarly, the schizoid person's apparent emotional indifference may hide an exquisite underlying sensitivity. For this reason, Ahktar and others (Livesley & West, 1986) have criticized the *DSM-III*'s description of schizoid personality disorder as an oversimplification that ignores the contradictions between superficial and "deeper" manifestations of the schizoid syndrome, as well as the *DSM-III*'s decision to categorize schizoid and avoidant personality disorders as separate diagnostic entities.

In contrast to the rich historical literature on schizoid personality disorder, little empirical research has been conducted on its pathogenesis. The few studies that have investigated the familial/genetic transmission of schizoid personality disorder have found little evidence that schizoid personality disorder is heritable, or that it is genetically related to schizophrenia (Baron et al., 1985; Gunderson, Siever, & Spaulding, 1983). Torgersen (1985) has reported that preliminary findings from a Norwegian twin study show negligible heritability for schizoid personality disorder. However, about one third of the variance in schizoid traits was attributable to family environmental factors, suggesting that schizoid personality disorder may indeed be familially related, but on a environmental rather than a genetic basis.

In contrast to the paucity of evidence for the heritability of schizoid personality disorder, there is ample evidence that schizotypal personality disorder is genetically transmitted, and that it is prevalent in the biological relatives of schizophrenics (Siever, Bernstein, & Silverman, 1991). As noted earlier, the major revision of the diagnostic nomenclature in the *DSM-III* created a new diagnostic category, schizotypal personality disorder, that encompassed some patients who would have formerly been considered "schizoid." These schizotypal individuals evinced emotional deficit (i.e., negative) symptoms that are similar to those seen in schizoid personality disorder, along with perceptual and ideational (i.e., positive) symptoms, such as perceptual illusions and ideas of reference. It seems plausible that some of the early clinical literature linking schizoid personality disorder to schizophrenia was based on observations of patients who would today be diagnosed as schizotypal. Nevertheless, further twin and adoption studies will be needed to definitively determine whether schizoid personality disorder as it is currently conceived lies on a "schizophrenia spectrum."

Millon (1981) has speculated that schizoid individuals may be temperamentally placid and underresponsive, and therefore evoke little reciprocal attention, affection, and stimulation from caregivers. The result is a negative feedback loop that reinforces the child's own innate tendency toward emotional detachment. Millon (1981) has also noted, however, that extreme emotional deprivation may lead to schizoid withdrawal, even in a child of normal temperament. Quoting a case described by Deutsch (1942), Millon (1981) noted that the experiential histories of schizoid individuals are often characterized by a virtual absence of parental warmth and affection. Unfortunately, there has been little attempt to confirm either of these developmental hypotheses. One recent study (Bernstein & Stein, 1997), however, suggests that schizoid personality disorder may in fact be linked to emotional deprivation in childhood. In a study of adult substance abusers, patients were asked to complete a series of self-report questionnaires including measures of childhood abuse and neglect and adult personality characteristics. Schizoid personality traits were specifically predicted by self-reported emotional deprivation in childhood; in contrast, other personality disorder characteristics (e.g., antisocial, borderline) were predicted by childhood abuse (physical, sexual, or emotional) rather than deprivation. Although the retrospective nature of this study limits the inferences that can be drawn about causality (it could be argued, for example, that schizoid individuals recall their parents as less emotionally available than they actually were), these findings provide some support for the emotional deprivation hypothesis.

Little longitudinal research has been done on the developmental course of schizoid personality disorder. In the only published study of its kind, Wolff and Chick (1980) followed 20 schizoid children (mean age = 10 years) and 20 matched controls from a child guidance clinic into early adulthood. Nearly all of the schizoid patients retained their initial diagnoses an average of 10 years later, despite an average of two years of psychotherapeutic treatment.In contrast, only one of the matched controls developed a schizoid personality disorder. Although some of the schizoid patients showed improvement in their educational or occupational functioning over time—particularly those patients with higher intelligence—most of them continued to display the same emotional and interpersonal deficits at follow-up as were seen during the initial evaluation. These findings suggest that the symptoms of schizoid personality disorder are relatively stable from childhood into early adulthood, even after children receive intensive psychotherapy.

Recent theorizing on the origins of avoidant personality disorder has been directed toward the role of innate temperament and early experience. Kagan (1989) contends that shyness and inhibition in unfamiliar situations can be traced to a temperamental style, "inhibited temperament," that is observable shortly after birth and has a genetic, physiological basis. His longitudinal research indicates that in the second year of life, approximately 15% of Caucasian children are timid, subdued, or fearful when they encounter unfamiliar adults or children. Moreover, this inhibition shows moderate stability from 2 to 7 years of age, with children who are very inhibited at first assessment being the most likely to maintain an inhibited style. About 75% of inhibited 7-year-olds in the study exhibited fears that were reminiscent of avoidant personality disorder or social phobia, such as speaking in class, attending summer camp, or going to bed alone at night. Kagan's research also suggests that temperamentally inhibited children have lower thresholds of limbic system reactivity, as indicated by increased heart rate, larger pupil diameters, greater motoric tension, and increased morning cortisol secretions. Kagan has suggested that his findings are more consistent with a qualitative rather than a quantitative distinction between inhibited and uninhibited temperamental types, implying that temperamental inhibition has a heritable basis that is analogous to a biological "strain." Nevertheless, since stability of inhibited temperament from infancy to childhood is only moderate, these heritable individual differences can be modified by experience.

Pilkonis (1995) has argued that both heritable temperamental vulnerability and early adverse experiences contribute to the development of avoidant personality disorder. While some individuals may be temperamentally shy, others may develop social fears owing to early narcissistic injuries. For the latter group, early experiences of being scorned and shamed lead to damaged feelings of self-worth and engender an expectation of further humiliation. A similar view has been advanced by Stravynski and colleagues (1989), who posited that parental "overprotection" (i.e., a combination of low parental affection and high parental control) fosters feelings of insecurity, dependency, and inferiority—core characteristics of avoidant personality disorder. However, a comparison of patients with avoidant personality disorder and matched controls on retrospective measures of caregiving provided only partial support for the overprotection hypothesis. Patients with avoidant personality disorder reported less parental affection and more guilt-engendering and rejecting parental behavior in childhood, but not more controlling behavior by parents (Stravynski et al., 1989). Consistent with these findings, other retrospective studies have supported a link between feelings of low self-esteem and childhood emotional/verbal abuse (Briere & Runtz, 1988; Gross & Keller, 1992), and one recent study found that symptoms of avoidant personality disorder were predicted by self-reported emotional abuse, but not by other forms of maltreatment (Bernstein & Stein, 1997). Thus, in contrast to schizoid personality disorder, which may be developmentally related to parental emotional deprivation, avoidant personality disorder may be linked to parental emotional abuse.

Conclusions

The distinction between schizoid and avoidant personality disorders remains a controversial one. A fundamental question is whether these disorders are truly separate or if they represent apparently contradictory traits—that is, superficial insensitivity and underlying hypersensitivity—that can be present in the same individuals. Although there is some empirical evidence supporting the discriminant validity of schizoid and avoidant personality disorders (Trull et al., 1987), only a few such studies have been conducted and further research is clearly needed. Anecdotal evidence (Livesley & West, 1986), including the case material included in this chapter, suggest that both schizoid and avoidant features can be discerned in the same individuals and that the manifestation of these disorders can change over time. At the very least, these case studies suggest the possibility of a mixed type in which schizoid and avoidant features co-occur, and the need for extended observation in some cases in order to formulate an accurate diagnosis. Another related question is whether schizoid personality disorder represents a lower level form of character pathology and can be differentiated from avoidant personality disorder on the basis of more primitive defenses, greater ego impairment, identity diffusion, and so on (Akhtar, 1987; Kernberg, 1984). If this formulation is correct, it would have clear prognostic implications, with schizoid patients expected to show poorer response to treatment. Unfortunately, no controlled studies comparing the treatment outcome of schizoid and avoidant patients have been conducted.

Ultimately, many of the criticisms of the *DSM* schizoid and avoidant diagnosis made by contemporary theorists (e.g., Livesley & West, 1986, Akhtar, 1987) raise fundamental issues about the nature of our nosology of mental disorders—specifically, whether a psychoanalytic, structural perspective on personality disorders that formed much of the historical basis for current descriptions of schizoid and avoidant personality disorders should be incorporated within the phenomenological framework espoused by the *DSM*.

References

Akhtar, S. (1987). Schizoid personality disorder: A synthesis of developmental, dynamic, and descriptive features. *American Journal of Psychotherapy, 41*, 499–518.

Alnaes, R., & Torgersen, S. (1988). DSM-III symptom disorders (Axis I) and personal disorders (Axis II) in an outpatient population. *Acta Psychiatrica Scandanavica, 78*, 348–355.

Baron, M., Gruen, R., Rainer, J. D., Kane, J., Asnis, L., & Lork, S. (1985). A family study of schizophrenic and normal control probands: Implications for the spectrum concept of schizophrenia. *American Journal of Psychiatry, 142*, 447–454.

Bernstein, D. P., Cohen, P., & Velez, N. (1993). Prevalence and stability of the DSM-III-R personality disorders in a community-based survey of adolescents. *American Journal of Psychiatry, 150*, 1237–1243.

Bernstein, D., & Stein, J. (1997). [Childhood trauma and personality disorders in substance abusing patients]. Unpublished raw data.

Bleuler, E. (1924). *Textbook of Psychiatry.* (A. A. Brill, Trans.). New York: Macmillan.

Briere, J., & Runtz, M. (1988). Multivariate correlates of childhood psychological and physical maltreatment among university women. *Child Abuse and Neglect, 12*, 331–341.

Deutsch, H. (1942). Some forms of emotional disturbance and their relationship to schizophrenia. *Psychoanalytic Quarterly, 11*, 301–321.

Fairbairn, W. R. D. (1952). *Psychoanalytic studies of the personality.* London: Routledge and Kegan Paul.

Fenichel, O. (1945). *The psychoanalytic theory of neurosis.* New York: Norton.

Gross, A. B., & Keller, H. R. (1992). Long-term consequences of childhood physical and psychological maltreatment. *Aggressive Behavior, 18*, 171–185.

Gunderson, J. G., Siever, L. J., & Spaulding, E. (1983). The search for a schizotype: Crossing the border again. *Archives of General Psychiatry, 40*, 15–22.

Guntrip, H. (1969). *Schizoid phenomena, object-relations and the self.* New York: International Universities Press.

Herbert, J., Hope, D., & Bellack, A. (1992). Validity of the distinction between generalized social phobia and avoidant personality disorder. *Journal of Abnormal Psychology, 101*, 332–339.

Kagan, J. (1989). Temperamental contributions to social behavior. *American Psychologist, 44*, 668–674.

Kalus, O., Bernstein, D., & Siever, L. (1993). Schizoid personality disorder: A review of current status and implications for DSM-IV. *Journal of Personality Disorders, 3*, 43–52.

Kass, F., Spitzer, R. L., & Williams, J. B. (1983). An empirical study of sex bias in the diagnostic criteria of DSM-III Axis II personality disorders. *American Psychologist, 38*, 799–801.

Kernberg, O. (1984). *Severe personality disorders*. New Haven: Yale University Press.

Kety, S. S., Rosenthal, D., Wender, P. H., & Schulsinger, F. (1971). Mental illness in the biological and adoptive families of adopted schizophrenics. *American Journal of Psychiatry, 128*, 302–306.

Klein, M. (1996). Notes on some schizoid mechanisms. *Journal of Psychotherapy Practice and Research, 5*, 164–179.

Kretschmer, E. (1925). *Physique and character.* New York: Harcourt Brace.

Livesley, J. W., & West, M. (1986). The DSM-III distinction between schizoid and avoidant personality disorders. *Canadian Journal of Psychiatry, 31*, 59–62.

MacKinnon, R. A., & Michels, R. (1971). *The psychiatric interview in clinical practice*. Philadelphia: W. B. Saunders.

Meehl, P. (1990). Toward an intergrated theory of schizotaxia, schizotypy, and schizophrenia. *Journal of Personality Disorders, 4*, 1–99.

Millon, T. (1981). *Disorders of personality: DSM-III, Axis II*. New York: Wiley-Interscience.

Millon, T., & Martinez, A. (1991). Avoidant personality disorder. *Journal of Personality Disorders, 5*, 353–362.

Olverholser, J. (1989). Differentiation between schizoid and avoidant personalities: An empirical test. *Canadian Journal of Psychiatry, 34* (8), 785–790.

Pilkonis, P. A. (1995). Commentary on avoidant personality disorder: Temperament, shame, or both? In J. Livesley (Ed.), *The DSM-IV personality disorders*, pp. 218–233. Washington, DC: American Psychiatric Association.

Rado, S. (1956). *Psychoanalysis of behavior: Collected papers*. New York: Grune and Stratton.

Reich, J. (1990). The relationship between DSM-III avoidant and dependent personality disorders. *Psychiatry Research, 34*, 218–292.

Siever, L., Bernstein, D., & Silverman, J. (1991). Schizoptypal personality disorder: A review of its current status. *Journal of Personality Disorders, 5*, 178–193.

Spitzer, R. L., Endicott J., & Givvon, M. (1979). Crossing the border into borderline personality and borderline schizophrenia: The development of criteria. *Archives of General Psychiatry, 36*, 17–24.

Stone, M. (1980). *The borderline syndromes: Constitution, personality, and adaptation*. New York: McGraw-Hill.

Stravynski, A., Elie, R., & Franche, R. L. (1989). Perception of early parenting by patients diagnosed avoidant personality disorder: A test of the overprotection hypothesis. *Acta Psychiatrica Scandinavica, 80*, 415–420.

Torgersen, S. (1985). Relationship of schizoptypal personality disorder to schizophrenia: Genetics. *Schizophrenia Bulletin, 11*, 554–563.

Trull, T. J., Widiger, T. A., & Frances, A. (1987). Covariation of criteria sets for avoidant, schizoid, and dependent personality disorder. *American Journal of Psychiatry, 144*, 767–772.

Turner, S. M., Beidel, D. C., Dancee, C. V., & Keys, D. J. (1986). Psychopathology of social phobia and comparison to avoidant personality disorder. *Journal of Abnormal Psychology, 95*, 389–394.

Weissman, M. (1993). The epidemiology of personality disorders: A 1990 Update. *Journal of Personality Disorders, 7* (Suppl.), 44–62.

Winnicott, D. W. (1991). Psychotherapy of character disorders. In M. Kets de Vries & S. Perzow (Eds.), *Handbook of Character Studies: Psychoanalytic Explorations* (pp. 461–475). Madison, CT: International Universities Press.

Wolff, S., & Chick, J. (1980). Schizoid personality in childhood: A controlled follow-up study. *Psychological Medicine, 10*, 85–100.

Zimmerman, M., & Coryell, W. (1989). DSM-III personality disorder diagnoses in a nonpatient sample. *Archives of General Psychiatry, 46*, 682–689.

21

Dependent and Histrionic Personality Disorders

ROBERT F. BORNSTEIN

Clinicians and researchers have long recognized that dependent personality disorder (DPD) and histrionic personality disorder (HPD) share at least one important feature: both are rooted in exaggerated, inflexible dependency needs. Dependency-related behaviors are present in both sets of diagnostic criteria as described in the *DSM-IV*. Moreover, both DPD and HPD have a long psychoanalytic history. Beginning with Freud (1905, 1915, 1923), and continuing with the work of Abraham (1927), Fenichel (1945), Reich (1933, 1949), and others (e.g., Kernberg, 1984; Kohut, 1971), psychoanalytic theorists and researchers have devoted considerable time and effort to exploring the intrapsychic dynamics that underly dependent and histrionic (or hysterical) personality traits. In fact, DPD and HPD have received a great deal of attention from clinicians of many different theoretical orientations, who have speculated on many occasions regarding the therapeutic approaches that are most (and least) effective in treating these disorders (see Beck & Freeman, 1990; Millon, 1981; Millon & Davis, 1996).

While DPD and HPD have much in common, there are also noteworthy differences. Most important, DPD and HPD individuals have very different presentation styles: HPD is typically associated with an active, seductive stance in interpersonal relationships, whereas DPD is generally associated with a more subservient, submissive quality. Beyond this, clinical researchers have shown much greater interest in DPD than HPD during the past two decades. Since the publication of the *DSM-III*, there have been many more studies examining the etiology and dynamics of DPD than of HPD.

This chapter reviews the theory, research, and clinical data bearing on the dependent and histrionic personality disorders. Definitional and diagnostic issues are discussed, and the literature on epidemiology and comorbidity is then reviewed. The most influential theoretical perspectives on each disorder are described, and research evidence related to these theoretical frameworks is assessed. Following these reviews of the DPD and HPD literature, suggestions for further research examining particular aspects of each disorder are offered.

Dependent Personality Disorder

A detailed review of the empirical literature suggests that dependency is best conceptualized as a personality style (or "type") characterized by four primary components (Bornstein, 1992): (1) *motivational* (i.e., a marked need for guidance, approval, and support from others); (2) *cognitive* (i.e., a perception of the self as relatively powerless, along with the belief that others are comparatively powerful and potent); (3) *affective* (i.e., a tendency to become anxious and fearful when required to function independently, especially when the products of one's efforts will be evaluated by others); and (4) *behavioral* (i.e., a tendency to seek help, support, approval, guidance, and reassurance from others). The eight symptoms of DPD listed in the *DSM-IV* focus primarily on two of these four components: behavioral (symptoms 1, 2, 4, and 5), and affective (symptoms 3, 6, 7, and 8). As will become apparent, the absence of any DPD symptoms capturing the cognitive aspects of dependency represents a significant problem for the *DSM-IV* DPD criteria. Without attention to these cognitive components it becomes difficult to conceptualize adequately or predict accurately the behavior of the dependent individual in laboratory, clinical, and field settings (Bornstein, 1995, 1997).

One other limitation of the DPD criteria warrants brief discussion in this context. As Livesley, Schroeder, and Jackson (1990) pointed out, the *DSM* criteria for DPD capture attachment-related behaviors (e.g., fear of disapproval by a significant caregiver/protector) in addition to the more generalized help-, support-, and nurturance-seeking orientation characteristic of dependency. To be sure, there is reason to expect that high levels of expressed dependency needs will be associated with an insecure attachment style (Sperling & Berman, 1991). Nonetheless, the inclusion of attachment-related behaviors in the DPD symptom criteria has implications for differential diagnosis and overlap between DPD and other Axis II personality disorders.

Diagnosis of DPD is complicated by the fact that the array of dependency-related symptoms and behaviors presented by the DPD patient vary markedly as a function of gender, ethnicity, and age. In general, men tend to express dependency-related symptoms and behaviors in a more indirect and disguised manner than women do (Ford & Widiger, 1989; Kaplan, 1983). Not surprisingly, men almost invariably obtain lower scores than women on dependency tests with high face validity, but women and men obtain comparable scores on dependency tests with low face validity (Bornstein, Rossner, Hill, & Stepanian, 1994). Paradoxically, however, even though women are more willing than men to acknowledge DPD characteristics, these characteristics are more noticeable in men than in women because they are inconsistent with the traditional male gender-role (Loring & Powell, 1988).

Ethnicity complicates DPD diagnosis further because there are profound cultural differences in attitudes regarding dependency and autonomy. In most Western societies autonomy and self-reliance are valued more strongly than interdependency and connectedness, so that dependent behaviors almost always carry a connotation of immaturity and pathology (Bornstein, 1994). In certain cultures, however—most notably Japan (Johnson, 1993) and India (Kaul, Mathur, & Murlidharan, 1982)—dependent behaviors and affiliative strivings in adults are not only tolerated but also actually expected (and in many instances rewarded). The higher levels of "normal" dependency expressed by individuals from these cultures can lead to inappropriate, excessive DPD diagnoses in members of various cultural groups.

The DPD symptom picture also varies as a function of age. Thus, the support that dependent persons solicit from others is often linked to their perceived vulnerabilities (e.g., instrumental, financial, medical). Such perceptions may, of course, be related to objective needs and deficits. For example, among individuals who experience health-related vulnerabilities, dependency is often expressed in terms of exaggerated expressions of need for health-oriented support. This is especially common in older adults (Baltes, 1996; Emery & Lesher, 1982).

Epidemiology and Comorbidity

Studies assessing the prevalence of DPD in various settings and populations have produced varying results. Some investigations (e.g., Alnaes & Torgerson, 1988) have found DPD prevalence rates as high as 47% among outpatients. Other similar studies have reported prevalence rates of only 2 to 4% (Stangler & Printz, 1980; Zimmerman & Coryell, 1989). Taken together, studies in this area suggest that DPD prevalence rates in most inpatient and outpatient settings average between 5 and 15% (Jackson, Rudd, Gazis, & Edwards, 1991; Piersma, 1987). DPD prevalence rates in the general adult population appear to range from about 2 to 8%, depending upon the sample surveyed and the diagnostic instruments used (Kass, Spitzer, & Williams, 1983; Zimmerman & Coryell, 1989).

The *DSM-IV* assertion that "the sex ratio of [DPD] is not significantly different than the sex ration of females within the respective clinical setting" (p. 667) is incorrect, and contradicted by a plethora of published investigations (Bornstein, 1996b). Studies consistently demonstrate that women receive DPD diagnoses at higher rates than men do. For example, Kass et al. (1983) found DPD prevalence rates of 11 and 5%, respectively, in women and men from a large community sample. Jackson et al. (1991) found that in a sample of psychiatric inpatients, 25% of women and 11% of men received DPD diagnoses. Other studies have produced similar results. Overall, women are far more likely than men to receive a DPD diagnosis, regardless of the type of setting in which diagnostic information is collected (Bornstein, 1997).

DPD shows substantial comorbidity with a variety of Axis I and Axis II disorders. On Axis I, DPD is associated with eating disorders (Tisdale, Pendleton, & Marler, 1990; Wonderlich, Swift, Slotnick, & Goodman, 1990), anxiety disorders (Alnaes & Torgerson, 1988, 1990), and somatization disorder (Hayward & King, 1990; Rost, Atkins, Brown, & Smith, 1992). Although there is some tendency for depressed patients to receive DPD diagnoses at higher rates than nondepressed patients, most studies examining the DPD-depression link have obtained inconclusive results (see Joffe, Swinson, & Regan, 1988; Maier, Lichtermann, Klingler, Heun, & Hallmeyer, 1992). On Axis II, DPD shows substantial comorbidity with schizoid, avoidant, schizotypal, borderline, and histrionic personality disorders (McCann, 1991; Zimmerman & Coryell, 1989).

Historical Perspectives

Neki (1976) pointed out that, although some societies condemn dependency while others embrace it, virtually every culture has recognized and described highly dependent individuals (see also Ainsworth, 1969; Parens & Saul, 1971). Modern thinking on the dependent personality can be traced to Kraepelin (1913) and Schneider (1923), who described precursors of what would eventually emerge as DPD in the *DSM* series. Although Kraepelin (1913) described the dependent person as "shiftless" while Schneider (1923) used the term "weak-willed," both theorists agreed that the dependent person was immature, compliant, gullible, and easily exploited by others.

Around the same time that Kraepelin (1913) and Schneider (1923) were describing the central features of pathological dependency, an independent stream of theoretical work was emerging in the psychoanalytic domain. First discussed by Freud (1905), and later elaborated by Abraham (1927), Fenichel (1945), and others, the psychoanalytic conceptualization of the "oral dependent" person bore a strong resemblance to contemporary viewpoints regarding dependency. Thus, Abraham (1927, p. 400) noted that dependent persons "are dominated by the belief that there will always be some kind person—a representative of the mother, of course—to care for them and give them everything they want. This optimistic belief condemns them to inactivity. . . . They make no kind of effort, and in some cases they even disdain to undertake a bread-winning occupation."

Neoanalytic theorists like Fromm (1947), Horney (1945), and Sullivan (1947) offered similar descriptions of dependent individuals. For example, speculating regarding the parental roots of dependency, Sullivan (1947, p. 84) suggested that "these people have been obedient children of a dominating parent. They go through life needing a strong person to make decisions for them. . . . [They] learned their helplessness and clinging vine adaptation from parental example."

The influence of Sullivan's work is evident in the *DSM-I* precursor of DPD, the "Passive-aggressive personality, passive-dependent type." Such individuals were characterized by "helplessness, indecisiveness, and a tendency to cling to others as a dependent child to a supporting parent" (p. 37). Strangely, the concept of the dependent personality received less attention in the *DSM-II*, where the passive-dependent personality was relegated to a "catch-all" category of Other Personality Disorders of Specified Types, a grouping that also included the "immature" personality.

Finally, a full-fledged category of DPD was included in the *DSM-III, DSM-III-R*, and *DSM-IV*. In the *DSM-III*, DPD was described in very general terms, and the central symptoms included: (1) an inability to function independently; (2) a willingness to subordinate one's needs to those of others; and (3) a lack of self-confidence. In contrast, the *DSM-III-R* and *DSM-IV* criteria for DPD are more detailed, including an array of behavioral and affective symptoms.

Contemporary Theoretical Perspectives

Although a wide variety of theoretical frameworks have been offered (Bornstein, 1992, 1993), three contemporary theoretical viewpoints have been particularly influential in the study of DPD. In the following sections I describe the psychoanalytic, biosocial-learning, and cognitive models of dependency, and review research testing each of these models.

The Psychoanalytic Perspective In classical psychoanalytic theory, dependency is inextricably linked to the infantile oral stage of development (Freud, 1905). Frustration or overgratification during the oral stage is hypothesized to result in oral "fixation" and an inability to resolve the developmental issues that characterize this stage (i.e., conflicts regarding dependency and autonomy). Thus, classical psychoanalytic theory postulates that the orally fixated (or "oral dependent") person will: (1) remain dependent on others for nurturance, guidance, and support; and (2) continue to exhibit behaviors in adulthood that reflect activities of the infantile oral stage (e.g., preoccupation with activities of the mouth, reliance on food and eating to cope with anxiety).

Early in his career Freud (1908, p. 167) discussed in general terms the links between "fixation" and the development of particular personality traits, noting that "one very often meets with a type of character in which certain traits are very strongly marked while at the same time one's attention is arrested by the behavior of these persons in regard to certain bodily functions." Subsequently, Freud (1938, p. 222) was more explicit in linking personality development to the feeding experience during infancy, arguing that "a child sucking at his mother's breast becomes the prototype of every relation of love." The evolution of Freud's thinking in this area paralleled what turned out to be, in retrospect, a pervasive trend in classical psychoanalytic theory, namely an ever-increasing emphasis on social rather than biological factors as key elements in personality development (Greenberg & Mitchell, 1983).

The object relations model of dependency extends the classical psychoanalytic model by emphasizing the internalization of mental representations of the parents (and other significant figures) as critical developmental tasks of infancy and early childhood (Bornstein, 1996a). By focusing on mental representations that are formed during the first few years of life, object relations theory alters the focus of psychoanalysis, shifting the theoretical emphasis from the study of Oedipal dynamics to the phenomenon of infantile dependency as a key factor in normal and pathological personality development (Greenberg & Mitchell, 1983; Kernberg, 1975).

In object relations theory, social exchange between caregiver and infant is viewed as the key to the development of a dependent personality orientation. During the past two decades, Blatt's (1974) theoretical framework has been one of the most influential perspectives in this area. Blatt and his colleagues (e.g., Blatt & Shichman, 1983) have argued that dependent personality traits result from the internalization of a mental representation of the self as weak and ineffectual. Such a self-representation leads the individual to: (1) look to others to provide protection, guidance, and support; (2) become preoccupied with fears of abandonment; and (3) behave in a dependent, help-seeking manner, especially toward potential nurturers and protectors (Blatt, Cornell, & Eshkol, 1993; Bornstein, 1992, 1993).

Studies testing the classical psychoanalytic model of dependency have generally produced weak results. There have been numerous studies assessing the relationships of various feeding and weaning variables to dependency levels in childhood, adolescence, and adulthood, but these investigations have failed to delineate any strong or consistent connection between feeding or weaning experiences and later dependency (see, e.g., Heinstein, 1963; Sears, 1963). To be sure, there have been some noteworthy methodological flaws in many of these investigations (see Bornstein, 1996a, for a review). Nonetheless, no published study conducted to date has provided unambiguous support for a feeding/weaning–dependency link. Experimental and factor-analytic studies examining the relationship between dependency and preoccupation with food- and mouth-related activities (e.g., thumb sucking, nail biting, pen chewing) also contradict the classical psychoanalytic model, finding only weak relationships between dependency scores and food/mouth preoccupation scores (Beckwith, 1986; Lazare, Klerman, & Armor, 1966, 1970; Mills & Cunningham, 1988).

A number of investigations have assessed the relationship between dependency and various "oral" psychopathologies (e.g., eating disorders, alcoholism, tobacco addiction). These studies produced mixed results. On the positive side, there is a predictable relationship between dependency and eating disorders: anorexic and bulimic individuals score higher than non–eating-disordered persons on objective and projective measures of dependency (Bornstein & Greenberg, 1991). Anorexics and bulimics also receive DPD diagnoses at higher rates than non–eating-disordered individuals (Jacobson & Robins, 1989; Lenihan & Kirk, 1990). Beyond this, studies have found a significant positive relationship between dependency and risk for tobacco addiction (Jacobs & Spilken, 1971; Veldman & Bown, 1969), and prospective findings indicate that high levels of dependency actually predispose individuals to cigarette smoking, rather than being a correlate or consequence of tobacco use (Vaillant, 1980).

However, studies show that—in contrast to predictions made by the classical psychoanalytic model—increases in dependent traits, attitudes, and behaviors follow (rather than precede) the onset of alcoholism (Jones, 1968; Vaillant, 1980). Despite numerous efforts to delineate a dependency–obesity link, there is no strong or consistent relationship between level of dependency and tendency to engage in pathological overeating during childhood, adolescence, or adulthood (Black, Goldstein, & Mason, 1992; Keith & Vandenberg, 1974).

Bornstein, Galley, and Leone (1986) tested the object relations model of dependency using Blatt, Wein, Chevron, and Quinlan's (1979) Parental Representations Scale to assess qualities of the maternal and paternal introjects (i.e., internalized mental representations of mother and father). Dependent subjects described maternal introjects that were less nurturant, warm, and constructively involved than the maternal introjects of nondependent subjects. However, the magnitudes of these relationships were small, and level of dependency was unrelated to qualities of the paternal introject. Similar findings were subsequently obtained by Sadeh, Rubin, and Berman (1993). Studies examining perceptions and memories of the parents in relation to level of dependency parallel those obtained in investigations where aspects of parental representations were assessed directly (see Head, Baker, & Williamson, 1991).

Using a modified version of the Parental Representations scale, Bornstein, Leone, and Galley (1988) assessed the relationship between level of dependency and qualities of the self-representation in a large sample of college students. Strong results were obtained, with dependent students' self-representations reflecting a view of the self as weak, submissive, and ineffectual. Other studies using different objective and projective self-concept measures (e.g., Birtchnell, 1988; Greenberg & Fisher, 1977) have generally produced results consistent with those of Bornstein et al. Overall, research testing object relations models of dependency suggests that a representation of the self as helpless and in need of support and guidance from others may be associated with exaggerated dependency needs in a variety of participant groups.

The Biosocial-Learning Perspective Millon's (1969, 1981, 1990) biosocial-learning model has probably been the most influential perspective on DPD during the past two decades. This interdisciplinary framework has roots in interpersonal theories of personality. Although interpersonal theories have a long history in psychology and psychiatry, contemporary thinking in this area can be traced largely to the work of Leary (1957) and others who, in different ways, attempted to map various personality styles as two- or three-dimensional spaces. Many variants of this general approach have emerged since the late 1950s, including Benjamin's (1974) Structural Analysis of Social Behavior (SASB) model, and Kiesler's (1982) Interpersonal Circle. Moreover, some researchers have used a modified interpersonal framework to locate dependency (and DPD) along the different dimensions of the five-factor model (e.g., Costa & McCrae, 1990; Shopshire & Craik, 1994).

Despite their surface differences, interpersonal theories share at least two fundamental assumptions: (1) that different personality types may be usefully conceptualized as styles of interacting with and relating to others; and (2) that different personality types can be reduced to some finite number of basic dimensions that—when combined—produce the major personality constellations identified by clinicians and researchers (Wiggins & Pincus, 1989). Beyond this, most interpersonal theories emphasize that personality traits are acquired and maintained through patterns of reward and punishment experienced in key relationships (see, e.g., Benjamin, 1974; Kiesler, 1982). This is an important consideration in the dynamics of dependency, insofar as interpersonal relationships are particularly salient for the dependent individual (Caspi, Bem, & Elder, 1989; Pincus & Gurtman, 1995).

Millon (1969, 1981) broadened interpersonal theory by emphasizing the interaction of organismic and environmental factors in the etiology and dynamics of personality traits and pathologies. Thus, biosocial-learning theory brings to the interpersonal framework a recognition that early learning and socialization experiences influence the strength and expression of the motives that underlie various personality dimensions, and combine with biological factors (e.g., temperament variables) to produce particular constellations of traits, motivations, and behaviors.

Millon (1990) undertook a major revision of his earlier model, linking personality traits and disorders to evolutionary theory. According to this view, different traits evolved and are maintained through natural selection processes. Even those traits that represent exaggerations of adaptive behavior patterns have evolutionary roots (thus, strong dependency needs may be an extreme variant of normal affiliative strivings).

Millon's (1990) interpersonal matrix combines four personality styles (*dependent, independent, ambivalent*, and *detached*) with two levels of activity (*active* versus *passive*). Dependency occupies the *dependent-passive* region, and is characterized by "a search for relationships in which one can lean on others for affection, security, and leadership. [The dependent] personality's lack of both initiative and autonomy was considered to be a consequence largely of parental overprotection. As a function of these early experiences, these individuals simply learned the comforts of assuming a passive role in interpersonal relations, accepting whatever kindness and support they found, and willingly submitting to the wishes of others in order to maintain their affection" (Millon & Davis, 1996, p. 68).

Research strongly supports Millon and Davis's (1996) contention that affection, security, and leadership seeking is a central component of the dependent personality. Studies show that dependent people seek physical contact and comfort more readily than nondependent people (Hollender, Luborsky, & Harvey, 1970); prefer nurturant, protective romantic partners to those that encourage autonomy and independence (Simpson & Gangestad, 1991); and subsume their needs to those of others in friendships and romantic relationships (Birtchnell, 1988; Birtchnell & Kennard, 1983). Other studies have shown that dependent individuals are highly suggestible (Tribich & Messer, 1974), tend to yield to others in interpersonal negotiations (Masling, Weiss, & Rothschild, 1968), and find comfort and reassurance in the presence of familiar people (Keinan & Hobfoll, 1989). Studies of infant-caregiver interactions and retrospective reports of parenting experiences converge to confirm that the children of overprotective parents score high on a wide variety of dependency measures (Head et al., 1991). Moreover, authoritarian parenting alone predicts later dependency in offspring (McPartland & Epstein, 1975). When parents exhibit both overprotectiveness and authoritarianism, high levels of dependency are particularly likely to result (Bornstein, 1993, 1996b). Parental overprotectiveness and authoritarianism serve simultaneously to: (1) reinforce dependent behavior; and (2) prevent the child from developing independent, autonomous behaviors (since the child is prevented from engaging in the kinds of trial-and-error learning that produce a sense of mastery and competence during childhood).

While research supports Millon's views regarding the relationships of the dependent person, and the parenting characteristics that lead to high levels of dependency, research does not support the notion that dependent individuals invariably "[assume] a passive role in interpersonal relations, accepting whatever kindness and support they found, and willingly submitting to the wishes of others in order to maintain their affection" (Millon & Davis, 1996, p. 68). In fact, studies show that the dependent person can be surprisingly assertive—even aggressive—in certain types of interpersonal transactions. Recent studies suggest that the dependent individual is not nearly as passive and compliant as we first thought.

The Cognitive Perspective Cognitive models emphasize the role of the self-concept, beliefs regarding other people, and expectations regarding self-other interactions (sometimes referred to as "internal working models") in the etiology and dynamics of normal and pathological personality traits. Cognitive theorists suggest that behavior can be understood and predicted with reference to an individual's core beliefs and salient interpersonal perceptions (see Mischel, 1973, 1979, 1984). Thus, Beck and Freeman (1990, p. 45) argued that the core belief of the dependent individual is "I am completely helpless," coupled with the sense that "I can function only if I have access to somebody competent." Beck and Freeman (1990, p. 290) further suggested that dependent persons "see the world as a cold, lonely, or even dangerous place that they could not possibly handle alone. . . . They conclude that the solution to the dilemma of being inadequate in a frightening world is to try to find someone who seems able to handle life and who will protect and take care of them."

Bornstein (1992, 1993, 1996a) extended traditional cognitive models of dependency by integrating into these models ideas and findings from object relations theory and developmental psychology. He contended that the etiology of DPD lies in two areas: overprotective, authoritarian parenting and sex-role socialization. Consistent with Millon's (1969, 1981) biosocial-learning view, Bornstein (1993) argued that overprotective, authoritarian parenting fosters dependency by preventing the child from developing a sense of mastery following successful learning experiences. Consistent with Blatt's (1974) framework, Bornstein (1996a) argued that parental overprotection and authoritarianism play a key role in the construction of a representation of the self as powerless, ineffectual, and weak. Beyond this, sex-role socialization experiences may further foster the development of a "dependent self-concept" in girls—and contribute to the higher rates of DPD diagnoses found in women relative to men—because traditional socialization practices encourage passivity and acquiescence in girls more strongly than in boys (Bornstein, Bowers, & Bonner, 1996).

Cognitive structures formed in response to early experiences within the family affect the motivations, behaviors, and affective responses of the dependent person in predictable ways (Bornstein, 1995, 1996a). A perception of the self as powerless and ineffectual will, first and foremost, have motivational effects: a person with such a self-concept will be motivated to seek guidance, support, protection, and nurturance from other people. These motivations in turn produce particular patterns of dependent behavior: the person who is highly motivated to seek the guidance, protection, and support of others will behave in ways that maximize the probability that they will obtain the protection and support they desire. Finally, a representation of the self as powerless and ineffectual will have important affective consequences (e.g., fear of abandonment, fear of negative evaluation; see Bornstein, 1992, 1993).

Cognitive models of dependency differ from other theoretical frameworks in at least one fundamental way: they posit that while the dependent person's self-concept (and self-concept based motivations) remains stable, the dependent individual's behavior may vary considerably from situation to situation, depending on the demands, constraints, and risks of that situation (Bornstein, 1993; Mischel, 1979). When behaving in a passive, submissive manner is likely to strengthen ties to potential nurturers and caregivers, the dependent person will behave passively and submissively. However, when active, assertive behavior seems more likely to strengthen important relationships, the dependent person becomes active and assertive.

Studies confirm that a view of the self as weak and ineffectual underlies a variety of problematic dependency-related behaviors in DPD-diagnosed patients and nonclinical participants (Bornstein, 1995; Coyne & Whiffen, 1995; Overholser, 1996). Other studies suggest that dysfunctional beliefs about the self and other people play a role in the dynamics of dependency (Baltes, 1996; Beck, Epstein, Harrison, & Emery, 1983), and furthermore help to propagate dependency-related attitudes and behaviors (Caspi et al., 1989). Developmental investigations indicate that dependency-related cognitions are central to help, support, and reassurance seeking in children, adolescents, and adults (Birtchnell, 1988).

Along somewhat different lines, recent research offers strong support for the "interactionist" component of contemporary cognitive models of dependency. In a series of experiments, Bornstein, Riggs, Hill, and Calabrese (1996) pitted the dependent person's desire to please a figure of authority with his or her motivation to get along with a peer. Highly consistent results were obtained: when a dependent individual was led to believe that the best way to strengthen ties to an important nurturer or caretaker was to behave in a passive, compliant manner, the dependent person behaved passively and allowed a peer to outperform him or her on an intellectual task. Led to believe that the best way to strengthen ties to a nurturing, protecting figure was to become active and assertive, the dependent person behaved in an active—even aggressive—manner, competing quite vigorously with a peer on this same intellectual task. Simply put, when forced to choose between pleasing an authority figure and getting along with a peer, the dependent person almost invariably opted to please the authority figure—the person best able to provide help and support over the long term.

These results suggest that the behavior of the dependent person can be quite variable, but that underlying this variability is a fundamental cognitive consistency: a view of the self as weak, coupled with a belief that the best way to survive and thrive is to cultivate relationships with figures of authority. To predict the behavior of the dependent person one must focus first on dependency-related cognitions, then consider the effects of these cognitions on dependency-related motivations, behaviors, and emotional responses.

Histrionic Personality Disorder

Clinicians and researchers do not always agree regarding the characteristics that distinguish HPD from other, ostensibly similar forms of personality pathology (e.g., narcissistic and borderline personality disorders). However, several traits emerge in many recent descriptions of histrionic traits and tendencies. The "core" components of HPD include egocentricity, seductiveness, theatrical emotionality, denial of anger and hostility, and a diffuse (or global) cognitive style (Pfohl, 1991). Among the other traits frequently associated with HPD are gregariousness, manipulativeness, low frustration tolerance, pseudo-hypersexuality, suggestibility, and somatizing tendencies (Andrews & Moore, 1991; Kantor, 1992; Millon & Davis, 1996).

The eight *DSM-IV* symptoms of HPD capture nicely these various traits and associated characteristics. Moreover, in contrast to the *DSM-IV* DPD criteria, which focus exclusively on the behavioral and affective correlates of dependency, the HPD criteria capture the cognitive components of HPD (symptoms 5 and 8) in addition to its affective (symptoms 1 and 3) and behavioral correlates (symptoms 2, 4, 6, and 7).

HPD is unique among the *DSM-IV* personality disorders in at least one respect: it is the only disorder explicitly tied to physical characteristics of the individual. Several researchers have noted that HPD tends to appear primarily in women and men who are above average in physical attractiveness (Apt & Hurlbert, 1994; Beck & Freeman, 1990; Char, 1985). In a sense this hypothesized link is not surprising. Clinicians and researchers agree that seductiveness is a key feature of the HPD individual's coping style, and physical appearance is an important feature of seductiveness. The *DSM-IV* captures nicely this component of HPD, noting that persons with HPD "consistently use physical appearance to draw attention to themselves . . . are overly concerned with impressing others by their appearance and expend an excessive amount of time, energy and money on clothes and grooming" (p. 655).

There has been relatively little research on gender differences in the expression of HPD symptoms, but what findings exist point to gender differences in at least two areas. First, clinicians agree that women more than men use overt sexual seductiveness to express histrionic needs in important interpersonal relationships (Lilienfeld, Van Valkenburg, Larntz, & Akiskal, 1986; Stone, 1993). Second, some clinical researchers have argued that HPD in men often overlaps—or is subsumed completely by—antisocial traits and behaviors. It has even been suggested that histrionic and antisocial personality disorders are two sides of the same coin, and some epidemiological and family history data support that assertion (Hamburger, Lilienfeld, & Hogben, 1996; Hart & Hare, 1989). According to this view, the antisocial male tends to manipulate others through active intimidation while the histrionic female achieves the same ends through seductive flirtation.

Although only one study has assessed directly the relationship of ethnicity and cultural background to HPD symptoms and diagnoses (Makaremi, 1990), it would appear that HPD is likely to be diagnosed more frequently in some cultural groups than in others (Love & Jackson, 1988). In particular, traditional socialization practices should lead to relatively low rates of HPD in many Asian cultures, where overt sexual seductiveness is often frowned upon (Johnson, 1993). Conversely, HPD should be diagnosed more frequently in Hispanic and Latin American cultures where vivid, uninhibited emotionality is expected, even valued, especially among women (see, e.g., Padilla, 1995).

The HPD symptom picture will also vary as a function of age. In children, histrionic tendencies are associated with overt manipulativeness, demandingness, and immaturity. The behavior of histrionic adolescents and adults is closest to the HPD prototype as described in the *DSM-IV*: in these age groups, HPD is associated with seductiveness, theatricality, and pseudo-hypersexuality (i.e., overt sexual seductiveness coupled with an underlying fear of sexuality). In older adults, sexual seductiveness will be a less effective means of obtaining gratification from others, so the primary interpersonal strategy of the older person with HPD may shift to a kind of maternal or paternal "seductiveness"—manipulation and coercion based on presentation of the self as a powerful, guilt-inducing maternal or paternal figure.

Epidemiology and Comorbidity

The prevalence of HPD varies from as low as 1% in some studies (e.g., Coryell & Zimmerman, 1989; Maier et al., 1992) to as high as 44% (Millon & Trignone, 1989) or even 63% (Morey, 1988) in others. As is true of most Axis II disorders, HPD occurs more frequently in psychiatric inpatients and outpatients than in college students or community subjects (Johnson, Bornstein, & Sherman, 1996). Following an extensive review of the epidemiological literature, Blashfield and Davis (1993) concluded that the frequency of HPD averaged about 24% in clinical samples, making it one of the most prevalent Axis II disorders.

Studies of gender differences in HPD prevalence rates have produced mixed results. Consistent with the *DSM-IV* assertion that in clinical settings men and women receive HPD diagnoses at approximately equal rates, several investigations have found no gender differences in HPD prevalence rates in psychiatric inpatients, outpatients, and nonclinical subjects (Bornstein, Greenberg, Leone, & Galley, 1990; Hamburger et al., 1996; Reich, 1987). However, other investigations using similar measures and methodologies have found that women receive HPD diagnoses significantly more frequently than men do (Schotte, de Doncker, Maes, Cluydts, & Cosyns, 1993; Zimmerman & Coryell, 1989). In fact, two recent investigations involving community subjects and university students found that women received 81% (Rubino, Saya, & Pezzarossa, 1992) and 100% (Stangler & Printz, 1980) of all HPD diagnoses in these nonclinical samples. Clearly additional data are needed before this issue may be resolved conclusively, but evidence suggests that in many settings women receive HPD diagnoses at higher rates than men do.

HPD shows substantial comorbidity with several Axis I pathologies, including anxiety disorders (Blashfield & Davis, 1993), somatization disorder (Reich, 1987), dissociative disorders (Boon & Draijer, 1993), and dysthymia (Pepper et al., 1995). On Axis II, HPD is associated with higher than expected rates of antisocial, narcissistic, borderline, and dependent personality disorders (Flick, Roy-Byrne, Cowley, Shores, & Dunner, 1993; Johnson & Bornstein, 1992; McCann, 1991). In a few investigations, HPD has also shown substantial comorbidity with paranoid, obsessive-compulsive, and avoidant personality disorders (Blashfield & Davis, 1993; Nestadt, Samuels, Romanowski, Folstein, & McHugh, 1994), but these are isolated studies that require replication before strong conclusions are drawn from their results (Johnson, Hyler, Skodol, Bornstein, & Sherman, 1995).

Historical Perspectives

The history of HPD has been characterized by two major trends: (1) a gradual evolution from physical to psychological models; and (2) a parallel change in descriptive terminology from *hysterical* (or *hysteroid*) to *histrionic*. Both trends are ongoing, and both are incomplete. Most (but not all) theoretical speculation regarding the etiology and dynamics of HPD focuses on psychological rather than physical processes. Many (but not all) clinicians and researchers today use the term *histrionic* in lieu of the term *hysterical* to describe individuals who would fulfill the *DSM-IV* DPD criteria (Merskey, 1995).

Among the earliest writings in this area are those of Hippocrates, who attributed hysterical traits and behaviors in women to a "wandering womb" that moved too close to the brain and thereby contaminated reason with emotion. Over time such physical explanations were gradually replaced with psychological theories, but the emphasis on emotionality remained. Thus, Sydenham (1682, pp. 88–89) noted that in this type of patient "tears and laughter succeed each other. . . . Fear, anger, jealousy, suspicion, and the worst passions of the mind arise without cause. . . . They love without measure those whom they will soon hate without reason. Now they will do this, now that; never receding from their purpose."

The 18th and 19th centuries saw a continued emphasis on sexuality in hysteria (a precursor of HPD), even prior to Freud's voluminous writings on this topic. Laycock (1840), Richer (1885), Janet (1907), and others helped solidify the link between "erotic passion" and hysterical traits and behaviors. During the first decades of the 20th century, theoretical writing on hysteria split into two independent streams, with psychoanalysts emphasizing the sexual origins of hysterical disorders, and descriptive psychiatrists like Kraepelin (1904) and Schneider (1923) focusing on the hysterical patient's immaturity and self-centeredness. Thus, while Freud (1931, p. 250) was asserting that "when persons of the erotic type fall ill they will develop hysteria," Kretschmer (1926, p. 26) was suggesting that hysterics show "a preference for what is loud and lively, a theatrical pathos, an inclination for brilliant roles . . . [and] a naive, sulky egotism."

Oddly, neither the hysterical or the histrionic personality appeared as a diagnostic category in the *DSM-I*, although the *DSM-I* description of the "emotionally unstable personality" captured some of the qualities that would emerge in later *DSM* descriptions of HPD. In the *DSM-II*, hysterical and histrionic personality disorders became one: the formal diagnostic category "hysterical personality" was followed in parentheses by the term "histrionic personality disorder." The *DSM-II* symptoms of hysterical personality, however, were much closer to modern conceptions of histrionicity than to contemporary models of hysteria.

Not everyone favored the merging of hysteria and histrionicity in the *DSM-II* (Gorton & Ahktar, 1990). Perhaps Kernberg (1984, 1986) has been the most vocal critic of this approach, arguing that these are separate and distinct disorders that should be diagnosed independently and studied in relation to each other. Stone (1993) offered an opposing view, contending that hysteria represents the most profoundly disturbed (i.e., most psychologically primitive) manifestation of HPD.

A separate category of HPD emerged for the first time in the *DSM-III*, and hysterical personality disorder disappeared completely from the diagnostic nomenclature (it has not reappeared in the *DSM-III-R* or *DSM-IV*). By this time, sexuality had dropped out of the HPD symptom picture, although the *DSM-III* noted that people with HPD were typically "attractive and seductive . . . [even though] the actual quality of their sexual relationships is variable" (p. 314).

In the *DSM-III*, the symptoms of HPD were divided into two broad, overlapping categories: (1) overly dramatic, intense behavior (e.g., self-dramatization); and (2) characteristic disturbances in interpersonal relationships (e.g., being perceived by others as shallow). The *DSM-III-R* and *DSM-IV* provided much more detailed (and more precise) descriptions of HPD, but both continued to emphasize the emotionality, attention seeking, and shallow, distorted relationships that have long been associated with histrionic personality traits.

Contemporary Theoretical Perspectives

Only a small number of contemporary theoretical frameworks have been used to describe the etiology and dynamics of HPD—a far smaller number of models than has been used to conceptualize DPD in recent years (Beck & Freeman, 1990; Blacker & Tupin, 1991; Kantor, 1992). Similarly, while there have been several hundred empirical studies of dependent personality traits since the early 1950s (Bornstein, 1993), there have been (at most) two or three dozen empirical investigations testing hypotheses regarding the etiology and dynamics of histrionic traits (Pfohl, 1991). In the following sections I describe three of the most influential contemporary models of HPD: the psychoanalytic, cognitive-dynamic, and biosocial-learning models.

The Psychoanalytic Perspective Although classical psychoanalytic theory got its start in Freud's treatment of hysterical patients (Breuer & Freud, 1895), early psychoanalytic theorists had little to say about hysterical personality traits, and even less to say about histrionicity per se. Freud's writings on this topic (and there were many) were limited almost entirely to speculation regarding hysterical conversion disorders (Kantor, 1992). It was Reich (1933, 1949) who provided the first detailed psychoanalytic description of hysterical personality traits. He argued that "coquetery in gait, look or speech betrays, especially in women, the hysterical character type. . . . We find fickleness of reactions, i.e., a tendency to change one's attitudes unexpectedly and unintentionally; a strong suggestibility, which never appears alone but is coupled with a strong tendency to reactions of disappointment. An attitude of compliance is usually followed by its opposite, swift deprecation and groundless disparagement" (1933, pp. 204–205).

A decade after Reich's initial work in this area, Fenichel (1945, pp. 527–528) linked hysterical and histrionic traits with "pseudo-hypersexuality," noting that these individuals "are inclined to sexualize all nonsexual relations. . . . The histrionic quality is a turning from reality to fantasy and probably also an attempt to master anxiety by 'acting' actively what otherwise might happen passively." Fenichel hinted at what psychodynamic theorists would later make explicit, namely that histrionicity is rooted in part in a rigid, maladaptive defensive style.

The assertive, attention-seeking behavior of the

histrionic, coupled with his or her pseudo-hypersexuality, seemed to make the origins of histrionic personality traits obvious and hard to miss: Abraham (1927), Freud (1931), Reich (1933), and Fenichel (1945) quibbled about the details, but all agreed that hysterical traits stemmed from Oedipal fixation, penis envy (in women), and castration anxiety (in men). It was not until Marmor's classic (1953) paper on orality in the hysterical personality that the possibility was raised that histrionic traits might be rooted in oral—rather than Oedipal—needs. In Marmor's view, histrionic theatricality and pseudo-hypersexuality were not direct expressions of Oedipal wishes. Instead, they served simultaneously as defenses and interpersonal coping strategies—defenses insofar as they kept underlying oral-dependent fantasies out of awareness, and coping strategies insofar as they enabled the histrionic person to obtain and maintain a network of gratifying, supportive relationships.

More recent psychoanalytic theorists have taken a compromise position regarding the oral-Oedipal dispute, suggesting that there is a spectrum of histrionic personality configurations, ranging from those that are primarily oral in nature to those that are primarily Oedipal (Easser & Lesser, 1965; Kernberg, 1975; Stone, 1993). The "oral histrionic" appears to be functioning at a more primitive level than the "Oedipal histrionic," with less ego strength, poorer impulse control, weaker reality testing, and more primitive, maladaptive ego defenses (e.g., repression and denial rather than displacement and rationalization).

There have been no empirical studies testing directly the links between HPD symptoms and oral or Oedipal traits. Factor-analytic investigations by Lazare et al. (1966, 1970) offer indirect support for an hypothesized relationship between histrionicity and orality, insofar as the "hysterical" personality factor that emerged in these two investigations included two oral traits (suggestibility and dependence) in addition to several histrionic traits (i.e., egocentricity, exhibitionism, emotionality, sexual provocativeness, and fear of sexuality). Subsequent factor-analyses by Vandenberg and Helstone (1975) and Torgerson (1980) generally supported Lazare et al.'s earlier findings, suggesting that certain oral traits tend to covary with histrionic traits and tendencies.

Studies of the defensive style of the HPD individual offer some support for psychoanalytic writings in this area. When Von der Lippe and Torgerson (1984) assessed the relationship between hysterical traits and a projective measure of repression in a sample of pregnant women, they found a small but marginally significant relationship between these variables. Rubino et al. (1992) subsequently obtained similar results using MCMI histrionicity scores and a behavioral index of repression in a large heterogenous sample of nonclinical participants.

Other studies of the histrionic person's defensive style used defense mechanism measures that did not include a separate repression index. Nonetheless, the results of these investigations are generally consistent with psychoanalytic speculation in this area. Bornstein et al. (1990) found that Lazare-Klerman hysteria scores (Lazare et al., 1966, 1970) were positively correlated with scores on the Defense Mechanisms Inventory (DMI) *projection* and *turning-against-other* scales (Ihilevich & Gleser, 1986). Johnson, Bornstein, and Krukonis (1992) found that Personality Diagnostic Questionnaire—Revised (PDQ-R) HPD scores (Hyler et al., 1988) were positively correlated with maladaptive defense scores and negatively correlated with adaptive (mature) defense scores on the Defense Styles Questionnaire (DSQ; Bond et al., 1989). Johnson et al.'s results suggest that HPD symptoms are associated with reliance on more primitive defenses such as regression, and with an inability to utilize more mature defenses such as sublimation.

The Cognitive-Dynamic Perspective The psychoanalytic hypothesis that histrionicity is associated with overreliance on denial and repression has important implications for understanding the cognitive style of the histrionic person. This issue did not come completely to the fore until David Shapiro (1965, pp. 111–112) argued that "hysterical cognition in general is global, relatively diffuse, and lacking in sharpness, particularly in sharp detail. In a word, it is impressionistic. . . . [T]he hysterical person tends cognitively to respond quickly and is highly susceptible to what is immediately impressive, striking, or merely obvious."

Subsequent theoretical analyses tended to follow Shapiro's lead and emphasize the dysfunctional aspects of histrionic cognition. However, there were a few notewothy exceptions to this trend. For example, Ortmeyer (1979) pointed out the links between a global cognitive style and creativity, while several theorists noted the relationship-faciliating functions of the histrionic's inattention to detail (Andrews & Moore, 1991). As Andrews (1984, p. 217) noted, the histrionic's "impressionistic approach facilitates the construction of conventionally idealized, oversimplified images of self and others . . . diverting attention away from displeasing realities, and [helping] maintain the pretense that everything in life is as 'nice' as it is supposed to be." This shift in emphasis from "histrionic cognition as deficit" to "histrionic cognition as both deficit and strength" parallels a similar shift (discussed earlier) in theorists' conceptualization of the interpersonal dynamics of dependency (Bornstein, 1995, 1996a).

Horowitz (1991) altered the focus of the cognitive-dynamic perspective by considering the internal dynamics that bridge the gap between histrionic perception and histrionic behavior. In his view, a key component of HPD is an underlying information-processing bias that is reflected in part in the histrionic person's global perceptual style, but manifested in other ways as well. As Horowitz noted, linking the various features of HPD is a *schema* (or mental representation) of the self as "sexy star, wounded hero, worthy invalid, or appealing but neglected waif" (1991, p. 6). Histrionic behavior is choreographed by a *role-relationship model* (or internalized script), in which others play the supporting roles of "interested suitor, devoted rescuer, or rueful and now responsible caretaker" (p. 6).

Beck and Freeman (1990) have offered the most purely cognitive view of HPD, although they too acknowledge the psychodynamic roots of most contemporary cognitive and cognitive-dynamic frameworks (see also Freeman & Leaf, 1989; Pfohl, 1991). Beck and Freeman (1990, p. 50) contend that the core beliefs of the HPD person include "Unless I captivate people I am nothing," "If I can't entertain people they will abandon me," and "If people don't respond to me they are rotten." One can see in this description echoes of Beck and Freeman's conceptualization of DPD, with one important difference: to the naive and succorant DPD person, relationships with nurturant caregivers are valued and cultivated, but to the more pessimistic HPD individual, potential caregivers are not to be trusted, so they must be manipulated instead.

Studies generally support the hypothesis that HPD is associated with a diffuse, impressionistic cognitive style. For example, McMullen and Rogers (1984) found that histrionic college students performed particularly well on intelligence and aptitude measures that tap global, impressionistic thinking, and relatively poorly on measures that assessed analytic thinking and attention to detail. Replicating and extending these results, Burgess (1992) found that HPD-diagnosed outpatients showed deficits on standardized tests of attention, memory, and behavior planning and sequencing. Along slightly different lines, Magaro, Smith, and Ashbrook (1983) found that histrionic female college students performed poorly on detailed visual search tasks involving focused attention and continuous tracking of stimuli. Studies that indicate that histrionic individuals tend to show right-hemisphere dominance are also consistent with the hypothesis that histrionicity is associated with global, impressionistic thinking, although these studies are open to several alternative interpretations (Andrews, 1984; Burgess, 1992; Smokler & Sherrin, 1979).

While most studies support the hypothesized link between HPD and impressionistic thinking, at least one investigation has produced the opposite pattern of results: Kaur and Kapur (1983) found that the Rorschach protocols of histrionic outpatients actually contained a greater number of detail responses than those of non-HPD patients. However, the quality of these responses was not assessed, leaving open the possibility that the Rorschach detail responses of HPD patients—while numerous—are idiosyncratic or inaccurate.

No empirical studies have tested directly Horowitz's (1991) hypothesis that HPD is associated with a predictable array of schemas and scripts. Similarly, Beck and Freeman's (1990) speculation regarding the core beliefs of the HPD patient remain unexamined. Perhaps the best we can conclude at this point is that HPD-diagnosed persons show a cognitive style consistent with that described by many cognitive-dynamic theorists, but that other hypotheses derived from this framework await empirical verification.

The Biosocial-Learning Perspective Interpersonal and circumplex analyses of HPD emphasize its active, receptive, attention-seeking qualities (McLemore & Brokaw, 1987; Wiggins & Pincus, 1989), a conclusion echoed—and confirmed empirically—by recent five-factor studies of histrionic traits and behaviors (Costa & McCrae, 1990). Consistent with the interpersonal view, Millon and Davis

(1996, p. 68) argued that the HPD person "shows an insatiable and indiscriminate search for stimulation and affection. This personality's sociable and capricious behaviors give the appearance of considerable independence of others, but beneath this guise lies a fear of autonomy and an intense need for signs of social approval and attention. Affection must be replenished constantly and must be obtained from every source of interpersonal contact."

According to the biosocial-learning framework, HPD may arise in part from inconsistent patterns of interpersonal reinforcement provided by parents and others (Millon & Davis, 1996). Like the infant whose caregivers do not respond until she screams at the top of her lungs, the histrionic child eventually learns that the way to get what she wants from others is to draw attention to herself through every means available—the more intrusive the better. Although the histrionic person's surface assertiveness belies an underlying insecurity and a tenuous, fragmented self-concept (Kernberg, 1984), over time the child who uses these attention- and nurturance-seeking strategies successfully may come to believe that she deserves special treatment, and that it will always be there if she continues to display manipulative, attention-demanding behaviors.

Like the psychoanalytic and cognitive-dynamic theories, Millon's (1990) biosocial-learning model also emphasizes the seductive and stimulation-seeking qualities of the HPD person. Consequently, within Millon's framework HPD occupies the *active-dependent* region. Emphasizing affiliation over individuation, and active modification of the environment over passive accommodation, the interpersonal style of the HPD person stands in marked contrast to the more solicitous, ingratiating style of the DPD individual.

Millon and Davis's (1996) discussion of self-perpetuation processes in HPD expands upon the earlier work of Horowitz (1991) in making explicit the self-defeating nature of histrionic exploitation. While recognizing that histrionic seductiveness brings its share of rewards—both internal and external—Millon and Davis (1996, p. 386) also note that "one consequence of these fleeting and erratic relationships is that histrionics can never be sure of securing the affection and support they crave. By moving constantly and by devouring the affections of one person then another, they place themselves in jeopardy of having nothing to tide them over the times in between. They may be left high and dry, alone and abandoned with nothing to do and no excitement with which to be preoccupied." If the central interpersonal risk of excessive dependency is abandonment and rejection, the central risk of histrionicity is alienation of others and a "sucking dry" of the surrounding interpersonal matrix—a histrionic "killing of the golden goose" (as it were) that results from indiscriminate, unmodulated manipulation of friends, supporters, and admirers (Birnbaum, 1987).

No studies have tested directly hypotheses derived from the biosocial-learning framework, but several empirical findings offer indirect support for Millon's model. For example, Baker, Capron, and Azorlosa (1996) found that the family dynamics of HPD individuals were characterized by a high degree of control but low cohesion—interaction patterns that would be expected to produce a histrionic self-presentation style later in life. Consistent with these results, Standage, Bilsbury, Jain, and Smith (1984) found that women with HPD showed impaired role- and perspective-taking skills and a lack of empathy: they had great difficulty assuming an objective, detached stance and seeing the world the way others might see it.

Along slightly different lines, studies offer some support for the notion that the HPD person's primary means of interpersonal influence is manipulation of others' needs and fears. Apt and Hurlbert (1994) found that HPD-diagnosed women showed overt sexual seductiveness in important interpersonal relationships, although underlying this "pseudo-hypersexuality" were powerful erotophobic feelings (see also Reise & Wright, 1996). Other investigations indicate that frustrated histrionics—like frustrated borderlines—are inclined to demand attention from others by making theatrical suicidal gestures directed toward therapists, friends, and romantic partners (see Fruensgaard & Hansen, 1988; Perry, 1989).

Taken together, studies of the family dynamics and interpersonal style of the HPD person confirm that HPD is rooted in inconsistent early reinforcement patterns, and that seductiveness and manipulativeness are central to the HPD person's interpersonal style. It is also clear that HPD represents a particularly primitive and maladaptive expression of underlying dependency needs—more self-destructive in certain respects than the overt, unmodulated expression of exaggerated dependency strivings.

Conclusion

Both DPD and HPD have a long history in psychology and psychiatry, but while research on DPD has reached maturity, research on HPD is still in its infancy. It is clear that a cognitive model best accounts for the etiology and dynamics of DPD, but for HPD the picture is less clear. The psychoanalytic, cognitive-dynamic, and biosocial-learning approaches have all received some empirical support, but no theoretical framework has been tested definitively, and none has yet emerged as the most heuristic HPD model. Clearly, one task for researchers during the coming years will be to assess empirically the many intriguing hypotheses regarding HPD that have been offered by clinicians and researchers.

It may be time to qualify the longstanding distinction frequently applied to DPD and HPD—namely the notion that DPD represents "passive dependency" while HPD represents "active dependency." While it is true that in general, the HPD individual tends to be more overtly aggressive and assertive than the DPD individual, there is considerable flexibility in the behavior of DPD and HPD persons. Just as the HPD individual is capable of assuming a passive-receptive stance to seduce others, the DPD person is capable of being competitive and aggressive to obtain and maintain nurturant, supportive relationships. Studies are needed to see exactly what situations and circumstances elicit active behavior in DPD and HPD individuals, and what situations and circumstances elicit passive behavior.

Perhaps a better way to contrast DPD and HPD is to focus on defenses and coping styles. While the DPD person expresses dependency needs directly, the HPD person displaces his or her needs for support and reassurance from a valued other to the world at large. Whereas the dependent person often recognizes anger and then directs it inward, the histrionic person relies more heavily on repression and denial to cope with unpleasant affect. Continued attention to the defenses and coping styles associated with DPD and HPD will allow clinicians and researchers to discover more meaningful distinctions between these two related disorders.

Extant research on DPD and HPD allows us to draw several other conclusions regarding the parallels between these two disorders, as well as their differences. These studies also point to several issues that warrant greater attention from clinicians and clinical researchers:

- *Gender differences*. Studies do not support the *DSM-IV* assertion that women and men receive DPD diagnoses at equal rates. Although there have been fewer studies of gender differences in HPD diagnoses, these data also tend to suggest that women receive HPD diagnoses more often than men. Future studies must address the sources of these gender differences and determine whether they represent genuine gender differences in symptom patterns, self-report bias on the part of patients, problems with the diagnostic criteria, or diagnostician bias.
- *DSM symptoms*. There have been no published studies assessing directly the external validity of the *DSM-IV* DPD or HPD criteria. Empirical studies of dependency in clinical and nonclinical populations suggest that several of the DPD criteria may be valid, but that others clearly are not. Additional research is needed in this area, and modifications of the DPD and HPD criteria may be warranted in future versions of the DSM.
- *Comorbidity issues*. Both DPD and HPD show substantial comorbidity with a number of Axis II disorders, so much so that the discriminant validity of both sets of criteria are called into question. It will be important to determine whether the high rates of DPD and HPD comorbidity reflect flaws in the symptom criteria themselves, or whether individuals with these disorders are actually at risk for a range of other personality disorders.
- *Underlying and expressed needs*. The DPD and HPD symptom criteria—like the symptom criteria for most psychological disorders—focus primarily on expressed (i.e., overt) needs, motivations, and behaviors. Studies show that in many instances underlying (or implicit) needs also play a key role in motivating and directing the behavior of normal and personality-disordered individuals. As the theoretical frameworks used to explain DPD and HPD are further refined, greater attention must be paid to the interrelationships of underlying and expressed needs.

To the extent that dependency needs are expressed in adaptive rather than maladaptive ways, the deleterious effects that these needs may have on social and occupational functioning should diminish. Although a number of therapeutic interventions have been developed to deal productively with dependency issues as they arise during the course of psychotherapy, there has been very little work addressing the question of how best to alter maladaptive, inflexible dependency-related defenses and coping strategies (Bornstein & Bowen, 1995). As Lerner (1983, p. 697) noted, "the struggle to achieve a healthy integration of dependent longings and active . . . strivings constitutes a lifelong task for both men and women." Although Lerner's analysis focused on helping individuals cope with passive and active dependency strivings in healthy social and romantic relationships, her conclusions apply to personality-disordered individuals as well.

References

Abraham, K. (1927). The influence of oral erotism on character formation. In C. A. D. Bryan & A. Strachey (Eds.), *Selected papers on psycho-analysis* (pp. 393–406). London: Hogarth.

Ainsworth, M. D. S. (1969). Object relations, dependency and attachment: A theoretical review of the infant-mother relationship. *Child Development, 40*, 969–1025.

Alnaes, R., & Torgerson, S. (1988). DSM-III symptom disorders and personality disorders in an outpatient population. *Acta Psychiatrica Scandinavica, 78*, 348–355.

Alnaes, R., & Torgerson, S. (1990). DSM-III personality disorders among patients with major depresion, anxiety disorders and mixed conditions. *Journal of Nervous and Mental Disease, 178*, 693–698.

Andrews, J. (1984). Psychotherapy with the hysterical personality: An interpersonal approach. *Psychiatry, 47*, 211–231.

Andrews, J., & Moore, S. (1991). Social cognition in the histrionic/overconventional personality. In P. A. Magaro (Ed.), *Cognitive bases of mental disorders* (pp. 11–76). Newbury Park, CA: Sage.

Apt, C., & Hurlbert, D. F. (1994). The sexual attitudes, behavior and relationships of women with histrionic personality disorder. *Journal of Sex and Marital Therapy, 20*, 125–133.

Baker, J. D., Capron, E. W., & Azorlosa, J. (1996). Family environment characteristics of persons with histrionic and dependent personality disorders. *Journal of Personality Disorders, 10*, 82–87.

Baltes, M. M. (1996). *The many faces of dependency in old age*. New York: Cambridge University Press.

Beck, A. T., Epstein, N., Harrison, R. P., & Emery, G. (1983). *Development of the Sociotropy-Autonomy Scale: A measure of personality factors in psychopathology.* Unpublished manuscript.

Beck, A. T., & Freeman, A. (1990). *Cognitive therapy of the personality disorders*. New York: Guilford Press.

Beckwith, J. B. (1986). Eating, drinking and smoking and their relationship in adult women. *Psychological Reports, 59*, 1089–1095.

Benjamin, L. S. (1974). A structural analysis of social behavior. *Psychological Review, 81*, 392–425.

Birnbaum, J. (1987). A replacement therapy for the histrionic personality disorder. *Transactional Analysis Journal, 17*, 24–28.

Birtchnell, J. (1988). Defining dependence. *British Journal of Medical Psychology, 61*, 111–123.

Birtchnell, J., & Kennard, J. (1983). What does the MMPI dependency scale really measure? *Journal of Clinical Psychology, 39*, 532–543.

Black, D. W., Goldstein, R. B., & Mason, E. E. (1992). Prevalence of mental disorder in 88 morbidly obese bariatric clinic patients. *American Journal of Psychiatry, 149*, 227–234.

Blacker, K. H., & Tupin, J. P. (1991). Hysteria and hysterical structures: Developmental and social theories. In M. J. Horowitz (Ed.), *Hysterical personality style and the histrionic personality disorder* (pp. 17–66). Northvale, NJ: Jason Aronson.

Blashfield, R. K., & Davis, R. T. (1993). Dependent and histrionic personality disorders. In P. B. Sutker & H. E. Adams (Eds.), *Comprehensive handbook of psychopathology* (pp. 395–409). New York: Plenum Press.

Blatt, S. J. (1974). Levels of object representation in anaclitic and introjective depression. *Psychoanalytic Study of the Child, 29*, 107–157.

Blatt, S. J., Cornell, C. E., & Eshkol, E. (1993). Personality style, differential vulnerability, and clinical course in immunological and cardiovascular disease. *Clinical Psychology Review, 13*, 421–450.

Blatt, S. J., & Shichman, S. (1983). Two primary configurations of psychopathology. *Psychoanalysis and Contemporary Thought, 6*, 187–254.

Blatt, S. J., Wein, S. J., Chevron, E. S., & Quinlan, D. M. (1979). Parental representations and depression in normal young adults. *Journal of Abnormal Psychology, 88*, 388–397.

Bond, M., Perry, J. C., Gautier, M., Goldenberg, M., Openheimer, J., & Simand, J. (1989). Validating the self-report of defense styles. *Journal of Personality Disorders, 3*, 101–112.

Boon, S., & Draijer, N. (1993). The differentiation of patients with MPD or DDNOS from patients with a Cluster B personality disorder. *Dissociation, 6*, 126–135.

Bornstein, R. F. (1992). The dependent personality: Developmental, social and clinical perspectives. *Psychological Bulletin, 112*, 3–23.

Bornstein, R. F. (1993). *The dependent personality.* New York: Guilford Press.

Bornstein, R. F. (1994). Adaptive and maladaptive aspects of dependency: An integrative review. *American Journal of Orthopsychiatry, 64*, 622–635.

Bornstein, R. F. (1995). Active dependency. *Journal of Nervous and Mental Disease, 183*, 64–77.

Bornstein, R. F. (1996a). Beyond orality: Toward an object relations/interactionist reconceptualization of the etiology and dynamics of dependency. *Psychoanalytic Psychology, 13*, 177–203.

Bornstein, R. F. (1996b). Sex differences in dependent personality disorder prevalence rates. *Clinical Psychology: Science and Practice, 3*, 1–12.

Bornstein, R. F. (1997). Dependent personality disorder in the DSM-IV and beyond. *Clinical Psychology: Science and Practice, 4*, 175–187.

Bornstein, R. F., & Bowen, R. F. (1995). Dependency in psychotherapy: Toward an integrated treatment approach. *Psychotherapy, 32*, 520–534.

Bornstein, R. F., Bowers, K. S., & Bonner, S. (1996). Relationships of objective and projective dependency scores to sex role orientation in college students. *Journal of Personality Assessment, 66*, 555–568.

Bornstein, R. F., Galley, D. J., & Leone, D. R. (1986). Parental representations and orality. *Journal of Personality Assessment, 50*, 80–89.

Bornstein, R. F., & Greenberg, R. P. (1991). Dependency and eating disorders in female psychiatric inpatients. *Journal of Nervous and Mental Disease, 179*, 148–152.

Bornstein, R. F., Greenberg, R. P., Leone, D. R., & Galley, D. J. (1990). Defense mechanism correlates of orality. *Journal of the American Academy of Psychoanalysis, 18*, 654–666.

Bornstein, R. F., Leone, D. R., & Galley, D. J. (1988). Rorschach measures of oral dependence and the internalized self-representation in normal college students. *Journal of Personality Assessment, 52*, 648–657.

Bornstein, R. F., Riggs, J. M., Hill, E. L., & Calabrese, C. (1996). Activity, passivity, self-denigration, and self-promotion: Toward an interactionist model of interpersonal dependency. *Journal of Personality, 64*, 637–673.

Bornstein, R. F., Rossner, S. C., Hill, E. L., & Stepanian, M. L. (1994). Face validity and fakability of objective and projective measures of dependency. *Journal of Personality Assessment, 63*, 363–386.

Breuer, J., & Freud, S. (1895). Studies on hysteria. *SE 2*, pp. 1–307. London: Hogarth.

Burgess, W. J. (1992). Neurocognitive impairment in dramatic personalities: Histrionic, narcissistic, borderline and antisocial disorders. *Psychiatry Research, 42*, 283–290.

Caspi, A., Bem, D. J., & Elder, G. H. (1989). Continuities and consequences of interactional styles across the life course. *Journal of Personality, 57*, 375–406.

Char, W. F. (1985). The hysterical spouse. *Medical Aspects of Human Sexuality, 19*, 123–133.

Coryell, W. H., & Zimmerman, M. (1989). Personality disorder in the families of depressed, schizophrenic, and never-ill probands. *American Journal of Psychiatry, 146*, 1131–1141.

Costa, P. T., & McCrae, R. R. (1990). Personality disorders and the five-factor model of personality. *Journal of Personality Disorders, 4*, 362–371.

Coyne, J. C., & Whiffen, V. E. (1995). Issues in personality as diathesis for depression: The case of sociotropy-dependency and autonomy-self-criticism. *Psychological Bulletin, 118*, 358–378.

Easser, R., & Lesser, S. (1965). Hysterical personality: A re-evaluation. *Psychoanalytic Quarterly, 34*, 390–402.

Emery, G., & Lesher, E. (1982). Treatment of depression in older adults. *Psychotherapy, 19*, 500–505.

Fenichel, O. (1945). *The psychoanalytic theory of neurosis*. New York: Norton.

Flick, S. N., Roy-Byrne, P. P., Cowley, D. S., Shores, M. M., & Dunner, D. L. (1993). DSM-III-R personality disorders in a mood and anxiety disorders clinic: Prevalence, comorbidity and clinical correlates. *Journal of Affective Disorders, 27*, 71–79.

Ford, M. R., & Widiger, T. A. (1989). Sex bias in the diagnosis of histrionic and antisocial personality disorders. *Journal of Consulting and Clinical Psychology, 57*, 301–305.

Freeman, A., & Leaf, R. C. (1989). Cognitive therapy applied to personality disorders. In A. Freeman, K. M. Simon, L. E. Beutler, & H. Arkowitz (Eds.), *Comprehensive handbook of cognitive therapy* (pp. 403–433). New York: Plenum Press.

Freud, S. (1905). Three essays on the theory of sexuality. *SE 7*, pp. 125–248. London: Hogarth.

Freud, S. (1908). Character and anal erotism. *SE 9*, pp. 167–176. London: Hogarth.

Freud, S. (1915). Some character types met with in psycho-analytic work. *SE 14*, pp. 310–333. London: Hogarth.

Freud, S. (1923). The ego and the id. *SE 21*, pp. 3–66. London: Hogarth.

Freud, S. (1931). Libidinal types. *SE 22*, pp. 310–333. London: Hogarth.

Freud, S. (1938). An outline of psychoanalysis. *SE 23*, pp. 125–248. London: Hogarth.

Fromm, E. (1947). *Man for himself*. New York: Rinehart.

Fruensgaard, K., & Hansen, H. F. (1988). Disease patterns sen in self-mutilating patients. *Nordisk Psykiatrisk Tidsskrift, 42*, 281–288.

Gorton, G., & Akhtar, S. (1990). The literature on personality disorders, 1985–1988: Trends, issues and controversies. *Hospital and Community Psychiatry, 41*, 39–51.

Greenberg, J. R., & Mitchell, S. J. (1983). *Object relations in psychoanalytic theory*. Cambridge, MA: Harvard University Press.

Greenberg, R. P., & Fisher, S. (1977). The relationship between willingness to adopt the sick role and attitudes toward women. *Journal of Chronic Disease, 30*, 29–37.

Hamburger, M. E., Lilienfeld, S. O., & Hogben, M. (1996). Psychopathy, gender and gender roles: Implications for antisocial and histrionic personality disorders. *Journal of Personality Disorders, 10*, 41–55.

Hart, S. D., & Hare, R. D. (1989). Discriminant validity of the Psychopathy Checklist in a forensic psychiatric population. *Psychological Assessment, 1*, 211–218.

Hayward, C., & King, R. (1990). Somatization and personality disorder traits in nonclinical volunteers. *Journal of Personality Disorders, 4*, 402–406.

Head, S. B., Baker, J. D., & Williamson, D. A. (1991). Family environment characteristics and dependent personality disorder. *Journal of Personality Disorders, 5*, 256–263.

Heinstein, M. I. (1963). Behavioral correlates of breast-bottle regimens under varying parent-infant relationships. *Monographs of the Society for Research in Child Development, 28*, 1–61.

Hollender, M. C., Luborsky, L., & Harvey, R. (1970). Correlates of the desire to be held in women. *Journal of Psychosomatic Research, 14*, 387–390.

Horney, K. (1945). *Our inner conflicts*. New York: Norton.

Horowitz, M. J. (1991). *Hysterical personality style and the histrionic personality disorder.* Northvale, NJ: Jason Aronson.

Hyler, S. E., Rieder, R. O., Williams, J. B. W., Spitzer, R. L., Hendler, J., & Lyons, M. (1988). The Personality Diagnostic Questionnaire: Development and preliminary results. *Journal of Personality Disorders, 2*, 229–237.

Ihilevich, D., & Gleser, G. C. (1986). *Defense mechanisms: Their classification, correlates and measurement with the Defense Mechanisms Inventory.* Owosso, MI: DMI Associates.

Jackson, H. C., Rudd, R., Gazis, J., & Edwards, J. (1991). Using the MCMI to diagnose personality disorders in inpatients: Axis I/Axis II associations and sex differences. *Australian Psychologist, 26*, 37–41.

Jacobs, M. A., & Spilken, A. Z. (1971). Personality patterns associated with heavy cigarette smoking in male college students. *Journal of Consulting and Clinical Psychology, 37*, 428–432.

Jacobson, R., & Robins, C. J. (1989). Social dependency and social support in bulimic and nonbulimic women. *International Journal of Eating Disorders, 8*, 665–670.

Janet, P. (1907). *The mental state of hystericals: A study of mental stigmata and mental accidents.* New York: Putnam.

Joffe, R. T., Swinson, R. P., & Regan, J. J. (1988). Personality features of obsessive-compulsive disordcr. *American Journal of Psychiatry, 145*, 1127–1129.

Johnson, F. A. (1993). *Dependency and Japanese socialization.* New York: New York University Press.

Johnson, J. G., & Bornstein, R. F. (1992). Utility of the Personality Diagnostic Questionnaire—Revised in a nonclinical population. *Journal of Personality Disorders, 6*, 450–457.

Johnson, J. G., Bornstein, R. F., & Krukonis, A. B. (1992). Defense styles as predictors of personality disorder symptomatology. *Journal of Personality Disorders, 6*, 408–416.

Johnson, J. G., Bornstein, R. F., & Sherman, M. F. (1996). A modified scoring algorithm for the PDQ-R: Psychiatric symptomatology and substance use in adolescents with personality disorders. *Educational and Psychological Measurement, 56*, 76–89.

Johnson, J. G., Hyler, S. E., Skodol, A. E., Bornstein, R. F., & Sherman, M. (1995). Personality disorder symptomatology associated with adolescent depression and substance abuse. *Journal of Personality Disorders, 9*, 318–329.

Jones, M. C. (1968). Personality correlates and antecedents of drinking patterns in adult males. *Journal of Consulting and Clinical Psychology, 32*, 2–12.

Kantor, M. (1992). *Diagnosis and treatment of the personality disorders*. St. Louis: Ishiyaku Euroamerica.

Kaplan, M. (1983). A woman's view of DSM-III. *American Psychologist, 38*, 786–792.

Kass, F., Spitzer, R. L., & Williams, J. B. W. (1983). An empirical study of the issue of sex bias in the diagnostic criteria of DSM-III Axis II personality disorders. *American Psychologist, 38*, 799–801.

Kaul, V., Mathur, P., & Murlidharan, R. (1982). Dependency and its antecedents: A review. *Indian Educational Review, 17*, 35–46.

Kaur, D., & Kapur, M. (1983). Rorschach study of hysteria. *Indian Journal of Clinical Psychology, 10*, 97–102.

Keinan, G., & Hobfoll, S. E. (1989). Stress, dependency and social support: Who benefits from husband's presence in delivery? *Journal of Social and Clinical Psychology, 8*, 32–44.

Keith, R. R., & Vandenberg, S. G. (1974). Relation between orality and weight. *Psychological Reports, 35*, 1205–1206.

Kernberg, O. F. (1975). *Borderline conditions and pathological narcissism*. New York: Jason Aronson.

Kernberg, O. F. (1984). *Severe personality disorders*. New Haven: Yale University Press.

Kernberg, O. F. (1986). Hysterical and histrionic personality disorders. In A. Cooper, A. Frances, & M. Sacks (Eds.), *Psychiatry, Volume 1: The personality disorders and neuroses* (pp. 267–286). New York: Basic Books.

Kiesler, D. J. (1982). Interpersonal theory for personality and psychotherapy. In J. C. Anchin & D. J. Kiesler (Eds.), *Handbook of interpersonal psychotherapy* (pp. 3–24). New York: Pergamon.

Kohut, H. (1971). *The analysis of the self*. New York: International Universities Press.

Kraepelin, E. (1904). *Lectures on clinical psychiatry*. New York: Wood.

Kraepelin, E. (1913). *Psychiatrie: Ein lehrbuch*. Leipzig: Barth.

Kretschmer, E. (1926). *Hysteria*. New York: Nervous and Mental Disease Publishers.

Laycock, T. (1840). *A treatise on the nervous disease of women: Composing an inquiry into the nature, causes and treatment of spinal and hysterical disorders*. London: Longmans, Orme, Brown, Green & Longmans.

Lazare, A., Klerman, G. L., & Armor, D. (1966). Oral, obsessive and hysterical personality patterns. *Archives of General Psychiatry, 14*, 624–630.

Lazare, A., Klerman, G. L., & Armor, D. (1970). Oral, obsessive and hysterical personality patterns: Replication of factor analysis in an independent sample. *Journal of Psychiatric Research, 7*, 275–290.

Leary, T. (1957). *Interpersonal diagnosis of personality*. New York: Ronald.

Lenihan, G. O., & Kirk, W. G. (1990). Personality characteristics of eating-disordered outpatients as measured by the Hand Test. *Journal of Personality Assessment, 55*, 350–361.

Lerner, H. E. (1983). Female dependency in context: Some theoretical and technical considerations. *American Journal of Orthopsychiatry, 53*, 697–705.

Lilienfeld, S. O., Van Valkenburg, C., Larntz, K., & Akiskal, H. S. (1986). The relationship of histrionic personality disorder to antisocial personality and somatization disorders. *American Journal of Psychiatry, 143*, 718–722.

Livesley, W. J., Schroeder, M. L., & Jackson, D. J. (1990). Dependent personality disorder and attachment problems. *Journal of Personality Disorders, 4*, 131–140.

Loring, M., & Powell, B. (1988). Gender, race and DSM-III: A study of the objectivity of psychiatric diagnostic behavior. *Journal of Health and Social Behavior, 29*, 1–22.

Love, A. W., & Jackson, H. J. (1988). The effects of diagnostic information in clinicians' impressions of an interviewee. *Australian Journal of Psychiatry, 40*, 53–59.

Magaro, P., Smith, P., & Ashbrook, R. (1983). Personality style differences in visual search performance. *Psychiatry Research, 10*, 131–138.

Maier, W., Lichtermann, D., Klingler, T., Heun, R., & Hallmayer, J. (1992). Prevalences of personality disorders (DSM-III-R) in the community. *Journal of Personality Disorders, 6*, 187–196.

Makaremi, A. (1990). Histrionic disorder among Iranian high school and college students. *Psychological Reports, 66*, 835–838.

Marmor, J. (1953). Orality in the hysterical personality. *Journal of the American Psychoanalytic Association, 1*, 656–671.

Masling, J. M., Weiss, L., & Rothschild, B. (1968). Relationships of oral imagery to yielding behavior and birth order. *Journal of Consulting and Clinical Psychology, 32*, 89–91.

McCann, J. T. (1991). Convergent and discriminant validity of the MCMI-II and MMPI personality disorder scales. *Psychological Assessment, 3*, 9–18.

McLemore, C. W., & Brokaw, D. W. (1987). Personality disorders as dysfunctional interpersonal behavior. *Journal of Personality Disorders, 1*, 270–285.

McMullen, L., & Rogers, D. (1984). WAIS characteristics of non-pathological obsessive and hysteric styles. *Journal of Clinical Psychology, 40*, 577–579.

McPartland, J. M., & Epstein, J. L. (1975). A comparison of continuous and episodic drinkers using the MCMI, MMPI, and ALCEVAL-R. *Journal of Clinical Psychology, 47*, 148–159.

Merskey, H. (1995). Commentary on histrionic personality disorder. In W. J. Livesley (Ed.), *The DSM-IV personality disorders* (pp. 193–200). New York: Guilford Press.

Millon, T. (1969). *Modern psychopathology: A biosocial approach to maladaptive learning and functioning*. Philadelphia: Saunders.

Millon, T. (1981). *Disorders of personality: DSM-III Axis 2*. New York: John Wiley.

Millon, T. (1990). *Toward a new personology: An evolutionary model*. New York: John Wiley.

Millon, T., & Davis, R. D. (1996). *Disorders of personality: DSM-IV and beyond*. New York: John Wiley.

Millon, T., & Tringone, R. (1989). [Co-occurrence and diagnostic efficiency statistics]. Unpublished raw data.

Mills, J. K., & Cunningham, J. (1988). Oral character and attitudes and behavior related to food and eating. *Psychological Reports, 63*, 15–18.

Mischel, W. (1973). Toward a cognitive social learning reconceptualization of personality. *Psychological Review, 80*, 252–283.

Mischel, W. (1979). On the interface of cognition and personality: Beyond the person-situation debate. *American Psychologist, 34*, 740–754.

Mischel, W. (1984). Convergences and challenges in the search for consistency. *American Psychologist, 39*, 351–364.

Morey, L. C. (1988). A psychometric analysis of the DSM-III-R personality disorder criteria. *Journal of Personality Disorders, 2*, 109–124.

Neki, J. S. (1976). An examination of the cultural relativism of dependence as a dynamic of social and therapeutic relationships. *British Journal of Medical Psychology, 49*, 1–10.

Nestadt, G., Samuels, J. F., Romanoski, A. J., Folstein, M. F., & McHugh, P. R. (1994). Obsessions and compulsions in the community. *Acta Psychiatrica Scandinavica, 89*, 219–224.

Ortmeyer, D. (1979). Interpersonal psychotherapy with the hysterical character. In G. Goldman & D. Millman (Eds.), *Parameters in psychoanalytic psychotherapy* (pp. 142–165). Dubuque, IA: Kendall/Hunt.

Overholser, J. C. (1996). The dependent personality and interpersonal problems. *Journal of Nervous and Mental Disease, 184*, 8–16.

Padilla, A. M. (1995). *Hispanic psychology: Critical issues in theory and research*. Newbury Park, CA: Sage.

Parens, H., & Saul, L. J. (1971). *Dependence in man*. New York: International Universities Press.

Pepper, C. M., Klein, D. N., Anderson, R. L., Riso, L. P., Ouimette, P. C., & Lizardi, H. (1995). DSM-III-R Axis II comorbidity in dysthymia and major depression. *American Journal of Psychiatry, 152*, 239–247.

Perry, J. C. (1989). Personality disorders, suicide and self-destructive behavior. In D. Jacobs & H. N. Brown (Eds.), *Suicide: Understanding and reporting* (pp. 157–169). Madison, CT: International Universities Press.

Pfohl, B. (1991). Histrionic personality disorder: A review of available data and recommendations for DSM-IV. *Journal of Personality Disorders, 5*, 150–166.

Piersma, H. L. (1987). The MCMI as a measure of DSM-III Axis II diagnoses: An empirical comparison. *Journal of Clinical Psychology, 43*, 478–483.

Pincus, A. L., & Gurtman, M. B. (1995). The three faces of interpersonal dependency: Structural analysis of self-report dependency measures. *Journal of Personality and Social Psychology, 69*, 744–758.

Reich, J. (1987). Sex distribution of DSM-III personality disorders in psychiatric outpatients. *American Journal of Psychiatry, 144*, 181–187.

Reich, W. (1933). *Charakteranalyse*. Leipzig: Verlag.

Reich, W. (1949). *Character analysis*. New York: Farrar, Straus and Giroux.

Reise, S. P., & Wright, T. M. (1996). Personality traits, Cluster B personality disorders and sociosexuality. *Journal of Research in Personality, 30*, 128–136.

Richer, P. (1885). *Etudes cliniques sur la grande hysterie, ou hystero-epilepsie*. Paris: Adrien Delahaye et Emile LeCrosnier.

Rost, K. M., Atkins, R. N., Brown, F. W., & Smith, G. R. (1992). The comorbidity of DSM-III-R personality disorders in somatization disorder. *General Hospital Psychiatry, 14*, 322–326.

Rubino, I. A., Saya, A., & Pezzarossa, B. (1992). Percept-genetic signs of repression in histrionic personality disorder. *Perceptual and Motor Skills, 74*, 451–464.

Sadeh, A., Rubin, S. S., & Berman, E. (1993). Parental and relationship representations and experiences of depression in college students. *Journal of Personality Assessment, 60*, 192–204.

Schneider, K. (1923). *Psychopathic personalities.* London: Cassell.

Schotte, C., De Donker, D., Maes, M., Cluydts, R., & Cosyns, P. (1993). MMPI assessment of DSM-III-R histrionic personality disorder. *Journal of Personality Assessment, 60,* 500–510.

Sears, R. R. (1963). Dependency motivation. In M. R. Jones (Ed.), *Nebraska symposium on motivation* (Vol. 11, pp. 25–64). Lincoln, NE: University of Nebraska Press.

Shapiro, D. (1965). *Neurotic styles.* New York: Basic Books.

Shopshire, M. S., & Craik, K. H. (1994). The five factor model of personality and the DSM-III-R personality disorders: Correspondence and differentiation. *Journal of Personality Disorders, 8,* 41–52.

Simpson, J. A., & Gangestad, S. W. (1991). Individual differences in sociosexuality: Evidence for convergent and discriminant validity. *Journal of Personality and Social Psychology, 60,* 870–883.

Smokler, I., & Sherrin, H. (1979). Cerebral lateralization and personality style. *Archives of General Psychiatry, 36,* 949–954.

Sperling, M. B., & Berman, W. H. (1991). An attachment classification of desparate love. *Journal of Personality Assessment, 56,* 45–55.

Standage, L., Bilsbury, C., Jain, S., & Smith, D. (1984). An investigation of role-taking in histrionic personalities. *Canadian Journal of Psychiatry, 29,* 407–411.

Stangler, R. S., & Printz, A. M. (1980). DSM-III: Psychiatric diagnoses in a university population. *American Journal of Psychiatry, 137,* 937–940.

Stone, M. H. (1993). *Abnormalities of personality.* New York: Norton.

Sullivan, H. S. (1947). *Conceptions of modern psychiatry.* Washington, DC: William Alanson White Institute.

Sydenham, T. (1982). Letter to Dr. Cole. In R. G. Latham (Ed.), *The works of Thomas Sydenham* (Vol. 2, pp. 88–89). London: New Sydenham Society.

Tisdale, M. J., Pendleton, L., & Marler, M. (1990). MCMI characteristics of DSM-III-R bulimics. *Journal of Personality Assessment, 55,* 477–483.

Torgerson, S. (1980). The oral, obsessive and hysterical personality syndromes: A study of hereditary and environmental factors by means of the twin method. *Archives of General Psychiatry, 37,* 1272–1277.

Tribich, D., & Messer, S. (1974). Psychoanalytic character type and status of authority as determiners of suggestibility. *Journal of Consulting and Clinical Psychology, 42,* 842–848.

Vaillant, G. E. (1980). Natural history of male psychological health, VIII: Antecedents of alcoholism and orality. *American Journal of Psychiatry, 137,* 181–186.

Vandenberg, P., & Helstone, F. (1975). Oral, obsessive and hysterical personality factors: A Dutch replication. *Journal of Psychiatric Research, 12,* 319–327.

Veldman, D. J., & Bown, O. H. (1969). Personality and performance characteristics associated with cigarette smoking among college freshmen. *Journal of Consulting and Clinical Psychology, 33,* 109–119.

Von der Lippe, A., & Torgerson, S. (1984). Character and defense: Relationships between oral, obsessive and hysterical character traits and defense mechanisms. *Scandinavian Journal of Psychology, 25,* 258–264.

Wiggins, J. S., & Pincus, A. L. (1989). Conceptions of personality disorders and dimensions of personality. *Psychological Assessment, 1,* 305–316.

Wonderlich, S. A., Swift, W. J., Slotnick, H. B., & Goodman, S. (1990). DSM-III-R personality disorders in eating disorder subtypes. *International Journal of Eating Disorders, 9,* 607–616.

Zimmerman, M., & Coryell, W. (1989). DSM-III personality disorder diagnoses in a nonpatient sample. *Archives of General Psychiatry, 46,* 682–689.

22

Psychopathy and Sadistic Personality Disorder

ROBERT D. HARE
DAVID J. COOKE
STEPHEN D. HART

At first blush, it may seem strange to review these two personality disorders (PDs) in a single chapter. In terms of empirical support, they could not be more different. A considerable body of scientific research supports the reliability and validity of the clinical construct of psychopathy, whereas the empirical support for sadistic PD (SPD) is very weak. Indeed, of all the PDs, psychopathy may be the best understood and SPD the least understood. The two concepts also have different histories in modern psychopathology: psychopathy has been recognized widely as a distinct form of PD since the mid- to late 1800s, predating the recognition of SPD by a hundred years.

Despite these differences, psychopathy and SPD share an important feature, namely—a predisposition to aggression and violence (e.g., Millon, 1981; Millon & Davis, 1996). This is not to say that all people with psychopathy or SPD are violent criminals, nor that all people convicted of serious violent crimes meet the criteria for psychopathy or SPD (Hart & Hare, 1997). However, the increased risk of violence associated with these disorders is sufficiently robust that it has important implications for theory, clinical practice, and social policy.

In the first section of this chapter, we review research on psychopathy. We begin with a discussion of assessment issues, emphasizing the distinction between psychopathy, as reflected in clinical tradition and in the Hare Psychopathy Checklist—Revised (PCL-R; Hare, 1991), and antisocial personality disorder (ASPD), as defined in *DSM-IV*. Next, we discuss research on the association between psychopathy and violence. We end the first section with an overview of some theories that may account for the increased risk of violence among psychopathic individuals. In the second section, we review research on SPD. This review is necessarily rather brief and speculative, but accurately reflects the sparse and inchoate nature of the relevant scientific literature. We conclude the chapter by highlighting some important similarities and differences between psychopathy and SPD with respect to clinical presentation, violence history, and possible etiology.

Psychopathy

The Concept and Its History

Psychopathy is a specific form of personality disorder with a distinctive pattern of interpersonal, affective, and behavioral symptoms (see Cleckley, 1976; Hare, 1970, 1991, 1993). It is related to, but not identical with, ASPD (see Hare, 1996; Widiger et al., 1996). Interpersonally, psychopaths are grandiose, arrogant, callous, superficial, and manipulative; affectively, they are short-tempered, unable to form strong emotional bond with others, and lacking in guilt or anxiety; and behaviorally, they are irresponsible, impulsive, and prone to delinquency and criminality (Hare, 1991). Even if one ignores behavioral symptoms, the interpersonal and affective features clearly put psychopaths at high risk for aggression and violence (Hare, 1993; Hart & Hare, 1997). Below, we provide a brief historical review of psychopathy that highlights the role of violence in the conceptualization of the disorder. More detailed accounts are available elsewhere (e.g., Berrios, 1996; McCord & McCord, 1964; Millon, 1981; Pichot, 1978).

The term *psychopathy* has had a variety of meanings over the past century (Millon, 1981; Pichot, 1978). Literally "disease of the mind," the term originally referred to mental disorder in general. In the 19th century and early 20th century, various types of mental disorder were described, some involving general disintegration or deterioration of mental functions ("total insanity"), and others more specific impairments of intellect, emotion, or volition (Berrios, 1996). Particularly interesting were conditions in which disturbances in emotion or volition occurred in the absence of intellectual deficits. The terms used to refer to such conditions included *manie sans délire*, monomania, moral insanity, and *folie lucide* (Millon, 1981; Pichot, 1978). Although not directly related to the modern conception of psychopathy (Whitlock, 1982), these case descriptions reinforced the notion that mental disorder could exist even when reasoning was intact.

One condition identified around this time is of particular relevance to the present discussion. *Impulsion* (or impulsive insanity) was conceptualized as a volitional disturbance characterized by unreflective or involuntary aggression and the absence of other symptoms. According to Berrios (1996), it "provided the kernel around which the notion of psychopathic personality was eventually to become organised" (p. 428). Part of the motivation for developing the concept of emotional or volitional disturbances in general, and more specifically the notion of impulsion, was forensic: for the testimony of clinicians to be legally relevant in criminal courts, their expertise had to extend beyond the realm of "total insanity" (Berrios, 1996).

In the first half of the 20th century, the concept of psychopathy was narrowed to refer to personality disorder in general. Personality disorder itself was defined as a chronic disturbance of emotion or volition, or a disturbance of their integration with intellectual functions, that resulted in socially disruptive behavior. As Blackburn (1993) noted, this represented a shift from viewing psychopaths as "damaged" to "damaging" (p. 80). Although there was little agreement among clinicians concerning the specific variants of personality disorder they identified, or in the names given to these disorders, there was consensus that one important cluster was characterized by impulsive, aggressive, and antisocial behavior. For example, Schneider described "labile," "explosive," "affectionless," and "wicked" psychopaths; Kahn described a cluster of "impulsive," "weak," and "sexual" psychopaths; and Henderson described a cluster of psychopaths with "predominantly aggressive" features (Berrios, 1996, pp. 431–433).

Over the past 50 years or so, the concept of psychopathy was narrowed further still and now refers to a specific form of PD. The development of this modern view has its roots in the psychodynamic formulations that characterized much of the first half of this century (see Meloy, 1988), and in the rich clinical descriptions provided in Cleckley's *The Mask of Sanity*, first published in 1941.

The importance of aggression and violence in psychopathic symptomatology has always been clear, and is well represented in current diagnostic criteria: those for ASPD in *DSM-IV*; those for dyssocial personality disorder (DSPD) in *ICD-10*; and those for psychopathy in the Hare PCL-R and the Screening Version of the PCL-R (PCL:SV; Hart, Cox, & Hare, 1995). Each set contains one criterion directly related to a history of irritability, hostility, and aggression, including overt physical violence. In addition, each set contains several criteria that are indirectly related to aggression or violence (e.g., callousness, lack of remorse). It is worth noting that the historical link between psychopathy and violence is not peculiar to Western psychiatry. Indeed, psychopathy is a disorder that apparently occurs in every culture, and the potential for violence usually is considered symptomatic of the disorder (Cooke, 1996, 1998; Tyrer & Ferguson, 1988).

It is important to recognize that psychopathy is not synonymous with criminality or violence; not all psychopaths engage in criminal activities and not all criminals are psychopaths. Some commentators use the term primary psychopathy for the construct described in this chapter, a term that recognizes the importance of genetic, biological, and tempermental predispositions. The terms secondary or neurotic psychopathy sometimes are used for individuals whose behavior appears to result from social or intrapsychic forces and experiences.

Some clinicians and researchers view the terms psychopathy and sociopathy as interchangeable, but, like Lykken (1995), we prefer to use the latter to refer to the products of poor socialization practices.

Although psychopaths clearly are prone to violate many of society's rules and expectations, some manage to avoid formal contacts with the criminal justice system (see Hare, 1993). Some are unreliable and untrustworthy employees; unscrupulous, predatory businessmen; corrupt politicians; or unethical and immoral professionals whose prestige and power are used to victimize their clients, patients, and the general public. Except for occasional news and anecdotal clinical reports, we know little about these individuals. Systematic research is needed to determine the prevalence of psychopathy in the general population, the varieties of criminal and noncriminal ways in which the disorder manifests itself, and the extent to which research with criminal psychopaths informs us about psychopaths in general. With respect to the latter issues, there are indications that the personality structure and propensity for unethical behavior probably are much the same in criminal and noncriminal psychopaths (e.g., Babiak, 1995; Cleckley, 1976; Forth, Brown, Hart, & Hare, 1996; Gustafson & Ritzer, 1995).

In this chapter we focus on the association between psychopathy and crime, particularly violent crime.

Assessment Issues: Two Diagnostic Traditions

It is clear now, despite occasional claims to the contrary, that traditional descriptions of psychopathy are in good agreement with current views of psychiatrists, psychologists, criminal justice personnel, experimental psychopathologists, and even the lay public (e.g., Livesley, 1986; Rogers, Duncan, Lynett, & Sewell, 1994; Tennent, Tennent, Prins, & Bedford, 1990). Nevertheless, there still is debate concerning the assessment of the disorder. Two major approaches have influenced clinical practice and empirical research (Hare, Hart, & Harpur, 1991; Lilienfeld, 1994). One stems naturally from the rich European and North American clinical tradition. It is reflected in the writings of Cleckley (1976), in the *ICD-10* diagnostic criteria for DSPD, and in the efforts of researchers to provide a sound conceptual and psychometric basis for assessing the disorder (Hare, 1991; Hart et al., 1995). The second approach, part of the neo-Kraepelinian movement in psychodiagnosis, is closely associated with research emanating from Washington University in St. Louis, Missouri (e.g., Feighner et al., 1972; Robins, 1966). It is reflected in the *DSM-III, DSM-III-R*, and *DSM-IV* criteria for ASPD.

Clinical Tradition and The Hare PCL-R An adequate diagnosis must be based on the full range of psychopathic symptomatology. According to this tradition, a focus on behavioral symptoms (e.g., irresponsibility, delinquency) to the exclusion of interpersonal and affective symptoms (e.g., callousness, grandiosity, deceitfulness) leads to the overdiagnosis of psychopathy in criminal populations and to underdiagnosis in noncriminals (Hare et al., 1991; Lilienfeld, 1994; Widiger & Corbitt, 1995). We have spent considerable effort over the past 15 years developing and validating rating scales for the assessment of the traditional construct of psychopathy. To ensure accurate diagnosis, our view is that psychopathy should be assessed using expert observer (i.e., clinical) ratings, based on a semistructured interview, a review of case history materials—such as criminal or psychiatric records, interviews with family members and employers, and so forth—and supplemented with behavioral observations whenever possible (Hare, 1991). Self-report personality inventories may be useful for research purposes and as supplements to clinical-behavioral methods (e.g., see Blackburn, 1993; Lilienfeld, 1994; Newman, 1998), and they may provide useful information about other aspects of personality. However, on their own, they are are inadequate measures of psychopathy (Hare, 1985, 1991; Hart et al., 1995).

The Hare PCL-R was designed to operationalize the traditional construct of psychopathy (Hare, 1991). It is a 20-item clinical construct rating scale completed on the basis of a semistructured interview and detailed collateral or file information. Each item is scored on a 3-point scale according to specific criteria. The total score, which can range from 0 to 40, provides an estimate of the extent to which a given individual matches the prototypical psychopath, as exemplified, for example, in the work of Cleckley (1976). The Hare PCL-R was developed primarily with data from male offenders and forensic patients, and its psychometric properties in these populations are well established (e.g.,

Cooke, Forth, & Hare, 1998; Cooke & Michie, 1997; Hare, 1991, 1996). Indeed, Fulero (1995) described the PCL-R as the "state of the art . . . both clinically and in research use" (p. 454). There now is increasing evidence of the reliability and validity of the PCL-R with female offenders, psychiatric patients, and substance abusers (e.g., Alterman, Cacciola, & Rutherford, 1993; Hart & Hare, 1989; Rutherford, Cacciola, Alterman, & McKay, 1996; Salekin, Rogers, & Sewell, 1997). With only slight modifications (see Forth, Hart, & Hare, 1990; Forth, Kosson, & Hare, in press), the PCL-R is proving as useful with adolescent offenders as with adult offenders (e.g., Brandt, Kennedy, Patrick, & Curtin, 1997; Forth, 1997).

Indices of internal consistency (alpha coefficient, mean inter-item correlation) and interrater reliability generally are high, and evidence for all aspects of validity is substantial. Cross-cultural research (see Cooke, 1998; Cooke & Michie, in press) attests to the generalizability of the construct of psychopathy and of the PCL-R as its operational measure.

The high internal consistency of the PCL-R indicates that it measures a unitary construct, yet factor analyses consistently reveal a stable two-factor structure (Harpur, Hare, & Hakstian, 1989; Hare, 1991). Factor 1 consists of items having to do with the affective/interpersonal features of psychopathy, such as egocentricity, manipulativeness, callousness, and lack of remorse—characteristics that many clinicians consider central to psychopathy. Factor 2 reflects those features of psychopathy associated with an impulsive, antisocial, and unstable lifestyle, or social deviance. The two factors are correlated about .5, but have different patterns of correlations with external variables. These patterns make theoretical and clinical sense. For example, Factor 1 is correlated positively with prototypicality ratings of narcissistic and histrionic PD, self-report measures of narcissism and Machiavellianism, risk for recidivism and violence, and unusual processing of affective material (see below). It is correlated negatively with self-report measures of empathy and anxiety. Factor 2 is most strongly correlated with diagnoses of ASPD, criminal and antisocial behaviors, substance abuse, and various self-report measures of psychopathy. It is also correlated negatively with socioeconomic level, education, and IQ. The PCL-R factors appear to measure two facets of a higher order construct, namely psychopathy. However, IRT analyses conducted by Cooke and Michie (1997) indicate that Factor 1 items are more discriminating and provide more information about the construct than do Factor 2 items. Factor 1 items occur at high levels of the construct and in the most extreme cases, whereas Factor 2 items are present at low levels of the construct. These analyses lend firm support for the clinical tradition that places interpersonal and affective features at the core of the disorder.

A 12-item screening version of the PCL-R (the Hare PCL:SV; Hart et al., 1995) was developed for use in the MacArthur Risk Assessment study (Steadman et al., 1994) and was the basis for one of the criteria sets used in the *DSM-IV* field trial for ASPD (see table 22.1). The Hare PCL:SV can serve as a screen for psychopathy in forensic populations or as a stand-alone instrument for research with noncriminals, including civil psychiatric patients.

Washington University Tradition: *DSM-III*, *DSM-III-R*, and *DSM-IV* criteria for ASPD The Washington University tradition is based on a number of influential works published by people who worked or trained at that institution. One of the fundamental

Table 22.1 Items in the Hare PCL-R

Item	Description	Factor Loading
1.	Glibness/superficial charm	1
2.	Grandiose sense of self-worth	1
3.	Need for stimulation/proneness to boredom	2
4.	Pathological lying	1
5.	Conning/manipulative	1
6.	Lack of remorse or guilt	1
7.	Shallow affect	1
8.	Callous/lack of empathy	1
9.	Parasitic lifestyle	2
10.	Poor behavioral controls	2
11.	Promiscuous sexual behavior	—
12.	Early behavioral problems	2
13.	Lack of realistic, long-term goals	2
14.	Impulsivity	2
15.	Irresponsibility	2
16.	Failure to accept responsibility for own actions	1
17.	Many short-term marital relationships	—
18.	Juvenile delinquency	2
19.	Revocation of conditional release	2
20.	Criminal versatility	—

SOURCE: From Hare (1991).

— = item doesn't load on either factor.

assumptions of this approach is that assessment should focus on publicly observable behaviors, as clinicians are incapable of reliably assessing interpersonal and affective characteristics (Robins, 1978). Another assumption is that early-onset delinquency is a cardinal symptom of ASPD, one that helps to differentiate it from adult antisocial behavior and from major mental illnesses. These assumptions account for the heavy emphasis on delinquent and antisocial behavior in criteria sets based on this tradition.

The content of the *DSM-III* ASPD criteria was decided by a committee of the American Psychiatric Association's *DSM-III* Task Force, and was revised slightly by another committee for the *DSM-III-R* (Widiger, Frances, Pincus, Davis, & First, 1991). The *DSM-IV* criteria also were decided by committee, based only to a very limited extent on the results of empirical research (Widiger & Corbitt, 1995; Hare & Hart, 1995). These criteria are less behaviorally focused than were those in *DSM-III-R* and, in this respect, resemble the criteria for the other *DSM-IV* PDs.

The ASPD criteria do not constitute a scale or test. They do not have a response format per se, they do not yield a score, and they do not have norms. Rather, the assessor determines if each (sub-) criterion is present/true or absent/false. The final decision is dichotomous: if the criteria are all present, then a lifetime diagnosis of ASPD is made; if one or more is absent, no such diagnosis is made. The *DSM* also does not specify a particular method for assessing ASPD. In the empirical literature, researchers have employed methods ranging from structured interview to semistructured interview plus a review of case history information to file review alone.

Although the interrater and test-retest reliability of *DSM-III-R* diagnoses of ASPD were good to excellent (Widiger & Corbitt, 1995), the *DSM-IV* criteria are too recent to have been the focus of much published research. Even the *DSM-IV* ASPD field trial (see table 22.1) provided little useful information in this respect because the ASPD criteria as they appear in *DSM-IV* were never actually tested in the field trial (Hare & Hart, 1995).

Association Between PCL-R and *DSM* Criteria Although here we have emphasized the conceptual differences between criteria sets based on the two traditions, the empirical associations between them are quite strong, and diagnostic agreement between the procedures typically is fair to good, at least in forensic settings (e.g., Hare, 1985; Widiger et al., 1996). However, in these settings, the disorders have very different prevalence rates. According to *DSM* criteria, anywhere between 50 and 80% of offenders and forensic patients are diagnosed as ASPD, whereas only about 15 to 30% of the same people meet the PCL-R criteria for psychopathy (Hare, 1985; Hare et al., 1991; Robins, Tipp, & Przybeck, 1991). Most psychopathic offenders and patients meet the criteria for ASPD, but most of those with ASPD are not psychopaths. *DSM-IV* (p. 647) suggsts that *in forensic settings* the formal criteria for ASPD may need to be supplemented by clinical inferences about the personality traits measured by Factor 1 of the PCL-R. This results in a peculiar situation where the diagnostic criteria for ASPD vary with the circumstances or location of the individual being diagnosed.

Because of the problems with the *DSM-III* and *DSM-III-R* diagnosis of ASPD, the American Psychiatric Association carried out a multisite field trial in preparation for *DSM-IV* (see Hare et al., 1991; Widiger et al., 1996; Widiger & Corbitt, 1995). The field trial evaluated three criteria sets: the *DSM-III-R* criteria for ASPD; a 10-item psychopathic personality disorder (PPD) criteria derived from the PCL-R and from an early draft of its screening version, the Hare PCL:SV; and the *ICD-10* criteria for DSPD, a category that is consistent with the traditional construct of psychopathy. A major goal of the field trial was to determine if personality traits could be included in the criteria for ASPD without reducing reliability, and thereby to bring the diagnosis of ASPD back into line with clinical tradition and *ICD-10*. The results of the field trial indicated that most of the personality traits that reflect the symptoms of psychopathy—exemplified by the PPD and the *ICD-10* items—were at least as reliable as the more behaviorally specific *DSM-III-R* items, thus invalidating the original premise for excluding personality from the diagnosis of ASPD/psychopathy (Widiger et al., 1996). Inclusion of these psychopathy (PCL-R Factor 1) items might have improved the validity of ASPD without sacrificing reliability. As it is, ASPD and the PCL-R may measure different constructs (Hare, 1996). Alternatively, if they do measure the same construct they may do so differently. IRT analyses (Cooke & Michie, 1997) indicate that the PCL-R measures the latent trait of psychopathy across its entire range. Similar analyses of the field trial data (Cooke, unpublished data) suggest that the ASPD criteria set was less discriminating of the trait than was the PPD criteria set, particularly at high levels of the trait.

Prevalence

Estimates of the prevalence of a disorder in any given population depend to a large extent on how it is defined and assessed, as well as on the ways in which samples are selected. Such estimates also are dependent on whether the disorder is considered to be dimensional or categorical in nature (see below), and are likely to be as arbitrary as the cutting scores used to diagnose the disorder.

For these reasons, and also because it is difficult to obtain assessments outside of forensic settings, only indirect estimates of the prevalence of psychopathy in the general population are possible at this time. For example, the ratio of ASPD to psychopathy (PCL-R) in forensic settings is about 3 : 1 (see previous section), and it is not unreasonable to hypothesize that much the same ratio applies to the general population. The 3% prevalence rate for ASPD in North American males (*DSM-IV*) therefore would translate into a 1% rate for psychopathy. Cooke (1998) noted that the prevalence of psychopathy appears to be somewhat lower in several European countries, perhaps because of differences in the manner in which the disorder is presented and expressed. These and other cross-cultural issues are discussed at length elsewhere (Cooke, 1998; Cooke & Michie, in press).

Comorbidity

Increasing our understanding of comorbidity can inform our understanding of causal processes (Rutter, 1997). However, our knowledge of the comorbidity of psychopathy with other psychiatric disorders is limited and confused. Many of the traits and behaviors that define psychopathy—impulsivity, egocentricity, callousness, irresponsibility, and so forth—can be found either singly or in various combinations in other individuals and disorders. In this respect, psychopathy is similar to the personality disorders defined in *DSM-IV*, where overlapping criteria are not uncommon (Shea, 1994). This is not peculiar to personality disorders; we have much the same situation in general medicine, where, for example, some cardiac and gastrointestinal disorders can present with similar symptoms. But this does not mean that a common disease underlies these symptoms; differential diagnosis must be based on the presence or absence of particular clusters of symptoms, on differential laboratory findings, on differential treatment response, and on differential associations with risk factors. As Rutter (1997) noted, "it cannot reasonably be expected that diagnosis can be made on the basis of non-overlapping patterns of symptoms" (p. 277).

The issue of comorbidity with respect to psychopathy, like that of prevalence, is complicated by the debate about whether psychopathy is better viewed as a dimensional construct (e.g., Blackburn, 1993; Jackson & Livesley, 1994; Widiger, 1998) or as a categorical entity (e.g., Hare, 1996; Harris, Rice, & Quinsey, 1994). This is a key issue that must be resolved before meaningful statements about comorbidity can be made. A artifactual comorbidity will occur "when the disorders are, in reality, based on quantitative dimensional features rather than qualitatively distinct categories" (Rutter, 1997, p. 267). The evidence that psychopaths are qualitatively different from nonpsychopaths remains unclear. If the dimensional model pertains, it is not surprising that there is substantial comorbidity of psychopathy with antisocial, narcissistic, histrionic, and borderline PD (Blackburn, 1998; Hare, 1991; Nedopil, Hollweg, Hartmann, & Jaser, 1998). In any case, one would expect comorbidity with substance-related disorders (Hemphill, Hart, & Hare, 1994; Nedopil et al., 1998).

Psychopathy and Crime

In the past few years there has been a dramatic change in role played by psychopathy in the criminal justice system. Formerly a prevailing view was that clinical diagnoses of psychopathy were of little value in understanding and predicting criminal behaviors. However, even a cursory inspection of the features that define psychopathy—callousness, impulsivity, egocentricity, grandiosity, irresponsibility, lack of empathy, guilt, or remorse, and so forth—indicates that psychopaths should be much more likely than other members of the general public to bend and break the rules and laws of society. Because they are emotionally unconnected to the rest of humanity, and because they callously view others as little more than objects, it should be relatively easy for psychopaths to victimize the vulnerable and to use violence as a tool to obtain what they want. Although there never has been a shortage of anecdotal reports and clinical speculations about the association between psychopathy and crime, it was not until the introduction and widespread adoption of the PCL-R that the putative association between psychopathy and crime began to gain empirical validity. There now is an extensive and robust research literature on this association (see Hemphill, Hare, & Wong, 1998; Salekin, Rogers, & Sewell, 1996). One of the interesting findings to emerge from this research is that in spite of their small numbers—perhaps 1% of the general population—psychopaths make up a significant proportion of our prison populations and are responsible for a markedly disproportionate amount of serious crime and social distress. The most dramatic evidence of their implication in crime—and the focus of this chapter—is the apparent ease with which psychopaths engage in dispassionate, instrumental violence, some of it cruel and sadistic. Below, we give some examples of this evidence.

Crime Across the Life Span Psychopathy is closely associated with antisocial and criminal behavior, but it should not be confused with criminality in general. Criminal behavior is much more common in society than is psychopathy. It may even be normative for people to engage in isolated instances of less serious criminal conduct (Blackburn, 1993). Psychopaths are qualitatively different from others who routinely engage in criminal behavior, different even from those whose criminal conduct is extremely serious and persistent. They have distinctive "criminal careers" with respect to the number and type of antisocial behaviors they commit, as well as the ages at which they commit them. Furthermore, it appears that the antisocial behavior of psychopaths is motivated by different factors than is that of nonpsychopaths, with the result that the behavioral topography of their criminal conduct (i.e., their victimology or modus operandi) also is different. The personality and social psychological factors that explain antisocial behavior in general may be less applicable to psychopaths.

Although the typical criminal career is relatively short, there are individuals who devote most of their adolescent and adult life to delinquent and criminal activites. Among these persistent offenders are psychopaths, who begin their antisocial and criminal activities at a relatively early age and continue to engage in these activities throughout much of the life (Forth & Burke, 1998; Hare, Forth, & Strachan, 1992).

Many of these "career" criminals become less grossly antisocial in middle age (Blumstein & Cohen, 1987; Robins, 1966). About half of the criminal psychopaths we have studied showed a relatively sharp reduction in criminality around age 35 or 40, primarily with respect to nonviolent offenses (Hare, McPherson, & Forth, 1988). This does not mean that they had given up crime completely, only that their level of general criminal activity had decreased to that of the average persistent offender. Moreover, it appears that the propensity for psychopaths to engage in violent and aggressive behavior decreased very little with age, a finding also reported by Harris, Rice, and Cormier (1991).

A question we might ask is this: Are age-related reductions in the criminality of psychopaths paralleled by changes in core personality traits, or have these individuals simply learned new ways of staying out of prison? Although we share the view of many clinicians that the personality structure of psychopaths is too stable to account for the behavioral changes that sometimes occur in middle age, empirical, longitudinal evidence is needed to resolve the issue. Meanwhile, a cross-sectional study of a large sample of male offenders provides a clue to what we might expect (Harpur & Hare, 1994). The offenders ranged in age from 16 to 70 at the time they were assessed with the PCL or the PCL-R. Scores on Factor 2 (socially deviant features) decreased sharply with age, whereas scores on Factor 1 (affective/interpersonal features) remained stable. These results are consistent with the view that age-related changes in the psychopath's antisocial behavior are not necessarily paralleled by changes in the egocentric, manipulative, and callous traits fundamental to psychopathy.

Violence: Postdictive Studies Several studies suggest that psychopaths have relatively high rates of violent offending in the community and in institutions. Hare (1981) examined past violent behavior in a large sample of adult male offenders. Psychopaths were more likely than were nonpsychopaths to have had at least one conviction for a violent offense; to have a high rate of conviction for armed robbery, robbery, and assault; and to have engaged in fights and aggressive homosexuality in prison.

Hare and McPherson (1984a) looked at the association between psychopathy and past violence in a large sample of adult male offenders. Compared with nonpsychopaths, the psychopaths had been convicted of about three times as many violent crimes (possession of weapons, robbery, assault, kidnapping, vandalism, and fighting), and had engaged in more institutional violence, including incidents of verbal abuse, verbal threats, irritability, belligerence, and fighting.

In a study of adult male offenders, Serin (1991) found that every psychopath, but only two thirds of the nonpsychopaths, had prior convictions for violence. Similar associations between psychopathy and violence have been reported in several other studies (e.g., Forth & Burke, 1998; Serin, Peters, & Barbaree, 1990).

Psychopathic offenders not only engage in more violence than do other offenders, they also seem to commit different types of violence acts. Williamson, Hare, and Wong (1987) examined police reports concerning the violent offenses of a random sample of adult male offenders. About two thirds of the victims of psychopaths were male strangers, whereas two thirds of the victims of nonpsychopaths were female family members or acquaintances. Furthermore, the violence of psychopaths seemed to be motivated primarily by revenge or retribution, whereas other offenders committed acts of violence while in a state of extreme emotional arousal.

Cornell et al. (1996) examined instrumental (i.e., predatory) versus reactive (i.e., hostile, impulsive) violence in two samples of adult male offenders. They found that almost all violent offenders had a history of reactive (i.e., expressive, impulsive, or emotional) violence, but that some also had a history of instrumental (i.e., goal-directed or predatory) violence. Instrumentally violent offenders had significantly higher scores on the PCL-R and the PCL:SV than did offenders who had committed only reactive violence. Similar findings recently were reported by Dempster et al. (1996; see also Hart & Dempster, 1997). In addition, Dempster et al. (1996) examined partial correlations between the PCL-R factor scores and ratings of instrumental versus reactive violence in a sample of mentally disordered offenders. PCL-R Factor 1 scores were correlated significantly with ratings of instrumental violence (after partialing Factor 2), whereas Factor 2 scores were correlated with ratings of reactive violence (after partialing Factor 1).

Cooke, Philip, Michie, and Carr (1997) found that PCL-R scores in a large sample of Scottish prisoners were strongly correlated with estimates of lifetime violence, as well as with the use of instrumental violence to either control the trade in illicit drugs or to gain goods or money with which to pay for illicit drugs.

Future Crime: Predictive Studies The significance of psychopathy as a risk factor for recidivism and violence is now well established. The empirical literature has been extensively reviewed in two recent meta-analyses of the PCL-R (Salekin et al., 1996; Hemphill et al., 1998), and only a summary and sampling of recent findings are provided here.

In the first study of its type, Hart, Kropp, and Hare (1988) found that the PCL-R made a significant contribution to the prediction of reoffending over and above the contribution made by relevant criminal-history and demographic variables. They also performed a survival analysis in which survival—that is, not being returned to prison—was plotted as a function of time following release. Within three years most of the psychopaths were back in prison, whereas most of the other offenders were still "on the street."

In a more recent study, Serin and Amos (1995) followed a large sample of male offenders for up to eight years after their release from a federal prison. Within three years, the psychopaths were more than twice as likely as the nonpsychopaths to have been convicted of a new crime, and about four times as likely to have been convicted of a violent crime. Similarly, Harris, Rice, and Quinsey (1993) found that the PCL-R was the single most important predictor of violent recidivism in a large sample of offenders released from a maximum security unit and a pretrial assessment center. In a Swedish study of a large sample of personality disordered offenders released into the community, Gran, Langström, Tengström, and Kullgren (in press) found that the risk for violent recidivism in a follow-up period that averaged more than four years was about four times higher among psychopaths (defined by a PCL-R cutoff score of 26 or more) than among nonpsychopaths (a PCL-R score below 26).

Although the prevalence of psychopathy is lower in forensic psychiatric populations than in offender populations, the presence of psychopathic attributes in forensic patients is as much a risk factor for recidivism and violence as it is in prison populations. For example, Rice and Harris (1992) found that scores on the PCL-R were as predictive of recidivism a sample of male not-guilty-by-reason-of-insanity schizophrenics as in a sample of nonpsychotic offenders. Hart and Hare (1989) found that only a small minority of consecutive admissions to a forensic psychiatric hospital were psychopaths, but that many patients exhibited a significant number of PCL-R symptoms. In a recent survival analysis of recidivism in this sample, Wintrup, Coles, Hart, & Webster (1994) found that psychopaths were about three times more likely to reoffend in a five-year period following release than were other patients. Tengström, Grann, Langström, and Kullgren (1999) used a PCL-R cutoff score of 26 to divide a large sample of violent schizophrenic offenders into psychopaths and nonpsychopaths. In the period following release into the community (an average of 51 months) the risk for a violent conviction was about four times higher among the psychopaths than among the nonpsychopaths, a ratio virtually the same as that reported by Grann et al. (in press) for personality disordered offenders (see previous paragraph).

Several studies have found that the PCL-R and the PCL:SV are predictive of institutional aggression and violence in forensic psychiatric hospitals (Hill, Rogers, & Bickford, 1996; Heilbrun et al., 1998). They also predict violence following release from a psychiatric institution. Douglas, Ogloff, and Nicholls (1997) assessed postrelease community violence in a large sample of male and female patients who had been involuntarily committed to a civil psychiatric facility. Although very few of the patients had a score high enough to warrant a diagnosis of psychopathy, the PCL:SV nevertheless was highly predictive of violent behaviors and arrests for violent crimes. When the distribution of PCL:SV scores was split at the median, the odds ratio for a violent crime was about 10 times higher for patients above the median than it was for those below it.

Although relatively little research has been conducted on psychopathy in female offenders, there are indications that recidivism rates among female psychopathic offenders may be higher than they are among other female offenders. Hare, Strachan, and Hemphill (1998) found that within one year of release from prison the recidivism rate for psychopaths (PCL-R) was more than twice the rate for nonpsychopaths. Salekin, Rogers, Ustad, and Sewell (1998) reported that at 50 days following release from prison the recidism rate for psychopaths (PCL-R) was almost seven times the rate for other offenders. However, after 50 days the difference between the groups disappeared.

Psychopathy is a strong predictor of recidivism and violence in adolescent offenders. Gretton, O'Shaughnessy, and Hare, 1998b examined the predictive validity of the PCL-R in a large sample of young offenders, age 12 to 18, who had been sent by the courts to a youth facility for psychological and psychiatric evaluation. Within five years after evaluation, the psychopaths were almost three times more likely than the nonpsychopaths to have committed at least one violent offence and to have attempted at least one escape from custody. Even when relevant demographic and criminal history variables were taken into account, the PCL-R made a substantial and significant contribution to the prediction of violent offending. Toupin Mercier, Déry, Côté, and Hodgins (1996) administered a French translation of the PCL-R (see Côté & Hodgins, 1996) to male adolescents receiving treatment in rehabilitation centers, day centers, or special educational programs. During a one-year follow-up period, PCL-R scores were significantly correlated with delinquency, aggressive behavior, alcohol use, and number of aggressive conduct disorder symptoms. Forth and Burke (1998) reported that violent recidivism in young offenders was significantly related to scores on the PCL-R. Similar results were obtained by Brandt et al. (1997) with a sample of mostly African-American young offenders.

These and other studies led Hemphill et al. (1998) to conclude that in the first year following release from prison psychopaths are three times more likely to reoffend, and four times more likely to violently reoffend, than are nonpsychopaths.

Sexual Violence It long has been recognized that psychopathic sex offenders present special problems for therapists and the criminal justice system. Indeed, some jurisdictions make provision for confining psychopathic sex offenders for indefinite terms in a forensic hospital. Prentky and Knight (1991) argued that rapists, on average, are significantly more psychopathic than are those who offend against children or adolescents. Several studies have examined this issue in more detail. Forth and Kroner (1994) looked at the PCL-R scores of a large sample of incarcerated adult male sex offenders. They found that the prevalence of psychopathy was 5.4% among incest offenders, 26.1%

among rapists, and 18.3% among "mixed" offenders (i.e., men who had offended against both children and adult women). Quinsey, Rice, and Harris (1995) examined a sample of sex offenders assessed or treated at a forensic psychiatric hospital and found a similar pattern of results. Miller, Geddings, Levenston, and Patrick (1994) found that among sex offenders in a treatment facility, rapists, those who had assaulted adolescents, and those who had assaulted children, had a base rate of psychopathy (PCL-R) of 76.5, 25.0, and 14.8%, respectively.

Within these broad categories of sex offenders, psychopathy is associated with specific motivational or behavioral offence characteristics. Two studies have examined the association between the PCL-R and the MTC:R3 classification system for rapists (see Prentky & Knight, 1991). The MTC: R3 system identifies four major types of rapists—vindictive, opportunistic, sadistic, and nonsadistic—that constitute nine subtypes. The primary motivation of the sadistic and nonsadistic types is sexual; and the primary motivation of the vindictive and opportunistic types is aggressive or hostile. Barbaree, Seto, Serin, Amos, and Preston (1994) used the MTC:R3 to classify a sample of incarcerated rapists. The mean PCL-R score was highest in the opportunistic and sadistic offenders, and lowest in the vindictive and nonsadistic offenders. Brown and Forth (1997) also used the MTC:R3 system in their study of rapists. They found that 81% of the psychopaths and 56% of the nonpsychopaths were classified as either opportunistic or vindictive.

Dixon, Hart, Gretton, McBride, and O'Shaughnessy (1995) examined the utility of the FBI's Crime Classification Manual (Douglas, Burgess, Burgess, & Ressler, 1992) in juvenile sex offenders. The mean PCL-R score for offenders who committed each type of sexual offence was as follows: anger and sadistic rape, 28.7 (4.0); domestic rape (e.g., incest, child abuse), 18.9 (7.6); entitlement rape (e.g., date rape, power-reassurance rape), 18.2 (7.5); and nuisance offenses (e.g., voyeurism, exhibitionism), 18.8 (8.7).

Psychopathy is related to the type and degree of violence committed during sexual offenses. Miller et al. (1994) found that sex offenders who used violence had significantly higher PCL-R scores than did those who did not use violence. Gretton, McBride, O'Shaughnessy, and Hare (1998a) found that adolescent sex offenders diagnosed as psychopaths (PCL-R) used more frequent and more severe violence during the commission of their acts than did nonpsychopathic sex offenders.

The studies on subtypes of sexual offenders cited above suggest that psychopathy may be associated with sexual sadism. Consistent with this view, two studies of adult sex offenders found that PCL-R scores were significantly correlated with sexual arousal to violent stimuli, as assessed by penile plethysmography (Quinsey et al., 1995; Serin, Malcolm, Khanna, & Barbaree, 1994). Also, Dempster and Hart (1996), in a sample of male juveniles charged with murder or attempted murder, found that those classified according to the Crime Classification Manual criteria as sexual homicide perpetrators had significantly higher PCL-R scores than did criminal enterprise, personal cause, or group excitement perpetrators.

Sex offenders generally are resistant to treatment (Quinsey, Harris, Rice, & Lalumiere, 1993), but it is the psychopaths among them who are most likely to recidivate early and often. For example, Quinsey et al. (1995), in a follow-up of treated rapists and child molesters, concluded that psychopathy functions as a general predictor of sexual and violent recidivism. They found that within six years of release from prison more than 80% of the psychopaths, but only about 20% of the nonpsychopaths, had violently recidivated. Many, but not all, of their offenses were sexual in nature. In a more recent follow-up of a large sample of sex offenders, Rice and Harris (1997) reported similar results. In addition, however, they found that sexual recidivism (as opposed to violent recidivism in general) was strongly predicted by a combination of a high PCL-R score and phallometric evidence of deviant sexual arousal, defined as any phallometric test that indicated a preference for deviant stimuli (children, rape cues, or nonsexual violence cues).

The implications of psychopathy are just as serious among adolescent sex offenders as among their adult counterparts. Gretton, O'Shaughnessy, and Hare (1998b) found that the reconviction rate for sexual offenses in the first five years following release was low (about 15%) and only moderately related to psychopathy (PCL-R). However, the pattern for other types of offenses was quite different. Thus, in the follow-up period, 51% of the offenders committed another crime; the rate of offending was more than three times as high in psychopaths as in nonpsychopaths. Psychopaths who exhibited phallometric evidence of deviant sexual arousal posed by far the highest risk of reoffending; about 90% of these individuals committed at least one offence in the follow-up period, whereas about 40% of the other offenders (including psychopaths who did not exhibit deviant sexual arousal) committed at least one offence. One conclusion from these results is that, following release, many adolescent sex offenders, and most psychopathic ones, were more likely to be convicted of a nonsexual than a sexual offense. Many of these individuals were not so much specialized sex offenders as they were offenders, and their misbehavior—sexual and otherwise—presumably was a reflection of a generalized propensity to violate social and legal expectations. If so, it may be as important to target their antisocial tendencies and behaviors as it is to treat their sexual deviancy.

Response to Treatment

Most clinicians and researchers are pessimistic about the treatability of psychopaths, with good reason. Unlike most other offenders, psychopaths suffer little personal distress, see little wrong with their attitudes and behavior, and seek treatment only when it is in their best interests to do so, such as when applying for probation or parole. It is therefore not surprising that they derive little benefit from traditional treatment programs, particularly those aimed at the development of empathy, conscience, and interpersonal skills (Dolan & Coid, 1993; Hare, 1993; Losel, 1998; Suedfeld & Landon, 1978). For example, Ogloff, Wong, and Greenwood (1990) reported that PCL-R psychopaths derived little benefit from an intensive therapeutic community program designed to treat personality disordered offenders. The psychopaths stayed in the program for a shorter time, were less motivated, and showed less clinical improvement than did other offenders. Hemphill and Wong (1991) reported that once released from prison, the reconviction rate in the first year was twice as high for the psychopaths (83%) as for the other offenders (42%).

Rice, Harris, and Cormier (1992) used file information to score the PCL-R and to code a variety of criminal history and other variables for offenders who previously had received at least two years (on average, more than five years) of intensive treatment in a therapeutic community program at a forensic hospital. This group included mentally ill and personality disordered offenders, as well as forensic patients who had been found not guilty by reason of insanity or incompetent to stand trial. The treated offenders were compared to a group of offenders who had been assessed at the hospital but, for a variety of reasons, not treated. The untreated controls were matched to the treated patients on variables that included age, index offense, and offense history, and both groups were subdivided into PCL-R psychopaths and nonpsychopaths. Progress in the treatment program was coded from institutional files.

Compard with other treated offenders, PCL-R psychopaths had more behavior problems while in the program, including more negative entries (concerning disruptive or counter-therapeutic behavior) recorded by treatment staff in the files during the first and last years in treatment, more incidents of seclusion for disruptive behavior during the first and last years of treatment, more referrals to a disciplinary subprogram, and a higher rate of misbehavior. Interesting, psychopaths also had as many positive entries recorded by treatment staff in their files as did nonpsychopaths.

Posttreatment general and violent recidivism (new charges, reincarceration, or rehospitalization due to criminal behavior) was examined in patients and controls over a follow-up period that averaged 10.5 years. The rate of general recidivism was 59% in the treated group and 68% in the controls; for violent recidivism, the rates were 40 and 46%, respectively. Thus, it appeared that treatment had little impact overall. However, when the recidivism rates of psychopaths and other offenders were examined, a surprising finding emerged: among psychopaths, the rates of general recidivism were equally high in the treated and untreated groups (87 and 90%, respectively); however, the rate of violent recidivism was significantly higher in the treated group than in the untreated group (77 and 55%). In contrast, the treated nonpsychopaths had significantly lower rates of general and violent recidivism (44 and 22%, respectively) than did the untreated nonpsychopaths (58 and 39%). Thus, although the therapeutic community appeared to be efficacious for nonpsychopaths, it actually may have been harmful for psychopaths.

But how could therapy make someone worse? The simple answer is that group therapy and insight-oriented programs may help psychopaths to develop better ways of manipulating, deceiving, and using people, but do little to help them to understand themselves. As a consequence, following release into the community they may be more likely than untreated psychopaths to continue to place themselves in situations where the potential for violence is high. However, before we spend too much effort in trying to determine why some therapies make psychopaths worse we need more evidence that they in fact become so. The findings by Rice et al. (1992), though intriguing and suggestive, were based on retrospective research with a particular population of mentally disordered offenders, and with an unusual, complex, and controversial treatment program.

At best, the results of these and other studies are discouraging. But we should emphasize that there is no conclusive evidence that psychopaths are completely untreatable or that their behavior cannot be modified. Major methodological weaknesses in the relevant literature include inadequate assessment procedures, poorly defined treatments, lack of posttreatment follow-ups, and lack of adequate control or comparison groups make it difficult to be certain that "nothing works." We need to mount a concerted effort to develop innovative procedures designed specifically for psychopathic offenders (Dolan & Coid, 1993; Hare, 1993; Losel, 1998). The broad outline of what such a program might look like has been provided by Hare (1992). In brief, he proposed that relapse-prevention techniques be integrated with elements of the best available cognitive-behavioral correctional programs. The program would be less concerned with developing empathy and conscience or effecting changes in personality than with convincing participants that they alone are responsible for their behavior and that they can learn more prosocial ways of using their strengths and abilities to satisfy their needs and wants. It would involve tight control and supervision, both in the institution and following release into the community, as well as comparisons with carefully selected groups of offenders treated in standard correctional programs. The experimental design would permit empirical evaluation of its treatment and intervention modules (what works and what doesn't work for particular individuals). That is, some modules or components might be effective with psychopaths but not with other offenders, and vice versa. Hare (1992) recognized that correctional programs are constantly in danger of erosion because of changing institutional priorities, community concerns, and political pressures. To prevent this from happening, he proposed stringent safeguards for maintaining the integrity of the program.

Recently, Losel (1998) provided an analysis of the issues involved in the treatment and management of offenders in general, and psychopathic offenders in particular, and has outlined the requirements for an effective program. Although arrived at independently, his conclusions and recommendations are consistent with those provided by Hare (1992).

The Etiology of Psychopathy

The etiology of psychopathy is unknown at present, and there exists no comprehensive theory that adequately accounts for the full range of clinical features and research findings. Below we describe several etiological and descriptive models, perhaps more accurately referred to as "mini-theories," hypotheses, or speculations (see Cooke et al., 1998, and Lykken, 1995, for more extended discussions). The lack of a comprehensive theory is not really surprising, given the limited empirical research on psychopathy (at least, limited in comparison to research on disorders such as schizophrenic, mood, and anxiety disorders). However, the situation is changing rapidly, and the near future should see the emergence of more general theories of psychopathy as the result of the integration of clinical insights, developmental psychopathology, cognitive neuroscience, neurobiology, behavioral genetics, and sociobiology.

Psychopathy as Adaptation: The Sociobiological Model Although psychopathy typically is considered to be a mental disorder, sociobiologists view it as only one of several possible adaptive strategies for passing on genes to the next generations (Mealey, 1995). While most humans have only a few children and care for them carefully, psychopaths use an adaptive "cheating" strategy in which they have large numbers of children and devote little time or effort to their care. Either strategy can be adaptive and successful, depending on a variety of social, economic, and environmental factors. A female psychopath, for example, might adopt a seductive mating strategy in which any offspring are quickly abandoned. For a male psychopath, the most effective way to have lots of children is to mate with a woman, quickly abandon her, and move on to the next woman. His goal of mating with a new woman is facilitated by deception, manipulation, cheating, and generally misrepresenting his status. "Of course, people who make a practice of lying and cheating usually get caught. Their effectiveness then is greatly reduced, so they quickly move on to other partners, groups, neighborhoods, or cities. The mobile, nomadic lifestyle of psychopaths, and the ease with which they adapt to new social environments, can be seen as part of a constant need for fresh breeding grounds" (Hare, 1993, p. 168). This "migration" hypothesis finds some support in the recent finding that the prevalence of psychopathy appears to be greater among Scottish criminals who emigrate to England than it is among those who remain in Scotland (Cooke & Michie, in press). However, Cooke and Michie caution that the search for fresh opportunities and victims is not the only reason psychopaths are nomadic. Impulsivity, a need for stimulation, lack of long-term goals, and so forth are all factors that impel the psychopath to move to new surroundings.

The sociobiology of psychopathy has been worked out in some detail by Mealey (1995). She argues that psychopaths have a genotype that results in an "inborn temperament or personality, coupled with a particular pattern of autonomic hypoarousal that, together, design the child to be selectively unresponsive to the cues necessary for normal socialization and moral development" (p. 536).

Psychopathy as Variant of Normal Personality: The Trait Model This model also does not discuss psychopathy as a distinct mental disorder. Rather, it suggests that what we call psychopathy is simply an extreme variation of basic traits of normal personality. Several investigators have attempted to understand psychopathy in terms of the five-factor model (FFM) of personality (Costa & McCrae, 1992). In most cases, this involved mapping the items of the PCL-R onto the FFM (Harpur, Hart, & Hare, 1994; Hart & Hare, 1994; Widiger, 1998). For example, Harpur et al. (1994) found that the PCL-R was significantly (negatively) correlated with agreeableness in a sample of male offenders, but was uncorrelated with neuroticism, extraversion, openness, or conscientiousness. At the facet level, the PCL-R was significantly correlated only with hostility and excitement seeking. Additional analyses indicated that a combination of the five factors was significantly related to scores on the PCL-R, but that the association was not strong enough for the factors to "produce" the personality of the psychopath. Harpur et al. (1994) suggested that a specific five-factor profile might represent a risk factor for psychopathy, but that "additional attributes or experiences that lie outside the sphere of traditional personality research" might be required to describe the full range of psychopathic symptomology. These additional factors include a variety of cognitive, affective, and neurobiological anomalies found in psychopaths (see the following sections).

In a more recent analysis, Widiger (1998) argued that the PCL-R and the FFM in fact mesh quite well, particularly when the analysis is conducted with the facets that underlie the five factors. He concluded that psychopathy may represent an extreme variant of common personality traits found in varying degrees in everyone, and that all the items in the PCL-R appeared to be contained within the FFM of normal personality. Widiger (1998) emphasized that the PCL-R and five-factor conceptualizations of psychopathy were complementary rather than contradictory. While the FFM enriches "the understanding of the syndrome of prototypic Psychopathy by placing it within the broader context of normal personality . . . the PCL-R in turn provides a vivid description of an especially problematic and even volatile constellation of personality traits. Identifying the constellation with a single term, Psychopathy, is then appropriate and very useful to clinical practice and empirical research" (pp. 64–65). Widiger's arguments are logical and compelling, but to our knowledge there are no empirical data demonstrating that a regression equation using the FFM factors and facets is effective in classifying PCL-R psychopaths.

Other investigators have focused on the relation between psychopathy and personality traits related to interpersonal style. For example, Blackburn (1993, 1998) has outlined a model of psychopathy based on the work of Leary (1957), Sullivan (1953), and Wiggins and his colleagues (e.g., Wiggins & Trapnell, 1996). He has conceived of psychopathy "as a dimension of personality disorder linked in turn to the structure of personality as it is currently understood. I have suggested that psychopathy can be understood primarily as the coercive control of interpersonal transactions, and that social cognitive processes may be a possible key to understanding" (Blackburn, 1998, p. 296). Specifically, Blackburn argued that psychopathy is primarily an interpersonal dimension asscociated with the hostile-dominant quadrant of the interpersonal circumplex and with the personality dimension of agreeableness. He also suggests that the behavior of psychopaths, though distasteful and "evil" to others, represents an attempt to make sense of the world as they see it.

Most trait models assume (at least implicitly) that personality is determined in part by genetic factors. A recent behavioral genetics (twin) study used a self-report scale of personality traits, The Dimensional Assessment of Personality Pathology (DAPP; Livesley & Jackson, 1998), to estimate the relative contributions of genes and environment to the expression of psychopathic symptoms (Livesley, 1998). The DAPP contains several factor scales related to psychopathy, including callousness, conduct problems, and narcissism. The heritability estimate for these scales was .56, .56, and .53, respectively. These heritability estimates are similar to those obtained for normal personality traits and antisocial behaviors (DiLalla, Carey, Gottesman, & Bouchard, 1996; Lykken, 1995).

Psychopathy as Brain Dysfunction: The Neurological Model A biological theory that has been around for a long time is that, for reasons unknown, some of the psychopath's brain structures mature at an abnormally slow rate (Hare, 1970). The basis for the theory is threefold: evidence that some parts of the brain, including frontal cortex and its associated neural pathways, continue to develop into early adulthood; reports of similarities between the recorded brain waves of adult psychopaths and those of normal adolescents; and similarities between some of the psychopath's characteristics—including egocentricity, impulsivity, selfishness, and unwillingness to delay gratification—and those of children. To some investigators, this suggests that psychopathy reflects little more than a developmental delay (Kegan, 1986).

These are interesting speculations, but the brain-wave characteristics in question are also associated with drowsiness or boredom in normal adults, and could as well result from the psychopath's sleepy disinterest in the routine procedures used to measure them as in a delay in brain development (Syndulko, 1978). Furthermore, it is unlikely that the egocentricity or impulsivity of children and psychopaths are really the same things. Few people would have any difficulty in distinguishing between the personality, motivations, and behavior of a normal 10-year-old and those of an adult psychopath, even after allowing for the difference in age.

A related biological model posits that psychopathy is associated with brain damage or dysfunction, especially in areas responsible for planning and executive processes (e.g., Gorenstein & Newman, 1980). This model is based on knowledge about frontal functions and on some apparent behavioral similarities between psychopaths and patients with damage to the frontal lobes of the brain (Damasio, 1994). These similarities include poor long-term planning, low frustration tolerance, shallow affect, irritability and aggressiveness, socially inappropriate behavior, and impulsivity. Evidence for frontal damage in psychopaths is equivocal (e.g., Gorenstein, 1982; Hare, 1984; Smith, Arnett, & Newman, 1992), and the similarities between psychopaths and frontal patients may be only superficial, or at least no more important than the differences. Still, several investigators have argued persuasively that some sort of frontal-lobe dysfunction—not necessarily involving structural damage—may underlie the psychopath's impulsivity and frequent failure to inhibit inappropriate behavior (Gorenstien & Newman, 1980; Newman & Wallace, 1993). Recent neurobiological research (see the following section on The Neurobiological Approach) is consistent with this argument.

Psychopathy as Early Adversity: The Attachment Model Perhaps the most common view of psychopathy is that it is related to, or the result of, early psychological traumas or adverse social experiences. It is certainly true that many adult psychological and behavioral problems are associated with a host of early experiences, including parental rejection, neglect, deprivation, and abuse. For example, one popular view is that when adverse experiences occur during the first two years of life they can disrupt the normal processes by which children become emotionally "attached" to their primary caregivers. These attachment failures are thought to play an important role in the development of a variety of psychological and behavioral problems, including psychopathy (Magid & McKelvey, 1989). However, there is little empirical research to support the relevance of this view to psychopathy. In fact, it might be argued that so-called attachment and socialization problems are more the result of psychopathic propensities than the cause of them (Hare, 1993; Lykken, 1995). As McCord put it, "Both parental rejection and inconsistent punitiveness have been implicated in the etiology of Psychopathy . . . (but) the data have been retrospective and the behavior of the psychopath might well have caused, rather than resulted from, parental rejection" (McCord, 1984).

This is not to say that early family and other social experiences play no role in the development of psychopathy, only that research on the issue is too limited to draw any reasonable conclusions at this time (but see the following section).

Psychopathy as Adult Expression of Early Pathology: The Developmental Model There is a rapidly developing research literature on the progression from childhood and adolescent disorders to adult antisocial behaviors and disorders. Until recently this research focused almost entirely on early social, medical, and environmental problems and stressors, with relatively little attention being paid to individual differences in personality (e.g., Moffitt, 1993). The situation is beginning to change, with recognition that theory and research on antisocial behaviors and disorders will always be incomplete without active consideration of interpersonal, intrapersonal, and affective traits and processes.

Investigators such as McBurnett and Pfiffner (1998), Lynam (1996), and Lahey and his colleagues (e.g., Lahey, Hart, Pliszka, Applegate, & McBurnett, 1993), have identified a small subset of children whose personality, psychophysiology, and behaviors are similar in many respects to those of adult psychopaths. At the diagnostic level, it now appears that these high-risk children tend to exhibit the symptoms of both attentional deficit hyperactivity disorder (ADHD) and conduct disorder (see McBurnett & Pfiffner, 1998; Lynam, 1996). Lynam (1996) has described children with both ADHD and CD as "fledgling psychopaths." McBurnett & Pfifner (1998) have recently suggested that the combination of these disorders "has the empirically validated advantages of concentrating behavioral and biological risks for Psychopathy, and it has better content validity for emergent Psychopathy than does CD or ADHD alone" (p. 200).

Frick (1998) has studied the emergence of psychopathic traits in very young children, using a specially developed, age-appropriate version of the PCL-R, the Psychopathy Screening Device (PSD). He concluded that a cluster of traits (similar to those in PCL-R Factor 1) described as callous-unemotional (e.g., callousness, absence of empathy, lack of guilt) develops out of a biologically based tendency toward low behavioral inhibition. These traits make socialization difficult, and "make a child more likely to act against parental and societal norms and to violate the rights of others" (Frick, 1998, p. 170). Frick further suggests that "dysfunctional parenting practices may play a major role in the development of conduct problems *primarily in children without (callous-emotional) traits*" (p. 179; emphasis in original). Presumably, children with these traits are quite capable of developing conduct problems more or less on their own. This suggestion is consistent with research on adolescents conducted by Forth and her colleaques (see review by Forth & Burke, 1998). They determined that the quality of family background is less of a factor in the development of criminal behaviors of psychopathic offenders than it is in other offenders. As Lykken (1995) put it, "By definition, a child whose innate temperament makes him or her a potential psychopath must remain at high risk unless the parents are unusually skillful or unless they have skilled help" (p. 228).

The most complex versions of the developmental model focus on nature-nurture interactions. For example, Hare (1993) has argued that psychopathy "emerges from a complex—and poorly understood—interplay between biological factors and social forces. . . . In effect, the elements needed for the development of Psychopathy . . . are provided in part by nature and possibly by some unknown biological influences on the developing fetus and neonate. As a result, the capacity for developing internal controls and conscience and for making emotional 'connections' with others is greatly reduced" (p. 173). Social forces and parenting practices may influence the way in which the disorder develops and is expressed in behavior, but they are not the sole or primary causes of the disorder (e.g., Lykken, 1995). This interactive model is consistent with mounting evidence that genetic factors contribute to the biological bases of brain function and to basic personality structure, which in turn influence the way the individual responds to, and interacts with, life experiences and the social environment. It also is in line with the results of behavioral genetics research described earlier (Livesley, 1998).

Psychopathy as Learning Deficit, I: The Fearlessness Model Beginning some 40 years ago, Lykken (1957) has argued that psychopaths are relatively fearless, a condition that makes it difficult for them to "learn to avoid antisocial behaviors and to inhibit forbidden impulses, through punishment and the conditioned fear it leaves behind" (Lykken, 1995, p. 135). This fearlessness may reflect an extreme variant of normality, presumably one with a substantial heritable component, rather than psychosocial stress or structural brain damage.

Lykken (1995) has provided compelling arguments for the viability of the fearlessnesss model in explaining a range of antisocial behaviors and laboratory findings. Indeed, much of the early laboratory research on psychopathy was based on the model (see reviews by Hare, 1978, and Lykken, 1995). A consistent finding was that psychopaths showed relatively small increases in palmar skin conductance (an electrodermal response mediated by the sympathetic nervous system) in anticipation of an unpleasant or painful event, a finding that implies they experienced relatively little anticipatory fear and that helps to explain their difficulty in learning to avoid punishment.

However, it is not clear how well the model accounts for the full range of psychopathic symptomatology. That fearlessness would result in impulsive behavior, or at least in lifestyle impulsivity, seems intuitively obvious, as Lykken (1995) points out. However, his attempts to explain symptoms like superficiality, egocentricity, and shallow emotions in terms of fearlessness appear less convincing. He must resort to disagreeing with clinical descriptions of psychopathy, or to extending fearlessness into something that resembles the more general cognitive-affective model described below. The fearlessness model generated a considerable amount of early experimental research on psychopathy, but, unfortunately, has received less attention from researchers in recent years. As Lykken (1995) has noted, this is probably because it can be subsumed within the framework of the weak behavioral inhibition models described in the next section.

Psychopathy as Learning Deficit, II: The Weak BIS Model Gray (e.g., 1987) has described a neurophysiological behavioral inhibition system (BIS) that controls the organism's response to signals of impending punishment or frustrative nonreward. Another system, the behavioral activation system (BAS), controls responses to signals of impending reward. Arousal of the BIS is experienced as negative affect and results in inhibition of motoric activity that might lead to the expected punishment or nonreward. Thus, a weak BIS can result in the failure to inhibit activity that may lead to punishment or frustrative nonreward (i.e., passive avoidance learning deficits).

Fowles and Missel (1994) hypothesized that psychopaths have a weak BIS, associated specifically with a deficit in anticipatory anxiety, that "produces impulsivity as a result of the failure of cues for potential punishment and frustration to inhibit reward-seeking behavior" (p. 278). There are some problems with the BIS model of psychopathy, however. First, like the fearlessness model, it has difficulty accounting for the interpersonal and affective symptoms of psychopathy. Second, within Gray's theoretical framework, psychopaths are not truly impulsive. As discussed by Newman and Wallace (1993), Gray's model provides several "pathways to disinhibition," including hyperresponsivity to reward due to a strong BAS and abnormal responsivity to punishment due to a deficient BIS (hyporesponsivity resulting from a weak BIS, and hyperresponsivity from a strong BIS). Gray himself linked impulsivity with a strong BAS (Newman & Wallace, 1993). Thus, according to his model, it would be more appropriate to describe the behavior of psychopaths as disinhibited rather than impulsive. Third, although the BIS model receives partial support from studies of electrodermal responsivity, fear conditioning, and passive avoidance learning in psychopaths (Fowles & Missel, 1994; Hare, 1978; Lykken, 1995), psychopaths may not be generally hyporesponsive to punishment; rather, their hyporesponsivity may be apparent only when they are faced with a competing reward contingency (Newman & Wallace, 1993).

Psychopathy as Learning Deficit, III: The Deficient Response Modulation Model Newman and his colleagues (e.g., Newman, 1998; Newman & Wallace, 1993) have developed a more sophisticated version of the BIS model, based on an impressive and systematic program of research. From this perspective, "the 'impulsive' behavior of Psychopaths appears to reflect difficulty in the automatic switching of attention which, in turn, interferes with their ability to assimilate unattended but potentially relevant information while they are engaged in the organization and implementation of goal-directed behavior" (Newman & Wallace, 1993, p. 712). That is, disinhibition in psychopaths is not attributable simply to a weak BIS, but rather to an attentional deficit that reduces input to the BIS once the BAS is activated.

As the fearlessness model can be subsumed within the weak BIS model, so can the latter be subsumed within the deficient response modulation model, which accounts for psychopathic symptomatology and empirical research findings as well as or better than does the weak BIS model. In addition, the deficient response modulation model can explain the finding that psychopaths exhibit hyporesponsivity to punishment only in specific contexts (Newman & Wallace, 1993). Finally, it may even be possible to explain psychopathic deficits in the processing of linguistic and emotional stimuli within the deficient response modulation framework (Newman, 1998; Newman & Wallace, 1993, pp. 711–712). The model is well thought out and the experiments designed to test it are ingenious and methodologically sophisticated. Perhaps its biggest weakness at the present time is that some of the experimental effects predicted by this model are not as strong or robust as one might hope (Lykken, 1995).

Psychopathy as Cognitive-Affective Dysfunction: The Neurobiolgical Approach Much of Hare's early work investigated anxiety and anxiety-mediated behaviors in psychopaths (Hare, 1970). He and his colleagues soon found that the fearlessness model, described above, was complicated by the finding that the small skin conductance responses shown by psychopaths in anticipation of an unpleasant stimulus were accompanied by relatively large increases in heart rate, whereas the large skin conductance responses exhibited by nonpsychopaths were accompanied by decreases in heart rate (see Hare, 1978). These apparently incongruous findings actually made psychophysiological sense, given what was known about the autonomic components of orienting and defensive responses. Thus, novel, interesting, or important events elicit an orienting response, which includes an increase in skin conductance and a decrease in heart rate, while unpleasant or threatening events elicit a defensive response, which includes an increase in both skin conductance and heart rate. Presumably, nonpsychopaths focus attention on the impending unpleasant stimulus and experience an increase in fear, whereas the psychopaths "tune out" the impending stimulus with little or no increase in fear. That is, rather than simply being incapable of experiencing anticipatory fear, psychopaths may have ready access to a dynamic protective mechanism that attenuates the psychological/emotional impact of cues associated with impending pain or punishment.

Other researchers have replicated and extended these findings (Larbig, Veit, Rau, Schlottke, & Birbaumer, 1992; Ogloff & Wong, 1990). Besides skin conductance and heart rate, Larbig et al. (1992) recorded slow cortical potentials (related to attentional processes) while their subjects (flagrant traffic violators in Germany assessed with the PCL-R) awaited delivery of a loud noise. The psychopaths gave much smaller cortical responses than did the other subjects, leading the authors to conclude that the former failed to focus attention on the impending noise.

More recently, Hare (1993, 1998) has postulated that psychopathy is associated with general difficulties in processing and understanding deep semantic and affective meaning, rather than simply with some relatively specific emotional deficit or dysfunction. This view is consistent with recent evidence that psychopathy is characterized by a wide range of cognitive and affective anomalies (see review by Hare, 1998). For example, Williamson et al. (1991) recorded reaction times and event-related brain potentials (ERPs) in a lexical decision task that required the subject to press a button as quickly and accurately as possible if a letter-string displayed on a computer screen formed a word. The letter-strings consisted of neutral and emotional words and pronounceable pseudowords. Lexical decision studies with noncriminals indicate that responses to both positive words and negative words are more accurate and faster than are those to neutral words. Further, over central and parietal sites the early and late components of the ERP are larger in response to affective words than to neutral words; the late components are thought to be indicative of enhanced elaborative processing of emotional words.

Williamson et al. (1991) found that, like noncriminals, nonpsychopathic criminals were sensitive to the affective manipulations of the lexical decision task. They responded faster to emotional words than to neutral words, and showed the expected ERP differentiation between the two word types. PCL-R psychopaths, on the other hand, failed to show any reaction time or ERP differences between neutral and emotional words. Further, the morphology of their ERPs was strikingly different from that of the nonpsychopaths. One of these differences involved the late components of the ERP; these components generally were relatively large and prolonged in nonpsychopaths, and relatively small and brief in psychopaths. Presumably the nonpsychopaths made a lexical decision and continued to process and to mentally "elaborate" the semantic and affective associations or networks of the word they had just seen. The psychopaths, on the other hand, presumably made a lexical decision but processed the information in a cursory, shallow manner. This interpretation is consistent with a recent brain-imaging study in which psychopathic (PCL-R) substance abusers showed less widespread cerebral activation during performance of a lexical decision task involving neutral and emotional words than did nonpsychopathic abusers (Intrator et al., 1997; also see Hare, 1998).

Kiehl, Hare, McDonald, and Brink (in press) found that the ERP anomalies of psychopaths are not specific to affective language. They found that nonpsychopaths, but not psychopaths, showed ERP differentiation between positive and negative words, and between concrete and abstract words. In addition, Kiehl et al. (in press) replicated a curious finding reported in the Williamson et al. (1991) study. This was the presence in psychopaths of an unusually large negative wave over frontal areas of the brain. Several tentative interpretations of this unusual wave were presented, including the possibility that it is a reflection, in psychopaths, of profound cognitive and affective processing anomalies.

Other recent studies lead to much the same conclusion. Thus, there is evidence that psychopaths have difficulties in the efficient processing of verbal and nonverbal affective material (e.g., Christianson et al., 1996; Patrick, 1994; Patrick, Cuthbert, & Lang, 1994; Williamson et al., 1991), tend to confuse the emotional significance (polarity) of events (Blair et al., 1995; Hare, Williamson, & Harpur, 1988; Hayes & Hare, 1998), exhibit unusual interhemispheric distribution (reduced asymmetry) of processing resources (e.g., Day & Wong, 1996; Hare & McPherson, 1984b; Hare & Jutai, 1988; Intrator et al., 1997; Mills, 1995; Raine, O'Brien, Smiley, Scerbo, & Chan, 1990), have difficulty in appreciating the subtle meanings and nuances of language (e.g., proverbs, metaphors; Gillstrom, 1995; Hayes & Hare, 1998), have poor olfactory discrimination, possibly because of orbito-frontal dysfunction (Lapierre, Braun, & Hodgins, 1995), and may have what appears to be a subclinical form of thought disorder characterized by a lack of cohesion and coherence in speech (Williamson, 1991).

These cognitive and affective anomalies are not readily explained by the models of psychopathy described above. However, recent advances in the neurobiology of cognition and affect provide some potentially fruitful leads. Clearly, we must pay particular attention to the interrelated functions of ventromedial prefrontal cortex, anterior temporal cortex, anterior cingulate cortex, and amygdala. These regions have rich afferent and efferent connections with each other and with other regions important in the processing and integration of semantic and affective information, planning, impulsivity, and the initiation and inhibition of behavior. Behavioral and neuroimaging studies indicate that damage to these regions can produce a dissociation of the logical/cognitive and affective components of thought not unlike that found in psychopaths (Damasio, 1994).

The issues of whether psychopathy is the result of brain dysfunction or disorganization, unusual cerebral asymmetry, or general difficulties in information processing are complex and poorly understood. However, recent advances in cognitive neuroscience have provided researchers with powerful tools for determining if psychopathy is the result of structural or functional anomalies, or disruptions in the normal transmission of information among the various parts of the brain responsible for the integration of cognition, affect, and behavior. Hare and his colleagues currrently are investigating the nature of these putative dysfunctions, using functional magnetic resonance imaging (fMRI) technology (Kiehl et al., 1998).

Sadistic Personality Disorder

Sadistic personality disorder (SPD) is underpinned by a cruel, demeaning, and aggressive approach to interactions with other people. As with all personality disorders, it starts early in life, it is long lasting, and it pervades most of the individual's interactions with others at school, work, socially, and within family relationships. Krafft-Ebing (1898) originally coined the term "sadism" to describe fantasies and behavior focused on inflicting pain during sexual interactions. Drawing on the writings of 18th-century author the Marquis de Sade, he argued that sadists experience sexual arousal as a consequence of exercising control and dominance, by inflicting pain and humiliation, and by degrading and punishing the object of their desire.

Over time, the construct of SPD has broadened within the clinical literature to include a wide range of personality traits and interpersonal behaviors that affect all social encounters, not merely sexual encounters. Recent clinical descriptions suggest that the features of the disorder are diverse and wide ranging—they span the behavioral, interpersonal, cognitive and affective domains (Feister & Gay, 1991, 1995; Millon & Davis, 1996).

At the behavioral level, sadistic individuals have poor behavioral controls—they are irritable and flare up easily in response to minor frustrations. They may use a variety of behaviors, from the hostile glance on the one hand to severe physical punishment on the other, in order to exercise control. Although they may engage in expressive violence—violence underpinned by emotions such as anger and frustration—much of their violence is instrumental, its purpose being to intimidate and control. Their intent is to harm and they derive gratification in the knowledge that suffering has occurred.

At the interpersonal level, these individuals are abrasive, or at least abrasive to those whom they do not perceive to be their superiors. The more social adept sadist may achieve satisfaction and control by derisive social comments and cutting remarks; others may achieve the same ends in a more overtly hostile manner, through the hectoring, threatening, coercing, or intimidation of others. They may exercise inappropriate control over others; the sadistic father may forbid his daughter to attend a desired social event, the sadistic husband may prevent his wife leaving the family home, while the sadistic boss may bully and exploit a subordinate (Millon & Davis, 1996).

At the cognitive level, sadistic individuals may display rigid and dogmatic cognitive style. Their values may be authoritarian and this may be evident through their social intolerance; for example, they may construe out-groups as being devoid of any value, their racism and prejudice is evident. They may have unusual interests. Brittain (1970), in his detailed clinical account of the sadistic murderer, argued that their interests may include concentration camps, atrocities, black magic, sexual perversions, toxicology, crime and criminals, murders and murderers. Many sadists will be familiar with the writings of de Sade, the more sophisticated with the writings of Nietzsche. Feister and Gay (1995) argued that they are apt to attribute malevolent intent to the behavior of others and are oversensitive to what they construe as the derisive behavior of others.

At the affective level, sadists share many of the critical features of the psychopath: they lack remorse for their controlling and exploitative behavior, they do not experience shame or guilt, and they are unable to empathize with their victims. They are cold-hearted.

It is important to emphasize that these characteristics can be expressed in differing ways in differing contexts. Perhaps the most obvious form are the tyrannical sadists who, in the workplace, choose their victims whom they abuse, intimidate, and humiliate in front of their colleagues; they obtain pleasure from the psychic pain and distress of those whom they subjugate. Sadists may seek and achieve social positions, which allow them to exercise control and to mete out punishment in socially sanctioned roles. They may include the judge who metes out punishment of a cruel and unusual severity, the army sergeant who brutalizes the new recruit, and the psychiatrist who misuses mental health legislation to incarcerate a patient.

The Nature of the Disorder

The concept of SPD can be seen to have emerged from constructs in the psychological, psychiatric, and psychoanalytic traditions (Widiger, Frances, Spitzer & Williams, 1988). Authors such as Millon (1981) argued that there was a need for systematic description to describe those individuals whose underlying temperament is domineering, intimidating, hostile, malicious, and who are short-tempered and prone to engage in physically cruel behavior. Widiger and Trull (1994) argued that this range of traits is not well described by either the criteria for ASPD or the criteria for psychopathy (Hare, 1991). For example, only one PCL-R item (poor behavioral controls) is directly focused on aggressive behavior. But this item is concerned primarily with disproportionately aggressive and violent responses to frustration, failure, or disputes. Thus, it is technically possible for an individual to be a PCL-R psychopath without displaying the range of sadistic traits described by Millon (1981).

An attempt was made to systemize the description of the disorder by introducing criteria for SPD in appendix A of *DSM-III-R*, "Proposed Diagnostic Categories Needing Further Study." These criteria are included in table 22.2 as they represent the criteria set for which there is most, albeit limited, empirical data. The disorder was excluded from *DSM-IV*.

The first seven features in Criterion A are conceptually coherent: they all relate to different methods for ensuring or exercising power and control over others. The eighth feature is likely a correlate rather than a core defining feature. There is an unfortunate emphasis on the behavioral rather than the affective and cognitive components of the disorder. Perhaps this reflects the misapprehension that clinicians cannot assess these domains reliably. This limitation in the definition of SPD thus parallels the limitation found in the definition of ASPD (Hart & Hare, 1995).

Given that the systematic description of this disorder is fairly recent, the disorder is comparatively rare, and the difficulty inherent in obtaining reliable information about its critical features, the literature available regarding its validity, prevalence, comorbidity, and demographic distribution is understandably very limited. Feister and Gay (1995) provide a valuable summary of what is known about this disorder.

Table 22.2 Diagnostic Criteria for Sadistic Personality Disorder

A. A pervasive pattern of cruel, demeaning, and aggressive behavior, beginning by early adulthood, as indicated by the repeated occurrence of at least four of the following:
  (1) has used physical cruelty or violence for the purpose of establishing dominance in a relationship (not merely to achieve some noninterpersonal goal, such as striking someone in order to rob him or her)
  (2) humiliates or demeans people in the presence of others
  (3) has treated or disciplined someone under his or her control unusually harshly, e.g., a child, student, prisoner, or patient
  (4) is amused by, or takes pleasure in, the psychological or physical suffering of others (including animals)
  (5) has lied for the purpose of harming or inflicting pain on others (not merely to achieve some other goal)
  (6) gets other people to do what he or she wants by frightening them (through intimidation or even terror)
  (7) restricts the autonomy of people with whom he or she has a close relationship, e.g., will not let spouse leave the house unaccompanied or permit teen-age daughter to attend social functions
  (8) is fascinated by violence, weapons, martial arts, injury, or torture

B. The behavior in A has not been directed towards only one person (e.g., spouse, one child) and has not been solely for the purpose of sexual arousal (as in Sexual Sadism).

Prevalence

Six empirical studies (three of which are unpublished and are quoted in Feister & Gay, 1995) provide some limited information about the prevalence of SPD in clinical and forensic populations. In a postal survey of forensic psychiatrists, around 2.5% of forensic psychiatric cases evaluated by their respondents in the previous year met the criteria for SPD. Unfortunately, it is difficult to generalize from this survey given the response rate of 20% in the study. In a sample of outpatients attending a mental health clinic in rural Georgia, 8% met *DSM-III-R* criteria for SPD. Gay (1989) examined a sample of adults who had been accused of child abuse. She found that approximately 5% met the diagnostic criteria of SPD. The unpublished data reported by Feister and Gay (1995) suggest there is considerable variance in the prevalence of the disorder. Freiman and Widiger (1989) assessed psychiatric hospital inpatients with the Personality Interview Questionnaire-II; 18% of the sample were diagnosed as having SPD. Not surprisingly, the prevelance of SPD among serial killers is extremely high. In a biographical analysis of serial killers, Stone (1998) reported that 90% in the sample met the *DSM-III-R* criteria for SPD. Other personality disorders in his sample with high prevelance were antisocial (81%), narcissistic (61%), and schizoid (48%) PD. An unpublished study by Berger (see Feister & Gay, 1995) found that the prevelance of SPD was also high (33%) in a small sample of pedophiles and rapists. Finally, Millon and Tringone (1989) found that the prevalence of SPD in a sample of outpatients was only 3%.

A number of factors—the paucity of studies, the inadequacy of sample size and sampling procedures, the variation in diagnostic procedures adopted—mitigate against the provision of any accurate estimate of the prevalence of this disorder. Both the clinical literature and the limited empirical literature available suggest that SPD is primarily a disorder of males (Freiman & Widiger, 1989; Gay, 1989; Spitzer, Feister, Gay, & Pfohl, 1991); no research has examined whether this difference could in part be attributed to gender bias in the individual diagnostic criteria.

Comorbidity

The absence of convincing and reliable prevalence data for this disorder means that it is inappropriate to provide quantitative estimates of the degree of comorbidity with other Axis II disorders. Taken as a whole the available studies suggest that there is clear comorbidity with ASPD and narcissistic PD (Freiman & Widiger, 1989; Gay, 1989; Millon & Tringone, 1989; Spitzer et al., 1991). Feister and Gay (1995) indicated that the high comorbidity of SPD with other disorders may call into question the discreteness of the category. Reviewing the characteristics alluded to above it is likely that SPD will demonstrate an asymmetric relationship with psychopathy as operationalized by the PCL-R; most sadists are likely to show significant psychopathic traits while not all psychopaths will necessarily meet clinical criteria for SPD. We are not aware of any data that address this issue directly in the general population or in forensic settings. However, in Stone's (1998) biographical analyis of serial killers, reported above, the prevelances for SPD and for PCL-R psychopathy were both about 90%, suggesting that the comorbidity of the two disorders in this sample was very high.

Problems in the Assessment of the Disorder

The nature of the defining features of SPD is such that those being assessed are likely to deny or minimize the presence of these features. It will be hard to get patients to admit to cruel, demeaning, and aggressive behavior, particularly when the demand characteristics of the situation—for example, a risk assessment for court—will militate against the patient being open (Dietz, Hazelwood, & Warren, 1990). Access to considerable collateral data would be necessary to ensure valid evaluation. The SPD criteria are essentially behaviorally based and fail to tap the cognitive or affective characteristic that the clinical descriptions of the disorder emphasize. Extensive research with the PCL-R demonstrates that it is possible for clinicians to assess related cognitive and affective features in a reliable and valid manner, and thus, the argument that clinicians are inherently incapable of achieving adequate assessments of these domains is untenable (Hare, 1991).

Deletion of the Sadistic Personality Disorder Criteria from DSM-IV

The criteria were included in the *DSM-III-R* appendix in response to those clinicians who observed this pattern of personality disturbance among spousal assaulters and child abusers (Widiger, 1995). The inclusion of SPD was not intended to establish it as an officially sanctioned disorder, but rather to stimulate more research directed at clarifying whether or not SPD should be recognized as a distinct disorder (Widiger, 1995). A range of considerations influenced the complete removal of the disorder from *DSM-IV*. The primary consideration was the lack of a coherent body of research concerning the validity and utility of the concept (Widiger, 1995). In addition, it was thought that enshrining the disorder in *DSM-IV*—thereby providing it with official status—could lead to the misuse of the diagnosis in forensic settings. Further, it is conceivable that those suffering from the disorder might endeavor to use the diagnosis to mitigate their responsibility for their violence against women and against. Indeed, 76% of the respondents to a survey of forensic psychiatrists held that the diagnosis had considerable potential for abuse (Spitzer et al., 1991). Nonetheless, it has been argued forcefully that the deletion of the SPD from the nomenclature of personality disorders is a major error underpinned by political, rather than scientific, considerations (Millon & Davis, 1996). Many diagnostic categories can be misused in forensic settings, yet this is not a good reason to obscure their existence and inhibit their study. It is the responsibility of the legal system—not those endeavoring to describe, measure, and understand the disorder—to determine the influence that expert testimony has on such issues as responsibility and risk.

Sexual Sadism

Unlike sadistic personality disorder, sexual sadism remains an official diagnosis in *DSM-IV*. The primary feature of this disorder is that the individual experiences intense sexual arousal as a consequence of fantasies, sexual urges, or behaviors that entail real—not simulated—acts whereby the victim is subjected to physical and psychological suffering. It is the suffering of the victim that leads to sexual arousal. It tends to be a chronic disorder with onset in adolescence or early adulthood. The behaviors exhibited by sexual sadists are varied, and may include forcing—by verbal means—the victim to say words of particular significance to the perpetrator, or to carry out particular acts. The sexual sadist's behavior may also include the use of physical methods—restraints, whipping, beating, burning, strangling, cutting, mutilation, and torture—to terrify and subjugate the victim. In the extreme case, sexual sadism can lead to murder (Dietz et al., 1990). Quinsey (1990) has emphasized the wide-ranging nature of the behaviors, indicating that most individuals who meet the diagnostic criteria for sexual sadism never physically damage another person. Indeed, the evidence available from the literture on pornography and from research on the sexual fantasies of "normal men" implies that sexually sadistic thoughts and fantasies are not uncommon (Crepault & Couture, 1980; Deitz et al., 1990).

Deviant sexual arousal and deviant sexual fantasies appear to underpin the development and maintenance of sexual sadism. In some early work, Abel, Becker, Blanchard, and Djenderedjian (1977) found that sexual sadists exhibited larger increases in penile volume in response to audiotaped descriptions of rapes than did nonsadistic rapists. Several investigators have used clinical case material to identify the power of the interplay between deviant fantasy and deviant arousal. For example, MacCulloch, Snowden, Wood, and Mills (1983) argued that as fantasies develop they may lose their ability to generate sufficient sexual arousal, the offender may begin to engage in behavioral "try-outs." He may track a female down a dark street, or pretend to bump into a victim and touch her private parts. Elements of the try-out are incorporated into fantasy material used during masturbation, and a downward cycle of progressively more serious offending continues. This is a powerful process. Prentky et al. (1989) argued, "Indeed, the selective reinforcement of deviant fantasies through paired association with masturbation over a protracted period may help to explain not only the power of fantasies but why they are so refractory to extinction" (p. 890).

Often by studying prototypical examples of a disorder we can grasp its essence. Dietz et al. (1990) provided a systematic account of cases from the most extreme end of the spectrum of sexual sadists, the sadistic murderer, described as a "sadist unencumbered by ethical, societal or legal inhibitions" (p. 163). They provide a quotation from a sadistic murderer that specifies the sine qua non of the disorder:

> Sadism: the wish to inflict pain on others is not the essence of sadism. One essential impulse: to have complete mastery over another person, to make him/her a helpless object of our will, to become the absolute ruler over her, to become her God, to do with her as one pleases. To humiliate her, to enslave her, are means to this end, and the most important radical aim is to make her suffer since there is no greater power over another person than that of inflicting pain on her to force her to undergo suffering without her being able to defend herself. The pleasure in the complete domination over another person is the very essence of the Sadistic drive. (p. 165)

Thus, many of the offenders described by Dietz et al. (1990) used methods of torture and humiliation to instill morbid fear in their victims; they exercised the ultimate control—the power of life and death—by resuscitating their near-dead victims in order to subject them to further torture.

The vast majority of these killers were known to be highly organized and to have planned their crimes carefully. They studied law enforcement techniques in order to minimize the possibility of detection, prepared their equipment (torture rooms, sound-proofed vans with disabled locks), collected the tools and supplies necessary for the disposal of the bodies, and acquired the means for recording their victims' suffering (tape recorders and video recorders) so they could relive their experiences and sharpen their fantasies after the killing. When committing the crimes, they did so in a highly methodical manner, one characterized by the lack of any emotion; this is reminiscent of psychopathic violence and contrasts markedly with the extreme emotional states that typifies most violent offences.

Sexual Sadism and Psychopathy It has been argued elsewhere (Hart & Hare, 1997) that there is likely to be an association between sexual sadism and psychopathy. Among serial killers this certainly appears to be so (Stone, 1998). More generally, two studies of adult male offenders have found significant correlations between PCL-R scores and degree of sexual arousal to violent stimuli, as measured by penile plethysmography (Quinsey et al., 1995; Serin et al., 1994). More recently, Dempster and Hart (1996) found that among male juveniles charged with murder or attempted murder, those who were classified as sexual homicide perpetrators had significantly higher PCL-R scores than other types of offenders.

The association between sexually deviant preferences and psychopathy may not be a simple relationship. Evidence from Rice and Harris (1997) suggests that there may be a synergistic relationship between these two characteristics and sexual recidivism. Psychopathic individuals who, on phallometric assessment, display strong sexual arousal to deviant stimuli—particularly stimuli that depict sexual behavior with children, and rape cues or violence cues of a nonsexual nature—had disproportionately higher rates of sexual recidivism than did other groups of offenders. Among adolescent sex offenders the combination of psychopathy and deviant sexual arousal is highly predictive of recidivism in general (Gretton, O'Shaughnessy, & Hare, 1998). These findings clearly have potential importance for risk assessments.

Conclusions

The nature and value of the construct of SPD remains elusive. The stage of development perhaps parallels that of the construct of psychopathy before the development of the PCL-R. It will be interesting to see if the deletion of SPD from *DSM* results in the extinction of the construct in the clinical and research literatures (Widiger, 1995). If the construct is to develop it must encompass the affective and cognitive aspects of the disorder that have been identified as central by the clinical literature (Feister & Gay, 1991, 1995; Millon & Davis, 1996). When sufficient data are available, the possibility that a latent trait underlies the disorder can be investigated, using modern psychometric procedures. The relevance of particular items, and the amount of information they contribute to the construct, can be evaluated directly through the use of Item Response Theory methods (e.g., Cooke & Michie, 1997). At the same time, it will be necessary to determine the convergent and divergent validity of the construct, and to determine its links within the nomological network of clinical variables.

References

Abel, G. G., Becker, J. V., Blanchard, E. B., & Djenderedjian, A. (1977). Differentiating sexual aggressives with penile measures. *Criminal Justice and Behavior, 5*, 315–332.

Alterman, A. I., Cacciola, J. S., & Rutherford, M. J. (1993). Reliability of the Revised Psychopathy Checklist in substance abuse patients. *Psychological Assessment: A Journal of Consulting and Clinical Psychology, 5*, 442–448.

Babiak, P. (1995). When psychopaths go to work: A case study of an industrial psychopath. *Applied Psychology: An International Review, 44*, 171–178.

Barbaree, H., Seto, M., Serin, R., Amos, N., & Preston, D. (1994). Comparisons between sexual and nonsexual rapist subtypes. *Criminal Justice and Behavior, 21*, 95–114.

Berrios, G. E. (1996). *The history of mental symptoms: Descriptive psychopathology since the nineteenth century.* Cambridge, UK: Cambridge University Press.

Blackburn, R. (1993). *The psychology of criminal conduct: Theory, research, and practice.* Chichester, England: John Wiley.

Blackburn, R. (1998). Psychopathy and personality disorder: Implications of interpersonal theory. In D. J. Cooke, A. E. Forth, & R. D. Hare (Eds.), *Psychopathy: Theory, research, and implications for society* (pp. 269–302). Dordrecht, The Netherlands: Kluwer.

Blair, R. J. R., Sellars, C., Strickland, I., Clark, F., Smith, M., & Jones, L. (1995). Emotional attributions in the psychopath. *Personality and Individual Differences, 19*, 431–437.

Brandt, J. R., Kennedy, W. A., Patrick, C. J., & Curtin, J. J. (1997). Assessment of psychopathy in a population of incarcerated adolescent offenders. *Psychological Assessment, 9*, 429–435.

Brittain, R. P. (1970). The sadistic murderer. *Medicine, Science and the Law, 10*, 198–207.

Brown, S. L., & Forth, A. E. (1997). Psychopathy and sexual assault: Static risk factors, emotional precursors, and rapist subtypes. *Journal of Consulting and Clinical Psychology, 65*, 848–857.

Christianson, S. A., Forth, A. E., Hare, R. D., Strachan, C., Lidberg, L., & Thorell, L. H.

(1996). Remembering details of emotional events: A comparison between psychopathic and nonpsychopathic offenders. *Personality and Individual Differences, 20*, 437–446.

Cleckley, H. (1976). *The mask of sanity*, 5th ed. St. Louis, MO: Mosby.

Cooke, D. J. (1996). Psychopathic personality in different cultures: What do we know? What do we need to find out? *Journal of Personality Disorders, 10*, 23–40.

Cooke, D. J. (1998). Psychopathy across cultures. In D. J. Cooke, A. E. Forth, & R. D. Hare (Eds.), *Psychopathy: Theory, research, and implications for society* (pp. 13–46). Dordrecht, The Netherlands: Kluwer.

Cooke, D. J., Forth, A. E., & Hare, R. D. (Eds.). (1998). *Psychopathy: Theory, research, and implications for society.* Dordrecht, The Netherlands: Kluwer.

Cooke, D. J., & Michie, C. (1997). An Item Response Theory evaluation of Hare's Psychopathy Checklist. *Psychological Assessment, 9*, 2–13.

Cooke, D. J., & Michie, C. (in press). Psychopathy across cultures: North America and Scotland compared. *Journal of Abnormal Psychology.*

Cooke, D. J., Philip, L., Michie, C., & Carr, E. (1997, October). *Dimensions of psychopathy and risk for instrumental and reactive violence.* Paper presented at the Seventh annual conference of the Division of Criminological and Legal Psychology of the British Psychological Society, September 29 to to October 1, 1997. University of Cambridge.

Cornell, D., Warren, J., Hawk, G., Stafford, E., Oram, G., & Pine, D. (1996). Psychopathy in instrumental and reactive violent offenders. *Journal of Consulting and Clinical Psychology, 64*, 783–790.

Costa, P. T., & McCrae, R. R. (1992). *Revised NEO Personality Inventory (NEO-PI-R) and NEO Five-Factor Inventory (NEO-FFI) Professional Manual.* Odessa, FL: Psychological Assessment Resources.

Côté, G., & Hodgins, S. (1996). *L'Échelle de psychopathie de Hare—Révisée: Éléments de la validation de la version française.* Toronto: Multi-Health Systems.

Crepault, C., & Couture, M. (1980). Men's erotic fantasies. *Archives of Sexual Behavior, 9*, 565–581.

Damasio, A. (1994). *Descartes' error: Emotion, reason, and the human brain.* New York: Putnam & Sons.

Day, R., & Wong, S. (1996). Anomalous perceptual asymmetries for negative emotional stimuli in the psychopath. *Journal of Consulting and Clinical Psychology, 105*, 648–652.

Dempster, R. J., & Hart, S. D. (1996, March). *Utility of the FBI's Crime Classification Manual: Coverage, reliability, and validity for adolescent murderers.* Paper presented at the Biennial Meeting of the American Psychology-Law Society (APA Div. 41), Hilton Head, South Carolina.

Dempster, R. J., Lyon, D. R., Sullivan, L. E., Hart, S. D., Smiley, W. C., & Mulloy, R. (1996, August). *Psychopathy and instrumental aggression in violent offenders.* Paper presented at the Annual Meeting of the American Psychological Association, Toronto, Ontario.

Dietz, P. E., Hazelwood, R. R., & Warren, J. (1990). The sexually sadistic criminal and his offenses. *Bulletin of the American Academy of Psychiatry and the Law, 18*, 163–178.

DiLalla, D. L., Carey, G., Gottesman, I. I., & Bouchard, T. J., Jr. (1996). Heritability of MMPI personality indicators of psychopathology in twins reared apart. *Journal of Abnormal Psychology, 105*, 491–499.

Dixon, M., Hart, S. D., Gretton, H., McBride, M., & O'Shaughnessy, R. (1995). Crime Classification Manual: Reliability and validity in juvenile sex offenders [Abstract]. *Canadian Psychology, 36*, 20.

Dolan, B., & Coid, J. (1993). *Psychopathic and antisocial personality disorders: Treatment and research issues.* London: Gaskell.

Douglas, J. E., Burgess, A. W., Burgess, A. G., & Ressler, R. K. (1992). *The Crime Classification Manual: A standard system for investigating and classifying violent crimes.* New York: Lexington.

Douglas, K. S., Ogloff, J. R., & Nicholls, T. L. (1997, June). *Personality disorders and violence in civil psychiatric patients.* In C. D. Websrer (Chair), Personality disorders and violence. Symposium conducted at the meeting of the Fifth International Congress on the Disorders of Personality. Vancouver, Canada.

Feighner, J. P., Robins, E., Guze, S. B., Woodruff, R. A., Winokur, G., & Munoz, R. (1972). Diagnostic criteria for use in psychiatric research. *Archives of General Psychiatry, 26*, 57–63.

Feister, S. J., & Gay, M. (1991). Sadistic personality disorder: A review of data and recommendations for DSM-IV. *Journal of Personality Disorders, 5*, 376–385.

Feister, S., & Gay, M. (1995). Sadistic Personality Disorder. In W. J. Livesley (Ed.), *The DSM-IV personality disorders* (pp. 329–340). New York: Guilford.

Forth, A. E., Brown, S. L., Hart, S. D., & Hare, R. D. (1996). The assessment of psychopathy in male and female noncriminals: Reliability and validity. *Personality and Individual Differences, 20*, 531–543.

Forth, A. E., & Burke, H. C. (1998). Psychopathy in adolescence: Assessment, violence, and developmental precursors. In D. J. Cooke, A. E. Forth, & R. D. Hare (Eds.), *Psychopathy: Theory, research, and implications for society* (pp. 205–229). Dordrecht, The Netherlands: Kluwer.

Forth, A. E., Hart, S. D., & Hare, R. D. (1990). Assessment of psychopathy in male young offenders. *Psychological Assessment: A Journal of Consulting and Clinical Psychology, 2*, 342–344.

Forth, A. E., Kosson, D., & Hare, R. D. (in press). *The Hare Psychopathy Checklist: Youth Version*. Toronto: Multi-health Systems.

Forth, A. E., & Kroner, D. (1994). *The factor structure of the Revised Psychopathy Checklist with incarcerated papist and incest offenders*. Unpublished manuscript.

Fowles, D. C., & Missel, K. (1994). Electrodermal hyporeactivity, motivation, and psychopathy: Theoretical issues. In D. Fowles, P. Sutker, & S. Goodman (Eds.), *Psychopathy and antisocial personality: A developmental perspective: Vol. 17. Progress in experimental personality and psychopathology research* (pp. 263–284). New York: Springer.

Freiman, K., & Widiger, T. A. (1989). *Co-occurence and diagnostic efficiency statistics*. Sadistic personality disorder. In W. J. Livesley (Ed.), *The DSM-IV personality disorders* (pp. 329–340). New York: Guilford.

Frick, P. J. (1998). Callous-emotional traits and conduct problems: Applying the two-factor model of Psychopathy to children. In D. J. Cooke, A. E. Forth, & R. D. Hare (Eds.), *Psychopathy: Theory, research, and implications for society* (pp. 161–187). Dordrecht, The Netherlands: Kluwer.

Fulero, S. M. (1995). Review of the Hare Psychopathy Checklist—Revised. In J. C. Conoley & J. C. Impara (Eds.), *Twelfth mental measurements yearbook* (pp. 453–454). Lincoln, NE: Buros Institute.

Gay, M. (1989, May). *Sadistic personality disorders among child abusers*. In R. Spitzer (Chair), Psychiatric diagnosis, victimization and women. Symposium presented at the 142nd annual meeting of the American Psychiatric Association, San Francisco.

Gillsttrom, B. (1995). *Abstract thinking in criminal psychopaths*. Unpublished doctoral dissertation, University of British Columbia, Vancouver, Canada.

Gorenstein, E. E. (1982). Frontal lobe functions in psychopaths. *Journal of Abnormal Psychology, 91*, 368–379.

Gorenstein, E. E., & Newman, J. P. (1980). Disinhibitory psychopathology: A new perspective and a model for research. *Psychological Review, 87*, 301–315.

Grann, M., Langström, N., Tengström, A., & Kullgren, G. (in press). Psychopathy (PCL-R) predicts violent recidivism among criminal offenders with personality disorders in Sweden. *Law and Human Behavior.*

Gray, J. A. (1987). *The neuropsychology of fear and stress*. New York: Cambridge University Press.

Gretton, H., McBride, M., O'Shaughnessy, R., & Hare, R. D. (1998). *A retrospective longitudinal study of recidivism in adolescent offenders*. Manuscript in preparation.

Gretton, H., McBride, M., O'Shaughnessy, R., & Hare, R. D. (1998b). *Psychopathy and recidivism in adolescent sex offenders*. Manuscript in preparation.

Gustaffson, S. B., & Ritzer, D. R. (1995). The dark side of normal: A psychopathy-linked pattern called aberrant self-promotion. *European Journal of Personality, 9*, 1–37.

Hare, R. D. (1970). *Psychopathy: Theory and research*. New York: John Wiley.

Hare, R. D. (1978). Electrodermal and cardiovascular correlates of psychopathy. In R. D. Hare & D. Schalling (Eds.), *Psychopathic behavior: Approaches to research* (pp. 107–143). Chichester, England: John Wiley.

Hare, R. D. (1981). Psychopathy and violence. In J. R. Hays, T. K. Roberts, & K. S. Soloway (Eds.), *Violence and the violent individual* (pp. 53–74). Jamaica, NY: Spectrum.

Hare, R. D. (1984). Performance of psychopaths on cognitive tasks related to frontal lobe functions. *Journal of Abnormal Psychology, 93*, 133–140.

Hare, R. D. (1985). A comparison of procedures for the assessment of psychopathy. *Journal of Consulting and Clinical Psychology, 53*, 7–16.

Hare, R. D. (1991). *The Hare Psychopathy Checklist—Revised*. Toronto, Ontario: Multi-Health Systems.

Hare, R. D. (1992). *A model program for offenders at high risk for violence*. Ottawa, Canada: Correctional Service of Canada.

Hare, R. D. (1993). *Without conscience: The disturbing world of the psychopaths among us*. New York: Simon & Schuster.

Hare, R. D. (1996). Psychopathy: A clinical construct whose time has come. *Criminal Justice and Behavior, 23*, 25–54.

Hare, R. D. (1998). Psychopathy, affect, and behavior. In D. J. Cooke, A. E. Forth, & R. D. Hare (Eds.), *Psychopathy: Theory, research, and implications for society* (pp. 105–137). Dordrecht, The Netherlands: Kluwer.

Hare, R. D., Forth, A. E., & Strachan, K. (1992). Psychopathy and crime across the lifespan. In R. DeV. Peters, R. J. McMahon, & V. L. Quinsey (Eds.), *Aggression and violence throughout the life span* (pp. 285–300). Newbury Park, CA: Sage.

Hare, R. D., & Hart, S. D. (1995). Commentary on antisocial personality disorder: The DSM-IV field trial. In W. J. Livesley (Ed.), *The DSM-IV personality disorders* (pp. 127–134). New York: Guilford.

Hare, R. D., Hart, S. D., & Harpur, T. J. (1991). Psychopathy and the DSM-IV criteria for antisocial personality disorder. *Journal of Abnormal Psychology, 100*, 391–398.

Hare, R. D., & Jutai, J. (1988). Psychopathy and cerebral asymmetry in semantic processing. *Personality and Individual Differences, 9*, 329–337.

Hare, R. D., & McPherson, L. M. (1984a). Violent and aggressive behavior by criminal psychopaths. *International Journal of Law and Psychiatry, 7*, 35–50.

Hare, R. D., & McPherson, L. M. (1984b). Psychopathy and perceptual asymmetry during verbal dichotic listening. *Journal of Abnormal Psychology, 93*, 140–149.

Hare, R. D., McPherson, L. E., & Forth, A. E. (1988). Male psychopaths and their criminal careers. *Journal of Consulting and Clinical Psychology, 56*, 710–714.

Hare, R. D., Strachan, C., & Hemphill, J. (1998). *Psychopathy in female offenders*. Manuscript in preparation.

Hare, R. D., Williamson, S. E., & Harpur, T. J. (1988). Psychopathy and language. In T. E. Moffitt & S. A. Mednick (Eds.), *Biological contributions to crime causation* (pp. 68–92). Dordrecht, The Netherlands: Martinus Nijhoff.

Harpur, T. J., & Hare, R. D. (1994). The assessment of psychopathy as a function of age. *Journal of Abnormal Psychology, 103*, 604–609.

Harpur, T. J., Hare, R. D., & Hakstian, R. A. (1989). A two-factor conceptualization of psychopathy: Construct validity and implications for assessment. *Psychological Assessment: A Journal of Consulting and Clinical Psychology, 1*, 6–17.

Harpur, T. J., Hart, S. D., & Hare, R. D. (1994). Personality of the psychopath. In P. T. Costa & T. A. Widiger (Eds.), *Personality disorders and the five-factor model of personality* (pp. 149–173). Washington, DC: American Psychological Association.

Harris, G. T., Rice, M. E., & Cormier, C. A. (1991). Psychopathy and violent recidivism. *Law and Human Behavior, 15*, 625–637.

Harris, G. T., Rice, M. E., & Quinsey, V. L. (1993). Violent recidivism of mentally disordered offenders: The development of a statistical prediction instrument. *Criminal Justice and Behavior, 20*, 315–335.

Harris, G. T., Rice, M. E., & Quinsey, V. L. (1994). Psychopathy as a taxon: Evidence that Psychopaths are a discrete class. *Journal of Consulting and Clinical Psychology, 62*, 387–397.

Hart, S. D., Cox, D. N., & Hare, R. D. (1995). *Manual for the Hare Psychopathy Checklist—Revised: Screening Version (PCL:SV)*. Toronto: Multi-Health Systems.

Hart, S. D., & Dempster, R, J. (1997). Impulsivity and psychopathy. In C. D. Webster & M. A. Jackson (Eds.), *Impulsivity in principle and practice* (pp. 212–232). New York: Guilford.

Hart, S. D., Forth, A. E., & Hare, R. D. (1990). Performance of criminal psychopaths on selected neuropsychological tests. *Journal of Abnormal Psychology, 99*, 374–379.

Hart, S. D., & Hare, R. D. (1989). Discriminant validity of the Psychopathy Checklist in a forensic psychiatric population. *Psychological Assessment: A Journal of Consulting and Clinical Psychology, 1*, 211–218.

Hart, S. D., & Hare, R. D. (1997). Psychopathy: Assessment and association with criminal conduct. In D. M. Stoff, J. Maser, & J. Brieling (Eds.), *Handbook of antisocial behaviour* (pp. 22–35). New York: John Wiley.

Hart, S. D., Hare, R. D., & Forth, A. E. (1994). Psychopathy as a risk marker for violence: Development and validation of a screening version of the Revised Psychopathy Checklist. In J. Monahan & H. Steadman (Eds.), *Violence and mental disorder: Developments in risk assessment* (pp. 81–98). Chicago: University of Chicago Press.

Hart, S. D., Kropp, P. R., & Hare, R. D. (1988). Performance of psychopaths following conditional release from prison. *Journal of Consulting and Clinical Psychology, 56*, 227–232.

Hayes, J., & Hare, R. D. (1998). *Psychopathy and the confusion of emotion in metaphorical statements*. Manuscript in preparation.

Heilbrun, K., Hart, S. D., Hare, R. D., Gustafson, D., Nunez, C., & White, A. (1998). Inpatient and post-discharge aggression in mentally disordered offenders: The role of psychopathy. *Journal of Interpersonal Violence, 13*, 514–527.

Hemphill, J. F., Hare, R. D., & Wong, S. (1998). Psychopathy and recidivism: A review. *Legal and Criminological Psychology, 3*, 141–172.

Hemphill, J., Hart, S. D., & Hare, R. D. (1994). Psychopathy and substance use. *Journal of Personality Disorders, 8*, 32–40.

Hemphill, J. F., & Wong, S. (1991). Efficacy of the therapeutic community for treating criminal Psychopaths [Abstract]. *Canadian Psychology, 32*, 206.

Hill, C. D., Rogers, R., & Bickford, M. E. (1996). Predicting aggressive and socially disruptive behavior in a maximum security forensic psychiatric hospital. *Journal of Forensic Sciences, 41*, 56–59.

Intrator, J., Hare, R., Strizke, P., Brichtswein, K., Dorfman, D., Harpur, T., Bernstein, D., Handelsman, L., Schaefer, C., Keilp, J., Rosen, J., & Machac, J. (1997). Brain imaging (SPECT) study of semantic and affective processing in psychopaths. *Biological Psychiatry, 42*, 96–103

Jackson, D. N., & Livesley, W. J. (1994). Possible contributions from personality assessment to the classification of personality disorders. In W. J. Livesley (Ed.), *The DSM-IV personality disorders* (pp. 459–481). New York: Guilford.

Kegan, R. (1986). The child behind the mask. In W. H. Reid, D. Dorr, J. I. Walker, & J. W. Bonner III (Eds.), *Unmasking the psychopath*. New York: W.W. Norton.

Kiehl, K. A., Hare, R. D., McDonald, J. J., & Brink, J. (in press). Semantic and affective processing in psychopaths: An event-related potential (ERP) study. *Psychophysiology*.

Kiehl, K. A., Smith, A. M., Forster, B. B., MacKay, A. L., Whittall, K., Hare, R. D., & Liddle, P. F. (1998). *A whole brain multi-subject functional MR comparison of EPI spin-echo, asymmetric spin-echo and gradient-echo sequences at 1.5 T*. Manuscript under review.

Krafft-Ebing, R. (1898). *Psychopathia sexualis* (10th ed.). Stuggart: Enke.

Lapierre, D., Braun, C. M. J., & Hodgins, S. (1995). Ventral frontal deficits in psychopathy: Neuropsychological test findings. *Neuropsychologia, 11*, 139–151.

Lahey, B. B., Hart, E. L., Pliszka, S., Applegate, B., & McBurnett, K. (1993). Neurophysiological correlates of conduct disorder. A rationale and a review of the literature. *Journal of Clinical Child Psychology, 22*, 141–153.

Larbig, W., Veit, R., Rau, H., Schlottke, P., & Birbaumer, N. (1992, October). *Cerebral and peripheral correlates in psychopaths during anticipation of aversive stimulation*. Paper presented at Annual Meeting of the Society for Psychophysiological Research, San Diego.

Leary, T. (1957). *Interpersonal diagnosis of personality*. New York: Ronald Press.

Lewis, A. (1974). Psychopathic personality: A most elusive category. *Psychological Medicine, 4*, 133–140.

Lilienfeld, S. O. (1994). Conceptual problems in the assessment of psychopathy. *Clinical Psychology Review, 14*, 17–38.

Livesley, W. J. (1986). Trait and behavioral prototypes of personality disorder. *American Journal of Psychiatry, 143*, 728–732.

Livesley, W. J. (1998). The phenotypic and genotypic structure of psychopathic traits. In D. J. Cooke, A. E. Forth, & R. D. Hare (Eds.), *Psychopathy: Theory, research, and implications for society* (pp. 69–79). Dordrecht, The Netherlands: Kluwer.

Livesley, W. J., & Jackson, D. N. (1998). *Dimensional assessment of personality disorder (DAPP-BQ)*. Port Huron, MI: Sigma Publications.

Losel, F. (1998). Treatment and management of psychopaths. In D. J. Cooke, A. E. Forth, & R. D. Hare (Eds.), *Psychopathy: Theory, research, and implications for society* (pp. 303–354). Dordrecht, The Netherlands: Kluwer.

Lykken, D. T. (1957). A study of anxiety in the sociopathic personality. *Journal of Abnormal and Social Psychology, 55*, 6–10.

Lykken, D. T. (1995). *The antisocial personalities*. Hillsdale, NJ: Erlbaum.

Lynam, D. R. (1996). Early identification of chronic offenders: Who is the fledgling psychopath? *Psychological Bulletin, 120*, 209–234.

MacCulloch, M. J., Snowden, P. R., Wood, P. J., & Mills, H. E. (1983). Sadistic fantasy, sadistic behaviour and offending. *British Journal of Psychiatry, 143*, 20–29.

Magid, K., & McKelvey, C. A. (1989). *High risk: Children without conscience*. New York: Bantam.

McBurnett, K., & Pfiffner, L. (1998). Comorbidities and biological correlates of conduct disorder. In D. J. Cooke, A. E. Forth, & R. D. Hare (Eds.), *Psychopathy: Theory, research, and implications for society* (pp. 189–203). Dordrecht, The Netherlands: Kluwer.

McCord, J. (July, 1984). *Family sources of crime*. Paper presented at the meeting of the International Society for Research on Aggression, Turku, Finland.

McCord, W., & McCord, J. (1964). *The psychopath: An essay on the criminal mind*. Princeton, NJ: Van Nostrand.

Mealey, L. (1995). The sociobiology of sociopathy: An integrated evolutionary model. *Behavioral and Brain Sciences, 18*, 523–599.

Meloy, J. R. (1988). *The psychopathic mind: Origins, dynamics, and treatments*. Northvale, NJ: Aronson.

Miller, M. W., Geddings, V. J., Levenston, G. K., & Patrick, C. J. (1994, March). *The personality characteristics of psychopathic and nonpsychopathic sex offenders*. Paper presented at the Biennial Meeting of the American Psychology-Law Society (Div. 41 of the American Psychological Association), Santa Fe, New Mexico.

Millon, T. (1981). *Disorders of personality.* New York: John Wiley.

Millon, T., & Davis, R. D. (1996). *Disorders of personality: DSM-IV and beyond* (2nd ed.). New York: John Wiley.

Millon, T., & Tringone, R. (1989). [Co-occurrence and diagnostic efficacy statistics]. Unpublished raw data.

Mills, R. (1995, April). *Unusual brain organization: A cause for psychopathy?* Paper presented at conference on Mental Disorder and Criminal Justice: Changes, Challenges, and Solutions, Vancouver, British Columbia, Canada.

Moffitt, T. E. (1993). Adolescent-limited and life-course-persistent antisocial behavior: A developmental taxonomy. *Psychological Review, 100*, 674–701.

Nedopil, N., Hollweg, M., Hartmann, J., & Jaser, R. (1998). Comorbidity of psychopathy with major mental disorders. In D. J. Cooke, A. E. Forth, & R. D. Hare (Eds.), *Psychopathy: Theory, research and implications for society* (pp. 257–268). Dordrecht, The Netherlands: Kluwer.

Newman, J. P. (1998). Psychopathic behavior: An information processing perspective. In D. J. Cooke, A. E. Forth, & R. D. Hare (Eds.), *Psychopathy: Theory, research, and implications for society* (pp. 81–104). Dordrecht, The Netherlands: Kluwer.

Newman, J. P., & Wallace, J. F. (1993). Psychopathy and cognition. In P. Kendall & K. Dobson (Eds.), *Psychopathology and cognition* (pp. 293–349). New York: Academic Press.

Ogloff, J. R., & Wong, S. (1990). Electrodermal and cardiovascular evidence of a coping response in Psychopaths. *Criminal Justice and Behavior, 17*, 231–245.

Ogloff, J. R. P., Wong, S., & Greenwood, A. (1990). Treating criminal psychopaths in a therapeutic community program. *Behavioral Sciences and the Law, 8*, 81–90.

Patrick, C. J. (1994). Emotion and psychopathy: Startling new insights. *Psychophysiology, 31*, 319–330.

Patrick, C. J., Cuthbert, B. N., & Lang, P. J. (1994). Emotion in the criminal psychopath: Fear image processing. *Journal of Abnormal Psychology, 103*, 523–534.

Pichot, P. (1978). Psychopathic behavior: A historical overview. In R. D. Hare & D. Schalling (Eds.), *Psychopathic behavior: Approaches to research* (pp. 55–70). Chichester, UK: John Wiley.

Prentky, R. A., Burgess, A. W., Rokous, F., Lee, A., Hartman, C., Ressler, R., & Douglas, J. (1989). The presumptive role of fantasy in serial sexual homicide. *American Journal of Psychiatry, 146*, 887–891.

Prentky, R. A., & Knight, R. A. (1991). Identifying critical dimensions for discriminating among rapists. *Journal of Consulting and Clinical Psychology, 59*, 643–661.

Quinsey, V. L. (1990). Sexual violence. In P. Bowden & R. Bluglass (Eds.), *Principles and practice of forensic psychiatry* (pp. 563–570). Edinburgh: Churchill Livingstone.

Quinsey, V. L., Harris, G. T., Rice, M. E., & Lalumiere, M. L. (1993). Assessing treatment efficacy in outcome studies of sex offenders. *Journal of Interpersonal Violence, 8*, 512–523.

Quinsey, V. L., Rice, M. E., & Harris, G. T. (1995). Actuarial prediction of sexual recidivism. *Journal of Interpersonal Violence, 10*, 85–105.

Raine, A., O'Brien, M., Smiley, N., Scerbo, A., & Chan, C. J. (1990). Reduced lateralization in verbal dichotic listening in adolescent psychopaths. *Journal of Abnormal Psychology, 99*, 272–277.

Rice, M. E., & Harris, G. T. (1992). A comparison of criminal recidivism among schizophrenic and nonschizophrenic offenders. *International Journal of Law and Psychiatry, 15*, 397–408.

Rice, M. E., & Harris, G. T. (1995). Psychopathy, schizophrenia, alcohol abuse, and violent recidivism. *International Journal of Law and Psychiatry, 18*, 333–342.

Rice, M. E., & Harris, G. T. (1997). Cross-validation and extension of the Violence Risk Appraisal Guide for child molesters and rapists. *Law and Human Behavior, 21*, 231–241.

Rice, M. E., Harris, G. T., & Cormier, C. A. (1992). An evaluation of a maximum security therapeutic community for psychopaths and other mentally disordered offenders. *Law and Human Behavior, 16*, 399–412.

Robins, L. N. (1966). *Deviant children grown up: A sociological and psychiatric study of sociopathic personality.* Baltimore, MD: Williams & Wilkins.

Robins, L. N. (1978). Aetiological implications in studies of childhood histories relating to antisocial personality. In R. D. Hare & D. Schalling (Eds.), *Psychopathic behavior: Ap-*

proaches to research (pp. 255–271). Chichester, England: John Wiley.

Robins, L. N., Tipp, J., & Przybeck, T. (1991). Antisocial personality. In L. N. Robins & D. Regier (Eds.), *Psychiatric disorders in America: The Epidemiologic Catchment Area study* (pp. 258–290). New York: Free Press.

Rogers, R., Duncan, J. C., Lynett, E., & Sewell, K. W. (1994). Prototypical analysis of antisocial personality disorder: DSM-IV and beyond. *Law and Human Behavior, 18*, 471–484.

Rutherford, M. J., Cacciola, J. S., Alterman, A. I., & McKay, J. R. (1996). Reliability and validity of the Revised Psychopathy Checklist in women methadone patients. *Assessment, 3*, 43–54.

Rutter, M. (1997) Comorbidity: concepts, claims and choices. *Criminal Behaviour and Mental Health, 7*, 265–285.

Salekin, R. T., Rogers, R., & Sewell, K. W. (1996). A review and meta-analysis of the Psychopathy Checklist and Psychopathy Checklist—Revised: Predictive validity of dangerousness. *Clinical Psychology: Science and Practice, 3*, 203–215.

Salekin, R. T., Rogers, R., & Sewell, K. T. (1997). Construct validity of psychopathy in a female offender sample: A multitrait-multimethod evaluation. *Journal of Abnormal Psychology, 106*, 576–585.

Salekin, R. W., Rogers, R., Ustad, K. L., & Sewell, K. W. (1998). Psychopathy and recidivism among female inmates. *Law and Human Behavior, 22*, 109–128.

Serin, R. C. (1991). Psychopathy and violence in criminals. *Journal of Interpersonal Violence, 6*, 423–431.

Serin, R. C., & Amos, N. L. (1995). The role of psychopathy in the assessment of dangerousness. *International Journal of Law and Psychiatry, 18*, 231–238.

Serin, R. C., Malcolm, P. B., Khanna, A., & Barbaree, H. E. (1994). Psychopathy and deviant sexual arousal in incarcerated sexual offenders. *Journal of Interpersonal Violence, 9*, 3–11.

Serin, R. C., Peters, R. D., & Barbaree, H. E. (1990). Predictors of psychopathy and release outcome in a criminal population. *Psychological Assessment: A Journal of Consulting and Clinical Psychology, 2*, 419–422.

Shea, M. T. (1994). Interrelationships among categories of personality disorders. In W. J. Livesley (Ed.), *The DSM-IV personality disorders* (pp. 127–134). New York: Guilford.

Smith, S. S., Arnett, P. A., & Newman, J. P. (1992). Neuropsychological differentiation of psychopathic and nonpsychopathic criminal offenders. *Personality and Individual Differences, 13*, 1233–1243.

Spitzer, R. L., Fiester, S. J., Gay, M., & Pfohl, B. (1991). Is sadisitic personality disorder a valid diagnosis? The results of a survey of forensic psychiatrists. *American Journal of Psychiatry, 148*, 875–879.

Steadman, H., Monahan, J., Applelbaum, P., Grisso, T., Mulvey, E., Roth, L., Robbins, P., & Klassen, D. (1994). Designing a new generation of risk assessment rsearch. In J. Monahan & H. Steadman (Eds.), *Violence and mental disorder: Developments in risk assessment* (pp. 287–318). Chicago: University of Chicago Press.

Stone, M. H. (1998, January). *Personality aberrations in serial killers.* Paper presented at the 41st Winter Meeting of the American Academy of Psychoanalysis, New York.

Suedfeld, P., & Landon, P. B. (1978). Approaches to treatment. In R. D. Hare & D. Schalling (Eds.), *Psychopathic behavior: Approaches to research* (pp. 347–376). Chichester, England: John Wiley.

Sullivan, H. S. (1953). *The interpersonal theory of psychiatry.* New York: Norton.

Sundulko, K. (1978). Electrocortical investigations of sociopathy. In R. D. Hare & D. Schalling (Eds.), *Psychopathic behavior: Approaches to research* (pp. 145–156). Chichester, England: John Wiley.

Tengström, A., Grann, M., Langström, N., & Kullgren, G. (1999). *Psychopathy (PCL-R) as a predictor of violent recidivism among criminal offenders with schizophrenia.* Manuscript under review.

Tennent, G., Tennent, D., Prins, H., & Bedford, A. (1990). Psychopathic disorder: A useful concept? *Medicine, Science, and the Law, 30*, 38–44.

Tyrer, P., & Ferguson, B. (1988). Development of the concept of abnormal personality. In P. Tyrer (Ed.), *Personality disorders: Diagnosis, management, and course* (pp. 1–11). London: Wright.

Sullivan, H. S. (1953). *The interpersonal theory of psychiatry.* New York: Norton.

Toupin, J., Mercier, H., Déry, M., Côté, G., & Hodgins, S. (1996). Validity of the PCL-R for adolescents. In D. J. Cooke, A. E. Forth, J. P. Newman, & R. D. Hare (Eds.), *Issues in criminological and legal psychology: No. 24, International perspectives on psychopathy* (pp. 143–145). Leicester, UK: British Psychological Society.

Whitlock, F. A. (1982). A note on moral insanity and psychopathic disorders. *Bulletin of the Royal College of Psychiatry, 6*, 57–59.

Widiger, T. A. (1995). Deletion of self-defeating and sadistic personality disorders. In W. J. Livesley (Ed.), *The DSM-IV personality disorders* (pp. 359–373). New York: Guilford.

Widiger, T. A. (1998). Psychopathy and normal personality. In D. J. Cooke, A. E. Forth, & R. D. Hare (Eds.), *Psychopathy: Theory, research, and implications for society* (pp. 47–68). Dordrecht, The Netherlands: Kluwer.

Widiger, T. A., Cadoret, R., Hare, R. D., Robins, L., Rutherford, M., Zanarini, M., Alterman, A., Apple, M., Corbitt, E., Forth, A. E., Hart, S. D., Kultermann, J., Woody, G., & Frances, A. (1996). DSM-IV antisocial personality disorder field trial. *Journal of Abnormal Psychology, 105*, 3–16.

Widiger, T. A., & Corbitt, E. M. (1995). Antisocial personality disorder in DSM-IV. In J. Livesley (Ed.), *DSM-IV personality disorders* (127–134). New York: Guilford.

Widiger, T. A., Frances, A. J., Pincus, H. A., Davis, W. W., & First, M. (1991). Toward an empirical classification for DSM-IV. *Journal of Abnormal Psychology, 100*, 280–288.

Widiger, T. A., Frances, R. J., Spitzer, R. L., & Williams, J. B. W. (1988). The DSM-IIIR personality disorders: An overview. *American Journal of Psychiatry, 145*, 786–795.

Widiger, T. A., & Trull, T. J. (1994). Personality disorders and violence. In J. Monahan & H. Steadman (Eds.), *Violence and mental disorder: Developments in risk assessment* (pp. 203–226). Chicago: University of Chicago Press.

Wiggins, J. S., & Trapnell, P. D. (1996). A dyadic-interactional pespective on the five-factor model. In J. S. Wiggins (Ed.), *The five-factor model of personality: Theoretical perspectives* (pp. 88–162). New York: Guilford.

Williamson, S. E. (1991). *Cohesion and coherence in the speech of psychopathic criminals.* Unpublished doctoral dissertation, University of British Columbia, Vancouver, British Columbia.

Williamson, S. E., Hare, R. D., & Wong, S. (1987). Violence: Criminal psychopaths and their victims. *Canadian Journal of Behavioral Science, 19*, 454–462.

Williamson, S. E., Harpur, T. J., & Hare, R. D. (1991). Abnormal processing of affective words by psychopaths. *Psychophysiology, 28*, 260–273.

Wintrup, A., Coles, M., Hart, S., & Webster, C. D. (1994). The predictive validity of the PCL-R in high-risk mentally disordered offenders [Abstract]. *Canadian Psychology, 35*, 47.

23

Obsessive-Compulsive and Negativistic Personality Disorders

JOSEPH T. MCCANN

The inquisitive reader will no doubt wonder why the obsessive-compulsive and negativistic personality disorders have been placed together in a single chapter. Indeed, one of the major goals of psychopathology is to create a sense of order and predictability that allows for greater understanding of various forms of psychological disturbance. Toward this end, various symptoms are grouped to form distinct diagnostic categories that are in turn grouped with other diagnoses that share common features.

Several themes and issues tie the obsessive-compulsive and negativistic personality disorders together. Both of these personality disorders have created a good deal of controversy in the labels utilized to describe them. The obsessive-compulsive personality disorder, for instance, has had a number of formal names, including "compulsive," "obsessive-compulsive," and "anankastic." Similarly, negativistic personality disorder is the current name for what used to be the passive-aggressive personality disorder. Much confusion surrounded "passive-aggressive" as a label because the term has also been used to refer to a defense mechanism, a specific personality trait, and a maladaptive coping style (Perry & Flannery, 1982).

Another common theme that connects these two personality disorders is the ambivalent and conflicted personality dynamics that are thought to underlie their presentation (Millon & Davis, 1996). Ambivalence has been conceptualized as a lack of certainty over the source of reinforcement in one's life. Accordingly, ambivalent individuals are conflicted over whether they should be dependent on others for reinforcing experiences or should rely on themselves. Thus, ambivalent individuals are conflicted over whether they should follow what others want them to do or follow their own needs and wishes. Millon and Davis have conceptualized the obsessive-compulsive and negativistic personality disorders as variants of an internally conflicted style, with the former style seen as more passive and accommodating in coping with this internal conflict and the latter more active in how that conflict is expressed.

In addition, these two personality disorders have historically been placed in the "anxious-fearful" cluster of *DSM* personality disorders, starting with *DSM-III*. Although validity of the *DSM* clusters has been questioned on theoretical and empirical grounds (Bagby, Joffe, Parker, & Schuller, 1993; Hyler & Lyons, 1988; Morey, 1988b, 1988c), the obsessive-compulsive and negativistic personality disorders have been grouped together because anxiety and tension are prominent symptoms associated with both.

In this chapter, the obsessive-compulsive and negativistic personality disorders are each reviewed separately in terms of the clinical characteristics that define each of them and the prevalence with which they occur in clinical populations. Various theoretical perspectives are also reviewed in terms of how obsessive-compulsive and negativistic personality disorders are conceptualized with respect to etiology, factors that maintain pathological tendencies, and other personality dynamics. In addition, some concluding remarks are offered with respect to some of the more controversial issues that continue to plague these two diagnostic entities. Finally, the chapter concludes with a brief discussion of major issues that will help to guide future research that will hopefully lead to greater refinement in future revisions of diagnostic criteria.

Obsessive-Compulsive Personality Disorder

Despite being recognized by most diagnostic classification systems and theoretical taxonomies, the obsessive-compulsive compulsive personality disorder (OCPD) has carried many different names (Pfohl & Blum, 1995). Original psychoanalytic writers referred to "anal character" types, the international classification systems (ICD) refer to an "anankastic" personality, and the *DSM* system has at various times defined a "compulsive" or "obsessive-compulsive" personality disorder. Remarkably, none of the official or theoretical diagnostic systems identifies obsessions or compulsions as symptoms of the personality disorder. However, there has been remarkable consistency in the specific personality traits that have been used to characterize this disorder.

The behavior of obsessive-compulsive individuals has been routinely characterized by extreme rigidity, preoccupation with details, and perfectionism (Pfohl & Blum, 1995; Pollack, 1987). Although orderliness and perfectionism are often viewed as desirable or adapative traits, in OCPD these traits often prevent the individual from completing important tasks because of extreme tension and worry over the need to have things perfect. In addition to perfectionistic, individuals with OCPD have been viewed as diligent and hard-working, but again the extreme forms of these traits render the person lacking in spontaneity, withholding, and unimaginative (Pollack, 1987).

Interpersonal relationships are also impaired. These individuals are seen as cold, distant, and authoritarian. Many of the problems in their relationships stem from their excessive need to control others. Relationships are typically identified as either subordinate or deferential. Those in authority are given respect, but there is underlying resentment or hostility that is extremely difficult to express. Those in subordinate positions often receive harsh, critical, and punitive comments. In short, interpersonal relationships are often conflicted due to the failure of others to meet the obsessive-compulsive individual's unrealistic personal demands and standards.

The inflexibility of such obsessive-compulsive traits is amplified by the self-image these individuals hold. They view themselves as conscientious, moralistic, industrious, and efficient. These perceptions are viewed as adaptive in work settings, and are often adopted in personal relationships as well. As such, there is little motivation to become more flexible. Compounding this inflexibility is a cognitive rigidity, identified by some theorists as a central feature of the disorder (Shapiro, 1965), that is seen both in the process and content of the person's thinking. There is a sharp and narrow focus on details that prevents a full grasp of the "big picture." For example, the fact that one's checkbook fails to balance leads to an intense focus on finding the error; time is wasted and important bills are late in getting paid. Moreover, obsessive-compulsives avoid unwelcome thoughts or impulses and frequently distract themselves by becoming unduly critical and judgmental of others. For example, the person will argue stubbornly with others in an attempt to change or devalue political or philosophical perspectives that are in opposition to his or her own.

A variety of proposals have been offered as to the essential "core feature" of the OCPD. Most theoretical and formal classification systems include rigidity, perfectionism, and restricted emotional expressivity as the main features of the disorder (Pfohl & Blum, 1995). Millon (1969, 1981; Millon & Davis, 1996) identifies intense ambivalence as the central feature; according to this perspective, the obsessive-compulsive harbors internal conflict over expressing self-oriented needs versus complying with the needs and wishes of others. Psychoanalytic theory views repressed anal eroticism as a central feature of the personality disorder (Kline, 1978).

The diagnostic construct of an OCPD has received some empirical support in factor analytic studies (Lazare, Klerman, & Armor, 1966, 1970; Torgersen, 1980). However, many studies on the validity of the construct have been based on self-report instruments. One of the major difficulties in using such methodologies to validate the obsessive-compulsive construct is that many of the external behavioral features of the disorder are highly correlated with social desirability (McCann, 1992). It has been suggested that the true core features of OCPD may be internalized dynamics such as conflict over unwanted thoughts, intense ambivalence, and psychic tension that may not lend themselves to measurement with self-report instruments (McCann, 1992).

In short, there is adequate support for the construct of an OCPD that is defined according to specific traits and characteristics through classical clinical formulations (Pollack, 1987). However, there has been no support for the superiority of one theoretical approach over another.

Another issue that has created confusion over the true nature of the personality disorder is the fact that some writers have proposed that obsessive-compulsive personality lies along a continuum of pathology that includes obsessive-compulsive neurosis (Goldstein, 1985). Others have proposed that the two are clinically and conceptually distinct from one another (Insel, 1982). As a result, confusion has arisen over how the personality disorder should be labeled and how it should be differentiated from other forms of psychopathology. As the following sections illustrate, many of these issues have yet to be resolved.

Prevalence

The prevalence of OCPD has been difficult to establish due to changes in the threshold of diagnostic criteria required to make the diagnosis (Pfohl & Blum, 1995). *DSM-III* criteria were very restrictive in that four out of five criteria were required to make the diagnosis, whereas *DSM-III-R* criteria were expanded to nine criteria, with five out of the nine needed to make the diagnosis. This led to a greater likelihood that obsessive-compulsive personality disorder would be diagnosed. Several research studies found a doubling or tripling of prevalence rates after the more inclusive criteria were adopted. Another factor influencing reported prevalence rates is the use of different assessment methods such as structured interviews and clinician rating forms.

Overall, the prevalence rate of OCPD has been reported to range from about 5 to 20% of psychiatric patient samples. Earlier studies using the more restrictive *DSM-III* criteria reported prevalence rates of 1% (Dahl, 1986), 2% (Kass, Skodol, Charles, & Sptizer, 1985; Widiger, Trull, Hurt, Clarkin, & Frances, 1987), and 9% (Frances, Clarkin, Gilmore, & Hurt, 1984). More recent studies have found the prevalence rate to be higher. For instance, Skodol, Rosnick, Kellman, Oldham, and Hyler (1988) found a prevalence rate of 18% in a patient sample, while a 20% prevalence rate was independently established by Alnaes and Torgersen (1988) and Standage and Ladha (1988).

According to data summarized by Pfohl and Blum (1995), there is a great deal of comorbidity between OCPD and other personality disorders, particularly paranoid, histrionic, borderline, narcissistic, and avoidant personalities. Some of the comorbid diagnoses make theoretical and conceptual sense, such as paranoid, avoidant, and narcissistic. The rigidity, tension, anxiety, and demandingness that characterize obsessive-compulsive personality are traits frequently associated with the defensive and guarded paranoid, socially anxious avoidant, and insensitive narcissist. However, some comorbid personality disorders found along with OCPD are not theoretically or conceptually expected. For instance, the obsessive-compulsive tends to be restrained in the expression of emotion, unlike the emotionally expressive or unstable histrionic and borderline personalities. The implication of these findings is that OCPD is not uncommon, but it does overlap to a large extent with other personality disorder diagnoses. As a result, revision of the diagnostic criteria for *DSM-IV* were directed at improving internal consistency, descriptive validity, and specificity (Pfohl & Blum, 1991). Future research will provide insight into whether these revisions have a significant impact on prevalence rates and comorbidity with other personality disorders.

There is special interest in the relationship between OCPD and Axis I obsessive-compulsive disorder (OCD) because the similarity in names implies that there should be some comparability in symptomatology. As the research illustrates, however, there is not a significant degree of overlap between these disorders (Pollack, 1979). For example, more recent studies cite fairly low prevalence rates of OCPD among patients with OCD. Black, Yates, Noyes, Pfohl, and Kelley (1989) found no compulsive personality disorders among a small group of patients with OCD; the more common personality disorders were histrionic, borderline, and dependent. Moreover, Baer, Jenike, and Riccardi (1990) found that only 6% of their sample of OCD's met criteria for OCPD. Therefore, the epidemiological research does not reveal higher prevalence rates of OCPD among patients with OCD; in fact, research suggests that the personality disorder is not common in this particular clinical population.

The relationship between OCPD and other Axis I clinical syndromes is even less clear. No studies have yet documented comorbidity trends (Pfohl & Blum, 1995).

Historical Perspectives

Perhaps no other personality disorder is as closely connected to a particular theoretical framework as is OCPD. Originally associated with classical psychoanalytic theory, this character type was seen as arising out of intense conflict during the anal stage of psychosexual development, prompting the early term the "anal character." According to early analytic theory, a child's wishes to have freedom and autonomy in controlling retention and elimination of bowel functions brought about clashes with parents who sought to impose social customs and standards for impulse control (Freud, 1908). Freud emphasized the conflict between the free gratification of bodily pleasure and the need to seek and obtain parental approval and love. As a result, the adult personality traits of orderliness, cleanliness, conscientiousness, and rigidity are seen as derivatives of conflict experienced during the anal period of psychosexual development (Pollack, 1987).

The terms "obsessive" and "compulsive," however, predate the analytic formulation of the personality disorder. In the 19th century, Kraft-Ebing first used the term "compulsion" to refer to constricted thought processes in individuals with severe depression, and the latter part of that century began to see application of the term to such traits as hidden emotions, incessant questioning, doubtfulness, and other characteristics that have come to be associated with the term "obsessive-compulsive" as it is used today (Millon & Davis, 1996). While OCPD has been used in the United States throughout the 20th century, the term "anankastic" has been used extensively in Europe and currently appears in recent versions of the *ICD* under the section on personality disorders. The term "anankastic" was used by Schneider (1923/1950) to describe a personality type that tends to conceal feelings of insecurity, compensates by adopting an overly correct or scrupulous demeanor, and uses control in most relationships.

Other early formulations of OCPD rested on notions of intrapsychic conflict and faulty constitutional mechanisms. Kretschmer, for instance, described a "sensitive" personality type in which the person experiences intense affect, but weakened methods for actively expressing such emotion, contributing to "pent up" mental activity (Millon & Davis, 1996). Kahn (1931) described extreme ambivalent tendencies characterizing a specific personality style, "ambitendency," in which the person avoids personal responsibility by avoiding decisions until all aspects of a situation have been appraised and some definite events have occurred. Kahn's formulation of the ambitent serves as a precursor to many of the contemporary formulations, particularly the passive-ambivalent type originally formulated by Millon (1969, 1981) and discussed later in this chapter.

Still, psychoanalytic theorists have provided most of the early formulations on the obsessive-compulsive personality. Expanding on Freud's early writing, Abraham detailed the anal character type as more obsessional in that the primary features were stubbornness, perseverence, and lack of initiative. Obsessional characters, according to Abraham, are seen as witholding in relationships and experience difficulty separating themselves from possessions. Reich (1949) expanded further on the compulsive character as a pervasive neurosis that is characterized by extreme attention to order, circumstantiality, rumination, indecision, and self-doubt. Analytic writers have thus been primarily responsible for much of the impetus behind research and clinical interest in what today we call the obsessive-compulsive personality disorder.

Contemporary Theoretical Perspectives

Psychoanalytic Perspectives The more contemporary psychoanalytic theorists and ego psychologists conceptualize the anal period not psychosexually but in terms of struggles over autonomy with parental figures, the quest for control and order in one's life, and intense conflict between defiance and obedience in interpersonal relationships. Toward this end, Erikson (1950) viewed the anal period as involving the child's struggle to gain autonomy and control not only over bowel functions but also over one's self and environment. Failure to successfully navigate the quest for autonomy results in shame and doubt. As a result, excessive parental criticism, punishment, and withdrawl of approval in this critical period can, according to Erikson, lead to development of strong defenses in which the child becomes invested in self-control, discipline, and control.

Other ego psychologists expanded on the role of parental standards and responses as critical factors. Rado (1959), for instance, viewed the mother's demandingness and intrusiveness into the child's bowel patterns as contributory to defiance and anger in response to parental boundary intrusions. The rage leads to battles between parent and child in which the parent makes the child feel guilty about expression of defiance, and an ambivalence develops between the child's anger over intense parental responses and guilt-inducing reactions from the parent. Other parental reactions during toilet training that have been posited as relevant, including the parent's self-righteous and authoritarian attitudes that are cloaked by a thin guise of fairness and support for the child (Ingram, 1982). The child is held to parental standards of right and wrong, yet later develops resentment and anger that is fostered by a shaky identity based more on parental standards and less on the child's own sense of self. Mallinger (1984) emphasized that parental rejection, authoritarian attitudes, and lack of respect for the child's growing sense of privacy all foster anxiety, tension, and feelings of vulnerability and unpredictability about the world. These feelings are repressed and defended against by an adoption of rigid convictions and exaggerated need for control.

More recent psychoanalytic formulations have expanded on a variety of features, including cognitive, interpersonal, and self-image components of the disorder. According to Salzman (1980) and Storr (1980), for example, the obsessive-compulsive experiences a pervasive threat to his or her security. There are constant threats from the outside world that seek to make life unpredictable or to change one's sense of order and stability in life. As a result, obsessive-compulsive character types become overly cautious, fearful of making a wrong decision, perfectionistic, and overly controlled in an attempt to provide greater stability and security. Expanding on the cognitive rigidity of this style, Gabbard (1994) noted that extreme perfectionism and the quest for certainty are driven by an underlying need for parental approval and affirmation that was lacking in early childhood. Because of parental withholding, the obsessive-compulsive often feels that he or she has not tried hard enough, and feelings of inadequacy and fears of being identified as inadequate drive the constant need for perfection.

Much of the research on psychoanalytic perspectives on the obsessive-compulsive style has been plagued by methodological difficulties. Because many of the etiological factors are internalized and often unconscious, traditional methodologies relying on self-report instruments or semistructured interviews cannot adequately tap intrapsychic processes that typically operate in this personality disorder (McCann, 1992). In addition, many of the measures designed to assess obsessive-compulsive personality traits either have questionable utility sometimes because they measure constructs (e.g., Type A personality, field independence) that are of questionable relevance (Pollack, 1987).

Several studies have examined the psychoanalytic construct of the anal character and found moderate support for many etiological factors. Using Kline's (1978, 1981) anality scale, Fischer and Juni (1982) found support for high levels of anality reflecting the withholding of emotions, excessive need for control, need for autonomy, defiance, and negativity. Additional studies have shown that undergraduates obtaining high scores on this scale experience greater hostility over intrusions by others (Juni & Rubenstein, 1982), perceive authority as separate and distinct from one's self, and avoid self-disclosure in interpersonal relationships (Juni & Semel, 1982).

Behavioral Perspectives Unlike the extensive coverage of OCPD in other theoretical frameworks, very little exists on the syndrome in behavior therapy literature. A behavioral approach eschews formal diagnosis in favor of the measurement of observable and objective behaviors (Turner & Turkat, 1988). In particular, treatment of OCPD uses two basic approaches. The first is a technological approach in which specific symptoms such as intense anxiety, perfectionistic behavior, and rigid behavior patterns are viewed as learned behaviors. Thus, treatment calls for specific protocols such as systematic desensitization, self-monitoring, contingency management, and flooding in order to alleviate specific behavior patterns. The technological approach assumes that if obsessive-compulsive personality propensities are learned they can be unlearned.

A second approach to conceptualizing the obsessive-compulsive character style is through a behavior case formulation method. As outlined by Turkat and his colleagues (Turkat & Levin, 1984; Turner & Turkat, 1988), this approach calls for the identification of specific problems, an analysis of possible etiological factors that maintain the problematic behavior, and prediction about future behavior. Interventions are then planned to yield new behaviors that are more adaptive and the efficacy of interventions are tested. Turkat and Maisto (1985) have pursued a formulation-based approach that suggests that difficulty in expressing adaptive emotions is common in patients with this personality disorder. They speculated further that obsessive-compulsive individuals learn maladaptive emotional reactions in homes that emphasize hard work and minimize close interpersonal relationships and the expression of emotions. As a result, patients with this style express anger and depression over not living up to personal expectations; moreover, excessive devotion to work, rigid ideas, laziness, and interpersonal difficulties are all common problems.

Based on the behavioral hypothesis that symptoms are learned within the context of a highly disciplined, yet withholding home, Turkat and Maisto (1985) identify a deficiency in social skills as a major component in OCPD. Therefore, social skills training is viewed as the most appropriate treatment. Because these patients are not particularly motivated or capable of sharing their feelings, self-management and anger control therapy are likely to be more acceptable than other forms of verbal therapy, according to Donat (1995). Indeed, "these patients [find] the idea of learning how to be more emotional and less rational to be rather frightening" (Turkat & Maisto, 1985, p. 523), and it is often difficult to maintain these individuals in treatment. Moreover, there are no large-scale research studies on the behavioral formulations discussed above. Future research is likely to focus on analysis of the individual case, a method for which behavioral perspectives are particularly well suited.

Cognitive Perspectives Beck and Freeman (1990) have been the major theorists writing about personality disorders from the cognitive perspective. According to these authors, obsessive-compulsives exhibit clear distortions in thinking that produce rigidity and perfectionism. The major errors in information processing that occur are tendencies to think in extreme all-or-nothing terms. The world is seen in black and white, causing procrastination due to the extreme need to avoid mistakes. In addition, obsessive-compulsive individuals are seen as engaging in the cognitive distortion of magnification and exaggeration. For example, minor errors, small deviations from standard procedures, and incidental changes in routine are given greater significance than is called for, and negative consequences are exaggerated beyond their true nature. Beck and Freeman (1990) further identified a set of rigid "musts" and "shoulds" that make for absolutistic and moralistic attitudes, creating the strict moralistic code of conduct and standards by which these individuals live. Such deeply ingrained beliefs as, "I must be in control," "You have to do it my way," "I must do virtually anything just right," and so forth are the factors that maintain the obsessive-compulsive style (Beck & Freeman, 1990, p. 47). These beliefs carry over into interpersonal relationships and account for the need for excessive control over others and the need to assume responsibility in order to get things done perfectly.

Since the extreme goal of perfectionism is a major component of the obsessive-compulsive style, one goal of cognitive therapy is to get the individual to see those strivings as unrealistic (Will, 1995). Moreover, the obsessive-compulsive character is viewed as having underdeveloped cognitive skills that permit spontaneous, innovative, and creative interpretation of everyday events. Treatment is often directed toward developing skills that permit flexible and playful patterns of thought, with a goal of achieving greater emotional sponteneity.

Interpersonal Perspectives One of the first interpersonal theorists to write on the OCPD was Leary (1957), who viewed this style as being defined by a strong set of actions that maintain conventionality and security. According to Leary, the obsessive-compulsive personality exhibits interpersonal behaviors that convey an appearance of success, maturity, and strength. In short, persons with this style avoid appearing weak and unconventional to others. There is evidence of maladaptive functioning when the person's sense of conventional security is shaken. Thus, OCPD may arise when anxiety and depression occur in response to developmental events in which the child feels weak, insecure, and isolated due to fears of appearing incompetent or imperfect.

Leary's (1957) model arranges interpersonal factors into two orthogonal dimensions: love/hostility and submissiveness/dominance (Kiesler, 1983; Wiggins, 1982; Widiger & Kelso, 1983). Obsessive-compulsive personality disorder is viewed as lying in the quadrant defined by high levels of dominance and love. Thus, the circumplex model sees this personality style as autocratic, responsible, hypernormal, and controlling.

More recent interpersonal approaches have included the Structural Analysis of Social Behavior (SASB) formulated by Benjamin (1974, 1993). According to this model, the obsessive-compulsive is guided by intense fears of making a mistake or being viewed as imperfect by others. As a result, the person is driven to maintain order and control by imposing perfectionistic needs on others. Excessive demands are made that others submit to the compulsive's methods for doing things. Failure to meet these unrealistic demands results in blame that is unfairly harsh or critical. The obsessive-compulsive is also deferential to those in authority, such that rules and principles are adhered to quite strictly. Within the SASB model, situational factors have an impact on interpersonal conduct in a given situation, thus accounting for some variability in behavior across situations.

While there has been much interest in interpersonal models in recent years, there has also been criticism. Endler and Edwards (1988) have argued that while interpersonal theories recognize the importance of situational factors, they are narrow in that they ignore complex person-situation interactions. Pincus and Wiggins (1990) evaluated the circumplex model of personality and found that obsessive-compulsive personality was not well represented by the model. These researchers proposed that interpersonal behaviors may not be the central source of maladjustment in OCPD; they suggest cognitive and emotional factors such as rigidity, isolation of affect, inflexible beliefs, and anxiety are more significant features of the disorder.

On the other hand, Sim and Romney (1990) found that research on the interpersonal circumplex model of OCPD is strongly influenced by the type of ratings made on interpersonal behavior. Using self-report instruments, these researchers found support for the circumplex model representations of the disorder as high on managerial-autocratic and responsible-hypernormal quadrants of the circumplex; these quadrants correspond to high levels of dominance and affiliation. However, Sim and Romney obtained very different results when others made ratings of the person's interpersonal behaviors: obsessive-compulsive individuals were rated high on rebellious-distrustful and self-effacing-masochistic dimensions (*low* on dominance and love and *high* on hostility and submissiveness). In short, there is some research to support interpersonal models of OCPD with self-report instruments, but these models tend to focus on a narrow range of features and traits that define the disorder. Another conclusion is that compulsives see themselves one way, while observers see them another. Thus discrepant findings do not reflect a failure of measures to converge, but rather an aspect of the substantive nature of the disorder, one which contributes to its perpetuation.

Factorial Perspectives One factorial approach to conceptualizing personality disorders is the five-factor model of personality, which uses the five dimensions of neuroticism, extraversion, openness to experience, agreeableness, and conscientiousness to classify personality traits (Costa & McCrae, 1992; Costa & Widiger, 1993; McCrae & Costa, 1990; Widiger, 1992). The OCPD is characterized as an extreme variant along the conscientiousness dimension (Costa & Widiger, 1993). Under normal expressions of this personality trait, individuals are seen as hardworking, well organized, ambitious, and disciplined, with strong commitment to goal-directed behavior. At the extreme elevations, conscientiousness leads to excessive devotion to work at the expense of spontaneity and interpersonal relationships. Likewise, perfectionism begins to interfere with completion of tasks, leading to rigidity and inflexibility.

There has been some empirical support for the five-factor model's formulation of the OCPD as lying at the extreme end of the conscientiousness dimension. Wiggins and Pincus (1989) found that OCPD traits, as measured by the Personality Adjective Checklist and MMPI, were positively related to conscientiousness as measured by the NEO-PI (Costa & McCrae, 1985, 1989), a major instrument used to assess the five-factor personality traits. In another study using different measures of personality disorders, including spouse and peer ratings and the MCMI, Costa and McCrae (1990) found strong relationships between self-reports of compulsive personality traits and conscientiousness. There were inconsistent findings on the relationship between obsessive-compulsive personality traits and neuroticism, suggesting no clear connection between this personality type and the negative expression of emotions. This finding is somewhat surprising given the extensive clinical theory that holds that the disorder is intrinsically conflicted. In short, the strongest evidence exists for a close relationship between the OCPD and extreme, maladaptive conscientiousness as defined by the five-factor model.

Other dimensional models of OCPD have been proposed. Some clustering methodologies have produced a typology where the obsessive-compulsive personality is identified as a moderately severe disturbance characterized by orderliness, rigidity, emotional constriction, and excessive controlling behavior (Walton, Foulds, Littman, & Presley, 1970; Walton & Presley, 1973a, 1973b). Other factor analytic studies of personality traits have consistently shown the OCPD to be described by traits involving rigidity, conscientiousness, and constricted emotional expressiveness (Tyrer, 1988).

While factorial approaches to the obsessive-compulsive personality are useful in providing consistent empirical support for the description commonly associated with this style, they are descriptive rather than explanatory (Millon & Davis, 1996). That is, they do not provide etiological explanations of how the obsessive-compulsive style develops, what the dynamics are in fostering and maintaining maladaptive functioning, and how it combines with other forms of psychopathology to produce unique variations in clinical presentation in the individual case.

Biological Perspectives There has been very limited attention given to the possible biological factors involved in OCPD. One possible reason for the lack of focus on the biological etiology of this disorder is that it has been conceptualized as belonging in the anxious cluster of personality disorders, and there is no support for a strong link between anxiety disturbances and that particular group of personality disorders (Weston & Siever, 1993). Therefore, what scant literature there is has focused on interesting, but untested speculative hypotheses.

Cloninger's (1987) neurobiological theory proposes that personality consists of three dimensions, namely novelty seeking, reward dependence, and harm avoidance. Compulsives exhibit low levels of novelty seeking, a dimension defined by an orientation to avoid change and to maintain stability. Likewise, the obsessive-compulsive exhibits well-developed neurobiological propensities to avoid harm and to have weakened reliance on rewards. Thus, the clinical picture is one of rigidity, unassertive behavior, preoccupation with order and safety, and excessive emotional control.

Millon and Davis (1996) also proposed some biological mechanisms that may play a role in the development of obsessive-compulsive personality pathology. These theorists speculated that neural connections in the limbic system that control fear and anger may contribute to the indecisiveness and excessive conflict that characterizes decision making in this personality style.

Integrative Models Each of the theoretical models reviewed thus far have focused on a particular domain of the obsessive-compulsive personality, such as interpersonal relationships or cognitive processing. To integrate each of these domains into a more comprehensive theory, Millon (1969, 1981; Millon & Davis, 1996) has offered an integrative formulation based on the principles of evolution.

According to Millon, OCPD can be conceptualized along three dimensions of personality that pertain to the specific aims of existence, strategies of replication, and instrumental modes of adapting to one's environment. Aims of existence are directed at enhancing (pleasure) and preserving (pain) life. Strategies of replication involve both individuation (self) and nurturance (other). Modes of adaptation may be directed at accommodating to (passive) or modifying (active) the environment. The obsessive-compulsive is viewed as a conflicted style that experiences intense ambivalence over needs for individuation and nurturance. Thus, there is guilt over seeking individual, self-centered needs but resistance to accepting direction from others. Therefore, the obsessive-compulsive passively adopts strict adherence to external rules and structure to cope with the ambivalence created by attempts to both individuate and seek nurturance from others.

Extending this underlying dimensional approach to OCPD, Millon and Davis (1996) have proposed clinical domain descriptions that integrate various theoretical approaches. Accordingly, the obsessive-compulsive is viewed as disciplined and highly structured in behavioral displays and respectful in interpersonal relationships. On a phenomenological level, this personality disorder presents a constricted cognitive style, and a conscientious and industrious self-image. Moreover, obsessive-compulsive individuals hide their true feelings and attitudes about important persons in their life. Their internal thoughts and feelings are compartmentalized so that mental structures are separate and unpleasant feelings and thoughts are avoided. On a biophysical level, the obsessive-compulsive is characterized by a solemn, tense, and serious mood in which emotions are tightly controlled. In short, the integrative approach proposed by Millon and his colleagues is designed to provide a framework for understanding the obsessive-compulsive personality disorder as a multidimensional construct with distinct features at all levels of personality.

In recent years there has been research supporting Millon's dimensional and integrative approach to personality disorders. For example, Strack, Lorr, and Campbell (1990) examined a circular model of personality disorders as predicted by Millon (1987) and found good support for the theoretical model. Moreover, McCann (1991) found good support for the dimensions proposed by Millon in factor analytic studies of the MCMI-II, with OCPD represented on a factor defined by interpersonal ambivalence in a fashion predicted by theory. Finally, Whyne-Berman and McCann (1995) examined Millon's proposed model of specific defense mechanisms being linked to specific personality disorders. While substantial method variance contributed to low overall correlations, the link between reaction formation and OCPD received moderate support.

To summarize, the integrative theory proposed by Millon is useful in combining various approaches to understanding personality disorders into a cohesive framework that broadens the theoretical and clinical understanding to include equally important facets of OCPD.

Concluding Reflections

Despite the consistency with which various theorists have defined OCPD, and despite the clinical utility the construct has had, several issues remain unresolved. Uncertainty remains as to the most appropriate name for the disorder. Given the poor theoretical and empirical support for a link between obsessive-compulsive neurosis and obsessive-compulsive personality disorder, it seems appropriate to rethink its designation. In addition, it appears that many of the core features that truly define this construct occur at a deeper level of personality than overt behavior, making direct clinical observations and self-report instruments of limited use in identifying the disorder. Various proposals have been drafted for broadening the criteria to include personality traits that reflect the internalized conflict that exists in obsessive-compulsive individuals (Pfohl & Blum, 1995). As diagnostic criteria are broadened and refined, our ability to empirically test various theoretical hypotheses will expand.

Negativistic Personality Disorder

Although the negativistic personality disorder (NPD) criteria include many features associated with the earlier notion of passive-aggressive personality, the current formulation constitutes a broader and much richer description of this personality disorder. Therefore, stubbornness, passive resistance to fulfilling routine demands, procrastination, and inefficiency all characterize the behavior of the negativistic personality. However, unlike passive-aggressive personality, NPD is also identified by sullen and irritable moods. While chronic dysphoria and irritability plague the negativistic's life, it is the facility with which they arouse or fall into these moods that characterizes their affective pattern, not the pervasiveness of these moods (McCann, 1988; Millon & Davis, 1996).

The anger and argumentative nature displayed by NPD individuals are closely connected to interpersonal relationships and cognitive style. They are quick to anger when pressures arise or demands are made by others; feelings of resentment and envy arise when others are viewed as being more fortunate. In relationships, anger and negative moods are difficult to accept because of underlying dependency needs. These unpleasant and dysphoric moods create intense conflict, causing negativistic persons to act in a contrary fashion, often adopting rapidly changing roles that only serve to baffle or confuse others. For instance, rejection from others is perceived as resentment and the individual may comment on the lack of virtue in all human beings. Yet at other times when people are accepting and supportive, the individual responds with skepticism and scorn.

Negativistic persons are often quickly identified by their cognitive style of intense skepticism, cynicism, and lack of trust in others. Positive events are met with disbelief, with the expectation that good things just do not last. When others encounter positive events, the negativistic person will find some way, either by action or verbal comment, to point out the negative aspects of the situation. Indeed, it could be said that negativistic personalities are masters at "raining on the parade" of other people. In keeping with the erratic and unpredictable nature of these individuals, the negative comments that defeat the joy experienced by others can be offered in one of two ways. On the one hand, negative and passive-aggressive comments may be made in an "innocent" and nonchalant manner. Often, however, the underlying negativity is perceived and the target responds with anger; this results in the negativistic person feeling misunderstood and unappreciated. On the other hand, sour and argumentative comments may be voiced in an irritable and prickly fashion. In some cases, comments may be generalized and have no target. Whatever the case, the individual's sour mood is spread to others until they too have lost enthusiasm and enjoyment.

The self-image of negativistic individuals is the result of a long history of disappointments, inconsistent parenting, and negative reactions from others (Millon & Davis, 1966). As such, they view themselves as misunderstood and unappreciated, and often feel demeaned, when, in fact, they typically provoke such a responses through their skeptical and cynical comments. Moreover, there are deep-seated, internalized, and contradictory attitudes due to unfulfilled dependency needs. Emotional outbursts, impulsive behavior, and interpersonal manipulation are often listed as associated features of NPD (Cloninger, 1987; Small, Small, Alig, & Moore, 1970).

Various theorists have offered different insights into the "core features" that characterize the negativistic personality. In Millon's (1969, 1981) model, active expression of internalized ambivalence is seen as a core feature leading to erratic behavior, sullen moods, and skeptical beliefs. Malinow (1981) considered indirect expression of hostility to be the major defining symptom. In past *DSM* revisions, a major factor involving passive resistance to demands was seen as the core defining feature. *DSM-IV* criteria have been broadened to reflect many of the characteristics discussed above. Included are passive-aggressive behavior, sullen and irritable moods, skeptical attitudes, feelings of being misunderstood, and conflicted and highly ambivalent moods and attachments.

Despite a core set of symptoms having been defined for NPD, there have been some difficulties in finding valid and reliable criteria for the disorder. One set of difficulties lies in the overlap between negativistic and other personality disorders. For instance, the irritable and sullen moods characteristic of negativistic individuals also pertains to other emotionally expressive personality disorders, including the borderline and histrionic (Millon, 1981; Millon & Davis, 1996). Moreover, the oppositional and obstructive actions of negativistic individuals are also found in antisocial personality disorder (Malinow, 1981). The skepticism evident in cognitive patterns of NPD are also similar to those seen in paranoid personality disorder. In fact, there is empirical support for a high degree of overlap between measures of passive-aggressive personality disorder and antisocial, borderline, dependent, and narcissistic personality disorders (Dubro & Wetzler, 1989; Morey, 1988a; Morey, Blashfield, Webb, & Jewell, 1988).

Problems in differential diagnosis have arisen in part because of narrow criteria that existed for passive-aggressive personality disorder in prior official classification systems. For example, passive-aggressive personality disorder had a number of apparently different criteria that were later shown empirically to be different examples of the same common trait, namely reisistance to demands for adequate performance (Livesley, Reiffer, Sheldon, & West, 1987; Pfohl, Coryell, Zimmerman, & Stangl, 1986). Nevertheless, attempts to remove the disorder completely from formal diagnostic nomenclature have been thwarted by the existence of research that is supportive of the diagnostic construct. Kass et al. (1985) found this personality disorder to load on a factor representative of anxious/fearful personality types, affective arousal that characterizes the passive-aggressive. Moreover, research has demonstrated that individuals given a diagnosis of passive-aggressive personality disorder exhibit severe disruptions in interpersonal relationships, self-image, ability to function at work, and cognitive problem solving (Drake & Vaillant, 1985; Livesley & Jackson, 1986). In spite of definitional problems, the *DSM-IV* work group on personality disorders thus saw fit to redefine the criteria and to broaden the construct, resulting in criteria for NPD.

Prevalence

An accurate determination of the prevalence rate of passive-aggressive/negativistic personality disorder has been extremely difficult. One major reason is that diagnostic criteria have undergone a rather significant change. Recall, for example, that the passive-aggressive personality disorder was the only diagnosis in *DSM-III* that could not be made when another personality disorder diagnosis was made. This severe restriction may have artificially lowered prevalence rates. Once this restriction was eliminated in *DSM-III-R*, passive-aggressive personality disorder could then be diagnosed along with other comorbid personality disorders. No epidemiological studies that have yet examined the prevalence of this disorder as currently conceived in *DSM-IV*.

Despite the difficulty in establishing a precise prevalence rate, there is sufficient evidence of the passive-aggressive diagnosis being useful to warrant its continued existence in formal taxonomies. Low prevalence rates have been cited by some researchers, such as 2% (Dahl, 1986; Kass et al., 1985), 5% (Standage & Ladha, 1988), 8% (Morey, 1988b), and even 0% in one study (Loranger, Susman, Oldham, & Russakoff, 1987). Other studies have found higher prevalence rates among larger patient populations. For example, Alnaes and Torgerson (1988) found a prevalence rate of 10%; Pfohl et al. (1986) found a rate of 14%; Zanarini, Frandenburg, Chauncy, and Gunderson (1987) found a rate of 19%; and Widiger et al. (1987) found a prevalence rate as high as 52% among a patient sample. Thus, despite concerns about the adequacy and precision of diagnostic criteria, passive-aggressive/negativistic personality disorder has been used frequently enough to be retained in formal diagnostic classification systems (Millon & Radovanov, 1995). It remains unclear as to whether or not expansion of diagnostic criteria will have any effect on established prevalence rates.

There is a fair degree of diagnostic overlap between passive-aggressive personality disorder and other types of character pathology. Expected comorbidity has been found between borderline, self-defeating, and sadistic personality disorder (Millon & Radovanov, 1995). Morey (1988b) found passive-aggressive personality disorder to be a frequent secondary diagnosis in antisocial personality disorder, pointing to common traits involving defiance and oppositionality. An unexpected connection has been identified linking passive-aggressive/negativistic personality disorder and narcissistic personality (Morey, 1988b). Again, it will be extremely interesting to see how recent revisions in diagnostic criteria will impact on the pattern of comorbidity with other personality disorders.

Very few data are available on the comorbidity between NPD and Axis I syndromes. Conceptually, the negativity, moodiness, and sour attitudes of this personality disorder suggest a link with mood disorders, particularly dysthymia and major depression. Results from studies of self-report measures of personality disorders support this link, suggesting major depression, cyclothymia, and dysthymia are very commonly diagnosed in NPD (Alnae & Torgersen, 1991). In addition, there have been conceptual links made between passive-aggressive/negativistic personality disorder in adulthood and oppositional-defiant disorder in adolescence (McCann, 1988). However, the presence of oppositional-defiant disorder in adolescence does not increase the likelihood of a passive-aggressive/negativistic personality disorder later on in adulthood (Rey, Morris-Yates, Singh, Andrews, & Stewart, 1995). In fact, both oppositional-defiant disorder and passive-aggressive/negativistic personality disorder have been shown to be unstable over long periods of time in adolescence (Mattanah, Becher, Levy, Edell, & McGlashen, 1995).

Historical Perspectives

The NPD, though new in *DSM-IV*, has a lengthy history due to its close connection to the passive-aggressive personality disorder. In fact, Millon (1993) noted that "the descriptive features that characterize the [negativistic personality] disorder have been portrayed in considerable detail by numerous distinguished clinicians for close to a century under a variety of different designations" (p. 78). In 1945, the War Department began using the passive-aggressive label to describe a distinct "immaturity reaction" in which soldiers became helpless and passive when demands were placed upon them (Malinow, 1981; Millon, 1981). Among the features of a passive-aggressive reaction were oppositional, resistant, and obstructive tendencies. Over the latter half of this century, passive-aggressive personality disorder has continued to be recognized in formal diagnostic classification systems. The *DSM-I* recognized a "pure" passive-aggressive subtype, as did the *DSM-II*. With the significant changes that took place in *DSM-III*, such as multiaxial diagnosis and greater precision in defining criteria, questions surfaced about the appropriateness of using the term "passive-aggressive" to define a distinct personality disorder. Preliminary drafts of the *DSM-III* omitted the passive-aggressive personality because of questions about whether passive-aggression described a syndrome of personality disturbance (Malinow, 1981).

In light of confusion that has surrounded its definition, it is not at all surprising that *DSM-IV* has attempted to completely revise diagnostic criteria for the disorder and to reconceptualize it under the more broadly defined negativistic personality. As such, passive-aggression is now viewed as one characteristic feature, involving stubbornness, resistance, and inefficiency. NPD introduces criteria that reflect important cognitive and affective features, providing a broader and richer description of the negativistic character type (Millon, 1993). That is, negativistic personalities are not only obstructive and erratic in their behavior but also moody, irritable, sullen, pessimistic, and cynical in their emotional and cognitive presentation.

Despite this recent history that has been punctuated with controversy and confusion, NPD has very strong ties to a number of early theoretical formulations that parallel the current definition (Millon & Davis, 1996). Early personality theorists included characterological styles in their taxonomy that resemble the negativistic personality as it is currently conceptualized. For instance, Kraeplin described individuals with unpleasant and sour constitutional predispositions that made them prone to exhibit fluctuating moods and to experience chronic frustration. Early theorists such as Bleuler, Schneider, and others described personality styles that were believed to have a biological predisposition toward an irritable and moody temperament. The work of Schneider in the early part of this century focused on the impact of various attachment styles on personality processes. His insecure type reflected deep-seated tendencies toward the development of poor self-image and irritable moods that correspond in many ways to the passive-aggressive personality disorder (Standage, 1986).

Other early theorists such as Aschaffenburg and Hellpach wrote of individuals who exhibited lifelong tendencies to feel constantly hurt or injured by others, leading to sour and fussy moods (Millon, 1993). All of these early formulations have as the central focus an irritable and unpleasant disposition that has its roots in biological tendencies for quick arousal of negative affect, erratic behavior, and oppositional attitudes. Some have speculated that negativistic personality tendencies are evident early on in difficult-to-manage infants who cry excessively and are extremely difficult to sooth (Millon, 1981).

Contemporary Theoretical Perspectives

Psychoanalytic Perspectives Traditional psychoanalytic approaches to understanding character pathology, and the more contemporary psychodynamic approaches to personality disorders, conceptualize early childhood development as the direct antecedent to the formation of mental structures and schemas, termed "internalized object relations," that guide interpersonal relationships and influence observable behavior (Stricker & Gold, 1988). The intense interpersonal ambivalence and conflict that characterize the relationships of negativistic individuals was first conceptualized by Karl Abraham. Abraham divided Freud's oral stage of psychosexual development into two distinct but related stages that were termed the biting and sucking stages (Millon & Davis, 1996; McCann, 1988). Within psychoanalytic theory, psychosexual development may proceed smoothly through various stages, or fixation can occur at any one stage when infants are either over indulged or frustrated in the attainment of developmental tasks. Fixation at the biting stage results in what Abraham referred to as the oral-sadistic character complex, defined by ambivalence over the need for nurturance on the one hand and oral aggression/teething on the other. This early developmental conflict generates hostile verbal behavior, negative and irritable moods, and obstructive patterns of communication in adulthood, which are all characteristic of NPD.

The psychoanalytic formulation of masochistic personality also informs some of the current thinking on NPD (McCann, 1988). Wilhelm Reich pointed out that masochistic character types experience chronic suffering, as seen in endless complaining, obstructive behavior, and thwarting of others' attempts at success. Reich's ideas obviously resonant with the characteristics of the negativistic personality already described. Recent theorists have distinguished between unpleasant moods and obstructive behavior that generate intense guilt (Kernberg, 1984), which is then externalized, as with the negativistic character and the masochistic character who internalizes guilt resulting in self-loathing and defeatist attitudes, resulting in overt irritability and active resistance.

Contemporary psychoanalytic formulations maintain many of the underlying principles formulated by early analytic writers. Expanding on the issue of frustrated oral dependency needs in early childhood, Sandler (1985) noted that the orally frustrated character assumes a pessimistic outlook that facilitates the experiencing of depression, irritability, and insecurity in relationships. Consequently, the orally frustrated character has strong needs for nurturance, but with a demanding, yet dissatisfied style. Many of the features of an orally frustrated character as outlined by Sandler are reflected in criteria for NPD.

Instead of focusing on frustrated psychosexual development, other psychoanalytic writers have emphasized early object relationships as possible etiological factors for negativistic character pathology. Stone (1993) has suggested that oppositional, verbally hostile, and sullen demeanor of the negativistic personality arises from the child's chronic power struggles with parents. Because the child is never able to directly "conquer" the parents, resentment and hostility grow as a result of unending nagging. Over time, says Stone, the individual becomes resentful, hypersensitive to criticism, and oppositional in the face of pressures or demands.

Another psychoanalytic perspective has been provided by the self psychology of Kohut (1971, 1977). In their seminal paper, Kohut and Wolf (1978) outlined disorders of the self and suggest that character pathology results from varying types of disruption in the responsiveness of other individuals to the person's needs to be affirmed, encouraged, and recognized as a worthwhile individual. McCann (1995) has interpreted various disorders of the self as outlined in psychoanalytic self psychology and has suggested that NPD parallels the overburdened self with strong merger-hungry needs as outlined by Kohut and Wolf (1978). Individuals with these deficits in self structure have difficulty soothing themselves when they experience unpleasant and disruptive moods. Their capacity for modulating intense affect is deficient, due primarily to the failure of early caregivers to respond to the infant's intense emotional reactions. Thus, negativistic character pathology results in hostile views of the world and strong needs to control others because of fears over separation and loss.

There is minimal empirical evidence for the various etiological hypotheses advanced by psychoanalytic theory. In one study, Whitman, Trosman, and Koenig (1954) found that a sample of passive-aggressive patients, when compared with a large sample of general psychiatric outpatients, experienced intense ambivalence. These researchers posited that strong feelings of guilt inhibited overt expression of anger and encouraged more passive dependent behavior that was difficult for the passive-aggressive individuals to handle, leading to indirect expressions of hostility. This early study suffers a number of methodological limitations, including the use of outdated diagnostic criteria.

Behavioral Perspectives As noted earlier, a behavioral approach to understanding and treating personality disorders requires specific criteria to be defined according to observable and measurable behavior. For this reason, behavioral formulations have relied less on formal diagnosis and more on technological and formulation-based approaches (Turkat & Levin, 1984; Turkat & Maisto, 1985; Turner & Turkat, 1988). Technical procedures such as systematic desensitization, contingency management, and self-monitoring are used to treat targeted symptoms such as procrastination, inefficiency, or skeptical thoughts and statements. In formulation-based behavior therapy, specific problems such as recurrent sullen moods or obstructive attitudes are identified and analyzed in terms of their relationship to one another. For example, feeling misunderstood or unappreciated may be caused by recurrent passive-aggressive comments and cynical opinions that are expressed openly. The etiology of these problems is examined and predictions are made concerning future behavior. Behavioral interventions are developed to prevent predicted negative outcomes and to enhance positive change.

Within a behavioral approach, negativistic behavior is viewed as the "expression of anger in social interactions in maladaptive verbal and nonverbal ways that do not lead to rewarding problem solving" (Perry & Flannery, 1982, p. 166). One of the major factors contributing to a negativistic personality style is the failure to learn appropriate assertive behavior. Chronic anger and irritability persist because passively hostile comments, procrastination, skeptical attitudes, and other features of this style prevent the taking of adaptive assertive actions to reduce angry feelings.

A number of behavioral interventions follow from technological and formulation-based approaches. Under technological strategies, progressive muscle relaxation, systematic desensitization, modeling, and flooding would all be appropriate for treating affective arousal (i.e., anger, anxiety), procrastination, and other targeted symptoms. Anger management, assertiveness training, modeling, and cognitive restructuring would all be appropriate for addressing poor assertivenss skills. The work of Small et al. (1970) showed verbal aggression, short-lived anger reactions, and anxiety and depression to be prominent characteristics of passive-aggressive individuals, providing indirect support for the lack of assertive behavior as a possible etiological factor as outlined in the behavioral approach. However, large-scale studies that strongly support the hypotheses generated in this approach are lacking at the present time.

Cognitive Perspectives Within a cognitive framework, negativistic persons are viewed as possessing automatic thoughts reflecting intense negativism, pessimism, and skepticism (Beck & Freeman, 1990). Simple requests from others may be distorted into intrusive demands, leading to internal ambivalence about whether the request should be followed. Similarly, irrational beliefs also contribute to faulty problem solving. As noted by Beck and Freeman (1990), the negativistic personality maintains conflicted beliefs such as, "I need authority to nurture and support me," and "I need to protect my identity" (p. 46). The need for authority and rules thus brings about a strong threat concerning loss of autonomy, producing a cognitive ambivalence that leads to erratic, vacillating moods and behaviors. This instability also results in the belief that others will take advantage because of the negativistic's feelings of low self-worth. Finally, a number of automatic thoughts foster the obstructive behavior, irritable moods, and resistant interpersonal conduct that defines the disorder. These include such ideas as, "Things just don't work out for me in life," "I'll do things my way," "I never get the credit I deserve for the good things I do in life," and similar statements (Will, 1995). These convictions are internal and infrequently expressed directly because of strong convictions that open and direct conflict is bad and will only lead to disapproval and rejection. Thus, negativistic individuals often submit to demands, but with mounting deep resentment that is displayed in indirect and passive-aggressive ways.

Interpersonal Perspectives Interpersonal theories of personality pathology place strong emphasis on maladaptive interpersonal behaviors and predispositions as the defining features of all personality disorder. Early interpersonal theorists such as Leary (1957) did not describe a passive-aggressive or NPD. Not until the 1980s did interpersonal perspectives on the disorder began to appear.

The interpersonal circumplex dimensions of affiliation and power have been very useful in understanding the passive-aggressive/negativistic style. Each major theorist utilizing the circumplex model has placed negativistic personality low on affiliation needs and indifferent on needs for power (Kiesler, 1983, 1986; Widiger & Kelso, 1983; Wiggins, 1982). As such, the defining features are intense anger and hostility that are accompanied by some needs for affiliation with others. Therefore, the person is erratic, often changing from irritable and quarrelsome to unwillingly cooperative and submissive.

Benjamin (1993) has conceptualized NPD as having extreme difficulty with power and control in relationships, viewing any attempt by others to exert influence as intrusive. Those in authority are seen as incompetent, unfair, and hostile. The resentment toward those who place demands on the individual fuels the resistance, stubbornness, and inefficiency that define the disorder. Benjamin has also noted that the negativistic person engages in excessive comparisons and appraisals between themselves and others. In particular, others are seen as having lighter work loads, better opportunities, and other advantages. In contrast, the view of oneself is of being treated unfairly and never having any rewards. Thus, the negativistic feels cheated and is convinced that they get a "raw deal" from life.

Research with the interpersonal circumplex has produced conflicting results. Sim and Romney (1990), for instance, found strong support for placement of passive-aggressive personality in quadrants involving both hostility and moderate submissiveness. These findings are consistent with the irritable and hostile, yet ambivalently guilty affect of negativistic personality disorder, and support the model outlined by Wiggins (1982) and Widiger and Kelso (1983). However, Pincus and Wiggins (1990) found that passive-aggressive personality was not adequately represented by the circumplex model. These researchers posited that interpersonal dysfunctions may not be a central component of this personality disorder and other difficulties in cognitive and affective realms of functioning may be more defining features. In short, there appears to be some support for interpersonal theories of NPD; however, the disorder appears to involve maladaptive functioning in many different domains of personality.

Factorial Perspectives Within the five-factor model, NPD is viewed as being low on the dimensions of agreeableness and conscientiousness and high on neuroticism (Costa & Widiger, 1993). This entails low levels of compliance and straightforwardness, making for oppositionality and irritability, with few competent behaviors, poor self-discipline, irritability, sulky behavior, and resentful emotional displays.

There is empirical support for this formulation. Wiggins and Pincus (1989) found passive-aggressive personality traits, as measured by the MMPI and Personality Adjective Checklist, to be associated with low levels of conscientiousness. Using peer and spousal ratings, Costa and McCrae (1990) found moderate negative correlations between passive-aggressive traits and conscientiousness. In this same study, strong correlations were also found between MCMI measures of passive-aggressive personality traits and neuroticism. Together these studies lend support to the five-factor model's view of negativistic personality as manifesting sullen and irritable mood, resistant and oppositional behavior, and poor self-discipline.

An intriguing dimensional model of negativistic/passive-aggressive personality disorder has been offered by Fine, Overholser, and Berkoff (1992). They proposed that this personality style is driven by two dimensions common to most forms of psychopathology and are thus nonspecific to NPD. These dimensions are rigidity and resentment, as characterized respectively by extreme difficulty in adjusting to change and by strong feelings of anger and hostility that are inhibited by feelings of shame. Rigidity and resentment then interact to produce three personality characteristics that are more specific to the negativistic style—resistance, reactance, and reversal of reinforcement. Resistance refers to stubbornness and refusal to submit to the demands of others; reactance is seen in procrastination, oppositional rebellion, and indirect displays of anger; reversal of reinforcement refers to the negativistic person's feeling of power and gratification that results when there has been success at creating problems for others or the efforts of others have been thwarted. One positive aspect of the dimensional model offered by Fine and colleagues is that, unlike some dimensional approaches, it formulates a dynamic connection between varying factors that helps to explain how maladaptive behaviors are maintained.

Biological Perspectives Very little attention has been given to the underlying biological processes that may potentially contribute to development of NPD (Weston & Siever, 1993). Of the literature that is available, there is only theoretical speculation or research on pharmacological responses of particular emotionally unstable syndromes that bear some similarity to NPD.

One interesting neurobiological perspective on personality has been posited by Cloninger (1987), who proposed that passive-aggressive individuals are characterized by high levels of novelty-seeking behavior in which biological inhibitory mechanisms are weakened, resulting in impulsivity, sudden unpredictable actions and rapid displays of anger. In addition to these features, Cloninger also postulated high harm-avoidance processes in which passive-aggressive individuals readily avoid active displays of anger and have well-developed mechanisms for maintaining dependence on rewards. Therefore, the individual is quick to anger but also maintains controls that result in indirect displays of moodiness and irritability.

Using similar constructs, Millon and Davis (1996) have hypothesized a number of neurobiological processes that may predispose an individual to NPD. While recognizing the speculative nature of their thesis, Millon and Davis have proposed that negativistic personality disorder develops in infants who are difficult to soothe and manage and who are inconsistent in their reactions to parents. Furthermore, there is increased excitation of the autonomic nervous system and possible hyperdensity in limbic structures of the brain that may contribute to the excessive emotionality that characterizes NPD.

Another approach to understanding the biological underpinnings of NPD has arisen from treatment of emotionally unstable character disorder with pharmacological agents (Klein, 1967; Kein, Gittleman, Quitkin, & Rifkin, 1980; Rifkin, Quitkin, Curillo, Blumberg, & Klein, 1972). Researchers in this area have generally viewed NPD to be of questionable clinical use and instead favor use of the term "emotionally unstable character." Despite the language differences, emotionally unstable personality shares many of the features of NPD, including rapid mood changes, problems with authority, conflict over dependency and intimacy, and poor frustration tolerance. Pharmacologic studies have shown chlorpromazine (Coccaro, 1993) and lithium (Rifkin et al., 1972) to be superior to antidepressants in managing mood swings and other clinical symptomatology in the emotionally unstable character type. As such, researchers in this area have conceptualized the emotionally unstable character as a form of bipolar illness, rather than a depressive illness.

Despite these interesting perspectives on NPD, the role of biological processes on etiology of the disorder remains untested and theoretically speculative at this time.

Integrative Models In an effort to incorporate various theoretical approaches to understanding NPD, Millon (1969, 1981; Millon & Davis, 1996) has formulated an integrative approach. Based on three personality dimensions that are derived from evolutionary theory, Millon's model views NPD as an active-ambivalent style. Accordingly, the negativistic has weakened orientation to pleasurable experiences and an average capacity to experience pain and discomfort. However, the primary dynamics of negativistic personality include an intense ambivalence in the source of reinforcing life experiences. That is, this personality style is characterized by strong resentment over having to follow the wishes of others while also experiencing strong guilt over asserting self-centered needs. Intense ambivalence is expressed actively in the form of obstructive behavior, sour moods, skeptical attitudes, and other indications of internalized conflict.

Expanding on the formulation of negativistic personality, Millon has identified a number of clinical features of the disorder that cut across several levels of personality. At the behavioral level, negativistic individuals are seen as resentful in their manner of expressive behavior and contrary in the way they handle interpersonal relationships. Their cognitive style is dominated by skeptical and untrusting attitudes, with discontented self-image and vacillating internal representations of significant others. At the intrapsychic level, the negativistic personality uses displacement as the primary means for regulating internal tension; anger and resentment are displaced onto others, with the indirect expression of anger serving to vent hostile feelings in an oppositonal manner. Finally, at the biophysical level, the prevailing mood and temperament are excessively irritable. In short, Millon's theoretical formulation integrates many of the major theoretical approaches into a unified framework.

Recently there have been empirical findings that lend support to the validity of Millon's integrative model. For instance, Strack et al. (1990) found good support for Millon's (1987) circular model of personality disorders using a series of self-report measures. On the MCMI-II, McCann (1991) found the passive-aggressive/negativistic scale to load on a factor with the obsessive-compulsive scale, though these two scales loaded in opposite directions. These findings support the negativistic and obsessive-compulsive as representing ambivalent personality styles as posited in Millon's theory, with the different directional factor loading reflecting the active (negativistic) versus passive (obsessive-compulsive) nature of these constructs. An additional study by Whyne-Berman and McCann (1995) examined Millon's theoretical model at the level of intrapsychic functioning and regulatory mechanisms. Results from this study provide moderate support for the theoretical link between negativistic personality disorder and externalizing defense mechanisms such as displacement.

Integrative approaches to understanding NPD are advantageous in several respects, particularly in that they encourage a broad, in-depth analysis of psychopathological features of the disorder. Moreover, integrative theories give attention to a number of different, but equally important pieces of information.

Concluding Reflections

The NPD has followed a unique path that distinguishes it from most other personality disorders. Although its predecessor, the passive-aggressive personality disorder, had almost been eliminated entirely from the formal classification system, recent attempts have been made to broaden and expand our understanding of this personality style. Research on NPD and its precursors has been thwarted by limitations in diagnostic criteria utilized and by major revisions in criteria. Nevertheless, this disorder has been shown to be a useful construct, regardless of the specific label or descriptor utilized to identify it. The *DSM-IV*'s attempt to broaden its criteria are apt to significantly advance research and clinical applications.

Summary and Conclusions

This chapter summarizes the various theoretical and empirical approaches to understanding and conceptualizing two very interesting personality disorders. The obsessive-compulsive and negativistic personality disorders share many common themes and issues. There has been confusion over the appropriate name to assign each; both have been questioned in terms of whether they represent points along a continuum of pathology or distinct clinical entities and they both share similar symptoms and features. Despite the controversies that have loomed, these personality disorders have continued to find a firm place in most formal classification systems and in various contemporary theoretical models. The longevity of these psychopathological constructs points to their utility. Current trends toward revising their criteria are likely to result in better applications in both research and clinical settings.

In addition, it appears that various theoretical models have focused on different aspects of personality functioning. The study of disorders of personality will be advanced by focusing on how these theories can be effectively integrated into broader and more complex formulations. That is, integrative approaches are likely to advance the field of psychopathology, particularly in the area of personality pathology.

References

Alnaes, R., & Torgersen, S. (1988). The relationship between DSM-III symptom disorders (Axis I) and personality disorders (Axis II) in an outpatient sample. *Acta Psychiatrica Scandinavica, 78*, 485–492.

Alnaes, R., & Torgersen, S. (1991). Personality and personality disorders among patients with various affective disorders. *Journal of Personality Disorders, 5*, 107–121.

Baer, L., Jenicke, M. A., & Riccardi, J. (1990). Standardized assessment of personality disorders in obsessive-compulsive disorder. *Archives of General Psychiatry, 47*, 826–830.

Bagby, R. M., Joffe, R. T., Parker, J. D. A., & Schuller, D. R. (1993). Re-examination of the evidence for DSM-III personality disorder clusters. *Journal of Personality Disorders, 7*, 320–328.

Beck, A. T., & Freeman, A. (1990). *Cognitive therapy of personality disorders.* New York: Guilford.

Benjamin, L. S. (1974). Structural analysis of social behavior. *Psychological Review, 81*, 392–425.

Benjamin, L. S. (1993). *Interpersonal diagnosis and treatment of personality disorders.* New York: Guilford.

Black, D. W., Yates, W. R., Noyes, R., Pfohl, B., & Kelley, M. (1989). DSM-III personality disorders in obsessive-compulsive study volunteers: A controlled study. *Journal of Personality Disorders, 3*, 58–62.

Cloninger, R. C. (1987). A systematic method for clinical description and classification of personality variants. *Archives of General Psychiatry, 44*, 573–588.

Coccaro, E. F. (1993). Psychopharmacologic studies in patients with personality disorders: Review and perspective. *Journal of Personality Disorders, 7*(Supp.), 181–192.

Costa, P. T., & McCrae, R. R. (1985). *The NEO personality inventory manual.* Odessa, FL: Psychological Assessment Resources.

Costa, P. T., & McCrae, R. R. (1989). *The NEO-PI/NEO-FFI manual supplement.* Odessa, FL: Psychological Assessment Resources.

Costa, P. T., & McCrae, R. R. (1990). Personality and the five-factor model of personality. *Journal of Personality Disorders, 4*, 362–371.

Costa, P. T., & McCrae, R. R. (1992). The five-factor model of personality and its relevance to personality disorders. *Journal of Personality Disorders, 6*, 343–359.

Costa, P. T., & Widiger, T. A. (1993). *Personality disorders and the five-factor model of personality.* Washington, DC: American Psychological Association.

Cloninger, R. C. (1987). A systematic method for clinical description and classification of personality variants. *Archives of General Psychiatry, 44*, 573–588.

Dahl, A. (1986). Some aspects of the DSM-III personality disorders illustrated by a consecutive sample of hospitalized patients. *Acta Psychiatrica Scandinavica, 73*, 61–66.

Donat, D. (1995). Use of the MCMI-III in behavior therapy. In P. D. Retzlaff (Ed.), *Tactical psychotherapy of the personality disorders: An MCMI-III-based approach* (pp. 40–65). Boston: Allyn and Bacon.

Drake, R. E., & Vaillant, G. E. (1985). A validity study of axis II of DSM-III. *American Journal of Psychiatry, 142*, 553–558.

Dubro, A. F., & Wetzler, S. (1989). An external validity study of the MMPI personality disorder scales. *Journal of Clinical Psychology, 45*, 570–575.

Endler, N. S., & Edwards, J. M. (1988). Personality disorders from an interactional perspective. *Journal of Personality Disorders, 2*, 326–333.

Erikson, E. H. (1950). *Childhood and society.* New York: Norton.

Fine, M. A., Overholser, J. C., & Berkoff, K. (1992). Diagnostic validity of the passive-aggressive personality disorder: Suggestions for reform. *American Journal of Psychotherapy, 46*, 470–484.

Fischer, R. E., & Juni, S. (1982). The anal personality: Self-disclosure, negativism, self-esteem, and superego severity. *Journal of Personality Assessment, 46*, 50–58.

Frances, A., Clarkin, J., Gilmore, M., Hurt, S., & Brown, R. (1984). Reliability of criteria for borderline personality disorder: A comparison of DSM-III and the diagnostic interview for borderline personality disorder. *American Journal of Psychiatry, 141*, 1080–1084.

Freud, S. (1908). Character and anal eroticism. In *The collected papers of Sigmund Freud.* London: Hogarth Press. (English translation, Vol. 2, 1925).

Gabbard, G. O. (1994). *Psychodynamic psychiatry in clinical practice.* Washington, DC: American Psychiatric Press.

Goldstein, W. N. (1985). Obsessive-compulsive behavior, DSM-III and a psychodynamic classification of psychopathology. *American Journal of Psychotherapy, 46*, 346–359.

Hyler, S., & Lyons, M. (1988). Factors analysis of the DSM-III personality disorder clusters: A replication. *Comprehensive Psychiatry, 29*, 304–308.

Ingram, D. H. (1982). Compulsive personality disorder. *American Journal of Psychoanalysis, 42*, 189–198.

Insel, T. R. (1982). Obsessive-compulsive disorder—Five clinical questions and a suggested approach. *Comprehensive Psychiatry, 23*, 241–251.

Juni, S., & Rubenstein, V. (1982). Anality and routine. *Journal of Personality Assessment, 46*, 142.

Juni, S., & Semel, S. R. (1982). Person perception as a function of orality and anality. *Journal of Social Psychology, 118*, 99–103.

Kahn, E. (1931). *Psychopathic personalities.* New Haven: Yale University Press.

Kass, F., Skodol, A. E., Charles, E., Spitzer, R. L., & Williams, J. B. W. (1985). Scaled ratings of DSM-III personality disorders. *American Journal of Psychiatry, 142*, 627–630.

Kernberg, O. (1984). *Severe personality disorders: Psychotherapeutic strategies.* New Haven: Yale University Press.

Kiesler, D. J. (1983). The 1982 interpersonal circle: A taxonomy for complimentarity inhuman transactions. *Psychological Review, 90*, 185–214.

Kiesler, D. J. (1986). The 1982 interpersonal circle: An analysis of DSM-III personality disorders. In T. Millon & G. L. Klerman (Eds.), *Contemporary directions in psychopathology: Toward the DSM-IV* (pp. 571–597). New York: Guilford.

Klein, D. F. (1967). Importance of psychiatric diagnosis in prediction of clinical drug effects. *Archives of General Psychiatry, 16*, 118–126.

Klein, D. F., Gittleman, R., Quitkin, F., & Rifkin, A. (1980). *Diagnosis and drug treatment of psychiatric disorders* (2nd ed.). Baltimore, MD: Williams & Wilkins.

Kline, P. (1978). The status of the anal character: A methodological and empirical reply to Hill. *British Journal of Medical Psychology, 51*, 87–90.

Kline, P. (1981). *Fact and fantasy in Freudian theory* (2nd ed.). London: Methuen.

Kohut, H., & Wolf, E. (1978). The disorders of the self and their treatment: An outline. *International Journal of Psychoanalysis, 59*, 413–425.

Lazare, A., Klerman, G., & Armor, D. J. (1966). Oral, obsessive and hysterical personality patterns. *Archives of General Psychiatry, 14*, 624–630.

Lazare, A., Klerman, G., & Aramor, D. J. (1970). Oral, obsessive and hysterical personality patterns: Replication of factor analysis in an independent sample. *Journal of Psychiatric Research, 7*, 275–279.

Leary, T. (1957). *Interpersonal diagnosis of personality.* New York: Ronald.

Livesley, W. J., & Jackson, D. N. (1986). The internal consistency and factorial structure of behaviors judged to be associated with DSM-III personality disorders. *American Journal of Psychiatry, 143*, 1473–1474.

Livesley, W. J., Reiffer, L. I., Sheldon, A. E. R., & West, M. (1987). Prototypical ratings of DSM-III criteria for personality disorders. *Journal of Nervous and Mental Disease, 175*, 395–401.

Loranger, A. Susman, V., Oldham, J., & Russakoff, L. (1987). The personality disorder examination: A preliminary report. *Journal of Personality Disorders, 1*, 1–13.

Malinow, K. L. (1981). Passive-aggressive personality. In J. R. Lion (Ed.), *Personality disorders: Diagnosis and management* (2nd ed.; pp. 121–132). Malabur, FL: Krieger.

Mallinger, A. E. (1984). The obsessive myth of control. *Journal of the American Academy of Psychoanalysis, 12*, 147–165.

Mattanah, J. J. F., Becker, D. F., Levy, K. N., Edell, W. S., & McGlashin, T. H. (1995). Diagnostic stability in adolescents followed up 2 years after hospitalization. *American Journal of Psychiatry, 152,* 889–894.

McCann, J. T. (1988). Passive-aggressive personality disorder: A review. *Journal of Personality Disorders,* 2, 170–179.

McCann, J. T. (1991). Convergent and discriminant validity fo the MCMI-II personality disorder scales. *Psychological Assessment, 3,* 9–18.

McCann, J. T. (1992). A comparison of two measures for obsessive-compulsive personality disorder. *Journal of Personality Disorders, 6,* 18–23.

McCann, J. T. (1995). The MCMI-III and treatment of the self. In P. D. Retzlaff (Ed.), *Tactical psychotherapy of the personality disorders: An MCMI-III-based approach* (pp. 137–157). Boston: Allyn & Bacon.

McCrae, R. R., & Costa, P. T. (1990). *Personality in adulthood.* New York: Guilford.

Millon, T. (1969). *Modern psychopathology.* Philadelphia: Saunders.

Millon, T. (1981). *Disorders of personality: DSM-III: Axis II.* New York: John Wiley.

Millon, T. (1987). *Millon clinical multiaxial inventory-II: Manual.* Minneapolis: National Computer Systems.

Millon, T. (1993). Negativistic (passive-aggressive) personality disorder. *Journal of Personality Disorders, 7,* 78–85.

Millon, T., & Davis, R. D. (1996). *Disorders of personality: DSM-IV and beyond.* New York: John Wiley.

Millon, T., & Radovanov, J. (1995). Passive-aggressive (negativistic) personality disorder. In W. J. Livesley (Ed.), *The DSM-IV personality disorders* (pp. 312–325). New York: Guilford.

Morey, L. C. (1988a). A psychometric analysis of the DSM-III-R personality disorder criteria. *Journal of Personality Disorders,* 2, 109–124.

Morey, L. (1988b). Personality disorder in DSM-III and DSM-III-R: Convergence, coverage, and internal consistency. *American Journal of Psychiatry, 145,* 573–577.

Morey, L. (1988c). The categorical representation of personality disorders: A cluster analysis of DSM-III-R personality features. *Journal of Abnormal Psychology, 97,* 314–321.

Morey, L. C., Blashfield, R. K., Webb, W. W., & Jewell, J. (1988). MMPI scales for DSM-III personality disorders: A preliminary validation study. *Journal of Clinical Psychology, 44,* 47–50.

Perry, J. C., & Flannery, R. B. (1982). Passive-aggressive personality disorder: Treatment implications of a clinical typology. *Journal of Nervous and Mental Disease, 170,* 164–173.

Pfohl, B., & Blum, N. (1991). Obsessive-compulsive personality disorder: A review of available data and recommendations for DSM-IV. *Journal of Personality Disorders, 5,* 363–375.

Pfohl, B., & Blum, N. (1995). Obsessive-compulsive personality disorder. In W. J. Livesley (Ed.), *The DSM-IV personality disorders* (pp. 261–276). New York: Guilford.

Pfohl, B., Coryell, W., Zimmerman, M., & Stangl, D. (1986). DSM-III personality disorders: Diagnostic overlap and internal consistency of individual DSM-III criteria. *Comprehensive Psychiatry,* 27, 21–34.

Pincus, A. L., & Wiggins, J. S. (1990). Interpersonal problems and conceptions of personality disorders. *Journal of Personality Disorders, 4,* 342–352.

Pollack, J. M. (1979). Obsessive-compulsive personality: A review. *Psychological Bulletin, 86,* 225–241.

Pollack, J. (1987). Obsessive-compulsive personality: Theoretical and clinical perspectives and recent research findings. *Journal of Personality Disorders, 1,* 248–262.

Rado, S. (1959). Obsessive behavior. In S. Arieti (Ed.), *American handbook of psychiatry* (Vol. 1, pp. 324–344). New York: Basic Books.

Reich, W. (1949). *Character analysis* (3rd ed.). New York: Farrar, Strous, & Giroux.

Rey, J. M., Morris-Yates, A., Singh, M., Andrews, G., & Stewart, G. W. (1995). Continuities between psychiatric disorders in adolescents and personality disorders in young adults. *American Journal of Psychiatry, 152,* 895–900.

Rifkin, A., Quitkin, F., Curillo, C., Blumberg, A. G., & Klein, D. F. (1972). Lithium carbonate in emotionally unstable character disorders. *Archives of General Psychiatry, 27,* 519–523.

Salzman, L. (1980). *Treatment of the obsessive personality.* New York: Jason Aronson.

Sandler, J. (1985). *The analysis of defense.* New York: International Universities Press.

Schneider (1923/1950). *Psychopathic personalities* (9th ed.). London: Cassell.

Shapiro, E. (1965). *Neurotic styles.* New York: Basic Books.

Sim, J. P., & Romney, D. M. (1990). The relationship between a circumplex model of interpersonal behaviors and personality disorders. *Journal of Personality Disorders, 4,* 329–341.

Skodol, A., Rosnick. L., Kellman, P., Oldham, J., & Hyler, S. (1988). Validating structured DSM-III-R personality disorder assessments with longitudinal data. *American Journal of Psychiatry, 145,* 1297–1299.

Small, I. F., Small, J. G., Alig, V. B., & Moore,

D. F. (1970). Passive-aggressive personality disorder: A search for a syndrome. *American Journal of Psychiatry, 126*, 973–981.

Standage, K. (1986). A clinical and psychometric investigation comparing Schneider's and DSM-III typologies of personality disorder. *Comprehensive Psychiatry, 27*, 35–46.

Standage, K., & Ladha, N. (1988). An examination of the reliability of the personality disorder examination and a comparison with other methods of identifying personality disorders in a clinical sample. *Journal of Personality Disorders, 2*, 267–271.

Stone, M. H. (1993). Etiology of borderline personality disorder: Psychobiological factors contributing to an underlying irritability. In J. Paris (Ed.), *Borderline personality disorder: Etiology and treatment* (pp. 87–101). Washington, DC: American Psychiatric Association.

Storr, A. (1980). *The art of psychotherapy.* New York: Metheun.

Strack, S., Lorr, M., & Campbell, L. (1990). An evaluation of Millon's circular model of personality disorders. *Journal of Personality Disorders, 4*, 353–361.

Stricker, G., & Gold, J. R. (1988). A psychodynamic approach to the personality disorders. *Journal of Personality Disorders, 2*, 350–359.

Torgersen, S. (1980). The oral, obsessive and hysterical personality syndromes: A study of hereditary and environmental factors by means of the twin method. *Archives of General Psychiatry, 37*, 1272–1277.

Turkat, I. D., & Levin, R. A. (1984). Formulation of personality disorders. In H. E. Adams & P. B. Sutker (Eds.), *Comprehensive handbook of psychotherapy* (pp. 495–522). New York: Plenum.

Turkat, I. D., & Maisto, S. A. (1985). Personality disorders: Applicaton of the experimental method to the formulation and modification of personality disorders. In D. H. Barlow (Ed.), *Clinical handbook of psychological disorders: A step-by-step treatment manual* (pp. 503–570). New York: Guilford.

Turner, S. M., & Turkat, I. D. (1988). Behavior therapy and the personality disorders. *Journal of Personality Disorders, 2*, 342–349.

Tyrer, P. (1988). What's wrong with DSM-III personality disorders? *Journal of Personality Disorders, 2*, 281–291.

Walton, H. J., Foulds, G. A., Littman, S. K., & Presley, A. S. (1970). Abnormal personality. *British Journal of Psychiatry, 116*, 497–510.

Walton, H. J., & Presley, A. S. (1973a). Dimensions of abnormal personality. *British Journal of Psychiatry, 122*, 269–276.

Walton, H. J., & Presley, A. S. (1973b). Use of a category system in the diagnosis of abnormal personality. *British Journal of Psychiatry, 122*, 259–263.

Weston, S. C., & Siever, L. J. (1993). Biologic correlates of personality disorder. *Journal of Personality Disorders, 7*(Supp.), 129–148.

Whitman, R. M., Trosman, H., & Koenig, R. (1954). Clinical assessment of passive-aggressive personality. *Archives of Neurology and Psychiatry, 72*, 540–549.

Whyne-Berman, S. M., & McCann, J. T. (1995). Defense mechanisms and personality disorders: An empirical test of Millon's theory. *Journal of Personality Assessment, 64*, 132–144.

Widiger, T. A. (1992). Categorical versus dimensional classification. *Journal of Personality Disorders, 6*, 287–300.

Widiger, T. A., & Kelso, K. (1983). Psychodiagnosis on Axis II. *Clinical Psychology Review, 3*, 491–590.

Widiger, T. A., Trull, T., Hurt, S., Clarkin, J., & Frances, A. (1987). A multidimensional scaling of the DSM-III personality disorders. *Archives of General Psychiatry, 44*, 557–563.

Wiggins, J. S. (1982). Circumplex models of interpersonal behavior in clinical psychology. In P. C. Kendall & J. N. Butcher (Eds.), *Handbook of research methods in clinical psychology* (pp. 183–221). New York: John Wiley.

Wiggins, J. S., & Pincus, A. L. (1989). Conceptions of personality disorders and dimensions of personality. *Psychological Assessment, 1*, 305–316.

Will, T. E. (1995). Cognitive therapy and the MCMI-III. In P. D. Retzlaff (Ed.), *Tactical psychotherapy of the personality disorders: An MCMI-III-based approach* (pp. 90–110). Needham Heights, MA: Allyn & Bacon.

Zanarini, M., Frankenburg, F., Chauncey, D., & Gundersen, J. (1987). The diagnostic interview for personality disorders: Interrater and test-retest reliability. *Comprehensive Psychiatry, 28*, 467–480.

24

Schizotypic Psychopathology

Theory, Evidence, and Future Directions

MARK F. LENZENWEGER

Schizotypic psychopathology has long intrigued researchers and clinicians. Beginning with early observations and speculations by Kraepelin and Bleuler, up through the most recent revisions of the American Psychiatric Association's official diagnostic nomenclature (e.g., *DSM-IV*) and the International Classification of Diseases (*ICD-10*), schizotypic psychopathology has posed a variety of challenges to classification, theory, and experimental approaches to psychopathology. In more recent years, schizotypic psychopathology has encompassed both paranoid and schizotypal personality disorder as defined by the *DSM-IV*. However, as will be discussed in this chapter, schizotypic psychopathology has been approached from a variety of theoretical and methodological vantage points, each offering useful insights into the fundamental nature of these pathologies. The variation in vantage points has generated alternative units of analysis with respect to schizotypic psychopathology that have not always conformed to prevailing nomenclatures, thus yielding challenges to consistency and organization for the purposes of a text such as the present one. On the other hand, theory and research in schizotypic psychopathology enjoys a spirited level of debate and development that is exceptional among the personality disorders.

Although relatively rare even through the early 1980s, research on schizotypic psychopathology has grown considerably in the past 10 years. Accordingly, the present review must be necessarily selective and makes no claim to be comprehensive. The reader should be aware that there will be topics or subareas that cannot be adequately detailed due to space constraints. The intention of this discussion is to introduce the reader to schizotypic psychopathology, as well as to identify several central theoretical and/or research issues and how they are confronted in this area of psychopathology research. Several extensive reviews on this topic are available (see Kotsaftis & Neale, 1993; Lenzenweger, 1993, 1994; Siever, Bernstein, & Silverman, 1991; Siever, Kalus, & Keefe, 1993). Likewise, excellent summary chapters can be found in specialty personality disorders texts (e.g., Millon & Davis, 1996; Stone, 1993).Finally, an entire volume has been devoted to the topic of schizotypal personality (Raine, Lencz, & Mednick, 1995). Although the present chapter will discuss research findings relevant to the *DSM-IV* schizotypal and paranoid personality disorders, it will *not* focus solely on these diagnostic entities as currently defined.

Schizotypic Psychopathology: Definitional Issues and Relevant Distinctions

To begin, it is important to draw upon and clarify several relevant distinctions in defining what is meant by *schizotypic*. Herein, the terms schizotypal and paranoid will be taken to imply the personality disorders as defined by the *DSM-IV*. It is important to note that schizotypal personality disorder (SPD) and paranoid personality disorder (PPD) are, by definition, merely sets of descriptors (signs and symptoms) since *DSM-IV* eschews any relationship to an explanatory framework for these disorders. Moreover, given their relatively high degree of comorbidity, shared phenomenologic features (e.g., suspiciousness), and relationship to clinical schizophrenia, they are often referred to as the "schizophrenia-related personality disorders." In contrast, the term *schizotypic* can be used to describe signs and symptoms that are the phenotypic manifestation of schizotypy, or a latent personality organization that derives from a liability for schizophrenia as conceptualized in Meehl's (1962, 1990) model (see below pp. 1311–1318). The term schizotypic can also serve as a generic shorthand descriptor of attenuated "schizophrenia-like" phenomenology that is stable and enduring, but is fundamentally nonpsychotic, without referring to Meehl's model. As will become evident, SPD and PPD can readily be conceived of as manifestations of schizotypy as well, but they are not isomorphic with the schizotypy construct. Schizotypic psychopathology is therefore adopted as a generic term for this general class of mental disturbance. A *schizotype* is one who evidences schizotypic psychopathology. In this context, note that schizoid personality disorder is not considered to be a schizophrenia-related personality disorder in light of available evidence and, therefore, is not viewed as an example of schizotypic psychopathology in this discussion.

A Clinical Vignette

The following case vignette presents an example of a schizotypic person. Consider the following:

Robin, a 24-year-old, single male graduate student in physics at a large midwestern research university, has a long history of exceedingly strong anxiety symptoms in response to social interactions. In fact, he describes the quality that social interaction has for him as similar to the feeling one experiences when one's "knuckles accidently scrape across a carrot grater." He has no interest in social interaction and leads a socially isolated life, does not seek out social contact, and many see him as a "loner." He has but one friend with whom he has talks about only highly esoteric topics and he refers to these discussions as "technicalizing." He frequently uses other words in a peculiar and vague manner. Aside from anxiety, he claims to feel no strong emotions such as joy or, even, sadness. He frequently thinks that neutral events have "special relevance" for him and he often seems to misperceive aspects of his body (e.g., he misjudges the length of his arms or legs). Despite having adequate financial resources, Robin's attire is often best described as "odd" or "eccentric," though clearly not stylish.

Three Ways to Define a Schizotype

Organization of Schizotypic Signs and Symptoms

As psychopathologists have come to learn that schizotypic psychopathology is likely to be related in a meaningful way to the liability for schizophrenia (see below), workers have sought to determine if the organization of schizotypic signs and symptoms bears any resemblance to what is known about the organization of schizophrenia phenomenology. In short, current exploratory (see Andreasen, Arnott, Alliger, Miller, & Flaum, 1995) and confirmatory (Lenzenweger & Dworkin, 1996) factor analytic studies suggest that schizophrenia symptoms are best organized into three factors: negative symptoms (flattened affect, avolition), reality distortion (hallucinations, delusions), and disorganization (thought disorder), with a fourth possible factor consisting of premorbid social impairment (see Lenzenweger & Dworkin, 1996). Factor analytic studies of schizotypic signs and symptoms yield solutions or conform to models that are broadly consistent with the picture observed for schizophrenia. For example, Raine et al. (1991) found a three-factor model, consisting of cognitive/perceptual, interpersonal, and disorganization components, that provided a good fit to observed data. Others have obtained convergent results (Claridge et al., 1996; Mason, 1995; Gruzelier, 1996). Thus, at the phenotypic level not only do schizotypic signs and symptoms appear as attenuated schizophrenia manifestations but they also appear organized in a similar fashion.

Methodological Approaches to Assessing Schizotypic Psychopathology Schizotypic psychopathology can be defined in one of three ways: clinically, in terms of deviance on reliable dimensional measures, or by virtue of having a first-degree biological relative affected with schizophrenia. The clinical approach implied in psychiatric diagnostic schemes involves, quite obviously, the use of explicit diagnostic criteria to identify either SPD or PPD (e.g., *DSM-IV*). Note that both SPD and PPD, while highly associated, constitute coherent syndromes. A second approach involves the use of reliable and valid psychometric measures of schizotypy to detect schizotypic psychopathology as defined by quantitative deviance on such measures. In this approach, psychometric scales designed to assess various schizotypic manifestations serve to define and measure the schizotypy construct; schizotypic status may be defined by deviance on one or more of such measures. The psychometric approach has been discussed and reviewed recently (Chapman, Chapman, & Kwapil, 1995; Edell, 1995; Lenzenweger, 1994). The hypothetical relations among these approaches in defining schizotypic psychopathology are depicted in figure 24.1. Clearly, all cases of schizophrenia must be direct reflections of true schizotypy (discounting phenocopies). Both psychometrically assessed schizotypy, SPD, and PPD are not perfectly related to an underlying genuine schizotypy construct and, therefore, they will both be considered fallible measures of true schizotypy. As depicted, SPD and PPD themselves overlap somewhat.

Finally, one can be concerned with the biologic relatives of schizophrenia patients and speak of "genotypic" schizotypes. Though many first-degree relatives of schizophrenia patients will not evidence their underlying genetic predisposition to the illness through schizotypic symptomatology, they are, as a group, at increased statistical risk for schizophrenia and can be spoken of as schizotypes. Some relatives of schizophrenia patients will, indeed, display schizotypic symptomatology (Kendler, 1985). It is essential to note that not all biologic relatives of schizophrenia patients will carry this liability (Hanson, Gottesman, & Meehl, 1977).

Prevalence of Schizotypic Psychopathology

Epidemiology of Personality Pathology: General Considerations No comprehensive, high-quality data speak to population prevalence rates of personality disorder according to either *DSM* or *ICD* definitions. No Epidemiologic Catchment Area (ECA; Robins et al., 1984) study or National Comorbidity Study (NCS; Kessler et al., 1994) equivalent has been conducted for personality disorders (PDs) other than antisocial PD (Robins et al., 1984). A rough estimate for the overall lifetime rate for *any* Axis II disorder was ventured to be in the range of 10 to 13% (Weissman, 1993). However, the data upon which this estimate was based were quite limited (i.e., few studies) and the studies from which the data derive suffered from various sampling defects or dubious methods of case ascertainment.

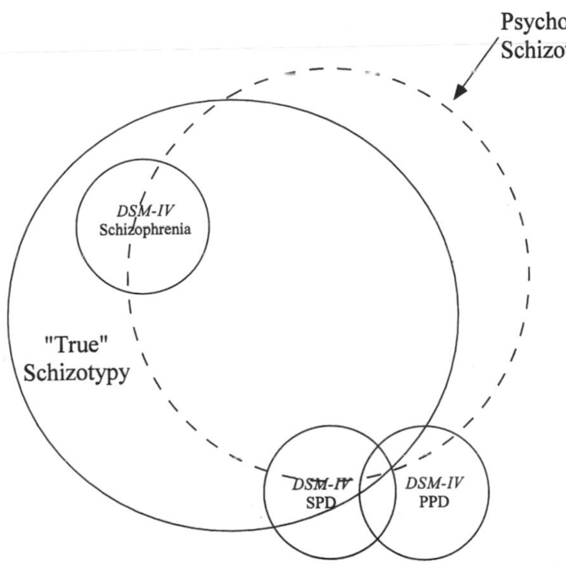

Figure 24.1 Hypothetical relations among constructs. All cases of schizophrenia (excluding phenocopies) are manifestations of "true schizotypy." *DSM-IV* schizotypal (SPD) and paranoid (PPD) personality disorders, which themselves overlap, are fallible manifestations of "true schizotypy." Psychometrically assessed schizotypy is also fallible and, therefore, partially overlaps with a "true schizotypy" as well as observed manifestations such as schizophrenia, SPD, and PPD.

How, then, best to proceed to generate quality prevalence estimates for personality disorders? Whereas reliable structured interviews for Axis II personality pathology have existed for some time (Loranger, 1988, 1991; Perry, 1992), these instruments typically require administration by clinically experienced diagnosticians and take several hours to complete in many instances, considerations which make the logistic requirements of epidemiologic study using them rather daunting. A related major obstacle to such epidemiologic work has been the cost of using experienced clinicians in contrast to lay interviewers to make PD diagnoses. It has been proposed that one way to curtail this expense might be to employ a two-stage design for case identification in which experienced clinicians would only interview screened positive cases and a random sample of negative ones drawn from a large sample screened with an effective self-report inventory. Lenzenweger, Loranger, Korfine, and Neff (1997) have implemented this research strategy and have reported on a PD screen that is quite efficient, in that it generated no false negatives as indexed against criterial interview diagnoses in a large randomly ascertained nonclinical sample. These authors have estimated the point prevalence of diagnosed PD to be approximately 11% (CI = 7.57 – 14.52%).

Epidemiology of Schizotypic Psychopathology As with other PDs, prevalence "estimates" for schizotypic psychopathology have been arrived at through indirect routes and are considered, at best, educated guesses. Genuine population-based epidemiological work in this area does not exist for contemporary notions of SPD and PPD. The *DSM-IV* suggests a prevalence of SPD of approximately 3% and PPD as 0.5 to 2.5% in the general population. Loranger (1990) reported, in a large series of consecutive psychiatric admissions to a university teaching hospital, 2.1% for *DSM-III* SPD and 1.2% for PPD. Zimmerman and Coryell (1990) reported, based on telephone interviews, that SPD was found to occur in 3.0% of their subjects and PPD was found in 0.4%. Maier, Lichtermann, Klingler, Heun, and Hallmayer (1992) found prevalence rates for SPD and PPD to be 0.7 and 1.8%, respectively, among the first-degree relatives of a sample of normal control subjects. Finally, Bernstein, Cohen, Skodol, Bezirganian, and Brook (1996) reported a 6.6% prevalence rate for *DSM-III-R* "Cluster A" PDs (which include SPD and PPD) in a community sample of adolescents. It is evident that schizotypic psychopathology as defined by the *DSM* system tends to appear in 5% or less of the population; however, great caution is needed in interpreting these data as none of them are drawn from an appropriately sampled general population. The prevalence estimates for the *DSM*-defined disorders necessarily reflects both the diagnostic threshold set for the disorder in the *DSM* system and the conservativeness of the diagnostic procedure used in any given study.

As noted, schizotypic psychopathology is broader than the contemporary definitions of SPD and PPD. Therefore, useful guidance on this epidemiologic question can be garnered from other sources as well. For example, Essen-Möller, Larsson, Uddenberg, and White (1956) reported from their landmark study of a rural Swedish population that schizoid personality, in the sense of "probably related to schizophrenia or to a schizophrenic taint" (sic) (p. 73), was found among 1.8% of women and 6.0% of men. Kety et al. (1994), in a recent report from their landmark Danish Adoption Study of schizophrenia, found that among the biological relatives of normal control adoptees 0.8% were paranoid personality, 3.3% schizoid personality, and 2.5% "latent schizophrenia," a pre-*DSM-III* diagnostic designation roughly akin to SPD. Kendler et al. (1994), in a secondary analysis of the Kety et al. (1994) data, found that, according to *DSM-III* criteria, from 3.1 to 3.7% of the relatives of the normal control adoptees had either SPD or a "schizophrenia spectrum" diagnosis (or, schizotypic psychopathology more generally). Generalization from family-based data to population prevalences must be done with great caution, however, owing to various constraints inherent in family data (Carey, Gottesman, & Robins, 1980). Finally, based on a consideration of familial risk rates, Meehl (1990) has argued that approximately 10% of the population are genotypically schizotypic, though not all manifest this predisposition in a highly visible manner; Meehl's conjecture is supported by empirical taxometric work (Lenzenweger & Korfine, 1992a; Korfine & Lenzenweger, 1995).

Comorbidity Among DSM-defined SPD and PPD Comorbidity as an issue for schizotypic psychopathology is usually concerned with the SPD and PPD *diagnoses* as observed in clinical samples. The *DSM* systems have allowed multiple diagnoses on

Axis II of the multiaxial system. This feature of the system complicates any discussion of comorbidity issues as observed comorbidity may represent little more than an artifact of the prevailing diagnostic system. Therefore, as opposed to the implication that two diseases are actually present in the same person (comorbidity), it may actually make greater sense to speak of "co-occurrence" of PD diagnoses within a *DSM* framework. Available data indicate that PPD appears to be present in 0 to 60% of SPD patients drawn from primarily clinical samples (Siever et al., 1991). SPD is present in 17 to 70% of patients diagnosed with PPD (Bernstein, Useda, & Siever, 1993). These co-occurrence rates may reflect (1) a system that allows multiple diagnoses, (2) shared diagnostic criteria, (3) sampling bias (e.g., more impaired individuals tend to seek treatment), and/or (4) a common underlying substrate (e.g., schizotypy as a latent liability for schizophrenia). Regarding shared diagnostic criteria, PPD and SPD share the features of suspiciousness and paranoia, but PPD lacks the cognitive and perceptual distortions included in the SPD criteria. The sampling bias issue is especially relevant here given that most SPD or PPD individuals probably never present for treatment, but when they do so they are likely to be in crisis and/or more impaired (Lenzenweger & Korfine, 1992b).

Available data also reveal that 33 to 91% of SPD diagnosed individuals tend to also receive the diagnosis of borderline personality disorder (BPD; Siever et al., 1991), though fewer BPD diagnosed cases have a co-occurring SPD diagnosis. This degree of co-occurrence may reflect, in part, the influence of the method used to derive the original SPD and BPD diagnostic criteria as well as less specific psychotic-like features that occur in both disorders (Siever et al., 1991) and the sampling issue noted previously. The issue of comorbidity is not directly relevant to schizotypic psychopathology as assessed by psychometric measures as these do not reflect a categorical approach to classification; measures of schizotypy, however, do tend to be intercorrelated (Chapman et al., 1995) as one would expect of valid indexes tapping a common underlying construct.

Brief Historical Overview of Schizotypic Psychopathology

Variants thought to be related to schizophrenia, or schizotypic pathology, have been identified in different ways across the years (see Siever & Gunderson, 1983, or Kendler, 1985, for reviews; see also Planansky, 1972). The difficult methodologic and conceptual issues attending research in this area have been carefully reviewed by Gottesman and colleagues (Gottesman, 1987; Shields, Heston, & Gottesman, 1975).

Both Kraepelin (1919/1971, p. 234) and Bleuler (1911/1950, p. 239) made note of what they termed latent schizophrenia, a personality aberration regarded as a quantitatively less severe expression of schizophrenia. Interestingly, because both Kraepelin and Bleuler believed that the signs and symptoms of the so-called latent schizophrenia were in fact continuous with the "principal malady" (Kraepelin, 1919/1971, p. 234) or "manifest types of the disease" (Bleuler, 1911/1950, p. 239), neither of these master phenomenologists provided extended clinical descriptions of such cases. Both suggested one merely envision schizotypic conditions as characterized by diminished schizophrenia signs and symptoms. In attending to schizotypic pathology, however, Kraepelin and Bleuler foreshadowed subsequent efforts to delineate the phenotypic boundaries of schizophrenia through exploration of the schizotypic states.

In reviewing the history of psychiatric developments that culminated in the diagnostic criteria for SPD in *DSM-III*, Kendler (1985) persuasively argued that much of the clinical literature dealing with schizotypic states can be organized along two major historical trends. The *familial* tradition emphasizes phenomenologic descriptions of nonpsychotic, but aberrant, personality states that occur in the biologic relatives of individuals suffering from clinical schizophrenia. The second tradition was termed *clinical* as it emphasizes the work of clinicians who described the symptomatology of their patients presenting schizotypic, or schizophrenia-like, features. As detailed by Kendler (1985), workers within the familial tradition (e.g., Kraepelin, Bleuler, Kretschemer, Kallmann, Slater) frequently used terms such as "latent schizophrenia," "schizoid personality or character," or "schizoform abnormalities" to describe some family members of schizophrenic patients. These early observers used terms like eccentric-odd, irritable-unreasonable, socially isolated, aloof/cold demeanor, and suspiciousness to describe the family members of schizophrenia patients (Kendler, 1985, p. 543, table 1).

In contrast, researchers and clinicians working

within the so-called clinical tradition (Kendler, 1985; e.g., Zilboorg, Deutsch, Hoch and Polatin, Rado, and Meehl) used terms such as "ambulatory schizophrenia," "as-if personality," "pseudoneurotic schizophrenia," and "schizotypal" to describe severely affected but nonpsychotic individuals. The patients described by these rubrics were observed to demonstrate "schizophrenia-like symptomatology" in their psychological and psychosocial functioning, and it was frequently hypothesized that a genuine schizophrenia-related process was driving the manifest pathology. Disordered ("primary process") thinking and the lack of deep interpersonal relations were the two features that occurred most frequently in the descriptions of schizotypic patients by clinical tradition workers (Kendler, 1985, p. 545, table 2). Kendler (1985) noted apparent basic agreement in the descriptions of schizotypic individuals across the two traditions in terms of interpersonal functioning impairments as well as broad overlap in other areas (e.g., disordered thinking, anxiety, anger, hypersensitivity). However, Kendler (1985) concluded, "although the syndromes described by these two traditions share certain important symptoms, they are *not* fundamentally the same" (p. 546).

Early depictions of schizotypic psychopathology, with the exception of those discussions by Rado and Meehl, were primarily descriptive and lacked any detailed etiologic or developmental consideration. While there was speculation about an association with schizophrenia and a possible hereditary connection, the precise pathway leading from the underlying liability for schizophrenia or schizophrenia-related pathology to the phenotypic expression of a clinical disorder was absent. Only Meehl (1962, 1964, 1990) offered a complex developmental model, setting him apart from other clinical researchers. Meehl's views are discussed in detail below (see pp. 1313–1318).

Perhaps the most influential evidence that helped to establish a link between schizotypic phenomenology and clinical schizophrenia came from the Danish Adoption Study of Schizophrenia (Kety, Rosenthal, Wender, & Schulsinger, 1968). Kety et al. (1968), using a definition of "borderline schizophrenia" heavily influenced by the clinical tradition described above, found elevated rates of borderline or latent schizophrenia in the biological relatives of schizophrenic adoptees. Kety et al. (1994) further confirmed these initial results through further study of adoptees from the entire Danish population. These early results provided compelling evidence derived from a rigorous adoption methodology for a genetically transmitted component underlying both manifest schizophrenia and the less severe schizophrenia-like disorders. The hypothesized continuity between the conditions was, thus, not merely phenomenologic but also genetic. The diagnostic framework used by Kety et al. (1968) to diagnose "borderline" schizophrenia was subsequently reexamined (Spitzer, Endicott, & Gibbon, 1979) for use in the Axis II section of the then forthcoming *DSM-III*. Note, however, that Spitzer and colleagues were not attempting to distill from the Kety et al. framework only symptoms that identified biological relatives of schizophrenics. Spitzer et al. (1979) proposed the following eight symptoms and signs for schizotypal personality disorder (SPD): magical thinking, ideas of reference, suspiciousness, recurrent illusions, social isolation, odd speech, undue social anxiety-hypersensitivity, and inadequate rapport (aloof/cold). These criteria were, in large part, adopted for use in the *DSM-III*. SPD was subsequently placed on Axis II, along with PPD and schizoid personality disorder, to constitute the so-called odd-eccentric personality disorders cluster. Both the *DSM-III* (and *DSM-III-R*) criteria for SPD remained essentially atheoretical in nature, reflecting merely a clustering of symptoms, denoting with no specification of etiology or development. The atheoretical nature of the *DSM-III* criteria for SPD stands in contrast to Meehl's model of schizotypy, a model that integrates etiologic, developmental, and phenomenologic considerations.

This overview provides a suggestion of the interest schizotypic conditions have enjoyed among clinical and research workers. Clearly, this interest has been sustained through a rich descriptive tradition and supported by findings indicating that schizotypic pathology is related genetically to schizophrenia per se (see Torgersen, 1985, 1994, for reviews). Moreover, with the advent of explicit diagnostic criteria for SPD in the *DSM-III* and a simultaneous narrowing of the definition of schizophrenia, there has been a marked decrease in the diagnosis of schizophrenia and a corresponding rise in diagnosis of Axis II schizophrenia-related personality disorders (Loranger, 1990). Such an effect generated by a shift in the nomenclature has surely facilitated the focus on schizotypic conditions. It is also reasonable to assume that interest in these conditions has been further augmented by the burgeoning of research work in personality disorders in general (cf. Loranger, 1988). Finally, nomenclature changes notwithstanding, a great deal of interest in the study of schizotypic pathology and schizophrenia has been generated by P. E. Meehl's genetic-developmental model of schizotypy and schizophrenia.

Contemporary Models of Schizotypic Psychopathology: Meehl's Integrative Model of Schizotypy

As noted above, many of the early depictions of schizotypic pathology were primarily descriptive in nature. While the peculiarities of the relatives of schizophrenics or the symptoms of schizophrenic-like outpatients were noted and thought to be related to schizophrenia in some manner (Kendler, 1985), none of the early workers advanced a model that unambiguously posited a genetic diathesis for schizophrenia and traced its influence through developmental psychobiologic and behavioral paths to a variety of clinical (and nonclinical) outcomes. Unlike his predecessors, Meehl (1962, 1990) proposed a model that was (and is) clearly developmental in nature.

The roots of Meehl's model can be found in the observations and psychodynamic formulations of Sandor Rado (1953, 1960). Working within the clinical tradition, Rado made initial strides toward an integrative model that sought to link genetic influences for schizophrenia and observed schizotypic personality functioning. In his two primary position papers on the topic, he argued from a psychodynamic position informed by an appreciation for genetics that schizotypal behavior derived from a fundamental liability to schizophrenia. Rado, in fact, coined the term *schizotype* to represent a condensation of "schizophrenic *pheno*type" (Rado, 1953, p. 410; Rado, 1960, p. 87). It is interesting to note that Rado did *not* suggest schizotype as a condensation of the terms schizophrenia and *geno*type (cf. Siever & Gunderson, 1983). Rado (1960) referred to the individual who possessed the schizophrenic phenotype as a schizotype, while the correlated traits deriving from this "type" were termed schizotypal organization and the overt behavioral manifestations of the schizotypal traits were termed schizotypal behavior (see p. 87).

For Rado, the causes of schizotypal "differentness" were to be found in two core psychodynamic features of such patients, both of which were thought to be driven by "mutated genes." The two core defects present in the schizotype's personality organization were: (1) a diminished capacity for pleasure, or pleasure deficiency, speculated to have a neurochemical basis deriving from an inherited pleasure potential coded in the infant's genes (Rado, 1960, p. 88); and (2) a proprioceptive (kinesthetic) diathesis that resulted in an aberrant awareness of the body (a feature giving rise to schizotypic body-image disortions (Rado, 1960, see pp. 88 and 90)). Rado believed the physiological nature of the proprioceptive diathesis was obscure and remained to be explored (1960, p. 88). According to Rado, integration of the "action self," a necessity of psychodynamic/psychological health, was endangered by both the diminished binding power of pleasure (p. 90) and the proprioceptive diathesis found in the schizotype. Consequently, Rado described the schizotype as struggling to retain a sense of personality integration through several compensatory mechanisms (see Rado, 1960, p. 90) and such mechanisms frequently manifest themselves as schizotypal traits and behaviors. An important feature of Rado's model concerned what he termed "developmental stages of schizotypal behavior," essentially a continuum view of clinical compensation (a view echoed later by Meehl, 1990, p. 25). Rado's continuum notion suggested that a common schizophrenia diathesis could lead to a variety of phenotypic outcomes ranging from compensated schizotypy to deteriorated schizophrenia; thus an etiologic unity was proposed as underlying a diversity of clinical manifestations.

Influenced by Rado's (1953, 1960) hypotheses, Meehl's model of schizotypy was first articulated in a now classic position paper, his 1962 presidential address to the American Psychological Association, titled "Schizotaxia, Schizotypy, Schizophrenia." In this paper, one that has been viewed as enormously transforming for schizophrenia research (cf. Holzman, 1990), Meehl laid out an integrative etiologic framework for schizophrenia. The model not only encompassed genetic factors, social learning influences, and clinical symptomatology but also contained hypotheses about the precise nature of the fundamental defect underlying schizotypic functioning and its interactions with what he came to term polygenic potentiators. Elaboration on and refinement of the original 1962 theory can be found in later papers (e.g., Meehl, 1972, 1974). The theory was recently updated and described fully in an extended position paper appearing in the *Journal of Personality Disorders* (Meehl, 1990). What follows is a distillation of the major points contained in Meehl's efforts to illuminate the development of schizophrenia. The reader, therefore, is encouraged to consult both Meehl's original position statement (Meehl, 1962) as well as his recent treatise (Meehl, 1990) for additional detail.

In brief, Meehl's (1962, 1990) model holds that a single major gene (the schizogene) exerts its influence during brain development by coding for a specific "functional parametric aberration of the synaptic control system" in the central nervous system (CNS; 1990, pp. 14–15). The aberration, present at the neuronal level, is termed *hypokrisia* and suggests a neural integrative defect characterized by an "insufficiency of separation, differentiation, or discrimination" in neural transmission. Meehl argues his conceptualization of schizotaxia should not be taken to represent a defect in basic sensory or information retrieval capacities (1990, p. 14), nor a CNS inhibitory function deficit (1990, p. 16). The defect in neural transmission amounts to the presence of "slippage" at the CNS synapse, and such slippage at the synapse has its behavioral counterparts (at the molar level) in the glaring clinical symptomatology of actual schizophrenia. In other words, just as the synaptic functioning in schizophrenia is characterized by slippage, so too are the symptoms of associative loosening and cognitive-affective aberrations observed in the schizophrenic patient. Hypokrisia is hypothesized to characterize the neuronal functioning throughout the brain of the affected individual, thus producing what amounts to a rather ubiquitous CNS anomaly (1990, p. 14) termed *schizotaxia.*

Thus, according to the model, schizotaxia is the "genetically determined integrative defect, predisposing to schizophrenia and a sine qua non for that disorder" (1990, p. 35) and is conjectured to have a general population base rate of 10% (see Meehl, 1990, for derivation). Note that schizotaxia essentially describes an aberration in brain functioning characterized by pervasive neuronal slippage in the CNS; it is *not* a behavior or observable personality pattern. The schizotaxic brain, however, becomes the foundation that other factors will build upon, and interact aversively with, to possibly produce clinically diagnosable schizophrenia. The other factors that interact with the schizotaxic brain, so to speak, and influence individual development (as well as clinical status) are the social learning history of an individual as well as other genetic factors, termed *polygenic potentiators.*

Meehl (1962, 1990) generally held that all (or nearly all) schizotaxic individuals develop schizotypy (i.e., a schizotypal personality organization) on essentially all existing social reinforcement schedules. Schizotypy, therefore, refers to the psychological and personality organization resulting from the schizotaxic individual interacting with and developing within the world of social learning influences. An individual who displays schizotypy is considered a schizotype. (Note that Meehl's "schizotypal personality organization" is *not* the same as the *DSM-III-R* or *DSM-IV* Axis II disorder schizotypal personality disorder.) Meehl (1990) considered the possibility that a schizotaxic individual might not develop schizotypy if reared in a sufficiently healthful environment, but viewed such an outcome as unlikely.

The second major set of factors influencing the development of clinical schizophrenia in the schizotypic individual is a class of genetically determined factors (or dimensions) termed polygenic potentiators. According to Meehl (1990), "a potentiator is any genetic factor which, given the presence of the schizogene *and therefore of the schizotypal personality organization,* raises the probability of clinical decompensation" (p. 39). Potentiators include personality dimensions independent of schizotaxia, such as social introversion, anxiety proneness, aggressivity, and hypohedonia. Such potentiators do *not* modify (in the technical genetic sense of the term) the expression of the putative schizogene, but rather interact with the established schizotypic personality organization and the social environment to facilitate (or, in some cases, "depotentiate") the development of decompensated schizotypy, namely schizophrenia. Meehl (1990) stated: "It's not as if the polygenes for introversion somehow 'get into the causal chain' between the schizogene in DNA and the parameters of social reinforcement" (p. 38), rather the potentiators push the schizotype toward psychosis. In this context it is interesting to note that Meehl's model encompasses the idea of a "mixed" model of genetic influence, namely a single major gene (i.e., an autosomal diallelic locus) operating against a background due to an additive polygenic (or cultural) component (Morton & MacLean, 1974). Thus, reviewing briefly, according to Meehl (1962, 1990), the development of clinically diagnosable schizophrenia is the result of a complex interaction among several crucial factors: (1) a schizotaxic brain characterized by genetically determined hypokrisia at the synapse; (2) environmentally mediated social learning experiences (that bring about a schizotypal personality organization); and (3) the polygenic potentiators.

Although the *modal* schizotype does not decompensate into diagnosable schizophrenia, Meehl suggests that their latent diathesis is detectable through aberrant psychological and social functioning. Meehl (1962) described four fundamental signs and symptoms of schizotypy: cognitive slippage (or mild associative loosening), interpersonal aversiveness (social fear), anhedonia (pleasure capacity deficit), and ambivalence. Later, in 1964, he developed a clinical checklist for schizotypic signs that included rich clinical descriptions of not only these four signs/symptoms, but also several others that he suggested were valid schizotypy indicators (see pp. 1321–1322). Basically, all aspects of the core clinical phenomenology and psychological functioning seen in the schizotype were hypothesized to derive fundamentally from aberrant CNS functioning (i.e., hypokrisia) as determined by the schizogene. For example, primary cognitive slippage gives rise to observable secondary cognitive slippage in thought, speech, affective integration, and behavior, while primary aversive drift, the steady developmental progression toward negative affective tone in personality functioning across the life span, gives rise to social fear, ambivalence, and anhedonia.

The role of anhedonia in Meehl's model has changed over the years. In the 1962 model, anhedonia was viewed as a fundamental, etiologically important factor in the development of schizotypy, actually falling somewhat "between" the genetic defect hypokrisia and the other schizotypic sign/symptoms interpersonal aversiveness, cognitive slippage, and ambivalence. In 1990, Meehl deemphasized anhedonia, relabeling it hypohedonia, casting it as a nontaxonic dimensional polygenic potentiator, one *not* deriving from the genetically determined schizophrenia diathesis). Furthermore, in the 1990 revision, Meehl strongly suggests associative loosening and aversive drift are those psychological processes (deriving from hypokrisia) that genuinely determine the behavioral and psychological characteristics of the schizotype (see Meehl, 1990, p. 28).

A most important assumption in Meehl's model is that schizotypy, as a *personality organization* reflective of a latent liability for schizophrenia, can manifest itself behaviorally and psychologically in various degrees of clinical compensation. Thus, following Rado (1960), Meehl (1962, 1990) argued that the schizotype may be highly compensated (showing minimal signs and symptoms of schizotypic functioning), or may reveal transient failures in compensation, or may be diagnosably schizophrenic. Schizotypes, therefore, can range clinically from apparent normality through psychosis, yet all share the schizogene and resultant schizotypic personality organization. A crucial implication of this assumption is that not all schizotypes develop diagnosable schizophrenia (i.e., one could genuinely be at risk yet never develop a psychotic illness), however all schizotypes will display some evidence of their underlying liability in the form of aberrant psychobiologic and/or psychological functioning. This particular implication of the model has guided nearly 30 years of research directed at developing methods for the valid and efficient detection of schizotypy (through clinical, psychometric, or other means). In short, if valid schizotypy detection strategies could be developed, samples of "high-risk" individuals (i.e., schizotypes) could be assembled and examined in various efforts to better illuminate the nature and development of both schizophrenia and related schizotypic conditions.

Several points merit emphasis: (1) schizotypy per se is *not* isomorphic with *DSM-IV* schizotypal personality disorder; (2) schizotypy as a personality organization is not heritable (rather, schizotaxia is heritable); (3) this model is *not* based on a latent schizophrenia conception akin to Hoch and Polatin notions (see Kendler, 1985); and (4) Meehl's model is not entirely "genetic." With respect to the last point, Meehl (1990) unambiguously reveals his support for environmental influences in statements such as, "environmental factors *must* be potent determiners of which schizotypes decompensate." (See Meehl, 1962, 1971, 1990), for descriptions of plausible causal chains in the development of schizophrenia that incorporate environmental influences.)

Although various efforts have been made to expand upon and refine his basic framework (e.g., see Nuechterlein & Subotnick, 1998; Lenzenweger & Dworkin, 1998), the core assumptions of contemporary liability models do not differ substantially from what Meehl in 1962. Contemporary neuroscience (e.g., Grace, 1991) and neurodevelopmental (Weinberger, 1987; Breslin & Weinberger, 1990) models for schizophrenia, albeit not wed to hypothetical processes such as *hypokrisia*, are nevertheless quite consistent with many of the major tenets of Meehl's framework for both schizotypic psychopathology and schizophrenia proper (cf. Siever et al., 1993). For example, both the Grace and Weinberger models speak to an underlying neurobiological dysregulation that impairs information processing and may lead to symptom formation (cf. Meehl, 1962).

Classification and Diagnostic Technology

Assessment of Schizotypy and Schizotypal Phenomena

This section focuses on the assessment of schizotypy and schizotypic phenomena with a brief review of clinical interviews and psychometric inventories that have been developed for either clinical or research work. An evaluation of psychometric measures conjectured to be putative schizotypy indicators developed before 1980 is available in Grove (1982). Not all of the assessment devices discussed below have been designed with Meehl's (1964) early effort in mind, though most have been influenced by his work. Some emerged from the increased interest in personality pathology that followed the introduction of *DSM-III* in 1980. All of the measures discussed below have been shown to have a reasonable degree of validity.

Clinical Interviews for Schizotypic Psychopathology

Three interviews have been developed to date specifically to assess schizotypic phenomena. A competent extended review of interviews available for the assessment of schizotypy can be found in Benishay and Lencz (1995).

Symptom Schedule for the Diagnosis of Borderline Schizophrenia (SSDBS) The SSDBS was developed by Khouri, Haier, Rieder, and Rosenthal (1980) to assess the symptoms of "borderline schizophrenia" as defined by Kety et al. (1968). The schedule was administered in an interview format, with eight symptoms rated on a 3-point scale (0 = no evidence, 1 = some evidence, 2 = clear evidence), including perceptual changes, body image aberrations, feelings of unreality, thought disturbances, ideas of reference, ideas of persecution, self-inflicted injuries, and preoccupation with perverse sexuality or violence. Inter-rater reliability for total scores was .83. Total scores of 2 or above appeared to accurately identify those individuals originally diagnosed "borderline schizophrenia" in the Danish Adoption Study sample (Khouri et al., 1980). The diagnostic criteria for "borderline schizophrenia" assessed by the SSDBS were influenced by the "clinical tradition" (cf. Kendler, 1985).

Schedule for Schizotypal Personalities (SSP) Developed by Baron and associates (Baron, Asnis, & Gruen, 1981), the SSP was designed to assess the diagnostic criteria for *DSM-III* SPD. The SSP assesses illusions, depersonalization/derealization, ideas of reference, suspiciousness, magical thinking, inadequate rapport, odd communication, social isolation, and social anxiety, the SSP also assesses delusions and hallucinations. Baron et al. (1981) report generally excellent interrater and test-rest reliabilities for the SSP scales. The kappa coefficient for the diagnosis of schizotypal personality disorder using the SSP was .88.

Structured Interview for Schizotypy (SIS) Kendler and colleagues (Kendler, Lieberman, & Walsh, 1989) developed the SIS to assess schizotypal signs and symptoms. The SIS consists of 19 sections, 18 to assess individual symptom dimensions and one to assess 36 separate schizotypal signs (Kendler et al., 1989). For example, the SIS includes social isolation, interpersonal sensitivity, social anxiety, ideas of reference, suspiciousness, and other schizotypal features. The SIS is intended to be given in conjunction with an Axis I assessment device. The interrater reliabilities associated with various aspects of the SIS are generally acceptable, with intraclass correlation coefficients typically above .70. Preliminary data based on the study of nonpsychotic relatives of schizophrenic patients support the criterion validity of the SIS as a measure of schizotypy (see Kendler et al., 1989). More recent results from the Roscommon Family Study of schizophrenia (Kendler et al., 1993) provide additional validation of the SIS. Unlike the SSP, the SIS assesses a broader range of schizotypic signs, going considerably beyond *DSM* schizotypal personality disorder, including some aspects of Meehl's construct of schizotypy.

Self-Report Psychometric Inventories for Schizotypy Detection

- *Chapman Psychosis Proneness Scales.* Guided by Meehl's model of schizotypy and his rich clinical descriptions of schizotypic signs (Meehl, 1964), Chapman and Chapman (1985, 1987) developed several objective self-report measures to assess traits reflective of a putative liability to psychosis, perhaps schizophrenia. (For recent reviews see Chapman, Chapman, & Kwapil, 1995, and Edell, 1995).

  Two of these scales, the Perceptual Aberration Scale (PAS; Chapman, Chapman, & Raulin, 1978) and the Magical Ideation Scale (MIS; Eckblad & Chapman, 1983), have been used extensively in recent research to detect schizotypy and assemble samples of subjects presumed to be at increased risk for psychosis from nonclinical populations. All of the Chapmans' psychosis proneness scales have been carefully constructed from the psychometric standpoint to minimize correlations with social desirability and acquiesence factors, while ensuring internal consistency, content validity, and construct validity. The PAS is a 35-item true-false measure of disturbances and distortions in perceptions of the body as well as other objects. It includes items like "Occasionally I have felt as though my body did not exist" (keyed *true*) and "I have never felt that my arms or legs have momentarily grown in size" (keyed *false*). Internal consistency analyses typically reveal coefficient alphas around .90 with short-term test-retest stability of.75 (Chapman & Chapman, 1985). Regarding the MIS, Chapman and Chapman (1985) defined magical ideation as a belief in forms of *causation* [italics added] that, by conventional standards of our society, are not valid but magical" (p. 164). The MIS includes items such as "I think I could learn to read other people's minds if I wanted to" (keyed *true*) and "At times I perform certain little rituals to ward off negative influences" (keyed *true*). Coefficient alphas run typically between .80 and .85. The PAS and MIS tend to be highly correlated (*r*'s at .68 to .70). As a result both measures are often used in conjunction to select schizotypic subjects from nonclinical populations. The PAS and MIS have been used extensively in schizotypy research and they are associated with an impressive body of empirical literature supportive of their validity.
- *Schizophrenia Liability Index.* Moldin and colleagues have reported on a schizophrenia liability index (SLI; Moldin, Gottesman, & Erlenmeyer-Kimling, 1987a, 1987b; Moldin, Gottesman, Erlenmeyer-Kimling, & Cornblatt, 1990; Moldin, Rice, Gottesman, & Erlenmeyer-Kimling, 1990a, 1990b) derived from the Minnesota Multiphasic Personality Inventory (MMPI). The index consists of a combination of 13 MMPI indicators known to be correlates of a liability for schizophrenia. Data available to date suggest: (1) deviance on the SLI characterizes children at risk for schizophrenia; (2) the latent structure of SLI values is consistent with a qualitative distribution of schizophrenia liability; and (3) deviance on the SLI is known to be familial.
- *Other Psychometric Measures of Schizotypy.* Several additional psychometric measures of schizotypy have been developed recently and should be mentioned. Unlike the PAS, MIS, and SLI, these other measures have not yet been shown to be associated with a *liability* for schizophrenia (i.e., schizotypy) through systematic family, twin, or adoption study, however available validity data suggest all are promising as schizotypy indicators. These measures include the Rust Inventory of Schizotypal Cognitions (RISC; Rust, 1988a, 1988b); the Referential Thinking Scale (Lenzenweger, Bennett, & Lilenfeld, 1997); the Social Fear Scale (Raulin & Wee, 1984); the schizotypal personality scale (STA; Claridge & Broks, 1984); the Schizotypal Questionnaire (Raine, 1992); the Schizophrenism Scale (Venables, 1990) and the schizoid, schizotypal, and paranoid personality disorder scales derived from the MMPI (Morey, Waugh, & Blashfield, 1985). Finally, Harkness, McNulty, and Ben-Porath (1995) have developed a five-scale dimensional system (the Personality Pathology Five-PSY-5), derived from MMPI-2 items, that can be used to describe personality and its disorders; one of the PSY-5 scales assesses psychoticism, a higher order construct of general relevance to schizotypy. Of these scales, only Lenzenweger et al.'s Referential Thinking Scale and Raulin and Wee's Social Fear Scale were designed specifically to assess aspects of Meehl's schizotypy construct.

Etiology, Development, and Pathogenesis

There have been two major research thrusts in the area of schizotypic psychopathology research. First, many investigators have studied the correlates of schizotypic psychopathology, through the study of either clinically defined SPD and PPD, psychometrically defined schizotypic persons, or first-degree biologic relatives of schizophrenia patients. The second thrust, which is really more of a theme through much of the research in this area, has been directed at illuminating the relationship between schizotypic psychopathology and schizophrenia per se, as well as development of a latent liability construct.

Given that the theme of relating schizotypic pathology to schizophrenia is so prominent in this area and that one of the guiding assumptions in this work concerns the theoretical notion of "latent liability," it seems appropriate to begin with a review of the need for such a construct. Following this discussion, empirical research related to schizotypic psychopathology will be discussed from the vantage points of (1) family history, (2) laboratory findings, (3) clinical phenomenology, and (4) follow-up studies. This section will be followed by a discussion of the delimitation of schizotypic psychopathology from other disorders at the latent (i.e., unobservable with the naked eye) level.

On the Need for a Latent Liability Construct

Much of the discussion above has *assumed* a common underlying liability for schizotypic psychopathology and schizophrenia. What is the empirical basis for such an assumption? As argued previously (Lenzenweger, 1993; Lenzenweger & Korfine, 1995), there is ample evidence in support of a latent liability conceptualization in schizophrenia that includes schizotypic psychopathology among other things. First, schizotypic psychopathology is linked, presumably via genetics (Torgersen, 1985), to schizophrenia (Kendler, 1985, Kendler et al., 1993). Perhaps the most influential evidence that helped to establish a link between schizotypic phenomenology and clinical schizophrenia came from the Danish Adoption Study of Schizophrenia (Kety et al., 1968), in which (as noted above) there were elevated rates of schizotypic psychopathology. These results provided compelling evidence for a genetically transmitted component underlying both manifest schizophrenia and the less severe schizophrenia-like disorders. The hypothesized continuity between the conditions was, thus, not merely phenomenologic but also genetic. Moreover, confirming the early Kety et al. findings, numerous family studies have found an excess of schizotypic disorders in the biological relatives of schizophrenic individuals (see Kendler et al., 1993). Clearly, the boundaries of the phenotypic expression of schizophrenia liability extend beyond manifest psychosis. Thus, liability manifestations are *not* isomorphic with expressed psychosis.

Second, the existence of a *clinically unexpressed* liability for schizophrenia has been confirmed (Gottesman & Bertelsen 1989; Lenzenweger & Loranger 1989a). Thus, liability can exist without obvious phenotypic, or symptomatic (i.e., psychotic), manifestations. Third, a well-established biobehavioral marker, namely eye tracking dysfunction (Holzman et al., 1988; Levy, Holzman, Matthysse, & Mendell, 1993), which bears no immediately discernible phenotypic connection to overt schizophrenia, is known to be associated with a latent diathesis for the illness. Thus, liability can manifest itself in an *alternative phenotypic form* (Lenzenweger, 1998). Finally, if the base rate of schizophrenia liability (or the schizotypy taxon) is, in fact, 10% as conjectured by Meehl (1990), then perhaps well over 50% of those carrying liability for schizophrenia may go clinically "undetected" across the life span (i.e., derived from the estimated combined prevalence of schizophrenia, SPD, and PPD of roughly 5% [cf. Loranger 1990]). Taken together, both theoretical and empirical considerations argue strongly for the plausibility of a complex latent liability construct in schizophrenia.

Given that *most* persons vulnerable to schizophrenia may never show flagrant psychosis or easily detectable signs and symptoms of schiztoypic personality functioning, researchers have sought ways to detect schizotypy using more sensitive laboratory and psychometric measures. Efforts have been made to discover valid objective indicators of schizotypy that function efficiently across a range of clinical compensation, as well as mental state, and are capable of detecting liability even in clinically unexpressed (nonsymptomatic) cases. Such indicators, psychometric and otherwise, are thought to assess an *endophenotype* (not visible to the unaided, "naked" eye; see Gottesman, 1991). Their inclusion in research investigations of the genetics and familiality of schizophrenia is likely to enhance those efforts even when the putative indicators are only modestly correlated with the latent liability (Smith & Mendell 1974; Moldin & Van Eerdewegh, 1995).

Empirical Findings Relevant to Development and Pathogenesis

Family History of Schizophrenia Overall, it is now generally established that schizotypic psychopathology does indeed occur in the biological first-degree relatives of schizophrenia affected persons at rates much higher that the population rate (for reviews see Kendler et al., 1993; Nigg & Goldsmith, 1994; Torgersen, 1994; Webb & Levinson, 1993). There is also evidence supportive of the familiality of schizophrenia and schizotypic psychopathology from studies that have found elevated rates of schizophrenia among the first-degree biologic relatives of schizotypic patients (Battaglia et al., 1991; Battaglia, Bernardeschi, Franchini, Bellodi, & Smeraldi, 1995; Kendler & Walsh, 1995).

Three studies have reported a significant excess of PPD in the relatives of schizophrenia probands (Baron et al., 1985; Kendler & Gruenberg, 1982; Kendler et al., 1993). However, PPD appears to be more prevalent in the first-degree relatives of those patients affected with Axis I delusional disorder, a psychotic illness (Kendler et al., 1985). One could argue that these data suggest a stronger link between PPD and the Axis I delusional disorder as opposed to schizophrenia, but more data would be required to resolve this issue.

From the "psychometric schizotypy" vantage point, Lenzenweger and Loranger (1989a) examined the lifetime expectancy (morbid risk) of treated schizophrenia, unipolar depression, and bipolar disorder in the biologic first-degree relatives of 101 nonpsychotic psychiatric patients (probands) who were classified as either "schizotypy-positive" or "schizotypy-negative" according to the Perceptual Aberration Scale (PAS). The relatives of schizotypy-positive probands were significantly more likely to have been treated for schizophrenia than the relatives of schizotypy-negative probands; the morbid risk for treated unipolar depression or bipolar disorder among the relatives of the two proband groups did *not* differ. Berenbaum and McGrew (1993) also reported that PAS deviance is familial. Of related interest, Battaglia et al. (1991) found in a study of the relatives of schizotypal patients that recurrent illusions (akin to perceptual aberrations) were found in every SPD patient with a positive family history of schizophrenia.

Twin and Adoption Studies Unfortunately there have not been any extensive twin studies of clinically defined schizotypic psychopathology beyond an initial study conducted by Torgersen (1994), which supported a heritable component to SPD. There are no known twin studies of PPD. Miller and Chapman (1993) demonstrated that the PAS has a substantial heritable component, and Kendler and Hewitt (1992) have found that "positive trait schizotypy" (of which perceptual aberration, among other features, is a component) is substantially heritable.

In terms of adoption studies, the most relevant research comes from the Danish Adoption Study conducted by Kety and colleagues (Kety et al., 1968; Kety et al., 1994) and the subsequent secondary analyses of these data by Kendler and colleagues (e.g., Kendler, Gruenberg, & Kinney, 1994). In short, whether working from the original data (Kety) or secondary analyses (Kendler), schizotypic psychopathology is found at greater rates among the biologic relatives of the schizophrenia affected adoptees. These data are also consistent with the family and twin data supporting both the familiality of schizotypic psychopathology and a heritable component to the pathology. There are no adoption studies of *DSM-III-R* or *DSM-IV* SPD or PPD.

Laboratory Studies of Schizotypic Psychopathology There have been a number of laboratory studies of schizotypic psychopathology. These studies have examined either clinical schizotypes (e.g., SPD/PPD), psychometrically identified schizotypes, or the first-degree relatives of schizophrenia patients. Only those findings related to the biobehavioral and neurocognitive processes that have received the greatest attention in the schizophrenia literature in recent years are reviewed here, namely sustained attention (Cornblatt & Keilp, 1994), eye tracking (Levy, Holzman, Matthysse, & Mendell, 1994), and various forms of executive functioning mediated by the prefrontal cortex (e.g., Gold & Harvey, 1993).

A deficit in sustained attention, a leading biobehavioral indicator of a possible schizophrenia liability, has been found in clinically defined schizotypic individuals (e.g., SPD) (e.g., Condray & Steinhauer, 1992; Harvey et al., 1996). Similar deficits were found among psychometrically identified schizotypic individuals by Lenzenweger, Cornblatt, and Putnick (1991). Replication of the Lenzenweger et al. (1991) results, using the same measure of sustained attention, have been reported by Obiols, Garcia-Domingo, de Trincheria, and Domenech (1993). Grove et al. (1991) have also reported a significant association between high PAS scores and poor sustained attention performance among the first-degree biological relatives of individuals with diagnosed schizophrenia. Finally, Cornblatt, Lenzenweger, Dworkin, and Erlenmeyer-Kimling (1992) found that attentional dysfunction that is detected in young children who are at risk for schizophrenia is correlated with schizotypic features in adulthood (assessed nearly 20 years later). There do not appear to have been any studies of sustained attention in PPD patients.

In terms of eye tracking dysfunction among individuals with schizotypic psychopathology, it appears that such deficits are found both among clinically defined schizotypes (e.g., Lencz et al., 1993; Siever et al., 1990; Siever et al., 1994; cf. Thaker, Cassady, Adami, & Moran, 1996) and psychometrically identified schizotypes (Simons & Katkin, 1985; O'Driscoll, Lenzenweger, & Holzman, 1998). Eye tracking dysfunction has also been found to aggregate in the biologic family members of schizophrenia patients across numerous studies (Levy et al., 1994). It is important to note that, just as sustained attention and eye tracking dysfunctions do not occur in all cases of schizophrenia, not all schizotypes evidence the dysfunctions either. Not only does the consistency in findings across both schizophrenia patients and individuals with schizotypic psychopathology inform us of the information processing and psychophysiological deficits found in schizotypes, but these very deficits further link the schizotype to schizophrenia. There are no reported studies of eye tracking dysfunction specifically in PPD patients.

Considerable recent attention has been focused on difficulties in abstract reasoning and novel problem solving in schizophrenia (Gold & Harvey, 1993), processes that are hypothesized to be mediated by the prefrontal cortex. Moreover, evidence has been presented that some schizophrenic symptoms may reflect a dysfunctional frontal system (e.g., Goldman-Rakic 1991; Levin 1984a, 1984b; Weinberger, Berman, & Zec, 1986). Much of this research has employed the Wisconsin Card Sorting Test (WCST) as a measure of abstraction ability and "executive functioning." Schizotypic subjects, identified through either a clinical or psychometric approach, have been found to display deficits on the WCST (Lenzenweger & Korfine, 1991, 1994; Raine, Sheard, Reynolds, & Lencz, 1992; Park, Holzman, & Lenzenweger, 1995), though not in all studies (Condray & Steinhauer, 1992). WCST findings for the biologic relatives of schizophrenia affected probands are mixed (Franke, Maier, Hardt, & Hain, 1993; Scarone, Abbruzzese, & Gambini, 1993). Clearly, the situation for WCST performance is somewhat inconsistent across mode of definition used in selecting subjects. Finally, in a more fine-grained assessment of the cognitive functions thought to be mediated frontally, Park et al. (1995) reported that psychometrically identified schizotypes revealed poorer "spatial working memory" performance, which is consistent with WCST deficits. Park, Holzman, and Levy (1993) have found that about half of the healthy relatives of schizophrenia patients also displayed impaired spatial working memory. There are no reported studies of working memory performance in PPD patients.

Schizophrenia-Related Deviance on Psychological Tests SPD and PPD patients are by definition schizotypic at the level of phenomenology and one would not necessarily anticipate using other measures of pathology to verify the presence of phenomenology already required by virtue of the *DSM* diagnostic criteria. However, psychometrically identified schizotypes have been selected as a function of deviance on a schizotypy measure and other measures of psychopathology have been used to inform the validity of their schizotypic "status," so to speak, of these subjects. For example, PAS-identified schizotypes reveal schizophrenia-related deviance on the Minnesota Multiphasic Personality Inventory (MMPI; Lenzenweger, 1991), schizophrenia-related personality disorder features (Lenzenweger & Korfine, 1992b), and thought disorder (Edell & Chapman, 1979; Coleman, Levy, Holzman, & Lenzenweger, 1995). See Edell (1995) or Chapman et al. (1995) for extensive reviews of the correlates of the Chapman psychosis-proneness scales.

Neuroimaging and Neurobiology of Schizotypic Psychopathology To date, neuroimaging studies of schizotypic psychopathology remain limited and it is somewhat premature to highlight major trends in this area (see Flaum & Andreasen, 1995; Gur & Gur, 1995). However, as this area of psychological science develops, it is anticipated that more and more studies using either positron emission tomography (PET), magnetic resonance imaging (MRI), or functional MRI (fMRI) will emerge. One especially interesting preliminary finding in this developing area is that of reduced hippocampal volume in relation to higher PAS scores (Flaum & Andreasen, 1995). The utility of PET methodology for illuminating the functional neuroanatomy of hallucination of schizophrenia has been demonstrated (Silbersweig et al., 1995), and further application of this technology to schizotypic psychopathology is welcome.

The neurobiology of schizophrenia has undergone major revisions within the past 10 years in response to greater knowledge regarding basic neurobiology (see Grace, 1991) and developmental neurobiology (Breslin & Weinberger, 1991), and psychopharmacology (Davis, Kohn, Ko, & Davidson, 1991). A more contemporary view of the dopaminergic (DA) dysfunction in schizophrenia emphasizes multiple processes and their dysfunction (Davis et al., 1991). For example, Weinberger (1987), among others, has suggested that there is a two-process DA dysfunction in schizophrenia with one process implicating the mesocortical DA pathway, underactivity in the prefrontal cortex, hypodopaminergia, and negative symptoms, whereas the other involves mesolimbic DA pathways, the striatum and related structures, hyperdopaminergia, and positive symptoms. Grace (1991) has further refined this model of DA dysfunction in schizophrenia by suggesting a glutamatergic dysfunction emanating from the prefrontal cortex affects both *tonic* and *phasic* DA processes in the striatum. Additionally, while there is a continued focus on the role of DA in schizophrenia, there is emerging interest in the role that serotonin plays in schizophrenia as well (Davis et al., 1991). Although there have not been systematic efforts to determine the precise correspondence between the neurobiological models for schizophrenia and schizotypic psychopathology, those efforts are surely on the horizon (Siever, 1995).

Clinical Phenomenology SPD and PPD patients are by definition schizotypic at the level of phenomenology, and one would not necessarily anticipate using other measures of pathology to confirm the phenomenology of such subjects. However, as noted previously, alternative methods of detecting schizotypes have been validated, in part, by examining the relations between schizotypic phenomenology as clinically assessed and, say, psychomteric measures of schizotypy. For example, Lenzenweger and Loranger (1989b) found that elevations on the PAS were most closely associated with schizotypal personality disorder symptoms and clinically assessed anxiety. Others have found that nonclinical subjects, identified as schizotypic through application of the psychometric approach, also reveal schizotypic and "psychotic-like" phenomenology (cf. Chapman, Edell, & Chapman, 1980; Chapman, Chapman, & Kwapil, 1995; Edell, 1995). From the standpoint of the first-degree biologic relatives of schizophrenia patients, Kendler et al. (1993) have shown that schizotypic features are found at higher levels among the relatives of schizophrenia cases versus the relatives of controls. However, it is important to note that not all psychometrically identified schizotypes or biologic relatives of schizophrenia patients will display levels of schizotypic phenomenology that would result in a diagnosis by *DSM-IV* criteria for SPD or PPD.

Follow-up Studies of Schizotypic Psychopathology

There are few long-term follow-up data available on schizotypic samples that would help to determine how many schizotypes move on to clinical schizophrenia. Moreover, given the relative absence of large-scale longitudinal studies of personality disorders that involve multiple assessments, with the exception of the study being conducted by the present author, it is difficult to examine the stability of schizotypic features over time. Fenton and McGlashan (1989) conducted a follow-up study of patients that had been non-psychotic at admission to the Chestnut Lodge Psychiatric Hospital. They found that 67% (12/18) of patients with a diagnosis of schizophrenia, located after a 15-year follow-up, were schizotypic (and non-psychotic) at their initial admission. The Chapman, Chapman, Kwapil, Eckblad, and Zinser (1994) 10-year follow-up of their "psychosis-prone" (i.e., schizotypic) subjects revealed that high scorers on the PAS and MIS revealed greater levels of psychotic illness and schizotypic phenomenology at follow-up. Interestingly, psychoticism, as a general schizotypy-relevant construct does *not* seem to predict heightened risk for psychosis (Chapman,

1994). A common question in this area of research is: "How many schizotypes go on to develop full-blown schizophrenia and how many stay compensated (non-psychotic) to one degree or another across the lifespan?" Meehl's model suggests that the modal schizotype never develops schizophrenia; this fascinating question awaits more empirical data from long-term follow-up study of schizotypic cases.

Delimitation from Other Disorders

Research on the delimitation of schizotypic psychopathology from other disorders has proceeded at both phenotypic and latent levels. The issue of delimitation at the latent level will be discussed here.

Assuming that schizotypy, as conceptualized by Meehl (1962, 1990), represents a *latent liability* construct and that current schizotypy indexes are valid, a basic question about the fundamental structure of schizotypy remains. Is it continuous (i.e., "dimensional") or is it truly discontinuous (or, "qualitative") in nature? For example, at the level of the gene, both Meehl's model (1962, 1990) and the "latent trait" model (Matthysse, Holzman, & Lange, 1986; Holzman et al., 1988) conjecture the existence of a qualitative discontinuity, whereas the polygenic multifactorial threshold model (Gottesman, 1991) predicts a continuous distribution of *levels* of liability. Clarification of the structure of schizotypy may help to resolve issues concerning appropriate genetic models for schizophrenia, and such information may aid in planning future studies in this area. Nearly all investigations of the structure of schizophrenia liability done to date have relied exclusively on fully expressed, diagnosable schizophrenia (see Gottesman, 1991), and the results of these studies have left the question of liability structure unresolved. Moreover, one surely cannot reason with confidence that a unimodal distribution of phenotypic schizotypic traits supports the existence of a continuum of liability either (e.g., Kendler, Ochs, Gorman, Hewitt, Ross, & Mirsky, 1991). In recent years, however, it has been proposed that a possible "expansion" of the schizophrenia phenotype to include other schizophrenia-related phenomena, such as eye tracking dysfunction (Holzman et al., 1988), might be helpful in efforts to illuminate the latent structure of liability in schizophrenia. In my laboratory, we have pursued such an approach, complementary to the "expanded phenotype" proposal, through the psychometric detection of schizotypy (see Lenzenweger, 1993). Thus, we have undertaken over the past several years a series of studies that begin to explore the latent structure of schizotypy. Our work has drawn extensively upon the theoretical formulations of Rado and Meehl, and we have used a well-validated measure of schizotypy, namely the Chapman's PAS, in these efforts.

We have explored the latent structure of schizotypy through application of Meehl's MAXCOV (Meehl, 1973, Meehl & Yonce, 1996) procedure to the covariance structure of scores on the PAS. Our samples have been randomly ascertained from nonclinical university populations and they have been purged of invalid responders and those with suspect test-taking attitudes. Using the MAXCOV procedure, we (Korfine & Lenzenweger, 1995; Lenzenweger & Korfine, 1992a) have found evidence that suggests that the latent structure of schizotypy, as assessed by the PAS, is taxonic (i.e., qualitative) in nature and, moreover, the base rate of the schizotypy taxon is approximately 5 to 10%. The taxon base rate figure is relatively consistent with the conjecture by Meehl that schizotypes can be found in the general population at a rate of 10%. In our work we have also conducted a variety of control analyses that have served to check the MAXCOV procedure and ensure that the technique does *not* generate spurious evidence of taxonicity. We (Korfine & Lenzenweger, 1995) have demonstrated that (1) MAXCOV detects a latent continuum when one is hypothesized to exist, (2) MAXCOV results based on dichotomous data do not automatically generate "taxonic" results, and (3) item endorsement frequencies do not correspond to our taxon base rate estimates (i.e., our base rate estimates are not a reflection of endorsement frequencies). Finally, in recent work (Lenzenweger, in press), MAXCOV analysis applied to three continuous measures of schizotypy reveals results that are highly consistent with our prior research in this area. Moreover, those individuals identified via taxometric analysis as putative taxon members do display, as a group, higher levels of deviance on a psychometric measure known to be associated with schziophrenia liability. These data, taken in aggregate, while they do not unambiguously confirm that the structure of schizotypy is qualitative, are clearly consistent with such a conjecture. This suggests that schizotypic psychopathology is discontinuous in its latent structure and raises interesting possibilities for future genetic research in this area.

Conclusions

Schizotypic psychopathology has long held the interest of researchers and clinicians alike, and it has been the subject of considerable theoretical discussion and empirical investigation. Continued study of this class of mental disturbance through the methods of experimental psychopathology, cognitive neuroscience, genetics, epidemiology, classification, and neurobiology will help to provide clues to the nature of schizophrenia, as well as the schizotypic disorders themselves. The multiplicity of vantage points that have been brought to bear on schizotypic psychopathology has helped to move this area of inquiry further, and the continued existence of alternative vantage points in both psychology and psychiatry in connection with these disorders will only serve to advance our knowledge.

References

Andreasen, N. C., Arndt, S., Alliger, R., Miller, D., & Flaum, M. (1995). Symptoms of schizophrenia: Methods, meanings, and mechanisms. *Archives of General Psychiatry, 52*, 341–351.

Baron, M., Asnis, L., & Gruen, R. (1981). The schedule for schizotypal personalities (SPP): A diagnostic interview for schizotypal features. *Psychiatry Research, 4*, 213–228.

Baron, M., Gruen, R., Rainer, J. D., Kanes, J., Asnis, L., & Lord, S. (1985). A family study of schizophrenic and normal control probands: Implications for the spectrum concept of schizophrenia. *American Journal of Psychiatry, 142*, 447–454.

Battaglia, M., Bernardeschi, L., Franchini, L., Bellodi, L., & Smeraldi, E. (1995). A family study of schizotypal disorder. *Schizophrenia Bulletin, 21*, 33–45.

Battaglia, M., Gasperini, M., Sciuto, G., Scherillo, P., Diaferia, G., & Bellodi, L. (1991). Psychiatric disorders in the families of schizotypal subjects. *Schizophrenia Bulletin, 17*, 659–68.

Benishay, D. S., & Lencz, T. (1995). Semistructured interviews for the measurement of schizotypal personality. In A. Raine, T. Lencz, & S. Mednick, (Eds.), *Schizotypal personality* (pp. 463–479). New York: Cambridge University Press.

Berenbaum, H., & McGrew, J. (1993). Familial resemblance of schizotypic traits. *Psychological Medicine, 23*, 327–333.

Bernstein, D. P., Cohen, P., Skodol, A., Bezirganian, S., & Brook, J. S. (1996). Childhood antecedents of adolescent personality disorders. *American Journal of Psychiatry, 153*, 907–913.

Bernstein, D. P., Useda, D., & Siever, L. J. (1993). Paranoid personality disorder: Review of the literature and resommendations for DSM-IV. *Journal of Personality Disorders, 7*, 53–62.

Bleuler, E. (1911/1950). *Dementia praecox or the group of schizophrenias*. (J. Zinkin, Trans.). New York: International Universities Press.

Breslin, N. A., & Weinberger, D. R. (1990). Schizophrenia and the normal functional development of the prefrontal cortex. *Development and Psychopathology, 2*, 409–424.

Carey, G., Gottesman, I., & Robins, E. (1980). Prevalence rates for the neuroses: Pitfalls in the evaluation of familiality. *Psychological Medicine, 10*, 437–443.

Chapman, J. P. (1994). Does the Eysenck Psychoticism Scale predict psychosis? A ten year longitudinal study. *Personality and Individual Differences, 17*, 369–375.

Chapman, L. J., & Chapman, J. P. (1973). *Disordered thought in schizophrenia*. New York: Appelton-Century-Crofts.

Chapman, L. J., & Chapman, J. P. (1985). Psychosis proneness. In M. Alpert (Ed.), *Controversies in schizophrenia: Changes and constancies* (pp. 157–172). New York: Guilford Press.

Chapman, L. J., & Chapman, J. P. (1987). The search for symptoms predictive of schizophrenia. *Schizophrenia Bulletin, 13*, 497–503.

Chapman, J., Chapman, L., & Kwapil, T. (1995). Scales for the measurement of schizotypy. In A. Raine, T. Lencz, & S. Mednick (Eds.), *Schizotypal personality* (pp. 79–106). New York: Cambridge.

Chapman, J. P., Chapman, L. J., & Kwapil, T. R. (1995). Scales for the measurement of schizotypy. In A. Raine, T. Lencz, & S. Mednick, (Eds.), *Schizotypal personality* (pp. 79–106). New York: Cambridge University Press.

Chapman, L. J., Chapman, J. P., Kwapil, T. R., Eckblad, M., & Zinser, M. C. (1994). Putatively psychosis-prone subjects 10 years later. *Journal of Abnormal Psychology, 103*, 171–183.

Chapman, L. J., Edell, W. S., & Chapman, J. P. (1980). Physical anhedonia, perceptual aberration, and psychosis proneness. *Schizophrenia Bulletin, 6*, 639–653.

Chapman, L. J., Chapman, J. P., & Raulin, M. L. (1978). Body-image aberration in schizophrenia. *Journal of Abnormal Psychology, 87*, 399–407.

Claridge, G. S., & Broks, P. (1984). Schizotypy and hemisphere function: I. Theoretical considerations and the measurement of schizotypy. *Personality and Individual Differences, 5*, 633–648.

Claridge, G., McCreery, C., Mason, O., & Bentall, R. (1996). The factor structure of "schizotypal" traits: A large replication study. *British Journal of Clinical Psychology, 35*, 103–115.

Claridge, G. S., McCreery, C., Mason, O., Bentall, R. P., Boyle, G., Slade, P. D., & Popplewell, D. (1996). The factor structure of 'schizotypal' traits: A large replication study. *British Journal of Clinical Psychology, 35*, 103–116.

Coleman, M. J., Levy, D. L., Lenzenweger, M. F., & Holzman, P. S. (1996). Thought disorder, perceptual aberrations, and schizotypy. *Journal of Abnormal Psychology, 105*, 469–473.

Condray, R., & Steinhauer, S. R. (1992). Schizotypal personality disorder in individuals with and without schizophrenic relatives: Similarities and contrasts in neurocognitive and clinical functioning. *Schizophrenia Research, 7*, 33–41.

Cornblatt, B. A., & Keilp, J. G. (1994). Impaired attention, genetics, and the pathophysiology of schizophrenia. *Schizophrenia Bulletin, 20*, 31–46.

Cornblatt, B. A., Lenzenweger, M. F., Dworkin, R. H., & Erlenmeyer-Kimling, L. (1992). Childhood attentional dysfunction predicts social isolation in adults at risk for schizophrenia. *British Journal of Psychiatry, 161* (Suppl. 18), 59–68.

Cronbach, L. J., & Meehl, P. E. (1955). Construct validity in psychological tests. *Psychological Bulletin, 52*, 281–302.

Davis, K. L., Kahn, R. S., Ko, G., & Davidson, M. (1991). Dopamine in schizophrenia: A review and reconceptualization. *American Journal of Psychiatry, 148*, 1474–1486.

Eckblad, M., & Chapman, L. J. (1983). Magical ideation as an indicator of schizotypy. *Journal of Consulting and Clinical Psychology, 51*, 215–225.

Edell, W. S. (1995). The psychometric measurement of schizotypy using the Wisconsin scales of psychosis-proneness. In G. A. Miller (Ed.), *The behavioral high-risk paradigm in psychopathology* (pp. 3–46). New York: Springer-Verlag.

Edell, W. S., & Chapman, L. J. (1979). Anhedonia, perceptual aberration, and the Rorschach. *Journal of Consulting and Clinical Psychology, 47*, 377–384.

Erlenmeyer-Kimling, L., Golden, R. R., & Cornblatt, B. A. (1989). A taxonometric analysis of cognitive and neuromotor variables in children at risk for schizophrenia. *Journal of Abnormal Psychology, 98*, 203–208.

Essen-Möller, Larsson, H., Uddenberg, C-E., & White, G. (1956). Individual traits and morbidity in a Swedish rural population. *Acta Psychiatrica et Neurologica Scandinavica* (Suppl. 100).

Everitt, B. S., & Hand, D. J. (1981). *Finite mixture distributions.* New York: Chapman & Hall.

Farmer, A., McGuffin, P., & Gottesman, I. I. (1990). Problems and pitfalls of the family history positive an negative dichotomy: Response to Dalen. *Schizophrenia Bulletin, 16*, 367–370.

Fenton, W. S., & McGlashan, T. H. (1989). Risk of schizophrenia in character disordered patients. *American Journal of Psychiatry, 146*, 1280–1284.

Flaum, M., & Andreasen, N. C. (1995). Brain morphology in schizotypal personality as assessed by magnetic resonance imaging. In A. Raine, T. Lencz, & S. Mednick, (Eds.), *Schizotypal personality* (pp. 385–405). New York: Cambridge University Press.

Franke, P., Maier, W., Hardt, J., & Hain, C. (1993). Cognitive functioning and anhedonia in subjects at risk for schizophrenia. *Schizophrenia Research, 10*, 77–84.

Franke, P., Maier, W., Hardt, J., & Hain, C. (1994). Attentional abilities and measures of schizotypy: Their variation and covariation in schizophrenic patients, their siblings, and normal control subjects. *Psychiatry Research, 54*, 259–272.

Gold, J. M., & Harvey, P. D. (1993). Cognitive deficits in schizophrenia. *Psychiatric Clinics of North America, 16*, 295–312.

Goldman-Rakic, P. S. (1991). Prefrontal cortical dysfunction in schizophrenia: The relevance of working memory. In B. Carroll (Ed.), *Psychopathology and the brain.* Raven Press: New York.

Gottesman, I. I. (1987). The psychotic hinterlands or the fringes of lunacy. *British Medical Bulletin, 43*, 557–569.

Gottesman, I. I. (1991). *Schizophrenia genesis: The origins of madness.* New York: W.H. Freeman.

Gottesman, I. I., & Bertelsen, A. (1989). Confirming unexpressed genotypes for schizophrenia: Risks in the offspring of Fischer's Danish identical and fraternal discordant twins. *Archives of General Psychiatry, 46*, 867–872.

Grace, A. A. (1991). Phasic versus tonic dopamine release and the modulation of dopamine system responsivity: A hypothesis for the etiology of schizophrenia. *Neuroscience, 41*, 1–24.

Grove, W. M. (1982). Psychometric detection of schizotypy. *Psychological Bulletin, 92*, 27–38.

Grove, W. M., Lebow, B. S., Clementz, B. A., Cerri, A., Medus, C., & Iacono, W. G. (1991). Familial prevalence and coaggregation of schizotypy indicators: A multitrait family study. *Journal of Abnormal Psychology, 100*, 115–121.

Gruzelier, J. H. (1996). The factorial structure of schizotypy: Part 1. Affinities with syndromes of schizophrenia. *Schizophrenia Bulletin, 22*, 611–620.

Gur, R. C., & Gur, R. E. (1995). The potential of physiological neuroimaging for the study of schizotypy: Experiences from applications to schizophrenia. In A. Raine, T. Lencz, & S. Mednick (Eds.), *Schizotypal personality* (pp. 406–425). New York: Cambridge University Press.

Halbreich, U., Bakhai, Y., Bacon, K. B., Goldstein, S., Asnis, G. M., Endicott, J., & Lesser, J. (1989). The normalcy of self-proclaimed "normal volunteers." *American Journal of Psychiatry, 146*, 1052–1055.

Hanson, D. R., Gottesman, I. I., & Meehl, P. E. (1977). Genetic theories and the validation of psychiatric diagnosis: Implications for the study of children of schizophrenics. *Journal of Abnormal Psychology, 86*, 575–588.

Harkness, A. R., McNulty, J. L., & Ben-Porath, Y. (1995). The personality pathology five (PSY-5): Constructs and MMPI-2 scales. *Psychological Assessment, 7*, 104–114.

Harvey, P. D., Keefe, R. S. E., Mitroupolou, V., DuPre, R., Roitman, S. L., Mohs, R., & Siever, L. J. (1996). Information-processing markers of vulnerability to schizophrenia: Performance of patients with schizotypal and nonschizotypal personality disorders. *Psychiatry Research, 60*, 49–56.

Holzman, P. S. (1982). The search for a biological marker of the functional psychoses. In M. J. Goldstein (Ed.), *Preventive intervention in schizophrenia: Are we ready?* (DHHS Publication No. ADM 82-1111, pp. 19–38). Washington, DC: U.S. Government Printing Office.

Holzman, P. S. (1990). Comments on Paul Meehl's "Toward an integrated theory of schizotaxia, schizotypy, and schizophrenia. *Journal of Personality Disorders, 4*, 100–105.

Holzman, P. S., Kringlen, E., Matthysse, S., Flanagan, S. D., Lipton, R. B., Cramer, G., Levin, S., Lange, K., & Levy, D. L. (1988). A single dominant gene can account for eye tracking dysfunctions and schizophrenia in offspring of discordant twins. *Archives of General Psychiatry, 45*, 641–647.

Kendler, K. S. (1985). Diagnostic approaches to schizotypal personality disorder: A historical perspective. *Schizophrenia Bulletin, 11*, 538–553.

Kendler, K., & Gruenberg, A. (1982). Genetic relationship between paranoid personality disorder and the "schizophrenic spectrum" disorders. *American Journal of Psychiatry*, 139, 1185–1186.

Kendler, K. S., Gruenberg, A. M., & Kinney, D. K. (1994). Independent diagnoses of adoptees and relatives as defined by DSM-III in the provincial and national samples of the Danish Adoption Study of Schizophrenia. *Archives of General Psychiatry, 51*, 456–468.

Kendler, K. S., & Hewitt, J. (1992). The structure of self-report schizotypy in twins. *Journal of Personality Disorders, 6*, 1–17.

Kendler, K. S., Lieberman, J. A., & Walsh, D. (1989). The structured interview for schizotypy (SIS): A preliminary report. *Schizophrenia Bulletin, 15*, 559–571.

Kendler, K. S., McGuire, M., Gruenberg, A. M., O'Hare, A., Spellman, M., & Walsh, D. (1993). The Roscommon Family Study: III. Schizophrenia-related personality disorders in relatives. *Archives of General Psychiatry, 50*, 781–788.

Kendler, K. S., Ochs, A. L., Gorman, A. M., Hewitt, J. K., Ross, D. E., & Mirsky, A. F. (1991). The structure of schizotypy: A pilot multitrait twin study. *Psychiatry Research, 36*, 19-36.

Kendler, K. S., Thacker, L., & Walsh, D. (1996). Self-report measures of schizotypy as indices of familial vulnerability to schizophrenia. *Schizophrenia Bulletin, 22*, 511–520.

Kendler, K. S., & Walsh, D. (1995). Schizotypal personality disorder in parents and risk for schizophrenia in siblings. *Schizophrenia Bulletin, 21*, 47–52.

Kessler, R., McGonagle, K., Zhao, S., Nelson, C., Hughes, M. Eshleman, S., Wittchen, H-U., & Kendler, K. (1994). Lifetime and 12-month prevalence of DSM-III-R psychiatric disorders in the United States: Results from the National Comorbidity Survey. *Archives of General Psychiatry, 51*, 8–19.

Kety, S. S., Rosenthal, D., Wender, P. H., & Schulsinger, F. (1968). The types and prevalence of mental illness in the biological and adoptive families of adopted schizophrenics. *Journal of Psychiatric Research, 6*, 345–362.

Kety, S. S., Wender, P. H., Jacobsen, B., Ingraham, L. J., Jansson, L., Faber, B., & Kinney, D. K. (1994). Mental illness in the biological and adoptive relatives of schizophrenic adoptees: Replication of the Copenhagen Study in the rest of Denmark. *Archives of General Psychiatry, 51*, 442–455.

Khouri, P. J., Haier, R. J., Rieder, R. O., & Rosenthal, D. (1980). A symptom schedule for the diagnosis of borderline schizophrenia: A first report. *British Journal of Psychiatry, 137*, 140–147.

Korfine, L., & Lenzenweger, M. F. (1995). The taxonicity of schizotypy: A replication. *Journal of Abnormal Psychology, 104*, 26–31.

Kotsaftis, A., & Neale, J. M. (1993). Schizotypal personality disorder I: The clinical syndrome. *Clinical Psychology Review, 13*, 451–472.

Kraepelin, E. (1919/1971). *Dementia praecox and paraphrenia* (R. M. Barclay, Trans., G. M. Robertson, Ed.). Huntington, NY: Krieger. (Original work published 1909–1913; original translation of selected portions published 1919.)

Lazarsfeld, P. F., & Henry, N. W. (1968). *Latent structure analysis.* New York: Houghton Mifflin.

Lencz, T., Raine, A., Scerbo, A., Redmon, M., Brodish, S., Holt, L., & Bird, L. (1993). Impaired eye tracking in undergraduates with schizotypal personality disorder. *American Journal of Psychiatry, 150*, 152–154.

Lenzenweger, M. F. (1991). Confirming schizotypic personality configurations in hypothetically psychosis-prone university students. *Psychiatry Research, 37*, 81–96.

Lenzenweger, M. F. (1993). Explorations in schizotypy and the psychometric high-risk paradigm. In L. J. Chapman, J. P. Chapman, & D. Fowles (Eds.), *Progress in experimental personality and psychopathology research*, #16 (pp. 66–116). New York: Springer.

Lenzenweger, M. F. (1994). The psychometric high-risk paradigm, perceptual aberrations, and schizotypy: An update. *Schizophrenia Bulletin, 20*, 121–135.

Lenzenweger, M. F. (1998). Schizotypy and schizotypic psychopathology: Mapping an alternative expression of schizophrenia liability. In M. F. Lenzenweger & R. H. Dworkin (Eds.), *Origins and development of schizophrenia: Advances in experimental psychopathology* (pp. 93–121). Washington, DC: American Psychological Association.

Lenzenweger, M. F. (in press). *Deeper into the schizotypy taxon: On the robust nature of MAXCOV analysis.* Manuscript submitted for publication. *Journal of Abnormal Psychology.*

Lenzenweger, M. F., Bennett, M. E., & Lilenfeld, L. R. (1997). The referential thinking scale as a measure of schizotypy: Scale development and initial construct validation. *Psychological Assessment, 9*, 452–463.

Lenzenweger, M. F., Cornblatt, B. A., & Putnick, M. E. (1991). Schizotypy and sustained attention. *Journal of Abnormal Psychology, 100*, 84–89.

Lenzenweger, M. F., & Dworkin, R. H. (Eds.). (1998). *Origins and development of schizophrenia: Advances in experimental psychopathology.* Washington, DC: American Psychological Association.

Lenzenweger, M. F., & Dworkin, R. H. (1996). The dimensions of schizophrenia phenomenology? Not one or not two, at least three, perhaps four. *British Journal of Psychiatry, 168*, 432–440.

Lenzenweger, M. F., & Korfine, L. (1991, December). *Schizotypy and Wisconsin Card Sorting Test performance.* Paper presented at the sixth annual meeting of the Society for Research in Psychopathology, Harvard University, Cambridge, MA.

Lenzenweger, M. F., & Korfine, L. (1992a). Confirming the latent structure and base rate of schizotypy: A taxometric analysis. *Journal of Abnormal Psychology, 101*, 567–571.

Lenzenweger, M. F., & Korfine, L. (1992b). Identifying schizophrenia-related personality disorder features in a nonclinical population using a psychometric approach. *Journal of Personality Disorders, 6*, 264–274.

Lenzenweger, M. F., & Korfine, L. (1994). Perceptual aberrations, schizotypy and the Wisconsin Card Sorting Test. *Schizophrenia Bulletin, 20*, 345–357.

Lenzenweger, M. F., & Korfine, L. (1995). Tracking the taxon: On the latent structure and base rate of schizotypy. In A. Raine, T. Lencz, & S. A. Mednick (Eds.), *Schizotypal personality* (pp. 135–167). New York: Cambridge University Press.

Lenzenweger, M. F., & Loranger, A. W. (1989a). Detection of familial schizophrenia using a psychometric measure of schizotypy. *Archives of General Psychiatry, 46*, 902–907.

Lenzenweger, M. F., & Loranger, A. W. (1989b). Psychosis proneness and clinical psychopathology: Examination of the correlates of schizotypy. *Journal of Abnormal Psychology, 98*, 3–8.

Lenzenweger, M. F., Loranger, A. W., Korfine, L., & Neff, C. (1997). Detecting personality disorders in a nonclinical population: Application of a two-stage procedure for case identification. *Archives of General Psychiatry, 54*, 345–351.

Lenzenweger, M. F., & Moldin, S. O. (1990). Discerning the latent structure of hypothetical psychosis proneness through admixture analysis. *Psychiatry Research, 33*, 243–257.

Levin, S. (1984a). Frontal lobe dysfunctions in schizophrenia-I. Eye movement impairments. *Journal of Psychiatric Research, 18*, 27–55.

Levin, S. (1984b). Frontal lobe dysfunctions in schizophrenia-II. Impairments of psychological brain functions. *Journal of Psychiatric Research, 18*, 57–72.

Levy, D. L., Holzman, P. S., Matthysse. S., & Mendell, R. (1993). Eye tracking dysfunction and schizophrenia: A critical perspective. *Schizophrenia Bulletin, 19*, 461–536.

Levy, D. L., Holzman, P. S., Matthysse, S., & Mendell, N. R. (1994). Eye tracking and schizophrenia: A selective review. *Schizophrenia Bulletin, 20*, 47–62.

Loranger, A. (1988). *The Personality Disorder Examination (PDE) manual*. Yonkers, NY: DV Communications.

Loranger, A. (1990). The impact of DSM-III on diagnostic practice in a university hospital: A comparison of DSM-II and DSM-III in 10,914 patients. *Archives of General Psychiatry, 47*, 672–675.

Loranger, A. (1991). Diagnosis of personality disorders: General considerations. In R. Michels, A. Cooper, S. Guze, L. Judd, G. Klerman, A. Solnit, & A. Stunkard (Eds.), *Psychiatry* (Rev. Ed.), (Vol. 1; pp. 1–14). New York: Lippincott.

Loranger, A., Lenzenweger, M., Gartner, A., Susman, V., Herzig, J., Zammit, G., Gartner, J., Abrams, R., & Young, R. (1991). Trait-state artifacts and the diagnosis of personality disorders. *Archives of General Psychiatry, 48*, 720–728.

Loranger, A. W., Sartorius, N., Andreoli, A., Berger, P., Channabasavanna, S. M., Coid, B., Dahl, A., Diekstra, R. F. W., Ferguson, B., Jacobsberg, L. B., Mombour, W., Pull, C., Ono, Y., & Regier, D. (1994). The International Personality Disorder Examination (IPDE): The World Health Organization/Alcohol, Drug Abuse, and Mental Health Administration International Pilot Study of Personality Disorders. *Archives of General Psychiatry, 51*, 215–224.

Loranger, A. W., Sartorius, N., & Janca, A. (Eds.), *Assessment and diagnosis of personality disorders: The International Personality Disorder Examination (IPDE)*. New York: Cambridge University Press.

Maier, W., Lichtermann, D., Klingler, T., Heun, R., & Hallmayer, J. (1992). Prevalences of personality disorders (DSM-III-R) in the community. *Journal of Personality Disorders, 6*, 187–192.

Mason, O. (1995). A confirmatory factor analysis of the structure of schizotypy. *European Journal of Personality, 9*, 271–281.

Matthysse, S., Holzman, P. S., & Lange, K. (1986). The genetic transmission of schizophrenia: Application of Mendelian latent structure analysis to eye tracking dysfunctions in schizophrenia and affective disorder. *Journal of Psychiatric Research, 20*, 57–67.

Meehl, P. E. (1962). Schizotaxia, schizotypy, schizophrenia. *American Psychologist, 17*, 827–838.

Meehl, P. E. (1964). *Manual for use with Checklist of Schizotypic Signs*. Minneapolis, MN: University of Minnesota.

Meehl, P. E. (1971). High school yearbooks: A reply to Schwarz. *Journal of Abnormal Psychology, 77*, 143–148.

Meehl, P. E. (1972). Specific genetic etiology, psychodynamics, and therapeutic nihilism. International *Journal of Mental Health, 1*, 10–27.

Meehl, P. E. (1973). MAXCOV-HITMAX: A taxonomic search method for loose genetic syndromes. In P. E. Meehl, *Psychodiagnosis: Selected papers* (pp. 200–224). Minneapolis, MN: University of Minnesota Press.

Meehl, P. E. (1974). Hedonic capacity: Some conjectures. *Bulletin of the Menninger Clinic, 39*, 295–307.

Meehl, P. E. (1990). Toward an integrated theory of schizotaxia, schizotypy, and schizophrenia. *Journal of Personality Disorders, 4*, 1–99.

Meehl, P. E. (1992). Factors and taxa, traits and types, differences of degree and differences in kind. *Journal of Personality, 60*, 117–174.

Meehl, P. E., & Yonce, L. J. (1996). Taxometric analysis: II. Detecting taxonicity using covariance of two quantitative indicators in successive intervals of a third indicator (MAXCOV procedure). *Psychological Reports* (Monograph Suppl. 1-V78).

Miller, M. B., & Chapman, J. P. (1993). *A twin study of schizotypy in college-age males*. Presented at the Eighth Annual meeting of the Society for Research in Psychopathology, Chicago, October 7–10.

Millon, T., & Davis, R. (1996). *Disorders of personality: DSM-IV and beyond* (2nd ed.). New York: John Wiley.

Moldin, S. O., Gottesman, I. I., & Erlenmeyer-Kimling, L. (1987a). Psychometric validation of psychiatric diagnoses in the New York High-Risk Study. *Psychiatry Research, 22*, 159–177.

Moldin, S. O., Gottesman, I. I., & Erlenmeyer-Kimling, L. (1987b). Searching for the psychometric boundaries of schizophrenia: Evidence from the New York High-Risk Study. *Journal of Abnormal Psychology, 96*, 354–363.

Moldin, S. O., Gottesman, I. I., Erlenmeyer-Kimling, L., & Cornblatt, B. A. (1990). Psychometric deviance in offspring at risk for schizophrenia: I. Initial delineation of a distinct subgroup. *Psychiatry Research, 32*, 297–310.

Moldin, S. O., Rice, J. P., Gottesman, I. I., & Erlenmeyer-Kimling, L. (1990a). Psychometric deviance in offspring at risk for schizophrenia: II. Resolving heterogeneity through admixture analysis. *Psychiatry Research, 32*, 311–322.

Moldin, S. O., Rice, J. P., Gottesman, I. I., & Erlenmeyer-Kimling, L. (1990b). Transmission of a psychometric indicator for liability to schizophrenia in normal families. *Genetic Epidemiology, 7*, 163–176.

Moldin, S. O., & Van Eerdewegh, P. (1995). Multivariate genetic analysis of an oligogenic disease. *Genetic Epidemiology, 12*, 801–806.

Morey, L. C., Waugh, M. H., & Blashfield, R. K. (1985). MMPI scales for DSM-III personality disorders: Their derivation and correlates. *Journal of Personality Assessment, 49*, 245–251.

Morton, N. E., & MacLean, C. J. (1974). Analysis of family resemblance. III. Complex segregation of quantitative traits. *American Journal of Human Genetics, 26*, 489–503.

Murphy, E. A. (1964). One cause? Many causes? The argument from the bimodal distribution. *Journal of Chronic Diseases, 17*, 301–324.

Neale, J. M., & Oltmanns, T. F. (1980). *Schizophrenia*. New York: John Wiley.

Nigg, J., & Goldsmith, H. (1994). Genetics of personality disorders: Perspectives from psychology and psychopathology research. *Psychological Bulletin, 115*, 346–380.

Nuechterlein, K. H. (1987). Vulnerability models for schizophrenia: State of the art. In H. Hfner, W. F. Gattaz, & W. Janzarik (Eds.), *Search for the causes of schizophrenia* (pp. 295–316). New York: Springer-Verlag.

Nuechterlein, K. H., Subotnik, K. L. (1998). The cognitive origins of schizophrenia and prospects for intervention. In T. Wykes, N. Tarrier, & S. Lewis (Eds.), *Outcome and innovation in psychological treatment of schizophrenia* (pp. 17–41). Chichester, England: John Wiley.

Nuechterlein, K. H., & Subotnik, K. L. (in press). The cognitive origins of schizophrenia and prospects for intervention. In T. Wykes, N. Tarrier, & S. Lewis (Eds.), *Outcome and innovation in the psychological treatment of schizophrenia*. Chichester, England: John Wiley.

Obiols, J. E., Garcia-Domingo, M., de Trincheria, I., & Domenech, E. (1993). Psychometric schizotypy and sustained attention in young males. *Personality and Individual Differences, 14*, 381–384.

O'Driscoll, G., Lenzenweger, M. F., & Holzman, P. S. (1998). Antisaccades and smooth pursuit eye tracking performance and schizotypy. *Archives of General Psychiatry, 55*, 837–843.

Park, S., Holzman, P. S., & Lenzenweger, M. F. (1995). Individual differences in working memory in relation to schizotypy. *Journal of Abnormal Psychology, 104*, 355–363.

Park, S., Holzman, P. S., & Levy, D. L. (1993). Spatial working memory deficit in the relatives of schizophrenic patients is associated with their smooth pursuit eye tracking performance. *Schizophrenia Research, 9*, 185.

Perry, J. (1992). Problems and considerations in the valid assessment of personality disorders. *American Journal of Psychiatry, 149*, 1645–1653.

Pfohl, B., Coryell, W., Zimmerman, M., & Stangl, D. (1986). DSM-III personality disorders: Diagnostic overlap and internal consistency of individual DSM-III criteria. *Comprehensive Psychiatry, 27*, 21–34.

Planansky, K. (1972). Phenotypic boundaries and genetic specificity in schizophrenia. In A. R. Kaplan (Ed.), Genetic factors in "schizophrenia" (pp. 141–172). Springfield, IL: Charles C. Thomas.

Rado, S. (1953). Dynamics and classification of disordered behavior. *American Journal of Psychiatry, 110*, 406–416.

Rado, S. (1960). Theory and therapy: The theory of schizotypal organization and its application to the treatment of decompensated schizotypal behavior. In S. C. Scher & H. R. Davis (Eds.), *The outpatient treatment of schizophrenia* (pp. 87–101). New York: Grune and Stratton.

Raine, A. (1991). The SPQ: A scale for the assessment of schizotypal personality disorder based on DSM-III-R criteria. *Schizophrenia Bulletin, 17*, 555–564.

Raine, A., Lencz, T., & Mednick, S. (1995). *Schizotypal personality*. New York: Cambridge University Press.

Raine, A., Reynolds, C., Lencz, T., Scerbo, A., Triphon, N., & Kim, D. (1994). Cognitive-perceptual, interpersonal, and disorganized features of schizotypal personality. *Schizophrenia Bulletin, 20*, 191–201.

Raine, A., Sheard, C., Reynolds, G., & Lencz, T. (1992). Pre-frontal structural and functional deficits associated with individual differences in schizotypal personality. *Schizophrenia Research, 7*, 237–247.

Raulin, M. L., & Wee, J. L. (1984). The development and initial validation of a scale to measure social fear. *Journal of Clinical Psychology, 40*, 780–784.

Robins, L., Helzer, J., Weissman, M., Orvaschel, H., Gruenberg, E., Burke, J., & Regier, D.

(1984). Lifetime prevalence of specific psychiatric disorders in three sites. *Archives of General Psychiatry, 41*, 949–958.

Rust, J. (1988a). *The handbook of the Rust Inventory of Schizotypal Cognitions (RISC)*. London: Psychological Corporation.

Rust, J. (1988b). The Rust Inventory of Schizotypal Cognitions (RISC). *Schizophrenia Bulletin, 14*, 317–322.

Scarone, S., Abbruzzese, M., & Gambini, O. (1993). The Wisconsin Card Sorting Test discriminates schizophrenic patients and their siblings. *Schizophrenia Research, 10*, 103–107.

Shields, J., Heston, L. I., & Gottesman, I. I. (1975). Schizophrenia and the schizoid: The problem for genetic analysis. In R. R. Fieve, D. Rosenthal, & H. Brill (Eds.), *Genetic research in psychiatry* (pp. 167–197). Baltimore: Johns Hopkins University Press.

Siever, L. J. (1995). Brain structure/function and the dopamine system in schizotypal personality disorder. In A. Raine, T. Lencz, & S. Mednick (Eds.), *Schizotypal personality* (pp. 272–286). New York: Cambridge University Press.

Siever, L. J., Bernstein, D. P., & Silverman, J. M. (1991). Schizotypal personality disorder: A review of its current status. *Journal of Personality Disorder, 5*, 178–193.

Siever, L. J., Friedman, L., Moskowitz, J., Mitropoulou, V., Keefe, R., Roitman, S. L., Merhige, D., Trestman, R., Silverman, J., & Mohs, R. (1994). Eye movement impairment and schizotypal psychopathology. *American Journal of Psychiatry, 151*, 1209–1215.

Siever, L. J., & Gunderson, J. G. (1983). The search for a schizotypal personality: Historical origins and current status. *Comprehensive Psychiatry, 24*, 199–212.

Siever, L. J., Keefe, R., Bernstein, D. P., Coccaro, E. F., Klar, H. M., Zemishlany, Z., Peterson, A. E., Davidson, M., Mahon, T., Horvath, T., & Mohs, R. (1990). Eye tracking impairment in clinically identified patients with schizotypal personality disorder. *American Journal of Psychiatry, 147*, 740–745.

Siever, L., Kalus, O., & Keefe, R. (1993). The boundaries of schizophrenia. *The Psychiatric Clinics of North America, 16*, 217–244.

Silbersweig, D. A., Stern, E., Frith, C., Cahill, C., Holmes, A., Grootoonk, S., Seaward, J., McKenna, P., Chua, S. E., Schnorr, L., Jones, T., & Frackowiak, R. S. J. (1995). A functional neuroanatomy of hallucinations in schizophrenia. *Nature, 378*, 176–179.

Simons, R. F., & Katkin, W. (1985). Smooth pursuit eye movements in subjects reporting physical anhedonia and perceptual aberrations. *Psychiatry Research, 14*, 275–289.

Smith, C., & Mendell, N. R. (1974). Recurrence risks from family history and metric traits. *Annuals of Human Genetics, 37*, 275–286.

Spitzer, R. L., Endicott, J., & Gibbon, M. (1979). Crossing the border into borderline personality and borderline schizophrenia: The development of criteria. *Archives of General Psychiatry, 36*, 17–24.

Stangl, D., Pfohl, B., Zimmerman, M., Bowers, W., & Corenthal, A. (1985). A structured interview for the DSM-III personality disorders: A preliminary report. *Archives of General Psychiatry, 42*, 591–596.

Stone, M. H. (1993). *Abnormalities of personality: Within and beyond the realm of treatment*. New York: Norton.

Thaker, G. K., Cassady, S., Adami, H., & Moran, M. (1996). Eye movements in spectrum personality disorder: Comparison of community subjects and relatives of schizophrenic patients. *American Journal of Psychiatry, 153*, 362–368.

Thaker, G. K., Moran, M., Lahti, A., Adami, H., & Tamminga, C. (1990). Psychiatric morbidity in research volunteers [letter]. *Archives of General Psychiatry, 47*, 980.

Torgersen, S. (1985). Relationship of schizotypal personality disorder to schizophrenia: Genetics. *Schizophrenia Bulletin, 11*, 554–563.

Torgersen, S. (1994). Personality deviations within the schizophrenia spectrum. *Acta Psychiatrica Scandinavica, 90*, (Suppl. 384), 40–44.

Venables, P. H. (1990). The measurement of schizotypy in Mauritius. *Personality and Individual Differences, 11*, 965–971.

Webb, C. T., & Levinson, D. F. (1993). Schizotypal and paranoid personality disorder in the relative of patients with schizophrenia and affective disorders: A review. *Schizophrenia Research, 11*, 81–92.

Weinberger, D. R. (1987). Implications of normal brain development for the pathogenesis of schizophrenia. *Archives of General Psychiatry, 44*, 660–669.

Weinberger, D. R., Berman, K. F., & Zec, R. F. (1986). Physiologic dysfunction ofdorsolateral prefrontal cortex in schizophrenics I. Regional cerebral blood flow evidence. *Archives of General Psychiatry, 43*, 114–124.

Weissman, M. (1993). The epidemiology of personality disorders: A 1990 update. *Journal of Personality Disorders, 7* (Suppl. spring), 44–62.

Zimmerman, M., & Coryell, W. (1990). Diagnosing personality disorders in the community: A comparison of self-report and interview measures. *Archives of General Psychiatry, 47*, 527–531.

25

Borderline Personality Disorder

JOEL PARIS

Borderline personality disorder (BPD) presents a serious challenge to clinicians. Its definition in *DSM-IV* requires the presence of five of nine specified criteria. Some of these describe impulsivity (unstable relationships, self-damaging actions, inappropriate anger, or suicidal threats), while others reflect emotional reactivity (affective instability, identity disturbance, emptiness or boredom, and frantic efforts to avoid abandonment). A new criterion, added only in *DSM-IV*, derives from a third domain, the cognitive or quasi-psychotic aspects of the syndrome (transient stress-related paranoid ideation or severe dissociative symptoms).

BPD is also included in *ICD-10*, but as a subtype of the larger category of emotionally unstable personality disorder. The *ICD* definition is very similar to that in *DSM*, but instead of counting a predetermined number of criteria, *ICD* describes the characteristic features of a disorder and asks the clinician to judge whether the patient's difficulties approximate this prototype.

Let us review the essential psychopathological features of BPD, which also reflect the underlying dimensions of the disorder:

- *Impulsivity* The most characteristic feature of borderline pathology is an impulsive reaction to dysphoria, usually associated with rebuffs or abandonment. Borderline patients relieve their dysphoria through action, often through self-cutting or overdosing. Although depressed patients may slash their wrists as part of a suicidal gesture or attempt, borderline patients cut repetitively. When blood flows, patients usually feel better for a while, probably because the distraction effectively reduces dysphoria (Leibenluft, Gardner, & Cowdry, 1987). Cutting oneself can therefore take on many of the characteristics of an addiction (Linehan, 1993). Similarly, patients may take pills after an altercation or an abandonment by a significant other. Overdoses are the most common reason for borderline patients to go to a hospital (Hull, Yeomans, Clarkin, Li, & Goodman, 1996). Other forms of impulsive action common in BPD include substance abuse, the destruction of property, reckless driving, eating binges, and sexual promiscuity.

  While the above are comparatively dramatic manifestations of the disorder, borderline impulsivity also takes more subtle interpersonal forms. Patients with BPD easily become involved with people, and just as easily become disappointed and disillusioned with them. These behaviors reflect the "image-distorting" defense styles, which have been shown to be particularly common in borderline patients (Bond, Paris, & Zweig-Frank, 1994). The most important of these is splitting (Kernberg, 1975), in which people are seen as all good or all bad, or in which the same person is seen as good or bad at different times. Clearly, such schemata interfere with stable attachments. As such, borderline patients tend to alternate between feeling totally abandoned and feeling engulfed by other people (Melges & Swartz, 1989). Their behavior in therapy reflects the same instability and impulsivity; the majority of borderline patients drop out of open-ended psychotherapeutic treatment within a few months (Skodol, Buckley, & Charles, 1983; Gunderson, Frank, Ronningstam, Wahter, Lynch, & Wolf, 1989).

- *Affective Instability* The moods of borderline patients can change radically, even in the course of a day. Patients can be suicidally depressed for a few hours, yet upon meeting someone who cheers them up, become almost euphoric. These rapid mood changes are sometimes mistaken by clinicians for bipolar mood disorder. However, the time scale of mood changes in BPD is not weeks to months, but hours. Unlike classical mood disorders, affect in BPD is highly responsive to environmental changes (Gunderson & Phillips, 1991). Borderline patients experience their emotions as determined by events they feel helpless to influence.

  Although borderline patients experience a great deal of anger and anxiety, their baseline mood is usually characterized by dysthymia and emptiness. Most patients describe this state as intolerable, and may act out impulsively to escape from it.
- *Cognitive Symptoms* A large number of borderline patients have cognitive symptoms (Zanarini, Gunderson, & Frankenburg, 1989a). Since many BPD patients hear voices, they may at times be mistaken for schizophrenics. Borderline patients, however, know that their hallucinations come from their own mind and do not respond to them with delusional elaboration. Voices may tell them that they are bad or be "command hallucinations" instructing them to commit suicide. Patients with BPD can sometimes have elaborate visual hallucinations, similar to those produced by hallucinogenic substances. A second type of cognitive disturbance involves paranoid ideas. Some borderline patients have brief psychotic episodes, but in most cases paranoid thinking remains at subdelusional levels. A third type of cognitive disturbance involves dissociative episodes. Although amnesias are rare, many patients describe a continuous feeling of painful depersonalization in which they feel estranged from themselves and their environment.

Case Examples

Let us exemplify the construct with brief clinical examples of three borderline patients who demonstrate many of the features described above:

Case 1: Jeanne was a high school student who requested treatment after the death her best friend, Carla, who had also been treated for borderline personality disorder at the same clinic, and had just jumped off a bridge. Although Jeanne refused to join in a suicide pact proposed by Carla, she had been suicidal in her own right for several years. She carried out recurrent wrist slashing and often fantasized about killing herself. Jeanne had an intense fantasy, bordering on a delusion, that her life was a dream and that she was living on another planet, where she had another existence and a real family. She thought that if she were dead, she would wake up and return to her true home. She would hear the voices of individual characters in this fantasy asking her to join them.

Jeanne had a very traumatic childhood. While the first five years of her life were spent in a foster home, this proved to be a positive atmosphere that protected her against later negative experiences. Upon returning to her parents, she had to cope with an alcoholic mother and a father who incestuously abused her. After attempting suicide by jumping off a balcony, she was seen in a child psychiatry clinic. Although she later ran away from home and lived with her older sister, both her parents remained disturbingly present in her life.

Although Jeanne had not had any relationships with men, she had formed a series of intense and unstable relationships with women. Her attachment to Carla was based largely on their shared suicidality and depression. Her moods were highly unstable and reactive, and she could be depressed, elated, anxious, or furious in the course of a single day, depending on the circumstances. Her impulsivity expressed itself through slashing her wrists every time something upsetting happened.

Case 2: Anne was a 22-year-old woman who presented for therapy because of intense suicidal ideation and disturbed interpersonal relationships. Although she was notably competent in her profession and had good friends, her intimate attachments with men were highly problematic. Several boyfriends were criminals, whom she would hide from the police at her apartment. She had become pregnant by one of these men and obtained an abortion about which, given her strong Catholic upbringing, she felt very guilty.

Anne had continuous ideas of suicide, which she readily communicated to other people, but did not act on. She also complained of depersonalization, continuous feelings of unreality about herself and the world around her. She found that her moods were strongly affected by events, particularly whether she felt cared for by others.

Anne's childhood was marked by the death of her mother when she was 7. Her alcoholic father was unable to look after her, and she entered foster care. Although her foster parents were religious and highly devoted people, she found them cold, and fantasized that her father would someday rescue her. When she at length decided to seek out her father, and found him to be a chronic alcoholic with little interest in her, she became depressed and briefly developed delusional ideas.

Case 3: Maxine, a 20-year-old woman, was admitted to the hospital after slashing her wrists and overdosing on aspirin. Although a brilliant student and an accomplished musician, she had never been able to achieve any meaningful relationships. Since childhood she had felt deeply alone in life. Her parents were well-meaning but insensitive, and had never been able to understand her emotional needs.

Most recently, Maxine had been abandoned by a boyfriend after a brief and unsuccessful love affair. Over the next few years, she attempted to obtain treatment from a variety of competent clinicians. Each time, she left therapy feeling angry and disappointed. She attended school and was able to obtain a good position after graduation, but continued to slash her wrists and take overdoses after disappointments in relationships.

Reliability and Validity of the Borderline Diagnosis

As these case examples show, the borderline construct describes a group of patients with a characteristic clinical presentation. However, the *DSM* definition has been criticized on several grounds: that it was written by a committee, that it combines several theoretical perspectives, and that it allows too many ways to reach the same diagnosis (Clarkin, Widiger, Frances, Hurt, & Gilmore, 1983). Some argue that empirical studies are needed to make each criterion more specific to the diagnosis (Gunderson, Zanarini, & Kisiel, 1991). Like most other Axis II disorders, BPD suffers from unclear boundaries.

Using the "gold standard" for the validity of any psychiatric diagnosis suggested by Robins and Guze (1970), BPD has been well studied phenomenologically and has a characteristic clinical course and outcome, but is not associated with specific biological markers, overlaps with other disorders on both Axis I and Axis II, and is not consistently familial (Paris, 1994a). However, hardly any of the diagnoses in *DSM* or *ICD* meet these stringent criteria, and the problems with the validity of BPD are endemic to *all* categories of mental illness. Mental disorders are best understood as "fuzzy sets," descriptive-level syndromes ranging in severity from normality to clear psychopathology.

One way to increase diagnostic reliability is to use semistructured interviews, such as the Structured Clinical Interview for Diagnosis, Axis II (SCID-II; Spitzer & Williams, 1986), the Structured Interview for Diagnosis of Personality Disorders (SIDP; Pfohl, Coryell, Zimmerman, & Stangl, 1986), the Personality Disorder Examination (PDE; Loranger, Susman, Oldham, & Russakoff, 1987), and the Diagnostic Interview for Personality Disorders (DIPD; Zanarini, Frankenburg, Chauncey, & Gunderson, 1987). Unfortunately, these measures appear to diagnose different subjects as borderline (Perry, 1992). Some researchers prefer the Diagnostic Interview for Borderlines (DIB; Gunderson & Kolb, 1978), an interview specifically designed to make a borderline diagnosis. In its revised version (DIB-R; Zanarini, Gunderson, & Frankenburg, 1989a), the answers to 136 questions are scored on four scales: affect, cognition, impulsivity, and interpersonal relationships, with a heavier weighting given to the latter two scales. The presence of BPD is then defined by achieving 8 out of a total 10-point scale.

Structured interviews, such as the DIB-R, can also discriminate BPD from depression, from schizophrenia, and from other personality disorders. Loranger et al. (1994), using an interview measure called the International Personality Disorders Examination (IDPE), have shown that BPD is the most common personality disorder in clinical settings around the world.

One of the potentially problematic characteristics of the DSM system is that there are no *required* criteria for any personality diagnosis. Making a diagnosis that is based on *any* 5 out of 9 possible criteria, as one is required for BPD, has been called a "Chinese menu" approach (Frances & Widiger, 1986). Clinicians diagnose personality disorders this way in practice, working with a *prototype* (Livesley, Schroeder, Jackson, & Jang, 1994), and looking for features that resemble it.

For example, the clinical prototype of BPD that most clinicians use (Morey & Ochoa, 1989) gives a stronger weighting to impulsive actions and unstable relationships than to other criteria. A definition of BPD based on this prototype would give stronger weight to its most typical features rather than simply listing and counting them, but clinicians cannot agree precisely on what the prototype of BPD should be. In the absence of strong empirical data, the criteria have remained unweighted. One recent change in the definition in *DSM-IV* is the addition of a criterion for the presence of micropsychotic or dissociative phenomena. These symptoms have been shown to discriminate BPD from other personality disorders (Zanarini, Gunderson, & Frankenburg, 1989b, 1990a, 1990b), and may be the only features that truly lie on a "borderline" with psychosis.

Some theorists (Costa & Widiger, 1994; Livesley et al., 1994) suggest that the problems with the validity of the diagnoses on Axis II might be solved by replacing categories with scores on personality dimensions. For research purposes, dimensions are often more useful, since they correlate better with biological factors (Siever & Davis, 1991). If we could define which personality traits or dimensions seen in normal individuals are abnormal in BPD, we would have a better grounding for a definition. In the absence of consistent data of this sort, the categories of mental disorder only provide meaningful clusters of symptoms about which clinicians can readily communicate.

Ultimately, however, until we understand the etiology of the personality disorders, all phenomenologically based classifications will continue to be inadequate. The present *DSM* criteria for BPD are a compromise, reflecting several clinical traditions. Thus, BPD is best viewed as a *syndrome*, the co-occurrence of symptoms that can be produced by many different psychopathological processes. A similar example from physical medicine is congestive heart failure. When present, it has a defined clinical course, but nevertheless arises from many etiological sources. In contrast, disorders such as myocardial infarction have a specific etiology as well as a specific course,. One might say that until we know the etiology of BPD, it is premature to call it a disorder. Unfortunately, this criticism applies to almost every category in DSM!

Future classifications of mental disorders should, and probably will derive from biological rather than phenomenological differences (Paris, 1999; Siever & Davis, 1991). Moreover, as we begin to understand the etiology and pathogenesis of BPD, it might be subdivided into homogeneous subgroups. In that case, clinicians and researchers might eventually discard the present construct. Alternatively, future research might provide support for the validity of BPD as a diagnostic entity. The best we can do now, until there is a better alternative, is to continue using the present classification.

Whatever the ultimate status of the borderline construct, it functions as a useful means of communication among clinicians. What the diagnosis needs is better discriminant validity, which should be reflected in improved *DSM* criteria. The problem is that doing so incurs a cost, since even the smallest change in criteria can cause major discontinuities in diagnosis, which then lead to disruptive effects on clinical research (Zimmerman, 1994). This is why in the most recent revision, *DSM-IV*, the authors left criteria essentially as they were unless there were strong empirical reasons to change them.

In spite of these problems, BPD is a sufficiently meaningful clinical construct so that therapists who work with personality disordered patients can sometimes make the diagnosis within minutes of meeting the patient. Moreover, in practice, a borderline diagnosis predicts important aspects of clinical course, as well as response to treatment.

Prevalence

Epidemiology

The prevalence of BPD was not determined in the ECA study, or in the recent National Comorbidity Survey. Other data (Swartz, Blazer, George, & Winfield, 1990; Ross, 1991; Reich, Yates, & Nduaguba, 1989), using either interview or questionnaire measures, have suggested that BPD affects between 1 and 2% of the general population.

Although Swartz et al. (1990) did not find a significant relationship between BPD and social class, Dohrenwend and Dohrenwend (1969) have described an overall relationship between personality pathology and social class. In general, severe personality disorders that arise early in life interfere with education and social competence. For example, in our follow-up sample of borderline patients (Paris, Brown, & Nowlis, 1987), more than half the cases fell in the lower socioeconomic levels, since so many failed to complete high school and did not resume their education.

Clinical observations (Gunderson, 1984), and community studies (Swartz et al., 1990) show that approximately three quarters of borderline patients are women. Although males and females with BPD have few differences in phenomenology (Paris, 1994a) or in risk factors (Paris, Zweig-Frank, & Guzder, 1994b), such gender differences require an explanation. Stone (1993) has suggested that since sexual abuse is more common in females, so is BPD. However, only a minority of women with BPD have experienced severe sexual abuse (Paris, 1994). Another possibility is that since the clinical prototype emphasizes an affective component (Kroll, 1988), and since depression is more common in women, we inevitably see more women with BPD. A third possibility is that BPD is a gender-linked subtype of a broader category. For example, antisocial personality is as predominantly male as borderline personality disorder is predominantly female (Robins & Regier, 1991). These two diagnoses might be aspects of the same underlying psychopathology, differentiated by the strength of their affective components, as well as by whether impulsivity is directed against other people or oneself (Paris, 1997).

Comorbidity

When substantial comorbidity is present, a question arises concerning whether one disorder is actually a subset or subtype of the other, or whether both represent aspects of a single larger disorder. For example, frequent Axis I comorbidity with the mood disorders could mean that borderline pathology is itself a form of depression (Akiskal, Chen, & Davis, 1985). However, in a recent review, Gunderson and Phillips (1991) rejected this hypothesis. First, although there is comorbidity between BPD and major depression or dysthymia, Axis I comorbidities exist for all other personality disorders. Second, BPD is infrequent among depressed patients, suggesting that the relationship between BPD and depression is nonspecific. Third, the phenomenology of depression is different in borderline and nonborderline patients, in that BPD patients describe more emptiness and loneliness, and have mood changes that are more environmentally responsive. Fourth, family history studies support a link between mood disorder and BPD only for cases with comorbid depression. Fifth, BPD patients do not respond to antidepressants in the same way as those with affective disorders do. Sixth, there are no clear-cut biological markers for BPD, and those shared with depression, such as decreased REM latency, are only present when the patient shows major depression or dysthymia. Finally, there is stronger evidence for environmental factors in the etiology of BPD than for mood disorders. On the basis of these findings, Gunderson and Phillips concluded that BPD and depression co-occur but are not otherwise related.

Researchers have often assumed that, when Axis I and Axis II disorders coexist, the Axis I disorder must have etiological primacy. Certainly depression exaggerates and distorts personality characteristics (Frances & Widiger, 1986). On the other hand, it is equally important to consider how personality disorders influence mood. Moreover, depression is not simply a function of biological vulnerability, but is elicited by environmental triggers, such as the pathological interpersonal relations seen in borderline patients.

Comorbidity can obscure the need for broader constructs that organize and give meaning to complex patterns of psychopathology. Undoubtedly, borderline patients have multiple Axis I comorbid diagnoses (Zanarini, Frankenburg, Dubo, & Sickel, 1998a). In fact, clinical experience suggests that the more Axis I diagnoses the patient has received in their chart, the more one should consider whether the patient has BPD. Yet, it may not be meaningful to make multiple diagnoses of anxiety disorders, mood disorders, and substance abuse in the same patient when a single organizing construct, BPD, makes sense of all the symptoms. Since its comorbid Axis I disorders appear to be a predictable consequence of the disorder, the borderline construct functions as a better predictor of treatment response.

Another challenge to the construct of BPD has come from trauma research. On the basis of studies showing that histories of child abuse are common in BPD, Herman and van der Kolk (1987) suggested that cases of BPD with such histories should be reclassified as chronic post-traumatic stress disorder (PTSD). This perspective has obtained a certain currency among clinicians. Kroll (1993) has even gone so far as to talk about "PTSD/borderline" patients. However, given our lack of knowledge about the etiology of BPD, this view is quite unjustified. PTSD is one of the few Axis I diagnoses in which a causal factor is built into its definition. To redefine BPD as a form of PTSD assumes we know the etiology of BPD, when in fact we do not. Moreover, as pointed out by Gunderson and Sabo (1993), there are important phenomenological differences between BPD and PTSD. The problem is that when patients present with a history of childhood trauma, clinicians may interpret characteristic features of borderline pathology as "posttraumatic."

What is more problematical is that BPD is highly comorbid with other Axis II diagnoses (Pfohl et al., 1986; Nurnberg, Raskin, Levine, Pollack, Siegel, & Prince 1991; Oldham, Skodol, Kellman, Hyler, Rosnick, & Davies, 1992; Zanarini, Frankenburg, Dubo, & Sickel, 1998b). However, this observation is likely an artifact of the diagnostic rules in *DSM*, which encourage rather than discourage multiple diagnoses. In practice, most clinicians do not entertain any other personality diagnosis once they recognize BPD in a patient (Morey & Ochoa, 1989; Westen, 1997). If we were to restrict multiple Axis II diagnoses, using only that diagnosis where the largest number of criteria were satisfied, comorbidity would markedly diminish.

Course and Outcome

Borderline personality is a disorder of youth. It begins in adolescence, peaks in young adulthood, and usually burns out by middle age.

The antecedents of borderline pathology in childhood are not known. Although child psychiatrists have described a category called the "borderline child" (Robson, 1983), and these children have risk factors similar to those seen in adult borderline patients (Goldman, D'Angelo, Demaso, & Mezzacappa, 1992; Guzder, Paris, Zelkowitz, & Marchessault, 1996; Guzder, Paris, Zelkowitz, & Feldman, in press), these children do not necessarily develop borderline pathology as adults. In fact, borderline children go on to develop a wide variety of personality disorders (Petti & Vela, 1990). In addition, most of these children are boys rather than girls, reversing the well-known gender distribution of BPD in adults.

On the other hand, when personality disorders are diagnosed in adolescence, they can be expected to continue into adulthood (Bernstein, Cohen, Skodol, Bezirganian, & Brook, 1996). Although the borderline diagnosis is not necessarily stable in adolescence, it seems to describe the same clinical phenomena as in adults (Pinto, Grapentine, Francis, & Piccariello, 1996). Four *DSM* criteria (anger, suicidal threats, identity disturbance, and emptiness) predict the continuance of borderline pathology in adolescents (Garnet, Levy, Mattanah, Edell, & McGlashan, 1994).

Many years ago, Schmideberg (1959) described the course of borderline personality as "stably unstable." Some recent evidence suggests that borderline patients in treatment can improve after a few years (Najavits & Gunderson, 1995; Sabo, Gunderson, Najavits, Chauncey, & Kiesel, 1995). However, at five-year follow-up, chronicity remains the rule, with most borderline patients showing very little change (Werble, 1970; Carpenter, Gunderson, & Strauss, 1977; Pope, Jonas, & Hudson, 1983).

Four research groups (McGlashan, 1985, 1986; Stone, 1990; Paris et al., 1987, Paris, Nowlis, & Brown, 1988; Plakun, Burkhardt, & Muller, 1986) have followed borderline patients for 15 years, and a fifth group (Silver & Cardish, 1991) has reported a 10-year follow-up. There was a remarkable concordance among all these studies, in spite of the fact that the samples were very different.

All these data show that, in the majority of cases, BPD remits by early middle age. After 15 years, the majority of patients no longer had acute symptoms, and most of them (75%) no longer met the diagnostic criteria for BPD (Paris et al., 1987). Although all of these follow-up studies were retrospective, a prospective study (Links, Mitton, Steiner, & Eppel, 1990) has largely confirmed their findings, with about a third of patients being no longer diagnosable after seven years, a rate of recovery that would have probably been higher with a longer follow-up.

This long-term improvement is most likely a naturalistic outcome, rather than a treatment effect. There have been no studies of the long-term effectiveness of any form of therapy in borderline patients, so that we do not know whether long courses of therapy are useful, or whether they are useful only in specific patient groups (Paris, 1994a). However, short-term improvements in BPD, involving declines in impulsive suicidal behavior have been described, both in uncontrolled trials (Najavits & Gunderson, 1995) and in controlled clinical trials (Linehan, 1993). On the other hand, other dimensions of the disorder, particularly affective dysphoria and pathological relationships, have not shown any striking improvements with these forms of treatment.

In summary, BPD patients show a striking but incomplete long-term recovery. Diagnosable BPD usually remits by middle age, but many patients remain prone to further mental disorders (McGlashan, 1986; Silver & Cardish, 1991; Links, Heselgrave, Mitton, van Reekum, & Patrick, 1995a).

BPD patients have a high rate of suicide completion. Both Stone (1990) and Paris (1993) described rates of 8 to 9%, and have observed additional suicides since their results were published. A lower rate of 3% reported by McGlashan (1986) may not be representative of the borderline population, since it is derived patients at a tertiary care residential facility. A recent Norwegian study (Kjelsberg, Eikeseth, & Dahl, 1991), and a Canadian study (Silver & Cardish, 1991) have confirmed that about 1 of 10 patients with BPD eventually commits suicide. This overall rate is similar to that in schizophrenia (Wilkinson, 1982) and in mood disorders (Guze & Robins, 1970). Most of these suicides occur in the first five years of follow-up.

It is difficult to predict which borderline patients are most at risk for completed suicide. This is not surprising, since suicides are rare events and always difficult to predict, even in large samples of patients (Pokorny, 1983). However, Stone (1990) found that borderline patients with substance abuse were more likely to complete suicide; substance abuse itself carries a high mortality by suicide (Rich, Fowler, Fogarty, & Young, 1983). Paris, Nowlis, and Brown (1989) reported that previous attempts predicted later completion, a finding confirmed by two other studies (Kjeslberg et al., 1991; Kullgren, 1988). Although there is a general relationship between the number of previous attempts and completions (Maris, 1981), suicide attempts by overdose should be distinguished from self-mutilation or wrist slashing, which involve little suicidal intent and which have not been shown to predict completed suicide (Kroll, 1993).

It is also difficult to predict from baseline variables which patients will have the best or the worst outcome. Neither demographic factors such as education, measures of functional level before treatment, clinical measures such as diagnostic criteria, or developmental factors such as traumatic events during childhood are strongly related to ultimate outcome (Paris, 1993). The impulsive symptom of greatest prognostic importance in BPD is substance abuse (Stone, 1993; Zanarini, 1993; Links, Heselgrave, Mitton, van Reekum, & Patrick, 1995b).

Patients with more education are somewhat more likely to commit suicide (Paris et al., 1988). A similar finding has been reported in schizophrenics by Drake and Gates (1984), in whom high social class and high expectations in conjunction with a serious mental illness are a "recipe" for suicide. Two studies (Kjelsberg et al., 1991; Lesage et al., 1993) have suggested that borderline patients who experience separation or loss early in life are more likely to complete suicide. However, in our follow-up (Paris et al., 1988), completed suicides had a somewhat less traumatic childhood overall, probably reflecting intercorrelations with higher education.

The "burn out" of BPD resembles the outcome for other impulsive disorders, including substance abuse (Vaillant, 1973, 1994; Robins & Regier, 1991), and antisocial personality disorder (Maddocks, 1970; Robins & Regier, 1991; Black, Baumgard, & Bell, 1995). In normal populations, impulsivity is associated with youth, and immature defenses are usually replaced by more mature defenses as people age (Vaillant, 1977; Bond, Gardner, Christian, & Sigal, 1983). Such normal changes with age could reflect the effects of brain maturation or of social learning, and are probably one of the main mechanisms of recovery in BPD.

Those patients who improve may do so by investing successfully in less intimate, and therefore less conflictual, areas of psychosocial functioning (McGlashan, 1993). Since intimate relationships are so often associated with the symptoms in BPD, patients can reduce their symptomatology by avoiding the situations they cannot tolerate. Stone (1993) found that borderline patients are less likely to marry or have children than most people. If they do have children, however, they may become less impulsive. In many cases, sublimations, such as involvement in work, can provide satisfying substitutes for intimacy. Recovered BPD cases remain susceptible to breakdown if they suffer losses in later life (McGlashan, 1993). We need 25-year and 35-year follow-up data to assess the continuing fragility of patients with a history of BPD.

Historical Perspectives

Diagnosis

Borderline personality is a term that continues to create confusion. What border are we talking about? The label is at best misleading, and at worst, meaningless. (It is, however, no worse than some better-known psychopathological constructs: schizophrenia has nothing to do with a split mind!)

The term "borderline" emerged from the psychoanalytic theory that some forms of mental illness lie on a border between neurosis and psychosis. The psychoanalyst Adolf Stern (1938), who introduced the term, first described phenomena that are still recognizable characteristics of these patients: narcissism, psychic bleeding, inordinate hypersensitivity, psychic rigidity, negative therapeutic reactions, feelings of inferiority, masochism, wound licking, somatic anxiety, projection, and difficulties in reality testing.

For the next 35 years, the concept of a borderline patient remained exclusive to the analytic literature, not appearing in either *DSM-I* or *DSM-II*. Patients with this form of psychopathology were treated under other labels, including "hysteria," or "pseudo-neurotic schizophrenia" (Hoch et al., 1962). Otto Kernberg (1975) was largely responsible for the revival of interest in the construct among psychoanalysts, although he used the term to describe a level of personality organization rather than a discrete, diagnosable syndrome.

Some of the earliest ideas about the causes of BPD derived the psychoanalytic theory of the primacy of early experience. In this view, the more severe the psychopathology, the earlier must be the events causing it. There is, unfortunately, little or no evidence base for this idea (Paris, 1999). Moreover, the "data" of psychoanalysis consist largely of reconstructions of childhood experience, in which the analyst's ideas shape the material provided by the patient (Grunbaum, 1984).

Some of the psychodynamic ideas proposing to explain the etiology of BPD have verged on the fantastic. For example, one theory, which obtained a vogue about 20 years ago. suggested that the source of borderline pathology was a mother who prevented children from psychologically separating in the second year of life (Masterson & Rinsley, 1975). No empirical evidence ever supported this hypothesis. Even if borderline patients sometimes act like 2-year-olds, this does not prove that they are "fixated" at the toddler stage.

An important turning point for the borderline construct occurred with the development of the first operational definition of BPD (Gunderson & Singer, 1975), leading to the finding that BPD could be reliably distinguished from other major mental disorders (Gunderson & Kolb, 1978). Once BPD could be reliably diagnosed, research grew exponentially. In 1980 the construct was solid enough to be included in *DSM-III*, and BPD became the most investigated of all the personality disorders.

There was some discussion among the editors of *DSM-III* as to what would be the best name for the disorder. Spitzer, Endicott, and Gibbon (1979) proposed the term "unstable personality disorder," and his group polled American psychiatrists to test the acceptability of this alternative. A majority of respondents were still most comfortable and familiar with "borderline personality," and the term was retained to reflect clinical usage.

In retrospect, this decision may have been a mistake. The fact that the term borderline had been closely associated with psychoanalytic concepts, and was associated with this theoretical perspective, had a negative impact on the acceptance of the construct among mental health professionals. Although other misleading terms, such as schizophrenia, also remain in the official classification, clinicians have often accepted novel terminology (e.g., bipolar mood disorder).

The diagnosis of borderline personality has met particularly strong resistance in Europe. Tyrer (1988) stated that the construct creates "bemusement" among British clinicians. Yet Kroll, Carey, and Sines (1982) showed that borderline patients form a sizable percentage of admissions in Britain, but are labeled "hysterical" or "inadequate" personality. Simonsen (1993) has also shown that, however labeled, borderline psychopathology is common in several European countries.

BPD was finally accepted into *ICD-10* under the name "emotionally unstable personality." This terminology is arguably superior, since it comes closer to capturing the crucial dimensions of BPD, its impulsivity and affective instability, and frees the construct from its previous theoretical baggage.

Only systematic research will solve the riddle of the etiology of BPD. Fortunately, in the last 20 years, a large body of empirical data has emerged that begin to shed light on this question.

Contemporary Theoretical Perspectives and Empirical Data Concerning the Etiology of BPD

We can apply a *biopsychosocial* model (Engel, 1980), or a *stress-diathesis* model (Monroe & Simons, 1991) to BPD. In doing so, we can distinguish between *necessary* and *sufficient* conditions for the disorder. Biological factors are probably necessary for psychopathology to take this particular form. However, genetic vulnerabilities do not, by themselves, cause BPD, since psychological and social factors determine whether vulnerable individuals develop overt disorders. A multidimensional model (Paris, 1994a, 1994b) is needed to shed light on these pathways.

Biological Factors

The strongest finding of family pedigree studies of BPD (Zanarini, 1993) is that the relatives of borderline patients are more likely to have other impulse spectrum disorders, such as antisocial personality disorder or substance abuse. There is also a greater frequency of affective disorders in the relatives of borderline patients, but only among those who also have comorbid depression. Thus, in a study that examined personality traits in the relatives of BPD probands, Silverman et al. (1991) found that they were characterized by either impulsivity or affective instability, precisely the traits that Siever and Davis (1991) consider the "core dimensions" of BPD. Although most BPD probands do not have any relatives with the disorder, there is a higher statistical frequency of BPD in relatives than in comparison groups (Links, Steiner, & Huxley, 1988b). No pedigree studies have found any specific pattern of inheritance. Of course, this method cannot separate genetic from environmental influences.

Torgersen (1984) has carried out the only twin studies of BPD. He originally found no monozygotic-dizygotic differences for the disorder, but the number of subjects was too small to make firm conclusions. However, in later work with a more extensive twin sample, Torgersen (1996) was able to establish that BPD has a large heritable component.

Studies on normal twin populations (Livesley, Jang, Schroeder, & Jackson, 1993; Jang, Livesley, Vernon, & Jackson, 1996) show that the basic dimensions of BPD—impulsivity, affective instability, and cognitive symptoms—are all heritable (see review in Plomin, DeFries, McClearn, & Rutter, 1997). There have been no adoption studies of BPD, although they are feasible, since borderline women were, at least in the past, likely to give up their children for adoption.

In general, research on the personality disorders suggests that traits are more heritable than disorders (McGuffin & Thapar, 1992; Nigg & Goldsmith, 1994). However, one would expect that disorders based on heritable traits would themselves show at least some degree of heritability.

A second approach to identifying biological factors in BPD involves biological markers. No biological markers have yet been found that are *specific* to BPD. Markers associated with depression, such as abnormal dexamethasone suppression or decreased REM latency, only appear in borderline patients who are also depressed (Gunderson & Phillips, 1991). Other markers are more specific to trait impulsivity than to BPD, such as serotonergic activity as measured by the fenfluramine challenge test (Coccaro et al., 1989; Martial et al., 1997). Moreover, levels of the serotonin metabolite 5-HIAA in cerebrospinal fluid are no lower in BPD than controls unless the borderline patients also have a history of suicide attempts (Gardner, Lucas, & Cowdry, 1990).

Other studies concern organization on the neurophysiological level. Although routine electroencephalography has not found changes specific to any of the major psychiatric illnesses, more sophisticated EEG studies of "P300" event-related potentials (Kutcher, Blackwood, Clair, Gaskell, & Muir, 1987) show abnormal responses, resembling those seen in schizophrenia. Thus far, there has been two reports of PET scan results in a small sample of BPD patients (Goyer, Konicki, & Schulz, 1994; Leyton et al., 1997), in which the strongest relationships were between brain activity and aggressive and/or impulsive traits.

Several studies (Andrulonis, Blueck, Stroebel, & Vogel, 1982; van Reekum, Links, & Boiago, 1993; O'Leary et al., 1991) suggest that borderline patients demonstrate "soft" neurological signs. It has also been theorized that the behavioral abnormalities of BPD patients might reflect effects of abnormalities in limbic activity and/or cortical modulation of the limbic system (Stone, 1993). One report (O'Leary, Blueck, Stroebel, & Vogel, 1991) has suggested that some of the clinical features in BPD could be associated with problems in the recall of complex learned material, a deficit that can be reversed by cueing.

Although the biological factors in BPD remain equivocal, theoretical considerations suggest that future research could be fruitful. A model developed by Siever and Davis (1991), which links the activity of neurotransmitter systems to both personality traits and personality disorders, could be heuristic for this purpose. This model hypothesizes that each of four systems—mood-affect, impulse-action, attention-cognition, and anxiety—is linked to mental disorders on Axes I and II, and associated with specific biological markers, as well as genetic markers.

The mood/affect system is associated with affective disorders on Axis I, but may also account, in part, for the phenomenology of BPD. The associated neurotransmitter is norepinephrine, which is important for behavioral activation. However, there are important differences between the biology of mood in the affective disorders and of the affective instability in the dramatic cluster personality disorders. The qualitative distinction between mood in BPD and in affective disorders lies in the environmental responsiveness of the borderline patient (Gunderson & Phillips, 1991). Siever and Davis (1991) have hypothesized that this lability might be explained by defects in cholinergic modulation.

There is some support for a role for the norepinephrine system in BPD. Catecholamine activity, given its role in behavioral activation, has been linked to impulsivity (Gurrera, 1990). Using platelet MAO activity as a biological marker, this system is also linked to traits of extraversion and novelty seeking (Zuckerman, 1979). These traits have also been measured in studies of cortical evoked potentials, in which an "augmenting" response reflects stimulus seeking, in contrast to a "reducing" response, which reflects a damping down of responsiveness when stimuli are presented (Buchsbaum, 1974).

The impulse/action system is associated with impulse disorders on Axis I, and with BPD or antisocial personality on Axis II. The associated neurotransmitter would be serotonin, which is associated with behavioral inhibition. If serotonin functions as "the brakes" on impulsive behavior, reductions in serotonergic activity would lead to an inability to stop behavioral responses, and would increase impulsivity and aggressivity. This is supported by earlier studies (Brown, Goodwin, Ballenger, Goyer, & Major, 1979; Asberg, Traksman, & Thoren, 1976), which showed that the level of a serotonin metabolite, 5-HIAA, in cerebrospinal fluid relates to impulsive aggressiveness, as well as to violent methods of suicide.

In Siever and Davis's (1991) model, it is the interaction of abnormalities in *multiple* neurotransmitter systems that increases the risk for developing personality disorders. BPD could also involve combined dysfunction, with serotonin less active and norepinephrine overactive. Abnormal levels of activation without behavioral inhibition could be the kind of combination which raises the risk of borderline psychopathology (Siever & Davis, 1991). Neurotransmitter activity would thus distinguish dramatic cluster disorders such as BPD, from anxious cluster disorders such as avoidant personality disorder, where affective instability is associated with anxiety rather than impulsivity, or from odd cluster disorders such as schizotypal personality disorder.

No doubt, even this theory will eventually be found to be too simple. Multiple receptors and multiple subsystems are associated with each neurotransmitter. Nevertheless, it is possible that this research will eventually pinpoint biological markers specific to disorders in the impulsive spectrum.

Other theorists who believe that a biological abnormality underlies BPD differ as to which dimensions are primary and which are secondary. Linehan (1993) has described the biological factor in BPD as "emotional vulnerability," a very similar construct to Siever's affective instability. Linehan has suggested that borderline patients are excessively sensitive to emotional input, and have intense and protracted reactions to even low levels of stimulation. The problem is that affective instability is not specific to BPD, but is seen in anxious cluster personality disorders, which lack the impulsive component seen in BPD. While the model developed by Siever and Davis emphasizes the interactions of multiple dimensions the cognitive symptoms associated with BPD are not accounted for by Siever's core dimensions, and may have entirely different biological roots.

Psychological Factors

The psychoanalytic emphasis on the primacy of early experience has led many clinicians to assume that childhood experiences must be the psychological factor in the etiology of BPD. However, there is no reason to discount the possibility that, at least in some cases, future BPD patients may be no worse off in early life than others without pathology, but are unable to overcome the developmental challenges of adolescence and early adulthood due to biological vulnerability.

In research using interviews and questionnaires, most borderline patients describe an unusually large number of negative events from their childhood. There are two questions we must raise about these findings. First, are these memories accurate or do they only reflect the borderline patient's tendency to split and to recall negative events selectively? Second, are these associations truly causal, or are constitutional factors in children associated with more negative life events?

Prospective studies, then, are needed to determine whether borderline patients have actually had a more negative childhood, or whether they simply remember their childhood in a more negative way. It would be useful, for example, to conduct follow-up research on high-risk samples of abused and neglected children to determine whether such individuals are more likely to develop BPD. At present, although there is a large literature on the psychological factors in BPD, the findings are, without exception, *retrospective*. Moreover, retrospective perceptions have also been shown to be influenced by heritable personality traits (Plomin & Bergeman, 1991).

Inaccuracies of memory may be particularly common among borderline patients, who are noted for their striking distortions of recent life events (Paris, 1995). It is a common observation in therapy, for example, that these patients externalize their problems, while perceiving the reactions of other people to their needs as unsympathetic. More problematically, borderline patients can react to their therapists in the same way. It is therefore not surprising that some borderline patients can be influenced by therapists to blame their families for their current difficulties. Moreover, they may be sufficiently suggestible to rewrite their childhood histories in accord with theories proposing that childhood trauma plays a crucial role in the etiology of BPD.

Even so, a second crucial issue remains: whether negative childhood experiences, however frequent, have real etiological significance. Developmental issues reported by borderline patients fall into three general categories: trauma, early separation or loss, and abnormal parenting. Individual cases can show a predominance of one risk factor or of all three together. Most individuals with these experiences either develop other mental disorders or have no mental disorder at all (Rutter, 1987). Psychological factors may therefore be *necessary* but not *sufficient* conditions for developing BPD.

With these caveats in mind, let us review the empirical literature.

Trauma Borderline patients report a high frequency of childhood sexual abuse (CSA). These studies (reviewed in Paris, 1994a; see also Laporte & Guttman, 1996; Zanarini et al., 1997) all show an overall rate of CSA between 50 and 70%. However, there are several problems in interpreting these findings. First, few studies systematically examined the *parameters* of sexual abuse, such as severity, frequency, duration, and the identity of the perpetrator. These parameters are known to be much more predictive of sequelae than the simple fact of abuse alone (Browne & Finkelhor, 1986). In particular, incest, abuse with penetration, and abuse of long duration are all associated with more severe outcomes. In contrast, milder forms of abuse usually leave no sequelae.

In our own study (Paris et al., 1994a, 1994b), although severe abuse, as measured by penetration and multiple perpetration, discriminated BPD patients from a control group with other personality disorders, only about a third of patients with BPD reported sexual abuse with parameters likely to lead to long-term sequelae. Another third reported only single episodes, nonincestuous perpetrators, and acts that did not involve penetration, which are types of CSA that have not been found in community studies to leave serious sequelae. Finally, a third of cases reported no trauma at all. We concluded that CSA plays an important etiological role only in the minority with severe trauma.

Second, childhood sexual abuse lacks *specificity* as a risk factor for BPD. In our own study, although CSA was more common in BPD, there was a large overlap with our non-BPD control group (71 vs. 46%). There is a very wide range of clinical symptoms seen in those who report trauma (Browne & Finkelhor, 1986). Thus, childhood trauma is probably more of a general risk factor for psychopathology than a specific cause of any one mental disorder.

Third, the effect size of the association between CSA and BPD is not very large. In a meta-analysis of 21 published studies, Fossati, Madeddu, and Maffei (in press) found only a moderate pooled correlation for this association, and a significant negative correlation between sample size and the strength of the association.

Fourth, most researchers have not examined intercorrelations between CSA and other psychological risk factors. Research shows that childhood sexual abuse is associated with a pathological family atmosphere (Finkelhor, Hotaling, Lewis, & Smith, 1990), and in one study (Nash, Hulsley, Sexton, Harraban, & Lambert, 1993), the long-term effects of CSA in community populations were accounted for by their intercorrelations with abnormalities in family functioning. These issues are particularly important for incest, since the pathological dynamics of these families amplify the trauma of intrafamilial sexual abuse (Burgess & Conger, 1978). Moreover, in the case of extrafamilial molestation, children who have been neglected by their families are probably more susceptible to being molested, since they are lonely and vulnerable, and are not able to protect their boundaries when approached by perpetrators. This explanation has been supported by a study of pedophiles (Conte, Wolf, & Smith, 1989), who report that they recognize potential victims by their obvious vulnerability, and then approach them selectively.

Fifth, research has not adequately considered interactions between childhood sexual abuse and constitutionally shaped personality traits. Childhood experiences have a different impact depending on how they are processed by the individual (Rutter, 1989). Finkelhor (1988) has suggested that the long-term effects of CSA are not adequately explained by posttraumatic mechanisms, but depend on cognitive factors, which he describes as sexualization, betrayal, stigmatization, and powerlessness. Individual differences in cognitive processing, which are largely related to personality traits, help to explain why even the most severe abuse is not consistently related to adult psychopathology.

Physical abuse (PA) in childhood has also been shown to increase the statistical risk for adult psychopathology. However, like sexual abuse, the long-term outcome of physical abuse depends on its parameters, such as frequency, duration and severity (Malinovsky-Rummell & Hansen, 1993). The type of abuse suffered by children differs strongly by gender. Epidemiological studies of community populations (Jason, Williams, Burton, & Rochat, 1982) show that sexual abuse is much more common among females, but that physical abuse is more common among males. Rutter and Madge (1976) also found that children with "difficult" temperaments are the most likely to be physically abused.

A number of studies have shown that PA is more frequently reported by borderline patients than by controls (Herman, Perry, & van der Kolk, 1989). However, some researchers (Zanarini, Gunderson, Marino et al., 1989; Ogata, Silk, & Goodrich, 1990) have not found such associations. In our own sample (Paris et al., 1994a, 1994b), the rate of physical abuse was significantly greater in females with BPD than in patients with other personality disorders, but there were no such differences in males. In our female sample, when we examined the parameters of PA, including frequency, duration, severity, and the relationship with the perpetrator, there were no differences between the groups, while in our male sample, only PA from fathers and PA of greater duration were significantly more common in the BPD patients.

Herman et al. (1989) also found that borderline patients also report more frequent episodes in which they have witnessed family violence, while Zanarini, Gunderson, Marino et al. (1989) reported verbal abuse to be a correlate of borderline pathology. Sexual, physical, and verbal abuse may have an impact on children that is ultimately similar. When Herman et al. (1989) combined all forms of abuse into a total trauma score, they obtained more substantial BPD-control differences than when each component alone was considered.

Borderline patients who report more severe abuse also have more severe symptoms (Silk, Lee, Hill, & Lohr, 1995). However, the hypothesis that certain specific symptoms, such as dissociation or self-mutilation, can be used to provide clues to a history of trauma remains controversial. Some theorists (Herman & van der Kolk, 1987; Terr, 1991) have proposed that children learn to use dissociative defenses when overwhelmed by abusive experiences. However, given the present state of evidence, clinicians should be advised to be very cautious in interpreting these, or any other symptoms, as proof of childhood trauma.

For example, in community populations, the link between CSA and dissociative phenomena has been shown to be largely mediated by family pathology (Nash et al., 1993). In clinical populations, some studies have found a relationship between dissociation and trauma (Chu & Dill, 1990; Ogata, Silk, Goodrich, & Lohr, 1990; Herman et al., 1989), but they failed to factor out the stronger relationship between dissociation and a borderline diagnosis. In our own research (Zweig-Frank, Paris, & Guzder, 1994), we found that on a standard measure, the Dissociative Experiences Scale (Bernstein & Putnam, 1986), scores were twice as high among BPD as compared to other personality disorders. But in multivariate analyses taking diagnosis into account, dissociation had no independent relationship to sexual abuse or its parameters, nor to any other psychological risk factors. Thus, the capacity to dissociate, which has a strong heritable component (Jang, Paris, Zweig-Frank, & Livesley, 1998) could well be a constitutional feature of BPD.

Borderline patients frequently self-mutilate, and Leibenluft et al. (1987) have suggested that one reason they act in this way is to cope with painful dissociative states. Van der Kolk, Perry, and Herman (1991) found that self-mutilation in BPD is related to histories of trauma and to dissociation. Brodsky, Cloitre, and Dulit (1995) also found that self-mutilation is most strongly correlated to dissociation. However, in our own research (Zweig-Frank, Paris, & Guzder, 1994), self-mutilation was not related to any of several psychological risk factors. The capacity to self-mutilate might also be a stronger reflection of the impulsive traits behind BPD rather than any particular life experience.

These conclusions seem to apply to other measures of traits in BPD. We used standard self-report measures of defense styles, and of hostility levels, and found that neither of these was related to psychological risk factors, but both were strongly to a borderline diagnosis (Paris, Zweig-Frank, Guzder, & Bond, 1996). Thus, the clinical features of borderline personality depend as much on underlying traits as on specific psychological experiences. This conclusion is in accord with a stress-diathesis model of the disorder.

Let us now summarize the relationship of trauma to BPD. About a third of borderline patients report severe abuse as children, and about a third report no abuse at all. The remaining patients describe less severe abuse. The most likely conclusion from these data is that trauma is an overall risk factor for BPD and carries a particular risk in certain subpopulations, but is far from the only etiological factor. Trauma probably has a different effect on individuals with personality trait profiles that make them vulnerable to develop impulsivity and affective instability.

These conclusions make even more sense when viewed in the context of community studies of childhood trauma. Research on CSA (Browne & Finkelhor, 1986) and on PA (Malinovsky-Rummel & Hansen, 1993) show the importance of resilience factors. Only about 20% of abused children go on to develop psychopathology as adults. Even among those with severe abuse, only a minority of these will develop psychopathology. There must, therefore, be interactions between abuse and other risk factors, including personality traits, nontraumatic adverse experiences, and the social context in which psychopathology develops.

Separation and Loss Several studies (Bradley, 1979; Soloff & Millward, 1983; Paris et al., 1988; Zanarini, Gunderson, Marino et al., 1989) have suggested that BPD patients have a higher frequency of early separation and loss from their parents during childhood than other psychiatric patients. However, Ogata, Silk, and Goodrich (1990) did not confirm these differences. The strength of the association seems to depend on the comparison group. In most reports supporting a relationship between separation and BPD, borderlines were compared to depressed patients. Yet, in our own study, when female BPD patients were compared to patients with other personality disorders (Paris et al., 1994a), histories of separation or loss before age 5 were frequent (21%), but no more so than in the controls. Separation or loss before age 16 was even more frequent (51%) in BPD, but, again, no more so than in other personality disorders. In our male sample, there were significantly more separations or losses before age 16 (43%) in BPD than in the non-BPD comparison group, although the rate of separations or losses in male BPD patients before age 5 (16%) was no greater than in non-BPD personality disorders.

A history of early separation and loss is not all that specific to any form of psychopathology, and is quite frequent in normal populations (Tennant, 1988). This does not mean that it plays no etiological role, only that it does not lead by itself to specific disorders. The impact of early loss on adult psychopathology has been shown to be influenced by a number of interacting variables, particularly levels of family dysfunction after the loss and the presence of buffering influences outside the family (Tennant, 1986; Rutter, 1989).

Parental Psychopathology The parents of borderline patients are themselves more likely to have some form of psychopathology, manifesting either as an overt psychiatric disorder or as personality traits that interfere with adequate parenting.

Links, Steiner, and Huxley (1988) carried out the most systematic study of psychiatric diagnoses in the parents of a cohort of borderline patients. The parents were either directly interviewed or assessed through information provided by another relative. The disorders with the greatest morbid risk in first-degree relatives were recurrent unipolar depression (27%), alcoholism (21%), BPD itself (15%), and antisocial personality disorder (10%). These findings are in accord with studies in which the parents were not directly interviewed (Zanarini, 1993).

When symptoms, rather than disorders, are measured, the first-degree relatives of BPD patients can be shown to have impulsive and affective personality traits (Silverman et al., 1991). These shared traits in families are consistent with common biological vulnerabilities. At the same time, impulsive and affective traits affect the quality of parenting. Thus, both parental substance abuse (West & Prinz, 1987), and depression (Downey & Coyne, 1990; Keitner & Miller, 1990) are known to lead to negative effects on children.

Parental Bonding One major clinical hypothesis about the etiology of BPD is that parents fail to provide a sufficiently supportive environment for their children (Adler, 1985). In an early study on the family environment associated with BPD, Gunderson, Kerr, and Englund (1980) measured relationships between borderline patients and their families using ratings of family interviews. As compared to controls, the parents of borderline patients appeared to be unresponsive and tended to scapegoat the patient. However, these findings might only be the result of living with a borderline child.

Ogata, Silk, and Goodrich (1990) gave adult borderline patients a standard self-report measure of family experience. As compared to a control group with depression, those with BPD described significantly lower family cohesion. Low family cohesion was also the main finding of a study of the children of borderline mothers (Feldman et al., 1995). Low cohesion points to poor boundary control, which could also be associated with trauma, loss, or emotional neglect.

Adler's (1985) theory that a failure of parental responsiveness leads to BPD assumes that children need parents to buffer their emotional distress, and only learn to accomplish this task for themselves when they internalize their relationship with a caring parent. Linehan's (1993) cognitive behavioral theory takes a similar view of parental failure, describing the parenting of the future borderline as creating an "invalidating environment" for emotions.

Emotional neglect is defined by a lack of sufficient emotional support for a child. One consequence of this neglect could be affective instability and dysphoria. Impulsive action could also be an attempt to cope with intense and unmodulated negative affects. Moreover, insecure attachment to parents is associated with clinging behaviors (Bowlby, 1973). Obviously, many of the phenomena associated with anxious attachment are also characteristic of BPD.

It is also possible that the parents of borderline patients have problems with the encouragement of autonomy and independence. Borderline patients certainly have trouble attaining autonomy, although it is not clear whether this is due to a constitutional deficit or to active parental interference. Masterson and Rinsley (1975) hypothesized that a mother with BPD might influence her child to develop the same disorder if she provided positive reinforcement only for responses maintaining a mother-child symbiosis, while negatively responding to responses leading to individuation. Yet the same outcome could derive from emotionally unresponsive parents who fail to recognize the affective states of their children (Feldman & Guttman, 1984), or from interactions between emotional vulnerability and an "invalidating environment" (Linehan, 1993).

These questions have been tested empirically using retrospective instruments in clinical samples. Interview data (Frank & Paris, 1981; Soloff & Millward, 1983; Zanarini et al., 1997), as well as self-report instruments (Paris, 1994a; Patrick, Hobson, Castle, Howard, & Maughan, 1994) suggest that borderline patients *perceive* having had abnormal bonding with their parents, including both neglectful and overprotective responses. If these perceptions are accurate, they would correspond to a style of parenting that Parker (1983) has called "affectionless control." There is a parallel between these parental bonding issues and the problems that borderline patients have with their adult attachments (Melges & Schwartz, 1989). One possible mechanism for this interaction between the dimensions of parenting and psychopathological sequelae is that when poor empathy is coupled with intrusive control, neglected children will have difficulty finding protective relationships outside the family.

One prospective community study offers support for Parker's ideas. Bezirganian, Cohen, and Brook (1993) used interview measures of parenting in a large sample of mothers to predict the development of personality disorders when the cohort reached adolescence, and found that only a combination of maternal overprotection and inconsistency was predictive of BPD.

In our own research (Zweig-Frank & Paris, 1991), we found that borderline patients described both their parents as neglectful and overprotective. We therefore proposed a theory that "biparental failure" is a psychological risk factor for BPD. Thus, when there are difficulties in bonding with both parents, the child cannot compensate for a bad relationship with one parent by a better relationship with the other.

However, as with all the other psychological risk factors for BPD, specificity depends on the nature of the comparison group. When we later compared BPD to non-BPD personality disordered groups (Paris et al., 1994a, 1994b), there were few differences, a finding similar to that found by Sullivan, Joyce, and Mulder (1994). We have therefore concluded that abnormal parental bonding lacks a specific relationship with BPD.

In summary, *none* of the psychological risk factors for BPD is very specific to the disorder. The specificity for BPD must lie elsewhere, most likely both in biological vulnerability and in the cumulative effects of multiple risk factors.

Social Factors

As discussed earlier in the chapter, there have been very few epidemiological studies of BPD. Therefore, we do not know its precise prevalence, or whether that prevalence varies with demographic, cultural, or social factors. Millon (1987, 1993) hypothesized that there has been a recent increase in the prevalence of BPD, and that this might be accounted for by social change. Millon has argued that rapid social change is a risk factor for BPD because it interferes with the intergenerational transmission of values and reduces the influence of the extended family and social community.

Although there is no direct epidemiological evidence of changes in the prevalence of BPD over time, indirect evidence supports Millon's conjecture that there are cohort effects in BPD (Paris, 1992, 1996). There has been a dramatic increase in the prevalence of several related diagnoses among young people: antisocial personality, depression, and substance abuse (Robins & Regier, 1991). In addition, there has been an increase in frequency in repeated parasuicide in young people (Weissman, 1974), a symptom that is particularly suggestive of borderline pathology (Zanarini et al., 1990b), and which has similar demographic characteristics to BPD (Maris, 1981). Weissman's finding, which is over 20 years old, has recently been confirmed in a study in Edmonton, Canada (Bland, Dyck, Newman, & Orn, 1998).

Also relevant is that the fact that the youth suicide rate has tripled over the last 25 years (Sudak, Ford, & Rushforth, 1984), and that studies using psychological autopsies (Runeson & Beskow, 1991; Lesage et al., 1994; Rich & Runeson, 1992; Martunnen, Aro, Henrikkson, & Lonnqvist, 1991) have found that about one third of youth suicides can be retrospectively diagnosed with BPD. Although the overall increase in suicide has occurred only in males, Martunnnen et al. (1995) found that 25% of adolescent female suicides in Finland can also be diagnosed as having had BPD.

This converging evidence for an increased prevalence of BPD points to dramatic shifts in behavioral symptomatology over short periods of time, suggesting changes in the social factors promoting these forms of psychopathology. The mechanism by which social factors play a role in the development of BPD most likely involves the influence of the social context on the quality of family life (Paris, 1996). At least one psychological risk factor is on the increase, since nuclear families dissolve more frequently due to separation and divorce. We do not know whether there have been cohort increases in the exposure of children to trauma or to neglect, although the higher rates of depression, substance abuse, and antisocial personality in the community are probably reducing the quality of parenting among those affected.

Fortunately, there can also be social influences that are protective against psychopathology. One of the main reason for resilience in children is that not all important relationships take place inside the family. The larger society offers alternative attachments that can buffer the effects of family pathology, and these relationships have been shown to have an important effect on personality development (Rutter, 1989). In particular, studies of resilient children (Kaufman, Grunebaum, Cohler, & Gamer, 1979) have consistently shown that attachments outside the family are protective against severe parental psychopathology. Societies that provide such relationships, and that offer readily accessible roles for young adults, protect the young against psychological risk factors that operate inside the family.

The construct of "social disintegration" (Leighton, Harding, & Macklin, 1963) is useful in understanding the social factors in both mental disorders in general and the personality disorders specifically. Social disintegration could have a particular relation to impulsive personality disorders, substance abuse, and youth suicide (Paris, 1996). Integrated societies offer structures that provide young people with a sense of identity. In disintegrated societies, these structures break down, with no buffering of family pathology, or for impulsive or affectively unstable personality traits. Moreover, integrated societies encourage repression rather than the acting out of conflicts (Murphy, 1982), while disintegrated social environments actually encourage those with impulsive traits to act out (Millon, 1993).

Linehan (1993) has hypothesized that high social demands, coupled with a relative absence of secure attachments in contemporary society, are increasing the levels of emotional dysregulation in children. On the other hand, traditional societies, by providing ready attachments, make borderline pathology less common (Paris, 1994a). Identity diffusion will not arise in societies that do not expect each generation to create its own identity de novo. Chaotic relationships will rarely develop in societies in which family and community play an active role in determining object choices.

A Multidimensional Theory of BPD

In understanding the pathways to BPD, we need to distinguish among temperament, traits, and disorders (Rutter, 1987). Traits, which are rooted in both temperament and social learning, develop into disorders through a process of *amplification* in which traits are used inappropriately and become maladaptive (Paris, 1996).

The core dimensions of BPD described by Siever and Davis (1991), impulsivity and affective instability, are the best candidates for the traits underlying BPD. Individuals with both these traits might be entirely normal: emotional, active, and engaging people who do things on the spur of the moment. Others might find them interesting, if a bit demanding. However, in the presence of psychological risk factors, such as trauma, loss, and parental failure, as well as social risk factors, these characteristics may be amplified. Emotional reactions become labile and dysphoric. Activity is used inappropriately to cope with dysphoria, and becomes impulsive acting out. Substance abuse, sexual activity, or chaotic interpersonal relationships may be used in an attempt to damp down the dysphoria. When dysphoria and impulsive action reinforce each other in a feedback loop, the pattern begins to resemble BPD.

In the absence of these underlying personality traits, no environmental stressor would produce the cluster of behaviors we call BPD. An introverted person who organizes life to stay out of harm's way might develop an avoidant or a dependent personality disorder under stress, but never BPD. Moreover, although those with impulsivity and affective instability would be more prone to BPD, they could also develop other impulsive disorders.

The impulsive cluster of personality disorders on Axis II probably reflects a continuum of psychopathology. The milder forms, histrionic and narcissistic personality disorders, would reflect the presence of less pathogenic environmental risk factors. The more severe forms, BPD and antisocial personality, would emerge only when environmental risk factors are strongly pathogenic. In fact, the risk factors for these two disorders are rather similar (Paris, 1997), and gender differences could be the strongest factor determining whether an individual has antisocial or borderline pathology.

The psychological stressors that mediate the process of amplification from traits to disorders need not be specific. The same end-point could be reached by any one or a combination of risk factors. In this view, there need be no specific constellation in the history of the borderline patient, but rather many pathways to a final common outcome.

There are three possible mechanisms that could determine whether traits such as impulsivity or affective instability go on to BPD: (1) the quantity of biological risk factors alone; (2) environmental factors alone; (3) the interaction of biology and environment. The first and second possibilities both seem unlikely, in view of the lack of specific relationships between either biological or psychological risk factors and BPD. The preferred mechanism would be the third possibility, a multidimensional and interactive model.

How would this interaction work? First, abnormal traits in children bring on negative responses from parents. Children who are impulsive and affectively labile overlap with Chess and Thomas' (1984) category of "difficult." They would therefore be more likely to face rejection and/or abuse if their impulsivity and emotionality makes them troublesome to their families (Rutter & Madge, 1976).

Second, psychopathological characteristics in the parents of the future BPD patient amplify personality traits in their children. The parents might themselves have personality disorders, or might be insensitive to the needs of their children, and fail to provide an adequate holding environment. Moreover, traumatic experiences in childhood, whether they occur inside or outside the family, are rooted in family dysfunction. Any of these factors would be experienced by the child as stressful and would amplify underlying personality traits.

Finally, the social environment could act as either a risk factor for BPD or a protective factor against BPD. Even in the presence of a biological predisposition and a traumatic or inadequate family environment, a positive social environment helps prevent the development of psychopathology by providing structures that buffer traits of impulsivity and affective instability. We would therefore predict that borderline personality disorder should be less frequent in highly integrated societies where family structures are stronger and where children have alternative sources of bonding that make them less emotionally dependent on what happens in the nuclear family. On the other hand, in societies with higher levels of social disintegration, many adolescents will have increased difficulty with the transition to adult roles. Those who are prone to borderline pathology will develop the characteristic features of the disorder.

The balance between risk factors and protective factors is the ultimate determinant of how likely it will be for any individual to develop BPD. Thus, the personality traits that increase the risk for BPD can be buffered by other traits which protect against BPD. Resilience research (Werner & Smith, 1992) has shown that intelligence and positive personality characteristics help children deal with adversity. Protective psychological factors might include positive experiences with secure attachment figures. Protective social factors, such as the presence of a supportive community to which children can bond, lead to resilience.

Future Directions

Further research on borderline personality might follow some of the following directions:

1. In the future, the validity of all psychiatric diagnoses will have to depend more and more on research identifying the specific biological factors associated with mental disorders. We will not develop a better definition of BPD until we understand its etiology.
2. Understanding the specific vulnerabilities in BPD will depend on significant advances in neurobiology. This will require both biological and genetic research.
3. The psychological factors in BPD need to be examined using prospective studies. We can either study large cohorts of children, or study children at risk as they become young adults.
4. To understand the social factors in BPD, we need more information about the prevalence of BPD: in more developed countries, in traditional societies, and in developing societies undergoing rapid transitions.
5. The best etiological model for this disorder will be multidimensional and multivariate.

References

Adler, G. (1985). *Borderline psychopathology and its Treatment*. New York: Jason Aronson.

Akiskal, H. S., Chen, S. E., & Davis, G. C. (1985). Borderline: An adjective in search of a noun. *Journal of Clinical Psychiatry, 46,* 41–48.

Andrulonis, P. A., Blueck, B. C., Stroebel, O. F., & Vogel, N. G. (1982). Borderline personality subcategories. *Journal of Nervous and Mental Diseases, 170,* 670–680.

Asberg, M., Traksman, L., & Thoren, P. (1976). 5-HIAA in the cerebrospinal fluid: A biochemical suicide predictor? *Archives General Psychiatry, 33,* 1193–1197.

Bernstein, E. M., & Putnam, F. W. (1986). Development, reliability, and validity of a dissociation scale. *Journal of Nervous and Mental Diseases, 174,* 727–734

Bezirganian, S., Cohen, P., & Brook, J. S. (1993). The impact of mother-child interaction on the development of borderline personality disorder. *American Journal of Psychiatry, 150,* 1836–1841.

Black, D. W., Baumgard, C. H., & Bell, S. E. (1995). A 16–45 year follow-up of 71 men with antisocial personality disorder. *Comprehensive Psychiatry, 36,* 130–140.

Bland, R. C., Dyck, R. J., Newman, S. C., & Orn, H. (1998). Attempted suicide in Edmonton. In A. A. Leenaars, S. Wenckstern, I. Sakinofsky, R. J. Dyck, M. J. Kral, & R. C. Bland (Eds.), *Suicide in Canada* (pp. 136–150). Toronto, University of Toronto Press.

Bond, M. P., Gardner, S., Christian, J., & Sigal, J. J. (1983). Empirical study of self-rated defense styles. *Archives of General Psychiatry, 40,* 333–338.

Bond, M., Paris, J., & Zweig-Frank, H. (1994). The Defense Style Questionaire in borderline personality disorder. *Journal of Personality Disorders, 8,* 28–31.

Bowlby, J. (1973). *Attachment and Loss: Separation.* London: Hogarth Press.

Bradley, S. J. (1979). The relationship of early maternal separation to borderline personality disorder in children and adolescents. *American Journal of Psychiatry, 136,* 424–426.

Brodsky, B. S., Cloitre, M., & Dulit, R. A. (1995). Relationship of dissociation to self-mutilation and childhood abuse in borderline personality disorder. *American Journal of Psychiatry, 152,* 1788–1792.

Brown, G. L., Goodwin, F. K., Ballenger, J. C., Goyer, P. F., & Major, L. F. (1979). Aggression in humans correlates with cerebrospinal fluid amine metabolites. *Psychiatry Research, 1,* 131–139.

Browne, A., & Finkelhor, D. (1986). Impact of child sexual abuse: A review of the literature. *Psychological Bulletin, 99,* 66–77.

Burgess, R. L., & Conger, P. D. (1978). Family interaction in abusive, neglectful and normal families. *Child Development, 49,* 1163–1173.

Buchsbaum, M. S. (1974). Average evoked response and stimulus intensity in identical and fraternal twins. *Physiological Psychology, 2,* 365–370.

Byrne, C. P., Cernovsky, A., Velamoor, V. R., Coretese, L., & Losztyn, S. (1990). A comparison of borderline and schizophrenic patients for childhood life events and parent-child relationships. *Canadian Journal of Psychiatry, 35,* 590–595.

Carpenter, W. T., Gunderson, J. G., & Strauss, J. S. (1977). Considerations of the borderline syndrome: A longitudinal comparative study of borderline and schizophrenic patients. In P. Hartocollis (Ed.), *Borderline Personality Disorders* (pp. 234–254). New York: International Universities Press.

Chess, S., & Thomas, A. (1984). *Origins and Evolution of Behavior Disorders: From infancy to adult life.* New York: Brunner/Mazel.

Chu, J. A., & Dill, D. L. (1990). Dissociative symptoms in relation to childhood physical and sexual abuse. *American Journal of Psychiatry, 147,* 887–892.

Clarkin, J. F., Widiger, T. A., Frances, A., Hurt, S. W., & Gilmore, M. (1983). Propotypic typology and the borderline personality disorder. *Journal of Abnormal Psychology, 92,* 263–275.

Cloninger, C. R., Martin, R. L., Guze, S. B., & Clayton, P. J. (1990). The empirical structure of psychiatric comorbidity and its theoretical significance. In J. D. Maser and C. R. Cloninger (Eds.), *Comorbidity of Anxiety and Depression* (pp. 439–462). Washington, D.C.: American Psychiatric Press.

Coccaro, E. F., Siever, L. J., Klar, H. M., Maurer, G., Cochrane, K., Cooper, T. B., Mohs, R. C., & Davis, K. L. (1989). Serotonergic studies in patients with affective and personality disorders. *Archives of General Psychiatry, 46,* 587–599.

Conte, J. R., Wolf, S., & Smith, T. (1989). What sexual offenders tell us about prevention strategies. *Child Abuse and Neglect, 13,* 293–301.

Costa, P. T., & McRae, R. R. (1992). The five-factor model of personality and its relevance to personality disorders. *Journal of Personality Disorders, 6,* 343–359.

Costa, P. T., Widiger, T. A., eds (1994): *Personality Disorders and the Five-Factor Model of Personality.* Washington, D.C., American Psychological Association

Dawson, D., & MacMillan, H. L. (1993). *Relationship Management of the Borderline Patient: From Understanding to Treatment.* New York: Brunner/Mazel.

Dorhenwend, B. P., & Dorhenwend, B. S. (1969). *Social Status and Psychological Disorder: A Causal Inquiry.* New York: John Wiley.

Downey, G., & Coyne, J. C. (1990). Children of depressed parents: an integrative review. *Psychological Bulletin, 108,* 50–76.

Drake, R. E., & Gates, C. (1984). Suicide among schizophrenics: Who is at risk? *Journal of Nervous and Mental Diseases, 172,* 613–617.

Dulit, R. A., Fyer, M. R., Miller, F. T., Sacks, M. H., & Frances, A. J. (1993). Gender differences in sexual preference and substance abuse of inpatients with borderline personality disorder. *Journal of Personality Disorders, 7,* 182–185.

Engel, G. L. (1980). The clinical application of the biopsychosocial model. *American Journal of Psychiatry, 137,* 535–544.

Eysenck, H. J. (1991). Genetic and environmental contributions to individual differences: The three major dimensions of personality. *Journal of Personality, 58,* 245–261.

Feldman, R. B., & Guttman, H. A. (1984). Families of borderline patients: Literal minded parents, borderline parents and parental protectiveness. *American Journal of Psychiatry, 141,* 1392–1396.

Feldman, R. B., Zelkowitz, P., Weiss, M., Heyman, M., Vogel, J., & Paris, J. (1995). A comparison of the families of borderline personality disorder mothers and the families of other personality disorder mothers. *Comprehensive Psychiatry, 36,* 157–163.

Finkelhor, D. (1988). The trauma of child sexual abuse: Two models. In G. E. Wyatt & G. J. Powell (Eds.), *Lasting Effects of Child Sexual Abuse* (pp. 61–82). Beverly Hills: Sage.

Finkelhor, D., Hotaling, G., Lewis, I. A., & Smith, C. (1990). Sexual abuse in a national survey of adult men and women: Prevalence characteristics and risk factors. *Child Abuse and Neglect, 14,* 19–28.

Fossati, A., Madeddu, F., & Maffei, C. (in press). Borderline personality disorder and childhood sexual abuse: A metanalytic study. *Journal of Personality Disorders.*

Frances, A. J., & Widiger, T. A. (1986). The classification of personality disorders: An overview of problems and solutions. *Psychiatry Annual Review, 5,* 240–257. Washington, D.C.: American Psychiatric Press.

Frank, A. F. (1992). The therapeutic alliances of borderline patients. In J. F. Clarkin, E. Marziali, & H. Munroe-Blum (Eds.), *Borderline Personality Disorder: Clinical and Empirical Perspectives* (pp. 220–247). New York: Guilford.

Frank, H., & Paris, J. (1981). Family experience in borderline patients. *Archives of General Psychiatry, 38,* 1031–1034.

Frank, H., & Hoffman, N. (1986). Borderline empathy: An empirical investigation. *Comprehensive Psychiatry, 27,* 387–395.

Gardner, D. L., Lucas, P. B., & Cowdry, R. W. (1990). CSF metabolites in borderline personality disorder compared with normal controls. *Biological Psychiatry, 28,* 247–254.

Garnet, K. E., Levy, K. N., Mattanah, J. J. F., Edell, W. S., & McGlashan, T. H. (1994). Borderline personality disorder in adolescents: Ubiquitous or specific? *American Journal of Psychiatry, 151,* 1380–1382.

Goldman, S. J., D'Angelo, E. J., Demaso, D. R., & Mezzacappa, E. (1992). Physical and sexual abuse histories among children with borderline personality disorder. *American Journal of Psychiatry, 149,* 1723–1726.

Goyer, P. F., Konicki, P. E., & Schulz, S. C. (1994). Brain imaging in personality disorders. In K. R. Silk (Ed.), *Biological and Neurobehavioral Studies of Borderline Personality Disorder* (pp. 109–127). Washington, D.C.: American Psychiatric Press.

Grunbaum, A. (1984). *The Foundations of Psychoanalysis: A Philosophical Critique.* Berkeley: University of California Press.

Gunderson, J. G. (1984). *Borderline Personality Disorder.* Washington, D.C.: American Psychiatric Press.

Gunderson, J. G., & Singer, M. T. (1975). Defining borderline patients: An overview. *American Journal of Psychiatry, 132,* 1–9.

Gunderson, J. G., & Kolb, J. E. (1978). Discriminating features of borderline patients. *American Journal of Psychiatry, 135,* 792–796.

Gunderson, J. G., Kerr, J., & Englund, D. W. (1980). The families of borderlines: A comparative study. *Archives of General Psychiatry, 37,* 27–33.

Gunderson, J. G., Frank, A. F., Ronningstam, E. F., Wahter, S., Lynch, V. J., & Wolf, P. J. (1989). Early discontinuance of borderline patients from psychotherapy. *Journal of Nervous and Mental Diseases, 177,* 38–42.

Gunderson, J. G., & Phillips, K. A. (1991). A current view of the interface between borderline personality disorder and depression. *American Journal of Psychiatry, 148,* 967–975.

Gunderson, J. G., Zanarini, M. C., & Kisiel, C. L. (1991). Borderline personality disorder: A review of data on DSM-III-R descriptions. *Journal Personality Disorders, 5,* 340–352.

Gunderson, J. G., & Sabo, A. N. (1993). The phenomenological and conceptual interface between borderline personality disorder and

PTSD. *American Journal of Psychiatry, 150*, 19–27.

Gurrera, R. (1990). Some biological and behavioral features associated with clinical personality types. *Journal of Nervous Mental Diseases, 178*, 556–566.

Gutheil, T. G. (1989). Borderline personality disorder, boundary violations and patient-therapist sex: Medicolegal pitfalls. *American Journal of Psychiatry, 146*, 597–602.

Guzder, J., Paris, J., Zelkowitz, P., & Marchessault, K. (1996). Risk factors for borderline personality disorder in children. *Journal of the American Academy of Child and Adolescent Psychiatry, 35*, 26–33.

Guzder, J., Paris, J., Zelkowitz, P., & Feldman, R. (in press). Psychological risk factors for borderline pathology in school-aged children. *Journal of the American Academy of Child Adolescent Psychiatry.*

Guze, J. B., & Robins, E. (1970). Suicide and primary affective disorders. *British Journal of Psychiatry, 117*, 437–438.

Herman, J. L., Perry, J. C., & van der Kolk, B. A. (1989). Childhood trauma in borderline personality disorder. *American Journal of Psychiatry, 146*, 490–495.

Herman, J., & van der Kolk, B. A. (1987). Traumatic antecedents of borderline personality disorder. In B. A. van der Kolk (Ed.), *Psychological Trauma* (pp. 111–126). Washington, D.C.: American Psychiatric Press.

Hoch, P. H., Cattell, J. P., Strahl, M. D., & Penness, H. H. (1962). The course and outcome of pseudoneurotic schizophrenia. *American Journal of Psychiatry, 119*, 106–115.

Hull, J. W., Yeomans, F., Clarkin, J., Li, C., & Goodman, G. (1996). Factors associated with multiple hospitalizations of patients with borderline personality disorder. *Psychiatric Services, 47*, 638–641.

Jang, K., Paris, J., Zweig-Frank, H., & Livesley, W. J. (in press). The heritability of dissociative experience. *Journal of Nervous and Mental Diseases.*

Jang, K. L., Livesley, W. J., Vernon, P. A., & Jackson, D. N. (1996). Heritability of personality traits: A twin study. *Acta Psychiatrica Scandinavica, 94*, 438–444.

Jason, J., Williams, S. L., Burton, A., & Rochat, R. (1982). Epidemiological differences between sexual and physical abuse. *Journal of the American Medical Association, 247*, 3344–3348.

Kaufman, C., Grunebaum, H., Cohler, B., & Gamer, E. (1979). Superkids: Competent children of schizophrenic mothers. *American Journal of Psychiatry, 136*, 1398–1402.

Keitner, I. G., & Miller, I. W. (1990). Family functioning and major depression: An overview. *American Journal of Psychiatry, 147*, 1128–1137.

Kernberg, O. F. (1975). *Borderline Conditions and Pathological Narcissism*. New York: Aronson.

Kessler, R. C., McGonagle, K. A., Nelson, C. B., Hughes, M., Eshelman, S., Wittchen, H. U., & Kendler, K. S. (1994). Lifetime and 12-month prevalence of DSM-III-R psychiatric disorders in the United States. *Archives of General Psychiatry, 51*, 8–19.

Kjeslberg, E., Eikeseth, P. H., & Dahl, A. A. (1991). Suicide in borderline patients—predictive factors. *Acta Psychiatrica Scandinavica, 84*, 283–287.

Kroll, J., Carey, K., & Sines, L. (1982). Are there borderlines in Britain? *Archives of General Psychiatry, 39*, 60–63.

Kroll, J. (1988). *The Challenge of the Borderline Patient*. New York: Norton.

Kroll, J. (1993). *PTSD/Borderlines in Therapy.* New York: Norton.

Kullgren, G. (1988). Factors associated with completed suicide in borderline personality disorder. *Journal of Nervous Mental Diseases, 176*, 40–44.

Kutcher, S. P., Blackwood, D. H. R., Clair, D., Gaskell, D. F., & Muir, W. J. (1987). Auditory P300 in borderline personality disorder and schizophrenia. *Archives of General Psychiatry, 44*, 645–650.

Laporte, L., & Guttman, H. (1996). Traumatic childhood experiences as risk factors for borderline and other personality disorders. *Journal of Personality Disorders, 10*, 247–259.

Leibenluft, E., Gardner, D. L., & Cowdry, R. W. (1987). The inner experience of the borderline self-mutilator. *Journal of Personality Disorders, 1*, 317–324.

Leighton, D. C., Harding, J. S., & Macklin, D. B. (1963). *The Character of Danger: Psychiatric Symptoms in Selected Communities*. New York: Basic.

Lesage, A. D., Boyer, R., Grunberg, F., Morisette, R., Vanier, C., Morrisette, R., Ménard-Buteau, C., & Loyer, M. (1994). Suicide and mental disorders: A case control study of young men. *American Journal of Psychiatry, 151*, 1063–1068.

Leyton, M., Diksic, M., Young, S. N., Okazawa, H., Nishizawa, S., Paris, J., Mzaengeza, S., & Benkelfat, C. (1997). Brain regional rate of 5HT synthesis in borderline personality disorder patients: PET study using ^{11}C-α-methyl-l-tryptophan. Presented to Society for Biological Psychiatry.

Linehan, M. M. (1993). *Cognitive Behavioral Therapy for Borderline Personality Disorder.* New York: Guilford.

Links, P. S., Steiner, M., Offord, D. R., & Eppel, A. (1988a). Characteristics of borderline personality disorder: A Canadian study. *Canadian Journal of Psychiatry, 33*, 336–340.

Links, P. S., Steiner, B., & Huxley, G. (1988b). The occurrence of borderline personality disorder in the families of borderline patients. *Journal of Personality Disorders, 2*, 14–20.

Links, P. S., Mitton, J. E., & Steiner, M. (1990). Predicting outcome for borderline personality disorder. *Comprehensive Psychiatry, 31*, 490–498.

Links, P. S, & van Reekum, R. (1993). Childhood sexual abuse, parental impairment, and the development of borderline personality disorder. *Canadian Journal of Psychiatry, 38*, 472–474.

Links, P. S., Heselgrave, R. J., Mitton, J. E., van Reekum, R., & Patrick, J. (1995a). Borderline psychopathology and recurrences of clinical disorders. *Journal of Nervous and Mental Diseases, 183*, 582–586.

Links, P. S., Heselgrave, R. J., Mitton, J. E., van Reekum, R., & Patrick, J. (1995b). Borderline personality disorder and substance abuse: Consequences of comorbidity. *Canadian Journal of Psychiatry, 40*, 9–14.

Livesley, W. J., Jang, K., Schroeder, M. L., & Jackson, D. N. (1993). Genetic and environmental factors in personality dimensions. *American Journal of Psychiatry, 150*, 1826–1831.

Livesley, W. J., Schroeder, M. L., Jackson, D. N., & Jang, K. (1994). Categorical distinctions in the study of personality disorder: Implications for classification. *Journal of Abnormal Psychology, 103*, 6–17.

Loranger, A. W., Susman, V. L., Oldham, J. M., Russakoff, L. M. (1987). The Personality Disorders Examination (PDE): A preliminary report. *Journal of Personality Disorders, 1*, 1–13.

Loranger, A. W., Sartori, N., Andreoli, A., Berger, P., Bucheim, P., & Channabasavanna, S. M. (1994). The International Personality Disorder Examination. *Archives of General Psychiatry, 51*, 215–224.

Malinovsky-Rummell, R., & Hansen, D. J. (1993). Long-term consequences of physical abuse. *Psychological Bulletin, 114*, 68–79.

Maris, R. (1981). *Pathways to Suicide*. Baltimore: Johns Hopkins Press.

Martial, J., Paris, J., Leyton, M., Zweig-Frank, H., Schwartz, G., Teboul, E., Thavuyandil, J., Larue, S., Ng, Y. J., & Nair, N. P. V. (1997). Neuroendocrine study of serotonergic sensitivity in female borderline personality disorder patients. *Biological Psychiatry, 42*, 737–739.

Martunnen, M., Aro, H. M., Henrikkson, M. M., & Lonnqvist, J. K. (1991). Mental disorder in adolescent suicide: DSM-III-R Axes I and II among 13 to 19 year olds. *Archives of General Psychiatry, 48*, 834–839.

Martunnen, M., Henrikkson, M. M., Aro, H. M., Heikkinen, M. E., Isometsa, E. T., & Lonnqvist, J. K. (1995). Suicide among female adolescents: Characteristics and comparison with males in the age group 13 to 22 years. *Journal of the American Academy of Child and Adolescent Psychiatry, 34*, 1297–1307.

Masterson, J., & Rinsley, D. (1975). The borderline syndrome: Role of the mother in the genesis and psychic structure of the borderline personality. *International Journal of Psychoanalysis, 56*, 163–177.

McGlashan, T. H. (1985). The prediction of outcome in borderline personality disorder. In T. H. McGlashan (Ed.), *The Borderline: Current Empirical Research* (pp. 61–98). Washington, D.C.: American Psychiatric Press.

McGlashan, T. H. (1986). The Chestnut Lodge follow-up study III: Long-term outcome of borderline personalities. *Archives of General Psychiatry, 43*, 2–30.

McGlashan, T. H. (1993). Implications of outcome research for the treatment of borderline personality disorder. In J. Paris (Ed.), *Borderline Personality Disorder: Etiology and Treatment* (pp. 235–260). Washington, D.C.: American Psychiatric Press.

McGuffin, P., & Thapar, A. (1992). The genetics of personality disorder. *British Journal of Psychiatry, 160*, 12–23.

Melges, F. T., & Swartz, M. S. (1989). Oscillations of attachment in borderline personality disorder. *American Journal of Psychiatry, 146*, 1115–1120.

Millon, T. (1987). On the genesis and prevalence of borderline personality disorder: A social learning thesis. *Journal of Personality Disorders, 1*, 354–372.

Millon, T. (1992). The borderline construct: Introductory notes on its history, theory, and empirical grounding. In J. F. Clarkin, E. Marziali, & H. Munroe-Blum (Eds.), *Borderline Personality Disorder: Clinical and Empirical Perspectives* (pp. 3–26). New York: Guilford.

Millon, T. (1993). Borderline personality disorder: A psychosocial epidemic. In J. Paris (Ed.), *Borderline Personality Disorder: Etiology and Treatment* (pp. 197–210). Washington, D.C.: American Psychiatric Press.

Monroe, S. M., & Simons, A. D. (1991). Diathesis-stress theories in the context of life stress research. *Psycholical Bulletin, 110*, 406–425.

Morey, L. C., & Ochoa, E. S. (1989). An investigation of adherence to diagnostic criteria: Clinical diagnosis of the DSM-III personality disorders. *Journal of Personality Disorders, 3*, 183–192.

Murphy, H. B. M. (1982). *Comparative Psychiatry.* New York: Springer-Verlag.

Najavits, L. M., & Gunderson, J. G. (1995). Better than expected: Improvements in borderline personality disorder in a 3 year prospective outcome study. *Comprehensive Psychiatry, 36*, 296–302.

Nash, M. R., Hulsely, T. L., Sexton, M. C., Harralson, T. L., & Lambert, W. (1993). Long-term effects of childhood sexual abuse: Perceived family environment, psychopathology, and dissociation. *Journal of Consulting and Clinical Psychology, 61*, 276–283.

Nigg, J. T., & Goldsmith, H. H. (1994). Genetics of personality disorders: Perspectives from personality and psychopathology research. *Psychological Bulletin, 115*, 346–380.

Nurnberg, H. G., Raskin, M., Levine, P. E., Pollack, S., Siegel, O., & Prince, R. (1991). The comorbidity of borderline personality disorder with other DSM-III-R Axis II personality disorders. *American Journal of Psychiatry, 148*, 1311–1317.

Ogata, S. N., Silk, K. R., Goodrich, S., Lohr, N. E., Westen, D., & Hill, E. M. (1990a). Childhood sexual and physical abuse in adult patients with borderline personality disorder. *American Journal of Psychiatry, 147*, 1008–1013.

Ogata, S. N., Silk, K. R., & Goodrich, S. (1990b). The childhood experience of the borderline patient. In P. S. Links (Ed.), *Family Environment and Borderline Personality Disorder* (pp. 85–104). Washington, D.C.: American Psychiatric Press.

Oldham, J. M., Skodol, A. E., Kellman, D., Hyler, S. E., Rosnick, L., & Davies, M. (1992). Diagnosis of DSM-III-R personality disorders by two structured interviews: Patterns of comorbidity. *American Journal of Psychiatry, 149*, 213–220.

O'Leary, K. M., Bouwers, P., Gardner, D. L., & Cowdry, R. W. (1991). Neuropsychological testing of patients with borderline personality disorder. *American Journal of Psychiatry, 148*, 106–111.

O'Leary, K. M., & Cowdry, R. W. (1994). Neuropsychological testing results with patients with borderline personality disorder. In K. R. Silk (Ed.), *Biological and Neurobehavioral Studies of Borderline Personality Disorder* (pp. 127–158). Washington, D.C.: American Psychiatric Press.

Paris, J. (1988). Follow-up studies of borderline personality: A critical review. *Journal of Personality Disorders, 2*, 189–197.

Paris, J. (1991). Personality disorders, parasuicide, and culture. *Transcultural Psychiatric Research Review, 28*, 25–40.

Paris, J. (1992). Social factors in borderline personality disorder: A review and a hypothesis. *Canadian Journal of Psychiatry, 37*, 510–515.

Paris, J. (1993). Long-term outcome of borderline personality disorder: Implications for treatment. *Canadian Journal of Psychiatry, 38*, S28–34.

Paris, J. (1994a). *Borderline Personality Disorder: A Multidimensional Approach.* Washington, D.C.: American Psychiatric Press.

Paris, J. (1994b). The etiology of borderline personality disorder: A biopsychosocial model. *Psychiatry, 57*, 300–307.

Paris, J. (1995). Memories of abuse in BPD: True or false? *Harvard Review Psychiatry, 3*, 10–17.

Paris, J. (1996). *Social Factors in the Personality Disorders: A biopsychosocial approach to etiology and treatment.* New York: Cambridge University Press.

Paris, J. (1997). Antisocial and borderline personality disorders: Two separate diagnoses or two aspects of the same psychopathology? *Comprehensive Psychiatry, 38*, 237–242.

Paris, J. (1999). *Nature and Nurture in Psychiatry: A Predisposition-Stress Model.* Washington, D.C.: American Psychiatric Press.

Paris, J., Brown, R., & Nowlis, D. (1987). Long-term follow-up of borderline patients in a general hospital. *Comprehensive Psychiatry, 28*, 530–535.

Paris, J., Nowlis, D., & Brown, R. (1988). Developmental factors in the outcome of borderline personality disorder. *Comprehensive Psychiatry, 29*, 147–15.

Paris, J., Nowlis, D., & Brown, R. (1989). Predictors of suicide in borderline personality disorder. *Canadian Journal of Psychiatry, 34*, 8–9.

Paris, J., & Zweig-Frank, H. (1992) A critical review of the role of childhood sexual abuse in the etiology of borderline personality disorder. *Canadian Journal of Psychiatry, 37*, 125–128.

Paris, J., Frank, H., Buonvino, M., & Bond, M. (1991). Recollections of parental behavior and Axis II cluster diagnosis. *Journal of Personality Disorders, 5*, 102–106.

Paris, J., & Braverman, S. (1995). Successful and unsuccessful marriages in borderline patients. *Journal of the American Academy of Psychoanalysis, 23*, 153–166.

Paris, J., & Zweig-Frank, H. (1993). Parental bonding in borderline patients. In J. Paris (Ed.), *Borderline Personality Disorder: Etiology and Treatment* (pp. 141–160). Washington, D.C.: American Psychiatric Press.

Paris, J., Zweig-Frank, H., & Guzder, J. (1993). Psychological risk factors and recovery from borderline personality disorder. *Comprehensive Psychiatry, 34*, 410–413.

Paris, J., Zweig-Frank, H., & Guzder, J. (1994a). Psychological risk factors for borderline personality disorder in female patients. *Comprehensive Psychiatry, 35*, 301–305.

Paris, J., Zweig-Frank, H., & Guzder, J. (1994b). Risk factors for borderline personality in male outpatients. *Journal of Nervous and Mental Diseases, 182*, 375–380.

Paris, J., Zweig-Frank, H., Bond, M., & Guzder, J. (1996). Defense styles, hostility, and psychological risk factors in male patients with personality disorders. *Journal of Nervous Mental Diseases, 184*, 155–160.

Parker, G. (1983). *Parental overprotection: A risk factor in psychosocial development.* New York: Grune and Stratton.

Patrick, M., Hobson, P., Castle, D., Howard, R., & Maughan, B. (1994). Personality disorder and the mental representation of early social experience. *Development and Psychopathology, 6*, 375–388.

Perry, J. C. (1992). Problems and considerations in the valid assessment of personality disorders. *American Journal of Psychiatry, 149*, 1645–1653.

Petti, T., & Vela, R. (1990). Borderline disorder of childhood: An overview. *Journal of the American Academy of Child and Adolescent Psychiatry, 29*, 327–337.

Pfohl, B., Coryell, W., Zimmerman, M., & Stangl, D. (1986). DSM-III personality disorders: Diagnostic overlap and internal consistency of individual DSM-III criteria. *Comprehensive Psychiatry, 27*, 21–34.

Pinto, A., Grapentine, W. L., Francis, G., & Piccariello, C. M. (1996). Borderline personality disorder in adolescence: Affective and cognitive features. *Journal of the American Academy of Child and Adolescent Psychiatry, 35*, 1338–1343.

Plakun, E. M., Burkhardt, P. E., & Muller, J. P. (1986). 14 year follow-up of borderline and schizotypal personality disorders. *Comprehensive Psychiatry, 27*, 448–455.

Plomin, R., & Bergeman, C. S. (1991). The nature of nurture: Genetic influence on "environmental" measures. *Behavioral and Brain Sciences, 14*, 373–427.

Plomin, R., DeFries, J. C., McClearn, G. E., & Rutter, M. M. (1997). *Behavioral Genetics: A Primer.* New York: W. H. Freeman.

Pokorny, A. D. (1983). Prediction of suicide in psychiatric patients: Report of a prospective study. *Archives of General Psychiatry, 40*, 23–40.

Pollock, V. E., Briere, J., Schneider, L., Knop, J., Mednick, S. A., & Goodwin, D. W. (1990). Childhood antecedents of antisocial behavior: Parental alcoholism and physical abusiveness. *American Journal of Psychiatry, 147*, 1290–1293.

Pope, H. G., Jonas, J. M., & Hudson, J. I. (1983). The validity of DSM-III borderline personality disorder. *Archives of General Psychiatry, 40*, 23–30.

Reich, J., Yates, W., & Nduaguba, M. (1989). Prevalence of DSM-III personality disorders in the community. *Social Psychiatry and Psychiatric Epidemiology, 24*, 12–16.

Rey, J. M., Morris-Yates, A., Singh, M., Andrews, G., & Stewart, G. W. (1995). Continuities between psychiatric disorders in adolescents and personality disorders in young adults. *American Journal of Psychiatry, 152*, 895–900.

Rich, C. L., Fowler, R. C., Fogarty, L. A., & Young, D. (1988). San Diego suicide study: Relationships between diagnoses and stressors. *Archives of General Psychiatry, 45*, 589–594.

Rich, C. L., & Runeson, B. S. (1992). Similarities in diagnostic comorbidity between suicide among young people in Sweden and the United States. *Acta Psychiatrica Scandinavica, 86*, 335–339.

Robins, E., & Guze, S. B. (1970). Establishment of diagnostic validity in psychiatric illness: Its application to schizophrenia. *American Journal of Psychiatry, 126*, 107–111.

Robins, L. N., & Regier, D. A. (Eds). (1991). *Psychiatric Disorders in America.* New York: Free Press.

Robson, K. R. (1983). *The Borderline Child.* New York: McGraw-Hill

Ross, C. (1991). Epidemiology of multiple personality and dissociation. *Psychiatric Clinics of North America, 14*, 503–518.

Runeson, B., & Beskow, J. (1991). Borderline personality disorder in young Swedish suicides. *Journal of Nervous and Mental Diseases, 179*, 153–156.

Rutter, M. (1987). Temperament, Personality, and Personality Disorders. *British Journal of Psychiatry, 150*, 443–448.

Rutter, M. (1989). Pathways from childhood to adult life. *Journal of Child Psychology and Psychiatry, 30*, 23–51.

Rutter, M., & Madge, N. (1976). *Cycles of disadvantage: A review of research*. London: Heinemann.

Sabo, A. N., Gunderson, J. G., Najavits, L. M., Chauncey, D., & Kiesel, C. (1995). Changes in self-destructiveness of borderline patients in psychotherapy: A prospective follow up. *Journal of Nervous and Mental Diseases, 183*, 370–376.

Schmideberg, M. (1959). The borderline patient. In S. Arieti (Ed.), *American Handbook of Psychiatry* (pp. 398–416), Volume 1, New York: Basic.

Siever, L. J., & Davis, K. L. (1991). A psychobiological perspective on the personality disorders. *American Journal of Psychiatry, 148*, 1647–1658.

Silk, K. R. (Ed.). (1994). *Biological and Neurobehavioral Studies of Borderline Personality Disorder.* Washington, D.C.: American Psychiatric Press.

Silk, K. R., Lee, S., Hill, E. M., & Lohr, N. E. (1995). Borderline personality disorder and severity of sexual abuse. *American Journal of Psychiatry, 152*, 1059–1064.

Silver, D., & Cardish, R. (1991). BPD outcome studies: Psychotherapy implications. Presented at the American Psychiatric Association. New Orleans, LA (May).

Silverman, J. M., Pinkham, L., Horvath, T. B., Coccaro, E. R., Klar, H., Schear, S., Apter, S., Davidson, M., Mohs, R. C., & Siever, L. J. (1991). Affective and impulsive personality disorder traits in the relatives of patients with borderline personality disorder. *American Journal of Psychiatry, 148*, 1378–1385.

Simonsen, E. (1993). Prevalence of BPD in Europe. Presented to American Psychiatric Association. San Francisco, CA (May).

Skodol, A. E., Buckley, P., & Charles, E. (1983). Is there a characteristic pattern to the treatment history of clinic patients with borderline personality disorder? *Journal of Nervous and Mental Diseases, 171*, 405–410.

Soloff, P. H., & Millward, J. W. (1983). Psychiatric disorders in the families of borderline patients. *Archives of General Psychiatry, 40*, 37–44.

Soloff, P. H., & Millward, J. W. (1983). Developmental histories of borderline patients. *Comprehensive Psychiatry, 23*, 574–588.

Spitzer, R. L., Endicott, J., & Gibbon, M. (1979). Crossing the border into borderline personality disorder. *Archives of General Psychiatry, 36*, 17–24.

Spitzer, R. L., & Williams, J. B.W. (1986). *Structured clinical Interview for DSM-III-R Personality Disorders*. New York: Biometric Research Department, New York State Psychiatric Institute.

Stern, A. (1938). Psychoanalytic investigation of and therapy in the borderline group of neuroses. *Psychoanalytical Quarterly, 7*, 467–489.

Stone, M. H. (1990). *The Fate of Borderline Patients*. New York: Guilford.

Stone, M. H. (1993). Etiology of borderline personality disorder: Psychobiological factors contributing to an underlying irritability. In J. Paris (Ed.), *Borderline Personality Disorder: Etiology and Treatment* (pp. 87–102). Washington, D.C.: American Psychiatric Press.

Sudak, H. S., Ford, A. B., & Rushforth, N. B. (Eds.). (1984). *Suicide in the Young*. Boston: John Wright.

Sullivan, P. F., Joyce, P. R., & Mulder, R. T. (1994). Borderline personality diosrder in major depression. *Journal of Nervous and Mental Diseases, 182*, 508–516.

Swartz, M., Blazer, D., George, L., & Winfield, I. (1990). Estimating the prevalence of borderline personality disorder in the community. *Journal of Personality Disorders, 4*, 257–272.

Swett, C., Surrey, J., & Cohen, C. (1990). Sexual and physical abuse histories among male psychiatric outpatients. *American Journal of Psychiatry, 147*, 632–636.

Tennant, C. (1988). Parental loss in childhood to adult life. *Archives of General Psychiatry, 45*, 1045–1050.

Terr, L. C. (1991). Childhood traumas: An outline and an overview. *American Journal of Psychiatry, 148*, 10–20.

Torgesen, S. (1984). Genetic and nosological aspects of schizotypal and borderline personality disorders: A twin study. *Archives of General Psychiatry, 35*, 153–155.

Torgersen, S. (1996). Personality disorders in our genes? Presentation to the *Second European Congress on Personality Disorders*. Milan (June).

Tyrer, P. (1988). *Personality disorders: Diagnosis, management, and course*. Boston: Wright.

Vaillant, G. E. (1973). A 20 year follow-up of New York narcotics addicts. *Archives of General Psychiatry, 29*, 237–241.

Vaillant, G. E. (1977). *Adaptation to Life*. Cambridge, MA: Little, Brown.

Vaillant, G. E. (1994). *The Natural History of Alcoholism*, second edition. Cambridge, MA: Harvard University Press.

van der Kolk, B. A., Perry, J. C., & Herman, J. L. (1991). Childhood origins of self-destructive behavior. *American Journal of Psychiatry, 148*, 1665–1671.

van Reekum, R., Links, P. S., & Boiago, I. (1993). Constitutional factors in borderline personality disorder. In J. Paris (Ed.), *Borderline Personality Disorder: Etiology and Treatment* (pp. 13–38). Washington, D.C.: American Psychiatric Press.

Weissman, M. W. (1974). The epidemiology of suicide attempts, 1960 to 1971. *Archives of General Psychiatry, 30*, 737–746.

Werble, B. (1970). Second follow-up study of borderline patients. *Archives of General Psychiatry, 23*, 3–7.

Werner, E. E., & Smith, R. S. (1992). *Overcoming the Odds: High Risk Children from Birth to Adulthood.* New York: Cornell University Press.

West, M. O., & Prinz, R. J. (1987). Parental alcoholism and childhood psychopathology. *Psychological Bulletin, 102*, 204–224.

Westen, D. (1985). *Self and Society: Narcissism, Collectivism and the Development of Morals.* New York: Cambridge University Press.

Westen, D. (1997). Divergences between clinical and research methods for assessing personality disorders. *American Journal of Psychiatry, 154*, 895–903.

Westen, D., Moses, M. J., Silk, K. R., Lohr, N. E., Cohen, R., & Segal, H. (1992). Quality of depressive experience in BPD and major depression. *Journal of Personality Disorders, 6*, 382–393.

Zanarini, M. C. (1993). Borderline personality as an impulse spectrum disorder. In J. Paris (Ed.), *Borderline Personality Disorder: Etiology and Treatment* (pp. 67–86). Washington, D.C.: American Psychiatric Press.

Zanarini, M. C., Frankenburg, F. R., Chauncey, D. L., & Gunderson, J. G. (1987). The diagnostic interview for personality disorders: Interrater and test-retest reliability. *Comprehensive Psychiatry, 28*, 467–480.

Zanarini, M. C., Gunderson, J. G., & Frankenburg, F. R. (1989a). The revised diagnostic interview for borderlines: Discriminating BPD from other Axis II disorders. *Journal of Personality Disorders, 3*, 10–18.

Zanarini, M. C., Gunderson, J. G., Marino, M. F., Schwartz, E. O., & Frankenburg, F. R. (1989b). Childhood experiences of borderline patients. *Comprehensive Psychiatry, 30*, 18–25.

Zanarini, M. C., Gunderson, J. G., & Frankenburg, F. R. (1989c). Axis I phenomenology of borderline personality disorder. *Comprehensive Psychiatry, 30*, 149–156.

Zanarini, M. C., Gunderson, J. G., & Frankenburg, F. R. (1990a). Cognitive features of borderline personality disorder. *American Journal of Psychiatry, 147*, 57–63.

Zanarini, M. C., Gunderson, J. G., & Frankenburg, F. R. (1990b). Discriminating borderline personality disorder from other Axis II disorders. *American Journal of Psychiatry, 147*, 161–167.

Zanarini, M. C., Williams, A. A., Lewis, R. E., Reich, R. B., Vera, S. C., Marino, M. F., Levin, A., Yong, L., & Frankenburg, F. R. (1997). Reported pathological childhood experiences associated with the development of borderline personality disorder. *American Journal of Psychiatry, 154*, 1101–1106.

Zanarini, M. C., Frankenburg, F. R., Dubo, E. D., & Sickel, A. E. (1998a). Axis I comorbidity of borderline personality disorder. *American Journal of Psychiatry, 155*, 1733–1739.

Zanarini, M. C., Frankenburg, F. R., Dubo, E. D., & Sickel, A. E. (1998b). Axis II comorbidity of borderline personality disorder. *Comprehensive Psychiatry, 39*, 296–302.

Zimmerman, M. (1994). Diagnosing personality disorders. *Archives of General Psychiatry, 51*, 225–245.

Zuckerman, J. (1979). *Sensation seeking: Beyond the optimum level of arousal.* Hillsdale, NJ: Erlbaum.

Zweig-Frank, H., & Paris, J. (1991). Recollections of emotional neglect and overprotection in borderline patients. *American Journal of Psychiatry, 148*, 648–651.

Zweig-Frank, H., Paris, J., & Guzder, J. (1994). Psychological risk factors for disssociation and self-mutilation in female patients with personality disorders. *Canadian Journal of Psychiatry, 39*, 259–265.

26

Depressive and Self-Defeating (Masochistic) Personality Disorders

DANIEL N. KLEIN
CARINA VOCISANO

In terms of historical development, the constructs of depressive and self-defeating (masochistic) personality disorder are intertwined and overlap to some degree. However, they can be distinguished on both conceptual and empirical grounds. This chapter begins by reviewing the clinical and empirical literature on depressive personality disorder. As self-defeating (masochistic) personality has been dropped from the current diagnostic nomenclature, it is reviewed more briefly. The chapter focuses on syndromal conceptualizations, rather than on dimensional and nonpathological conceptualizations of depressive and self-defeating or masochistic personality traits (Akiskal, Hirschfeld, & Yerevanian, 1983; Baumeister, 1988; Baumeister & Sher, 1988; Clark, Watson, & Mineka, 1994).

Depressive Personality Disorder

Individuals with depressive personality disorder are predisposed to interpret the events in their lives, whether trivial or important, in an overwhelmingly pessimistic way. They view themselves as inadequate and worthless, and act as their own prosecutor and tormentor. Minor mistakes result in bouts of self-criticism, self-blame, and self-depreciation. Even when faced with achievements that others find rewarding, these individuals focus on their own failures and shortcomings. People with depressive personality disorder are often overly conscientious and extend their perfectionistic expectations to others. Family members, friends and coworkers may be judged critically and harshly.

People with depressive personality take life too seriously. They shun opportunities for enjoyment because they feel undeserving of happiness. Joy in the present does not offer refuge from their pessimism, and neither does review of the past. Looking back, individuals with depressive personality disorder dwell on failures and experience guilt and remorse about what they did, and failed to do. Hope for the future is similarly truncated; they worry a great deal and anticipate the worst.

These characteristics cause moderate impairment, particularly in social functioning. Although individuals with depressive personality appear to be vulnerable to developing mood disorders, they do not evidence vegetative symptoms, and their symptoms tend to be less severe than is evidenced in major depressive and dysthymic disorder.

The "depressive temperament" was described by Kraepelin in 1921, and since then the concept has been widely used in the clinical literature. However, the empirical literature on the epidemiology, etiology, course, and development of depressive personality disorder is limited. The paucity of empirical studies may be due to the fact that, until recently, clear and consistent definitions of the central characteristics of depressive personality disorder had not been established. The inclusion of a depressive personality disorder category in the appendix of *DSM-IV* should facilitate research on this condition. The available theoretical and empirical literature on the construct of depressive personality disorder is reviewed in the first part of this chapter. Other recent reviews of this topic are available in Phillips, Gunderson, Hirschfeld, and Smith (1990) and Phillips, Hirschfeld, Shea, and Gunderson (1995).

Historical Background

Until the 1960s, discussion of depressive personality disorder was largely limited to the German phenomenological literature. In 1921, Emil Kraepelin described individuals with "depressive temperament" as "characterized by a permanent gloomy emotional stress in all the experiences of life," and as despairing and despondent, lacking self-confidence, burdened with guilt and self-reproach, ruminative and indecisive, anxious, quiet and shy, easily fatigued, lacking in vitality and initiative, and particularly susceptible to the difficulties and disappointments of life.

Kraepelin believed that the depressive temperament was inherited, and was generally evident by childhood or adolescence. He noted that the course tended to be stable, although many cases progressed to full-blown major mood disorders. Indeed, Kraepelin argued that the depressive temperament represented one of the "fundamental states" underlying the major mood disorders, a rudimentary form of mood disorder from which major affective episodes "rise like mountain peaks from a structurally similar plain" (Slater & Roth, 1969).

Kretschmer (1925) expressed similar ideas in his book *Physique and Character*. He described several affective personality types, including a depressive temperament that was characterized by many of the same traits observed by Kraepelin. Kretschmer noted that the predominant mood in persons with depressive personality is not sadness. Rather, they tend to be less cheerful and joyous than others, and more easily affected by sad conditions. Like Kraepelin, Kretschmer believed that the affective personality types were constitutional in origin and predisposed to the development of major mood disorders.

Kurt Schneider's (1958) description of "depressive psychopathy" is also similar to Kraepelin's depressive temperament. (Schneider used the term "psychopathy" as a general term for personality disorder, rather than to refer to what is currently called antisocial personality disorder.) According to Schneider, the depressive psychopath tends to be gloomy and pessimistic, quiet and self-effacing, duty-bound, anxious, and lacking a capacity for frank enjoyment. Schneider also noted that these individuals often overvalue themselves, viewing those with more happy, lighted-hearted natures as superficial. According to Schneider, they frequently see suffering as meritorious, and "there is a tendency to establish an aristocracy of discomfort." Schneider also suggested that depressive psychopathy may be more common in males. Like Kraepelin and Kretschmer, Schneider noted that the onset was typically in childhood or adolescence. However, he rejected the argument that there was a biogenetic link between depressive personality and the major mood disorders. Interestingly, Schneider observed that while it is sometimes helpful for people with depressive personality to "talk things out," "work is their best friend and the wisest therapy is to help them along these lines" (p. 84).

Tellenbach (1961) described a constellation of traits similar to earlier concepts of the depressive personality, which he referred to as "typus melancholicus." He reported that many of the same characteristics described by Kraepelin were common in the premorbid personalities of patients who had recovered from full-blown episodes of melancholic depression. However, Tellenbach placed greater emphasis on compulsive features, such as orderliness, conscientiousness, devotion to duty, scrupulousness, and achievement orientation, as well as on interpersonal dependency.

Psychoanalytic investigators have generally focused on premorbid personality traits (especially oral, or passive-dependent, and anal, or obsessive-compulsive features) that were thought to predispose individuals to develop depressive episodes, rather than on the depressive personality per se. However, in the 1960s and 1970s, a number of psychoanalytic investigators, such as Berliner (1966), Laughlin (1967), Kahn (1975), and Bemporad (1976) made important contributions to the literature on depressive personality disorder. These theorists tended to view the depressive personality as developing in the context of disturbed early relationships, rather than being due to constitutional factors. Despite the significant differences between the German phenomenologists' and the psychoanalysts' views of the etiology of depressive personality, their descriptions of clinical features were quite similar.

The leading contemporary psychoanalytic theorist in this area is Otto Kernberg (1984, 1988). Influenced by Freud's writings on moral masochism, Kernberg proposed a broader construct of depressive personality that included masochistic, as well as depressive, traits. According to Kernberg, the core underlying features of depressive-masochistic character disorder are an excessively punitive super-ego, difficulty expressing aggression, and overdependence on others. Owing to their harsh superegos, individuals with depressive-masochistic personality disorder tend to be overly serious, responsible, conscientious, and concerned about work performance, as well as somber, humorless, and critical of themselves and others. When they fail to meet their own high standards, they become depressed. They also tend to be overdependent on others' support, love, and acceptance. This can produce vicious cycles of excessive demandingness, feelings of rejection, and an unconscious tendency to make others feel guilty. This, in turn, may result in actual rejection by others, which can trigger depressive episodes related to the loss of love. Kernberg also noted that individuals with depressive-masochistic character disorders tend to inhibit angry, critical thoughts and feelings to the point of appearing overly agreeable and polite. Following Freud, Kernberg hypothesized that these aggressive feelings are turned inward via the process of introjection, leading to depression.

The concept of depressive-masochistic character disorder has been criticized by Simons (1986), who argued that masochistic and depressive personality disorders are really distinct conditions. According to Simons, patients with depressive personality disorder internalize their conflicts in the form of self punishment and self-blame. In contrast, individuals with masochistic personality disorder externalize their "inner struggle" by unconsciously provoking retaliation by others that reflects their own self-disdain.

It is interesting to note that much of the theoretical and empirical work on the psychological processes underlying Axis I depression in recent years is consonant with the clinical literature on depressive personality. For example, most cognitive theories of depression, beginning with Beck (1967) and Seligman (1975), emphasize the role of traitlike factors that predispose to depression, most of which were described in the classic writings on the depressive personality (e.g., the tendency to view the self, future, and world in a negative light; a propensity to feel helpless and hopeless). Moreover, a variety of theorists from both the psychoanalytic and cognitive traditions have recently emphasized the roles of dependent and self-critical personality styles in the vulnerability to major depressive episodes (Ouimette & Klein, 1993).

Classification

While neither *DSM-I* nor *DSM-II* included a category for depressive personality, both included a category for cyclothymic (or affective) personality, noting that it could assume predominantly hypomanic, depressive, and alternating forms. In *DSM-III* and *DSM-III-R*, depressive personality was subsumed under the rubric of dysthymic disorder. However, in light of evidence that criteria for depressive personality and dysthymia identified different, albeit overlapping, groups (see section on Comorbidity: Mood Disorders below), depressive personality disorder was included in the *DSM-IV* appendix as a condition requiring further study.

There are currently three sets of explicit diagnostic criteria for depressive personality. Based on Schneider's (1958) descriptive work, Akiskal (1983) proposed a set of criteria that included five of the following groups of traits: (1) quiet, introverted, passive, and nonassertive; (2) gloomy, pessimistic, serious, and incapable of fun; (3) self-critical, self-reproaching, and self-derogatory; (4) skeptical, critical of others, and hard to please; (5) conscientious, responsible, and self-disciplining; (6) brooding and given to worry; and (7) preoccupied with negative events, feelings of inadequacy, and personal shortcomings.

Gunderson, Phillips, Triebwasser, and Hirschfeld (1994) developed a comprehensive semistructured interview, the Diagnostic Interview for Depressive Personality (DIDP), to assess most of the traits associated with depressive personality in the descriptive and psychoanalytic literatures. The interview consists of 30 traits in four general areas: depressive/negativistic (e.g., gloomy, pessimistic, remorseful, low self-esteem, worried, critical of others, self-critical), introverted/tense (e.g., introverted, quiet, constricted, serious, difficulty having fun), unassertive/passive (e.g., unassertive, passive, dependent, hypersensitive), and masochistic (e.g., moralistic, self-denying). The scores for the items are totaled, and a diagnosis of depressive personality is made based on a predetermined cutoff.

Finally, the *DSM-IV* criteria require five or more of the following traits: usual mood is dominated by dejection, gloominess, cheerlessness, joylessness, unhappiness; self-concept centers around beliefs of inadequacy, worthlessness, and low self-esteem; is critical, blaming, and derogatory toward self; is brooding and given to worry; is negativistic, critical and judgmental toward others; is pessimistic; and is prone to feeling guilty or remorseful.

Although these three criteria sets overlap substantially, they vary somewhat in content and breadth. Using the *DSM-IV* Mood Disorders Field Trial sample, Hirschfeld and Holzer (1994) found that the *DSM-IV* criteria for depressive personality were the most inclusive, diagnosing 41% of the sample. Gunderson et al.'s criteria were intermediate, diagnosing 37% of the sample. Finally, Akiskal's criteria were the narrowest, diagnosing 31% of the sample. Based on data reported in the paper, it is possible to calculate the concordance among the three criteria sets. Kappa for the concordance between the *DSM-IV* and Akiskal criteria was .57; for *DSM-IV* and the Gunderson et al. criteria, it was .64; and for the Gunderson and Akiskal criteria it was .60.

Internal Construct Validity

Hirschfeld and Holzer (1994) also conducted a principal components analysis of the DIDP. They reported a four-factor solution that corresponded fairly closely to the a priori structure of the DIDP: depressive/negativistic, introverted/tense, passive/unassertive, and conscientious/moralistic.

Several studies have examined the item characteristics of specific definitions of depressive personality (Gunderson et al., 1994; Klein, 1990; Klein & Miller, 1993). These studies have yielded consistent results indicating that traits like gloominess, joylessness, pessimism, self-criticism, feelings of inadequacy, low self-esteem, brooding, and remorse are at the core of the depressive personality construct. Introversion and passivity also appear to be important, but are less central to the construct. Conscientiousness is not correlated with the other features of depressive personality, and therefore may not be an integral component. Finally, the role of being skeptical and critical of others remains unclear. Interestingly, the *DSM-IV* criteria primarily consist of the core traits, and do not include most of the less central features. However, these non-core features may still play a role in contributing to discriminant and predictive validity, as discussed in the section on "Relationship to Normal Personality Dimension" on page 660.

Interrater Reliability and Mood-State Effects

Four studies have examined the interrater reliability of depressive personality using a paired-rater design. Kappas for presence or absence of depressive personality disorder ranged from .62 to .82, with a median of .75 (Gunderson et al., 1994; Klein, 1990; Klein, Clark, Dansky, & Margolis, 1988; Klein & Miller, 1993).

There have been two test-retest reliability studies of depressive personality. Using 6- and 14-month test-retest intervals, respectively, Klein (1990) and Gunderson et al. (1994) both reported Kappas of .41 for the diagnosis of depressive personality.

In order to examine the effects of mood state on the assessment of depressive personality, Klein (1990) compared the number of depressive personality traits in a group of outpatients when they were in a major depressive episode and again after they had been fully recovered for at least two months. The means were almost identical, and the difference did not approach statistical significance, suggesting that assessments of depressive personality are not biased by current mood state.

Epidemiology

No data on the prevalence of depressive personality disorder in the general population are available. Klein (1990) found that the prevalence of depressive personality disorder in a large sample of consecutive outpatients was 26% using a cutoff of six of the seven traits in Akiskal's (1983) critera. However, Klein (1990) also noted that the prevalence varied considerably depending on the particular cutoff employed.

Consistent differences have not been reported between persons with and without depressive personality disorder on sex, age, race, marital status, education, or socioeconomic status (Hirschfeld & Holzer, 1994; Klein, 1990; Klein & Miller, 1993; Perugi, Musetti, Simonini, Piagentini, Cassano, & Akiskal, 1990; Phillips, Gunderson, Kimball, Triebwassser, & Faedda, 1992). The lack of consistent sex differences is noteworthy in light of the higher rates of major depressive and dysthymic disorder in women (Weissman et al., 1996). While these data fail to support Schneider's (1958) observation that depressive personality is more common in males, they do suggest that there may be a relative male preponderance when compared to Axis I depressive conditions. More direct support for this point comes from a study by Klein (1990), who found a higher prevalence of males among subjects with depressive personality but no diagnosis of dysthymia, compared to subjects with dysthymia but no diagnosis of depressive personality. This finding may also be relevant to Kretschmer's (1925) observation that many individuals with depressive personality are clearly unhappy, but do not experience sadness. Sad mood is not required in any of the current criteria for depressive personality disorder (see section on Differential Diagnosis below). If women are more likely to experience or express sadness than men, this may explain why males are more likely than females to meet criteria for depressive personality but not dysthymic disorder.

Differential Diagnosis and Comorbidity

The theoretical literature is replete with observations and arguments about where depressive personality should be conceptualized in relation to other mood and personality disorders. In contrast, empirical data on these issues are more limited. A few studies provide data on the diagnostic boundaries between depressive personality disorder and the mood disorders. The relationship between depressive personality and other personality disorders, however, remains even more poorly charted.

Differential Diagnosis: Mood Disorders The most difficult condition to differentiate from depressive personality disorder is dysthymic disorder, particularly the early-onset (before age 21) subtype. Indeed, the relationship between the two disorders has been very controversial. As reviewed below, recent empirical studies suggest that depressive personality disorder and dysthymia are overlapping, but not identical, constructs. The two conditions share a number of clinical features (e.g., low self-esteem, pessimism/hopelessness), and both are persistent and longstanding. However, they also differ in a number of respects. First, the *DSM-IV* requires persistent depressed mood for a diagnosis of dysthymia, and includes several vegetative symptoms (e.g., sleep and appetite disturbance) in its list of associated symptoms. In contrast, none of the criteria for depressive personality require, or even include, depressed mood or any vegetative symptoms. Rather, depressive personality is defined in terms of personality traits or dispositions, often of a cognitive nature. Second, dysthymic disorder is a more severe condition that causes greater distress and impairment. Third, depressive personality is evident by young adulthood and is assumed to be a lifelong condition, while dysthymic disorder can develop at any age and may be as short as two years in duration. Finally, individuals with depressive personality view their depressive traits as part of their characteristic personalities. While many persons with dysthymic disorder also see their depressive symptoms as part of their usual selves, others view their symptoms as "ego-dystonic," and a departure from their true personality.

Depressive personality disorder is more easily distinguished from major depressive disorder. Unlike depressive personality, the core features of major depressive disorder include persistent depressed mood, psychomotor, sleep, and appetite disturbances, difficulty concentrating or making decisions, and suicidal ideation or behavior. Major depressive episodes can be as brief as two weeks in duration, and the majority of persons with major depressive disorder remit within one year. Finally, major depressive disorder is characterized by discrete episodes of mood disturbance that cause much greater impairment than is typically associated with depressive personality disorder. However, it may be more difficult to distinguish depressive personality disorder from a major depressive episode that is chronic or has only partially remitted.

Comorbidity: Mood Disorders The five studies that have examined the relationship between depressive personality and the mood disorders have yielded fairly consistent results, despite using a variety of subject populations and criteria for depressive personality (Hirschfeld & Holzer, 1994; Klein, 1990; Klein & Miller, 1993; Klein & Shih, 1998; Phillips et al., 1992). In all but one of these studies (Phillips et al., 1992) there was a significant association between depressive personality and dysthymia; however the magnitude of the associations has been quite modest. For example, Kappas for the association between depressive personality and dysthymic disorder ranged from .09 to .42, with a median of .25. The association between depressive personality and the early-onset subtype of dysthymia was slightly higher in one study (Klein, 1990), but lower in another (Hirschfeld & Holzer, 1994).

These data suggest that, although there is significant overlap between depressive personality and dysthymic disorder, the two constructs are not identical. A significant number of individuals who meet criteria for depressive personality do not meet criteria for dysthymic disorder, and vice versa. The distinction between these constructs is further supported by evidence that depressive personality and dysthymic disorder have differing clinical correlates. Klein (1990) compared a group of outpatients with depressive personality but not dysthymia to a group with dysthymia but not depressive personality. As noted above, there was a higher proportion of males in the depressive personality group. In contrast, patients with dysthymia had a higher level of depressive symptoms, both at entry into treatment and at six-month follow-up, and a higher rate of depression in their first-degree relatives. In addition, there was a trend for a higher rate of borderline personality disorder in the dysthymic group, suggesting that dysthymia may be more heterogeneous with respect to personality style. This last finding is consistent with Akiskal's (1983) hypothesis that dysthymia consists of two distinct subgroups: one characterized by a depressive personality style and the other characterized by an unstable (e.g., cluster B) personality style.

While these data support the distinctiveness of depressive personality and dysthymia, further work is necessary in order to rule out the possibility that the modest overlap and differing correlates between depressive personality and dysthymia are due to such factors as diagnostic unreliability and minor differences in diagnostic algorithms. The former possibility appears unlikely, as the studies reviewed above have generally documented good interrater reliability. However, the latter set of factors may play a greater role. According to current criteria, individuals with loss of interest but not depressed mood can be diagnosed as having depressive personality disorder, but not dysthymic disorder. It would be of interest to determine whether these individuals would meet criteria for dysthymia if the diagnostic criteria for dysthymic disorder were changed to allow loss of interest/pleasure to substitute for depressed mood, as it does in the criteria for major depressive disorder. It would also be of interest to see if such a change eliminated the excess of males in the group meeting criteria for depressive personality but not dysthymia.

While rates of current and lifetime major depression are higher among persons with depressive personality, they are also high in most comparison groups, resulting in fairly weak associations. Thus, some studies have found significant differences in rates of major depression between subjects with and without depressive personality (Hirschfeld & Holzer, 1994; Klein & Miller, 1993), while others have not (Klein, 1990; Phillips et al., 1992), and among the studies reporting significant differences, the magnitudes of the associations have been weak, with Kappas ranging from .12 to .18.

These data suggest that the degree of overlap between depressive personality disorder and major depressive disorder is fairly minimal. In addition, they suggest that mistaking major depressive episodes in partial remission for depressive personality disorder is not a substantial problem.

Differential Diagnosis: Personality Disorders The differential diagnosis of depressive personality and the Axis II disorders is most difficult for avoidant, dependent, obsessive-compulsive, borderline, passive-aggressive (negativistic), and self-defeating (masochistic) personality (Hirschfeld & Shea, 1994; Millon & Kotik-Harper, 1995; Phillips, Hirschfeld, Shea, & Gunderson, 1993; Phillips et al., 1995). However, there are important conceptual distinctions between depressive personality and each of these conditions.

The core characteristics of avoidant personality disorder include social inhibition, avoidance of interpersonal contact, feelings of inadequacy, and hypersensitivity to negative evaluation. While individuals with depressive personality share many of these characteristics, they tend to be less reluctant to enter into relationships with others, and to have a wider range of interpersonal contacts. In addition, their most prominent affects are depression and apathy, rather than fear, and their feelings of inadequacy extend beyond interpersonal situations.

Individuals with dependent personality disorder have an excessive need to be taken care of, fear separation, and engage in clinging behavior. Persons with depressive personality are often overly dependent on others for approval (Kernberg, 1988), but they are not usually overtly clingy. Also, they are less likely to remain in relationships in which their dependency needs are not being met.

Obsessive-compulsive personality disorder is characterized by a pervasive pattern of preoccupation with orderliness, perfectionism and control, at the expense of flexibility and efficiency. In contrast to individuals with obsessive-compulsive personality who are constricted in their expression of affect and interpersonally controlling, those with depressive personality are dejected and unassertive (Kernberg, 1988). Some of the features of obsessive-compulsive personality, such as conscientiousness, devotion to duty, and excessive self-discipline, are included in some conceptualizations of depressive personality (Schneider, 1958; Kernberg, 1988). However, as noted above, these tend to be only weakly related to other features of the construct.

The central characteristics of borderline personality disorder are instability of interpersonal relationships, self-image, and affect, and marked impulsivity. While individuals with borderline personality experience reactive mood shifts of which dysphoria is one of many states, those with depressive personality are more persistently dysphoric. Borderlines often express and "act out" feelings of aggression and hostility, while these feelings tend to be inhibited and internalized in depressive personality. The interpersonal relationships of the borderline are marked by alternations between idealization and devaluation of others. In contrast, individuals with depressive personality tend to have more stable relationships, and their views of others, while often characterized by skepticism and criticism, tend to be more consistent. In terms of identity, a clear self-image is absent or disturbed in borderline personality disorder, whereas the identity of persons with depressive personality is stable and characterized by feelings of inadequacy and worthlessness. Finally, individuals with depressive personality tend to be responsible and conscientious, rather than impulsive like those with borderline personality.

Passive-aggressive personality disorder was included in *DSM-III* and *DSM-III-R*, but dropped from *DSM-IV*. However, negativistic personality disorder, a broader variant of passive-aggressive personality, was included in the *DSM-IV* appendix. Individuals with passive-aggressive personality resent and passively resist demands for adequate performance, particularly when these are made by authority figures. Unlike passive-aggressive individuals, persons with depressive personality are no more critical of authority figures than they are of others. Moreover, when individuals with depressive personality feel critical of others, they are more likely to inhibit than express these feelings.

As discussed below, the construct of self-defeating personality disorder was derived from the clinical literature on masochistic personality. It was included in the appendix in *DSM-III-R*, but was dropped from *DSM-IV*. Individuals with self-defeating personality disorder exhibit a lifelong pattern of failure in multiple areas, tend to reject opportunities for pleasure, and react negatively to positive events. In contrast, those with depressive personality are often successful in one or more spheres (particularly work), and tend to be gloomy and joyless across situations. Moreover, as Simons (1986) has observed, individuals with self-defeating personality disorder unconsciously torture others, provoking retaliation, so their "inner struggle is externalized and then acted out with the external world." Persons with depressive personality, on the other hand, internalize their conflict, leading to self-torture in the absence of provoked retaliation by others.

Comorbidity: Personality Disorders Data on the comorbidity between depressive personality and other personality disorders can help to clarify the boundaries between these constructs. Even more important, such data are necessary to evaluate the possibility that there is so much overlap that the construct of depressive personality is redundant and unnecessary.

Several studies have investigated the relationship between depressive personality and the Axis II disorders using either a very small sample (Standage, 1986) or investigating a very limited range of personality disorders (Klein, 1990; Klein & Miller, 1993). These studies have found some evidence for associations between depressive personality and avoidant personality disorder (Standage, 1986) and schizotypal personality disorder (Klein, 1990; Klein & Miller, 1993).

There have also been two larger, more comprehensive studies of this issue. Using semistructured diagnostic interviews, Phillips et al. (1992, 1995) examined the relationship between depressive personality and the full range of *DSM-III* personality disorders in a sample of subjects with mild, chronic depressive symptoms. Of the subjects with depressive personality disorder, 13% met criteria for a cluster A disorder (none with schizotypal personality); 19% met criteria for a cluster B disorder (including 10% with borderline personality); and 48%

met criteria for a cluster C disorder (including 29% with avoidant, 13% with obsessive-compulsive, 10% with dependent, and 10% with passive-aggressive personality disorder). Only 13% met criteria for self-defeating personality disorder. Subjects with depressive personality did not have significantly elevated rates of any specific personality disorder compared to subjects without depressive personality, although subjects with depressive personality were significantly more likely to have at least one of the personality disorders.

Finally, Klein and Shih (1998) examined the comorbidity between depressive personality disorder, as defined by Akiskal's (1983) criteria, and the *DSM-III-R* personality disorders. Two samples were employed: a large group of outpatients with dysthymia, major depression, and/or personality disorders, and their first-degree relatives. In both samples, there were a number of significant associations between depressive personality and specific *DSM-III-R* personality disorders. However, the magnitude of these associations was quite modest. In the patient sample, Kappas ranged from –.01 to .18, with a median of .07. In the sample of relatives, Kappas ranged from .04 to .34, with a median of .13. The two most common personality disorders in subjects with depressive personality in both samples were avoidant and borderline personality; however, these were also the most common personality disorders in both samples as a whole. In general, depressive personality did not appear to be redundant with any of the *DSM-III-R* personality disorders, as less than 30% of subjects with depressive personality in each sample met criteria for any specific Axis II condition. Moreover, only 9 to 10% of subjects with depressive personality also met criteria for self-defeating personality disorder.

Taken together, these studies suggest that avoidant personality is probably the Axis II condition with the greatest overlap with depressive personality. However, there does not appear to be a particularly high degree of overlap between depressive personality and any of the personality disorders.

Relationship to Normal Personality Dimensions

It is also of interest to consider the relationship between depressive personality and normal dimensions of personality. This provides information on the convergent validity of depressive personality, and may be useful in elaborating the meaning of the construct (Shea & Hirschfeld, 1996). In addition, it is reasonable to ask whether the construct of depressive personality adds anything to existing models from the normal personality literature. For example, McLean and Woody (1995) have argued that depressive personality is equivalent to a high level of negative affectivity (or neuroticism), and is therefore an unnecessary construct.

While there are several competing models of normal personality structure, Tellegen's (1985) model includes the three most widely agreed-upon dimensions, and the dimensions that appear to be most relevant to depressive personality: negative affectivity (which is similar to neuroticism in the Eysenck and five-factor models; John, 1990), positive affectivity (which is similar to extraversion in the Eysenck and five-factor models), and constraint (which is similar to conscientiousness in the five-factor model, and the opposite of impulsivity in other models). McLean and Woody (1995) indicate that depressive personality is equivalent to a high level of negative affectivity, or neuroticism. In contrast, others have argued that the depressive temperament corresponds to a low level of positive affectivity, in addition to a high level of negative affectivity (Clark, Watson, & Mineka, 1994; Shea & Hirschfeld, 1996). Moreover, some descriptions and criteria sets for depressive personality (i.e., those including the traits of conscientiousness and self-discipline) suggest that the construct also implies a high level of constraint.

Klein (1990) and Phillips et al. (1992) both examined the relationship between measures of these three personality dimensions and a diagnosis of depressive personality disorder using the Akiskal et al. (1983) and Gunderson et al. (1994) criteria, respectively. In both studies, subjects with depressive personality disorder obtained significantly higher scores on negative affectivity, and significantly lower scores on positive affectivity, than controls. However, the groups did not differ on measures of constraint in either study.

As a more direct comparison of the McLean and Woody (1995) and Clark et al. (1994) models, Klein and Shih (1998) recently examined whether low positive affectivity was still associated with a diagnosis of depressive personality disorder after controlling for negative affectivity. In multiple logistic regression analyses with samples of outpatients and their first-degree relatives, they found that both dimensions were independently associated with a depressive personality diagnosis in both samples.

Taken together, these studies support the convergent validity of the construct of depressive personality disorder. In addition, these results are consistent with the data discussed above indicating that conscientiousness is not closely related to the depressive personality construct.

Dimensional models of personality are also useful in comparing competing concepts of, and criteria for, depressive personality. As Shea and Hirschfeld (1996) have noted, the *DSM-IV* criteria place more exclusive emphasis on negative affectivity than earlier definitions. Only one of the seven *DSM-IV* criteria even partially reflects low positive affectivity ("usual mood dominated by dejection, gloominess, cheerlessness, unhappiness"), and none of the items taps the constraint dimension. While the data reviewed above suggest that this should maximize the internal consistency of the criteria, it may be at the cost of discriminant validity. The recent theoretical and empirical literature indicates that high negative affectivity is psychopathologically nonspecific, characterizing depressive, anxiety, somatoform, and many personality (e.g., borderline) disorders (Clark et al., 1994; Tellegen, 1985; Widiger & Costa, 1994). In contrast, low positive affectivity appears to be critical in distinguishing depression from at least some of these conditions, such as the anxiety disorders (Clark et al., 1994; Tellegen, 1985). Hence, an exclusive emphasis on negative affectivity may result in identifying an overly broad and nonspecific group of dysphoric individuals.

Finally, critics have questioned whether the depressive personality category contributes anything beyond existing models of normal personality dimensions (McLean & Woody, 1995). Klein and Shih (1998) have recently reported data indicating that it does. They found that even after controlling for negative and positive affectivity, depressive personality made a unique contribution in predicting a lifetime history of mood disorder in a sample of relatives of patients with mood and personality disorders. Similarly, in a 30-month follow-up of depressed outpatients, Klein and Shih (1998) found that after controlling for baseline levels of positive and negative affectivity, depressive personality was significantly associated with depressive symptomatology at outcome.

Stability Over Time

A key assumption underlying the construct of depressive personality is that it is relatively stable over time. In studies with follow-up intervals of 6 and 12 months, respectively, Klein (1990) and Gunderson et al. (1994) both reported stability estimates of K = .41. Finally, in a 30-month study of depressed outpatients, Klein and Shih (1998) found that the concordance between blind diagnoses of depressive personality at baseline and follow-up was 67% (K = .37). When diagnoses at follow-up were broadened to include probable cases (one criterion short of meeting full criteria), Kappa was .49. Most discrepancies were due to patients who met criteria for depressive personality at baseline but no longer met full criteria at follow-up. The intraclass correlation between the number of depressive personality traits rated as present at the two assessments was .56. While these data indicate that depressive personality is only modestly stable over time, it is quite similar to the stability of most other personality disorder diagnoses (McDavid & Pilkonis, 1996).

Impairment and Treatment

By definition, personality disorders should result in impaired functioning. Both Hirschfeld and Holzer (1994) and Klein and Miller (1993) reported that subjects with depressive personality exhibited significantly greater impairment than subjects without depressive personality. In addition, Klein and Miller (1993) found that college students with depressive personality were significantly more likely to have sought treatment from a mental health professional. After controlling for a history of mood disorder, Klein and Miller (1993) found that the groups still differed significantly on impairment. However the effect for treatment disappeared, suggesting that individuals with depressive personality are unlikely to seek treatment unless it is complicated by major depression or dysthymia.

Etiology and Development

The leading theoretical perspective on the etiology of depressive personality stems from Kraepelin

(1921), and, more recently, Akiskal (1989). This view holds that depressive personality is a genetically transmitted temperament that predisposes individuals to develop major mood disorders. Alternative views include Schneider's (1958) argument that depressive personality is the extreme end of a dimension of normal personality that is unrelated to the major mood disorders, and psychoanalysts' emphasis on the role of disturbances in the parent-child relationship that lead to a harsh superego and excessive dependency.

The only systematic data on etiological and developmental factors that directly bear on depressive personality disorder stem from family and family history studies. However, there are some suggestive findings in the areas of developmental psychopathology and psychophysiology that may provide some useful leads.

Family History There are currently no data available on whether depressive personality disorder aggregates in families. However, there have been three family history studies in which groups of probands with and without depressive personality were interviewed regarding lifetime Axis I disorders in their first-degree relatives (Cassano, Akiskal, Perugi, Musetti, & Savino, 1992; Klein, 1990; Klein & Miller, 1993), and two family studies in which the relatives of probands with mood disorders and controls were assessed for depressive personality (Klein, Clark, et al., 1988; Klein, in press).

Klein (1990) reported that the first-degree relatives of outpatients with depressive personality had significantly higher rates of bipolar disorder and mood disorders severe enough to have required hospitalization than the first-degree relatives of outpatients without depressive personality. The groups did not differ on rates of nonbipolar depression, alcoholism, or antisocial personality in relatives. Interestingly, outpatients with dysthymia but not depressive personality had a significantly higher rate of nonbipolar depression in their relatives than outpatients with depressive personality but not dysthymia. This suggests that dysthymic disorder is associated with a greater familial liability for mood disorders than depressive personality disorder.

Klein and Miller (1993) reported that college students with depressive personality had significantly higher rates of any affective disorder and major depression in their first-degree relatives than subjects without depressive personality. The groups did not differ on rates of bipolar disorder, alcoholism, drug abuse, or antisocial personality in relatives. Importantly, the rate of affective disorders in relatives was elevated even in the group of probands with depressive personality disorder but no lifetime history of mood disorder, indicating that the findings were not attributable to comorbid mood disorders in the probands.

Summarizing the results of unpublished analyses, Cassano et al. (1992) reported that outpatients with both depressive personality and major depressive disorder had higher rates of mood disorder in their relatives than patients with major depression alone.

In the first of the two family studies, Klein, Clark et al. (1988) found an increased rate of depressive personality in the adolescent and young adult offspring of patients hospitalized with major depressive disorder compared to the offspring of patients hospitalized for chronic medical conditions and the offspring of healthy controls. Finally, Klein (in press) recently reported an increased rate of depressive personality in the first-degree relatives of outpatients with early-onset dysthymic disorder (with or without superimposed major depressive episodes) compared to the relatives of normal controls. Interestingly, the rate of depressive personality was also higher in the relatives of outpatients with dysthymia than in the relatives of outpatients with episodic (nonchronic) major depression.

Taken together, these data are consistent with the idea that there is a spectrum of mood disorders ranging from depressive personality to at least some forms of major depressive disorder, and including dysthymia, all of which share a common familial (possibly genetic) liability (Akiskal, 1989). The conditions included in this spectrum tend to be chronic, have an early onset, and are associated with particularly high levels of familial aggregation (Cassano et al., 1992; Klein, Clark et al., 1988; Klein, Taylor, & Harding, 1988; Klein et al., 1995). It is currently unclear where (or whether) episodic and late-onset forms of major depression fit within this conceptualization.

Early Home Environment There are no systematic data on the role of the early home environment in the etiology of depressive personality. However, a number of retrospective studies have documented associations between parental behavior and the related dimensions of dependency and self-criticism (Blatt & Homann, 1992).

Development Since Kraepelin (1921), clinicians have noted that many patients with major depressive disorder exhibit depressive premorbid personalities. More recently, von Zerssen, Tauscher, and Possl (1994) confirmed these observations using blind assessments of case history data in a sample of inpatients with major mood disorders. In this study, patients with major depressive and bipolar 2 disorders were significantly more likely to be classified as having had a melancholic personality, while patients with bipolar 1 disorder were more likely to have had a manic personality. However, retrospective studies have a number of limitations, including the possibility that data on premorbid personality are colored by the experience of a major mood disorder, and the fact that there is no information about the individuals with depressive personality who were not hospitalized with major psychiatric disorders. Unfortunately, there have not been any prospective studies of the development of depressive personality.

While not directly addressing depressive personality disorder per se, several recent developmental studies have produced provocative findings that may be of some relevance. In a doctoral dissertation, Neff (1993) conducted in-depth interviews and home observations of depressed and nondepressed mothers from the community and their 2- to 3-year-old children. There were several intriguing findings. The largest difference between the offspring of depressed and normal mothers in the home observation data was on a factor labeled behavioral/affective impoverishment. Scores on this factor were bimodally distributed in the offspring of depressives, with the mode reflecting greater impoverishment falling completely outside the range of the offspring of normal controls. Interestingly, behavioral/affective impoverishment in the toddlers of depressives was highly correlated with chronic depressive symptoms and depressive personality traits in the mothers.

In a longitudinal study of a large birth cohort in New Zealand, Caspi, Moffitt, Newman, and Silva (1996) reported that children who were classified as inhibited (e.g., socially reticent, inhibited, and easily upset by strangers) based on behavioral observations at age 3 were significantly more likely to meet criteria for major depressive disorder in structured diagnostic interviews at age 21 than noninhibited children. Moreover, this relationship was quite specific; inhibited children were not at increased risk for anxiety disorders, alcoholism, or antisocial personality disorder. Finally, in a longitudinal study of a large birth cohort in England, van Os, Jones, Lewis, Wadsworth, and Murray (1997) reported that ratings of behavioral apathy at ages 6 to 11 predicted persistent, but not nonpersistent, affective disorders in middle adulthood.

The measures of behavioral/affective impoverishment, inhibition, and behavioral apathy in these studies do not correspond directly to depressive personality. However, they all appear to be tapping a similar phenomenon that may be a more direct reflection of a basic affective/motivational temperamental style. It is reasonable to speculate that this style may undergo substantial elaboration (particularly in the cognitive and social realms) over the course of development, resulting in depressive personality traits in adulthood.

Psychophysiology Davidson (1992, 1993) has hypothesized that the left and right frontal regions of the cortex are associated with approach and withdrawal behavioral systems, respectively, which can be assessed using scalp-recorded measures of cortical electrical activity. There is evidence that these differing patterns of frontal EEG activation are temporally stable, present within a few days after birth, and associated with characteristic styles of temperament, mood, and psychopathology. In particular, a pattern of decreased left, as compared to right, frontal activation is thought to reflect a deficit in approach behavior. Interestingly, the concept of an approach deficit appears to be very similar to the concepts of behavioral/affective impoverishment, inhibition, and behavioral apathy in the developmental studies reviewed above, particularly in light of recent studies reporting strong associations between frontal EEG asymmetry and measures of positive and negative emotionality (Tomarken, Davidson, Wheeler, & Doss, 1992) and behavioral activation and inhibition (Harmon-Jones & Allen, 1997; Sutton & Davidson, 1997).

Several studies have examined frontal EEG asymmetry in depressives. Henriques and Davidson (1991) reported decreased left frontal activation in patients with major depression. Moreover, Henriques and Davidson (1990) reported similar findings in patients who had recovered from a major depressive episode, suggesting that this is a trait, rather than state, marker. Finally, a similar pattern of frontal EEG asymetry has been reported in the infants of mothers with elevated depressive symptoms (Dawson, Klinger, Panagiotides, Hill, & Spieker, 1992). Taken together, these data suggest that decreased left frontal activation may be a biological marker for a pattern of traits that appear to be temperamental in origin, and may be related to depressive personality disorder.

Conclusions

There is a longstanding and rich clinical literature on depressive personality disorder that tends to yield a consistent picture of individuals who are habitually gloomy, pessimistic, critical of themselves and others, lacking in self-esteem, worried, remorseful, introverted, passive, anergic, and anhedonic. In recent years, several sets of explicit criteria for depressive personality disorder have been introduced, and depressive personality disorder is now included as a category needing further study in the appendix of *DSM-IV*. The construct appears to have reasonable internal consistency and interrater reliability, and is moderately stable over time.

Depressive personality disorder overlaps significantly with dysthymic disorder, particularly the early-onset subtype. However, depressive personality is less symptomatic and more trait oriented than dysthymic disorder. In addition, the two constructs have distinctive correlates and identify somewhat different populations. Depressive personality disorder also shares some features with a number of the personality disorders, particularly avoidant personality. However, the rates of comorbidity between depressive personality and the personality disorders are fairly low. Depressive personality disorder is associated with significant psychosocial impairment, and elevated rates of mood disorders in relatives. The family history data indicate that although depressive personality can be distinguished from dysthymic and major depressive disorder, it is probably best conceptualized as a milder condition along a spectrum of mood disorders. Finally, there are data raising the possibility that a rudimentary form of depressive personality is evident at an early age, and may be associated with an increased risk for developing major depressive disorder, particularly of a chronic nature.

Further work is necessary in a number of areas. First, it is important to compare the validity of different definitions of the depressive personality disorder construct, and to explore the consequences of retaining or eliminating criteria tapping positive affectivity and constraint. Second, it is also important to determine the degree to which the overlap with dysthymic disorder varies as a function of minor changes in diagnostic algorithms, such as the inclusion of loss of interest as a defining feature of dysthymia. Third, it is important to extend the limited work on the epidemiology, course, and developmental and psychobiological origins of depressive personality disorder. Finally, it would be of interest to examine whether depressive personality influences the presentation and course of mood disorders (pathoplasticity). For example, Cassano et al. (1992) have indicated that depressive personality is associated with greater symptom severity, an earlier onset, and a greater number of episodes in patients with major depressive disorder.

Self-Defeating (Masochistic) Personality Disorder

The term *masochism* has been used to refer to both sexual masochism and masochistic, or self-defeating, personality disorder. While some theorists have argued that self-defeating behavior is a derivative of sexual drives, and is consciously or unconsciously pleasurable (e.g., Brenner, 1959), most investigators view masochism and masochistic personality as separate and distinct concepts. Masochism refers to the need for pain in order to experience sexual gratification, while masochistic personality refers to a lifelong pattern of self-defeating behaviors in multiple contexts and areas of functioning. Individuals with self-defeating personality disorder tend to avoid or undermine pleasurable experiences, are drawn to situations or relationships that will result in suffering, and will not allow others to help them.

The concept of masochistic personality disorder is primarily derived from the psychoanalytic literature. Despite great controversy, it was introduced into the diagnostic nomenclature in *DSM-III-R*, where it was included under the rubric of self-defeating personality disorder in the appendix as a condition warranting further study. However, it was subsequently dropped from the *DSM-IV*, and is not included in the current diagnostic nomenclature. More extensive reviews of masochistic/self-defeating personality disorder can be found in Asch (1986), Fiester (1991), Glickauf-Hughes and Wells (1991), and Widiger and Frances (1989).

Historical Background

Freud (1924/1961) introduced the concept of moral masochism, referring to a tendency to unconsciously set oneself up for disappointment or failure and then castigate oneself owing to an excessively harsh superego. Freud also introduced the related concept of "female masochism," later elaborated by Deutsch (1944), which was based on the idea that since women naturally experience pain as a result of childbirth and the menstrual cycle, they may have inherent masochistic tendencies.

Wilhelm Reich (1933/1976) described individuals with masochistic character disorder as long-suffering, demanding, complaining, provocative, tormenting, and self-abasing. According to Reich, these individuals use their suffering as a means of demanding and extracting love. Horney (1939) portrayed the masochistic personality as characterized by a sense of inadequacy and worthlessness, combined with clinging dependency. She believed that this pattern was more common in women than men. More recently, Asch (1986) described the masochistic personality as characterized by a lifelong pattern of unconsciously arranged difficulties or failures in multiple domains, and noted that these individuals repeatedly manage to wrest failure from the teeth of success. Asch also indicated that people with masochistic personality disorder are unable to appreciate their own role in thwarting success, and perceive failure as a defeat by an external agency, such as fate. In addition, while individuals with masochistic personality tend to be submissive, they flaunt their humiliations and misfortunes and use them as a means of provoking guilt. In psychotherapy, these patients are likely to sabotage treatment and have negative therapeutic reactions.

As discussed earlier, Kernberg (1984, 1988) viewed masochistic and depressive personality traits as being closely related, and combined them under the rubric of depressive-masochistic character disorder. He believed that this is one of the higher functioning personality disorders, and can be distinguished from more severely disturbed personality types that also exhibit masochistic traits, particularly those with prominent narcissistic and borderline features. Finally, as noted above, Simons (1986) rejected the concept of depressive-masochistic personality disorder, arguing that these are distinct conditions. According to Simons, the critical distinction is that individuals with masochistic personality disorder provoke others into rejecting and punishing them, whereas individuals with depressive personality punish themselves.

Classification

An initial draft of criteria for masochistic personality disorder was formulated in 1983, and underwent a number of revisions in response to preliminary studies and criticisms of the nature and potential implications of the diagnosis. In addition, owing to its association with the psychoanalytic theory of female masochism, and the implication that the masochist derives unconscious pleasure from suffering, the name of the category was changed to self-defeating personality disorder. Ultimately, self-defeating personality disorder was included in the *DSM-III-R* appendix as a category warranting further study (Kass, Spitzer, Williams, & Widiger, 1989).

The final criteria required five of the following: chooses people and situations that lead to disappointment, failure, or mistreatment even when better options are available; rejects or renders ineffective the attempts of others to help; following positive personal events responds with depression, guilt, or a behavior that produces pain; incites angry or rejecting responses from others and then feels hurt, defeated, or humiliated; rejects opportunities for pleasure, or is reluctant to acknowledge enjoying him/herself; fails to accomplish tasks crucial to his/her personal objectives despite demonstrated ability to do so; is uninterested in or rejects people who consistently treat him/her well; and engages in excessive self-sacrifice that is unsolicited by the intended recipients. In addition, these features cannot occur exclusively in response to, or anticipation of, being abused or only when the person is depressed. Self-defeating personality disorder was subsequently omitted from *DSM-IV* owing to continuing controversy and a lack of sufficient data supporting its utility or validity (Fiester, 1991).

Before reviewing the empirical literature on self-defeating personality disorder, it should be noted that many of these studies suffer from several limitations. First, the majority have consisted of surveys asking clinicians to rate prototypical case histories or criteria, rather than real patients (e.g., Blashfield & Breen, 1989; Heisler, Lyons, & Goethe, 1995; Huprich & Fine, 1996), or requesting clinicians to nominate and rate one or two patients from their own practices, rather than systematically sampling subjects (e.g., Kass, 1987; Kass, MacKinnon, & Spitzer, 1986; Spitzer, Williams, Kass, & Davies, 1989). The response rates in these surveys have generally been low, and the clinician-subjects have not been blind to the purpose of the study. In addition, many of these studies have used early versions of the criteria for the disorder that vary substantially from the final criteria set (e.g., only 4 of the original 10 criteria are represented in the final set of 8 criteria). Hence, it is difficult to compare studies and to extrapolate the results to the final set of diagnostic criteria. Finally, several studies relied on self-report measures of personality disorders (e.g., Dowson, 1994; Reich, 1987, 1990), which are only minimally related to diagnoses based on semi-structured interviews (Perry, 1992; Zimmerman, 1994).

Internal Construct Validity

In several studies, the internal consistency of the masochistic and self-defeating personality disorder criteria sets was moderate, ranging from .59 to .76 (Kass et al., 1986; Skodal et al., 1994; Spitzer et al., 1989). In three studies, item-total correlations generally ranged from the .20s to the .40s (Kass et al., 1986; Kass, 1987; Skodal et al., 1994).

The discriminant validity of the criteria appear to be more problematic. In a factor analysis of the criteria for borderline, dependent and self-defeating personality disorder, Spitzer et al. (1989) found that independent factors emerged for borderline and dependent, but not for self-defeating, personality. In addition, Dowson (1994) reported that every self-defeating personality disorder criterion correlated more highly with the sum of the criteria for avoidant, borderline, or dependent personality disorder than with the sum of the other self-defeating personality items.

Interrater Reliability

The two available interrater reliability studies have yielded discrepant results. Loranger et al. (1994) examined the six-month test-retest reliability of the Personality Disorder Examination, with both assessments generally being conducted by the same interviewer. Kappa for a diagnosis of definite or probable self-defeating personality disorder was .71. In contrast, First et al. (1995) examined the 1- to 14-day test-retest reliability of the Structured Clinical Interview for DSM-III-R Personality Disorders in both a clinical and nonclinical sample, with the assessments being conducted by different interviewers. Kappas for self-defeating personality disorder were .40 in the clinical, and .12 in the nonclinical sample.

Epidemiology

There are no adequate data on the prevalence of self-defeating personality disorder in the general population. Prevalence estimates in outpatients have ranged between 7% and 26% (Dowson, 1994; Kass, 1987; Nurnberg et al., 1993; Skodal et al., 1994). As discussed below, there has been considerable controversy regarding potential sex biases in the diagnosis. However, most (Kass et al., 1986; Nurnberg et al., 1993; Reich, 1987; Skodal et al., 1994), but not all (Spitzer et al., 1989), studies have failed to find differences in the rates of self-defeating personality disorder in males and females. Finally, self-defeating personality disorder does not appear to be correlated with age, marital status, or education (Reich, 1987; Skodal et al., 1994).

The Issue of Sex Bias

The category of self-defeating personality disorder has been highly controversial, largely owing to concerns about sex bias and the potential for misuse. The two major sets of criticisms have been that: (1) the category pathologizes behavior that is part of normal female socialization in this culture; and (2) it will be inappropriately applied to women in abusive relationships, and increase the chances that the victim of violence rather than the perpetrator will be seen as the person with psychopathology (Caplan, 1987; Rosewater, 1987; Walker, 1987).

The issue of testing potential sex biases in the diagnostic criteria for personality disorders is complex (Widiger & Spitzer, 1991). However, at this point there does not appear to be much evidence supporting the existence of sex biases in either the criteria for self-defeating personality disorder, or their clinical application, although further research is still necessary (Widiger & Frances, 1989).

As noted above, the majority of studies have not found sex differences in the prevalence of self-defeating personality disorder (Kass et al., 1986; Nurnberg et al., 1993; Reich, 1987; Skodal et al., 1994). However, even if there were differences in prevalence, this would not necessarily indicate bias, as gender may be a valid correlate of a disorder (e.g., the fact that alcoholism and antisocial personality disorder are more common in males is probably real, rather than a function of bias).

One approach to evaluating bias in a test or set of diagnostic criteria is to determine whether a subset of items differs between groups (Hale, 1983). Evidence for sex biases in the individual items in the criteria for self-defeating personality disorder is mixed. One study using an outpatient sample reported sex differences on approximately half the items (Kass, 1987). However, another study using a nonclinical sample did not find differences on any of the items (Heisler et al., 1995). Alternative approaches to examining bias include determining whether the factorial structure of the criteria set differs as a function of sex, and whether the criteria are differentially associated with external correlates, such as course or treatment response, for males and females (Hale, 1983). Unfortunately, no studies have employed either of these approaches.

Several studies have examined whether there are sex biases in the application of the criteria for self-defeating personality disorder by asking clinicians to make diagnoses from case vignettes (Fuller & Blashfield, 1989; Heisler et al., 1995; Huprich & Fine, 1996). There was little evidence of diagnostic bias as a function of the sex of either the patient or clinician in any of these studies.

One study addressed the issue of whether the criteria for self-defeating personality disorder reflect normative female behavior in our culture. Sprock, Blashfield, and Smith (1990) asked college students to rate the criteria for all Axis II disorders on the basis of how characteristic they were of each sex. The self-defeating personality disorder criteria were not viewed as being more characteristic of either sex, and the ratings were similar for male and female raters.

Finally, only one study has examined the relationship between self-defeating personality disorder and adult victimization. In a nonclinical sample, Heisler et al. (1995) reported that there was no association between self-defeating personality disorder and a history of having been in a physically abusive adult relationship.

Differential Diagnosis and Comorbidity

Critics of the construct of self-defeating personality disorder have questioned whether it is sufficiently delimited from other disorders to warrant a distinct category. One issue concerns its overlap with the mood disorders (Liebowitz, 1987). A second concerns the overlap with other personality disorders, particularly dependent, avoidant, borderline, and passive-aggressive/negativistic personality (Millon & Kotik-Harper, 1995; Vaillant & Perry, 1985).

Like the mood disorders, self-defeating personality disorder is often characterized by a lack of interest in potentially pleasurable activities, and dysphoria in the context of positive events. However, unlike self-defeating personality, major depressive disorder and dysthymic disorder are characterized by persistent depressed mood and vegetative symptoms, and major depression generally has an episodic course. In addition, in self-defeating personality disorder, self-defeating behaviors are evident even in the absence of depression.

Individuals with dependent and self-defeating personality disorder both tend to sacrifice their own needs for those of others, and often choose to remain in relationships in which they are mistreated. However, individuals with dependent personality do not typically exhibit self-defeating behavior in noninterpersonal contexts, and do not reject people who treat them well, offers of help, and opportunities for pleasure.

Like persons with avoidant personality disorder, individuals with self-defeating personality avoid some interpersonal situations. However, in avoidant personality, this is a general pattern, while in self-defeating personality it tends to be limited to positive situations and relationships. In addition, persons with avoidant personality rarely engage in the kind of provocative behavior that is characteristic of self-defeating personality disorder.

Borderline and self-defeating personality disorder both share a penchant for interpersonal conflict, dysphoria, and self-injurious behavior. However, persons with self-defeating personality lack the impulsivity and unstable self-image that is characteristic of individuals with borderline personality, and their self-injurious behavior does not typically assume a physical form, such as self-mutilation or suicide attempts.

Finally, individuals with passive-aggressive/negativistic and self-defeating personality disorder both tend to foil others' attempts to help them, often fail to accomplish important tasks, frequently complain about their misfortunes, and incite angry, rejecting responses from others. However, persons with passive-aggressive personality are not typically uninterested in people who treat them well, and rarely engage in unsolicited self-sacrifice.

Data on comorbidity between self-defeating personality disorder and the Axis I disorders are very limited. In two studies, the Axis I diagnoses that co-occurred most frequently with self-defeating personality disorder were the mood disorders (Reich, 1987; Skodal et al., 1994).

Several studies have examined whether self-defeating personality disorder can be distinguished from other personality disorders by asking clinicians to make diagnoses from case vignettes or sort diagnostic criteria for personality disorders into the correct Axis II categories. The results have been mixed. Two studies found that clinicians were able to apply diagnostic criteria for self-defeating personality disorder to case histories fairly accurately (Fuller & Blashfield, 1989; Heisler et al., 1995). Huprich and Fine (1996) also reported that clinicians could diagnose case histories of self-defeating personality disorder patients with better-than-chance accuracy, but that their diagnostic accuracy was substantially lower than for the other personality disorders studied. Blashfield and Haymaker (1988) reported that clinicians were unable to sort the majority of self-defeating personality disorder criteria into the correct diagnostic category, suggesting that the criteria were not uniquely descriptive of a particular personality disorder type. However, in a second study, Blashfield and Breen (1989) reported that clinicians could sort the criteria with reasonable accuracy.

Several studies have examined the relationship between self-defeating and other personality disorders in real patients. Reich (1987) found that a high proportion of patients with masochistic personality disorder also met criteria for dependent, avoidant, and borderline personality disorders. Spitzer et al. (1989) reported that the number of self-defeating personality traits correlated .55 with the number of borderline, and .56 with the number of dependent traits. Nurnberg et al. (1993) found that 67% of outpatients with self-defeating personality disorder had other Axis II diagnoses, and that the overlap was greatest for avoidant, dependent, and obsessive-compulsive personality disorder. However, the Axis II comorbidity for self-defeating personality was no greater than that for most of the personality disorders. Skodal et al. (1994) reported that there was significant comorbidity between self-defeating personality and most of the other personality disorders in an outpatient sample, with the greatest overlap occurring with borderline and dependent personality disorder. Finally, Dowson (1994) reported that there was modest, but significant, overlap between self-defeating personality disorder and avoidant and passive-aggressive personality disorder using a self-report measure of Axis II traits.

Taken together, these studies indicate that self-defeating personality disorder exhibits substantial overlap with the mood disorders and other personality disorders, particularly dependent, avoidant, and borderline personality. However, it is unclear whether the degree of overlap is greater for self-defeating personality than for other Axis II disorders.

Course

Like all personality disorders, self-defeating personality disorder is assumed to be manifested by mid- to late-adolescence, and to follow a chronic course. However, there are no data available on the onset, stability, or course of this condition.

Etiology

The major theoretical perspective on the etiology of self-defeating personality disorder derives from the psychoanalytic literature, where it has been hypothesized that individuals with self-defeating personality internalize rejecting, punitive, and inconsistent parental behavior. Feeling that they deserve to be treated badly, and seeking to heal their narcissistic injury by making critical, rejecting partners love and approve of them, these individuals tend to seek partners who will replicate their early relationships (Asch, 1986; Glickhauf-Hughes & Wells, 1991).

There are few data testing this, or any alternative, etiological theory. Norden, Klein, Donaldson,

Pepper, and Klein (1995) examined the relationship between individuals' retrospective reports of their early home environments and the *DSM-III-R* personality disorders in a large sample of outpatients with definite or probable Axis II conditions. Self-defeating traits were significantly associated with a poorer relationship with both parents and with childhood sexual abuse. Interestingly, the only Axis II condition that exhibited as strong a set of associations with childhood adversity was borderline personality disorder. Using a self-report measure of self-defeating personality traits in college student samples, Schill, Beyler, Morales, and Ekstrom (1991) and Williams and Schill (1993) found significant correlations between self-defeating traits and perceptions of the family environment as unsupportive and lacking in cohesion, and with anxious and avoidant attachments to mothers.

Finally, one study has examined the familial aggregation of self-defeating personality disorder. Using a self-report measure and a very small sample, Reich (1990) found an increased rate of both self-defeating and schizotypal personality disorders in the relatives of outpatients with self-defeating personality compared to the relatives of normal controls.

Conclusion

Self-defeating (masochistic) personality disorder has a long clinical tradition and is perceived as a useful construct by a number of clinicians. However, it continues to be the subject of intense controversy and has not gained widespread acceptance as a useful and valid diagnostic category.

A number of critical questions remain. In particular, there is a need for data on the long-term stability and course of self-defeating personality disorder, and whether it is limited to periods of victimization or depression. In addition, it remains unclear whether it is a distinct condition or represents a heterogeneous collection of traits that are also characteristic of other personality disorders, such as dependent, borderline, avoidant, and passive-aggressive/negativistic personality (Millon & Kotik-Harper, 1995; Vaillant & Perry, 1985). Further work testing sex biases in the criteria for self-defeating personality disorder is also needed. Finally, if future studies support the stability and distinctiveness of self-defeating personality disorder, further research on the developmental, psychosocial, and biological origins of this condition would be indicated.

References

Akiskal, H. S. (1983). Dysthymic disorder: Psychopathology of proposed chronic depressive subtypes. *American Journal of Psychiatry, 140*, 11–20.

Akiskal, H. S. (1989). Validating affective personality types. In L. Robins & J. Barrett (Eds.), *The validity of psychiatric diagnosis* (pp. 217–227). New York: Raven Press.

Akiskal, H. S., Hirschfeld, R. M. A., & Yerevanian, B. I. (1983). The relationship of personality to affective disorders: A critical review. *Archives of General Psychiatry, 40*, 801–810.

Asch, S. S. (1986). The masochistic personality. In A. M. Cooper, A. J. Frances, & M. H. Sacks (Eds.), *Psychiatry: Volume 1. The personality disorders and neuroses* (pp. 291–299). Philadelphia: J.P. Lippincott.

Baumeister, R. F. (1988). Masochism as escape from self. *Journal of Sex Research, 25*, 28–59.

Baumeister, R. F., & Sher, S. J. (1988). Self-defeating behavior patterns among normal individuals: Review and analysis of common self-destructive tendencies. *Psychological Bulletin, 104*, 3–22.

Beck, A. T. (1967). *Depression: Causes and treatment*. Philadelphia: University of Pennsylvania Press.

Bemporad, J. (1976). Psychotherapy of the depressive character. *Journal of the American Academy of Psychoanalysis, 4*, 347–372.

Berliner, B. (1966). Psychodynamics of the depressive character. *Psychoanalytic Forum, 1*, 244–251.

Blashfield, R. K., & Breen, M. J. (1989). Face validity of the DSM-III-R personality disorders. *American Journal of Psychiatry, 146*, 1575–1579.

Blashfield, R. K., & Haymaker, D. (1988). A prototype analysis of the diagnostic criteria for DSM-III-R personality disorders. *Journal of Personality Disorders, 2*, 272–280.

Blatt, S. J., & Homann, E. (1992). Parent-child interaction in the etiology of dependent and self-critical depression. *Clinical Psychology Review, 12*, 47–91.

Brenner, C. (1959). The masochistic character: Genesis and treatment. *Journal of the American Psychoanalytic Association, 7*, 197–225.

Caplan, P. J. (1987). The psychiatric association's failure to meet its own standards: The dangers of self-defeating personality disorder as a category. *Journal of Personality Disorders, 1*, 178–182.

Caspi, A., Moffitt, T. E., Newman, D. L., & Silva, P. A. (1996). Behavioral observations at age 3 years predict adult psychiatric disorders: Longitudinal evidence from a birth cohort. *Archives of General Psychiatry, 53*, 1033–1039.

Cassano, G. B., Akiskal, H. S., Perugi, G., Musetti, L., & Savino, M. (1992). The importance of measures of affective temperaments in genetic studies of mood disorders. *Journal of Psychiatric Research, 26*, 257–268.

Clark, L. A., Watson, D., & Mineka, S. (1994). Temperament, personality, and the mood and anxiety disorders. *Journal of Abnormal Psychology, 103*, 103–116.

Davidson, R. J. (1992). Emotion and affective style: Hemispheric substrates. *Psychological Science, 3*, 39–43.

Davidson, R. J. (1993). Parsing affective space: Perspectives from neuropsychology and psychophysiology. *Neuropsychology, 7*, 464–475.

Dawson, G., Klinger, L. G., Panagiotides, H., Hill, D., & Spieker, S. (1992). Frontal lobe activity and affective behavior of infants of mothers with depressive symptoms. *Child Development, 63*, 725–737.

Deutsch, H. (1944). *The psychology of women.* New York: Grune and Stratton.

Dowson, J. H. (1994). DSM-III-R self-defeating personality disorder criteria evaluated by patients' self-report questionnaire: Relationships with other personality disorders and positive predictive powers of the individual criteria. *Acta Psychiatrica Scandinavica, 90*, 32–37.

Fiester, S. J. (1991). Self-defeating personality disorder: A review of data and recommendations for DSM-IV. *Journal of Personality Disorders, 5*, 194–209.

First, M. B., Spitzer, R. L., Williams, J. B. W., Davies, M., Borus, J., Howes, M. J., Kane, J., Pope, Jr., H. G., & Rounsaville, B. (1995). The Structured Clinical Interview for DSM-III-R Personality Disorders (SCID-II). Part II: Multi-site test-retest reliability study. *Journal of Personality Disorders, 9*, 92–104.

Freud, S. (1924/1961). The economic problem of masochism. In J. Strachey (Ed.), *The standard edition of the complete psychological works of Sigmund Freud* (vol. 19, pp. 157–174). London: Hogarth Press.

Fuller, A. K., & Blashfield, R. K. (1989). Masochistic personality disorder: A prototype analysis of diagnosis and sex bias. *Journal of Nervous and Mental Disease, 177*, 168–172.

Glickauf-Hughes, C., & Wells, M. (1991). Current conceptualizations on masochism: Genesis and object relations. *American Journal of Psychotherapy, 45*, 53–68.

Gunderson, J. G., Phillips, K. A., Triebwasser, J. T., & Hirschfeld, R. M. A. (1994). The Diagnostic Interview for Depressive Personality. *American Journal of Psychiatry, 151*, 1300–1304.

Hale, R. L. (1983). Intellectual assessment. In M. Hersen, A. E. Kazdin, & A. S. Bellack (Eds.), *The clinical psychology handbook* (pp. 345–376). New York: Pergamon Press.

Harmon-Jones, E., & Allen, J. J. B. (1997). Behavioral activation sensitivity and resting frontal EEG asymmetry: Covariation of putative indicators related to risk for mood disorders. *Journal of Abnormal Psychology, 106*, 159–163.

Heisler, L. K., Lyons, M. J., & Goethe, J. W. (1995). Self-defeating personality disorder: A cross-national study of clinical utility. *Journal of Nervous and Mental Disease, 183*, 214–221.

Henriques, J. B., & Davidson, R. J. (1990). Regional brain electrical asymmetries discriminate between previously depressed and healthy control subjects. *Journal of Abnormal Psychology, 99*, 22–31.

Henriques, J. B., & Davidson, R. J. (1991). Left frontal hypoactivation in depression. *Journal of Abnormal Psychology, 100*, 535–545.

Hirschfeld, R. M. A., & Holzer, III, C. E. (1994). Depressive personality disorder: Clinical implications. *Journal of Clinical Psychiatry, 55*, 10–17.

Hirschfeld, R. M. A., & Shea, M. T. (1994). Personality. In E. S. Paykel (Ed.), *Handbook of affective disorders*, 2nd ed. (pp. 185–194). New York: Guilford Press.

Horney, K. (1939). *New ways in psychoanalysis.* New York: Norton.

Huprich, S. K., & Fine, M. A. (1996). Self-defeating personality disorder: Diagnostic accuracy and overlap with dependent personality disorder. *Journal of Personality Disorders, 10*, 229–246.

John, O. P. (1990). The "Big Five" factor taxonomy: Dimensions of personality in the natural language and in questionnaires. In L. A. Pervin (Ed.), *Handbook of personality: Theory and research* (pp. 66–100). New York: Guilford Press.

Kahn, E. (1975). The depressive character. *Folia Psychiatrica et Neurologica Japonica, 29*, 291–303.

Kass, F. (1987). Self-defeating personality disorder: An empirical study. *Journal of Personality Disorders, 1*, 43–47.

Kass, F., MacKinnon, R. A., & Spitzer, R. L. (1986). Masochistic personality: An empirical study. *American Journal of Psychiatry, 143*, 216–218.

Kass, F., Spitzer, R. L., Williams, J. B. W., & Widiger, T. (1989). Self-defeating personality disorder and DSM-III-R: Development of the diagnostic criteria. *American Journal of Psychiatry, 146*, 1022–1026.

Kernberg, O. F. (1984). *Severe personality disorders: Psychotherapeutic strategies*. New Haven: Yale University Press.

Kernberg, O. F. (1988). Clinical dimensions of masochism. *Journal of the American Psychoanalytic Association, 36*, 1005–1029.

Klein, D. N. (1990). Depressive personality: Reliability, validity, and relation to dysthymia. *Journal of Abnormal Psychology, 99*, 412–421.

Klein, D. N. (in press). Depressive personality in the relatives of outpatients with dysthymic disorder and episodic major depressive disorder, and normal controls. *Journal of Affective Disorders*.

Klein, D. N., Clark, D. C., Dansky, L., & Margolis, E. T. (1988). Dysthymia in the offspring of parents with primary unipolar affective disorder. *Journal of Abnormal Psychology, 97*, 265–274.

Klein, D. N., & Miller, G. A. (1993). Depressive personality in nonclinical subjects. *American Journal of Psychiatry, 150*, 1718–1724.

Klein, D. N., Riso, L. P., Donaldson, S. K., Schwartz, J. E., Anderson, R. L., Ouimette, P. C., Lizardi, H., & Aronson, T. A. (1995). Family study of early-onset dysthymia: Mood and personality disorders in relatives of outpatients with dysthymia and episodic major depression and normal controls. *Archives of General Psychiatry, 52*, 487–496.

Klein, D. N., & Shih, J. (1998). Depressive personality: Thirty-month stability and relationships to DSM-III-R personality disorders and normal personality dimensions. *Journal of Abnormal Psychology, 107*, 319–327.

Klein, D. N., Taylor, E. B., S., & Harding, K. (1988). Primary early-onset dysthymia: Comparison with primary nonbipolar nonchronic major depression on demographic, clinical, familial, personality, and socioenvironmental characteristics and short-term outcome. *Journal of Abnormal Psychology, 97*, 387–398.

Kraepelin, E. (1921). *Manic depressive insanity and paranoia*. Edinburgh, E. & S. Livingstone.

Kretschmer, E. (1925). *Physique and character*. New York: Harcourt, Brace.

Laughlin, H. P. (1967). *The neuroses*. Washington, D.C.: Butterworths.

Liebowitz, M. R. (1987). Commentary on the criteria for self-defeating personality disorder. *Journal of Personality Disorders, 1*, 197–199.

Loranger, A., Sartorius, N., Andreoli, A., Berger, P., Buchheim, P., Channabasavanna, S. M., Coid, B., Dahl, A., Diekstra, R. F. W., Ferguson, B., Jacobsberg, L. B., Mombour, W., Pull, C., Ono, Y., & Regier, D. A. (1994). The International Personality Disorder Examination. *Archives of General Psychiatry, 51*, 215–224.

McDavid, J. D., & Pilkonis, P. A. (1996). The stability of personality disorder diagnoses. *Journal of Personality Disorders, 10*, 1–15.

McLean, P., & Woody, S. (1995). Commentary on depressive personality disorder: A false start. In W. S. Livesley (Eds.), *DSM-IV personality disorders* (pp. 303–311). New York: Guilford Press.

Millon, T., & Kotik-Harper, D. (1995). The relationship of depression to disorders of personality. In E. E. Beckham & W. R. Leber (Eds.), *Handbook of depression*, 2nd ed. (pp. 107–146). New York: Guilford Press.

Neff, C. (1993). *Chronic maternal depression: Its impact on maternal behavior, the caregiving environment, and offspring functioning in toddlerhood*. Unpublished doctoral dissertation, University of Illinois at Champaign-Urbana.

Norden, K. A., Klein, D. N., Donaldson, S. K., Pepper, C. M., & Klein, L. M. (1995). Reports of the early home environment in DSM-III-R personality disorders. *Journal of Personality Disorders, 9*, 213–223.

Nurnberg, H. G., Siegel, O., Prince, R., Levine, P. E., Raskin, M., & Pollack, S. (1993). Axis-II comorbidity of self-defeating personality disorder. *Journal of Personality Disorders, 7*, 10–21.

Ouimette, P. C., & Klein, D. N. (1993). Convergence of psychoanalytic and cognitive-behavioral theories of depression: An empirical review and new data on Blatt's and Beck's models. In J. M. Masling & R. F. Bornstein (Eds.), *Psychoanalytic perspectives on psychopathology* (pp. 191–224). Washington, D.C.: American Psychological Association.

Perry, J. C. (1992). Problems and considerations in the valid assessment of personality disorders. *American Journal of Psychiatry, 149*, 1645–1653.

Perugi, G., Musetti, L., Simonini, E., Piagentini, F., Cassano, G. B., & Akiskal, H. S. (1990). Gender-mediated clinical features of depressive illness: The importance of temperamental differences. *British Journal of Psychiatry, 157*, 835–841.

Phillips, K. A., Gunderson, J. G., Hirschfeld, R. M. A., & Smith, L. E. (1990). A review of the depressive personality. *American Journal of Psychiatry, 147*, 830–837.

Phillips, K. A., Gunderson, J. G., Kimball, C. R., Triebwasser, J., & Faedda, G. (1992). *An empirical study of depressive personality.* Presented at the 145th Annual Meeting of the American Psychiatric Association, Washington, D.C., May.

Phillips, K. A., Hirschfeld, R. M. A., Shea, M. T., & Gunderson, J. G. (1993). Depressive personality disorder: Perspectives for DSM-IV. *Journal of Personality Disorders, 7*, 30–42.

Phillips, K. A., Hirschfeld, R. M. A., Shea, M. T., & Gunderson, J. G. (1995). Depressive Personality Disorder: Perspectives For DSM-IV. In W. S. Livesly (Ed.), *DSM-IV personality disorders.* New York: Guilford Press.

Reich, J. (1987). Prevalence of DSM-III-R self-defeating (masochistic) personality disorder in normal and outpatient populations. *Journal of Nervous and Mental Disease, 175*, 52–54.

Reich, J. (1990). Familiality of DSM-III self-defeating personality disorder. *Journal of Nervous and Mental Disease, 178*, 597–598.

Reich, W. (1933/1976). *Character analysis.* New York: Pocket Books.

Rosewater, L. B. (1987). A critical analysis of the proposed self-defeating personality disorder. *Journal of Personality Disorders, 1*, 190–196.

Schill, T., Beyler, J., Morales, J., & Ekstrom, B. (1991). Self-defeating personality and perceptions of family environment. *Psychological Reports, 69*, 744–746.

Schneider, K. (1958). *Psychopathic personalities.* London: Cassell.

Seligman, M. E. P. (1975). *Helplessness: On depression, development, and death.* San Francisco: W.H. Freeman.

Shea, M. T., & Hirschfeld, R. M. A. (1996). Chronic mood disorder and depressive personality. *Psychiatric Clinics of North America, 19*, 103–120.

Simons, R. C. (1986). Psychoanalytic contributions to psychiatric nosology: Forms of masochistic behavior. *Journal of the American Psychoanalytic Association, 35*, 583–608.

Skodal, A. E., Oldham, J. M., Gallaher, P. E., & Bezirganian, S. (1994). Validity of self-defeating personality disorder. *American Journal of Psychiatry, 151*, 560–567.

Slater, E., & Roth, M. (1969). *Clinical psychiatry* (3rd ed.). Baltimore: Williams & Wilkins.

Spitzer, R. L., Williams, J. B. W., Kass, F., & Davies, M. (1989). National field trial of the DSM-III-R diagnostic criteria for self-defeating personality disorder. *American Journal of Psychiatry, 146*, 1561–1567.

Sprock, J., Blashfield, R. K., & Smith, B. (1990). Gender weighting of DSM-III-R personality disorder criteria. *American Journal of Psychiatry, 147*, 586–590.

Standage, K. F. (1986). A clinical and psychometric investigation comparing Scheider's and the DSM-III typologies of personality disorders. *Comprehensive Psychiatry, 27*, 35–46.

Sutton, S. K., & Davidson, R. J. (1997). Prefrontal brain asymmetry: A biological substrate of the behavioral approach and inhibition systems. *Psychological Science, 8*, 204–210.

Tellegen, A. (1985). Structures of mood and personality and their relevance to assessing anxiety, with an emphasis on self-report. In A. H. Tuma & J. D. Maser (Eds.), *Anxiety and the anxiety disorders* (pp. 681–706). Hillsdale, NJ: Lawrence Erlbaum.

Tellenbach, H. (1961). *Melancholy: History of the problem, endogeneity, typology, pathogenesis, clinical considerations.* Pittsburgh: Duquesne University Press.

Tomarken, A. J., Davidson, R. J., Wheeler, R. E., & Doss, R. C. (1992). Individual differences in anterior brain asymmetry and fundamental dimensions of emotion. *Journal of Personality and Social Psychology, 62*, 676–687.

Vaillant, G., & Perry, J. (1985). Personality disorders. In H. Kaplan & B. Sadock (Eds.), *Comprehensive textbook of psychiatry*, 4th ed. (vol. 1, pp. 958–986). Baltimore: Williams & Wilkins.

Van Os, J., Jones, P., Lewis, G., Wadsworth, M., & Murray, R. (1997). Developmental precursors of affective illness in a general population birth cohort. *Archives of General Psychiatry, 54*, 625–631.

Walker, L. E. A. (1987). Inadequacies of the masochistic personality disorder diagnosis for women. *Journal of Personality Disorders, 1*, 183–189.

Weissman, M. M., Bland, R. C., Canino, G. J., Faravelli, C., Greenwald, S., Hwu, H.-G., Joyce, P. R., Karam, E. G., Lee, C.-K., Lellouch, J., Lepine, J.-P., Newman, S. C., Rubio-Stipec, M., Wells, J. E., Wickramaratne, P., Wittchen, H.-U., & Yeh, E.-K. (1996). Cross-national epidemiology of major depression and bipolar disorder. *Journal of the American Medical Association, 276*, 293–299.

Widiger, T. A., & Costa, Jr., P. T. (1994). Personality and personality disorders. *Journal of Abnormal Psychology, 103*, 78–91.

Widiger, T. A., & Frances, A. J. (1989). Controversies concerning the self-defeating personality disorder. In R. Curtis (Ed.), *Self-defeating behaviors: Experimental, research, and clini-*

cal impressions, and practical implications (pp. 289–309). New York: Plenum.

Widiger, T. A., & Spitzer, R. L. (1991). Sex bias in the diagnosis of personality disorders: Conceptual and methodological issues. *Clinical Psychology Review, 11*, 1–22.

Williams, D., & Schill, T. (1993). Attachment histories for people with characteristics of self-defeating personality. *Psychological Reports, 73*, 1232–1234.

Von Zerssen, D., Tauscher, R., & Possl, J. (1994). The relationship of premorbid personality to subtypes of an affective illness: A replication study by means of an operationalized procedure for the diagnosis of personality structures. *Journal of Affective Disorders, 32*, 61–72.

Zimmerman, M. (1994). Diagnosing personality disorders. *Archives of General Psychiatry, 51*, 225–245.

27

Narcissistic Personality Disorder

ELSA RONNINGSTAM

Until recently, most knowledge about the narcissistic personality disorder (NPD) and pathological narcissism was based on psychoanalytic conceptions. Clinical observations of such patients contributed to a growing database on the complexity of narcissistic pathology and its broad range of characterological and symptomatic expressions. The inclusion of NPD in *DSM-III* in 1980 established its status as an official diagnostic category, with overt and identifiable criteria amenable to more rigorous empirical study. Recently, NPD has been conceptualized through other traditions, including the biopsychosocial, the cognitive, and the interpersonal perspectives. This chapter provides an overview of the essential theoretical, clinical, and empirical views of NPD. Major theoretical and clinical controversies regarding the definition and diagnosis of NPD are reviewed, and further diagnostic clarifications for this complex disorder are suggested.

Definition

NPD is linked to the psychoanalytic concept of narcissism that over the past century has acquired several meanings. The various theoretical and clinical definitions of narcissism were reviewed by Pulver (1970), who noted that the term was referring to a perversion, a developmental stage, a mood of relating to objects, and levels of self-esteem. Stolorow (1975) proposed a functional definition, stating that narcissism was expressed in "activities aiming at maintaining cohesiveness and stability of the self-representations." On a descriptive level, narcissism is defined as "a concentration of psychological interest upon the self" (More & Fine, 1968).

Presently, the most accepted psychoanalytic definition states that narcissism refers to the libidinal investment of the self (O. Kernberg, 1975). This conception has gradually become differentiated from its clinical meaning and usage, and from the definition of pathological narcissism and the clinical diagnosis of NPD. On a clinical level, narcissism refers to the process of self-esteem regulation, and is closely related to affect regulation, superego functioning, interpersonal relations, and cognitive functioning. In turn, all of these are important components of self-esteem regulation (O. Kernberg, 1975).

Normal narcissism refers to all aspects of normal self-esteem within a normally functioning self-structure. This would include not only self-preservation, self-regard, and a positive feeling from the body self (health and attractiveness; P. Kernberg, 1998) but also self-assertiveness with normal levels of entitlement and competitiveness, and affiliativeness with empathy and compassion (Stone, 1998). The construct validity of normal narcissism and narcissistic personality traits have been extensively investigated by Raskin and colleagues using the

Narcissistic Personality Inventory (NPI), a self-report questionnaire (Raskin & Hall, 1979; Raskin & Terry, 1988). Fifty-four items relate to four behavioral factors: leadership/authority, superiority/arrogance, exploitiveness/entitlement, and self-absorption/self-admiration (Emmons, 1987). Relations between the NPI and measures of egocentrism, as indicated by use of the first-person pronoun (Raskin & Shaw, 1988), self-esteem and grandiosity (Raskin, Novacek, & Hogan, 1991), sensation seeking (Emmons, 1981), lack of empathy (Watson, Grisham, Trotter, & Biderman, 1984; Watson & Morris, 1991), and anger (McCann & Biaggio, 1989) have been empirically established.

In pathological narcissism, the self-esteem is disturbed and regulated through a distorted self-structure with a pathological grandiose self (P. Kernberg, 1989, 1998). This contributes to a fragile self-esteem that requires different expressive or defensive regulatory processes. NPD is hence the characterological constellation that sustains pathological self-esteem regulation.

Clinical Description

In *DSM-IV*, NPD is described as "a pervasive pattern of grandiosity, need for admiration, and lack of empathy." In addition, the *DSM* acknowledges the associated features of vulnerable self-esteem, sensitivity, intense reactions of humiliation, emptiness or disdain to criticism or defeat, and vocational irregularities owing to difficulties tolerating criticism or competition. Feelings of shame, intense self-criticism, and social withdrawal are also acknowledged. Patients presenting such secondary characteristics may on the surface appear quite different compared to those captured in the *DSM* criteria set. Narcissistic patients can also present with specific antisocial characteristics, and those functioning on a lower level sometimes show similarities with borderline patients. Additional characteristics such as high achievement and success, masochism, promiscuity, excessive rage, and suicidal behavior have also been acknowledged in the clinical literature.

NPD encompasses a range of clinical presentations with conspicuous and pervasive personality trait—that is, arrogance, shyness, antisocial behavior, and borderline features. A descriptive overview of these most acknowledged clinical presentations of NPD follows below. Clinical features are described in terms of five areas of functioning: grandiosity, interpersonal relations, reactivity, affects and mood states, and social or moral adaptation (Ronningstam & Gunderson, 1990).

The Arrogant Narcissist

Grandiosity is usually the most outstanding and discriminating feature of individuals with NPD. Grandiosity can be expressed in an unrealistic overvaluation of talents and ability; preoccupation with fantasies of unlimited beauty, power, wealth or success; and a belief in unrealistic superiority and uniqueness. This is usually accompanied by boastful, pretentious, self-centered and self-referential behavior.

Incapacity to maintain satisfactory, mutual, and enduringly committed relations with others is the most prognostically important feature of narcissistic individuals. They often see others either as means of ego inflation and support for their self-esteem, or as stepping stones in the pursuit of their own goals. They have a strong need for admiring attention, and they actively seek opportunities whereby attention will be forthcoming. A deep sense of entitlement leads them to expect or demand special treatment from others, and they become surprised, hurt, or even enraged if expectations are not being met. Narcissistic people exploit others, usually in a passive, indirect, or manipulative way with no intention of reciprocity. A condescending and devaluating manner toward others is often combined with arrogance and haughtiness. Some may appear snobbish, supercilious, or patronizing. They reluctantly admit that they actually envy others' possessions, talents, or success, but more often they believe that others envy them because of their specialness or talents, and they can react with suspiciousness and intense feelings of rage when perceiving others' envy.

Narcissistic individuals have intense reactions to criticism, defeats, losses, and counteractions. Although many chose to remain indifferent on the surface, they still experience strong feelings of disdain, humiliation, or emptiness. Overt reactions range from dismissal and minimizing of the criticism, to verbal counterattacks, or revengeful plans or actions. In more severe cases, episodes of depression, psychosomatic reactions or syndromes, periodic substance abuse, or suicidal ideations or actions may occur.

Although on the surface seemingly actively engaged, narcissistic individuals struggle with sustained or recurrent feelings of worthlessness, emptiness, meaninglessness, hollowness, and futility. Depression and dysthymia are the most common psychiatric symptoms, especially occurring in the middle age with the awareness of limitations or lost opportunities.

The Shy Narcissist

A different clinical presentation of NPD, recently highlighted in the clinical literature (Akhtar, 1989; Gabbard, 1989; Gersten, 1991; Cooper & Ronningstam, 1992) as well as by *DSM-IV*, is characterized by hypervigilance, shyness, and social withdrawl. These persons appear clinically quite different from arrogant narcissists because of their sensitivity, inhibitions, vulnerability, and shame-ridden and social withdrawal. Nevertheless, these individuals possess the same pathological grandiose self-image, although their grandiose desires are seldom expressed overtly, but performed at the fantasy level. These patients usually have a secret self-awareness about the discrepancies between their grandiose self-experience and their actual capacity and limitations. Whereas the arrogant narcissist seldom reveals feelings of inferiority and shame, the shy narcissist admits the experience of intense self-criticism, fear of failure in living up to aspirations, and low self-regard. Although these individuals can appear empathic and interested in others, they are nevertheless often unable to genuinely respond to others' needs. These patients suffer from inner shame because of their narcissistic wishes and pursuits, and guilt because of their awareness of the inability to genuinely and mutually care for other people. The shy narcissists are extremely attentive and sensitive to the reactions of others, and observant of slights and criticism toward them. Accordingly, they may avoid social life because of fear of rejection and humiliation. Diagnostically, this subtype reflects characteristics of both the narcissistic, avoidant, and masochistic personality disorders. As their presentation is not easily recognizable, correct diagnosis usually requires several interviews or a period of psychotherapy.

Case Vignettes

Mr. P., a 27-year-old unmarried man with a degree in business, sought treatment because of increased drug and alcohol abuse, and suicidal ideation. Mr. P. was a masculine, flamboyant, very intelligent, and outgoing young man, who immediately gave an impression of confidence and experience. In the clinical interview he was easily engageable and initially enjoyed talking about himself. However, when the clinician tried to get a closer contact, Mr. P. became anxious. He broke eye contact, lost interest in continuing, and his responses to further inquires were abrupt, arrogant, and even provocative or hostile.

Mr. P.'s drug and alcohol abuse started in college when he moved away from his family. He soon developed a reckless habit of drunk driving, got into several car accidents, became involved in occasional cocaine transactions, and began missing lectures and failing his courses. After graduation six years later, he started his own business with substantial financial assistance from his family. Initially very successful, Mr. P. was involved in serious confrontations with two senior business colleagues. Mr. P. denied his own misjudgments or faults, and blamed the conflict and his own business failure on the senior colleagues, whom he saw as authoritarian and deliberately undermining of his successful progress. He then became suicidal, intensified his cocaine abuse, and turned to his family for help.

Ms. S., a 42-year-old unmarried woman who worked as a research librarian, sought psychiatric consultation after a severe anxiety attack. Ms. S. was an intelligent, hardworking, conscientious, women with strong work ethics and professional standards. She was pleasant and polite, discreetly but well dressed, soft spoken, and articulate. She was concerned about having to bother the clinician with her problems, and excused herself by stressing that this was the first time she had experienced such severe symptoms. She was observant and sensitive to the clinician's reactions, but had difficulty understanding and remembering the clinician's questions or comments. Once when the clinician was late, she described feeling deeply humiliated when having to wait in front of the other clients and not being promptly attended to.

Ms. S. was the oldest of four daughters. Her father was an influential lawyer. In high school she also wanted to become a lawyer, but her father advised against it, stating that women had difficulty becoming good lawyers. Ms. S. entered her choice of profession with great enthusiasm and ambition. After a few years, however, she noticed that she became increasingly upset by the unprofessional and sometimes sloppy behavior she observed in her colleagues and the way the library was managed. She complained about the director's lack of ethics, efficiency, and long-term plans, as well as his lack of communication with the employees. As a result, she felt increasingly powerless, frustrated, and inferior. She became irritated and snapped at her colleagues who she experienced as having less serious ambitions or taking personal and professional advantage of the workplace. Ms. S. stated with pride that she did not like nor need much social interaction, and she socialized only with a few carefully chosen female friends and her parents. She prided herself on her ability to read others and respond to their needs, interests, and wishes.

In psychotherapy, the therapist was somewhat puzzled by Ms. S.'s contradictory presentation. Although she was proud and slightly pretentiousness, she also exhibited a deep sense of inferiority and vulnerability to humiliation. After several months, she revealed with some embarrassment her intense wish to become famous and influential like her father. She felt entitled as his oldest daughter to continue on his track, and had expected more support and acknowledgment for her contributions to her professional field.

NPD with Antisocial or Borderline Features

Within the psychoanalytic frame of reference, mental disorders are categorized according to their level of personality organization—that is, neurotic, borderline (O. Kernberg, 1975), referring to their capacity to maintain a sense of reality and identity and their level of defense system. People functioning on a neurotic level have intact reality testing, stable sense of their identity, and high level defenses such as repression. People with a psychotic personality organization have disturbed reality testing, identity diffusion, and low-level defense such as projective identification and splitting. Most patients with NPD are capable of high functioning owing to their fairly stable although pathological ego structure—that is, they normally do not lose their sense of reality or become psychotic. In addition, their sense of their own identity, although unrealistically grandiose, usually does not vary except under extraordinary circumstances. People with NPD may vary in terms of their level of superego pathology. Some have an intact superego with normal moral functioning not influenced by their narcissistic pathology. Some can even be moral perfectionists and incorporate their high ethical and moral standards as part of their sense of superiority while condemning others. However, corrupt behavior, lack of commitment, irresponsibility, and more active and deliberately exploitive and ruthless behavior are not uncommon in people with NPD. There are specifically two types of NPD whose clinical presentations are strongly influenced by severe superego and ego pathology—NPD with antisocial trends and NPD with borderline features.

Except for those with advanced drug abuse who finance their addiction through regular criminal behavior, narcissistic individuals are seldom involved in recurrent antisocial behavior (Ronningstam & Gunderson, 1995b). However, they can occasionally commit one or a few crimes under the circumstances of being enraged or as a mean of avoiding defeat. The grandiose self-image is infiltrated by the idea of criminal acts, as either revenge or an ultimate experience of superiority and control.

A specific group of narcissistic patients with malignant narcissism (O. Kernberg, 1984) or psychopathy (Hart & Hare, 1998; Meloy, 1988) do evince more sustained antisocial trends and are diagnostically closely related to individuals with antisocial personality disorder. Pathological lying, manipulativeness, and lack of guilt are outstanding features in these individuals. They can also show extremely sadistic interpersonal behavior, paranoid features, passive parasitic behavior, or chronic suicidal behavior. Some act as authoritarian, ideological group leaders; others are found within the forensic psychiatric system.

NPD patients functioning on a borderline level possess a grandiose but poorly integrated ego. Since the ego coordinates activities and inputs from the superego, id, and external world, these people are more influenced by impulses and are unable to delay gratification and coordinate resources toward a premeditated goal. They have low anxiety tolerance and are prone to intense, uncontrolled rage, and primary process thinking (O. Kernberg, 1975).

NPD and Axis I Syndromes

Narcissistic individuals usually display few psychiatric symptoms. However, when they come to treatment it is usually because of acute depression after experiencing failures, losses, or other severe narcissistic injuries. Dysthymia, another frequently occurring symptom in narcissistic patients, characterized by a chronic state of boredom, emptiness, aloneness, stimulus hunger, dissatisfaction, and meaninglessness (Millon, 1981), is often a reaction to a repeated failures and gradual disillusionment.

Although most suicide attempts and actual suicides occur in patients with major mental illnesses, such as depression, schizophrenia, or substance abuse disorders, there is a clinical agreement that narcissistic patients are specifically prone to suicidal behavior (Perry, 1990; Maltsberger, 1998). Painful reactions to failure, criticism, and humiliation can make the narcissistic patient specifically vulnerable to suicide. Comorbid NPD in BPD is related to a higher frequency of suicide rates compared to pure BPD patients (Stone, 1989; McGlashan & Heinssen 1989). Postmortem diagnosis of a group of young men who committed suicide showed that over 20% had a narcissistic personality type (Apter et al., 1993).

Both O. Kernberg (1984) and Kohut (1971) related suicide in narcissistic patients to specific types of self-directed aggression—egosyntonic sadism in malignant narcissism and narcissistic rage in response to narcissistic injuries. They also agreed that suicidal behavior in narcissistic patients is not necessarily related to depressed states with accompanying guilt, but contrary, can increase the narcissist's self-esteem and induce a sense of power, freedom from fear, control over life, and triumph over death (O. Kernberg, 1984). Suicidal acts can also be understood as attempts to eliminate the self in order to erase a reality that is filled with disappointments and failures (Kohut, 1971). Late middle age is particularly critical for narcissists, when hopelessness, empty depression, and the realization that life events are irreversible can evoke a strong wish to end unbearable feelings of mortification and shame due to failure (Kohut, 1977). A specific type of sudden deadly suicidal behavior in response to interpersonal stress or threats can be found in nondepressed narcissists who are grandiose, vulnerable, and impulsive. Such individuals have impaired capacity to identify, experience, and contain feelings (Ronningstam & Maltsberger, 1998).

Affect intolerance and vulnerability have been highlighted as important predisposing personality factors in the development of substance abuse and dependency (Vaillant, 1988). Wurmser (1974) identified narcissistic disturbances as a precondition for addictive behavior, and Khantzian (1979, 1982) has pointed to the self-medicating effect of drugs, such as cocaine, that can diminish the disorganizing influence of rage and overwhelming feelings of depression, and contribute to a sense mastery, control and grandeur, and increased the sense of self-sufficiency.

Although no evidence implicates a significant relationship between NPD and bipolar disorder, a complex comorbid interaction can sometimes be found in patients with the two disorders. As the self-regulatory functions are impaired, depression and mania can for these patients reflect a narcissistic balance directing feelings of rage and shame (Aleksandrowicz, 1980; Morrison, 1989). Patients in hypomanic or acute manic phase can show affective, experiential, and behavioral similarities with, and actually meet several of the discriminating characteristics for, NPD (Ronningstam, 1996; Stormberg, Ronningstam, Gunderson, & Tohen, 1998). These patients often highly value their manic phase as a means to overcome inferiority, limitations, an attitude that can highly decrease motivation for treatment.

Empirical Studies of the Diagnostic Criteria of NPD

Empirical studies have confirmed the diagnostic validity of some of the overt characteristics of NPD as represented in the *DSM-III-R* and *DSM-IV* criteria sets, such as grandiosity, grandiose fantasy (Morey, 1988a, 1988b, 1998), desire for uniqueness, a need for admiring attention, and arrogant haughty behavior (Ronningstam & Gunderson, 1990).

Empirical studies have also focused on the validity and usefulness of other NPD characteristics besides those included in the *DSM*. Using the Diagnostic Interview for Narcissism (DIN; Gunderson, Ronningstam, & Bodkin, 1990), a semistructured interview that evaluates 33 characteristics for pathological narcissism, Ronningstam and Gunderson (1990) found the following features to significantly discriminate narcissistic patients from all other psychiatric patients: (1) boastful and pretentious behavior—that is, the tendency to brag and behave ostentatiously, as if assuming the interest or naiveté of other people; (2) self-centered and self-referential behavior—that is, notable self-preoccupation and tendencies to personalize meanings of facts and events; and (3) reactions to the envy of others—that is, the belief that other people envy them because of their special talents or unique qualities occurring with hostile and suspicious reactions to the perception of such envy.

Based on detailed studies of the construct validity of NPD and internal consistency of the present criteria for NPD using the Personality Assessment Inventory (PAI; Morey, 1991), Morey (1998) suggested the following set of monothetic criteria for improving the diagnostic efficiency and the discriminant validity of the diagnosis: First, inflated self-esteem and marked affective reactions (such as rage or depression) to assaults to self-esteem. This criterion takes into account both unrealistic grandiose characteristics and the vulnerability of the narcissist's self-esteem. It also highlights the narcissist's proneness to intense reactions due to hypersensitivity and vulnerability. Second, marked need for interpersonal control. This criterion emphasizes an important underlying aspect of the narcissistic person's interpersonal relatedness—that is, the unempathic, detached self-serving involvement. Third, noteworthy expressions (either active or passive) of interpersonal hostility, with the degree and type of hostility varying from less obvious passive-aggressive behavior to overtly blithering, exploitive, or sadistic behavior, especially toward subordinates. Fourth, lack of overtly self-destructive tendencies. Narcissistic patients are usually not involved in impulsive or controlled self-damaging or self-mutilating behavior. This criterion is especially important for differentiating narcissistic and borderline patients.

Prevalence

Most diagnostic instruments for evaluating personality disorders developed during the past decade have included NPD. Empirical studies on the prevalence and comorbidity of personality disorders (Gunderson, Ronningstam, & Smith, 1991; Ronningstam, 1996) using the *DSM-III-R* criteria for NPD have estimated the prevalence rate in the adult clinical population to be between 2% (Dahl, 1986) and 22% (Morey, 1988a). A substantial increase in prevalence occurred with the shift from *DSM-III* (6.2% among inpatients) to *DSM-III-R* (22%; Morey, 1988a). In the general population, the prevalence is estimated to be less than 1% (Reich, Yates, & Ndvaguba, 1989; Zimmerman & Coryell, 1990), although individuals exhibiting a narcissistic personality style or significant narcissistic traits are considered common in Western culture (Stone, 1993; Sperry, 1995).

The prevalence of NPD seems to vary according to the type of clinical practice. The diagnosis of NPD is used differently depending on the psychiatric setting. In some settings, ambiguity in defining and interpreting the criteria lead to a reluctance use the diagnosis. In others, a broader interest in psychoanalytic and psychodynamic formulations stimulates increased interest in the construct and more frequent usage of the diagnosis (Cooper & Ronningstam, 1992). In private practice and small clinics providing outpatient individual or couples treatment the diagnosis is likely to be used more frequently than in larger psychiatric hospital clinics and inpatient services (Gunderson et al., 1991).

Gender and Age Differences

Research reports disagree on the gender distribution of NPD. Some studies support the idea that NPD is more common in males than in females (Ronningstam & Gunderson, 1990; Millon, 1990), while others believe NPD is equally prevalent in both sexes (Plakun, 1990). *DSM-IV* claims that 50 to 75% of those diagnosed with NPD are male. One study of gender differences found that men and women express narcissistic issues in different ways, and the authors claimed that the present conceptualization of narcissism reflects predominantly male expressions of the disorder. Men manifest a greater sense of uniqueness, more interpersonal exploitiveness, entitlement, and lack of empathy, while women show more intense reactiveness to slights from others (Reichman & Flaherty, 1990).

Narcissistic disturbances are frequent among people in their late teens and early twenties, due mainly to the specific developmental challenges in the transition from adolescence to adulthood. Such disturbances are usually corrected through developmental life experiences and normally do not develop into adult NPD (Ronningstam & Gunderson, 1995a). However, the presence of NPD in both children and adolescence have been empirically verified (Abrams, 1993; Bardenstein, 1994; P. Kernberg, Hajal, & Normandin, 1998).

Unlike other dramatic cluster disorders, narcissistic personality disorder does not necessarily remit with advanced age. In fact, middle age is an especially critical period for the development or worsening of NPD. The challenge of facing personal and professional limitations, lost opportunities, loss of parents, increased independence of own children, and so on can reinforce specific pathological or defensive narcissistic traits, leading to chronic denial, emptiness, devaluation, guilt, and cynicism (O. Kernberg, 1980). Significant narcissistic pathology and personality disorder have also been found in elderly people (Berezin, 1977; O. Kernberg, 1977).

Sociocultural Factors

The concept of narcissism and the diagnosis of narcissistic personality disorder have been particularly prone to cultural contextualization and sociopolitical analysis. Lasch (1979) presented the idea that the modernization of Western society, with its social changes and disintegration, and its increased demands for individual achievement, productivity, autonomy, mobility, and adaptation, has contributed to the development of a narcissistic personality style. Individual accomplishment and detachment are expected and valued traits in modern society, in contrast to the values of attachment, dependency, and cohesion found in more traditional cultures and societies. Although there is no evidence that these factors have a direct causal relationship with the increased prevalence of NPD, the connection between individual development and culture raise questions about how self-esteem is influenced by society.

In addition, the predominant values and traditions in each social environment influence an individual's possibility of developing a normal and adapted sense of self-esteem, as expressed through normal narcissistic functions such as assertiveness, pride, status, power, value, and attraction (Stone, 1998). Certain societies or cultures encourage healthy self-esteem regulation and normal narcissistic development, including pride, constructive self-assertiveness, and competition, while others do not. On the other hand, some cultures generate more covert narcissistic disorders and specific culturally determined narcissistic vulnerabilities. The fact that NPD is not included in the *ICD* system, and that some countries actually consider it to be a disorder with very low prevalence (E. Simonsen, personal communication; Millon, 1998) might reflect such social and cultural differences.

Comorbidity

Despite considerable improvements in the NPD criteria from *DSM-III* to *DSM-III-R*, substantial comorbidity with other Axis II disorders continues. Patients who meet criteria for NPD often also meet criteria for other personality disorders as well. In fact, NPD has one of the highest rates of diagnostic overlap among the Axis II disorders, especially with disorders in the dramatic cluster (Gunderson et al., 1991). The most commonly overlapping personality disorders are histrionic (53%), borderline (47%), paranoid (36%), avoidant (36%), passive-aggressive (28%), and antisocial (16%; Morey, 1988a). Revisions of the NPD criteria in *DSM-IV* were aimed particularly at addressing this problem.

Studies investigating the co-occurrence of Axis I and Axis II disorders have reported somewhat higher prevalence among bipolar patients (11–47%) and substance abusers (12–38%). However, no consistent evidence was provided indicating the presence of a significant relation between NPD and any Axis I disorder (Ronningstam, 1996). In clinical samples of NPD, the most frequently co-occurring Axis I disorders were major depression or dysthymia (42–50%) followed by substance abuse (24–50%) and bipolar disorder (5–12%; Ronningstam, 1993). An integrative analysis of available theoretical, clinical, and empirical data suggests comorbidity between NPD and substance use disorder, bipolar disorder, depression, and anorexia nervosa (Ronningstam, 1996).

Differential Diagnosis

The high comorbidity of NPD with other personality disorders makes differential diagnoses essential. The relations between NPD and antisocial and borderline personality disorders have received both theoretical and empirical attention, providing reliable differential diagnostic guidelines. In addition, histrionic, obsessive-compulsive, paranoid, and schizoid personality disorders sometimes manifest narcissistic features. Even some Axis I states can resemble NPD, including hypomania and mania, and psychotic states with severe grandiose delusions.

NPD versus Antisocial Personality Disorder (ASPD)

A strong conceptual and clinical relationship between NPD and ASPD has been reported by several authors (O. Kernberg, 1989; Ronningstam & Gunderson, 1995b; Hart & Hare, 1998; Morey, 1998), and empirical studies have indicated a relationship between some NPD criteria and psychopathy (Morey, 1998; Hart & Hare, 1998). O. Kernberg (1989) outlined a structural relation between NPD and ASPD. More specifically, he suggested that "all patients with an antisocial personality disorder present typical features of the narcissistic personality disorder plus a specific pathology of their internalized systems of morality (their 'superego functions') and a particular deterioration in their world of internalized object relations" (p. 553). In other words, all antisocials are assumed to have a narcissistic personality structure, but not all narcissists are antisocial. The most important differential features are the more severe superego pathology—that is, lack of concern and understanding of moral functions, and the impaired capacity to be involved in mutual, nonexploitive relationships found in ASPD. Interpersonal and affective manifestations (anxiety and depression) are more pronounced in NPD, while psychopaths show more acting out, particularly with drug and alcohol abuse. Narcissists are usually more grandiose, while ASPD patients are exploitive, have a superficial value system, and are involved in recurrent antisocial activities (Ronningstam & Gunderson, 1995b). Exploitiveness in antisocial patients is probably more likely to be consciously and actively related to materialistic or sexual gain, while exploitive behavior in narcissistic patients is more passive, serving to enhance self-image by attaining praise or power.

NPD versus Borderline Personality Disorder (BPD)

The differential diagnosis between NPD and BPD has received substantial clinical attention (O. Kernberg, 1975; Adler, 1981; Masterson, 1981; Plakun, 1987; Ronningstam & Gunderson, 1991). Several similarities between NPD and BPD have been identified, and as mentioned earlier, some patients with severe forms of NPD function on a borderline level. However, people with NPD have a more cohesive self-structure while borderlines are prone to severe regression, identity diffusion, and impulsivity (O. Kernberg, 1975). Narcissists are more capable of high, sustained achievement and usually have a better work record (Ronningstam & Gunderson, 1991; Akhtar, 1989). The most important discriminators are the various manifestations of grandiosity, including exaggeration of talent, grandiose fantasies, and a sense of uniqueness in NPD (Akhtar, 1989; Morey, 1988b; Plakun, 1987; Ronningstam & Gunderson, 1991). While narcissistic patients are less overtly self-destructive and less preoccupied with dependency and abandonment concerns (*DSM IV*; Morey, 1998), they show more passive-aggressive features (Morey, 1988b), arrogance, and haughtiness. Both groups regard attention as important, but while borderlines seek nurturing attention because they need it, narcissists feel they deserve admiring attention because of their superiority (Ronningstam & Gunderson, 1991).

Other Important Differential Diagnostic Issues

- *NPD vs. histrionic personality disorder*. Both narcissistic and histrionic individuals demonstrate exhibitionistic, dramatic, and seductive behavior. However, while the histrionic is capable of warmth, dependency, and genuine concern and commitment, the narcissist is more cold, exploitive, manipulative, and aggressive (Morey, 1998; O. Kernberg, 1975; Millon, 1981). The histrionic person can appear spontaneous, without ulterior motives, and seemingly sympathetic for all the trouble he or she causes, while the narcissistic individual is more controlled, calculating, and relentless.

- *NPD vs. obsessive-compulsive personality disorder (OCD).* Perfectionism is a common characteristic in both obsessive-compulsive and narcissistic patients (Akhtar, 1989; Rothstein, 1980). Both sometimes appear emotionally cold, with a strong need for control. Similar to histrionics but different from narcissists, however, the obsessive-compulsive is capable of mutually deep relationships and commitments. Furthermore, OCD individuals show empathy and guilt, and their perfectionism is not associated with the devaluation, haughtiness, and demandingness found in narcissistic patients (Vaillant & Perry, 1980; Akhtar, 1989; O. Kernberg, 1975).
- *NPD vs. paranoid personality disorder (PAR).* Both NPD and paranoid personalities display grandiose features. However, the paranoid person's grandiosity is usually connected to self-righteousness and self-justifying argumentation, and his or her anger is unrelated to exploitiveness or envy (O. Kernberg, 1990). Narcissistic and paranoid individuals can also share devaluation, sensitivity to criticism, and lack of empathy (Akhtar, 1989). However, narcissists are more exploitive, envious, attention seeking, arrogant, and not pervasively mistrustful or in search of hidden motives. NPD patients sometimes show brief paranoid ideations, usually related to the belief that other people envy them and want to hurt them, or spoil their achievements (Ronningstam & Gunderson, 1990). People functioning on a lower level with malignant narcissism or borderline features can nevertheless manifest sustained paranoid features.
- *NPD vs. schizoid personality disorder.* Emotional aloofness and lack of mutual interpersonal relations or genuine deep interest in other people are common characteristics in both schizoid and narcissistic personality disorders. While narcissists are ambitious and high achieving, more actively in pursuit of advantageous or admiring relations, and more exploitive, the schizoid individual is passive, withdrawn, and resigned (Akhtar, 1989). However, contrary to narcissists, schizoid individuals actually show a capacity to empathize with other people and to observe, describe, and evaluate others with depth and differentiation (O. Kernberg, 1990). In addition, a sense of superiority (Guntrip 1952/1969); inclinations toward a cognitive, intellectual style (as contrary to an emotional, bodily anchored style); and the presence of compensatory internal life and grandiose fantasies can be found in both personality disorders. While narcissists can appear flamboyant and charming, schizoid persons are indifferent, and colorless.
- *NPD vs. mania and hypomania.* Patients in the hypomanic and acute manic phase can appear quite similar to narcissistic patients and actually expose most of the core characteristics for NPD (Akhtar, 1989; Stormberg et al., 1998). However, the active search for admiring attention and profound envy of others in narcissistic patients are not found in manics.
- *NPD vs. paranoid psychosis or schizophrenia with grandiose delusions.* Although grandiosity occurs in both NPD and psychotic disorders, the presence of psychotic illness and loss of reality testing contraindicate a diagnosis of NPD (O. Kernberg, 1990).

Historical Perspectives

Long known in literature and poetry (Winge, 1967), the term *narcissism* was introduced to psychiatry a century ago by Ellis (1898) in a psychological study of male autoeroticism, and by Näcke (1899) in a description of sexual perversions. Freud first mentioned narcissism in a footnote added in 1910 to "Three Essays on the Theory of Sexuality" (Freud, 1905/1957), as a phase in the development of homosexuality, and in (1911/1957) he referred to narcissism as the choice of self as a libidinal object, a normal stage in libidinal development.

Rank (1911) published the first psychoanalytic paper on narcissism, in which he discussed different aspects of self-love. In his main paper, "On Narcissism" (1914/1957), Freud presented definitions of primary and secondary narcissism, identified narcissistic object-choice, and suggested methods for studying narcissism through the studies of organic disease, hypochondria, and human erotic life. In 1925, Waelder outlined essential narcissistic characteristics, discussed different manifestations of narcissism, and suggested a treatment strategy aimed at the "sublimation of narcissism." In 1931/1961, Freud for the first time described the "narcissistic libidinal character type," and in 1933,

Wilhelm Reich specified the "phallic-narcissistic character," in which narcissism is used as a defense against threats to self-esteem and well-being.

The connection between narcissism and self-esteem regulation was first alluded to by Freud in his discussion of self-regard and the development of the ego-ideal (1914/1957). Horney (1939), Anne Reich (1960, 1964/1973), and Pulver (1970) added substantially to the definition and differentiation of healthy self-esteem and pathological self-esteem regulation, and to understanding of the complex interrelation between narcissism and self-esteem.

The origin of NPD as a diagnostic category is more difficult to establish. Terms like narcissistic neurosis, schizophrenia, and psychosis have often been used interchangeably, reflecting the initial close interrelation between narcissism and these illnesses. The theory of narcissistic and auto-erotic regression (Freud, 1911/1957, 1914/1957) explained schizophrenic symptoms as a libidinal withdrawal from the object world and regression to a narcissistic stage. In addition, the observation that the capacity to develop classical transference during psychoanalysis was absent in patients diagnosed with narcissistic neurosis (Freud, 1914/1957) further connected narcissism and psychosis or schizophrenia.

In addition, portrayals of various narcissistic individuals highlighting different aspects of narcissistic pathology have been valuable contributions to the definition and understanding of this character disorder. These include the "God complex" (Jones, (1913/1951), the "Don Juan of achievement" (Fenichel, 1945), the "Nobel Prize complex" (Tartakoff, 1966), the "Icarus complex" (Murray, 1955; Weinberg & Muller, 1974), and the "Glass-bubble fantasy" (Volkan, 1979). In an attempt to classify different narcissistic personalities (Bursten, 1973) identified carving, paranoid, manipulative, and phallic types.

The concepts "narcissistic personality structure" and "narcissistic personality disorder" were first introduced in the 1960s by O. Kernberg (1967) and Kohut (1968). Both O. Kernberg and Kohut made radical reformulations of the nature of narcissistic transference that enabled the development of different psychoanalytic treatment strategies for NPD. Their work stimulated an enormous debate during the 1970s and 1980s regarding theoretical standpoints and definitions of the origin and nature of narcissistic disorders and the pathological grandiose self, and the psychoanalytic techniques for treating these disorders. Currently, both are enormously influential on psychiatry, psychoanalysis, and personality disorder treatment and research.

In an attempt to integrate the extensive and divergent psychoanalytic literature on narcissistic personality disorder, Akhtar (Akhtar & Thomson, 1982; Akhtar, 1989) developed the first comprehensive diagnostic system distinguishing a broad range of overt and covert features of NPD. In his classification, Akhtar highlighted the diagnostic importance of less apparent narcissistic characteristics, indicating the complexity of narcissistic personality disorder and capturing both its conspicuous and hidden natures. He also pointed out that the full range and complete nature of this disorder often requires a long time to explore and accurately diagnose. Clinical features were grouped into six areas of functioning: self-concept; interpersonal relations; social adaptation; ethics, standards and ideals; love and sexuality; and cognitive style.

Contemporary Theoretical Perspectives and Controversies

Few disorders have as many theoretical and clinical antecedents as NPD. Although there is substantial agreement about some basic diagnostic features and etiology, areas of disagreement still remain. Contemporary psychoanalytic formulations diverge concerning the origin of the pathological grandiose self and the roles of aggression, envy, and primitive shame in the early development. The issue of stability or cohesion of the pathological grandiose self and even the overt characteristics of narcissistic patients are subject to dispute. Another perspective, the biosocial learning theory, has influenced the empirical research on NPD. This perspective highlights environmental and parental influence on the development of an inflated self characterized by egotism, self-sufficiency, and learned entitled and exploitive behavior. A cognitive model for understanding NPD is the most recent contribution, instigating new treatment approaches outside the psychoanalytic realm.

The Psychoanalytic Perspective

Within psychoanalysis, several schools have made contributions to contemporary conceptions of NPD and pathological narcissism, especially ego-psychology (Jacobson, 1964; Hartman, 1964) and the Kleinian school (Klein, 1957; Rosenfeldt, 1964, 1971). To some extent, representatives for both British (Winnicott, 1953, 1965; Fairbairn, 1952; Balint, 1952) and French psychoanalysis (Grundberger, 1975; Chasseguet-Smirgel, 1985; McDougall, 1985) have been important as well. Besides the two most influential theoretical perspectives—that is, those of O. Kernberg and Kohut—a more recent interest in the development of the self and the role of shame in character pathology has broaden our understanding of narcissistic functioning and its descriptive features.

Ego-Psychology and Object Relation Theory

O. Kernberg's (1975, 1980) conception of NPD is based on ego-psychology and object relations theory. Kernberg differentiates pathological narcissism from both normal adult narcissism and a regression to infantile narcissism in adult individuals. Accordingly to Kernberg, the central etiological factor is the presence of unintegrated early rage, which caused the splitting and projection of devalued self and object representations from idealized ones. Together, the idealized self and object representations form the pathological grandiose self. Consequently, a dysfunctional superego develops that tends to be overly aggressive, and often dissociated and projected. He outlined three areas where narcissistic character traits are manifested: (1) pathological self-love expressed in grandiosity, superiority, emotional shallowness, and in a discrepancy between exaggerated talents and ambitions, and actual capacity and achievements; (2) pathological object-love characterized by envy and devaluation of others, exploitative behavior, lack of empathy, and inability to depend on others; and (3) superego pathology that can be expressed as an inability to experience depression, severe mood swings, shame regulated self-esteem, and superficial or self-serving values. More severe superego pathology leads to the syndrome of malignant narcissism mentioned above. Kernberg's conceptualization has been highly influential on the definition of NPD in the DSM system.

Self-Psychology Perspective

Kohut (1971, 1972), founder of the self-psychological school, identified narcissistic pathology as an arrest in normal narcissistic and self-object development. According to Kohut, narcissism represents a separate developmental line originating from an archaic grandiose self and moving toward the internalization of an ego ideal and into increased self-cohesion and more mature transformations of narcissism including healthy self-esteem. Empathic failures lead to arrests in the normal development of narcissism. Based on extensive psychoanalytic work with narcissistic patients, Kohut identified two themes that represent needs, fantasies, and expectations derived from an arrested developmental stage dominated by an archaic grandiose self. In therapy these themes are represented by two major types of transference: first, a mirror transference representing a need for affirmation and approval; and second, an idealizing transference in which the therapist is idealized. In this stage the narcissistic individual is left searching for such mirroring and idealized self-objects.

Kohut defined primary and secondary types of self-disorders based upon the level of self-cohesion—that is, the degree to which the self is stabel vs. fragile. Among the primary self-disorders he identified as analyzable (1) the narcissistic behavior disorder, which features temporary breakups or distortions of the self, with reversible symptoms; and (2) the narcissistic personality disorder, also with temporary self-distortions, but with symptoms that involve the person's entire psychological state. Kohut's focus was on understanding the specific logic of the patient's inner experiences. The emphasis on empathy as the observational method and central in treatment has made his work very influential in developing techniques for treating narcissistic patients.

Studies on the Role of Shame

The role of shame in pathological narcissism and the development of the self has been specifically integrated by Cooper (1998). The grandiose self in narcissistic patients is suggested to develop out of primitive shame experiences (Broucek, 1982). Intense shame can cause a disruption of normal narcissistic functioning and is experienced as hurtful, with feelings of anger and a lowering of the self-esteem (Levin 1982; Morrison, 1989). Cooper defined NPD as an attempt to defend and compensate against unstable self-esteem and changes in self-experience. Such attempts can be observed in behaviors related to (1) fragile self-representations—that is, when the person is facing his or her own needs or deficiences, he or she experiences excessive feelings of shame, embarrassment, humiliation, or hypochondriasis; (2) grandiosity, such as fantasies of being special, exhibitionistic tendencies, and perfectionism; and (3) superego functioning, such as strong rules against desires to be assertive or exhibitionistic and harsh demands for perfection (Cooper & Ronningstam, 1992; Cooper, 1998). Cooper (1988) also analyzed the connection between masochism and narcissism. He observed that both arrogant and shy narcissistic patients had masochistic and self-defeating tendencies. In humiliating interpersonal interactions, the narcissistic person gets grandiose fantasies of controlling the humility and experiences satisfaction from believeing that he or she is mastering the humiliations. Cooper's work has been specifically important for specifying the discrepancy between the clinical usage of the NPD diagnosis and the DSM criteria.

Etiology

Etiological accounts of NPD have traditionally focused on the origins and development the pathological grandiose self (O. Kernberg, 1990). Although constitutional and temperamental factors have also been considered important (Torgersen, 1994), no significant efforts were made to incorporate these into a more comprehensive theory.

Recently there has been a connection between studies of early infant interaction and research on neurphysiological development. Findings show that certain types of interaction between caregiver and child are essential for the character formation, and that this interaction also influences the child's biopsychological development, especially during the second year of life (Schore, 1994). Of specific importance for the development of NPD are the neurophysiological origins of hypersensitivity, strong aggressive drive, low anxiety or frustration tolerance, and defects in affect regulation. Under normal circumstances, the caregiver helps the child to handle intense and stressful affects. The child's inner representations of the caregiver promote normal psychobiological affect regulation (which includes both the bodily and the psychological systems). This helps the child to neutralize grandiosity, modulate narcissistic distress, and regulate both excitement and self-esteem. However, inconsistent attunement between caregiver and child, and the caregiver's failure to help the child to modulate positive and negative hyperaroused states such as excitement, anger, or anxiety, as well as low aroused states such as shame and depression, can lead to failure to develop adequate affect regulation.

Schore identified two types of caregiver-child interactional patterns that lead to the development of the arrogant and shy types of NPD. An "insecure-resistant" attachment contributes to states of hyperactivation and affect underregulation, resulting in overt grandiosity, entitlement, arrogance, and aggressive reactions to others. A "depressed-hypoarousing" attachment contributes to an affect overregulation, leading to inhibition, shyness, and predominant shame, which hides grandiose strivings (Schore, 1994).

The psychodynamic account holds that developmental experiences contribute to the formation of NPD (O. Kernberg, 1990). Theorists agree that while the family environment may be ostensibly structured and even admiring, parents are cold, unempathic, and emotionally unavailable. O. Kernberg (1975, 1984) believes that an integrated but highly pathological grandiose self develops some time between ages 3 and 5, and helps to defend toward early projected rage and envy. The pathological grandiose self interferes with normal ego and superego development, as well as with the formation of internal and external object relations. In contrast, Kohut (1971, 1972) suggests that parental empathic failure to support normal narcissistic development results in a developmental arrest at the stage of an archaic (pre stage) grandiose self. Parents' empathic interaction with the child stimulates the normal narcissistic development and integration toward healthy self-esteem.

In addition, certain types of family interaction create specific risks for development of NPD (P. Kernberg, 1989). A family constellation where narcissistic parents give their children roles or functions beyond or inconsistent with what normally is expected of the child can contribute to the preservation of the grandiose self. Children of divorced parents who develop the function of replacing the missing parent, or adopted children who have experienced being chosen by the adoptive parents in addition to being abandoned by their biological parents, are specifically at risk. Abused children can create a merger with the idealized parent image in order to protect themselves from a sadistically abusive real parent, thus giving foundation to a pathological grandiose self. The overindulged or wealthy child who is considered special develops a strong sense of entitlement and omnipotent control (infantile narcissism and grandiosity) that later in life, when combined with frustration and anger, can turn into a pathological character style. In addition, the child develops a social handicap with very little capacity for mutual interaction, cooperation, sharing, and empathic understanding.

The Biosocial-Learning Perspective

Based on a biosocial learning perspective, Millon (1981, 1998) outlined a matrix of narcissistic personality characteristics capturing several clinical domains including both overt (expressive, cognitive, and interpersonal) and hidden areas of functioning (self-image, and defensive functions). He also elaborated a set of narcissistic personality subtypes ordered in sequence of severity. Influenced by Freud's description of the narcissistic libidinal type and Reich's conceptualization of the phallic-narcissistic disorder, Millon highlighted the narcissistic individual's inflated sense of self-worth and self-admiration, his or her confident, haughty, and exploitative interpersonal style, expansive cognitive functioning, and tendency to rationalize and to return to a compensatory and comforting fantasy world when faced with failures or obstacles. The narcissistic subtypes include: (1) a normal narcissistic type characterized by self-assurance and competitiveness; (2) the unprincipled narcissist, who is deceitful, vengeful, and lacks loyalty; (3) the amorous narcissist, who is seductive and erotic; (4) the compensatory narcissist, whose underlying insecurity and past wounds force a constant seeking of support for self-esteem; (5) the elitist narcissist, who is self-assertive, arrogant, and intrusive; and (6) the fanatical narcissist, whose paranoid ideations and illusional omnipotence cause repetitive and painful collisions with the real environment. Millon's conceptualization of NPD, organized in itemized characteristics in the diagnostic self-report MCMI (Millon, 1983), has stimulated empirical research on NPD.

Cognitive Perspective

Based on Beck's (Beck & Freeman, 1990) cognitive theory on dysfunctional schemes in personality disorders, Young (1994, 1998) suggested three core operating schema moods in narcissistic individuals: entitlement, emotional deprivation, and defectiveness. Additional secondary schemas include approval seeking, unrelenting standards, subjugation, mistrust, and avoidance. These maladaptive schemas are further grouped into three clusters that represent separate aspects of the self. In the "special self" mood the narcissist is superior, entitled, critical, and unempathic. The "vulnerable child" mood is triggered by aloneness, criticism, and failures. Here, the special self is lost, and the narcissist feels empty, humiliated, and ignored, and can even become demoralized, self-critical, and depressed. The "self-soother" mood provides a means of avoiding the negative affect of the vulnerable self and serves to detach or numb the narcissist through drugs, excessive work, sex, gambling, or fantasies. The narcissistic patient is assumed to alternate among these three modes when reacting to changes and events in the environment.

Course and Prognosis

NPD has been considered highly resistant to change. The perpetuation of narcissistic patterns, especially in interpersonal relations, leads to poor prognosis of NPD. Denial of problems and factors in the environment that interfere with grandiosity and narcissistic pursuits, combined with a compensatory fantasy life and the opportunities for gratifying support of grandiose self-experience, are some of the contributing factors. NPD may worsen over the years, with more severe envy, disillusionment, and contempt (Millon, 1981; O. Kernberg, 1980). Profound narcissistic pathology can persist past middle age and has even been reported in older geriatric subjects (Berezin, 1977; O. Kernberg, 1977). The presence of severe superego pathology, malignant narcissism, sexual deviations, and overt borderline functioning worsens the prognoses for NPD patients, while tolerance for depression and mourning, and capacity for feeling and the ability to tolerate guilt, improve prognosis (O. Kernberg, 1975). On the other hand, in some narcissistic individuals reaching middle age an increased motivation for changes has been found, making treatment efforts more favorable and improving prognosis (O. Kernberg, 1980).

Empirical studies have provided moderate support for the poor prognosis of narcissistic patients.

In a retrospective longitudinal study conducted over 14 years, Plakun (1989) found that narcissistic patients have a lower level of social and global functioning with higher rates of rehospitalizations than the comparison group of borderlines. Two studies (Stone, 1989; McGlashan & Heinssen, 1989) compared patients with comorbid narcissistic and borderline personality pathology with a group of BPD only. Narcissistic comorbidity did not generally influence outcome, except for the subgroup of narcissistic borderlines with profound antisocial features who had a poor outcome (Stone, 1989).

Pathological Narcissism and Corrective Life Events

Contrasting empirical findings (Ronningstam & Gunderson, 1995a) have shown that NPD patients with less severe narcissistically disturbed object relations may have a better prognosis and actually improve over time. Improvements were not due to treatment experiences but were related to three types of corrective life events involving achievements, interpersonal relations, and disillusionments.

Corrective Achievement

Achievements are the most common corrective life event contributing to improvement in pathological narcissism. Graduations, promotions, recognitions, and acceptance to schools, programs, or positions applied for often reduce the need for unrealistic grandiose fantasies and exaggerations of talents and personal qualities. That also leads to changes in interpersonal relations—for example, decreased arrogance and devaluation. Consider the following case vignette:

Mr. A., an extremely intelligent, reserved but arrogant 25-year-old college student, had suffered from depression for several years. Although an exceptionally competent student, he constantly felt unappreciated. He described himself as extraordinarily superior, with feelings of disdain and confusion toward people whose values and standards were different from his own. He also described himself as intellectually unique, stressing his specific theoretical and philosophical perspective and high academic standards. He liked to give the teachers and professors a hard time by criticizing them and by asking "impossible" questions. He had close friends among his male peers, but felt shy and insecure in relating to young women.

Mr. A. came from a very competitive and successful family background. His father, with whom he had a complicated relationship, was a famous lawyer. He both admired and idealized his father, felt deeply misunderstood by him, and despised him for his demands, values, and expectations. While he envied his father and fantasized about becoming as successful as he was, he also felt inferior and took every opportunity to protest against him. After successfully graduating from college, Mr. A. decided to work as a pizza deliverer, a decision that he considered in line with his "unique life approach."

Three years later, Mr. A. reported several important developments. Individual psychotherapy (1½ years) had focused specifically on depression and insecurity. A new job as a university teacher contributed to important changes in his behavior and attitudes toward himself and others. He had developed techniques for teaching that his former teachers were unable to apply. He had learned to interact with people and appreciate people with different ideas and values, and he described himself as more tolerant of criticism. His sense of pride reflected more realistic self-appraisals and diminished arrogance. The relationship with his father remained conflicted, but a sincere desire to identify with his competent and successful father had also surfaced. Relations with women were improved, with his girlfriend of two years greatly contributing to his esteem. As Mr. A.'s experiences of realistic competence and independent, goal-oriented, professional responsibility increased, his narcissistic self-inflation and antagonizing and devaluating behavior toward others decreased, and his capacity for mutual interpersonal relations could develop.

Corrective Relationships

In addition to achievements, interpersonal relationships can reduce levels of pathological narcissism. Prior interpersonal characteristics such as devaluation, entitlement, exploitive behavior, and arrogance apparently had served defensive purposes and were not characterologically ingrained. The corrective relationship is typically long term, close, and mutual, as reflected in the following vignette:

Miss B., an attractive, intelligent, self-assertive, and articulate research assistant in her thirties, was caught stealing drugs at her workplace. Over the last five years she had been using increasing amounts of drugs, recently on a daily basis. Miss B. described herself as superior. In contrast to other abusers, she had been able to keep herself "clean" and use more sophisticated methods to gain access to drugs. Although hard to please, she usually got what she wanted. She dreamed about becoming a famous journalist and loved to drive her car recklessly. Although she had honored the high expectations of her working-class parents by graduating magna cum laude, they would not support her through graduate school. She experienced this as treachery. After graduation, three problems gradually emerged. A feeling of indecisiveness and uncertainty made it difficult for her to find purpose and direction in life. Her relationships, especially with boyfriends, never went beyond quick intense involvements, followed by abrupt withdrawal when the relationships could develop. She especially feared close interactions and intimacy. Finally, she recognized a increasing fear of becoming bored and failing at work, despite high competence.

At follow-up, Miss B. described several notable changes. After six months of detoxification and treatment for drug abuse, and two years of psychotherapy, her drug dependency was in remission. She had acknowledged how her extremely low self-esteem and feelings of inferiority had contributed to her interpersonal problems, boredom, and drug abuse. She had been accepted to graduate school and was studying business. However, according to Miss B., the most important change was her close relation with a man with whom she was in love for the first time, and she planned to get married. In contrast to previous boyfriends, she felt accepted by her husband-to-be, sensed that he was stronger than her without putting her down. This enabled her to feel secure and develop in their relationship. Her self-description was more realistic and diversified. Whereas she before had felt different and misunderstood, she realized that her tough, independent, and self-sufficient demeanor alienated others in her life. Her ability to tolerate and enjoy intimacy obviously led to increased self-esteem. Grandiose fantasies remained, but were related to the field she was now studying. In addition, she still had strong feelings of envy and difficulty empathizing with the sadness of others, which made her feel helpless and disgusted.

Corrective Disillusionment

The final corrective experience is termed corrective disillusionment. Here, incompatible experiences challenge the previous grandiose self-experience, bringing the view of self into greater congruence with actual talents, abilities, and status. Such experiences may reflect the realization of personal, intellectual, or vocational limitations; failure to achieve life goals or conform to narcissistically determined ideals and standards; or even reflect personal losses or lost opportunities in life. However, the impact of such experiences must not be too adverse. If especially severe and experienced without support, narcissistic pathologies may actually worsen.

Mr. C., a manager in his mid-forties, considered himself to be goal oriented and super intelligent, with strong puritan values, quick reasoning skills, and extraordinary leadership capacity. Although happily married with two teenage sons and a younger daughter, he viewed himself as a loner, not interested in wasting time with meaningless social activities. As a top manager in a small company, he was bragging, self-praising, and self-centered. He consistently devaluated the social acumen of others, but did admit that he envied their social belonging. In his early forties he experienced two significant changes: his company suddenly underwent a major expansion and Mr. C. was sent to a very challenging business schools for continuing education to meet the company's new needs. In addition, his adolescent sons developed a lifestyle with values and interests Mr. C. found threatening and disgusting. Yet, he found no reasonable way to influence or even communicate with his sons. He considered himself a failure as a parent and struggled with intense aggressive impulses to punish them or even disown them. Used to being the most intellectually accomplished, Mr. C. was stunned at discovering the exceptionally high intellectual level among the other graduate students. With humbleness, admiration, and some envy, he accepted and submitted to his own B+ grades.

At follow-up, Mr. C. was in the process of returning to a new position in his company. He described feeling remarkably more humble with less intense aggressive, bragging, and self-inflating behavior. In his own appraisal, he had reached the maximum of his personal and professional capacity. Although satisfied with his results in graduate school, he felt dethroned and incompetent as a father, realizing that he could not change his sons' values. However, he had now more realistic ambitions to become their friend and supporter. Facing personal and professional limitations was enormously challenging for Mr. C.'s self-esteem. With the sustained support of his loyal wife and his own personal flexibility and capacity to integrate initially unacceptable aspects of himself, he was able to bring a grandiose self-image more in line with realistic assessments.

Conclusions

Although pathological narcissism and narcissistic personality disorder are among the most studied and debated phenomena in clinical psychiatry and psychology, and in psychoanalysis, during the past century, a number of unexplored and unresolved issues still remain. The recent influences of other disciplines, such as psychiatric empirical research, neurobiological and psychological studies, academic psychological theory and research, and infant research, have added extremely valuable information to our knowledge and understanding of pathological narcissism and narcissistic personality disorder. However, the clinical usage of the NPD diagnosis is quite variable. The official diagnostic category of NPD as outlined in *DSM-IV* is much improved but does not fully capture the variable nature and clinical complexity of NPD. The development of empirical methods and instruments for diagnosing signs of both covert and overt narcissism is necessary.

References

Abrams, D. M. (1993). Pathological narcissism in an eight year old boy: An example of Bellak's TAT and CAT diagnostic system. *Psychoanalytic Psychology, 10*, 573–591.

Adler, G. (1981). The borderline-narcissistic personality disorder continuum. *American Journal of Psychiatry, 138*, 46–50.

Akhtar, S. (1989). Narcissistic personality disorder: Descriptive features and differential diagnosis. *Psychiatric Clinic of North America, 2*(3), 505–530.

Akhtar, S., & Thomson, J. A. (1982). Overview: Narcissistic personality disorder. *American Journal of Psychiatry, 139*, 12–20.

Alexandrowicz, D. R. (1980). Psychoanalytic studies of mania. In R. Belmaker & H. M. Van Praag (Eds), *Mania—an evolving concept* (pp. 309–322). Utrecht: MTP.

Apter, A., Bleich, A., King, R., Kron, S., Fluch, A., Kotler, M., & Cohen, D. (1993). Death without warning? A clinical postmortem study of suicide in 43 Israeli Adolescent Males. *Archive of General Psychiatry, 50*, 138–142.

Balint, M. (Ed). (1952). *Primary love and psychoanalytic technique*. London: Hogarth Press.

Bardenstein, K. (1994). *Rorschach features of narcissistic children*. Paper presented at the Annual Conference of the Society for Personality Assessment, Chicago, IL.

Beck, A., & Freeman, A. (1990). *Cognitive therapy of personality disorders*. New York: Guilford Press.

Berezin, M. (1977). Normal psychology of the aging process, revisited II. The fate of narcissism in old age: Clinical case reports. *Journal of Geriatric Psychiatry, 10*, 9–26.

Broucek, F. J. (1982). Shame and its relationship to early narcissistic developments. *International Journal of Psychoanalysis, 63*, 369–378.

Bursten, B. (1973). Some narcissistic personality types. *International Journal of Psychoanalysis, 54*, 287–300.

Chasseguet-Smirgel, J. (1985). *Creativity and perversions*. New York: Norton.

Cooper, A. (1988). The Narcissistic-masochistic character. In R. A. Glick & D. I. Meyers (Eds.), *Masochism: Current psychoanalytic perspectives* (pp. 117–138). Hillsdale, NJ: The Analytic Press.

Cooper, A. (1998). Further developments of the diagnosis of narcissistic personality disorder. In E. Ronningstam (Ed.), *Disorders of narcissism: Diagnostic, clinical, and empirical implications* (pp. 53–74). Washington, DC: American Psychiatric Press.

Cooper, A. M., & Ronningstam, E. (1992). Narcissistic personality disorder. In A. Tasman & M. Riba (Eds.), *American Psychiatric Press Review of Psychiatry* (vol. 11; pp. 80–97). Washington, DC: American Psychiatric Press.

Dahl, A. (1986). Some aspects of DSM-III personality disorders illustrated by a consecutive sample of hospitalized patients. *Acta Psychiatrica Scandinavica, 73*, 61–66.

Ellis, H. (1898). Auto-erotism: A psychological study. *Alienist and Neurologist, 19*, 260–299.

Emmons, R. A. (1981). Relationship between narcissism and sensation seeking. *Psychological Reports, 48*, 247–250.

Emmons, R. A. (1987) Narcissism: Theory and measurement. *Journal of Personality and Social Psychology, 52*, 11–17.

Fairbairn, W. R. D. (1952). *An object relations theory of the personality.* New York: Basic Books.

Fenichel, O. (1945): *The psychoanalytic theory of neurosis.* New York: Norton.

Freud, S. (1905/1957). Three essays on the theory of sexuality. In J. Strachey (Ed. and Trans.), *The standard edition of the complete psychological works of Sigmund Freud* (vol. 7; pp. 125–243). London: Hogarth Press.

Freud, S. (1911/1957). Psychoanalytic notes on an autobiographical account of a case of paranoia. In J. Strachey (Ed. and Trans.), *The standard edition of the complete psychological works of Sigmund Freud* (vol. 12; pp. 9–82). London: Hogarth Press.

Freud, S. (1914/1957). On narcissism. In J. Strachey (Ed. and Trans.), *The standard edition of the complete psychological works of Sigmund Freud* (vol. 14; pp. 66–102). London: Hogarth Press.

Freud, S. (1931/1961). Libidinal types. In J. Strachey (Ed. and Trans.), *The standard edition of the complete psychological works of Sigmund Freud* (vol. 21; pp. 217–220). London: Hogarth Press.

Gabbard, G. O. (1989). Two subtypes of narcissistic personality disorder. *Bulletin of the Menninger Clinic, 53*, 527–532.

Gersten, P. (1991). Narcissistic personality disorder consists of two distinct subtypes. *Psychiatric Times, 8*, 25–26.

Grundberger, B. (1975). *Narcissism: Psychoanalytic essays.* New York: International Universities Press.

Gunderson, J., Ronningstam, E., & Bodkin, A. (1990). The diagnostic interview for narcissistic patients. *Archives of General Psychiatry, 47*, 676–680.

Gunderson, J., Ronningstam, E., & Smith, L. (1991). Narcissistic personality disorder: A review of data on DSM-III-R descriptions. *Journal of Personality Disorder, 5*, 167–77.

Guntrip, H. (1952/1969). The schizoid personality and the external world. In H. Guntrip (Ed.), *Schizoid phenomena, object relations and self.* New York: International Universities Press.

Hart, S. D., & Hare, R. D. (1998). The association between psychopathy and narcissism: Theoretical views and empirical evidence. In E. Ronningstam (Ed.), *Disorders of narcissism: Diagnostic, clinical and empirical implications* (pp. 415–436). Washington, DC: American Psychiatric Press.

Hartman, H. (1964). *Essays on ego psychology.* New York: International Universities Press.

Horney, K. (1939). *New ways in psychoanalysis.* New York: Norton.

Jacobson, E. (1964). *The self and the object world.* New York: International Universities Press.

Joffe, W. G., & Sandler, J. (1967). Some conceptual problems involved in the consideration of disorders of narcissism. *Journal of Child Psychotherapy, 2*, 56–66.

Jones, E. (1913/1951). The God Complex. In E. Jones (Ed.), *Essays in applied psychoanalysis* (vol. 2; pp. 244–265). London: Hogarth Press.

Kernberg, O. F. (1967): Borderline personality organization. *Journal of American Psychoanalytical Association, 15*, 641–685.

Kernberg, O. F. (1975). *Borderline conditions and pathological narcissism.* New York: Jason Aronson.

Kernberg, O. F. (1977). Normal psychology of the aging process, revisited II. Discussion. *Journal of Geriatric Psychiatry, 10*, 27–45.

Kernberg, O. F. (1980). *Internal world and external reality.* New York: Jason Aronson.

Kernberg, O. F. (1984). *Severe personality disorders.* New Haven: Yale University Press.

Kernberg, O. F. (1989). The narcissistic personality disorder and the differential diagnosis of antisocial behavior. *Psychiatric Clinic of North America, 12*, 553–570.

Kernberg, O. F. (1990). Narcissistic personality disorder. In Michaels (Ed.), Psychiatry, Chapter 18. Philadelphia: Lippincott-Raven.

Kernberg, P. (1989). Narcissistic personality disorder in childhood. *Psychiatric Clinic of North America, 12*, 671–694.

Kernberg, P. (1998). Developmental aspects of normal and pathological narcissism. In E. Ronningstam (Ed.),*Disorders of narcissism: Diagnostic, clinical and empirical implications* (pp. 103–120). Washington, DC: American Psychiatric Press.

Kernberg, P., Hajal, F., & Normandin, L. (1998). Narcissistic personality disorder in adolescent inpatients—A retrospective record review study of descriptive characteristics. In E. Ronningsstam (Ed.), *Disorders of narcissism: Diagnostic, clinical and empirical implications* (pp. 437–456). Washington, DC: American Psychiatric Press.

Khantzian, E. J. (1979). Impulse problems in addictions: Cause and effect relationships. In H. Wishnie (Ed.), *Working with the impulsive person.* New York: Plenum.

Khantzian, E. J. (1982). Psychological (structural) vulnerabilities and the specific appeal to narcotics. *Annals of New York Academy of Science, 398*, 24–32.

Klein, M. (1957). *Envy and gratitude.* New York: Basic Books.

Kohut, H. (1968). The psychoanalytic treatment of narcissistic personality disorder. *Psychoanalytic Study of the Child, 23*, 86–113.

Kohut, H. (1971). *The analysis of the self.* New York: International Universities Press.

Kohut, H. (1972). Thoughts on narcissism and narcissistic rage. *Psychoanalytic Study of the Child, 27*, 360–400.

Kohut, H. (1977). *The restoration of the self.* New York: International Universities Press.

Lasch, C. (1979). *The culture of narcissism.* New York: Norton.

Levin, S. (1982). *The psychoanalysis of shame.* Unpublished manuscript.

Maltsberger, J. T. (1998). Pathological narcissism and self-regulatory processes in suicidal states. In E. Ronningstam (Ed.), *Disorders of narcissism: Diagnostic, clinical and empirical implications* (pp. 327–344). Washington, DC: American Psychiatric Press.

Masterson, J. F. (1981). *The narcissistic and borderline disorders.* New York: Brunner/Mazel.

McCann, J. T., & Biaggio, M. K. (1989). Narcissistic personality features of self-reported anger. *Psychological Reports, 64*, 55–58.

McDougall, J. (1985). *Theaters of the mind.* New York: Basic Books.

McGlashan, T., & Heinssen, R. (1989). Narcissistic, antisocial and noncomorbid subgroups of borderline patients. *Psychiatric Clinics of North America, 12*, 653–671.

Meloy, J. R. (1988). *The psychopathic mind.* Northvale, NJ: Jason Aronson.

Millon, T. (1981). *Disorders of personality DSM-III: Axis II.* New York: John Wiley.

Millon, T. (1983). *Millon Clinical Multiaxial Inventory*, 3rd ed. Minneapolis: National Computer Systems.

Millon, T. (1990). The avoidant personality. In R. Michaels, J. O. Cavenar, H. K. H. Brodie, A. M. Cooper, S. B. Guze, & L. L. Judd (Eds.), *Psychiatry* (vol. 1; chap. 18). Philadelphia: Lippincott.

Millon, T. (1998). The DSM narcissistic personality—Historical reflections and future directions. In E. Ronningstam (Ed.), *Disorders of narcissism: Diagnostic, clinical and empirical implications* (pp. 75–102). Washington, DC: American Psychiatric Press.

More, B. E., & Fine, B. D. (1968). *A glossary of psychoanalytic terms and concepts*, 2nd ed. New York: American Psychoanalytic Association.

Morey, L. C. (1988a). Personality disorders in DSM-III and DSM-III-R: An examination of convergence, coverage, and internal consistency. *American Journal of Psychiatry, 145*, 573–577

Morey, L. C. (1988b). A psychometric analysis of the DSM-III-R personality disorder criteria. *Journal of Personality Disorders, 2*, 109–124.

Morey, L. C. (1991). *The personality assessment inventory professional manual.* Odessa, FL: Psychological Assessment Resources.

Morey, L. C. (1998). Empirical studies of the construct validity of narcissistic personality disorder. In E. Ronningstam (Ed.), *Disorders of narcissism: Diagnostic, clinical and empirical implications* (pp. 351–376). Washington, DC: American Psychiatric Press.

Morrison, P. (1989). *Shame: The underside of narcissism.* Hillsdale, NJ: The Analytic Press.

Murray, H. (1955). American Icarus. In A. Burton & R. Harris (Eds.), *Clinical studies in personality* (vol. 2; pp. 615–641). New York: Harper.

Näcke, P. (1899). Die sexuellen Perversitäten in der Irrenanstalt. *Psychiatriche en Neurologische Bladen, 3.*

Perry, C. (1990). Personality disorders, suicide and self-destructive behavior. In D. Jacobs, H. Brown, & C. T. Madison (Eds.), *Suicide—Understanding and responding.* International Universities Press.

Plakun, E. M. (1987). Distinguishing narcissistic and borderline personality disorder. *Comprehensive Psychiatry, 26*, 448–455.

Plakun, E. M. (1989). Narcissistic personality disorder: A validity study and comparison to borderline personality disorder. *Psychiatric Clinics of North America, 12*, 653–671.

Plakun, E. M. (1990). Empirical overview of narcissistic personality disorder. In E. M. Plakun (Ed.), *New perspectives on narcissism* (pp. 101–149). Washington, DC: American Psychiatric Press.

Pulver, S. E. (1970). Narcissism: The term and the concept. *Journal of American Psychoanalytical Association, 18*, 319–341.

Rank, O. (1911). Ein Beitrag zum Narzissismus. *Jahrbuch fur Psychoanalytische und Psychopathologische Forschungen, 3*, 401–426.

Raskin, R. N., & Hall, C. S. (1979). A narcissistic personality inventory. *Psychological Reports, 45*, 590.

Raskin, R., Novacek, J., & Hogan, R. (1991). Narcissism, self-esteem, and defensive self-enhancement. *Journal of Personality, 59*, 19–38.

Raskin, R. N., & Terry, H. (1988). A principal-component analysis of the narcissistic personality inventory and further evidence of its construct validity. *Journal of Personality and Social Psychology, 54*, 890–902.

Raskin, R. N., & Shaw, R. (1988) Narcissism and the use of personal pronouns. *Journal of Personality, 56*, 393–404.

Reich, A. (1960). Pathological forms of self-esteem regulation. *Psychoanalytic Study of the Child, 15*, 215–232.

Reich, A. (1964/1973). Masturbation and self-esteem. In A. Reich (Ed.), *Psychoanalytic contributions*. New York: International Universities Press.

Reich, J., Yates, W., & Ndvaguba, M. (1989). Prevalence of DSM-III personality disorders in the community. *Social Psychiatry and Psychiatric Epidemiology, 24*, 12–16.

Reich, W. (1933/1949). *Character analysis*. (T. P. Wolfe, Trans.). New York: Orgone Institute Press.

Reichman, J., & Flaherty, J. (1990). Gender differences in narcissistic styles. In E. M. Placun (Ed.), *New perspective on narcissism* (pp. 71–100). Washington, DC: American Psychiatric Press.

Ronningstam, E. (1996). Pathological narcissism and narcissistic personality disorder in Axis I disorders. *Harvard Review of Psychiatry, 3*, 326–340.

Ronningstam, E. (1993). [Co-occurrence of Axis I diagnosis in two samples of NPD patients at McLean Hospital]. Unpublished data.

Ronningstam, E., & Gunderson, J. (1990). Identifying criteria for narcissistic personality disorder. *American Journal of Psychiatry, 147*, 918–922.

Ronningstam, E., & Gunderson, J. (1991). Differentiating borderline personality disorder from narcissistic personality disorder. *Journal of Personality Disorder, 5*, 225–232.

Ronningstam, E., & Gunderson, J. (1995a). Changes in pathological narcissism. *American Journal of Psychiatry, 152*, 253–257.

Ronningstam, E., & Gunderson, J. (1995b). *Differentiating narcissist and antisocial personality disorders*. Paper presented at American Psychiatric Association Annual Meeting, Miami.

Ronningstam, E., & Maltsberger, J. (1998). Suicide attempts in patients with pathological affect regulation and narcissistic disorders. *Suicide and Life Threatening Behavior, 28*, 261–271.

Rosenfeldt, H. (1964). On the psychopathology of narcissism: A clinical approach. *International Journal of Psychoanalysis, 45*, 332–337.

Rosenfeldt, H. (1971). A clinical approach to the psychoanalytic theory of life and death instinct: An investigation into the aggressive aspects of narcissism. *International Journal of Psychoanalysis, 52*, 169–178.

Rothstein, A. (1980). *The narcissistic pursuit for perfection*. New York: International Universities Press.

Schore, A. (1994). *Affect regulation and the origin of the self. The neurobiology of emotional development*. Hillsdale, NJ: Lawrence Erlbaum.

Sperry, L. (1995). *Handbook of diagnosis and treatment of the DSM-IV personality disorders*. New York: Brunel Mazel.

Stolorow, R. D. (1975). Toward a functional definition of narcissism. *International Journal of Psychoanalysis, 56*, 179–185.

Stone, M. (1989). Long-term follow-up of narcissistic boderline patients. *Psychiatric Clinics of North America, 12*, 621–642.

Stone, M. (1993). *Abnormalities of personality. Within and beyond the realm of treatment*. New York: Norton.

Stone, M. (1998). Normal narcissism—An etiological and ethological perspective. In E. Ronningstam (Ed.), *Disorders of narcissism: Diagnostic, clinical and empirical implications* (pp. 7–28). Washington, DC: American Psychiatric Press.

Stormberg, D., Ronningstam, E., Gunderson, J., & Tohen, M. (1998). Pathological narcissism in bipolar patients. *Journal of Personality Disorders, 12*, 179–185.

Tartakoff, H. (1966). The normal personality in our culture and the Nobel Prize complex. In R. M. Lowenstein, L. M. Newman, M. Schure, et al. (Eds.), *Psychoanalysis: A general psychology* (pp. 222–252). New York: International Universities Press.

Torgerson, S. (1994). Genetics in borderline conditions. *Acta Psychiatrica Scandinavica, 89* (Suppl. 379), 19–25.

Vaillant, G. E. (1988). The alcohol-dependent and drug-dependent person. In A. M. Nicholi (Ed.), *The Harvard guide to modern psychiatry*. 2nd ed. Cambridge, MA: Harvard University Press.

Vaillant, G. E., & Perry, C. P. (1980). Personality disorders. In H. Kaplan, A. Freedman, & G. Sadoch (Eds.), *The comprehensive textbook of psychiatry*, 3rd ed. (vol. 1; pp. 974–985). Baltimore: Williams & Wilkins.

Volkan, V. D. (1979). The "Glass Bubble" of the narcissistic patient. In J. LeBoit & A. Capponi (Eds.), *Advances in the psychotherapy of the borderline patient* (pp. 405–432). New York: Jason Aronson.

Waelder, R. (1925). The psychosis, their mechanisms and accessibility to influence. *International Journal of Psychoanalysis, 6*, 259–281.

Watson, P. J., Grisham, S. O., Trotter, M. V., & Biderman, M. D. (1984). Narcissism and empathy: validity evidence for the narcissistic personality inventory. *Journal of Personality Assessment, 48*, 301–305.

Watson P. J., & Morris, J. R. (1991). Narcissism, empathy and social desirability. *Personality and Individual Differences, 12*, 575–579.

Weinberger, J. L., & Muller, J. J. (1974). The American Icarus revisited: Phallic narcissism and boredom. *International Journal of Psychoanalysis, 55*, 581–585.

Winge, L. (1967). *The narcissus theme in western European literature up to the early 19th century.* Stockholm, Sweden: Glerups.

Wink, P. (1991). Two faces of narcissism. *Journal of Personality and Social Psychology, 61*, 590–597.

Winnicott, D. W. (1953). Transitional objects and transitional phenomena: A study of the first not me possession. *International Journal of Psychoanalysis, 43*, 89–97.

Winnicott, D. W. (1965). *The maturational processes and the facilitating environment.* New York: International Universities Press.

Wurmser, L. (1974). Psychoanalytic considerations of the etiology of compulsive drug use. *Journal of American Psychoanalytic Association, 22*, 820–843.

Young, J. (1994). *Cognitive therapy for personality disorders: A schema-focused approach.* Rev. ed. Sarasota, FL: Professional Resource Press.

Young, J. (1998). Schema-focused therapy for narcissistic patients. In E. Ronningstam (Ed.), *Disorders of narcissism: Diagnostic, clinical and empirical implications* (pp. 239–268). Washington, DC: American Psychiatric Press.

Zimmerman, M., & Coryell, W. (1990). Diagnosing personality disorders in the community. *Archives of General Psychiatry, 47*, 527–531.

Index

AA. *See* autonomic arousal
Äärelä, E., 459
abandonment fears, 538, 541
abbreviations, neurobiological, table of, 167
Abel, G. G., 422, 424, 576
Abel, J. L., 119
aberrant beliefs (delusionlike ideas), 346–47
abnormal illness behavior, 458–59
ABO blood types, 189
Abraham, K., 32, 204, 495–96, 535, 537, 545, 588, 596
Abramson, L. Y., 210–11, 213, 215, 216–17
abstract reasoning, 618
abuse. *See* childhood physical/sexual abuse; violence
acamprosate, 262
acetylcholine (ACH), 167, 172–73, 191
achievement
  as corrective narcissistic disorder factor, 687
  orientation, 654
  striving, 45–46
ACTH (adrenocorticotropic hormone), 153, 177, 180
acute pain, definition of, 449
acute stress disorder, 468
  posttraumatic stress disorder vs., 30
adaptive behaviors
  discrimination and, 41
  evolutionary, 512
  extinction of, 41–42
  fear as, 87–88, 100
  personality traits and, 540
  psychopathy as, 566–67
  reinforcement patterns and, 498
addiction
  diagnostic questions, 228, 230
  strength of nicotinic effects, 264
  withdrawal biochemistry, 261, 262–63
  withdrawal sleep/wake disturbances, 402, 403
  withdrawal symptoms, 228, 229, 241
  See also substance abuse; *specific substances*
Addiction Severity Index, 229
addictive personality, 258, 369
additive genetic effects, 61
adenylate cyclase, 174
ADHD
  psychopathology and, 569
  substance-related disorders and, 239, 256, 259, 265, 266
ADIS-R
  generalized anxiety disorder and, 119
  obsessive-compulsive disorder and, 128
Adler, G., 641, 681
adolescence
  alcohol and drug expectancies and, 234, 264
  alcohol use and, 253
  anorexia nervosa and, 367, 376
  body dysmorphic disorder and, 454
  borderline personality disorder and, 633, 642
  depression onset and, 206
  dissociative disorders prevalence, 470
  female substance abuse and, 235
  gender definition and, 43
  obsessive-compulsive disorder and, 127, 128
  oppositional-defiant disorder and, 595
  peer-influenced substance use, 233–34
  psychopathic sex offenders, 564–65, 577
  psychopathy as criminal recidivism predictor, 563, 565
  schizophrenia onset and, 277, 295–96
  schizophrenic high-risk social functioning, 320
  social-evaluative fears and, 83
  substance abuse and, 252, 253, 256
  substance use-related cognitive impairment and, 237
  suicide and, 642, 643
adoption studies, 63–64
  alcohol abuse, 258–59
  bipolar disorders, 189
  cautionary notes, 63–64
  schizophrenia, 63–64, 283–84, 524, 610, 616, 617
  shared environments and, 65
adrenal cortex, 153, 177
adrenal gland, 168, 433
adrenal steroids (adrenergic receptors), 178, 295. *See also* HPA axis
adrenocorticotropic hormone, 153, 177, 180
AEQ (Alcohol Expectancy Questionnaire), 234
affect
  borderline personality instability, 629, 641, 643, 644
  labile, 497, 643
  low positive. *See* anhedonia
  narcissistic personality disorder inflation, 679
  schizophrenic flattening, 279, 317, 318, 326, 330, 606
  See also negative affectivity
affectionless control, parental, 642
affective disorders, biological aspects of, 166–93
  borderline personality and, 637
  chronobiology and, 183–84
  electroencephalographic sleep studies, 175–76
  gender differences and, 190–91
  genetics and, 188–90
  neurobiology, 167–73
  neuroendocrine abnormalities, 176–80
  neuroradiological abnormalities, 181–83

psychopathy and, 572–82
second messenger systems, 173–75
summary of findings, 191–93
affective lability, 497, 643
African Americans
mistrust linked with depression, 344
substance abuse rates, 231, 232
substance-use initiation risks, 233–34
age
alcoholism onset and, 231
body dysmorphic disorder onset and, 454
borderline personality disorder and, 633, 634
breathing-related sleep disorders and, 395
conversion disorder onset and, 449
depression onset and, 190, 192
depression rates and, 206–7
depressive personality disorder onset and, 654
eating disorders and, 367
erectile dysfunction and, 416
gender identity disorder and, 429
generalized anxiety disorder and, 115–16
generalized anxiety disorder onset and, 117–18
histrionic personality disorder and, 542–43
hypochondriasis onset, 452
insomnia and, 391
life-span perspective on psychopathology and, 29
narcissistic personality disorder and, 678, 680, 686
nightmare disorder and, 396, 397
obsessive-compulsive disorder onset and, 127
panic disorder onset and, 95
paraphilias onset and, 423, 424, 425
pedophilia and, 424
phobia onset and, 83
primary insomnia and, 392, 393
schizophrenia onset and, 277, 295–96, 316
sexual arousal disorders and, 416
sexual sadism onset and, 576
sleep continuity disturbances and, 175, 393
somatization disorder onset and, 446, 447
substance abuse rates and, 231
See also adolescence; childhood *headings*; elderly people
age-of-risk profiles, 70–71
aggression
depression and, 211
dissociative identification with, 473
narcissistic self-directed, 678
obsessive impulses, 129
psychopathy and, 555, 556
sadistic personality disorder and, 555, 572–73
substance abuse and, 236–37, 254, 265
See also hostility; violence
agitation
cocaine use and, 236
depression and, 211
substance withdrawal and, 241
agonists
definition of, 168, 292
See also neurotransmitters; *specific types*
agoraphobia, 81, 82, 84, 85
DSM-IV classification, 91
eating disorder comorbidity, 369
historical perspectives, 99–100
ICD-10 classification, 91
lifetime prevalence rate, 83
panic disorder associated with, 82, 90–91, 93–95, 98–99, 104–5, 128, 341
paranoid conditions and, 341, 356
predictors of, 94
prevalence of, 95
Agras, S., 451
agreement studies, diagnostic, 13
Ahrens, A. H., 218
Ainser, M. C., 71
AIPSS (Assessment of Interpersonal Problem-Solving Skills), 315, 323, 325
Akhtar, S., 531, 533, 681, 682, 683
Akiskal, H. S., 35, 655, 656, 658, 660, 662, 664, 240
alcohol abuse
ADHD adults and, 239
aggression and, 236–37
alcohol availability and, 252
biochemistry of, 260, 261, 262, 263
cognitive impairment from, 237
comorbid psychopathology, 238–41, 257–58
cultural variations and, 253, 254
dependent traits and, 539
DSM diagnostic grouping, 227
eating disorder comorbidity, 369, 373
expectancies and, 234, 253, 264–65
expressed emotion and, 328
family history and, 69, 231, 232, 252f, 253, 255, 256, 260, 265, 267f
in gateway model hierarchy, 255
genetic factors, 258–60
historical, 250
naltrexone treatment, 263
neurophysiological factors, 69, 231, 233
neuropsychological dysfunction and, 266
panic disorder comorbidity, 96–97
paraphilias and, 427t
peer influences and, 233–34
personality profile of, 258
posttraumatic stress disorder comorbidity, 148, 153, 155, 257
predispositional risk factors, 267f
prenatal effects of, 256
prevalence of, 231–32
schizoidlike characteristics of, 526
sexual functioning and, 237–38, 416, 417
sleep/wake disorder and, 402, 403
social modeling and, 255
tension-reduction hypothesis and, 97, 240–41, 257–58
tolerance and, 228, 229, 233
typologies, 229–31
underdiagnosis and treatment of, 250–51
women's patterns of, 235–36, 256
Alcohol Dependence Scale, 229
Alcohol Expectancy Questionnaire, 234
Alcoholics Anonymous, 250
aldehyde dehydrogenas, 259
alexithymia, 459
Alfano, M. S., 212, 213
Alford, B. A., 505
Alig, V. B., 598
Allen, L. S., 430
Alliger, R., 279
Alloy, L. B., 125, 213, 215, 216–17
Allport, G. W., 491, 493
Allred, K. D., 208
Almagor, M., 493–94
Alnaes, R., 587, 595
alogia, 279
Alpert, J. L., 432
Alpert, N. M., 155–56
alpha alcoholism, 230t
alpha-2-adrenoceptor antagonist, 102, 152
alpha waves, 68, 69
Alsobrook, J. P., 130
Alterman, A., 555
alternative form method, 13, 14
alter personalities. *See* dissociative identity disorder
Altman, B., 152
Alzheimer's dementia, 263, 342, 356
sleep/wake disorders and, 400–401
Amador, X. F., 357n.3
ambiguity, paranoid intolerance of, 340
ambitendency, 588
ambivalence
definition of, 585
obsessive-compulsive/negativistic personality disorders and, 585, 586, 589, 594, 597, 598, 512
as personality style, 540
ambulatory schizophrenia, 610
Amen, M., 14
"American dream," 45
American Educational Research Association, 15
American Psychiatric Association, 6, 9. *See also Diagnostic and Statistical Manual of Mental Disorders*; *DSM headings*
American Psychological Association, 15, 611
Ames, G., 252–53
Amin, Idi, 355
amino acids
bipolar disorder and, 186
depression and, 173, 192
schizophrenia and, 294
amnesias. *See* dissociative amnesia; memory deficits
Amos, N. L., 562, 564
amphetamines
aggression and, 236, 237
cerebral metabolic lowering by, 265
dopaminergic system and, 261, 293
dysphoric withdrawal effects, 240
psychiatric disorder mimic, 239
sleep-wake disturbances and, 402–3
teratogenic effects of, 256
amygdala, 157, 170, 180, 181, 262, 572
AN. *See* anorexia nervosa
anal character type (obsessive-compulsive), 586, 588, 589
analgesic response, 153
analogue studies, 65–66, 53
analogue to digital (A/D) converter, 67
anal stage, 495, 588–89
anankastic personality (obsessive-compulsive), 585, 586, 587
Anastasiades, P., 101
ancient civilizations
depression descriptions in, 3, 204
eating disorders in, 467
humors medical doctrine, 506
hysteria description in, 447
substance abuse in, 240–50

Anderson, A., 419
Anderson, D. J., 123
Anderson, G., 471
Anderson, L. R., 234
Anderson, S. M., 350
Andia, A. N., 316
Andreasen, N. C., 278, 279, 286, 291
Andreoli, A., 630, 666
Andreski, P., 146, 147, 149, 240
Andrews, J., 546
androgen, 430, 431, 433
anergia, 168, 170, 324
anesthetic personality traits, 529
anger
  borderline personality and, 633
  cocaine use and, 236
  negativistic personality disorder and, 593, 597, 598, 599, 600
  paranoid conditions and, 340, 354, 355
Angermeyer, M. C., 316
Angleinter, A., 490–91
anhedonia
  neurophysiological basis, 168, 170
  schizoid personality and, 523, 613
  schizophrenia and, 279, 317, 318
  in tripartite model of anxiety and depression, 121, 122
animal model studies
  anxiety, 103
  behavior genetics, 61, 64
  chronic uncontrollable stressors exposure, 152
  depression, 172, 173
  dissociation memory, 466
  genetic vulnerability to alcoholism, 260
  posttraumatic stress disorder, 152, 156–57
  preparedness theory, 87
  psychopathology research design, 53–54
  substance abuse, 249, 261, 263, 264
animal phobias, 82, 83, 84, 89
anorexia nervosa, 365–66
  biological factors, 372–74
  body-image disturbances and, 377
  cross-cultural study, 372
  dependency personality and, 538–39
  depression and, 368
  family history and, 373
  family systems theory and, 378–79, 380
  introduction of term, 367
  narcissistic personality disorder and, 680
  neurobiology, 374
  obsessive-compulsive comorbidity, 369
  personality disorders comorbidity, 370
  personality type, 373, 376
  stereotype of, 374–75
  substance abuse comorbidity, 369
anorgasmia, 418–19
Anson, A. M., 122
antagonists
  definition of, 168
  opiate, 153, 156, 263
anterior commissure, 430
anticipatory anxiety
  alcohol used to reduce, 97
  generalized anxiety vs., 115
  panic disorder with agoraphobia and, 90, 100
  psychopath's deficit in, 570, 571
  spontaneous panic attacks vs., 99
  See also anxious apprehension
anticonvulsants, as bipolar disorder treatment, 186, 187, 188
antidepressant medication, 168, 171, 172–73, 178, 179, 181, 191
  gender differences and, 190
  for obsessive-compulsive disorder, 130
  rapid-cycling bipolar disorder and, 188
  for seasonal affective disorder, 188
  second-messenger systems and, 174
  sites of action, 193
  sleep continuity improvement by, 175
antihypertensive drugs, 417
antimanic drugs, 193
antipsychiatry movement, 7, 8
antipsychotic agents, 186, 249, 261, 293, 294
  "atypical," 295
antisocial personality disorder, 555
  ADHD comorbidity, 239
  borderline personality and, 497, 498f, 642, 643
  developmental pathogenesis theorists, 32
  dissociative personality disorder and, 475t, 476
  DSM criteria, 557, 558–59, 574
  DSM-I grouping, 227
  epidemiological study of, 57, 560
  fearlessness and, 570
  functional and structural attributes of personality, 517ff
  histrionic personality disorder and, 542, 543
  narcissistic personality disorder and, 675, 677, 680, 681
  negativistic personality disorder and, 594
  paranoid conditions and, 341–42
  posttraumatic stress disorder comorbidity, 148
  prevalence of, 560
  psychopathy and, 555, 556, 558, 560
  superego and, 496
Antony, M. M., 100
anxiety disorders, 81–105
  agoraphobia, 82, 90–91, 93–95, 98–99, 104–5
  anxious apprehension and, 118
  biological vulnerability of, 125
  dependent personality disorder and, 537
  dissociation and, 468
  dissociative identity disorder and, 469
  eating disorder comorbidity, 368, 369
  fears and phobias, 81–90
  Freudian concept of, 99
  gender and, 95
  generalized anxiety disorder differentiations from, 120–21, 122
  histrionic personality disorder and, 543
  life events and, 208
  neuroses reclassification under, 445
  obsessive-compulsive disorder and, 125, 126, 127, 128, 129, 131, 134
  panic disorder and, 81, 99–105
  paranoid conditions and, 341
  paraphilias comorbidity, 427, 427t
  as posttraumatic stress disorder risk factor, 146, 148, 257
  preoccupational somatoform disorders and, 445
  prevalence of, 95–96
  primary insomnia with, 392, 393
  sexual arousal disorders and, 417, 433
  sleep/wake disorders and, 399–400, 403–4, 392, 393
  somatoform disorders and, 457–58, 445
  substance-related comorbidity, 236, 238, 239, 240–41, 257, 262
  tripartite model of, 121–23
  See also generalized anxiety disorder
Anxiety Disorders Interview Schedule, 116, 119
anxiety neurosis, 99, 114
anxiety sensitivity, 89–90, 102, 118
  as alcohol abuser trait, 258
  obsessive-compulsive/negativistic personality disorders and, 585
Anxiety Sensitivity Index, 89, 102
anxiolytics, 262, 267f
anxious apprehension, 100
  content variations, 118
  definition of, 118
  generalized anxiety disorder as exemplification of, 123
  high negative affect and, 118
  hypochondrias vs. somatization disorder, 456
  See also anticipatory anxiety
apathy, 156, 318
apnea, 395, 400
apocrine glands, 67
Appelo, M. T., 318
appetite, 187
Apple, M., 555
Applegate, B., 569
apprehension. *See* anticipatory anxiety; anxious apprehension
Apt, C., 547
Apter, S., 636
Araetus of Cappadocia, 204
Ardon, A. M., 83
Arieti, S., 342
Aristotle, 449
Armor, D., 545
Arndt, S., 279
Aro, H. M., 642
arousal increase
  conversion disorder, 449
  posttraumatic stress disorder, 145
arrested developmental stage, 684, 685
Arrindell, W. A., 83, 84
arrogance
  narcissistic, 675–76, 678, 681, 682, 685
  psychopathic, 555
AS. *See* anxiety sensitivity
Asahara, Shoko, 355
Asch, S. S., 665
ASDC. *See* Association of Sleep Disorders Center
a7-nicotinic receptor gene, 300
Ash, P., 6
Ashbrook, R., 546
Asher, R., 455
Asherson, P., 351

Asians, 207, 259, 445, 542
as-if personality, 530, 610
Asmundson, G. J., 81, 104
Asnis, L., 614
ASPD. *See* antisocial personality disorder
assertiveness training, 598
Assessment of Interpersonal Problem-Solving Skills, 315, 323, 325
assessments, respondent-based vs. investigator-based, 208
association disturbances, schizophrenic, 287
associationism, 497
Association of Sleep Disorders Center, 390–91
association studies, 189
assortative matings, 64
atrocities, posttraumatic stress disorder and, 146
attachment, 42
  avoidant personality problems with, 523
  borderline personality and, 641–42, 643, 644
  childhood insecure, 125
  dependent personality disorder and, 535–36
  dissociative identity disorders and, 476, 477
  psychopathy and adverse, 568–69
  schizoid personality problems with, 523
attentional impairment, schizophrenia and, 279, 287, 299–300, 302, 321–22, 323
attention deficit disorder without hyperactivity, 9
attention deficit/hyperactivity disorder. *See* ADHD
attention seeking
  borderline personality vs. narcissistic, 681
  histrionic personality, 544–45, 547
  narcissistic personality, 675, 682
attributional style, depression and, 216–17
auditory hallucinations, 279, 351, 469, 471, 479, 629
auditory stimuli, alcoholism and, 233
Auerbach, J. G., 302
authoritarianism, 540, 541, 573, 586, 591
authority figures, 41, 42
  "anal" characters and, 495
  dependent personality and, 541
  histrionic personality disorder and, 542–43
  obsessive-compulsive personality disorder and, 586, 589, 591
autobiographical memory disturbance, 150–51, 155
autoerotic asphyxiation, 425, 426
autoeroticism, 682
autogynephilia, 425
autonomic arousal
  generalized anxiety symptoms and, 120–22, 124
  posttraumatic stress disorder and, 151
  psychopathy and, 571
  tripartite model of anxiety and depression and, 122–23
Autonomic Hyperactivity cluster, 121
autonomy
  dependent personality disorder and, 536, 540
  depression triggers, 217
  eating disorders and, 378, 380
  interpersonal development of, 42–43, 46
  obsessive-compulsive personality disorder and, 588–89
  paranoid's perceived insufficiency in, 349
autopsy, 69
aversive conditioning, 87, 156, 157
avoidance behavior
  confirmation and, 88
  as defense mechanism, 530
  obsessive-compulsive, 131
  panic expectancy and, 94
  pathological worry as, 124
  posttraumatic stress disorder and, 144–45
  two-factor theory of, 131
avoidant personality disorder, 523–33
  characterization of, 524, 527, 529, 658
  clinical description, 525–28
  contemporary views of, 532–33
  dependent personality disorder and, 524, 528, 529
  depressive personality disorder and, 658, 660, 664
  diagnositic comorbidity, 528–29
  diagnostic boundaries, 524, 525–26, 528, 533
  functional attributes of personality, 517ff
  historical perspective, 530
  histrionic personality disorder and, 543
  narcissistic personality disorder and, 680
  obsessive-compulsive disorder comorbidity, 128
  obsessive-compulsive personality disorder comorbidity, 587
  paranoid conditions and, 341, 356
  schizoid personality disorder diagnostic boundary, 524
  self-defeating (masochistic) personality disorder and, 667
  structural attributes of personality, 517ff
Axis I and II, 10–11
  borderline comorbidities, 632, 633
  distinction between, 11, 33–36
  etiological primacy, 632
  personality disorders boundaries, 485
  taxonomy and pathogenesis, 30–33
Ayur-Veda, 3
Azorlosa, J., 547

Babor, T. F., 229, 230
Bach, D., 459
Bach, M., 459
Bachman, J. G., 264
BACs (blood alcohol concentrations), 235, 236
Baddeley, A., 351
Baer, L., 133, 587–88
Baker, J. D., 547
Baker, L., 378
Balian, L., 50
Balint, M., 684
Ball, S. A., 239
Balter, M. B., 403
Bancroft, J. H., 415, 418, 424, 429
Bandura, A., 217
Barbaree, H., 564
barbiturates, 256, 262
Barch, D., 322
Barlow, D. H., 54, 84, 91, 92, 93, 94, 100–101, 105, 116, 117–18, 119, 120, 121, 122, 123, 124, 125, 134, 460
Barnard, P. J., 214
Barnett, M. C., 97, 453
Baron, M., 430, 614
Barraclough, B., 285
Barsky, A. J., 97, 452, 453, 458
Bartko, J. J., 279, 319
Bartlett, F. C., 504
basal ganglia, 134, 168, 170, 181, 182
  schizophrenia and, 291–92
BAS (behavioral activation system), 570, 571
base rate, 58
Basoğlu, M., 147–48, 158
Bass, C. M., 92, 456, 459, 460
Bassett, A. S., 285
Bateson, G., 60, 327
Battaglia, M., 617
battered-child syndrome, 454
"battle fatigue" diagnosis, 144
Bauer, D. H., 83
Bauer, L., 234
Bauer, M., 454
Baumeister, R. F., 377
Bavly, L., 229
BDD. *See* body dysmorphic disorder
Beam-Goulet, J., 322
Beauvais, F., 255
Beck, A. T., 6, 116, 122, 131, 205, 213–16, 217, 504–5, 515, 535, 540–51, 546, 590, 598, 655, 686
Beck, J. G., 118, 411, 414
Beck, J. S., 122
Beck Depression Inventory, 16
Becker, J. V., 422, 576
Beckham, E. E., 204
Beckner, M., 22
Beck's Cognitive Theory of Depression, 213–16
Bedford, A., 23
Bedford College Life Events and Difficulties Schedule, 208, 209
bedwetting, 402
beer, 250, 265
Begleiter, H., 232
Behar-Mitrani, V., 218
behavioral activation system, 570, 571
behavioral compulsions, 125, 126, 129, 130
behavioral inhibition system, 570, 571
behavioral models
  alcoholism and, 231
  cognitive model contrasted with, 503–4
  concept history, 498–99
  depression and, 210–13
  dissociative identity disorder and, 473
  of fears and phobias, 85–86, 88–90, 131, 156–57
  formal characteristics, 498
  generalization and discrimination, 41
  genetic influences on, 60–64
  high-risk paradigm, 70, 71–72
  hypochondriasis and, 452

behavioral models (*continued*)
negativistic personality disorder and, 597–98, 600
obsessive-compulsive disorder and, 125, 126, 129, 131
obsessive-compulsive personality disorder and, 589–90
of pain, 449–50
of paranoid conditions, 340
of paraphilias, 426
of pathological worry, 124
of personality development, 40–42, 46, 490, 495, 497–99, 515
posttraumatic stress disorder and, 156–57
of primary insomnia, 393
psychopathy and, 555–56, 570–71
sadistic personality disorder and, 573
vaginismus and, 421, 433
See also learned helplessness
behavioral therapies
negativistic personality disorder and, 597–98
obsessive-compulsive personality disorder and, 589, 590
phobias and, 82
psychopathy and, 566
somatization disorder and, 447
behavior genetics, 60–64, 65, 73
Beidel, D. C., 529
beliefs, delusions vs., 347–48, 350
Belknap, J., 260
Bell, M., 322
Bellack, A. S., 314, 315, 316, 317, 318, 324, 329, 529
Bellodi, L., 617
Bemporad, J., 654
Benedict, R. H. B., 330
Benes, F. M., 294, 296
Benishay, D. S., 614
Benjamin, L. S., 33, 340, 501–2, 503f, 508–9, 510, 515, 539, 591, 598
Bennett, M. E., 314, 315, 318, 615
Ben-Porath, Y., 615
Bentall, R. P., 324, 349, 350, 352
Benton, M. K., 329
benzodiazepines, 257, 262, 265, 266, 402
Berchick, R. J., 116
bereavement, 204
Berenbaum, H., 322, 326, 328, 617
Berezin, M., 80, 686
Berger, P., 630, 666
Bergner, R. M., 349
Berkoff, K., 599
Berkson, J., 60
Berksonian bias, 60
Berlin, B., 19–20
Berlin, F. S., 427
Berliner, B., 654
Berman, E., 539
Berman, K. F., 298
Bermond, B., 459
Berner, P., 353
Bernstein, D. P., 608
Bernstein, G., 320
Berrios, G. E., 556
Bertelson, A., 283
Bertillon, Jacques, 6
Bertillon Classification of Causes of Death, The, 6
Besyner, J. K., 149
beta alcoholism, 230t
beta endorphin, 263
Beyler, J., 669
Bezirganian, S., 608, 642, 668
BFM. *See* Big Five Model
bias
fear acquisition theory and, 86
potential research, 59–60, 61
Bible, 204
Biebl, W., 381
Biederman, J., 239
Big Five Model (personality), 490, 491–92, 491t, 493
Big Seven Model, 491t, 493–94, 509
Bilsbury, C., 547
binge eating disorder, 366, 377, 378, 379
binge/purge syndromes, 365, 366, 368, 370, 374, 375, 376, 379, 380
biobehavioral markers, 297, 298, 299–302
biochemistry. *See* neurotransmitters
biological classification, 4, 5, 10, 17–20, 24
biological models
affective disorders, 166–93
bipolar disorder, 174–75, 185–87, 190, 191, 192–93
borderline personality disorder, 636–38
eating disorders, 372–74, 381, 383t
gender identity disorder, 429–31, 433
generalized anxiety disorder, 125
inescapable shock, 156
negativistic personality disorder, 599–600
obsessive-compulsive disorder, 133–34
panic disorder, 101, 102–3
panic provocation, 102–4
paraphilias, 427–28
personality development, 38–40, 46, 506–10
posttraumatic stress disorder, 151–56, 158
primary insomnia, 393
psychopathy, 568
schizophrenia, 67, 279, 296–99, 616, 619
sexual arousal disorders, 416–17, 418
sexual pain disorders, 420
substance abuse, 258–64
See also biological studies; neurophysiological factors; sociobiology
biological rhythms. *See* circadian rhythms
biological studies, 66–70
gender differences in affective disorders, 190–91
biological vulnerability. *See* genetic factors
biopsychosocial models. *See* psychophysiology
biosocial learning theory
dependent personality disorder and, 539–40, 541
histrionic personality disorder and, 546–47
narcissistic disorders and, 683, 686–89
bipolar disorder
biological aspects, 174–75, 185–87, 190, 191, 192–93
bipolar I vs. bipolar II, 188, 189
chronobiology and, 183, 185
construct validity, 56
corticol changes, 181
depressive personality and, 663
family tendency, 188–89
gender and, 190
genetic factors, 39, 188–89
grandiose delusions and, 339, 346
iatrogenic dissociative identity disorder and, 477
imaging studies, 182–83
Kraepelin diagnosis, 5–6, 204, 278
life event stressors, 353
narcissistic personality disorder and, 678, 680
paraphilias and, 427t
posttraumatic stress disorder comorbidity, 148
rapid-cycling, 188, 192
schizophrenia probands and, 617
seasonal affective disorder and, 187, 188
second-messenger system and, 192–93
sleep/wake disorders and, 398
substance-disorder comorbidity, 240
thyroid dysfunction and, 179–80
bipolar II disorder, 188, 189
Birbaumer, N., 450, 459, 460, 571
birth abnormalities
obsessive-compulsive disorder and, 134
teratogenic drug effects, 256, 257f, 259
See also prenatal environment
birth order, 431
BIS (behavioral inhibition system), 570, 571
biting stage, 596
Bixler, E., 14, 391, 393
Bjornson, L., 471
Blackburn, R., 556, 567–68
Blackwood, D., 81
Blanchard, E. B., 92, 116, 151, 576
Blanchard, J. J., 318, 324, 326
Blashfield, R. K., 543, 667, 668
Blatt, S. J., 217, 538, 539, 541
Blazer, D., 117, 632
Bleich, A., 149
Bleuler, E., 278, 287, 311, 523, 529, 596, 605, 609
Block, J., 492
Bloem, W. D., 315
blood alcohol concentration, 235, 236
blood-injection-injury phobia, 82, 83, 84, 85, 89
Blum, N., 586, 587, 588, 593
BN. *See* bulimia nervosa
Boardman, A. P., 445
boastful behavior, 679
Bodkin, A., 679
Bodner, E., 352–53
body dysmorphic disorder, 453–54
anxiety disorder and, 457
delusional intensity symptoms and, 346
differential diagnosis, 457
dissociative identity disorder and, 474
DSM-IV classification, 445
eating disorders and, 377, 380
obsessive-compulsive disorder and, 130, 458
personality disorder and, 458
sexual arousal disorder and, 417
body-image disturbances. *See* body dysmorphic disorder

body temperature, 184, 185
body type, personality linked with, 488, 507
Boegner, F., 454
Bohman, M., 230, 232, 258, 259
Boisoneau, D., 154
Bolk, J. H., 444
bone density, 235
Bonett, D., 280
bootstrapping, 71
Bootzin, R. R., 53
borderline personality disorder, 628–44
  case vignettes, 629–30
  characteristics, 594, 628–29, 633, 635, 643, 659
  clinical prototype, 631
  contemporary theoretical perspectives, 636–44
  course and outcome, 633–35
  dependent personality disorder and, 537
  depressive personality disorder and, 659, 660
  developmental pathogenesis theorists, 32
  diagnosis reliability and validity, 630–31
  dissociative identity disorder and, 469, 475t, 477
  dissociative symptoms, 468, 629, 630, 631
  dysthymic disorder and, 629, 658
  ego identity and, 497
  factitious disorder and, 455
  first operational definition of, 635
  functional and structural attributes of personality, 517ff
  historical perspectives, 635–36
  histrionic personality disorder and, 543
  multidimensional theory of, 643–44
  narcissistic personality disorder and, 675, 677–78, 680, 681, 687
  negativistic personality disorder and, 594, 595
  obsessive-compulsive personality disorder comorbidity, 587
  organizational levels, 497, 498f
  prevalence of, 631–32, 642
  psychopathy and, 497, 560
  psychosexual stages and, 496
  schizoid personality and, 531
  self-defeating (masochistic) personality disorder and, 667–68
  splitting and, 497, 531, 628–29
  suicide risk and, 634
borderline schizophrenia, 610, 614
Borkovec, T. D., 119, 120, 124, 125
Borman Spurrell, E. B., 378
Bornstein, R. F., 539, 541, 545
Borus, J., 666
Bosnia, 344
Botvin, G. J., 237
Boudewyns, P. A., 153
Boulet, J., 422
bowel functions, 588, 589
Bowen, L., 315, 323, 330
Bowen-Jones, K., 350
Bower, G. H., 214
Boyd, J. H., 90
Bozman, A. W., 414
BPD. *See* borderline personality disorder
Bradford, J. M. W., 422
Bradley, S. J., 430, 431, 432–33
Bradwein, J., 103
Brady, J. P., 319
Braff, D. L., 316
Braginsky, Y., 341
brain
  affective disorders and, 181, 192
  alcoholic impairment of, 265
  aversive conditioning and, 157
  borderline personality disorder and, 636–37
  clinical neuropsychology and, 287–89
  computer simulation and, 72
  depression and, 168–73, 181, 186, 192
  depressive personality and, 663–64
  dissociative identity disorder and, 474
  eating disorders and, 374
  EEG studies. *See* EEG waves
  gender identity, 430
  imaging technology, 69–70, 73, 181–83, 187, 188, 191, 265, 290–91, 293, 302–3, 474, 572, 618–19
  metabolism in affective disorders, 181, 187, 188, 191
  metabolism in alcoholism, 265
  neural circuits, 295–96
  obsessive-compulsive disorder and, 134
  organizational propensity of, 49
  panic disorder and, 102, 104
  paraphilias and, 427–28
  pathological worry and, 124, 125
  personality as function of, 38–39, 46
  posttraumatic stress disorder and, 155–56, 157
  psychopathy as dysfunction of, 568, 571–72
  schizogene and, 612
  schizophrenic abnormality, 181, 279, 286–92, 295–96, 298, 618–19
  sexual orientation and, 430
  substance abuse and, 260–67
  thyroid dysfunction and, 179
  See also central nervous system; cognitive models; neurophysiological factors; neurotransmitters
brain lesion, 296, 297, 302–3
brain waves. *See* EEG record
Branch Davidians, 344
Brandt, J. R., 563
Brave New World (Huxley), 250
breast cancer, 235
breathing-related sleep disorder, 391, 395, 400, 401
Breen, M. J., 668
Breitmeyer, B., 300
Brennan, J. H., 352
Brenner, C., 664
Breslau, N., 146, 147, 149, 240
Breuer, J., 544
Brewin, C. R., 150–51
Brief Psychiatric Rating Scale, 324
brief psychotic disorder, 339, 353
bright light therapy, 187–88
Brink, J., 572
Briquet's syndrome, 447
Brittain, R. P., 573
Broca's area, 156
Brodsky, B. S., 640
Bromet, E., 146, 147, 148, 149
Brook, J. S., 608, 642
Brookings, J. B., 380
Brooks-Gunn, J., 369
Brown, G., 116
Brown, G. W., 204, 208, 209, 327
Brown, R., 634
Brown, S. A., 234, 240
Brown, S. L., 564
Brown, T. A., 92, 116, 117–18, 119, 120, 121, 122, 123
Brown, T. M., 153
Brownell, K. D., 378
BRSD (breathing-related sleep disorder), 391, 395, 400, 401
Bruch, H., 374–75
Bryant, K. J., 228
Brynjolfsson, J., 64, 285
Brzustowicz, L. M., 285
Bucheim, P., 630, 666
Buck, K., 260
bulimia nervosa, 366, 367, 368
  binge episodes, 377–78
  body-image disturbances and, 377
  dependent personality and, 538, 539
  dissociative disturbances comorbidity, 370
  family models, 378, 379–81
  impulsivity and, 376–77, 378
  mood disorders comorbidity, 373
  neurobiology of, 374
  obsessive-compulsive comorbidity, 369
  personality disorders comorbidity, 370
  personality traits, 376–77
  stereotype, 375
  substance abuse comorbidity, 369
bupropion, 175
Burchill, S. A., 211
Burgess, A. W., 576
Burgess, P. M., 318
Burgess, W. J., 546
Burke, H. C., 563, 569
Burke, J. D., 58, 59
Burnam, M. A., 446
Burroughs, J., 372, 373
Burroughs, M., 373
Bursten, B., 683
Buysse, D. J., 14, 391, 393

Cadoret, R. J., 232, 259, 555
caffeine, 402, 403
Cahoon, B. J., 151
Calabrese, C., 541
calcium-calmodulin, 173
Calderbank, S., 447
callousness, 555, 556, 558, 560, 568
Camatta, C. D., 240
Camberwell Family Interview, 327
Cameron, N., 341
Campbell, C. H., 357n.2
Campbell, D. T., 16
Campbell, I. M., 318
Campbell, L., 593, 600
Campbell, P., 134
Campbell, S. B., 40, 44
cAMP (cyclic adenosine monophosphate), 173, 174, 182
Canestrari, R., 93
Canetti, L., 148
cannabis. *See* marijuana
Capgras syndrome, 346, 354
Caplan, R. D., 208
Cappell, H., 241
Capron, E. W., 547
carbamazepine, 186, 188
carbohydrate craving, 187

cardiophobia, 457
cardiorespiratory distress, 92, 94
cardiotachometer, 68
cardiovascular disease, 417
Cardno, A. G., 351
"career" criminals, 561
caregiver. *See* parenting style
Carey, G., 13
Carey, K., 635
Carey, M. P., 238, 421
Carlisle, J. M., 426
Carmichael, H. T., 6
Carpenter, J. A., 233
Carpenter, W. B., 229
Carpenter, W. T., Jr., 279, 319, 341
Carr, A. T., 131
Carr, E., 562
Carroll, K. M., 228, 239
Carstairs, G. M., 327
Carter, M. J., 315
Carter, W. R., 124
Cartesian dualism, 445–46, 449, 456
Carver, C. S., 218
case-control method, 58–59
case-study methodology, 50–61
Casper, R., 373, 375
Caspi, A., 663
Cassano, G. B., 662, 664
castration anxiety, 427, 545
cataplexy, 394
catastrophic misinterpretations, panic disorder and, 101–2, 103–4
catatonic motor behavior, 279
catecholamines, 167, 191, 292, 395
categorical diagnoses system, 17, 21–22, 23, 122
  personality disorders and, 32, 33, 487–89, 487t
categorical variable, 51
categorization. *See* classification
Cates, R., 232–33
CAT scans, 69–70, 181
Cattell, R. B., 84, 491, 492
Caucasians
  eating disorders and, 367
  genetics of alcoholism vulnerability, 259
  substance abuse rates, 231, 232
  substance-use initiation risks, 233
caudate nucleus, 181
causality
  cognitive illusions and, 49–50
  correlation caution and, 65
  depression and, 205, 207, 208–9, 219
  experimental vs. quasi-experimental design, 52
  phobia typologies, 84
  in psychopathology research, 51, 53, 73
  substance abuse, 250–67
cautiousness, 589
cave art, 249
CCK-4 (cholecystokinin tetrapetide), 103
CCK (cholecystokinin), 373, 374
CD. *See* conduct disorder; conversion disorder
Center for Alcohol Studies (Rutgers), Research Diagnostic Project, 228–29
central nervous system, 167–73, 192
  circadian rhythms and, 183–84
  kindling and, 157, 186
  narcolepsy and, 394–95
  nicotine effects on, 264
  schizogene and, 612
  thyroid dysfunction effects on, 179
  See also brain; neurotransmitters; sympathetic nervous system
cerebellum, 264
cerebral cortex, 168, 177
cerebral metabolism. *See* brain
cerebrovascular disease, 181
Cernovsky, Z. Z., 419
Cerny, J. A., 92
Cerri, A., 618
certainty
  obsessive-compulsive personality need for, 589
  paranoid need for, 340
Cervone, D., 217
CFT (chronic fatigue syndrome), 459
cGMP (cyclic guanine monophosphate), 173, 182
challenge paradigm, 54
  panic provocation, 103–4
Channabasavanna, S. M., 630, 666
Chapman, J. P., 50, 52, 66, 70, 71, 346–47, 351, 615, 617, 618, 619–20
Chapman, L. J., 50, 52, 66, 70, 71, 346–47, 351, 615, 618, 619–20
Chapman Psychosis Proneness Scales, 615
character, colloquial vs. psychoanalytic usage of term, 495
"character armor," 495
character pathologies. *See* personality disorders
Charcot, J.-M., 448
Charisiou, J., 318
charismatic paranoia, 344
Charles, E., 594
Charney, D. S., 152, 157
Chasseguet-Smirgel, J., 684
Chassin, L., 232
Chaturvedi, S. K., 457
Chauncy, D., 595
checking compulsion, 125, 126, 127, 129, 133, 399
cheerlessness, 656
Chen, J. J., 149
Chermack, S. T., 236–37
Chess, S., 644
Chevron, E. S., 539
Chick, J., 532
Child and Adolescent Psychiatric Clinics of North America (journal), 473
childhood disorders
  borderline personality, 633
  dissociative amnesia, 478
  dissociative identity, 472–73, 474, 475–76, 477
  five-axes classification of, 10
  gender identity, 428, 433
  hypochondriasis, 452–53
  obsessive-compulsive, 128
childhood neglect
  borderline personality and, 638, 641
  definition of, 475–76
childhood-onset insomnia, 393, 394
childhood personality development. *See* personality development
childhood physical/sexual abuse
  as alcohol problem predictor, 235, 257
  borderline personality disorder and, 629, 632–33, 634, 638–40
  childhood neglect vs., 475–76
  differing developmental reactions to, 44
  dissociative personality disorder and, 370, 469, 470, 471–72, 472–73, 474, 475, 475t, 477, 478
  eating disorders and, 380–81
  factitious disorder and, 455
  gender identity disorder and, 432
  generalized anxiety disorder and, 125
  hippocampi size effects of, 155
  hypoactive sexual desire disorder and, 415
  hypochondriasis and, 453
  memory deficits and, 151
  Münchhausen-by-proxy syndrome and, 454
  pain disorder and, 451
  paraphilias and, 426
  pedophilia as, 424–25
  as posttraumatic stress disorder risk factor, 147, 155, 156, 157
  psychopathy and, 564, 568–69
  as reportable sex crime, 422
  sadistic personality disorder diagnosis and, 575
  self-defeating (masochistic) personality disorder and, 669
  sexual arousal disorders and, 417, 433
  somatization disorder and, 447
  substance abuse and, 256, 257
  superego development and, 496
  vaginismus and, 421, 433
Childress, K., 236
chlorpromazine, 600
cholecystokinin, 373, 374
cholecystokinin tetrapetide, 103
choline, 186
cholinergic neurons, 172, 173, 186, 192, 395, 401
Chorpita, B. F., 122, 124, 125
Christiansen, B. A., 234
chromosomal abnormalities, 433. *See also* genetic factors
chromosome 5, 285
chronic fatigue syndrome, 459
chronic pain
  biopsychological theory of, 450–51, 459
  definition of, 449
  See also pain disorder
chronic worry, 118, 119–20
chronobiology
  affective disorders and, 183–85
  See also circadian rhythms; REM sleep
Chua, S. E., 351
Chung, T., 229
cigarette smoker typology. *See* smoking
cingulate gyrus, 170, 181
circadian rhythms, 168, 170, 177, 179, 180, 187, 188, 192
  bipolar II disorder, 188, 191, 192
  function and maintenance of, 183–84
  primary insomnia and, 393
  seasonal affective disorder and, 187, 188, 192
  serotonin and, 261
  sleep/wake schedule disorders and, 391, 395–96
circannual rhythms, 183
cirrhosis, 235
cladistics, 17, 19, 22, 24
Clancy, J., 123
Clancy, S. A., 151
Clark, D. A., 121, 122, 123, 125
Clark, D. M., 90, 98, 101–2, 104
Clark, L. A., 84, 492, 494, 660–61, 662

Clarkin, J., 492, 595
Clarkson, C., 123
class (biological classification), 17
classical conditioning, 41
  definition of, 84
  fear aquisition and, 85
  See also behavioral models
classical systematics (set theory), 17–18, 19, 23
classification, 3–25
  in ancient civilizations, 3, 204
  biological, 4, 5, 10, 17–20
  criticisms of, 7
  different models of, 22–23
  dimensional vs. categorical, 21, 122
  evaluative components of, 10, 13–17
  formal components of, 9–10, 17–24
  further directions for, 24–25
  hierarchical structure, 20, 23–24
  history of, 5–9
  Kraepelin, 5
  multiaxial system, 9, 10–11
  personality disorders and issues of, 485–87
  purpose of, 4–5
  "splitters" vs. "lumpers," 5
  substantive components of, 9–13
  taxonomy and pathogenesis, 30–33
  theory-based, 486
  variations within systems, 14–15
  See also diagnoses; taxonomy; *specific conditions*
class (social). *See* cultural factors; socioeconomic status
claustrophobia, 84
cleaning compulsion, 129, 133
cleanliness, 588
Cleary, P. D., 97, 453
Cleckley, H., 492, 556, 557
Clements, C. M., 125
Clementz, B. A., 67, 618
clinical depression. *See* depression
clinical interview, 14, 614
clinical neuropsychology, 287–89
clinical selection bias, 60
Cloitre, M., 640
clomipramine, 133
clonidine, 191
Cloninger, C. R., 230, 231, 232, 258, 259
Cloninger, R. C., 33, 507, 508f, 510, 592, 599
clozapine, 295
Clum, G. A., 94
cluster analysis, 18, 21, 57
cluster sampling, 59
CNS. *See* central nervous system
cocaine
  ADHD history and, 239
  cerebral metabolic lowering by, 265
  dopaminergic system and, 261
  dysphoric withdrawal effects of, 240
  effect expectancies, 234, 264
  euphoric effects of, 264
  in gateway model hierarchy, 255
  interpersonal aggression and, 236, 237
  narcissistic personality disorder and, 678
  paranoia induced by, 356
  paraphilias and, 427t
  prenatal effects of, 256
  psychiatric disorder mimic, 239
  serotonergic system and, 262
  sexual risk taking and, 238
  sleep/wake disturbances and, 402–3
Cocaine Negative Consequences Checklist, 236
coca leaves, 250
Coccaro, E. R., 636
Coffey, H. S., 500
cognitive development, 43–44
  classical theories of, 32
  schizophrenic, 279, 297
  See also biosocial learning theory
cognitive illusions, 49–50, 265–66
cognitive models
  behavioral model contrasted with, 503–4
  body dysmorphic disorder, 453
  borderline personality, 629
  computer simulation of, 72
  delusions and, 351–52, 356
  dependent personality disorder, 540–42, 548
  depression, 192, 209, 211, 213–18, 219
  diagnostic ranking and, 23
  dissociation and, 466–67
  dissociative identity disorder, 473–74
  eating disorders, 374
  fears and phobias, 88–90
  histrionic personality disorder, 545–46
  hypochondriasis, 452
  narcissistic personality disorder, 686
  negativistic personality disorder, 593–94, 598, 600
  noradrenergic systems and, 168
  obsessive-compulsive disorder, 125, 129, 131–33, 134, 135
  obsessive-compulsive personality disorder, 586, 590
  pain behavior, 450
  panic attacks, 92, 94, 100–102
  panic disorder vs. hyponchondriasis, 97–98
  paranoid conditions, 349, 352, 356
  pathological worry, 124, 125
  personality development, 43–44, 490, 503–6, 515, 516
  posttraumatic stress disorder, 149–51, 158
  psychopathy, 571–72
  sadistic personality disorder, 573
  schizophrenia, 286–92, 297, 298, 299, 303, 321–26, 357n.4, 618
  schizophrenic interpersonal dysfunction, 321–26, 330
  sexual arousal disorders, 417
  social phobia, 90
  substance abuse impairment, 237, 264–67
  See also information processing
cognitive psychology
  definition of, 286
  general systems theory, 467
cognitive style. *See* information processing
cognitive therapy, 503–5
Cohen, J. A., 54
Cohen, J. D., 72
Cohen, N. J., 466, 474
Cohen, P., 608, 642
Coid, B., 666
Colby, K. M., 348
cold-heartedness, 573, 586
Coles, M., 563
Coles, M. G., 69
Colussi, K., 419
combat
  dissociative amnesia and, 468
  as traumatic stressor, 145, 150, 155
Comer, R. J., 445
communal paranoia, 344
comorbidity
  avoidant personality disorder, 528–29
  borderline personality disorder, 632–33, 634
  categorical diagnosis systems and, 21
  as clinical or Berksonian selection bias result, 60
  dependent personality disorder, 537, 548
  depression, 96, 98, 117, 128
  depressive personality disorder, 657–60
  dissociative identity disorder, 469
  eating disorders, 368–71
  generalized anxiety disorder's high rate of, 115, 116–17, 118, 124, 125, 135
  histrionic personality disorder, 543, 548
  mood disorders, 117, 128
  narcissistic personality disorder, 677–78, 680, 681
  negativistic personality disorder, 595
  obsessive-compulsive disorder's high rate of, 128, 130
  panic disorder, 96–99
  panic disorder with agoraphobia, 90, 96, 98–99
  panic disorder with generalized anxiety disorder, 91
  paranoid conditions, 341–42, 608–9
  paraphilias, 427, 427t
  personality disorders, 512–13
  posttraumatic stress disorder, 149, 158
  primary insomnia, 393
  psychopathy, 560
  sadistic personality disorder, 575
  schizotypal personality disorder, 508–9, 528
  schzoid personality disorder, 528–29
  self-defeating (masochistic) personality disorder, 668
  sleep disorders, 398–401, 403–4
  social phobia, 98–99, 458
  somatoform disorders, 456–58
  of substance-related disorders, 96–97, 117, 236, 238–41, 251, 261
comparison group
  at-risk profile and, 71
  behavior-genetic paradigms, 62, 63
  definition of, 58
compensation, paranoid, 349
competition, 45–46
complication model, 35
compulsions
  cognitive appraisal models, 131
  common types, 129–30
  definition of, 125, 126, 129
  first use of term, 588
  personality type and, 506
  sexual, 421
  See also obsessive-compulsive disorder; paraphilias
compulsive personality disorder. *See* obsessive-compulsive personality disorder
computational models, of depression, 218

computerized axial tomography (CAT scan), 69, 181
computerized tomographic scans, 290, 291
computer simulations, 72–73
concentration problems
  generalized anxiety disorder and, 114, 120
  neurophysiological basis, 170
  sleep apnea and, 395
concordance rate, 62–63
concurrent validity, 55
conditioned stimulus (CS), 85, 86, 88–89, 131, 153
  deviant arousal and, 426
  hypochondriasis and, 452
  primary insomnia and, 392–93
  sensory pain and, 449
  two-factor theory, 85–86, 131, 156–57
  vaginismus and, 421
conditioning. *See* behavioral models
condom use, 238
conduct disorder, 569
conflict avoidance, anorexics and, 378–79
congenital adrenal hyperplasia, 430, 433
Conger, J. J., 241
Connolly, P. J., 453
Connors, M., 381
Conrod, P., 266
conscientiousness
  depressive personality disorder, 653, 656, 659, 660, 661
  obsessive-compulsive personality disorder, 586, 588, 591, 592
consistency studies, 13, 54
consistency of support, 42
conspicuousness, 340
conspiracy theories, 344
constraint, 84, 660
construct validity, 16–17, 24, 55–56
  computer simulations and, 72, 73
contamination obsessions, 129, 131
content validity, 15
context of discovery, 51
context of justification, 51
Continuous Performance Test tasks, 72, 299, 321, 323, 330
contrast set, 17
control group
  definition of, 58
  matching, 71
  random sampling and, 59
controlling personality, 586, 588, 589, 590, 591, 659
conversational skills. *See* speech patterns
conversion disorder, 445, 448–49, 456, 457, 468, 544
convulsions, pseudoneurological, 448
Cook, B. L., 123
Cook, M., 87, 88
Cooke, D. J., 558, 560, 562, 567
Coon, H., 300
Cooper, A., 684, 685
Cooper, A. F., 356
Cooper, A. J., 419
Cooper, J. E., 7
Copeland, J. R. M., 7
Copernicus, N., 508
coping styles, 10
  dependent personality, 548
  depression onset and, 211
  gender and, 97, 190
  histrionic personality, 542, 545, 548
  pain perception and, 450
  panic prevention, 97
  passive-aggressive, 585
coprophilia, 426
Corbitt, E., 555, 557, 559
Corcoran, R., 325
Cormier, C. A., 561, 565, 566
Cornblatt, B. A., 285, 299, 320, 323, 615, 618
Cornell, C. E., 538
Cornell, D., 562
Cornet, F. C., 83
corrective images, compulsive, 129
correlational studies, 65, 490
correlation coefficient, 54
Corrigan, P. W., 318, 324, 325
corticotropin-releasing hormone, 153, 177
cortisol
  circadian rhythms and, 184
  depression and rhythm of, 177–78, 180, 184, 185, 186
  dissociative identity disorder and, 474
  posttraumatic syndrome and lowered level of, 153–54, 155, 156, 474
  schizophrenia and, 295
Coryell, W., 16, 240, 449, 595
Cosentino, C. E., 432
Costa, P. T., 21, 490, 492, 591–92, 599, 631
costs. *See* economic costs
Cotard's syndrome, 346
Côté, G., 563
Coté, S., 266
Cotton, N. S., 232
counting obsession-compulsion, 126, 129, 130
course (multiaxial classification component), 10
courtship disorder, paraphilia as, 426
coverage (evaluative component), 10
Cowan, N., 290
Cowdry, R. W., 640
Cox, B. J., 81, 84, 93, 94, 95, 97, 103, 104
Cox, D. N., 556, 557
Coyle, J., 263
Coyne, J., 210, 211–13, 219
Coyne's Interpersonal Model of Depression, 211–13
CPT (Continuous Performance Test), 72, 299, 321, 323, 330
Crabbe, J., 260
Craig, T. K. J., 445
Craigen, D., 68
Craske, M. G., 92, 93, 94
CRH (corticotropin-releasing hormone), 153, 177, 178, 180
criminality
  antisocial personality disorder and, 57
  criminal behavior vs. psychopathy, 561
  heart rates and, 68
  narcissistic grandiosity and, 677
  paranoid conditions and, 355
  psychopath recidivism, 562–63, 564, 565, 577
  psychopathy and, 555, 556, 557, 559, 560–65
  sadistic personality disorder and, 574, 575, 576
  sex offenders and, 421–22, 563–65
  sexual sadism and, 576
  See also violence
Crisp, A. H., 375, 378
criterion-related validity, 15, 55
criticism, personal. *See* expressed emotions
Cronbach, L. J., 55
cross-dressing
  gender identity disorder and, 429
  as transvestite fetishism, 425
cross-sectional taxonomies, 30, 31, 33, 47
Crothers, T., 229
Crow, T. J., 279, 286
Crowe, R. R., 123
CS. *See* conditioned stimulus
CT scans, 290–91
Cullen, William, 5
cultural factors
  beliefs vs. delusions and, 347–48, 350–51
  borderline personality disorder and, 643, 644
  definition of pathology and, 36–37
  dependent personality disorder and, 536, 537
  depression and, 207
  dissociative identity model and, 473, 479
  dissociative possession and, 472
  eating disorders and, 367, 371–72, 372, 381
  familial expressed emotions and, 328
  fear acquisition and, 87
  gender differences in depression rate and, 190
  histrionic personality disorder and, 542
  narcissistic personality disorder and, 680
  nightmare attribution and, 397
  personality development and, 38, 45–46
  personality factor models and, 493, 494
  psychopathy's universality and, 556
  schizophrenia and, 277
  sexual normality, abnormality, or perversion and, 410, 421, 424
  substance abuse and, 231, 232, 251–54
  substance-use initiation risks, 233–34
  trust and mistrust and, 344, 350–51
  See also African Americans; Hispanics: Asians; socieconomic status
Cunningham-Rathner, J., 422
Curtin, J. J., 563
Cutting, J., 289, 324
cutting of self. *See* self-mutilation
cyclic adenosine monophosphate, 173, 174, 182
cyclic guanine monophosphate, 173, 182
cyclothymia, 183, 188, 189, 191, 204, 595, 655
cynicism
  negativistic personality and, 593, 594
  paranoid conditions and, 340

DA. *See* dopamine
DaCosta, M., 365, 366
Dahl, A., 666
Daly-Jones, O., 445
Damielak, M. H., 380

Dancee, C. V., 529
Daniels, L., 394
Danish Adoption Study of Schizophrenia. *See* adoption studies, schizophrenia
Dansky, L., 662
DAP (Draw-a-Person) test, 50
DAPP-BQ (Dimensional Assessment of Personality Pathology—Basic Questionnaire), 493
DAPP (Dimensional Assessment of Personality Pathology), 568
Davey, G. C. L., 87, 88, 90
Davidson, M., 636
Davidson, R. J., 663–64
Davies, M., 104, 666, 668
Davis, A., 300
Davis, D., 301–2
Davis, G. C., 146, 147, 149
Davis, K. L., 636, 637–38, 643
Davis, M., 157
Davis, R. D., 340, 512, 535, 540, 546–47, 547, 555, 573, 575, 577, 585, 586, 592–93, 594, 596, 599, 600
Davis, R. T., 543
Davis, W. W., 99
Dawes, R. M., 71
daytime sleepiness, 394, 395, 396, 398
DCSAD (Diagnostic Classification of Sleep and Arousal Disorders), 390–91
DD. *See* delusional disorder
DDIS (Dissociative Disorders Interview Schedule), 470, 478
DDNOS (dissociative disorder not otherwise specified), 466, 476, 477–78
DDs. *See* dissociative disorders
Dean, J. D., 447
Deckel, A. W., 234
declarative memory, 466–67
de Clérambault's syndrome (erotomanic delusions), 341, 346
defense mechanisms, 10
  associative identity disorder, 473
  avoidance as, 530
  borderline personality, 628
  character formation and, 495–96, 515
  histrionic personality, 545
  obsessive-compulsive personality disorder, 589
  paranoid conditions and, 348, 349, 350, 356
  paraphilias as, 426, 427
  passive-aggressive behavior as, 585
  schizoid personality, 531
  somatoform symptoms as, 448
Defense Mechanisms Inventory, 545
Defense Styles Questionnaire, 545
deficient response modulation model, 570–71
definitions
  classical set theory, 18
  syndrome refinement, 55
  See also diagnosis; *specific conditions*
DeFries, J. C., 61
Degraded-Stimulus CPT, 323, 325
Deiter, P. J., 453
dejection, 656
de Jong, J. B., 152
Delany, W., 252–53
Del Boca, F., 230
Deleon, J., 324
delirium, 204
delta alcoholism, 230t
delta waves, 68, 69
delusional disorder, 339, 340, 341, 344
  body dysmorphic disorder seen as, 458
  obsessive-compulsive disorder and, 130, 134
  subtypes, 345–47
delusions, 345–52
  Alzheimer's dementia and, 356
  criteria for, 347–48
  deficit approach to, 351–52
  emotional commitment to, 347
  grandiose manic, 346
  legal aspects of, 354–55
  misattributional model of, 350–51
  motivational approach to, 348–50
  narcissistic personality disorder and, 681
  obsessions vs., 126–27, 135n.2
  panic associated with, 341
  paranoid conditions and, 339, 340, 341, 342, 345–47, 353
  schizophrenic, 278, 279, 287, 317, 318, 346, 351, 355, 357n.4, 606
  social isolation and, 356
  See also persecutory delusions
demagoguery, 344
dementia
  paranoia and, 342, 356
  sleep/wake disorders and, 400–401
  See also Alzheimer's dementia
dementia praecox
  Kraepelin diagnosis, 5–6, 278, 296, 342
  See also schizophrenia
demogogues, 344
demonic possession, 471
Dempster, R. J., 562, 564, 577
Dennert, J. W., 279
dependence theory, 228
dependency needs
  depression and, 209
  depressive personality disorder, 654, 655
  negativistic personality, 593, 594
  self-defeating (masochistic) personality, 665
dependent personality disorder, 535–42, 548–49
  avoidant personality disorder and, 524, 528, 529
  central components, 540, 548
  contemporary theoretical perspectives, 537–42, 548
  depressive personality disorder and, 658, 660
  diagnosis, 536
  dissociative identity disorder and, 475t, 477
  functional and structural attributes of personality, 517ff
  historical perspectives, 537
  histrionic personality disorder comorbidity, 537, 543
  histrionic personality disorder vs., 535, 546, 548
  negativistic personality disorder and, 594
  obsessive-compulsive disorder comorbidity, 128
  other orientation and, 512
  self-defeating (masochistic) personality disorder and, 667
depersonalization, 466, 471, 478
depressants
  in gateway model hierarchy, 255
  psychiatric disorder mimics, 239, 241
depression, 203–19
  age and cohort effects, 206–7
  alcohol use and, 236, 240, 257–58
  anxiety and, 125
  behavioral and interpersonal models, 210–13
  biological aspects of, 168–73, 176–80, 185–87, 191–93
  biological vulnerability of, 125
  borderline personality disorder comorbidity, 632, 636, 642
  brain imaging, 70, 179, 181
  circadian rhythms and, 184–85
  cognitive models, 213–18, 219, 655
  comorbidities, 96, 98, 117, 128
  complication model, 35
  computational models of, 218
  criterion validity, 16
  definitional issues, 204–5, 206
  depressive personality and, 663, 664
  depressive personality disorder vs., 655, 657, 658, 660
  diagnosis criteria, 204, 205
  dissociative identity disorder and, 460, 473
  duration of episodes, 206
  eating disorders and, 368, 371
  EEG finding, 69
  endogenous vs. reactive, 204
  as endstate anxiety, 125
  ethnicity and nationality effects, 207
  female alcohol abuse comorbidity, 236, 257–58
  gender differences, 190, 206, 207, 209, 238, 657
  gender identity disorder and, 433
  generalized anxiety disorder vs., 121, 122, 123
  genetic factors, 123, 188–90
  historical overview, 203–4
  hypoactive sexual desire and, 414–15
  information-processing models, 214–16
  learned helplessness and, 216–17, 219
  life event models, 207–10, 211
  memory deficits and, 151, 215
  models of, 207–18, 219
  narcissistic personality disorder and, 676, 678, 680
  negativistic personality disorder and, 595
  neuroendocrine abnormalities and, 176–80
  neuroradiological abnormalities and, 181–83
  obsessive-compulsive disorder and, 128
  onset and maintenance of, 205
  pain disorder and, 451
  panic disorder comorbidity, 96
  paranoid conditions as variant, 349–50
  paraphilias and, 427t
  postpartum, 180
  posttraumatic stress disorder comorbidity, 148
  prevalence of, 205–7
  as recurrent, 206
  schizophrenia probands and, 617
  self-defeating (masochistic) personality disorder and, 667
  self-regulatory approaches to, 217–18
  seriousness and toll of, 203

depression (*continued*)
sexual dysfunction and, 412, 417, 421, 433
sleep dysfunctions and, 175–76, 178, 186, 191, 192, 398, 401, 403–4
social phobia comorbidity, 98
somatoform disorders and, 457
substance-related comorbidity, 236, 238, 240
subtype distinctions, 204
subtype prevalence, 206
as symptom, 205
symptoms of, 211
as syndrome, 205
thyroid dysfunction and, 179
tripartite model of, 121–23
vulnerability factors, 35, 209–10, 210–12, 213, 217–18, 655
See also bipolar disorder; depressive personality disorder
depressive-masochistic character disorder, 655, 665
depressive personality disorder, 485, 653–64
characteristics and core feature, 653, 654, 655, 656, 664
classification, 655–56
diagnostic criteria, 655
differential diagnosis, 657–60, 664
etiology, 661–63
functional and structural attributes of personality, 517ff
historical background, 654–55
impairment and treatment, 661
interrater reliability, 656
normal personality and, 660–61
prevalence of, 656–57
self-defeating traits and, 655, 659, 660, 665
stability over time, 661
depressive temperament, 653, 654, 660, 662
DePress, J. A., 124
depth-of-processing model of depression, 214
Déry, M., 563
Descartes, R., 445–46, 449, 456, 497
description, classification and, 4
DES (diethylstilbesterol), 430
DES (dissociative experiences) scale, 467, 470, 475, 475t, 477
de Silva, P., 87, 125
desipramine, 180, 187
details, preoccupation with, 586
deterministic genes, probabilistic genes vs., 39
de Trincheria, I., 618
Deutch, A. Y., 157
Deutsch, H., 531, 665
Deutsch, S. I., 352
developmental model. *See* personality development
developmental pathogenesis, 29–47
Axis I, 30–31
Axis II, 32–33
Axis I vs. Axis II, 33–36
by domains of personality, 38–44
definition of pathogenesis, 29
ecology of, 36–37
developmental psychology
classical theories of, 32
life-span perspective, 29
Dewey, M. E., 350
dexamethasone, 154
suppression test, 176–77, 178, 186–87
diabetes, 417
diacylglycerol, 173
Diaferia, G., 617
diagnosis
behavior-genetic studies, 61–62
classification history, 5–12, 24–25, 60, 204
construct validity criteria, 55–56
criteria establishment, 8, 9, 11–12
criteria validity, 15–16
developmental criteria, 30, 46
differing standards of, 7, 11
evaluation of, 25
existing controversies over, 3–4, 6–8
formal components, 20–24
hierarchical ranking, 23
information retrieval and, 4
medical model and, 7–8
narrowing of, 56–57
neo-Kraepelianian view of, 8
operational definitions, 11–12
overlap, 15, 17, 23
reliability studies, 7, 13–15, 54–55, 116
sex bias and, 666–67
stigma of psychiatric, 7
substance abuse criteria, 227–31
taxonomy and, 30–33, 489
time duration and, 30
validity, 15–17, 25, 630
"waste basket" categories, 15, 17
See also Axis I and Axis II; *Diagnostic and Statistical Manual*; *DSM* headings; multiaxial classification system; *specific conditions*
Diagnostic and Statistical Manual of Mental Disorders, 3
categories, 18, 24
criteria overlap, 490
as cross-sectional taxonomy example, 30, 31, 33, 47
definition of mental disorder, 12–13
evaluations of, 25
exhaustive coverage by, 15, 17
formal components of, 20–24
generalized anxiety disorder definitions revisions, 114, 118
hierarchical structure, 20, 23, 24
major problems, 15
multiaxial classification, 10–11
new categories, 9
nomenclature criticisms, 91
operational definitions, 11–12
panic and agoraphobia classifications, 91–92
paranoid disorders, 342
personality disorders classifications, 485, 631
polythetic categories, 22
reliability of diagnoses, 14–15, 17, 24
revision process, 12, 25
specific editions. *See DSM* headings
substance abuse groupings, 227–28
"waste basket" categories, 15
Diagnostic Classification of Sleep and Arousal Disorders, 390–91
Diagnostic Interview for Borderlines, 630
Diagnostic Interview for Borderlines—Revised, 630
Diagnostic Interview for Depressive Personality, 655, 656
Diagnostic Interview for Narcissism, 678–79
Diagnostic Interview for Personality Disorders, 630
Diagnostic Interview Schedule, 12
Diagnostic model, 22–23
Diagnostic overlap, 10
Dial, T., 81
diastolic phase (heart), 68
diathesis-stress model, 51, 219, 281, 295, 297, 298, 329
DiBartolo, P. M., 122
DID. *See* dissociative identity disorder
DIDP (Diagnostic Interview for Depressive Personality), 544, 656
Diehl, S. R., 282–83
Diekstra, R. F. W., 666
diethylstilbesterol, 430
Dietz, P. E., 576
Diforio, J. F., 295
Digit Span Distractibility Test, 323, 325
Dignam, J. M., 490–91
Dillard, J. P., 212
Dimberg, U., 87
Dimensional Assessment of Personality Pathology, 568
Dimensional Assessment of Personality Pathology—Basic Questionnaire, 493
dimensional diagnosis system, 21, 23, 122
depression and, 205
personality disorders and, 487–88, 487t, 489–90
dimensional variable, 51
DIMS (disorders of initiating and maintaining sleep), 390–91
DiNardo, P. A., 92, 116, 119
DIN (Diagnostic Interview for Narcissism), 678–69
direct conditioning, fear acquisition and, 86
directional fractionation, 68
disappointments, 594
disease, illness vs., 446
Disease Concept of Alcoholism (Jellinek), 230
disease phobia, 457, 458
Dishion, T. J., 32
disinhibited behaviors, 185
disorders of excessive daytime somnolence, 391
disorders of initiating and maintaining sleep, 390–91
displacement, 600
DIS-Q (Dissociation Questionnaire), 470
dissociation, 466–68, 629, 631, 633
Dissociation Questionnaire, 470
dissociative amnesia, 466, 468, 471, 478, 479
dissociative disorders, 466–79
borderline personality disorder and, 631, 640
complex comorbidities and, 469
developmental pathogenesis, 475–77
differential diagnosis, 468–70, 478–79
eating disorder comorbidity, 369–70
five *DSM-IV* categories, 466, 477–78
historical perspectives, 471–72
histrionic personality disorder and, 543
neuroses reclassification under, 445
prevalence of, 470–71
See also dissociative identity disorder
Dissociative Disorders Interview Schedule, 470, 478

Dissociative Disorders Program, 475, 477
Dissociative Experiences Scale, 467, 470, 477
dissociative fugue, 466, 478
dissociative identity disorder, 278, 369, 466–79
characteristics, 471, 479
contemporary models, 472–77
developmental pathogenesis, 475–77
historical antecedents, 471
reality debates on, 472, 473, 478
divalproex, 173, 185, 188
divorce, 208
Dixon, M., 564
dizygotic twins (fraternal)
alcoholism studies, 259
depression studies, 189
eating disorders studies, 372
obsessive-compulsive disorder rate, 130
posttraumatic stress disorder study, 155
schizophrenia studies, 62–63, 283
See also monozygotic twins
Djenderedjian, A., 576
DMI (Defense Mechanisms Inventory), 545
DNA markers, 189
DNA sequences, 259, 260
DNA transcription, 174
Dobbs, M., 64, 285
DOES (disorders of excessive daytime somnolence), 391
Dohrenwend, B. P., 208, 632
Dohrenwend, B. S., 632
Dolinsky, Z., 230
Domenech, E., 618
Donahoe, C. P., 315
Donaldson, S. K., 668–69
Donat, D., 590
Donchin, E., 69
Dongier, M., 266
"Don Juan of achievement," 683
Doonan, R., 324
dopamine (dopaminergic system), 156
affective disorders and, 167, 192
alcoholism and, 231
bipolar disorder and, 185–86, 187
depression and, 170, 171, 172, 178, 180
function of, 231, 292–93
nicotine and, 264
opioid receptors, 263
pathways, 293
personality traits and, 407
schizophrenia and, 72, 279, 292–94, 293–94, 295, 619
substance abuse and, 259, 260, 261, 263, 264
substance withdrawal and, 240, 241
Dorner, G., 430
double awareness, paranoid, 341
double bind, 60, 327
doubting obsession, 129
Douglas, J., 576
Douglas, K. S., 563
Douglas, M. S., 316
Downey, K. K., 238
Downs, W. R., 235
Down's syndrome, 39
Dowson, J. H., 666, 668
DPD. *See* dependent personality disorder
Drake, H., 445
Drake, R. E., 634
dramatic behavior, 681
Draw-A-Person (DAP) test, 50
dreams. *See* nightmares
drive theory, 496
drug abuse
ADHD adults and, 239
biochemistry of, 260–64
cognitive aspects, 264–67
cognitive impairment and, 237
comorbid psychopathology, 238–41
craving and withdrawal factors, 261
cultural factors, 251–54
DSM diagnostic grouping, 227
expectancies and, 234, 264
family history and, 232, 255–56
historical, 249–50
narcissistic personality disorder and, 678
neuroimagery, 265
paranoid reactions, 356
peer influences, 233–34
prevalence increase, 231
psychotic symptoms, 293
sexual risk taking and, 238
sleep disorders and, 402–3
use vs., 250
See also specific drugs
drug culture, 254
Dryfoos, J. G., 254
DS-CPT (Degraded-Stimulus CPT), 323, 325
DSDT (Digit Span Distractibility Test), 323, 325
DSM. *See Diagnostic and Statistical Manual of Mental Disorders*
DSM-I, 6, 9, 485
cyclothymic personality, 655
dependency personality disorder precursor, 537
emotionally unstable personality, 544
gross stress reaction, 144
groupings, 227
paranoid disorders, 342
passive-aggressive subtype, 595
DSM-II, 6, 9, 342
anxiety neurosis, 114
cyclothymic personality, 655
dependent personality, 537
hysterical (histrionic) personality disorder, 544
obsessive-compulsive neurosis, 126
passive-aggressive subtype, 595
substance abuse, 227
transitional situational disturbance, 144
DSM-III, 5, 8–9, 10–11, 12, 24, 468
antisocial personality disorder, 557, 558–60
anxiety disorders, 81, 91, 100, 115, 116, 118, 123
anxiety states subcategory, 126
atheoretical position of, 486, 524, 610
avoidant personality disorder, 523, 524, 528, 529, 530, 531
borderline personality disorder, 635
dependent personality disorder, 537
descriptive diagnosis criteria introduced in, 54, 56
dysthymic disorder, 655
factitious disorder, 455
gender identity, 428
histrionic personality disorder, 544
narcissistic personality disorder, 674
obsessive-compulsive disorder, 114, 126, 127, 128
obsessive-compulsive personality disorders, 585, 587
panic disorder and agoraphobia, 91, 114
passive-aggresive (negativistic) personality disorder, 585, 587, 595–96, 659
personality disorder, 492, 513, 523
polythetic definitions, 22
posttraumatic stress disorder, 144, 146, 147, 158
schizoid personality, 523, 524, 529, 530, 531, 609
schizophrenia narrowed diagnostic, 56, 331n.3
schizotypal personality disorder, 524, 528, 608, 609, 610, 614
self-defeating personality disorder, 664, 665
sexual dysfunctions and disorders categories, 413
social phobia as official category, 90
substance abuse, 227, 228
DSM-III-R, 9, 12, 15, 96
agoraphobia classification with panic disorder, 91–92, 95
antisocial personality disorder, 557, 558–60
borderline personality disorder, 468
dependent personality disorder, 537
dissociative identity disorder, 470, 471, 472
dysthymic disorder, 655
gender identity disorders, 428
generalized anxiety disorder, 115, 116, 119, 120, 123, 135n.1
histrionic personality disorder, 544
induced psychotic disorder, 343
Motor Tension and Vigilance and Scanning clusters, 120, 121
narcissistic personality disorder, 678–79, 684
obsessive-compulsive disorder, 126, 128
obsessive-compulsive personality disorder, 587
passive-aggressive personality disorder, 595, 659
personality disorder, 493, 513, 660
phobias, 84, 98, 99
posttraumatic stress disorder, 144, 146
sadistic personality disorder, 485, 574, 575
schizoid diagnostic, 528
schizotypal personality disorder, 610, 612
self-defeating personality disorder, 659, 669
sexual dysfunctions and disorders categories, 413
sleep/wake disorders, 391
social phobias, 524, 529
somatization disorder, 446–47
Structured Clinical Interview, 469
substance abuse, 227
DSM-IV, 10, 12, 22, 47, 267
agoraphobia classification with panic disorder, 91
antisocial personality disorder, 555, 556, 557, 558–60
anxiety disorders, 91
avoidant personality disorder, 527
borderline personality disorder, 468, 485, 628, 631, 633

DSM-IV, (*continued*)
brief psychotic disorder description, 339
categorical approach, 20, 21, 32, 33
as cross-sectional taxonomy, 31, 33
dependent personality disorder, 536, 537, 648
depression, 203, 204, 205
depressive personality disorder, 485, 654, 655, 656, 664
diagnostic overlap, 15
discriminant validity, 122
dissociation definition, 468
dissociative disorder, 466, 468–70, 478
dissociative identity disorder, 369, 471
dysthymic disorder, 657
eating disorders classification, 366
evolutionary theory of fear, 87
female orgasmic disorder, 418
gender identity disorders, 428, 429, 433–34n.1
generalized anxiety disorder as formal diagnosis, 114, 115, 118, 119, 121, 122
hierarchical structure, 23
histrionic personality disorder, 542, 543, 544, 548
narcissistic personality disorder, 675, 676, 678–79, 680, 684, 685
negativistic personality disorder, 595, 596, 600, 659
obsessive-compulsive disorder, 125–27, 128, 129–30, 135n.2
obsessive-compulsive personality disorder, 587
panic disorder, 95, 99
panic disorder with social phobia, 98
paranoid disorders classification, 231, 339, 340, 344, 346, 351, 353, 357n.3
paranoid personality, 605, 606
paraphilias, 422, 423–24, 425, 426
personality disorders, 32, 33, 487, 488, 497, 507, 513, 519, 528
personality traits definition, 503
phobia classification, 82, 83
posttraumatic stress disorder, 144, 145, 147, 158
sadistic personality disorder removed from, 575, 577
schizotypal personality, 605, 606, 612, 614
self-defeating personality disorder removed from, 664
sexual dysfunction classification, 411, 413, 419, 420, 422, 423–24, 425, 428, 429
sexual sadism diagnosis, 575–76
sleep/wake disorders, 391, 392, 393, 395, 402
somatoform disorders classification, 444–45, 446, 447, 448, 451, 454, 455, 456, 457, 458, 460, 468
substance abuse, 227–29, 231
Substance Use Disorders Work Group, 227–28
DSM-V, design of, 229
DSPD. *See* dyssocial personality disorder
DSQ (Defense Styles Questionnaire), 545
DST (dexamethasone suppression test), 176–77, 178, 186–87
D2 receptors, 261, 264
dual personality. *See* dissociative identity disorder
Dugas, M. J., 132
Dulit, R. A., 640
Dunham, H. W., 58
Durant, W., 267
Dutch Hunger Winter (1944–45), 280–81
Dutton, D. G., 354
Dworkin, R. H., 316, 318, 319, 320, 323, 618
Dwyer, P. D., 20
Dyck, M. J., 214
Dyer, D. C., 355
Dykman, B. M., 215
dyspareunia. *See* sexual pain disorders
dysphoria
borderline impulsivity reaction to, 628, 641, 643, 659
CNS stimulants withdrawal and, 240
depression and, 192, 210, 211, 215, 217, 218
depressive personality disorder and, 659
gender identity and, 429
negativistic personality disorder and, 593
panic disorder with agoraphobia and, 90
self-defeating (masochistic) personality disorder and, 667
sleep apnea and, 395
dyssocial personality disorder, 556, 557
dyssomnias, 391, 392–96
dysthymia, 191, 204, 485
borderline personality and, 629, 658
characteristics, 657
classification, 655
comorbidities, 117, 128, 457, 657
depressive personality disorder and, 657–58, 660, 664
generalized anxiety disorder vs., 121
histrionic personality disorder and, 543
narcissistic personality disorder and, 675, 678
negativistic personality order and, 595
obsessive-compulsive disorder and, 128
paraphilia and, 427t
sleep disorders and, 398, 403
substance abuse comorbidity, 240
DZ twins. *See* dizygotic twins

E. *See* epinephrine
early morning awakening, depression and, 398
eating disorders, 365–84
biological factors, 372–73
childhood traumata and, 380–81
comorbidity, 368–71, 373
defining characteristics, 365–66
dependent personality disorder and, 537, 538–39
dietary restraint as factor, 377–78
dissociative personality disorder and, 469
epidemiology, 367–68
etiology, 371–84
expressed emotion and, 328
family dynamics and, 378–80
historical references to, 366–67
integrated etiological concept, 381–84
psychological and developmental factors, 374–78
risk factors, 383t
sociocultural context, 371–72
Eaves, L. J., 84–85, 123, 232, 232–33, 259, 373
ECA. *See* Epidemiological Catchment Area study
Eckblad, M., 71, 619–20
ecology
definition of, 36, 46
of development, 36–37, 44–46
See also environmental factors
economic costs
of schizophrenia, 277
of substance abuse, 231
ectomorphy, 488, 507
Edell, W. S., 70, 71, 356, 618
Edelstein, C. K., 370–71
Edinger, J. D., 391
EDs. *See* eating disorders
Edwards, G., 227
Edwards, J. M., 537, 591
Edwards, K., 456
EE. *See* expressed emotion
EEG record (brain waves), 67, 68–69
borderline personality disorder and, 636
depressive personality and, 663–64
familial alcoholism and, 265
sleep abnormalities in depression, 175–76, 178, 180
sleep studies in bipolar disorder, 186, 187
ego, 495
ego boundaries, 397
egocentricity
histrionic personality disorder and, 542, 545
narcissism and, 675
psychopathy and, 558, 560, 568, 570
ego-ideal, 683
ego identity, 496, 497, 530
ego pathology, 677–68
ego psychology, 588–89, 684
egosyntonic sadism, 678
Egypt, ancient, 3, 249, 250
Ehrhardt, A. A., 428, 429, 430
Eichenbaum, H., 466, 474
Eifert, G. H., 456
Einfeld, S. L., 14
Eisen, J. L., 129
Eisen, S. A., 154–55
ejaculation
delayed, 419
premature, 411, 418, 419–20, 433
Eke, M., 102
EKG (electrocardiogram), 68
Ekstrom, B., 669
elderly people
breathing-related sleep disorders and, 395
dementia and, 342
depression and, 181, 192, 206
generalized anxiety disorder and, 115–16
insomnia and, 392
narcissistic pathology and personality disorder and, 680
REM sleep disturbances and, 176
sleep continuity disturbances and, 175, 401
electrocardiogram, 68

electrodes
definition of, 67
heart rate measurement, 68
electroencephalogric studies. *See* EEG record
electrophysiology. *See* EEG record
Eliason, M. J., 236
Elie, R., 532
Ellason, J. W., 471
Ellis, H., 682
EMDs. *See* eye-movement dysfunctions
Eme, R. F., 380
Emery, G., 504
Emmelkamp, P. M. G., 318
emotional blandness, 525
emotional bonding lack, 555
emotional constriction, 586, 587, 588, 589, 590, 592
emotional disorders. *See* mood disorders
emotional expressivity, 327, 459
emotionally unstable personality, 599–600, 635
emotional numbing, 145, 153, 156
emotional reactivity, 628
emotional shallowness, 570, 576, 684
emotional Stroop paradigm, 149–50
emotion recognition, 324
emotive biasing, 157
empathy lack
narcissistic personality disorder and, 675, 676, 682, 684, 685
psychopathy and, 555, 560
sadistic personality disorder and, 573
Empedocles, 506
empiricism-rationalism duality, 497–98
emptiness, borderline personality and, 628, 633
encephalitis, obsessive-compulsive disorder and, 134
Endicott, J., 54–55, 116, 240, 610, 635
Endler, N. S., 94, 97, 591
endogenous opioids, 263, 264
endomorphy, 488, 507
endophenotype, 616–17
endorphins, 263, 369, 473
Engel, G. E., 451
Englund, D. W., 641
entitlement, narcissistic feeling of, 675, 685
entroencephalographic sleep studies, 175–76
environmental factors
as addiction reinforcement, 261
affective disorders and, 184, 189
alcoholism and, 231
as behaviorism basis, 498
bipolar disorders and, 189
circadian rhythm as, 183–84
definition of, 73n.6
diathesis-stress model, 51
generalized anxiety disorder and, 123, 125
genetic stimulation by, 39, 60, 63, 65, 73, 174
historical attribution of psychopathology to, 60
nonshared influences, 65, 71, 85
paranoid conditions and, 356
personality development and, 36–37, 38, 40–42, 44–46, 60
phobias and, 85
psychopathy and, 569–70
research study design, 65–66
schizophrenia research, 280–81, 326–27
shared influences, 65, 85, 155
somatoform disorders and, 445
stressors as diagnostic category, 9
temperament and, 40
twin studies and, 63, 71
See also family history and system; life event models; prenatal environment; social environment
envy
narcissism and, 675, 679, 682, 684, 686
negativistic personality disorder and, 593
Epictetus, 449
Epidemiological Catchment Area study
anxiety disorders, 81
major depression lifetime prevalence, 206, 207
panic disorder with agoraphobia, 95, 96
posttraumatic stress disorder, 146
schizophrenia/substance abuse comorbidity rate, 239
sleep disorder/psychiatric disorder comorbidity, 403, 404
somatization disorder, 446–47
epidemiology
alcohol abuse or dependency, 231–32, 402
analogue studies of, 65–66
anorgasmia, 419
avoidant personality disorder, 528
borderline personality disorder, 631–32, 642
circadian rhythms sleep disorders, 396
classic studies of, 57–58
concepts and terms, 58–59
conversion disorder, 448
correlational studies, 65
definition of, 57, 58
dependent personality disorder, 536–37
depression, 205–7
depressive personality disorder, 656–57
dissociative disorders, 470–71
eating disorders, 367–68
factitious disorder, 454–55
gender identity disorder, 429
generalized anxiety disorder, 115–16
genetic factors research, 60–65
histrionic personality disorder, 543
hypoactive sexual desire disorder, 413–14
hypochondriasis, 451
male orgasmic disorder, 419
narcissistic personality disorder, 679
narcolepsy, 394
negativistic personality disorder, 594–95
nightmare disorder, 396
obsessive-compulsive disorder, 127–28
obsessive-compulsive personality disorder, 587–88
panic disorder, 95–96
paraphilias, 422
phobias, 83
posttraumatic stress disorder, 146–47
potential biases, 59–60
premature ejaculation, 419
psychopathy and antisocial personality disorder, 560
research methods, 57–60, 73
schizoid personality disorder, 528
schizophrenia, 277
schizotypic psychopathology, 607–8, 620
self-defeating (masochistic) personality disorder, 666
sexual arousal disorder, 416
sleep walking, 397
somatization disorder, 446–47
somatoform disorders, 445
vaginismus, 420
EPI (Eysenck Personality Inventory), 375, 660
epilepsy
dissociative identity disorder mimic, 469
obsessive-compulsive disorder and, 134
sleep-related seizures, 402
epinephrine, 167, 178, 292
Epstein, R., 430
erectile problems. *See* penile erections
Erikson, E. H., 32, 588–89
Erlenmeyer-Kimling, L., 320, 323, 615, 618
Ernst, D., 214
erotomanic delusions, 341, 346, 349
ERP studies (event-related potential), 69, 233, 265, 571, 572
Escobar, J. I., 446
Eshkol, E., 538
Essen-Möller, E., 10, 608
estrogens, 180, 190, 430
ethnicity. *See* cultural factors; *specific groups*
ethnobiological classification, 17, 19–20, 21
etiology
body dysmorphic disorder, 454
borderline personality, 636–44
classification and, 6
conversion disorder, 449
definition of, 29
dependent personality disorder, 541, 548
depressive personality disorder, 661–63
eating disorders, 371–84
epidemiological studies and, 57–60
factitious disorder, 455
hypoactive sexual desire disorder, 414–15
hypochondriasis, 452–53
as multiaxial classification component, 10
narcissistic personality disorder, 685–86
nonshared environmental influences and, 65
pain disorder, 451
paraphilias, 426–28
parasomnias, 397–98
posttraumatic stress disorder, 145
primary insomnia theory, 392
psychopathy, 566–72
sadistic personality disorder, 574–75
schizophrenia, 279–86
schizotypic psychopathology, 616–17
sexual arousal disorder, 416–17
somatization disorder, 447–48
somatoform disorders, 445
euphoria, 185, 264
event-related potential, 69, 233, 265, 571, 572
evironotype, 36

evoked potentials, 265
evoked responses, 68–69
evolutionary theory, 37–38
biological classification and, 19, 24
fear acquisition and, 87–88, 100
personality and, 511–19, 540
spontaneous panic and, 99–100
exaggeration, 590
excessive daytime sleepiness, 394, 395, 396, 398
excessive worry. *See* generalized anxiety disorder
exemplars (diagnostic protoypes), 22
exhibitionism
histrionic, 545
narcissistic, 681, 685
paraphilic, 421, 422, 423, 423t, 427
expectations, fears and, 88
experiential openness, 591
experimental design, 52, 53
experimental psychology, 289–90
experiments of nature, 53
exploitiveness
antisocial vs. narcissistic, 681
narcissistic, 682, 684
sadistic, 573
expressed emotion (criticism)
families of anorexics, 379
families of schizophrenics, 327–29
expressive acts, 515–16
extensional definitions, 18
extraversion, 147
in Five-Factor Model, 591
levels of personality organization and, 497f
eye-movement dysfunctions, 67, 298, 299, 300–301, 302, 616, 618, 620
Eysenck, H. J., 21, 38, 660
Eysenck Personality Inventory, 375, 660

Faber, B., 608, 610, 617
Facial Emotion Identification Test, 324
factitious disorder, 454–55, 458
dissociative identity disorder and, 475t, 476–77
factor analytic studies
anxiety disorders, 91
dimensions of fear, 83, 84
negativistic personality disorder, 599
obsessive-compulsive personality disorder, 586–87, 591–92
personality, 490–94
schizotypic signs and symptoms, 606
Faedda, G., 659–60
Fagot, B. L., 431–32
Fairbairn, W. R. B., 39, 530, 684
Fairbank, J. A., 148, 151
fallacy of positive instances, 50
"false self" concept, 530
family (biological classification), 17
family history and system
affective disorders and, 188–90
antisocial personality disorder and, 57
bipolar disorder and, 188–89
borderline personality disorder and, 636, 639, 640–41, 642–43
depression and, 189–90
depressive personality disorder and, 662, 663, 664
dissociative identity disorder and, 474, 475–76
eating disorder/mood disorder overlap, 368
eating disorders and, 372, 373, 378–82
expressed emotions and, 327–29
factitious disorder and, 455
gender identity disorder and, 431–32
generalized anxiety disorder and, 123
high-risk paradigms and, 70–72
histrionic personality disorder and, 547
mood disorders and, 662
narcissistic personality disorder and, 685
obsessive-compulsive disorder and, 130
paranoid conditions and, 353–54
personality development and, 41–46, 60
as posttraumatic stress disorder factor, 147
as research diagnostic approach, 61, 62, 63
sadistic personality disorder and, 573
schizophrenia and, 60, 280, 281–83, 299, 300, 326–29, 330, 524, 608, 609, 617, 618
self-defeating (masochistic) personality disorder and, 669
shared psychotic disorder and, 343–44
shared vs. nonshared environmental influences and, 65
somatoform disorders and, 445
substance abuse and, 69, 231–34, 251, 252f, 253, 255–56, 258, 265, 267f
See also childhood physical/sexual abuse; environmental factors; genetic factors; parenting styles
fantasies
dissociative, 476, 629
narcissistic, 684, 685, 686
schizoid, 497
sexual. *See* paraphilias
Faraone, S. V., 239, 286, 352
Farber, N. B., 294
Faris, R. E. L., 58
Farmer, M. E., 239
Farooq, S., 445
FAS (fetal alcohol syndrome), 256, 259
fatigability
generalized anxiety disorder and, 114, 120
psychobiological theories of, 459
Fava, G. A., 93, 459
fearless familiarity, 86
fearlessness model (psychopathy), 570, 571
fear-relevant stimuli, 87
fears. *See* phobias and fears
Feighner, J. P., 11, 557
Feinberg, I., 296
Feister, S. J., 573, 574, 575, 577
female masochism (psychoanalytic theory), 665
female orgasmic disorder, 418–19
female sexual arousal disorder, 415, 416, 417
Fenichel, O., 530, 535, 537, 544, 545, 683
Fenigstein, A., 340, 348, 352–53
Fenton, W. S., 619
Ferguson, B., 666
Fernandez, E., 450
fetal alcohol syndrome, 256, 259
fetal development. *See* prenatal environment
fetishism. *See* paraphilias
FFM. *See* Five-Factor Model
Fichter, M. M., 457
Fiester, S. J., 575, 665
"fight or flight" response, 100, 156, 168
Fine, M. A., 599, 668
Fink, P., 455
Finkelhor, D., 639
Finland, 6
Finlay-Jones, R., 208
Fins, A. I., 391
Fint, M. B., 55
First, M. B., 666
Fischer, M., 283
Fischer, R. E., 589
Fischman, F. J., 155–56
Fish, B., 301, 302
Fishbain, D. A., 448, 456
Fisher, M. M., 97
Fiske, D. W., 16
Fisler, R. E., 155–56
Fitts, S. N., 453
5-alpha reductase deficiency (5-ARD), 431
5HT. *See* serotonin
Five-Factor Model (personality), 490, 491t, 493, 503, 509, 539, 567, 660
histrionic personality disorder, 546–47
negativistic personality disorder, 599
obsessive-compulsive personality disorder, 591–92
Flach, A., 379
Flaherty, J. A., 206, 207
flashbacks, 149, 153, 157
Flaum, M., 279
Fleiss, J. L., 13
Flint, A. J., 116
Flor, F., 450, 459, 460
Florentine Codex, 250
Flor-Henry, P., 288, 289
Florin, I., 133
fluoxetine, 175
fluvoxamine, 103
fly agaric, 249
fMRI (functional MRI), 70, 619
Foa, E. B., 89, 90, 126, 127, 129–30, 148, 156, 158
FOD. *See* female orgasmic disorder
folie à deux, 343
folie à famille, 344
folie à quatre, 343
folie à trois, 343
folie lucide, 556
folk classification. *See* ethnobiological classification
Folks, D. G., 448–49
Fonagy, P., 16
Fontaine, V., 266
Ford, C. V., 448–49
Ford, D. E., 403, 404, 405
Fordyce, W. E., 449–50
Forgue, D. F., 152
Forsythe, A., 446
Forth, A. E., 555, 563–64, 569
Fossati, A., 639
fotteurism, 422
Foucault, M., 7
Foulds, G. A., 23
Fourier transformation, 68
Fowles, D. C., 570
France, R. D., 457
Frances, A., 99, 500, 528–29, 555, 595, 665, 667

Franche, R. L., 532
Frank, E., 419
Frankenburg, F. R., 595, 639
Fraser, G. A., 471
fraternal twins. *See* dizygotic twins
Frazer, N. L., 456
Freed, S., 93
Freedman, M. B., 500
Freedman, R., 300
Freedy, J. R., 147
Freeman, A., 504–5, 535, 540–41, 546, 590, 598, 686
Freeman, C. P., 376
Freeman, J., 59
Freeston, D. S., 132
Freiman, K., 574, 575
French, D. C., 32
Frenkel, M., 458
Freud, S., 5, 32, 37, 99, 204, 348, 357n.2, 448, 451, 478, 486, 488, 495, 500, 535, 537, 538, 543–44, 545, 588, 596, 655, 665, 682–83, 686
Freund, K., 426
Frick, P. J., 569
Friedmann, R., 323
Frieze, I. H., 235
Frith, C. D., 325, 357n.4
Fromm, E., 45, 537
Fromm-Reichmann, F., 60, 280, 326–27
frontal cortex, 291, 568
frontal lobe, 181, 182–83, 192, 266
  schizophrenic underactivity, 298
Frost, R. O., 133
frotteurism, 422, 423t, 424, 426
FSAD. *See* female sexual arousal disorder
Fuchs, D., 471
fugue state. *See* dissociative fugue
Fulero, S. M., 558
functional domains, 515–16
  listing of, 518
functional MRI, 70, 619
functional somatic symptoms, 446
fundamental fears, 89
Fyer, A. J., 54, 98, 116

GABA-benzodiazepine, 125
GABA (gamma-aminobutyric acid), 180
  bipolar disorder and, 186, 191
  depression and, 173, 191
  schizophrenia and, 294
  substance abuse and, 262, 265
Gabbard, G. O., 589
Gabriel, E., 353
GAD. *See* generalized anxiety disorder
Gagnon, J. H., 418, 419, 421
Gahir, M. S., 445
Gaines, R., 432
Galen, 367, 506
Gallaher, P. E., 668
Galley, D. J., 539, 545
Gallops, M. S., 116
gambling, 427t
gamma alcoholism, 230t
gamma-aminobutyric acid. *See* GABA
Ganellen, R. J., 218
gangs, 43
Garb, R., 149
Garcia-Domingo, M., 618
Gardner, D. L., 640
Garety, P. A., 352
Garfinkel, P., 372, 381
Garner, D., 372, 381
Garside, R. F., 356
Garske, J. P., 321
Garvey, M. J., 123
Gasperini, M., 617
gastroesophageal reflux, 400
Gates, C., 634
gateway model (substance abuse), 255
Gavira, F. M., 206
Gay, M., 565, 573, 574, 575, 577
Gazis, J., 537
Geddings, V. J., 564
Geer, J. H., 83
Geissner, E., 457
Gelder, M., 90, 101
gender differences
  alcoholism heritability, 259
  antisocial personality disorder, 57
  avoidant personality disorder, 528, 529
  biology of affective disorders, 190–91
  bipolar disorder, 190
  borderline personality disorder, 632, 633, 639
  breathing-related sleep disorders, 395
  conversion disorder, 448
  coping mechanisms, 97, 190
  definition of gender vs. sex, 428
  dependency-related symptoms, 536, 541
  in dependent personality disorder diagnoses, 529, 536–37, 541, 548
  depression, 190, 206, 207, 209, 238, 657
  depression/alcoholism comorbidity, 257–58
  depressive personality disorder, 654, 656, 657, 658
  diagnostic sex bias, 666–67
  eating disorders, 367, 371, 380
  factitious disorder, 454
  generalized anxiety disorder, 115
  histrionic personality disorder, 542, 543, 548
  hypoactive sexual desire disorder, 413–15
  hypochondriasis, 451
  identity disorder, 429, 430, 432, 433
  insomnia, 392
  narcissistic personality disorder, 679
  nightmare disorder, 396–97
  night terrors, 397
  obsessive-compulsive disorder, 127
  orgasmic disorders, 418
  panic disorder with agoraphobia, 95, 97, 99
  paraphilias, 422, 423, 428
  pedophilia, 424
  posttraumatic stress disorder, 146, 147, 148, 154
  psychopath criminal recidivism, 563
  rapid-cycling bipolar disorder, 188
  sadistic personality disorder, 575
  sadomasochism, 425
  schizoid personality disorder, 528
  schizophrenia, 277
  schizophrenic interpersonal functioning, 313, 316–17, 319, 320–21, 326, 330
  self defeating (masochistic) personality, 665, 667
  self-definition, 43
  sexual arousal disorders, 415, 416–18, 433
  sexual pain disorder, 420–21, 433
  sexual victimization, 422
  smoking, 232
  sociobiological strategies, 512
  somatization disorder, 446
  somatoform disorders, 445, 448
  substance abuse, 231, 232, 234–36, 257–58
  transvestic fetishism, 425
  See also women
gender identity disorders, 410, 428–32
  biological factors, 429–31
  characterization of, 428, 429, 433
gender role, definition of, 428
gene linkage. *See* linkage (gene) studies
generalized anxiety disorder, 114–25
  anticipatory anxiety vs., 115
  characterization of, 124, 125
  comorbidity, 115, 116–17, 118, 124, 125, 135
  conceptual models, 121, 123–25
  defining differentiation from other emotional disorders, 118, 119–20, 121–22, 123
  definition of, 114, 118
  as diagnostic category, 114, 118–25
  diagnostic reliability, 116
  early and gradual onset of, 123
  eating disorder comorbidity, 369
  epidemiology, 115–16
  family and genetic studies, 123
  fluctuations in course of, 117
  future research directions, 134–35
  high comorbidity rate of, 116–17, 118, 124, 135
  measures of worry, 118, 119–20
  obsessive-compulsive disorder linked with, 122, 126, 130
  overview and history of, 114–15
  panic disorder comorbidity, 91
  panic disorder vs., 100
  paraphilias and, 427t
  pathological worry models, 124–25
  posttraumatic stress disorder comorbidity, 148
  residual nature of, 114
  significant impairment from, 116
  sleep/wake disorders and, 399–400, 403, 404
  symptoms associated with, 120–21
  treatment resistance of, 124
  vs. other anxiety disorders, 119, 120–21
  See also anxiety disorders
general systems theory, dissociation and, 467
generic rank (folk classification), 19–20
genetic diseases, 39
genetic factors
  affective disorders and, 188–90
  alcohol dependence/abuse and, 158–59, 230–31, 232, 258–60
  alcohol dependence vulnerability and, 258–59
  as behavior influence, 60–61, 65, 73
  bipolar I and II distinctions, 188
  borderline personality disorder and, 636
  of common fears, 84
  definition of, 61
  depression and, 123, 188–90
  depressive personality and, 662
  diathesis-stress model, 51
  eating disorders and, 372–73
  environmental factors and, 39, 60, 63, 65, 73, 174
  gender and bipolar disorder transmission, 190

genetic factors (*continued*)
  gender identity disorder and, 430
  generalized anxiety disorder and, 123
  high-risk paradigm, 70–71
  homosexuality and, 430
  linkage studies, 64–65, 285–86
  narcolepsy and, 394
  obsessive-compulsive disorder and, 130, 134
  panic vulnerability and, 100
  parasomnias and, 397
  personality development and, 39, 46, 60–65
  personality traits rate, 64
  phobias and, 84–84
  posttraumatic stress disorder and, 154–55
  psychopathy and, 568, 569–70
  research approach, 61–65
  schizophrenia and, 39, 60, 62–64, 70–71, 281–86, 297–98, 300, 302, 327, 489, 524, 616, 617
  schizophrenic mode of transmission, 284–85
  schizotypal personality disorder and, 531
  schizotypic psychopathology and, 607, 610, 611, 612, 613
  second-messenger systems and, 174
  serotonergic system and, 169
  substance abuse disorders and, 258–60
genetic mapping, 285
genital stage, 496
genotype
  definition of, 283
  psychopathy theory, 567
  schizophrenia and schizotypal personality disorder, 524, 607, 611, 612, 620
genus (biological classification), 17, 19
George, L., 117, 632
Gerardi, R. J., 151
Gerken, K., 236
Gersh, T. L., 391
Ghana, depression rate, 207
GH (growth hormone), 180, 186, 191
Giancola, P. R., 236
Gibbon, M., 55, 610, 635
Gibson, P., 453
GID. *See* gender identity disorder
Gilbertson, M. W., 155
Giller, E. L., 154
Gilligan, C., 512
Gillin, J. C., 240
Gilovich, T., 49, 50
Gipson, M., 453
"glass-bubble fantasy," 683
Glick, M., 349
Glickauf-Hughes, C., 665
gloominess, 654, 655, 656, 664
glove anaesthesia, 448
glucocorticoids, 153, 154, 155, 172, 178, 192, 264
glucose metabolism, 182–83
glutamate
  depression and, 173, 178
  schizophrenia and, 294, 619
  substance abuse and, 262–63
glycine
  depression and, 173
  schizophrenia and, 294
Glynn, S. M., 315, 323, 330
Gnys, M., 231
"God complex," 683
Goeke, J. M., 391
Goethe, J. W., 667
Gold, D. D., 317
Gold, E. O., 233
Goldberg, J., 154–55
Goldberg, L. R., 490–92
Goldberg, M., 448, 456
Goldberg, R. L., 352
Golden, R. R., 57
Golding, J. M., 446
Goldman, M. S., 234
Goldstein, H. J., 378–79
Goldstein, J. M., 316, 352
Goldstein, M. J., 330
Goldstein, W. N., 587
gonadal hormones, 414
Good, T., 326, 328
Goodman, W., 130
Goodrich, S., 640, 641
Goodwin, D. W., 56, 232, 258
Goodwin, F. K., 239
Gordis, E., 260
Gordon, C. M., 238
Gordon, R., 256
Gorelick, D., 259
Gorenstein, E. E., 60
Gorman, J. M., 54, 116
Gorski, R. A., 430
Gostfriend, D., 263
Gotlib, I. H., 215, 219
Gottesman, I. I., 13, 51, 56, 57, 60, 61–62, 63, 64, 71, 281–82, 283, 284, 285, 609, 615
Gourlay, A. J., 7
G-protein functions, 173, 174, 175
Grace, A. A., 614, 619
grandiosity
  biological aspects of, 185
  delusions of, 339, 341, 346, 356, 681, 682
  Freudian view of, 348
  narcissistic, 675, 676, 677, 678, 681, 683, 684, 685–86
  narcissistic vs. borderline disorder, 681
  narcissistic vs. paranoid, 682
  narcissistic vs. paranoid and schizophrenic, 682
  paranoid conditions and, 340, 341, 344, 346
  psychopathy and, 555, 560
Grandi, S., 93
Grann, M., 562, 563
Grant, B. F., 238
gratification delay, 568
Gray, J. A., 570
Great Britain, 6, 7
Greece, ancient, 3
  depression theories in, 204
  eating disorders reported in, 367
  humors doctrine, 506
  hysteria description, 447
  psychopharmacology in, 249, 250
Green, M. F., 300, 318, 322, 323, 330
Green, R., 431, 432
Green, S., 256
Green, S. R., 320
Greenbaum, P. E., 234
Greenberg, M. S., 153
Greenberg, R. P., 545
Greenwood, A., 565
gregariousness, 542
Gregg, J. R., 10
Gretton, H., 563, 564–65
Grim, R., 459
Gross, M. M., 227
"gross stress reaction" diagnosis, 144
group psychotherapy, 528
Grove, W. M., 614, 618
growth hormone, 180, 186, 191
Gruen, R., 614
Gruenberg, A. M., 282–83, 284, 608, 617, 619
Grundberger, B., 684
guanine nucleotide-binding proteins (G-proteins), 173
guardedness, paranoid conditions and, 340
Guenther, V., 381
guilt
  depressive personality disorder and, 654
  narcissism and, 677, 678
  obsessive-compulsive personality disorder and, 589
guilt, lack of
  psychopathy and, 555, 560
  sadistic personality disorder and, 573
Gull, W., 367
gullibility, 343, 344
Gunderson, J., 595, 632, 633, 635, 639, 641, 654, 655, 656, 659–60, 661, 677, 679, 680, 681, 682, 687
Guntrip, H., 530, 682
Gurland, B. J., 7
Gurling, H., 64, 285
Gursky, M., 89
Gurvits, T. V., 155
Guze, S. B., 11, 55–56, 232, 258, 447, 557, 630

Haack, L. J., 215
Haaga, D. A., 214
Haas, G., 329
habit disorders, 130
Hackmann, A., 101
Haddad, J., 456
Hagen, R., 432
Haier, R. J., 614
Halberstadt, L. J., 216
Haley, J., 60, 327
Hall, C. S., 674–75
Hallam, R. S., 94
Hallmayer, J., 608
hallucinations
  borderline personality, 629
  dissociative, 469, 471, 479
  hypnagogic, 394
  narcoleptic, 400
  schizophrenic, 278, 279, 287, 317, 318, 351, 400, 606
  See also auditory hallucinations
hallucinogens
  comorbid depression, 238
  cultural use of, 252
  in gateway model hierarchy, 255
  glutamate receptors and, 263
  historical use of, 249, 250
  serotonergic receptors and, 262
Halmi, K. A., 365, 366
Hamer, D. H., 430
Hamilton Rating Scale for Depression, 16
Hammen, C. L., 205, 209
Hammond, D. C., 415
hand washing, 125
Hannan, P., 232
Hans, S. L., 302
Hardin, T. S., 216
Harding, B., 378

Hare, R. D., 60, 68, 69, 555, 556, 557, 559, 561, 561–62, 563, 564–65, 566, 567, 568, 569–72, 574, 576–77, 677, 681
Hare PCL-R, 555, 556, 557–60, 561, 564, 577
  childhood psychopathic traits and, 569
  as criminal recidivism predictor, 562, 563
  DSM criteria and, 559–60
  five-factor model of personality and, 567
  high internal consistency, 558
  item description, 558t
  sadistic personality disorder and, 573–74, 575
  treatment prognosis, 565
Hare PCL:SV, 558, 559, 562
Harford, T. C., 238
Harkness, A. R., 493, 615
Harlow, H., 42
harm avoidance, 507, 508f, 599
Harper, D. J., 342, 344
Harpur, T. J., 557, 567, 571–72
Harris, A. E., 330
Harris, G. T., 561, 562–63, 564, 565, 566, 577
Harris, T., 204, 208, 209
Harris, T. R., 235
Harrow, M., 347
Hart, E. L., 569
Hart, S. D., 555, 556, 557, 558, 559, 562, 563, 564, 567, 574, 576–77, 577, 677, 681
Hartl, T. L., 133
Hartman, C., 576
Hartman, H., 684
Hartshorn, J., 378
Harvey, P. D., 353
Hasin, D., 240
Hass, W., 430
Hastrup, J. L., 67, 68, 69
Hatfield, A. B., 326
Hauri, P., 14, 391, 393
Hautzinger, M., 211
Hawk, G., 562
Haymaker, D., 668
Haynes, S. N., 357n.5
Hazelwood, R. R., 576
Hazlett, R. L., 117, 118
headaches, chronic, 117
head trauma, 134
health care systems, classification and, 5
hearing voices. *See* auditory hallucinations
heart disease, 235
heart rate
  blood-injection-injury phobia and, 82
  fears and phobias and, 82
  generalized anxiety disorder and, 121
  measures of, 67, 68
  posttraumatic stress disorder and, 151, 152
  psychopathy and, 571
Heath, A. C., 84–85, 123, 155, 232, 232–33, 259, 373
Heatherton, T. F., 377
Heaton, R. K., 316
Hedeker, D., 375
Hedlund, S., 216
Heikkinen, M. E., 642
Heimberg, R. G., 90
Heinrichs, D. W., 279
Heinrichs, R., 31
Heisler, L. K., 667
helplessness
  dependent personality's feelings of, 537, 540
  depression and feelings of, 211, 655
  See also learned helplessness
Helstone, F., 545
hembene, 250
hemispheric asymmetry, schizophrenic, 292
Hempel, C. G., 11
Hemphill, J. F., 561, 563, 565
Hemsley, D. R., 352
Henderson, B., 81
Henderson, W. G., 154
Hengeveld, M. W., 444
Heninger, G. R., 152
Hennig, W., 19
Henrikkson, M. M., 642
Henriques, J. B., 663–64
Herbert, J., 529
heredity. *See* genetic factors
heritability. *See* genetic factors
Herman, C. P., 366, 377
Herman, J. L., 633, 639, 640
Hermansen, L., 232, 258
hermaphroditism, 431
Herodutus, 250
heroin
  endogenous opioid system and, 263
  in gateway model hierarchy, 255
Hertzberg, M., 149
Herz, L. R., 152
Hesselbrock, M. N., 236
Hesselbrock, V., 230, 234, 236, 241
Hesselink, J., 316
Heston, L. L., 283–84, 609
Heumann, K. A., 21
Heun, R., 608
Hewitt, J., 232–33, 617
Heywood, E., 232
hierarchical structure
  biological classification, 17, 18, 20
  of fears, 84, 85
  mental disorders classification, 20, 23–24
high-magnitude stressors, 145–46, 147
high-risk research paradigm, 70–72
Hill, E. L., 541
Hill, J. L., 369
Hill, S. Y., 231, 232, 236, 258
Hiller, J. B., 328
Hiller, W., 457
Himmelfarb, S., 115
hippocampus
  affective disorders and, 168, 170, 177, 178, 180
  dissociative identity disorder and, 466, 474
  posttraumatic stress disorder and, 153, 155
  procedural vs. declaration memory and, 466
  schizophrenia and, 291, 294, 295
  schizotypic psychopathology and, 619
Hippocrates, 204, 500, 506, 543
Hirsch, G. L., 315
Hirschfeld, R. M. A., 654, 655, 656, 659–60, 661
Hispanics
  depressive symptom clusters, 207
  histrionic personality disorder and, 542
  substance abuse rates, 231
histrionic personality disorder, 9, 468, 469, 506, 542–47, 548
  charactristics and core components, 542, 545, 546, 547, 548, 594
  contemporary theory perspectives, 544–49
  dependent personality disorder comorbidity, 537, 543
  dependent personality disorder vs., 535, 546, 548
  functional and structural attributes of personality, 517ff
  historical perspectives, 543–44
  narcissistic personality disorder and, 680, 681–82
  obsessive-compulsive disorder comorbidity, 128
  obsessive-compulsive personality disorder comorbidity, 587
  physical attractiveness as aspect of, 542
  psychopathy and, 560
  self-perpetuation processes in, 547
Hite, S., 418
Hitler, Adolf, 355
HIV-related illenesses, 32
H.M. case, 466
Ho, P., 372
hoarding compulsion, 129, 130
Hoberman, H., 211
Hodgins, S., 563
Hoehn-Saric, R., 117, 118
Hofmann, M., 230
Hogan, M. E., 216–17
Hogan, R., 675
Hokama, H., 155
Holderness, C., 369
Holland, A. J., 372
Hollander, E., 458
Holle, C., 214, 215
Hollon, S. D., 205
Holloway, W., 102
Holocaust survivors
  dissociative amnesia and, 468
  low rates of dream recall, 153
  posttraumatic stress disorder and, 146, 154
Holzer, C. E., III, 656, 661
Holzman, P. S., 618
homeless people, 277
homosexuality, 3, 13, 36
  birth order/sibling sex ratio, 431
  childhood cross-gender behavior and, 429, 433
  cross-dressing and, 425
  Freudian linking of narcissism with, 682
  Freudian linking of paranoia with, 348
  genetic factors, 430
  historical views of, 421
  sexual disorder diagnosis, 433–34n.1
homovanillic acid, 293
Hooley, J. M., 328
Hope, D., 90, 529
hopelessness theory of depression, 211, 213, 219, 655
Hopi Indians, 207
hormone replacement therapy, 414
hormones, 179, 180
  disorders, 414, 416–17, 427
  prenatal effects, 430
  See also specific glands and hormones
Horney, K., 537, 665, 683
Hornig, C. D., 96

Horowitz, L. M., 215
Horowitz, M. J., 546, 547
horrific images, 129
Horvath, T. B., 636
hostility
  toward depressed person, 212
  depression and, 211
  narcissistic personality disorder and, 679
  negativistic personality disorder and, 594, 596, 597, 598, 599, 600
  obsessive-compulsive personality disorder and, 586
  paranoia and, 348, 356
  psychopathy and, 556
  See also hostility
Houck, P. R., 14
Hough, R. L., 148
Houpt, J. L., 457
Howes, M. J., 666
HPA axis (hypothalamic-pituitary-adrenocortical)
  biological workings of, 168, 169, 191, 192
  bipolar disorder and, 186–87
  bipolar II disorder and, 188
  depression and, 171, 172, 173, 176–78, 186–87, 192
  feedback inhibition system, 177–78
  gender differences and, 190
  posttraumatic stress disorder and, 153–54, 158
  schizophrenia and, 295
HPD. *See* histrionic personality disorder
HPO axis (hypothalamic-pituitary-ovarian), 190
HPT axis (hypothalamic-pituitary-thyroid)
  biological workings of, 179, 187
  depression and, 179–80
  gender differences and, 190
HR. *See* heart rate
HSDD. *See* hypoactive sexual desire disorder
Hsiao, C.-Y., 232
Hsu, L. K. G., 372, 377, 378
Hu, N., 430
Hu, S., 125, 430
Hudson, J. L., 346
Hughes, D., 117
Hughes, M., 146, 147, 148, 149
Hughlings-Jackson, J., 278–79
Human Genome Project, 64–65
human relationships. *See* interpersonal models
human sexuality. *See* sexual dysfunctions and disorders
Hume, D., 497
humorlessness, paranoid conditions and, 340, 348
humors (early medical doctrine), 204, 506
Humphrey, L. L., 373, 378, 379
Huntington's disease, 39, 51, 263
Huprich, S. K., 668
Hurlbert, D. F., 547
Hurt, S., 595
Huska, J. A., 149
Huttunen, M. O., 280
Huxley, A., 250
Huxley, G., 641
Hyler, S. E., 370–71, 587
hymenal scarring, 420
hyperactivity, 185
hyperaesthetic personality traits, 529, 530
hyperarousal, depression and, 175
hypersensitivity, 523, 524, 528, 529, 533, 685
hypersexuality, 185
hypersomnia, 391
  depression and, 175, 186, 187, 398
  substance-induced, 402, 403, 404
hyperthyroidism, 179
hyperventilation, 104
hypervigilance, 118, 157
  narcissistic, 676
  paranoid, 343, 351, 356
hypnagogic hallucinations, 394
hypoactive sexual desire disorder, 411–12, 413–15
hypochondriasis, 444, 445, 451–53
  anxiety disorder and, 457
  differential diagnosis, 456, 457
  four dimensions of, 457
  obsessive-compulsive disorder comorbidity, 130
  panic disorder comorbidity, 97–98
  personality disorder and, 458
hypofrontality, 298
hypohedonia, 613
hypokrisia, 612, 613
hypomanias, 187, 681, 682
hypomanic personality disorder, 497
hypothalamic-pituitary-adrenocortical axis. *See* HPA axis
hypothalamic-pituitary-ovarian axis. *See* HPO axis
hypothalamic-pituitary-thyroid axis. *See* HPT axis
hypothalamus, 153, 157, 168, 170, 177, 179, 180, 184, 187
  sexual orientation and cell volume theory, 430
hypothyroidism, 179, 187, 188, 190
hypoxia (autoerotic asphyxiation), 425
hysteria
  as borderline label, 635
  conversion symptoms and, 468
  cultural content and, 37
  historical descriptions of, 3, 447, 451, 543
  as histrionic personality disorder precursor, 543–44
  hypochondriasis associated with, 451
  psychoanalytic theory on, 543
  somatization disorder as, 447, 448
  See also conversion disorder; dissociative amnesia; histrionic personality disorder; somatization disorder
hysterical conversion disorders, 544
hysterical personality disorder
  DSM-II definition of, 11
  personality development level and, 497
  See also histrionic personality disorder
hysterical somatoform disorders, 445

Iacono, W. G., 618
"Icarus complex," 683
ICD. See International Classification of Diseases and Related Health Problems
ICD-6, 11
ICD-8, 6
ICD-9, 12
ICD-10, 12, 15, 23
  agoraphobia, 91
  anankastic personality, 588
  borderline personality disorder, 628
  conversion disorder, 468
  dyssocial personality disorder, 556, 557, 559
  emotionally unstable personality, 635
  as most sensitive diagnostic system, 228
  paranoid conditions, 340, 353
  substance abuse, 228
ICSD. *See International Classification of Sleep Disorders*
id, 495
IDD (Inventory to Diagnose Depression), 16
ideal types, 22
identical twins. *See* monozygotic twins
identity diffusion, 473, 497
identity disturbances. *See* dissociation; dissociative disorders
identity fragmentation, 369
identity transformation. *See* dissociative identity disorder
idiographic research design, 50–51
idiopathic insomnia, 393, 394
illness
  disease vs., 446
  medical model of, 7–8, 24, 487
illness behavior, 459
illusory correlations, 59
image-distorting defense style, 628
imagery
  obsessive-compulsive, 129, 131
  psychotic vs. obsessive-compulsive, 127
  worry as avoidance of, 124
imaginary world, 476
imaging technology
  neuroimagery, 265
  and reduced false positive diagnoses of somatization disorder, 456
  schizotypic psychopathology, 618–19
  See also brain, imaging technology; *specific types*
imipramine, 99, 100, 168, 171
impaired attention. *See* attention impairment
imposter delusion, 346, 354
impotence, 416
impressionistic thinking, 546
imprinting, paraphilias and, 426
impulse disorder, paraphilias and, 427t
impulsivity
  borderline personality disorder and, 628–29, 631, 634, 636, 637, 641, 643, 644
  eating disorders and, 369, 376–77, 378
  infantile hysterical personality and, 497
  paraphilias and, 421, 427
  psychopathy and, 555, 556, 558, 560, 568, 570
  social disintegration construct and, 643
  substance dependence vulnerability and, 266, 369
Inaba, R. K., 240
Incas, 250
incest, 422, 423t, 424, 468
  borderline personality disorder and, 638
  dissociative identity disorder and, 473
  psychopathy and, 563–64

Incesu, C., 147–48
incidence, prevalence vs., 58
incidental learning, 41
incompetence (legal), paranoid disorders and, 354
indecision, 132
index of reliability, 54
India, ancient, 3, 249–50
indirect evidence, 55
individual interview approach, 61–62
induced psychotic disorder, 343
inefficiency, 593
inescapable shock, 156
infantile narcissism, 684, 686
infantile personality, 497
inflexibility, obsessive-compulsive, 586
influenza virus, 280, 327
information processing
 cognitive models and, 503, 504
 depression models and, 214–16, 218
 paranoid conditions and, 352–53
 posttraumatic stress disorder models and, 157–58
 procedural memory and, 466
 schizophrenia and, 289–90
 schizophrenic interpersonal relations and, 321–23
information retrieval, 4
Ingraham, L. J., 608, 610, 617
Ingram, R. E., 205, 214, 215, 216
inheritance. *See* genetic factors
inhibited sexual desire. *See* hypoactive sexual desire
inhibited temperament, 532, 663
initial values, law of, 68
initiative lack, 588
Inn, A., 234
inner-city problems, 253
inner fantasy world, 476
inositol, 173
insanity defense, 355
insect phobias, 82, 83, 84
insight
 obsessive-compulsive disorder and, 126, 127, 135n.2
 paranoid lack of, 341
insomnia. *See* primary insomnia; sleep/wake disorders
instructional transmission, fear acquisition and, 86
instrumental conditioning, 156–57
insufficient learning, 42
intake-rejection hypothesis, 68
intensional definitions, 18
intermediate rank (folk classification), 19
internal consistency
 measures, 13, 14
 reliabiliy, 54
internal representational models, 42
International Classification of Causes of Death, 6
International Classification of Diseases and Related Health Problems, 6
 DSM vs., 9, 91, 228
 editions of, 3, 6, 9, 11. *See also pecific ICD* headings
 hierarchical ranking, 23
 operational definitions, 11–12
 reliability estimates, 15
International Classification of Sleep Disorders, 391, 393, 394, 396
International Personality Disorders Examination, 630
International Statistical Institute, 6
Interpersonal CheckList, 509
Interpersonal Circle, 501–3, 502f, 509, 539
interpersonal models
 attachment and autonomy, 42–43, 46
 avoidant personality disorder, 523, 524, 525, 529
 borderline personality, 497, 628, 634, 659
 dependent personality disorder, 535, 539–40, 541
 depression, 209, 210–13, 217
 depressive personality disorder, 659
 histrionic personality disorder, 535, 544, 547
 imbalanced and conflicted personalities, 513f
 innate temperment and personality development, 40
 interpersonal circles, 501–3, 502f, 509, 539
 narcissistic personality disorder, 675, 677, 679, 682, 686, 687–88
 negativistic personality disorder, 593–94, 596, 598–99
 obsessive-compulsive personality disorders, 586, 588, 589, 590–91
 orgasmic disorders, 419
 paranoid mistrust, 340–41, 342–45
 paraphilias, 421, 426
 personality and, 490, 499–503, 509, 510, 515, 516, 539–40
 psychopathy and, 555, 558, 567–68
 sadistic personality disorder, 572–77
 schizoid personality disorder, 523–24, 525
 schizophrenia, 311–31
 self-defeating (masochistic) personality disorder, 667
 sexual arousal disorders, 417, 418–19
 sexual desire disorders, 415
 sexual pain disorders, 421
 See also withdrawal, social
interpersonal problem solving, 314–16
interpersonal trust, 340–41, 342–45
inter-rater reliability, 54
intersex conditions, 431, 433
interviews, diagnostic, 12, 14
intimidation, 542
intoxication. *See* substance abuse
intracellular calcium metabolism, 174
introversion
 depressive personality disorder and, 655
 environmental vs. genetic factors, 39
 levels of personality organization and, 498f
 social phobias and, 84
intrusive thoughts
 boundary between obsessive and normal, 131–32, 134
 neutralization efforts, 132
 posttraumatic stress disorder recollections as, 144, 145
Inventory to Diagnose Depression, 16
investigator-based assessment, 208
involuntary commitment, 355–56
involutary motor activity, 170
Inz, J., 124
IPDE (International Personality Disorders Examination), 630
IQ scores, posttraumatic stress disorder and, 146, 147, 155
irresponsibility, 555
irritability
 cocaine use and, 236
 depression and, 192, 211
 eating disorders and, 371
 generalized anxiety disorder and, 114, 120, 121
 negativistic personality disorder and, 593, 594, 596, 598, 599
 posttraumatic stress disorder and, 157
 psychopathy and, 556
 sleep apnea and, 395
irritable bowel syndrome, 117
Irving, L. M., 380
Irwin, M. R., 240
Isometsa, E. T., 642
Item Response Theory, 577

Jackson, D., 327
Jackson, D. D., 60
Jackson, D. J., 536
Jackson, D. N., 25, 492–93, 494, 631
Jackson, H. C., 537
Jackson, H. L., 318
Jacobs, C., 372, 373
Jacobsberg, L. B., 666
Jacobsen, B., 63, 608, 610, 617
Jacobson, E., 684
Jain, S., 547
James, W., 351
Janet, P., 543
Jang, K., 631
Jansson, L., 608, 610, 617
Jaspers, K., 22, 23
jealousy, paranoid conditions and, 340, 345, 346, 354
Jellinek, E. M., 229, 230
Jenike, M. A., 155–56, 587–88
Jensen, J., 353
Jernigan, T., 316
Jerome, E. A., 352
Jessor, R., 254
Jessor, S. L., 254
jet lag, 192, 391, 395
John, O. P., 490–91
Johnson, C., 375, 378, 379, 381
Johnson, D., 152
Johnson, J. G., 35, 545
Johnson, M. C., 124
Johnson, M. E., 380
Johnson, M. K., 351
Johnson, V. E., 410, 412, 413, 417, 418, 419, 420
Johnston, J. C., 88
Johnston, L. D., 264
Johnston, R., 317
Joiner, T. E., Jr., 212, 213, 216
Jolesz, F. A., 155
Jones, B., 285
Jones, E., 683
Jones, Jim, 355
Jones, L. A., 351
Jones, P., 301, 663
Jones-Webb, R. J., 232
Jordan, B. K., 148
Jørgensen, P., 353
Josephson, S., 458
Joshua, S. D., 318
Jourden, F., 53
Joyce, P. R., 642
joylessness, 656
Judd, L. L., 239
judgmentalism, 586, 653, 655, 664
Juni, S., 589
Jutai, J. W., 69

Kabat, L. G., 350
Kaczinski, Ted, 347, 355, 357n.1
Kaelber, C. T., 15
Kagan, J., 532
Kahn, E., 556, 588, 654
Kales, A., 14, 391, 393
Kallman, F. J., 60
Kaloupek, D. G., 151
Kamerow, D. B., 403, 404, 405
Kane, J., 666
Kaney, S., 349, 350, 352
Kant, Immanuel, 204
Kantor, M., 544
Kaplan, H. E., 277
Kaplan, H. S., 410, 412, 413, 414, 417, 419, 420, 426, 427
Kaplansky, L. M., 320, 323
kappa coefficent, 54, 614
kappa (statistic), 14, 15
Kapur, M., 546
Karno, M., 446
Kass, F., 537, 594, 666, 668
Kassel, J. D., 231
Kathol, R. G., 97
Katkin, E. S., 67, 68, 69
Kaur, D., 546
Kay, D. W. K., 356
Keane, T. M., 149, 151
Keck, P. E., 346
Keefe, R. S. E., 285, 353
Keith, S. J., 239
Keller, H., 46
Keller, M. B., 240
Kelley, M., 587
Kellman, P., 587
Kellner, R., 444, 445, 446, 447, 449, 451, 452, 456
Kelly, K. A., 125
Kelso, K., 598
Kemp, L. L., 355
Kendall, P. C., 205
Kendell, R. E., 7, 11, 13, 16, 21, 23
Kendler, K. S., 84–85, 123, 232, 259, 282–83, 284, 373, 608, 609–10, 614, 617, 619
Kennedy, H. G., 355
Kennedy, W. A., 563
Kent, D. A., 449
Kenyon, F. E., 451
Kern, R. S., 330
Kernberg, O. F., 496–97, 498f, 531, 533, 535, 544, 545, 547, 635, 655, 658, 659, 665, 674, 677–78, 680, 681, 682, 683, 684, 685, 686
Kernberg, P., 674
Kerr, J., 641
Kerr, N., 229
Kessler, R. C., 84–85, 123, 146, 147, 148, 149, 232, 259, 373
Kety, S. S., 61–62, 63, 284, 524, 608, 610, 614, 616, 617
Keys, D. J., 529
Khantzian, E. J., 678
Khot, V., 302
Khouri, P. J., 614
Kieffer, W., 353
Kiehl, K. A., 572
Kiesler, D. J., 501, 502f, 509, 515, 539
Kikinis, R., 155
Kilbey, M. M., 240
Kilpatrick, D. G., 147
Kimball, C. R., 659–60
Kinderman, P., 349
kindling, 157, 186, 192
King, D., 430
King, N. J., 83
kingdom (classification rank), 17, 19, 20
Kinney, D. K., 608, 610, 617
Kinsey, A. C., 421
Kinzl, J. F., 381
Kirisci, L., 237
Kirk, S. A., 7
Kirkpatrick, B., 357n.3
Klar, H., 636
Klassen, A. D., 235
Klauminzer, G. W., 151
Klein, D. F., 96, 98, 99–100, 104, 116
Klein, D. N., 656, 657, 658, 660–61, 662, 668–69
Klein, K., 35
Klein, L. M., 669
Klein, M., 529–30, 684
kleptomania, paraphilias and, 427t
Klerman, G. L., 6–7, 96, 452, 545
Kley, I. B., 299
Kline, P., 586, 589
Klinefelter's syndrome, 433
Klingler, T., 608
klismaphilia, 426
Knecht, G., 353
Knight, R. A., 424, 563
Knight, R. P., 229–30, 230
Knowles, S. L., 94
Koenig, R., 597
Kog, E., 379–80
Kohlberg, L., 32
Kohut, H., 535, 597, 678, 683, 684, 685
Kolb, J. E., 635
Kolb, L. C., 151
Koopman, C., 238
Koreen, A. R., 293, 294
Koresh, David, 355
Korfine, L., 608
Kosslyn, S. M., 156
Koszycki, D., 103
Kotler, M., 148, 149
Kozak, M. J., 89, 90, 126, 127, 129–30
Kraepelin, E., 5, 35, 204, 278, 286, 287, 296, 311, 342, 537, 543–44, 596, 605, 609, 653, 654, 661–62, 663
  neo-Kraepelinians and, 7–9, 557
Krafft-Ebing, R., 426, 573, 588
Kramer, R. M., 352
Krasner, L., 448
Kreitman, N., 14–15
Krell, L., 430
Kremen, W. S., 352
Kretschmer, E., 35, 488, 506–7, 524, 529, 530, 544, 588, 654, 657
Krishnan, K. R. R., 457
Kroll, J., 633, 635
Kroner, D., 563–64
Kropp, P. R., 562
Krukonis, A. B., 545
Krystal, A. D., 391
Krystal, J. H., 152, 157
K-strategy, 512
Kuch, K., 93, 99
Kuck, J., 316
Kuehenl, T. G., 315, 323, 330
Küfferle, B., 353
Kuhl, J., 218
Kuhn, L., 316
Kuhn, T., 508
Kuiper, N. A., 214
Kulka, R. A., 148
Kullgren, G., 562, 563
Kultermann, J., 555
Kupfer, D. J., 14, 391, 393, 398, 399
Kutchins, H., 7
Kuyken, W., 150–51
Kwapil, T. R., 71, 618, 619–20
Kwee, M. G. T., 84

laam (L-alpha-acetylmethadol), 263
Laasi, N., 315
labeling theory, 7, 8
Labouvie, E., 229
Lacey, B. C., 68
Lacey, J. I., 68
Ladha, B., 587
Ladouceur, R., 132
Lahey, B., 256, 569
Lakatos, I, 508, 515
Lamacz, M., 427–28
lamotrigine, 173
Lampert, C., 372, 373
Landsverk, J., 370–71
Lang, P. J., 83, 157, 499
Langenbucher, J. W., 229, 241
Langevin, R., 426
Langström, N., 562, 563
language
  cognitive development and, 44
  depression and, 210
  psychopathy and processing deficits, 572
  schizophrenia and, 316, 318, 322
Larbig, W., 571
Larsson, H., 608
laryngospasm, 400
Lasch, C., 680
Lasègue, C., 367
Lasko, N. B., 151, 155, 156
latent inhibition, 86
latent schizophrenia, 609, 620
Lauerman, R. J., 229
Laughlin, H. P., 654
Laumann, E. O., 418, 419, 421
La Voie, L., 218
Lavori, P. W., 240
law of initial values, 68
laxative abuse, 365, 366
Laycock, T., 543
Lazare, A., 545
Lazare-Klerman hysteria score, 545
laziness, 590
learned alarms. *See* panic disorder
learned helplessness
  analogue studies, 53, 65
  animal models, 53, 156
  depression and, 168, 190, 216–17, 219
  gender and, 190
  noradrenergic projections and, 168
learning. *See* behavioral models; biosocial learning theory; cognitive development; cognitive models
Leary, T., 33, 500–502, 506, 509, 539, 567, 590–91, 598
Leber, W. R., 204
Lebow, B. S., 618
Leckman, J. F., 130
LEDS (Bedford College Life Events and Difficulties Schedule), 208, 209
Lee, A., 576
Lee, S., 372
legal system, 354–56
Leibenluft, E., 640
Leibniz, G. W., 497
Leiguarda, R., 356
Leinbach, M. D., 431–32

Lelliott, P., 92, 93
Lencz, T., 605, 606, 614
Lenzenweger, M. F., 608, 615, 617, 618, 619
Leone, D. R., 539, 545
Lerer, B., 149
Lerner, H. E., 549
Letarte, H., 132
leukocyte antigens, 189
Leung, F., 380
LeVay, S., 430
Levengood, R. A., 154
Levenston, G. K., 564
Leventhal, B., 256
Levin, B., 149
Levin, R. A., 590
Levine, M. P., 380, 381
Levine, P. E., 668
Levy, A., 347
Levy, D. L., 618
Lewine, R. J., 320
Lewinsohn, Peter, 210–11
Lewis, G., 663
Lewis, J. A., 320, 323
Lewis, V. G., 430
Lewisohn Revised Integrative Model of Depression, 211
Lewisohn's Behavioral Model of Depression, 210–11
lexical hypothesis (personality factor models), 490–94
Ley, R., 92, 104
L'Heureux, F., 369
libido, 451, 682, 685
Lichtermann, D., 608
Lieberman, J. A., 293, 294, 614
Liebowitz, M. R., 54, 90, 98, 116, 123, 458
Lief, H., 413
life event models (stress-related)
  bipolar disorder and, 353
  borderline personality disorder and, 640–44
  conversion disorder and, 448, 449
  depression and, 125, 190, 192, 207–10, 211–13, 217
  dissociative fugue and, 478
  eating disorders and, 368
  gender and, 190
  generalized anxiety disorder and, 117, 125
  narcolepsy and, 395
  obsessive-compulsive disorder and, 127, 131–32, 134
  panic attacks and, 93
  paranoid conditions and, 353, 356
  primary insomnia and, 392, 393
  schizophrenia and, 353
  somatization disorder and, 447
  substance abuse and, 256, 257–58
  traumatic. *See* traumatic stressor
life form rank (folk classification), 19
lifestyle impairment
  generalized anxiety disorder and, 116–17
  obsessive-compulsive disorder and, 127
life-threatening event. *See* traumatic stressor
Lilenfeld, L. R., 615
Lilienfeld, S. O., 557
limbic system, 168, 170, 177, 180, 184
  borderline personality disorder and, 637
  generalized anxiety disorder and, 125
  kindling and, 157
  posttraumatic stress disorder and, 155, 156, 157
  schizophrenia and, 295, 296
Lin, R., 148
Linehan, M. M., 637, 641, 643
Link, B. G., 208
linkage (gene) studies, 64–65, 285–86, 302
  attentional marker deficits, 300
Links, P. S., 641
Linnaeus, Carolus, 4, 5
Lipowsky, Z. J., 446
Lipscomb, T. R., 233
Lipsitz, J. D., 320
lithium, 175, 180, 185, 186, 188
litigiousness, paranoid, 354–55
Litke, A., 232
Litz, B. T., 149
liver disease, 235
Livesley, W. J., 25, 96, 340, 492–93, 494, 525, 533, 536, 631
Locke, B. Z., 239
Locke, J., 232, 497, 498
locus ceruleus, 102, 152, 156, 168, 170, 171, 178, 180
"locus of control" shift, 474
Loeber, R., 256
Loehlin, J. C., 64, 65
Loevinger, J., 16–17
Loftus, E., 467
Loma Prima earthquake (1989), 53
longitudinal studies
  advantages of, 70, 71
  for borderline personality, 633
  for generalized anxiety disorder, 134–35
  high-risk paradigm alternative, 70–72
  incidence and, 58
  pathogenesis and, 30
  for schizoid personality disorder, 532
Lonnqvist, J. K., 642
Lopatka, C., 133
Loranger, A. W., 313, 608, 617, 619, 630, 666
Lord, F. M., 52
Lorr, M., 593, 600
Losel, F., 566
loss events
  borderline personality disorder and, 640–41
  depression and, 208–9, 217
Louis XVI, king of France, 416
Louro, C. E., 89
Louwens, J. W., 318
Loveman, C., 379
low extraversion. *See* introversion
low positive affect. *See* anhedonia
low sexual desire. *See* hypoactive sexual desire disorder
Lowy, M. T., 154
LSD, 295
L-tryptophan, 171
Luchins, D. L., 59–60
Lukach, B. M., 145
Luria, A. R., 264
Lutz, G. M., 236
Lutzker, J. R., 315, 323, 330
Lydiard, R. B., 120
lying, pathological, 677
Lykken, D. T., 66, 67, 557, 569, 570
lymphocyte glucocorticoid receptors, 154
Lynam, D. R., 569
Lyon, D. R., 562
Lyonfields, J. D., 124
Lyons, M. J., 155, 286, 667
Lysaker, P., 322

MacArthur Risk Assessment study, 558
MacCulloch, M. J., 576
MacDonald, M. R., 214
Mace, C. J., 449
Machon, R. A., 280
MacKinnon, R. A., 530
Macklin, M. L., 156
Madakasira, S., 420
Madeddu, F., 639
Madge, N., 639
Maffei, C., 639
Magaro, P., 546
Magical Ideation Scale, 615
magnetic resonance imaging, 69–70, 155, 181, 182, 265, 290–91, 474, 572, 619
magnification, 590
Magnuson, V. L., 430
Maher, B. A., 350, 351, 352
Maier, S. F., 156
Maier, W., 608
Maisto, S. A., 590
maladaptive behaviors, reinforcement patterns of, 498
Malan, J., 95
male erectile disorder, 415–17, 433
male orgasmic disorder, 418, 419, 433
malingering
  abnormal illness behavior and, 458
  dissociative disorders and, 474, 478
  factitious disorder vs., 454
Malinow, K. L., 594
Malleus Maleficarum, 471
Mallinger, A. E., 589
malnutrition
  from eating disorders, 368–69, 371, 374
  maternal prenatal, 280–81, 327
Maltbie, A. A., 457
managed care, 5
Mandeli, J., 237–38, 414
mandrake root, 250
Manfredi, R., 14, 391, 393
mania
  ancient descriptions of, 3
  manic-depressive syndrome similarity, 56
  narcissistic personality disorder and, 681, 682
  neuroendocrine abnormalities, 186–87, 191
manic-depressive psychosis
  Kraepelin labeling of, 5–6, 204, 278
  See also bipolar disorder
manie sans dédlire, 556
manipulativeness
  dependent personality disorder and, 542
  dissociative identity disorder and, 476
  histrionic personality disorder and, 546, 547
  narcissism and, 675, 677
  psychopathy and, 555, 558
Manning, D., 99
Mannuzza, S., 98, 116
MAOI tranylcypromine, 175
Marcus, J., 302
Margolis, E. T., 662
Marie Antoinette, queen of France, 416

marijuana
biochemistry of, 261, 263–64
comorbid depression, 238
differing intoxicating experience, 253
effect expectancies, 234, 264
experimentation with, 255
in gateway model hierarchy, 255
historical use of, 249–50
paraphilias and, 427t
sexual risk taking and, 238
Marino, M. F., 639
marital problems, 208–9
Markow, T., 330
Markowitz, J. S., 96
Marks, I., 90, 93, 99, 105, 147–48
Marmer, C. R., 148
Marmor, J., 545
Marmot, M., 301
Marshall, E., 430
Marten, P. A., 120, 121, 122
Martin, C. E., 421
Martin, F., 237
Martin, L. Y., 116
Martin, N. G., 232–33
Martinez, A., 528, 529
Martunnen, M., 642
Maser, J. D., 81, 104
Masius, W. G., 430
Mask of Sanity, The (Cleckley), 556
masochism
definition of, 664
masochistic personality vs., 664
narcissism and, 685
sexual, 422, 425
See also sadomasochism
masochistic personality disorder. *See* self-defeating (masochistic) personality disorder
Mason, H., 266
Mason, J. W., 154
Masserman, J. H., 6, 241
Masssachusetts Male Aging Study, 416
Masters, W. H., 410, 412, 413, 417, 418, 419, 420
Masterson, J., 641, 681
Mastropaola, J., 352
masturbation, 418, 419, 421
paraphilic fantasy rehearsal, 426, 576
public, 423, 423t
transvestic fetishism, 425
matching (quasi-experimental designs), 52, 71
Maudsley, Henry, 5
Maudsley Obsessional Compulsive Inventory, 119
Maudsley Twin Register, 63
Mayou, R., 459, 460
McBride, M., 563, 564–65
McBurnett, K., 569
McCall, W. V., 391
McCann, J. T., 587, 589, 593, 596, 597, 600
McCanne, T. R., 381
McCarley, R. W., 155
McChesney, C. M., 123
McClearn, G. E., 61
McClough, J. F., 375
McCluskey-Fawcett, K., 380
McCord, J., 569
McCormick, J. A., 330
McCrae, R. R., 490, 492, 591–92, 599
McDonald, J. J., 572
McDougall, J., 684
McDowell, J. J., 450
McElroy, S. L., 346
McFall, M. E., 131
McFall, R. M., 314
McFarland, R. E., 149
McFarlane, A. C., 158, 474
McGillivray, B. C., 285
McGlashan, T. H., 619, 634
McGrew, J., 617
McGuffin, P., 284, 351
McGuire, L. S., 426
McGuire, M., 619
McHugh, P. R., 15
McKenna, P., 351
McLean, P., 660–61
McLeod, D. R., 117, 118
McMillan, D. K., 391
McMullen, L., 546
McNally, R. J., 87, 88, 89, 91, 93, 94, 95, 96, 100, 101, 102, 103, 105, 133, 145, 149–50, 151, 156
McNamee, G., 93
McNamera, H., 379
McNulty, J. L., 493, 615
McPherson, L. M., 561–62
Mealey, L., 566, 567
Means-Ends Problem Solving, 314
measurement model
diagnostic, 22, 23
psychometric research, 54–55
MED. *See* male erectile disorder
medial dorsal nucleus, 170
medial forebrain bundle, 168, 185
mediational model, 35
medical disorder
as diagnostic category, 9
disease vs. illness distinction, 446
generalized anxiety disorder comorbidity, 117
paranoid conditions and, 342, 350
sexual dysfunction from, 411, 417, 418, 419
sick role and, 446, 447, 452, 454, 458–59, 476
sleep disorders and, 401–2
See also somatoform disorders
medical model of illness, 7, 487
classification and, 24
neo-Kraepelinians and, 7–8
See also biological classification
Mednick, S. A., 70, 71, 280, 299, 605
medulla, 168
Medus, C., 618
Meehl, P. E., 38, 39, 51, 52, 55, 57, 58, 60, 71, 489, 606, 608, 610, 611–14, 615, 616, 620
melancholia
ancient descriptions of, 3, 204
diagnostic characterization, 204
hypochondriasis and, 451
Kraepelin classification, 5
mood disorder classification and, 204
melatonin, 184, 187
Mellinger, G. D., 403
Meloy, J. R., 556, 677
Meltzer, H. Y., 295
memory
declarative vs. procedural, 466–67
dissociations, 466–67
dopamine and, 294
fears fueled by, 88, 157
paranoid delusions and, 345, 351
posttraumatic stress disorder and, 150, 155, 156
memory deficits
autobiographical memory and, 150–51, 155
borderline personality disorder and, 638
compulsive checking and, 133
depression and, 151, 215
dissociative disorders and, 369
paranoid schizophrenics and, 352
schizophrenic social skills impairment and, 322–23
sleep apnea and, 395
Mendelian model, 39, 285
meningitis, 134
menopause. *See* postmenopausal women
mental compulsions and obsessions, 125, 126, 127, 129, 130, 131–33
mental diseases and disorders
classification, 13
definition of, 12–13
psychopathy historically as synonym for, 556
mental health professionals, 8
mental ilnesses, 13
MEPS (Means-Ends Problem Solving), 314
Mercer, G., 325
Mercier, H., 563
Merckelbach, H., 83
meritorious, 654
Mesiano, D., 391, 393
mesocortical system, 293, 619
mesocorticolimbic system, 170, 173, 181, 192
bipolar disorder and, 185–86, 192–93
mesolimbic system, 293
drug effects on, 261, 264
mesomorphy, 488, 507
messenger-RNA translation, 174, 177, 178
Messick, S., 16
Messing, M. L., 149
metabolites, 167
Metalsky, G. I., 212, 213, 215, 216
methadone, 263
Metten, P., 260
Metzger, L. J., 151, 156
Meyer, J., 232–33
Meyer, R., 230
Meyer-Bahlburg, H. F. L., 429, 430, 432
MHPG (3-methoxy-r-hydroxy-henylglycol), 102–3, 170, 171, 178
bipolar I disorder and, 185
bipolar II disorder and, 188
Michael, A., 457
Michael, R. T., 418, 419, 421
Michaels, S., 418, 419, 421
Michels, R., 530
Michie, C., 558, 562, 567
Mick, E., 239
Middleton, H., 101
Miele, G. M., 99
Migiorelli, R., 356
"migration" hypothesis, 567
Mikulincer, M., 352–53
Milberger, S., 239
Miller, B. A., 235
Miller, D., 279
Miller, D. A., 380
Miller, G. A., 506, 661, 662
Miller, M. P., 617
Miller, M. W., 564
Miller, S. D., 471

Millon, T., 11, 33, 38, 44, 45, 340, 458, 511, 512, 515, 523, 525, 528, 529, 530, 531, 535, 539–40, 541, 546–47, 547, 555, 556, 573, 574, 575, 577, 585, 586, 588, 592–93, 594, 595, 596, 599, 600, 642, 679, 680, 686
Millon Clinical Multiaxial Inventory-II, 577
Mills, H. E., 576
Mills, K., 445
Minas, I. H., 318
mind-body dualism, 445–46, 449, 456
Mineka, S., 84, 87, 88, 90, 121, 122, 123, 125, 660–61
Minnesota Multiphasic Personality Inventory, 373, 375, 489, 501, 545, 591, 599, 615, 618
Minuchin, S., 378
Mirotznik, J., 208
misidentification syndome, 346
misinterpretations, paranoid, 345, 354
MIS (Magical Ideation Scale), 615
Missel, K., 570
mistrust
  avoidant personality disorder and, 341
  cultural factors, 344, 350–51
  depression and, 344
  negativistic personality disorder and, 593, 600
  paranoid conditions and, 340–41, 342–45
  sexual arousal disorder and, 417
  sexual desire disorders and, 415
Mitchell, J. E., 368
Mitchell, J. N., 432
Mittelman, M., 422
MMPI. *See* Minnesota Multiphasic Personality Inventory
M'Naughton rule, 355
MOD. *See* male orgasmic disorder
modeling
  conversion symptoms and, 448
  as fear acquisition pathway, 86
  hypochondriasis and, 453
  pain behavior and, 450
  personality development and, 41
  substance abuse and, 255–56
Moffitt, T. E., 663
Mohs, R. C., 636
Moldin, S. O., 615
molecular biology, 189, 285, 298
Mollen, N., 232, 258
Mombour, W., 666
Monck, E. M., 327
Money, J., 426, 427–28, 428, 429, 430, 431, 433
mongoloidism, 31
monoamaine oxidase, 189
monoamine abnormalities
  depression and, 170–73
  See also dopamine; norepinephrine; serotonin
monoamine oxidase inhibitors, 175
monomania, 556
monothetic categories, 17, 22
monozygotic twins (identical)
  alcoholism studies, 259
  bipolar disorder studies, 189
  discordance rate and, 65
  eating disorders studies, 372
  homosexuality studies, 430
  nonshared environment and, 65, 71
  obsessive-compulsive disorder rate, 130
  posttraumatic stress disorder studies, 154–55
  schizophrenia studies, 57, 62–63, 65, 71, 282, 283
Monroe, M., 371
Monroe, S. M., 209
mood disorders
  comorbidities, 117, 128, 130, 368–69, 632
  depressive personality disorder and, 657–58, 664
  depressive temperament and, 654, 661, 664
  as diagnostic category, 204
  dissociative identity disorder and, 460
  diversity of, 203
  eating disorders and, 368–69, 373
  expressed emotion and, 328
  familial liability to, 662
  generalized anxiety disorder and, 114, 121–22, 123–24, 125
  hierarchical ranking, 23
  negativistic personality disorder and, 595
  neuroses reclassification under, 445
  obsessive-compulsive disorder as variant of, 128, 130
  paraphilia comorbidity, 427, 427t
  as posttraumatic stress disorder risk factor, 146, 148
  schizophrenic diagnostic boundaries with, 286
  self-defeating (masochistic) personality disorder and, 667
  sleep/wake disorders and, 398–99, 404
  substance-related comorbidity, 240
  tripartite model of, 121–23
  See also bipolar disorder; depression; dysthymia
mood fluctuations, 190–91
mood-temperament, personality disorders and, 517ff, 518–19
Moore, D., 316, 598
moral development, classical theories of, 32
Morales, J., 669
moral insanity, 556
moral masochism, 655, 665
Moras, K., 116, 119
Morey, L. C., 14, 21, 230, 595, 681
Morgan, C. A., 152
Morganville, J., 316
Morgenstern, J., 229
Moridaira, J., 313
Morokoff, P. J., 418–19
morphine, 264, 265
morphologic organization, 518
Morrell, W., 372, 373
Morrison, J., 447
Morrison, R. L., 314, 316, 317, 318, 324, 329
Morselli, E., 453
Morton, T., 367
Moss, H. B., 237
motor development dysfunction, 301–2
motor symptoms, pseudoneurological, 448
Motor Tension and Vigilance and Scanning clusters, 120, 121
Mowrer, O. H., 85, 131, 156
MPQ. *See* Multidimensional Personality Questionnaire
MRI (magnetic resonance imaging), 69–70, 155, 181, 182, 265, 290–91, 474, 572, 619
Mueller, T. I., 240
Mueser, K. T., 313, 315, 316, 317, 318, 324, 329
Mulder, R. T., 642
Muller, J. J., 683
Mulloy, R., 562
multiaxial classification system, 9, 10–11
  Axis I vs. Axis II, 11, 33–36
  taxonomic pathogenesis and, 30–36
Multidimensional Personality Questionnaire, 375, 376
multiple personality. *See* dissociative identity disorder
multiple sclerosis, 181
multiple syndromes, construct validity, 56
multitrait-multimethod matrix, 16
Münchhausen by-proxy syndrome, 454
Münchhausen syndrome, 454, 455
Munoz, R., 11, 557
Munro, J., 376
murderers, psychopathic and sadistic, 574, 575, 576, 577
Murphy, D., 324
Murphy, D. L., 369
Murphy, K. C., 351
Murphy, M. R., 455
Murray, H., 683
Murray, R., 301, 663
Murrell, S. A., 115
muscle tension, 114, 120, 121
Musetti, L., 662, 664
mushrooms, hallucinogenic, 249, 250
mutilation. *See* self-mutilation
mutilation anxiety, 427
myhrr, 250
Myles-Worsley, M., 300
MZ twins. *See* monozygotic twins

NA. *See* noradrenergic system
Näcke, P., 682
Nagoshi, C. T., 240
Nagy, L. M., 152
naloxone, 153, 263
naltrexone, 263
Nanko, S., 313
Napolean Bonaparte, 416
narcissistic personality disorder, 674–89
  age and, 678, 680
  antisocial features of, 677
  biosocial-learning theory and, 683, 686–89
  borderline features of, 497, 677–78, 681
  case vignettes, 676–77, 687, 688–89
  clinical description of, 675
  clinical presentations of, 675–78, 679
  comorbidity, 680, 681
  corrective factors, 687–89
  course and prognosis, 686–87
  definition of, 674–75
  diagnosis, 676, 678–79, 683
  diagnostic overlap, 680
  differential diagnosis, 681–82
  functional and structural attributes of personality, 517ff
  gender and, 679
  historical perspectives, 682–83
  histrionic personality disorder and, 543
  negativistic personality disorder and, 594, 595
  normal narcissism vs., 674, 684
  obsessive-compulsive personality disorder and, 512, 587, 681, 682

narcissistic personality disorder (*continued*)
paranoid conditions and, 341
personality types and, 683, 685
prevalence of, 679
psychoanalytic perspective, 683–86
psychopathy and, 560, 568
sadistic personality disorder and, 575
self orientation and, 512
subtypes, 686
superego and, 496
symptoms, 678
Narcissistic Personality Inventory, 675
narcolepsy, 391, 394–95, 398, 400
narrow heritability, definition of, 61
Nasca culture, 250
Nash, J. F., 295
Nathan, P. E., 229, 233, 236, 241
National Alcohol Survey (1984), 232
National Comorbidity Survey, 95, 157, 206
generalized anxiety disorder, 115, 116, 117
posttraumatic stress disorder, 146, 147, 148–49
National Council on Measurement in Education, 15
nationality, depression and, 207
National Longitudinal Alcohol Epidemiologic Study (1992), 232
National Survey of Psychotherapeutic Drug Use, 403
National Vietnam Veterans Readjustment Study, 146–47, 148
natural disasters, 53, 145, 468
natural environment phobias, 82, 83
nature vs. nurture. *See* environmental factors; family history and system; genetic factors
NCS. *See* National Comorbidity Survey
NE. *See* norepinephrine
Neale, J. M., 348
Neale, M. C., 84–85, 123, 232, 232–33, 259, 373
necrophilia, 426
neediness, 524
nefazodone, 175
Neff, C., 608, 663
negative affectivity
in anxiety and depression tripartite model, 121, 122–23
anxious apprehension and, 118, 123
depressive personality as, 660
generalized anxiety disorder and, 114, 121, 123, 124, 125, 135
as obsessive byproduct, 132
See also neuroses and neuroticism
negative information processing, depression and, 211, 213–15, 216, 218
negative life events. *See* life events model
negativistic personality disorder (passive-aggressive), 593–600
ambivalence and, 512
characteristics and core features, 593–94, 596, 597
contemporary theoretical perspectives, 596–600
depressive personality disorder and, 659, 660
differential diagnosis, 594
functional and structural attributes of personality, 517ff
historical perspectives, 595–96
internally conflicted style, 585
narcissistic personality disorder and, 680, 681
obsessive-compulsive personality disorder and, 512, 585–86, 601
prevalence of, 594–95
self-defeating (masochistic) personality disorder and, 667, 668
neglect cases. *See* childhood neglect
Neki, J. S., 537
Nelson, C. B., 146, 147, 148, 149
neo-conditioning, fears and phobias, 88–89, 90
neocortex, 156, 294
neo-Kraepelinian movement, 7–9, 557
NEO Personality Inventory, 492, 493, 591
Neufeld, R. W. J., 352
neural circuits, 157, 181, 295–96, 568
neurobiological perspective. *See* biological model
neurochemicals. *See* neurotransmitters; *specific types*
neurocognition, schizophrenia and, 286–92, 321–26, 357n.4
neurogenetic mode of, alcoholism, 230–31, 232, 234
neuroimagery, 265, 618–19
neuroleptic drugs, 293, 302
neurology, 5, 448
neuromotor abnormality, 299, 301–2
neuromuscular deconditioning, 459
neurons, 507
neuropeptides, 192
neurophysiological factors, 73, 167–73
abbreviations table, 167
anxiety and depression and, 125
borderline personality disorder and, 637–38
conversion disorder and, 449
narcissistic personality disorder and, 685
obsessive-compulsive disorder and, 133–34
panic disorder and, 100, 103–4
of personality and temperament, 506–10
psychopathy and, 568, 570, 571–72
substance abuse and, 233, 234
neuropsychology
cognition and, 287–92
definition of, 286
dissociative identity disorder and, 474
eating disorders and, 374
schizophrenia model, 357n.4
substance abuse studies, 265–66
neuroradiological abnormalities, 181–83
neuroreceptors, 166, 167, 292, 294
second-messenger systems and, 173–75, 192
neuroses and neuroticism
addictive personality and, 258
borderline level, 496, 635, 677
depressive personality and, 660
DSM reclassification, 444–45
as earlier somatoform disorder classification, 444–45, 448
fears and, 84
in Five-Factor model, 591, 599
hierarchical ranking, 23
hysterical personality and, 497
introduction of concept, 5
negativistic personality disorder and, 599
panic attacks and, 93
paraphilia and, 427
as personality organization level, 258, 496–97, 498f
posttraumatic stress disorder and, 147
substance abuse and, 258
See also negative affectivity
neurotransmitters, 46, 73, 231, 241
affective disorders and, 166, 167–73
definition of, 167, 292
eating disorder/mood disorder overlap and, 368
eating disorders and, 373–74
endogenous cannaboid, 264
generalized anxiety disorder and, 125
obsessive-compulsive disorder and, 133
panic disorder and, 102–3
personality disorders and, 637
personality trait dispositions and, 507
schizophrenia and, 292–94
schizotypal personality, 612, 619
second-messenger systems and, 173–75, 192
See also specific types
neutralizing behavior, obsessive-compulsive, 131, 132–33
Neville, D., 458
Newhill, C. E., 343
Newlin, D., 259
Newman, D. L., 663
Newman, J. P., 570–71
Newman, L., 324
Newton, J. R., 376
New York High Risk Project, 300, 320, 323
New Zealand, 6
depression rate, 207
NGRI (not guilty by reason of insanity), 355
Nicholls, T. L., 563
Nichols, J. M., 237
Nicolaou, A., 152
nicotine
dependence, 231, 264, 265
as highly addictive, 264
receptor gene-schizophrenia link, 300
sleep/wake disturbances and, 402, 403
See also smoking
Nietzsche, F. W., 573
Nigeria, depression rate, 207
nightmares
cause-and-effect relations research, 53
as diagnostic disorder, 391, 396–98
posttraumatic stress disorder and, 144, 149, 153, 157, 400
night terrors, 391, 397–98
alcohol abuse and, 402
nocturnal panic vs., 93, 400
nigrostriatal system, 170, 293
NIMH Epidemiologic Catchment Area Study (1984), 231–32
Nisenson, L., 326, 328
Nishith, P., 324
NMDA receptor (N-methyl-D-aspartate), 173, 263, 294
"Nobel prize complex," 683
nocturnal myoclonus, 153
nocturnal panic, 93, 400

nocturnal penile tumescence, 414, 417
Nolen-Hoeksema, S., 53, 190
nomenclature, 4, 6
nomological network, 55–56
nomothetic research design, 50, 51
nonadditive genetic influences, 61
non-REM sleep, nocturnal panic and, 93, 400
nonsensical images and impulses, 129
nonshared environmental influences, 65, 71, 85
noradrenergic system
  bipolar I depression and, 185, 186
  depression and, 168, 171
  generalized anxiety disorder and, 125
  hyperactivity and panic disorder and, 102–3
  pathway, 169f
  posttraumatic stress disorder and, 152–53, 156
Norden, K. A., 668–69
norepinephrine, 292
  affective disorders and, 167, 192, 637
  alcoholism and, 231
  bipolar depression and, 185
  bipolar II disorder and, 188
  depression and, 168, 170–71, 178, 179, 180, 368
  eating disorders and, 368, 373–74
  panic disorder and, 102
  posttraumatic stress disorder and, 152, 156
  receptors, 156
  schizophrenia and, 294
normality
  boundary between illness and, 8
  developmental pathogenesis and, 29, 498f
  psychoanalytic concept of, 496
North, C. S., 469
Norton, G. R., 81, 95, 97, 104, 471
NOS diagnosis, 15
"not guilty by reason of insanity," 355
Novacek, J., 675
novelty seeking. *See* sensation-seeking trait
Nowak, J., 155
Nowlis, D., 634
Noyes, R., 97, 123, 587
NPD. *See* narissistic personality disorder
NPI (Narcissistic Personality Inventory), 675
nucleus accumbens, 170, 180, 261, 263, 264, 295
Nuechterlein, K. H., 300, 315, 323, 330
nuisance variables, 52
numerical taxonomy, 17, 18–19, 22
Nurnberg, H. G., 668
NVVRS (National Vietnam Veterans Readjustment Study), 146–47, 148

Obiols, J. E., 618
object relations theory, 500, 684
  dependency model, 538, 539
  dissociative identity disorder and, 473
  negativistic personality disorder and, 597
  schizoid concept, 529–30
object representations, 518
O'Brien, G. T., 116
obscene phone calls, 423t, 426
obsessional slowness, 129
obsessions
  characterization and common types of, 129
  cognitive appraisal models, 131
  criteria for, 127
  definition of, 125, 126
  delusional, 134
  delusions vs., 126–27, 135n.2
  first use of term, 588
obsessive-compulsive disorder (Axis I), 125–35
  anxiety reduction and, 120
  body dysmorphic disorder and, 130, 458
  characterization of, 129–30
  cognitive styles of, 132–33, 135
  comorbidities, 128, 130, 458
  conceptual models of, 131–34
  definition of, 125–26
  depression linked with, 128
  diagnosis criteria, 126–27
  diagnostic reliability, 128
  eating disorder structural similarity, 369, 371
  empirical basis for, 130
  epidemiology, 127–28
  future research directions, 134–35
  generalized anxiety disorder autonomic symptoms vs., 120
  generalized anxiety disorder as closest construct, 122, 130
  generalized anxiety disorder differentiated from, 119–20
  genetic factors, 130, 134
  gradual onset of, 127
  nightmare content and, 396
  obsessive-compulsive personality disorder vs., 587–88, 593
  overview and history of, 125–27, 131
  paraphilias and, 421, 427, 427t
  self-recognition factor, 126
  sleep/wake disorders and, 399
  subclinical symptoms, 127
  symptoms, 127, 130, 133
  "waxing and waning" course of, 127
obsessive-compulsive personality disorder (Axis II), 586–93
  characteristic traits of, 585, 586, 588, 589, 590, 593, 659
  contemporary theoretical perspectives, 588–93
  core feature of, 586, 587
  depressive personality disorder and, 659, 660
  functional and structural attributes of personality, 517ff
  historical perspectives, 588
  histrionic personality disorder and, 543
  internally conflicted style of, 585
  narcissistic personality disorder and, 512, 587, 681, 682
  negativistic personality disorder and, 512, 585–86, 601
  obsessive-compulsive disorder vs., 587–88, 593
  prevalence of, 587–88
obstructive actions, 594
obstructive sleep apnea, 395
Obuchowski, M., 299
occupational factors, pain syndromes and, 451
OCD. *See* obsessive-compulsive disorder
Ochoa, E., 353
OCPD. *See* obsessive-compulsive personality disorder
Odbert, H. S., 491, 493
odd-eccentric personality disorders cluster, 610
O'Donnell, J. P., 84
Oedipal fixation, 545
Oetting, E. R., 255
Ogata, S. N., 640, 641
Ogloff, J. R. P., 563, 565
O'Gorman, T. W., 232
O'Hara, B., 259
O'Hare, A., 619
Ohman, A., 87
Ohta, H., 155
Okyere, E., 445
Oldham, J. M., 587, 668
O'Leary, T. A., 117–18
Olincy, A., 300
Olinger, L. J., 214
Oliveau, D., 451
Ollendick, T. H., 83
Olmsted, M., 381
Olney, J. W., 294
Olsen, S. A., 279
Oltmanns, T. F., 347
O'Malley, P. M., 264
"On Narcissism" (Freud), 682–83
Ono, Y., 666
ontogenetic parade, 82
operant conditioning, 41
  deviant arousal and, 426
  fear maintenance and, 85–86, 88
  psychological pain and, 449, 450
opiate antagonists, 153, 156, 263
opiates
  paraphilias and, 427t
  See also drug abuse; *specific kinds*
opioid-mediated stress-induced analgesia, 153
opioid receptors, 263
opium, 149, 249, 250, 263
oppositional-defiant disorder, 595
oral dependent person, 537, 538, 597
orality, histrionicity and, 545
oral-sadistic character complex, 596
oral stage, 495, 496, 538, 596
Oram, G., 562
orbitofrontal cortex, 134, 170, 181
order (biological classification), 17
orderliness
  depressive personality disorder and, 654, 659
  obsessive-compulsive personality disorder and, 586, 588, 589, 592, 659
Orford, D. H., 509
orgasmic disorders, 410, 411, 412–13, 418–20, 433
Orr, S. P., 152, 153, 155–56, 157
Orr-Urtreger, A., 300
Orsillo, S. M., 149
Ortmeyer, D., 545
Osborn, C., 422
O'Shaughnessy, R., 563, 564–65
Osler, William, 249
Ossorio, A. G., 500
Ost, L.-G., 87
Ostendorf, F., 490–91
Østergard, L., 63
Othello syndrome, 345

other orientation, 512
Ottosson, J. O., 10
Ouellette, R., 96
overarousal, chronic, 118
overdoses, borderline personality and, 628, 634
overeating, bulimic, 366
Overholser, J. C., 528, 599
overprotected children
  avoidant personality disorder and, 527–28, 532
  dependent personality disorder and, 540, 541
  eating disorders and, 368, 378
  hypochondriasis and, 452
  personality development of, 43
over-the-counter medications, 254, 402
Owen, M. J., 351
Oyebode, F., 445
Ozmen, E., 147–48

pain
  chronic, biopsychological theory of, 450–51, 459
  chronic vs. acute, 449
  major depression relationship, 457
  serotonin and perception of, 261
  sexual disorders marked by, 411, 420–21, 433
  as somatization disorder symptom, 446, 456, 457
pain behavior, 450
pain disorder, 444, 445, 449–51, 456, 457, 458, 459
Paker, M., 147–48
Paker, Ö., 147–48
Palazolli, M., 378
Pallmeyer, T. P., 151
Palmer, R, 367
Pålson, N., 451
pandysmaturation index, 301
panic attacks
  difinition and characterization of, 90
  fear of, 91, 118
  Freudian description of, 99
  nocturnal vs. wakefulness, 400
  posttraumatic stress disorder yohimbine-induced, 152
  prevalence of, 95
  provocation experiment, 100
  social phobias and, 98
  suffocation false alarm and, 104
  vs. panic disorder, 95
panic disorder, 81, 91–105
  with agoraphobia, 82, 90–91, 93–95, 98–99, 104–5, 128
  as alcoholism risk, 257
  anxiety sensitivity and, 89–90, 102, 115, 118
  comorbidities, 96–99, 117, 124, 128, 257, 262, 341
  contemporary approaches to, 100–104
  diagnostic criteria, 95
  eating disorder comorbidity, 369
  generalized anxiety disorder autonomic symptoms vs., 120, 121
  generalized anxiety disorder comorbidity, 117, 124
  generalized anxiety disorder familial aggregation vs., 123
  generalized anxiety disorder onset vs., 117
  hallmark feature of, 91
  heterogeneity issue, 92
  historical perspective, 99–100
  nocturnal, 93
  obsessive-compulsive disorder and, 128
  obsessive features of, 120
  onset of, 93, 95
  paranoid conditions and, 341
  paraphilias and, 427t
  posttraumatic stress disorder comorbidity, 148
  prevalence and course, 95–96
  sleep/wake disorders and, 399–400
  somatoform disorder diagnostic overlap, 457–58
  spontaneity of onset, 93, 94, 95, 99, 104
  traumatic stressor and, 145
Pantzar, J. T., 285
Panzarella, C., 326
paralinguistic behaviors. *See* speech patterns
parallel distributed processing (PDP) models, 72
paralysis, pseudoneurological, 448
paranoid conditions, 339–56
  amphetamine abuse and, 236
  ancient descriptions of, 3
  antisocial personality disorder and, 341–42
  anxiety and, 341
  avoidant personality disorder and, 341
  case vignette, 345
  cocaine abuse and, 356
  comorbidities, 341, 609
  delusions and, 345–52
  descriptive and behavioral features, 339–40, 355
  diagnostic boundaries, 342–45, 347–48
  differential diagnosis and history, 340–42
  "double awareness phase," 341
  family factor, 353–54
  forensic issues, 354–56
  functional and structural attributes of personality, 517ff
  histrionic personality disorder and, 543
  medical conditions as contributing factor to, 342
  multiple pathways to, 356
  narcisstic personality disorder and, 341, 680, 681, 682
  obsessive-compulsive personality disorder and, 587
  phenomenology of, 619
  risk factors, 356
  sadistic personality disorder and, 573
  schizophrenia probands and, 617
  stress and, 353
  theoretical perspectives, 348–54
paranoid personality disorder, 606, 607
paraphilias, 410, 421–23
  description of, 422–23, 433
  DSM-I grouping, 227
  etiological and developmental factors, 426–28
  narcissism linked with, 682
  psychopathy and, 563–66, 577
  sadistic personality disorder and, 573, 574, 576–77
parasomnias, 391, 396–98, 402
Parental Representations Scale, 539
parentheses, 426
parenting styles
  avoidant personality disorder and, 527–28, 532
  borderline personality disorder and, 641–42, 643, 644
  childhood conduct problems and, 569
  dependent personality disorder and, 537, 538, 539, 540
  depressive personality and, 663
  eating disorders and, 378–80
  gender identity disorder and, 432
  histrionic personality disorder and, 547
  hypochondriasis and, 452–53
  narcissistic personality disorder and, 685
  negativistic personality disorder and, 594, 597
  obsessive-compulsive personality disorder and, 589, 590
  paranoid conditions and, 353
  personality development and, 40, 41, 42–43, 44–45, 46, 497, 529–30
  psychogenic mid-twentieth-century attributions to, 60, 280
  schizoid personality disorder and, 531–32
  schizophrenia and, 60, 280, 326–27
  self-defeating (masochistic) personality disorder and, 669
  as shared vs. nonshared environmental influences, 65
  somatoform disorders and, 445
  substance abuse and, 256
  superego development and, 496
  See also childhood physical/sexual abuse; overprotected children
Paris, J., 32, 634
Park, S., 618
Parker, D. A., 238
Parkinson, L., 125
Parkinsonian symptoms, 279, 293
partialism, 424
PAS. *See* Perceptual Aberration Scale; Premorbid Adjustment Scale
"passing" (sexual), 429
passive-aggressive label, 537, 585, 594, 595, 596
passive-aggressive personality disorder. *See* negativistic personality disorder
passive resistance, 593
passivity, 525, 541, 655, 540
pathogenesis. *See* developmental pathogenesis
pathological lying, narcissistic, 677
pathological personality domain. *See* personality disorders
pathological worry
  boundary between normal and, 119
  generalized anxiety disorder and, 121, 123–25
  models of nature and functions of, 124–25
  models of origins of, 125
  See also anxiety disorders; generalized anxiety disorder
pathoplasty model, 35–36
Patrick, C. J., 563, 564
Pattatucci, A. M., 430
Patterson, G. R., 32
Paty, J., 231
Pauls, D. L., 130
Pavlov, I. P., 85, 86, 498

Pawlak, A., 422
Paykel, E. S., 208
PCL-R. *See* Hare PCL-R
PCP (phencycladine), 263, 294
PDA. *See* panic disorder, with agoraphobia
PDE (Personality Disorders Examination), 630, 666
PDP models, 72
PDQ-R (Personality Diagnostic Questionnaire—Revised), 545
PDs. *See* personality disorders
PE. *See* premature ejaculation
Peabody, D., 492
Peake, P. K., 217
Pearson, J. S., 299
pedophilia, 421, 422, 423t, 424–25, 427
  sadistic personality disorder and, 574
peer group norms, 43, 233–34, 254–55
Pelcovitz, D., 147
pelvic inflammatory disease, 420
penile erection, 410, 411, 412
  male erectile disorder, 415–16, 433
penis envy, 545
Penn, D. L., 324, 325
Pennebaker, J. W., 452
Penn State Worry Questionnaire, 119, 121
Pepper, C. M., 669
Perceptual Aberration Scale, 615, 618, 619
Perdue, S., 302
perfectionism
  body dysmorphic disorder and, 454
  depression and, 218
  depressive personality disorder and, 653, 659
  narcissistic, 685
  narcissistic and obsessive-compulsive, 682
  obsessive-compulsive personality disorder and, 586, 589, 590, 591, 659
performance anxiety (sexual), 417, 419
performance standards, depression and, 217
period prevalence, 58
Peri, T., 148
periventricular area, 181
Perley, M. J., 447
Perris, C., 10
Perry, C. P., 682
Perry, J. C., 639, 640
Perry, W., 316
persecutory delusions
  Alzheimer's patients and, 356
  dissociative identity disorder and, 474
  litigousness and, 355
  misattributional, 350–51
  paranoid condition and, 346, 347, 349
  paranoid criterion, 348
  schizophrenia and, 279
  shared psychotic disorder, 343–44
  violence and, 355
Persian Gulf War, 145–46
Persico, A., 259
persistent anxiety. *See* generalized anxiety disorder
personality
  categorical vs. dimensional models of, 487–90, 487t
  definition of, 33, 510, 519
  depressive personality and normal dimensions, 660–61
  domains of, 37–46, 513–19
  factor models of, 490–94, 567, 591
  five levels of, 509
  historical meanings of, 510
  imbalanced, 513
  normal characterization, 496
  organizational levels, 497, 498f
  personology vs., 511
  profile, 489
  theoretical perspectives, 494–510
  See also personality development; personality disorders; personality traits; personality type
Personality Adjective Checklist, 591
Personality Assessment Inventory, 679
personality development, 36–47
  alternative attachments and, 643
  assessment methodology, 490–94
  attachment and autonomy, 42–43
  behavioral models, 40–42, 46, 490, 496, 497–99, 515
  biophysical influences, 38–40, 46, 60–64
  cognitive models, 43–44, 490, 503–6, 515, 516
  competition and, 45–46
  dual influences on, 60, 64
  ecological factors and, 36–37, 44–46
  evolutionary theory of, 37–38, 511–19, 540
  fears and, 82–83
  gender identity disorder and, 433
  generalization and discrimination, 41
  incidental learning, 41
  innate temperament and, 40
  insufficient learning, 42
  interpersonal aspects, 42–43, 490, 499–503, 509, 510, 515, 516
  modeling and, 41
  narcissistic personality disorder and, 685–86
  obsessive-compulsive disorder vulnerability and, 134
  obsessive-compulsive personality disorder and, 588–89
  psychodynamic models, 495–97, 529–30
  psychopathy and, 569–70
  self-image and, 43, 46
  temperament and, 39–40, 506
Personality Diagnostic Questionnaire—Revised, 545
Personality Disorder Examination, 630, 666
personality disorders, 485–519
  assessment methodology, 490–94
  assessment reliability, 21
  Axis I boundaries and, 485
  classifications controversies, 32, 33, 485–86
  cognitive models and, 505–6
  cognitive therapies and, 504–5
  complexity of development of, 37–38
  definitional history, 556
  depressive personality disorder and, 658–60, 664
  developmental relationship between Axis I and II, 33–36
  diagnostic boundaries and criteria disagreement, 485
  diagnostic criteria and sex biases, 666–67
  diagnostic prototypes, 22, 25, 32, 33, 487–90
  DSM-IV overlap diagnoses, 15, 32
  eating disorder high-rate comorbidity, 368, 370–71
  factitious disorder and, 455
  factor models, 491t, 492–94
  generalized anxiety disorder associated with, 117
  hierarchical dignostic clusters, 23
  interpersonally imbalanced and conflicted, 513, 513f
  mechanism, content, and taxonomy, 32–36
  models of, 35, 495–510, 513f
  narcissistic comorbidity, 680–81
  narcissistic subtypes, 683, 686
  negativistic, 585–86, 593–601
  neurobiological model, 507–8, 508f
  neurotic vs. psychotic, 677
  obsessive-compulsive, 585–93
  obsessive-compulsive disorder comorbidity, 128
  paraphilias and, 427
  paraphilias formerly classified as, 421
  polarity model, 514f, 515
  psychodynamic models, 495–97
  psychopathy and, 555–72
  psychosexual development and, 496
  sadistic personality disorder, 572–77
  somatoform disorders and, 458
  See also paranoid conditions; schizotypic psychopathology
Personality Disorders Examination, 323
Personality Pathology Five-PSY-5, 615
personality traits
  definition of, 37, 489, 503
  dimensional model and, 489–90
  etiology research, 37
  factor models, 490–94, 540, 591
  Freudian psychosexual developmental stages and, 495
  histrionic, 542
  lexical hypothesis, 494
  neurobiological models, 506–10
  obsessive-compulsive, 586, 587, 588, 589, 590–91
  passive-aggressive, 586
  psychopathy as variant, 567–68
  substance abuse and, 258
personality type
  addictive, 258, 369
  alcoholic subtypes and, 231, 234
  classification levels, 496
  dependent personality disorder and, 535–36
  depressive temperament and, 654
  depressive vulnerability and, 217–18
  as diagnostic category, 9, 488–89
  eating disorders and, 369, 373, 375–76
  evolutionary theory and, 512
  expressed emotions and, 328–29
  of food- and drug-abusers, 369
  interpersonal theory and, 490, 499–503, 509, 510, 515, 516, 539–40
  pain-prone, 451
  paraphilias and, 427
  pedophilia and, 424
  phobia specificity and, 84
  primary insomnia and, 393
  schizotypy and, 613
  substance abuse and, 258
  temperament as basis of, 39–40, 506

personalization, paranoid conditions and, 340
personal relations. *See* interpersonal models
Peru, 6
Perugi, G., 662, 664
pervasive worry. *See* generalized anxiety disorder
perversions. *See* paraphilias
pessimism
 depression and, 214
 depressive personality disorder and, 653, 654, 655, 664
 negativistic personality and, 597, 598
 pain-prone personality and, 451
Peterson, E., 146, 147, 149
Peterson, J., 266
Peterson, R. A., 89
Petracca, G., 356
PET scans, 70, 155–56, 181, 265, 293, 474, 619
Pett, M. A., 415
Petursson, H., 64, 285
peyote, 250, 253
Peyronie's disease, 420
Pezzarossa, B., 545
Pfiffner, L., 569
Pfohl, B., 575, 586, 587, 588, 593, 595
phallic stage, 496
phantom limb syndrome, 3351
phencycladine, 263, 294
phenocopies, 39
 definition of, 284
phenotype, definition of, 283
Philip, L., 562
Phillips, B. M., 97
Phillips, K. A., 346, 632, 654, 655, 656, 659–60, 661
phobias and fears, 81–90
 anxiety sensitivity and, 89–90, 115
 common, 82–83
 dissociative identity disorder as, 473
 fundamental fears, 89
 generalized anxiety disorder autonomic symptoms vs., 120
 generalized anxiety disorder comorbidity, 117
 genetic and environmental factors, 84–85
 hypochondriasis and, 457–58
 nonrandom distribution of, 88
 obsessive-compulsive, 128, 129, 130, 131
 panic attacks and, 100, 104
 prevalence and course, 82–84
 theories of, 85–90, 131, 156–58
 types and subtypes, 82, 89
 weight-gain, 365, 369, 378
 See also agoraphobia; panic disorder
"phobic character," 530
phosphatidylinositol, 173, 182
phosphoinositide hydrolysis, 174
phospholipid, 174
phosphorus metabolism, 182
phrenology, 39
phrenophobia, 89
phylum, 17
physical abuse. *See* childhood physical/sexual abuse; violence
Physical Anhedonia Scale, 318
physical characteristics
 gender identity disorder and, 431
 histrionic personality disorder related with, 542
 psychopathology related with, 506–7
physical compulsions, 125
physical conditions. *See* medical disorder
physical symptoms. *See* somatoform disorders
physiological hyperarousal, anxiety disorders and, 121
physiological psychology. *See* psychophysiology
Physique and Character (Kretschmer), 654
Piaget, J., 32, 504
Pickens, R., 259
Pickersgill, M. J., 83
Piggott, T. A., 369
Pihl, R., 266
Pilkonis, P. A., 532
Pilowsky, I., 457, 458–59
Pincus, A. L., 500, 591, 598–99
Pincus, H. A., 81, 99
pineal gland, 184, 187
Pine, D., 104, 562
Pinkham, L., 636
Pitman, R. K., 151, 152, 153, 155–56, 157
pituitary gland, 153, 173, 177, 180, 414
Plakun, E. M., 679, 681, 687
Planansky, K., 317
Planck, M. K. E. L., 515
Plato, 486
Platt, J. J., 314–15
pleasure deficiency, 611
Pliszka, S., 569
Plomin, R., 61
pneumoencephalogram, 69
point prevalence, 58
political dissidents, 146, 147–48, 158
political paranoia, 344
Polivy, J., 366, 377, 381
Pollack, J., 586, 587, 589
Pollack, S., 668
Pol Pot, 355
polygenic potentiators, 612
polygenic transmissions, 284–85
polygraph, definition of, 66–67
polythetic categories, 17, 22, 23
Pomerleau, C. S., 238
Pomerleau, O. F., 238
Pomeroy, W. B., 421
Pope, H. G., Jr., 346, 666
Popper, K., 72, 508
population genetics, 64–65
Porjesz, B., 232
pornography, 576
positron emission tomagraphy, 70, 155–56, 181, 265, 293, 474, 619
possession states, 471–72
Possl, J., 663
Post, J. M., 344, 348
Post, R. M., 157
posterior temporal gyrus, 291
postmenopausal women, 190–91, 192
 sexual arousal problems, 416
postpartum depression, 180, 190
postpartum thyroid dysfunction, 190
posttraumatic stress disorder, 144–59
 as alcoholism risk factor, 148, 153, 155, 257
 biological aspects, 151–56, 474
 borderline personality disorder and, 633
 cognitive aspects of, 149–51
 comorbidity, 149, 153, 158, 257
 dissociation and, 468
 longitudinal course of, 148–49
 as normal vs. abnormal response, 158–59
 onset of, 148
 prevalence of, 146–47
 qualifying stressor, 145–46, 147
 risk factors, 147–48
 signs and symptoms, 144–45
 sleep disturbances and, 144, 145, 149, 153, 400
 theoretical models, 156–59
 time factor in diagnosis of, 30
Potter, M., 64, 285
poverty. *See* socioeconomic status
PPD. *See* paranoid conditions; paranoid personality disorder
prediction
 as classification function, 4
 validity of, 55
prefrontal cortex, 170, 177, 180, 181, 192, 572, 618, 619
premature ejaculation, 411, 418, 419–20, 433
premenstrual dysphoric disorder, 4
premenstrual syndrome, 4
Premorbid Adjustment Scale, 319
prenatal environment
 drug abuse effects, 256, 257f, 259
 gender identity and, 430, 433
 schizophrenic risk factors, 280–81, 298, 327
 sexual orientation and, 430
Prentky, R. A., 424, 563, 576
preoccupation disorders, somatoform, 445
preparedness theory, phobias and, 86–88
Present State Examination, 12
Presson, C. C., 232
Preston, D., 564
pretentious behavior, 679
Pretzer, J. L., 505
prevalence, definition of, 58. *See also* epidemiology
Pribor, E. F., 447
Price, R. H., 208
primary anorgasmia, 418–19
primary insomnia, 392–94, 399, 403
primary premature ejaculation, 419–20
Prince, R., 668
Prins, A., 151
probabilistic genes, 39
 deterministic genes vs., 39
problem behavior syndrome, 254–55
problem solving
 depression and problems with, 192
 worry as avoidance of, 124
procedural memory, 466–67
procrastination, 590, 593, 597
progesterone, 190
Prohibition, 252
projection
 narcissistic personality and, 677
 paranoia and, 348–49
 schizoid personality and, 531
prolactin, 170, 180
prostate surgery, 417
protein kinases, 173–74
protein phosphyorylation, 174
prototypes, 22
Pruzinsky, T., 124
Przybeck, T. R., 507
PS. *See* schizophrenia, paranoid type
PSD (Psychopathy Screening Device), 569

pseudohermaphroditism, 433
pseudologia phantastica, 454
pseudoneurological symptoms, 448
pseudoneurotic schizophrenia, 610, 635
PSY-5, 493
psychoanalytic theory
borderline personality and, 635
classification and, 8
conversion disorder and, 448
dependent personality disorder and, 535, 537, 539
depressive personality disorder and, 654–55
dissociative identity disorder and, 473, 538–39
histrionic personality disorder and, 535, 543, 544–45
hypochondriasis and, 451
hysteria and, 543
medical model and, 7
narcissistic disorders and, 682–83, 683–86
negativistic personality disorder and, 596–97
of neurotic borderline, 677
nightmare attribution, 397
normality concept, 496
obsessive-compulsive personality disorder and, 586, 588–89
paranoid conditions and, 348, 357n.2
paraphilias and, 426, 427
personality models and, 495–97, 515, 529–30
schizoid personality disorder and, 527
self-defeating (masochsitic) personality disorder and, 664, 665, 668
psychodynamic models of personality, 495–97, 515, 529–30
schizotypic psychopathology, 611–14
psychogenic paranoid psychosis, 353
psychological tests
dimensional model and, 489
reliability evaluation, 13
validity evaluation, 15–16
psychometrics, 54–55
anorexia nervosa studies, 375–76
schizotypy, 607, 607f, 615, 617, 618
psychopathy, 555–72
as adaptation, 566–67
assessment of, 557–60, 577
attachment model, 568–69
as brain dysfunction, 568
as cognitive-affective disorder, 571–72
concept and history, 555–57
criminal behavior vs., 561
defining features of, 555, 556, 558, 560, 568
developmental model, 569–70
fearlessness model, 570, 571
as learning deficit, 570–71
personality organization and, 497
prevalence of, 560
sadistic personality disorder and, 572, 573, 574, 575, 576–77
sociopathy vs., 557
trait model of, 567–68
treatment response, 565–66
Psychopathy Checklist—Revised, 555, 556, 557–60
Psychopathy Screening Device, 569
psychopharmacology
historical, 249–50
as substance-abuse treatment, 261
See also specific drugs and drug types
psychophysiological (psychosomatic) medicine, 66, 412
psychophysiology
depressive personality disorder and, 663–64
eating disorders theory, 381–84
generalized anxiety disorder vulnerability and, 125
hypoactive sexual desire disorder and, 414–15
narcissistic personality disorder and, 685
obsessive-compulsive disorder and, 134
orgasmic disorders and, 419
panic disorder misinterpretations, 101–2, 104
physiological psychology vs., 66
posttraumatic stress disorder and, 151–56, 153–54, 156–57, 158
psychophysiology vs., 66
research methods, 66–70, 73
sexual dysfunctions and, 412, 418
sexual pain disorders and, 420–21
somatization and, 446, 459–60
vs. psychophysiological medicine, 66
psychosexual development
classical theories of, 32
fixation and, 588, 589, 596
personality models and, 495
psychosis. *See* psychotic disorders
Psychosomatic Circle of Sex model, 418
psychosomatic disorders
alexithymia and, 459
traditional definition of, 446
See also somatoform disorders
psychosomatic medicine. *See* psychophysiological (psychosomatic) medicine
psychotherapy, biological boundary of, 191
psychotic disorders
attribution models, 60
borderline personality and, 496, 629, 631, 635
dissociative identity disorder and, 469
melancholia and, 204
narcissism and, 683
obsessive-compulsive disorder vs., 127
personality organization characteristics, 497, 498f, 677
proneness scale, 615
sleep/wake disorders and, 400
See also schizophrenia
psychotic paranoid condition, 341
psychotic-spectrum OCD, 134
psychotropic drugs, 168, 193, 254, 347
sexual arousal disorders and, 417
P3 amplitude, 265
P300 marker
alcohol use and, 69, 233, 237
borderline personality disorder and, 636
functional significance of, 69
PTSD. *See* posttraumatic stress disorder
Puentes-Neuman, G., 380
Pull, C., 666
Pulver, S. E., 674, 683
punitive superego, 655
pupillometer, 67
Putnick, M. E., 618
pyromania, paraphilias and, 427t
Quality of Life Scale, 313–14
Qualtrough, T., 414
quasi-experimental design, 52–53, 54
adoption studies as, 63
Quigley, J. F., 35
Quinlan, D. M., 539
Quinsey, V. L., 562, 564, 576
QUTL mapping, 259

race. *See* African Americans; cultural factors
Racenstein, J. M., 324
Rachman, S., 85, 86, 87, 88, 125, 132, 133
Rado, S., 530, 589, 610, 611, 613, 620
Radovanov, J., 595
Rae, D. S., 15, 239
rage
narcissistic, 678
paranoid conditions and, 340
Raine, A., 605, 606
Ramachandran, G., 232
random sampling, 59
Rank, O., 682
ranks (folk biological classification), 19–20
rape
dissociative amnesia and, 468
paraphilic, 422, 423, 426, 427
psychopathy and, 563, 564
sadistic personality disorder and, 574, 576
sexual desire difficulties, 415
as traumatic stressor, 145, 147, 149, 150, 158
Rapee, R. M., 94, 116
rapid-cycling bipolar disorder, 188, 190, 192
Raskin, M., 668
Raskin, R. N., 674–75
Rasmussen, S. A., 129, 130
Råstam, M., 371
rationalism-empiricism duality, 497–98
Rattenbury, F., 347
Rau, H., 571
Rauch, S. L., 155–56, 156
Raulin, M. L., 615
Raulin, M. R., 70, 71
Rayner, R., 85
RDP (Research Diagnostic Project), 228–29
reaction formation, 496–97
reactive delusional psychosis, 353
reactive gliosis, 296
Reagor, P., 471
reality distortion. *See* delusions; hallucinations
reasoning, distorted, 214
reassurance seeking, 129, 212, 213
receptors. *See* neuroreceptors
records review approach, 61, 62
Redding, C. A., 453
reductionism to the whole, 37
Reed, D., 325
Reeves, P. C., 380
Referential Thinking Scale, 615
Regan, W. M., 448–49
Regier, D. A., 15, 58, 59, 239, 666
regulatory mechanisms, personality and, 516
Reich, J., 341, 529, 666, 668, 669
Reich, R., 683
Reich, W., 32, 495–96, 535, 544, 545, 588, 596, 665, 683, 686
Reichenbach, H., 51

Reichman, J. T., 93
Reiss, S., 89, 102
rejection
avoidant personality fear of, 524, 525
of depressed people, 212, 213
as depression trigger, 217
relationship factors. *See* interpersonal models
reliability
of classification, 13–15, 17, 24
dimensional diagnosis system, 21
as evaluative component, 10
measurement of, 13
psychological test assessment, 13–14
as psychometric issue, 54–55
of respondent-based assessments, 208
three major types, 54–55
religious beliefs
drug use and, 254
medieval holy anorexics, 367
obsessive-compulsive disorder and, 132, 134
pain and, 449
persecution delusions and, 344
sexual dysfunctions and disorders and, 417, 421
remorse, lack of, 556, 558, 560, 573
REM sleep, 153, 173
alcohol use and, 402
bipolar disorder and, 186, 191
cycle duration, 183, 184
depression and, 175, 176, 185, 191, 192, 398–99, 401
general anxiety disorder and, 399
nightmares and, 396
posttraumatic stress disorder and, 400
schizophrenia and, 400
stimulants and, 403
repetitive behaviors, 125, 129, 130
reproduction, 512
reptile phobias, 82, 83
Rescorla, R. A., 88
research, psychopathology
biological aspects of, 166–93
case study methodology, 50–51
cause and effect in, 51–52, 53
cognitive illusions pitfall, 50
computer simulations, 72–73
diagnostic criteria and, 9
epidemiological studies, 57–60
experimental vs. quasi-experimental design, 52–54
GAD and OCD future directions, 134–35
high-risk approaches, 70–72, 297, 298–99, 300, 320–21, 323
longitudinal studies, 30
necessity for designs, 49–50
psychometric issues, 54–55
psychophysiological methods, 66–70
syndrome definition refinement, 55–57
See also animal model studies; longitudinal studies; twin studies; *specific conditions*
Research Diagnostic Project, 228–29
resentment
of depressed person, 212
negativistic personality and, 593, 597, 598, 599, 600
obsessive-compulsive personality and, 586, 589
reserpine, 249
resiliance research, 643, 644
resistance (Freudian term), 357n.2
Resnick, H. S., 147
Resnick, P., 147
respondent-based assessment, 208
response-contingent reinforcement, 210, 211
responsibility
depressive personality, 659
obsessive-compulsive personality, 591
obsessive's inflated sense of, 132–33
Ressler, R., 576
restlessness, generalized anxiety disorder and, 114, 120
restricter eater/binger distinction, 366, 370, 375, 376, 379, 380
restriction fragment length polymorphisms, 285
retina, 184, 187
reuptake, 292
reward dependence, 507, 508f
Rey Auditory Learning Test, 325
Reynolds, C. F., 14, 391, 393, 398, 399
Reynolds, G., 606
RFLPs (restriction fragment length polymorphisms), 285
Rhéaume, J., 132
Riccardi, J., 587–88
Ricci, D. A., 469
Rice, J. P., 155, 240, 615
Rice, M. E., 561, 562–63, 564, 565, 566, 577
Richards, H. C., 379
Richer, P., 543
Rieder, R. O., 614
Rief, W., 457
Riggs, J. M., 541
rigidity
eating disorders/personality disorder and, 371, 378
negativistic personality disorder and, 599
obsessive-compulsive personality disorder and, 586, 587, 588, 589, 590, 592
paranoid conditions and, 340, 587
sadistic personality disorder and, 573
Rinaldi, A., 320, 323
Rinsley, D., 641
Rios, B., 353
Risch, N. J., 286
RISC (Rust Inventory of Schizotypal Cognitions), 615
risk avoidance, 343
risk factors
alcoholism, 258–59, 265, 266, 267f
avoidant and schizoid personality disorders, 527
bipolar disorder, 188
definition of, 29
depression, 188
drug abuse, 254, 256
eating disorders, 383t
high-risk research paradigm, 70–72
paranoid conditions, 356
posttraumatic stress disorder, 147–48, 157, 158
schizophrenia, 280–86, 298–301, 319, 327, 489, 606, 607, 613, 615
Riskind, J. H., 116
risk overestimation, 132
Ritter, J., 216
ritualistic behaviors
anorexic eating habits, 365
obsessive-compulsive, 129, 130, 131–32, 134
rivalry, paranoid conditions and, 340
Robins, E., 11, 54–56, 557, 630
Robins, L. N., 555, 557, 559
Robins, R. S., 344, 348
Robinson, E., 124
Rodgers, B., 301
Rodin, G. M., 454–55
Rofaifo (people), 20
RO15-4513 (experimental drug), 262
Rogers, D., 546
Rogers, R., 561, 563
Rohde, W., 430
Rokous, F., 576
role impairment (diagnostic category), 9
role models, 43
role-playing techniques, 314, 316, 318
Romney, D. M., 591, 598
Ronningstam, E., 677, 679, 680, 681, 682, 687
Rooijmans, H. G. M., 444
Roosevelt, Eleanor, 344
Roosevelt, Franklin Delano, 344
Roper, M. T., 15
Rorschach test, 50
Rosario, M., 238
Roscommon Family Study, 614
Rose, J. S., 232
Rosen, A., 58
Rosen, J. C., 453–54
Rosen, R. C., 411
Rosenfeldt, H., 684
Rosenhan, D., 7, 53
Rosenstock, I. M., 238
Rosenthal, D., 61–62, 63, 524, 610, 614, 616, 617
Rosman, B. L., 378
Rosnick, L., 587
Ross, C. A., 471
Rosse, R. B., 352
Roth, A., 16
Roth, S., 147
Roth, T., 14, 391, 393
Rothbaum, B. O., 89, 148, 156, 158
Rotheram-Borus, M. J., 238
Rothstein, A., 682
Rouleau, J. L., 422, 424
Rounsaville, B., 228, 230, 239, 666
routines, compulsive, 129
R spike (EKG), 68
r-strategy, 512
Rubenstein, C. S., 369
Rubin, S. S., 539
Rubino, I. A., 545
Rubinstein, D., 419
Rudd, R., 537
Rude, S. S., 216
Rudgley, R., 249, 250
rules, compulsive following of, 129
Rush, A. J., 504
Rushton, J. P., 512
Russell, G., 367
Russo, A. J., 429
Rust Inventory of Schizotypal Cognitions, 615
Rutgers University, 228
Rutherford, M., 555
Rutter, M., 10, 57, 59, 560, 639
Rwanda, 344, 355
Ryall, J., 469
Ryan, P., 151

Saarijävi, S., 459
Sabe, L., 356
Sabo, A. N., 633
Sacks, M. H., 341

Sackson, S. W., 166
SAD. *See* seasonal affective disorder; sexual aversion disorder
Sade, Marquis de, 573
Sadeh, A., 539
sadism
coining of term, 573
narcissistic, 677, 678
sexual, 422, 423t, 425, 564, 572, 573, 575–77
sadistic personality disorder, 555, 572–77
assessment difficulty, 575
diagnostic criteria, 574t, 575
DSM-IV dropping of, 488
functional and structural attributes of personality, 517f
negativistic personality disorder, 595
Sadock, B. J., 277
sadomasochism, 422, 425, 564, 573
safe-sex practices, 238
Sahin, D., 147–48
St. Lawrence, J. S., 420
Salapatek, P., 83
Salekin, R. W., 563
Salkin, B., 373
Salkovskis, P. M., 98, 101, 131, 132, 133, 134, 135, 452, 457
Salminen, J. K., 459
Salmon, P., 447
Salzman, L., 589
Sameroff, A. J., 36
sampling methods, 58, 59, 61
Sanderson, C., 492
Sanderson, W. C., 96, 98
Sandler, J., 597
SANS. *See* Scale for the Assessment of Negative Symptoms
Sarkstein, S. E., 356
Sartori, N., 630
Sartorius, N., 15, 666
SASB. *See* Structural Analysis of Social Behavior
Satel, S. L., 356
satiety, 373, 374
Savage, C. R., 155–56
Savino, M., 662, 664
Savoie, T., 301–2
Saya, A., 545
Sayers, M., 315, 318
Sayers, S. L., 314, 329
SC. *See* skin conductance
Scale for the Assessment of Negative Symptoms (schizophrenia), 279, 318
Scale for the Assessment of Positive Symptoms (schizophrenia), 279
scam artists, 476
scar model. *See* complication model
Scarr, S., 83
Schaaf, K. K., 381
Schafer, J., 234
Schafer, P. C., 235
Schanda, H., 353
Schear, S., 636
Schedule for Non-adaptive and Adaptive Personality, 492
Schedule for Schizotypal Personalities, 614
Scheier, L. M., 237
schemas, 504
Scherillo, P., 617
Schiavi, R. C., 237–38, 414
Schiffman, S., 231
Schill, T., 669
schizogene, 612
schizoid personality disorder, 523–33
avoidant personality disorder diagnostic boundary, 515, 525–26, 528, 529, 533
categorization, 610
clinical description, 525–28, 609, 610
contemporary views, 531–32
dependent personality disorder and, 537
diagnositic comorbidity, 528–29
diagnostic label, 523
functional and structural attributes of personality, 517ff
historical perspectives, 529–30
schizotypal personality disorder and, 524
schizotypic psychopathology vs., 606
schizomimetic conditions, 66, 523–33
schizophrenia, 277–303, 311–31
adoption studies, 63–64, 283–84, 524, 610, 616, 617
behavioral high-risk paradigm, 71–72
biobehavioral marker, 297, 298, 299–302
borderline personality vs., 629
brain abnormalities and, 181, 279, 286–92, 295–96, 298, 618–19
causality fallacy of positive instances and, 50
contemporary clinical views of, 278–79
diagnosis, 5, 7, 56, 286, 311, 346
diagnosis decrease, 610
diathesis-stress model, 51, 219, 281, 295, 297, 298
dimensional diagnosis models, 21
dissociative identity disorder vs., 469, 478
dopamine hypothesis and, 292, 293–94
DSM classification, 20, 31
EEG findings, 69
epidemiology, 277
etiology, 279–86, 302–3, 326–27, 353
expressed emotion and, 327–29
eye-movement dysfunction and, 67, 298, 299, 300–301, 302, 616, 618, 620
family study paradigm, 62, 66, 71, 281–83, 326–30, 524, 617, 618
gender and, 217, 313, 316–17, 319, 320–21, 326, 330
genetic factors, 39, 60, 62–64, 70–71, 281–86, 297–98, 300, 302, 327, 489, 524, 616, 617
genetic high-risk paradigm, 70–71
hierarchical diagnostic ranking, 23
high-risk research, 297, 298–301, 320–21, 323
historical attribution, 60, 287–88, 326–27, 342, 609
historical diagnostic categorization, 204, 278, 286
interpersonal functioning in, 311–31
liability constructs, 615, 616–17, 620–21
Meehl integrative model, 611–14, 620
neurochemical aspects, 292–96
neurocognition and, 286–92, 321–26, 357n.4
neurodevelopmental vs. neurodegenerative models, 296–99
neuromotor abnormalities, 301–2
nicotine receptor gene and, 300
obsessive-compulsive disorder and, 128, 130
paranoid type, 339, 340, 341, 342, 344, 349, 352, 353, 355, 357n.3
patients' subjective reports, 311, 312–13, 322
PDP study models, 72–73
polygenic/multifactorial model of, 285
premorbid social function in, 319–21
psychosocial treatment approaches, 329–30
range of expression of, 298
relapse factors, 327–29, 331
risk of, 298–99, 319, 606
schizoid personality disorder and, 529, 610
schizotypal personality disorder and, 524, 531, 610
schizotypes and development of, 613
schizotypic psychopathology and, 606, 609–10, 616–18
sleep/wake disorders and, 400
social cognition and, 324–26
spectrum disorders, 62
substance abuse comorbidity, 239
symptom fluctuation, 286
symptom hierarchy, 287
symptoms, 278–79, 286, 287, 317, 351, 606
symptoms relationship with social functioning, 317–19
taxometrics and, 489
twin studies, 57, 62–63, 65, 71, 282, 283, 319, 617
two-syndrome model of, 278–79, 286, 318
as weakly taxonic, 31–32
See also schizoid personality disorder; schizotypal personality disorder; schizotypic psychopathology
Schizophrenia Liability Index, 615
Schizophrenism Scale, 615
"schizophrenogenic mother," 60, 280, 326–27
schizotaxia, 612, 613
"Schizotaxia, Schizotypy" (Meehl), 611–12
schizotypal personality disorder
aberrant beliefs and, 347
attention deficits and, 300
borderline personality level and, 497, 498f
categorization, 485, 610
characteristics, 610
dependent personality disorder and, 537
depressive personality disorder and, 659
as descriptor set, 606, 607
diagnostic boundary, 286
diathesis-stress model, 298
eye-movement dysfunction and, 301
functional attributes of personality, 517f
gender and interpersonal functioning, 326
genetic factor, 531, 612
narcissistic personality disorder and, 681, 682, 683
obsessive-compulsive disorder comorbidity, 128
pandysmaturation index as predictor of, 301
phenomenology of, 619

schizotypal personality disorder (*continued*)
 schizoid diagnosis and, 524, 528
 schizophrenia and, 524, 531
 schizotypic psychopathology and, 605, 611–14, 619
 schizotypy and, 613
 SSP diagnostic scale, 614
 structural attributes of personality, 517f
Schizotypal Personality Scale, 615
Schizotypal Questionnaire, 615
schizotypic psychopathology, 283, 605–21
 case vignette, 606
 classification and diagnosis, 614–20
 contemporary models, 611–14
 definitions and distinctions, 605–7
 delimitation from other disorders, 620–21
 development and pathogenesis, 617–18
 etiology, 616–17
 follow-up studies, 619–20
 historical overview, 609–11
 laboratory stories, 617–18
 prevalence of, 607–8, 620
schizotypy, 612–15, 617, 618, 620
Schlenger, W. E., 148
Schlottke, P., 571
Schmideberg, M., 633
Schmidt, U., 379
Schneider, K., 537, 543–44, 556, 588, 596, 654, 655, 657, 662
Schneier, F. R., 90
Schofield, W., 50
Schore, A., 685
Schott, G., 430
Schreiber, S., 148
Schreiner-Engel, P., 414
Schroeder, H. E., 329
Schroeder, M. L., 340, 492–93, 494, 536, 631
Schuckit, M. A., 232, 233, 238–39, 240, 241
Schulsinger, F., 61–62, 63, 70, 71, 232, 258, 524, 614, 616, 617
Schulsinger, P. H., 610
Schwartz, B. L., 352
Schwartz, D. A., 349
Schwartz, E. O., 639
Schwartz, M., 430
SCID-D. *See* Structured Clinical Interview for DSM-IV Dissociative Disorders
Science (journal), 7
Sciuto, G., 617
SCN (suprachiasmatic nucleus), 168, 184, 187
scopophilia (scoptophilia). *See* voyeurism
Scott, L. C., 351
Scott, W. D., 217
SCRT (Social Cue Recognition Test), 324
scrupulousness, 654
seasonal affective disorder, 183, 185, 187–89, 192
 bulimia nervosa comorbidity, 368
 family studies, 189
 sleep/wake disorders and, 398
second messenger systems, 166, 171, 173–75, 182, 191, 192–93
sedative hypnotic medications. *See* benzodiazepines
seduction theory, 478
seductive behavior, 542, 544, 547, 681
Segal, Z. V., 216
Segrin, C., 210–11, 212, 213
Seidel, K., 430
Seidman, L. J., 352
seizures, 157
 pseudoneurological, 448
selection bias, 59
selective serotonin reuptake inhibitors, 374
Selekin, R. T., 561
self, sense of. *See* ego identity
self-absorption
 depression and, 214
 narcissism and, 674, 679
 paranoid conditions and, 350, 352, 354
self-beliefs
 dependent personality and, 540–41
 depression and, 211, 217
 paranoia and, 349
self-blame
 depressive personality disorder and, 653, 654, 655, 656
 obsessive-compulsive disorder and, 132, 133
self-consciousness
 paranoid, 352
 social phobias and, 89–90
self-containment, 340
self-control, anorexic, 376, 378
self-criticism
 avoidant personality and, 523, 525, 527
 depressive personality and, 653, 655, 656, 664
 narcissistic personality and, 675, 676
self-defeating (masochistic) personality disorder, 664–69
 characteristics, 655, 659, 665, 667
 classification, 13, 485, 665–66
 depressive personality disorder vs., 655, 659, 660, 665
 differential diagnosis and comorbidity, 595, 667–68
 epidemiology, 666
 etiology, 668–69
 functional and structural attributes of personality, 517ff
 historical background, 665
 internal construct validity, 666
 interrater reliability, 666
 masochism vs., 664
 passive-aggresive personality disorder and, 595
 sex bias issue, 666–67
self-disclosure
 depression and, 210
 obsessive-compulsive personality and, 589
self-doubt, obsessive-compulsive disorder and, 132
self-efficacy
 depression and appraisal of, 217, 218
 temperament and development of, 40
self-esteem
 avoidant personality and low, 528
 depression linked with loss of, 209
 ego identity and, 496
 narcissism as regulator of, 674–75, 676, 678, 679, 680, 683, 684–85
 projection and, 348
 substance abuse and, 258
self-image
 development of, 43, 46
 eating disorders and, 371, 372, 377
 of negativistic individuals, 594
 obsessive-compulsive personality and, 586
 personality development and, 517–18
self-importance, paranoid conditions and, 340, 357n.5
selfishness, psychopathy and, 568
self-justification, paranoid conditions and, 340, 682
self-mutilation
 borderline personality disorder and, 628, 629, 630, 634
 dissociative identity patients and, 473, 474
 reaction formation and, 496–97
self-orientation, 512
self-protection, paranoid conditions and, 349, 356
self-psychology school, 597, 684
self-punishment
 depression and, 215
 depressive personality disorder and, 655
 See also self-mutilation
self-recognition, as obsessive-compulsive disorder criterion, 126, 127
self-referent encoding task, 215
self-regulatory models, depression and, 217–18
self-report measures
 depression assessment, 208
 dissociation studies, 467
 dissociative disorders, 470
 fears, 84
 panic attacks, 95
 schizotypy psychometric inventories, 615
 smoking typology, 231
self-righteousness, paranoid, 340, 349, 355, 357n.5, 682
self-schema
 depressive, 213–14
 gender identity disorder, 432–33
self-starvation syndromes, 365–66, 367
Seligman, M. E. P., 53, 86–87, 88, 156, 216, 655
semistructured interviews, 12, 208
sensation-seeking trait
 eating disorder-substance abuse comorbidity, 369
 narcissistic personality disorder and, 675
 negativistic personality disorder and, 599
 neurobiologic basis, 507, 508f
 as substance abuse factor, 258, 259–60, 266–67
sensory symptoms and deficits, pseudoneurological, 448
separation problems, 82, 378, 497, 524, 640–51
septal-hippocampal system, 125
septum, 168
Serban-Schreiber, D., 72
serial killers, 574, 575, 577
Serin, R. C., 562, 564
serotonergic drugs, 133, 175, 187–88
serotonin (serotonergic system; 5-HT), 167, 175, 178, 179, 180, 181, 190, 192, 231, 241
 bipolar I disorder and, 185

borderline personality disorder and, 637
depression and, 168–69, 171–72, 188, 368
eating disorders and, 368, 369, 373, 374
functions of, 168–69, 261–62
general anxiety disorder and, 125
obsessive-compulsive disorder and, 133, 134, 369
panic and, 103
pathway, 169f, 294
personality traits and, 507
schizophrenia and, 294–95, 619
seasonal affective disorder and, 187
substance abuse and, 261–62, 369
Seto, M., 564
setraline, 103
set theory, 17–18, 19, 23
Seven-Factor Model. *See* Big Seven Model
Sewell, K. W., 561, 563
sex, gender vs., 428
sex assignment, gender identity and, 431
sex bias, self-defeating personality category and, 666–67
sex crimes, 421–22, 563–65. *See also* paraphilias; rape; sexual sadism
sex differences. *See* gender differences
sex offenders. *See* sex crimes
sex-role socialization, 541
sexual abuse. *See* childhood physical/sexual abuse; rape; sexual sadism
sexual arousal disorders, 411, 412, 415–18
sexual aversion disorder, 411, 413, 414, 415
sexual compulsivity. *See* paraphilias
sexual desire disorders, 411, 413–15
sexual deviations. *See* paraphilias
sexual dysfunctions and disorders, 410–34
case vignettes, 412, 415–16
diagnostic subjectivity, 412, 419
dysfunctions definition, 410–11
gender identity disorders, 428–33
orgasmic disorders, 418–20, 433
paraphilias, 421–23
serotonin and, 261
sexual arousal disorders, 411, 412, 415–18, 433
sexual desire disorders, 411, 413–15, 433
sexual pain disorders, 411, 420–21, 433
substance abuse and, 237–38, 411, 416
three major categories, 410
sexual harassment, 422
sexual masochism, 422, 425
sexual obsessive images or impulses, 129
sexual orientation, 433–34n.1
gender identity vs., 428, 429
prenatal hormone exposure and, 430
See also homosexuality
sexual pain disorders (dyspareunia), 411, 420–21, 433
sexual perversions. *See* paraphilias
sexual response cycle, 410–11
phases and associated dysfunctions, 411t
sexual risk taking, 238, 628
sexual sadism, 422, 423t, 425, 564, 572, 573, 575–77
sexual violence, 421–22, 563–65
Shafer, E., 501–2
Shaffer, D., 10
Shafran, R., 132
Shalev, A. Y., 148, 152, 157
shamans, 277
shame
narcissism and, 675, 676, 678, 684–85
sadistic personality disorder and absence of, 573
Shapiro, D., 340, 348, 545
Shapiro, E., 586
shared environmental influences, 65, 85, 155
shared psychotic disorder, 343–44
Sharma, I., 339
Sharpe, L., 7
Sharpe, M., 456, 459, 460
Shaw, B. F., 504
Shaw, R., 675
Shea, C. A., 98
Shea, M. T., 35, 654, 659, 661
Shear, M .K., 120
Sheard, C., 606
Sheikh, A. J., 445
Sheldon, W. H., 488, 507
"shell shock" diagnosis, 144
Shenton, M. E., 155
Sheperd, M., 10
Sher, K., 258
Sherman, M. F., 35
Sherman, S. J., 232
Sherrington, R., 64, 285
Shichman, S., 538
Shields, J., 60, 61–62, 63, 64, 71, 609
shift work, 391, 395, 396
Shih, J., 660–61
Shilliday, C., 323
Shin, L. M., 156
Shrout, P. E., 208
Shulman, I. D., 93
shyness
avoidant personality disorder and, 532
fear development and, 82
narcissistic, 675, 676–77, 685
SIA (Structured Interview for Schizotypy), 614
sick role, 446, 447, 452, 454, 458–59, 476
Siegel, O., 668
Sierles, F. S., 149
Siever, L. J., 154, 636, 637–38, 643
Sifneos, P. E., 459
Sights, J. R., 379
Sigvardsson, S., 230, 232, 258, 259
Silk, K. R., 640, 641
Silva, P. A., 663
Silverman, J. M., 636
Silvestri, J. M., 104
Sim, J. P., 591, 598
similarity, concept of, 18
Simmelweis, I., 347–48
Simon, R., 7
Simon, W., 421
Simons, A. D., 209
Simons, R. C., 655, 659, 665
Simonsen, E., 635, 680
Sines, L., 635
Singer, M., 477
single-subject experimental design, 54
Situational Confidence Questionnaire, 229
situational orgasmic dysfunction, 418, 419
situational phobias, 83, 84
Sixteen Personality Factor (16PF) inventory, 491, 492
skepticism, 593, 594, 597, 598, 600, 655, 656, 659
skin conductance, 67–68, 571
Skinner, B. F., 498, 515
Skinner, H. A., 16, 230
Skinstad, A. H., 236
Skodol, A. E., 208, 587, 594, 608, 668
Slater, S. L., 320
Slavney, P. R., 15
Sledge, W. H., 14
sleep apnea, 395, 400
sleep choking, 400
sleep paralysis, 394
sleep-state misperception (subjective insomnia), 393–94
sleep terrors. *See* night terrors
sleep-wake cycles. *See* circadian rhythms
sleep/wake disorders, 390–405
bipolar disorder and, 186, 191
breathing-related sleep disorders, 391, 395, 400, 401
classification, 390–92
comorbidities, 398–401, 403–4
depression and, 175–76, 178, 186, 191, 192, 398, 401, 403–4
diagnoses reliability test, 14
as diagnostic category, 9, 390
generalized anxiety disorder and, 114, 120
in medical disorders context, 401–2
narcolepsy, 391, 394–95, 398, 400
other mental disorders linked with, 398–401, 403–4
parasomnias, 391, 396–98, 402
posttraumatic stress disorder and, 144, 145, 149, 153, 400
primary insomnia, 392–94, 399, 403
psychological symptoms in wake of, 404
research needs, 405
substance abuse and, 391, 402–3
See also REM sleep
sleep/wake schedule disorders, 391
sleep walking, 391, 397–98, 402
SLI (Schizophrenia Liability Index), 615
slimness, 365, 371–72
Slooff, C. J., 318
slow wave sleep, depression and, 175–76, 191
Small, I. F., 598
Small, J. G., 598
Small, N. E. M., 320
Smiley, W. C., 562
Smith, B., 667
Smith, D., 547
Smith, G. T., 234
Smith, L., 679
Smith, L. E., 654
Smith, M. A., 157
Smith, M. R., 279
Smith, P., 546
Smith, S., 259
Smith, T. L., 232, 233
Smith, T. W., 208
smoking, 231, 232–33
ADHD comorbidity, 239
cultural controls and, 252
dependent personality and, 539
depression comorbidity, 240
family history and, 255–56
in gateway model hierarchy, 255

smoking (*continued*)
  nicotine as psychoactive substance, 264
  prenatal effects of, 256
  sexual arousal disorder and, 416, 417
  See also nicotine
Smolak, L., 380, 381
smooth pursuit eye movement dysfunction, 67
snakeroot, 249
Sneath, P. H. A., 18
Snow, J., 57–58
Snowden, P. R., 576
Sobkiewicz, T. A., 377
Social Anhedonia Scale, 318
social cognition, schizophrenia and, 324–26
social competence
  depression and, 210, 213
  obsessive-compulsive personality and, 590
  schizophrenia and, 313–14, 316, 317, 318
  See also social phobias; social skills
Social Competency Index, 313, 316
Social Cue Recognition Test, 324
social disintegration, 643
social environment
  abnormal illness behavior and, 458–59
  adaptive vs. functional paranoia, 343
  borderline personality disorder and, 642–43, 644
  depression and, 190, 211–13, 217, 219
  eating disorders and, 371–72, 381, 383t
  fears and, 82–83, 84
  gender identity disorder and, 431–33
  narcissistic personality disorder and, 676–77, 680
  personality development and, 36–37, 41, 42–43, 45–46
  schizophrenia and, 326–29, 331
  substance abuse and, 251–58
  unstable and contradictory social standards, 46
  See also environmental factors; interpersonal models; life event models
Social Fear Scale, 615
social functioning. *See* interpersonal models
social isolation. *See* withdrawal, social
social modeling. *See* modeling
social phobias, 81, 82, 83, 84, 85
  anxious apprehension and, 118
  avoidant personality disorder and, 524, 529
  body dysmorphic disorder and, 458
  comorbidities, 98–99, 117, 118, 148, 369, 458
  eating disorders and, 369
  generalized anxiety disorder autonomic symptoms vs., 120
  heightened self-consciousness and, 89–90
  panic disorder and, 98–99
  paraphilias and, 427t
  posttraumatic stress disorder and, 148
  prevalence of, 95
  schizoid personality disorder and, 529
social relations. *See* interpersonal models
social skills
  deficit theory of depression, 210, 213
  definition of, 314
  obsessive-compulsive personality behavior as deficit in, 590
social skills training, 329–30, 590
social values, 46
social withdrawal. *See* withdrawal, social
sociobiology
  of gender differences, 512
  of psychopathy, 566–67
socioeconomic status
  antisocial personality disorder and, 57
  borderline personality disorder and, 632
  conversion disorder and, 448, 449
  eating disorders and, 368
  social standards and, 46
  substance abuse and, 231, 232, 253
sociopathic personality disturbances, 227
  paraphilias formerly classified as, 421
sociopathy, psychopathy vs., 557
sodium lactate, 93, 101
Sokal, R. R., 18
Solomon, L., 259
Solomon, Z., 148
soma, 250
somatic delusions, 346
somatization disorder, 445, 446–48, 456, 468
  dependent personality disorder and, 537
  dissociative identity disorder and, 469
  histrionic personality disorder and, 543
  personality disorder and, 458
somatoform disorders, 444–61
  body dysmorphic disorder, 453–54
  comorbidities, 456–58
  conversion disorder, 445, 448–49, 468
  diagnostic problems, 460
  differentiating among, 456–57
  dissociation and, 468
  dissociative identity disorder and, 476
  factitious disorder, 454–55, 476
  general models of, 458–60
  historical perspectives, 445–46, 447, 448, 449, 451
  hypochondriasis, 444, 445, 451, 453
  illness-affirming vs. illness denying, 445, 458–59
  neuroses reclassification under, 445
  obsessive-compulsive disorder and, 130
  overview of, 445
  pain disorder, 444, 445, 449–51
  sick role and, 446, 447, 452, 455, 458–59, 476
  somatization disorder, 445, 446–48
somatosensory amplification, 447, 452
somatostatin, 180, 186, 191
somatotype, 488
Sonnega, A., 146, 147, 148, 149
Southwick, S. M., 152, 154, 157
Span of Apprehension, 321, 330
Span of Attention, 300
Spaulding, W. D., 325
SPD. *See* sadistic personality disorder; schizotypal personality disorder; shared psychotic disorder
species (biological), 17, 19, 87
specific rank (folk classification), 19
spectrum model, 35
speech patterns
  depression and, 210
  schizophrenia and, 316, 318, 322
  See also language
Spellman, M., 619
SPEM (smooth pursuit eye movement dysfunction), 67
Spencer, T. J., 239
spider phobia, 82
Spinoza, B., 497
Spitzer, M., 350
Spitzer, R. G., 54–55
Spitzer, R. L., 13, 15, 55, 537, 575, 594, 610, 635, 666, 668
Spivak, G., 314–15
"split personality," 278
"splitting," 497, 529–30, 531, 628–29
spousal abuse, 575
Spratt, K. F., 236
Sprock, J., 667
SRET (self-referent encoding task), 215
SSDBS (Symptom Schedule for the Diagnosis of Borderline Schizophrenia), 614
SSP (Schedule for Schizotypal Personalities), 614
SSRIs (selective serotonin reuptake inhibitors), 103
SST. *See* social skills training
Staats, A. W., 499
Stafford, E., 562
Stahl, F., 430
Staley, A. A., 84
Stalin, Joseph, 344, 355
Standage, K., 587
Standage, L., 547
Standards for Educational and Psychological Testing (APA manual), 15
Stangl, D., 595
Stanley, M. A., 118
Stapf, D. M., 14
Starcevic, V., 121
startle responses, 152, 157
starvation
  anorexia nervosa and, 365–66, 371
  prenatal maternal-schizophrenia link, 280–81, 327
statistical methods
  biological classification, 18–19
  diagnosis and classification, 8
  diagnostic reliability and, 14
  epidemiology and, 57
  experimental vs. quasi-experimental, 52–54
  population genetics, 64–65
  stratified random sampling, 59
Steer, R. A., 116
Steiger, H., 380
Stein, J., 54
Stein, M. B., 90, 98
Steinberg, H. R., 149
Steiner, B., 641
Steiner, J. L., 14
Steinhauer, S., 232
Steketee, G., 89, 158
Stelson, F. W., 238
Stengel, E., 6, 11
Stepanski, E., 14, 391, 393

step-function model, 51
Stern, A., 635
steroid receptors, 154
Stevens, J., 295
Stevens, S. S., 507
Stewart, M. A., 240
Stewart, S., 257, 266
stigmatization, paranoid feelings of, 349
Stiles, W. B., 211
Stimmel, B. B., 237–38
stimulants, 186, 239, 240, 260
  in gateway model hierarchy, 255
  sleep/wake disturbances and, 402–3
  See also amphetamines; cocaine; nicotine
Stoll, F., 347
Stoller, R. J., 426, 428, 432
Stolorow, R. D., 674
Stone, M. H., 544, 574, 575, 597, 632, 634
Stormberg, D, 682
Storr, A., 589
Strachen, C., 563
Strack, S., 593, 600
stratified random sampling, 59
Strauss, J. S., 10, 279, 319, 341
Stravynski, A., 532
stressful events. *See* life events model; posttraumatic stress disorder; tension; traumatic stressor
stress response dampening, 257
stress symptoms
  generalized anxiety disorder comorbidity, 117
  See also posttraumatic stress disorder
striatum, 181, 295, 619
Strober, M., 372, 373, 375, 376, 381
Stroop Effect, 72, 149–50
Structural Analysis of Social Behavior, 501–3, 503f, 508–9, 539, 591
structural domains, 516–19
  listing of, 518
structural organization
  development and, 36–37
  personality type classification and, 496
Structured Clinical Interview for Diagnosis, Axis II, 630
Structured Clinical Interview for DSM-IV Dissociative Disorders, 470
Structured Clinical Interview for the DSM-III-R, 12, 469, 666
Structured Clinical Interview for the DSM-IV, 55
structured diagnostic interview, 54–55, 630
Structured Interview for Schizotypy, 614
Structured Interview for the Diagnosis of Personality, 12, 530, 630
Stuart, F. M., 415
stubbornness, 588, 593
Stueve, A., 208
Sturt, E., 284
subcortical neural circuits, 157, 181, 295–96
subjective insomnia, 393–94
substance abuse, 227–41, 249–67
  biochemistry of, 260–64
  borderline personality disorder and, 628, 634, 642, 643
  cognitive aspects, 264–67
  cognitive impairment and, 237
  comorbid disorders, 96–97, 117, 236, 238–41, 251, 368, 369, 373
  cultural variations and, 251–54
  diagnostic history, 227–31
  dissociative disorders and, 469, 470
  eating disorder comorbidity, 368, 369, 373
  epidemiology, 231–32
  etiological considerations, 250–67
  family history and, 69, 231, 232–33, 234, 251, 252f, 253, 255–56, 267f
  gateway model of, 255
  gender differences, 231, 232, 234–36, 257–58
  genetic factors, 258–60
  historical overview, 249–51
  narcissistic personality disorder and, 678, 680
  panic disorder comorbidity, 96–97
  paraphilias and, 427, 427t
  peer group and, 254–55
  personality and, 258
  psychopathology, 236–38
  psychopathy and, 560
  rate decline, 234
  reinforcing effects of, 261
  risk markers, 232–34
  sexual dysfunction and, 237–38, 411, 416
  sleep/wake disorders and, 391, 402–3
  social disintegration construct and, 643
  somatization disorder and, 448
  stress and affective factors, 257–58
  See also alcohol abuse; drug abuse; smoking; *specific substances*
substance abuse syndrome, 227
sucking stage, 596
Suelzer, M., 97, 123
suffocation false alarm, 104
suggestibility
  borderline patients, 638
  dependent personality, 540
suicide
  borderline personality disorder and, 628, 629, 630, 633, 634, 636, 637, 642
  cohort trends, 207
  depression and, 192
  histrionic personality threats of, 547
  narcissistic personality disorder vulnerability, 677, 678
  panic disorder and, 96
  youth, 642, 643
sullenness, 593, 594, 597
Sullins, E., 381
Sullivan, H. S., 33, 500, 515, 537, 567
Sullivan, L. E., 562
Sullivan, M., 325
Sullivan, P. F., 642
Sumeria, 250
sundown syndrome, 401
superego, 495, 496, 655, 665, 677, 681, 684, 685, 686
superficiality, 555, 570
superiority feelings, 684
support, consistent, 42
suppression, obsessive-compulsive symptoms and, 133
suprachiasmatic nucleus, 168, 184, 187
suspiciousness
  cocaine use and, 236
  paranoid conditions and, 340, 344, 348, 354, 609
  paranoid vs. adaptive behavior and, 343
  schizoid personality disorder and, 609
Sutherland, A. J., 454–55
Svrakic, D. M., 507
Swartz, A., 240
Swartz, M., 632
sweat glands, 67
Sweeney, J. A., 67
Swinson, R. P., 93, 94, 97, 99
SWS. *See* slow wave sleep
Sydenham, Thomas, 24, 451, 543
Sylvester, D., 451
symmetry, obsessive-compulsive need for, 129, 130
sympathetic nervous system, 168, 570
symptoms
  depression, 205
  developmental pathogenesis and, 30
  as diagnostic category, 9
  factitious disorder, 454
  familial expressed emotions and, 328
  generalized anxiety disorder, 114, 115, 117, 120–21
  hypochondriasis-panic disorder comorbidity, 97
  hysterical vs. preoccupational disorders, 445
  manic, 185
  as multiaxial classification component, 10
  obsessive-compulsive disorder, 127, 130, 133
  panic attacks, 90, 92, 99, 104
  paranoid conditions, 339–40
  physical, fabricated/exaggerated, 454, 476
  physical, misattribution of, 452
  physical, unexplained, 444, 445, 446, 447, 455
  positive and negative factors, 57
  posttraumatic stress disorder, 144–45
  presentation as classification function, 4
  pseudoneurological, 448
  schizophrenia, 278–79, 286, 287, 317–19
Symptom Schedule for the Diagnosis of Borderline Schizophrenia, 614
synapomorphies, 19
synaptic pruning, 296
syndrome, definition and definition refinement approach, 55–57
systolic phase (heart), 68
Szasz, T. S., 7, 8

Taiwan, depression rate, 207
Tanofsky, M. B., 378
Tartakoff, H., 683
Tauscher, R., 663
Taweger, C., 381
taxonicity, definition of, 31
taxonomy
  cross-sectional, 30, 31, 33, 47
  environmental influences and, 36
  factor models, 490
  manifest and latent similarity, 30–31
  methodology of, 489
  numerical, 17–18, 18–19, 22
  pathogenesis, Axis I and II, and, 30–36
  as simplification, 35
  substantive vs. formal, 10
  theory-based, 486
Taylor, L., 216
Taylor, M. A., 149
Taylor, S., 89, 91, 96
Taylor, S. W. P., 236–37

Teasdale, J. D., 214, 216
Tebes, J. K., 14
Teicher, M. H., 154
telephone scatalogia, 423t, 426
Tellegen, A., 493–94, 660
Tellenbach, H., 654
temperament, 38, 433
  depressive, 653, 654, 660, 662
  historical views of, 506–7
  neurobiology and, 506–10
  personality disorders and, 517ff, 518–19, 532
  as personality foundation, 39–40, 506
temporal cortex, 291, 572
temporal lobe epilepsy, 469
Tengström, A., 562, 563
tension
  generalized anxiety disorder and, 114, 121
  obsessive-compulsive and negativistic personality disorders and, 585, 600
tension-reduction hypothesis, substance abuse and, 240–41, 257–58
teratogenic drug effects, 256, 257f, 259
Teri, L., 211
Terry, H., 674–75
Tesón, A., 356
testosterone, 414, 417, 430, 431
test-retest method, 13–14, 54
tetrhydrocanabinol, 264
Thailand, 6
thalamus, 157, 168, 170, 181, 291, 293
theatrical emotionality, 542
theoretical model (diagnostic), 22, 24
theory development, 4, 19, 24
thermister, 67
thermoregulatory abnormalities, 187
theta waves, 69
thinness, 364, 365, 371–72, 381
Third World, 12
Thomas, A., 644
Thompson, R. N., 456
Thompson, W. L., 156
Thomson, J. A., 683
Thordarson, D. S., 132
Thorndike, Edward, 498, 515
Thornton, A., 351
Thorpy, M. J., 14, 391, 393
thought disorder
  paranoid, 339–56
  psychopathy and, 572
  schizophrenic, 279, 318, 606
  See also delusions
threat-related stimuli, 118
"Three Essays on the Theory of Sexuality" (Freud), 682
3-methoxy-r-hydroxyhenylglycol. *See* MHPG
threshold effect, 51
thyroid dysfunction, 179–80, 187, 188, 190
thyroid stimulating hormone, 179, 180
thyrotropin-releasing hormone, 179, 180, 187, 191
thyroxine, 179
tic disorders, obsessive-compulsive comorbidities, 128, 130, 134
Tiefer, L., 411
Tierney, A., 329
Tillemanns, A., 126
Tiller, J., 379
Timberlawn Health System (Dallas, Texas), 475
tinnitis, 3351
tobacco use. *See* nicotine; smoking
Tobena, A., 93
Tohen, M., 682
toilet training, 43, 588, 589
tolerance, substance abuse and, 228, 229, 233
Tomasson, K., 449
tonic autonomic arousal, 151
Toomey, R., 318, 325
Torgersen, S., 445, 531, 545, 587, 595, 617, 636
torture, 146, 147–48, 158, 576
Toupin, J., 563
Tourette's syndrome
  genetic factor, 39
  obsessive-compulsive disorder and, 128, 130, 134
TPQ (Tridimensional Personality Questionnaire), 375, 376
trance states, dissociative, 471, 479
tranquilizers, 256
transducers, definition of, 67
transference, psychoanalytic, 683
"transitional situational disturbance" diagnosis, 144
transsexualism, 429, 432
transvestic fetishism, 421, 422, 423t, 425, 427, 429
Trapnell, P. D., 567
traumatic stressor
  criteria for, 145
  cue reactions, 151–52
  dissociative amnesia and, 468, 478, 479
  as drug abuse risk, 257
  introversion and, 39
  normal vs. abnormal responses to, 158–59
  parasomnias, 397
  See also childhood physical/sexual abuse; posttraumatic stress disorder; rape
Treasure, J., 372, 379
treatment
  nicotine addiction's resistance to, 264
  prediction of responses to, 56
  psychopathy prognosis, 565–66
  See also specific conditions
tree diagram, 18
Trestman, R. L., 154
TRH. *See* tension-reduction hypothesis
TRH (thyrotropin-releasing hormone), 179, 180, 187, 191
trichotillomania, 130
tricyclic antidepressants, 188
Tridimensional Personality Questionnaire, 375, 376
Triebwasser, J. T., 655, 656, 659–60, 661
triiodythyonine, 179
Trimble, M. R., 449
Tringone, R., 574
triphosphate, 173
Trosman, H., 597
Troughton, E., 232
True, W. R., 154–55
Trull, T. J., 258, 492, 528–29, 573–74, 595
trust, 42, 342–43, 344. *See also* mistrust
tryptophan, 180, 294. *See also* serotonin
Tsai, G., 263
TSH (thyroid stimulating hormone), 179, 180, 187, 190
Tsuang, M. T., 286, 352
tuberoinfundibula system, 170
Turk, D. C., 450, 459, 460
Turkat, I. D., 589, 590
Turner, S. M., 529, 589
Turner's syndrome, 433
Turovsky, J., 124, 125
twin studies
  alcoholism, 259
  bipolar disorder, 189
  borderline personality disorder, 636
  depression, 189
  eating disorders, 372
  epidemiological methods, 57, 62–63, 64, 65, 71
  generalized anxiety disorder, 123
  homosexuality, 430
  obsessive-compulsive disorder, 130
  phobias, 84–85
  posttraumatic stress disorder, 154–55
  schizophrenia, 57, 62–63, 65, 71, 282, 283, 617
  schizophrenic social functioning, 319
  somatoform disorders, 445
two-factor theory of fear, 85–86, 131, 156–57
Tyrer, P., 635
tyrosine, 292

UCRs. *See* unconditioned responses
UCS. *See* unconditioned stimulus
Uddenberg, C.-E., 608
Uhde, T. W., 98
Uhl, G., 259
Uhlenhuth, E. H., 403
U.K./U.S. Diagnostic Project, 7
Ullmann, L., 448
ultrardian rhythms, 183, 184
Unabomber, 347
uncertainty, obsessive-compulsive intolerance of, 132
unconditioned responses, 85
unconditioned stimulus, 85, 86, 88–89, 131, 145, 157
  hypochondriasis and, 452
uncontrollability
  generalized anxiety disorder and, 118, 119–20, 124, 125
  posttraumatic stress disorder and, 156, 158
unhappiness, 656, 657
unipolar depression. *See* depression
United Kingdom, 6, 7
unrealistic worry. *See* generalized anxiety disorder
unreliability, 557
unscrupulousness, 557
untrustworthiness, 557
upregulation, definition of, 167–68
urophilia, 426
Usher, M., 215
usnea, 249
Ustad, K. L., 563

vaginal lubrication, 410, 416, 417, 420
vaginismus, 411, 420, 421
Vaillant, G. E., 539, 678, 682
Val, E. R., 206
validity
  classification, 15–17, 25, 630
  construct, 55, 122
  criterion-related, 55
  definition of, 16, 55
  as evaluative component, 10
  research design and, 55
  of self-reports, 208

Vanable, P. A., 352
Vandenberg, P., 545
van der Ende, J., 84
Vandereycken, W., 370, 379–80
van der Kolk, B. A., 147, 153, 155–56, 474, 633, 639, 640
Vanderlinden, J., 370
van Dyk, R., 370
Van Heck, G. L., 459
Van Hemert, A. M., 444
van Nieuwenhuizen, C. J., 318
van Os, J., 663
variables
  correlation and, 65, 490
  factor models and, 490
  illusory correlations of, 50, 65
  matching and, 52–53
  reliability tests, 54
variance, diagnostic interview, 14
varietal rank (folk classification), 19
Varma, S. L., 339
vasovagal reactions, 82
Veit, R., 571
Velten, E., 53
Venable, P. A., 340
Venables, P. H., 67
Vendenbroucke, J. P., 444
ventral tegmental area, 170, 261, 263
ventricular enlargement, schizophrenic, 292, 296
verbal skills, 314
Vermilyea, B. B., 92
Vermilyea, J. A., 92
Vertommen, H., 370, 379–80
VES (Vietnam Experience Study), 146
Vgontzas, A., 14, 391, 393
Vicente, N., 353
victimization
  dissociative identity disorder and, 474
  paranoid feelings of, 340, 341, 344, 352–53, 354
  self-fulfilling, 344
Vietnam Era Twin registry, 154–55
Vietnam Experience Study, 146
Vietnam War, 144, 146, 149, 150, 151, 152, 153, 154–55, 257
vigilance, 323, 325, 343, 351
Vingerhoets, A. J. J. M., 459
Vinokur, A. D., 208
violence
  borderline personality disorder and, 639–40
  drug-induced, 236
  paranoid delusions and, 353–54, 355
  psychopathy and, 555, 556–57, 560–61, 561–65
  sadistic personality disorder and, 555, 573
  sexual, 421–22, 563–65, 576–77
  See also childhood physical/sexual abuse; criminality
viral infection, 280, 327
Vlahor, D., 259
Vogeltanz, N. D., 235
"voices." *See* auditory hallucinations
Volkan, V. D., 683
vomiting, induced, 365, 366
Von der Lippe, A., 545
von Zerssen, D., 663
voyeurism, 422, 423t, 425, 426
vulnerability
  anxious apprehension, 100
  bipolar disorder, 188
  definition of, 29
  diathesis-stress model, 51
  generalized anxiety disorder, 124, 125
  genetics of alcoholism, 259–60
  negative life event-related depression, 209
  panic attacks, 93
  personality disorder and depression model, 35
  posttraumatic stress disorder, 158
  primary insomnia, 392
  schizophrenia, 320, 351
  women and depression, 190
vulvar vestibulitis, 420

Waddell, M. T., 116
Wade, J. H., 314, 316, 317, 318, 329
Wadsworth, M., 663
Waelder, R., 682
Wagman, A. M. I., 279
Wagner, A. R., 88
Wakefield, J. C., 158, 418
Wakschlay, L., 256
Walker, E., 295, 301–2, 320
Walker, M. L., 14
Wallace, C. J., 315, 323, 324, 330
Wallace, J. F., 570–71
Waller, G., 379
Waller, N. G., 493–94
Walsh, D., 614, 619
Walters, E. E., 85, 373
war on drugs, 252
Warner, M. L., 320
Warren, J., 562, 576
Warren, M., 369
Warshaw, M., 240
Warwick, H. M. C., 452, 457
washing compulsion, 126, 129, 131
Washington University (St. Louis), 557, 558–59
Wasmuth, J., 64, 285
Watson, D., 22, 84, 121, 122, 123, 660–61
Watson, J. B., 85, 498, 515
Watson, R., 426
Watt, J. A. G., 339
WCST (Wisconsin Card Sorting Test), 322, 323, 325, 618
Weakland, J., 60, 327
Weathers, F. W., 149
Webster, C. D., 563
Wechsler Memory Scale, 133
Wee, J. L., 615
Weese-Mayer, D. E., 104
Wegner, D. M., 133
weight-gain phobia. *See* anorexia nervosa
Wein, S. J., 539
Weinberger, D. R., 296, 297, 298, 614, 619
Weinberger, J. L., 683
Weisath, L., 474
Weiss, D. S., 148
Weiss, S. R. B., 157
Weissman, M. M., 96
Weissman, M. W., 642
Wells, A., 90
Wells, M., 665
Welner, J., 63
Wender, P. H., 61–62, 63, 524, 608, 610, 614, 616, 617
Wessely, S., 352, 459
West, M., 525–26, 533
Westphal, C., 99
Wetzel, R. D., 447, 469
Wetzler, S., 96, 98
Whitaker, A. H., 104
White, D., 237–38, 414
White, G., 608
White, R. W., 42
Whitman, R. M., 597
Whorf, B., 44
Whyne-Berman, S. M., 593, 600
Widiger, T. A., 21, 99, 490, 492, 528–29, 555, 557, 559, 567, 573–74, 575, 577, 591, 595, 598, 599, 631, 665, 666, 667
Wiggins, J. S., 515, 567, 591, 598–99
Wilens, T., 239
Wilfley, D. E., 378
Wilhelm, S., 133
Williams, D., 669
Williams, J., 351
Williams, J. B. W., 13, 15, 55, 537, 594, 666, 668
Williamson, S. E., 562, 571–72
will validity, 354
Wilsnack, R. W., 235
Wilsnack, S. C., 235
Wilson, E. O., 512
Wilson, J. F., 380
Wincze, J. P., 421
wine, 250, 265
Winfield, I., 632
Wing, J. K., 327
Wingfield, H., 229
Winnicott, D. W., 530, 684
Winokur, G., 11, 232, 258, 557
Winters, K. C., 348
Wintrup, A., 563
Wisconsin Card Sorting Test, 322, 323, 325, 618
withdrawal, addictive substance
  biochemistry of, 261, 262–63
  sleep/wake disturbances and, 402, 403
  symptoms of, 228, 229, 241
withdrawal, social
  avoidant personality and, 523
  depression and, 204, 211
  narcissistic personality disorder and, 675, 676
  paranoid conditions and, 356
  schizoid personality and, 497, 523, 524, 525, 526
  schizophrenia and, 311, 524
  See also social phobias
Wixted, J. T., 318
Wohlfahrt, S., 10
Wolf, E., 597
Wolff, S., 532
Wollersheim, J. P., 131
Wolpe, J., 83, 85
women
  body ideal, 371–72
  depression in, 190, 206, 209, 238, 657
  eating disorders and, 367, 369, 371, 372, 380
  generalized anxiety disorder correlates, 115
  historical linkage between uterus and somatoform disorders, 447, 448, 543
  insomnia and, 392
  nightmare disorder and, 396–97
  orgasmic disorder and, 418–19
  panic disorder with agoraphobia and, 95
  postmenopausal, 190–91, 192, 416
  posttraumatic stress disorder and, 146, 147, 155, 156, 158

women (*continued*)
 psychoanalytic theory of masochism in, 665
 rapid-cycling bipolar disorder and, 188, 190
 schizophrenic advantages in, 316–17
 sex bias in diagnosis of self-defeating personality disorder in, 666–67
 sexual arousal disorder and, 415, 416, 417
 sexual pain disorder and, 420–21
 somatoform disorders and, 445
 substance abuse by, 234–36, 238, 256
 See also gender differences; prenatal environment
Wong, S., 561, 562, 563, 565
Wood, J. M., 53
Wood, P. J., 576
Woodman, C., 97, 123
Woodruff, R. A., 11, 557
Woody, G., 555
Woody, S. R., 132, 660–61
Wool, C., 453
Woonings, F. M. J., 318
Wörgöttner, G., 353
World Health Organization, 6. *See also International Classification of Diseases and Related Health Problems*
World War I, 144
World War II
 differing psychopathology classifications, 6
 posttraumatic stress disorder, 144, 146, 148
Wormworth, J. A., 493
worry
 boundary between normal and pathological, 119
 measures of, 119–20
 mature and function of, 124–25
 pathological, 121, 123–25
 uncontrollability of, 118, 119–20, 124, 125
 See also anxiety disorders; generalized anxiety disorder; panic disorder
Wozney, K., 471
Wundt, Wilhelm, 5, 287, 494
Wurmser, L., 678
Wyatt, R. J., 302
Wyshak, G., 452

Yager, J., 370–71
Yates, W. R., 123, 587
Yehuda, R., 154, 158
yohimbine, 102, 152–53
Youll, L. K., 204
Young, B. G., 426
Young, J., 686
Young, M. L., 352
Yugoslavia, 355
Yum, K. S., 241
Yutzy, S. H., 447

Zanarini, M., 555, 595, 639
Zborowski, M. J., 321
Zebb, B. J., 118
Zeichner, A., 236
zeitgebers, 184
Zettler-Segal, M., 231
Zigler, E., 349
Zimbardo, P. G., 350
Zimmerman, M., 16, 595, 608
Zinbarg, R. E., 84, 91, 119, 156
Zinser, M. C., 619–20
Ziolko, H.-U., 367
Zisook, S., 316
zoophilia, 426
Zubin, J., 13
Zucker, K. J., 430, 431, 432–33
Zucker, R. A., 230
Zuroff, D. C., 217